ESSENTIALS OF
Abnormal Psychology

V. Mark Durand

University of South Florida–St. Petersburg

David H. Barlow

Boston University

 **WADSWORTH**
CENGAGE Learning

Australia • Brazil • Japan • Korea • Mexico • Singapore • Spain • United Kingdom • United States

Essentials of Abnormal Psychology,
Sixth Edition
V. Mark Durand and David H. Barlow

Publisher: Jon-David Hague

Development Editor: Tangelique Williams

Freelance Development Editor: Carolyn Smith

Assistant Editor: Paige Leeds

Editorial Assistant: Jessica Alderman

Media Editor: Lauren Keyes

Marketing Manager: Christine Sosa

Marketing Communications Manager:
Laura Localio

Marketing Assistant: Janay Pryor

Senior Content Project Manager: Pat Waldo

Design Director: Rob Hugel

Senior Art Director: Vernon Boes

Manufacturing Planner: Judy Inouye

Rights Acquisitions Specialist: Don Schlotman

Production Service: Megan Greiner,
Graphic World Inc.

Text Designer: Ellen Pettengill

Photo Researcher: Wendy Granger/Bill Smith
Group

Text Researcher: Pablo D'Stair

Copy Editor: Graphic World Inc.

Cover Designer: Paula Goldstein

Cover Image: Digital Vision/Getty Images

Compositor: Graphic World Inc.

For product information and technology assistance, contact us at
Cengage Learning Customer & Sales Support, 1-800-354-9706

For permission to use material from this text or product,
submit all requests online at **www.cengage.com/permissions**
Further permissions questions can be emailed to
permissionrequest@cengage.com

Library of Congress Control Number: 2011934458

Student Edition (SE):
ISBN-13: 978-1-111-83698-6
ISBN-10: 1-111-83698-1

Paperbound Edition:
ISBN-13: 978-1-111-83729-7
ISBN-10: 1-111-83729-5

Loose-Leaf Edition:
ISBN-13: 978-1-111-83735-8
ISBN-10: 1-111-83735-X

Wadsworth
20 Davis Drive
Belmont, CA 94002-3098
USA

Cengage Learning is a leading provider of customized learning solutions with office locations around the globe, including Singapore, the United Kingdom, Australia, Mexico, Brazil, and Japan. Locate your local office at **www.cengage.com/global**

Cengage Learning products are represented in Canada by Nelson Education, Ltd.

To learn more about Wadsworth, visit **www.cengage.com/wadsworth**

Purchase any of our products at your local college store or at our preferred online store **www.CengageBrain.com**

Printed in Canada
2 3 4 5 6 7 15 14 13

V. Mark Durand

V. Mark Durand is known worldwide as an authority in the area of autism spectrum disorders. He is a professor of psychology at the University of South Florida–St. Petersburg, where he was the founding Dean of Arts & Sciences and Vice Chancellor for Academic Affairs. Dr. Durand is a fellow of the American Psychological Association. He has received over $4 million in continuous federal funding since the beginning of his career to study the nature, assessment, and treatment of behavior problems in children with disabilities. Before moving to Florida, he served in a variety of leadership positions at the University at Albany, including associate director for clinical training for the doctoral psychology program from 1987 to 1990, chair of the psychology department from 1995 to 1998, and interim dean of Arts and Sciences from 2001 to 2002. There he established the Center for Autism and Related Disabilities at the University at Albany, SUNY. He received his B.A., M.A., and Ph.D.—all in psychology—at the State University of New York–Stony Brook.

Dr. Durand was awarded the University Award for Excellence in Teaching at SUNY–Albany in 1991 and was given the Chancellor's Award for Excellence in Research and Creative Scholarship at the University of South Florida–St. Petersburg in 2007. Dr. Durand is currently a member of the Professional Advisory Board for the Autism Society of America and is on the board of directors of the International Association of Positive Behavioral Support. He is co-editor of the *Journal of Positive Behavior Interventions*, serves on a number of editorial boards, and has over 100 publications on functional communication, educational programming, and behavior therapy. His books include *Severe Behavior Problems: A Functional Communication Training Approach*, *Sleep Better! A Guide to Improving Sleep for Children with Special Needs*, *Helping Parents with Challenging Children: Positive Family Intervention*, and most recently, *Optimistic Parenting: Hope and Help for You and Your Challenging Child*.

Dr. Durand developed a unique treatment for severe behavior problems that is currently mandated by states across the country and is used worldwide. He also developed an assessment tool that is used internationally and has been translated into more than 15 languages. Most recently he developed an innovative approach to help families work with their challenging child (Optimistic Parenting), which was validated in a 5-year clinical trial. He has been consulted by the departments of education in numerous states and by the U.S. Departments of Justice and Education. His current research program includes the study of prevention models and treatments for such serious problems as self-injurious behavior.

In his leisure time, he enjoys long-distance running and has just completed his third marathon.

David H. Barlow

David H. Barlow is an internationally recognized pioneer and leader in clinical psychology. A professor of psychology and psychiatry at Boston University, Dr. Barlow is Founder and Director Emeritus of the Center for Anxiety and Related Disorders, one of the largest research clinics of its kind in the world. From 1996 to 2004, he directed the clinical psychology programs. From 1979 to 1996, he was distinguished professor at the University at Albany–State University of New York. From 1975 to 1979, he was professor of psychiatry and psychology at Brown University, where he also founded the clinical psychology internship program. From 1969 to 1975, he was professor of psychiatry at the University of Mississippi, where he founded the Medical School psychology residency program. Dr. Barlow received his B.A. from the University of Notre Dame, his M.A. from Boston College, and his Ph.D. from the University of Vermont.

A fellow of every major psychological association, Dr. Barlow has received many awards in honor of his excellence in scholarship, including the National Institute of Mental Health Merit Award for his long-term contributions to the clinical research effort; the 2000 Distinguished Scientist Award for applications of psychology from the American Psychological Association; the Distinguished Scientist Award from the Society of Clinical Psychology of the American Psychological Association; and a certificate of appreciation from the APA section on the clinical psychology of women for "outstanding commitment to the advancement of women in psychology." In 2004, he received the C. Charles Burlingame Award from the Institute of Living and was awarded an Honorary Doctorate of Humane Letters degree from the Massachusetts School of Professional Psychology. He also received career contribution awards from the Massachusetts, Connecticut, and California Psychological Asso-

ciations and, in 2000, was named Honorary Visiting Professor at the Chinese People's Liberation Army General Hospital and Postgraduate Medical School in Beijing, China. In addition, the annual Grand Rounds in Clinical Psychology at Brown University was named in his honor, and he was awarded the first graduate alumni scholar award at the University of Vermont. During the 1997–1998 academic year, he was Fritz Redlich Fellow at the Center for Advanced Study in the Behavioral Sciences in Menlo Park, California. His research has been continually funded by the National Institute of Mental Health for over 40 years.

Dr. Barlow has edited three journals, has served on the editorial boards of 19 different journals and is currently editor in chief of the "Treatments That Work" series for Oxford University Press.

He has published more than 500 scholarly articles and written over 65 books and clinical manuals, including *Anxiety and Its Disorders,* 2nd edition, Guilford Press; *Clinical Handbook of Psychological Disorders: A Step-by-Step Treatment Manual,* 4th edition, Guilford Press; *Single-Case Experimental Designs: Strategies for Studying Behavior Change,* 3rd edition, Allyn & Bacon (with Matthew Nock and Michael Hersen); *The Scientist–Practitioner: Research and Accountability in the Age of Managed Care,* 2nd edition, Allyn & Bacon (with Steve Hayes and Rosemery Nelson); and *Mastery of Your Anxiety and Panic,* Oxford University Press (with Michelle Craske). The book and manuals have been translated in over 20 languages, including Arabic, Chinese, and Russian.

Dr. Barlow was one of three psychologists on the task force that was responsible for reviewing the work of more than 1,000 mental health professionals who participated in the creation of *DSM-IV*. He also chaired the APA Task Force on Psychological Intervention Guidelines, which created a template for clinical practice guidelines. His current research program focuses on the nature and treatment of anxiety and related emotional disorders.

At leisure he plays golf, skis, and retreats to his home in Nantucket, where he loves to write, walk on the beach, and visit with his island friends.

BRIEF CONTENTS

CONTENTS

3 Clinical Assessment, Diagnosis, and Research in Psychopathology 69

4 Anxiety Disorders 116

5   Somatoform and Dissociative Disorders   164

10 Substance-Related and Impulse-Control Disorders   370

11 Personality Disorders   412

12 Schizophrenia and Other Psychotic Disorders 450

13 Developmental and Cognitive Disorders 484

14 Mental Health Services: Legal and Ethical Issues 536

PREFACE

Science is a constantly evolving field, but every now and then something groundbreaking occurs that alters our way of thinking. For example, evolutionary biologists, who long assumed that the process of evolution was gradual, suddenly had to adjust to evidence that says evolution happens in fits and starts in response to such cataclysmic, environmental events as meteor impacts. Similarly, geology has been revolutionized by the discovery of plate tectonics.

Until recently, the science of psychopathology had been compartmentalized, with psychopathologists examining the separate effects of psychological, biological, and social influences. This approach is still reflected in popular media accounts that describe, for example, a newly discovered gene, a biological dysfunction (chemical imbalance), or early childhood experiences as a "cause" of a psychological disorder. This way of thinking still dominates discussions of causality and treatment in some psychology textbooks: "The psychoanalytic views of this disorder are . . . ," "the biological views are . . . ," and, often in a separate chapter, "psychoanalytic treatment approaches for this disorder are . . . ," "cognitive behavioral treatment approaches are . . . ," or "biological treatment approaches are . . ."

In the first edition of this text, we tried to do something very different. We thought the field had advanced to the point that it was ready for an integrative approach in which the intricate interactions of biological, psychological, and social factors are explicated in as clear and convincing a manner as possible. Recent explosive advances in knowledge confirm this approach as the only viable way of understanding psychopathology. To take just two examples, Chapter 2 describes a study demonstrating that stressful life events can lead to depression but that not everyone shows this response. Rather, stress is more likely to cause depression in individuals who already carry a particular gene that influences serotonin at the brain synapses. Similarly, Chapter 7 describes how the pain of social rejection activates the same neural mechanisms in the brain as physical pain. On the other hand, the entire section on genetics has been rewritten to highlight the new emphasis on gene–environment interaction, along with recent thinking from leading behavioral geneticists that the goal of basing the classification of psychological disorders on the firm foundation of genetics is fundamentally flawed. Descriptions of the emerging field of epigenetics, or the influence of the environment on gene expression, is also woven into the chapter, along with new studies on the seeming ability of extreme environments to largely override the effects of genetic contributions. Studies elucidating the mechanisms of epigenetics or specifically how environmental events influence gene expression are described.

These results confirm the integrative approach in this book: psychological disorders cannot be explained by genetic or environmental factors alone but rather from their interaction. We now understand that psychological and social factors directly affect neurotransmitter function and even genetic expression. Similarly, we cannot study behavioral, cognitive, or emotional processes without appreciating the contribution of biological and social factors to psychological and psychopathological expression. Instead of compartmentalizing psychopathology, we use a more accessible approach that accurately reflects the current state of our clinical science.

As colleagues, you are aware that we understand some disorders better than others. But we hope you will share our excitement in conveying to students both what we currently know about the causes and treatment of psychopathology and how far we have yet to go in understanding these complex interactions.

Integrative Approach

As noted earlier, the first edition of *Abnormal Psychology* pioneered a new generation of abnormal psychology textbooks, which offer an integrative and multidimensional perspective. (We acknowledge such one-dimensional approaches as biological, psychosocial, or supernatural as historic trends.) We include substantial current evidence of the reciprocal influences of biology and behavior and of psychological and social influences on biology. Our examples hold students' attention; for example, we discuss genetic contributions to divorce, the effects of early social and behavioral experience on later brain function and structure, new information on the relation of social networks to the common cold, and new data on psychosocial treatments for cancer. We emphasize the fact that in the phenomenon of implicit memory and blind sight, which may have parallels in dissociative experiences, psychological science verifies the existence of the unconscious (although it does not much resemble the seething caldron of conflicts envisioned by Freud). We present new evidence confirming the effects of psychological treatments on neurotransmitter flow and brain function. We acknowledge the often neglected area of emotion theory for its rich contributions to psychopathology (e.g., the effects of anger on cardiovascular disease). We weave scientific findings from the study of emotions together with behavioral, biological, cognitive, and social discoveries to create an integrated tapestry of psychopathology.

Life-Span Developmental Influences

No modern view of abnormal psychology can ignore the importance of life-span developmental factors in the manifestation and treatment of psychopathology. In this edition, for the first time, studies highlighting developmental windows for the influence of the environment on gene expression are highlighted. Accordingly, although we include a developmental disorders chapter (Chapter 13), we consider the importance of development throughout the text; we discuss childhood and geriatric anxiety, for example, in the context of the anxiety disorders chapter. This organization, which is for the most part consistent with *DSM-IV*, helps students appreciate the need to study each disorder from childhood through adulthood and old age. We note findings on developmental considerations in separate sections of each disorder chapter and, as appropriate, discuss how specific developmental factors affect causation and treatment.

Scientist–Practitioner Approach

We go to some lengths to explain why the scientist-practitioner approach to psychopathology is both practical and ideal. Like most of our colleagues, we view this as something more than simple awareness of how scientific findings apply to psychopathology. We show how every clinician contributes to general scientific knowledge through astute and systematic clinical observations, functional analyses of individual case studies, and systematic observations of series of cases in clinical settings. For example, we explain how information on dissociative phenomena provided by early psychoanalytic theorists remains relevant today. We also describe the formal methods used by scientist–practitioners and show how abstract research designs are actually implemented in research programs.

Clinical Cases of Real People

We have enriched the book with authentic clinical histories to illustrate scientific findings on the causes and treatment of psychopathology. We have both run active clinics for years, so 95% of the cases are from our own files, and they provide a fascinating frame of reference for the findings we describe. Most chapters begin with a case description, and most of the discussion of the latest theory and research is related to these very cases.

Disorders in Detail

We cover the major psychological disorders in 10 chapters, focusing on three broad categories: clinical description, causal factors, and treatment and outcomes. We pay considerable attention to case studies and *DSM-IV* criteria, and we include statistical data, such as prevalence and incidence rates, sex ratio, age of onset, and the general course or pattern for the disorder as a whole. Because one of us (DHB) is an appointed advisor to the *DMS-5* task force, we are able to include likely revisions to the diagnostic criteria and the reasons why. Throughout, we explore how biological, psychological, and social dimensions may interact to cause a particular disorder. Finally, by covering treatment and outcomes within the context of specific disorders, we provide a realistic sense of clinical practice.

Treatment

One of the best received innovations in the first five editions is that we discuss treatment in the same chapter as the disorders themselves instead of in a separate chapter, an approach that is supported by the development of specific psychosocial and pharmacological treatment procedures for specific disorders. We have retained this integrative format and have improved upon it, and we include treatment procedures in the key terms and glossary.

Legal and Ethical Issues

In our closing chapter, we integrate many of the approaches and themes that have been discussed throughout the text. We include case studies of people who have been involved directly with many legal and ethical issues and with the delivery of mental health services. We also provide a historical context for current perspectives so students will understand the effects of social and cultural influences on legal and ethical issues.

Diversity

Issues of culture and gender are integral to the study of psychopathology. Throughout the text we describe current thinking about which aspects of the disorders are culturally specific and which are universal and about the strong and sometimes puzzling effects of gender roles. For instance, we discuss the current information on topics, such as the gender imbalance in depression, how panic disorders are expressed differently in various Asian cultures, the ethnic differences in eating disorders, treatment of schizophrenia across cultures, and the diagnostic differences of attention deficit/hyperactivity disorder (ADHD) in boys and girls. Clearly, our field will grow in depth and detail as these subjects and others become standard research topics. For example, why do some disorders overwhelmingly affect females and others appear predominantly in males? And why does this apportionment sometimes change from one culture to another? In answering questions like these, we adhere closely to science, emphasizing that gender and culture are each one dimension among several that constitute psychopathology.

New to This Edition

A Thorough Update

This exciting field moves at a rapid pace, and we take particular pride in how our book reflects the most recent developments. Therefore, once again, every chapter has been carefully revised to reflect the latest research studies on psychological disorders. Hundreds of new references from 2008 to 2011 (and some still "in press") appear for the first time in this edition, and some of the information they contain stuns the imagination. Nonessential material has been eliminated, some new headings have been added, and *DSM-IV* criteria are included in their entirety as tables in the appropriate disorder chapters.

The chapters on Anxiety Disorders (Chapter 4), Mood Disorders and Suicide (Chapter 6), Physical Disorders and Health Psychology (Chapter 7), Eating and Sleep Disorders (Chapter 8), Substance-Related and Impulse-Control Disorders (Chapter 10), Schizophrenia and Other Psychotic Disorders (Chapter 12), and Developmental and Cognitive Disorders (Chapter 13) have been the most heavily revised to reflect new research, but all chapters have been significantly updated and freshened. Some highlights of the changes include:

› In Chapter 2, An Integrative Approach to Psychopathology, the entire section on genetics has been rewritten to highlight the new emphasis on gene–environment interaction. The emerging field of epigenetics is integrated throughout the chapter. Also included are new studies on the relative contribution of genetic factors and environmental factors to both variability and stability in important human traits, as well as new evidence on the ability of early childhood experiences to override genetic influences in the development of behavior.

› Chapter 3, Clinical Assessment, Diagnosis, and Research in Psychopathology, now presents updated research findings on labeling and stigma and their relation to potential changes in the *DSM-5*, as well as examples of more fully developed conceptually satisfying dimensional approaches to diagnosis and reasons why these will probably not make an appearance until the *DSM-6*.

› Chapter 3 also introduces a new concept that is now the focus of intense study—endophenotypes. Another new section describes clinical trials and defines the differences among clinical trials, randomized clinical trials, and randomized control trials. The section "Studying Behavior over Time" is completely rewritten, with a new example of prospective longitudinal research on the development of autism, as is the section "The Power of a Program of Research," using all new examples to illustrate different research strategies and how these are used to answer complex questions in abnormal psychology.

› Chapter 4, Anxiety Disorders, now includes the conceptual basis of description on how a future diagnostic system using dimensional approaches for emotional disorders might work, as well as data supporting a possible new category of separation anxiety disorder in adults.

› Chapter 4 also describes consideration of the likely new names for several anxiety disorders in *DSM-5*, as well as likely changes to definitions.

› Descriptions of new major clinical trials for both adults and children with GAD evaluating the effects of psychological treatments and drugs are also presented in Chapter 4.

› Finally, Chapter 4 provides a description of a new disorder under consideration for inclusion in *DSM-5* called "olfactory reference syndrome."

› Chapter 5, Somatoform and Dissociative Disorders, describes a potential new *DSM-5* reorganization where the disorders of hypochondriasis, somatization disorder, and (somatoform) pain disorders are grouped together as varying examples of medically unexplained physical symptoms (MUPS) with a potential label of complex somatic symptom disorder. Chapter 5 also includes an updated review of the latest evidence on the induction of false memories and the role that false memory may play in various presentations of dissociation and psychopathology.

› Chapter 6, Mood Disorders and Suicide, is thoroughly rewritten and reorganized, with approximately 40% new material and 149 new references. Existing material has been streamlined and reorganized to facilitate reading and comprehension, resulting in a chapter that is shorter and more succinct than in previous editions. Chapter 6 also includes data underscoring the combination of depression with impulse control problems as causal factors in suicide, as well as new data on the ability to detect implicit or out-of-awareness suicidal ideation as a possible powerful risk factor for depression.

› In Chapter 7, Physical Disorders and Health Psychology, updated information is presented on the worldwide epidemic of AIDS, as well as new information on the effectiveness of psychological treatments for AIDS on immune functioning and survival time. Chapter 7 also includes updated information on the role of psychological factors on the progression and treatment of cancer, including new randomized controlled trials demonstrating increases in survival time from psychological treatments, as well as new hypotheses on the causes and maintenance factors of chronic fatigue syndrome.

> Chapter 8, Eating and Sleep Disorders, includes an update on the status of binge-eating disorder and the reasons why it will almost certainly be included as a disorder in the *DSM-5*, as well as new data on the disappointing follow-up of anti-obesity drugs for binge-eating disorder. Chapter 8 also presents recent results from a transdiagnostic psychological approach to the treatment of eating disorders, illustrating the importance of conceptualizing eating disorders on a dimension or spectrum.

> Chapter 8 also presents research that suggests that the effects of jet lag on circadian rhythms can be quite serious—at least among older adults.

> Chapter 9, Sexual and Gender Identity Disorders, includes prevalence, social and psychological determinants, treatments, and likely changes to *DSM-5* for sexual dysfunction. Also presented is new information on the malleability of sexual identities relative to sexual arousal patterns, particularly in women, and new information on the very loose connections between gender nonconforming behavior in children and sexual orientation and gender identity as an adult.

> Chapter 10, Substance-Related and Impulse-Control Disorders, includes a discussion of a new longitudinal study that shows that hard drug use in high school predicts poorer job outcomes in young adults (younger than 29 years of age). The section on medical marijuana use is also completely revised and now describes its application in routine medical care in Canada. Chapter 10 also provides a revised section on fetal alcohol syndrome and updated data on cultural variations in binge drinking.

> In addition to updated coverage of changes being discussed for *DSM-5*, Chapter 11, Personality Disorders, describes a large and important longitudinal study that finds impaired fear conditioning at age 3 predicts criminal status at age 23, which suggests a gene–environment interaction in the development of antisocial personality disorder. Chapter 11 also discusses a new prospective study, which shows that a history of abuse and neglect does predict later development of borderline personality disorder. Updated research on the medical treatment of borderline personality disorder is also provided.

> Chapter 12, Schizophrenia and Other Psychotic Disorders, now includes coverage of the outcomes from two large drug studies conducted in the United States (called the Clinical Antipsychotic Trials of Intervention Effectiveness or CATIE) and in the U.K. (called the Cost Utility of the Latest Antipsychotic Drugs in Schizophrenia Study or CUtLASS). These studies find that newer, second-generation drugs are no more effective or better tolerated than the older drugs.

> In Chapter 13, Developmental and Cognitive Disorders, a great deal of new information on ADHD is presented, including a new section on ADHD comorbidity; new information on global ADHD prevalence; significantly expanded coverage of genetics, including the only gene–environment interaction study; updated material on brain structural differences in children with ADHD; and a new discussion of the overlap among ADHD and opposition defiant disorder (ODD), conduct disorder, and bipolar disorder. Also, the section previously titled "Mental Retardation" is completely revised to recognize the use of the more acceptable term *intellectual disability*.

> Chapter 13 also includes a new section on Spectra and Dimensions, which describes the changes proposed for *DSM-5* to use two types of "Neurocognitive Disorders" (Major and Minor) to indicate their dimensional quality. Chapter 13 also provides updated information on the progress being made in the early identification of Alzheimer's disease (the Alzheimer's Disease Neuroimaging Initiative or ADNI), as well as an added discussion of the controversial nature of vascular dementia as different from dementia of the Alzheimer's type. New data are also presented on sex differences in dementia across developed and developing countries.

○ New Features

In addition to the changes highlighted earlier, we have added two new features to the sixth edition:

> New *Student Learning Outcomes* at the start of each chapter assist instructors in accurately assessing and mapping questions throughout the chapter. The outcomes are mapped to the core APA goals and are integrated throughout the instructor resources and testing program.

> At the end of every disorder chapter is another new feature called *On the Spectrum*, which examines

cutting-edge developments in the gradual but inexorable movement toward a more multidimensional approach to studying psychopathology. Examples include new transdiagnostic assessment schemes and treatment for emotional disorders; previews of disorders in the *DSM-5*, where more dimensional approaches will be adopted; and the adoption of cross-cutting dimensional measures of, for example, anxiety or features of distorted reality for every patient to provide a richer description of psychopathology.

Much has been said about the mix of political and scientific considerations that resulted in *DSM-IV*, and naturally we have our own opinions. (DHB had the interesting experience of sitting on the task force.) Psychologists are often concerned about turf issues in what has become, for better or worse, the nosological standard in our field, and with good reason: in previous *DSM* editions, scientific findings sometimes gave way to personal opinions.

However, for *DSM-IV*, most professional biases were left at the door while the task force almost endlessly debated the data. This process produced enough new information to fill every psychopathology journal for a year with integrative reviews, reanalysis of existing databases, and new data from field trials. From a scholarly point of view, the process was both stimulating and exhausting. This book contains highlights of various debates that created the nomenclature, as well as recent updates. For example, we summarize and update the data and discussion of premenstrual dysphoric disorder and mixed anxiety depression, two disorders that did not make it into the final criteria. Students can thus see the process of making diagnoses, as well as the mix of data and inferences that are part of it.

In 2000, the American Psychiatric Association published a revision of the text accompanying the *DSM-IV* diagnostic criteria, which updated the scientific literature and changed some of the criteria themselves, mostly in minor ways. Several senior clinical investigators from one of our (DHB) research centers participated in the text revision, and this information is included. For example, the text revision (*DSM-IV-TR*) discusses the intense continuing debate on categorical and dimensional approaches to classification.

We describe some of the compromises the task force made to accommodate data, such as why it does not yet seem possible to dimensionalize personality disorders even though almost everyone agrees that when we can, we will prefer to do so.

Now *DSM-5* is nearing completion with a publication date of May 2013, and one of us (DHB) is an appointed advisor to the *DSM-5* task force. The first phase of this massive project involved a joint effort by the National Institute of Mental Health and the American Psychiatric Association in focusing on delineating needed research efforts to provide crucial information for the *DSM-5* process. Research planning workgroups were formed in areas, such as neuroscience, problems/gaps in the current system, cross-cultural issues, and developmental issues with the charge of producing "white papers" outlining the required research agenda. The white papers, along with an article summarizing important recommendations, were published in 2002 with an update in 2008. The planning committee then organized a series of conferences to further these efforts. Eleven conferences were held from 2004 to 2007, chaired by members of the American and international research communities on topics such as externalizing disorders of childhood, personality disorders, and stress-induced and fear circuitry disorders. In 2007, the *DSM-5* task force and the major committees covering large classes of disorders (anxiety, mood, schizophrenia, and so on) were appointed. Field trials testing proposed changes to the criteria are underway and will continue into early 2012. It is already clear that *DSM-5* will incorporate a somewhat more dimensional approach to classification. Likely changes along these lines are presented in Chapter 3 and in the disorder chapters. For this reason, as noted previously, we now end each disorder chapter with a special feature entitled *On the Spectrum*, highlighting new scientific findings illustrating and supporting a more dimensional approach to psychopathology.

Prevention

Looking into the future of abnormal psychology as a field, it seems our ability to prevent psychological disorders may help the most. Although this has long been a goal of many, we are now at the precipice of what appears to be the beginning of a new age in prevention research. Numerous scientists from all over the globe are developing the methodologies and techniques that may at long last provide us with the means to interrupt the debilitating toll of emotional distress caused by the disorders chronicled in this book. We therefore highlight these cutting-edge prevention efforts—such as preventing eating disorders, suicide, and health problems, such as HIV and injuries—in appropriate chapters as a means to celebrate these important events, as well as to spur on the field to continue this important work.

Retained Features

Video Concept Reviews

VMD's *Video Concept Reviews*—more than 200—are video clips that review challenging topics that typically need more than one explanation. A list of these clips appears in every chapter, and the actual videos can be found within CourseMate.

Visual Summaries

At the end of each disorder chapter is a colorful, two-page visual overview that succinctly summarizes the causes, development, symptoms, and treatment of each disorder covered in that chapter. Our integrative approach is instantly evident in these diagrams, which show the interaction of biological, psychological, and social factors in the etiology and treatment of disorders. The visual summaries will help instructors wrap up discussions, and students will appreciate them as study aids.

Pedagogy

Each chapter contains several Concept Checks, which let students verify their comprehension at regular intervals. Answers are listed at the end of each chapter, along with a more detailed Summary; the Key Terms are listed in the order they appear in the text and thus form a sort of outline that students can study. Finally, each chapter concludes with two elements: a link to *Psychology CourseMate*, which includes chapter-specific interactive learning tools including the *Abnormal Psychology Videos*, and a link to the *CengageNOW* online study tool, which includes pre- and posttests and VMD's *Video Concept Reviews* on challenging topics.

Discussing Diversity

Each chapter features *Discussing Diversity* boxes, which highlight diversity and discuss important research about how gender and culture impact the presentation and treatment of disorders.

Learning Aids for the Student

Abnormal Psychology Videos

The *Abnormal Psychology Videos*, which include video clips of actual clients discussing their disorders, are available online through *Psychology CourseMate* (www.cengagebrain.com). Each video clip has specific questions written around it, and students can write their responses on the screen, as well as print them out. By chapter, the videos include:

› **Chapter 2, An Integrative Approach to Psychopathology:** Integrative Approach
› **Chapter 3, Clinical Assessment, Diagnosis, and Research in Psychopathology:** Arriving at a Diagnosis; Psychological Assessment; Research Methods
› **Chapter 4, Anxiety Disorders:** Panic Disorder: Steve; Virtual Reality Therapy: A New Technique on the Treatment of Anxiety Disorders; Rapid Behavioral Treatment of a Specific Phobia (Snakes); Obsessive-Compulsive Disorder: Chuck
› **Chapter 5, Somatoform and Dissociative Disorders:** Dissociative Identity Disorder: Rachel; Body Dysmorphic Disorder: Doug
› **Chapter 6, Mood Disorders and Suicide:** Major Depressive Disorder: Barbara; Major Depressive Disorder: Evelyn; Bipolar Disorder: Mary
› **Chapter 7, Physical Disorders and Health Psychology:** Social Support/HIV: Orel; The Immune System,

Effects of Stress and Emotion; Cancer: Education and Support Groups
› **Chapter 8, Eating and Sleep Disorders:** Anorexia Nervosa: Susan; Anorexia Nervosa/Bulimia: Twins; Weight Control: The Obesity Epidemic; Sleep Cycle
› **Chapter 9, Sexual and Gender Identity Disorders:** Erectile Dysfunction: Clark; Changing Over: Jessica
› **Chapter 10, Substance-Related and Impulse-Control Disorders:** Substance Use Disorder: Tim; Nicotine Dependence
› **Chapter 11, Personality Disorders:** Antisocial Personality Disorder: George; Borderline Personality Disorders; Dialectical Behavior Therapy
› **Chapter 12, Schizophrenia and Other Psychotic Disorders:** Schizophrenia: Etta; Positive versus Negative Symptoms; Common Symptoms of Schizophrenia
› **Chapter 13, Developmental and Cognitive Disorders:** ADHD: Sean; Edward: ADHD in a Gifted Student; Life Skills Training; Bullying Prevention; Autism: The Nature of the Disorder; Autism: Christina; Rebecca: A First-Grader with Autistic Disorder; Lauren: A Kindergartner with Down Syndrome; Alzheimer's Disease: Tom; Amnestic Disorder: Mike; Amnestic Patient Interview: Endel Tulving; Neural Networks: Cognition and Dementia
› **Chapter 14, Mental Health Services: Legal and Ethical Issues:** False Memory Research

Teaching Aids for the Instructor

PowerLecture

PowerLecture instructor resources are a collection of book-specific lecture and class tools on either CD or DVD. The fastest and easiest way to build powerful, customized media-rich lectures, PowerLecture assets include chapter-specific PowerPoint presentations, images, animations and videos, instructor manuals, test banks, useful web links, and more. PowerLecture media-teaching tools are an effective way to enhance the educational experience.

Instructor's Manual

Written by Fred Whitford of Montana State University, the Instructor's Manual helps you streamline and maximize the effectiveness of your course preparation using such resources as learning objectives, chapter outlines, classroom activities, handouts, and annotated supplementary reading lists and video resources.

Test Bank

Simplify testing and assessment using this printed selection of more than 1,500 questions. Choose from multiple-choice and essay questions in the test bank by David W. Alfano, Community College of Rhode Island.

CENGAGENOW CengageNOW is an online teaching and learning resource that gives you more control in less time and delivers better outcomes—NOW. And only CengageNOW for Accounting identifies and reports content as it relates to AACSB, AICPA, and IMA, and specific Principles of Accounting Course Outcomes allows you to track student assessment outcomes throughout your accounting course.

CourseMate Cengage Learning's new Psychology CourseMate includes interactive teaching and learning tools including an integrated eBook, quizzes, flashcards, videos, learning modules, and more. It also features Engagement Tracker, a first-of-its-kind tool that monitors student engagement in the course.

aplia Aplia™ is an online interactive learning solution that improves comprehension and outcomes by increasing student effort and engagement. Founded by a professor to enhance his own courses, Aplia provides automatically graded assignments that were written to make the most of the web medium and contains detailed, immediate explanations on every question. Our easy-to-use system has been used by more than 1,000,000 students at over 1,800 institutions.

WebTUTOR "Jumpstart your course with customizable, rich, text-specific content within your Course Management System.

> Jumpstart—Simply load a WebTutor cartridge into your Course Management System.
> Customizable—Easily blend, add, edit, reorganize, or delete content.
> Content—Rich, text-specific content, media assets, quizzing, web links, discussion topics, interactive games and exercises, and more."

Videos

> *Abnormal Psychology: Inside/Out,* Volume I 0-534-20359-0
> *Abnormal Psychology: Inside/Out,* Volume II 0-534-36480-2
> *Abnormal Psychology: Inside/Out,* Volume III 0-534-50759-X
> *Abnormal Psychology: Inside/Out,* Volume IV 0-534-63369-2
> ABC Video: Abnormal Psychology, Volume I 0-495-59639-6
> ABC Video: Abnormal Psychology, Volume II 0-495-60494-1

Additional Resources

> *Looking into Abnormal Psychology: Contemporary Readings*, by Scott O. Lilienfeld, is a fascinating 234-page reader comprised of 40 articles from popular magazines and journals. Each article explores ongoing controversies regarding mental illness and its treatment. 0-534-35416-5
> *Casebook in Abnormal Psychology*, 4th edition, by Timothy A. Brown and David H. Barlow, is a comprehensive casebook that reflects the integrative approach, which considers the multiple influences of genetics, biology, and familial and environmental factors into a unified model of causality, as well as maintenance and treatment of the disorder. The casebook reflects treatment methods that are the most effective interventions developed for a particular disorder. It also presents three undiagnosed cases in order to give students an appreciation for the complexity of disorders. The cases are strictly teaching/learning exercises, similar to what many instructors use on their examinations. 0-495-60438-0

Acknowledgments

Finally, this book in all of its editions would not have begun and certainly would not have been finished without the inspiration and coordination of our senior editor at Cengage, Jaime Perkins, who always keeps his eye on the ball. A special note of thanks to Carolyn Smith and senior developmental editor Tangelique Williams for their attention to detail and organization. The book is much better for their efforts. We hope to work with you on many subsequent editions. We appreciate the expertise of marketing manager Christine Sosa. Lauren Keyes did an outstanding job on the media products. Paige Leeds and Jessica Alderman were hardworking, enthusiastic, and organized from beginning to end.

In the production process, many individuals worked as hard as we did to complete this project. In Boston, Meredith Elkins assisted enormously in typing and integrating a vast amount of new information into each chapter. Her ability to find missing references and track down information was remarkable. It is an understatement to say we couldn't have done it without you. In St. Petersburg, Marly Sadou's quiet professionalism and attention to detail helped smooth this process immensely. At Wadsworth/Cengage, Vernon Boes guided the design down to the last detail. Pat Waldo coordinated all of the production details with grace under pressure. To production manager Megan Greiner at Graphic World Inc. and copy editor Margo Harris, let's just say your attention to detail puts the folks at CSI to shame. We thank Wendy Granger with Bill Smith Group for her commitment to finding the best photos possible.

Numerous colleagues and students provided superb feedback on the previous editions, and to them we express our deepest gratitude. Although not all comments were favorable, all were important. Readers who take the time to communicate their thoughts offer the greatest reward to writers and scholars.

Finally, you share with us the task of communicating knowledge and discoveries in the exciting field of psychopathology, a challenge that none of us takes lightly. In the spirit of collegiality, we would greatly appreciate your comments on the content and style of this book and recommendations for improving it further.

Reviewers

Creating this book has been both stimulating and exhausting, and we could not have done it without the valuable assistance of colleagues who read one or more chapters and provided extraordinarily perceptive critical comments, corrected errors, pointed to relevant information, and, on occasion, offered new insights that helped us achieve a successful, integrative model of each disorder. We thank the following reviewers of the sixth edition of *Essentials of Abnormal Psychology*:

Pamela G. Costa, *Tacoma Community College*
Kurt R Emmerling, *Carlow University*
Maria A. Gartstein, *Washington State University*
Ellen I. Koch, *Eastern Michigan University*
John Ramirez, *Middlesex County College*
Sandra Terneus, *Tennessee Tech University*
Terry S. Trepper, *Purdue University Calumet*
Cynthia L. Turk, *Washburn University*

We also thank the reviewers of previous editions:

Kerm O. Almos, *Capital University*
Frank Andrasik, *University of West Florida*
Robin Apple, *Stanford University Medical Center*
Jim Backlund, *Kirkland Community College*
Joe S. Bean, *Shorter College*
Dorothy Bianco, *Rhode Island College*
Cheryl Bluestone, *Queensborough Community College*
Susan Blumenson, *City University of New York, John Jay College of Criminal Justice*
Robert Bornstein, *Gettysburg College*
Edwin Boundreaux, *Louisiana State University*
James Calhoun, *University of Georgia*
Glenn M. Callagan, *San Jose State University*
Montie Campbell, *Oklahoma Baptist University*
Antonio Cepeda-Benito, *Texas A & M University*
Sheree Dukes Conrad, *University of Massachusetts at Boston*

Eric J. Cooley, *Western Oregon State University*
Laurie Rotando Corey, *Westchester Community College*
Lenore DeFonson, *Indiana-Purdue University–Fort Wayne*
Andrew L. Dickson, *University of Southern Mississippi*
Joan B. Doolittle, *Anne Arundel Community College*
Juris Draguns, *Pennsylvania State University*
Mitchell Earlywine, *University of Southern California*
Raymond Eastman, *Stephen F. Austin State University*
Elizabeth Epstein, *Rutgers University*
Donald Evans, *Drake University*
Ronald G. Evans, *Washburn University*
Anthony Fazio, *University of Wisconsin–Milwaukee*
Mark A. Fine, *University of Missouri at Columbia*
Diane Finley, *Towson State University*
Sheila Fling, *Southwest Texas State University*
Karen E. Ford, *Mesa State College*
John R. Foust, *Parkland College*
Allen Frances, *Duke University*
David Gard, *San Francisco State University*
Andrew Getzfeld, *New Jersey City University*
David Gleaves, *Texas A & M University*
Frank Goodkin, *Castleton State College*
Irving Gottesman, *University of Virginia*
Peter Gram, *Pensacola Junior College*
Ron Hallman, *Emmanuel Bible College*
Marjorie Hardy, *Muhlenberg College*
Brian Hayden, *Brown University*
Holly Hazlett-Stevens, *University of Nevada–Reno*
Shaine Henert, *Chicago State University*
Stephen Hinshaw, *University of California–Berkeley*
Debra L. Hollister, *Valencia Community College*
Steven Huprich, *Baylor University*
William Iacono, *University of Minnesota*
Heidi M. Inderbitzen-Nolan, *University of Nebraska–Lincoln*
Ken Ishida, *California State University–Bakersfield*
Thomas Jackson, *University of Arkansas*

Boaz Kahana, *Cleveland State University*
Stephen R. Kahoe, *El Paso Community College*
Ricki E. Kantrowitz, *Westfield State College*
Susan Kashubeck, *Texas Tech University*
Arthur Kaye, *Virginia Commonwealth University*
Christopher Kearney, *University of Nevada–Las Vegas*
Ernest Keen, *Bucknell University*
Elizabeth Klonoff
Ellen I. Koch, *Eastern Michigan University*
Ann Kring, *Vanderbilt University*
Julie Kuehnel, *California Lutheran*
Marvin Kumler, *Bowling Green State University*
Thomas Kwapil, *University of North Carolina–Greensboro*
Michael Lambert, *Brigham Young University*
Kristi Lane, *Winona State University*
Travis Langley, *Henderson State University*
Cynthia Ann Lease, *Virginia Polytechnic Institute and State University*
Richard Leavy, *Ohio Weslyan University*
Scott Lilienfeld, *Emory University*
Karsten Look, *Columbus State Community College*
Mark Lukin, *University of Nebraska–Lincoln*
Michael Lyons, *Boston University*
Jerald Marshall, *Valencia Community College*
Charles Mate-Kole, *Central Connecticut State University*
Janet Matthews, *Loyola University*
Dena Matzenbacher, *McNeese State University*
Dennis McChargue, *University of Nebraska–Lincoln*
Edward McEntee, *Community College of Rhode Island*
Dean McKay, *Fordham University*
Mary McNaughton-Cassill, *University of Texas at San Antonio*
Thomas Miller, *Murray State University*
Scott Monroe, *University of Oregon*
Laura A. Negel, *University of Tennessee*
Bridget Nelson, *Hocking Technical College*
Sumie Okazaki, *University of Wisconsin–Madison*
John W. Otey, *South Arkansas University*
Gregory Page, *University of Pittsburgh–Bradford*

Victoria Pederson, *Southwestern Community College*
Diane J. Pfahler, *California State University, San Bernardino*
Ralph G. Pifer, *Sauk Valley College*
P. B. Poorman, *University of Wisconsin–Whitewater*
Gene Ritter, *Santa Fe Community College*
Carole Rothman, *City University of New York, Herbert H. Lehman College*
Deborah Roundtree, *University of Michigan–Dearborn*
Mary Bower Russa, *Grand Valley State College*
David A. Santogrossi, *Purdue University*
Evelyn Schliecker, *Gordon College*
William B. Scott, *College of Wooster*
Charles Seidel, *Mansfield University*
John Shepherd, *New Mexico Junior College*
Richard Siegel, *University of Massachusetts–Lowell*
David Skinner, *Valencia Community College*
Jerome Small, *Youngstown State University*
Brian Stagner, *Texas A & M University*
Irene Staik, *University of Montevallo*
Tome Stuber, *Itasca Community College*
Chris Tate, *Middle Tennessee State University*
Lisa Terre, *University of Missouri–Kansas City*
Susan Troy, *Northeast Iowa Community College*
Doug Uselding, *Marian College*
Michael Vasey, *Ohio State University*
John Velasquez, *University of the Incarnate Word*
Larry Ventis, *College of William and Mary*
Richard Viken, *Indiana University*
Philip Watkins, *Eastern Washington University*
Marcia Wehr, *Santa Fe Community College*
Kim Weikel, *Shippensburg University of Pennsylvania*
Michael Wierzbicki, *Marquette University*
John Wincze, *Brown University*
Bradley Woldt, *South Dakota State University*
Guy Wylie, *Western Nebraska Community College*
Ellen Zaleski, *Fordham University*
Raymond Zurawski, *St. Norbert College*

CULTURE INDEX

GENDER INDEX

CHAPTER 1

Abnormal Behavior in Historical Context

Characterize the nature of psychology as a discipline.	› Explain why psychology is a science (APA SLO 1.1.a) *(see textbook pages 4–6)*.
Demonstrate knowledge and understanding representing appropriate breadth and depth in selected content areas of psychology.	› Know the history of psychology, including the evolution of methods of psychology, its theoretical conflicts, and its sociocultural contexts (APA SLO 1.2.b) *(see textbook pages 6–22)*.
Use the concepts, language, and major theories of the discipline to account for psychological phenomena.	› Use theories to explain and predict behavior and mental processes (APA SLO 1.3.d) *(see textbook pages 7–22)*. › Integrate theoretical perspectives to produce comprehensive and multifaceted explanations (APA SLO 1.3.e) *(see textbook page 23)*.
Explain major perspectives of psychology (e.g., behavioral, biological, cognitive, evolutionary, humanistic, psychodynamic, and sociocultural).	› Explain major perspectives in psychology (APA SLO 1.4a) *(see textbook pages 7–22)*.

*Portions of this chapter cover learning outcomes suggested by the American Psychological Association (2007) in their guidelines for the undergraduate psychology major. Chapter coverage of these outcomes is identified by APA Goal and APA Suggested Learning Outcome (SLO).

Understanding Psychopathology

› **How do psychologists define a psychological disorder?**
› **What is a scientist–practitioner?**

Today you may have gotten out of bed, had breakfast, gone to class, studied, and enjoyed the company of your friends before dropping off to sleep. It probably did not occur to you that many people are not able to do some or any of these things. What they have in common is a **psychological disorder**, a psychological dysfunction associated with distress or impairment in functioning and a response that is not typical or culturally expected. Before examining exactly what this means, let's look at one individual's situation.

Judy | The Girl Who Fainted at the Sight of Blood

Judy, a 16 year old, was referred to our anxiety disorders clinic after increasing episodes of fainting. About 2 years earlier, in Judy's first biology class, the teacher showed a movie of a frog dissection.

This was a graphic film, with vivid images of blood, tissue, and muscle. About halfway through, Judy felt lightheaded and left the room. But the images did not leave her. She continued to be bothered by them and occasionally felt queasy. She began to avoid situations in which she might see blood or injury. She found it difficult to look at raw meat, or even Band-Aids, because they brought the feared images to mind. Eventually, anything anyone said that evoked an image of blood or injury caused Judy to feel lightheaded. If one of her friends exclaimed, "Cut it out!" she felt faint.

Beginning about 6 months before her visit to the clinic, Judy fainted when she encountered something bloody. Physicians could find nothing wrong with her. By the time she was referred to our clinic she was fainting 5 to 10 times a week, often in class. Clearly, this was problematic and disruptive; each time Judy fainted, the other students flocked around her, trying to help, and class was interrupted. The principal finally concluded that she was being manipulative and suspended her from school, even though she was an honor student.

Judy was suffering from what we now call *blood–injury–injection phobia*. Her reaction was severe, thereby meeting the criteria for **phobia**, a psychological disorder characterized by marked and persistent fear of an object or situation. But many people have similar reactions that are not as severe when they receive an injection or see someone who is injured. For people who react as severely as Judy, this phobia can be disabling. They may avoid certain careers, such as medicine or nursing, and their fear of injections may put their health at risk.

psychological disorder Psychological dysfunction associated with distress or impairment in functioning that is not a typical or culturally expected response.
phobia Psychological disorder characterized by marked and persistent fear of an object or situation.

Jerry Cooke/Time & Life Pictures/Getty Images

What Is a Psychological Disorder?

A psychological disorder, or **abnormal behavior**, is a psychological dysfunction that is associated with distress or impairment in functioning and a response that is not typical or culturally expected (■ Figure 1.1). These three criteria may seem obvious, but they were not easily arrived at and it is worth a moment to explore what they mean.

Psychological Dysfunction

Psychological dysfunction refers to a breakdown in cognitive, emotional, or behavioral functioning. For example, if you are on a date, it should be fun. But if you experience severe fear all evening, even though there is nothing to be afraid of, and the fear happens on every date, your emotions are not functioning properly. However, if your friends agree that the person who asked you out is dangerous in some way, it would not be dysfunctional to be fearful.

A dysfunction was clearly present for Judy. But many people experience a mild version of this reaction (feeling queasy at the sight of blood) without meeting the criteria for the disorder. Drawing the line between normal and abnormal dysfunction is often difficult. For this reason, these problems are often considered to be on a continuum or a dimension rather than either present or absent. This, too, is a reason why just having a dysfunction is not enough to meet the criteria for a psychological disorder.

Personal Distress

That the behavior must be associated with distress to be classified as abnormal seems clear: The criterion is satisfied if the individual is extremely upset. We can certainly say that Judy was distressed. But remember, by itself this criterion does not define abnormal behavior. It is often normal to be distressed—for example, if someone close to you dies. Suffering and distress are very much part of life. Furthermore, for some disorders, by definition, suffering and distress are absent. Consider the person who feels elated and may act impulsively as part of a manic episode. As you will see in Chapter 6, one of the major difficulties with this problem is that some people enjoy the manic state so much they are reluctant to receive treatment for it.

▲ Distress and suffering are a natural part of life and do not in themselves constitute a psychological disorder.

Thus, defining psychological disorder by distress alone doesn't work.

The concept of *impairment* is useful, although it is not entirely satisfactory. For example, many people consider themselves shy or lazy. This doesn't mean they're abnormal. But if you are so shy that you find it impossible to interact with people even though you would like to have friends, your social functioning is impaired.

Judy was clearly impaired by her phobia, but many people with less severe reactions are not impaired. This difference again shows that most psychological disorders are extreme expressions of otherwise normal emotions, behaviors, and cognitive processes.

Atypical or Not Culturally Expected

The criterion that the response be *atypical* or *not culturally expected* is also insufficient to determine abnormality by itself. At times, something is considered abnormal because it deviates from the average. The greater the deviation, the more abnormal it is. You might say that someone is abnormally short or abnormally tall, but this obviously isn't a definition of a disorder. Many people's behavior is far from average, but we call them talented or eccentric, not disordered. For example, it's not normal to plan to have blood spurt from your clothes, but when Lady Gaga did this while performing it only enhanced her celebrity. In most cases, the more productive you are in the eyes of society, the more eccentricities society will tolerate. Therefore, "deviating from the average" doesn't work as a definition for abnormal behavior.

Another view is that your behavior is abnormal if you are violating social norms. This definition is useful in considering cultural differences in psychological disorders. For example, to enter a trance state and believe you are possessed reflects a psychological disorder in most Western cultures but not in many other societies, where the behavior is accepted and expected (see Chapter 5). An example is provided by Robert Sapolsky (2002), a neurosci-

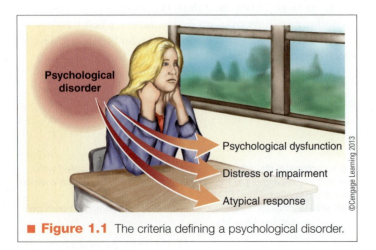

Psychological disorder

Psychological dysfunction

Distress or impairment

Atypical response

©Cengage Learning 2013

■ **Figure 1.1** The criteria defining a psychological disorder.

entist who worked closely with the Masai tribe in East Africa. One day, Sapolsky's Masai friend Rhoda asked him to bring his jeep to the village where a woman had been acting aggressively and hearing voices. The woman had killed a goat with her own hands. Sapolsky and several Masai were able to subdue her and transport her to a local health center. Sapolsky and Rhoda had the following discussion:

"So, Rhoda," I began laconically, "what do you suppose was wrong with that woman?"

She looked at me as if I was mad.

"She is crazy."

"But how can you tell?"

"She's crazy. Can't you just see from how she acts?"

"But how do you decide that she is crazy? What did she do?"

"She killed that goat."

"Oh," I said with anthropological detachment, "but Masai kill goats all the time."

She looked at me as if I were an idiot. "Only the men kill goats," she said.

▲ We accept extreme behaviors by entertainers, such as Lady Gaga, that would not be tolerated in other members of our society.

"Well, how else do you know that she is crazy?"

"She hears voices."

Again, I made a pain of myself. "Oh, but the Masai hear voices sometimes." (At ceremonies before long cattle drives, the Masai trance-dance and claim to hear voices.) In one sentence, Rhoda summed up half of what anyone needs to know about cross-cultural psychiatry:

"But she hears voices at the wrong time." (p. 138)

A social standard of *normal* can be misused. Consider the practice of committing political dissidents to mental institutions because they protest the policies of their government, which was common in Iraq before the fall of Saddam Hussein. Although such behavior violates social norms, it should not be cause for commitment.

Jerome Wakefield (1992, 1999, 2009) uses the shorthand definition of harmful dysfunction. A related concept is whether the behavior is out of the individual's control (Widiger & Sankis, 2000). Variants of these approaches are most often used in current diagnostic practice, as outlined in the American Psychological Association's (APA's) *Diagnostic and Statistical Manual (DSM)*.

An Accepted Definition

In conclusion, it is difficult to define "normal" and "abnormal" (Lilienfeld & Marino, 1995, 1999)—and the debate continues (Clark, 1999; Houts, 2001; Klein, 1999; Spitzer, 1999; Wakefield, 2003, 2009). The most widely accepted definition describes behavioral, psychological, or biological dysfunctions that are unexpected in their cultural context and associated with present distress and impairment in functioning or increased risk of suffering, death, pain, or impairment. This definition can be useful across cultures if we pay attention to what is dysfunctional (or out of control) in a given society. But it is never easy to decide what represents dysfunction, and some scholars have argued that we can never satisfactorily define *disease* or *disorder* (see, for example, Lilienfeld & Marino, 1995, 1999). The best we may be able to do is to consider how the apparent disease or disorder matches a "typical" profile of a disorder—for example, major depression or schizophrenia. We call this typical profile a *prototype*, and, as described in Chapter 3, the diagnostic criteria found throughout this book are all prototypes. This means that the patient may have only some symptoms of the disorder and still meet criteria for the disorder because those symptoms are close to the prototype.

Creation of the *fifth edition of the DSM (DSM-5)* is in progress, with publication due May 2013. But the basic definition of psychological disorder will be largely unchanged.

abnormal behavior Actions that are unexpected and often evaluated negatively because they differ from typical or usual behavior.

▲ Some religious behaviors may seem unusual to us but are culturally or individually appropriate.

The Science of Psychopathology

Psychopathology is the scientific study of psychological disorders. Within this field are clinical and counseling psychologists, psychiatrists, psychiatric social workers, psychiatric nurses, marriage and family therapists, and mental health counselors. *Clinical* and *counseling psychologists* receive the PhD degree (or sometimes an EdD, doctor of education, or PsyD, doctor of psychology) and follow a course of graduate-level study, lasting approximately 5 years, that prepares them to conduct research into the causes and treatment of psychological disorders and to diagnose, assess, and treat these disorders. Counseling psychologists tend to study and treat adjustment and vocational issues encountered by relatively healthy individuals, and clinical psychologists usually concentrate on more severe psychological disorders. Psychologists with other specialty training, such as experimental and social psychologists, investigate the basic determinants of behavior but do not assess or treat psychological disorders.

Psychiatrists first earn an MD degree in medical school and then specialize in psychiatry during residency training that lasts 3 to 4 years. Psychiatrists also investigate the nature and causes of psychological disorders, make diagnoses, and offer treatments. Many psychiatrists emphasize drugs or other biological treatments, although most also use psychosocial treatments.

Psychiatric social workers typically earn a master's degree in social work as they develop expertise in collecting information about the social and family situation of the individual with a psychological disorder. Social workers also treat disorders, often concentrating on family problems. *Psychiatric nurses* have advanced degrees and specialize in the care and treatment of patients with psychological disorders, usually in hospitals as part of a treatment team.

Finally, *marriage and family therapists* and *mental health counselors* typically spend 1–2 years earning a master's degree and are employed to provide clinical services by hospitals or clinics.

The Scientist–Practitioner

The most important recent development in psychopathology is the adoption of scientific methods to learn more about psychological disorders, their causes, and their treatment. Many mental health professionals take a scientific approach to their clinical work and therefore are called **scientist–practitioners** (Barlow, Hayes, & Nelson, 1984; Hayes, Barlow, & Nelson-Gray, 1999). Mental health practitioners function as scientist–practitioners in three ways (■ Figure 1.2). First, they keep up with the latest developments in their field and therefore use the most current diagnostic and treatment procedures. In this sense, they are consumers of the science of psychopathology.

Second, they evaluate their own assessments or treatment procedures to see whether they work. They are accountable not only to their patients, but also to government agencies and insurance companies, so they must demonstrate that their treatments work. Third, they conduct research that produces new information about disorders or their treatment. Such research attempts three basic things: describe psychological disorders, determine their causes, and treat them (■ Figure 1.3). These three categories compose an organizational structure that recurs throughout this book. A general overview of them will give you a clearer perspective on our efforts to understand abnormality.

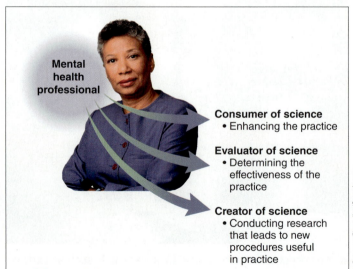

Mental health professional

Consumer of science
• Enhancing the practice

Evaluator of science
• Determining the effectiveness of the practice

Creator of science
• Conducting research that leads to new procedures useful in practice

■ **Figure 1.2** Functioning as a scientist–practitioner.

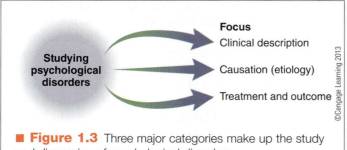

Figure 1.3 Three major categories make up the study and discussion of psychological disorders.

Clinical Description

In hospitals and clinics, we often say that a patient "presents" with a specific problem or we discuss the **presenting problem**. Describing Judy's presenting problem is the first step in determining her **clinical description**, the unique combination of behaviors, thoughts, and feelings that make up a specific disorder. The word *clinical* refers both to the types of disorders you would find in a clinic or hospital and to the activities connected with assessment and treatment.

An important function of the clinical description is to specify what makes the disorder different from normal behavior or from other disorders. Statistical data may also be relevant. For example, how many people in the population as a whole have the disorder? This figure is called the **prevalence** of the disorder. Statistics on how many new cases occur during a given period, such as a year, represent the **incidence** of the disorder. Other statistics include the *sex ratio*—that is, what percentage of males and females have the disorder—and the typical age of onset, which often differs from one disorder to another.

In addition, most disorders follow a particular pattern, or **course**. Some, such as schizophrenia (see Chapter 12), follow a *chronic course,* meaning that they tend to last a long time. Others, like mood disorders (see Chapter 6), follow an *episodic course,* in that the individual is likely to recover within a few months only to suffer a recurrence of the disorder at a later time. Still other disorders may have a *time-limited course,* meaning they will improve without treatment in a relatively short period.

Closely related to differences in course of disorders are differences in onset. Some disorders have an *acute onset,* meaning they begin suddenly; others develop gradually over an extended period, which is sometimes called an *insidious onset.* It is important to know the typical course of a disorder so we can know what to expect and how best to deal with the problem. For example, if someone is suffering from a mild disorder with acute onset that we know is time limited, we might advise the individual not to bother with expensive treatment. However, if the disorder is likely to last a long time (become chronic), the individual might want to seek treatment. The anticipated course of a disorder is called the **prognosis**. Age is an important part of the clinical description. A disorder occurring in childhood may present differently from the same disorder in adulthood or old age. Children experiencing severe anxiety often assume they are

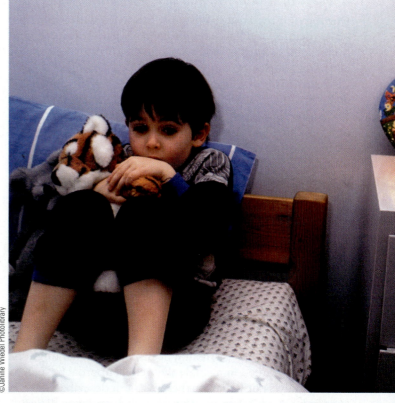

▲ Children experience panic and anxiety differently from adults, so their reactions may be mistaken for symptoms of physical illness.

physically ill. Because their thoughts and feelings are different from those experienced by adults with anxiety, children are often misdiagnosed and treated for a medical disorder.

We call the study of changes in behavior over time *developmental psychology,* and we refer to the study of changes in abnormal behavior as *developmental psychopathology.* Because we change throughout our lives, researchers study development in children, adolescents, adults, and older adults. Study of abnormal behavior across the entire age span is referred to as *life-span developmental psychopathology.*

psychopathology Scientific study of psychological disorders.
scientist–practitioner Mental health professional expected to apply scientific methods to his or her work. A scientist–practitioner must know the latest research on diagnosis and treatment, must evaluate his or her methods for effectiveness, and may generate research to discover information about disorders and their treatment.
presenting problem Original complaint reported by the client to the therapist. The actual treated problem may be a modification derived from the presenting problem.
clinical description Details of the combination of behaviors, thoughts, and feelings of an individual that make up a particular disorder.
prevalence Number of people displaying a disorder in the total population at any given time (compare with incidence).
incidence Number of new cases of a disorder appearing during a specific period (compare with prevalence).
course Pattern of development and change of a disorder over time.
prognosis Predicted development of a disorder over time.

Causation, Treatment, and Etiology Outcomes

Etiology, or the study of origins, has to do with why a disorder begins and includes biological, psychological, and social dimensions. Chapter 2 is devoted to this key aspect of abnormal psychology.

Treatment is also important to the study of psychological disorders. If a new drug or psychosocial treatment is successful in treating a disorder, it may give us some hints about the nature of the disorder and its causes. For example, if a drug with a specific effect within the nervous system alleviates a specific disorder, we know that something in that part of the nervous system might either be causing the disorder or helping maintain it. As you will see in the next chapter, psychology is rarely simple because the *effect* does not necessarily imply the *cause*. To use a common example, you might take an aspirin to relieve a headache you developed while taking an exam. If you then feel better, that does not mean the headache was caused by a lack of aspirin. Nevertheless, many people seek treatment for psychological disorders, and treatment can provide hints about the nature of the disorder.

In the past, textbooks emphasized treatment approaches in a general sense, with little attention to the disorder being treated. For example, a mental health professional might be thoroughly trained in a single theoretical approach, such as psychoanalysis or behavior therapy (both described later in the chapter), and then use that approach on every disorder. More recently, as our science has advanced, we have developed specific effective treatments that do not always adhere neatly to one theoretical approach or another but that have grown out of a deeper understanding of the disorder in question. For this reason, there are no separate chapters in this book on such types of treatment approaches as psychodynamic, cognitive behavioral, or humanistic. Rather, the latest and most effective drug and psychosocial treatments (nonmedical treatments that focus on psychological, social, and cultural factors) are described in the context of specific disorders in keeping with our integrative multidimensional perspective.

We now survey many early attempts to describe and treat abnormal behavior and to comprehend its causes. In Chapter 2 we examine contemporary views of causation and treatment. In Chapter 3 we discuss efforts to classify abnormal behavior and review research methods. In Chapters 4 through 13 we examine specific disorders. Finally, in Chapter 14 we examine legal, professional, and ethical issues relevant to psychological disorders and their treatment.

Historical Conceptions of Abnormal Behavior

How have people viewed abnormal behavior? For thousands of years, humans have tried to explain and control problematic behavior. But our efforts always derive from the theories or models of behavior popular at the time. The purpose of these models is to explain why someone is "acting like that." Three major models that have guided us date back to the beginnings of civilization.

Humans have always supposed that agents outside our bodies and environment influence our behavior, thinking, and emotions. These agents, which might be divinities, demons, spirits, or other phenomena such as magnetic fields or the moon or the stars, are the driving forces behind the *supernatural model*. In addition, the mind has often been called the *soul* or the *psyche* and considered separate from the body. Although many have thought that the mind can influence the body and, in turn, the body can influence the mind, most philosophers looked for causes of abnormal behavior in one or the other. This split gave rise to two traditions of thought about abnormal behavior: the *biological model* and the *psychological model*.

Concept Check 1.1

Part A

Write the letter for any or all of the following definitions of abnormality in the blanks: (a) societal norm violation, (b) impairment in functioning, (c) dysfunction, (d) distress.

1. Miguel recently began feeling sad and lonely. Although still able to function, he finds himself feeling down much of the time and worries about what is happening to him. Which definitions of abnormality apply to Miguel's situation? _____

2. Three weeks ago, Jane, a 35-year-old business executive, stopped showering, refused to leave her apartment, and started watching television talk shows. Threats of being fired have failed to bring Jane back to reality. Which of the definitions seems to describe Jane's behavior? _____

Part B

Match the following words that are used in clinical descriptions with their corresponding examples: (a) presenting problem, (b) prevalence, (c) incidence, (d) prognosis, (e) course, (f) etiology.

3. Maria should recover quickly with no intervention. Without treatment, John will deteriorate rapidly. _____

4. Three new cases of bulimia have been reported in this county during the past month and only one in the next county. _____

5. Elizabeth visited the campus mental health center because of her increasing feelings of guilt and anxiety. _____

6. Biological, psychological, and social influences all contribute to a variety of disorders. _____

7. The pattern a disorder follows can be chronic, time limited, or episodic. _____

8. How many people in the population as a whole suffer from obsessive–compulsive disorder? _____

What supernatural influences were formerly believed to explain abnormal behavior? For much of our recorded history, deviant behavior has been considered a reflection of the battle between good and evil. When confronted with unexplainable, irrational behavior, people perceived evil.

Demons and Witches

One strong current of opinion put the causes and treatment of psychological disorders squarely in the realm of the supernatural. During the last quarter of the 14th century, religious and lay authorities supported these popular superstitions and society as a whole began to believe more strongly in the existence and power of demons and witches.

The bizarre behavior of people afflicted with psychological disorders was seen as the work of the devil and witches. It followed that individuals "possessed" by evil spirits were probably responsible for any misfortune experienced by the townspeople, which inspired drastic action against the possessed. Treatments included **exorcism**, in which various religious rituals were performed to rid the victim of evil spirits. Other approaches included shaving the pattern of a cross in the hair of the victim's head and securing sufferers to a wall near the front of a church so that they might benefit from hearing Mass.

The conviction that sorcery and witches are causes of madness and other evils continued into the 15th century, and evil continued to be blamed for unexplainable behavior, as evidenced by the Salem, Massachusetts, witch trials.

Stress and Melancholy

An equally strong opinion reflected the view that insanity was a natural phenomenon, caused by mental or emotional stress, and was curable (Alexander & Selesnick, 1966; Maher & Maher, 1985a). Mental depression and anxiety were recognized as illnesses (Kemp, 1990; Schoeneman, 1977), although the church identified symptoms such as despair and lethargy with the sin of *acedia*, or sloth (Tuchman, 1978). Common treatments were rest, sleep, and a healthy environment. Other treatments included baths, ointments, and various potions. Indeed, during the 14th and 15th centuries, people with insanity, along with those

▲ During the Middle Ages, individuals with psychological disorders were sometimes thought to be possessed by evil spirits that had to be exorcised through rituals.

with physical deformities or disabilities, were often moved from house to house in medieval villages as neighbors took turns caring for them. We now know that keeping people with psychological disturbances in their own community is beneficial (see Chapter 12).

One of the chief advisers to the king of France, Nicholas Oresme, suggested that melancholy (depression) was the source of some bizarre behavior, rather than demons. Oresme pointed out that much of the evidence for the existence of sorcery and witchcraft, particularly among those considered insane, was obtained from people who were tortured and who, quite understandably, confessed to anything.

These conflicting natural and supernatural explanations for mental disorders are represented more or less strongly in historical works, depending on the sources consulted by historians. Some assumed that demonic influences were the predominant explanations of abnormal behavior during the Middle Ages (for example, Zilboorg & Henry, 1941); others believed that the supernatural had little or no influ-

etiology Cause or source of a disorder.
exorcism Religious ritual that attributes disordered behavior to possession by demons and seeks to treat the individual by driving the demons from the body.

ence. As we see in the handling of the severe psychological disorder experienced by late-14th-century King Charles VI of France, both influences were strong, sometimes alternating in the treatment of the same case.

Charles VI ◆ The Mad King

In the summer of 1392, King Charles VI of France was under a great deal of stress. As he rode with his army to the province of Brittany, a nearby aide dropped his lance with a loud clatter and the king, thinking he was under attack, turned on his own army, killing several prominent knights before being subdued from behind. The army immediately marched back to Paris. The king's lieutenants and advisers concluded that he was mad.

During the following years, at his worst, the king hid in a corner of his castle believing he was made of glass or roamed the corridors howling like a wolf. At other times he couldn't remember who or what he was. He became fearful and enraged whenever he saw his own royal coat of arms and would try to destroy it if it was brought near him.

▲ King Charles VI

The people of Paris were devastated by their leader's apparent madness. Some thought it reflected God's anger, but most thought it was caused by sorcery, a belief strengthened by a great drought that dried up the ponds and rivers, causing cattle to die of thirst. Merchants claimed their worst losses in 20 years.

Naturally, the king was given the best care available. The most famous healer in the land was a 92-year-old physician whose treatment program included moving the king to one of his residences in the country where the air was thought to be the cleanest in the land. The physician prescribed rest, relaxation, and recreation. After some time, the king seemed to recover. Unfortunately, the physician died and the insanity of King Charles VI returned more seriously than before. This time, however, he came under the influence of the conflicting crosscurrent of supernatural causation. "An unkempt evil-eyed charlatan and pseudo-mystic named Arnaut Guilhem was allowed to treat Charles on his claim of possessing a book given by God to Adam by means of which man could overcome all affliction resulting from original sin" (Tuchman, 1978, p. 514). Guilhem insisted that the king's malady was caused by sorcery.

Various remedies and rituals of all kinds were tried, but none worked. High-ranking officials and doctors of the university called for the "sorcerers" to be discovered and punished. "On one occasion, two Augustinian friars, after getting no results from magic incantations and a liquid made from powdered pearls, proposed to cut incisions in the king's head. When this was not allowed by the king's council, the friars accused those who opposed their recommendation of sorcery" (Tuchman, 1978, p. 514). Even the king himself, during his lucid moments, came to believe that the source of madness was evil and sorcery.

Treatments for Possession

Exorcisms at least have the virtue of being relatively painless. Interestingly, they sometimes work, as do other forms of faith healing, for reasons we explore in subsequent chapters. But what if they did not? In the Middle Ages if exorcism failed, some authorities thought that steps were necessary to make the body uninhabitable by evil spirits, and many people were subjected to confinement, beatings, and other forms of torture (Kemp, 1990).

Somewhere along the way, a creative "therapist" decided that hanging people over a pit full of poisonous snakes might scare the evil spirits right out of their bodies. Strangely, this approach sometimes worked; the most disturbed individuals would suddenly come to their senses, if only temporarily. Many other treatments based on the hypothesized therapeutic element of shock were developed, including dunkings in ice-cold water.

Mass Hysteria

Another fascinating phenomenon is characterized by large-scale outbreaks of bizarre behavior. During the Middle Ages they lent support to the notion of possession. In Europe whole groups of people were simultaneously compelled to run out in the streets, dance, shout, rave, and jump around in patterns as if they were at a particularly wild party (called a *rave* even then) but without the

L'hydrothérapie.

▲ In hydrotherapy, patients were shocked back to their senses by being submerged in ice-cold water.

Adriana is an 18-year-old woman who has become concerned about her increasingly excessive nervousness, irritability, loss of appetite, and insomnia. According to the biological tradition of abnormal behavior, what is the best explanation for Adriana's experiences? How should they be treated?

As the understanding of human biology has changed over time, so too have the biological models that guide the conceptualization and treatment of psychopathology. Unfortunately, some approaches to understanding and treating psychopathology have been unfavorable for women. An interesting and relevant case is the diagnosis of hysteria to describe general psychological complaints among women. In ancient times, the Greek physician Hippocrates would have attributed Adriana's symptoms to a biological condition known as "wandering womb," or the movement of Adriana's uterus around her body because of a lack of sexual intercourse. Hippocrates often prescribed marriage as an effective treatment for hysteria. Although this idea may seem absurd in retrospect, hysteria was a popular diagnosis for a range of psychological complaints expressed by women. As recently as the late 19th century, Adriana's complaints still would have been attributed to hysteria, although by that time the idea of a wandering womb had been replaced with the belief that hysteria was caused by sexual dissatisfaction. As a result, the prescribed treatment often was vaginal massage to enhance sexual satisfaction.

In the early 20th century, Sigmund Freud (1856–1939) proposed that hysteria actually worked in the opposite direction and suggested that many general physical complaints reported by young women in the 1900s were the result of the "conversion" of unacceptable sexual fantasies into more acceptable outlets. This was an influential theory and one that ultimately led to the inclusion of a diagnosis of conversion hysteria in the DSM.

More recent scientific advances have abandoned the concept of hysteria, which has been replaced with more objective, specific, and gender-neutral diagnoses such as anxiety disorders, depressive disorders, and somatoform disorders. As a result of research on genetics and neuroscience, simple biological explanations such as the wandering womb theory also have been replaced with more sophisticated models of biological influences on psychopathology. Despite these modern-day advances, history suggests that our current approaches to conceptualizing and treating psychopathology will someday be looked on as primitive and naïve. In the meantime, psychologists continue to use currently available science as a guide to explaining and treating psychopathology.

music. This behavior was known by several names, including Saint Vitus's Dance and tarantism. Several reasons were offered in addition to possession. One reasonable guess was reaction to insect bites. Another possibility was what we now call *mass hysteria*. Consider the following example.

Modern Mass Hysteria

One Friday afternoon an alarm sounded over the public address system of a community hospital calling all physicians to the emergency room. Arriving from a local school in a fleet of ambulances were 17 students and 4 teachers who reported dizziness, headache, nausea, and stomach pains. Some were vomiting; most were hyperventilating.

All the students and teachers had been in four classrooms, two on each side of the hallway. The incident began when a 14-year-old girl reported a smell that seemed to be coming from a vent. She fell to the floor, crying and complaining that her stomach hurt and her eyes stung. Soon, many of the students and most of the teachers in the four adjoining classrooms, who could see and hear what was happening, experienced similar symptoms. Of 86 susceptible people (82 students and 4 teachers in the four classrooms), 21 patients (17 students and 4 teachers) experienced symptoms severe enough to be evaluated at the hospital. Inspection of the school building by public health authorities revealed no apparent cause for the reactions, and physical examinations revealed no physical abnormalities. All the patients were sent home and quickly recovered (Rockney & Lemke, 1992).

Mass hysteria may simply demonstrate the phenomenon of *emotion contagion,* in which the experience of an emotion seems to spread to those around us (Hatfield, Cacioppo, & Rapson, 1994; Wang, 2006). If someone nearby becomes frightened or sad, chances are that for the moment you also will feel fear or sadness. When this kind of experience escalates into full-blown panic, whole communities are affected (Barlow, 2002). People are also suggestible when they are in states of high emotion. Therefore, if one person identifies a "cause" of the problem, others will probably assume that their own reactions have the same source. In popular language, this shared response is sometimes referred to as *mob psychology.*

The Moon and the Stars

Paracelsus, a Swiss physician who lived from 1493 to 1541, rejected notions of possession by the devil, suggesting instead that the movements of the moon and stars had profound effects on people's psychological functioning. This influential theory inspired the word *lunatic,* which is derived from the Latin word for moon, *luna.* You might hear some of your friends explain something crazy they did last night by saying, "It must have been the full moon." Despite much ridicule, millions of people around the world are convinced that their behavior is influenced by the stages of the moon or the position of the stars. This belief is most noticeable today in followers of astrology, who hold that their behavior and the major events in their lives can be predicted by their day-to-day relationship to the position of the planets. However, no serious evidence has ever confirmed such a connection.

Comments

The supernatural tradition in psychopathology is alive and well, although it is relegated, for the most part, to small religious sects and primitive cultures. Members of organized religions look to psychology and medical science for help with psychological disorders; in fact, the Roman Catholic Church requires that all health-care resources be exhausted before spiritual solutions such as exorcism can be considered. Miraculous cures are sometimes achieved by exorcism, rituals, and other methods that seem to have little connection with modern science. But such cases are relatively rare, and almost no one would advocate supernatural treatment for severe psychological disorders except, perhaps, as a last resort.

▲ Emotions are contagious and can escalate into mass hysteria.

AP Photo/Hatem Moussa

The Biological Tradition

› **What are the underlying assumptions of the biological approach to understanding abnormal behavior?**

Physical causes of mental disorders have been sought since antiquity. Important to the biological tradition are a man, Hippocrates; a disease, syphilis; and the early consequences of believing that psychological disorders are biologically caused.

Hippocrates and Galen

The Greek physician Hippocrates (460–377 B.C.) is considered the father of modern Western medicine. In a body of work called the *Hippocratic Corpus,* written between 450 and 350 B.C. (Maher & Maher, 1985a), he and others suggested that psychological disorders could be treated like any other disease. They did not limit their search to the general area of "disease"; they believed psychological disorders might also be caused by brain pathology or head trauma and could be influenced by heredity (genetics). Hippocrates considered the brain to be the seat of wisdom, consciousness, intelligence, and emotion. Therefore, disorders involving these functions would logically be located in the brain.

Hippocrates also recognized the importance of psychological and interpersonal contributions to psychopathology.

The Roman physician Galen (approximately 129–198 A.D.) adopted these ideas and developed them further, creating an influential school of thought that extended well into the 19th century. One of the more interesting legacies of the Hippocratic–Galenic approach is the *humoral theory* of disorders. Hippocrates assumed that normal brain functioning was related to four bodily fluids or *humors:* blood, black bile, yellow bile, and phlegm. Blood came from the heart, black bile from the spleen, phlegm from the brain, and choler or yellow bile from the liver. Physicians believed that disease resulted from too much or too little of one of the humors; for example, too much black bile was thought to cause melancholia (depression). In fact, the term *melancholy,* from *melancholer,* which means black bile, is still used to refer to aspects of depression. The humoral theory was, perhaps, the first example of associating psychological disorders with a "chemical imbalance," an approach that is widespread today.

▲ Bloodletting, the extraction of blood from patients, was intended to restore the balance of humors in the body.

The four humors were related to the Greeks' conception of the four basic qualities: heat, dryness, moisture, and cold. Each humor was associated with one of these qualities. Terms derived from the four humors are still sometimes applied to personality traits. For example, *sanguine* (red, like blood) describes someone who is ruddy in complexion and cheerful and optimistic, although insomnia and delirium were thought to be caused by excessive blood in the brain. *Melancholic* means depressive (depression was thought to be caused by black bile flooding the brain). A *phlegmatic* personality (from the humor phlegm) indicates apathy and sluggishness but can also mean being calm under stress. A *choleric* person (from yellow bile or choler) is hot tempered (Maher & Maher, 1985a).

Excess humors were treated by regulating the environment to increase or decrease heat, dryness, moisture, or cold. One reason King Charles VI's physician moved him to the countryside was to restore the balance in his humors (Kemp, 1990). In addition to rest, good nutrition, and exercise, two treatments were developed. In one, *bleeding* or *bloodletting*, a carefully measured amount of blood was removed from the body, often with leeches. The other was to induce vomiting; indeed, in a well-known treatise on depression published in 1621, *Anatomy of Melancholy*, Robert Burton recommended eating tobacco and a half-boiled cabbage to induce vomiting (Burton, 1621/1977). If Judy had lived 300 years ago, she might have been diagnosed with an illness, a brain disorder, or some other physical problem, perhaps related to excessive humors, and been given the proper medical treatments of the day, including bed rest, a healthful diet, and exercise.

In ancient China and throughout Asia, a similar idea existed. But rather than "humors," the Chinese focused on

the movement of air or "wind" throughout the body. Unexplained mental disorders were caused by blockages of wind or the presence of cold, dark wind (yin) as opposed to warm, life-sustaining wind (yang). Treatment involved restoring proper flow of wind through various methods, including acupuncture.

Hippocrates also coined the word *hysteria* to describe a concept he learned from the Egyptians, who had identified what we now call the *somatoform disorders*. In these disorders, symptoms, such as paralysis and some kinds of blindness, appear to be the result of a problem for which no physical cause can be found. Because these disorders occurred primarily in women, physicians assumed that they were restricted to women. They also presumed a cause: The empty uterus wandered to various parts of the body in search of conception (the Greek for uterus is *hysteron*). Numerous physical symptoms reflected the location of the wandering uterus. The prescribed cure might be marriage or, occasionally, fumigation of the vagina to lure the uterus back to its natural location (Alexander & Selesnick, 1966). Knowledge of physiology eventually disproved the wandering uterus theory; however, the tendency to stigmatize dramatic women as hysterical continued into the 1970s. As you will learn in Chapter 5, somatoform disorders are not limited to one sex.

The 19th Century

The biological tradition waxed and waned during the centuries after Hippocrates and Galen but was reinvigorated in the 19th century because of two factors: the discovery of the nature and cause of syphilis and strong support from the well-respected American psychiatrist John P. Grey.

Syphilis

Behavioral and cognitive symptoms of what we now know as *advanced syphilis,* a sexually transmitted disease caused by a bacterial microorganism entering the brain, include believing that everyone is plotting against you (delusion of persecution) or that you are God (delusion of grandeur). Although these symptoms are similar to those of *psychosis*—psychological disorders characterized in part by beliefs and/or perceptions that are not based in reality—researchers recognized that a subgroup of apparently psychotic patients deteriorated steadily, becoming paralyzed and dying within 5 years of onset. This course of events contrasted with that of most psychotic patients, who remained fairly stable. In 1825, the condition was designated a disease, *general paresis,* because it had consistent symptoms (presentation) and a consistent course that resulted in death. The relationship between general paresis and syphilis was only gradually established. Louis Pasteur's germ theory of disease, around 1870, facilitated the identification of the microorganism that caused syphilis.

Of equal importance was the discovery of a cure for general paresis. Physicians observed a surprising recovery in patients with general paresis who had contracted malaria, so they injected other patients with blood from a soldier who was ill with malaria. Many recovered because the high fever "burned out" the syphilis bacteria. Obviously, this type of experiment would not be ethically possible today. Ultimately, investigators discovered that penicillin cures syphilis, but with the malaria cure, "madness" and associated symptoms for the first time were traced directly to a curable infection. Many mental health professionals assumed that comparable causes and cures might be discovered for all psychological disorders.

John P. Grey

The champion of the biological tradition in the United States was the most influential American psychiatrist of the time, John P. Grey (Bockoven, 1963). In 1854, Grey was appointed superintendent of the Utica State Hospital in New York and became editor of the *American Journal of Insanity*, the precursor of the *American Journal of Psychiatry*. Grey held that the causes of insanity were *always* physical. Therefore, mentally ill patients should be treated as if they were physically ill, with treatment including rest, diet, and proper room temperature and ventilation. Grey even invented the rotary fan to ventilate his large hospital.

Under Grey's leadership, conditions in hospitals improved and they became more humane institutions. But in subsequent years they also became so large that individual attention was not possible.

In fact, leaders in psychiatry became alarmed at the increasing size and impersonality of mental hospitals and recommended that they be downsized. It was almost 100 years before the community mental health movement was successful in reducing the population of mental hospitals with the controversial policy of deinstitutionalization, in which patients were released into their communities. Unfortunately, this practice has as many negative consequences as positive ones, including a large increase in the number of homeless patients on city streets.

The Development of Biological Treatments

Renewed interest in the biological origin of psychological disorders led to greatly increased understanding of biological contributions to psychopathology and to the development of new treatments. In the 1930s, electric shock and brain surgery were often used. Their effects, and the effects of new drugs, were discovered by accident. For example, insulin was occasionally given to stimulate appetite in psychotic patients who were not eating, but it also seemed to calm them down. In 1927, a Viennese physician, Manfred Sakel, began using increasingly higher dosages until, finally, patients convulsed and became temporarily comatose (Sakel, 1958). Some actually recovered their mental health, and their recovery was attributed to the convulsions. The procedure became known as *insulin shock therapy*, but it was abandoned because it often resulted in coma or death. Other methods of producing convulsions had to be found.

In the 1920s, Hungarian psychiatrist Joseph von Meduna observed that schizophrenia was rarely found in individu-

als with epilepsy. Some of his followers concluded that induced brain seizures might cure schizophrenia. Following suggestions on the possible benefits of applying electric shock directly to the brain—notably, by two Italian physicians, Ugo Cerletti and Lucio Bini, in 1938—a surgeon in London treated a depressed patient by sending six small shocks directly through his brain, producing convulsions (Hunt, 1980). The patient recovered. Although greatly modified, shock treatment is still used. The controversial modern uses of *electroconvulsive therapy* are described in Chapter 6. During the 1950s, the first effective drugs for severe psychotic disorders were developed in a systematic way. Before that time, a number of medicinal substances, including opium, had been used as sedatives, along with countless herbs and folk remedies (Alexander & Selesnick, 1966). With the discovery of *Rauwolfia serpentine* (later renamed *reserpine*) and another class of drugs called *neuroleptics* (major tranquilizers), for the first time hallucinatory and delusional thought processes could be diminished in some patients; these drugs also controlled agitation and aggressiveness. Other discoveries included *benzodiazepines* (minor tranquilizers), which seemed to reduce anxiety. By the 1970s, the benzodiazepines (such as Valium and Librium) were among the most widely prescribed drugs in the world. As drawbacks of tranquilizers became apparent, prescriptions decreased somewhat (we discuss the benzodiazepines in more detail in Chapters 4 and 10).

Throughout the centuries, as Alexander and Selesnick point out, "[t]he general pattern of drug therapy for mental illness has been one of initial enthusiasm followed by disappointment" (1966, p. 287). For example, bromides, a class of sedating drugs, were used at the end of the 19th century and beginning of the 20th century to treat anxiety and other psychological disorders. By the 1920s, they were reported as being effective for many serious psychological and emotional symptoms. When their side effects became widely known and experience began to show that their overall effectiveness was modest, bromides largely disappeared from the scene.

Neuroleptics have also been used less as attention has focused on side effects such as tremors and shaking. However, the positive effects of these drugs on some patients' psychotic symptoms revitalized the search both for biological contributions to psychological disorders and for new and more powerful drugs.

Consequences of the Biological Tradition

In the late 19th century, Grey and his colleagues ironically reduced interest in treating mental patients because they thought mental disorders were the result of some as-yet-undiscovered brain pathology and were therefore incurable. The only available course of action was to hospitalize these patients. Around the turn of the century, some nurses documented clinical success in treating mental patients but were prevented from treating others for fear of raising hopes of a cure among family members. In place of treatment, interest centered on diagnosis and the study of brain pathology itself.

Emil Kraepelin (1856–1926) was the dominant figure during this period. He was influential in advocating the major ideas of the biological tradition, but he was little involved in treatment. His lasting contribution was in the area of diagnosis and classification. Kraepelin (1913) was one of the first to distinguish among various psychological disorders, seeing that each may have a different age of onset, different symptoms, and probably a different cause.

By the end of the 1800s, a scientific approach to psychological disorders and their classification had begun with the search for biological causes. Furthermore, treatment was based on humane principles. However, there were many drawbacks, the most unfortunate being that treatment was all but eliminated in some settings, despite the availability of some effective approaches. It is to these that we now turn.

Concept Check 1.2

Check your understanding of these historical theories and match them to the treatments used to "cure" abnormal behavior: (a) bloodletting; induced vomiting; (b) patient placed in socially facilitative environments; and (c) exorcism; burning at the stake.

1. Supernatural causes; evil demons took over victims' bodies and controlled their behaviors. _____

2. The humoral theory reflected the belief that normal functioning of the brain required a balance of four bodily fluids or humors. _____

3. Maladaptive behavior was caused by poor social and cultural influences within the environment. _____

The Psychological Tradition

› How do the psychological approaches of psychoanalysis, humanism, and behaviorism explain abnormal behavior?

It is a long leap from evil spirits to brain pathology as the cause of psychological disorders. In the intervening centuries, how did psychological development come to be viewed in an interpersonal and social context? In fact, this approach has a long tradition. Plato, for example, thought that the two causes of maladaptive behavior were the social and cultural influences in one's life and the learning that took place in that environment. If something was wrong in the environment, such as abusive parents, one's impulses and emotions would overcome reason. The best treatment was to reeducate the individual so that reason would predominate (Maher & Maher, 1985a). This was a precursor to modern **psychosocial treatment** approaches to the treatment of pyschopathology, which focus not only on psychological factors, but also on social and cultural ones. Other early philosophers, including Aristotle, also emphasized the influence of social environment and early learning on later psychopathology. They wrote about the importance of fantasies, dreams, and cognitions and thus anticipated later developments in psychoanalytic thought and cognitive science. They also advocated humane care for individuals with psychological disturbances.

Moral Therapy

During the first half of the 19th century, a psychosocial approach called **moral therapy** became influential. (The term *moral* meant emotional or psychological rather than a code of conduct.) Its tenets included treating patients as normally as possible in a setting that encouraged social interaction (Bockoven, 1963). Relationships were carefully nurtured. Individual attention emphasized positive consequences for appropriate behavior, and restraint and seclusion were eliminated.

As with the biological tradition, the principles of moral therapy date back to Plato and beyond. For example, the Greek Asclepiad Temples of the 6th century B.C. housed the chronically ill, including those with psychological disorders. Here, patients were well cared for, massaged, and provided with soothing music. Similar practices were evident in Muslim countries in the Middle East (Millon, 2004). But moral therapy as a system originated with the French psychiatrist Philippe Pinel (1745–1826) and his associate Jean-Baptiste Pussin (1746–1811), the superintendent of the Parisian hospital La Bicêtre (Gerard, 1997; Zilboorg & Henry, 1941).

When Pinel arrived in 1791, Pussin had already removed chains used to restrain patients and instituted humane psychological interventions. Pussin persuaded Pinel to go along with the changes. Much to Pinel's credit, he did, first at La Bicêtre and then at the women's hospital

psychosocial treatment Treatment practices that focus on social and cultural factors (such as family experience), as well as psychological influences. These approaches include cognitive, behavioral, and interpersonal methods.

moral therapy Psychosocial approach in the 19th century that involved treating patients as normally as possible in normal environments.

Salpétrière (Gerard, 1997; Maher & Maher, 1985b; Weiner, 1979).

After William Tuke (1732–1822) followed Pinel's lead in England, Benjamin Rush (1745–1813), often considered the founder of American psychiatry, introduced moral therapy at Pennsylvania Hospital. *Asylums* had appeared in the 16th century, but they were more like prisons than hospitals. It was the rise of moral therapy in Europe and the United States that made asylums habitable and even therapeutic.

In 1833, Horace Mann, chairman of the board of trustees of the Worcester State Hospital, reported on 32 patients who had been given up as incurable. These patients were treated with moral therapy, cured, and released to their families. Of 100 patients who were viciously assaultive before treatment, no more than 12 continued to be violent a year after beginning treatment. Before treatment, 40 patients had routinely torn off clothes provided by attendants; only 8 continued this behavior after treatment. These statistics would be remarkable even today (Bockoven, 1963).

Asylum Reform and the Decline of Moral Therapy

After the mid-19th century, humane treatment declined. It was widely recognized that moral therapy worked best when the number of patients in an institution was 200 or fewer, allowing for a great deal of individual attention. But after the Civil War, enormous waves of immigrants arrived in the United States, and patient loads in existing hospitals increased to 1,000 or 2,000, and even more. Because immigrants were thought not to deserve the same privileges as native-born Americans (whose ancestors had immigrated perhaps only 50 or 100 years earlier!), they were not given moral treatments even when there were sufficient hospital personnel.

A second reason for the decline of moral therapy has an unlikely source. Dorothea Dix (1802–1887) campaigned for reform in the treatment of insanity. Having worked in various institutions, she had firsthand knowledge of the deplorable conditions imposed on patients with insanity, and she made it her life's work to inform the American public of these abuses. Her work became known as the **mental hygiene movement**.

In addition to improving the standards of care, Dix worked hard to make sure everyone who needed care received it. Through her efforts, humane treatment became more widely available.

▲ Patients with psychological disorders were freed from chains and shackles as a result of the influence of Philippe Pinel (1745–1826), a pioneer in making mental institutions more humane.

▲ Dorothea Dix (1802–1887) began the mental hygiene movement and spent much of her life campaigning for reform in the treatment of the mentally ill.

An unforeseen consequence of Dix's heroic efforts was a substantial increase in the number of mental patients. This influx led to a rapid transition from moral therapy to custodial care. Dix reformed our asylums and inspired the construction of numerous new institutions here and abroad. But even her tireless efforts could not ensure sufficient staffing to allow the individual attention necessary to moral therapy. A final blow was the decision, in the middle of the 19th century, that mental illness was caused by brain pathology and, therefore, was incurable.

The psychological tradition lay dormant for a time, only to reemerge in several different schools of thought in the 20th century. The first major approach was **psychoanalysis**, based on Sigmund Freud's (1856–1939) theory of the structure of the mind and the role of unconscious processes in determining behavior. The second was **behaviorism**, associated with John B. Watson, Ivan Pavlov, and B. F. Skinner, which focuses on how learning and adaptation affect the development of psychopathology.

Psychoanalytic Theory

Have you ever felt as if someone cast a spell on you? Have you ever been mesmerized by a look across the classroom from a beautiful man or woman or a stare from a rock musician as you sat down in front at a concert? If so, you have something in common with the patients of Anton Mesmer (1734–1815) and with millions of people who have been hypnotized. Mesmer suggested to his patients that their problem was caused by an undetectable fluid found in all living organisms called "animal magnetism," which could become blocked.

Mesmer had his patients sit in a dark room around a large vat of chemicals with rods extending from it and touching them. Dressed in flowing robes, he might then identify and tap various areas of their bodies where their "animal magnetism" was blocked, while suggesting strongly that they were being cured. Because of his unusual techniques, Mesmer was considered an oddity and strongly opposed by the medical establishment (Winter, 1998). Many scientists and physicians were interested in Mesmer's powerful methods of suggestion. One of the best known, Jean-Martin Charcot (1825–1893), was head of the Salpêtrière Hospital in Paris, where Philippe Pinel had introduced psychological treatments several generations earlier. Charcot demonstrated that some techniques of mesmerism were effective with a number of psychological disorders, and he did much to legitimize the practice of hypnosis. In 1885 a young man named Sigmund Freud came from Vienna to study with Charcot.

After returning from France, Freud teamed up with Josef Breuer (1842–1925), who had experimented with a somewhat different hypnotic procedure. While his patients were in the highly suggestible state of hypnosis, Breuer asked them to describe their problems, conflicts, and fears. Breuer observed two important phenomena during this

▲ Jean Charcot (1825–1893) studied hypnosis and influenced Sigmund Freud to consider psychosocial approaches to psychological disorders.

process. First, patients often became extremely emotional as they talked and felt relieved and improved after emerging from the hypnotic state. Second, seldom would they have gained an understanding of the relationship between their emotional problems and their psychological disorder. In fact, it was difficult or impossible for them to recall some details they had described under hypnosis. In other words, the material seemed to be beyond the awareness of the patient. With this observation, Breuer and Freud had "discovered" the **unconscious** mind and its apparent influence on the production of psychological disorders.

They also discovered that it is therapeutic to recall emotional trauma that has been made unconscious and to release the accompanying tension. This release of emotional material became known as **catharsis**. A fuller understanding of the relationship between current emotions and earlier events is referred to as *insight*. As you shall see throughout this book, the existence of "unconscious" memories and feelings and the importance of processing emotion-filled information have been verified.

Freud and Breuer's theories were based on case observations. An example is Breuer's description of his treatment

▲ Anton Mesmer (1734–1815) and other early therapists used strong suggestions to cure their patients, who were often hypnotized.

mental hygiene movement Mid-19th-century effort to improve care of the mentally disordered by informing the public of their mistreatment.
psychoanalysis Assessment and therapy pioneered by Sigmund Freud that emphasizes exploration of, and insight into, unconscious processes and conflicts.
behaviorism Explanation of human behavior, including dysfunction, based on principles of learning and adaptation derived from experimental psychology.
unconscious Part of the psychic makeup that is outside the awareness of the person.
catharsis Rapid or sudden release of emotional tension thought to be an important factor in psychoanalytic therapy.

of "hysterical" symptoms in Anna O. in 1895 (Breuer & Freud, 1957). Anna O. was a bright, attractive young woman who was perfectly healthy until she reached 21 years of age. Shortly before her problems began, her father developed a chronic illness that led to his death. Throughout his illness, Anna O. had cared for him, spending endless hours at his bedside. Five months after her father became ill, Anna noticed that during the day her vision blurred and that from time to time she had difficulty moving her right arm and both legs. Soon she began to experience difficulty speaking, and her behavior became unpredictable. Shortly thereafter, she consulted Breuer.

In a series of treatment sessions, Breuer dealt with one symptom at a time through hypnosis and subsequent "talking through," tracing each symptom to its hypothetical causation in circumstances surrounding the death of Anna's father. One at a time her "hysterical" ailments disappeared, but only after treatment was administered for each respective behavior. This process of treating one behavior at a time fulfills a basic requirement for drawing scientific conclusions about the effects of treatment in an individual case study. Freud expanded these basic observations into the **psychoanalytic model**, the most comprehensive theory yet constructed on the development and structure of our personalities. He also speculated on where this development could go wrong and produce psychological disorders. Although many of Freud's views changed over time, the basic principles of mental functioning that he originally proposed remained constant through his writings and are still applied by psychoanalysts today.

Although most of it remains unproven, psychoanalytic theory has had a strong influence, and it is important to be familiar with its basic ideas; what follows is a brief outline of the theory. We focus on its three major facets: (1) the structure of the mind and the distinct functions of personality that sometimes clash with one another; (2) the defense mechanisms with which the mind defends itself from these conflicts; and (3) the stages of psychosexual development that contribute to our inner conflicts.

▲ Bertha Pappenheim (1859–1936), famous as Anna O., was described as "hysterical" by Breuer.

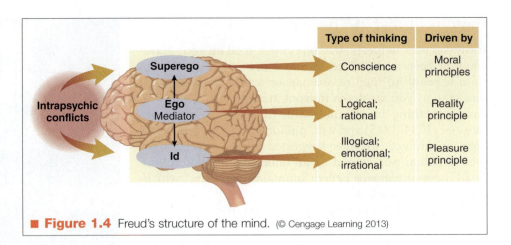

	Type of thinking	Driven by
Superego	Conscience	Moral principles
Ego Mediator	Logical; rational	Reality principle
Id	Illogical; emotional; irrational	Pleasure principle

■ **Figure 1.4** Freud's structure of the mind. (© Cengage Learning 2013)

The Structure of the Mind

The mind, according to Freud, has three major parts: the id, ego, and superego (■ Figure 1.4). Although you may have heard these terms, you may not be aware of their meaning. The **id** is the source of our strong sexual and aggressive feelings or energies. It is, basically, the animal within us; if totally unchecked, it would make us all rapists or killers. The energy or drive within the id is the *libido*. Even today, some people explain low sex drive as an absence of libido. A less important source of energy is the death instinct, or *thanatos*. These two basic drives, toward life and fulfillment on the one hand and death and destruction on the other, are continually in opposition.

The id operates according to the *pleasure principle*, trying to maximize pleasure and eliminate any associated tension or conflicts. The goal of pleasure, which is particularly prominent in childhood, often conflicts with social rules. The id has its own characteristic way of processing information; referred to as the *primary process*, this type of thinking is emotional; irrational; illogical; filled with fantasies; and preoccupied with sex, aggression, selfishness, and envy.

Fortunately for all of us, in Freud's view, the id's selfish and sometimes dangerous drives do not go unchecked. In fact, only a few months into life, we know we must find ways to meet our basic needs without offending everyone around us. Put yet another way, we must act realistically. The part of our mind that ensures that we act realistically is called the **ego**, and it operates according to the *reality principle*. The cognitive operations or thinking styles of the ego are characterized by logic and reason and are referred to as the *secondary process*, as opposed to the illogical and irrational primary process of the id.

The third important structure within the mind, the **superego**, or conscience, represents the *moral principles* instilled in us by our parents and our culture. It is the voice within us that nags at us when we know we're doing something wrong. Because the purpose of the superego is to counteract the potentially dangerous aggressive and sexual drives of the id, the basis for conflict is apparent.

▲ Sigmund Freud (1856–1939) is considered the founder of psychoanalysis.

The role of the ego is to mediate conflict between the id and the superego. The ego is often referred to as the executive or manager of our minds. If it mediates successfully, we can go on to higher intellectual and creative pursuits. If it is unsuccessful and the id or superego becomes too strong, conflict will overtake us and psychological disorders will develop. Because these conflicts are all within the mind, they are referred to as **intrapsychic conflicts**.

Defense Mechanisms

The ego fights a continual battle to stay on top of the warring id and superego. Occasionally, their conflicts produce anxiety. The anxiety alerts the ego to marshal **defense mechanisms**, unconscious protective processes that keep emotions associated with conflicts in check so that the ego can continue to function. Although Freud first conceptualized defense mechanisms, it was his daughter, Anna Freud, who developed the ideas more fully.

Defense mechanisms may be adaptive or maladaptive. Have you ever done poorly on a test because the grading was unfair, and when you got home you yelled at your brother or perhaps your dog? This is an example of the defense mechanism of *displacement*. The ego adaptively decides that expressing anger at your professor might not be in your best interest. Because your brother and your dog don't have the authority to affect you in an adverse way, your anger is displaced to one of them. Some people may redirect energy from conflict or underlying anxiety into a more constructive outlet such as work. This process is called *sublimation*.

More severe internal conflicts that produce a lot of anxiety or other emotions can trigger self-defeating defensive processes or symptoms. Phobic and obsessive symptoms are common self-defeating defensive reactions that, according to Freud, reflect an inadequate attempt to deal with such conflicts. Phobic symptoms typically incorporate elements of the conflict. For example, a dog phobia may be connected to an infantile fear of castration; that is, a man's internal conflict involves a fear of being attacked and castrated, a fear that is consciously expressed as a fear of being attacked and bitten by a dog, even if he knows the dog is harmless.

Examples of defense mechanisms include the following (based on *DSM-IV-TR*, APA, 2000):

Denial: Refuses to acknowledge some aspect of objective reality or subjective experience that is apparent to others

▲ Anna Freud (1895–1982), here with her father, contributed the concept of defense mechanisms to the field of psychoanalysis.

Displacement: Transfers a feeling about, or a response to, an object that causes discomfort onto another, usually less-threatening, object or person

Projection: Falsely attributes own unacceptable feelings, impulses, or thoughts to another individual or object

Rationalization: Conceals the true motivations for actions, thoughts, or feelings through elaborate reassuring or self-serving but incorrect explanations

Reaction formation: Substitutes behavior, thoughts, or feelings that are the direct opposite of unacceptable ones

Repression: Blocks disturbing wishes, thoughts, or experiences from conscious awareness

Sublimation: Directs potentially maladaptive feelings or impulses into socially acceptable behavior

psychoanalytic model Complex and comprehensive theory originally advanced by Sigmund Freud that seeks to account for the development and structure of personality, as well as the origin of abnormal behavior, based primarily on inferred inner entities and forces.

id In psychoanalysis, the unconscious psychic entity present at birth representing basic drives.

ego In psychoanalysis, the psychic entity responsible for finding realistic and practical ways to satisfy id drives.

superego In psychoanalysis, the psychic entity representing the internalized moral standards of parents and society.

intrapsychic conflicts In psychoanalytic theory, a struggle among the id, ego, and superego.

defense mechanisms Common pattern of behavior, often an adaptive coping style when it occurs in moderation, observed in response to a particular situation. Psychoanalytic theory suggests that defense mechanisms are unconscious processes originating in the ego.

Psychosexual Stages of Development

Freud also theorized that during infancy and early childhood we pass through a number of **psychosexual stages of development**. The stages—oral, anal, phallic, latency, and genital—represent distinctive patterns of gratifying our basic needs and satisfying our drive for physical pleasure. For example, the oral stage (birth to about age 2), is characterized by a focus on the need for food. In the act of sucking, necessary for feeding, the lips, tongue, and mouth become the focus of libidinal drives and, therefore, the principal source of pleasure. Freud hypothesized that if we did not receive appropriate gratification during a specific stage or if a specific stage left a particularly strong impression (which he termed *fixation*), an individual's personality would reflect the stage throughout adult life. For example, fixation at the oral stage might result in excessive thumbsucking and emphasis on oral stimulation through eating, chewing pencils, or biting fingernails. Adult personality characteristics theoretically associated with oral fixation include dependency and passivity or, in reaction to these tendencies, rebelliousness and cynicism.

One of the more controversial psychosexual conflicts occurs during the phallic stage (from age 3 to age 5 or 6), which is characterized by early genital self-stimulation. This conflict is the subject of the Greek tragedy *Oedipus Rex*, in which Oedipus is fated to kill his father and, unknowingly, to marry his mother. Freud asserted that all young boys relive this fantasy when genital self-stimulation is accompanied by images of sexual interactions with their mothers. These fantasies, in turn, are accompanied by strong feelings of envy and perhaps anger toward their fathers, with whom they identify but whose place they wish to take. Furthermore, strong fears develop that the father may punish that lust by removing the son's penis—thus, the phenomenon of **castration anxiety**. This fear helps the boy keep his lustful impulses toward his mother in check. The battle of the lustful impulses on the one hand and castration anxiety on the other creates a conflict that is internal, or intrapsychic, called the *Oedipus complex*. The phallic stage passes uneventfully only if several things happen. First, the child must resolve his ambivalent relationship with his parents. If this happens, he may channel his libidinal impulses into heterosexual relationships while retaining harmless affection for his mother.

The counterpart conflict in girls, called the *Electra complex*, is even more controversial. Freud viewed the young girl as wanting to replace her mother and possess her father. Central to this possession is the girl's desire for a penis—hence the term *penis envy*. According to Freud, the conflict is resolved when females develop heterosexual relationships and look forward to having a baby, which he viewed as a healthy substitute for having a penis. Needless to say, this particular theory has provoked marked consternation over the years as being sexist and demeaning. It is important to remember that it is theory, not fact; no systematic research exists to support it.

In Freud's view, all nonpsychotic psychological disorders resulted from unconscious conflicts, the anxiety that resulted from those conflicts, and the implementation of defense mechanisms. Freud called such disorders **neuroses**, or *neurotic disorders*.

Later Developments in Psychoanalytic Thought

Freud's original psychoanalytic theories have been modified and developed in a number of different directions. Some theorists simply took one component of psychoanalytic theory and developed it more fully. Others broke with Freud and went in entirely new directions.

Anna Freud (1895–1982), Freud's daughter, concentrated on how defense mechanisms determine behavior. In so doing, she was the first proponent of the modern field of **ego psychology**. According to Anna Freud, the individual slowly accumulates adaptational capacities, skill in reality testing, and defenses. Abnormal behavior develops when the ego is deficient in regulating such functions as controlling impulses or in marshaling appropriate defenses to internal conflicts. In another modification of Freud's theories, Heinz Kohut (1913–1981) focused on the formation of self-concept and the attributes of the self that allow an individual to progress toward health or develop neurosis. This psychoanalytic approach became known as **self psychology** (Kohut, 1977).

A related area is **object relations**, the study of how children incorporate the images, the memories, and sometimes the values of a person to whom they were (or are) emotionally attached. *Object* in this sense refers to these important people, and the process of incorporation is called *introjection*. Introjected objects can become an integrated part of the ego or may assume conflicting roles in determining the identity, or self. For example, your parents may have conflicting views on relationships or careers, which, in turn, may differ from your own. To the extent that these varying positions have been incorporated, the potential for conflict arises. One day you may feel one way about your career direction, and the next day you may feel quite different. According to object relations theory, you tend to see the world through the eyes of the person incorporated into your self. Object relations theorists focus on how these disparate images come together to make up a person's identity.

Carl Jung (1875–1961) and Alfred Adler (1870–1937) were students of Freud who formed their own schools of thought. Jung, rejecting many of the sexual aspects of Freud's theory, introduced the concept of the collective unconscious, a wisdom that is stored deep in individual memories and passed down from generation to generation. Jung also suggested that spiritual and religious drives are as much a part of human nature as are sexual drives; this emphasis and the idea of the **collective unconscious** continue to draw the attention of mystics.

Adler focused on feelings of inferiority and the striving for superiority; he created the term *inferiority complex*. Unlike Freud, both Jung and Adler believed that the basic quality of human nature is positive and that there is a drive toward self-actualization (realizing one's full potential). They believed that by removing barriers to both internal and external growth the individual would flourish.

Others emphasized development over the life span and the influence of culture and society. Karen Horney (1885–

1952) and Erich Fromm (1900–1980) are associated with these ideas, but the best-known theorist is Erik Erikson (1902–1994). Erikson's greatest contribution was his theory of development across the life span, in which he described the crises and conflicts that accompany eight specific stages. For example, in the *mature stage,* beginning about age 65, individuals review their lives, experiencing both satisfaction at having completed some goals and despair at having failed at others. Scientific developments have borne out the wisdom of considering psychopathology from a developmental point of view.

Psychoanalytic Psychotherapy

Many techniques of psychoanalytic psychotherapy, or psychoanalysis, are designed to reveal the nature of unconscious mental processes through catharsis and insight. Freud developed techniques of **free association**, in which patients are instructed to say whatever comes to mind. Free association is intended to reveal material that may be repressed because it is too painful or threatening to bring into consciousness. Freud's patients lay on a couch, and he sat behind them so they would not be distracted. Other techniques include **dream analysis** (still quite popular), in which the therapist interprets the content of dreams, supposedly reflecting the primary-process thinking of the id, and relates the dreams to symbolic aspects of unconscious conflicts. This procedure is often difficult because the patient may resist the efforts of the therapist to uncover repressed conflicts and may deny the interpretations. The goal of this stage of therapy is to help the patient gain insight into the nature of the conflicts.

The relationship between the therapist, called the **psychoanalyst**, and the patient is important. In the context of this relationship, the therapist may discover the nature of the patient's intrapsychic conflict because, in a phenomenon called **transference**, patients come to relate to the therapist much as they did to important figures in their childhood. Patients who resent the therapist but cannot give a reason may be re-enacting childhood resentment toward a parent. More often, the patient falls in love with the therapist, reflecting strong positive feelings for a parent. In the phenomenon of *counter-transference,* therapists project some of their own feelings, usually positive, onto the patient. Therapists are trained to deal with their own feelings in addition to those of their patients, and relationships outside therapy are forbidden.

Classical psychoanalysis requires therapy 4 to 5 times a week for 2 to 5 years to analyze unconscious conflicts, resolve them, and restructure the personality to put the ego back in charge. Reduction of symptoms (psychological disorders) is less important because they are only expressions of intrapsychic conflicts that arise from psychosexual development. Thus, eliminating a phobia or depressive episode would be of little use unless the underlying conflict was dealt with because another set of symptoms would probably emerge *(symptom substitution).* Because of the huge expense of classical psychoanalysis, and the lack of evidence that it is effective, this approach is seldom used today.

Psychoanalysis is still practiced, but many psychotherapists use a loosely related set of approaches referred to as **psychodynamic psychotherapy**. Although conflicts and unconscious processes are still emphasized and efforts are made to identify trauma and defense mechanisms, therapists use a mixture of tactics, including (1) a focus on affect and the expression of patients' emotions; (2) exploration of patients' attempts to avoid topics or hinder the progress of therapy; (3) identification of patterns in patients' actions, thoughts, feelings, experiences, and relationships; (4) an emphasis on past experiences; (5) a focus on interpersonal experiences; (6) an emphasis on the therapeutic relationship; and (7) exploration of patients' wishes, dreams, or fantasies (Blagys & Hilsenroth, 2000). Two additional features characterize psychodynamic psychotherapy. First, it is significantly briefer than classical psychoanalysis. Second, psychodynamic therapists deemphasize the goal of personality reconstruction, focusing instead on relieving the suffering associated with psychological disorders.

Comments

Classical psychoanalysis as a treatment has been diminishing in popularity for years. A major criticism of psychoanalysis is that it is unscientific, relying on reports by the patient of events that happened years ago. These events have been filtered through the experience of the observer and then interpreted by the psychoanalyst in ways that could be questioned and might differ from one analyst to the next. Finally, there has been no careful measurement of

psychosexual stages of development Psychoanalytic concept of the sequence of phases a person passes through during development. Each stage is named for the location on the body where id gratification is maximal at that time.

castration anxiety In psychoanalysis, the fear in young boys that they will be mutilated genitally because of their lust for their mothers.

neurosis (neuroses *plural*) Obsolete psychodynamic term for a psychological disorder thought to result from an unconscious conflict and the anxiety it causes. Plural is *neuroses.*

ego psychology Psychoanalytic theory that emphasizes the role of the ego in development and attributes psychological disorders to failure of the ego to manage impulses and internal conflicts. Also known as self-psychology.

object relations Modern development in psychodynamic theory involving the study of how children incorporate the memories and values of people who are close and important to them.

collective unconscious Accumulated wisdom of a culture collected and remembered across generations, a psychodynamic concept introduced by Carl Jung.

free association Psychoanalytic therapy technique intended to explore threatening material repressed into the unconscious. The patient is instructed to say whatever comes to mind without censoring.

dream analysis Psychoanalytic therapy method in which dream content is examined as symbolic of id impulses and intrapsychic conflicts.

psychoanalyst Therapist who practices psychoanalysis after earning either an M.D. or a Ph.D. degree and receiving additional specialized postdoctoral training.

transference Psychoanalytic concept suggesting that clients may seek to relate to the therapist as they do to important authority figures, particularly their parents.

psychodynamic psychotherapy Contemporary version of psychoanalysis that still emphasizes unconscious processes and conflicts but is briefer and more focused on specific problems.

any of these phenomena and no obvious way to prove or disprove the basic hypotheses of psychoanalysis. This is important because measurement and the ability to prove or disprove a theory are the foundations of the scientific approach.

Nevertheless, psychoanalytic concepts and observations have been valuable. Scientific studies have supported the observation of unconscious mental processes, the notion that emotional responses are often triggered by hidden or symbolic cues, and the understanding that memories can be repressed and avoided in a variety of ways. The relationship of the therapist and the patient, called the *therapeutic alliance*, is an important area of study. These concepts, along with the importance of various coping styles or defense mechanisms, will appear throughout this book.

Freud's revolutionary idea that pathological anxiety emerges in connection with some of our deepest and darkest instincts brought us a long way from witch trials and ideas of incurable brain pathology. Before Freud, the source of good and evil and of urges and prohibitions was conceived as external and spiritual, usually in the form of demons confronting the forces of good. Since Freud, we ourselves have become the battleground for these forces.

Humanistic Theory

We have already seen that Jung and Adler broke sharply with Freud. Their fundamental disagreement concerned the very nature of humanity. Freud portrayed life as a battleground where we are continually in danger of being overwhelmed by our darkest forces. Jung and Adler, by contrast, emphasized the positive, optimistic side of human nature. Jung talked about setting goals, looking toward the future, and realizing one's fullest potential. Adler believed that human nature reaches its fullest potential when we contribute to other individuals and to society as a whole. He believed that we all strive to reach superior levels of intellectual and moral development. Nevertheless, both retained many of the principles of psychodynamic thought. Their philosophies were adopted by personality theorists and became known as *humanistic psychology*.

This movement emphasized **self-actualizing**. It assumed that all of us could reach our highest potential if only we had the freedom to grow. A variety of conditions may block our actualization, usually originating outside the individual. Difficult living conditions or stressful experiences may move you away from your true self.

Abraham Maslow (1908–1970) postulated a *hierarchy of needs*, beginning with our needs for food and sex and ranging upward to our needs for self-actualization, love, and self-esteem. Social needs such as friendship fall somewhere between. Maslow hypothesized that we cannot progress up the hierarchy until we have satisfied the needs at lower levels.

Carl Rogers (1902–1987) is the most influential humanist. Rogers (1961) originated client-centered therapy, later known as **person-centered therapy**. In this approach, the therapist takes a passive role, making as few interpretations as possible. The point is to give the individual a chance to develop, unfettered by threats to the self. **Unconditional positive regard**, the complete acceptance of most of the client's feelings and actions, is critical to this approach. *Empathy* is the sympathetic understanding of the individual's view of the world. The hoped-for result of person-centered therapy is that clients will be more straightforward and honest with themselves and will access their innate tendencies toward growth.

The humanistic approach has had a substantial effect on theories of interpersonal relationships. For example, the human potential movements so popular in the 1960s and 1970s were a direct result of humanistic theorizing. This approach also emphasized the importance of the therapeutic relationship in a way quite different from Freud's approach. Rather than seeing the relationship as a means to an end (transference), humanistic therapists believed that relationships, including the therapeutic relationship, were the most positive influence in facilitating human growth. Nevertheless, the humanistic model contributed relatively little new information to the field of psychopathology. One reason for this is that its proponents, with some exceptions, had little interest in doing research that would discover or create new knowledge. Rather, they stressed the unique, nonquantifiable experiences of the individual, emphasizing that people are more different than alike. As Maslow noted, the humanistic model found its greatest application among individuals without psychological disorders. The application of person-centered therapy to more severe psychological disorders has decreased substantially over the decades.

The Behavioral Model

The **behavioral model**, also known as the *cognitive–behavioral model* or *social learning model*, brought a more scientific approach to psychological aspects of psychopathology.

Pavlov and Classical Conditioning

In examining why dogs salivate before the presentation of food, physiologist Ivan Pavlov (1849–1936) of St. Petersburg, Russia, initiated the study of **classical conditioning**, a type of learning in which a neutral stimulus is paired with a response until it elicits that response. Conditioning is one way in which we acquire new information. This process can be automatic. Here's an example.

Chemotherapy, a common treatment for some forms of cancer, has side effects including severe nausea and vomiting. But pa-

▲ Ivan Pavlov (1849–1936) identified the process of classical conditioning, which is important to many emotional disorders.

©Hulton Archives/Getty Images

tients often experience these effects when they merely see the person who administered the chemotherapy or any equipment associated with the treatment (Morrow & Dobkin, 1988). For some patients, this reaction becomes associated with stimuli that evoke people or things present during chemotherapy—anybody in a nurse's uniform or even the sight of the hospital. This phenomenon is called *stimulus generalization* because the response generalizes to similar stimuli. Psychologists have had to develop specific treatments to overcome this response (Redd & Andrykowski, 1982).

Whether the stimulus is food or chemotherapy, the classical conditioning process begins with a stimulus that would elicit a response in almost anyone and requires no learning; no conditions must be present for the response to occur. This is the *unconditioned stimulus (UCS)*. The unlearned response to this stimulus—in these cases, salivation or nausea—is the *unconditioned response (UCR)*. Now the learning comes in. As we have seen, any person or object associated with the unconditioned stimulus (food or chemotherapy) acquires the power to elicit the same response, but now the response, because it was elicited by the conditional or *conditioned stimulus (CS)*, is termed a *conditioned response (CR)*. Thus, the nurse associated with the chemotherapy becomes a conditioned stimulus. The nauseous sensation (on seeing the nurse), which is almost the same as that experienced during chemotherapy, becomes the conditioned response.

With unconditioned stimuli as powerful as chemotherapy, a conditioned response can be learned in one trial. However, most learning of this type requires repeated pairing of the unconditioned stimulus and the conditioned stimulus. When Pavlov began studying this phenomenon, he substituted a metronome for the footsteps of his assistants so he could quantify the stimulus more accurately. He found that presentation of the conditioned stimulus (for example, the metronome) *without* the food for a long enough period would eventually eliminate the conditioned response to the food. In other words, the dog learned that the metronome no longer meant that a meal might be on the way. This process was called **extinction**.

Because Pavlov was a physiologist, it was natural for him to study these processes in a laboratory. This required precision in measuring and observing relationships and in ruling out alternative explanations. Although this scientific approach is common in biology, it was uncommon in psychology at that time. For example, it was impossible to measure unconscious conflicts precisely or even observe them. Even early experimental psychologists such as Edward Titchener (1867–1927) emphasized the study of **introspection**. Subjects reported their thoughts and feelings after experiencing certain stimuli, but the results of this "armchair" psychology were inconsistent.

Watson and the Rise of Behaviorism

American psychologist John B. Watson (1878–1958) is considered the founder of behaviorism. Watson decided that to base psychology on introspection was to head in the wrong direction—that psychology could be made as scientific as physiology (Watson, 1913).

Most of Watson's time was spent developing behavioral psychology as an empirical science, but he did dabble briefly in the study of psychopathology. In 1920, he and a student, Rosalie Rayner, presented an 11-month-old boy named Albert with a fluffy white rat to play with. Albert was not afraid of the small animal and enjoyed playing with it. However, every time Albert reached for the rat, the experimenters made a loud noise behind him. After only five trials, Albert showed signs of fear if the white rat came near. The experimenters then determined that Albert displayed mild fear of any white furry object, even a Santa Claus beard. You may not think this is surprising, but keep in mind that this was one of the first examples ever recorded in a laboratory of producing fear of an object not previously feared. Of course, this experiment would be considered unethical by today's standards.

Another student of Watson's, Mary Cover Jones (1896–1987), thought that if fear could be conditioned in this way, perhaps it could also be unlearned or extinguished. She worked with a boy named Peter, who at 2 years, 10 months old was already afraid of furry objects. Jones decided to bring a white rabbit into the room where Peter was playing for a short time each day. She also arranged for other children, who did not fear rabbits, to be in the same room. Peter's fear gradually diminished. Each time it diminished, Jones brought the rabbit closer. Eventually Peter was touching and even playing with the rabbit (Jones, 1924a, 1924b).

The Beginnings of Behavior Therapy

The implications of Jones's research were largely ignored for two decades, but in the late 1940s and early 1950s, South African psychiatrist Joseph Wolpe (1915–1997) became dissatisfied with psychoanalytic interpretations of psychopathology. He turned to the field of behavioral psychology and

self-actualizing Process emphasized in humanistic psychology in which people strive to achieve their highest potential against difficult life experiences.

person-centered therapy Therapy method in which the client, rather than the counselor, primarily directs the course of discussion, seeking self-discovery and self-responsibility.

unconditional positive regard Acceptance by the counselor of the client's feelings and actions without judgment or condemnation.

behavioral model Explanation of human behavior, including dysfunction, based on principles of learning and adaptation derived from experimental psychology.

classical conditioning Fundamental learning process first described by Ivan Pavlov. An event that automatically elicits a response is paired with another stimulus event that does not (a neutral stimulus). After repeated pairings, the neutral stimulus becomes a conditioned stimulus that by itself can elicit the desired response.

extinction Learning process in which a response maintained by reinforcement in operant conditioning or pairing in classical conditioning decreases when that reinforcement or pairing is removed; also the procedure of removing that reinforcement or pairing.

introspection Early, nonscientific approach to the study of psychology involving systematic attempts to report thoughts and feelings that specific stimuli evoked.

developed a variety of behavioral procedures for treating his patients, many of whom suffered from phobias. His best-known technique was termed **systematic desensitization**. It was similar to the treatment of little Peter: Individuals were gradually introduced to the objects or situations they feared so that their fear could extinguish. They could test reality and see that nothing bad happened in the presence of the phobic object or scene. Wolpe also had his patients do something that was incompatible with fear while they were in the presence of the dreaded object or situation. Because he could not always reproduce the phobic object in his office, Wolpe had his patients *imagine* the phobic scene while relaxing. For example, Wolpe treated a young man with a phobia of dogs by training him first to relax deeply and then imagine he was looking at a dog across the park. Gradually, he could imagine the dog across the park and remain relaxed, experiencing little or no fear. Wolpe then had him imagine that he was closer to the dog. Eventually, the young man imagined that he was touching the dog while maintaining a relaxed, almost trancelike state.

Wolpe reported great success with systematic desensitization, one of the first wide-scale applications of the new science of behaviorism to psychopathology. Wolpe, working with fellow pioneers Hans Eysenck and Stanley Rachman in London, called this approach **behavior therapy**. Although Wolpe's procedures are seldom used today, they paved the way for modern-day procedures in which severe phobias can be eliminated in as little as 1 day (see Chapter 4).

B. F. Skinner and Operant Conditioning

Freud's influence extended far beyond psychopathology into many aspects of cultural and intellectual history. Only one other behavioral scientist has made a similar impact: Burrhus Frederic (B. F.) Skinner (1904–1990). In 1938 he published *The Behavior of Organisms,* in which he laid out the principles of *operant conditioning,* a type of learning in which behavior changes as a function of what follows it. Skinner was strongly influenced by Watson's conviction that a science of human behavior must be based on observable events; he was also influenced by the work of psychologist Edward L. Thorndike (1874–1949).

▲ Mary Cover Jones (1896–1987) was one of the first psychologists to use behavioral techniques to free a patient from a phobia.

Archives of the History of American Psychology/University of Akron

Thorndike is known for the *law of effect,* which states that behavior is either strengthened (likely to occur more frequently) or weakened (likely to occur less frequently) depending on its consequences. Skinner took the simple notions that Thorndike had tested in animals, using food as a reinforcer, and developed them in a variety of ways to apply to much of our behavior. For example, if a 5-year-old boy starts shouting at the top of his lungs in McDonald's, it is unlikely that his behavior was automatically elicited by an unconditioned stimulus. Also, he will be less likely to do it in the future if his parents scold him, take him out to the car, or consistently reinforce more appropriate behavior. If the parents think his behavior is cute and laugh at it, chances are he will do it again.

Skinner coined the term *operant conditioning* because behavior operates on the environment and changes it in some way. For example, the boy's behavior affects his parents' behavior and probably the behavior of other customers. Most things that we do socially provide the context for other people to respond to us, thereby providing consequences for our behavior. The same is true of our physical environment, although the consequences may be long term (polluting the air eventually will poison us). Skinner preferred the term **reinforcement** to "reward" because it connotes the effect on the behavior. He pointed out that all our behavior is governed to some degree by reinforcement, which can be arranged in a variety of *schedules of reinforcement* (Ferster & Skinner, 1957). He also believed that using punishment as a consequence is relatively ineffective and that the primary way to develop new behavior is to positively reinforce desired behavior. Skinner did not deny the influence of biology or the existence of subjective states of emotion or cognition; he simply explained them as side effects of a particular history of reinforcement.

The subjects of Skinner's research were usually pigeons or rats. Skinner taught the animals a variety of tricks, including dancing, playing ping-pong, and playing a toy piano. To do this he used **shaping**, a process of reinforcing successive approximations to a final behavior. If you want a pigeon to play ping-pong, first you provide it with a pellet of food every time it moves its head slightly toward a ping-pong ball tossed in its direction. Gradually you require the pigeon to move its head ever closer to the ball until it touches it. Finally, receiving the food pellet is contingent on the pigeon hitting the ball with its head.

▲ B. F. Skinner (1904–1990) studied operant conditioning, a form of learning that is central to psychopathology.

©Bettmann/Corbis

Comments

The behavioral model has contributed greatly to the

understanding and treatment of psychopathology. Nevertheless, this model is inadequate to account for what we now know about psychopathology. In the past, there was little or no room for biology in behaviorism. The model also fails to account for development of psychopathology across the life span. Recent advances in our knowledge of how information is processed have added a layer of complexity. Integrating all these dimensions requires a new model of psychopathology.

An Integrative Approach

Why is the scientific method so important in studying abnormal behavior? We have reviewed three traditions or ways of thinking about causes of psychopathology: supernatural, biological, and psychological (further subdivided into two major historical components: psychoanalytic and behavioral).

Supernatural explanations of psychopathology are still with us. However, this tradition has little influence on scientists and other professionals. Biological, psychoanalytic, and behavioral models, by contrast, continue to further our knowledge of psychopathology.

Each tradition has failed in important ways. First, scientific methods were not often applied to the theories and treatments within a tradition, mostly because methods that would have produced the evidence necessary to confirm or disprove them had not been developed. Lacking such evidence, various fads were widely accepted that ultimately proved to be useless. New fads often superseded truly useful procedures. King Charles VI was subjected to a variety of procedures, some of which have since been proved useful and others that were mere fads or even harmful. How we use scientific methods to confirm or disconfirm findings in psychopathology is described in Chapter 3. Second, health professionals tend to look at psychological disorders from their own point of view. Grey assumed that psychological disorders were the result of brain disease. Watson assumed that all behaviors, including disordered behavior, were the result of psychological and social influences.

In the 1990s, two developments came together to shed light on the nature of psychopathology: (1) the increasing sophistication of scientific methodology and (2) the realization that no influence ever occurs in isolation. Every time we think, feel, or do something, the brain and the rest of the body are hard at work. Perhaps not as obvious, however, is that our thoughts, feelings, and actions influence the function and even the structure of the brain. In other words, our behavior, both normal and abnormal, is the product of a continual interaction of psychological, biological, and social influences.

By 2000, the young fields of cognitive science and neuroscience were growing rapidly as we learned more about the brain and about how we process, remember, and use information. At the same time, new findings from behavioral science revealed the importance of early experience in determining later development. It was clear that a new model was needed that would consider biological, psychological, and social influences on behavior and findings from our rapidly growing understanding of how we experience life during different developmental periods. In 2010, the National Institute of Mental Health (NIMH) undertook to support research on the interrelationship of these factors with the aim of translating research findings to treatment settings (Insel, 2009). In the remainder of this book, therefore, we explore the reciprocal influences among neuroscience, cognitive science, behavior science, and developmental science and demonstrate that the only currently valid model of psychopathology is multidimensional and integrative.

Concept Check 1.3

Match the treatment with the corresponding theory:
(a) behavioral model, (b) moral therapy, (c) psychoanalytic theory, (d) humanistic theory.

1. Treating institutionalized patients as normally as possible and encouraging social interaction and relationship development. _____

2. Hypnosis, psychoanalysis-like free association and dream analysis, and balance of the id, ego, and superego. _____

3. Person-centered therapy with unconditional positive regard. _____

4. Classical conditioning, systematic desensitization, and operant conditioning. _____

systematic desensitization Behavioral therapy technique to diminish excessive fears, involving gradual exposure to the feared stimulus paired with a positive coping experience, usually relaxation.

behavior therapy Array of therapeutic methods based on the principles of behavioral and cognitive science, as well as principles of learning as applied to clinical problems. It considers specific behaviors rather than inferred conflicts as legitimate targets for change.

reinforcement In operant conditioning, consequences for behavior that strengthen it or increase its frequency. Positive reinforcement involves the contingent delivery of a desired consequence. Negative reinforcement is the contingent escape from an aversive consequence. Unwanted behaviors may result from reinforcement of those behaviors or the failure to reinforce desired behaviors.

shaping In operant conditioning, the development of a new response by reinforcing successively more similar versions of that response. Both desirable and undesirable behaviors may be learned in this manner.

Summary

Understanding Psychopathology

How do psychologists define a psychological disorder?

> A psychological disorder is (1) a psychological dysfunction that is (2) associated with distress or impairment in functioning and (3) a response that is not typical or culturally expected. No single criterion has been identified that defines the essence of abnormality.

> Psychopathology is concerned with the study of psychological disorders. Mental health professionals range from clinical and counseling psychologists to psychiatrists and psychiatric social workers and nurses. Each profession requires a specific type of training.

What is a scientist–practitioner?

> Mental health professionals can function as scientist–practitioners. They not only keep up with the latest findings, but also use scientific data to evaluate their own work, and they often conduct research within their clinics or hospitals.

> Research about psychological disorders falls into three categories: description, causation, and treatment and outcomes.

The Supernatural, Biological, and Psychological Traditions

What supernatural influences were formerly believed to explain abnormal behavior?

What are the underlying assumptions of the biological approach to understanding abnormal behavior?

How do the psychological approaches of psychoanalysis, humanism, and behaviorism explain abnormal behavior?

> Historically, there have been three approaches to abnormal behavior. In the supernatural tradition, abnormal behavior is attributed to outside agents such as demons or spirits; this tradition has been largely replaced by biological and psychological perspectives. In the biological tradition, disorders are attributed to disease or biochemical imbalances; in the psychological tradition, abnormal behavior is attributed to faulty psychological development and to social context.

> Each tradition has its own forms of treatment. Supernatural treatments include exorcism to rid the body of the supernatural spirits. Biological treatments emphasize physical care and medical cures, especially drugs. Psychological approaches use psychosocial treatments, beginning with moral therapy and including modern psychotherapy.

> Sigmund Freud, the founder of psychoanalytic therapy, offered an elaborate conception of the unconscious mind. In therapy, Freud focused on tapping into the unconscious through such techniques as catharsis, free association, and dream analysis.

> One outgrowth of Freudian therapy is humanistic psychology, which focuses more on human potential and self-actualizing. Therapy that has evolved from this approach is known as person-centered therapy; the therapist shows almost unconditional positive regard for the client's feelings and thoughts.

> The behavioral model moved psychology into the realm of science. Both research and therapy focus on things that are measurable, including such techniques as systematic desensitization, reinforcement, and shaping.

An Integrative Approach

Why is the scientific method so important in studying abnormal behavior?

> With new knowledge from cognitive science, behavioral science, and neuroscience, we now realize that no contribution to psychological disorders occurs in isolation. Behavior is a product of a continual interaction of psychological, biological, and social influences.

Key Terms

psychological disorder, 1
phobia, 1
abnormal behavior, 2
psychopathology, 4
scientist–practitioner, 4
presenting problem, 5
clinical description, 5
prevalence, 5
incidence, 5
course, 5
prognosis, 5
etiology, 6
exorcism, 7
psychosocial treatment, 13

moral therapy, 13
mental hygiene movement, 14
psychoanalysis, 14
behaviorism, 14
unconscious, 15
catharsis, 15
psychoanalytic model, 16
id, 16
ego, 16
superego, 16
intrapsychic conflicts, 17
defense mechanisms, 17
psychosexual stages of development, 18

castration anxiety, 18
neurosis (neuroses *plural*), 18
ego psychology, 18
object relations, 18
collective unconscious, 18
free association, 19
dream analysis, 19
psychoanalyst, 19
transference, 19
psychodynamic psychotherapy, 19
self-actualizing, 20
person-centered therapy, 20
unconditional positive regard, 20
behavioral model, 20

Answers to Concept Checks

1.1

Part A

1. d; 2. b, c

Part B

3. d; 4. c; 5. a; 6. f; 7. e; 8. b

1.2

1. c; 2. a; 3. b

1.3

1. b; 2. c; 3. d; 4. a

Media Resources

Log in to CengageBrain to access the resources your instructor requires. For this book, you can access:

CourseMate brings course concepts to life with interactive learning, study, and exam preparation tools that support the printed textbook. A textbook-specific website, Psychology CourseMate includes an integrated interactive eBook and other interactive learning tools including quizzes, flashcards, videos, and more.

CENGAGENOW CengageNow is an easy-to-use online resource that helps you study in less time to get the grade you want—NOW. Take a pre-test for this chapter and receive a personalized study plan based on your results that will identify the topics you need to review and direct you to online resources to help you master those topics. Then take a post-test to help you determine the concepts you have mastered and what you will need to work on. If your textbook does not include an access code card, go to CengageBrain.com to gain access.

> Visit www.cengagebrain.com to access your account and purchase materials.

aplia If your professor has assigned Aplia homework:

1. Sign in to your account.

2. Complete the corresponding homework exercises as required by your professor.
3. When finished, click "Grade It Now" to see which areas you have mastered, which need more work, and for detailed explanations of every answer.

Video Concept Reviews

CengageNOW also contains Mark Durand's *Video Concept Reviews* on these challenging topics:

> Concept Check—Abnormality
> Psychopathology
> Mental Health Professions
> The Scientist–Practitioner
> Presenting Problem
> Prevalence
> Incidence
> Course
> Prognosis
> Supernatural Views—Historical
> Supernatural Views—Current
> Emotion Contagion
> Hippocrates
> Bodily Humors
> Moral Therapy
> Concept Check—Integrative Approach

Chapter Quiz

1. Dr. Roberts, a psychiatrist, often prescribes medication to his patients for their psychological problems. Dr. Roberts has what type of degree?
   a. PhD
   b. MD
   c. PsyD
   d. EdD

2. All of the following are part of a clinical description EXCEPT:
   a. thoughts
   b. feelings
   c. causes
   d. behaviors

3. The _____ describes the number of people in a population who have a disorder, whereas the _____ describes how many new cases of a disorder occur within a given period.
   a. ratio; prevalence
   b. incidence; ratio
   c. incidence; prevalence
   d. prevalence; incidence

4. Which of the following is NOT a historical model of abnormal behavior?
   a. the psyche model
   b. the supernatural model
   c. the biological model
   d. the psychological model

5. During the 19th century, the biological tradition of psychological disorders was supported by the discovery that a bacterial microorganism, _____, could result in psychotic symptoms and bizarre behaviors in advanced stages.
   a. malaria
   b. yellow fever
   c. dengue
   d. syphilis

6. Which of the following describes the order in which biological treatments for mental disorders were introduced?
   a. neuroleptic drug therapy, insulin therapy, electroconvulsive therapy
   b. insulin therapy, electroconvulsive therapy, neuroleptic drug therapy
   c. electroconvulsive therapy, neuroleptic drug therapy, insulin therapy
   d. electroconvulsive therapy, insulin therapy, neuroleptic drug therapy

7. _____ is the release of tension following the disclosure of emotional trauma, whereas _____ is the increased understanding of current feelings and past events.
   a. Insight; catharsis
   b. Catharsis; insight
   c. Catharsis; mediation
   d. Mediation; catharsis

8. Which of the following is an example of the Freudian defense mechanism known as displacement?
   a. Terry despises the fact that his brother is a star athlete. Instead of letting his brother know how he feels, Terry cheers him on at every game.
   b. Erika is attracted to her friend's husband and flirts with him. When her friend confronts her, Erika disagrees and refuses to believe what her friend is saying.
   c. Adam is criticized by his teacher in front of other students. When he goes home, his dog runs to him, and Adam kicks the dog.
   d. Judith feels uncomfortable around people with ethnic backgrounds different from her own. During a group discussion at work, she tells a coworker that his ideas are racist.

9. Before feeding her dog, Anna always gets his food out of the pantry. When she opens the pantry door, her dog begins to salivate. The dog's salivation is a(n):
   a. unconditioned stimulus
   b. unconditioned response
   c. conditioned stimulus
   d. conditioned response

10. B. F. Skinner is known for introducing the concept of _____, the belief that behavior can influence and change the environment.
    a. classical conditioning
    b. systematic desensitization
    c. operant conditioning
    d. extinction
    (See Appendix A for answers.)

Timeline of Significant Events

400 B.C.–1825

©Mary Evans Picture Library/the Image Works

©National Library of Medicine

©Mary Evans Picture Library/The Image Works

400 B.C.: Hippocrates suggests that psychological disorders have both biological and psychological causes.

1300s: Mental disorders are blamed on demons and witches; exorcisms are performed to rid victims of evil spirits.

1400–1800: Bloodletting and leeches are used to rid the body of unhealthy fluids and restore balance.

1793: Philippe Pinel introduces moral therapy and makes French mental institutions more humane.

400 B.C.	1300s	1500s	1825–1875

200 B.C.: Galen suggests that normal and abnormal behavior are related to four bodily fluids, or humors.

1400s: View that insanity is caused by mental or emotional stress gains momentum, and depression and anxiety are again regarded as disorders.

1500s: Paracelsus suggests that the moon and the stars affect people's psychological functioning.

1825–1875: Syphilis is differentiated from other types of psychosis in that it is caused by a specific bacterium; penicillin is found to cure syphilis.

1930–1968

1930: Insulin shock therapy, electric shock treatments, and brain surgery are used to treat psychopathology.

1943: The Minnesota Multiphasic Personality Inventory is published.

1950: The first effective drugs for severe psychotic disorders are developed. Humanistic psychology (based on ideas of Carl Jung, Alfred Adler, and Carl Rogers) gains some acceptance.

1958: Joseph Wolpe treats patients with phobias using systematic desensitization based on principles of behavioral science.

1930	1943	1950	1968

1938: B. F. Skinner publishes *The Behavior of Organisms*, which describes the principles of operant conditioning.

1946: Anna Freud publishes *Ego and the Mechanisms of Defense*.

1952: The first edition of the *Diagnostic and Statistical Manual (DSM-I)* is published.

1968: *DSM-II* is published.

©Bettmann/Corbis

©Imagno Hulton Archive/Getty Images

1848–1920

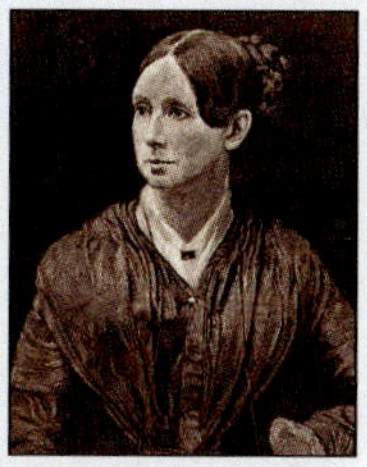

The Granger Collection, NYC—All rights reserved.

1848: Dorothea Dix campaigns for more humane treatment in American mental institutions.

1870: Louis Pasteur develops his germ theory of disease, which helps identify the bacterium that causes syphilis.

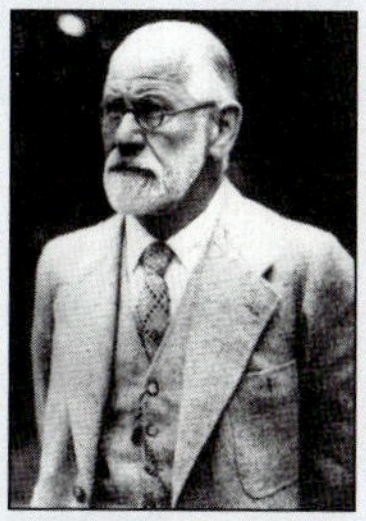

AP Photos

1900: Sigmund Freud publishes *The Interpretation of Dreams.*

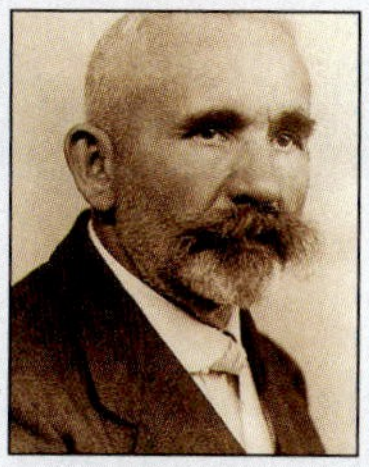

The Granger Collection, NYC—All rights reserved.

1913: Emil Kraepelin classifies various psychological disorders from a biological point of view and publishes work on diagnosis.

1848 | **1870** | **1900** | **1920**

1854: John P. Grey, head of New York's Utica Hospital, believes that insanity is the result of physical causes, thus deemphasizing psychological treatments.

1895: Josef Breuer treats the "hysterical" Anna O., leading to Freud's development of psychoanalytic theory.

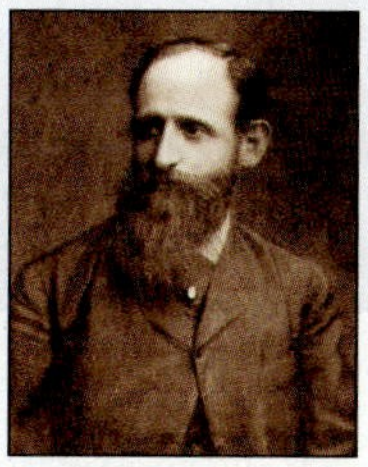

©Mary Evans Picture Library/Alamy

1904: Ivan Pavlov identifies conditioned reflexes in dogs.

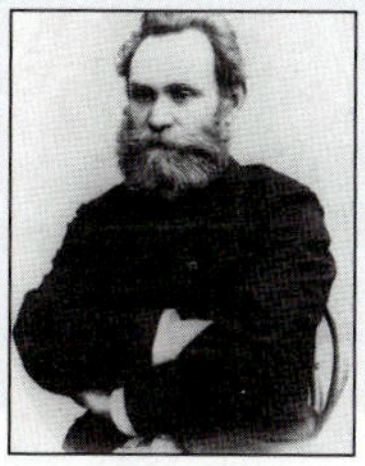

©Hulton Archive/Getty Images

1920: John B. Watson experiments with conditioned fear in Little Albert using a white rat.

1980–2000

1980: *DSM-III* is published.

1990s: Increasingly sophisticated research methods are developed; no one influence—biological or environmental—is found to cause psychological disorders in isolation from the other.

2000: *DSM-IV-TR* is published.

1980 | **1990s** | **2000**

1987: *DSM-III-R* is published.

1994: *DSM-IV* is published.

An Integrative Approach to Psychopathology

1.2 Demonstrate knowledge and understanding representing appropriate breadth and depth in selected content areas of psychology.	› Learning and cognition (APA SLO 1.2.a [1]) *(see textbook pages 53–56)* › Biological bases of behavior and mental processes, including physiology, sensation, perception, comparative, motivation, and emotion (APA SLO 1.2.a [3]) *(see textbook pages 34–53, 57–60)* › Developmental changes in behavior and mental processes across the life span (APA SLO 1.2.a [4]) *(see textbook pages 63–64)* › The interaction of heredity and environment (APA SLO 1.2.d [1]) *(see textbook pages 36–40)*
1.3 Use the concepts, language, and major theories of the discipline to account for psychological phenomena.	› Integrate theoretical perspectives to produce comprehensive and multifaceted explanations (APA SLO 1.3.e) *(see textbook pages 31–33, 63–64)*
1.4 Explain major perspectives of psychology (e.g., behavioral, biological, cognitive, evolutionary, humanistic, psychodynamic, and sociocultural). (APA SLO 1.4) *(see textbook pages XXX)*	› Compare and contrast major perspectives (APA SLO 1.4.a) *(see textbook pages 35–37, 53–55, 61–63)*

*Portions of this chapter cover learning outcomes suggested by the American Psychological Association (2007) in their guidelines for the undergraduate psychology major. Chapter coverage of these outcomes is identified by APA Goal and APA Suggested Learning Outcome (SLO).

Remember Judy from Chapter 1? We knew she suffered from blood–injury–injection phobia, but we did not know why. Here, we address the issue of causation. This chapter examines the components of a **multidimensional integrative approach** to psychopathology (■ Figure 2.1). Biological dimensions include causal factors from the fields of genetics and neuroscience. Psychological dimensions include causal factors from behavioral and cognitive processes, including learned helplessness, social learning, prepared learning, and even unconscious processes. Emotional influences contribute in a variety of ways, as do social and interpersonal influences. Finally, developmental influences figure in any discussion of causes of psychological disorders. Remember that no influence operates in isolation. Each dimension is strongly influenced by the others and by development, and they weave together in intricate ways to create a psychological disorder.

Here, we explain briefly why we have adopted a multidimensional integrative model of psychopathology. Then we preview various causal influences and interactions, using Judy's case as background. After that, we look more deeply at specific causal influences in psychopathology.

Zigy Kaluzny/Getty Images

multidimensional integrative approach Approach to the study of psychopathology that holds psychological disorders are always the products of multiple interacting causal factors.

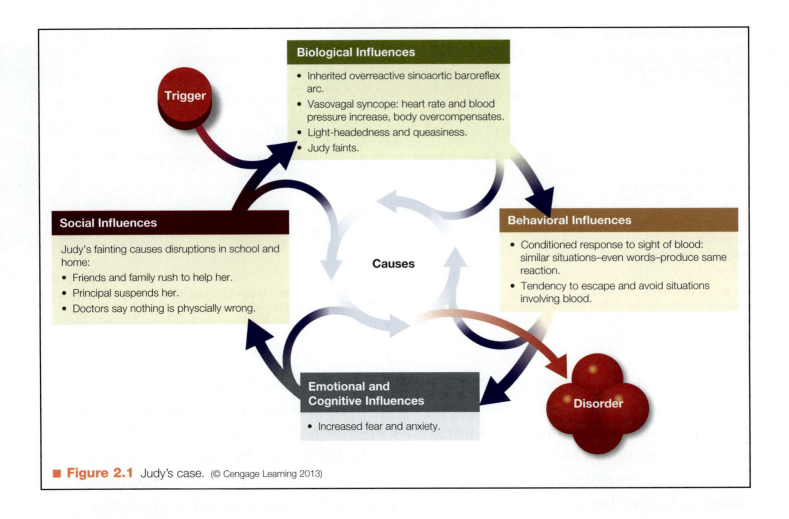

Biological Influences

- Inherited overreactive sinoaortic baroreflex arc.
- Vasovagal syncope: heart rate and blood pressure increase, body overcompensates.
- Light-headedness and queasiness.
- Judy faints.

Trigger

Social Influences

Judy's fainting causes disruptions in school and home:

- Friends and family rush to help her.
- Principal suspends her.
- Doctors say nothing is physcially wrong.

Causes

Behavioral Influences

- Conditioned response to sight of blood: similar situations–even words–produce same reaction.
- Tendency to escape and avoid situations involving blood.

Emotional and Cognitive Influences

- Increased fear and anxiety.

Disorder

■ **Figure 2.1** Judy's case. (© Cengage Learning 2013)

One-Dimensional versus Multidimensional Models

> How does a multidimensional model of causality differ from a unidimensional model?
> What are the key influences comprising the multidimensional model of abnormal behavior?

To say that psychopathology is caused by a single cause is to accept a linear or one-dimensional model. A linear causal model might hold that schizophrenia is caused by a chemical imbalance. However, most scientists and clinicians believe abnormal behavior results from multiple influences. It may have independent inputs at many points, but as each input becomes part of the whole it can no longer be considered independent. This perspective is *systemic;* it implies that no influence contributing to psychopathology can be considered out of context—that is, the biology and behavior of the individual and the cognitive, emotional, social, and cultural environment. In this multidimensional model, each component of the system inevitably affects the other components.

What Caused Judy's Phobia?

From a multidimensional perspective, let's look at what might have caused Judy's phobia (see Figure 2.1).

Behavioral Influences

The cause of Judy's phobia might seem obvious. She saw a movie with graphic scenes of blood and injury and had a bad reaction to it. Her reaction, an unconditioned response, became associated with situations similar to the scenes in the movie. But Judy's reaction reached such an extreme that even hearing someone say "Cut it out!" evoked queasiness. Is Judy's phobia a straightforward case of classical conditioning? It might seem so, but why didn't the other kids in Judy's class develop the same phobia?

Biological Influences

We now know that more is involved in blood–injury–injection phobia than a simple conditioning experience (Antony & Barlow, 2002; Ayala, Meuret, & Ritz, 2009; Exeter-Kent & Page, 2006; Page, 1994, 1996). Physiologically, Judy experienced a *vasovagal syncope,* a common cause of fainting. When she saw the film, she became mildly distressed, and her heart rate and blood pressure increased. Then her body took over, immediately compensating by decreasing her vascular resistance, lowering her heart rate and, eventually, lowering her blood pressure. The amount of blood reaching her brain diminished until she lost consciousness. *Syncope* means "sinking feeling" or "swoon" caused by low blood pressure in the head.

A possible cause of the vasovagal syncope is an overreaction of the *sinoaortic baroreflex arc,* which compensates for sudden increases in blood pressure by lowering it. This tendency to overcompensate seems to be inherited. Do you feel queasy at the sight of blood? If so, chances are your mother, your father, or someone else in your immediate family has the same reaction. In one study, 61% of the family members of individuals with this phobia had a similar condition (Öst, 1992). You might think, then, that we have discovered the cause of blood–injury–injection phobia. But many people with severe syncope reaction tendencies do *not* develop phobias. They cope with their reaction in various ways, including tensing their muscles whenever they are confronted with blood. Tensing the muscles quickly raises blood pressure and prevents the fainting response. Furthermore, some people with little or no syncope reaction develop the phobia anyway (Öst, 1992). Therefore, the cause of blood–injury–injection phobia is more complicated than it seems. If we said the phobia is caused by a biological dysfunction (an overactive vasovagal reaction) or a traumatic experience (seeing a gruesome film) and subsequent conditioning, we would be partly right on both counts, but we would miss the most important point: To cause blood–injury–injection phobia, a complex *interaction* must occur between behavioral and biological factors. Inheriting a strong syncope reaction definitely puts a person at risk for developing this phobia, but other influences also are at work.

Emotional Influences

Judy's case is a good example of biology influencing behavior. But behavior can also influence biology. What role did Judy's fear play in the development of her phobia? Emotions can affect physiological responses such as blood pressure, heart rate, and respiration, particularly if we know there is nothing to fear, as Judy did. In her case, rapid increases in heart rate, caused by her emotions, may have triggered a stronger and more intense baroreflex. Emotions also changed the way she thought about situations involving blood and injury and motivated her to avoid all situations connected with blood and injury, even if it was important not to avoid them.

Social Influences

Social and cultural factors contribute to biology and behavior. Judy's friends and family rushed to her aid when she fainted. Did their support help or hurt? Her principal dismissed her problem. What effect did this behavior have on her phobia? Rejection, particularly by authority figures, can make psychological disorders worse than they other-

▲ People who experience the same traumatic event will have different long-term reactions.

wise would be. Then again, being supportive only when somebody is experiencing symptoms is not always helpful because the attention may actually increase the frequency and intensity of the reaction.

Developmental Influences

As time passes, many things about ourselves and our environments change in important ways, causing us to react differently at different ages. At certain times we may enter a *developmental critical period* when we are more or less reactive to a given situation than at other times. To go back to Judy, it is possible she was previously exposed to other situations involving blood. Why did this problem develop when she was 16 and not before? Is it possible that her susceptibility to having a vasovagal reaction was highest in her teenage years? It may be that the timing of her physiological reaction, along with viewing the disturbing film, provided just the right combination to initiate her phobic response.

Outcome and Comments

Fortunately for Judy, she responded well to treatment at one of our clinics and was back in school within 7 days. Judy was gradually exposed to words, images, and situations describing or depicting blood and injury while a sudden drop in blood pressure was prevented. We began with something mild, such as the phrase "cut it out!" By the end of the week Judy was witnessing surgical procedures at the local hospital.

As you can see, finding the causes of abnormal behavior is a complex process. Focusing on biological or behavioral factors would not have given us a full picture of the causes of Judy's disorder; we had to consider other influences and how they might interact. We now examine the research underlying the many biological, psychological, and social influences that give rise to psychological disorders.

Genetic Contributions to Psychopathology

> **How do genes interact with environmental factors to affect behavior?**
> **What kinds of models have been proposed to describe this interaction?**

What causes you to look like one or both of your parents or, perhaps, your grandparents? Obviously, the genes you inherit are from your parents and from your ancestors before them. **Genes** are long molecules of deoxyribonucleic acid (DNA) at various locations on chromosomes within the cell nucleus. Physical characteristics are determined—or at least strongly influenced—by our genetic endowment. However, other factors in the environment influence our physical appearance. While our genes provide some boundaries to our development, exactly where we go within these boundaries depends on environmental influences.

Although this is true for most of our characteristics, it is not true for all of them. Some of our characteristics are strongly determined by one or more genes, including hair and eye color. A few rare disorders are also determined in this way, including Huntington's disease, a degenerative brain disease that appears in early to middle age. This disease has been traced to a genetic defect that causes deterioration in a specific area of the brain, the basal ganglia. It causes broad changes in personality, cognitive functioning, and motor behavior. We have not yet discovered a way to environmentally influence the course of Huntington's disease. Except for identical twins, every person has a unique set of genes. Because there is plenty of room for the environment to influence our development within the constraints set by our genes, there are many reasons for the development of individual differences.

What about our behavior and traits? Do genes influence personality and, by extension, abnormal behavior? This question of nature (genes) versus nurture (upbringing and other environmental influences) is age old, and the answers beginning to emerge are fascinating. Before discussing them, let's review briefly what we know.

The Nature of Genes

We have known for a long time that each normal human cell has 46 chromosomes arranged in 23 pairs. One chromosome in each pair comes from the father and one from the mother.

The first 22 pairs of chromosomes provide programs or directions for the development of the body and brain, and the last pair, called the *sex chromosomes*, determines an individual's sex. In females, both chromosomes in the 23rd pair are *X chromosomes*. In males, the mother contributes an X chromosome but the father contributes a *Y chromosome*. Abnormalities in the sex chromosomal pair can cause ambiguous sexual characteristics.

The DNA molecules that contain genes have a certain structure, a double helix. The shape of a helix is like a spiral staircase. A double helix is two spirals intertwined, turning in opposite directions. Located on this double spiral are simple pairs of molecules bound together and arranged in different orders. The ordering of these pairs influences how the body develops and works.

A *dominant gene* is one of a pair of genes that strongly influences a particular trait, and we only need one of them to determine, for example, our eye or hair color. A *recessive gene*, by contrast, must be paired with another (recessive) gene to determine a trait. Gene dominance occurs when one member of a gene pair is consistently expressed over the other (for example, a brown-eyed gene is dominant over a blue-eyed gene). When we have a dominant gene, we can predict fairly accurately how many offspring will develop a certain trait, characteristic, or disorder, depending on whether one or both of the parents carry that dominant gene.

Most of the time, predictions are not so simple. Much of our development and most of our behavior, personality, and even intelligence quotient (IQ) score are probably *polygenic*—that is, influenced by many genes, each contributing only a tiny effect, all of which, in turn, may be influenced by the environment. And because the human *genome*, or an individual's complete set of genes, is composed of more than 20,000 genes (U.S. Department of Energy Office of Science, 2009), polygenic interactions can be complex. For this reason, most genetic scientists now use sophisticated procedures such as quantitative genetics and molecular genetics that allow them to look for patterns of influence across many genes (Kendler, 2006; Plomin & Davis, 2009; Rutter, Moffitt, & Caspi, 2006; Thapar & McGuffin, 2009). *Quantitative genetics* sums up all the tiny effects across many genes without telling us which genes are responsible for which effects. *Molecular genetics* examines the structure of genes with advanced technologies such as *DNA microarrays;* these technologies allow scientists to analyze thousands of genes at once and identify broad networks of genes that may be contributing to a particular trait (Plomin & Davis, 2009). Such studies have indicated that hundreds of genes can contribute to the heritability of a single trait (Gottesman, 1997; Hariri et al., 2002; Plomin et al., 1995; Rutter et al., 2006). Research also continues to identify specific genes that contribute to individual differences in traits or temperament, such as shyness or impulsivity (for example, Gershon, Kelsoe, Kendler, & Watson, 2001).

Genes influence our bodies and behavior through a series of steps that produce proteins. Although all cells contain our entire genetic structure, only a small proportion of the genes in any one cell are "turned on" or expressed. In this way, cells become specialized. Environmental factors, in the form of social and cultural influences, can determine whether genes are "turned on." To take one example, in

▲ Scientists can now isolate DNA for study.

studies with rat pups, researchers have found that the absence of normal maternal behavior of "licking and grooming" prevents the genetic expression of a glucocorticoid receptor that modulates stress hormones. This means rats with inadequate maternal care have greater sensitivity to stress (Meaney & Szyf, 2005). There is evidence that a similar model may be relevant in humans (Hyman, 2009).

New Developments in the Study of Genes and Behavior

Scientists have identified, in a preliminary way, the genetic contribution to psychological disorders and related behavioral patterns. The best estimates attribute about half of our enduring personality traits and cognitive abilities to genetic influence (Rutter, 2006). For example, McClearn et al. (1997) compared 110 Swedish identical twin pairs, at least 80 years old, with 130 same-sex fraternal twin pairs of a similar age and found heritability estimates for specific cognitive abilities, such as memory, ranged from 32% to 62%. This work built on earlier twin studies, with different age groups showing similar results (for example, Bouchard, Lykken, McGue, Segal, & Tellegen, 1990). Furthermore, a study of more than 1,200 twins spanning 35 years confirmed that during adulthood genetic factors determined stability in cognitive abilities, whereas environmental factors determined any changes (Lyons et al., 2009). In other studies, the same heritability calculation for personality traits such as shyness ranges between 30% and 50% (Bouchard et al., 1990; Kendler, 2001; Loehlin, 1992; Rutter, 2006; Saudino & Plomin, 1996; Saudino, Plomin, & DeFries, 1996).

It has also become clear that adverse events such as a "chaotic" childhood can overwhelm the influence of genes

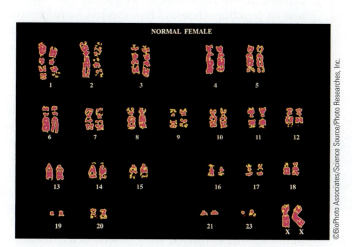

▲ A normal female has 23 pairs of chromosomes.

genes Long deoxyribonucleic acid (DNA) molecule, the basic physical unit of heredity that appears as a location on a chromosome.

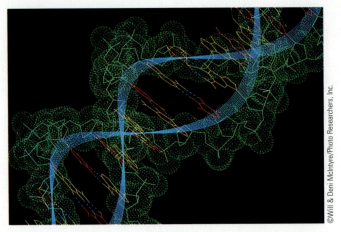

▲ A DNA molecule, which contains genes, resembles a double spiral, or helix.

(Turkheimer, Haley, Waldron, D'Onofrio, & Gottesman, 2003). For example, one member of a set of twins in the Lyons et al. (2009) study showed marked change in cognitive abilities if his or her environment changed dramatically from the other twin's because of some stressful event such as death of a loved one.

For psychological disorders, the evidence indicates that genetic factors contribute to all disorders but account for less than half of the explanation. If one of a pair of identical twins has schizophrenia, there is a less than 50% likelihood that the other twin will also have the illness (Gottesman, 1991). Similar or lower rates exist for other psychological disorders (Kendler & Prescott, 2006; Plomin, DeFries, McClearn, & Rutter, 1997; Rutter, 2006).

Behavioral geneticists have concluded that specific genes or small groups of genes may ultimately be found to be associated with certain psychological disorders. But much of the evidence suggests that contributions to psy-

chological disorders come from many genes, each having a relatively small effect (Flint, 2009; Rutter, 2006). Advances in gene mapping, molecular genetics, and linkage studies help us track the genes implicated in various disorders (for example, Gershon et al., 2001; Hettema, Prescott, Myers, Neale, & Kendler, 2005; Plomin et al., 1997). In linkage studies, scientists study individuals who have the same disorder, such as bipolar disorder, and also share other features, such as eye color; because the location of the gene for eye color is known, this allows scientists to "link" known gene locations with the possible location of a gene contributing to the disorder (Flint, 2009).

It is increasingly clear that genetic contributions cannot be studied in the absence of interactions with events that "turn on" specific genes (Rutter, 2010). It is to this fascinating topic that we now turn.

The Interaction of Genes and the Environment

In 1983, neuroscientist Eric Kandel speculated that the process of learning affects more than behavior. He suggested that the genetic structure of cells may change as a result of learning if genes that were inactive interact with the environment in such a way that they become active. In other words, the environment may occasionally turn on certain genes. This type of mechanism may lead to changes in the number of receptors at the end of a neuron, which, in turn, would affect biochemical functioning in the brain.

Most of us assume that the brain, like other parts of the body, may be influenced by environmental changes during development. But we also assume that once maturity is reached, the structure and function of most of our physiology are set or, in the case of the brain, hardwired. The competing idea is that the brain and its functions are subject to continual change in response to the environment, even at the genetic level. Now there is evidence supporting that view (Kolb, Gibb, & Robinson, 2003; Landis & Insel, 2008; Owens, Mulchahey, Stout, & Plotsky, 1997; Robinson, Fernald, & Clayton, 2008).

With these new findings in mind, we can now explore gene–environment interactions as they relate to psychopathology. Two models have received the most attention: the diathesis–stress model and reciprocal gene–environment model (or gene–environment correlations).

The Diathesis–Stress Model

According to this **diathesis–stress model**, individuals inherit tendencies to express certain traits or behaviors, which may be activated under conditions of stress (■ Figure 2.2). Each inherited tendency is a *diathesis*, a condition that makes someone susceptible to developing a disorder. When the right kind of event, such as a certain type of stressor, comes along, the disorder develops. For example, according to the diathesis–stress model, Judy inherited a *tendency* to faint at the sight of blood. This tendency is the dia-

▲ Genetic contributions to behavior are evident in twins who were raised apart. When these brothers were finally reunited, they were both firefighters and they discovered many other shared characteristics and interests.

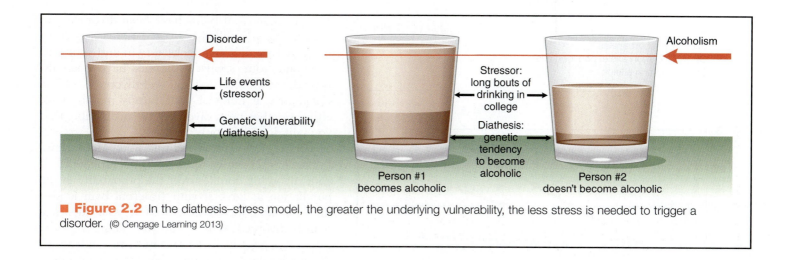

■ **Figure 2.2** In the diathesis–stress model, the greater the underlying vulnerability, the less stress is needed to trigger a disorder. (© Cengage Learning 2013)

thesis, or **vulnerability**. It would not become prominent until certain environmental events occurred. For Judy, this event was the sight of an animal being dissected when she was in a situation in which escape was not acceptable. The stress of seeing the dissection under these conditions activated her tendency to faint. Together, these factors led to her developing a disorder. If she had not taken biology, she might have gone through life without knowing she had the tendency, at least to such an extreme, although she might have felt queasy about minor cuts. In short, the "diathesis" is genetically based and the "stress" is environmental, but they must interact to produce a disorder.

We might also take the case of someone who inherits a vulnerability to alcoholism. During college, both this person and a friend who lacks the tendency engage in drinking bouts, but only the individual with the so-called addictive genes begins the downward spiral into alcoholism. Having a particular vulnerability doesn't mean you will develop the associated disorder. The smaller the vulnerability, the greater the stress required to produce the disorder; conversely, with greater vulnerability, less stress is required.

This relationship has been demonstrated in a landmark study by Caspi et al. (2003), who have been studying a group of 847 individuals in New Zealand for more than 2 decades. They noted whether the participants, at age 26, had been depressed during the past year. Overall, 17% had experienced a major depressive episode and 3% felt suicidal. The investigators also identified the genetic makeup of the individuals and, in particular, a gene that produces a *chemical transporter* that affects the transmission of serotonin in the brain. Serotonin, a neurotransmitter, is implicated in depression and related disorders. But the gene that Caspi et al. were studying comes in two common versions, or *alleles:* one long and one short. There was reason to believe, from work with animals, that individuals with at least two copies of the long allele (LL) were able to cope better with stress than individuals with two copies of the short allele (SS).

Because the investigators have been recording stressful events in these individuals most of their lives, they were able to test this relationship. In people with two S alleles, the risk for having a major depressive episode doubled if they had at

least four stressful events, compared with participants experiencing four stressful events who had two L alleles. Moreover, in people with the SS alleles, severe maltreatment during childhood more than doubled their risks of depression in adulthood compared to individuals carrying the SS alleles who were not maltreated (63% versus 30%). For individuals carrying the LL alleles, however, stressful childhood experiences did not affect the incidence of depression in adulthood; 30% of this group became depressed whether they had experienced stressful childhoods or not. (This relationship is shown in ■ Figure 2.3.) Therefore, unlike this SS group, depression in the LL allele group seems related to stress in their recent past rather than childhood experiences. This study was important in demonstrating that neither genes nor life experiences (environmental events) can solely explain the onset of a disorder such as depression. It takes a complex interaction of the two factors. Other studies have replicated or supported these findings (Binder et al., 2008; Kilpatrick et al., 2007; Rutter et al., 2006).

The Reciprocal Gene–Environment Model

With increased study, the web of interrelationships between genes and environment has been found to be even more complex. Some evidence now indicates that genetic endowment may *increase the probability* that an individual will experience stressful events (for example, Kendler, 2001, 2006; Rutter, 2006, 2010; Saudino, Pedersen, Lichtenstein, McClearn, & Plomin, 1997; Thapar & McGuffin, 2009). For example, people with a genetic vulnerability to develop a certain disorder, such as blood–injury–injection phobia, may also have a personality trait—say, impulsiveness—that makes them more likely to be involved in minor accidents that would result in their seeing blood. In other words, they may be accident prone because they are continually rushing without regard for their safety. These people, then,

diathesis–stress model Hypothesis that both an inherited tendency (a vulnerability) and specific stressful conditions are required to produce a disorder.
vulnerability Susceptibility or tendency to develop a disorder.

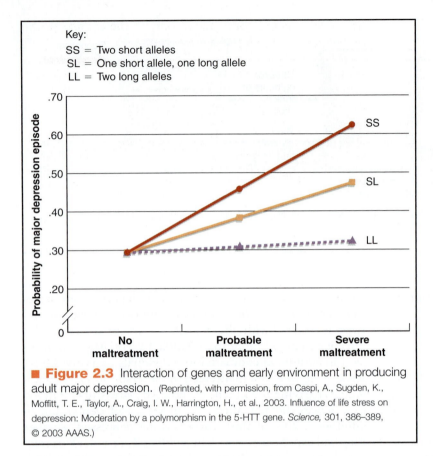

Figure 2.3 Interaction of genes and early environment in producing adult major depression. (Reprinted, with permission, from Caspi, A., Sugden, K., Moffitt, T. E., Taylor, A., Craig, I. W., Harrington, H., et al., 2003. Influence of life stress on depression: Moderation by a polymorphism in the 5-HTT gene. *Science*, 301, 386–389, © 2003 AAAS.)

Key:
SS = Two short alleles
SL = One short allele, one long allele
LL = Two long alleles

might have a genetically determined tendency to create the environmental factors that trigger their vulnerability to blood–injury–injection phobia.

This is the **reciprocal gene–environment model** or gene–environment correlation model (Kendler, 2001; Thapar & McGuffin, 2009) (■ Figure 2.4). Some evidence indicates that it applies to depression because some people may tend to seek out difficult relationships or other circumstances that lead to depression (Bebbington et al., 1988; Kendler et al., 1995; McGuffin, Katz, & Bebbington, 1988). McGue and Lykken (1992) have applied the reciprocal gene–environment model to the divorce rate. For example, if you and your spouse each have an identical twin

and both identical twins have been divorced, the chance that you will also divorce increases greatly. Furthermore, if your identical twin and your parents and your spouse's parents have been divorced, the chance that you will divorce is 77.5%. Conversely, if none of your family members on either side has been divorced, the probability that you will divorce is only 5.3%.

This is the extreme example, but McGue and Lykken (1992) demonstrated that the probability of your divorcing doubles over the probability in the population at large if your fraternal twin is also divorced and increases sixfold if your identical twin is divorced. Why would this happen? To the extent it is genetically determined, the tendency to divorce is almost certainly related to various inherited traits, such as being impulsive or short tempered, that make someone hard to get along with (Jockin, McGue, & Lykken, 1996). Another possibility is that an inherited trait makes you more likely to choose an incompatible spouse. If you are unassertive, you may choose a dominant mate who turns out to be impossible to live with. You get divorced but then find yourself attracted to another individual with the same traits, who is also impossible to live with. Some people would attribute this pattern to poor judgment. Nevertheless, there's no doubt that social, interpersonal, psychological, and environmental factors play major roles in whether we stay married, and it's quite possible that our genes contribute to how we create our own environment.

Epigenetics and the Nongenomic "Inheritance" of Behavior

Recent reports suggest that studies to date have overemphasized the extent of genetic influence on our personalities, our temperaments, and their contribution to psychological disorders (Moore, 2001; Turkheimer & Waldron, 2000). Several lines of evidence have come together to buttress this conclusion.

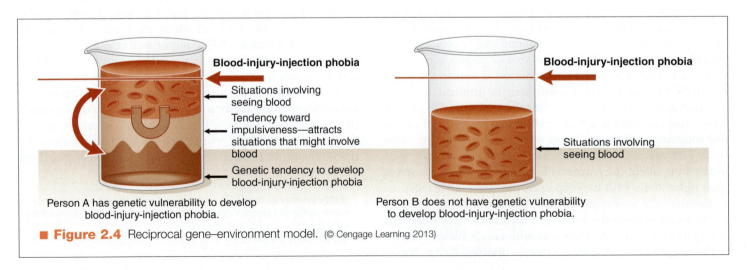

Figure 2.4 Reciprocal gene–environment model. (© Cengage Learning 2013)

For example, behavioral geneticists Crabbe, Wahlsten, and Dudek (1999) conducted an experiment in which three types of mice with different genetic makeups were raised in virtually identical environments at three sites. Each mouse of a given type was genetically indistinguishable from all other mice of that type at each site. The experimenters made sure the environments were the same at each site. For example, each site had the same kind of sawdust bedding that was changed on the same day of the week. If the animals had to be handled, all of them were handled at the same time by experimenters wearing the same kind of glove. If genes determine the behavior of the mice, then mice with virtually identical genetic makeup (type A) should have performed the same at all three sites on a series of tests, as should have type B and type C mice. But this did not happen. Although a certain type of mouse might perform similarly on a specific test across all three sites, on other tests that type of mouse performed differently. Robert Sapolsky, a prominent neuroscientist, concluded, "[G]enetic influences are often a lot less powerful than is commonly believed. The environment, even working subtly, can still mold and hold its own in the biological interactions that shape who we are" (Sapolsky, 2000, p. 15).

In research with rats (Cameron et al., 2005; Francis, Diorio, Liu, & Meaney, 1999; Weaver et al., 2004), investigators studied stress reactivity and how it is passed through generations, using a procedure called *cross-fostering*, in which a rat pup born to one mother is assigned to another mother for rearing. They first demonstrated that maternal behavior affected how the young rats tolerated stress. If the mothers were calm, their rat pups were better able to tolerate stress. But we don't know if this effect results from genetic influences or from being raised by calm mothers. Francis et al. (1999) took some newly born rat pups of easily stressed mothers and placed them with calm mothers. Other young rats remained with their easily stressed mothers. They found that calm and supportive behavior by the mothers could be passed down through generations of rats *independent of genetic influences* because rats born to easily stressed mothers but reared by calm mothers grew up more calm and supportive. The authors concluded,

> these findings suggest that individual differences in the expression of genes in brain regions that regulate stress reactivity can be transmitted from one generation to the next through behavior. . . . The results . . . suggest that the mechanism for this pattern of inheritance involves differences in maternal care. (p. 1158)

Strong effects of the environment have also been observed in humans. For example, Tienari et al. (1994) found that children of parents with schizophrenia who were adopted away as babies tended to develop psychiatric disorders (including schizophrenia) themselves only if they were adopted into dysfunctional families. Children adopted into functional families with high-quality parenting did not develop the disorders. Thus, it is simplistic to say the genetic contribution to a personality trait or psychological disorder is approximately 50%. We can talk of a

heritable (genetic) contribution only in the context of the individual's past and present environment.

In support of this conclusion, Suomi (2000) demonstrated that for young monkeys with a specific genetic pattern associated with a highly reactive temperament (emotional or susceptible to the effects of stress), early maternal deprivation (disruptions in mothering) will have a powerful effect on their neuroendocrine functioning and their later emotional reactions. However, for animals without this genetic characteristic, maternal deprivation will have little effect, just as was found in the New Zealand study in humans by Caspi et al. (2003), and it is likely this effect will be carried down through the generations. But chaotic early environments can override genetic factors and alter neuroendocrine function to increase the likelihood of later behavioral and emotional disorders (Ouellet-Morin et al., 2008).

How does this work? It seems that genes are turned on or off by cellular material that is located just outside of the genome ("epi," as in the word *epigenetics*, means on or around) and that stress, nutrition, or other factors can affect this epigenome, which is passed down to the next generation and maybe for several generations (Arai, Li, Hartley, & Feig, 2009). The genome itself isn't changed, so if the stressful environment disappears, eventually the epigenome will fade. Thus, it seems that environmental manipulations, particularly early parenting influences, may override the genetically influenced tendency to develop undesirable behavioral and emotional reactions (Cameron et al., 2005; Collins et al., 2000; Ouellet-Morin et al., 2008).

Nowhere is the complexity of the interaction of genetic and environmental influences more apparent than in the famous cases of Chang and Eng, identical twins born in Thailand in 1810 (known as Siam at the time) who were joined at the chest. These individuals, who became successful entertainers, were the source of the name "Siamese twins." They obviously shared identical genes, and nearly identical environments throughout their lives. Thus, we would expect them to behave in similar ways when it comes to personality features, temperaments, and psychological disorders. But these twins had distinct personalities. Chang was prone to moodiness and depression and started drinking heavily. Eng was more cheerful, quiet, and thoughtful (Moore, 2001).

In summary, a complex interaction between genes and the environment plays a role in every psychological disorder (Kendler, 2001; Rutter, 2006, 2010; Turkheimer, 1998). Our genes contribute to our behavior, emotions, and cognitive processes and constrain the influence of environmental factors, such as upbringing, on our later behavior. Environmental events, in turn, seem to affect our genes by determining

reciprocal gene–environment model Hypothesis that people with a genetic predisposition for a disorder may also have a genetic tendency to create environmental risk factors that promote the disorder.
epigenetics The study of factors other than inherited DNA sequence, such as new learning or stress, that alter the phenotypic expression of genes.

whether certain genes are activated or not (Gottlieb, 1998; Landis & Insel, 2008). Furthermore, strong environmental influences alone may be sufficient to override genetic diatheses. Thus, neither nature (genes) nor nurture (environmental events) alone, but a complex interaction of the two, influences the development of our behavior and personalities.

Concept Check 2.2

Determine whether these statements are true (T) or false (F).

1. ___ The first 20 pairs of chromosomes program the development of the body and brain.

2. ___ No individual genes have been identified that cause psychological disorders.

3. ___ According to the diathesis–stress model, people inherit a vulnerability to express certain traits that may be activated under certain conditions.

4. ___ The idea that individuals' genes may increase the probability that they will experience stressful events and therefore trigger a vulnerability is in accordance with the diathesis–stress model.

5. ___ Environmental events alone influence the development of our behavior and personalities.

Neuroscience and Its Contributions to Psychopathology

> **What are neurotransmitters, and how are they involved in abnormal behavior?**
> **What are the functions of different brain regions, and what are their roles in psychopathology?**

Knowing how the nervous system works is central to understanding behavior, emotions, and cognitive processes. This is the focus of **neuroscience**. To comprehend research in this field, we first need an overview of how the brain and the nervous system function. The human nervous system includes the *central nervous system,* consisting of the brain and the spinal cord, and the *peripheral nervous system,* consisting of the somatic nervous system and the autonomic nervous system (■ Figure 2.5).

The Central Nervous System

The central nervous system processes information received from our sense organs. It sorts out what is relevant, such as a certain taste or a new sound, from what isn't, such as a familiar view or ticking clock; checks memory to determine why the information is relevant; and implements the right reaction, whether it is to answer a question or to play a Mozart sonata. This is a lot of exceedingly complex work. The spinal cord is part of the central nervous system, but its primary function is to facilitate the sending of messages to and from the brain, which is the other major component of the central nervous system (CNS). The brain uses an average of 140 billion nerve cells, called **neurons**, to control thoughts and actions. Neurons transmit information throughout the nervous system.

The typical neuron contains a central cell body with two kinds of branches. One kind is a *dendrite*. Dendrites have numerous *receptors* that receive messages from other nerve cells in the form of chemical impulses, which are converted into electrical impulses. The other kind of branch, an *axon*, transmits these impulses to other neurons. Any nerve cell may have multiple connections to other neurons. The brain has billions of nerve cells.

Neurons are not actually connected to each other. There is a small space through which the impulse must pass to get to the next neuron. The space between the axon of one neuron and the dendrite of another is called the **synaptic cleft** (■ Figure 2.6). The biochemicals that are released from one neuron and transmit the impulse to another neuron are called **neurotransmitters**. Using increasingly sensitive equipment and techniques, scientists have identified many types of neurotransmitters.

The nervous system also contains glia (or glial) cells. For many years scientists believed that they merely served to connect and insulate neurons (Koob, 2009). More recently, scientists have discovered that glia (which are 10 times more numerous than neurons) play active roles in neural activity. It is now known that there are different types of glia cells, some of which serve to modulate neurotransmitter activity (Allen & Barres, 2009; Perea & Araque, 2007). Better understanding the role of glia cells is an important new area of research. To date, however, most neuroscience research in psychopathology focuses on neurons.

Major neurotransmitters relevant to psychopathology include norepinephrine (also known as noradrenaline), serotonin, dopamine, gamma-aminobutyric acid (GABA), and glutamate. Excesses or insufficiencies in some neurotransmitters are associated with different groups of psychological disorders. For example, reduced levels of GABA

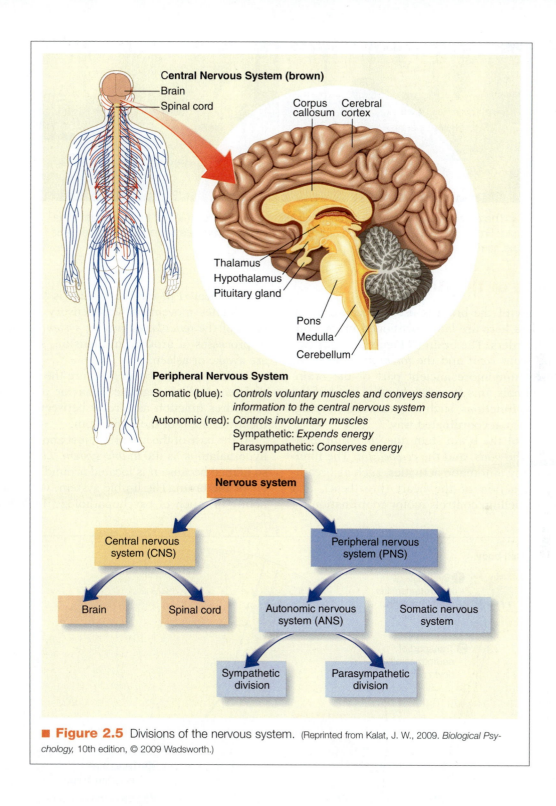

Central Nervous System (brown)
— Brain
— Spinal cord

Corpus callosum   Cerebral cortex

Thalamus
Hypothalamus
Pituitary gland

Pons
Medulla
Cerebellum

Peripheral Nervous System

Somatic (blue): *Controls voluntary muscles and conveys sensory information to the central nervous system*
Autonomic (red): *Controls involuntary muscles*
    Sympathetic: *Expends energy*
    Parasympathetic: *Conserves energy*

Nervous system

Central nervous system (CNS)

Peripheral nervous system (PNS)

Brain

Spinal cord

Autonomic nervous system (ANS)

Somatic nervous system

Sympathetic division

Parasympathetic division

■ **Figure 2.5** Divisions of the nervous system. (Reprinted from Kalat, J. W., 2009. *Biological Psychology*, 10th edition, © 2009 Wadsworth.)

were initially thought to be associated with excessive anxiety (Costa, 1985). Early research (Snyder, 1976, 1981) linked increases in dopamine activity to schizophrenia. Other early research found correlations between depression and high levels of norepinephrine (Schildkraut, 1965) and, possibly, low levels of serotonin (Siever, Davis, & Gorman, 1991). However, more recent research indicates that these early interpretations were simplistic. We return to the subject of neurotransmitters shortly.

neuroscience Study of the nervous system and its role in behavior, thoughts, and emotions.
neuron Individual nerve cell responsible for transmitting information.
synaptic cleft Space between nerve cells where chemical transmitters act to move impulses from one neuron to the next.
neurotransmitters Chemical that crosses the synaptic cleft between nerve cells to transmit impulses from one neuron to the next. Relative excess or deficiency of neurotransmitters is involved in several psychological disorders.

▲ The central nervous system screens out information that is irrelevant to the current situation. From moment to moment we notice what moves or changes more than what remains the same.

The Structure of the Brain

Having an overview of the brain is useful because many structures described here are later mentioned in the context of specific disorders. The brain (■ Figure 2.7) has two main parts—the *brain stem* and the *forebrain*. The brain stem is the lower and more ancient part of the brain. Found in most animals, this structure handles most of the essential automatic functions, such as breathing, sleeping, and moving around in a coordinated way.

The lowest part of the brain stem, the *hindbrain*, contains the *medulla*, the *pons*, and the *cerebellum*. The hindbrain regulates many automatic activities, such as breathing, the pumping action of the heart (heartbeat), and digestion. The cerebellum controls motor coordination.

Also located in the brain stem is the *midbrain*, which coordinates movement with sensory input and contains parts of the *reticular activating system*, which contributes to processes of arousal and tension, such as whether we are awake or asleep.

At the top of the brain stem are the *thalamus* and *hypothalamus*, which regulate behavior and emotion. These structures function as a relay between the forebrain and the lower areas of the brain stem.

At the base of the forebrain, just above the thalamus and hypothalamus, is the *limbic system*. *Limbic* means border, so named because it is located around the edge of the center of the brain. The limbic system, which figures prominently in much of psychopathology, includes such struc-

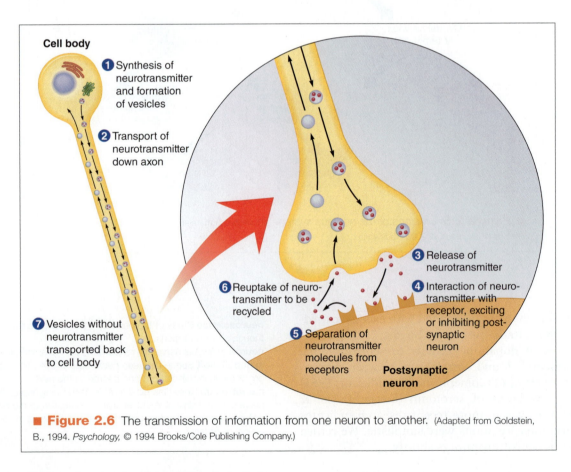

Cell body

1 Synthesis of neurotransmitter and formation of vesicles

2 Transport of neurotransmitter down axon

7 Vesicles without neurotransmitter transported back to cell body

6 Reuptake of neurotransmitter to be recycled

5 Separation of neurotransmitter molecules from receptors

3 Release of neurotransmitter

4 Interaction of neurotransmitter with receptor, exciting or inhibiting postsynaptic neuron

Postsynaptic neuron

■ **Figure 2.6** The transmission of information from one neuron to another. (Adapted from Goldstein, B., 1994. *Psychology*, © 1994 Brooks/Cole Publishing Company.)

tures as the *hippocampus* (sea horse), *cingulated gyrus* (girdle), *septum* (partition), and *amygdala* (almond), all of which are named for their shapes. This system helps regulate emotion and, to some extent, our ability to learn and to control our impulses. It is also involved with the basic drives of sex, aggression, hunger, and thirst.

The *basal ganglia*, also at the base of the forebrain, include the *caudate* (tailed) *nucleus*. Because damage to these structures may make us change our posture or twitch or shake, they are believed to control motor activity.

The largest part of the forebrain is the *cerebral cortex*, which contains more than 80% of all neurons in the central

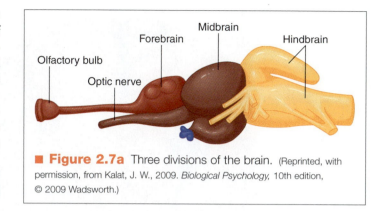

■ **Figure 2.7a** Three divisions of the brain. (Reprinted, with permission, from Kalat, J. W., 2009. *Biological Psychology*, 10th edition, © 2009 Wadsworth.)

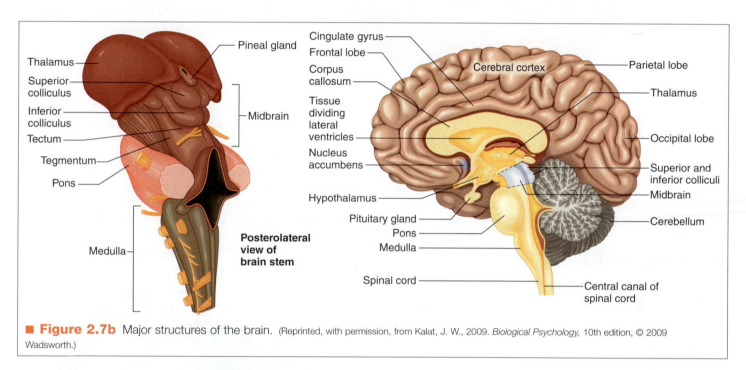

■ **Figure 2.7b** Major structures of the brain. (Reprinted, with permission, from Kalat, J. W., 2009. *Biological Psychology*, 10th edition, © 2009 Wadsworth.)

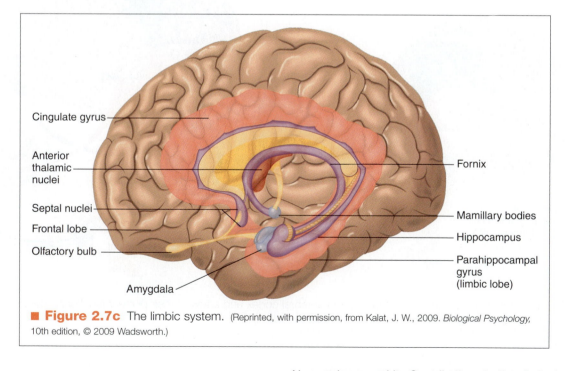

■ **Figure 2.7c** The limbic system. (Reprinted, with permission, from Kalat, J. W., 2009. *Biological Psychology*, 10th edition, © 2009 Wadsworth.)

Neuroscience and Its Contributions to Psychopathology   **43**

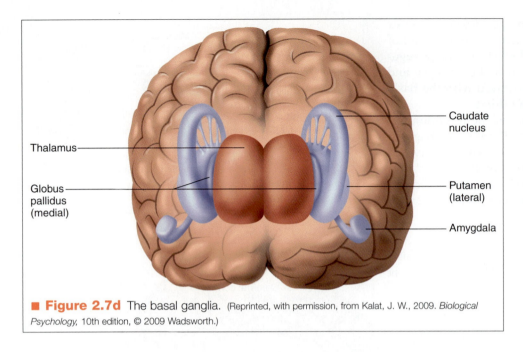

■ **Figure 2.7d** The basal ganglia. (Reprinted, with permission, from Kalat, J. W., 2009. *Biological Psychology*, 10th edition, © 2009 Wadsworth.)

Thalamus

Globus pallidus (medial)

Caudate nucleus

Putamen (lateral)

Amygdala

specialties. The left hemisphere seems to be chiefly responsible for verbal and other cognitive processes. The right hemisphere seems to be better at perceiving and creating images. The hemispheres may play differential roles in specific disorders. For example, current theories about dyslexia (a learning disability involving reading) suggest that it may be a result of problems in processing information in the left hemisphere and that the right hemisphere may attempt to compensate by involving visual cues from pictures while reading (Shaywitz, 2003).

Each hemisphere consists of four *lobes:* temporal, parietal, occipital, and frontal (■ Figure 2.8). Each lobe is associated with different processes: the *temporal lobe*

nervous system. It gives us our distinctly human qualities, allowing us to plan, reason, and create. It is divided into two hemispheres. Although the hemispheres look alike and operate relatively independently (both are capable of perceiving, thinking, and remembering), each has different

with recognizing sights and sounds and with long-term memory storage; the *parietal* lobe with recognizing sensations of touch and monitoring body positioning; the *occipital lobe* with making sense of visual inputs. These three lobes, located toward the back (posterior) of the brain, work

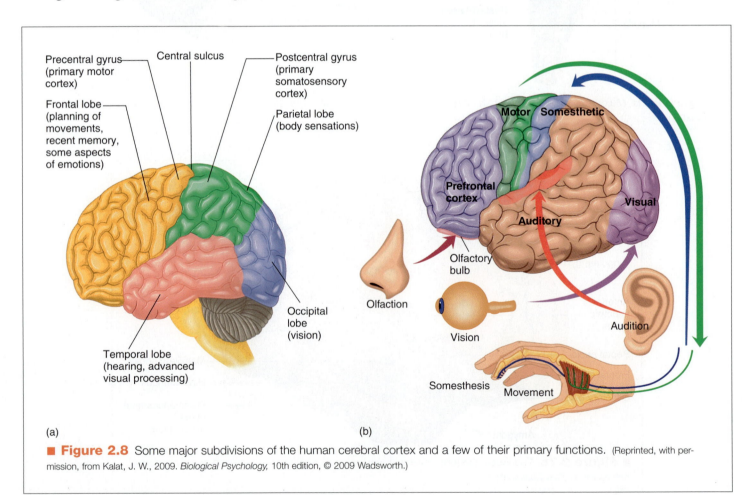

Precentral gyrus (primary motor cortex)

Central sulcus

Postcentral gyrus (primary somatosensory cortex)

Frontal lobe (planning of movements, recent memory, some aspects of emotions)

Parietal lobe (body sensations)

Occipital lobe (vision)

Temporal lobe (hearing, advanced visual processing)

(a)

Motor   Somesthetic

Prefrontal cortex

Visual

Auditory

Olfactory bulb

Olfaction

Vision

Somesthesis

Movement

Audition

(b)

■ **Figure 2.8** Some major subdivisions of the human cerebral cortex and a few of their primary functions. (Reprinted, with permission, from Kalat, J. W., 2009. *Biological Psychology*, 10th edition, © 2009 Wadsworth.)

together to process sight, touch, hearing, and other signals from our senses.

The front (or anterior) of the frontal lobe is called the *prefrontal cortex* and is responsible for higher cognitive functions such as thinking and reasoning, planning for the future, and long-term memory. It synthesizes information received from other parts of the brain and decides how to respond. It is what enables us to relate to the world around us. When studying the brain for clues to psychopathology, most researchers focus on the frontal lobe of the cerebral cortex in addition to the limbic system and the basal ganglia.

The Peripheral Nervous System

The peripheral nervous system coordinates with the brain stem to make sure the body is working properly. It consists of the *somatic nervous system* and the *autonomic nervous system*. The somatic nervous system controls the muscles. The autonomic nervous system includes the *sympathetic nervous system* and the *parasympathetic nervous system*. The autonomic nervous system regulates the cardiovascular and endocrine systems and performs various other functions, as shown in ■ Figure 2.9.

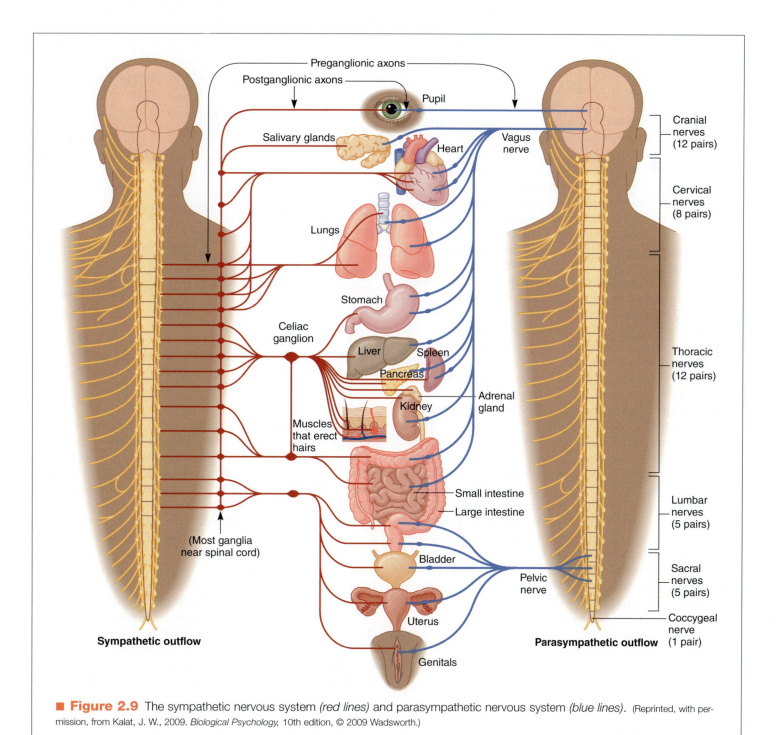

■ **Figure 2.9** The sympathetic nervous system *(red lines)* and parasympathetic nervous system *(blue lines)*. (Reprinted, with permission, from Kalat, J. W., 2009. *Biological Psychology*, 10th edition, © 2009 Wadsworth.)

The *endocrine system* includes a number of glands, each of which produces a chemical messenger, called a **hormone**, and releases it into the bloodstream. The adrenal glands produce *epinephrine* (also called *adrenaline*) in response to stress and salt-regulating hormones; the thyroid gland produces *thyroxine*, which facilitates energy metabolism and growth; the pituitary produces a variety of regulatory hormones; and the gonadal glands produce sex hormones such as estrogen and testosterone. The endocrine system is implicated in a variety of disorders. In addition to contributing to stress-related physical disorders, endocrine regulation may play a role in depression, anxiety, and schizophrenia. Recent studies have found, for example, that depressed patients may respond better to an antidepressant medication if it is administered in combination with a thyroid hormone (Nierenberg et al., 2006). This interdisciplinary area of research is termed *psychoneuroendocrinology* and is a growing subfield.

The sympathetic and parasympathetic nervous systems operate in a complementary fashion. The sympathetic system mobilizes the body during times of stress or danger by rapidly activating the organs and glands under its control. The heart beats faster, thereby increasing the flow of blood to the muscles; respiration increases, allowing more oxygen to get into the blood and brain; and the adrenal glands are stimulated. All these changes help mobilize us for action. When you read in the newspaper that a woman lifted a heavy object to free a trapped child, you can be sure her sympathetic nervous system was working overtime. This system mediates a substantial part of our "emergency" or "alarm" reaction, discussed later in this chapter and in Chapter 4.

One of the functions of the parasympathetic system is to balance the sympathetic system. In other words, because we could not operate in a state of hyperarousal forever, the parasympathetic system takes over after the sympathetic system has been active for a while, normalizing arousal and facilitating the storage of energy by helping the digestive process.

As we noted previously, surges of epinephrine tend to energize us, arouse us, and get our bodies ready for threat or challenge. When athletes say their adrenaline was really flowing, they mean they were highly aroused and up for the competition. The cortical part of the adrenal glands also produces the stress hormone cortisol. This system is called the *hypothalamic–pituitary–adrenocortical axis*, or *HPA axis* (■ Figure 2.10); it has been implicated in several psychological disorders and is mentioned in Chapters 4, 6, and 8.

This brief overview should give you a general sense of the structure and function of the brain and nervous system. New procedures for studying brain structure and function that involve photographing the working brain are discussed in Chapter 3. Here, we focus on what these studies reveal about psychopathology.

Neurotransmitters

Neurotransmitters are receiving intense attention by psychopathologists (Bloom & Kupfer, 1995; Bloom, Nelson, & Lazerson, 2001; LeDoux, 2002; Iverson, 2006; Nestler, Hy-

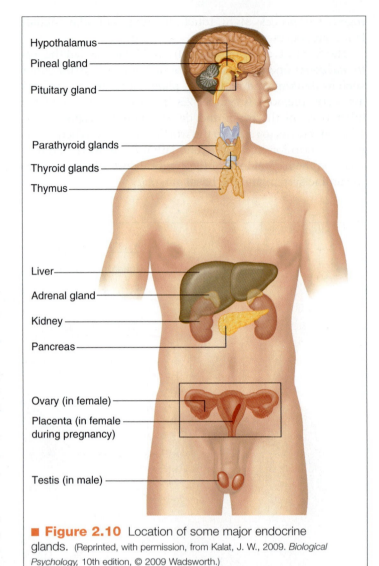

■ **Figure 2.10** Location of some major endocrine glands. (Reprinted, with permission, from Kalat, J. W., 2009. *Biological Psychology*, 10th edition, © 2009 Wadsworth.)

man, & Malenka, 2008; Secko, 2005). Current estimates suggest that more than 100 different neurotransmitters, each with multiple receptors, are functioning in various parts of the nervous system (Borodinsky et al., 2004; Sharp, 2009). One way to think of neurotransmitters is as narrow currents flowing through the ocean of the brain. Sometimes they run parallel with other currents. Often they meander, looping back on themselves before moving on. Neurons that are sensitive to one type of neurotransmitter cluster together and form paths from one part of the brain to the other.

Often these paths overlap with the paths of other neurotransmitters but end up going their separate ways (Bloom et al., 2001; Dean, Kelsey, Heller, & Ciaranello, 1993). There are thousands, perhaps tens of thousands, of these **brain circuits** (Arenkiel & Ehlers, 2009). Neuroscientists have identified several neural pathways that seem to play roles in psychological disorders (Fineberg et al., 2010; LeDoux, 2002; Stahl, 2008; Tau & Peterson, 2010).

You may still read reports that certain psychological disorders are "caused" by biochemical imbalances, excesses, or deficiencies in certain neurotransmitter systems. For example, abnormal activity of the neurotransmitter serotonin is often described as causing depression. However, increasing evidence indicates that this is an enormous oversimplification. We are now learning that the effects of neurotransmitter activity are less specific. They often seem to be related to the way we process information (Bloom et al., 2001; Depue, Luciana, Arbisi, Collins, & Leon, 1994; Harmer et al., 2009; Kandel, Schwartz, & Jessell, 2000; LeDoux, 2002; Sullivan & LeDoux, 2004). Changes in neurotransmitter activity may make people more or less likely to exhibit certain kinds of behavior in certain situations without causing the behavior directly. In addition, broad-based disturbances in our functioning are almost always associated with interactions of the various neurotransmitters rather than with alterations in the activity of any one system (Depue & Spoont, 1986; Depue & Zald, 1993; Fineberg et al., 2010; LeDoux, 2002; Owens et al., 1997; Secko, 2005; Stahl, 2008; Xing, Zhang, Russell, & Post, 2006). In other words, the currents intersect so often that changes in one result in changes in the other, often in a way scientists are not yet able to predict.

Research on neurotransmitter function focuses primarily on what happens when activity levels change. We can study this in several ways. We can introduce substances called **agonists** that effectively *increase* the activity of a neurotransmitter by mimicking its effects; substances called **antagonists** that *decrease,* or block, a neurotransmitter; or substances called **inverse agonists** that produce effects *opposite* to those produced by the neurotransmitter. By manipulating the production of a neurotransmitter in different parts of the brain, we can learn more about its effects. Most drugs could be classified as either agonistic or antagonistic—that is, they work by either increasing or decreasing the flow of specific neurotransmitters. Some drugs inhibit the production of a neurotransmitter. Others increase the production of competing biochemical substances that may deactivate the neurotransmitter. Yet others do not affect neurotransmitters directly but prevent the chemical from reaching the next neuron by closing down, or occupying, the receptors in that neuron. After a neurotransmitter is released, it is quickly drawn back from the synaptic cleft into the same neuron. This process is called **reuptake**. Some drugs work by blocking the reuptake process, thereby causing continued stimulation along the brain circuit.

Two types of neurotransmitters, *monoamines* and *amino acids,* have been most studied in regard to psychopathology. These are considered the "classic" neurotransmitters because they are synthesized in the nerve. Neurotransmitters in the monoamine class include norepinephrine (also known as noradrenaline), serotonin, and dopamine. Amino acid neurotransmitters include gamma-aminobutyric acid (GABA) and glutamate.

Glutamate and GABA

Two major neurotransmitters affect much of what we do. The first, **glutamate**, is an excitatory transmitter that "turns on" many different neurons, leading to ac-

tion. The second, **gamma-aminobutyric acid**, or **GABA** for short, is an inhibitory neurotransmitter. Its job is to inhibit (or regulate) the transmission of information and action potentials. Glutamate and GABA operate relatively independently, but the relative balance of each in a cell will determine whether the neuron is activated (fires) or not.

Another characteristic of these "chemical brothers" (LeDoux, 2002) is that they are fast acting. For example, some people who are sensitive to glutamate may have experienced a few adverse reactions right after eating Chinese food. These are to the result of an additive, monosodium glutamate (MSG), that can increase the amount of glutamate in the body, causing headaches, ringing in the ears, or other physical symptoms in some people.

As noted earlier, GABA reduces postsynaptic activity, which, in turn, inhibits a variety of behaviors and emotions. Its best-known effect is to reduce anxiety (Charney & Drevets, 2002; Davis, 2002; Sullivan & LeDoux, 2004). A particular class of drugs, the *benzodiazepines,* or minor tranquilizers, makes it easier for GABA molecules to attach themselves to the receptors of specialized neurons. Thus, the higher the level of benzodiazepine, the more GABA becomes attached to neuron receptors and the calmer we become (to a point). Because benzodiazepines have addictive properties, scientists are working to identify other substances that may modulate levels of GABA; these include certain natural steroids in the brain (Eser, Schule, Baghai, Romeo, & Rupprecht, 2006; Gordon, 2002; Rupprecht et al., 2009).

As with other neurotransmitter systems, we now know that GABA's effect is not specific to anxiety but has a broader influence. The GABA system rides on many circuits distributed widely throughout the brain. GABA seems to reduce overall arousal somewhat and to temper our emotional responses. For example, in addition to reducing anxiety, minor tranquilizers have an anticonvulsant effect, relaxing muscle groups that may be subject to spasms. Drug compounds that increase GABA are also under evalu-

---

hormone Chemical messenger produced by the endocrine glands.
brain circuits Neurotransmitter current or neural pathway in the brain.
agonist In neuroscience, a chemical substance that effectively increases the activity of a neurotransmitter by imitating its effects.
antagonist In neuroscience, a chemical substance that decreases or blocks the effects of a neurotransmitter.
inverse agonist In neuroscience, a chemical substance that produces effects opposite those of a particular neurotransmitter.
reuptake Action by which a neurotransmitter is quickly drawn back into the discharging neuron after being released into a synaptic cleft.
glutamate Amino acid neurotransmitter that excites many different **neurons**, leading to action.
gamma-aminobutyric acid (GABA) Neurotransmitter that reduces activity across the synaptic cleft and thus inhibits a range of behaviors and emotions, especially generalized anxiety.

ation as treatments for insomnia (Sullivan & Guilleminault, 2009; Walsh et al., 2008). Furthermore, the GABA system seems to reduce levels of anger, hostility, aggression, and perhaps even positive emotional states such as eager anticipation and pleasure, making GABA a generalized inhibiting neurotransmitter, much as glutamate has a generalized excitatory function (Bond & Lader, 1979; Lader, 1975; Sharp, 2009).

Serotonin

The technical name for **serotonin** is 5-hydroxytryptamine (5HT). It is in the monoamine category of neurotransmitters. Approximately six major circuits of serotonin spread from the midbrain, looping around its various parts (Azmitia, 1978) (■ Figure 2.11). Serotonin is believed to influence much of our behavior, particularly the way we process information (Depue & Spoont, 1986; Harmer, 2008; Merens, Willem Van der Does, & Spinhoven, 2007; Spoont, 1992). It was genetically influenced dysregulation in this system that contributed to depression in the New Zealand study described earlier (Caspi et al., 2003).

The serotonin system regulates our behavior, moods, and thought processes. Extremely low levels of serotonin are associated with less inhibition and with instability, impulsivity, and the tendency to overreact. Low serotonin activity has been associated with aggression, suicide, impulsive overeating, and excessive sexual behavior. However, these behaviors do not *necessarily* happen if serotonin activity is low. Other currents in the brain, or other psychological or social influences, may compensate. Therefore, low serotonin activity may make us more vulnerable to certain problematic behavior without directly causing it. On the other end, high levels of serotonin may interact with GABA to counteract glutamate.

Several classes of drugs primarily affect the serotonin system, including the tricyclic antidepressants such as imipramine (known by its brand name, Tofranil). However, the serotonin-specific reuptake inhibitors (SSRIs), including fluoxetine (Prozac) (■ Figure 2.12), affect serotonin more directly than other drugs, including the tricyclic antidepressants. SSRIs are used to treat a number of psychological disorders, particularly anxiety, mood, and eating disorders. The herbal medication St. John's wort, available in health food stores, also affects serotonin levels.

Norepinephrine

A third neurotransmitter system in the monoamine class is **norepinephrine** (also known as **noradrenaline**) (■ Figure 2.13 on page 50).

Norepinephrine seems to stimulate at least two groups of receptors called *alpha-adrenergic* and *beta-adrenergic receptors*. A widely used class of drugs called *beta-blockers* are used to treat hypertension or difficulties with regulating heart rate. These drugs block the beta-receptors so that their response to a surge of norepinephrine is reduced, which keeps blood pressure and heart rate down. A number of norepinephrine circuits have been identified. One major circuit begins in the hindbrain, an area that controls

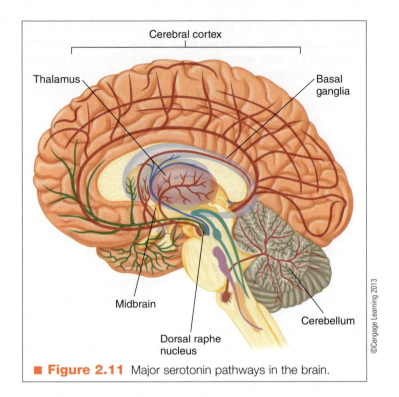

■ **Figure 2.11** Major serotonin pathways in the brain.

©Cengage Learning 2013

basic bodily functions such as respiration. Another circuit appears to influence emergency reactions or alarm responses (Charney & Drevets, 2002; Gray, 1987; Gray & McNaughton, 1996; Sullivan & LeDoux, 2004), suggesting that norepinephrine may bear some relationship to states of panic (Charney et al., 1990; Gray & McNaughton, 1996). More likely, however, is that this system acts in a more general way to regulate certain behavioral tendencies and is not directly involved in specific patterns of behavior or in psychological disorders.

Dopamine

Finally, **dopamine** is a major neurotransmitter in the monoamine class. Dopamine has been implicated in schizophrenia (■ Figure 2.14 on page 50) and disorders of addiction (LeFoll, Gallo, LeStrat, Lu, & Gorwood, 2009). New research also indicates it may play a significant role in depression (Dunlop & Nemeroff, 2007) and attention deficit hyperactivity disorder (Volkow et al., 2009). Remember the wonder drug reserpine that reduced psychotic behaviors associated with schizophrenia? This drug and more modern antipsychotic treatments affect a number of neurotransmitter systems, but their greatest impact may be that they block specific dopamine receptors, thus lowering dopamine activity (see, for example, Snyder, Burt, & Creese, 1976).

In its various circuits throughout specific regions of the brain, dopamine also seems to have a more general effect, best described as a switch that turns on various brain circuits possibly associated with certain types of behavior. Once the switch is turned on, other neurotransmitters may then inhibit or facilitate emotions or behavior (Armbruster et al., 2009; Oades, 1985; Spoont, 1992; Stahl, 2008). Dopamine circuits merge and cross with serotonin circuits at

How Neurotransmitters Work
Neurotransmitters are stored in tiny sacs at the end of the neuron **A**. An electric jolt makes the sacs merge with the outer membrane, and the neurotransmitter is released into the synapse **B**. The molecules diffuse across the gap and bind receptors, specialized proteins, on the adjacent neuron **C**. When sufficient neurotransmitter has been absorbed, the receptors release the molecules, which are then broken down or reabsorbed by the first neuron and stored for later use **D**.

How Serotonin Drugs Work
Prozac enhances serotonin's effects by preventing it from being absorbed **E**. Redux and fenfluramine (antiobesity drugs) cause the release of extra serotonin into the synapse **F**.

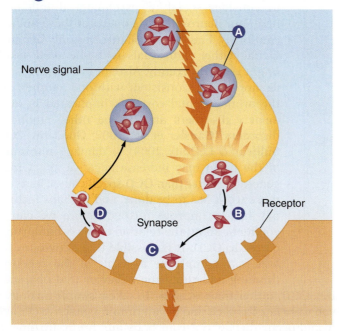

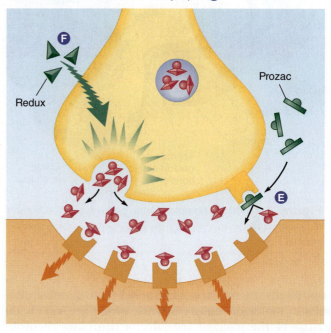

Receptor Variation
There are at least 15 different serotonin receptors, each associated with a different function. This schematic shows how some of them may work.

■ **Figure 2.12** Manipulating serotonin in the brain. (© Cengage Learning 2013)

many points and therefore influence many of the same behaviors. For example, dopamine activity is associated with exploratory, outgoing, pleasure-seeking behaviors (Elovainio, Kivimaki, Viikari, Ekelund, & Keltikangas-Jarvinen, 2005), and serotonin is associated with inhibition and constraint; thus, in a sense they balance each other (Depue et al., 1994).

Researchers have thus far discovered at least five different receptor sites that are selectively sensitive to dopamine (Owens et al., 1997; Girault & Greengard, 2004). One of a class of drugs that affects the dopamine circuits specifically is L-dopa, a dopamine agonist (increases levels of dopamine). One of the systems that dopamine switches on is the locomotor system, which regulates ability to move in a coordinated way and, once turned on, is influenced by serotonin activity. Because of these connections, deficiencies in dopamine have been associated with disorders such as Parkinson's disease, in which a marked deterioration in motor behavior includes tremors, rigidity of muscles, and difficulty with judgment. L-dopa has been successful in reducing some of these motor disabilities.

Implications for Psychopathology

Psychological disorders typically mix emotional, behavioral, and cognitive symptoms, so lesions (or damage) in specific structures of the brain do not, for the most part,

serotonin Neurotransmitter involved in processing of information and coordination of movement, as well as inhibition and restraint. It also assists in the regulation of eating, sexual, and aggressive behaviors, all of which may be involved in different psychological disorders. Its interaction with dopamine is implicated in schizophrenia.

norepinephrine (also noradrenaline) Neurotransmitter active in the central and peripheral nervous systems, controlling heart rate, blood pressure, and respiration, among other functions. Because of its role in the body's alarm reaction, it may also contribute generally and indirectly to panic attacks and other disorders. Also known as *noradrenaline*.

dopamine Neurotransmitter whose generalized function is to activate other neurotransmitters and to aid in exploratory and pleasure-seeking behaviors (thus balancing serotonin). A relative excess of dopamine is implicated in schizophrenia (although contradictory evidence suggests the connection is not simple), and its deficit is involved in Parkinson's disease.

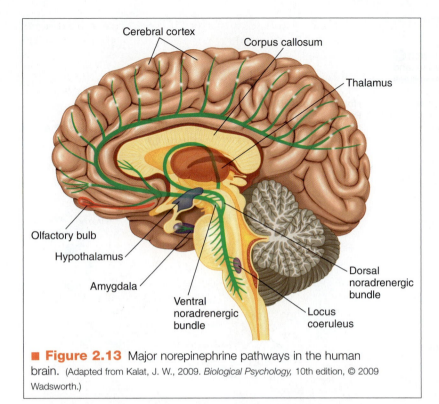

■ **Figure 2.13** Major norepinephrine pathways in the human brain. (Adapted from Kalat, J. W., 2009. *Biological Psychology*, 10th edition, © 2009 Wadsworth.)

gaging in uncontrollable compulsive rituals. He spent his days washing, dressing, and rearranging things in the single room where he lived. In other words, he had classic obsessive-compulsive symptoms. Removal of the tumor had damaged a small area of his orbital frontal cortex.

This information seems to support a biological cause for OCD. You might think there is no need to consider social or psychological influences here, but neuroscientists interpret these findings cautiously. First, this case involves only one individual. Other individuals with the *same* lesion might react differently. Also, brain-imaging studies are often inconsistent with one another, and the orbital frontal cortex is implicated in other anxiety disorders and maybe other emotional disorders (Gansler et al., 2009; Goodwin, 2009; Sullivan & LeDoux, 2004), so damage in this area of the brain may increase negative affect more generally rather than OCD specifically. Therefore, more work has to be done, and perhaps technology has to improve further, before we can be confident about the relation of the orbital frontal cortex to OCD. It is possible that activity in this area may simply be a result of the repetitive thinking and ritualistic behavior that characterizes OCD, rather than a cause. To take a simple analogy, if you were late for class and began running, massive changes would occur throughout your body and brain. If someone who did not know that you had just sprinted to class then

cause the disorders. Even widespread damage most often results in motor or sensory deficits, which are usually the province of the medical specialty of neurology; neurologists often work with neuropsychologists to identify specific lesions. But psychopathologists are focusing on the more general role of brain function in the development of personality, with the goal of considering how different types of personalities might be more vulnerable to certain types of disorders. For example, genetic contributions might lead to patterns of neurotransmitter activity that influence personality. Thus, some impulsive risk takers may have low serotonin activity and high dopamine activity.

Remember that one of the roles of serotonin seems to be to moderate our reactions. Eating behavior, sexual behavior, and aggression are under better control with adequate levels of serotonin. Research, mostly on animals, demonstrates that lesions (damage) that interrupt serotonin circuits seem to impair the ability to ignore irrelevant external cues, making the organism overactive. Thus, if we were to experience damage or interruption in this brain circuit, we might find ourselves acting on every thought or impulse that enters our heads.

Thomas Insel (1992) described a case originally reported by Eslinger and Damasio (1985) of a man who had been successful as an accountant, husband, and father of two before undergoing surgery for a brain tumor. He made a good recovery from surgery, but in the following year his business failed and he separated from his family. Although his scores on IQ tests were as high as ever and all his mental functions were intact, he was unable to keep a job or even be on time for an appointment. Instead, he was en-

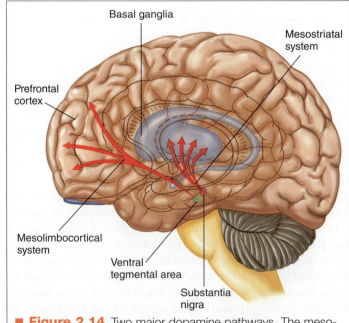

■ **Figure 2.14** Two major dopamine pathways. The mesolimbic system is apparently implicated in schizophrenia; the path to the basal ganglia contributes to problems in the locomotor system, such as tardive dyskinesia, which sometimes results from use of neuroleptic drugs. (Adapted from Kalat, J. W., 2009. *Biological Psychology*, 10th edition, © 2009 Wadsworth.)

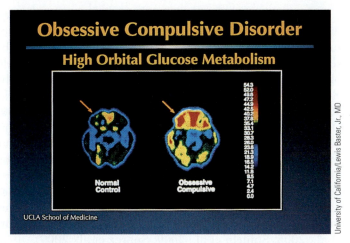

Obsessive Compulsive Disorder

High Orbital Glucose Metabolism

Normal Control

Obsessive Compulsive

UCLA School of Medicine

University of California/Lewis Baster, Jr., MD

▲ Brain function is altered in people with obsessive-compulsive disorder, but it normalizes after effective psychosocial treatment.

examined you with brain scans, your brain functions would look different from those of the brain of a person who had walked to class. If you were doing well in the class, the scientist might conclude, wrongly, that your unusual brain function "caused" your intelligence.

Psychosocial Influences on Brain Structure and Function

Sometimes the effects of treatment tell us something about the nature of psychopathology. For example, if a clinician thinks OCD is caused by a specific brain dysfunction or by learned anxiety, this view would determine choice of treatment. Directing a treatment at one or the other of these theoretical causes and observing whether the patient gets better will prove or disprove the accuracy of the theory. This common strategy has one overriding weakness. Successfully treating a patient's toothache with aspirin does not mean the toothache was caused by an aspirin deficiency because an effect does not imply a cause. Nevertheless, this line of evidence gives us some hints about causes of psychopathology, particularly when it is combined with other experimental evidence.

If you knew that someone with OCD might have a faulty brain circuit, what treatment would you choose? Maybe you would recommend brain surgery, or neurosurgery. Neurosurgery to correct severe psychopathology (called "psychosurgery") is still done on occasion, particularly in the case of OCD when the suffering is severe and other treatments have failed (Aouizerate et al., 2006; Dougherty et al., 2002; Jenike et al., 1991; see also Chapter 4). For the accountant described previously, removal of his tumor seems to have eliminated an inhibitory part of the brain circuit implicated in OCD. Precise surgical lesions might dampen the runaway activity that seems to occur in or near this area of the brain. This result would probably be welcome if all other treatments have failed, although psychosurgery is used seldom and has not been studied systematically.

Nobody wants to do surgery if less intrusive treatments are available. To use the analogy of a television set that has developed the "disorder" of going fuzzy, if you had to rearrange wires on the circuit board every time the disorder occurred, the correction would be a major undertaking. If you could simply push some buttons on the remote and eliminate the fuzziness, the correction would be simpler and less risky. The development of drugs affecting neurotransmitter activity has given us one of those buttons. We now have drugs that seem to be beneficial in treating OCD. As you might suspect, most of them act by increasing serotonin activity.

But is it possible to get at this brain circuit without either surgery or drugs? Could psychological treatment be powerful enough to affect the circuit directly? The answer seems to be yes. Lewis R. Baxter and his colleagues used brain imaging on patients who had not been treated, then treated the patients with a cognitive-behavioral therapy known to be effective in OCD called *exposure and response prevention*, and then repeated the brain imaging (Baxter et al., 1992). They discovered that the brain circuit had been changed (normalized) by a psychological intervention. They replicated the experiment with a different group of patients and found the same changes in brain function (Schwartz, Stoessel, Baxter, Martin, & Phelps, 1996).

In other examples, investigators noted changes in brain function after successful psychological treatment for depression (Brody et al., 2001; Martin, Martin, Rai, Richardson, & Royall, 2001), posttraumatic stress disorder (Rabe, Zoellner, Beauducel, Maercker, & Karl, 2008), and specific phobia, which they termed "re-wiring the brain" (Paquette et al., 2003). In another intriguing study, Leuchter, Cook, Witte, Morgan, and Abrams (2002) treated patients with major depressive disorder with either antidepressant medications or placebo medications. (Remember that it is common for inactive placebo medications, which are just sugar pills, to result in behavioral and emotional changes in patients, presumably as a result of psychological factors such as increasing hope and expectations.) Measures of brain function showed that both antidepressant medications and placebos changed brain function but in somewhat different parts of the brain, suggesting different mechanisms of action for these two interventions. It would seem that psychological treatments are another button on the remote with which we can directly change brain circuits.

Another area of research is exploring the specific ways in which drug or psychological treatments work in terms of changes in brain function. Are the changes similar or different? Kennedy et al. (2007) treated individuals with major depressive disorder with either a psychological treatment, cognitive-behavioral therapy (CBT), or the antidepressant drug venlafaxine. Although some brain changes were similar among the three treatment groups, differences were also noted, primarily in the way in which CBT facilitated changes in thinking patterns in the cortex that, in turn, affected the emotional brain. Sometimes this is called a "top down" change because it originates in the cortex and works its way down into the lower brain.

Drugs, however, often seem to work more in a "bottom up" manner, reaching higher areas of the cortex (where thinking occurs) last. Many similar studies are now in progress. Because we know that some people respond better to psychological treatments, and others respond better to drugs, this research provides hope that we will one day be able to choose the best treatments or better combine treatments based on an analysis of the individual's brain function.

Interactions of Psychosocial Factors with Brain Structure and Function

Several experiments illustrate the interaction of psychosocial factors and brain function. Some even indicate that psychosocial factors directly affect levels of neurotransmitters. For example, Insel, Scanlan, Champoux, and Suomi (1988) raised two groups of rhesus monkeys identically except for their ability to control things in their cages. One group had free access to toys and food treats, but the second group got these toys and treats only when the first group did. In other words, members of the second group had the same number of toys and treats but could not choose when they got them. Thus, the monkeys in the first group grew up with a sense of control over things in their lives and those in the second group didn't.

Later in their lives, all these monkeys were administered a benzodiazepine inverse agonist, a neurochemical that has the *opposite* effect of the neurotransmitter GABA; the effect is an extreme burst of anxiety. The monkeys that had been raised with little control over their environment ran to a corner of their cage where they crouched and displayed signs of severe anxiety and panic. But the monkeys that had a sense of control did not seem anxious. Rather, they seemed angry and aggressive, even attacking other monkeys near them. Thus, the same level of a neurochemical substance, acting as a neurotransmitter, had different effects, depending on the psychological and environmental histories of the monkeys.

Other experiments suggest that psychosocial influences directly affect the functioning and perhaps even the structure of the central nervous system. Scientists have observed that psychosocial factors change the activity levels of many neurotransmitter systems, including norepinephrine and serotonin (Cacioppo et al., 2007; Coplan et al., 1996, 1998; Heim & Nemeroff, 1999; Ladd et al., 2000; Ouellet-Morin et al., 2008; Roma, Champoux, & Suomi, 2006; Sullivan, Kent, & Coplan, 2000). It also seems that the structure of neurons themselves, including the number of receptors on a cell, can be changed by learning and experience (Gottlieb, 1998; Kandel, 1983; Kandel, Jessell, & Schacter, 1991; Ladd et al., 2000; Owens et al., 1997) and that these effects continue throughout our lives (Cameron et al., 2005; Spinelli et al., 2009; Suarez et al., 2009).

We are beginning to learn how psychosocial factors affect brain function and structure (Kolb, Gibb, & Robinson, 2003; Kolb & Whishaw, 1998). William Greenough and his associates (Greenough, Withers, & Wallace, 1990) discovered that the nervous systems of rats raised in a rich environment requiring a lot of learning and motor behavior develop differently from those in rats that were "couch potatoes." The active rats had many more connections between nerve cells in the cerebellum and grew many more dendrites. In a follow-up study, Wallace, Kilman, Withers, and Greenough (1992) reported that these structural changes in the brain began in as little as 4 days. Similarly, stress during early development can lead to changes in the functioning of the HPA axis (described earlier in this chapter) that, in turn, make primates more or less susceptible to stress later in life (Barlow, 2002; Coplan et al., 1998; Gillespie & Nemeroff, 2007; Spinelli et al., 2009; Suomi, 1999). It may be something similar to this mechanism that was responsible for the effects of early stress on the later development of depression in genetically susceptible individuals in the New Zealand study described earlier (Caspi et al., 2003). So, we can conclude that early psychological experience affects the development of the nervous system and thus determines vulnerability to psychological disorders later in life. It seems that the very structure of the nervous system is constantly changing as a result of learning and experience, and that some of these changes become permanent (Kolb, Gibb, & Gorny, 2003; Suárez et al., 2009).

Scientists have begun to pin down the complex interaction among psychosocial factors, brain structure, and brain function as reflected in neurotransmitter activity. Yeh, Fricke, and Edwards (1996) studied two male crayfish battling to establish dominance in their social group. When one of the crayfish won the battle, serotonin made a specific set of neurons more likely to fire; but in the animal that lost the battle, serotonin made the same neurons less likely to fire. Thus, Edwards et al. discovered that naturally occurring

▲ Rhesus monkeys injected with a specific neurotransmitter react with anger or fear, depending on their early psychological experiences.

Thomas Insel/1986 study/National Institute of Mental Health

▲ William Greenough and his associates raised rats in a complex environment that required significant learning and motor behavior, which affected the structure of the rat's brains. This supports the role of psychological factors on biological development.

neurotransmitters have different effects depending on the organism's previous psychosocial experience. Furthermore, this experience directly affects the structure of neurons at the synapse by altering the sensitivity of serotonin receptors. The researchers also discovered that the effects of serotonin are reversible if the losers again become dominant. Similarly, Suomi (2000) demonstrated in primates that early stressful experiences produced deficits in serotonin in genetically susceptible individuals, deficits that did not occur in the absence of early stress.

Comments

The brain circuits involved in psychological disorders are complex systems identified by pathways of neurotransmitters traversing the brain. The existence of these circuits suggests that the structure and function of the nervous system play major roles in psychopathology. But other research suggests that the circuits are influenced, perhaps even created, by psychological and social factors. Furthermore, both biological interventions, such as drugs, and

psychological interventions or experience seem capable of altering the circuits. Therefore, we cannot consider the nature of psychological disorders without examining both biological and psychological factors. We now turn to an examination of psychological factors.

Concept Check 2.3

Match each of the following with its description below: (a) frontal lobe, (b) brain stem, (c) GABA, (d) midbrain, (e) serotonin, (f) dopamine, (g) norepinephrine, and (h) cerebral cortex.

1. Movement, breathing, and sleeping depend on this ancient part of the brain, which is present in most animals. _____

2. Which neurotransmitter binds to neuron receptor sites, inhibiting postsynaptic activity and reducing overall arousal? _____

3. Which neurotransmitter is a switch that turns on various brain circuits? _____

4. Which neurotransmitter seems to be involved in emergency reactions or alarm responses? _____

5. This area contains part of the reticular activating system and coordinates movement with sensory output. _____

6. Which neurotransmitter is believed to influence the way we process information and moderate or inhibit our behavior? _____

7. More than 80% of the neurons in the human central nervous system are contained in this part of the brain. _____

8. This area is responsible for most of our memory, thinking, and reasoning capabilities and makes us social animals. _____

Behavioral and Cognitive Psychology

› **What are the key differences between behavioral and cognitive explanations of the origins of mental illness?**

Enormous progress has been made in understanding behavioral and cognitive influences in psychopathology. Some new information has come from the field of **cognitive science**, which is concerned with how we acquire and process information and how we store and ultimately retrieve it (one of the processes involved in memory). Scientists have also discovered that a great deal goes on inside our heads of

which we are not necessarily aware. Because, technically, these cognitive processes are unconscious, some findings

cognitive science Field of study that examines how humans and other animals acquire, process, store, and retrieve information.

recall the unconscious mental processes that are so much a part of Sigmund Freud's theory of psychoanalysis (although they do not look much like the ones he envisioned). Following is a brief account of current thinking on what happens during the process of classical conditioning.

Conditioning and Cognitive Processes

During the 1960s and 1970s, behavioral scientists in animal laboratories began to uncover the complexity of the basic processes of classical conditioning (Bouton, 2005; Bouton, Mineka, & Barlow, 2001; Eelen & Vervliet, 2006; Mineka & Zinbarg, 1996, 1998). Robert Rescorla (1988) concluded that simply pairing two events closely in time (such as the meat powder and the metronome in Pavlov's laboratories) is not what's important in this type of learning. Rather, a variety of judgments and cognitive processes combine to determine the final outcome of this learning, even in lower animals such as rats.

To take just one example, Pavlov would have predicted that if the meat powder and the metronome were paired, say, 50 times, a certain amount of learning would take place. But Rescorla and others discovered that if one animal never saw the meat powder except for the 50 trials following the metronome sound, whereas the meat powder was brought to a second animal many times *between* the 50 times it was paired with the metronome, the two animals would learn different things—that is, even though the metronome and the meat powder were paired 50 times for each animal, the metronome was less meaningful to the second animal (■ Figure 2.15). Put another way, the first animal learned that the sound of the metronome meant meat powder came next; the second animal learned that the meat sometimes came after the sound and sometimes without the sound. That two different conditions produce two different learning outcomes is a commonsense notion, but it demonstrates that basic conditioning facilitates the learning of the relationship among events in the environment.

This type of learning enables us to develop working ideas about the world that allow us to make appropriate judgments. We can then respond in a way that will benefit or at least not hurt us. In other words, complex cognitive, and emotional, processing of information is involved when conditioning occurs, even in animals.

Learned Helplessness

Along similar lines, Martin Seligman and his colleague Steven Maier, also working with animals, described the phenomenon of **learned helplessness**, which occurs when ani-

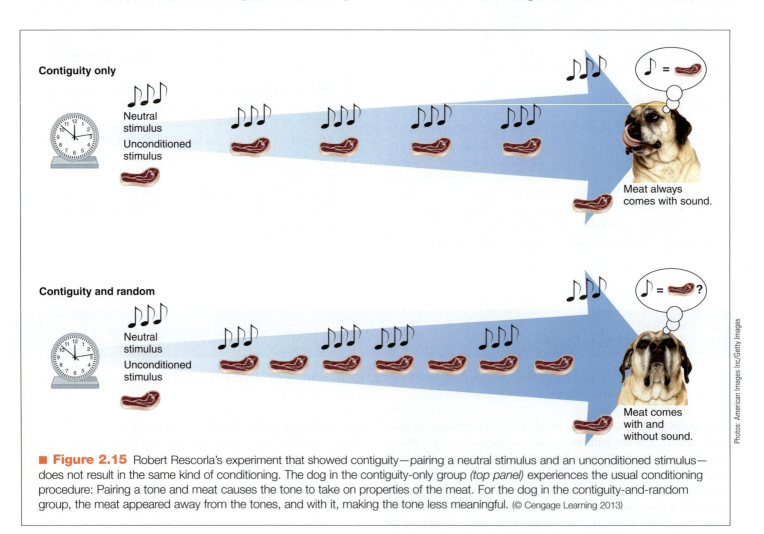

■ **Figure 2.15** Robert Rescorla's experiment that showed contiguity—pairing a neutral stimulus and an unconditioned stimulus—does not result in the same kind of conditioning. The dog in the contiguity-only group *(top panel)* experiences the usual conditioning procedure: Pairing a tone and meat causes the tone to take on properties of the meat. For the dog in the contiguity-and-random group, the meat appeared away from the tones, and with it, making the tone less meaningful. (© Cengage Learning 2013)

mals encounter conditions over which they have no control (Maier & Seligman, 1976). If rats are confronted with a situation in which they receive occasional foot shocks, they can function well if they learn to cope with these shocks by doing something to avoid them (say, pressing a lever). But if the animals learn that their behavior has no effect on their environment—sometimes they get shocked and sometimes they don't, no matter what they do—they become "helpless"; they give up attempting to cope and seem to develop the animal equivalent of depression.

Seligman theorized that the same phenomenon may happen with people who are faced with uncontrollable stress. Subsequent work revealed this to be true under one important condition: People become depressed if they "decide" or "think" they can do little about the stress in their lives, even if it seems to others that there is something they could do. People make an *attribution* that they have no control, and they become depressed (Abramson, Seligman, & Teasdale, 1978; Miller & Norman, 1979). This finding illustrates, again, the necessity of recognizing that different people process information about events in different ways. These cognitive differences are an important component of psychopathology.

Lately, Seligman has turned his attention to a different set of attributions, which he terms *learned optimism* (Seligman, 1998, 2002). If people faced with considerable stress and difficulty in their lives nevertheless display an optimistic, upbeat attitude, they are likely to function better. Consider an example: In a study by Levy, Slade, Kunkel, & Kasl (2002), individuals between ages 50 and 94 who had positive views about themselves and positive attitudes toward aging lived 7.5 years longer than those without such attitudes. This connection was still true after the investigators controlled for age, sex, income, loneliness, and physical capability to engage in household and social activities. This effect exceeds the 1 to 4 years of added life associated with other factors, such as low blood pressure, low cholesterol levels, and no history of obesity or cigarette smoking. Studies such as this have created interest in *positive psychology,* in which investigators explore factors that account for positive attitudes and happiness (Diener, 2000; Lyubomirsky, 2001).

Social Learning

Another influential psychologist, Albert Bandura (1973, 1986), observed that organisms do not have to experience certain events in their environment to learn effectively. They can learn just as much by observing what happens to someone else in a given situation, a process termed **modeling** or **observational learning**. Even in animals, this type of learning requires integration of the experiences of others with judgments of what might happen to oneself; in other words, even an animal such as a monkey must make a decision about the conditions under which its own experiences would be similar to those of the animal it is observing. Bandura concluded that behavior, cognitive factors, and environmental influences converge to produce the complex-

ity of behavior that confronts us. He also emphasized the social context of learning—that is, much of what we learn depends on our interactions with people around us. These ideas have been integrated with findings on the genetic and biological bases of social behavior in a new field of study called social neuroscience (Cacioppo et al., 2007).

The basic idea here is that careful analysis of cognitive processes may produce the most accurate predictions of behavior. Concepts of probability learning, information processing, and attention have become increasingly important in psychopathology (Barlow, 2002; Craighead, Ilardi, Greenberg, & Craighead, 1997; Davey, 2006; Lovibond, 2006; Mathews & MacLeod, 1994).

Prepared Learning

It is clear that biological factors influence what we learn. This conclusion is based on the fact that we learn to fear some objects more easily than others (Mineka & Sutton, 2006; Morris, Öhman, & Dolan, 1998; Öhman, Flykt, & Lundqvist, 2000; Öhman & Mineka, 2001; Rakison, 2009). Why might this be? According to the concept of **prepared learning**, we have become highly prepared for learning about certain types of objects or situations over the course of evolution because this knowledge contributes to the survival of the species (Mineka, 1985; Seligman, 1971). Even without any contact, we are more likely to learn to fear snakes or spiders than rocks or flowers, even if we know the snake or spider is harmless (for example, Fredrikson, Annas, & Wik, 1997; Pury & Mineka, 1997). In the absence of experience, however, we are less likely to fear guns or electrical outlets, even though they are potentially deadlier.

Why do we so readily learn to fear snakes or spiders? One possibility is that when our ancestors lived in caves, those who avoided snakes and spiders survived in greater numbers to pass down their genes to us, thus contributing to the survival of the species. In fact, recent research has found that a sex difference may exist for this type of learning: females are particularly sensitive to this learning and, unlike males, demonstrate it as early as 11 months of age (Rakison, 2009). Thus, "prepared learning" may account for the greater incidence of snake and spider phobias in adult women (see Chapter 4). According to this theory it would have been more important for women, in their roles as foragers and gatherers, to develop a tendency to avoid snakes and spiders than for males, in their roles as risk-taking hunters (Rakison, 2009).

learned helplessness Martin Seligman's theory that people become anxious and depressed when they make an attribution that they have no control over the stress in their lives (whether or not they actually have control).

modeling (also observational learning) Learning through observation and imitation of the behavior of other individuals and consequences of that behavior.

prepared learning Ability adaptive for evolution, allowing certain associations to be learned more readily than others.

In any case, something within us recognizes the connection between a certain signal and a threatening event. If you've ever gotten sick on cheap wine or bad food, chances are you won't make the same mistake again. This quick or "one-trial" learning also occurs in animals that eat something that tastes bad, causes nausea, or may contain poison. It is easy to see that survival is associated with quickly learning to avoid poisonous food. If animals are shocked instead of poisoned when eating certain foods, however, they do not learn this association nearly as quickly, probably because in nature shock is not a consequence of eating, whereas being poisoned may be. Perhaps these selective associations are also facilitated by our genes (Barlow, 2002; Cook, Hodes, & Lang, 1986; Garcia, McGowan, & Green, 1972).

Cognitive Science and the Unconscious

Advances in cognitive science have revolutionized our conceptions of the unconscious. We are not aware of much of what goes on inside our heads, but our unconscious is not necessarily the seething cauldron of primitive emotional conflicts envisioned by Freud. Rather, we simply seem able to process and store information, and act on it, without being aware of the information or why we are acting on it (Bargh & Chartrand, 1999; Uleman, Saribay, & Gonzalez, 2008). Is this surprising? Consider two examples.

Lawrence Weiskrantz (1992) describes a phenomenon called *blind sight* or *unconscious vision.* He relates the case of a young man who, for medical reasons, had a small section of his visual cortex (the center for the control of vision in the brain) surgically removed. Although the operation was considered a success, the young man became blind in both eyes. Later, during routine tests, a physician raised his hand to the left of the patient, who reached out and touched it. Subsequently, scientists determined that he could not only reach accurately for objects but could also distinguish among objects and perform most of the functions usually associated with sight. Yet, when asked about his abilities, he would say, "I couldn't see anything, not a darn thing," and that all he was doing was guessing.

The phenomenon in this case is associated with real brain damage. However, the same thing seems to occur in healthy individuals who have been hypnotized (Hilgard, 1992; Kihlstrom, 1992)—that is, normal individuals, given hypnotic suggestions that they are blind, are able to function visually but have no awareness or memory of their visual abilities. This condition, which illustrates a process of *dissociation* between behavior and consciousness, is the basis of the dissociative disorders discussed in Chapter 5.

A second example, more relevant to psychopathology, is called **implicit memory** (Bowers & Marsolek, 2003; Craighead et al., 1997; Graf, Squire, & Mandler, 1984; Kihlstrom, Barnhardt, & Tataryn, 1992; McNally, 1999; Schacter, Chiu, & Ochsner, 1993). Implicit memory is apparent when someone clearly acts on the basis of things

that have happened in the past but can't remember the events. (A good memory for events is called *explicit memory.*) But implicit memory can be selective for only certain events or circumstances. An example of implicit memory at work is the story of Anna O., the classic case first described by Breuer and Freud (1895/1957) to demonstrate the existence of the unconscious. It was only after therapy that Anna O. remembered events surrounding her father's death and the connection of these events to her paralysis. Thus, Anna O.'s behavior (occasional paralysis) was evidently connected to implicit memories of her father's death. Several methods for studying the unconscious have been made possible by advances in technology. One of them is the Stroop color-naming paradigm.

In the Stroop paradigm, participants are shown a variety of words, each printed in a different color. They are shown these words quickly and asked to name the colors in which they are printed while ignoring their meaning. Color naming is delayed when the meaning of the word attracts the participant's attention, despite efforts to concentrate on the color—that is, the meaning of the word interferes with the participant's ability to process color information. For example, experimenters have determined that people with certain psychological disorders, like Judy, are much slower at naming the colors of words associated with their problem (for example, *blood, injury,* and *dissect*) than the colors of words that have no relation to the disorder. Thus, psychologists can now uncover emotionally significant patterns, even if the participant cannot verbalize them or is not even aware of them.

These developments in our understanding of the nature of psychopathology will come up repeatedly as we discuss specific disorders. Again, note that these findings support Freud's theories about the unconscious, up to a point. But no assumptions are made about an elaborate structure existing within the mind that is continually in conflict (Freud's id, ego, and superego); at present, there is no evidence to support the existence of an unconscious with such a complex structure and array of functions.

1.	RED	6.	GREEN	11.	BLUE
2.	PURPLE	7.	PURPLE	12.	PURPLE
3.	GREEN	8.	BROWN	13.	BROWN
4.	BLUE	9.	BLUE	14.	RED
5.	BROWN	10.	RED	15.	GREEN

The Stroop paradigm. Have someone keep time as you name the colors of the words, not the words themselves, and again as you name the words and colors together.
(© Cengage Learning 2013)

> ## What role do emotions play in psychopathology?

Emotions can contribute in major ways to the development of psychopathology (Gross, 2007; Kring & Sloan, 2010; Rottenberg & Johnson, 2007). Consider fear. Have you ever found yourself in a really dangerous situation? Have you ever almost crashed your car and known for several seconds beforehand what was going to happen? Have you ever been swimming in the ocean and realized you were out too far or caught in a current? Have you ever almost fallen from a height, such as a cliff or a roof? In such instances, you would have felt an incredible surge of arousal. As Charles Darwin (1872) pointed out more than 100 years ago, this kind of reaction seems to be programmed in all animals, including humans, which suggests that it serves a useful function. The alarm reaction that activates during potentially life-threatening emergencies is called the **flight or fight response**. If you are caught in an ocean current, you are likely to struggle toward shore. You might realize that you're best off just floating until the current runs its course. Yet the instinct for survival won't let you relax, even though struggling against the ocean will only wear you out and increase your chance of drowning. Still, this kind of reaction might momentarily give you the strength to lift a car off your trapped brother or fight off an attacker. The whole purpose of the physical rush of adrenaline that we feel in extreme danger is to mobilize us to escape the danger (flight) or fend it off (fight).

▲ Charles Darwin (1809–1882) drew this cat frightened by a dog to show the flight or fight reaction.

The Physiology and Purpose of Fear

How do physical reactions prepare us to respond this way? According to physiologist Walter Cannon (1929), fear activates your cardiovascular system. Your blood vessels constrict, thereby raising arterial pressure and decreasing blood flow to your extremities (fingers and toes). Excess blood is redirected to the skeletal muscles, where it is available to the organs that may be needed in an emergency. Often people seem "white with fear"—that is, they turn pale as a result of decreased blood flow to the skin. "Trembling with fear," with your hair standing on end, may be the result of shivering and piloerection (in which body hairs stand erect), reactions that conserve heat when your blood vessels are constricted.

These defensive adjustments can also produce the hot-and-cold spells that often occur during extreme fear. Breathing becomes faster and, usually, deeper to provide oxygen to rapidly circulating blood. Increased blood circulation carries oxygen to the brain, stimulating cognitive processes and sensory functions, which make you more alert and able to think more quickly. An increased amount of glucose (sugar) is released from the liver into the bloodstream, further energizing crucial muscles and organs, including the brain. Pupils dilate; hearing becomes more acute; and digestive activity is suspended, resulting in a reduced flow of saliva (the "dry mouth" of fear). In the short term, voiding the body of all waste material and eliminating digestive processes further prepare the organism for concentrated action and activity, so there is often pressure to urinate and defecate and, occasionally, to vomit.

Emotional Phenomena

The **emotion** of fear is a subjective feeling of terror, a strong motivation for behavior (escaping or fighting), and a complex physiological or arousal response. Most theorists agree that emotion is an *action tendency* (Barlow, 2002; Lang, 1985, 1995; Lang, Bradley, & Cuthbert, 1998)— that is, a tendency to behave in a certain way (for example, escape), elicited by an external event (a threat) and a feel-

implicit memory Condition of memory in which a person cannot recall past events despite acting in response to them.
flight or fight response Biological reaction to alarming stressors that musters the body's resources (for example, blood flow and respiration) to resist or flee a threat.
emotion Pattern of action elicited by an external event and a feeling state, accompanied by a characteristic physiological response.

ing state (terror) and accompanied by a (possibly) characteristic physiological response (Fairholme, Boisseau, Ellard, Ehrenreich, & Barlow, 2010; Gross, 2007; Izard, 1992; Lazarus, 1991, 1995). One purpose of a feeling state is to motivate us to carry out a behavior: If we escape, our terror, which is unpleasant, will be decreased (Campbell-Sills & Barlow, 2007; Gross, 2007; Öhman, 1996). As Öhman (1996; Öhman, Flykt, & Lundquist, 2000) points out, the principal function of emotions can be understood as a means to get us to do what we have to do to pass on our genes to coming generations. How do you think this works with anger or love? What is the feeling state? What is the behavior?

Emotions are usually temporary states lasting from several minutes to several hours, occurring in response to an external event. **Mood** is a more persistent period of affect or emotionality. Thus, in Chapter 6 we describe enduring or recurring states of depression or excitement (mania) as *mood disorders*. But *anxiety disorders*, described in Chapter 4, are characterized by enduring or chronic anxiety and, therefore, could also be called *mood disorders*. Alternatively, both anxiety disorders and mood disorders could be called *emotional disorders*, a term not formally used in psychopathology. This is only one example of the occasional inconsistencies in the terminology of abnormal psychology. A related term you will see occasionally is **affect**, which usually refers to the momentary emotional tone that accompanies what we say or do. For example, if you just got an A+ on your test but look sad, your friends might think your reaction strange because your affect is not appropriate. The term *affect* can also be used to summarize commonalities among emotional states characteristic of an individual. Thus, someone who tends to be fearful, anxious, and depressed is experiencing negative affect.

Components of Emotion

Emotion is composed of three related components—*behavior, physiology,* and *cognition*—but most emotion theorists tend to concentrate on one component or another (■ Figure 2.16). Those who concentrate on behavior think basic emotions differ in fundamental ways; for example, anger may differ from sadness not only in how it feels, but also behaviorally and physiologically. They also emphasize that emotion is a way of communicating between one member of the species and another. One function of fear is to motivate immediate action, such as running away. But if you look scared, your facial expression will communicate the possibility of danger to your friends, who may not have been aware of it. Your facial communication increases their chance for survival because they can respond more quickly to the threat. This may be one reason emotions are contagious (Hatfield, Cacioppo, & Rapson, 1994; Wang, 2006).

Other scientists have concentrated on the physiology of emotions. Cannon (1929) viewed emotion as primarily a brain function. Some physiological research suggests that areas of the brain associated with emotional expression are

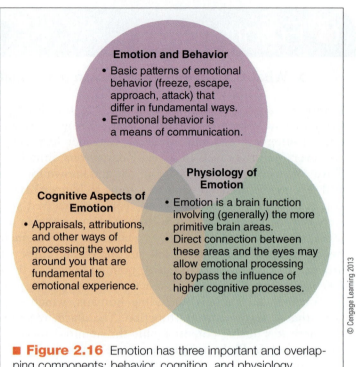

Emotion and Behavior
• Basic patterns of emotional behavior (freeze, escape, approach, attack) that differ in fundamental ways.
• Emotional behavior is a means of communication.

Cognitive Aspects of Emotion
• Appraisals, attributions, and other ways of processing the world around you that are fundamental to emotional experience.

Physiology of Emotion
• Emotion is a brain function involving (generally) the more primitive brain areas.
• Direct connection between these areas and the eyes may allow emotional processing to bypass the influence of higher cognitive processes.

© Cengage Learning 2013

■ **Figure 2.16** Emotion has three important and overlapping components: behavior, cognition, and physiology.

more ancient and primitive than areas associated with higher cognitive processes, such as reasoning. Other research demonstrates direct neurobiological connections between emotional centers of the brain and parts of the eye (the retina) or the ear that allow emotional activation without the influence of higher cognitive processes (LeDoux, 1996, 2002; Öhman, Flykt, & Lundqvist, 2000; Zajonc, 1984, 1998). In other words, you may experience various emotions quickly and directly without thinking about them or being aware of why you feel the way you do.

Finally, some theorists concentrate on cognitive aspects of emotion. Notable among them was the late Richard S. Lazarus (for example, 1968, 1991, 1995), who proposed that changes in a person's environment are appraised in terms of their potential impact on that person, and the type of appraisal made determines the emotion experienced. For example, if you see somebody holding a gun in a dark alley, you will probably appraise the situation as dangerous and experience fear. You would make a different appraisal if you saw a tour guide displaying an antique gun in a museum. Lazarus would suggest that thinking and feeling cannot be separated, but other cognitive scientists suggest that, although cognitive and emotional systems interact, they are fundamentally separate (Teasdale, 1993). All components of emotion—behavior, physiology, and cognition—are important, and their interaction is a subject of much current research (Barrett, 2009; Gendron & Barrett, 2009; Gross, 2007).

Anger and Your Heart

When we discussed Judy's blood phobia, we observed that behavior and emotion may influence biology. This is especially true of anger. We have known for years that negative

▲ Our emotional reaction depends on context. Fire, for example, can be threatening or comforting.

emotions such as hostility and anger increase a person's risk of developing heart disease (Chesney, 1986; MacDougall, Dembroski, Dimsdale, & Hackett, 1985). Sustained hostility with angry outbursts, and repeatedly and continually suppressing anger, contribute more strongly to death from heart disease than other well-known risk factors, including smoking, high blood pressure, and high cholesterol levels (Finney, Stoney, & Engebretson, 2002; Harburg, Kaciroti, Gleiberman, Julius, & Schork, 2008; Suarez, Lewis, & Kuhn, 2002; Williams, Haney, Lee, Kong, & Blumenthal, 1980).

Why is this, exactly? Ironson and colleagues (1992) asked people with heart disease to recall something that made them angry in the past. Sometimes these events had occurred many years earlier. In one case, an individual who had spent time in a Japanese prisoner-of-war camp during World War II became angry every time he thought about it, especially when he thought about reparations paid by the U.S. government to Japanese Americans who had been held in internment camps during the war. Ironson and associates compared the experience of anger to stressful events that increased heart rate but were not associated with anger. For example, some participants imagined making a speech to defend themselves against a charge of shoplifting. Others tried to solve difficult arithmetic problems within a time limit. Heart rates during angry and stressful situations were then compared to heart rates that increased as a result of exercise (riding a stationary bicycle). The investigators found that the ability of the heart to pump blood efficiently through the body dropped significantly during anger but not during stress or exercise. In fact, remembering being angry was sufficient to cause the anger effect. If participants were really angry, their heart-pumping efficiency dropped even more.

This study was the first to prove that anger affects the heart through decreased pumping efficiency, at least in people who already have heart disease. Other studies, such as one by Williams and colleagues (1980), demonstrated that anger also affects people without heart disease. Medical students who were often angry were 7 times more likely

to die by the age of 50 than students in the same class who had lower levels of hostility. Suarez et al. (2002) demonstrated how anger may cause this effect. Inflammation produced by an overactive immune system in particularly hostile individuals may contribute to clogged arteries (and decreased heart-pumping efficiency). Shall we conclude that too much anger causes heart attacks? This would be another example of one-dimensional causal modeling. Increasing evidence, including the studies just mentioned, suggests that anger and hostility contribute to heart disease, but so do many other factors, including a genetically determined biological vulnerability. We discuss cardiovascular disease in Chapter 7.

Emotions and Psychopathology

We now know that suppressing almost any kind of emotional response increases sympathetic nervous system activity, which may contribute to psychopathology (Barlow, Allen, & Choate, 2004; Campbell-Sills & Barlow, 2007; Fairholme et al., 2010). Some emotions seem to have a more direct effect. In Chapter 4, we study the phenomenon of *panic* and its relationship to anxiety disorders. One interesting possibility is that a panic attack is simply the normal emotion of fear occurring at the wrong time, when there is nothing to be afraid of (Barlow, 2002). Some patients with mood disorders become overly excited and joyful. They think they can do anything they want and spend as much money as they want because everything will turn out all right. These individuals are suffering from *mania*, which is part of a serious mood disorder called *bipolar disorder*, discussed in Chapter 6. People who suffer from mania usually alternate periods of excitement with periods of extreme sad-

mood Enduring period of emotionality.
affect Conscious, subjective aspect of an emotion that accompanies an action at a given time.

ness and distress, when they feel that the world is a gloomy and hopeless place. If hopelessness becomes acute, they are at risk for suicide. This emotional state is *depression*, a defining feature of many mood disorders.

Thus, basic emotions of fear, anger, sadness or distress, and excitement may contribute to many psychological disorders and even define them. Emotions and mood also affect our cognitive processes: If your mood is positive, your interpretations and impressions also tend to be positive (Bower, 1981; Diener, Oishi, & Lucas, 2003). Your impression of people you first meet and even your memories of past events are colored to a great extent by your current mood. If you are consistently negative or depressed, then your memories of past events are likely to be unpleasant. The person who is pessimistic or depressed sees the bottle as half empty. In contrast, the cheerful optimist is said to see the world through rose-colored glasses and to see the bottle as half full. This is a rich area of investigation for cognitive and emotion scientists (Eysenck, 1992; Rottenberg & Johnson, 2007; Teasdale, 1993), particularly those interested in the interconnection of cognitive and emotional processes (Barlow et al., 2004; Campbell-Sills & Barlow, 2007; Gross, 2007; Kring & Sloan, 2010).

Concept Check 2.4

Check your understanding of behavioral and cognitive influences by identifying the descriptions. Choose your answers from (a) learned helplessness, (b) modeling, (c) prepared learning, and (d) implicit memory.

1. Karen noticed that every time Tyrone behaved well at lunch, the teacher praised him. Karen decided to behave better to receive praise herself. _____

2. Josh stopped trying to please his father because he never knows whether his father will be proud or outraged. _____

3. Greg fell into a lake as a baby and almost drowned. Even though he does not remember the event, he hates to be around large bodies of water. _____

4. Juanita was scared to death of the tarantula, even though she knew it wasn't likely to hurt her. _____

Discussing Diversity Fear: Evolutionary and Social Influences

Fear and phobias are universal, occurring across all countries and cultures. Some fears are evolutionarily ingrained and found in people from all different cultures. However, other fears are learned and only are present within specific cultures.

Perhaps the most salient example of evolutionarily ingrained fear that people from all cultures experience is that related to physical illness from food and subsequent fear or repulsion at the site of similar food in the future. Have you ever eaten at a new restaurant only to go home and become physically ill after your dining experience? Chances are if this has happened to you, then you are highly unlikely to return to the same restaurant and almost certainly not going to order the dish associated with your physical illness. The strong aversion to foods that make us ill was first written about by Garcia, Ervin, & Koelling (1966) and is referred to as conditioned taste aversion. These researchers found that unlike other negative stimuli (e.g., electric shock); this type of aversion is learned from a single pairing of food with illness. Once you have become physically ill, your brain says, "No way! I am not taking a chance on that food

again." This evolutionarily based phenomenon can be used to the advantage of farmers desiring to protect their sheep from hungry coyotes. Farmers will feed coyotes sheep meat containing enough lithium salts to cause illness to the coyotes. After becoming ill from the tainted sheep meat, coyotes generally will not attack a farmer's sheep (fearing the illness) and instead will hunt rabbits or other animals (Gustavson, Kelly, Sweeney, & Garcia, 1976). Whereas this is an evolutionarily ingrained fear that affects all people (and animals) similarly despite cultural backgrounds, there also are fears that are uniquely influenced by culture/social learning.

An interesting example of a socially learned fear is that of "Koro" seen in parts of Asia (with the first epidemic appearing in Southern China in 1865). Koro refers to a fear that the penis will shrink or retract into one's abdomen, with some people even fearing that this will result in death (Garlipp, 2006). Although the perceived cause of Koro has changed over time, it has long been attributed to social influences such as witchcraft and sorcery. Moreover, reports of mass episodes of

Koro suggest that beliefs about the possibility of one's genitals shrinking or retracting into the body are spread through social means (such as word-of-mouth or people reading about other cases). In addition to the extreme fear associated with episodes of Koro, this condition can lead to dangerous physical consequences from efforts to prevent genital retraction, such as tying or asking male family members and friends to grasp the penis to prevent retraction (Cheng, 1997). Treatment often includes providing education about the impossibility of spontaneous genital retraction, as well as treatment for the anxiety associated with this condition.

Cases of Koro are rare in the United States, where episodes of sudden and intense anxiety generally are not accompanied by concerns about genital retraction (American Psychiatric Association, 2000). Instead, anxiety in Americans often occurs along with concerns about more widely accepted medical concerns, including that the person is having a heart attack or "going crazy." What seems to be an unbelievable fear in one culture can appear quite reasonable to people in other cultures.

> › How do cultural, social, and interpersonal factors influence abnormal behavior?

Given the welter of neurobiological and psychological variables impinging on our lives, is there any room for the influence of social, interpersonal, and cultural factors? Studies are beginning to demonstrate the substantial power and depth of such influences. Consider the following example.

Voodoo, the Evil Eye, and Other Fears

In many cultures, individuals may suffer from *fright disorders,* which are characterized by exaggerated startle responses, and other observable fear and anxiety reactions. One example is the Latin American *susto,* which describes various anxiety-based symptoms, including insomnia, irritability, phobias, and the marked somatic symptoms of sweating and increased heart rate (tachycardia). But *susto* has only one cause: The individual becomes the object of black magic, or witchcraft. In some cultures, the sinister influence is called the *evil eye* (Good & Kleinman, 1985; Tan, 1980), and the resulting fright disorder can be fatal. Cannon (1942), examining the Haitian phenomenon of voodoo death, suggested that the sentence of death by a medicine man may create an intolerable autonomic arousal in the participant, who has little ability to cope because there is no social support—that is, friends and family ignore the individual after a brief period of grieving because

they assume death has already occurred. Ultimately, the condition leads to damage to internal organs and death. Thus, from all accounts, an individual who is from a physical and psychological point of view functioning in a perfectly healthy and adaptive way suddenly dies because of marked changes in the social environment.

Gender

Gender roles have a strong and sometimes puzzling effect on psychopathology (Kistner, 2009; Rutter, Caspi, & Moffitt, 2006). The likelihood of your having a particular phobia is powerfully influenced by your gender. For example, someone who complains of an insect or small-animal phobia severe enough to prohibit field trips or visits to friends in the country is almost certain to be female, as are 90% of the people with this phobia (possible reasons for this were mentioned earlier in this chapter). But a social phobia strong enough to keep someone from attending parties or meetings affects men and women equally.

We think these substantial differences have to do with, at least in part, cultural expectations of men and women, or our *gender roles.* For example, an equal number of men and women may have an experience that could lead to an insect or small-animal phobia, such as being bitten by one, but in our society it isn't always acceptable for a man to show or even admit fear. So a man is more likely to hide or endure the fear until he gets over it. It is more acceptable for women to acknowledge fearfulness, so a phobia develops. It is also more acceptable for a man to be shy than to show fear, so he is more likely to admit social discomfort.

Bulimia nervosa, the severe eating disorder, occurs almost entirely in young females. Why? As you will see in Chapter 8, a cultural emphasis on female thinness plagues our society and, increasingly, societies around the world. The pressures for males to be thin are less apparent, and of the few males who develop bulimia, a substantial percentage are gay; for these individuals, cultural imperatives to be thin are present in many specific instances (Rothblum, 2002).

Finally, Taylor (2002, 2006; Taylor et al., 2000) described a unique way in which females in many species respond to stress in their lives. This response is called "tend and befriend" and refers to protecting themselves and their young through nurturing behavior (tend) and forming alliances with larger social groups, particularly other females (befriend). Taylor et al. (2000) supposed that this response fits better with the way females respond to stress because it builds on the brain's attachment–

▲ A "possessed" person receives treatment in a voodoo ritual.

THONY BELIZAIRE/AFP/Getty Images

caregiving system and leads to nurturing and affiliative behavior. Furthermore, the response is characterized by identifiable neurobiological processes in the brain that are gender specific.

Our gender doesn't cause psychopathology. But because gender role is a social and cultural factor that influences the form and content of a disorder, we attend closely to it in the chapters that follow.

Social Effects on Health and Behavior

Many studies have demonstrated that the greater the number and frequency of social relationships and contacts, the longer you are likely to live. Conversely, the lower you score on a social index that measures the richness of your social life, the shorter your life expectancy. Studies documenting this finding have been reported in the United States (Berkman & Syme, 1979; House, Robbins, & Metzner, 1982; Schoenbach, Kaplan, Fredman, & Kleinbaum, 1986), Sweden, and Finland. They take into account existing physical health and other risk factors for dying young, such as high blood pressure, high cholesterol levels, and smoking habits, and they still produce the same result. Studies also show that social relationships seem to protect individuals against many physical and psychological disorders, such as high blood pressure, depression, alcoholism, arthritis, the progression to AIDS, and bearing low birth weight babies (Cobb, 1976; House, Landis, & Umberson, 1988; Leserman et al., 2000; Thurston & Kubzanksy, 2009).

Even whether or not we come down with a cold is strongly influenced by the quality and extent of our social network. Cohen, Doyle, Skoner, Rabin, and Gwaltney (1997) used nasal drops to expose 276 healthy volunteers to one of two different rhinoviruses (cold viruses), then quarantined the participants for a week. The researchers measured the extent of participation in 12 types of social relationships (for example, spouse, parent, friend, and col-

league), and other factors, such as smoking and poor sleep quality, that are likely to increase susceptibility to colds. The surprising results were that the greater the extent of social ties, the smaller the chance of catching a cold, even after all other factors were taken into consideration (controlled for). Those with the fewest social ties were more than 4 times more likely to catch a cold than those with the greatest number of ties. Thus, we cannot study psychological and biological aspects of psychological disorders (or physical disorders, for that matter) without taking into account the social and cultural context of the disorder.

How do social relationships have such a profound impact on physical and psychological characteristics? We don't know for sure, but there are some intriguing hints (Cacioppo et al., 2007). Some people think interpersonal relationships give meaning to life and that people who have something to live for can overcome physical deficiencies and even delay death. You may have known an elderly person who far outlived his or her expected time to witness a significant family event, such as a grandchild's graduation from college. Once the event has passed, the person dies. A common observation is that if one spouse in a longstanding marriage dies, the other often dies soon after, regardless of health status. It is also possible that social relationships facilitate health-promoting behaviors, such as restraint in the use of alcohol and drugs, getting proper sleep, and seeking appropriate health care (House, Landis, & Umberson, 1988; Leserman et al., 2000).

Sometimes social upheaval is an opportunity for studying the impact of social networks on individual functioning. For example, whether you live in a city or the country may be associated with your chances of developing schizophrenia, a severe disorder. Lewis, David, Andreasson, and Allsbeck (1992) found that the incidence of schizophrenia was 38% greater in men who had been raised in cities than in those raised in rural areas. We have known for a long time that more schizophrenia exists in the city than in the country, but researchers thought people with schizophrenia who drifted to cities *after* developing schizophrenia or other endemic urban factors, such as drug use or unstable family relationships, might account for the disparity. But Lewis and associates carefully controlled for such factors, and it now seems something about cities beyond those influences may contribute to the development of schizophrenia (Pedersen & Mortensen, 2006). We do not yet know what it is. This finding, if it is replicated and shown to be true, may be important in view of the mass migration of individuals to overcrowded urban areas, particularly in less developed countries.

The effect of social and interpersonal factors may differ with age (Charles & Carstensen, 2010; Gallagher-Thompson & Holland, in press). Grant, Patterson, and Yager (1988) studied 118 men and women 65 years or older who lived independently. Those with fewer meaningful contacts and less social support from relatives had consistently higher levels of depression and more reports of unsatisfac-

▲ A long and productive life usually includes strong social relationships and interpersonal relations.

Yellow Dog Productions/Digital Vision/JupiterImages

▲ In developing countries, personal upheaval because of political strife affects mental health.

the unfortunate soldiers earn scorn. Often, a patient with a psychological disorder does not seek health insurance reimbursement for fear a coworker might learn about the problem. With far less social support than for physical illness, there is less chance of full recovery.

Global Incidence of Psychological Disorders

Behavioral and mental health problems in developing countries are exacerbated by political strife, technological change, and massive movements from rural to urban areas. An important study from the World Health Organization (WHO) reveals that 10% to 20% of all primary medical services in poor countries are sought by patients with psychological disorders, principally anxiety and mood disorders (including suicide attempts), alcoholism, drug abuse, and childhood developmental disorders (WHO, 2001). Record numbers of young men are committing suicide in Micronesia. Alcoholism levels among adults in Latin America have risen to 20%. Treatments for disorders such as depression and addictive behaviors that are successful in the United States can't be administered in countries where mental health care is limited. Even in the United States, where approximately 200,000 mental health professionals serve almost 300 million people, only one in three people with a psychological disorder has ever received treatment of any kind (Institute of Medicine, 2001). These statistics suggest that in addition to their role in causation, social and cultural factors help maintain disorders because most societies have not yet developed the social context for alleviating them. Changing societal attitudes is just one of the challenges facing us as the century unfolds.

tory quality of life. However, if these individuals became physically ill, they had more substantial support from their families than those who were not physically ill. This finding raises the unfortunate possibility that it may be advantageous for elderly people to become physically ill because illness allows them to reestablish the social support that makes life worth living. If further research confirms this finding, we will know for fact what seems to make intuitive sense: Involvement with their families before they become ill might help elderly people maintain their physical health.

Social Stigma

Psychological disorders continue to carry a stigma in our society (Hinshaw & Stier, 2008). To be anxious or depressed is to be weak and cowardly. To be schizophrenic is to be unpredictable and crazy. For physical injuries in times of war, we award medals. For psychological injuries,

Life-Span Development

> **Why should psychological disorders be considered from a life-span developmental perspective?**

We tend to look at psychological disorders from a snapshot perspective: We focus on a particular point in a person's life and assume it represents the whole person. The inadequacy of this way of looking at people should be clear. The person you were, say, 3 years ago, is different from the person you are now, and the person you will be 3 years from now will have changed in important ways. To understand psychopathology, we must appreciate how experiences during different periods of development may influence our vulnerability to stress or to psychological disorders (Charles & Carstensen, 2010; Rutter, 2002).

Important developmental changes occur at all points in life. Erik Erikson (1982) suggested that we go through eight major crises during our lives, each determined by our biological maturation and the social demands made at particular times. Unlike Freud, who envisioned no developmental stages beyond adolescence, Erikson believed that we grow and change throughout life, even in old age. During older adulthood, for example, we look back and view our lives either as rewarding or as disappointing.

Although aspects of Erikson's theory have been criticized as vague and not supported by research (Shaffer, 1993), it demonstrates the comprehensive approach to human development advocated by life-span developmental psychologists. Research confirms the importance of this approach. In one experiment, Kolb, Gibb, and Gorny (2003) placed animals in complex environments as juveniles, as adults, or in old age. They found that the environment had different effects on the brains of these animals depending on their developmental stage. Basically, the complex and challenging environments increased the size and complexity of neurons in the motor and sensory cortical regions in the adult and aged animals; however, unlike the older groups, in young animals the challenging environments decreased the size and complexity of neurons in the spine. Nevertheless, this decrease was associated with enhanced motor and cognitive skills when the animals became adults, indicating that stimulating environments can affect brain function in a positive way at any age. Even prenatal experience seems to affect brain structure because the offspring of an animal housed in a rich environment during the term of her pregnancy have the advantage of more complex cortical brain circuits after birth (Kolb, Gibb, & Robinson, 2003). Thus, we can infer that the individual's developmental stage and prior experience have a substantial impact on the development of psychological disorders, an inference that is receiving confirmation from life-span developmental psychologists such as Laura Carstensen (Carstensen, Charles, Isaacowitz, & Kenney, 2003; Charles & Carstensen, 2010; Isaacowitz, Smith, & Carstensen, 2003). For example, in depressive (mood) disorders, children and adolescents do not receive the same benefit from antidepressant drugs as do adults (Hazell, O'Connell, Heathcote, Robertson, & Henry, 1995; Santosh, 2009), and for many of them these drugs pose risks that are not present in adults (Santosh, 2009). Also, the gender distribution in depression is approximately equal until puberty, when it becomes more common in girls (Compas et al., 1997; Hankin, Wetter, & Cheely, 2007).

Like a fever, a particular behavior or disorder may have a number of causes. The principle of **equifinality** is used to indicate that we must consider a number of paths to a given outcome (Cicchetti, 1991). There are many examples of this principle. A delusional syndrome may be an aspect of schizophrenia, but it can also arise from amphetamine abuse. Delirium, which involves difficulty focusing attention, often occurs in older adults after surgery, but it can also result from thiamine deficiency or renal (kidney) disease. Autism can sometimes occur in children whose mothers are exposed to rubella during pregnancy, but it can also occur in children whose mothers experience difficulties during labor.

Different paths can also result from the interaction of psychological and biological factors during various stages of development. How someone copes with impairment resulting from physical causes may have a profound effect on that person's overall functioning. For example, people with brain damage of approximately equal severity may have different levels of disorder. Those with healthy systems of social support, consisting of family and friends, and highly adaptive personality characteristics, such as confidence in their abilities to overcome challenges, may experience only mild behavioral and cognitive disturbance despite physical (organic) pathology. Those without comparable support and personality may be incapacitated. This may be clearer if you think of people you know with physical disabilities. Some, paralyzed from the waist down by accident or disease (paraplegics), have nevertheless become superb athletes or accomplished in business or the arts. Others with the same condition are depressed and hopeless; they have withdrawn from life or, even worse, ended their lives. Even the content of delusions and hallucinations that may accompany a disorder, and the degree to which they are frightening or difficult to cope with, is partly determined by psychological and social factors.

Researchers are exploring not only what makes people experience particular disorders, but also what protects others from having the same difficulties. If you were interested in why someone would be depressed, for example, you would first look at people who display depression. But you could also study people in similar situations and from similar backgrounds who are not depressed. An excellent example of this approach is research on "resilient" children, which suggests that social factors may protect some children from being hurt by stressful experiences, such as one or both parents suffering a psychiatric disturbance (Cooper, Feder, Southwick & Charney, 2007; Garmezy & Rutter, 1983; Hetherington & Blechman, 1996; Weiner, 2000). The presence of a caring adult friend or relative can offset the negative stresses of this environment, as can the child's own ability to understand and cope with unpleasant situations. More recently, scientists are discovering strong biological differences in responsiveness to trauma and stress as a result of protective factors such as social support or having a strong purpose in life (Alim et al., 2008; Charney, 2004; Ozbay et al., 2007). Perhaps if we better understand why some people do not encounter the same problems as others in similar circumstances, we can better understand particular disorders, assist those who suffer from them, and even prevent some cases from occurring.

Conclusions

In this overview of modern approaches to psychopathology, we have seen that contributions from (1) psychoanalytic theory, (2) behavioral and cognitive science, (3) emotional influences, (4) social and cultural influences, (5) genetics, (6) neuroscience, and (7) life-span developmental factors all must be considered when we think about psychopathology. Even though our knowledge is incomplete, you can see why we could never resume the one-dimensional thinking typical of the various historical traditions described in Chapter 1.

Yet, books about psychological disorders and news reports in the popular press often describe the causes of these disorders in one-dimensional terms. For example, how many times have you heard that a psychological disorder such as depression, or perhaps schizophrenia, is caused by a "chemical imbalance" without considering other possible causes? When you read that a disorder is *caused* by a chemical imbalance, it sounds like nothing else really matters and all you have to do is correct the imbalance in neurotransmitter activity to "cure" the problem.

There is no question that psychological disorders are associated with altered neurotransmitter activity and other aspects of brain function (a chemical imbalance). But you have learned in this chapter that a "chemical imbalance" could, in turn, be caused by psychological or social factors such as stress, strong emotional reactions, difficult family interactions, changes caused by aging, or—most likely—some interaction of all these factors. Therefore, it is inaccurate and misleading to say that a psychological disorder is "caused" by a chemical imbalance, even though chemical imbalances almost certainly exist.

Similarly, how many times have you heard that alcoholism or other addictive behaviors were caused by "lack of willpower," implying that if these individuals simply developed the right attitude they could overcome their addiction? There is no question that people with severe addictions may have faulty cognitive processes as indicated, for example, by attributing their problems to stress in their lives or some other "bogus" excuse. They may also misperceive the effects alcohol has on them, and these cognitions and attitudes all contribute to developing addictions. But considering only cognitive processes without considering other factors, such as genes and brain physiology, as causes of addictions would be as incorrect as saying that depression is caused by a chemical imbalance. Interpersonal, social, and cultural factors also contribute to the development of addictive behaviors. To say, then, that addictive behaviors such as alcoholism are caused by lack of willpower is just plain wrong.

If you learn one thing from this book, it should be that psychological disorders have many causes—which interact with one another—and we must understand this interaction to appreciate fully the origins of psychological disorders. To do this requires a multidimensional integrative approach. In chapters covering specific psychological disorders, we return to cases like Judy's and consider them from this multidimensional integrative perspective. But first we must explore the processes of assessment and diagnosis used to measure and classify psychopathology.

Concept Check 2.5

Fill in the blanks to complete the following statements.

1. What we _____ is influenced by our social environments.

2. The likelihood of your having a particular phobia is influenced by your _____.

3. Studies have demonstrated that the greater the number and frequency of _____ relationships and _____, the longer you are likely to live.

4. The effect of social and interpersonal factors on the expression of physical and psychological disorders may differ with _____.

5. The principle of _____ is used to indicate that we must consider a number of paths to a given outcome.

equifinality Developmental psychopathology principle that a behavior or disorder may have several causes.

Summary

One-Dimensional versus Multidimensional Models

How does a multidimensional model of causality differ from a unidimensional model?

> The causes of abnormal behavior are complex. You can say that psychological disorders are caused by nature (biology) and by nurture (psychosocial factors), and you would be right on both counts—but also wrong on both counts.

What are the key influences comprising the multidimensional model of abnormal behavior?

> To identify the causes of various psychological disorders, we must consider the interaction of all relevant dimensions: genetic contributions, the role of the nervous system, behavioral and cognitive processes, emotional influences, social and interpersonal influences, and developmental factors. Thus, we have arrived at a multidimensional approach to the causes of psychological disorders.

Genetic Contributions to Psychopathology

How do genes interact with environmental factors to affect behavior?

> The genetic influence on much of our development and most of our behavior, personality, and even IQ score is polygenic—that is, influenced by many genes. This is assumed to be the case in abnormal behavior also, although research has identified specific small groups of genes that relate to some psychological disorders.

What kinds of models have been proposed to describe this interaction?

> In studying casual relationships in psychopathology, researchers look at the interactions of genetic and environmental effects. In the diathesis–stress model, individuals are assumed to inherit certain vulnerabilities that make them susceptible to a disorder when the right kind of stressor comes along. In the reciprocal gene–environment, or gene–environment correlation, model, genetic vulnerability toward a certain disorder may make it more likely that the person will experience the stressor that, in turn, triggers the vulnerability and thus the disorder. In epigenetics, the immediate effects of the environment (such as early stressful experiences) influence cells that turn certain genes on or off. This effect may be passed down through several generations.

Neuroscience and Its Contributions to Psychopathology

What are neurotransmitters, and how are they involved in abnormal behavior?

> Within the nervous system, levels of neurotransmitter and neuroendocrine activity interact in complex ways to regulate emotions and behavior and contribute to psychological disorders.

What are the functions of different brain regions, and what are their roles in psychopathology?

> Critical to our understanding of psychopathology are the neurotransmitter currents called brain circuits. Of the neurotransmitters that may play a key role, we investigated five: serotonin, gamma-aminobutyric acid (GABA), glutamate, norepinephrine, and dopamine.

Behavioral and Cognitive Science

What are the key differences between behavioral and cognitive explanations of the origins of mental illness?

> The field of cognitive science provides a valuable perspective on how behavioral and cognitive influences affect the learning and adaptation each of us experience throughout life. Clearly, such influences not only contribute to psychological disorders, but also may directly modify brain functioning, brain structure, and even genetic expression. We examined some research in this field by looking at learned helplessness, modeling, prepared learning, and implicit memory.

Emotions

What role do emotions play in psychopathology?

> Emotions have a direct and dramatic impact on our functioning and play a central role in many disorders. Mood, a persistent period of emotionality, is often evident in psychological disorders.

Cultural, Social, and Interpersonal Factors

How do cultural, social, and interpersonal factors influence abnormal behavior?

> Social and interpersonal influences profoundly affect both psychological disorders and biology.

Life-Span Development

Why should psychological disorders be considered from a life-span developmental perspective?

> The principle of equifinality reminds us that we must consider the various paths to a particular outcome, not just the result.

Key Terms

multidimensional integrative
   approach, 31
genes, 34
diathesis–stress model, 36
vulnerability, 37
reciprocal gene–environment model,
   38
epigenetics, 39
neuroscience, 40
neuron, 40
synaptic cleft, 40
neurotransmitters, 40

hormone, 46
brain circuits, 46
agonist, 47
antagonist, 47
inverse agonist, 47
reuptake, 47
glutamate, 47
gamma-aminobutyric acid (GABA),
   47
serotonin, 48
norepinephrine (also noradrenaline),
   48

dopamine, 48
cognitive science, 53
learned helplessness, 54
modeling (also observational
   learning), 55
prepared learning, 55
implicit memory, 56
flight or fight response, 57
emotion, 57
mood, 58
affect, 58
equifinality, 64

Answers to Concept Checks

2.1

1. b; 2. a (best answer) or c; 3. e; 4. a
(initial), c (maintenance)

2.2

1. F (first 22 pairs); 2. T; 3. T; 4. F (reciprocal gene–environment model);

5. F (complex interaction of both nature and nurture)

2.3

1. b; 2. c; 3. f; 4. g; 5. d; 6. e; 7. h; 8. a

2.4

1. b; 2. a; 3. d; 4. c

2.5

1. fear; 2. gender; 3. social, contacts;
4. age; 5. equifinality

Media Resources

Log in to CengageBrain to access the resources your instructor requires. For this book, you can access:

 CourseMate brings course concepts to life with interactive learning, study, and exam preparation
tools that support the printed textbook. A textbook-
specific website, Psychology CourseMate includes an integrated interactive eBook and other interactive learning
tools including quizzes, flashcards, videos, and more.

Abnormal Psychology Videos

Integrative Approach: This clip summarizes the integrative
approach, showing how psychological factors affect our
biology and our brain influences our behavior.

CENGAGENOW CengageNow is an easy-to-use online
resource that helps you study in less time to get the grade
you want—NOW. Take a pre-test for this chapter and receive a personalized study plan based on your results that
will identify the topics you need to review and direct you
to online resources to help you master those topics. Then
take a post-test to help you determine the concepts you
have mastered and what you will need to work on. If your
textbook does not include an access code card, go to
CengageBrain.com to gain access.

> Visit www.cengagebrain.com to access your account
   and purchase materials.

aplia If your professor has assigned Aplia homework:
1. Sign in to your account.
2. Complete the corresponding homework exercises as required by your professor.
3. When finished, click "Grade It Now" to see which areas
   you have mastered, which need more work, and for detailed explanations of every answer.

Video Concept Reviews

CengageNOW also contains Mark Durand's *Video Concept
Reviews* on these challenging topics:
> Multidimensional Models
> Genetics: Phenotype and Genotype
> Genetics: Nature of Genes
> Genetics: Dominant versus Recessive Genes
> Genetics: Polygenic
> Diathesis–Stress Model
> Concept Check—Reciprocal Gene–Environment Model
> Neuroscience
> Neuroimaging
> Neurons
> Neurotransmitters/Reuptake
> Agonist/Antagonist
> Implicit Memory/Stroop Test
> Emotion

Chapter Quiz

1. Which approach to psychopathology considers biological, social, behavioral, emotional, cognitive, and developmental influences?

   a. genetic

   b. multidimensional

   c. interpersonal

   d. psychodynamic

2. Much of our development and most of our behavior, personality, and IQ are influenced by many genes, each contributing only a portion of the overall effect. This type of influence is known as:

   a. reciprocal

   b. polygenic

   c. integrative

   d. recessive

3. Behavioral genetics research has concluded that:

   a. genetic factors do not contribute to most psychological disorders

   b. genetic factors that contribute to psychological disorders account for most of the explanation

   c. for any one psychological disorder there is probably one gene that explains most of its development

   d. genetic factors that contribute to psychological disorders account for less than half of the explanation

4. Which portion of the brain is responsible for complex cognitive activities such as reasoning, planning, and creating?

   a. limbic system

   b. basal ganglia

   c. hindbrain

   d. cerebral cortex

5. John is startled by a loud crash in his apartment. His heart immediately starts beating rapidly and the pace of his breathing increases. What part of the nervous system is responsible for this physiological response?

   a. central nervous system

   b. sympathetic nervous system

   c. limbic system

   d. parasympathetic nervous system

6. Which neurotransmitter appears to reduce overall arousal and dampen emotional responses?

   a. serotonin

   b. gamma-aminobutyric acid

   c. norepinephrine

   d. dopamine

7. Martin Seligman noted that when rats or other animals encounter conditions over which they have no control, they give up attempting to cope and seem to develop the animal equivalent of depression. This is referred to as:

   a. learned depression

   b. learned fear

   c. learned helplessness

   d. learned defenselessness

8. Which concept explains why fears of snakes and heights are more common (or more easily learned) than fears of cats and flowers?

   a. equifinality

   b. vulnerability

   c. prepared learning

   d. observational learning

9. Recent research on implicit memory suggests that:

   a. people can recall colors more quickly than words

   b. memories can change based on the implicit structures of the brain

   c. implicit memory is more relevant to psychopathology than explicit memory

   d. memories outside our awareness may influence psychopathology, just as Freud speculated

10. Emotion comprises all of the following components EXCEPT:

    a. behavior

    b. cognition

    c. genetics

    d. physiology

    (See Appendix A for answers.)

Clinical Assessment, Diagnosis, and Research in Psychopathology

CHAPTER 3

Stockbyte/Royalty Free/age fotostock

Demonstrate knowledge and understanding of selected content areas of psychology:	› Biological bases of behavior and mental processes, including physiology, sensation, perception, comparative, motivation, and emotion (APA SLO 1.2.a [3]) *(see textbook pages 81–83)*
	› The history of psychology, including the evolution of methods of psychology, its theoretical conflicts, and its sociocultural contexts (APA SLO 1.2.b) *(see textbook pages 87–91)*
Identify applications of psychology in solving problems, such as:	› Psychological tests and measurements (APA SLO 4.2.c) *(see textbook pages 71–82, 84–91)*
Explain different research methods used by psychologists.	› Describe how various research designs address different types of questions and hypotheses (APA SLO 2.2.a) *(see textbook pages 95–103)*
	› Articulate strengths and limitations of various research designs, including distinguishing between qualitative and quantitative methods (APA SLO 2.2.b) *(see textbook pages 103–109)*
Design and conduct basic studies to address psychological questions using appropriate research methods.	› Recognize that theoretical and sociocultural contexts and personal biases may shape research questions, design, data collection, analysis, and interpretation (APA SLO 2.4.f) *(see textbook pages 107–109)*

*Portions of this chapter cover learning outcomes suggested by the American Psychological Association (2007) in their guidelines for the undergraduate psychology major. Chapter coverage of these outcomes is identified by APA Goal and APA Suggested Learning Outcome (SLO).

Assessing Psychological Disorders

› **What are clinical assessment and diagnosis?**
› **What are the main methods used in clinical assessment?**

The processes of clinical assessment and diagnosis are central to the study of psychopathology. **Clinical assessment** is the evaluation and measurement of psychological, biological, and social factors in an individual with a possible psychological disorder. **Diagnosis** is the process of determining whether the problem afflicting the individual meets all criteria for a psychological disorder, as set forth in the fourth edition, text revision, of the *Diagnostic and Statistical Manual of Mental Disorders,* or *DSM-IV-TR* (American Psychiatric Association, 2000). In this chapter, we examine the development of the *DSM* into a widely used classification system for abnormal behavior. Then we review the assessment techniques available to clinicians. Finally, we turn to diagnostic issues and the challenges of classification.

Frank ⦁ Young, Serious, and Anxious

Frank was referred to one of our clinics for evaluation and possible treatment of severe distress and anxiety centering on his marriage. He reported that he was 24 years old and that this was the first time he had ever seen a mental health professional. He wasn't sure that he needed to be there, but he felt he was beginning to "come apart" because of his marital difficulties. He figured that it wouldn't hurt to come once to see whether we could help. What follows is a transcript of parts of this first interview.

THERAPIST: What sorts of problems have been troubling you during the past month?

FRANK: I'm beginning to have a lot of marital problems. I was married about 9 months ago, but I've been really tense around the house and we've been having a lot of arguments.

THERAPIST: Is this something recent?

FRANK: Well, it wasn't too bad at first, but it's been worse lately. I've also been really uptight in my job, and I haven't been getting my work done.

Note that we always begin by asking the patient to describe the difficulties that brought him or her to the office. When dealing with adults, or children old enough (or verbal enough) to tell us their story, this strategy tends to break the ice. After Frank described this problem in some detail, we asked him about his marriage, his job, and other current life circumstances. Frank reported that he had worked in an auto body repair shop for the past 4 years and that, 9 months previously, he had married a 17-year-old woman. After getting a better picture of his current situation, we returned to his feelings of distress and anxiety.

THERAPIST: When you feel uptight at work, is it the same kind of feeling you have at home?

FRANK: Pretty much. I just can't seem to concentrate, and lots of times I lose track of what my wife's saying to me, which makes her mad and then we'll have a big fight.

THERAPIST: Are you thinking about something when you lose your concentration, such as your work or maybe other things?

FRANK: Oh, I don't know. I guess I just worry a lot.

THERAPIST: What do you find yourself worrying about most of the time?

FRANK: Well, I worry about getting fired and then not being able to support my family. A lot of the time I feel like I'm going to catch something—you know, get sick and not be able to work. Basically I guess I'm afraid of getting sick and then failing at my job and in my marriage and having my parents and her parents both telling me what an ass I was for getting married in the first place.

During the first few minutes of the interview, Frank seemed tense and anxious and often looked down while he talked, glancing up only occasionally to make eye contact. Sometimes his right leg twitched a bit. Although it was not easy to see at first because he was looking down, Frank was also closing his eyes tightly for a period of 2 to 3 seconds. It was during these periods when his eyes were closed that his right leg would twitch.

The interview proceeded for the next half hour, exploring marital and job issues. It became increasingly clear that Frank was feeling inadequate and anxious about handling situations in his life. By this time, he was talking freely and looking up a little more at the therapist, but he continued to close his eyes and twitch his right leg slightly.

THERAPIST: Are you aware that once in a while you're closing your eyes while you're telling me this?

FRANK: I'm not aware all the time, but I know I do it.

THERAPIST: Do you know how long you've been doing that?

FRANK: Oh, I don't know, maybe a year or two.

THERAPIST: Are you thinking about anything when you close your eyes?

FRANK: Well, actually I'm trying not to think about something.

THERAPIST: What do you mean?

FRANK: Well, I have these really frightening and stupid thoughts, and . . . it's hard to even talk about it.

THERAPIST: The thoughts are frightening?

FRANK: Yes, I keep thinking I'm going to take a fit, and I'm just trying to get that out of my mind.

THERAPIST: Could you tell me more about this fit?

FRANK: Well, you know, it's those terrible things where people fall down and they froth at the mouth,

and their tongues come out, and they shake all over. You know, seizures. I think they call it epilepsy.

THERAPIST: And you're trying to get these thoughts out of your mind?

FRANK: Oh, I do everything possible to get those thoughts out of my mind as quickly as I can.

THERAPIST: I've noticed you moving your leg when you close your eyes. Is that part of it?

FRANK: Yes, I've noticed if I really jerk my leg and pray real hard for a little while the thought will go away.

(Excerpt from Nelson, R. O., & Barlow, D. H. Behavioral assessment: Basic strategies and initial procedures. In D. H. Barlow, Ed., *Behavioral assessment of adult disorders*. Copyright ©1981 Guilford Publications, Inc. Reprinted by permission.)

What's wrong with Frank? The first interview reveals an insecure young man experiencing substantial stress as he questions whether he is capable of handling marriage and a job. He reports that he loves his wife and wants the marriage to work and is attempting to be conscientious on his job, from which he derives a lot of satisfaction. Also, for some reason, he is having troubling thoughts about seizures.

How do we determine whether Frank has a psychological disorder or is simply suffering the normal stresses of a new marriage and could benefit from marital counseling? The purpose of this chapter is to illustrate how mental health clinicians address these types of questions to make diagnoses and plan treatment.

Key Concepts in Assessment

The process of clinical assessment has been likened to a funnel (Antony & Barlow, 2010; Hunsley & Mash, 2011). The clinician begins by collecting information across a broad range of the individual's functioning. Then the clinician narrows the focus by ruling out problems in some areas and concentrating on areas that seem most relevant.

Three basic concepts help determine the value of clinicians' assessments: reliability, validity, and standardization (Bagby & Ayearst, 2010) (■ Figure 3.1). One of the more important requirements of these assessments is that they be reliable: that they actually do what they are designed to do. **Reliability** is the degree to which a measurement is

clinical assessment Systematic evaluation and measurement of psychological, biological, and social factors in a person presenting with a possible psychological disorder.

diagnosis Process of determining whether a presenting problem meets the established criteria for a specific psychological disorder.

reliability Degree to which a measurement is consistent—for example, over time or among different raters.

▲ During their first meeting, the mental health professional focuses on the problem that brought the person to treatment.

consistent. Imagine how irritated you would be if you had stomach pain and you went to four physicians and got four different diagnoses and four different treatments. The diagnoses would be said to be unreliable because two or more "raters" (the physicians) did not agree on the conclusion. We expect that presenting the same symptoms to different physicians will result in similar diagnoses. One way psychologists improve their reliability is by carefully designing their assessment devices and then conducting research on them to ensure that two or more raters will get the same answers (called *interrater reliability*). They also determine whether these assessment techniques are stable across time. In other words, if you go to a clinician on

Tuesday and are told you have an IQ of 110, you should expect a similar result if you take the same test again on Thursday. This is known as *test–retest reliability*.

Validity is whether something measures what it is designed to measure. Comparing the results of an assessment measure under consideration with the results of others that are better known helps determine the validity of the first measure. This comparison is called *concurrent* or *descriptive validity*. For example, if the results from a standard, but long, IQ test were essentially the same as the results from a new, brief version, you could conclude that the brief version had concurrent validity. *Predictive validity* is how well your assessment tells you what will happen in the future. For example, does it predict who will succeed in school, which is one of the goals of an IQ test?

Standardization is the process by which a certain set of standards or norms is determined for a technique to make its use consistent across different measurements. The standards might apply to the procedures of testing, scoring, and evaluating data. For example, the assessment might be given to large numbers of people who differ on important factors such as age, race, and gender; their scores would be pooled with those of other individuals like them and then be used as a standard, or norm, for comparison purposes. If you are an African American male, 19-years-old, and from a middle-class background, your score on a psychological test should be compared to those of others like you and not to those of women of Asian descent in their 60s from working-class backgrounds. Reliability, validity, and standardization are important to all forms of psychological assessment.

Clinical assessment consists of procedures that help clinicians acquire the information they need to understand their patients. These procedures include a clinical interview and, within the context of the interview, a mental status exam that can be administered either formally or informally; often a thorough physical examination; a behavioral observation and assessment; and psychological tests (if needed).

The Clinical Interview

The clinical interview is used by psychologists, psychiatrists, and other mental health professionals. It gathers information on current and past behavior, attitudes, and emotions and a detailed history of the individual's life in general and of the presenting problem. Clinicians determine when the specific problem started and identify other events that might have occurred about the same time. In addition, most clinicians gather at least some information on the patient's current and past interpersonal and social history, including family makeup, and on the individual's upbringing. Information on sexual development, religious attitudes (current and past), relevant cultural concerns (such as stress induced by discrimination), and educational history is also collected. To organize information obtained during an interview, many clinicians use a **mental status exam**.

Value of assessment depends on:

Reliability → The degree to which a measurement is consistent

Validity → The degree to which a technique measures what it is designed to measure

Standardization → Application of certain standards to ensure consistency across different measurements

■ **Figure 3.1** Concepts that determine the value of clinical assessments. (© Cengage Learning 2013)

The Mental Status Exam

A mental status exam involves the systematic observation of an individual's behavior. We all perform mental status exams whenever we interact with others, but clinicians must organize their observations in a way that gives them sufficient information to determine whether a psychological disorder might be present (Nelson & Barlow, 1981). Mental status exams can be structured and detailed (Wing, Cooper, & Sartorius, 1974), but mostly they are performed relatively quickly in the course of interviewing or observing a patient. The exam covers five categories:

1. *Appearance and behavior.* The clinician notes any overt physical behaviors, such as Frank's leg twitch, and the individual's dress, general appearance, posture, and facial expression. For example, slow and effortful motor behavior, sometimes referred to as *psychomotor retardation*, may indicate severe depression.

2. *Thought processes.* When clinicians listen to a patient talk, they're getting a good idea of that person's thought processes. What is the rate or flow of speech? Does the person talk quickly or slowly? What about continuity? Does the patient make sense when talking, or are ideas presented with no apparent connection? In some patients with schizophrenia, a disorganized speech pattern, referred to as *loose association* or *derailment*, is noticeable. Clinicians sometimes ask specific questions. If the patient shows difficulty with continuity or rate of speech, a clinician might ask, "Can you think clearly, or do your thoughts tend to be mixed up or come slowly?" What about the content of speech? Is there evidence of *delusions* (distorted views of reality)? Typical delusions are *delusions of persecution,* in which someone thinks people are after him and out to get him all the time, or *delusions of grandeur,* in which someone thinks she is all-powerful. The individual might also have *ideas of reference,* in which everything everyone else does somehow relates back to the individual. The most common example is thinking a conversation between two strangers on the other side of the room must be about you. *Hallucinations* are things a person sees or hears when those things really aren't there.

3. *Mood and affect.* Determining mood and affect is an important part of the mental status exam. *Mood* is the predominant feeling state of the individual. Does the person appear to be down in the dumps or continually elated? Does the individual talk in a depressed or hopeless fashion? How pervasive is this mood? *Affect,* by contrast, refers to the feeling state that accompanies what we say at a given point. Usually our affect is "appropriate"—that is, we laugh when we say something funny or look sad when we talk about something sad. If a friend just told you his mother died and is laughing about it, you would think it strange, to say the least. A mental health clinician would note that your friend's affect is "inappropriate." Then again, you might observe your friend talking about a range of happy and sad things with no affect whatsoever. In this case, a

mental health clinician would say the affect is "blunted" or "flat."

4. *Intellectual functioning.* Clinicians make a rough estimate of others' intellectual functioning just by talking to them. Do they seem to have a reasonable vocabulary? Can they talk in abstractions and metaphors? How is the person's memory? Clinicians usually make a rough estimate of intelligence that is noticeable only if it deviates from normal.

5. *Sensorium.* The term *sensorium* refers to our general awareness of our surroundings. Does an individual know the date and time, who and where he or she is, and who you are? Most of us are fully aware of these facts. People with brain damage or dysfunction may not know the answer to these questions. If the patient knows who he is and who the clinician is and has a good idea of the time and place, the clinician would say that the patient's sensorium is "clear" and is "oriented times three" (to person, place, and time).

What can we conclude from these observations? Basically, they allow the clinician to make a preliminary determination of which areas of the patient's behavior should be assessed in more detail. If psychological disorders remain a possibility, the clinician may begin to hypothesize which disorders might be present.

Returning to our case, what have we learned from this mental status exam (■ Figure 3.2)? Observing Frank's persistent motor behavior in the form of a twitch led to the discovery of a connection (functional relationship) with his troublesome thoughts regarding seizures. Beyond this, his appearance was appropriate, and the flow and content of his speech was reasonable; his intelligence was well within normal limits, and he was oriented times three. He did display an anxious mood; however, his affect was appropriate to what he was saying. These observations suggested that we attempt to identify the possible existence of a disorder characterized by intrusive, unwanted thoughts and the attempt to resist them—in other words, *obsessive-compulsive disorder (OCD).* Later we describe some assessment strategies we would use with Frank.

Patients usually have a good idea of their major concerns in a general sense ("I'm depressed" or "I'm phobic"); occasionally, the problem reported by the patient may not be the major issue. The case of Frank illustrates this point well: He complained of distress relating to marital problems, but the clinician decided that the principal difficul-

validity Degree to which a technique measures what it purports to measure.

standardization Process of establishing specific norms and requirements for a measurement technique to ensure it is used consistently across measurement occasions. This includes instructions for administering the measure, evaluating its findings, and comparing these to data for large numbers of people.

mental status exam Relatively coarse preliminary test of a client's judgment, orientation to time and place, and emotional and mental state; typically conducted during an initial interview.

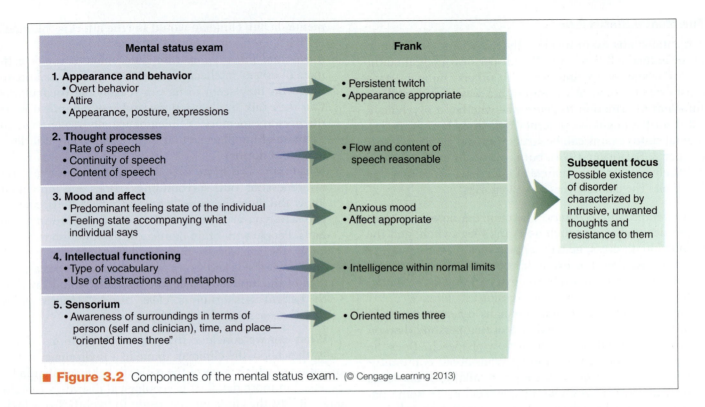

Mental status exam	Frank
1. Appearance and behavior • Overt behavior • Attire • Appearance, posture, expressions	• Persistent twitch • Appearance appropriate
2. Thought processes • Rate of speech • Continuity of speech • Content of speech	• Flow and content of speech reasonable
3. Mood and affect • Predominant feeling state of the individual • Feeling state accompanying what individual says	• Anxious mood • Affect appropriate
4. Intellectual functioning • Type of vocabulary • Use of abstractions and metaphors	• Intelligence within normal limits
5. Sensorium • Awareness of surroundings in terms of person (self and clinician), time, and place— "oriented times three"	• Oriented times three

Subsequent focus
Possible existence of disorder characterized by intrusive, unwanted thoughts and resistance to them

■ **Figure 3.2** Components of the mental status exam. (© Cengage Learning 2013)

ties lay elsewhere. Frank wasn't attempting to hide anything from the clinician. Frank just didn't think his intrusive thoughts were the major problem; in addition, talking about them was difficult for him because they were quite frightening.

This example illustrates the importance of conducting the clinical interview in a way that elicits the patient's trust and empathy. Psychologists and other mental health professionals are trained in methods that put patients at ease and facilitate communication, including nonthreatening ways of seeking information and appropriate listening skills. Information provided by patients to psychologists and psychiatrists is protected by laws of "privileged communication" or confidentiality in most states. The only exception occurs when the clinician judges that some harm or danger to either the patient or someone else is imminent. At the outset of the initial interview, the therapist should inform the patient of the confidential nature of their conversation and the (rare) conditions under which that confidence would not hold.

Despite these assurances of confidentiality and the clinician's interview skills, patients sometimes find it difficult to volunteer sensitive information. In our own files is the case of a man in his early 20s who came to therapy once a week for 5 months. He wanted help with what he viewed as deficient interpersonal skills and anxieties that were impeding his ability to relate to other people. Only after 5 months, and by chance, did he reveal his secret. He was strongly sexually attracted to small boys and confessed that he found their feet and associated objects such as socks and shoes to be nearly irresistible. Although he had never actually approached any young boys, he had hidden in his home a large collection of small socks and shoes. Confiden-

tiality had been assured, and the therapist was there to help. Nevertheless, the patient found it almost impossible to volunteer this information.

Semistructured Clinical Interviews

Unstructured interviews follow no systematic format. *Semistructured interviews* are made up of questions that have been carefully phrased and tested to elicit useful information in a consistent manner so that clinicians can be sure they have inquired about the most important aspects of particular disorders (Summerfeldt, Kloosterman, & Antony, 2010). Clinicians may also depart from set questions to follow up on specific issues—thus the label "semistructured." Because the wording and sequencing of questions has been worked out over a number of years, the clinician can feel confident that a semistructured interview will accomplish its purpose. The disadvantage is that it robs the interview of some of the spontaneous quality of two people talking about a problem. Also, if applied too rigidly, a semistructured interview may inhibit the patient from volunteering information that is not directly relevant to the questions being asked. Because of these few drawbacks, structured interviews administered wholly by a computer have not caught on, although they are used in some settings.

An increasing number of mental health professionals, however, do routinely use semistructured interviews. Some are quite specialized. For example, Frank's clinician might use the *Anxiety Disorders Interview Schedule for DSM-IV (ADIS-IV)* (DiNardo, Brown, & Barlow, 1994). According to this interview schedule, the clinician first asks if the patient is bothered by thoughts, images, or impulses (obsessions) or feels driven to experience some behavior or thought repeatedly (compulsions). Based on an 8-point rating scale that ranges from "never" to "constantly," the clinician then asks the patient to rate each obsession on two measures: persistence–distress (how often it occurs and how much distress it causes) and resistance (types of attempts the patient makes to get rid of the obsession). For compulsions, the patient provides a rating of their frequency.

Physical Examination

Many patients with problems first go to a family physician. If the patient presenting with psychological problems has not had a physical exam in the past year, a clinician might recommend one. Many problems presenting as disorders of behavior, cognition, or mood may have a clear relationship to a temporary toxic state. This toxic state could be caused by bad food, the wrong amount or type of medicine, or onset of a medical condition. For example, thyroid difficulties, particularly hyperthyroidism (overactive thyroid gland), may produce symptoms that mimic certain anxiety disorders, such as generalized anxiety disorder. Withdrawal from cocaine often produces panic attacks, but many patients presenting with panic attacks are reluctant to volunteer information about their addiction, which may lead to an inappropriate diagnosis and improper treatment.

If a current medical condition or substance abuse situation exists, the clinician must ascertain whether it is merely coexisting or is causal, usually by looking at the onset of the problem. If a patient has suffered from severe bouts of depression for the past 5 years but within the past year has also developed hypothyroid problems or begun taking a sedative drug, then the clinician would not conclude the depression was caused by the medical or drug condition. If the depression developed simultaneously with the initiation of sedative drugs and diminished considerably when the drugs were discontinued, the clinician would be likely to conclude the depression was part of a substance-induced mood disorder.

Behavioral Assessment

The mental status exam is one way to begin to sample how people think, feel, and behave and how these actions might contribute to or explain their problems. **Behavioral assessment** takes this process one step further by using direct observation to assess an individual's thoughts, feelings, and behavior in specific contexts. Behavioral assessment may be more appropriate than any interview in terms of assessing individuals who are not old enough or skilled enough to report their problems and experiences.

In behavioral assessment, target behaviors are identified and observed with the goal of determining the factors that seem to influence them. It may seem easy to identify what is bothering a particular person (that is, the target behavior), but even this aspect of assessment can be challenging. For example, when the mother of a 7-year-old child with a severe conduct disorder came to one of our clinics for assistance, she told the clinician, after much prodding, that her son "didn't listen to her" and he sometimes had an "at-

titude." The boy's schoolteacher, however, painted a different picture. She spoke candidly of his threats toward other children and to herself. To get a clearer picture of the situation at home, the clinician visited one afternoon. Approximately 15 minutes after the visit began, the boy got up from the kitchen table without removing the drinking glass he was using. When his mother meekly asked him to put the glass in the sink, he picked it up and threw it across the room, sending broken glass throughout the kitchen. He giggled and went into his room to watch television. "See," she said. "He doesn't listen to me!"

Obviously, this mother's description of her son's behavior at home didn't portray what he was really like. It also didn't accurately describe her response to his violent outbursts. Clearly this was more than simple disobedience. We developed strategies to teach the mother how to make requests of her son and how to follow up if he was violent.

Getting back to Frank and his anxiety about his marriage, what would we find if we observed Frank and his wife interacting in their home or if they had a typical conversation in front of us in a clinical setting? Most clinicians assume that a complete picture of a person's problems requires direct observation in naturalistic environments. But going into a person's home, workplace, or school isn't always possible or practical, so clinicians sometimes arrange *analog*, or similar, settings (Haynes, Yoshioka, Kloezeman, & Bello, 2009). For example, one of us studies children with autism (a disorder characterized by social withdrawal and communication problems). The reasons for self-hitting (called *self-injurious*) behavior are discovered by placing the children in simulated classroom situations, such as sitting alone at a desk, working in a group, or being asked to complete a difficult task (Durand & Hieneman, 2008). Observing how the children behave in these different situations helps determine why they hit themselves. Other researchers are using hypnosis to produce analog assessments (conditions that mimic real-life clinical symptoms or situations) by inducing symptoms of psychopathology in healthy individuals to study these characteristics in a more controlled way (Oakley & Halligan, 2009). In one example, researchers studied delusions (a symptom of schizophrenia) while conducting brain scans in volunteers by hypnotizing them to believe some other force was controlling their arm movement (Blakemore, Oakley, & Frith, 2003). As you can see, researchers are using a variety of new creative techniques to study psychological disorders.

The ABCs of Observation

Observational assessment is usually focused on the here and now. Therefore, the clinician's attention is usually directed to the immediate behavior, its antecedents (what happened just before the behavior), and its consequences

behavioral assessment Measuring, observing, and systematically evaluating (rather than inferring) the client's thoughts, feelings, and behavior in the actual problem situation or context.

(what happened afterward) (Haynes et al., 2009). To use the example of the violent boy, an observer would note that the sequence of events was (1) his mother asking him to put his glass in the sink (antecedent), (2) the boy throwing the glass (behavior), and (3) his mother's lack of response (consequence). This antecedent–behavior–consequence sequence (the ABCs) might suggest that the boy was being reinforced for his violent outburst by not having to clean up his mess. And because there was no negative consequence for his behavior (his mother didn't scold or reprimand him), he will probably act violently the next time he doesn't want to do something (■ Figure 3.3).

This is an example of a relatively *informal observation*. A problem with this type of observation is that it relies on the observer's recollection, and interpretation, of the events. *Formal observation* involves identifying specific behaviors that are observable and measurable (called an *operational definition*). For example, it would be difficult for two people to agree on what "having an attitude" looks like. An operational definition, however, clarifies this behavior by specifying that this is "any time the boy does not comply with his mother's reasonable requests." Once the target behavior is selected and defined, an observer writes down each time it occurs, along with what happened just before (antecedent) and just after (consequence). The goal of collecting this information is to see whether there are any obvious patterns of behavior.

Self-Monitoring

People can also observe their own behavior to find patterns, a technique known as **self-monitoring** or *self-observation* (Haynes et al., 2009). People trying to quit smoking may write down the number of cigarettes they smoke and the times when and places where they smoke. This observation can tell them exactly how big their problem is and what situations lead them to smoke more (for example, talking on the phone) (Piasecki, Hufford, Solhan, & Trull, 2007). When behaviors occur only in private (such as purging by people with bulimia), self-monitoring is essential.

A more formal and structured way to observe behavior is through checklists and *behavior rating scales*, which are used as assessment tools before treatment and then periodically during treatment to assess changes in the person's behavior (Blacker, 2005; Myers & Collett, 2006). Of the many such instruments for assessing a variety of behaviors, the *Brief Psychiatric Rating Scale* (Clarkin, Howieson, & McClough, 2008), assesses 18 general areas of concern. Each symptom is rated on a 7-point scale from 0 (not present) to 6 (extremely severe). The rating scale screens for moderate to severe psychotic disorders and includes such items as somatic concern (preoccupation with physical health, fear of physical illness), guilt feelings (shame, remorse for past behavior), and grandiosity (exaggerated self-opinion, conviction of unusual power or abilities) (American Psychiatric Association, 2006).

A phenomenon known as *reactivity* can distort any observational data. Any time you observe how people behave, the mere fact of your presence may cause them to change their behavior (Haynes et al., 2009). To test reactivity, you can tell a friend you are going to record every time she says the word *like*. Just before you reveal your intent, however, count the times your friend uses this word in a 5-minute period. You will probably find that your friend uses the word less often when you are recording it. The same phenomenon occurs if you observe your own behavior, or self-monitor. Behaviors people want to increase, such as talking more in class, tend to increase, and behaviors people want to decrease, such as smoking, tend to decrease when they are self-monitored (for example, Hufford, Shields, Shiffman, Paty, & Balabanis, 2002).

Psychological Testing

We are confronted with so-called psychological tests in the popular press almost every week: "12 Questions to Test Your Relationship," "Every Guy's Private Marriage Checklist," "Are You a Type 'Z' Personality?" Many such tests are no more than entertainment. They are typically made up for the purposes of the article and include questions that, on the surface, seem to make sense. In reality, they usually tell us little.

In contrast, the tests used to assess psychological disorders must meet the strict standards we have noted: They must be reliable and valid.

Psychological tests include specific tools to determine cognitive, emotional, or behavioral responses that might be associated with a specific disorder and more general ones that assess long-standing personality features, such as a tendency to be suspicious. Specialized areas include intelligence testing to determine the structure and patterns of cognition. Neuropsychological testing determines the possible contribution of brain damage or dysfunction to the patient's condition. Neuroimaging uses sophisticated technology to assess brain structure and function.

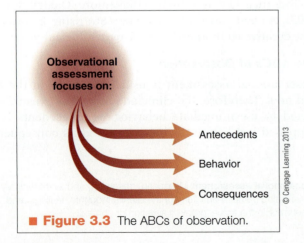

Observational
assessment
focuses on:

Antecedents

Behavior

Consequences

© Cengage Learning 2013

■ **Figure 3.3** The ABCs of observation.

Projective Testing

To assess unconscious processes in psychological disorders, psychoanalysts have developed assessment measures known as **projective tests**. They include a variety of methods in which ambiguous stimuli, such as pictures of people or things, are presented to people who are asked to describe what they see. The theory here is that people project their own personality and unconscious fears onto other people and things—in this case, the ambiguous stimuli—and, without realizing it, reveal their unconscious thoughts to the therapist.

Because these tests are based in psychoanalytic theory, they are controversial. Even so, the use of projective tests is common, with a majority of clinicians administering them at least occasionally (Butcher, 2009). Three of the more widely used are the Rorschach inkblot test, the Thematic Apperception Test, and the sentence-completion method.

The *Rorschach inkblot test* is one of the early projective tests. In its current form, the test includes 10 inkblot pictures that serve as the ambiguous stimuli (■ Figure 3.4). The examiner presents the inkblots one by one to the person being assessed, who responds by telling what he or she sees. Unfortunately, much of the early use of the Rorschach is extremely controversial because of the lack of data on reliability or validity, among other things. Until relatively recently, therapists administered the test any way they saw fit, although one of the most important tenets of assessment is that the same test be given in the same way

each time—that is, according to standardized procedures. If you encourage someone to give more detailed answers during one testing session but not during a second session, you may get different responses as the result of your administering the test differently on the two occasions—not because of problems with the test or administration by another person (interrater reliability).

To respond to the concerns about reliability and validity, John Exner developed a standardized version of the Rorschach inkblot test, called the *Comprehensive System* (Exner, 2003). Exner's system of administering and scoring the Rorschach specifies how the cards should be presented, what the examiner should say, and how the responses should be recorded (Clarkin et al., 2008). Varying these steps can lead to varying responses by the patient. Still, critics of the Rorschach question whether research on the Comprehensive System supports its use for people with psychological disorders (Garb, Wood, Lilienfeld, & Nezworski, 2005; Hunsley & Mash, 2011).

The *Thematic Apperception Test (TAT)* is perhaps the best-known projective test after the Rorschach (Clarkin et al., 2008). It consists of a series of 31 cards: 30 with pictures on them and 1 blank card, although only 20 cards are typically used during each administration. The instructions ask the person to tell a dramatic story about the picture. The tester presents the pictures and tells the patient, "This is a test of imagination, one form of intelligence." The person being assessed can "let your imagination have its way, as in a myth, fairy story, or allegory" (Stein, 1978, p. 186). Again like the Rorschach, the TAT is based on the notion that people will reveal their unconscious mental processes in their stories about the pictures.

Several variations of the TAT have been developed for different groups, including a Children's Apperception Test (CAT) and a Senior Apperception Technique (SAT). In addition, modifications of the test have evolved for use with a variety of racial and ethnic groups (Bellak, 1975; Dana, 1996). These modifications have included changes not only in the appearance of people in the pictures, but also in the situations depicted. Like the Comprehensive System used with the Rorschach, researchers have developed formal scoring systems for TAT stories, including the Social Cognition and Object Relations Scale (Westen, 1991).

Unfortunately, the TAT and its variants continue to be used inconsistently. How the stories people tell about these pictures are interpreted depends on the examiner's frame of reference and what the patient may say. It is not surpris-

■ **Figure 3.4** This inkblot resembles the ambiguous figures presented in the Rorschach test. (© Cengage Learning 2013)

self-monitoring The action by which clients observe and record their own behaviors as either an assessment of a problem and its change or a treatment procedure that makes them more aware of their responses. Also known as *self-observation*.

projective tests Psychoanalytically based measure that presents ambiguous stimuli to clients on the assumption that their responses can reveal their unconscious conflicts. Such tests are inferential and lack high reliability and validity.

ing, therefore, that questions remain about its use in psychopathology (Hunsley & Mash, 2011).

Most clinicians who use projective tests have their own methods of administration and interpretation. When used to get people to open up and talk about how they feel, the ambiguous stimuli in these tests can be valuable tools. However, their relative lack of reliability and validity makes them less useful as diagnostic tests.

Personality Inventories

The questions in psychological tests published in mainstream magazines typically make sense when you read them. This is called having *face validity:* The wording of the questions seems to fit the type of information desired. But is this necessary? Paul Meehl (1945) pointed out that what is necessary from these types of tests is not whether the questions make sense on the surface but, rather, what the answers predict. If we find that people who have schizophrenia tend to respond "true" to "I have never been in love with anyone," then it doesn't matter whether we have a theory of love and schizophrenia. What matters is if people with certain disorders tend, as a group, to answer a variety of questions in a certain way, this pattern may predict who else has this disorder. The content of the questions becomes irrelevant. This insight gave rise to a whole field of study on **personality inventories**.

Although many personality inventories are available, the most widely used personality inventory in the United States is the *Minnesota Multiphasic Personality Inventory (MMPI)*, which was developed in the late 1930s and early 1940s and first published in 1943 (Hathaway & McKinley, 1943). In stark contrast to projective tests, which rely heavily on theory for an interpretation, the MMPI and similar inventories are based on an *empirical* approach—that is, the collection and evaluation of data. The administration of the MMPI is straightforward. The individual being assessed reads statements and answers either "true" or "false." Following are some statements from the MMPI:

Cry readily
Often happy for no reason
Am being followed
Fearful of things or people that can't hurt me

There is little room for interpretation of MMPI responses. A problem with administering the MMPI, however, is the time and tedium of responding to the 550 items on the original version and now the 567 items on the MMPI-2 (published in 1989). A version of the MMPI that is appropriate for adolescents is also available—MMPI-A (published in 1992)—and other versions are being adapted for people in different cultures (Okazaki, Okazaki, & Sue, 2009). Individual responses on the MMPI are not examined; instead, the pattern of responses is reviewed to see whether it resembles patterns from groups of people who have specific disorders. Each group is represented on separate standard scales (Butcher & Perry, 2008) (Table 3.1).

Fortunately, clinicians can have these responses scored by computer; the program also includes an interpretation of the

results, thereby reducing problems of reliability. One concern that arose early in the development of the MMPI was the potential of some people to answer in ways that would downplay their problems; skilled individuals would ascertain the intent of statements such as "Worry about saying things that hurt people's feelings" and fake the answers. To assess this possibility, the MMPI includes additional scales that determine the validity of each administration. For example, on the Lie scale, a statement such as "Have hurt someone when angry," when answered "false" might be an indication that the person may be falsifying answers to look good. The other scales are the Infrequency scale, which measures false claims about psychological problems or determines whether the person is answering randomly, and the Subtle Defensiveness scale, which assesses whether the person sees herself in unrealistically positive ways (Butcher & Perry, 2008).

■ Figure 3.5 is an MMPI *profile* or summary of scores from an individual being clinically assessed. Before we tell you why this 27-year-old man (we'll call him James S.) was being evaluated, let's see what his MMPI profile tells us about him (note that these scores were obtained on the original version of the MMPI). The first three data points represent scores on the validity scales; the high scores on these scales were interpreted to mean that James S. made a naive attempt to look good for the evaluator and may have been trying to fake an appearance of having no problems. Another important part of his profile is the very high score on the psychopathic deviation scale, which measures the tendency to behave in antisocial ways. The interpretation of this score from the assessing clinician is that James S. is "aggressive, unreliable, irresponsible; unable to learn from experience; may initially make a good impression but then psychopathic features will surface in longer interactions or under stress."

James S. was a young man with a criminal record that began in his childhood. He was evaluated as part of his trial for kidnapping, raping, and murdering a middle-aged woman. Throughout his trial, he made up a number of contradictory stories to make himself look innocent (remember his high scores on the validity scales). However, there was overwhelming evidence of his guilt, and he was sentenced to life in prison. His answers on the MMPI resembled those of others who act in violent and antisocial ways.

The MMPI is one of the most extensively researched assessment instruments in psychology (Cox, Weed, & Butcher, 2009). The original standardization sample—the people who first responded to the statements and set the standard for answers—included many people from Minnesota who had no psychological disorders and several groups of people who had particular disorders. The more recent versions of this test, the MMPI-2 and the MMPI-A, eliminate problems with the original version (Ranson, Nichols, Rouse, & Harrington, 2009). For example, some questions were sexist. One item on the original version asks the respondent to say whether she has ever been sorry she is a girl (Worell & Remer, 1992). Another item states, "Any man who is willing to work hard has a good chance of succeeding" (Hathaway & McKinley, 1943). The MMPI-2 has also been

Table 3.1 Scales of the MMPI-2

Validity Scales	Characteristics of High Scorers
"Cannot say" score	Reading difficulties, guardedness, confusion and distractibility, depression, rebellion, or obsessiveness
Response inconsistency	Responding to questions in a manner inconsistent with psychological disorder
Infrequency	Exhibit randomness of responses or psychotic psychopathology
The back side F	Changing the way the questions are answered at the end of the test
Psychiatric infrequency	Claiming more psychiatric symptoms than expected
Lie	Dishonest, deceptive, and/or defended
Subtle defensiveness	Defensive through presenting themselves as healthier than they are
Superlative self-presentation	Claiming extreme positive characteristics and high moral values, and denying adjustment problems
Clinical Scales	**Characteristics of High Scorers**
Hypochondriasis	Somatizers, possible medical problems
Depression	Dysphoric, possibly suicidal
Hysteria	Highly reactive to stress, anxious, and sad at times
Psychopathic deviate	Antisocial, dishonest, possible drug abusers
Masculinity–femininity	Exhibit lack of stereotypical masculine interests, aesthetic and artistic
Paranoia	Exhibit disturbed thinking, ideas of persecution, possibly psychotic
Psychasthenia	Exhibit psychological turmoil and discomfort, extreme anxiety
Schizophrenia	Confused, disorganized, possible hallucinations
Mania	Manic, emotionally labile, unrealistic self-appraisal
Social introversion	Very insecure and uncomfortable in social situations, timid

*Excerpted from the MMPI(R)-2 (Minnesota Multiphasic Personality Inventory (R)-2) Manual for Administration. Copyright © 2001 by the Regents of the University of Minnesota. Used by permission of the University of Minnesota Press. All rights reserved. "MMPI-2" and "Minnesota Multiphasic Personality Iventory-2" are trademarks owned by the Regents of the University of Minnesota.

standardized with a sample that reflects the 1980 U.S. Census figures, including African Americans and Native Americans for the first time. In addition, new items have been added that deal with contemporary issues such as type A personality, low self-esteem, and family problems.

Intelligence Testing

In 1904 a French psychologist, Alfred Binet, and his colleague, Théodore Simon, were commissioned by the French government to develop a test that would identify "slow learners" who would benefit from remedial help. The two psychologists identified a series of tasks that presumably measured the skills children need to succeed in school, including tasks of attention, perception, memory, reasoning, and verbal comprehension. Binet and Simon gave their original series of tasks to a large number of children; they then eliminated tasks that did not separate the slow learners from the children who did well in school. After several revisions and sample administrations, they had a test that was relatively easy to administer and that did what it was designed to do—predict academic success. In 1916, Lewis Terman of Stanford University translated a

revised version of this test for use in the United States; it became known as the *Stanford-Binet test*.

The test provided a score known as an **intelligence quotient**, or **IQ**. Initially, IQ scores were calculated by using the child's *mental age*. For example, a child who passed all questions on the 7-year-old level and none of the questions on the 8-year-old level received a mental age of 7. This mental age was then divided by the child's *chronological age* and multiplied by 100 to get the IQ score. However, there were problems with using this type of formula for calculating an IQ score. Current tests use what is called a *deviation IQ*. A person's score is compared only to scores of others of the same age. The IQ score, then, is an estimate of how much a child's performance in school will deviate

personality inventories Self-report questionnaire that assesses personal traits by asking respondents to identify descriptions that apply to themselves.

intelligence quotient (IQ) Score on an intelligence test estimating a person's deviation from average test performance.

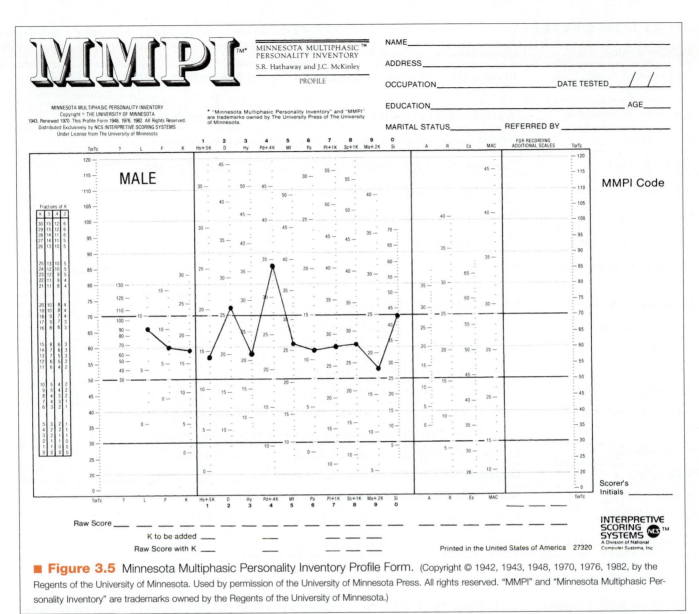

■ Figure 3.5 Minnesota Multiphasic Personality Inventory Profile Form. (Copyright © 1942, 1943, 1948, 1970, 1976, 1982, by the Regents of the University of Minnesota. Used by permission of the University of Minnesota Press. All rights reserved. "MMPI" and "Minnesota Multiphasic Personality Inventory" are trademarks owned by the Regents of the University of Minnesota.)

from the average performance of others of the same age (Gottfredson & Saklofske, 2009).

In addition to the revised version of the Stanford-Binet (*Stanford-Binet V;* Roid & Pomplun, 2005), there is another widely used set of intelligence tests, developed by psychologist David Wechsler. The Wechsler tests include versions for adults (*Wechsler Adult Intelligence Scale,* third edition, or *WAIS-III*), children (*Wechsler Intelligence Scale for Children,* fourth edition, or *WISC-IV*), and young children (*Wechsler Preschool and Primary Scale of Intelligence,* third edition, or *WPPSI-III*). All these tests contain *verbal scales* (which measure vocabulary, knowledge of facts, short-term memory, and verbal reasoning skills) and *performance scales* (which assess psychomotor abilities, nonverbal reasoning, and ability to learn new relationships) (Hunsley & Mash, 2011).

One of the biggest mistakes nonpsychologists make is to confuse IQ with intelligence. An IQ score significantly higher than average means the person has a significantly greater than average chance of doing well in our educa-

tional system. By contrast, a score significantly lower than average suggests the person will probably not do well in school. Does a lower-than-average IQ score mean a person is not intelligent? Not necessarily. First, there are numerous reasons for a low score. For example, if the IQ test is administered in English and that is not the person's native language, the results will be affected.

Perhaps more important, however, is the continued development of models that answer the question "What constitutes intelligence?" Remember that the IQ tests measure abilities such as memory, reasoning, and verbal comprehension. But do these skills represent the totality of what we consider intelligence? Some recent theorists believe that what we think of as intelligence involves more, including the ability to adapt to the environment, the ability to generate new ideas, and the ability to process information efficiently (Gottfredson & Saklofske, 2009). In general, however, IQ tests tend to be reliable, and to the extent that they predict academic success, they are valid assessment tools.

▲ This child is concentrating on a standard psychological assessment test.

Neuropsychological Testing

Sophisticated tests now exist that can pinpoint the location of brain dysfunction. Fortunately, these techniques are generally available and relatively inexpensive, and technological advances in interactive teleconferencing have led to efforts to conduct such assessments for people in remote areas (Swanda & Haaland, 2009). **Neuropsychological tests** measure abilities in areas such as receptive and expressive language, attention and concentration, memory, motor skills, perceptual abilities, and learning and abstraction.

A fairly simple neuropsychological test often used with children is the *Bender Visual–Motor Gestalt Test* (Brannigan & Decker, 2006). A child is given a series of cards on which are drawn various lines and shapes. The task is for the child to copy what is drawn on the card. The errors on the test are compared to test results of other children of the same age; if the number of errors exceeds a certain amount, brain dysfunction is suspected. Two advanced tests of organic (brain) damage that allow more precise determinations of the location of the problem are the *Luria-Nebraska Neuropsychological Battery* (Golden, Hammeke, & Purisch, 1980) and the *Halstead-Reitan Neuropsychological Battery* (Reitan & Davison, 1974). These tests assess a variety of skills in adolescents and adults. For example, the Halstead-Reitan Neuropsychological Battery includes the *Rhythm Test* (which asks the person to compare rhythmic beats, thus testing sound recognition, attention, and concentration), the *Strength of Grip Test* (which compares the grips of the right and left hands), and the *Tactile Performance Test* (which requires the test taker to place wooden blocks in a form board while blindfolded, thus testing learning and memory skills) (McCaffrey, Lynch, & Westervelt, 2011).

Research on the validity of neuropsychological tests suggests they may be useful for detecting organic damage. One study found that the Halstead-Reitan and the Luria-Nebraska test batteries were equivalent in their abilities to detect damage and were about 80% correct (Goldstein &

Shelly, 1984). However, these types of studies raise the issue of **false positives** and **false negatives**. For any assessment strategy, there will be times when the test shows a problem when none exists (false-positive results) and times when no problem is found even though some difficulty is present (false-negative results). Neuropsychological tests therefore are used primarily as screening devices and are routinely paired with other assessments to improve the likelihood that real problems will be found.

Neuroimaging: Pictures of the Brain

In recent years we have developed the ability to look inside the brain and take increasingly accurate pictures of its structure and function using a technique called **neuroimaging** (Kim, Schulz, Wilde, & Yudofsky, 2008). Neuroimaging can be divided into two categories: (1) procedures that examine the structure of the brain, such as the size of various parts and whether there is any damage, and (2) procedures that examine the actual functioning of the brain by mapping blood flow and other metabolic activity.

Images of Brain Structure

The first neuroimaging technique, developed in the early 1970s, uses multiple X-ray exposures of the brain from different angles. As with any X ray, these are partially blocked or attenuated more by bone and less by brain tissue. The degree of blockage is picked up by detectors in the opposite side of the head. A computer then reconstructs pictures of various slices of the brain. This procedure, which takes about 15 minutes, is called a *computerized axial tomography (CAT) scan* or *CT scan*. CT scans are particularly useful in locating brain tumors, injuries, and other structural and anatomical abnormalities. One difficulty, however, is that these scans, like all X rays, involve repeated X radiation, which poses some risk of cell damage (Kim et al., 2008).

Several more recently developed procedures give greater accuracy than a CT scan without the inherent risks of X-ray tests. In nuclear *magnetic resonance imaging (MRI)*, the patient's head is placed in a high-strength magnetic field through which radio-frequency signals are transmitted. These signals "excite" the brain tissue, altering the protons in the hydrogen atoms. The alteration is measured, along with the time it takes the protons to "relax" or return to normal. Where there are lesions or damage, the signal is lighter or darker (Kim et al., 2008). Technology now exists that allows the computer to view the brain in

neuropsychological testing Assessment of brain and nervous system functioning by testing an individual's performance on behavioral tasks.
false positive Assessment error in which pathology is reported (that is, test results are positive) when none is actually present.
false negative Assessment error in which no pathology is noted (that is, test results are negative) when one is actually present.
neuroimaging Sophisticated computer-aided procedure that allows nonintrusive examination of nervous system structure and function.

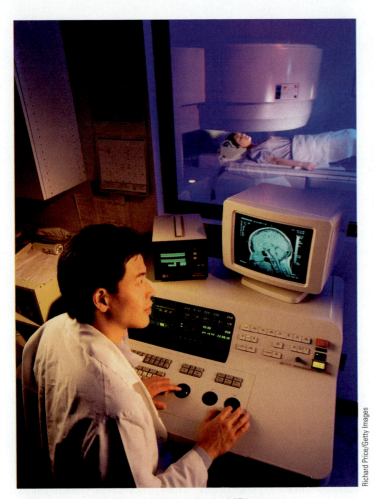

▲ The patient is being positioned for an MRI scan.

increasingly to look at varying patterns of metabolism that might be associated with different disorders. Recent PET scans have demonstrated that many patients with early Alzheimer's-type dementia show reduced glucose metabolism in the parietal lobes. Other intriguing findings have been reported for obsessive-compulsive disorder and bipolar disorder. Because PET scanning is expensive, these facilities are available only in large medical centers.

A second procedure used to assess brain functioning is called *single photon emission computed tomography (SPECT)*. It works much like PET, although a different tracer substance is used and this procedure is somewhat less accurate. It is also less expensive, however, and requires far less sophisticated equipment to pick up the signals. Therefore, SPECT is used more often than PET scans.

The most exciting advances involve MRI procedures that have been developed to work more quickly than the regular MRI (Kim et al., 2008). These procedures take only milliseconds and therefore can actually take pictures of the brain at work, recording its changes from one second to the next. Because these procedures measure the functioning of the brain, they are called *functional MRI,* or *fMRI.* fMRI procedures have largely replaced PET scans in the leading brain-imaging centers because they allow researchers to see the immediate response of the brain to a brief event, such as seeing a new face. BOLD-fMRI (Blood-Oxygen-Level-Dependent fMRI) is currently the most common fMRI technique used to study psychological disorders (Kim et al., 2008).

Psychophysiological Assessment

Yet another method for assessing brain structure and function specifically and nervous system activity generally is called **psychophysiological assessment**. As the term implies, *psychophysiology* refers to measurable changes in the nervous system that reflect emotional or psychological events. The measurements may be taken either directly from the brain or peripherally from other parts of the body.

Frank feared that he might have seizures. If we had any reason to suspect he might have periods of memory loss or

layers, which enables precise examination of the structure. Although an MRI is more expensive than a CT scan and originally took as long as 45 minutes, this is changing as technology improves. Another disadvantage of MRI at present is that someone undergoing the procedure is totally enclosed inside a narrow tube with a magnetic coil surrounding the head. People who are somewhat claustrophobic often cannot tolerate an MRI.

Images of Brain Functioning

Several widely used procedures are capable of measuring the actual functioning of the brain. The first is called *positron emission tomography (PET) scan.* Subjects undergoing a PET scan are injected with a tracer substance attached to radioactive isotopes, or groups of atoms that react distinctively. This substance interacts with blood, oxygen, or glucose. When parts of the brain become active, blood, oxygen, or glucose rushes to these areas of the brain, creating "hot spots" picked up by detectors that identify the location of the isotopes. Thus, we can learn what parts of the brain are working and what parts are not. These images can be superimposed on MRI images to show the precise location of the active areas. PET scans are used

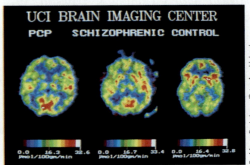

▲ The PET scans compare activity in the brain of a drug abuser *(left),* a person with schizophrenia *(center),* and in a normal brain *(right).*

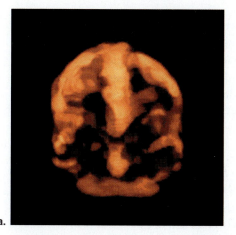 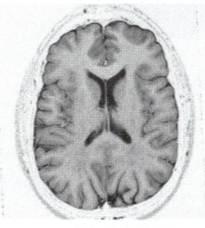 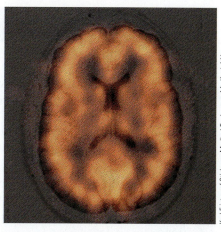

a.   b.   c.

▲ A horizontal brain section (a) in a SPECT image clearly reveals parietal lobe damage in a person with schizophrenia. Images (b) and (c) are MRI photographs. SPECT images show metabolic activity and thus indicate the relationship between the person's brain and the person's behavior. The higher-resolution MRI images show tissue variations.

exhibit bizarre, trancelike behavior, if only for a short period, it would be important for him to have an **electroencephalogram (EEG)**. Measuring electrical activity in the head related to the firing of a specific group of neurons reveals brain wave activity; brain waves come from the low-voltage electrical current that runs through the neurons. In an EEG, electrodes are placed directly on various places on the scalp to record the different low-voltage currents.

We have learned much about EEG patterns in the past decades (Kim et al., 2008). Usually we measure ongoing electrical activity in the brain. When brief periods of EEG patterns are recorded in response to specific events, such as hearing a psychologically meaningful stimulus, the response is called an *event-related potential (ERP)* or *evoked potential*. EEG patterns are often affected by psychological or emotional factors and can be an index of these reactions.

In a normal, healthy, relaxed adult, waking activities are characterized by a regular pattern of changes in voltage termed *alpha waves*. Many types of stress-reduction treatments attempt to *increase* the frequency of the alpha waves, often by relaxing the patients in some way. The alpha wave pattern is associated with relaxation and calmness. During sleep, we pass through several stages of brain activity, at least partially identified by EEG patterns. During the deepest, most relaxed stage, typically occurring 1 to 2 hours after a person falls asleep, EEG recordings show a pattern of *delta waves*. These brain waves are slower and more irregular than the alpha waves, which is normal for this stage of sleep. If frequent delta wave activity occurred during the waking state, it might indicate dysfunction of localized areas of the brain.

Psychophysiological assessment of other bodily responses may also play a role in assessment. These responses include heart rate, respiration, and *electrodermal responding*, formerly referred to as *galvanic skin response (GSR)*, which is a measure of sweat gland activity con-

trolled by the peripheral nervous system. Assessing psychophysiological response to emotional stimuli is important in many disorders, one being posttraumatic stress disorder. Stimuli such as sights and sounds associated with the trauma evoke strong psychophysiological responses, even if the patient is not fully aware that this is happening.

Physiological measures are also important in the assessment and treatment of conditions such as headaches and hypertension (Nicassio, Meyerowitz, & Kerns, 2004); they form the basis for the treatment we call *biofeedback*. In biofeedback, levels of physiological responding, such as blood pressure readings, are fed back to the patient (provided on a continuous basis) by meters or gauges so that the patient can try to regulate these responses.

Physiological assessment requires a great deal of skill and some technical expertise. Even when administered properly, the measures sometimes produce inconsistent results because of procedural or technical difficulties or the nature of the response itself. Therefore, only clinicians specializing in certain disorders in which these measures are particularly important are likely to make extensive use of psychophysiological recording equipment, although more straightforward applications, such as monitoring heart rate during relaxation exercises, are more common. More sophisticated psychophysiological assessment is most often used in theoretical investigations of the nature of certain psychological disorders, particularly emotional disorders (Barlow, 2002; Ovsiew, 2005).

psychophysiological assessment Measurement of changes in the nervous system reflecting psychological or emotional events such as anxiety, stress, and sexual arousal.

electroencephalogram (EEG) Measure of electrical activity patterns in the brain, taken through electrodes placed on the scalp.

◉ Diagnosing Psychological Disorders

> **How is psychiatric diagnosis carried out?**

Thus far, we have looked at Frank's functioning on an individual basis—that is, we have closely observed his behavior, cognitive processes, and mood, and we have conducted semistructured interviewing, behavioral assessment, and psychological tests. These operations tell us what is unique about Frank, not what he may have in common with other individuals.

Learning how Frank may resemble other people in terms of the problems he presents is important for several reasons. If in the past people came in with similar problems or psychological profiles, we can go back and find a lot of information from their cases that might be applicable to Frank's case. We can see how the problems began for those other individuals, what factors seemed influential, and how long the problem or disorder lasted. Did the problem in the other cases just go away on its own? If not, what kept it going? Did it need treatment? Most important, what treatments seemed to relieve the problem for those other individuals? These general questions are useful because they evoke a wealth of clinical and research information that enables the investigator to make certain inferences about what will happen next and what treatments may work. In other words, the clinician can form general conclusions and establish a *prognosis,* a term we discussed in

Chapter 1 that refers to the likely future course of a disorder under certain conditions.

Both strategies are essential in the study and treatment of psychopathology. If we want to determine what is unique about an individual's personality, cultural background, or circumstances, we use what is known as an **idiographic strategy**. This information lets us tailor our treatment to the person. But to take advantage of the information already accumulated on a particular problem or disorder, we must be able to determine a general class of problems to which the presenting problem belongs. This is known as a **nomothetic strategy**. When we identify a specific psychological disorder, we are making a diagnosis. We can also identify a general class or grouping of problems by determining a particular personality profile on a psychological test such as the MMPI. Before proceeding, let's define some additional terms more precisely.

The term **classification** itself is broad, referring simply to any effort to construct groups or categories and to assign objects or people to these categories on the basis of their shared attributes or relations—a nomothetic strategy. If the classification is in a scientific context, it is most often called **taxonomy**, which is the classification of entities for scientific purposes, such as insects, rocks, or—if the subject is psychology—behaviors. If you apply a taxonomic system to psychological or medical phenomena or other clinical areas, you use the word **nosology**. All diagnostic systems used in health-care settings, such as those for infectious diseases, are nosological systems. The term **nomenclature** describes the names or labels of the disorders that make up the nosology (for example, anxiety or mood disorders). Most mental health professionals use the classification system contained in the *DSM-IV-TR* (American Psychiatric Association, 2000). During the past several years, there have been enormous changes in how psychopathology is classified. Because these developments affect so much of what clinicians do, we examine carefully the processes of classification and diagnosis as they are used in psychopathology. We look first at different approaches, examine the concepts of reliability and validity as they pertain to diagnosis, and then discuss our current system of classification, the *DSM-IV*.

Classification Issues

Classification is at the heart of any science, and much of what we have said about it is common sense. When we are dealing with human behavior or human behavioral disorders, however, the subject of classification becomes controversial. Some people have questioned whether it is proper or ethical to classify human behavior. Even among those who recognize the necessity of classification, major controversies have arisen in several areas. Within psychopathology, for example, definitions of "normal" and "abnormal" are questioned, as is the assumption that a behavior or cognition is part of one disorder and not another. Some would prefer to talk about behavior and feelings on a continuum from happy to sad or fearful to nonfearful rather than to create such categories as mania, depression, and phobia. For better or worse, classifying behavior and people is something we all do. Few of us talk about our own emotions or those of our friends by using a number on a scale (where 0 is totally unhappy and 100 is totally happy), although this approach might be more accurate. ("How do you feel about that?" "About 65.") Rather, we talk about being happy, sad, angry, depressed, fearful, and so on.

Categorical and Dimensional Approaches

How can we classify human behavior? We have already alluded to two possibilities. We can have distinct categories of disorders that have little or nothing in common with one another; for example, you either hear voices talking to you from the refrigerator (auditory hallucination) and have other symptoms of schizophrenia or you don't. Alternatively, we can quantify the various attributes of a psychological disorder along several dimensions, coming up with a composite score. An MMPI profile is a good example; another is "dimensionalizing" a disorder—for example, depression—on a continuum of severity, from feeling mildly depressed in the morning (something most of us experience once in a while) to feeling so deeply depressed and hopeless that suicide is the only solution. Each system

has both strengths and faults (Brown & Barlow, 2005; Helzer et al., 2008; Widiger & Edmundson, 2011; Widiger & Samuel, 2005).

The **classical** (or pure) **categorical approach** to classification assumes that every diagnosis has a clear underlying pathophysiological cause, such as a bacterial infection or a malfunctioning endocrine system, and that each disorder is unique. When diagnoses are thought of in this way, the causes could be psychological or cultural instead of pathophysiological, but there is still only one set of causative factors per disorder, which does not overlap with those of other disorders. Because each disorder is fundamentally different from every other, we need only one set of defining criteria, which everybody in the category has to meet. If the criteria for a major depressive episode are (1) the presence of depressed mood, (2) significant weight loss or gain when not dieting, (3) diminished ability to think or concentrate, and seven additional specific symptoms, then, to be diagnosed with depression, an individual would have to meet all of the criteria. In that case, according to the classical categorical approach, the clinician would know the cause of the disorder.

Classical categorical approaches are useful in medicine. It is extremely important for a physician to make accurate diagnoses. If a patient has a fever accompanied by stomach pain, the doctor must determine quickly whether the cause is stomach flu or an infected appendix. To understand the cause of symptoms (infected appendix) is to know what treatment will be effective (surgery). But if someone is depressed or anxious, is there a similar type of underlying cause? Probably not. Most psychopathologists believe psychological and social factors interact with biological factors to produce a disorder. Therefore, the mental health field has not adopted a classical categorical model of psychopathology (Frances & Widiger, 1986; Helzer et al., 2008; Regier, Narrow, Kuhl, & Kupfer, 2009; Widiger & Edmundson, 2011).

A second strategy is a **dimensional approach**, in which we note the variety of cognitions, moods, and be-

---

idiographic strategy A close and detailed investigation of an individual emphasizing what makes that person unique. (Compare with *nomothetic strategy*.)

nomothetic strategy Identification and examination of large groups of people with the same disorder to note similarities and develop general laws.

classification Assignment of objects or people to categories on the basis of shared characteristics.

taxonomy System of naming and classification (for example, of specimens) in science.

nosology Classification and naming system for medical and psychological phenomena.

nomenclature In a naming system or nosology, the actual labels or names that are applied. In psychopathology, these include mood disorders and eating disorders.

classical categorical approach Classification method founded on the assumption of clear-cut differences among disorders, each with a different known cause. Also known as *pure categorical approach*.

dimensional approach Method of categorizing characteristics on a continuum rather than on a binary, either-or, or all-or-none basis.

haviors with which the patient presents and quantify them on a scale. For example, on a scale of 1 to 10, a patient might be rated as severely anxious (10), moderately depressed (5), and mildly manic (2) to create a profile of emotional functioning (10, 5, 2). Although dimensional approaches have been applied to psychopathology, they have been relatively unsatisfactory until now (Brown & Barlow, 2009; Frances, 2009; Regier et al., 2009; Widiger & Edmundson, 2011). Most theorists have not been able to agree on how many dimensions are required: some say 1 dimension is enough; others have identified as many as 33 (Millon, 1991, 2004).

A third strategy for organizing and classifying behavioral disorders has found increasing support in recent years. It combines some features of each of the former approaches. Called a **prototypical approach**, this alternative identifies certain essential characteristics of an entity so that you (and others) can classify it, but it also allows certain nonessential variations that do not necessarily change the classification. For example, if someone were to ask you to describe a dog, you could easily give a general description, but you might not exactly describe a specific dog. Dogs come in different colors, sizes, and even species, but they all share certain doggish characteristics that allow you to classify them separately from cats. Thus, requiring a certain number of prototypical criteria and only some of an additional number of criteria is adequate. This system is not perfect because there is a greater blurring at the boundaries of categories, and some symptoms apply to more than one disorder. However, it has the advantage of fitting best with the current state of our knowledge of psychopathology, and it is relatively user-friendly.

▲ Despite their wide physical variation, all dogs belong to the same class of animals.

DSM-IV-TR

When a prototypical approach is used in classifying a psychological disorder, many possible features or properties of the disorder are listed and any candidate must meet enough of them to fall into that category. Consider the *DSM-IV-TR* criteria defining a major depressive episode.

As you can see, the criteria include many nonessential symptoms, but if you have either depressed mood or marked loss of interest or pleasure in most activities and at least four of the remaining eight symptoms, you come close enough to the prototype to meet the criteria for a major depressive episode. One person might have depressed mood, significant weight loss, insomnia, psychomotor agitation, and loss of energy, whereas another person who also meets the criteria for major depressive episode might have markedly diminished interest or pleasure in activities, fatigue, feelings of worthlessness, difficulty thinking or concentrating, and ideas of committing suicide. Although both have the requisite five symptoms that bring them close to the prototype, they look different because they share only one symptom. This is a good example of a prototypical category. The *DSM-IV-TR* is based on this approach.

Reliability

Any system of classification should describe specific subgroups of symptoms that are clearly evident and can be readily identified by experienced clinicians. If two clinicians interview the patient at separate times on the same day (and assuming the patient's condition does not change during the day), the two clinicians should see, and perhaps measure, the same set of behaviors and emotions. The psychological disorder can thus be identified reliably. If the disorder is not readily apparent to both clinicians, the resulting diagnoses might represent bias. For example, someone's clothes might provoke some comment. One of your friends might later say, "She looked kind of sloppy tonight." Another might comment, "No, that's just a real funky look—she's right in style." Perhaps a third friend would say, "Actually, I thought she was dressed kind of neatly." You might wonder if they had

---

DSM **Disorder Criteria Summary**
Major Depressive Episode

Features of a major depressive episode include the following:

❯ Depressed mood most of the day (or irritable mood in children or adolescents)

❯ Markedly diminished interest or pleasure in most daily activities

❯ Significant weight loss when not dieting or weight gain, or significant decrease or increase in appetite

❯ Ongoing insomnia or hypersomnia

❯ Psychomotor agitation or retardation

❯ Fatigue or loss of energy

❯ Feelings of worthlessness or excessive guilt

❯ Diminished ability to think or concentrate

❯ Recurrent thoughts of death, suicide ideation, or suicide attempt

Source: Based on DSM-IV-TR. Reprinted with permission from *Diagnostic and Statistical Manual of Mental Disorders* (4th ed., text revision). © 2000 American Psychiatric Association.

all seen the same person. In any case, there would be no reliability to their observations. Getting your friends to agree about someone's appearance would require a careful set of definitions that they all accept.

As we noted before, unreliable classification systems are subject to bias by clinicians making diagnoses. One of the most unreliable categories in current classification is the area of personality disorders—chronic, traitlike sets of inappropriate behaviors and emotional reactions that characterize a person's way of interacting with the world. Although great progress has been made, particularly with certain personality disorders, determining the presence or absence of this type of disorder during one interview is still difficult.

Validity

In addition to being reliable, a system of nosology must be valid. Earlier we described *validity* as whether something measures what it is designed to measure. There are several types of diagnostic validity. For one, the system should have *construct validity*. This means the signs and symptoms chosen as criteria for the diagnostic category are consistently associated and what they identify differs from other categories. Someone meeting the criteria for depression should be discriminable from someone meeting the criteria for social phobia. This discriminability might be evident not only in presenting symptoms, but also in the course of the disorder and possibly in the choice of treatment. It may also predict **familial aggregation**, the extent to which the disorder would be found among the patient's relatives (Blashfield & Livesley, 1991; Cloninger, 1989; Kupfer, First, & Regier, 2002).

In addition, a valid diagnosis tells the clinician what is likely to happen with the prototypical patient; it may predict the course of the disorder and the likely effect of one treatment or another. This type of validity is referred to often as *predictive validity* and sometimes as *criterion validity*, when the outcome is the criterion by which we judge the usefulness of the diagnostic category. Finally, there is *content validity*, which simply means that if you create criteria for a diagnosis of, say, social phobia, it should reflect the way most experts in the field think of social phobia, as opposed to, say, depression. In other words, you need to get the label right.

Diagnosis before 1980

Early efforts to classify psychopathology arose out of the biological tradition, particularly the work of Kraepelin. Kraepelin first identified what we now know as the disorder of schizophrenia. His term for the disorder at the time was *dementia praecox*. Dementia praecox refers to deterioration of the brain that sometimes occurs with advancing age (dementia) and develops earlier than it is supposed to, or "prematurely" (praecox). This label (later changed to *schizophrenia*) reflected Kraepelin's belief that brain pathology is the cause of this particular disorder. Kraepelin's landmark 1913 book (*Psychiatry: A Textbook for Students and Physicians*) described not only dementia praecox but also bipolar disorder, then called *manic depressive psychosis*. Kraepelin also described a variety of organic brain syndromes. Other well-known figures in their time, such as French psychiatrist Philippe Pinel, characterized psychological disorders, including depression (melancholia), as separate entities, but Kraepelin's theorizing that psychological disorders are basically biological disturbances had the greatest impact on the development of our nosology and led to an early emphasis on classical categorical strategies.

It was not until 1948 that the World Health Organization (WHO) added a section classifying mental disorders to the sixth edition of the *International Classification of Diseases and Related Health Problems (ICD)*. However, this early system did not have much influence. Nor did the first *Diagnostic and Statistical Manual (DSM-I)*, published in 1952 by the American Psychiatric Association. Only in the late 1960s did systems of nosology begin to have some real influence on mental health professionals. In 1968 the American Psychiatric Association published a second edition of its *Diagnostic and Statistical Manual (DSM-II)*. In 1969, WHO published the eighth edition of the *ICD*. Nevertheless, these systems lacked precision, often differing substantially from one another and relying heavily on unproven theories of etiology not widely accepted by all mental health professionals. To make matters worse, the systems had little reliability. In these countries, the same disorders would be labeled and interpreted differently.

DSM-III and DSM-III-R

The year 1980 brought a landmark in the history of nosology: the third edition of the *Diagnostic and Statistical Manual (DSM-III)* (American Psychiatric Association, 1980). *DSM-III* departed radically from its predecessors. Three changes stood out. First, *DSM-III* relied on precise descriptions of the disorders as they presented to clinicians rather than on psychoanalytic or biological theories of etiology. For example, rather than classifying phobia under the broad category "neurosis," defined by intrapsychic conflicts and defense mechanisms, it was assigned its own category within a new broader group, "anxiety disorders."

The second major change in *DSM-III* was that the specificity and detail with which the criteria for identifying a disorder were listed made it possible to study their reliability and validity. Although not all categories in *DSM-III* achieved perfect reliability and validity, this system was a vast improvement over what was available before. Third, *DSM-III* allowed individuals with possible psychological disorders to be rated on five dimensions, or axes. The disorder itself, such as schizophrenia or mood disorder, was represented only on the first axis. More enduring (chronic)

prototypical approach System for categorizing disorders using both essential, defining characteristics and a range of variation on other characteristics.
familial aggregation The extent to which a disorder would be found among a patient's relatives.

disorders of personality were listed on Axis II. Axis III consisted of any physical disorders and conditions that might be present. On Axis IV the clinician rated, in a dimensional fashion, the amount of psychosocial stress the person reported, and the current level of adaptive functioning was indicated on Axis V. This framework, called the *multiaxial system*, allowed the clinician to gather information about the individual's functioning in a number of areas rather than limiting information to the disorder itself.

DSM-IV and DSM-IV-TR

By the late 1980s, clinicians and researchers realized the need for a consistent, worldwide system of nosology. The 10th edition of the *International Classification of Diseases (ICD-10)* would be published in 1993, and the United States is required by treaty obligations to use the *ICD-10* codes in all matters related to health. To make the *ICD-10* and *DSM* as compatible as possible, work proceeded more or less simultaneously on both the *ICD-10* and the fourth edition of the *DSM (DSM-IV)* published in 1994. The *DSM-IV* task force attempted to review the literature in all areas pertaining to the diagnostic system (Widiger et al., 1996, 1998) and to identify large sets of data that might have been collected for other reasons but that, with reanalysis, would be useful to *DSM-IV*. Finally, 12 independent studies or field trials examined the reliability and validity of alternative sets of definitions or criteria and, in some cases, the possibility of creating a new diagnosis.

Perhaps the most substantial change in *DSM-IV* is that the distinction between organically based disorders and psychologically based disorders that was present in previous editions has been eliminated. Even disorders associated with known brain pathology are substantially affected by psychological and social influences. Similarly, disorders previously described as psychological in origin have biological components.

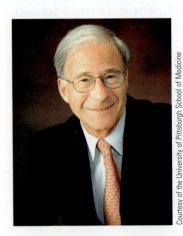

▲ David Kupfer is the chair of the task force for the 5th edition of the *Diagnostic and Statistical Manual of Mental Disorders (DSM)*, which is due to appear in 2013.

The Multiaxial Format in DSM-IV

The multiaxial system remained in *DSM-IV*, with some changes in the five axes. Specifically, only personality disorders and mental retardation were now coded on Axis II. Pervasive developmental disorders, learning disorders, motor skills disorders, and communication disorders, previously coded on Axis II, were now all coded on Axis I. Axis IV, which rated the patient's amount of psychosocial stress, was not useful and was replaced. The new Axis IV is used for reporting psychosocial and environmental problems that might have an impact on the disorder. Axis V was essentially unchanged.

In 2000 a committee updated the text that describes the research literature accompanying the *DSM-IV* diagnostic category and made minor changes to some of the criteria themselves to improve consistency (First & Pincus, 2002; American Psychiatric Association, 2000). This text revision *(DSM-IV-TR)* helped clarify many issues related to the diagnosis of psychological disorders.

The use of dimensional axes for rating—for example, severity of the disorder in a uniform manner across all disorders—will be greatly expanded in *DSM-5* (Regier et al., 2009). A variety of proposals for creating these crosscutting or superordinate dimensions are currently under evaluation. Another proposal, for example, is to rate the presence of anxiety in a global sense across disorders. Thus, one might diagnose bipolar disorder and provide a dimensional rating of the degree of anxiety also present because a greater degree of anxiety seems to predict a poorer response to treatment (Howland et al., 2009).

DSM-IV and Frank

In Frank's case, initial observations indicate an anxiety disorder on Axis I, specifically obsessive-compulsive disorder. However, he might also have long-standing personality traits that lead him to avoid social contact. If so, there might be a diagnosis of schizoid personality disorder on Axis II. Unless Frank has an identifiable medical condition, there is nothing on Axis III. Job and marital difficulties would be coded on Axis IV, where clinicians note psychosocial or environmental problems that are not part of the disorder but might make it worse. Frank's difficulties with work would be noted by checking "occupational problems" and specifying "threat of job loss"; for "problems with primary support group," "marital difficulties" would be noted. On Axis V, the clinician would rate the highest overall level of Frank's current functioning on a 0-to-100 scale (100 indicates superior functioning in a variety of situations). At present, Frank's score is 55, which indicates moderate interference with functioning at home and at work.

It is important to emphasize that impairment is a crucial determination in making any diagnosis. For example, if someone, such as Frank, has all of the symptoms of obsessive-compulsive disorder but finds them only mildly annoying because the intrusive thoughts are not severe and don't occur that often, that person would not merit criteria for a psychological disorder. It is essential that the various behaviors and cognitions comprising the diagnosis interfere with functioning in some substantial manner. Thus, the criteria for disorders include the provision that the disorder must cause clinically significant distress or impairment in social, occupational, or other important areas of functioning. As noted earlier, one change in *DSM-5* will be to make this judgment of severity and impairment more systematic by using a dimensional scale. In one of our own clinics, we have been doing something similar to this—that is, in addition to rating overall impairment on Axis V, impairment specifically associated with the Axis I disorder (if present) is also rated. A scale of 0 to 8 is used, where 0 is no impairment and 8 is severely disturbing or disabling (usually housebound and barely functional). The disorder must be rated at least a 4 in severity (definitely disturbing or disabling) to meet criteria for a psychological disorder. Many times, disorders such as obsessive-compulsive disorder would be rated a 2 or 3, meaning that all of the symptoms are there but in too mild a form to impair functioning; in this case, the disorder would be termed *subthreshold*. Using Frank as an example again, the severity of his obsessive-compulsive disorder would be rated 5. In a diagnostic report, a summary of Frank's profile based on the multiaxial formulation of *DSM-IV* would look like this:

Axis I   Obsessive-compulsive disorder
Axis II   Schizoid personality disorder
Axis III   None
Axis IV   Occupational problems: threat of job loss; problems with primary support group: marital difficulties
Axis V   55 (current)

Social and Cultural Considerations in DSM-IV

By emphasizing levels of stress in the environment, *DSM-III* and *DSM-IV* facilitate a more complete picture of the individual. Furthermore, *DSM-IV* corrects a previous omission by including a plan for integrating important social and cultural influences on diagnosis. The plan, referred to as the "cultural formulation guidelines," allows the disorder to be described from the perspective of the patient's personal experience and in terms of the primary social and cultural group, such as Hispanic or Chinese. Answering the following suggested culture-related questions will help accomplish these goals (Mezzich et al., 1993, 1999):

1. What is the primary cultural reference group of the patient? For recent immigrants to the country, and other ethnic minorities, how involved are they with their "new" culture versus their old culture? Have they mastered the language of their new country, or is language a continuing problem?
2. Does the patient use terms and descriptions from his or her "old" country to describe the disorder? For example, *ataques de nervios* in the Hispanic subculture is a type of anxiety disorder close to panic disorder. Does the patient accept Western models of disease or disorder for which treatment is available in health-care systems, or does the patient also have an alternative health-care system in another culture (for example, traditional herbal doctors in Chinese subcultures)?
3. What does it mean to be "disabled"? Which kinds of "disabilities" are acceptable in a given culture and which are not? For example, is it acceptable to be physically ill but not to be anxious or depressed? What are the typical family, social, and religious supports in the culture? Are they available to the patient?

These cultural considerations must not be overlooked in making diagnoses and planning treatment, and they are assumed throughout this book. But, as yet, there is no research supporting the use of these cultural formulation guidelines (Alarcon et al., 2002). The consensus is that we have a lot more work to do in this area to make our nosology truly culturally sensitive, and *DSM-5V* has commissioned a number of reviews addressing cultural variations (for example, Lewis-Fernandez et al., 2009).

Criticisms of DSM-IV and DSM-IV-TR

DSM-IV (and the closely related *ICD-10* mental disorder section) is the most advanced, scientifically based system of nosology ever developed. Nevertheless, any nosological system should be considered a work in progress (Brown & Barlow, 2005; Millon, 2004; Regier et al., 2009; Smith & Oltmanns, 2009). We still have "fuzzy" categories that blur at the edges. As a consequence, individuals are often diagnosed with more than one psychological disorder at the same time, which is called **comorbidity**. How can we conclude anything definite about the course of a disorder, the response to treatment, or the likelihood of associated problems if we are dealing with combinations of disorders (Brown & Barlow, 2009; Follette & Houts, 1996; Kupfer et al., 2002)? Is there a way to identify essential features of comorbid disorders and, perhaps, rate them dimensionally (Brown & Barlow, 2009; Helzer et al., 2008)?

Criticisms center on two other aspects of *DSM-IV* and *ICD-10*. First, the systems strongly emphasize reliability, sometimes at the expense of validity. This is understandable because reliability is so difficult to achieve unless you are willing to sacrifice validity. If the sole criterion for establishing depression were to hear the patient say at some point during an interview, "I feel depressed," the clinician could theoretically achieve perfect reliability. But this achievement would be at the expense of validity because many people with differing psychological disorders, or none, occasionally say they are depressed. Thus, clinicians could agree that the statement occurred, but it would be of little use (Carson, 1991; Meehl, 1989). Second, as Carson (1996) points out, methods of constructing a nosology of mental disorders have a way of perpetuating definitions handed down to us from past decades. It might be better to start fresh once in a while and create a new system of disorders based on emerging scientific knowledge rather than to simply fine-tune old definitions, but this is unlikely to happen because of the enormous effort and expense involved and the necessity of discarding the accumulated wisdom of previous versions.

A Caution About Labeling and Stigma

A related problem that occurs any time we categorize people is **labeling**. You may remember Kermit the Frog from *Sesame Street* sharing with us that "it's not easy being

---

comorbidity Presence of two or more disorders in an individual at the same time.
labeling Applying a name to a phenomenon or a pattern of behavior. The label may acquire negative connotations or be applied erroneously to the person rather than that person's behaviors.

green." Something in human nature causes us to use a label, even one as superficial as skin color, to characterize the totality of an individual ("He's green . . . he's different from me"). We see the same phenomenon among psychological disorders ("He's a schizo"). Furthermore, if the disorder is associated with an impairment in cognitive or behavioral functioning, the label itself has negative connotations and contributes to stigma, which is a combination of stereotypic negative beliefs, prejudices, and attitudes resulting in reduced life opportunities for the devalued group in question, such as individuals with mental disorders (Hinshaw & Stier, 2008).

Once labeled, individuals with a disorder may identify with the negative connotations associated with the label (Hinshaw & Stier, 2008). This affects their self-esteem. We have to remember that terms in psychopathology do not describe people but identify patterns of behavior that may or may not occur in certain circumstances. Thus, whether the disorder is medical or psychological, we must resist the temptation to identify the person with the disorder: Note

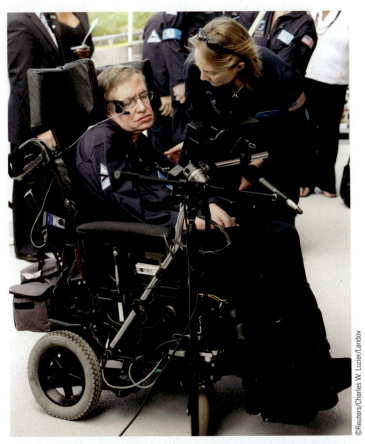

©Reuters/Charles W. Luzier/Landov

▲ Would we label this man? Stephen Hawking, one of the world's leading physicists, is severely disabled by amyotrophic lateral sclerosis, a rare progressive degenerative disease of the spinal cord. Because he cannot activate his voice box or move his lips, Hawking types his words into an electronic voice synthesizer that "speaks" for him. He uses his thumbprint to autograph his books. "I have been lucky," he says, "I don't have anything to be angry about."

the different implications of "John is a diabetic" and "John is a person who has diabetes."

Beyond *DSM-IV:* Dimensions and Spectra

The process of changing the criteria for existing diagnoses and creating new ones will continue as our science advances. New findings on brain circuits, cognitive processes, and cultural factors that affect our behavior could date diagnostic criteria relatively quickly.

Now the process to create the fifth edition of the *Diagnostic and Statistical Manual of Mental Disorders (DSM-5)* that began formally in 2006 is nearing completion, with publication scheduled for May 2013. The *DSM-5* task force has set clear criteria for reviewing diagnostic categories currently in the appendix in *DSM-IV.* After each category is reviewed, one of the following actions is to be taken for each included disorder: (1) delete the disorder from the appendix, (2) "promote" it to the main manual, or (3) retain it in the appendix. The criteria for one decision or another would be based primarily on new research that would be either sufficient to establish the validity of the diagnosis or not (Kendler, Kupfer, Narrow, Phillips, & Fawcett, 2009). In addition, it is now clear to most professionals involved in this process that an exclusive reliance on discrete diagnostic categories has not achieved its objective in achieving a satisfactory system of nosology (Krueger, Watson, & Barlow, 2005). In addition to problems noted earlier with comorbidity and the fuzzy boundary between diagnostic categories, little evidence has emerged validating these categories, such as discovering specific underlying causes associated with each category (Regier et al., 2009). In fact, not one biological marker, such as a laboratory test, that would clearly distinguish one disorder from another has been discovered (Frances, 2009; Widiger & Samuel, 2005). It is also clear that the current categories lack treatment specificity—that is, certain treatments such as cognitive behavioral therapies or specific antidepressant drugs are effective for a large number of diagnostic categories that are not supposed to be all that similar.

It may therefore be time for a new approach. Most people agree that this approach will incorporate a dimensional strategy to a much greater extent than in *DSM-IV* (Krueger et al., 2005; Kupfer et al., 2002; Widiger & Coker, 2003; Widiger & Sankis, 2000). The term "spectrum" is another way to describe groups of disorders that share certain basic biological or psychological qualities or dimensions. For example, in Chapter 13 you will read about the proposal in *DSM-5* to eliminate the term "Asperger's syndrome" (a mild form of autism) and combine it with autistic disorder into a new category of "autism spectrum disorder." It is also clear at this point that research is not sufficiently advanced to attempt a wholesale switch to a dimensional or spectrum approach, so the proposed categories in *DSM-5* look very much like the categories in *DSM-IV* with some updated language and increased precision and clarity. One more substantial change may be the creation of the cross-cutting or superordinate dimensional ratings that we described earlier in the chapter. But, sparked by research and conceptual advances during the process of creating *DSM-5,* more conceptually substantial and consistent dimensional approaches are in development and may be ready for the sixth edition of the *DSM* in 10 to 20 years.

For example, in the area of personality disorders, Livesley, Jang, and Vernon (1998) concluded that these disorders were not qualitatively distinct from the personalities of normal-functioning individuals in community samples. Instead, personality disorders simply represent maladaptive, and perhaps extreme, variants of common personality traits (Widiger & Edmundson, 2011; Widiger, Livesley & Clark, 2009; Widiger & Samuel, 2005). For the anxiety and mood disorders, Brown and Barlow (2009) have proposed a new dimensional system of classification based on previous research (Brown, Chorpita, & Barlow, 1998) demonstrating that anxiety and depression have more in common than previously thought and may best be represented as points on a continuum of negative affect or a spectrum of emotional disorders (see Barlow, 2002; Brown & Barlow, 2005, 2009; Clark, 2005; Mineka, Watson, & Clark, 1998; Watson, 2005). Even for severe disorders with seemingly stronger genetic influences, such as schizophrenia, it appears that dimensional classification strategies or spectrum approaches might prove superior (Charney et al., 2002; Lenzenweger & Dworkin, 1996; Toomey, Faraone, Simpson, & Tsuang, 1998; Widiger & Edmundson, 2011; Widiger, 1997; Widiger & Samuel, 2005).

At the same time, exciting new developments from the area of neuroscience relating to brain structure and function will provide enormously important information on the nature of psychological disorders. This information could then be integrated with more psychological, social, and cultural information into a diagnostic system. But even neuroscientists are abandoning the notion that groups of genes or brain circuits will be found that are specifically associated with *DSM-IV* diagnostic categories. Rather, it is now assumed that neurobiological processes will be discovered that are associated with specific cognitive, emotional, and behavioral patterns or traits

(for example, behavioral inhibition) that do not necessarily correspond closely with current diagnostic categories.

With this in mind, we can turn our attention to the current state of our knowledge about a variety of major psychological disorders. Beginning with Chapter 4, we attempt to predict the next major scientific breakthroughs affecting diagnostic criteria and definitions of disorders. Toward this end, we introduce a new section at the end of each disorder chapter entitled "On the Spectrum" detailing recent work that anticipates important changes in the years to come in how we think about psychological disorders. But first we review the all-important area of research methods and strategies used to establish new knowledge of psychopathology.

Concept Check 3.2

Identify each of the following statements as either true (T) or false (F).

1. ___ The classical categorical approach to classification assumes there is only one set of causative factors per disorder with no overlap between disorders, and the prototypical approach uses essential, defining features and a range of other characteristics.

2. ___ As in earlier versions, *DSM-IV* retains a distinction between organically and psychologically based disorders.

3. ___ The *DSM-IV* eradicated the problem of comorbidity, the identification of two or more disorders in an individual at one time, which was previously caused by imprecise categories.

4. ___ If two or more clinicians agree on a patient's classification, the assessments are said to be valid.

5. ___ A danger in psychological classification is that a diagnostic label might be used to characterize personally the total individual.

Conducting Research in Psychopathology

> **What are the basic components of research in psychopathology?**
> **Why are ethical principles so important in the research process?**

As you have already seen, abnormal behavior is a challenging subject because of the interaction of biological and psychological dimensions. Rarely are there any simple answers to such questions as "Why do some people have hallucinations?" or "How do you treat someone who is suicidal?"

In addition to the obvious complexity of human nature, another factor that makes an objective study of abnormal behavior difficult is the inaccessibility of many important aspects of this phenomenon. We can't get inside the minds of people except indirectly. Fortunately, some creative individuals have accepted this challenge and have developed many ingenious methods for studying scientifically what behaviors constitute problems, why people suffer from behavioral disorders, and how to treat these problems. Some of you will ultimately contribute to this important field by applying the methods described in this chapter. Many critical questions regarding abnormal behavior have yet to be answered, and we hope that some of you will be inspired to take them on. However, understanding research methods is extremely important for everyone. You or someone close to you may need the services of a psychologist, psychiatrist, or other mental health provider. You may have questions such as these:

> Should childhood aggression be cause for concern, or is it a phase my child will grow out of?
> The *Today* show just reported that increased exposure to sunlight alleviates depression. Instead of seeing a therapist, should I buy a ticket to Hawaii?
> My brother has been in therapy for 3 years but doesn't seem to be any better. Should I tell him to look elsewhere for help?
> My mother is still in her 50s but seems to be forgetting things. Friends tell me this is natural as you grow older. Should I be concerned?

To answer such questions, you need to be a good consumer of research. When you understand the correct ways of obtaining information—that is, research methodology—you will know when you are dealing with fact and not fiction.

Basic Components of a Research Study

The basic research process is simple. You start with an educated guess, called a hypothesis, about what you expect to find. When you decide how you want to test this **hypothesis**, you formulate a **research design** that includes the aspects you want to measure in the people you are studying (the dependent variable) and the influences on their behaviors (the independent variable). Finally, two forms of validity are specific to research studies: internal validity and external validity. **Internal validity** is the extent to which you can be confident that the independent variable is causing the dependent variable to change. **External validity** refers to how well the results relate to things outside your study—in other words, how well your findings describe similar individuals who were not among the study participants. Although we discuss a variety of research strategies, they all have these basic elements. Table 3.2 shows the essential components of a research study.

Hypothesis

Human beings look for order and purpose. We want to know why the world works as it does and why people behave the way they do. Robert Kegan (cited in Lefrancois, 1990) describes us as "meaning-making" organisms, constantly striving to make sense of what is going on around us. In an attempt to make sense of these phenomena, be-

Table 3.2 The Basic Components of a Research Study

Component	Description
Hypothesis	An educated guess or statement to be supported by data
Research design	The plan for testing the hypothesis, affected by the question addressed, by the hypothesis, and by practical considerations
Dependent variable	Some aspect of the phenomenon that is measured and is expected to be changed or influenced by the independent variable
Independent variable	The aspect manipulated or thought to influence the change in the dependent variable
Internal validity	The extent to which the results of the study can be attributed to the independent variable
External validity	The extent to which the results of the study can be generalized or applied outside the immediate study

havioral scientists construct hypotheses and then test them. Hypotheses are nothing more than educated guesses about the world. You may believe that watching violent television programs will cause children to be more aggressive. You may think that bulimia is influenced by media depictions of supposedly ideal female body types. You may suspect that someone abused as a child is likely to abuse his or her significant other or child. These concerns are all testable hypotheses.

Once a scientist decides what to study, the next step is to put it in words that are unambiguous and in a form that is testable. Consider a study of how one's self-esteem (how you feel about yourself) affects depression. Ulrich Orth from the University of California–Davis and his colleagues from around the world gathered information from more than 4,000 people over a number of years (Orth, Robins, Trzesniewski, Maes, & Schmitt, 2009). They knew from previous research that at least over a short period of time, having feelings of low self-esteem seems to put people at risk for later depression. In their study, these researchers posed the following hypothesis: "Prior low self-esteem will be a predictor of later depression across all age groups of participants." The way the hypothesis is stated suggests the researchers already know the answer to their question. They won't know what they will find until the study is completed, but phrasing the hypothesis in this way makes it testable. If, for example, people with high self-esteem are at equal risk for later depression, then other influences must be studied. This concept of **testability** (the ability to support the hypothesis) is important for science because it allows us to say that in this case, either (1) low self-esteem signals later depression, so maybe we can use this information for prevention efforts, or (2) there is no relationship between self-esteem and depression, so let's look for other early signs that might predict who will become depressed. The researchers did find a strong relationship between early self-esteem and depression for people in all age groups, which may prove useful for detecting people at risk for this debilitating disorder (Orth et al., 2009).

When they develop an experimental hypothesis, researchers also specify dependent and independent variables. A **dependent variable** is what is expected to change or be influenced by the study. Psychologists studying abnormal behavior typically measure an aspect of the disorder, such as overt behaviors, thoughts, and feelings, or biological symptoms. In the study by Orth and colleagues, the main dependent variable (level of depression) was measured using the person's responses on a questionnaire about their depression (Center for Epidemiologic Studies Depression Scale). Independent variables are those factors thought to affect the dependent variables. The **independent variable** in the study was measured using responses on a questionnaire on self-esteem (the Rosenberg Self-Esteem Scale). In other words, changes in self-esteem over the years were thought to influence later levels of depression.

Internal and External Validity

The researchers in the study on self-esteem and depression used responses on the questionnaires collected from two very large studies conducted in the United States and Germany. Suppose they found that, unknown to them, most people who agree to participate in these types of studies have higher self-esteem than people who do not participate. This would have affected the data in a way that would limit what they could conclude about self-esteem and depression and would change the meaning of their results. This situation, which relates to internal validity, is called a **confound** (or **confounding variable**), defined as any factor occurring in a study that makes the results uninterpretable because a variable (in this instance, the type of population being studied) other than the independent variable (having high or low self-esteem) may also affect the dependent variable (depression).

Scientists use many strategies to ensure internal validity in their studies, three of which we discuss here: control groups, randomization, and analog models. In a **control group**, people are similar to the experimental group in every way except that members of the experimental group are exposed to the independent variable and those in the control group are not. Because researchers can't prevent people from being exposed to many things around them that could affect the outcomes of the study, they try to compare people who receive the treatment with people who go through similar experiences except for the treatment (control group). Control groups help rule out alternative explanations for results, thereby strengthening internal validity.

Randomization is the process of assigning people to different research groups in such a way that each person has an equal chance of being placed in any group. Researchers can, for example, randomly place people in groups but still end up with more of certain people (for example, people with more severe depression) in one group than another. Placing people in groups by flipping a coin or using a random number table helps improve internal validity by eliminating any systematic bias in assignment, but it does not necessarily eliminate bias in your group. You will see later that people sometimes "put themselves in groups," and this self-selection can affect study results.

Analog models create in the controlled conditions of the laboratory aspects that are comparable (analogous) to the phenomenon under study. Bulimia researchers could ask volunteers to binge eat in the laboratory, questioning them before they ate, while they were eating, and after they finished to learn whether eating in this way made them feel more or less anxious, guilty, and so on. If they used volunteers of any age, gender, race, or background, the researchers could rule out influences on the participants' attitudes about eating that they might not be able to dismiss if the group contained only people with bulimia. In this way, such "artificial" studies help improve internal validity.

In a research study, internal and external validity often seem to be in opposition. On the one hand, we want to be able to control as many things as possible to conclude that the independent variable (the aspect of the study we ma-

---

hypothesis Educated guess or statement to be tested by research.

research design Plan of experimentation used to test a hypothesis.

internal validity Extent to which the results of a study can be attributed to the independent variable after confounding alternative explanations have been ruled out.

external validity Extent to which research findings generalize, or apply, to people and settings not involved in the study.

testability Ability of a hypothesis, for example, to be subjected to scientific scrutiny and to be accepted or rejected, a necessary condition for the hypothesis to be useful.

dependent variable In an experimental study, the phenomenon that is measured and expected to be influenced (compare with independent variable).

independent variable Phenomenon manipulated by the experimenter in a study and expected to influence the dependent variable.

confound Any factor occurring in a study that makes the results uninterpretable because its effects cannot be separated from those of the variables being studied.

confounding variable Variable in a research study that was not part of the intended design and that may contribute to changes in the dependent variable.

control group Group of individuals in a study who are similar to the experimental subjects in every way but are not exposed to the treatment received by the experimental group. Their presence allows for a comparison of the differential effects of the treatment.

randomization Method for placing individuals into research groups that assures each an equal chance of being assigned to any group, thus eliminating any systematic differences across groups.

analog model Approach to research that employs subjects who are similar to clinical clients, allowing replication of a clinical problem under controlled conditions.

▲ Studying people as part of a group sometimes masks individual differences.

nipulated) was responsible for the changes in the dependent variables (the aspects of the study we expected to change). On the other hand, we want the results to apply to people other than the participants of the study and in other settings; this is **generalizability**, the extent to which results apply to everyone with a particular disorder. If we control all aspects of a study so that only the independent variable changes, the result is not relevant to the real world. For example, if you reduce the influence of gender issues by only studying males, and if you reduce age variables by only selecting people from 25 to 30 years of age, and finally, if you limit your study to those with college degrees so that education level isn't an issue—then what you study (in this case, 25- to 30-year-old male college graduates) may not be relevant to many other populations. Internal and external validity are in this way often inversely related. Researchers constantly try to balance these two concerns and, as you will see later in this chapter, the best solution for achieving both internal and external validity may be to conduct several related studies.

Statistical versus Clinical Significance

In psychological research, statistical significance typically means the probability of obtaining the observed effect by chance is small. As an example, consider a study evaluating whether a drug (naltrexone)—when added to a psychological intervention—helps those with alcohol addiction stay sober longer (Anton et al., 2006). The study found that the combination of medication and psychotherapy helped people stay abstinent 77 days on average and those receiving a placebo stayed abstinent 75 days on average. This difference was statistically significant. But is it an important difference? The difficulty is in the distinction between **statistical significance** (a mathematical calculation about the difference between groups) and **clinical significance**

(whether or not the difference was meaningful for those affected) (Thirthalli & Rajkumar, 2009).

Closer examination of the results leads to concern about the size of the effect. Because this research studied a large group of people dependent on alcohol (1,383 volunteers), even this small difference (75 versus 77 days) was statistically different. However, few of us would say staying sober for 2 extra days was worth taking medication and participating in extensive therapy.

Fortunately, concern for the clinical significance of results has led researchers to develop statistical methods that address not just that groups are different, but also how large these differences are, or **effect size**. Calculating the actual statistical measures involves fairly sophisticated procedures that take into account how much each treated and untreated person in a research study improves or worsens (Reichardt, 2006). In other words, instead of just looking at the results of the group as a whole, individual differences also are considered. Some researchers have used more subjective ways of determining whether truly important change has resulted from treatment. The late behavioral scientist Montrose Wolf (1978) advocated the assessment of what he called *social validity*. This technique involves obtaining input from the person being treated, and from significant others, about the importance of the changes that have occurred. In the example here, we might ask the participants and family members if they thought the treatment led to truly important improvements in alcohol abstinence. If the effect of the treatment is large enough to impress those who are directly involved, the treatment effect is clinically significant.

The "Average" Client

Too often we look at results from studies and make generalizations about the group, ignoring individual differences. Kiesler (1966) labeled the tendency to see all participants as one homogeneous group the **patient uniformity myth**. This myth leads researchers to make inaccurate generalizations about disorders and their treatments. To continue with our previous example, what if the researchers studying the treatment of alcoholism concluded that the experimental treatment was a good approach? And suppose we found that, although some participants improved with treatment, others worsened. Such differences would be averaged out in the analysis of the group as a whole, but for the person whose drinking increased with the experimental treatment, it would make little difference that "on the average" people improved. Because people differ in such ways as age, cognitive abilities, gender, and history of treatment, a simple group comparison may be misleading.

In each of the statements provided, fill in the blanks with one of the following: hypothesis, dependent variable, independent variable, internal validity, external validity, or confound.

1. In a treatment study, the introduction of the treatment to the participants is referred to as the _____.

2. After the treatment study was completed, you found that many people in the control group received treatment outside of the study. This is called a _____.

3. A researcher's guess about what a study might find is labeled the _____.

4. Scores on a depression scale improved for a treatment group after therapy. The change in these scores would be referred to as a change in the _____.

5. A relative lack of confounds in a study would indicate good _____, whereas good generalizability of the results would be called good _____.

Types of Research Methods

> **What methods are used to conduct research on the causes of behavior?**

Researchers who study human behavior use several forms of research when studying the causes of behavior. We now examine individual case studies, correlational research, experimental research, and single-case experimental studies.

Studying Individual Cases

Consider the following scenario: A psychologist thinks she has discovered a new disorder. She has observed several men who seem to have similar characteristics. All complain of a specific sleep disorder: falling asleep at work. Each man has obvious cognitive impairments that were evident during the initial interviews, and all are similar physically, each with significant hair loss and a pear-shaped physique. Finally, their personality styles are extremely egocentric, or self-centered. On the basis of these preliminary observations, the psychologist has come up with a tentative name, the Homer Simpson disorder, and she has decided to investigate this condition and possible treatments. But what is the best way to begin exploring a relatively unknown disorder? One method is to use the **case study method**, investigating intensively one or more individuals who display the behavioral and physical patterns (Borckardt et al., 2008).

One way to describe the case study method is by noting what it is not. It does not use the scientific method. Few efforts are made to ensure internal validity and, typically, many confounding variables are present that can interfere with conclusions. Instead, the case study method relies on a clinician's observations of differences among one person or one group with a disorder, people with other disorders, and people with no psychological disorders. The clinician usually collects as much information as possible to obtain a detailed description of the person. Historically, interview-

ing the person under study yields a great deal of information on personal and family background, education, health, and work history in addition to the person's opinions about the nature and causes of the problems being studied.

Case studies are important in the history of psychology. Sigmund Freud developed psychoanalytic theory and the methods of psychoanalysis on the basis of his observations of dozens of cases. Freud and Josef Breuer's description of Anna O. (see Chapter 1) led to development of the clinical technique known as free association. Sexuality researchers Virginia Johnson and William Masters based their work on many case studies and helped shed light on numerous myths regarding sexual behavior (Masters & Johnson, 1966). Joseph Wolpe, author of the landmark book *Psychotherapy by Reciprocal Inhibition* (1958), based his work with systematic desensitization on more than 200 cases. As our knowledge of psychological disorders has grown, psychological researchers' reliance on the case study method has gradually decreased.

generalizability Extent to which research results apply to a range of individuals not included in the study.

statistical significance Small probability of obtaining the observed research findings by chance.

clinical significance Degree to which research findings have useful and meaningful applications to real problems.

effect size A statistical process that estimates how large a change in measures occurred. Often used before and after a clinical treatment to determine its relative success.

patient uniformity myth Tendency to consider all members of a category as more similar than they are, ignoring their individual differences.

case study method Research procedure in which a single person or small group is studied in detail. The method does not allow conclusions about cause-and-effect relationships, and findings can be generalized only with great caution (contrast with single-case experimental design).

Research by Correlation

One of the fundamental questions posed by scientists is whether two variables relate to each other. A statistical relationship between two variables is called a **correlation**. For example, is schizophrenia related to the size of ventricles (spaces) in the brain? Are people with depression more likely to have negative attributions (negative explanations for their own and others' behavior)? Is the frequency of hallucinations higher among older people? The answers depend on determining how one variable (for example, number of hallucinations) is related to another (for example, age). Unlike experimental designs, which involve manipulating or changing conditions, correlational designs are used to study phenomena just as they occur. The result of a correlational study—whether variables occur together—is important to the ongoing search for knowledge about abnormal behavior.

One of the clichés of science is that correlation does not imply causation. In other words, two things occurring together do not necessarily mean that one caused the other. For example, the occurrence of marital problems in families is correlated with behavior problems in children (Erath, Bierman, & Conduct Problems Prevention Research Group, 2006). If you conduct a correlational study in this area, you will find that in families with marital problems you tend to see children with behavior problems; in families with fewer marital problems you are likely to find children with fewer behavior problems. The most obvious conclusion is that having marital problems will cause children to misbehave. If only it were as simple as that! The nature of the relationship between marital discord and childhood behavior problems can be explained in a number of ways. It may be that problems in a marriage cause disruptive behavior in the children. However, some evidence suggests the opposite may be true: The disruptive behavior of children may cause marital problems (Rutter & Giller, 1984). In addition, evidence suggests genetic influences may play a role in conduct disorders and in marital discord (D'Onofrio et al., 2006; Lynch et al., 2006).

This example points out the problems in interpreting the results of a correlational study. We know that variable A (marital problems) is correlated with variable B (child behavior problems). We do not know from these studies whether A causes B (marital problems cause child problems), whether B causes A (child problems cause marital problems), or whether some third variable, C, causes both (genes influence both marital problems and child problems).

The association between marital discord and child problems represents a **positive correlation**. This means that great strength or quantity in one variable (a great deal of marital distress) is associated with great strength or quantity in the other variable (more child disruptive behavior). At the same time, lower strength or quantity in one variable (marital distress) is associated with lower strength or quantity in the other (disruptive behavior). If you have trouble conceptualizing statistical concepts, you can think about this mathematical relationship in the same way you would a social relationship. Two people who are getting along well tend to go places together: "Where I go, you will go!" The correlation (or **correlation coefficient**) is represented as +1.00. The plus sign means there is a positive relationship, and the 1.00 means that it is a "perfect" relationship, in which the people are inseparable. Obviously, two people who like each other do not go everywhere together. The strength of their relationship ranges between 0.00 and +1.00 (0.00 means no relationship exists). The higher the number, the stronger the relationship, whether the number is positive or negative (for example, a correlation of +0.80 is "stronger" than a correlation of +0.75). You would expect two strangers, for example, to have a relationship of 0.00 because their behavior is not related; they sometimes end up in the same place together, but this occurs rarely and randomly. Two people who know each other but do not like each other would be represented by a negative sign, with the strongest negative relationship being −1.00, which means, "Anywhere you go, I won't be there!"

Using this analogy, marital problems in families and behavior problems in children have a relatively strong positive correlation represented by a number around +0.50. They tend to go together. However, other variables are strangers to each other. Schizophrenia and height are not related, so they don't go together and probably would be represented by a number close to 0.00. If A and B have no correlation, their correlation coefficient would approximate 0.00. Other factors have negative relationships: As one increases, the other decreases. (See ■ Figure 3.6 for an illustration of positive and negative correlations.) We used an example of **negative correlation** in Chapter 2, when we discussed social supports and illness. The more social supports that are present, the less likely it is that a person will become ill. The negative relationship between social supports and illness could be represented by a number such as −0.40.

Epidemiological Research

Scientists often think of themselves as detectives, searching for the truth by studying clues. One type of correlational research that is much like the efforts of detectives is called **epidemiology**, the study of the incidence, distribution, and consequences of a particular problem or set of problems in one or more populations. Epidemiologists expect that by tracking a disorder among many people they will find important clues as to why the disorder exists. One strategy involves determining *prevalence*, the number of people with a disorder at any one time. For example, the prevalence of binge drinking (having five or more drinks in a row) among U.S. college students is about 40% (Beets et al., 2009). A related strategy is to determine the *incidence* of a disorder, the estimated number of new cases during a specific period. For example, incidence of binge drinking among college students has lowered only slightly from 1980 until the present (Substance Abuse and Mental Health Services Administration, 2006), suggesting that despite ef-

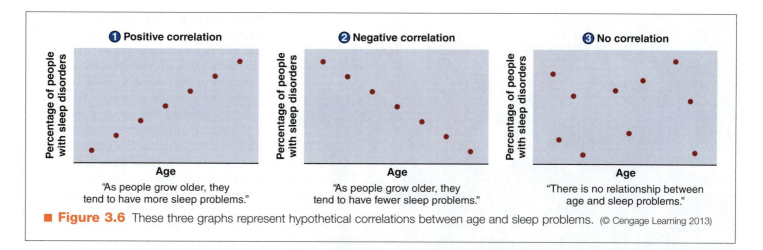

① Positive correlation

Percentage of people with sleep disorders / Age

"As people grow older, they tend to have more sleep problems."

② Negative correlation

Percentage of people with sleep disorders / Age

"As people grow older, they tend to have fewer sleep problems."

③ No correlation

Percentage of people with sleep disorders / Age

"There is no relationship between age and sleep problems."

■ **Figure 3.6** These three graphs represent hypothetical correlations between age and sleep problems. (© Cengage Learning 2013)

forts to reduce such heavy drinking, it continues to be a problem. Epidemiologists study the incidence and prevalence of disorders among different groups of people. For instance, data from epidemiological research indicate that the prevalence of alcohol abuse among African Americans is lower than that among whites (Substance Abuse and Mental Health Services Administration, 2006).

Although the primary goal of epidemiology is to determine the extent of medical problems, it is also useful in the study of psychological disorders. In the early 1900s, a number of Americans displayed symptoms of a strange mental disorder. Its symptoms were similar to those of organic psychosis, which is often caused by mind-altering drugs or great quantities of alcohol. Many patients appeared to be catatonic (immobile for long periods) or exhibited symptoms similar to those of paranoid schizophrenia. Victims were likely to be poor and African American, which led to speculation about racial and class inferiority. However, using the methods of epidemiological research, researcher Joseph Goldberger found correlations between the disorder and diet, and he identified the cause of the disorder as a deficiency of the B vitamin niacin among people with poor diets. The symptoms were successfully eliminated by niacin therapy and improved diets among the poor. A long-term, widespread benefit of Goldberger's findings was the introduction of vitamin-enriched bread in the 1940s (Colp, 2009).

Researchers have used epidemiological techniques to study the effects of stress on psychological disorders. On the morning of September 11, 2001, approximately 3,000 people died from three separate terrorist attacks in lower Manhattan, at the Pentagon, and in Pennsylvania. DeLisi and colleagues (DeLisi et al., 2003) interviewed 1,009 men and women throughout Manhattan to assess their long-term emotional reactions to the attacks, especially given their proximity to the destroyed World Trade Center towers. These researchers found that individuals who had the most negative reactions to this traumatic event were those who had preexisting psychological disorders, those who had the greatest exposure to the attack (for example, being evacuated from the World Trade Center), and women. The most common negative reactions included anxiety and

painful memories. This is a correlational study because the investigators did not manipulate the independent variable. (The attack was not part of an experiment.)

Like other types of correlational research, epidemiological research can't tell us conclusively what causes a particular phenomenon. However, knowledge about the prevalence and course of psychological disorders is extremely valuable to our understanding because it points researchers in the right direction.

Research by Experiment

An **experiment** involves the manipulation of an independent variable and the observation of its effects. We manipulate the independent variable to answer the question of causality. If we observe a correlation between social supports and psychological disorders, we can't conclude which of these factors influenced the other. We can, however, change the extent of social supports and see whether there is an accompanying change in the prevalence of psychological disorders—in other words, do an experiment.

What will this experiment tell us about the relationship between these two variables? If we increase social supports

correlation Degree to which two variables are associated. In a positive correlation, the two variables increase or decrease together. In a negative correlation, one variable decreases as the other increases.

positive correlation Association between two variables in which one increases as the other increases.

correlation coefficient Computed statistic reflecting the strength and direction of any association between two variables. It can range from 21.00 through 0.00 (indicating no association) to 11.00, with the absolute value indicating the strength and the sign reflecting the direction.

negative correlation Association between two variables in which one increases as the other decreases.

directionality Possibility that when two variables, A and B, are correlated variable A causes variable B or variable B causes variable A.

epidemiology Psychopathology research method examining the prevalence, distribution, and consequences of disorders in populations.

experiment Research method that can establish causation by manipulating the variables in question and controlling for alternative explanations of any observed effects.

▲ The more social supports people have, the less likely it is that they will become ill.

Wang, 2011). A clinical trial is an experiment used to determine the effectiveness and safety of a treatment or treatments. The term clinical trial implies a level of formality with regard to how it is conducted. As a result, a clinical trial is not a design by itself but rather a method of evaluation that follows a number of generally accepted rules. For example, these rules cover how you should select the research participants, how many individuals should be included in the study, how they should be assigned to groups, and how the data should be analyzed—and this represents only a partial list. Also, treatments are usually applied using formal protocols to ensure that everyone is treated the same.

and find no change in the frequency of psychological disorders, it may mean that lack of such supports does not cause psychological problems. However, if we find that psychological disorders diminish with increased social support, we can be more confident that nonsupport does contribute to psychological disorders. However, because we are never 100% confident that our experiments are internally valid—that no other explanations are possible—we must be cautious about interpreting our results. In the following section, we describe different ways in which researchers conduct experiments and consider how each one brings us closer to understanding abnormal behavior.

Group Experimental Designs

With correlational designs, researchers observe groups to see how different variables are associated. In group experimental designs, researchers are more active. They actually change an independent variable to see how the behavior of the people in the group is affected. Suppose researchers design an intervention to help reduce insomnia in older adults, who are particularly affected by the condition (Ancoli-Israel & Ayalon, 2009). They treat a number of individuals and follow them for 10 years to learn whether their sleep patterns improve. The treatment is the independent variable—that is, it would not have occurred naturally. They then assess the treated group to learn whether their behavior changed as a function of what the researchers did. Introducing or withdrawing a variable in a way that would not have occurred naturally is called *manipulating a variable*.

Unfortunately, a decade later the researchers find that the older adults treated for sleep problems still, as a group, sleep less than 8 hours per night. Is the treatment a failure? Maybe not. The question that can't be answered in this study is what would have happened to group members if they hadn't been treated. Perhaps their sleep patterns would have been worse. Fortunately, researchers have devised ingenious methods to help sort out these complicated questions.

A special type of group experimental design is used more and more frequently in the treatment of psychological disorders and is referred to as a *clinical trial* (Durand &

Control Groups

One answer to the what-if dilemma is to use a control group—people who are similar to the experimental group in every way except they are not exposed to the independent variable. In the previous study looking at sleep in older adults, suppose another group who didn't receive treatment was selected. Further suppose that the researchers also follow this group of people, assess them 10 years later, and look at their sleep patterns over this time. They probably observe that, without intervention, people tend to sleep fewer hours as they get older (Cho et al., 2008). Members of the control group, then, might sleep significantly less than people in the treated group, who might themselves sleep somewhat less than they did 10 years earlier. The control group allows the researchers to see that their treatment did help the treated participants keep their sleep time from decreasing further.

Ideally, a control group is nearly identical to the treatment group in such factors as age, gender, socioeconomic backgrounds, and the problems they are reporting. Furthermore, a researcher would do the same assessments before and after the independent variable manipulation (for example, a treatment) to people in both groups. Any later differences between the groups after the change would, therefore, be attributable only to what was changed.

People in a treatment group often expect to get better. When behavior changes as a result of a person's expectation of change rather than as a result of any manipulation by an experimenter, the phenomenon is known as a **placebo effect** (from the Latin, which means "I shall please"). Conversely, people in the control group may be disappointed that they are not receiving treatment. Depending on the type of disorder they experience (for example, depression), disappointment may make them worse. This phenomenon would also make the treatment group look better by comparison.

One way researchers address the expectation concern is through **placebo control groups**. The word *placebo* typically refers to inactive medications such as sugar pills.

The placebo is given to members of the control group to make them believe they are getting treatment (Wampold, Minami, Tierney, Baskin, & Bhati, 2005). A placebo control in a medication study can be carried out with relative ease because people in the untreated group receive something that looks like the medication administered to the treatment group. In psychological treatments, however, it is not always easy to devise something that people believe may help them but does not include the component the researcher believes is effective. Clients in these types of control groups are often given part of the actual therapy—for example, the same homework as the treated group—but not the portions the researchers believe are responsible for improvements.

Note that you can look at the placebo effect as one portion of any treatment (Kendall & Comer, 2011). If someone you provide with a treatment improves, you would have to attribute the improvement to a combination of your treatment and the client's expectation of improving (placebo effect). Therapists want their clients to expect improvement; this helps strengthen the treatment. However, when researchers conduct an experiment to determine what portion of a particular treatment is responsible for the observed changes, the placebo effect is a confound that can dilute the validity of the research. Thus, researchers use a placebo control group to help distinguish the results of positive expectations from the results of actual treatment.

The **double-blind control** is a variant of the placebo control group procedure. As the name suggests, not only are the participants in the study "blind," or unaware of what group they are in or what treatment they are given (single blind), but so are the researchers or therapists providing treatment (double blind). This type of control eliminates the possibility that an investigator might bias the outcome. For example, a researcher comparing two treatments who expected one to be more effective than the other might "try harder" if the "preferred" treatment wasn't working as well as expected. However, if the treatment that wasn't expected to work seemed to be failing, the researcher might not push as hard to see it succeed. This reaction might not be deliberate, but it does happen. This phenomenon is referred to as an *allegiance effect* (Leykin & DeRubeis, 2009). If, however, both the participants and the researchers or therapists are "blind," there is less chance that bias will affect the results.

Comparative Treatment Research

As an alternative to using no-treatment control groups to help evaluate results, some researchers compare different treatments. In this design, the researcher gives different treatments to two or more comparable groups of people with a particular disorder and can then assess how or whether each treatment helped the people who received it. This is called **comparative treatment research**. In the sleep study we discussed, two groups of older adults could be selected, with one group given medication for insomnia, the other given a cognitive-behavioral intervention, and the results compared.

The process and outcome of treatment are two important issues to be considered when different approaches are studied. *Process research* focuses on the mechanisms responsible for behavior change, or "why does it work?" In an old joke, someone goes to a physician for a new miracle cold cure. The physician prescribes the new drug and tells the patient the cold will be gone in 7 to 10 days. As most of us know, colds typically improve in 7 to 10 days without so-called miracle drugs. The new drug probably does nothing to further the improvement of the patient's cold. The process aspect of testing medical interventions involves evaluating biological mechanisms responsible for change. Does the medication cause lower serotonin levels, for example, and does this account for the changes we observe? Similarly, in looking at psychological interventions, we determine what is "causing" the observed changes. This is important for several reasons. First, if we understand what the "active ingredients" of our treatment are, we can often eliminate aspects that are not important, thereby saving clients' time and money. For an example, one study of insomnia found that adding a relaxation training component to a treatment package provided no additional benefit—allowing clinicians to reduce the amount of training and focus on only those aspects that really improve sleep (for example, cognitive-behavioral therapy) (Harvey, Inglis, & Espie, 2002). In addition, knowing what is important about our interventions can help us create more powerful, newer versions that may be more effective.

Outcome research focuses on the positive or negative (or both) results of the treatment. In other words, does it work? Remember, *treatment process* involves finding out why or how your treatment works. In contrast, treatment outcome involves finding out what changes occur after treatment.

Single-Case Experimental Designs

B. F. Skinner's innovations in scientific methodology were among his most important contributions to psychopathology. Skinner formalized the concept of **single-case experimental designs**. This method involves the systematic study

placebo effect Behavior change resulting from the person's expectation of change rather than from the experimental manipulation itself.
placebo control group In outcome research, a control group that does not receive the experimental manipulation but is given a similar procedure with an identical expectation of change, allowing the researcher to assess any placebo effect.
double-blind control Procedure in outcome research that prevents bias by ensuring that neither the subjects nor the providers of the experimental treatment know who is receiving treatment and who is receiving a placebo.
comparative treatment research Outcome research that contrasts two or more treatment methods to determine which is most effective.
single-case experimental design Research tactic in which an independent variable is manipulated for a single individual, allowing cause-and-effect conclusions but with limited generalizability (contrast with case study method).

of individuals under a variety of experimental conditions. Skinner thought it was much better to know a lot about the behavior of one individual than to make only a few observations of a large group for the sake of presenting the "average" response. Psychopathology is concerned with the suffering of specific people, and this methodology has greatly helped us understand the factors involved in individual psychopathology (Barlow, Nock, & Hersen, 2009). Many applications throughout this book reflect Skinnerian methods.

Single-case experimental designs differ from case studies in their use of various strategies to improve internal validity, thereby reducing the number of confounding variables. As you will see, these strategies have strengths and weaknesses in comparison with traditional group designs. Although we use examples from treatment research to illustrate the single-case experimental designs, they, like other research strategies, can help explain why people engage in abnormal behavior and how to treat them.

Repeated Measurements

One of the more important strategies used in single-case experimental design is **repeated measurement**, in which a behavior is measured several times instead of only once before you change the independent variable and once afterward. The researcher takes the same measurements repeatedly to learn how variable the behavior is (how much does it change from day to day?) and whether it shows any obvious trends (is it getting better or worse?). Suppose a young woman, Wendy, comes into the office complaining about feelings of anxiety. When asked to rate the level of her anxiety, she gives it a 9 (10 is the worst). After several weeks of treatment, Wendy rates her anxiety at 6. Can we say that the treatment reduced her anxiety? Not necessarily.

Suppose we had measured Wendy's anxiety each day during the weeks before her visit to the office (repeated measurement) and observed that it differed greatly. On particularly good days, she rated her anxiety from 5 to 7. On bad days, it was up between 8 and 10. Suppose further that, even after treatment, her daily ratings continued to range from 5 to 10. The rating of 9 before treatment and 6 after treatment may only have been part of the daily variations she experienced normally. Wendy could just as easily have had a good day and reported a 6 before treatment and then had a bad day and reported a 9 after treatment, which would imply that the treatment made her worse.

Repeated measurement is part of each single-subject experimental design. It helps identify how a person is doing before and after intervention and whether the treatment accounted for any changes. ■ Figure 3.7 summarizes Wendy's anxiety and the added information obtained by repeated measurement. The top graph shows Wendy's original before-and-after ratings of her anxiety. The middle graph shows that with daily ratings her reports are variable and that just by chance the previous measurement was probably misleading. She had good and bad days both before and after treatment and doesn't seem to have changed much.

The bottom graph shows a different possibility: Wendy's anxiety was on its way down before the treatment, which would also have been obscured with just before-and-after measurements. Maybe she was getting better on her own and the treatment didn't have much effect. Although the middle graph shows how the **variability** from day to day could be important in an interpretation of the effect of treatment, the bottom graph shows how the **trend** itself can also be important in determining the cause of any change. The three graphs illustrate important parts of repeated measurements: (1) the **level** or degree of behavior change with different interventions *(top)*; (2) the variability or degree of change over time *(middle)*; and (3) the trend or direction of change *(bottom)*. Again, before-and-after scores alone do not necessarily show what is responsible for behavioral changes.

Withdrawal Designs

One of the more common strategies used in single-subject research is a **withdrawal design**, in which a researcher tries to determine whether the independent variable is responsible for changes in behavior. The effect of Wendy's treatment could be tested by stopping it for some time to see whether her anxiety increased. A simple withdrawal design has three parts. First, a person's condition is evaluated before treatment to establish a **baseline**. Then comes the change in the independent variable—in Wendy's case, the beginning of treatment. Last, treatment is withdrawn ("return to baseline") and the researcher assesses whether Wendy's anxiety level changes again as a function of this last step. If with the treatment her anxiety reduces in comparison to baseline and then worsens after treatment is withdrawn, the researcher can conclude the treatment has reduced Wendy's anxiety.

How is this design different from a case study? An important difference is that the change in treatment is designed specifically to show whether treatment caused the changes in behavior. Although case studies often involve treatment, they don't include any effort to learn whether the person would have improved without the treatment. A withdrawal design gives researchers a better sense of whether or not the treatment itself caused behavior change.

Despite their advantages, withdrawal designs are not always appropriate. The researcher is required to remove what might be an effective treatment, a decision that is sometimes difficult to justify for ethical reasons. In Wendy's case, a researcher would have to decide there was a sufficient reason to risk making her anxious again. A withdrawal design is also unsuitable when the treatment can't be removed. Suppose Wendy's treatment involved visualizing herself on a beach on a tropical island. It would be difficult—if not impossible—to stop her from imagining something. Similarly, some treatments involve teaching people skills, which might be impossible to unlearn. If Wendy learned how to be less anxious in social situations, how could she revert to being socially apprehensive?

Several counterarguments support the use of withdrawal designs (Barlow et al., 2009). Treatment is routinely withdrawn when medications are involved. *Drug holidays* are periods when the medication is withdrawn so that cli-

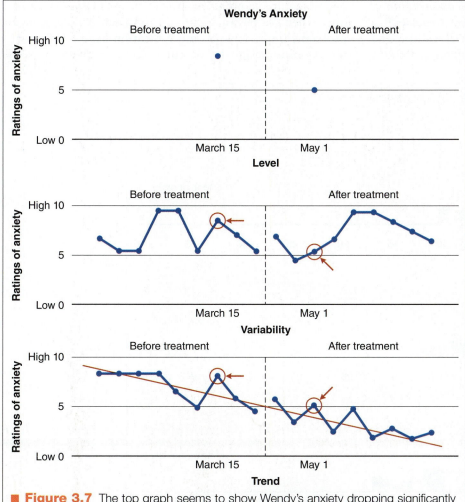

Figure 3.7 The top graph seems to show Wendy's anxiety dropping significantly after treatment (measuring level). However, when you look at repeated measures before and after treatment, the middle graph reveals little change because her anxiety fluctuated a great deal (measuring variability). A different scenario is illustrated in the bottom graph (measuring trend), where her anxiety also varied. In general, there was a downward movement (improved anxiety) even before treatment, suggesting that she might have improved without help. Examining variability and trend can provide more information about the true nature of the change. (© Cengage Learning 2013)

could begin at work. If she improves only at home after beginning treatment but improves at work after treatment is used there also, we could conclude the treatment was effective. This is an example of using a multiple baseline across settings.

Suppose a researcher wanted to assess the effectiveness of a treatment for a child's problem behaviors. Treatment could focus first on the child's crying, then on a second problem, such as fighting with siblings. If the treatment was first effective only in reducing crying and effective for reducing fighting only after the second intervention, the researcher could conclude that the treatment, not something else, accounted for the improvements. This is a multiple baseline conducted across behaviors.

Single-case experimental designs are sometimes criticized because they tend to involve only a small number of cases, leaving their external validity in doubt. In other words, we can't say the results we saw with a few people would be the same for everyone. However, although they are called *single-case* designs, researchers can and often do use them with several people at once, in part to address the issue of external validity. One of us studied the effectiveness of a treatment for the severe behavior problems of children with autism (Durand, 1999) (■ Figure 3.8). We taught the children to communicate instead of misbehave, using

nicians can determine whether it is responsible for the treatment effects. Any medication can have negative side effects, and unnecessary medication should be avoided. Sometimes treatment withdrawal happens naturally. Withdrawal does not have to be prolonged; a brief withdrawal may still clarify the role of the treatment.

Multiple Baseline

Another single-case experimental design strategy used often that doesn't have some of the drawbacks of a withdrawal design is the **multiple baseline**. Rather than stopping the intervention to see whether it is effective, the researcher starts treatment at different times across settings (home versus school), behaviors (yelling at spouse/partner or boss), or people. After waiting for a while and taking repeated measures of Wendy's anxiety both at home and at her office (the baseline), the clinician could treat her first at home. When the treatment begins to be effective, intervention

repeated measurement When responses are measured on more than two occasions (not just before and after intervention) to assess trends.
variability Degree of change in a phenomenon over time.
trend Direction of change of a behavior or behaviors (for example, increasing or decreasing).
level Degree of behavior change with different interventions (for example, high or low).
withdrawal design Removing a treatment to note whether it has been effective. In single-case experimental designs, a behavior is measured (baseline), an independent variable is introduced (intervention), and then the intervention is withdrawn. Because the behavior continues to be measured throughout (repeated measurement), any effects of the intervention can be noted.
baseline Measured rate of a behavior before introduction of an intervention that allows comparison and assessment of the effects of the intervention.
multiple baseline Single-case experimental design in which measures are taken on two or more behaviors or on a single behavior in two or more situations. A particular intervention is introduced for each at different times. If behavior change is coincident with each introduction, this is strong evidence the intervention caused the change.

a procedure known as *functional communication training.* Using a multiple baseline, we introduced this treatment to a group of five children. Our dependent variables were the incidence of the children's behavior problems and their newly acquired communication skills. As Figure 3.8 shows, only when we began treatment did each child's behavior problems improve and communication begin. This multiple baseline design let us rule out coincidence or some

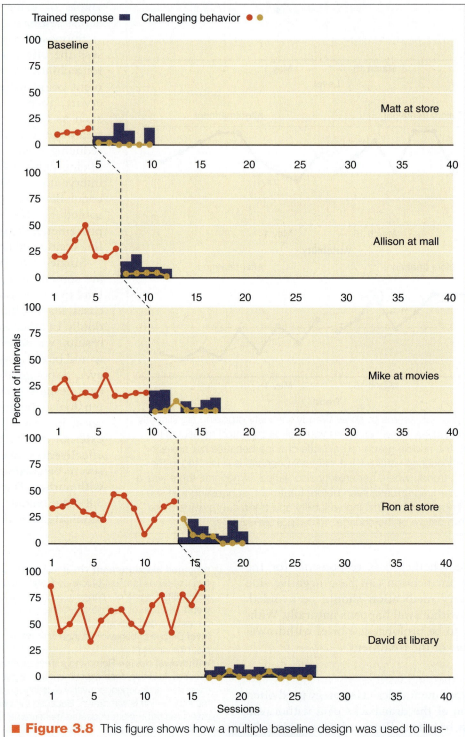

■ **Figure 3.8** This figure shows how a multiple baseline design was used to illustrate that the treatment—functional communication training—was responsible for improvements in the children's behaviors. The circles represent how often each child exhibited behavior problems (called challenging behavior), and the blue-shaded areas show how often they communicated without help from the teacher (referred to as unprompted communication). (From Durand, V. M., 1999. Functional communication training using assistive devices: recruiting natural communities of reinforcement, *Journal of Applied Behavior Analysis, 32(3),* 247–267. Reprinted by permission of the Society for the Experimental Analysis of Human Behavior.)

other change in the children's lives as explanations for the improvements.

Among the advantages of the multiple baseline design in evaluating treatments is that it does not require withdrawal of treatment, and, as you've seen, withdrawing treatment is sometimes difficult or impossible. Furthermore, the multiple baseline typically resembles the way treatment would naturally be implemented. A clinician can't help a client with numerous problems simultaneously but can take repeated measures of the relevant behaviors and observe when they change. A clinician who sees predictable and orderly changes related to where and when the treatment is used can conclude the treatment is causing the change.

Concept Check 3.4

Check your understanding of research methods by indicating which would be most appropriate in each of the following situations. Choose from (a) case study, (b) correlation, (c) randomized clinical trials, (d) epidemiology, (e) experiment, (f) single-case experimental design.

1. A researcher changes the level of noise several times to see how it affects concentration in a group of people. _____

2. A group of researchers uses chance assignment to include participants in one of two treatment groups and uses published protocols to make sure treatment is applied uniformly. _____

3. A researcher wants to investigate the hypothesis that as children go through adolescence they listen to louder music. _____

4. A researcher is interested in studying a woman who had no contact with civilization and created her own language. _____

5. A researcher wants to know how different kinds of music will affect a 5-year-old who has never spoken. _____

Genetics and Behavior across Time and Cultures

> How do researchers study the interaction between environment and genetics?
> Why do researchers study behavior over time and across cultures?

Examining the origin and strategies for treating an individual's behavior problem or disorder requires several factors to be considered so that multiple possible influences are taken into account. The factors include determining any inherited influences, how behavior will change or remain the same over time, and the effects of culture.

Studying Genetics

We tend to think of genetics in terms of what we inherit from our parents: "He has his mother's eyes." "She's thin just like her dad." "She's stubborn like her mother." This simple view of how we become the people we are suggests that how we look, think, feel, and behave is predetermined. Yet we now know that the interaction between our genetic makeup and our experiences is what determines how we will develop. The goal of behavioral geneticists (people who study the genetics of behavior) is to tease out the role of genetics in these interactions.

Genetic researchers examine **phenotypes**, the observable characteristics or behavior of the individual, and **genotypes**, the unique genetic makeup of individual people. For example, a person with Down syndrome typically has some level of mental retardation and a variety of other physical characteristics, such as slanted eyes and a thick tongue.

These characteristics are the phenotype. The genotype is the extra chromosome (21) that causes Down syndrome.

Beginning in 1990, scientists around the world, in a coordinated effort, began the **human genome project** (*genome* means all the genes of an organism). Using the latest advances in molecular biology, scientists working on this project completed a rough draft of the mapping of the approximately 25,000 human genes. This work identified hundreds of genes that contribute to inherited diseases. These exciting findings represent truly astounding progress in deciphering the nature of genetic endowment and its role in psychological disorders.

What follows is a brief review of the research strategies scientists use as they study the interaction between environment and genetics in psychological disorders: family studies, adoption studies, twin studies, genetic linkage analysis, and association studies.

phenotype Observable characteristics or behaviors of an individual.
genotype Specific genetic makeup of an individual.
human genome project Ongoing scientific attempt to develop a comprehensive map of all human genes.

Family Studies

In **family studies**, scientists simply examine a behavioral pattern or emotional trait in the context of the family. The family member with the trait singled out for study is called the **proband**. If there is a genetic influence, presumably the trait should occur more often in first-degree relatives (parents, siblings, or offspring) than in second-degree or more distant relatives. The presence of the trait in distant relatives, in turn, should be somewhat greater than in the population as a whole. In Chapter 1 you met Judy, the adolescent with blood–injury–injection phobia who fainted at the sight of blood. The tendency of a trait to run in families, or familial aggregation, is as high as 60% for this disorder—that is, 60% of the first-degree relatives of someone with blood–injury–injection phobia have the same reaction to at least some degree.

The problem with family studies is that family members tend to live together and there might be something in their shared environment that causes the high familial aggregation. For example, Mom might have developed a bad reaction to blood as a young girl after witnessing a serious accident. Every time she sees blood she has a strong emotional response. Because emotions are contagious, the young children watching Mom probably react similarly. In adulthood, they pass it on, in turn, to their own children.

Adoption Studies

How do we separate environmental from genetic influences in families? One way is through **adoption studies**. Scientists identify adoptees who have a particular behavioral pattern or psychological disorder and attempt to locate first-degree relatives who were raised in different family settings. Suppose a young man has a disorder and scientists discover his brother was adopted as a baby and brought up in a different home. The researchers would then examine the brother to see whether he also displays signs of the disorder. If they can identify enough sibling pairs (and they usually do after a lot of hard work), they can assess whether siblings brought up in different families display the disorder to the same extent as the original participant. If the siblings raised with different families have the disorder more often than would be expected by chance, the researchers can infer that genetic endowment is a contributor.

Twin Studies

Nature presents an elegant experiment that gives behavioral geneticists their closest possible look at the role of genes in development: identical (monozygotic) twins (Johnson, Turkheimer, Gottesman, & Bouchard Jr., 2009). These twins not only look alike, but also have identical genes. Fraternal (dizygotic) twins, however, come from different eggs and have only about 50% of their genes in common, as do all first-degree relatives. In **twin studies**, the obvious scientific question is whether identical twins share the same trait—say, fainting at the sight of blood—more often than fraternal twins. Determining whether a trait is shared is easy with some physical traits, such as height. As Plomin (1990) points out, correlations in height are 0.45 for both first-degree relatives and fraternal twins and 0.90 for identical twins. These findings show that heritability of height is about 90%, so approximately 10% of the variance is the result of environmental factors. But the case of conjoined identical twins with different personalities reminds us that the 90% estimate is the *average* contribution. An identical twin who was severely physically abused or selectively deprived of proper foods might be substantially different in height from the other twin.

Michael Lyons and his colleagues (1995) conducted a study of antisocial behavior among members of the Vietnam Era Twin Registry. The individuals in the study were about 8,000 twin men who served in the military from 1965 to 1975. The investigators found that among identical twins there was a greater degree of resemblance for antisocial traits than among fraternal twins. The difference was greater for adult antisocial behavior—that is, identical twins' behavior was more similar than fraternal twins' behavior in adulthood—than for juvenile antisocial behavior (meaning that nonadult identical and fraternal twin pairs were more similar in childhood than in adulthood). The researchers concluded that the family environment is a stronger influence than genetic factors on juvenile antisocial traits and that antisocial behavior in adulthood is more strongly influenced by genetic factors. In other words, after the individual grew up and left the family of origin, early environmental influences mattered less and less.

This way of studying genetics is not perfect. You can assume identical twins have the same genetic makeup and fraternal twins do not. However, a complicating concern is whether identical twins have the same experiences or environment as fraternal twins. Some identical twins are dressed alike and are even given similar names. Yet the twins themselves influence each other's behavior, and in some cases, identical twins may affect each other more than fraternal twins (Johnson et al., 2009). One way to address this problem is by combining the adoption study and twin study methods. If you can find identical twins, one or both of whom was adopted as an infant, you can estimate the relative roles of genes and the environment (nature versus nurture) in the development of behavioral patterns.

Genetic Linkage Analysis and Association Studies

The results of a series of family, twin, and adoption studies may suggest that a particular disorder has a genetic component, but they can't provide the location of the implicated gene or genes. To locate a defective gene, there are two general strategies: genetic linkage analysis and association studies (Fears, Mathews, & Freimer, 2009).

The basic principle of **genetic linkage analysis** is simple. When a family disorder is studied, other inherited characteristics are assessed at the same time. These other characteristics—called **genetic markers**—are selected because we know their exact location. If a match or link is discovered between the inheritance of the disorder and the inheritance of a genetic marker, the genes for the disorder and the genetic marker are probably close together on the same chromosome. For example, bipolar disorder (manic

▲ Although family members often resemble one another, genetics has to do with far more than what we inherit from our parents.

depression) was studied in a large Amish family (Egeland et al., 1987). Researchers found that two markers on chromosome 11—genes for insulin and a known cancer gene— were linked to the presence of mood disorder in this family, suggesting that a gene for bipolar disorder might be on chromosome 11. Unfortunately, although this is a genetic linkage study, it also illustrates the danger of drawing premature conclusions from research. This linkage study and a second study that purported to find a linkage between bipolar disorder and the X chromosome (Biron et al., 1987) have yet to be replicated; that is, different researchers have not been able to show similar linkages in other families (Craddock & Jones, 2001).

The second strategy for locating specific genes, **association studies**, also uses genetic markers. Whereas linkage studies compare markers in a large group of people with a particular disorder, association studies compare such people to people without the disorder. If certain markers occur significantly more often in the people with the disorder, it is assumed the markers are close to the genes involved with the disorder. This type of comparison makes association studies better able to identify genes that may only weakly be associated with a disorder. Both strategies for locating specific genes shed new light on the origins of specific disorders and may inspire new approaches to treatment (Fears et al., 2009).

Studying Behavior over Time

Sometimes we want to ask, "How will a disorder or behavior pattern change (or remain the same) over time?" This question is important for several reasons. First, the answer helps us decide whether to treat a particular person. For example, should we begin an expensive and time-consuming program for a young adult who is depressed over the loss of a grandparent? You might not if you knew that with normal social

supports the depression is likely to diminish over the next few months without treatment. However, if you have reason to believe a problem isn't likely to go away on its own, you might decide to begin treatment. For example, aggression among young children does not usually go away naturally and should be dealt with as early as possible.

It is also important to understand the developmental changes in abnormal behavior because sometimes these can provide insight into how problems are created and how they become more serious. For example, you will see that some researchers identify newborns who are at risk for autism because they are siblings of a child with autism and then follow them through infancy until some develop the disorder themselves. This type of study is showing us that the pattern of the onset of this disorder is actually much different than parents report after the fact (they tend to remember drastic changes in the child's behavior when, in fact, the changes occur gradually) (Rogers, 2009).

Prevention Research

An additional reason for studying clinical problems over time is that we may be able to design interventions and services to prevent these problems. Clearly, preventing mental health difficulties would save countless families significant emotional distress, and the financial savings could be substantial. Prevention research has expanded over the years to include a broad range of approaches. These different methods can be viewed in four broad categories: positive development strategies (health promotion), universal prevention strategies, selective prevention strategies, and indicated prevention strategies (Daniels, Adams, Carroll, & Beinecke, 2009). *Health promotion* or *positive development strategies* involve efforts to blanket entire populations of people—even those who may not be

family studies Genetic study that examines patterns of traits and behaviors among relatives.

proband In genetics research, the individual displaying the trait or characteristic being studied.

adoption studies In genetics research, the study of first-degree relatives reared in different families and environments. If they share common characteristics, such as a disorder, this finding suggests that those characteristics have a genetic component.

twin studies In genetics research, the comparison of twins with unrelated or less closely related individuals. If twins, particularly monozygotic twins who share identical genotypes, share common characteristics such as a disorder, even if they were reared in different environments, then strong evidence of genetic involvement in those characteristics exists.

genetic linkage analysis Study that seeks to match the inheritance pattern of a disorder to that of a genetic marker. This helps researchers establish the location of the gene responsible for the disorder.

genetic marker Inherited characteristic for which the chromosomal location of the responsible gene is known.

association studies Research strategy for comparing genetic markers in groups of people with and without a particular disorder.

at risk—to prevent later problems and promote protective behaviors. For example, the Seattle Social Development Program targets young children in public elementary schools in the Seattle school system that are in high-crime areas, providing intervention with teachers and parents to engage the children in learning and positive behaviors. Although this approach does not target one particular problem (for example, drug use), long-term follow-up of these children suggests multiple positive effects in achievement and reductions in delinquency (Bailey, 2009; Lonczak, Abbott, Hawkins, Kosterman, & Catalano, 2002). *Universal prevention strategies* focus on entire populations and target certain specific risk factors (for example, behavior problems in inner-city classrooms) without focusing on specific individuals. The third approach to prevention intervention— *selective prevention*—specifically targets whole groups at risk (for example, children who have parents who have died) and designs specific interventions aimed at helping them avoid future problems. Finally, *indicated prevention* is a strategy for those individuals who are beginning to show signs of problems (for example, depressive symptoms) but do not yet have a psychological disorder.

To evaluate the effectiveness of each of these approaches, the research strategies used in prevention research for examining psychopathology across time combine individual and group research methods, including both correlational and experimental designs. We look next at two of the most often used: cross-sectional and longitudinal designs.

Cross-Sectional Designs A variation of correlation research is to compare different people at different ages. For a **cross-sectional design**, researchers take a cross section of a population across the different age groups and compare them on some characteristic. For example, if they were trying to understand the development of alcohol abuse and dependence, they could take groups of adolescents at 12, 15, and 17 years of age and assess their beliefs about alcohol use. In an early comparison, Brown and Finn (1982) made some interesting discoveries. They found that 36% of the 12-year-olds thought the primary purpose of drinking was to get drunk. This percentage increased to 64% with 15-year-olds, but dropped again to 42% for the 17-year-old students. The researchers also found that 28% of the 12-year-olds reported drinking with their friends at least sometimes, a rate that increased to 80% for the 15-year-olds and to 88% for the 17-year-olds. Brown and Finn used this information to develop the hypothesis that the reason for excessive drinking among teens is a deliberate attempt to get drunk rather than a mistake in judgment once they are under the influence of alcohol.

In cross-sectional designs, the participants in each age group are called **cohorts**; Brown and Finn studied three cohorts: 12-year-olds, 15-year-olds, and 17-year-olds. The members of each cohort are the same age at the same time and thus have all been exposed to similar experiences. Members of one cohort differ from members of other cohorts in age and in their exposure to cultural and historical experiences. You would expect a group of 12-year-olds in the early 1980s to have received a great deal of education about drug and alcohol use ("Just Say No"), whereas the 17-year-olds may not have. Differences among cohorts in their opinions about alcohol use may be related to their respective cognitive and emotional development at these different ages and to their dissimilar experiences. This **cohort effect**, the confounding of age and experience, is a limitation of the cross-sectional design.

Researchers prefer cross-sectional designs to study changes over time partly because they are easier to use than longitudinal designs (discussed next). In addition, some phenomena are less likely to be influenced by different cultural and historical experiences and therefore less susceptible to cohort effects. For example, the prevalence of Alzheimer's disease among people at ages 60 and 70—assumed to be strongly influenced by biology—is not likely to be greatly affected by different experiences among the study participants.

One question not answered by cross-sectional designs is how problems develop in individuals. For example, do children who refuse to go to school grow up to have anxiety disorders? Researchers cannot answer this question simply by comparing adults with anxiety problems and children who refuse to go to school. They could ask the adults whether they were anxious about school when they were children, but this **retrospective information** (looking back) is usually less than accurate. To get a better picture of how individuals develop over the years, researchers use longitudinal designs.

Longitudinal Designs Rather than looking at different groups of people of differing ages, researchers may follow one group over time and assess change in its members directly. The advantages of **longitudinal designs** are that they do not suffer from cohort effect problems and they allow the researchers to assess individual change. (■ Figure 3.9 illustrates both longitudinal and cross-sectional designs.) Researchers in Australia, for example, conducted a longitudinal study of adolescents who had some symptoms of depression (Sheffield et al., 2006). They compared different prevention strategies—including universal and indicated prevention strategies—to assess if they could prevent these mildly depressed youth from becoming more depressed by giving them problem-solving skills. They followed 2,479 depressed ninth-graders in 34 schools over a 12-month period and found, surprisingly, that the interventions had no significant impact compared to no treatment. Although these results are disappointing, they show the value of longitudinal designs when assessing the durability of treatment.

Imagine conducting a major longitudinal study. Not only must the researcher persevere over months and years, but so must the people who participate in the study. They must remain willing to continue in the project, and the researcher must hope they will not move away or die. Longitudinal research is costly and time consuming. Finally, longitudinal designs can suffer from a phenomenon similar to the cohort effect on cross-sectional designs. The **cross-generational effect** involves trying to generalize the findings to groups whose experiences are different from those of the study par-

▲ Longitudinal studies can be complicated by the cross-generational effect; for example, young people in the 1960s shared experiences that were different from those of young people today.

ticipants. For example, the drug-use histories of people who were young adults in the 1960s and early 1970s are vastly different from those of people born in the 1990s.

Sometimes psychopathologists combine longitudinal and cross-sectional designs in a strategy called **sequential design**, which involves repeated study of different cohorts over time. As an example, we will look at work by Laurie Chassin and her colleagues, who study children's beliefs

about cigarette smoking (Chassin, Presson, Rose, & Sherman, 2001). These researchers have followed 10 cohorts of middle- and high-school-age children (cross-sectional design) since the early 1980s (longitudinal design). Through questionnaires, they have tracked how these children (and later, adults) viewed the health risks associated with smoking from their youth into their mid-30s. The results suggest that as middle schoolers (ages 11–14) the children viewed smoking as less risky to them personally and believed that there were positive psychological benefits (for example, making them appear more mature). These beliefs changed as the children went into high school and entered adulthood, but they point to the importance of targeting smoking prevention programs during the middle-school period (Chassin et al., 2005; Chassin et al., 2001).

Studying Behavior across Cultures

Researchers in Malaysia—where psychological disorders are commonly believed to have supernatural origins—have described a disorder they call *sakit gila,* which has some features of schizophrenia but differs in important ways

Longitudinal design

2015
25 years
old

2005
15 years
old

1995
5 years
old

1990

Same people followed across time

Cross-sectional design

25 yrs.

15 yrs.

5 yrs.

People of different ages viewed at the same time

■ **Figure 3.9** Two research designs. (© Cengage Learning 2013)

cross-sectional design Methodology to examine a characteristic by comparing individuals of different ages (contrast with longitudinal design).

cohort Participants in each age group of a study with a cross-sectional design.

cohort effect Observation that people of different age groups differ in their values and experiences.

retrospective information Literally "the view back"; data collected by examining records or recollections of the past. It is limited by the accuracy, validity, and thoroughness of the sources.

longitudinal design Systematic study of changes in the same individual or group examined over time (contrast with cross-sectional design).

cross-generational effect Limit on the generalizability of longitudinal research because the group under study may differ from others in culture and experience.

sequential design Combination of cross-sectional and longitudinal designs involving repeated study of different cohorts over time.

(Barrett et al., 2005). Could we learn more about schizophrenia (and *sakit gila*) by comparing the disorders themselves and the cultures in which they are found? Increasing awareness of the limited cultural scope of our research is creating a corresponding increase in cross-cultural research on psychopathology.

The designs we have described are adapted for studying abnormal behavior across cultures. Some researchers view the effects of different cultures as though they were different treatments (Hobfoll, Canetti-Nisim, & Johnson, 2006). In other words, the independent variable is the effect of different cultures on behavior, rather than, say, the effect of cognitive therapy versus simple exposure for the treatment of fears. The difference between looking at culture as a "treatment" and our typical design, however, is important. In cross-cultural research, we can't randomly assign infants to different cultures and observe how they develop. People from varying cultures can differ in any number of important ways—their genetic backgrounds, for one—that could explain variations in their behavior for reasons other than culture.

The characteristics of different cultures can also complicate research efforts. Symptoms, or descriptions of symptoms, can be dissimilar in different societies (Gaw, 2008; Marsella & Kaplan, 2002). Nigerians who are depressed complain of heaviness or heat in the head, crawling sensations in the head or legs, burning sensations in the body, and a feeling that the belly is bloated with water (Ebigno, 1982). In contrast, people in the United States report feeling worthless, being unable to start or finish anything, losing interest in usual activities, and thinking of suicide. Natives of China, however, are less likely to report feeling depressed or losing interest in favorite things but may have thoughts of suicide or worthlessness (Phillips et al., 2007). These few examples illustrate that applying a standard definition of depression across different cultures will result in vastly different outcomes.

An additional complicating factor is varying tolerances, or thresholds, for abnormal behavior. If people in different cultures see the same behaviors differently, researchers will have trouble comparing incidence and prevalence rates. Lambert and colleagues (1992) found that Jamaican parents and teachers report fewer incidents of abnormal child behavior than do their American counterparts. Does this represent a biological or environmental difference in the children themselves, the effects of different thresholds of tolerance in the societies, or a combination of both? Understanding cultural attitudes and customs is essential to such research (Kohn, Wintrob, & Alarcón, 2009).

Finally, treatment research is also complicated by cross-cultural differences. Cultures develop treatment models that reflect their own values. In Japan, psychiatric hospitalization is organized in terms of a family model, with caregivers assuming parental roles. A family model was common in psychiatric institutions in 19th-century North America until it was replaced with the medical model common today (Colp, 2009). In Saudi Arabia, women are veiled when outside the home, which prevents them from uncovering their faces in the presence of therapists; custom thus complicates efforts to establish a trusting and intimate therapeutic client–therapist relationship (Dubovsky, 1983). Because in the Islamic view medicine and religion are inseparable, medical and religious treatments are combined (Baasher, 2001). As you can see, something as basic as comparing treatment outcomes is highly complex in a cross-cultural context.

The Power of a Program of Research

When we examine different research strategies independently, as we have done here, we often have the impression that some approaches are better than others. It is important to understand that this is not true. Depending on the type of question you are asking and the practical limitations inherent in the inquiry, any of the research techniques would be appropriate. Significant issues often are resolved not by one perfectly designed study but rather by a series of studies that examine different aspects of the problem—in a program of research. The research of one of this book's authors will be used to illustrate how complex research questions are answered with a variety of different research designs.

One of us (Durand) studies why children with autism spectrum disorders display seemingly irrational behaviors such as self-injury (hitting or biting yourself) or aggression. The expectation is that the more we understand why these behaviors occur, the better the chances of de-

▲ The same behavior—in this case a woman baring her legs and having her head uncovered in public—would be acceptable in some cultures but not in others.

©Paul Springett/Alamy

signing an effective treatment. In an early study we used a single-subject design (withdrawal design) to test the influence of adult attention and escaping from unpleasant educational tasks on these problem behaviors (Carr & Durand, 1985). We found that some children hit themselves more when people ignore them, and others will hit themselves to get out of school assignments that are too difficult, showing that these disturbing behaviors can be understood by looking at them as primitive forms of communication (for example, "Please come here" or "This is too hard."). This led us to consider what would happen if we taught these children to communicate with us more appropriately (Durand, 1990). The next series of studies again used single-subject designs and demonstrated that teaching more acceptable ways of getting attention or help from others did significantly reduce these challenging behaviors (e.g., Durand & Carr, 1992). Several decades of research on this treatment (called functional communication training) demonstrates its value in significantly improving the lives of people with these once severe behavior problems by reducing the severity of the misbehavior through improving communication skills (Durand, 2011).

One of the questions that researchers face in this area is why some children develop more severe forms of these behavior problems and others do not. To begin to answer this question we conducted a 3-year prospective longitudinal study on more than 100 children with autism to see what factors might cause more problems (Durand, 2001). We studied the children at age 3 and later at age 6 to determine what about the child or the family led to more severe problems. We found the following two factors to be the most important indicators of severe behavior problems in the children: (1) if the parents were pessimistic about their ability to help their child or (2) if the parents were doubtful about their child's ability to change. These parents would "give up" and allow their child to dictate many of the routines around the house (for example, eating dinner in the living room or not going out to the movies because it would cause tantrums) (Durand, 2001).

This important finding then led to the next question: Could we make pessimistic parents more optimistic, and would this help prevent their children from developing more severe behavior problems? To answer this question we next relied on a randomized clinical trial to see if adding a cognitive behavior intervention (described in more detail in the later chapters on the individual disorders) would help make pessimistic parents more optimistic. We wanted to teach these parents to examine their own pessimistic thoughts ("I have no control of my child." "My child won't improve because of his/her autism.") and replace them with more hopeful views of their world ("I can help my child." "My child can improve his/her behavior."). We hypothesized that this cognitive intervention would help them carry out the parenting strategies we offer them (including functional communication training) and in turn improve the outcomes of our behavioral interventions. We randomly assigned groups of pessimistic parents who also had a child with very severe behavior problems to either a group that taught them how to work with their child or a group that used the same techniques but also helped them explore their pessimistic thinking and helped them view themselves and their child in a better light. The treatments were applied formally, using written protocols to make sure that each group received the treatment as designed (Durand & Hieneman, 2008). What we found was that addition of the cognitive behavioral intervention had the expected effect—improving optimism and improving child outcomes (Durand, Hieneman, Clarke, & Zona, 2009).

As this example indicates, research is conducted in stages, and a complete picture of any disorder and its treatment can be seen only after looking at it from many perspectives. An integrated program of research can help researchers explore various aspects of abnormal behavior.

Replication

Scientists in general, and behavioral scientists in particular, are never really convinced something is "true." Replicating findings is what makes researchers confident that what they are observing isn't a coincidence.

The strength of a research program is in its ability to replicate findings in different ways to build confidence in the results. If you look back at the research strategies we have described, you will find that replication is one of the most important aspects of each. The more times researchers repeat a process (and the behavior they are studying changes as expected), the more certain they are about what caused the changes.

Research Ethics

An important final issue involves the ethics of doing research in abnormal psychology. For example, the appropriateness of a clinician's delaying treatment to people who need it, just to satisfy the requirements of an experimental design, is often questioned. One single-case experimental design, the withdrawal design, can involve removing treatment for some time. Treatment is also withheld when placebo control groups are used in group experimental designs. Researchers across the world—in an evolving code of ethics referred to as the Declaration of Helsinki—are developing guidelines to determine just when it would be appropriate to use placebo-controlled trials (Roberts, Hoop, & Dunn, 2008). The fundamental question is this: When does a scientist's interest in preserving the internal validity of a study outweigh a client's right to treatment?

One answer to this question involves **informed consent**— a research participant's formal agreement to cooperate in a study following full disclosure of the nature of the research

informed consent Ethical requirement whereby research subjects agree to participate in a study only after they receive full disclosure about the nature of the study and their own role in it.

and the participant's role in it (Lubit, 2009). In studies using some form of treatment delay or withdrawal, the participant is told why it will occur and the risks and benefits, and permission to proceed is then obtained. In placebo control studies, participants are told they may not receive an active treatment (all participants are blind to or unaware of which group they are placed in), but they are usually given the option of receiving treatment after the study ends.

True informed consent is at times elusive. The basic components are competence, voluntarism, full information, and comprehension on the part of the participant (Bankert & Madur, 2006). In other words, research participants must be capable of consenting to participation in the research, they must volunteer or not be coerced into participating, they must have all the information they need to make the decision, and they must understand what their participation will involve. In some circumstances, all these conditions are difficult to attain. Children, for example, often do not fully appreciate what will occur during research. Similarly, individuals with cognitive impairments such as mental retardation or schizophrenia may not understand their role or their rights as participants. In institutional settings, participants should not feel coerced into taking part in research.

Research in university and medical settings must be approved by an institutional review board (IRB) (Lubit, 2009). These are committees made up of university faculty and nonacademic people from the community, and their purpose is to see that the rights of research participants are protected. The committee structure allows people other than the researcher to look at the research procedures to determine whether sufficient care is being taken to protect the welfare and dignity of the participants.

To safeguard those who participate in psychological research and to clarify the responsibilities of researchers, the American Psychological Association has published *Ethical Principles of Psychologists and Code of Conduct*, which includes general guidelines for conducting research (American Psychological Association, 2002). People in research experiments must be protected from both physical and psychological harm. In addition to the issue of informed consent, these principles stress the investigators' responsibility for the research participants' welfare because the researcher must ensure that the welfare of the research participants is given priority over any other consideration, including experimental design.

Psychological harm is difficult to define, but its definition remains the responsibility of the investigators. Researchers must hold in confidence all information obtained from participants, who have the right to concealment of their identity on all data, either written or informal. Whenever deception is considered essential to research, the investigator must satisfy a committee of peers that this judgment is correct. If deception or concealment is used, participants must be debriefed—that is, told in language

Discussing Diversity — Do Psychological Disorders Look the Same across Countries?

Since the end of World War II, researchers have been conducting national surveys to determine what percentages of people in the population have different psychological disorders. In such surveys, researchers typically conduct household, face-to-face diagnostic interviews with a large (approximately 5,000), randomly selected group of people within a given country and use the information obtained to make inferences about what percentage of people in that country have each psychological disorder. (This is similar to the strategy used in political election polls in which a small but randomly selected group of people are polled regarding who they plan to vote for and that information is used to generalize about how the entire population will vote.) Surveys like these are how we know what percentage of the population has the psychological disor-

ders you learn about later in this book, such as anxiety disorders, mood disorders, and eating disorders. Most of these surveys are done only within individual countries and so have not been able to address whether psychological disorders occur at the same rate or look the same across different countries.

To address such questions, in the late 1990s researchers from 28 countries came together and began a series of coordinated and rigorously implemented population surveys designed to estimate the prevalence of psychological disorders around the world and to identify risk, protective factors, and treatments used for each disorder. This large project, which is called the World Health Organization (WHO) World Mental Health Survey Initiative and is led by Ronald Kessler at Harvard Medical School and T. Bedirhan

Üstün of WHO, is ongoing but already has yielded some noteworthy findings. Of note, the rates of each psychological disorder vary significantly across the 28 countries; however, when they occur, disorders look similar across the countries. For instance, when disorders are present, their age of onset is remarkably consistent cross-nationally, and approximately half of all disorders begin before adulthood in each country. The results of this historic study suggest that despite differences in rates and in the manifestation of different disorders (as discussed in Chapter 2), many characteristics of anxiety, mood, eating, and other psychological disorders look the same across many countries around the world. To learn more about this study and its findings, go to www.hcp.med.harvard.edu/wmh.

they can understand the true purpose of the study and why it was necessary to deceive them.

The Society for Research in Child Development (2007) has endorsed ethical guidelines for research that address some issues unique to research on children. For example, these guidelines not only call for confidentiality, protection from harm, and debriefing but also require informed consent from children's caregivers and from the children themselves if they are age 7 or older. These guidelines specify that the research must be explained to children in language they can understand so that they can decide whether they wish to participate. Many other ethical issues extend beyond protection of the participants, including how researchers deal with errors in their research, fraud in science, and the proper way to give credit to others. Doing a study involves more than selecting the appropriate design. Researchers must be aware of numerous concerns that involve the rights of the people in the experiment, as well as their own conduct.

A final and important development in the field that will help to "keep the face" on psychological disorders is the involvement of consumers in important aspects of this research—referred to as participatory action research (Kindon, Pain, & Kesby, 2007). The concern over not only how people are treated in research studies but also how the information is interpreted and used has resulted in many government agencies providing guidance on how the people who are the targets of the research (for example, those with schizophrenia, depression, or anxiety disorders) should be involved in the process. The hope is that if people who experience these disorders are partners in designing, running, and interpreting this research, the relevance of the research and the treatment of the participants in these studies, will be markedly improved.

Summary

Assessing Psychological Disorders

What are clinical assessment and diagnosis?

> Clinical assessment is the systematic evaluation and measurement of psychological, biological, and social factors in an individual with a possible psychological disorder; diagnosis is the process of determining that those factors meet all criteria for a specific psychological disorder.

> Reliability, validity, and standardization are important components in determining the value of a psychological assessment.

What are the main methods used in clinical assessment?

> To assess various aspects of psychological disorders, clinicians may first interview and take an informal men-

tal status exam of the patient. More systematic observations of behavior are called behavioral assessment.

> A variety of psychological tests can be used during assessment, including projective tests, in which the patient responds to ambiguous stimuli by projecting unconscious thoughts; personality inventories, in which the patient takes a self-report questionnaire designed to assess personal traits; and intelligence testing, which provides a score known as an intelligence quotient (IQ).

> Biological aspects of psychological disorders may be assessed through neuropsychological testing designed to identify possible areas of brain dysfunction. Neuroimaging can be used more directly to identify brain structure and function. Finally, psychophysiological assessment refers to measurable changes in the nervous

system, reflecting emotional or psychological events that might be relevant to a psychological disorder.

Diagnosing Psychological Disorders

How is psychiatric diagnosis carried out?

> The term *classification* refers to any effort to construct groups or categories and to assign objects or people to the categories on the basis of their shared attributes or relations. Methods of classification include classical categorical, dimensional, and prototypical approaches. Our current system of classification, the *Diagnostic and Statistical Manual*, fourth edition, text revision *(DSM-IV)*, and in the forthcoming fifth edition *(DSM-5)* is based on a prototypical approach in which certain essential characteristics are identified but certain "nonessential" variations do not necessarily change the classification. The *DSM-IV-TR* categories are based on empirical findings to identify the criteria for each diagnosis. Although this system is the best to date in terms of scientific underpinnings, it is far from perfect, and research continues on the most useful way to classify psychological disorders.

Conducting Research in Psychopathology

What are the basic components of research in psychopathology?

> Research involves establishing a hypothesis that is then tested. In abnormal psychology, research focuses on hypotheses meant to explain the nature, the causes, or the treatment of a disorder.

Why are ethical principles so important in the research process?

> Ethics are important to the research process, and ethical guidelines are spelled out by many professional organizations in an effort to ensure the well-being of research participants.
> Ethical concerns are being addressed through informed consent and through the inclusion of consumers in research design, implementation, and interpretation.

Types of Research Methods

What methods are used to conduct research on the causes of behavior?

> The individual case study is used to study one or more individuals in depth. Although case studies have an important role in the theoretical development of psychology, they are not subject to experimental control and must necessarily be suspect in terms of both internal and external validity.
> Research by correlation can tell us whether a relationship exists between two variables, but it does not tell us if that relationship is a causal one. Epidemiological research is a type of correlational research that reveals the incidence, distribution, and consequences of a particular problem in one or more populations.
> Research by experiment can follow one of two designs: group or single case. In both designs, a variable (or variables) is manipulated and the effects are observed to determine the nature of a causal relationship.

Genetics and Behavior across Time and Cultures

How do researchers study the interaction between environment and genetics?

> Genetic research focuses on the role of genetics in behavior. These research strategies include family studies, adoption studies, twin studies, genetic linkage analyses, and association studies.
> Research strategies that examine psychopathology across time include cross-sectional and longitudinal designs. Both focus on differences in behavior or attitudes at different ages, but the former does so by looking at different individuals at different ages and the latter looks at the same individuals at different ages.
> Prevention research can be viewed in four broad categories: health promotion or positive development strategies, universal prevention strategies, selective prevention strategies, and indicated prevention strategies.

Why do researchers study behavior over time and across cultures?

> The clinical picture, causal factors, and treatment process and outcome can all be influenced by cultural factors.
> The more the findings of a research program are replicated, the more they gain in credibility.

Key Terms

clinical assessment, 70
diagnosis, 70
reliability, 71
validity, 72
standardization, 72
mental status exam, 72

behavioral assessment, 75
self-monitoring, 76
projective tests, 77
personality inventories, 78
intelligence quotient (IQ), 79
neuropsychological testing, 81

false positive, 81
false negative, 81
neuroimaging, 81
psychophysiological assessment, 82
electroencephalogram (EEG), 83
idiographic strategy, 84

Answers to Concept Checks

3.1

Part A

1. thought processes; 2. appearance and behavior; 3. sensorium; 4. mood and affect; 5. intellectual functioning

Part B

6. R, V; 7. NR, NV; 8. R, V; 9. NR, NV

3.2

1. T; 2. F; 3. F (still a problem); 4. F (reliable); 5. T

3.3

1. independent variable; 2. confound; 3. hypothesis; 4. dependent variable; 5. internal validity, external validity

3.4

1. e; 2. c; 3. b; 4. a; 5. f

3.5

Part A

1. L; 2. CS; 3. L; 4. CS; 5. L; 6. CS

Part B

7. T; 8. F; 9. T; 10. T; 11. F

Media Resources

Log in to CengageBrain to access the resources your instructor requires. For this book, you can access:

CourseMate brings course concepts to life with interactive learning, study, and exam preparation tools that support the printed textbook. A textbook-specific website, Psychology CourseMate includes an integrated interactive eBook and other interactive learning tools including quizzes, flashcards, videos, and more.

Abnormal Psychology Videos

> *Arriving at a Diagnosis:* A team discusses how it arrived at the conclusion that a patient has a panic disorder.
> *Psychological Assessment:* The psychological team discusses factors in dysfunctional beliefs, family relationships, and behavior patterns that might be contributing to a woman's major depressive disorder.

> *Research Methods:* David Barlow discusses the protocols and procedures in doing ethical research on clients with psychological problems. He explains the safeguards and the changes in the practices over time.

CENGAGENOW CengageNow is an easy-to-use online resource that helps you study in less time to get the grade you want—NOW. Take a pre-test for this chapter and receive a personalized study plan based on your results that will identify the topics you need to review and direct you to online resources to help you master those topics. Then take a post-test to help you determine the concepts you have mastered and what you will need to work on. If your textbook does not include an access code card, go to CengageBrain.com to gain access.

> Visit www.cengagebrain.com to access your account and purchase materials.

Video Concept Reviews

CengageNOW also contains Mark Durand's *Video Concept Reviews* on these challenging topics:

> Clinical Assessment
> Reliability/Validity
> Standardization
> Mental Status Exam
> Behavioral Assessment
> Projective Tests
> Concept Check—Data-Based Approach
> Neuropsychological Testing
> False Positive/False Negative
> Psychophysiological Assessment
> Diagnosis/Classification
> Taxonomy/Nosology/Nomenclature
> Concept Check—Categorical Versus Dimensional
> Classification Systems
> *DSM-IV*
> Hypothesis/Testability
> Independent/Dependent Variables
> Internal/External Validity
> Statistical Versus Clinical Significance
> Case Study Method
> Correlational Research
> Correlation Coefficient
> Experiment
> Placebo Control Group
> Double-Blind Control
> Single-Case Experimental Design (Repeated Measures)
> Genetic Research (Family and Adoptee Studies)
> Genetic Research (Twin, Genetic Linkage, and Association Studies)
> Longitudinal and Cross-Sectional Designs

Chapter Quiz

1. During a clinical interview a psychologist notes that a client is not aware of what the date is or even where she is. The psychologist has gained information about what aspect of the client's mental status?
   a. reliability
   b. affect
   c. sensorium
   d. intellectual functioning

2. One criticism of the Rorschach inkblot test and other projective assessment techniques is that different therapists administer and interpret them in different ways. Because of that variability, the tests lack what key attribute?
   a. random sampling
   b. standardization
   c. validity
   d. testability

3. What type of test would you use to explore whether an individual might have some sort of brain damage or injury?
   a. neuropsychological test
   b. projective test
   c. electrodermal test
   d. personality test

4. Measuring electrical activity in the brain with an electroencephalogram (EEG) would be most appropriate to answer which of the following questions?
   a. Will this client perform at the same level with his peers in school?
   b. Does this client have excessive fears and worries?
   c. Is this client well suited to pursue a career in the creative arts?
   d. Is this client benefiting from relaxation training?

5. Which approach to diagnostic classification identifies both essential characteristics of a disorder that everyone with the disorder shares and nonessential characteristics that might vary from person to person?
   a. prototypical
   b. standardized
   c. dimensional
   d. categorical

6. Despite improvements in *DSM-IV* and *DSM-IV-TR*, which of the following criticisms can still be leveled at that classification system?

   a. It provides no opportunity to describe biological or social factors that might influence psychological health.

   b. It relies on a purely dimensional approach, and the number of relevant dimensions on which to describe clients is infinite.

   c. The system emphasizes validity at the expense of reliability.

   d. It categorizes and labels people, which can be pejorative or even self-fulfilling.

7. In most experiments, researchers explore the expected influence of the _____ on the _____.

   a. incidence; prevalence

   b. independent variable; dependent variable

   c. external validity; internal validity

   d. testability; generalizability

8. When behavior change occurs because of a person's expectation of change rather than (or in addition to) the result of any manipulation by the experimenter, it is known as the:

   a. clinical significance

   b. cohort effect

   c. placebo effect

   d. prevalence

9. What type of research design is used if an experiment examines life satisfaction in different groups of 20-, 40-, and 60-year-olds to draw conclusions about age differences?

   a. cross-sectional

   b. longitudinal

   c. multiple baseline

   d. case study

10. One way that participants in research projects are protected from harm is by making sure they are not coerced into participating and that they have full knowledge of what their participation will involve. What is that ethical protection called?

   a. internal validity

   b. positive correlation

   c. informed consent

   d. clinical significance

   (See Appendix A for answers.)

CHAPTER 4

Anxiety Disorders

Demonstrate knowledge and understanding representing appropriate breadth and depth in selected content areas of psychology:	❯ Biological bases of behavior and mental processes, including physiology, sensation, perception, comparative, motivation, and emotion *(see textbook pages 119–121)*
Use the concepts, language, and major theories of the discipline to account for psychological phenomena.	❯ Describe behavior and mental processes empirically, including operational definitions *(see textbook pages 117–119, 123–125, 127–130, 135–139, 141–143, 145–148, 152–155)*
Identify appropriate applications of psychology in solving problems, such as:	❯ Origin and treatment of abnormal behavior *(see textbook pages 125–127, 131–135, 139–141, 143–145, 148–151, 155–156)*

*Portions of this chapter cover learning outcomes suggested by the American Psychological Association (2007) in their guidelines for the undergraduate psychology major. Chapter coverage of these outcomes is identified by APA Goal and APA Suggested Learning Outcome (SLO).

The Complexity of Anxiety Disorders

> **What are the similarities and differences among anxiety, fear, and panic attacks?**

Anxiety is complex and mysterious. In some ways, the more we learn about it, the more baffling it seems. "Anxiety" is a specific type of disorder, but it is more than that. It is an emotion implicated so heavily across the full range of psychopathology that we begin by exploring its general nature, both biological and psychological. Next, we consider fear, a somewhat different but clearly related emotion. Related to fear is panic attack, which we propose is fear that occurs when there is nothing to be afraid of and, therefore, at an inappropriate time. With these important ideas clearly in mind, we focus on specific anxiety disorders.

Anxiety, Fear, and Panic: Some Definitions

Have you ever experienced anxiety? That is a silly question, you might say, because most of us feel some anxiety almost every day of our lives. Did you have a test in school today for which you weren't "perfectly" prepared? Did you have a date last weekend with somebody new? And how about that job interview coming up? Even thinking about that might make you nervous. But have you ever stopped to think about the nature of anxiety? What is it? What causes it?

Anxiety is a negative mood state characterized by bodily symptoms of physical tension and by apprehension about the future (American Psychiatric Association, 2000; Barlow, 2002). In humans it can be a subjective sense of

unease, a set of behaviors (looking worried and anxious or fidgeting), or a physiological response originating in the brain and reflected in elevated heart rate and muscle tension. Because anxiety is difficult to study in humans, much of the research has been done with animals. But is the animals' experience of anxiety the same as that of humans? It seems to be similar, but we don't know for sure. Thus, anxiety remains a mystery, and we are only beginning our journey of discovery. Anxiety is also closely related to depression (Barlow, 2000, 2002; Brown & Barlow, 2005, 2009; Clark, 2005; Wilamowska et al., 2010), so much of what we say here is relevant to Chapter 6.

Surprisingly, anxiety is good for us, at least in moderate amounts. Psychologists have known for more than a century that we perform better when we are a little anxious (Yerkes & Dodson, 1908). You would not have done so well on that test the other day if you had had no anxiety. You were a little more charming and lively on that date last weekend because you were anxious. And you will be better prepared for that job interview coming up if you are anxious. In short, social, physical, and intellectual perfor-

anxiety Mood state characterized by marked negative affect and bodily symptoms of tension in which a person apprehensively anticipates future danger or misfortune. Anxiety may involve feelings, behaviors, and physiological responses.

John Moore/Getty Images

is an immediate emotional reaction to current danger characterized by strong escapist action tendencies and, often, a surge in the sympathetic branch of the autonomic nervous system (Barlow, Brown, & Craske, 1994; Craske et al., 2010).

What happens if you experience the alarm response of fear when there is nothing to be afraid of—that is, if you have a false alarm? Consider the case of Gretchen, who appeared at one of our clinics.

mances are driven and enhanced by anxiety. Without it, few of us would get much done. Howard Liddell (1949) first proposed this idea when he called anxiety the "shadow of intelligence." He thought the human ability to plan in some detail for the future was connected to that gnawing feeling that things could go wrong and we had better be prepared for them. This is why anxiety is a future-oriented mood state. If you were to put it into words, you might say, "Something might go wrong, and I'm not sure I can deal with it, but I've got to be ready to try. Maybe I'd better study a little harder (or check the mirror one more time before my date, or do a little more research on that company before the interview)."

But what happens when you have too much anxiety? You might actually fail the exam because you can't concentrate on the questions. All you can think about when you're too anxious is how terrible it will be if you fail. You might blow the interview for the same reason. On that date with a new person, you might spend the evening perspiring profusely, with a sick feeling in your stomach, unable to think of even one reasonably interesting thing to say. Too much of a good thing can be harmful, and few sensations are more harmful than severe anxiety that is out of control. What makes the situation worse is that severe anxiety usually doesn't go away—that is, even if we "know" there is nothing to be afraid of, we remain anxious.

All the disorders discussed in this chapter are characterized by excessive anxiety, which takes many forms. In Chapter 2 you saw that **fear** is an immediate alarm reaction to danger. Like anxiety, fear can be good for us. It protects us by activating a massive response from the autonomic nervous system (increased heart rate and blood pressure, for example), which, along with our subjective sense of terror, motivates us to escape (flee) or, possibly, to attack (fight). As such, this emergency reaction is often called the flight or fight response.

There is much evidence that fear and anxiety reactions differ psychologically and physiologically (Barlow, 2002; Bouton, 2005; Craske et al., 2010; Waddell, Morris, & Bouton, 2006). As noted earlier, anxiety is a future-oriented mood state, characterized by apprehension because we cannot predict or control upcoming events. Fear, however,

Gretchen | Attacked by Panic

I was 25 when I had my first attack. It was a few weeks after I'd come home from the hospital. I had had my appendix out. The surgery had gone well, and I wasn't in any danger, which is why I don't understand what happened. But one night I went to sleep and I woke up a few hours later—I'm not sure how long—but I woke up with this vague feeling of apprehension. Mostly I remember how my heart started pounding. And my chest hurt. It felt like I was dying—that I was having a heart attack. And I felt kind of queer, as if I were detached from the experience. It seemed like my bedroom was covered with a haze. I ran to my sister's room, but I felt like I was a puppet or a robot who was under the control of somebody else while I was running. I think I scared her almost as much as I was frightened myself. She called an ambulance (Barlow, 2002).

This sudden overwhelming reaction came to be known as **panic**, after the Greek god Pan who terrified travelers with bloodcurdling screams. In psychopathology, a **panic attack** is defined as an abrupt experience of intense fear or acute discomfort, accompanied by physical symptoms that usually include heart palpitations, chest pain, shortness of breath, and (possibly) dizziness.

Three basic types of panic attacks are described in *DSM-IV*: situationally bound, unexpected, and situationally predisposed. If you know you are afraid of high places or of driving over long bridges, you might have a panic attack in these situations but not anywhere else; this is a *situationally bound (cued) panic attack*. By contrast, you might experience *unexpected (uncued) panic attacks* if you don't have a clue when or where the next attack will occur. The third type of panic attack, the *situationally predisposed panic attack*, is between these two types. You are more likely to, but will not inevitably, have an attack where you have had one before (for example, in a large mall). If you don't know whether it will happen today and it does, the attack is situationally predisposed (this type of panic attack may be dropped in *DSM-5* just to make differentiation simpler). We mention these types of attacks because they play a role in several anxiety disorders. Unexpected and situationally predisposed attacks are important in panic disorder. Situationally bound attacks are more common in specific phobias or social phobia (see ■ Figure 4.1).

Remember that fear is an intense emotional alarm accompanied by a surge of energy in the autonomic nervous system that motivates us to flee from danger. Does Gretchen's panic attack sound like it could be the emotion of fear? A variety of evidence suggests it is (Barlow, 2002; Barlow, Chorpita, & Turovsky, 1996; Bouton, 2005), including similarities in reports of the experience of fear and panic, similar behavioral tendencies to escape, and similar underlying neurobiological processes.

Causes of Anxiety Disorders

You learned in Chapters 1 and 2 that excessive emotional reactions have no simple one-dimensional cause but come from multiple sources. Next, we explore the biological, psychological, and social contributors and how they interact to produce anxiety disorders. (See the Discussing Diversity box.)

Biological Contributions

Increasing evidence shows that we inherit a tendency to be tense, uptight, and anxious (Clark, 2005; Eysenck, 1967; Gray & McNaughton, 1996). The tendency to panic also

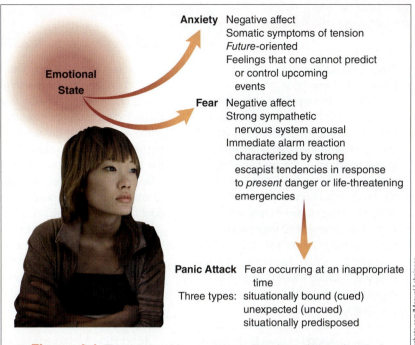

■ Figure 4.1 The relationships among anxiety, fear, and panic attack.

Emotional State

Anxiety Negative affect
Somatic symptoms of tension
Future-oriented
Feelings that one cannot predict or control upcoming events

Fear Negative affect
Strong sympathetic nervous system arousal
Immediate alarm reaction characterized by strong escapist tendencies in response to *present* danger or life-threatening emergencies

Panic Attack Fear occurring at an inappropriate time
Three types: situationally bound (cued)
unexpected (uncued)
situationally predisposed

iStockphoto.com/Manuel Lohninger

seems to run in families and probably has a genetic component that differs somewhat from genetic contributions to anxiety (Barlow, 2002; Craske, 1999; Craske & Barlow, 2008; Kendler et al., 1995). As with almost all emotional traits and psychological disorders, no single gene seems to cause anxiety or panic. Instead, contributions from collections of genes in several areas on chromosomes make us vulnerable when the right psychological and social factors are in place. Furthermore, a genetic vulnerability does not cause anxiety and/or panic directly—that is, stress or other factors in the environment can "turn on" these genes, as we reviewed in Chapter 2 (Gelernter & Stein, 2009; Kendler, 2006; Rutter, Moffitt, & Caspi, 2006; Schumacher et al., 2005; Smoller, Block, & Young, 2009).

Anxiety is also associated with specific brain circuits and neurotransmitter systems. For example, depleted levels of gamma-aminobutyric acid (GABA), part of the GABA–benzodiazepine system, are associated with increased anxiety, although the relationship is not quite so direct. The noradrenergic system has also been implicated in anxiety, and evidence from basic animal studies, and studies of normal anxiety in humans, suggest the serotonergic neurotransmitter system is also involved (Lesch et al., 1996; Maier, 1997; Stein, Schork, & Gelernter, 2007). But increasing attention is focusing on the role of the corticotropin-releasing factor (CRF) system as central to

---

DSM **Disorder Criteria Summary**
Panic Attack

A panic attack involves experiencing four or more of the following symptoms during a specific period:

> Palpitations, pounding heart, or accelerated heart rate

> Sweating

> Trembling or shaking

> Sensations of shortness of breath or smothering

> Feeling of choking

> Chest pain or discomfort

> Nausea or abdominal distress

> Feeling dizzy, unsteady, lightheaded, or faint

> Derealization (feelings of unreality) or depersonalization (being detached from oneself)

> Fear of losing control or going crazy

> Fear of dying

> Paresthesias (numbness or tingling sensations)

> Chills or hot flushes

Source: Based on *DSM-IV-TR.* Reprinted with permission from *Diagnostic and Statistical Manual of Mental Disorders* (4th ed., text revision). © 2000 American Psychiatric Association.

---

fear Emotion of an immediate alarm reaction to present danger or life-threatening emergencies.
panic Sudden, overwhelming fright or terror.
panic attack Abrupt experience of intense fear or discomfort accompanied by several physical symptoms, such as dizziness or heart palpitations.

Anxiety is experienced by people all over the world. However, significant differences are found in the reported rates of anxiety disorders and how people experience them across different countries. When asked whether they had suffered from an anxiety disorder in the past year, approximately 3% of those in China reported having an anxiety disorder, whereas 18% of those in the United States reported such a disorder (WHO World Mental Health Survey Consortium, 2004). This could reflect a true difference in the rate of anxiety across these countries but may largely result from how anxiety is experienced and reported.

For instance, the criteria used to assess the presence of anxiety disorders around the world typically are based on the Western conceptualization of each disorder. In the case of panic disorder, this includes the experience of extreme physiological distress (such as heart racing and sweating), along with fears that one is going crazy or losing control. The physiological symptoms associated with panic appear to be universal and are reported in virtually all countries. However, the psychological manifestations of panic differ across countries, and this may lead to lower numbers of people in other countries meeting diagnostic criteria for panic disorder as defined by Western standards. In many third-world countries, for example, anxiety and mood disorders are experienced as bodily sensations but symptoms like fear and dread are not reported (Hinton, Chhean, Fama, Pollack, & McNally, 2007).

In addition to differences in the experience of anxiety, some people may be more willing to report anxiety than others. This appears to be the explanation behind the large sex differences in the prevalence of anxiety disorders in the United States—that is, women consistently report higher rates of fears and phobias, whereas men are less inclined to admit to such disorders (Arrindell et al., 2003a). So what happens to men with severe anxiety that goes unnoticed and untreated? A large portion of them seem to cope with their anxiety by drinking alcohol, often leading to the development of an alcohol use disorder (Kushner, Abrams, & Borchardt, 2000).

Although more is known about sex differences in rates of anxiety disorders, researchers are just beginning to learn how cultural factors can influence the experience and reporting of anxiety disorders. It will be important for future work to continue to enhance our ability to understand and treat anxiety disorders around the world.

the expression of anxiety (and depression) and the groups of genes that increase the likelihood that this system will be turned on (Heim & Nemeroff, 1999; Khan, King, Abelson, & Liberzon, 2009; Ladd, et al., 2000; Smoller, Yamaki, & Fagerness, 2005; Sullivan, Kent, & Coplan, 2000). This is because CRF activates the hypothalamic–pituitary–adrenocortical (HPA) axis, which is part of the CRF system, and this CRF system has wide-ranging effects on areas of the brain implicated in anxiety, including the emotional brain (the limbic system), particularly the hippocampus and the amygdala; the locus coeruleus in the brain stem; the prefrontal cortex; and the dopaminergic neurotransmitter system. The CRF system is also directly related to the GABA–benzodiazepine system and the serotonergic and noradrenergic neurotransmitter systems.

The area of the brain most often associated with anxiety is the limbic system (Britton & Rauch, 2009; Charney & Drevets, 2002; Gray & McNaughton, 1996; LeDoux, 1996, 2002; see Figure 2.7c), which acts as a mediator between the brain stem and the cortex. The more primitive brain stem monitors and senses changes in bodily functions and relays these potential danger signals to higher cortical processes through the limbic system. The late Jeffrey Gray, a prominent British neuropsychologist, identified a brain circuit in the limbic system of animals that seems heavily involved in anxiety (Gray, 1982, 1985; McNaughton & Gray, 2000) and may be relevant to humans. This circuit leads from the septal and hippocampal area in the limbic system to the frontal cortex. The system that Gray calls the **behavioral inhibition system (BIS)** is activated by signals from the brain stem of unexpected events, such as major changes in body functioning that might signal danger. Danger signals in response to something we see that might be threatening descend from the cortex to the septal–hippocampal system. The BIS also receives a big boost from the amygdala (Davis, 1992; LeDoux, 1996, 2002). When the BIS is activated by signals that arise from the brain stem or descend from the cortex, our tendency is to freeze, experience anxiety, and apprehensively evaluate the situation to confirm that danger is present.

The BIS circuit is distinct from the circuit involved in panic. Gray (1982; Gray & McNaughton, 1996) and Graeff (1987, 1993; Deakin & Graeff, 1991) identified what Gray calls the **fight/flight system (FFS)**. This circuit originates in the brain stem and travels through several midbrain structures, including the amygdala, the ventromedial nucleus of the hypothalamus, and the central gray matter. When stimulated in animals, this circuit produces an immediate alarm-and-escape response that looks very much like panic in humans (Gray & McNaughton, 1996). Gray and McNaughton (1996) and Graeff (1993) think the FFS is activated partly by deficiencies in serotonin.

It is likely that factors in your environment can change the sensitivity of these brain circuits, making you more or less susceptible to developing anxiety and its disorders, a finding that has been demonstrated in several laboratories (Francis, Diorio, Plotsky, & Meaney, 2002; Stein et al., 2007). For example, one important study suggested that cigarette smoking as a teenager is associated with greatly increased risk for developing anxiety disorders as adults, particularly panic disorder and generalized anxiety disorder (Johnson et al., 2000). One possible explanation is that chronic exposure to nicotine, an addictive drug that increases somatic symptoms, and respiratory problems, triggers additional anxiety and panic, thereby increasing biological vulnerability to develop severe anxiety disorders.

Research into the neurobiology of anxiety and panic is still new, but we have made exciting progress by implicating two seemingly different brain systems and confirming the crucial role of the CRF system and the amygdala. Brain-imaging procedures will undoubtedly yield more information in the years to come, and this has already begun to happen (Britton & Rauch, 2009; Charney & Drevets, 2002). For example, there is now general agreement that in people with anxiety disorders the limbic system, including the amygdala, is overly responsive to stimulation or new information (abnormal bottom-up processing); at the same time, controlling functions of the cortex that would down-regulate the hyperexcitable amygdala are deficient (abnormal top-down processing), consistent with Gray's BIS model (Britton & Rauch, 2009; Ochsner et al., 2009).

Psychological Contributions

Evidence is accumulating (see, for example, Barlow, 2002; Suárez, Bennett, Goldstein, & Barlow, 2009) that supports an integrated model of anxiety involving a variety of psychological factors. In childhood we may acquire an awareness that events are not always in our control (Chorpita & Barlow, 1998). The continuum of this perception may range from total confidence in our control of all aspects of our lives to deep uncertainty about ourselves and our ability to deal with upcoming events. If you are anxious about schoolwork, you may worry you will do poorly on the next exam, even though all your grades have been As and Bs. A general "sense of uncontrollability" may develop early as a function of upbringing and other disruptive or traumatic environmental factors.

Interestingly, the actions of parents in early childhood seem to do a lot to foster this sense of control or a sense of uncontrollability (Chorpita & Barlow, 1998; Gunnar & Fisher, 2006). Generally, it seems that parents who interact in a positive and predictable way with their children by responding to their needs, particularly when the child communicates needs for attention, food, relief from pain, and so on, perform an important function. These parents teach their children that they have control over their environment and their responses have an effect on their parents and their environment. In addition, parents who provide a "secure home base" but allow their children to explore their world and develop the necessary skills to cope with unexpected occurrences enable their children to develop a healthy sense of control (Chorpita & Barlow, 1998). In contrast, parents who are overprotective and overintrusive and who "clear the way" for their children, never letting them experience any adversity, create a situation in which children never learn how to cope with adversity

when it comes along. Therefore, these children don't learn that they can control their environment. A variety of evidence has accumulated supporting these ideas (Barlow, 2002; Chorpita & Barlow, 1998; Chorpita, Brown, & Barlow, 1998; Gunnar & Fisher, 2006; Lieb et al., 2000; Nolen-Hoeksema, Wolfson, Mumme, & Guskin, 1995; White, Brown, Somers, & Barlow, 2006). A sense of control (or lack of it) that develops from these early experiences is the psychological factor that makes us more or less vulnerable to anxiety in later life.

Most psychological accounts of panic (as opposed to anxiety) invoke conditioning and cognitive explanations that are difficult to separate (Bouton, Mineka, & Barlow, 2001). Thus, a strong fear response initially occurs during extreme stress or perhaps as a result of a dangerous situation in the environment (a true alarm). This emotional response then becomes associated with a variety of external and internal cues. In other words, these cues, or conditioned stimuli, provoke the fear response and an assumption of danger, even if the danger is not actually present (Bouton, 2005; Bouton et al., 2001; Martin, 1983; Mineka & Zinbarg, 2006; Razran, 1961), so it is really a learned or false alarm. This is the conditioning process described in Chapter 2. External cues are places or situations similar to the one where the initial panic attack occurred. Internal cues are increases in heart rate or respiration that were associated with the initial panic attack, even if they are now the result of normal circumstances, such as exercise. Thus, when your heart is beating fast you are more likely to think of and, perhaps, experience a panic attack than when it is beating normally. Furthermore, you may not be aware of the cues or triggers of severe fear—that is, they are unconscious.

Social Contributions

Stressful life events trigger our biological and psychological vulnerabilities to anxiety. Most are social and interpersonal in nature—marriage, divorce, difficulties at work, death of a loved one, pressures to excel in school, and so on. Some might be physical, such as an injury or illness.

The same stressors can trigger physical reactions such as headaches or hypertension and emotional reactions such as panic attacks (Barlow, 2002). The particular way we react to stress seems to run in families. If you get headaches when under stress, chances are other people in your family also get headaches. If you have panic attacks, other members of your family probably do also. This finding suggests a possible genetic contribution, at least to initial panic attacks.

---

behavioral inhibition system (BIS) Brain circuit in the limbic system that responds to threat signals by inhibiting activity and causing anxiety.

fight/flight system (FFS) Brain circuit in animals that when stimulated causes an immediate alarm-and-escape response resembling human panic.

An Integrated Model

Putting the factors together in an integrated way, we have described a theory of the development of anxiety and related disorders called the *triple vulnerability theory* (Barlow, 2000, 2002; Suárez et al., 2009). The first vulnerability (or diathesis) is a *generalized biological vulnerability*. We can see that a tendency to be uptight or high-strung might be inherited. But a generalized biological vulnerability to develop anxiety is not sufficient to produce anxiety itself. The second vulnerability is a *generalized psychological vulnerability*—that is, you might also grow up believing the world is dangerous and out of control and you might not be able to cope when things go wrong based on your early experiences. If this perception is strong, you have a generalized psychological vulnerability to anxiety. The third vulnerability is a *specific psychological vulnerability* in which you learn from early experience, such as being taught by your parents that some situations or objects are fraught with danger (even if they really aren't). Possible examples are dogs if one of your parents is afraid of dogs, or being evaluated negatively by others if this is something your parents worry about. These triple vulnerabilities are presented in ■ Figure 4.2. If you are feeling a lot of pressure, particularly from interpersonal stressors, a given stressor could activate your biological tendencies to be anxious and your psychological tendencies to feel you might not be able to deal with the situation and control the stress. Once this cycle starts, it tends to feed on itself, so it might not stop even when the particular life stressor has long since passed. Anxiety can be general, evoked by many aspects of your life, but it is usually focused on one area, such as social evaluations or grades (Barlow, 2002).

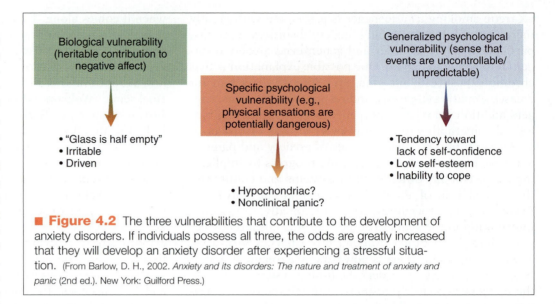

■ **Figure 4.2** The three vulnerabilities that contribute to the development of anxiety disorders. If individuals possess all three, the odds are greatly increased that they will develop an anxiety disorder after experiencing a stressful situation. (From Barlow, D. H., 2002. *Anxiety and its disorders: The nature and treatment of anxiety and panic* (2nd ed.). New York: Guilford Press.)

Comorbidity of Anxiety Disorders

Before describing the specific anxiety disorders, it is important to note that they often co-occur. As we described in Chapter 3, the co-occurrence of two or more disorders in a single individual is referred to as *comorbidity*. The high rates of comorbidity among anxiety disorders (and depression) emphasize how all of these disorders share the common features of anxiety and panic described here. They also share the same vulnerabilities, biological and psychological, to develop anxiety and panic. The various anxiety disorders differ only in what triggers the anxiety and, perhaps, the patterning of panic attacks. Of course, if each patient with an anxiety disorder also had every other anxiety disorder, there would be little sense in distinguishing among the specific disorders. But this is not the case, and, although

rates of comorbidity are high, they vary somewhat from disorder to disorder (Allen et al., 2010; Bruce et al., 2005; Tsao, Mystkowski, Zucker, & Craske, 2002). A large-scale study completed at one of our centers examined the comorbidity of *Diagnostic and Statistical Manual of Mental Disorders*, fourth edition *(DSM-IV-TR)* anxiety and mood disorders (Brown & Barlow, 2002; Brown, Campbell, Lehman, Grisham, & Mancill, 2001). Data were collected from 1,127 patients. If we examine just rates of comorbidity at the time of assessment, the results indicate that 55% of the patients who received a principal diagnosis of an anxiety or depressive disorder had at least one additional anxiety or depressive disorder at the time of the assessment. If we consider whether the patient met criteria for an additional diagnosis at any time in his or her life, rather than just at the time of the assessment, the rate increases to 76%.

By far, the most common additional diagnosis for all anxiety disorders was major depression, which occurred in 50% of the cases over the course of the patient's life. This becomes important when we discuss the relationship of anxiety and depression later in this chapter. Also important is the finding that additional diagnoses of depression or alcohol or drug abuse makes it less likely that you will recover from an anxiety disorder and more likely that you will relapse if you do recover (Bruce et al., 2005; Huppert, 2009).

Concept Check 4.1

Complete the following statements about anxiety and its causes with the following terms: (a) comorbidity, (b) panic attack, (c) situationally bound, (d) neurotransmitter, (e) brain circuits, and (f) stressful.

1. A _____ is an abrupt experience of intense fear or acute discomfort accompanied by physical symptoms, such as chest pain and shortness of breath.

2. A _____ panic attack often occurs in certain situations but not anywhere else.

3. Anxiety is associated with specific _____ (for example, behavioral inhibition system or fight/flight system) and _____ systems (for example, noradrenergic).

4. The rates of _____ among anxiety disorders are high because they share the common features of anxiety and panic.

5. _____ life events can trigger biological and psychological vulnerabilities to anxiety.

Generalized Anxiety Disorder

› **What are the essential features, possible causes, and available treatment approaches for generalized anxiety disorder?**

Specific anxiety disorders are complicated by panic attacks or other features that are the focus of the anxiety. In generalized anxiety disorder, the focus is generalized to the events of everyday life. Therefore, we consider generalized anxiety disorder first.

Clinical Description

Most of us worry to some extent. As we have said, worry can be useful. It helps us plan for the future, make sure that we're prepared for that test, or double-check that we've thought of everything before we head home for the holidays. But what if you worry indiscriminately about everything? Furthermore, what if worrying is unproductive? No matter how much you worry, you can't seem to decide what to do about an upcoming problem or situation. And what if you can't stop worrying, even if you know it is doing you no good and probably making everyone else around you miserable? These features characterize **generalized anxiety disorder (GAD)**. Consider the case of Irene.

Irene · Ruled by Worry

Irene, a 20-year-old college student, came to the clinic complaining of excessive anxiety and general difficulties in controlling her life. Everything was a catastrophe for Irene. Although she carried a 3.7 grade point average, she was convinced she would flunk every test she took.

Irene worried until she dropped out of the first college she attended after 1 month. She felt depressed for a while, then decided to take a couple of courses at a local junior college, believing she could handle the work there better. After achieving straight As at the junior college for 2 years, she enrolled once again in a 4-year college as a junior. After a short time, she began calling the clinic in a state of extreme agitation, saying she had to drop this or that course because she couldn't handle it. With great difficulty, her therapist and parents persuaded her to stay in the courses and to seek further help. In any course Irene completed, her grade was between an A and a B-minus, but she still worried about every test and every paper.

Irene was also concerned about relationships with her friends, and whenever she was with her new boyfriend she feared making a fool of herself and losing his interest. She reported that each date went extremely well but she knew the next one would probably be a disaster. As the relationship progressed and some sexual contact seemed natural, Irene was worried sick that her inexperience would make her boyfriend consider her naive and stupid. Nevertheless, she reported enjoying the early sexual contact and admitted that he seemed to enjoy it also, but she was convinced that the next time a catastrophe would happen.

Irene was also concerned about her health. She had minor hypertension, probably because she was somewhat overweight. She then approached every meal as if death itself might result if she ate the wrong types or amounts of food. She became reluctant to have her blood pressure checked for fear it would be high or to weigh herself for fear she was not losing weight. She severely restricted her eating and as a result had an occasional episode of binge eating.

Although Irene had an occasional panic attack, this was not a major issue to her. As soon as the panic subsided, she focused on the next possible catastrophe. In addition to high blood pressure, Irene had tension headaches and a "nervous stomach,"

generalized anxiety disorder (GAD) Anxiety disorder characterized by intense, uncontrollable, unfocused, chronic, and continuous worry that is distressing and unproductive, accompanied by physical symptoms of tenseness, irritability, and restlessness.

with a lot of gas, occasional diarrhea, and some abdominal pain. Irene's life was a series of impending catastrophes. Her mother reported that she dreaded a phone call from Irene, let alone a visit, because she knew she would have to see her daughter through a crisis. For the same reason, Irene had few friends.

Irene suffered from GAD. The *DSM-IV-TR* criteria specify that at least 6 months of excessive anxiety and worry (apprehensive expectation) must be ongoing more days than not. Furthermore, it must be difficult to turn off or control the worry process. Most of us worry for a time but can set the problem aside and go on to another task. Even if the upcoming challenge is a big one, as soon as it is over the worrying stops. For Irene, it never stopped. She turned to the next crisis as soon as the current one was over.

The physical symptoms associated with generalized anxiety and GAD differ somewhat from those associated with panic attacks and panic disorder (covered next). Whereas panic is associated with autonomic arousal, presumably as a result of a sympathetic nervous system surge (for instance, increased heart rate, palpitations, perspiration, and trembling), GAD is characterized by muscle tension, mental agitation (Brown, Marten, & Barlow, 1995), susceptibility to fatigue (probably the result of chronic excessive muscle tension), some irritability, and difficulty sleeping. Focusing attention is difficult as the mind quickly switches from crisis to crisis. People with GAD mostly worry about minor, everyday life events, a characteristic that distinguishes GAD from other anxiety disorders. When asked, "Do you worry excessively about minor things?" 100% of individuals with GAD respond "yes" compared to approximately 50% of individuals whose anxiety disorder falls within other categories (Barlow, 2002). Such a difference is statistically significant. Major events quickly become the focus of anxiety and worry, too. Adults typically focus on possible misfortune to their children, family health, job responsibilities, and more minor things such as household chores or being on time for appointments. Children with GAD most often worry about competence in academic, athletic, or social performance and about family issues (Albano & Hack, 2004; Furr, Tiwari, Suveg, & Kendall, 2009; Weems, Silverman, & La Greca, 2000). Older adults tend to focus, understandably, on health (Ayers, Thorp, & Wetherell, 2009; Beck & Averill, 2004; Person & Borkovec, 1995); they also have difficulty sleeping, which seems to make the anxiety worse (Beck & Stanley, 1997).

Statistics

Although worry and physical tension are common, the severe generalized anxiety experienced by Irene is rare. Approximately 3.1% of the population meets criteria for GAD during a given 1-year period (Kessler, Chiu, Demler,

DSM Disorder Criteria Summary
Generalized Anxiety Disorder

Features of generalized anxiety disorder include the following:

› Excessive anxiety and worry (apprehensive expectation), occurring more days than not for at least 6 months about a number of events or activities

› Difficulty in controlling the worry

› At least three of these symptoms: (1) restlessness or feeling keyed up or on edge; (2) being easily fatigued; (3) difficulty concentrating or mind going blank; (4) irritability: (5) muscle tension; (6) sleep disturbance

› Significant distress or impairment

› Anxiety is not limited to one specific issue

Source: Based on *DSM-IV-TR.* Reprinted with permission from Diagnostic and Statistical Manual of Mental Disorders (4th ed., text revision). © 2000 American Psychiatric Association.

& Walters, 2005) and 5.7% at some point during their lifetime (Kessler, Berglund, Demler, Jin, & Walters, 2005). This is still a large number, making GAD one of the most common anxiety disorders. Similar rates are reported from around the world—for example, from rural South Africa (Bhagwanjee, Parekh, Paruk, Petersen, & Subedar, 1998). However, relatively few people with GAD come for treatment compared to patients with panic disorder. Anxiety clinics like ours report that only approximately 10% of their patients meet criteria for GAD compared to 30% to 50% for panic disorder. This may be because most patients with GAD seek help from their primary care doctors, where they are found in large numbers (Roy-Byrne & Katon, 2000).

About two-thirds of individuals with GAD are female in both clinical samples (Woodman, Noyes, Black, Schlosser, & Yagla, 1999; Yonkers, Warshaw, Massion, & Keller, 1996) and epidemiological studies (where individuals with GAD are identified from population surveys), which include people who do not necessarily seek treatment (Blazer, George, & Hughes, 1991; Carter, Wittchen, Pfister, & Kessler, 2001; Wittchen, Zhao, Kessler, & Eaton, 1994). But this sex ratio may be specific to developed countries. In the South African study mentioned here, GAD was more common in males.

Some people with GAD report onset in early adulthood, usually in response to a life stressor. Nevertheless, most studies find that GAD is associated with an earlier and more gradual onset than most other anxiety disorders (Anderson, Noyes, & Crowe, 1984; Barlow, 2002; Brown et al., 1994; Sanderson & Barlow, 1990; Woodman et al., 1999). The median age of onset based on interviews is 31 (Kessler, Berglund, et al., 2005), but like Irene, many people have felt anxious and tense all their lives. Once it develops, GAD, like most anxiety disorders, follows a chronic course, characterized by waxing and waning of symptoms.

GAD is prevalent among older adults. In the large national comorbidity study, GAD was found to be most common in the group over 45 years of age and least common in the youngest group, ages 15 to 24 (Wittchen et al., 1994).

Flint (1994) reported prevalence rates of GAD in older adults to be as high as 7%. We also know that the use of minor tranquilizers in the elderly is high, ranging from 17% to 50% in one study (Salzman, 1991). It is not entirely clear why drugs are prescribed with such frequency for the elderly. One possibility is that the drugs may not be entirely intended for anxiety. Prescribed drugs may be primarily for sleeping problems or other secondary effects of medical illnesses. In any case, benzodiazepines (minor tranquilizers) interfere with cognitive function and put the elderly at greater risks for falling down and breaking bones, particularly their hips (Barlow, 2002). In a classic study, Rodin and Langer (1977) demonstrated that older adults may be particularly susceptible to anxiety about failing health or other life situations that begin to diminish whatever control they retain over events in their lives. This increasing lack of control, failing health, and gradual loss of meaningful functions may be a particularly unfortunate by-product of the way the elderly are treated in Western culture. The result is substantial impairment in quality of life in older adults with GAD (Wetherell et al., 2004). If it were possible to change our attitudes and behavior, we might well reduce the frequency of anxiety, depression, and early death among our elderly citizens.

Causes

What causes GAD? We have learned a great deal in the past several years. As with most anxiety disorders, there seems to be a generalized biological vulnerability, as is reflected in studies examining a genetic contribution to GAD. This conclusion is based on studies showing that GAD tends to run in families (Noyes, Clarkson, Crowe, Yates, & McChesney, 1987; Noyes et al., 1992). Twin studies strengthen this suggestion (Kendler, Neale, Kessler, Heath, & Eaves, 1992). Kendler and colleagues (1995; Hettema, Prescott, Myers, Neale, & Kendler, 2005) confirmed that what seems to be inherited is the tendency to become anxious rather than GAD itself.

For years, clinicians thought that people who were generally anxious had simply not focused their anxiety on anything specific. Thus, such anxiety was described as "free floating." But now scientists have looked more closely and have discovered some interesting distinctions from other anxiety disorders.

The first hints of difference were found in the physiological responsivity of individuals with GAD. It is interesting that individuals with GAD do not respond as strongly to stressors as individuals with anxiety disorders in which panic is more prominent. Several studies have found that individuals with GAD show *less responsiveness* on most physiological measures, such as heart rate, blood pressure, skin conductance, and respiration rate (Borkovec & Hu, 1990; Hoehn-Saric, McLeod, & Zimmerli, 1989; Roemer, Orsillo, & Barlow, 2002), than do individuals with other anxiety disorders. Therefore, people with GAD have been called *autonomic restrictors* (Barlow et al., 1996; Thayer, Friedman, & Borkovec, 1996).

When individuals with GAD are compared to nonanxious "normal" participants, the one physiological measure that consistently distinguishes the anxious group is muscle tension (Marten et al., 1993). People with GAD are chronically tense. For this reason, one proposal for *DSM-5* is to highlight muscle tension as the principal physical symptom in diagnosing GAD (Andrews et al., 2010). To understand this phenomenon of chronic muscle tension, we may have to know what's going on in the minds of people with GAD. With new methods from cognitive science, we are beginning to uncover the sometimes-unconscious mental processes ongoing in GAD (McNally, 1996).

There is evidence that individuals with GAD are highly sensitive to threat in general, particularly to a threat that has personal relevance—that is, they allocate their attention more readily to sources of threat than do people who are not anxious (Aikins & Craske, 2001; Barlow, 2002; Bradley, Mogg, White, Groom, & de Bono, 1999; MacLeod, Mathews, & Tata, 1986; Mathews, 1997). This high sensitivity may have arisen in early stressful experiences where they learned that the world is dangerous and out of control, and they might not be able to cope (generalized psychological vulnerability). Furthermore, this acute awareness of potential threat seems to be entirely automatic or unconscious. Using the Stroop color-naming task described in Chapter 2, MacLeod and Mathews (1991) presented threatening words on a screen for only 20 milliseconds and still found that individuals with GAD were slower to name the colors of the words than were nonanxious individuals. Remember that in this task words in colored letters are presented briefly and participants are asked to name the *color* rather than the word. The fact that the colors of threatening words were named more slowly suggests the *words* were more relevant to people with GAD, which interfered with their naming the color—even though the words were not present long enough for the individuals to be conscious of them.

How do mental processes link up with the tendency of individuals with GAD to be autonomic restrictors? Tom Borkovec and his colleagues noticed that although the peripheral autonomic arousal of individuals with GAD is restricted, they showed intense cognitive processing in the frontal lobes as indicated by EEG activity, particularly in the left hemisphere. This finding would suggest frantic, intense thought processes or worry without accompanying images (which would be reflected by activity in the right hemisphere of the brain rather than the left) (Borkovec, Alcaine, & Behar, 2004). Borkovec suggests that this kind of worry may be what causes these individuals to be autonomic restrictors (Borkovec, Shadick, & Hopkins, 1991; Roemer & Borkovec, 1993)—that is, they are thinking so hard about upcoming problems that they don't have the attentional capacity left for the all-important process of creating images of the potential threat, images that would elicit more substantial negative affect and autonomic activity. They *avoid* images associated with the threat (Borkovec et al., 2004; Craske, 1999; Fisher & Wells, 2009). But from the point of view of therapy, it is important to "process" the images and negative affect associated with anxiety (Craske & Barlow,

2006; Zinbarg, Craske, & Barlow, 2006). Because people with GAD do not seem to engage in this process, they may avoid much of the unpleasantness and pain associated with the negative affect and imagery, but they are never able to work through their problems and arrive at solutions. Therefore, they become chronic worriers, with accompanying autonomic inflexibility and severe muscle tension. In summary, some people inherit a tendency to be tense (generalized biological vulnerability), and they develop a sense early on that important events in their lives may be uncontrollable and potentially dangerous (generalized psychological vulnerability). Significant stress makes them apprehensive and vigilant. This sets off intense worry with resulting physiological changes, leading to GAD (Roemer et al., 2002; Turovsky & Barlow, 1996). This model is consistent with our view of anxiety as a future-oriented mood state focused on potential danger or threat, as opposed to an emergency or alarm reaction to actual present danger. A model of the development of GAD is presented in ■ Figure 4.3.

Treatment

GAD is quite common, and available treatments, both drug and psychological, are reasonably effective. Benzodiazepines are most often prescribed for generalized anxiety, and the evidence indicates that they give some relief, at least in the short term. Few studies have looked at the effects of these drugs for a period longer than 8 weeks (Mathew & Hoffman, 2009). But the therapeutic effect is relatively modest. Furthermore, benzodiazepines carry some risks. First, they seem to impair both cognitive and motor functioning (see, for example, Hindmarch, 1986, 1990; O'Hanlon, Haak, Blaauw, & Riemersma, 1982; van Laar, Volkerts, & Verbaten, 2001). The drugs may impair driving, and in older adults they seem to be associated with falls (Ray, Gurwitz, Decker, & Kennedy, 1992; Wang, Bohn, Glynn, Mogun, & Avorn, 2001). More important, benzodiazepines seem to produce both psychological and physical dependence, making it difficult for people to stop taking them (Mathew & Hoffman, 2009; Noyes, Garvey, Cook, & Suelzer, 1991; Rickels, Schweizer, Case, & Greenblatt, 1990). There is reasonably wide agreement that the optimal use of benzodiazepines is for the short-term relief of anxiety associated with a temporary crisis or stressful event, such as a family problem (Craske & Barlow, 2006). Under these circumstances, a physician may prescribe a benzodiazepine until the crisis is resolved but for no more than a week or two. There is stronger evidence for the usefulness of antidepressants in the treatment of GAD; these drugs may prove to be a better choice (Brawman-Mintzer, 2001; Mathew & Hoffman, 2009).

In the short term, psychological treatments seem to confer about the same benefit as drugs in the treatment of GAD, but psychological treatments are probably more effective in the long term (Barlow, Allen, & Basden, 2007; Barlow & Lehman, 1996; Borkovec, Newman, Pincus, & Lytle, 2002; Roemer et al., 2002). Recent reports of innovations in brief psychological treatments are encouraging.

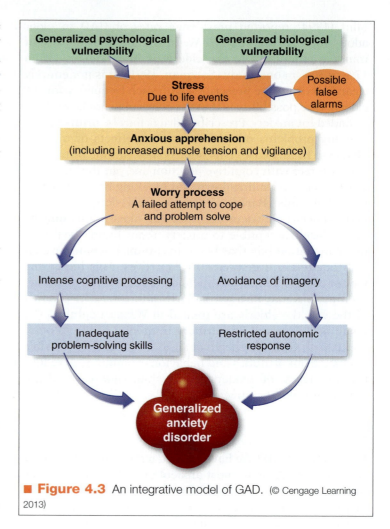

■ **Figure 4.3** An integrative model of GAD. (© Cengage Learning 2013)

Because we now know that individuals with GAD seem to avoid "feelings" of anxiety and the negative affect associated with threatening images, clinicians have designed treatments to help patients with GAD process the threatening information on an emotional level, using images, so that they will feel (rather than avoid feeling) anxious. In the early 1990s, we developed a cognitive-behavioral treatment (CBT) for GAD in which patients evoke the worry process during therapy sessions and confront anxiety-provoking images and thoughts head-on. The patient learns to use cognitive therapy and other coping techniques to counteract and control the worry process (Craske & Barlow, 2006; Wetherell, Gatz, & Craske, 2003). In a major study, a brief adaptation of this treatment was also used successfully to decrease anxiety and improve quality of life in a primary care office (family doctors and nurses) where GAD is a frequent complaint (Rollman, Belnap, & Mazumdar, 2005). Studies indicate that brief psychological treatments such as these alter the sometimes-unconscious cognitive biases associated with GAD (Mathews, Mogg, Kentish, & Eysenck, 1995; Mogg, Bradley, Millar, & White, 1995).

Despite this success, it is clear we need more powerful treatments, both drug and psychological, for this chronic, treatment-resistant condition. Recently, a new psychological treatment for GAD has been developed that incorporates procedures focusing on acceptance rather than avoidance of distressing thoughts and feelings in addition to cognitive therapy. Meditational approaches help teach the patient to be more tolerant of these feelings (Orsillo, Roemer, & Barlow, 2003; Roemer & Orsillo, 2002; Roemer et al., 2002). Preliminary results are encouraging (Roemer & Orsillo, 2007).

There is particularly encouraging evidence that psychological treatments are effective with children who suffer from generalized anxiety (Albano & Hack, 2004; Furr et al., 2009). Kendall and colleagues (1997) randomly assigned 94 children from 9 to 13 years of age to CBT or a wait-list control group. The majority of the children were diagnosed with GAD, but some had social phobia or separation anxiety. Based on teacher ratings, 70% of the treated children were functioning normally after treatment, gains maintained for at least 1 year. In a major clinical trial with children, CBT and the antidepressant drug sertraline (Zoloft) were equally effective immediately following treatment compared to taking placebo pills for children with GAD and other related disorders, but the combination of CBT and sertraline was even better, with 80% showing substantial improvement versus 24% on placebo (Walkup et al., 2008). Progress is also being made in adapting psychological treatments for older adults (Beck & Stanley, 1997; Stanley et al., 2003; Wetherell, Lenze, & Stanley, 2005). One large clinical trial demonstrated very clearly the efficiency of this treatment for adults over 60 compared to the usual care they received (Stanley et al., 2009).

After trying a number of different drugs, Irene was treated with the CBT approach developed at our clinic and found herself more able to cope with life. She completed college and graduate school, married, and is successful in her career as a counselor in a nursing home. But even now Irene finds it difficult to relax and stop worrying. She continues to experience mild to moderate anxiety, particularly when experiencing stress; she occasionally takes minor tranquilizers to support her psychological coping skills.

Concept Check 4.2

True (T) or false (F)?

1. ___ GAD is characterized by muscle tension, mental agitation, irritability, sleeping difficulties, and susceptibility to fatigue.
2. ___ Most studies show that in the majority of cases of GAD, onset is early in adulthood as an immediate response to a life stressor.
3. ___ GAD is prevalent in the elderly and in females in our society.
4. ___ GAD has no genetic basis.
5. ___ Cognitive-behavioral treatment and other psychological treatments for GAD are probably better than drug therapies in the long run.

Panic Disorder with and without Agoraphobia

> **What are the essential features of panic disorder?**

Did you have a relative, an eccentric aunt, for example, who never seemed to leave the house? Family reunions or visits always had to be at her house. She never went anywhere else. Most people attributed their old aunt's behavior to her being a little odd or perhaps just not fond of travel. She was warm and friendly when people came to visit, so she retained contact with the family.

Your aunt may not have been just odd or eccentric. She may have suffered from a debilitating anxiety disorder called **panic disorder with agoraphobia (PDA)**, in which individuals experience severe, unexpected panic attacks; they may think they're dying or otherwise losing control. Because they never know when an attack might occur, they develop **agoraphobia**, fear and avoidance of situations in which they would feel unsafe in the event of a panic attack or symptoms. These situations include those from which it would be hard or embarrassing to escape to get home or to a hospital. In severe cases, people with PDA are unable to leave the house, sometimes for years on end, as in the example of Mrs. M.

Mrs. M. | Self-Imprisoned

Mrs. M. was 67 years old and lived in a second-floor walk-up apartment in a lower-middle-class section of the city. Her adult daughter, one of her few remaining contacts with the world, had requested an evaluation with Mrs. M.'s consent. I rang the bell and entered a narrow hallway; Mrs. M. was nowhere in sight. Knowing that she lived on the second floor, I walked up the stairs and knocked on the door at the top. When I heard Mrs. M. ask me to come in, I opened the door.

panic disorder with agoraphobia (PDA) Fear and avoidance of situations the person believes might induce a dreaded panic attack.
agoraphobia Anxiety about being in places or situations from which escape might be difficult.

She was sitting in her living room, and I could quickly see the layout of the rest of the apartment. The living room was in the front; the kitchen was in the back, adjoining a porch. To the right of the stairs was the one bedroom, with a bathroom opening from it.

Mrs. M. was glad to see me and friendly, offering me coffee and homemade cookies. I was the first person she had seen in 3 weeks. Mrs. M. had not left that apartment in 20 years, and she had suffered from PDA for more than 30 years.

As she told her story, Mrs. M. conveyed vivid images of a wasted life. And yet she continued to struggle in the face of adversity and to make the best she could of her limited existence. Even areas in her apartment signaled the potential for terrifying panic attacks. She had not answered the door herself for the past 15 years because she was afraid to look into the hallway. She could enter her kitchen and go into the areas containing the stove and refrigerator, but for the past 10 years she had not been to the part of the room that overlooked the backyard or out onto the back porch. Thus, her life for the past decade had been confined to her bedroom, her living room, and the front half of her kitchen. She relied on her adult daughter to bring groceries and visit once a week. Her only other visitor was the parish priest, who came to deliver communion every 2 to 3 weeks when he could. Her only other contact with the outside world was through the television and the radio. Her husband, who had abused both alcohol and Mrs. M., had died 10 years earlier of alcohol-related causes. Early in her stressful marriage she had her first terrifying panic attack and had gradually withdrawn from the world. As long as she stayed in her apartment, she was relatively free of panic. Therefore, and because in her mind there were few reasons left near the end of her life to venture out, she declined treatment.

Clinical Description

At the beginning of the chapter, we talked about the related phenomena of anxiety and panic. In PDA, anxiety and panic are combined with *phobic avoidance* in an intricate relationship that can become as devastating as it was for Mrs. M. Many people who have panic attacks do not necessarily develop panic disorder. Similarly, many people experience anxiety and panic without developing agoraphobia. In those cases, the disorder is called **panic disorder without agoraphobia (PD)**.

To meet criteria for panic disorder (with or without agoraphobia), a person must experience an unexpected panic attack and develop substantial anxiety over the possibility of having another attack or about the implications of the attack or its consequences. In other words, the person must think that each attack is a sign of impending death or incapacitation. A few individuals do not report concern about another

attack but still change their behavior in a way that indicates the distress the attacks cause them. They may avoid going to certain places or neglect their duties around the house for fear an attack might occur if they are too active.

The Development of Agoraphobia

Many people with panic disorder develop agoraphobia. The term *agoraphobia* was coined in 1871 by Karl Westphal, a German physician, and, in the original Greek, refers to fear of the marketplace. This is an appropriate term because the *agora*, the Greek marketplace, was a busy, bustling area. One of the most stressful places for individuals with agoraphobia today is the shopping mall, the modern-day agora.

Almost all agoraphobic avoidance behavior is simply a complication of severe, unexpected panic attacks (Barlow, 2002; Craske & Barlow, 1988, 2008). Simply put, if you have had unexpected panic attacks and are afraid you may have another one, you want to be in a safe place or at least with a safe person who knows what you are experiencing if another attack occurs so that you can quickly get to a hospital or at least go into your bedroom and lie down (the home is usually a safe place). We know that anxiety is diminished for individuals with agoraphobia if they think a location or person is "safe," even if there is nothing effective the person could do if something bad did happen. For these reasons, when they do venture outside their homes, people with agoraphobia always plan for rapid escape (for example, by sitting near the door). A list of typical situations commonly avoided by someone with agoraphobia is found in Table 4.1.

Although agoraphobic behavior almost always is closely tied to the occasions of panic initially, it can become relatively independent of panic attacks (Craske & Barlow, 1988; Craske, Rapee, & Barlow, 1988; White & Barlow, 2002). In other words, an individual who has not had a panic attack for years may still have strong agoraphobic avoidance, like Mrs. M. Agoraphobic avoidance seems to be determined for the most part by the extent to which you think or expect you might have another attack rather than by how many attacks you actually have or how severe they are. Thus, agoraphobic avoidance is simply one way of coping with unexpected panic attacks.

Other methods of coping with panic attacks include using (and eventually abusing) drugs and/or alcohol. Some individuals do not avoid agoraphobic situations but endure them with "intense dread." For example, people who must go to work each day or, perhaps, travel as part of the job will suffer untold agonies of anxiety and panic simply to achieve their goals. Thus, *DSM-IV-TR* notes that agoraphobia may be characterized either by avoiding the situations or by enduring them with marked distress. More recently, epidemiological surveys have identified a group of people who seem to have agoraphobia without ever having a panic attack or any fearful spells whatsoever (Wittchen, Gloster, Beesdo-Baum, Fava, & Craske, 2010). Further research is needed to confirm this condition.

Most patients with severe agoraphobic avoidance (and some with little) also display another cluster of avoidant behaviors that we call *interoceptive avoidance*, or avoid-

Table 4.1 Typical Situations Avoided by People with Agoraphobia

Shopping malls	Being far from home
Cars (as driver or passenger)	Staying at home alone
Buses	Waiting in line
Trains	Supermarkets
Subways	Stores
Wide streets	Crowds
Tunnels	Planes
Restaurants	Elevators
Theaters	Escalators

Source: Adapted, with permission, from Barlow, D. H., & Craske, M. G. (2007). *Mastery of your anxiety and panic* (4th ed., p. 5). New York: Oxford University Press.

ance of internal physical sensations (Barlow & Craske, 2007; Brown, White, & Barlow, 2005; Craske & Barlow, 2008; Shear et al., 1997). These behaviors involve removing yourself from situations or activities that might produce the physiological arousal that somehow resembles the beginnings of a panic attack. Some patients might avoid exercise because it produces increased cardiovascular activity or faster respiration that reminds them of panic attacks and makes them think one might be beginning. Other patients might avoid sauna baths or any rooms in which they might perspire. Psychopathologists are beginning to recognize that this cluster of avoidance behaviors is every bit as important as more classical agoraphobic avoidance.

Statistics

PD or PDA is fairly common. Approximately 2.7% of the population meet criteria for PD or PDA during a given 1-year period (Kessler, Chiu, et al., 2005; Kessler, Chiu, Jin, et al., 2006) and 4.7% met them at some point during their lives, two-thirds of them women (Eaton, Kessler, Wittchen, & Magee, 1994; Kessler, Berglund, et al., 2005). Another smaller group (1.4% at some point during their lives) develops agoraphobia without ever having a full-blown panic attack. Typically, these individuals will have only one or two severe symptoms, such as dizziness, rather than the minimum of four required to be called a panic attack. This condition is called *agoraphobia without a history of panic disorder,* but it looks much the same as PDA and is treated with the same treatments (Craske & Barlow, 2008; Kessler, Chiu, Jin, et al., 2006). Onset of panic disorder usually occurs in early adult life—from midteens through about 40 years of age. The median age of onset is between 20 and 24 (Kessler, Berglund, et al., 2005). Most initial unexpected panic attacks begin at or after puberty. Furthermore, many prepubertal children who are seen by general medical practitio-

ners have symptoms of hyperventilation that may well be panic attacks. However, these children do not report fear of dying or losing control—perhaps because they are not at a stage of their cognitive development where they can make these attributions (Nelles & Barlow, 1988).

Important work on anxiety in the elderly suggests that health and vitality are the primary focus of anxiety in the elderly population (Wisocki, 1988; Wolitzky-Taylor, Castriotta, Lenze, Stanley, & Craske, 2010). Lindesay (1991) studied 60 confirmed cases of phobic disorder in the elderly and found that they differed from younger adults in several ways, such as age of onset and prevalence. The primary phobia in this group was agoraphobia, which had a late onset (after age 50) and was often related to a stressful life event, usually an illness or injury. In general, the prevalence of PD or PDA decreases among the elderly, from 5.7% at ages 30–44 to 2.0% or less after age 60 (Kessler, Berglund, et al., 2005).

As we have said, most (75% or more) of those who suffer from agoraphobia are women (Barlow, 2002; Myers et al., 1984; Thorpe & Burns, 1983). The most logical explanation is cultural (Arrindell et al., 2003a; Wolitzky-Taylor et al., 2010). It is more accepted for women to report fear and to avoid numerous situations. Men, however, are expected to be stronger and braver—to "tough it out." The higher the severity of agoraphobic avoidance, the greater the proportion of women. For example, in our clinic, out of a group of patients suffering from panic disorder with mild agoraphobia, 72% were women; but if the agoraphobia was moderate, the percentage was 81%. Similarly, if agoraphobia was severe, the percentage was 89%.

What happens to men who have severe unexpected panic attacks? Is cultural disapproval of fear in men so strong that most of them simply endure panic? The answer seems to be

DSM Disorder Criteria Summary
Panic Disorder with Agoraphobia

Features of panic disorder with agoraphobia include the following:

> Recurrent unexpected panic attacks

> One or more of the following during the month after a panic attack: (1) persistent concern about having additional attacks; (2) worry about the implications of the attack; (3) a significant change in behavior related to the attacks.

> Anxiety about being in places or situations from which escape might be difficult or embarrassing, such as being in a crowd, traveling on a bus, or waiting in line.

Source: Based on *DSM-IV-TR.* Reprinted with permission from Diagnostic and Statistical Manual of Mental Disorders (4th ed., text revision). © 2000 American Psychiatric Association.

panic disorder without agoraphobia (PD) Panic attacks experienced without development of agoraphobia.

"no." A large proportion of males with unexpected panic attacks cope in a culturally acceptable way: They consume large amounts of alcohol. The problem is that they become dependent on alcohol, and many begin the long downward spiral into serious addiction. Thus, males may end up with an even more severe problem than PDA.

Cultural Influences

Panic disorder exists worldwide, although its expression may vary from place to place. In Lesotho, Africa, the prevalence of panic disorder (and GAD) was found to be equal to or greater than in North America (Hollifield, Katon, Spain, & Pule, 1990). In a more comprehensive study, prevalence rates for panic disorder were remarkably similar in the United States, Canada, Puerto Rico, New Zealand, Italy, Korea, and Taiwan, with only Taiwan showing somewhat lower rates (Horwath & Weissman, 1997). Rates are also similar among different ethnic groups in the United States, including African Americans. Furthermore, black and white patients with panic disorder show no significant differences in symptoms (Friedman, Paradis, & Hatch, 1994). However, note that panic disorder often co-occurs with hypertension in African American patients (Neal, Nagle-Rich, & Smucker, 1994; Neal-Barnett & Smith, 1997).

Somatic symptoms of anxiety may be emphasized in Third World cultures. Subjective feelings of dread or angst may not be a part of some cultures—that is, individuals in these cultures do not attend to these feelings and do not report them, focusing more on bodily sensations (Asmal & Stein, 2009; Lewis-Fernández et al., 2010). An anxiety-related, culturally defined syndrome prominent among Hispanic Americans, particularly those from the Caribbean, is called *ataques de nervios* (Hinton, Chong, Pollack, Barlow, & McNally, 2008; Hinton, Lewis-Fernández, & Pollack, 2009; Liebowitz et al., 1994). The symptoms of an *ataque* seem similar to those of a panic attack, although such manifestations as shouting uncontrollably or bursting into tears may be associated more often with *ataque* than with panic.

Finally, Devon Hinton, a psychiatrist/anthropologist, and his colleagues have recently described a fascinating manifestation of panic disorder among Khmer (Cambodian) and Vietnamese refugees in the United States. Both of these groups seem to suffer from a high rate of panic disorder. But a substantial number of these panic attacks are associated with orthostatic dizziness (dizziness if one stands up quickly) and "sore neck." What Hinton's group discovered is that the Khmer concept of *kyol goeu* or "wind overload" (too much wind or gas in the body, which may cause blood vessels to burst) becomes the focus of catastrophic thinking during panic attacks (Hinton & Good, 2009; Hinton, Pollack, Pich, Fama, & Barlow, 2005; Hinton, Hofmann, Pitman, Pollack, & Barlow, 2008).

Nocturnal Panic

Think back to the case of Gretchen, whose panic attack was described earlier. She was sound asleep when it happened. Approximately 60% of the people with panic disorder have experienced such nocturnal attacks (Craske & Rowe, 1997;

Uhde, 1994). In fact, panic attacks occur more often between 1:30 A.M. and 3:30 A.M. than any other time (Taylor et al., 1986). In some cases, people are afraid to go to sleep at night. What's happening to them? Are they having nightmares? Research indicates they are not. Nocturnal attacks are studied in a sleep laboratory. Patients spend a few nights sleeping while attached to an electroencephalograph machine that monitors their brain waves (see Chapter 3). We all go through various stages of sleep that are reflected by different patterns on the electroencephalogram. We have learned that nocturnal panics occur during delta wave or slow wave sleep, which typically occurs several hours after we fall asleep and is the deepest stage of sleep. People with panic disorder often begin to panic when they start sinking into delta sleep, then they awaken amid an attack. Because there is no obvious reason for them to be anxious or panicky when they are sound asleep, most of these individuals think they are dying (Craske & Barlow, 1988; Craske & Rowe, 1997).

What causes nocturnal panic? Currently, our best information is that the change in stages of sleep to slow wave sleep produces physical sensations of "letting go" that are frightening to an individual with panic disorder (Craske, Lang, Mystkowski, Zucker, & Bystritsky, 2002). This process is described more fully later when we discuss causes of panic disorder. Several other events also occur during sleep that resemble nocturnal panic and are mistakenly thought by some to be the cause of nocturnal panic. Initially, these events were thought to be nightmares, but nightmares and other dreamlike activity occur only during a stage of sleep characterized by rapid eye movement (REM) sleep, which typically occurs much later in the sleep cycle. Therefore, people are not dreaming when they have nocturnal panics, a conclusion consistent with patient reports. A related phenomenon occurring in children is called *sleep terrors*, which we describe in more detail in Chapter 8 (Durand, 2006). Often children scream and get out of bed as if something were after them. However, they do not wake up and have no memory of the event in the morning. In contrast, individuals experiencing nocturnal panic attacks do wake up and later remember the event clearly. Sleep terrors also tend to occur at a later stage of sleep (stage 4 sleep), a stage associated with sleepwalking.

Finally, there is a fascinating condition called *isolated sleep paralysis* that seems culturally determined. Isolated sleep paralysis occurs during the transitional state between sleep and waking, when a person is either falling asleep or waking up but mostly when waking up. During this period, the individual is unable to move and experiences a surge of terror that resembles a panic attack; occasionally, there are also vivid hallucinations. One possible explanation is that REM sleep is spilling over into the waking cycle. This seems likely because one feature of REM sleep is lack of bodily movement. Another is vivid dreams, which could account for the experience of hallucination. Paradis, Friedman, and Hatch (1997) confirmed that the occurrence of isolated sleep paralysis was significantly higher in African Americans with panic disorder (59.6%) as compared with other groups (see ■ Figure 4.4). More recently, Ramsawh and colleagues (2008) replicated this finding and discovered that African Americans with isolated sleep paralysis had a history of trauma and more frequent diagnoses of panic disorder and post-traumatic stress disorder than African Americans without isolated sleep paralysis.

Causes

It is not possible to understand panic disorder (with or without agoraphobia) without referring to the triad of contributing factors mentioned throughout this book: biological, psychological, and social. Strong evidence indicates that agoraphobia, for the most part, develops after a person has unexpected panic attacks (or panic-like sensations); but whether agoraphobia develops and how severe it becomes seem to be socially and culturally determined, as we noted earlier. Panic attacks and panic disorder, however, seem to be related most strongly to biological and psychological factors and their interaction.

According to the triple vulnerability model (Bouton et al., 2001; Bouton, 2005; Suárez et al., 2009; White & Barlow, 2002), we all inherit—some more than others—a vulnerability to stress, which is a tendency to be generally neurobiologically overreactive to the events of daily life (generalized biological vulnerability). But some people are also more likely than others to have an emergency alarm reaction (unexpected panic attack) when confronted with stress-producing events. (Remember that other people might be more likely to have headaches or high blood pres-

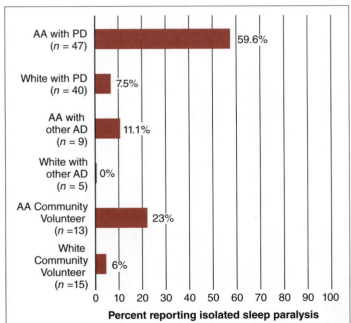

■ **Figure 4.4** Isolated sleep paralysis in African Americans (AA) and Caucasian Americans with panic disorder (PD), other anxiety disorder (AD) but not panic disorder, and community volunteers with no disorder. (Adapted from Paradis, C. M., Friedman, S., & Hatch, M., 1997. Isolated sleep paralysis in African-Americans with panic disorder. *Cultural Diversity & Mental Health, 3,* 69–76.)

sure in response to the same kinds of stress.) Particular situations quickly become associated in an individual's mind with external and internal cues that were present during the panic attack (Bouton et al., 2001). The next time the person's heart rate increases during exercise, she might assume she is having a panic attack (conditioning). Harmless exercise is an example of an internal cue or a conditioned stimulus for a panic attack. Being in a movie theater when panic first occurred would be an external cue that might become a conditioned stimulus for future panics. Because these cues become associated with a number of different internal and external stimuli through a learning process, we call them *learned alarms*.

But none of this would make much difference without the next step. An individual must be susceptible to developing anxiety over the possibility of having another panic attack (a generalized psychological vulnerability)—that is, he or she thinks the physical sensations associated with the panic attack mean something terrible is about to happen, perhaps death. This is what creates panic disorder. This tendency to believe that unexpected bodily sensations are dangerous reflects a specific psychological vulnerability to develop panic and related disorders. This causal sequence is depicted in ■ Figure 4.5.

Approximately 8% to 12% of the population has an occasional unexpected panic attack, often during a period of intense stress during the past year (Kessler et al., 2006; Mattis & Ollendick, 2002; Norton, Harrison, Hauch, & Rhodes, 1985; Suárez et al., 2009; Telch, Lucas, & Nelson, 1989). Most of these people do not develop anxiety (Telch et al., 1989). They seem to attribute the attack to events of the moment, such as an argument with a friend, something they ate, or a bad day, and go on with their lives.

The influential cognitive theories of David Clark (1986, 1996) explicate in more detail some cognitive processes that may be ongoing in the development of panic disorder. Clark emphasizes the specific psychological vulnerability of people with this disorder to interpret normal physical sensations in a catastrophic way. In other words, although we all typically experience rapid heartbeat after exercise, if you have a psychological or cognitive vulnerability, you might interpret the response as dangerous and feel a surge of anxiety. This anxiety, in turn, produces more physical sensations because of the action of the sympathetic nervous system, you perceive these additional sensations as even more dangerous, and a vicious cycle begins that results in a panic attack. Thus, Clark emphasizes the cognitive process as most important in panic disorder.

Treatment

As we noted in Chapter 1, research on the effectiveness of new treatments is important to psychopathology. Responses to certain specific treatments, whether drug or psychological, may indicate the causes of the disorder. We now discuss the benefits and some drawbacks of medication, psychological interventions, and a combination of these two treatments.

Virtual Reality Therapy: A New Technique on the Treatment of Anxiety Disorders

"I just feel really closed in, I feel like my heart is going to start beating really fast. . . . I won't be able to get enough air, I won't be able to breathe, and I'll pass out."

Go to Psychology CourseMate at www.cengagebrain.com to watch this video.

Medication

A large number of drugs affecting the noradrenergic, serotonergic, or GABA–benzodiazepine neurotransmitter systems or some combination seem effective in treating panic disorder, including high-potency benzodiazepines, the newer serotonin-specific reuptake inhibitors (SSRIs) such as Prozac and Paxil, and the closely related serotonin-norepinephrine reuptake inhibitors (SNRIs) such as venlafaxine (Barlow, 2002; Barlow & Craske, 2007; Pollack, 2005; Pollack & Simon, 2009; Spiegel, Wiegel, Baker, & Greene, 2000).

Each class of drugs has advantages and disadvantages too. SSRIs are currently the indicated drug for panic disorder based on all available evidence, although sexual dysfunction seems to occur in 75% or more of people taking these medications (Lecrubier, Bakker, et al., 1997; Lecrubier, Judge, et al., 1997). However, high-potency benzodiazepines such as alprazolam (Xanax), commonly used for panic disorder, work quickly but are hard to stop taking because of psychological and physical dependence and addiction. Therefore, they are not recommended as strongly as the SSRIs. Nevertheless, benzodiazepines remain the most widely used class of drugs in practice (Bruce et al., 2003). Also, all benzodiazepines adversely affect cognitive and motor functions to some degree. Therefore, people taking them in high doses often find their ability to drive a car or study somewhat reduced.

Approximately 60% of patients with panic disorder are free of panic as long as they stay on an effective drug

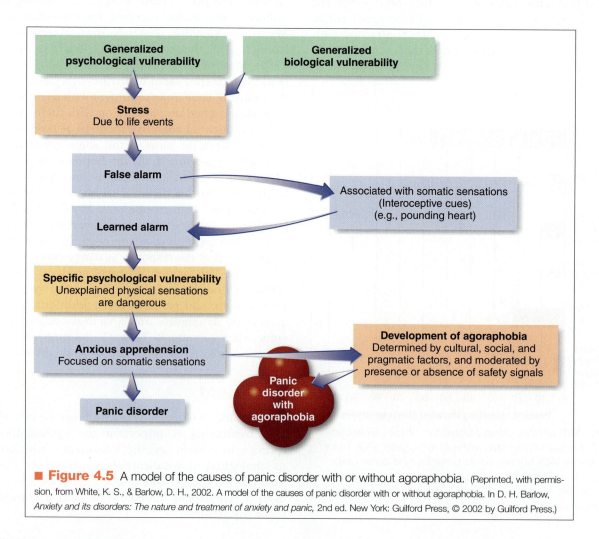

■ Figure 4.5 A model of the causes of panic disorder with or without agoraphobia. (Reprinted, with permission, from White, K. S., & Barlow, D. H., 2002. A model of the causes of panic disorder with or without agoraphobia. In D. H. Barlow, *Anxiety and its disorders: The nature and treatment of anxiety and panic,* 2nd ed. New York: Guilford Press, © 2002 by Guilford Press.)

(Lecrubier, Bakker, et al., 1997; Pollack & Simon, 2009), but 20% or more stop taking the drug before treatment is done (Otto, Behar, Smits, & Hofmann, 2009), and relapse rates are high (approximately 50%) once the medication is stopped (Hollon et al., 2005; Spiegel et al., 2000). The relapse rate is closer to 90% for those who stop taking benzodiazepines (see, for example, Fyer et al., 1987).

Psychological Intervention

Psychological treatments have proved effective for panic disorder. Originally, such treatments concentrated on reducing agoraphobic avoidance, using strategies based on exposure to feared situations. The strategy of exposure-based treatments is to arrange conditions in which the patient can gradually face the feared situations and learn there is nothing to fear. Sometimes the therapist accompanies the patients on their exposure exercises. At other times, the therapist simply helps patients structure their own exercises and provides them with a variety of psychological coping mechanisms to help them complete the exercises, which are typically arranged from least to most difficult. A sample of these is listed in Table 4.2.

Gradual exposure exercises, sometimes combined with anxiety-reducing coping mechanisms such as relaxation or breathing retraining, have proved effective in helping patients overcome agoraphobic behavior. As many as 70% of patients undergoing these treatments substantially improve as their anxiety and panic are reduced and their agoraphobic avoidance is greatly diminished. Few, however, are cured because many still experience some anxiety and panic attacks, although at a less severe level.

Effective psychological treatments have recently been developed that treat panic attacks directly (Barlow & Craske, 2007; Clark et al., 1994; Craske & Barlow, 2008; Klosko, Barlow, Tassinari, & Cerny, 1990). **Panic control treatment (PCT)** developed at one of our clinics concentrates on exposing patients with panic disorder to the cluster of interoceptive (physical) sensations that remind them of their panic attacks. The therapist attempts to create "mini" panic attacks in the office by having the pa-

tients exercise to elevate their heart rates or perhaps by spinning them in a chair to make them dizzy. A variety of exercises have been developed for this purpose. Patients also receive cognitive therapy. Basic attitudes and perceptions concerning the dangerousness of the feared but objectively harmless situations are identified and modified. Follow-up studies of patients who receive PCT indicate that most of them remain better after at least 2 years (Craske & Barlow, 2008; Craske, Brown, & Barlow, 1991). Remaining agoraphobic behavior can then be treated with more standard exposure exercises. Although these treatments are quite effective, they are relatively new and not yet available to many individuals who suffer from panic disorder because administering them requires therapists to have advanced training (Barlow, Levitt, & Bufka, 1999; McHugh & Barlow, 2010).

Combined Psychological and Drug Treatments

Partly because primary care physicians are usually the first clinicians to treat those suffering from panic disorder and psychological treatments are not available in those settings, when patients do get referred for psychological treatment, they are often already taking medications. So, important questions are as follows: How do these treatments compare to each other? And do they work together? One major study sponsored by the National Institute of Mental Health looked at the separate and combined effects of psychological and drug treatments (Barlow, Gorman, Shear, & Woods, 2000). In this double-blind study, 312 carefully screened patients with panic disorder were treated at four sites, two known for their expertise with medication treatments and two known for their expertise with psychological treatments. The purpose of this arrangement was to control for any bias that might affect the results because of the allegiance of investigators committed to one type of treatment or the other. Patients were randomly assigned into five treatment conditions: psychological treatment alone (CBT); drug treatment alone (imipramine—IMI—a tricyclic antidepressant, was used because this study was begun before the SSRIs were available); a combined treatment condition (IMI + CBT); and two "control" conditions, one using placebo alone (PBO), and one using PBO + CBT (to determine the extent to which any advantage for combined treatment was caused by placebo contribution).

■ Figure 4.6 shows the results in terms of the percentage of patients who had responded to treatment by the end of 3 months of active treatment (termed the acute response), during which patients were seen weekly. Data were based on the judgment of an independent evaluator using the Panic Disorder Severity Scale and include patients who

Table 4.2 Situation-Exposure Tasks
(From Least to Most Difficult)

Shopping in a crowded supermarket for 30 minutes alone
Walking five blocks away from home alone
Driving on a busy highway for 5 miles with spouse and alone
Eating in a restaurant, seated in the middle
Watching a movie while seated in the middle of the row

Source: Adapted, with permission, from Barlow, D. H., & Craske, M. G. (2007). *Mastery of your anxiety and panic* (4th ed., p. 133). New York: Oxford University Press.

panic control treatment (PCT) Cognitive–behavioral treatment for panic attacks, involving gradual exposure to feared somatic sensations and modification of perceptions and attitudes about them.

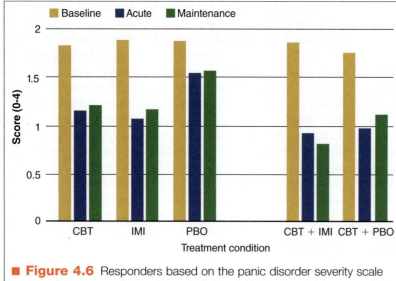

■ **Figure 4.6** Responders based on the panic disorder severity scale average item score after acute and after maintenance conditions. (Adapted from Barlow, D. H., Gorman, J. M., Shear, K. M., & Woods, S. W., 2000. Cognitive-behavioral therapy, imipramine, or their combination for panic disorder: A randomized controlled trial. *Journal of the American Medical Association, 283*(19), 2529–2536.)

dropped out along the way and were counted as failures. The data indicate that all treatment groups were significantly better than placebo, with some evidence that, among those who responded to treatment, people taking the drug alone did a little better than those receiving the CBT alone, but approximately the same number of patients responded to both treatments. Combined treatment was no better than individual treatments.

Figure 4.6 also presents the results after 6 additional months of maintenance treatment (9 months after treatment was initiated), during which patients were seen once per month. At this point, the results looked much as they did after initial treatment, except there was a slight advantage for combined treatment at this point and the number of people responding to placebo had diminished. Six months after treatment was discontinued, patients on medication, whether combined with CBT or not, had deteriorated somewhat, and those receiving CBT without the drug had retained most of their gains. Thus, psychological treatments seemed to perform better in the long run (six months after treatment had stopped).

Most studies show that drugs, particularly benzodiazepines, may interfere with the effects of psychological treatments (Craske & Barlow, 2008). Because of this, our multisite collaborative team asked whether a sequential strategy where one treatment was delayed until later and only given to those patients who didn't do as well as hoped would work better than giving both treatments at the same time. In this study, currently in preparation for publication, 256 patients with PD or PDA completed 3 months of initial treatment with CBT. Fifty-eight of those patients did not reach an optimal level of functioning (high end-state functioning) and entered a trial where they either received

continued CBT or paroxetine. The paroxetine was administered for up to 1 year, whereas the CBT was delivered for 3 months. At the end of the 1-year period, there was a strong suggestion, represented as a statistical trend, that more of the patients receiving paroxetine responded compared to those receiving continued CBT. Looking at it the other way, another study (Craske et al., 2005) found that in the primary care setting, adding CBT to the treatment of patients already on medications resulted in significant further improvement compared to those patients on medication who did not have CBT added. This suggests that a "stepped-care" approach, where one treatment, such as a psychological treatment, is offered first, followed by a second treatment, such as a drug treatment, for those patients who do not respond adequately, may be superior to combining treatments from the beginning.

Investigation is beginning on a different drug that, unlike existing drugs, looks like it might enhance the effects of the best psychological interventions. This drug, an antibiotic, is called D-cycloserine (DCS). Neuroscientists such as Michael Davis at Emory University have made some interesting discoveries about this drug. Davis found that when rats who had learned a fear response, such as when a light was paired with a brief electric shock, were put into extinction trials in which the light that they had learned to fear was no longer paired with a frightening electric shock, the animals gradually learned not to fear the light (their fear extinguished), as expected. However, giving them DCS during these extinction trials made extinction work faster and last longer (Walker, Ressler, Lu, & Davis, 2002). Further research indicated that this drug works in the amygdala, a structure in the brain involved in the learning and unlearning of fear and anxiety. DCS affects neurotransmitter flow in a way that strengthens the extinction process (Hofmann, 2007).

Most recently, several investigators have used this drug with humans suffering from social anxiety disorder or panic disorder. DCS is given approximately an hour before the extinction or exposure trial, and the individual does not take the drug on an ongoing basis. For example, Michael Otto and his colleagues in one of our clinics (Otto et al., 2010) administered the most effective cognitive-behavioral intervention to patients with panic disorder either with or without the drug. (That is, one group got the drug and the other group got a placebo, and neither the patients nor the therapists knew which group was getting the drug and which was not, making it a double-blind experiment.) The people who got the drug improved significantly more during treatment than those who didn't get the drug. This is particularly noteworthy because the feared cues for people with panic disorder are physical sensations, and the drug DCS helped extinguish anxiety triggered by sensations such as increased heart rate or respiration. Stefan Hofmann and colleagues

(2006) found a similar result with social anxiety disorder. If these results are replicated, we may have an important advance in treating anxiety disorders.

Concept Check 4.3

True (T) or false (F)?

1. ___ PD is a disorder in which an individual experiences anxiety and panic with phobic avoidance of what that person considers an "unsafe" situation.

2. ___ About 40% of the population meet the criteria for panic disorder at some point in their lives.

3. ___ Some individuals with panic disorder are suicidal, have nocturnal panic, and/or are agoraphobic.

4. ___ Psychological treatments such as PCT or CBT are highly effective for treating panic disorder.

Specific Phobia

> **What are the principal causes of specific phobia?**
> **What strategies are typically used to treat specific phobia?**

Remember Judy in Chapter 1? When she saw a film of the frog being dissected, Judy began feeling queasy. Eventually she reached the point of fainting if someone simply said "Cut it out". Judy has what we call a specific phobia.

Clinical Description

A **specific phobia** is an irrational fear of a specific object or situation that markedly interferes with an individual's ability to function. Many of you might be afraid of something that is not dangerous, such as going to the dentist, or have a greatly exaggerated fear of something that is only slightly dangerous, such as driving a car or flying. Surveys indicate that specific fears of a variety of objects or situations occur in a majority of the population (Myers et al., 1984). But the very commonness of fears, even severe fears, often causes people to trivialize the psychological disorder known as a specific phobia. These phobias, in their severe form, can be extremely disabling, as we saw with Judy.

For many people, phobias are a nuisance—sometimes an extremely inconvenient nuisance—but people can adapt to life with a phobia by simply working around it somehow. In upstate New York and New England, some people are afraid to drive in the snow. We have had people come to our clinics who have been so severely phobic that during the winter they were ready to uproot, change their jobs and their lives, and move south. That is one way of dealing with a phobia. We discuss some other ways at the end of this chapter.

Judy's phobia meets the *DSM-IV* criterion of marked and persistent fear that is set off by a specific object or situation. She recognized that her fear and anxiety are excessive or unreasonable and went to considerable lengths to avoid situations in which her phobic response might occur.

DSM Disorder Criteria Summary
Specific Phobia

Features of specific phobia include the following:

> Persistent, excessive or unreasonable fear of a specific object or situation (e.g., heights, animals, seeing blood) with a duration of at least 6 months

> Immediate anxious or fearful response upon exposure to the phobic object or situation

> Recognition that the fear is excessive or unreasonable, or marked distress about having the phobia

> The phobic situation or object is avoided or is endured with intense anxiety or distress

Source: Based on *DSM-IV-TR.* Reprinted with permission from Diagnostic and Statistical Manual of Mental Disorders (4th ed., text revision). © 2000 American Psychiatric Association.

There are as many phobias as there are objects and situations. The variety of Greek and Latin names contrived to describe phobias stuns the imagination. Table 4.3 gives only the phobias beginning with the letter "a" (Maser, 1985).

Before the publication of *DSM-IV* in 1994, no meaningful classification of specific phobias existed. However, we have now learned that distinct types of specific phobia differ in major ways. Four major subtypes of specific phobia

specific phobia Unreasonable fear of a specific object or situation that markedly interferes with daily life functioning.

Table 4.3 Phobias Beginning with "A"

Term	Fear of:
Acarophobia	Insects, mites
Achluophobia	Darkness, night
Acousticophobia	Sounds
Acrophobia	Heights
Aerophobia	Air currents, drafts, wind
Agoraphobia	Open spaces
Agyiophobia	Crossing the street
Aichmophobia	Sharp, pointed objects; knives; being touched by a finger
Ailurophobia	Cats
Algophobia	Pain
Amathophobia	Dust
Amychophobia	Laceration; being clawed, scratched
Androphobia	Men (and sex with men)
Anemophobia	Air currents, wind, drafts
Anginophobia	Angina pectoris (brief attacks of chest pain)
Anthropophobia	Human society
Antlophobia	Floods
Apeirophobia	Infinity
Aphephobia	Physical contact, being touched
Apiphobia	Bees, bee stings
Astraphobia	Thunderstorms, lightning
Ataxiophobia	Disorder
Atephobia	Ruin
Auroraphobia	Northern lights
Autophobia	Being alone, solitude, oneself, being egotistical

Source: Reprinted, with permission, from Maser, J. D. (1985). List of phobias. In A. H. Tuma & J. D. Maser (Eds.), *Anxiety and the anxiety disorders* (p. 805). Mahwah, NJ: Erlbaum, © 1985 Lawrence Erlbaum Associates.

have been identified: blood–injury–injection type, situational type (such as planes, elevators, or enclosed places), natural environment type (for example, heights, storms, and water), and animal type. A fifth category, "other," includes phobias that do not fit any of the four major subtypes (for example, situations that may lead to choking, vomiting, or contracting an illness or, in children, avoidance of loud sounds or costumed characters). Although this subtyping strategy is useful, we also know that most people who suffer from phobia tend to have multiple phobias of several types (Hofmann, Lehman, & Barlow, 1997). This fact weakens the utility of subtyping, but subtyping remains useful enough to most likely be retained in *DSM-5* (LeBeau et al., 2010).

Blood–Injury–Injection Phobia

How do phobia subtypes differ from each other? We have already seen one major difference in the case of Judy. Rather than the usual surge of activity in the sympathetic nervous system and increased heart rate and blood pressure, Judy experienced a marked drop in heart rate and blood pressure and fainted as a consequence. Many people who suffer from phobias and experience panic attacks in their feared situations report that they feel like they are going to faint, but they never do because their heart rate and blood pressure are actually increasing. Therefore, those with **blood–injury–injection phobias** almost always differ in their physiological reaction from people with other types of phobia (Barlow & Liebowitz, 1995; Craske, Antony, & Barlow, 2006; Hofmann, Alpers, & Pauli, 2009; Öst, 1992). We also noted in Chapter 2 that blood–injury–injection phobia runs in families more strongly than any phobic disorder we know. This is probably because people with this phobia inherit a strong vasovagal response to blood, injury, or the possibility of an injection, all of which cause a drop in blood pressure and a tendency to faint. The phobia develops over the possibility of having this response. The average age of onset for this phobia is approximately 9 years (Antony, Brown, & Barlow, 1997a; LeBeau et al., 2010; Öst, 1989).

Situational Phobia

Phobias characterized by fear of public transportation or enclosed places are called **situational phobias**. Claustrophobia, a fear of small enclosed places, is situational, as is a phobia of flying. Psychopathologists first thought that situational phobia was similar to panic disorder with agoraphobia (PDA). Both situational phobia and PDA tend to emerge from midteens to mid-20s (Antony et al., 1997a; Craske et al., 2006; LeBeau et al., 2010) and have been shown to run in families (Curtis, Hill, & Lewis, 1990; Curtis, Himle, Lewis, & Lee, 1989; Fyer et al., 1990). But some analyses do not support the similarity as anything more than superficial (Antony et al., 1997a; Antony, Brown, & Barlow, 1997b). The main difference between situational phobia and PDA is that people with situational phobia never experience panic attacks outside the context of their phobic object or situation. Therefore, they can relax when they don't have to confront their phobic situation. People with panic disorder, in contrast, might experience unexpected, uncued panic attacks at any time.

Natural Environment Phobia

Sometimes very young people develop fears of situations or events occurring in nature. These fears are called **natural environment phobias**. The major examples are heights, storms, and water. These fears also seem to cluster together (Antony & Barlow, 2002; Hofmann et al., 1997): If

▲ People who develop a natural environment phobia intensely fear such places as heights and events such as lightning.

you fear one situation or event, such as deep water, you are likely to fear another, such as storms. Many of these situations have some danger associated with them and, therefore, mild to moderate fear can be adaptive. It is entirely possible that we are somewhat prepared to be afraid of these situations; as we discussed in Chapter 2, something in our genes makes us sensitive to these situations if any sign of danger is present. In any case, these phobias have a peak age of onset of about 7 years. They are not phobias if they are only passing fears. They have to be persistent and to interfere substantially with the person's functioning, leading to avoidance of boat trips or summer vacations in the mountains where there might be a storm.

Animal Phobia

Fears of animals and insects are called **animal phobias**. Again, these fears are common and become phobic only if severe interference with functioning occurs. For example, we have seen cases in our clinic in which people with snake or mice phobias are unable to read magazines for fear of unexpectedly coming across a picture of one of these animals. These people are unable to go many places, even if they want to very much, such as to the country to visit someone. The fear experienced by people with animal phobias is different from an ordinary mild revulsion. The age of onset for these phobias, like that of natural environment phobias, peaks around 7 years (Antony et al., 1997a; LeBeau et al., 2010; Öst, 1987).

Separation Anxiety Disorder

All anxiety disorders described in this chapter may occur during childhood (Rapee, Schniering, & Hudson, 2009), and there is one additional anxiety disorder that is identified more closely with children. **Separation anxiety disorder** is characterized by children's unrealistic and persistent worry that something will happen to their parents or other important people in their life or that something will hap-

pen to the children themselves that will separate them from their parents (for example, they will be lost, kidnapped, killed, or hurt in an accident). Children often refuse to go to school or even to leave home, not because they are afraid of school but because they are afraid of separating from loved ones. These fears can result in refusing to sleep alone and may be characterized by nightmares involving possible separation and by physical symptoms, distress, and anxiety (Barlow, Pincus, Heinrichs, & Choate, 2003).

All young children experience separation anxiety to some extent; this fear usually decreases as they grow older. Therefore, a clinician must judge whether the separation anxiety is greater than would be expected at that particular age (Barlow et al., 2003; Ollendick & Huntzinger, 1990). It is also important to differentiate separation anxiety from school phobia. In school phobia, the fear is clearly focused on something specific to the school situation; the child can leave the parents or other attachment figures to go somewhere other than school. In separation anxiety, the act of separating from the parent or attachment figure provokes anxiety and fear.

There is now evidence that separation anxiety, if untreated, can extend into adulthood in approximately 35% of cases (Shear, Jin, Ruscio, Walters, & Kessler, 2006). Furthermore, very recent evidence suggests that this disorder occurs in approximately 6.6% of the adult population over the course of a lifetime (Shear et al., 2006). In some cases, the onset is in adulthood rather than carrying over from childhood. The focus of anxiety in adults is the same: that harm may befall loved ones during separation (Manicavasagar et al., 2010; Silove, Marnane, Wagner, Manicavasagar, & Rees, 2010).

Statistics

Specific fears occur in a majority of people. The ones most commonly found in the population at large, categorized by Agras, Sylvester, and Oliveau (1969), are presented in Table 4.4. Not surprisingly, fears of snakes and heights rank near the top. Few people who report specific fears qualify as hav-

blood–injury–injection phobia Unreasonable fear and avoidance of exposure to blood, injury, or the possibility of an injection. Victims experience fainting and a drop in blood pressure.
situational phobia Anxiety involving enclosed places (for example, claustrophobia) or public transportation (for example, fear of flying).
natural environment phobia Fear of situations or events in nature, especially heights, storms, and water.
animal phobia Unreasonable, enduring fear of animals or insects that usually develops early in life.
separation anxiety disorder Excessive, enduring fear in some children that harm will come to them or their parents while they are apart.

▲ A child with separation anxiety disorder persistently worries that parting with an important person drastically endangers either the loved one or the child.

last for several years. At age 10, children may fear evaluation by others and feel anxiety over their physical appearance. Generally, reports of fear decline with age, although performance-related fears of such activities as taking a test or talking in front of a large group may increase with age. Specific phobias seem to decline with old age (Ayers et al., 2009; Blazer et al., 1991; Sheikh, 1992).

The prevalence of specific phobias varies from one culture to another (Hinton & Good, 2009). Hispanics are two times more likely to report specific phobias than white Americans (Magee et al., 1996) for reasons not entirely clear. A variant of phobia in Chinese cultures is called *Pa-leng*, sometimes *frigo phobia* or "fear of the cold." *Pa-leng* can be understood only in the context of traditional ideas—in this case, the Chinese concepts of *yin* and *yang* (Tan, 1980). Chinese medicine holds that there must be a balance of yin and yang forces in the body for health to be maintained. Yin represents the cold, dark, windy, energy-sapping aspects of life; yang refers to the warm,

ing a phobia, but for approximately 12.5% of the population, their fears become severe enough to earn the label "phobia." During a given 1-year period the prevalence is 8.7%. This is a high percentage, making specific phobia one of the most common psychological disorders in the United States and around the world (Arrindell et al., 2003b; Kessler, Berglund et al., 2005). In addition, 4.1% of children have separation anxiety at a severe enough level to meet criteria for a disorder (Shear et al., 2006). As with common fears, the sex ratio for specific phobias is, at 4:1, overwhelmingly female; this is also consistent around the world (Arrindell et al., 2003b; Craske et al., 2006; LeBeau et al., 2010).

Even though phobias may interfere with an individual's functioning, only the most severe cases come for treatment because more mildly affected people tend to work around their phobias; for example, someone with a fear of heights arranges her life so she never has to be in a tall building or other high place. People with situational phobias of such things as driving, flying, or being in small enclosed places most often come for treatment.

Once a phobia develops, it tends to last a lifetime (run a chronic course) (see, for example, Antony et al., 1997a; Barlow, 2002; Kessler, Berglund, et al., 2005); thus, the issue of treatment, described shortly, becomes important.

Although most anxiety disorders look much the same in adults and in children, clinicians must be aware of the types of normal fears and anxieties experienced throughout childhood so that they can distinguish them from specific phobias (Albano et al., 1996; Silverman & Rabian, 1993). Infants, for example, show marked fear of loud noises and strangers. At 1 to 2 years of age, children quite normally are anxious about separating from parents, and fears of animals and the dark also develop and may persist into the fourth or fifth year of life. Fear of various monsters and other imaginary creatures may begin about age 3 and

Table 4.4 Prevalence of Intense Fears and Phobias

Intense Fear	Prevalence per 1,000 Population	Sex Distribution	SE by Sex
Snakes	253	M: 118 F: 376	M: 34 F: 48
Heights	120	M: 109 F: 128	M: 33 F: 36
Flying	109	M: 70 F: 144	M: 26 F: 38
Enclosures	50	M: 32 F: 63	M: 18 F: 25
Illness	33	M: 31 F: 35	M: 18 F: 19
Death	33	M: 46 F: 21	M: 21 F: 15
Injury	23	M: 24 F: 22	M: 15 F: 15
Storms	31	M: 9 F: 48	M: 9 F: 22
Dentists	24	M: 22 F: 26	M: 15 F: 16
Journeys alone	16	M: 0 F: 31	M: 0 F: 18
Being alone	10	M: 5 F: 13	M: 7 F: 11

SE, standard error.

Source: Adapted, with permission, from Agras, W. S., Sylvester, D., & Oliveau, D. (1969). The epidemiology of common fears and phobias. *Comprehensive Psychiatry, 10*, 151–156, © 1969 Elsevier.

▲ Chinese medicine is based on the concept that *yin* (dark, cold, enervating forces) and *yang* (bright, warm, energizing forces) must harmonize in the body. In this traditional representation of the yin–yang balance, note that each aspect contains something of the other.

bright, energy-producing aspects of life. Individuals with *Pa-leng* have a morbid fear of the cold. They ruminate over loss of body heat and may wear several layers of clothing even on a hot day. They may complain of belching and flatulence (passing gas), which indicate the presence of wind and therefore of too much yin in the body.

Causes

For a long time, we thought that most specific phobias began with an unusual traumatic event. For example, if you were bitten by a dog, you would develop a phobia of dogs. We now know this is not always the case (Barlow, 2002; Craske et al., 2006; Öst, 1985; Rachman, 2002). This is not to say that traumatic conditioning experiences do not result in subsequent phobic behavior. Almost every person with a choking phobia has had some kind of a choking experience. An individual with claustrophobia who recently came to our clinic reported being trapped in an elevator for an extraordinarily long period. These are examples of phobias acquired by *direct experience,* where real danger or pain results in an alarm response (a true alarm). This is one way of developing a phobia, and there are at least three others: *experiencing* a false alarm (panic attack) in a specific situation; *observing* someone else experience severe fear (vicarious experience); or, under the right conditions, *being told* about danger.

Studies show that many people with a phobia do not necessarily experience a true alarm resulting from real danger at the onset of their phobia. Many initially have an un-expected panic attack in a specific situation, perhaps related to current life stress. A phobia of that situation may then develop. Munjack (1984; Mineka & Zinbarg, 2006) studied people with specific phobias of driving. He noted that about 50% of the people who could remember when their phobia started had experienced a true alarm because of a traumatic experience such as a car accident. The others had had nothing terrible happen to them while they were driving, but they had experienced an unexpected panic attack during which they felt they were going to lose control of the car. Their driving was not impaired, and their catastrophic thoughts were simply part of the panic attack.

We also learn fears vicariously. Seeing someone else have a traumatic experience or endure intense fear may be enough to instill a phobia in the watcher. Remember, we noted earlier that emotions are contagious. If someone you are with is either happy or fearful, you will probably feel a tinge of happiness or fear also. Öst (1985) describes how a severe dental fear developed in this way. An adolescent boy sat in the waiting room at the school dentist's office partly observing, but fully hearing, his friend who was being treated. Evidently, the boy's reaction to pain caused him to move suddenly, and the drill punctured his cheek. The boy in the waiting room who overhead the accident bolted from the room and developed a severe and long-lasting fear of dental situations. Nothing actually happened to the second person, but you can certainly understand why he developed his phobia. Sometimes just being warned repeatedly about a potential danger is sufficient for someone to develop a phobia. Öst (1985) describes the case of a woman with an extremely severe snake phobia who had never encountered a snake. Rather, she had been told repeatedly while growing up about the dangers of snakes in the high grass. She was encouraged to wear high rubber boots to guard against this imminent threat—and she did so even when walking down the street. We call this mode of developing a phobia *information transmission.*

Terrifying experiences alone do not create phobias. As we have said, a true phobia also requires anxiety over the possibility of another extremely traumatic event or false alarm and we are likely to avoid situations in which that terrible thing might occur. If we don't develop anxiety, our reaction would presumably be in the category of normal fears experienced by more than half the population. Normal fear can cause mild distress, but it is usually ignored and forgotten. This point is best illustrated by Peter DiNardo and his colleagues (1988), who studied a group of dog phobics and a matched group who did not have the phobia. Like Munjack's (1984) driving phobics, about 50% of the dog phobics had had a frightening encounter with a dog, usually involving a bite. However, in the other group of individuals who did not have dog phobia, about 50% had also had a frightening encounter with a dog. Why hadn't they become phobics? They had not developed anxiety about another encounter with a dog, unlike the people who did become phobic (reflecting a generalized psychological vulnerability). A diagram of the etiology of specific phobia is presented in ■ Figure 4.7.

In summary, several things have to occur for a person to develop a phobia. First, a traumatic conditioning experience often plays a role (even hearing about a frightening event is sufficient for some individuals). Second, fear is more likely to develop if we are "prepared"—that is, we seem to carry an inherited tendency to fear situations that have always been dangerous to the human race, such as being threatened by wild animals or trapped in small places (see Chapter 2).

Third, we also have to be susceptible to developing anxiety about the possibility that the event will happen again. We have discussed the biological and psychological reasons for anxiety and have seen that at least one phobia, blood–injury–injection phobia, is highly heritable (Öst, 1989; Page & Martin, 1998). Patients with blood phobia probably also inherit a strong vasovagal response that makes them susceptible to fainting. This alone would not be sufficient to ensure their becoming phobic, but it combines with anxiety to produce strong vulnerability.

Several years ago, Fyer and colleagues (1990) demonstrated that approximately 31% of the first-degree relatives of people with specific phobias also had a phobia, compared with 11% of the first-degree relatives of "normal" controls. More recently, in a collaborative study between Fyer's clinic and our center, we replicated these results, finding a 28% prevalence in the first-degree relatives of patients with phobia compared to 10% in relatives of con-trols. More interestingly, it seems that each subtype of phobia "bred true," in that relatives were likely to have identical types of phobia. Kendler, Karkowski, and Prescott (1999a and b) and Page and Martin (1998) found relatively high estimates for heritability of individual specific phobias. We do not know for sure whether the tendency for phobias to run in families is caused by genes or by modeling, but the findings are at least suggestive of a unique genetic contribution to specific phobia (Antony & Barlow, 2002; Hettema et al., 2005; Smoller et al., 2005).

Finally, social and cultural factors are strong determinants of who develops and reports a specific phobia. In most societies, it is almost unacceptable for males to express fears and phobias. Thus, the overwhelming majority of reported specific phobias occur in women (Arrindell et al., 2003b; LeBeau et al., 2010). What happens to men? Possibly they work hard to overcome their fears by repeatedly exposing themselves to their feared situations. A more likely possibility is that they simply endure their fears without telling anyone about them and without seeking treatment (Antony & Barlow, 2002).

Treatment

Although the development of phobias is relatively complex, the treatment is fairly straightforward. Almost everyone agrees that specific phobias require structured and consis-

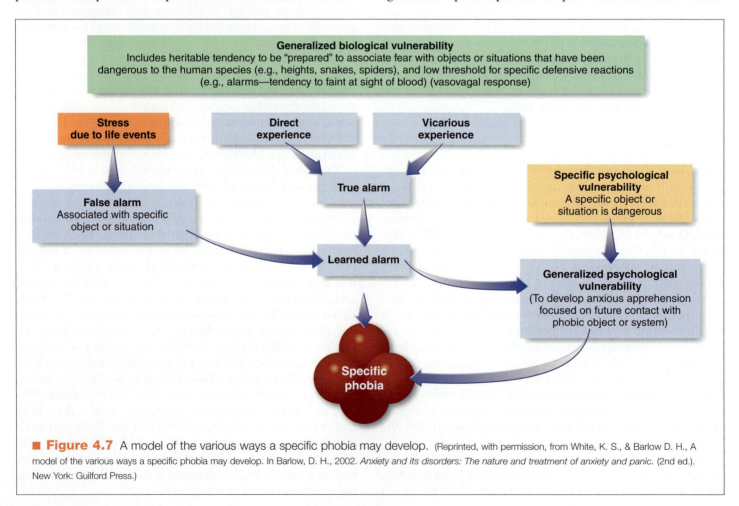

■ **Figure 4.7** A model of the various ways a specific phobia may develop. (Reprinted, with permission, from White, K. S., & Barlow D. H., A model of the various ways a specific phobia may develop. In Barlow, D. H., 2002. *Anxiety and its disorders: The nature and treatment of anxiety and panic.* (2nd ed.). New York: Guilford Press.)

tent exposure-based exercises (Barlow, Moscovitch, & Micco, 2004; Craske et al., 2006). Nevertheless, most patients who expose themselves gradually to what they fear must be under therapeutic supervision. Individuals who attempt to carry out the exercises alone often attempt to do too much too soon and end up escaping the situation, which may strengthen the phobia. In addition, if they fear having another unexpected panic attack in this situation, it is helpful to direct therapy at panic attacks in the manner described for panic disorder (Antony, Craske, & Barlow, 2006; Craske et al., 2006). For separation anxiety, parents are often included to help structure the exercises and also to address parental reaction to childhood anxiety (Choate, Pincus, Eyberg, & Barlow, 2005). More recently, an intensive 1-week program for girls ages 8 to 11 developed at one of our clinics in which the girls end up having a sleepover at the clinic has proven highly successful (Pincus, Santucci, Ehrenreich, & Ryberg, 2008; Santucci, Ehrenreich, Trosper, Bennett, & Pincus, 2009).

Finally, in cases of blood–injury–injection phobia, where fainting is a real possibility, graduated exposure-based exercises must be done in specific ways. Individuals must tense various muscle groups during exposure exercises to keep their blood pressure sufficiently high to complete the practice (Ayala, Meuret, & Ritz, 2009; Öst & Sterner, 1987). New developments make it possible to treat many specific phobias, including blood phobia, in a single, daylong session (see, for example, Antony & Barlow, 2002; Antony et al., 2006; Craske et al., 2006; Öst, Ferebee, & Furmark, 1997; Öst, Svensson, Hellström, & Lindwall, 2001). Basically, the therapist spends most of the day with the individual, working through exposure exercises with the phobia object or situation. The patient then practices approaching the phobic situation at home, checking in occasionally with the therapist. It is interesting that in these cases not only does the phobia disappear, but the tendency to experience the vasovagal response at the sight of blood also lessens considerably. It is also now clear based on brain-imaging work that these treatments change brain functioning by modifying neural circuitry— that is, these treatments "rewire" the brain (Paquette et al., 2003).

Social Phobia (Social Anxiety Disorder)

> **What are the principal causes of social phobia?**
> **What strategies are used to treat social phobia?**

Are you shy? If so, you have something in common with 20% to 50% of college students, depending on which survey you read. A much smaller number of people, who suffer severely around others, have **social phobia**, also called social anxiety disorder (SAD), which most likely will be the name adopted in the *DSM-5*. Consider the case of Billy, a 13-year-old boy.

Billy | Too Shy

Billy was the model boy at home. He did his homework, stayed out of trouble, obeyed his parents, and was generally so quiet and reserved he didn't attract much attention. However, when he got to junior high school, something his parents had noticed earlier became painfully evident. Billy had no friends. He was unwilling to attend social or sporting activities connected with school, even though most of the other kids in his class went to these events. When his parents decided to check with the guidance counselor, they found that she had been about to call them. She reported that Billy did not socialize or speak up in class and was sick to his stomach all day if he knew he was going to be called on. His teachers had difficulty getting anything more than a yes-or-no answer from him. More troublesome was that he had been found hiding in a stall in the boy's restroom during lunch, which he said he had been doing for several months instead of eating. After Billy was referred to our clinic, we diagnosed a severe case of social phobia, an irrational and extreme fear of social situations. Billy's phobia took the form of extreme shyness. He was afraid of being embarrassed or humiliated in the presence of almost everyone except his parents.

Clinical Description

SAD is more than exaggerated shyness (Bögels et al., 2010; Hofmann et al., 2009; Schneier et al., 1996). The cases described here are typical of many that appear occasionally in the press over the years.

---

social phobia Extreme, enduring, irrational fear and avoidance of social or performance situations.

Rapid Behavioral Treatment of a Specific Phobia (Snakes)

"Since I remember, I remember being afraid of snakes. . . . I have dreams of snakes; it's horrible."

Go to Psychology CourseMate at www.cengagebrain.com to watch this video.

Abnormal Psychology Inside Out. produced by Ira Wohl. Only Child Motion Pictures

---

Steve and Chuck ♦ Star Players?

In the second inning of an All-Star game, Los Angeles Dodger second baseman Steve Sax fielded an easy grounder, straightened up for the lob to first, and bounced the ball past first baseman Al Oliver, who was less than 40 feet away. It was a startling error even in an All-Star game studded with bush-league mishaps. But hard-core baseball fans knew it was one more manifestation of a leading mystery of the 1983 season: Sax, 23, the National League Rookie of the Year, could not seem to make routine throws to first base. (Of his first 27 errors that season, 22 were bad throws.)

Chuck Knoblauch won the Golden Glove Award in 1997 but led the league in errors in 1999 with 26, most of them throwing errors. Announcers and reporters observed that his throws would be hard and on target to first base if he made a difficult play and had to quickly turn and throw the ball "without thinking about it." But if he fielded a routine ground ball and had time to think about the accuracy of his throw, he would throw awkwardly and slowly—and often off target. The announcers and reporters concluded that, because his arm seemed fine on the difficult plays, his problem must be "mental." For the 2001 season, he was moved to left field to avoid having to make that throw and by 2003 was out of baseball.

Whereas Knoblauch continued to struggle, Sax overcame his problem. Many other athletes are not so fortunate. This problem is not limited to athletes but is also experienced by well-known lecturers and performers. Actress Scarlett Johansson avoided doing Broadway for many years because of intolerable performance anxiety. The inability of a skilled athlete to throw a baseball to first base or a seasoned performer to appear on stage certainly does not match the concept of "shyness" with which we are all familiar. What holds these seemingly different conditions together within the category of social anxiety disorder? Billy, Knoblauch, Sax, and Johansson all experienced marked and persistent anxiety focused on one or more social or performance situations. In Billy's case, these situations were any in which he might have to interact with people. For Knoblauch and Johansson, they were specific to performing some special behavior in public. Individuals with performance anxiety usually have no difficulty with social interaction, but when they must do something specific in front of people, anxiety takes over and they focus on the possibility that they will embarrass themselves.

The most common type of performance anxiety, to which most people can relate, is public speaking. Other situations that commonly provoke performance anxiety are eating in a restaurant or signing a paper in front of a clerk. Anxiety-provoking physical reactions include blushing; sweating; trembling; or, for males, urinating in a public restroom ("bashful bladder" or paruresis). Males with this problem must wait until a stall is available, a difficult task at times. What these examples have in common is that the individual is very anxious only while others are present and maybe watching and, to some extent, evaluating their behavior. This is truly social anxiety disorder because the people have no difficulty eating, writing, or urinating in private. Only when others are watching does the behavior deteriorate.

Individuals who are extremely and painfully shy in almost all social situations meet *DSM-IV-TR* criteria for the subtype *social phobia generalized type*. It is particularly prominent in children. In the child program in one of our clinics, 100% of children and adolescents with social phobia met criteria for the generalized type (Albano, DiBartolo, Heimberg, & Barlow, 1995), as did Billy in the example above (Schneier et al., 1996). Because most people with SAD meet criteria for this subtype to at least some degree, it may be dropped in *DSM-5* as being unnecessary (Bögels et al., 2010).

Statistics

As many as 12.1% of the general population suffer from social phobia at some point in their lives (Kessler, Berglund, et al., 2005). In a given 1-year period, the prevalence is 6.8% (Kessler, Chiu, et al., 2005). This makes social phobia second only to specific phobia as the most prevalent anxiety disorder, afflicting more than 35 million people in the United States alone, based on current population estimates. Many more people are shy, but not severely enough to meet criteria for social phobia. Unlike other anxiety disorders for which females predominate (Hofmann et al., 2009; Magee et al., 1996), the sex ratio for social phobia is nearly 50:50 (Hofmann & Barlow, 2002; Marks, 1985). Overall, 45.6% of people suffering from social phobia sought professional help in a recent 12-month period (Wang et al., 2005). Social phobia usually begins during adolescence, with a peak age of onset around 13 years (Kessler, Berglund, et al., 2005). Social phobia also tends to be more prevalent in people who are young (18–29 years), undereducated, single, and of low socioeconomic class. It is less than half as prevalent among individuals older than age 60 (6.6%) as it is among individuals 18–29 (13.6%) (Kessler, Berglund, et al., 2005).

Considering their difficulty meeting people, it is not surprising that a greater percentage of individuals with social phobia are single than in the population at large. Social phobias distribute relatively equally among different ethnic groups (Magee et al., 1996). In Japan, the clinical presentation of anxiety disorders is best summarized under the label *shinkeishitsu.* One of the most common subcategories is referred to as *taijin kyofusho* (Hofmann et al., 2009; Kirmayer, 1991; Kleinknecht, Dinnel, Kleinknecht, Hiruma, & Harada, 1997). Japanese people with this form of social phobia strongly fear looking people in the eye and are afraid that some aspect of their personal presentation (blushing, stuttering, body odor, and so on) will appear reprehensible. Thus, the focus of anxiety in this disorder is on offending or embarrassing others rather than embarrassing oneself as in social phobia, although these two disorders overlap considerably (Dinnel, Kleinknecht, & Tanaka-Matsumi, 2002). Japanese males with this disorder outnumber females by a 3:2 ratio (Takahasi, 1989). More recently it has been established that this syndrome is found in many cultures around the world, including North America. The key feature once again is preoccupation with a belief that one is embarrassing oneself and offending others with a foul body odor. This set of symptoms is now called "olfactory reference syndrome" and has been proposed as a possible new disorder pending further study to be published in the appendix of *DSM-5* (Feusner, Phillips, & Stein, 2010).

Causes

We have noted that we seem to be prepared by evolution to fear certain wild animals and dangerous situations in the natural environment. Similarly, it seems we are also prepared to fear angry, critical, or rejecting people (Blair et al., 2008; Mineka & Zinbarg, 1996, 2006; Mogg, Philippot, & Bradley, 2004; Öhman, 1986). In a series of studies, Öhman and colleagues (see, for example, Dimberg & Öhman, 1983; Öhman & Dimberg, 1978) noted that we learn more quickly to fear angry expressions than other facial expressions, and this fear diminishes more slowly than other types of learning. Lundh and Öst (1996) demonstrated that people with social phobia who saw a number of pictures of faces were likely to remember critical expressions; Mogg and colleagues (2004) showed that socially anxious individuals more quickly recognized angry faces than "normals," whereas "normals" remembered the accepting expressions (Navarrete et al, 2009). Fox and Damjanovic (2006) demonstrated that the eye region specifically is the threatening area of the face.

Why should we inherit a tendency to fear angry faces? Our ancestors probably avoided hostile, angry, domineering people who might attack or kill them. In all species, dominant, aggressive individuals, high in the social hierarchy, tend to be avoided. Jerome Kagan and his colleagues (see, for example, Kagan, 1994, 1997; Kagan, Reznick, & Snidman, 1988; Kagan & Snidman, 1991, 1999) have demonstrated that some infants are born with a temperamental profile or trait of inhibition or shyness that is evident as early as 4 months of age. Four-month-old infants with this trait become more agitated and cry more frequently when presented with toys or other age-appropriate stimuli than infants without the trait. There is now evidence that individuals with excessive behavioral inhibition are at increased risk for developing phobic behavior (Biederman et al., 1990; Essex, Klein, Slattery, Goldsmith, & Kalin, 2010; Hirschfeld et al., 1992).

A model of the etiology of social phobia would look somewhat like models of panic disorder and specific phobia. Three pathways to social phobia are possible, as depicted in ■ Figure 4.8.

First, someone could inherit a generalized biological vulnerability to develop anxiety, a biological tendency to be socially inhibited, or both. The existence of a generalized psychological vulnerability—such as the belief that events, particularly stressful events, are potentially uncontrollable—would increase an individual's vulnerability. When under stress, anxiety and self-focused attention could increase to the point of disrupting performance, even in the absence of a false alarm (panic attack). Second, when under stress, someone might have an unexpected panic attack in a social situation that would become associated (conditioned) to social cues. The individual would then become anxious about having additional panic attacks in the same or similar social situations. Third, someone might experience a real social trauma resulting in a true alarm. Anxiety would then develop (be conditioned) in the same or similar social situations. Traumatic social experiences may also extend back to difficult periods in childhood. Early adolescence—usually ages 12 through 15—is when children may be brutally taunted by peers who are attempting to assert their own dominance. This experience may produce anxiety and panic that are reproduced in future social situations. For example, McCabe, Anthony, Summerfeldt, Liss,

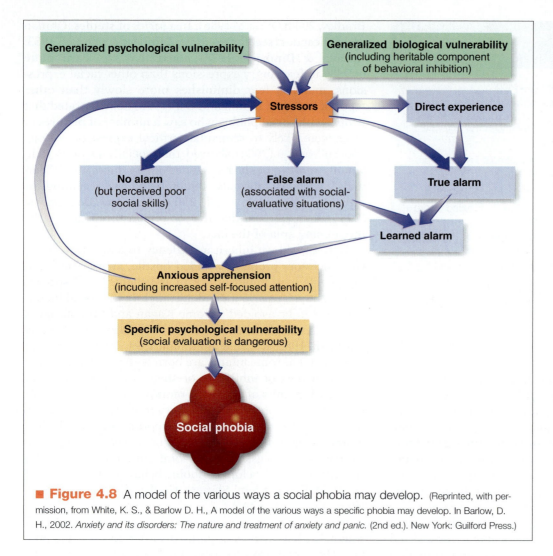

Treatment

Effective treatments have been developed for social phobia only in the past several years (Barlow & Lehman, 1996; Hofmann, 2004; Taylor, 1996; Turk, Heimberg, & Magee, 2008). Rick Heimberg and colleagues developed a cognitive-behavioral group therapy (CBGT) program in which groups of patients rehearse or role-play their socially phobic situations in front of one another (Heimberg et al., 1990; Turk et al., 2008). The group members participate in the role-playing, for example, acting as audience for someone who has extreme difficulty giving a speech. At the same time, the therapist conducts rather intensive cognitive therapy aimed at uncovering and changing the automatic or unconscious perceptions of danger that the socially phobic client assumes to exist. These treatments have proved to be more effective than comparison treatments involving education about anxiety and social phobia and social support

■ **Figure 4.8** A model of the various ways a social phobia may develop. (Reprinted, with permission, from White, K. S., & Barlow D. H., A model of the various ways a specific phobia may develop. In Barlow, D. H., 2002. *Anxiety and its disorders: The nature and treatment of anxiety and panic.* (2nd ed.). New York: Guilford Press.)

and Swinson (2003) noted that 92% of adults with social phobia in their sample experienced severe teasing and bullying in childhood, compared to only 35% to 50% among people with other anxiety disorders.

But one more factor must fall into place to make it a social anxiety disorder. The individual with the vulnerabilities and experiences just described must also have learned growing up that social evaluation in particular can be dangerous, creating a specific psychological vulnerability to develop social anxiety. Evidence indicates that some people with social phobia are predisposed to focus their anxiety on events involving social evaluation. Some investigators (Bruch & Heimberg, 1994; Rapee & Melville, 1997) suggest that the parents of patients with social phobia are significantly more socially fearful and concerned with the opinions of others than are the parents of patients with panic disorder and that they pass this concern on to their children (Lieb et al., 2000). Fyer, Mannuzza, Chapman, Liebowitz, and Klein (1993) reported that the relatives of people with social phobia had a significantly greater risk of developing it than the relatives of individuals without social phobia (16% versus 5%)—thus, the specific psychological vulnerability depicted in Figure 4.8. As you can see, a combination of biological and psychological events seems to lead to the development of social phobia.

for stressful life events. More important, a follow-up after 5 years indicates that the therapeutic gains are maintained (Heimberg, Salzman, Holt, & Blendell, 1993). Clark and colleagues (2006) evaluated a new and improved cognitive therapy program that emphasized more real-life experiences during therapy to disprove automatic perceptions of danger. This program substantially benefited 84% of individuals receiving treatment, and these results were maintained at a 1-year follow-up.

We have adapted these protocols for use with adolescents, directly involving parents in the group treatment process. Preliminary results suggest that severely socially phobic adolescents can attain relatively normal functioning in school and other social settings (Albano & Barlow, 1996) and that including the parents in the treatment process produces better outcomes than treating the adolescents alone (Albano, Pincus, Tracey, & Barlow, in preparation).

Effective drug treatments also have been discovered (Van Ameringen, Mancini, Patterson, & Simpson, 2009). Tricyclic antidepressants and, particularly, monoamine oxidase (MAO) inhibitors have been found to be more effective than placebo in the treatment of severe social anxiety (Liebowitz et al., 1992). Since 1999 the SSRIs Paxil, Zoloft, and Effexor have received approval from the Food and Drug Administration for treatment of social anxiety disorder based on studies showing effectiveness compared to placebo (see, for example, Stein et al., 1998).

Several major studies have compared psychological and drug treatments. One large and important study compared MAO inhibitors to the psychological treatments described earlier. In this study (Heimberg et al., 1998; Liebowitz et al., 1999) 133 patients were randomly assigned to phenelzine (the MAO inhibitor), CBGT, a placebo drug, or an educational-supportive group therapy that served as a placebo for the psychological treatment because it did not contain the cognitive-behavioral component. Results show that both active treatments are highly and equally effective compared to the two placebo conditions but that relapse tends to be more common after treatment stops among those taking medication. Another impressive study compared Clark's cognitive therapy described earlier to the SSRI drug Prozac, along with instructions to the patients with generalized social phobia to attempt to engage in more social situations (self-exposure). A third group received placebo plus instructions to attempt to engage in more social activities. Assessments were conducted before the 16-week treatment, at the midpoint of treatment, posttreatment, and then after 3 months of booster sessions. Finally, researchers followed up with patients in the two treatment groups 12 months later (Clark et al., 2003). Both treatments did well, but the psychological treatment was substantially better at all times. This study is also notable because of the *extent* of change in treatment (most patients were cured or nearly cured with few remaining symptoms).

The evidence is mixed on the usefulness of combining SSRIs or related drugs with psychological treatments. Davidson, Foa, and Huppert (2004) found that a cognitive-behavioral treatment and an SSRI were comparable in efficacy but that the combination was no better than the two individual treatments; Blanco and colleagues (2010), however, did find an additive effect. As noted earlier, an exciting study suggests that adding the drug D-cycloserine (DCS) to

cognitive-behavioral treatments significantly enhances the effects of treatment (Hofmann et al., 2006). Unlike SSRIs, this drug is known to facilitate the extinction of anxiety, an important part of cognitive-behavioral treatments, by modifying neurotransmitter flow in the glutamate system as described in Chapter 2.

Concept Check 4.4

Identify the following specific phobias: (a) blood–injury–injection, (b) acrophobia, (c) animal, (d) social, (e) natural environment, and (f) other. The same phobia may apply to more than one statement.

1. Mark had no friends at school and hid in the boys' bathroom during both lunch and recess. _____

2. Dennis fears and strenuously avoids storms. Not surprisingly, on his first oceangoing cruise, he found that deep water terrified him, too. _____

3. Rita was comfortable at the zoo until the old terror gripped her at the insect display. _____

4. Armando would love to eat fish with his fishing buddies, but he experiences an inordinate fear of choking on a bone. _____

5. John had to give up his dream of becoming a surgeon because he faints at the sight of blood. _____

6. Rachel turned down several lucrative job offers that involved public speaking and took a low-paying desk job instead. _____

7. Farrah can't visit her rural friends because of her fear of snakes. _____

Posttraumatic Stress Disorder

> **What are the essential features and possible causes of posttraumatic stress disorder?**
> **What treatment approaches are available for posttraumatic stress order?**

In recent years, we have heard a great deal about the severe and long-lasting emotional disorders that can occur after a variety of traumatic events. For Americans, perhaps the most notorious traumatic events have been war, the tragedy of the World Trade Center and the Pentagon on September 11, 2001, or Hurricane Katrina in 2005. Still, emotional disorders also occur after physical assault (particularly rape), car accidents, natural catastrophes, or the sudden death of a loved one. One emotional disorder that

follows a trauma is known as **posttraumatic stress disorder (PTSD)**.

posttraumatic stress disorder (PTSD) Enduring, distressing emotional disorder that follows exposure to a severe helplessness- or fear-inducing threat. The victim reexperiences the trauma, avoids stimuli associated with it, and develops a numbing of responsiveness and an increased vigilance and arousal.

Clinical Description

DSM-IV-TR describes the setting event for PTSD as exposure to a traumatic event during which someone feels fear, helplessness, or horror. Afterward, victims reexperience the event through memories and nightmares. When memories occur suddenly accompanied by strong emotion and the victims find themselves reliving the event, they are having a *flashback*. Victims most often avoid anything that reminds them of the trauma. They display a characteristic restriction or numbing of emotional responsiveness, which may be disruptive to interpersonal relationships. They are sometimes unable to remember certain aspects of the event. It is possible that victims unconsciously attempt to avoid the experience of emotion itself, like people with panic disorder, because intense emotions could bring back memories of the trauma. Finally, victims typically are chronically overaroused, easily startled, and quick to anger.

Consider the case of the Joneses from one of our clinics.

The Joneses ¦ One Victim, Many Traumas

Mrs. Betty Jones and her four children arrived at a farm to visit a friend. (Mr. Jones was at work.) Jeff, the oldest child, was 8 years old. Marcie, Cathy, and Susan were 6, 4, and 2 years of age. Mrs. Jones parked the car in the driveway, and they all started across the yard to the front door. Suddenly Jeff heard growling somewhere near the house. Before he could warn the others, a large German shepherd charged and leapt at Marcie, the 6-year-old, knocking her to the ground and tearing viciously at her face. The family, too stunned to move, watched the attack helplessly. After what seemed like an eternity, Jeff lunged at the dog and it moved away. The owner of the dog, in a state of panic, ran to a nearby house to get help. Mrs. Jones immediately put pressure on Marcie's facial wounds in an attempt to stop the bleeding. The owner had neglected to retrieve the dog, and it stood a short distance away, growling and barking at the frightened family. Eventually, the dog was restrained and Marcie was rushed to the hospital. Marcie, who was hysterical, had to be restrained on a padded board so that emergency room physicians could stitch her wounds.

This case is unusual because not only did Marcie develop PTSD but so did her 8-year-old brother. In addition, Cathy, 4, and Susan, 2, although quite young, showed symptoms of the disorder, as did their mother (Table 4.5) (Albano, Miller, Zarate, Côté, & Barlow, 1997). Jeff evidenced classic survivor guilt symptoms, reporting that he should have saved Marcie or at least put himself between Marcie and the dog. Both Jeff and Marcie regressed developmentally, wetting the bed (nocturnal enuresis) and experi-

encing nightmares and separation fears. In addition, Marcie, having been strapped down and given a local anesthetic and stitches, became frightened of any medical procedures and even of such routine daily events as having her nails trimmed or taking a bath. Furthermore, she refused to be tucked into bed, something she had enjoyed all her life, probably because it reminded her of the hospital board. Jeff started sucking his fingers, which he had not done for years. These behaviors, along with intense separation anxiety, are common, particularly in younger children (Eth, 1990; Silverman & La Greca, 2002). Cathy, the 4-year-old, displayed considerable fear and avoidance when tested but denied having any problem when she was interviewed by a child psychologist. Susan, the 2-year-old, also had some symptoms, as shown in Table 4.5, but was too young to talk about them. However, for several months following the trauma she repeatedly said, without provocation, "Doggy bit sister."

Table 4.5 Symptoms of Posttraumatic Stress Disorder (PTSD) Evidenced by Marcie and Her Siblings

Symptoms	Jeff	Marcie	Cathy	Susan
Repetitive play—trauma themes		X	X	X
Nightmares	X	X	X	X
Reexperiencing	X			
Distress at exposure to similar stimuli	X	X	X	X
Avoidance of talk of trauma	X	X		
Avoidance of trauma recollections	X			
Regressive behavior	X	X		
Detachment	X	X		
Restricted affect	X	X		
Sleep disturbance	X	X	X	X
Anger outbursts	X	X		
Hypervigilance	X	X		
Startle response	X	X		
DSM-III-R PTSD diagnosis met	X	X		

Source: From Albano, A. M., Miller, P. P., Zarate, R., Côté, G., & Barlow, D. H. (1997). Behavioral assessment and treatment of PTSD in prepubertal children: Attention to developmental factors and innovative strategies in the case study of a family. *Cognitive and Behavioral Practice, 4,* 245–262.

As indicated in the criteria, PTSD is subdivided into acute and chronic. *Acute PTSD* can be diagnosed 1 month after the event occurs. When PTSD continues longer than 3 months, it is considered chronic. *Chronic PTSD* is usually associated with more prominent avoidance behaviors (Davidson, Hughes, Blazer, & George, 1991) and with the more frequent co-occurrence of additional diagnoses, such as social phobia. In *PTSD with delayed onset* individuals show few or no symptoms immediately after a trauma, but later, perhaps years afterward, they develop full-blown PTSD. Why onset is delayed in some individuals is not yet clear.

As we noted, PTSD cannot be diagnosed until a month after the trauma. New to *DSM-IV-TR* is a disorder called **acute stress disorder**. This is really PTSD occurring within the first month after the trauma, but the different name emphasizes the severe reaction that some people have immediately. PTSD-like symptoms are accompanied by severe dissociative symptoms, such as amnesia for all or part of the trauma, emotional numbing, and derealization, or feelings of unreality. According to one study, 63% to 70% of individuals with acute stress disorder from motor vehicle accidents went on to develop PTSD up to 2 years after the trauma. In addition, 13% who did not meet criteria for acute stress disorder went on to develop PTSD. If the victim experienced strong arousal and emotional numbing as part of acute stress disorder, the likelihood of later developing PTSD was greater (Harvey & Bryant, 1998).

Statistics

A number of studies have demonstrated the remarkably low prevalence of PTSD in populations of trauma victims. Rachman (1978), in a classic study, reported on the British citizenry who endured numerous life-threatening air raids during Word War II. He concluded that "a great majority of people endured the air raids extraordinarily well, contrary to the universal expectation of mass panic. Exposure to repeated bombings did not produce a significant increase in psychiatric disorders. Although short-lived fear reactions were common, surprisingly few persistent phobic reactions emerged" (Rachman, 1991, p. 162). Similar results have been observed from classic studies following disastrous fires, earthquakes, and floods (e.g., Green, Grace, Lindy, Titchener, & Lindy, 1983).

Phillip Saigh (1984) made some interesting observations when he was teaching at the American University in Beirut, Lebanon, just before and during the Israeli invasion in the early 1980s. Saigh had been collecting questionnaires measuring anxiety among university students just before the invasion. When the invasion began, half these students escaped to the surrounding mountains and were safe. The other half endured intense shelling and bombing for a period. Saigh continued administering the questionnaires and found a surprising result. There were no significant long-term differences between the group in the mountains and the group in the city, although a few students in the city who were closely exposed to danger and death did develop emotional reactions that progressed into PTSD.

DSM Disorder Criteria Summary
Posttraumatic Stress Disorder

Features of PTSD include the following:

> Exposure to a traumatic event in which the person experienced, witnessed, or was confronted by a situation involving death, threatened death, or serious injury, in response to which the person reacted with intense fear, helplessness, or horror

> The traumatic event is persistently reexperienced in one or more of the following ways: (1) recurrent and intrusive distressing recollections of the event, including images, thoughts, or perceptions; (2) recurrent distressing dreams of the event; (3) a sense that the traumatic event is recurring, including illusions, hallucinations, and dissociative flashbacks; (4) intense psychological distress at exposure to internal or external cues that call to mind the event; (5) physiological reaction to cues that call to mind the event

> Persistent avoidance of stimuli associated with the trauma and numbing of general responsiveness

> Persistent symptoms of increased arousal, such as difficulty sleeping, irritability, and hypervigilance

> Clinically significant distress or impairment in social, occupational, or other important areas of functioning

> Duration of the disturbance for more than 1 month

Source: Based on *DSM-IV-TR.* Reprinted with permission from *Diagnostic and Statistical Manual of Mental Disorders* (4th ed., text revision). © 2000 American Psychiatric Association.

In contrast, some studies have found a high incidence of PTSD after trauma. Kilpatrick and colleagues (1985) sampled more than 2,000 adult women who had personally experienced such trauma as rape, sexual molestation, robbery, and aggravated assault. Participants were asked whether they had thought about suicide after the trauma, had attempted suicide, or had a *nervous breakdown* (a lay term that has no meaning in psychopathology but is commonly used to refer to a severe psychological upset). The authors also analyzed the results based on whether the attack was completed or attempted. Rape had the most significant emotional impact. Compared to 2.2% of nonvictims, 19.2% of rape victims had attempted suicide and 44% reported suicidal ideation at some time following the rape. Similarly, Resnick, Kilpatrick, Dansky, Saunders, and Best (1993) found that 32% of rape victims met criteria for PTSD at some point in their lives. Taylor and Koch (1995) found that 15% to 20% of people experiencing severe auto accidents developed PTSD. Other surveys indicate that among the population as a whole, 6.8% have experienced PTSD at some point in their life (Kessler, Berglund, et al.,

acute stress disorder Severe reaction immediately following a terrifying event, often including amnesia about the event, emotional numbing, and derealization. Many victims later develop posttraumatic stress disorder.

2005) and 3.5% during the past year (Kessler, Chiu, et al., 2005), and combat and sexual assault are the most common precipitating traumas (Kessler, Sonnega, Bromet, Hughes, & Nelson, 1995). The fact that a diagnosis of PTSD predicts suicidal attempts independently of any other problem, such as alcohol abuse, has recently been confirmed (Wilcox, Storr, & Breslau, 2009).

What accounts for the discrepancies between the low rate of PTSD in citizens who endured bombing and shelling in London and Beirut and the relatively high rate in victims of crime? Investigators have now concluded that during air raids many people may not have directly experienced the horrors of dying, death, and direct attack. Close exposure to the trauma seems to be necessary to developing this disorder (Friedman, 2009; Keane & Barlow, 2002; King, King, Foy, & Gudanowski, 1996). But this is also evident among Vietnam veterans, where 18.7% developed PTSD, with prevalence rates directly related to amount of combat exposure (Dohrenwend, Turner, & Turse, 2006). Surveys of 76 victims of Hurricane Katrina also report a doubling of severe mental illness (Kessler, Galea, Jones, & Parker, 2006). The connection between proximity to the traumatic event and the development of PTSD was starkly evident following the tragedy of 9/11. Galea and colleagues (2002) contacted a representative sample of adults living south of 110th Street in Manhattan and found that 7.5% reported symptoms consistent with a diagnosis of acute stress disorder or PTSD. But among respondents who lived close to the World Trade Center (south of Canal Street) the prevalence of the disorder was 20%. Again, those who experienced the disaster most personally and directly seemed to be the ones most affected.

But is this the whole story? It seems not. Some people experience the most horrifying traumas imaginable and emerge psychologically healthy. For others, even relatively mild stressful events are sufficient to produce a full-blown disorder. To understand how this can happen, we must consider the etiology of PTSD.

Causes

PTSD is the one disorder for which we know the cause at least in terms of the precipitating event. Someone personally experiences a trauma and develops a disorder. However, whether a person develops PTSD is a surprisingly complex issue involving biological, psychological, and social factors. David Foy and his colleagues (Foy, Sipprelle, Rueger, & Carroll, 1984) concluded that the intensity of combat exposure contributed to the etiology of PTSD in a group of Vietnam War veterans, a finding recently confirmed, as noted earlier (Dohrenwend et al., 2006; Friedman, 2009), but did not account for all of it. For example, approximately 67% of prisoners of war developed PTSD (Foy, Resnick, Sipprelle, & Carroll, 1987). This means that 33% of the prisoners who endured long-term deprivation and torture *did not* develop the disorder; perhaps the best known among the group is Senator John McCain. Similarly, Resnick and colleagues (1993) demonstrated that the percentage of female crime victims who developed PTSD increased as a function of the severity of the trauma (see ■ Figure 4.9). Finally, children experiencing severe burns are likely to develop PTSD in proportion to the severity of the burns and the pain associated with them (Saxe et al., 2005). At lower levels of trauma, some people develop PTSD, but most do not. What accounts for these differences?

As with other disorders, we bring our own generalized biological and psychological vulnerabilities with us. The greater the vulnerability, the more likely we are to develop PTSD. If certain characteristics run in your family, you have a much greater chance of developing the disorder (Davidson, Swartz, Storck, Krishnan, & Hammett, 1985; Foy et al., 1987). A family history of anxiety suggests a generalized biological vulnerability for PTSD. True and colleagues (1993) reported that, given the same amount of combat exposure and one twin with PTSD, a monozygotic (identical) twin was more likely to develop PTSD than a dizygotic (fraternal) twin. The correlation of symptoms in identical twins was between 0.28 and 0.41, whereas for fraternal twins it was between 0.11 and 0.24, which suggests some genetic influence in the development of PTSD. Nevertheless, as with other disorders, there is little or no evidence that genes directly cause PTSD (Norrholm & Ressler, 2009). Rather, genetic factors predispose individuals to be easily stressed and anxious, which then may make it more likely that a traumatic experience will result in PTSD.

▲ Exposure to a traumatic event may create profound fear and helplessness. People who suffer from PTSD may reexperience such feelings in flashbacks, involuntarily reliving the horrifying event.

Andy Nelson/The Christian Science Monitor via Getty Images

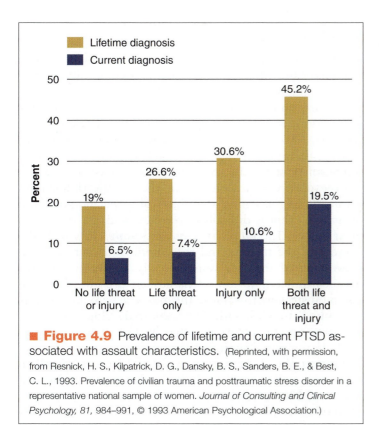

Figure 4.9 Prevalence of lifetime and current PTSD associated with assault characteristics. (Reprinted, with permission, from Resnick, H. S., Kilpatrick, D. G., Dansky, B. S., Sanders, B. E., & Best, C. L., 1993. Prevalence of civilian trauma and posttraumatic stress disorder in a representative national sample of women. *Journal of Consulting and Clinical Psychology, 81,* 984–991, © 1993 American Psychological Association.)

Breslau, Davis, and Andreski (1995) demonstrated among a random sample of 1,200 individuals that characteristics such as a tendency to be anxious, and factors such as minimal education, predict exposure to traumatic events in the first place and therefore an increased risk for PTSD. Breslau, Lucia, and Alvarado (2006) elaborated on this finding by showing that 6-year-old children with externalizing (acting out) problems were more likely to encounter trauma (such as assaults), probably because of their acting out, and later develop PTSD. Higher intelligence predicted decreased exposure to these types of traumatic events—that is, personality and other characteristics, some of them at least partially heritable, may predispose people to the experience of trauma by making it likely that they will be in (risky) situations where trauma is likely to occur (Norrholm & Ressler, 2009). Also, there seems to be a generalized psychological vulnerability described in the context of other disorders based on early experiences with unpredictable or uncontrollable events. Foy and colleagues (1987) discovered that at high levels of trauma, these vulnerabilities did not matter as much because the majority (67%) of prisoners of war they studied developed PTSD. However, at low levels of stress or trauma, vulnerabilities matter a great deal in determining whether the disorder will develop. Family instability is one factor that may instill a sense that the world is an uncontrollable, potentially dangerous place (Chorpita & Barlow, 1998; Suárez et al., 2009), so it is not surprising that individuals from unstable families are at increased risk for developing PTSD if they experience trauma. Family instability was found to be a prewar risk factor for the development of PTSD in a study

of more than 1,600 male and female Vietnam veterans (King et al., 1996).

Finally, social factors play a major role in the development of PTSD (see, for example, Carroll, Rueger, Foy, & Donahoe, 1985). The results from a number of studies are consistent in showing that, if you have a strong and supportive group of people around you, it is much less likely you will develop PTSD after a trauma (Friedman, 2009). These factors seem to be true around the world because the reaction to trauma is similar across cultures, as a study comparing American and Russian adolescents demonstrated (Ruchkin et al., 2005). In a particularly interesting study, Vernberg, La Greca, Silverman, and Prinstein (1996) studied 568 elementary school children 3 months after Hurricane Andrew hit the coast of south Florida. More than 55% of these children reported moderate to severe levels of PTSD symptoms, a typical result for this type of disaster (La Greca & Prinstein, 2002). When the authors examined factors contributing to who developed PTSD symptoms and who didn't, social support from parents, close friends, classmates, and teachers was an important protective factor. Similarly, positive coping strategies involving active problem solving seemed to be protective, whereas becoming angry and placing blame on others were associated with higher levels of PTSD. The broader and deeper the network of social support, the less chance of developing PTSD.

Why is this? As you saw in Chapter 2, we are all social animals, and something about having a loving, caring group of people around us directly affects our biological and psychological responses to stress. A number of studies show that support from loved ones reduces cortisol secretion and hypothalamic–pituitary–adrenocortical (HPA) axis activity in children during stress (see, for example, Nachmias, Gunnar, Mangelsdorf, Parritz, & Buss, 1996). It seems clear that PTSD involves a number of neurobiological systems, particularly elevated corticotropin-releasing factor (CRF), which indicates heightened activity in the HPA axis, as described earlier in this chapter and in Chapter 2 (Amat et al., 2005; Charney, Deutch, Krystal, Southwick, & Davis, 1993; Gunnar & Fisher, 2006; Heim & Nemeroff, 1999; Ladd et al., 2000; Shin et al., 2004; Shin et al., 2009; Sullivan et al., 2000). You may remember that primates studied in the wild under extreme stress also have elevated levels of CRF and cortisol, the stress hormones. Chronic activation of stress hormones in these primates seems to result in permanent damage to the hippocampus, which regulates the stress hormones. Thus, chronic arousal and some other symptoms of PTSD may be directly related to changes in brain function and structure (Bremner, 1999; Bremner et al., 1997; McEwen & Magarinos, 2004). Evidence of damage to the hippocampus has appeared in groups of patients with war-related PTSD (Gurvits et al., 1996; Wang et al., 2010), adult survivors of childhood sexual abuse (Bremner et al., 1995), and firefighters exposed to extreme trauma (Shin et al., 2004). The hippocampus is a part of the brain that plays an important role in learning and memory. Thus, if there is damage to the hippocampus, we might expect some disruptions in learning and memory. Disruptions in memory functions, including short-term memory and recalling events, have been demonstrated in patients with PTSD (Sass et al., 1992). Bremner, Vermetten, Southwick, Krystal, and Charney (1998) suggest that the fragmentation of memory often seen in patients with PTSD may account for difficulties in recalling at least some aspects of their trauma.

Earlier we described a panic attack as an adaptive fear response occurring at an inappropriate time. We have speculated that the "alarm reaction" that is a panic attack is similar in both panic disorder and PTSD but that in panic disorder the alarm is false. In PTSD, the initial alarm is true in that real danger is present (Jones & Barlow, 1990; Keane & Barlow, 2002). If the alarm is severe enough, we may develop a conditioned or learned alarm reaction to stimuli that remind us of the trauma (for example, being tucked into bed reminded Marcie of the emergency room board). We may also develop anxiety about the possibility of additional uncontrollable emotional experiences (such as flashbacks, which are common in PTSD). Whether or not we develop anxiety partly depends on our vulnerabilities. This model of the etiology of PTSD is presented in ■ Figure 4.10.

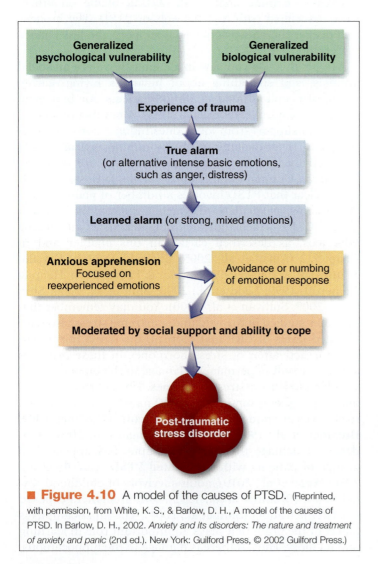

■ **Figure 4.10** A model of the causes of PTSD. (Reprinted, with permission, from White, K. S., & Barlow, D. H., A model of the causes of PTSD. In Barlow, D. H., 2002. *Anxiety and its disorders: The nature and treatment of anxiety and panic* (2nd ed.). New York: Guilford Press, © 2002 Guilford Press.)

Treatment

From the psychological point of view, most clinicians agree that victims of PTSD should face the original trauma, process the intense emotions, and develop effective coping procedures to overcome the debilitating effects of the disorder (Barlow & Lehman, 1996; Keane & Barlow, 2002; Najavits, 2007; Resick, Monson, & Rizvi, 2008). In psychoanalytic therapy, reliving emotional trauma to relieve emotional suffering is called *catharsis*. The trick is in arranging the reexposure so that it will be therapeutic rather than traumatic again. Unlike the object of a specific phobia, a traumatic event is difficult to recreate, and few therapists want to try. Therefore, *imaginal exposure,* in which the content of the trauma and the emotions associated with it are worked through systematically, has been used for decades under a variety of names. At present, the most common strategy to achieve this purpose with adolescents or adults is to work with the victim to develop a narrative of the traumatic experience that is then reviewed extensively in therapy. Cognitive therapy to correct negative assumptions about the trauma, such as blaming oneself in some way, feeling guilty, or both, is often part of treatment (Najavits, 2007; Resick et al., 2008).

Another complication is that trauma victims often repress the emotional side of their memories of the event and sometimes, it seems, the memory itself. This happens automatically and unconsciously. Occasionally, with treatment, the memories flood back and the patient dramatically relives the episode. Although this may be frightening to both patient and therapist, it can be therapeutic if handled appropriately. Evidence is now accumulating that early, structured interventions delivered as soon after the trauma as possible to those who require help are useful in preventing the development of PTSD (Bryant, Moulds, & Nixon, 2003; Ehlers et al., 2003; Litz, Gray, Bryant, & Adler, 2002). For example, in the study by Ehlers and colleagues (2003) of patients who had experienced a scary car accident and were clearly at risk for developing PTSD, only 11% developed PTSD after 12 sessions of cognitive therapy, compared with 61% of those receiving a detailed self-help booklet or 55% of those who were just assessed repeatedly over time but had no intervention. All patients who needed it were then treated with cognitive therapy. However, there is evidence that subjecting trauma victims to a single debriefing session, in which they are forced to express their feelings whether they are distressed or not, can be harmful (Ehlers & Clark, 2003).

Both Marcie, the young girl bitten by the dog, and her brother were treated simultaneously at our clinic. The primary difficulty was Marcie's reluctance to be seen by a doctor or to undergo any physical examinations, so a series of experiences was arranged from least to most intense (Table 4.6). Mildly anxiety-provoking procedures for Marcie included having her pulse taken, lying on an examination table, and taking a bath after accidentally cutting herself. The most intense challenge was being strapped on a restraining board. First Marcie watched her brother go

Table 4.6 Fear and Avoidance Hierarchy for Marcie

	Pretreatment Fear Rating	Posttreatment Fear Rating
Being strapped on a board	4	0
Having an electrocardiogram	4	0
Having a chest X ray	4	0
Having doctor listen to heart with stethoscope	3	0
Lying on examination table	3	0
Taking a bath after sustaining an accidentally inflicted cut	3	0
Allowing therapist to put bandage on a cut	2	0
Letting therapist listen to heart with stethoscope	1	0
Having pulse taken	1	0
Allowing therapist to examine throat with tongue depressor	1	0

Source: From Albano, A. M., Miller, P. P., Zarate, R., Côté, G., & Barlow, D. H. (1997). Behavioral assessment and treatment of PTSD in prepubertal children: Attention to developmental factors and innovative strategies in the case study of a family. *Cognitive and Behavioral Practice, 4,* 254, © 1997 Association for Advancement of Behavior Therapy.

through these exercises. He was not afraid of these particular procedures, although he was anxious about being strapped to a board because of Marcie's terror at the thought. After she watched her brother experience these situations with little or no fear, Marcie tried each one in turn. The therapist took instant photographs of her that she kept after completing the procedures. Marcie was also asked to draw pictures of the situations. The therapist and her family warmly congratulated her as she completed each exercise. Because of Marcie's age, she was not adept at imaginatively recreating memories of the traumatic medical procedures. Therefore, her treatment offered experiences designed to alter her current perceptions of the situations. Marcie's PTSD was successfully treated, and her brother's guilt was greatly reduced as a function of helping in her treatment.

Drugs can also be effective for symptoms of PTSD (Dent & Bremner, 2009). Some of the drugs, such as SSRIs (e.g., Prozac and Paxil), that are effective for anxiety disorders in general have been shown to be helpful for PTSD, perhaps because they relieve the severe anxiety and panic attacks so prominent in this disorder.

Concept Check 4.5

Match the correct preliminary diagnosis with the following cases: (a) acute posttraumatic stress disorder, (b) acute stress disorder, and (c) delayed onset posttraumatic stress disorder.

1. Judy witnessed a horrific tornado level her farm 3 weeks ago. Since then, she's had many flashbacks of the incident, trouble sleeping, and a fear of going outside in storms. _____

2. Jack was involved in a car accident 6 weeks ago in which the driver of the other car was killed. Since then, Jack has been unable to get into a car because it brings back the horrible scene he witnessed. Nightmares of the incident haunt him and interfere with his sleep. He is irritable and has lost interest in his work and hobbies.

_____

3. Patricia was raped at the age of 17, which was 30 years ago. Just recently, she has been having flashbacks of the event, difficulty sleeping, and fear of sexual contact with her husband. _____

Obsessive-Compulsive Disorder

> ### What are the symptoms of obsessive-compulsive disorder?

A client with an anxiety disorder who needs hospitalization is likely to have **obsessive-compulsive disorder (OCD)**. A client referred for psychosurgery (neurosurgery for a psychological disorder) because every psychological and pharmacological treatment has failed and the suffering is unbearable probably has OCD. OCD is the devastating culmination of the anxiety disorders. It is not uncommon for someone with OCD to experience severe generalized anxiety, recurrent panic attacks, debilitating avoidance, and major depression, all occurring simultaneously with obsessive-compulsive symptoms.

Clinical Description

In other anxiety disorders the danger is usually in an external object or situation—or at least in the memory of one. In OCD the dangerous event is a thought, image, or impulse that the client attempts to avoid as completely as someone with a snake phobia avoids snakes (Clark & O'Connor, 2005). For example, has anyone ever told you not to think of pink elephants? If you really concentrate on not thinking of pink elephants, using every mental means possible, you will realize how difficult it is to suppress a suggested thought or image. Individuals with OCD fight this battle all day, every day, sometimes for most of their lives, and they usually fail miserably. In Chapter 3 we discussed the case of Frank, who experienced involuntary thoughts of epilepsy or seizures and prayed or shook his leg to try to distract himself. **Obsessions** are intrusive and mostly nonsensical thoughts, images, or urges that the individual tries to resist or eliminate. **Compulsions** are the thoughts or actions used to suppress the obsessions and provide relief. Frank had both obsessions and compulsions, but his disorder was mild compared to the case of Richard.

Richard ⚬ Enslaved by Ritual

Richard, a 19-year-old college freshman majoring in philosophy, withdrew from school because of incapacitating ritualistic behavior. He abandoned personal hygiene because the compulsive rituals that he had to carry out during washing or cleaning were so time consuming that he could do nothing else. Almost continual showering gave way to no showering. He stopped cutting and washing his hair and beard, brushing his teeth, and changing his clothes. He left his room infrequently and, to avoid rituals associated with the toilet, defecated on paper towels, urinated in paper cups, and stored the waste in the closet. He ate

only late at night when his family was asleep. To be able to eat he had to exhale completely, making a lot of hissing noises, coughs, and hacks, and then fill his mouth with as much food as he could while no air was in his lungs. He would eat only a mixture of peanut butter, sugar, cocoa, milk, and mayonnaise. All other foods he considered contaminants. When he walked he took small steps on his toes while continually looking back, checking and rechecking.

Like everyone with OCD, Richard experienced intrusive and persistent thoughts and impulses; in his case they were about sex, aggression, and religion. His various behaviors were efforts to suppress sexual and aggressive thoughts or to ward off the disastrous consequences he thought would ensue if he did not perform his rituals. Compulsions can be either behavioral (handwashing or checking) or mental (thinking about certain words in a specific order, counting, praying, and so on) (Foa et al., 1996; Purdon, 2009; Steketee & Barlow, 2002). The important thing is that they are believed to reduce stress or prevent a dreaded event. Compulsions are often "magical" in that they often bear no logical relation to the obsession.

Types of Obsessions and Compulsions

Based on statistically associated groupings, there are four major types of obsessions (Bloch, Landeros-Weisenberger, Rosario, Pittenger, & Leckman, 2008; Mathews, 2009) and each is associated with a pattern of compulsive behavior. Symmetry obsessions account for most obsessions (26.7%), followed by "forbidden thoughts or actions" (21%), cleaning and contamination (15.9%), and hoarding (15.4%) (Bloch et al., 2008). Symmetry refers to keeping things in perfect order or doing something in a specific way. As a child, were you careful not to step on cracks in the sidewalk? You and your friends might have kept this up for a few minutes before tiring of it. But what if you had to spend your whole life avoiding cracks, on foot or in a car, to prevent something bad from happening? You wouldn't have much fun. People with aggressive (forbidden) obsessive impulses may feel they are about to yell out a swear word in church. One patient of ours, a young and moral woman, was afraid to ride the bus for fear that if a man sat down beside her she would grab his crotch! In reality, this would be the last thing she would do, but the aggressive urge was so horrifying that she made every attempt possible to suppress it and to avoid riding the bus or similar situations where the impulse might occur.

Certain kinds of obsessions are strongly associated with certain kinds of rituals (Bloch et al., 2008; Calamari et al., 2004; Leckman et al., 1997). For example, forbidden thoughts or actions seem to lead to checking rituals. Checking rituals serve to prevent an imagined disaster or catastrophe. Many are logical, such as repeatedly checking the stove to see whether you turned it off, but severe cases can be illogical. For example, Richard thought that if he did not eat in a certain way he might become possessed. If he didn't take small steps and look back, some disaster might happen to his family. A mental act, such as counting, can also be a compulsion. Obsessions with symmetry lead to ordering and arranging or repeating rituals; obsessions with contamination lead to washing rituals that may restore a sense of safety and control (Rachman, 2006). Like Richard, many patients have several kinds of obsessions and compulsions.

▲ People with obsessive-compulsive hoarding are so afraid they may throw something important away that clutter piles up in their homes.

Tic Disorder and OCD

It is also common for tic disorder, characterized by involuntary movement (sudden jerking of limbs, for example), to co-occur in patients with OCD (particularly children) or in their families (Grados et al., 2001; Leckman et al., 2010). More complex tics with involuntary vocalizations are referred to as Tourette's disorder (Leckman et al., 2010; see Chapter 13). In some cases, these movements are not tics but may be compulsions, as they were in the case of Frank in Chapter 3 who kept jerking his leg if thoughts of seizures entered his head. Approximately 10% to 40% of children and adolescents with OCD also have had tic disorder at some point, leading to a suggestion that tic-related OCD be categorized as a subtype of OCD in *DSM-5* (Leckman et al., 2010). The obsessions in tic-related OCD are almost always related to symmetry.

Hoarding

Recently, a group of patients have come to the attention of specialty clinics because they compulsively hoard things, fearing that if they throw something away, even a 10-year-old newspaper, they then might urgently need it (Frost, Steketee, & Williams, 2002; Grisham & Barlow, 2005; Samuels et al., 2002; Steketee & Frost, 2007a, 2007b). It is not uncommon for some patients' houses and yards to come to the attention of public health authorities. One patient's house and yard was condemned because junk was piled so high it was both unsightly and a fire hazard. Among her hoard was a 20-year collection of used sanitary napkins!

Basically, these individuals usually begin acquiring things during their teenage years and often experience great pleasure, even euphoria, from shopping or otherwise collecting various items. Shopping or collecting things may be a re-

---

DSM Disorder Criteria Summary
Obsessive-Compulsive Disorder

Features of OCD include the following:

> Obsessions: Recurrent and persistent thoughts, impulses, or images that are experienced as intrusive and inappropriate and cause marked anxiety or distress; more than just excessive worries about real-life problems; the person attempts to ignore or suppress or neutralize them; the person recognizes that the thoughts, impulses, or images are a product of his or her own mind

> Compulsions: Repetitive behaviors (e.g., frequent handwashing or checking) or mental acts (e.g., praying or counting) that the person feels driven to perform in response to an obsession or according to rules that must be applied rigidly

> Recognition that the obsessions or compulsions are excessive or unreasonable

> The thoughts, impulses, or behaviors cause marked distress, consume more than an hour a day, or significantly interfere with the person's normal functioning or relationships

Source: Based on DSM-IV-TR. Reprinted with permission from Diagnostic and Statistical Manual of Mental Disorders (4th ed., text revision). © 2000 American Psychiatric Association.

---

obsessive-compulsive disorder (OCD) Anxiety disorder involving unwanted, persistent, intrusive thoughts and impulses, as well as repetitive actions intended to suppress them.

obsessions Recurrent intrusive thought or impulse the client seeks to suppress or neutralize while recognizing it is not imposed by outside forces.

compulsions Repetitive, ritualistic, time-consuming behavior or mental act a person feels driven to perform.

©WR Publishing/Alamy

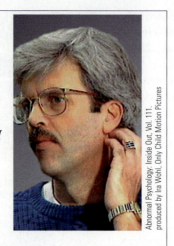

Abnormal Psychology: Inside Out, Vol. 111, produced by Ira Wohl, Only Child Motion Pictures

for example, when sitting in class. Gail Steketee and her colleagues collected examples of thoughts from ordinary people who do not have OCD. Some of these thoughts are listed in Table 4.7.

Have you had any of these thoughts? Most people do, but they are passing worries. Certain individuals, however, are horrified by such thoughts, considering them signs of an alien, intrusive, evil force. The majority of individuals with OCD are female, but the per-

sponse to feeling down or depressed and is sometimes called, facetiously, "retail therapy." But unlike most people who like to shop or collect, these individuals then experience strong anxiety and distress about throwing anything away because everything has either some potential use or sentimental value in their minds, and their homes or apartments may become almost impossible to live in. Most of these individuals don't consider that they have a problem until family members or authorities insist that they receive help. The average age when these people come for treatment is approximately 50, after many years of hoarding (Grisham, Frost, Steketee, Kim, & Hood, 2006). Often they live alone.

Recent careful analysis of the rapidly increasing knowledge of hoarding suggests that it has both similarities and differences with OCD as well as with impulse control disorders, and that, perhaps, it should be listed as a separate disorder in *DSM-5* (Mataix-Cols et al., 2010). This is unlikely, although it may be assigned to the appendix of *DSM-5* for further study. New treatments are in development at our clinic that teach people to assign different values to objects and to reduce anxiety about throwing away items that are somewhat less valued (Steketee & Frost, 2007a). Preliminary results are promising, but more information on long-term effects of these treatments is needed.

Statistics

The lifetime prevalence of OCD is approximately 1.6% (Kessler, Berglund, et al., 2005), and in a given 1-year period the prevalence is 1% (Kessler, Chiu, et al., 2005). Not all cases meeting criteria for OCD are as severe as Richard's. Obsessions and compulsions can be arranged along a continuum, like most clinical features of anxiety disorders. Intrusive and distressing thoughts are common in nonclinical ("normal") individuals (Boyer & Liénard, 2008; Clark & Rhyno, 2005; Fullana et al., 2009). Spinella (2005) found that 13% of a "normal" community sample of people had moderate levels of obsessions or compulsions that were not severe enough to meet diagnostic criteria for OCD.

It would also be unusual *not* to have an occasional intrusive or strange thought. Many people have bizarre, sexual, or aggressive thoughts, particularly if they are bored—

Table 4.7 Obsessions and Intrusive Thoughts Reported by Nonclinical Samples*

Harming
Impulse to jump out of high window
Idea of jumping in front of a car
Impulse to push someone in front of train
Wishing a person would die
While holding a baby, having a sudden urge to kick it
Thoughts of dropping a baby
The thought that if I forget to say goodbye to someone, they might die
Thought that thinking about horrible things happening to a child will cause it
Contamination or Disease
Thought of catching a disease from public pools or other public places
Thoughts I may have caught a disease from touching toilet seat
Idea that dirt is always on my hand
Inappropriate or Unacceptable Behavior
Idea of swearing or yelling at my boss
Thought of doing something embarrassing in public, like forgetting to wear a top
Hoping someone doesn't succeed
Thought of blurting out something in church
Thought of "unnatural" sexual acts
Doubts About Safety, Memory, and So On
Thought that I haven't locked the house up properly
Idea of leaving my curling iron on the carpet and forgetting to pull out the plug
Thought that I've left the heater and stove on
Idea that I've left the car unlocked when I know I've locked it
Idea that objects are not arranged perfectly

*Examples were obtained from Rachman and deSilva (1978) and from unpublished research by Dana Thordarson, PhD, and Michael Kyrios, PhD (personal communications, 2000). *Source:* Reprinted, with permission, from Steketee, G., & Barlow, D. H. (2002). Obsessive-compulsive disorder. In D. H. Barlow, *Anxiety and its disorders: The nature and treatment of anxiety and panic* (2nd ed., p. 529), © 2002 Guilford Press.

centage is not as large as for some other anxiety disorders. Rasmussen and Tsuang (1984, 1986) reported that 55% of 1,630 patients with OCD were female. An epidemiology study noted 60% females in their sample of people with OCD (Karno & Golding, 1991). Interestingly, in children the sex ratio is reversed, with more males than females (Hanna, 1995). This seems to be because boys tend to develop OCD earlier. By mid-adolescence, the sex ratio is approximately equal before becoming predominantly female in adulthood (Albano et al., 1996). Age of onset ranges from childhood through the 30s, with a median age of onset of 19 (Kessler, Berglund, et al., 2005). The age of onset peaks earlier in males (at 13 to 15) than in females (at 20 to 24) (Rasmussen & Eisen, 1990). Once OCD develops, it tends to become chronic (Eisen & Steketee, 1998; Steketee & Barlow, 2002).

OCD looks remarkably similar across cultures. Insel (1984) reviewed studies from England, Hong Kong, India, Egypt, Japan, and Norway and found essentially similar types and proportions of obsessions and compulsions, as did Weissman and colleagues (1994) reviewing studies from Canada, Finland, Taiwan, Africa, Puerto Rico, Korea, and New Zealand.

Causes

Many of us sometimes have intrusive, even horrific, thoughts and occasionally engage in ritualistic behavior, especially when we are under stress (Parkinson & Rachman, 1981a, 1981b). But few of us develop OCD. Again, as with panic disorder and PTSD, someone must develop anxiety focused on the possibility of having additional intrusive thoughts.

The repetitive, intrusive, unacceptable thoughts of OCD may well be regulated by the hypothetical brain circuits described in Chapter 2. However, the tendency to develop anxiety over having additional compulsive thoughts may have the same generalized biological and psychological precursors as anxiety in general (Suárez et al., 2009).

Why would people with OCD focus their anxiety on the occasional intrusive thought rather than on the possibility of a panic attack or some other external situation? One hypothesis is that early experiences taught them that some thoughts are dangerous and unacceptable because the terrible things they are thinking might happen and they would be responsible. These early experiences would result in a specific psychological vulnerability to develop OCD. When clients with OCD equate thoughts with the specific actions or activity represented by the thoughts, this is called *thought–action fusion*. Thought–action fusion may, in turn, be caused by attitudes of excessive responsibility and resulting guilt developed during childhood when even a bad thought is associated with evil intent (Clark & O'Connor, 2005; Salkovskis, Shafran, Rachman, & Freeston, 1999; Steketee & Barlow, 2002). They may learn this through the same process of misinformation that convinced the person with snake phobia that snakes were dangerous and could be everywhere. One patient believed thinking about abortion was the moral equivalent of having an abortion. Richard finally admitted to having strong homosexual impulses that were unacceptable to him and to his minister father, and he believed the impulses were as sinful as actual acts. Many people with OCD who believe in the tenets of fundamental religions, whether Christian, Jewish, or Islamic, present with similar attitudes of inflated responsibility and thought–action fusion. Several studies showed that the strength of religious belief, but not the type of belief, was associated with thought–action fusion and severity of OCD (Rassin & Koster, 2003; Steketee, Quay, & White, 1991). Of course, most people with fundamental religious beliefs do not develop OCD. But what if the most frightening thing in your life was not a snake or speaking in public but a terrible thought that happened to pop into your head? You can't avoid it as you would a snake, so you resist this thought by attempting to suppress it or "neutralize" it using mental or behavioral strategies, such as distraction, praying, or checking. These strategies become compulsions, but they are doomed to fail in the long term, because these strategies backfire and actually increase the frequency of the thought (Purdon, 1999; Wegner, 1989).

Again, generalized biological and psychological vulnerabilities must be present for this disorder to develop. Believing some thoughts are unacceptable and therefore must be suppressed (a specific psychological vulnerability) may put people at greater risk of OCD (Amir, Cashman, & Foa, 1997; Parkinson & Rachman, 1981b; Salkovskis & Campbell, 1994). A model of the etiology of OCD that is somewhat similar to other models of anxiety disorders is presented in ■ Figure 4.11.

Treatment

Studies evaluating the effects of drugs on OCD are showing some promise (Steketee & Barlow, 2002; Stewart, Jenike, & Jenike, 2009). The most effective seem to be those that specifically inhibit the reuptake of serotonin, such as clomipramine or the SSRIs, which benefit up to 60% of patients with OCD, with no particular advantage to one drug over another. However, the average treatment gain is moderate at best (Greist, 1990), and relapse often occurs when the drug is discontinued (Lydiard, Brawman-Mintzer, & Ballenger, 1996).

Highly structured psychological treatments work somewhat better than drugs, but they are not readily available. The most effective approach is called *exposure and ritual prevention (ERP)*, a process whereby the rituals are actively prevented and the patient is systematically and gradually exposed to the feared thoughts or situations (Barlow & Lehman, 1996; Franklin & Foa, 2008; Steketee & Barlow, 2002). Richard, for example, would be systematically exposed to harmless objects or situations that he thought were contaminated, including certain foods and household chemicals, and his washing and checking rituals would be prevented. Usually this can be done by simply working closely with patients to see that they do not wash or check. In severe cases, patients may be hospitalized and the faucets removed

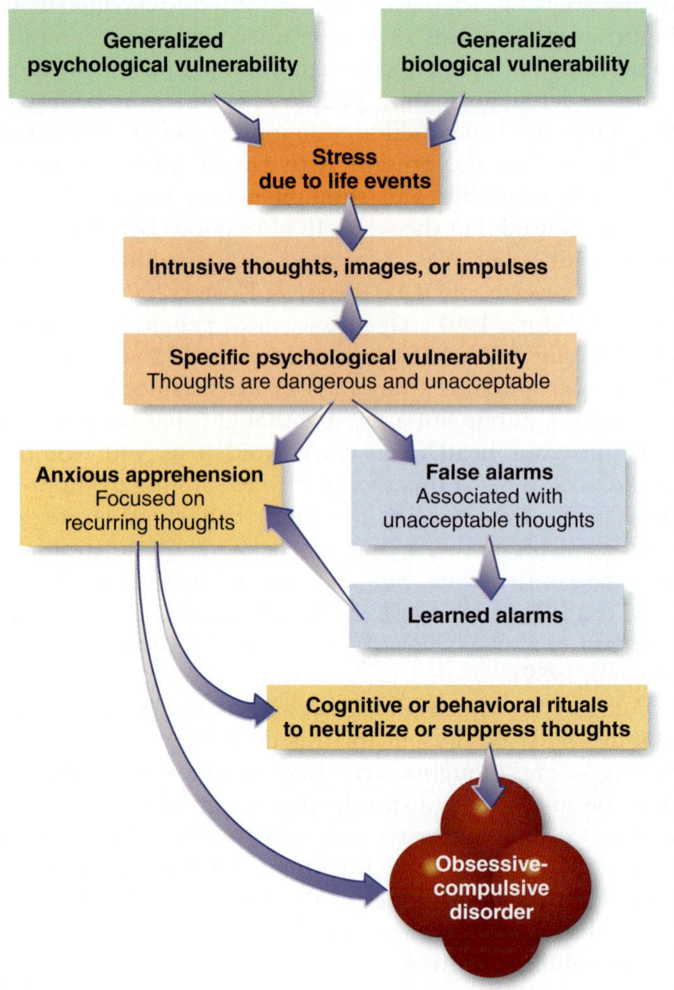

Generalized psychological vulnerability
Generalized biological vulnerability
Stress due to life events
Intrusive thoughts, images, or impulses
Specific psychological vulnerability
Thoughts are dangerous and unacceptable
Anxious apprehension
Focused on recurring thoughts
False alarms
Associated with unacceptable thoughts
Learned alarms
Cognitive or behavioral rituals to neutralize or suppress thoughts
Obsessive-compulsive disorder

Figure 4.11 A model of the causes of obsessive-compulsive disorder. (Reprinted, with permission, from White, K. S., & Barlow, D. H., A model of the causes obsess-compulsive disorder. In Barlow, D. H., *Anxiety and its disorders: The nature and treatment of anxiety and panic* (2nd ed., p. 536). New York: Guilford Press, © 2002 Guilford Press.)

from the bathroom sink for a period to discourage repeated washing. However the rituals are prevented, the procedures seem to facilitate "reality testing," because the client soon learns, at an emotional level, that no harm will result whether he carries out the rituals or not.

Studies are now available examining the combined effects of medication and psychological treatments. In one large study (Foa et al., 2005) ERP was compared to the drug clomipramine, as well as to a combined condition. ERP, with or without the drug, produced superior results to the drug alone, with 86% responding to ERP alone versus 48% to the drug alone. Combining the treatments did not produce any additional advantage. Also, relapse rates were high from the medication-only group when the drug was withdrawn.

Psychosurgery is one of the more radical treatments for OCD. "Psychosurgery" is a misnomer that refers to neurosurgery for a psychological disorder. Jenike and colleagues (1991) reviewed the records of 33 patients with OCD, most of them extremely severe cases who had failed to respond to either drug or psychological treatment. After a specific surgical lesion to the cingulate bundle (cingulotomy), approximately 30% benefited substantially. Similarly, Rück et al. (2008) performed a related surgery (capsulotomy) on 25 patients who had not responded to 5 years of previous treatment; 35% (9 patients) benefited substantially, but 6 of those 9 patients suffered from serious adverse side effects of the surgery. Considering that these patients seemed to have no hope from other treatments, surgery deserves consideration as a last resort.

Concept Check 4.6

Fill in the blanks to form facts about OCD.

1. ____________ are intrusive and nonsensical thoughts, images, or urges an individual tries to eliminate or suppress.
2. The practices of washing, counting, and hoarding to suppress obsessions and provide relief are called ____________________.
3. The lifetime prevalence of OCD is approximately ____________ or even lower.
4. ____________ is a radical treatment for OCD involving a surgical lesion to the cingulate bundle.

On the Spectrum Emerging Views of Anxiety Disorders

In Chapter 3 we introduced the idea that emerging conceptions of psychopathology move us away from an emphasis on categorical (individual) diagnoses to a consideration of larger dimensions, or spectra, in which similar and related diagnoses might be grouped. One such spectrum consists of what some call emotional disorders, including anxiety and depression (Leyfer & Brown, 2011). But how would this dimensional approach to psychopathology change the way we make diagnoses? Recently, we speculated on how a future diagnostic system using dimensional approaches for emotional disorders might work (Brown & Barlow, 2009). To illustrate this approach, let's first consider a case from our clinic.

Mr. S was a high school teacher in his midfifties who had been in a very serious car accident several months before coming in and was suffering from symptoms related to that accident. These included intrusive memories of the crash, "flashbacks" of the accident itself that were very intense emotionally, and images of the cuts and bruises on his wife's face. He also had a strong startle reaction to any cues that reminded him of the accident and avoided driving in certain locations that were somewhat similar to where he had his accident. These symptoms intermingled with a similar set of symptoms emerging from a series of traumatic experiences that had occurred during his service in the Vietnam War. In addition to these trauma symptoms, he also spent a lot of his day worrying about various life events including his own health and that of his family. He also worried about his performance at work and whether he would be evaluated poorly by other staff members, despite the fact that he received consistently high evaluations for his teaching.

After considering everything he said and evaluating him clinically, it was clear that he met criteria for PTSD. He also met criteria for GAD given his substantial worry that was occurring every day about life events unrelated to the trauma. In addition he had some mild depression, perhaps due in part to all of the anxiety he was experiencing. In summary, the patient could be diagnosed with PTSD, although he had substantial features of GAD and depression. But what would it look like if we attempted to describe his symptoms on a series of dimensions rather than on whether they meet criteria for one category or another? ■ Figure 4.12 displays a simplified version of one possible dimensional system (Brown & Barlow, 2009). In this dimensional scheme, "anxiety" (AN) is represented on the left because all individuals with anxiety or depressive disorders have some level of anxiety. Many individuals, but not all, are also depressed (DEP) (as was Mr. S). Mr. S would score fairly high on anxiety and somewhat lower on depression. Looking to the far right of the figure, Mr. S displayed a lot of behavioral avoidance and avoidance of physical sensations (interoceptive avoidance) (AV-BI). Mostly he was having difficulty driving and also would avoid cues connected with his earlier trauma by refusing if at all possible to engage in activities or conversations associ-

ated with the war. Another related type of avoidance is when you avoid experiencing intense emotions or thoughts about emotional experiences. We call this cognitive and emotional avoidance (AV-CE) and Mr. S also scored relatively high on this aspect of avoidance.

But what was the focus of Mr. S's anxiety? Here we look at five characteristics that currently categorize anxiety disorder diagnoses. Looking first at trauma (TRM) focus, obviously, this earned the highest score on Mr. S's profile. He also was suffering from frequent flashbacks to his traumatic experiences, which as you may remember, are similar to panic attacks and consist of strong autonomic surges, such as rapidly increasing heart rate. Thus, he scored high on panic and related autonomic surges (PAS). Other kinds of intrusive obsessive thoughts were not present and he scored low on this dimension (IC). His worry about his health and the health of his family caused him to score moderately high on somatic anxiety (SOM), but social anxiety (SOC) was not particularly high.

As you can see, this dimensional profile provides a more complete picture of Mr. S's clinical presentation than simply noting that he met criteria for PTSD. This is because the profile captures the relative severity of a number of key features of anxiety and mood disorders that are often present together in patients who might meet criteria for only a single diagnosis in the current categorical system. This profile also captures the fact that Mr. S had some depression that was below the severity threshold to meet criteria for mood disorder. Knowing all of this by glancing at Mr. S's profile in Figure 4.12 should help clinicians match therapy more closely to his presenting problems.

This is just one possible example, but it does provide some idea of what a diagnostic system might look like in the future. Although this system would not be ready for *DSM-5* (to be published in 2013) because we would need to do much more research on how best to make it work, a system like this might be ready for *DSM-6*.

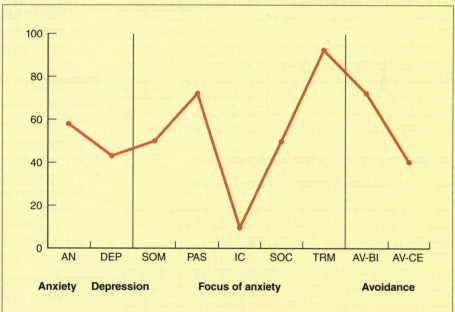

■ **Figure 4.12** Proposed *DSM-5* (or 6) Dimensional Diagnosis of a Patient with PTSD. *AN,* anxiety; *DEP,* unipolar depression; *SOM,* somatic anxiety; *PAS,* panic and related autonomic surges; *IC,* intrusive cognitions; *SOC,* social evaluation; *TRM,* past trauma; *AV-BI,* behavioral and interoceptive avoidance; *AV-CE,* cognitive and emotional avoidance. Higher scores on the *y*-axis (0–100) indicate higher levels of the *x*-axis dimension, but otherwise the *y*-axis metric is arbitrary and is used for illustrative purposes. (Adapted from Brown, T. A., & Barlow, D. H., 2009. A proposal for a dimensional classification system based on the shared features of the DSM-IV anxiety and mood disorders: Implications for assessment and treatment. *Psychological Assessment, 21*(3), 267. © 2009 by American Psychological Association. Reprinted with permission.)

Summary

The Complexity of Anxiety Disorders

What are the similarities and differences among anxiety, fear, and panic attacks?

> Anxiety is a future-oriented state characterized by negative affect in which a person focuses on the possibility of uncontrollable danger or misfortune; in contrast, fear is a present-oriented state characterized by strong escapist tendencies and a surge in the sympathetic branch of the autonomic nervous system in response to current danger.

> A panic attack represents the alarm response of real fear, but there is no actual danger.

> Panic attacks may be (1) unexpected (without warning), (2) situationally bound (always occurring in a specific situation), or (3) situationally predisposed (likely but unpredictable in a specific situation).

> Panic and anxiety combine to create different anxiety disorders.

Generalized Anxiety Disorder

What are the essential features, possible causes, and available treatment approaches for generalized anxiety disorder (GAD)?

> In generalized anxiety disorder, anxiety focuses on minor everyday events, not one major worry or concern.

> Both genetic and psychological vulnerabilities seem to contribute to the development of GAD.

> Although drug and psychological treatments may be effective in the short term, drug treatments are no more effective in the long term than placebo treatments. Successful treatment may help individuals with GAD focus on what is really threatening to them in their lives.

Panic Disorder With and Without Agoraphobia

What are the essential features of panic disorder?

> In panic disorder with or without agoraphobia (a fear and avoidance of situations considered to be "unsafe"), anxiety is focused on the next panic attack.

> We all have some genetic vulnerability to stress, and many of us have had a neurobiological overreaction to some stressful event—that is, a panic attack. Individuals who develop panic disorder then develop anxiety over the possibility of having another panic attack.

> Both drug and psychological treatments have proved successful in the treatment of panic disorder. One psychological method, panic control treatment, concentrates on exposing patients to clusters of sensations that remind them of their panic attacks.

Specific Phobia

What are the principal causes of specific phobia?

> In phobic disorders, the individual avoids situations that produce severe anxiety, panic, or both. In specific phobia, the fear is focused on a particular object or situation.

> Phobias can be acquired by experiencing some traumatic event; they can also be learned vicariously or even be taught.

What strategies are typically used to treat specific phobia?

> Treatment of phobias is rather straightforward, with a focus on structured and consistent exposure-based exercises.

Social Phobia

What are the principal causes of social phobia?

> Social phobia is a fear of being around others, particularly in situations that call for some kind of "performance" in front of other people.

What strategies are used to treat social phobia?

> Although the causes of social phobia are similar to those of specific phobias, treatment has a different focus that includes rehearsing or role-playing socially phobic situations. In addition, drug treatments have been effective.

Posttraumatic Stress Disorder

What are the essential features and possible causes of posttraumatic stress disorder?

> Posttraumatic stress disorder (PTSD) focuses on avoiding thoughts or images of past traumatic experiences.

> The precipitating cause of PTSD is obvious—a traumatic experience. But mere exposure to trauma is not enough. The intensity of the experience seems to be a factor in whether an individual develops PTSD; biological vulnerabilities, as well as social and cultural factors, appear to play a role as well.

What treatment approaches are available for posttraumatic stress disorder?

> Treatment involves reexposing the victim to the trauma and reestablishing a sense of safety to overcome the debilitating effects of PTSD.

Obsessive-Compulsive Disorder

What are the symptoms of obsessive-compulsive disorder?

› Obsessive-compulsive disorder (OCD) focuses on avoiding frightening or repulsive intrusive thoughts (obsessions) or neutralizing these thoughts through the use of ritualistic behavior (compulsions).

› As with all anxiety disorders, biological and psychological vulnerabilities seem to be involved in the development of OCD.

› Drug treatment seems to be only modestly successful in treating OCD. The most effective treatment approach is a psychological treatment called exposure and ritual prevention (ERP).

Key Terms

anxiety, 117
fear, 118
panic, 118
panic attack, 118
behavioral inhibition system (BIS), 120
fight/flight system (FFS), 120
generalized anxiety disorder (GAD), 123

panic disorder with agoraphobia (PDA), 127
agoraphobia, 127
panic disorder without agoraphobia (PD), 128
panic control treatment (PCT), 133
specific phobia, 135
blood–injury–injection phobia, 136
situational phobia, 136
natural environment phobia, 136

animal phobia, 137
separation anxiety disorder, 137
social phobia, 141
posttraumatic stress disorder (PTSD), 145
acute stress disorder, 147
obsessive-compulsive disorder (OCD), 152
obsessions, 152
compulsions, 152

Answers to Concept Checks

4.1

1. b; 2. c; 3. e, d; 4. a; 5. f

4.2

1. T; 2. F (more gradual); 3. T; 4. F; 5. T

4.3

1. F (with agoraphobia); 2. F (3.5%); 3. T; 4. T

4.4

1. d; 2. e; 3. c; 4. f; 5. a; 6. d; 7. c

4.5

1. b; 2. a; 3. c

4.6

1. obsessions; 2. compulsions; 3. 1.6%; 4. psychosurgery

Media Resources

Log in to CengageBrain to access the resources your instructor requires. For this book, you can access:

CourseMate brings course concepts to life with interactive learning, study, and exam preparation tools that support the printed textbook. A textbook-specific website, Psychology CourseMate includes an integrated interactive eBook and other interactive learning tools including quizzes, flashcards, videos, and more.

Abnormal Psychology Videos

› *Steve, a Patient with Panic Disorder:* Steve discusses how panic attacks have disrupted his life.
› *Chuck, a Client with Obsessive-Compulsive Disorder:* Chuck discusses how his obsessions affect his everyday life, going to work, planning a vacation, and so on.
› *Virtual Reality Therapy:* A virtual reality program helps one woman overcome her fear of riding the subway.

› *Snake Phobia Treatment:* A demonstration of exposure therapy helps a snake phobic overcome her severe fear of snakes in just 3 hours.

CENGAGENOW CengageNow is an easy-to-use online resource that helps you study in less time to get the grade you want—NOW. Take a pre-test for this chapter and receive a personalized study plan based on your results that will identify the topics you need to review and direct you to online resources to help you master those topics. Then take a post-test to help you determine the concepts you have mastered and what you will need to work on. If your textbook does not include an access code card, go to CengageBrain.com to gain access.

› Visit www.cengagebrain.com to access your account and purchase materials.

aplia If your professor has assigned Aplia homework:

1. Sign in to your account.
2. Complete the corresponding homework exercises as required by your professor.
3. When finished, click "Grade It Now" to see which areas you have mastered, which need more work, and for detailed explanations of every answer.

Video Concept Reviews

CengageNOW also contains Mark Durand's *Video Concept Reviews* on these challenging topics.

> Anxiety
> Fear

Chapter Quiz

1. _____ is a psychological experience characterized by concern about future events, and _____ is characterized by concern about current circumstances.
   a. Panic; anxiety
   b. Fear; anxiety
   c. Anxiety; fear
   d. Depression; anxiety

2. In an integrated model of anxiety, which childhood experience appears to make an individual more vulnerable to anxiety in adulthood?
   a. negative and inconsistent attention from parents
   b. exposure to situations that reinforce a rigid sense of personal control
   c. interactions with peers that are violent
   d. academic failures in preschool

3. Which of the following is true about generalized anxiety disorder?
   a. It is most common in individuals aged 15–24 years.
   b. Its course tends to be chronic.
   c. It is the least common of the anxiety disorders.
   d. It is more common in men.

4. Why are the majority of people who suffer from agoraphobia women?
   a. Chromosomal features related to sensitivity of the hypothalamus–pituitary axis are more common in women.
   b. Women are more likely to use cognitive distortions in which they appraise events as threatening.
   c. The hormonal system in women sensitizes the female nervous system to stress.
   d. Cultural factors make it more acceptable for women to avoid situations and to report their fears.

5. Marty has a fear of dogs. Which of the following suggests that his fear qualifies as a specific phobia rather than just an everyday fear?
   a. Marty's fear of dogs comes and goes following an episodic pattern.
   b. Marty owns a cat but no dog.
   c. Marty believes that his fear of dogs is reasonable and appropriate.
   d. Marty will only work night shifts, a time when he thinks all dogs will be safely inside.

6. Which technique appears to be the most effective treatment for phobias?
   a. exposure to the feared stimulus under therapeutic supervision
   b. rapid and repeated exposure to the feared stimulus followed by immediate escape
   c. hypnosis during which fear-related conflicts are banished from the unconscious
   d. challenging the client to see that the fears are irrational, unrealistic, and excessive

7. Which of the following is the most essential characteristic of social phobia?
   a. fear of being in public places
   b. fear of being left alone
   c. fear of evaluation by other people
   d. fear of having a panic attack

8. Which feature differentiates posttraumatic stress disorder from acute stress disorder?
   a. the time since the traumatic event occurred
   b. the severity of the symptoms
   c. the nature of the symptoms
   d. the presence of emotional numbing

9. Every morning when he leaves for work Anthony has recurring doubts about whether he locked his front door. He continues thinking about this throughout the day, to the distraction of his work. Anthony is experiencing:
   a. obsession
   b. derealization
   c. panic
   d. compulsion

10. When a person believes that thinking about hurting someone is just as bad as actually hurting someone, that person is experiencing:
    a. obsession
    b. a false alarm
    c. a panic attack
    d. thought-action fusion

Exploring Anxiety Disorders

People with anxiety disorders:

❯ Feel overwhelming tension, apprehension, or fear when there is no actual danger

❯ May take extreme action to avoid the source of their anxiety

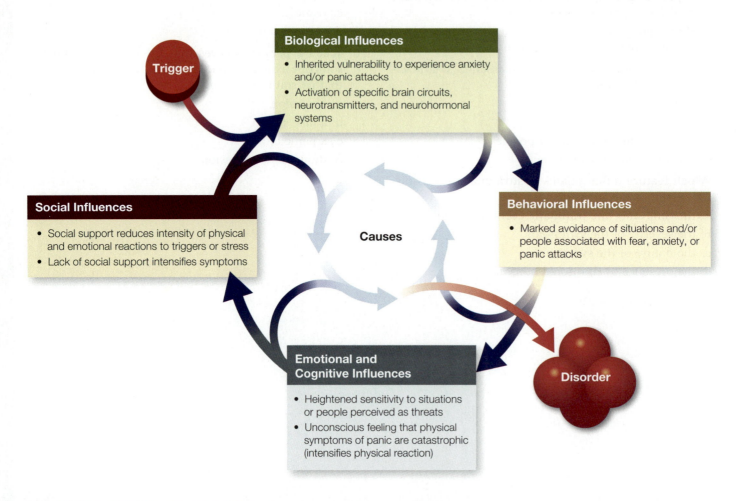

Trigger

Biological Influences
- Inherited vulnerability to experience anxiety and/or panic attacks
- Activation of specific brain circuits, neurotransmitters, and neurohormonal systems

Social Influences
- Social support reduces intensity of physical and emotional reactions to triggers or stress
- Lack of social support intensifies symptoms

Causes

Behavioral Influences
- Marked avoidance of situations and/or people associated with fear, anxiety, or panic attacks

Emotional and Cognitive Influences
- Heightened sensitivity to situations or people perceived as threats
- Unconscious feeling that physical symptoms of panic are catastrophic (intensifies physical reaction)

Disorder

TREATMENT FOR ANXIETY DISORDERS

Cognitive-Behavioral Therapy
- Systematic exposure to anxiety-provoking situations or thoughts
- Learning to substitute positive behaviors and thoughts for negative ones
- Learning new coping skills: relaxation exercises, controlled breathing, etc.

Drug Treatment
- Reduces the symptoms of anxiety disorders by influencing brain chemistry
  —antidepressants (Tofranil, Paxil, Effexor)
  —benzodiazepines (Xanax, Klonopin)

Other Treatments
- Managing stress through a healthy lifestyle: rest, exercise, nutrition, social support, and moderate alcohol or other drug intake

TYPES OF ANXIETY DISORDERS

Panic

People with panic disorders have had one or more panic attacks and are anxious and fearful about having future attacks.

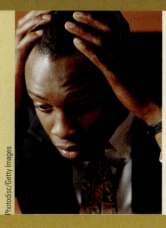

Photodisc/Getty Images

What is a panic attack?
A person having a panic attack feels:
- Apprehension leading to intense fear
- Sensation of "going crazy" or of losing control
- Physical signs of distress: racing heartbeat, rapid breathing, dizziness, nausea, or sensation of heart attack or imminent death

When/why do panic attacks occur?
Panic attacks can be:
- Situationally bound: Always occurring in the same situation, which may lead to extreme avoidance of triggering people, places, or events (see specific and social phobias)
- Unexpected: Can lead to extreme avoidance of any situation or place felt to be unsafe (agoraphobia)
- Situationally predisposed: Attacks may or may not occur in specific situations (between situationally bound and unexpected)

Phobias

People with phobias avoid situations that produce severe anxiety and/or panic. There are three main types:

Eyewire/Getty Images

Agoraphobia
- Fear and avoidance of situations, people, or places where it would be unsafe to have a panic attack: malls, grocery stores, buses, planes, tunnels, etc.
- In the extreme, inability to leave the house or even a specific room
- Begins after a panic attack but can continue for years even if no other attacks occur

Specific Phobia
- Fear of specific object or situation that triggers attack: heights, closed spaces, insects, snakes, or flying
- Develops from personal or vicarious experience of traumatic event with the triggering object or situation or from misinformation

Social Phobia
- Fear of being called for some kind of "performance" that may be judged: speaking in public, using a public restroom (for males), or generally interacting with people

Other Types

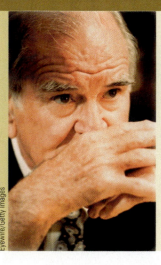

Eyewire/Getty Images

Generalized Anxiety
- Uncontrollable unproductive worrying about everyday events
- Feeling impending catastrophe even after successes
- Inability to stop the worry–anxiety cycle: e.g., Irene's fear of failure about school relationships and health even though everything seemed fine
- Physical symptoms of muscle tension

Posttraumatic Stress
- Fear of reexperiencing a traumatic event: rape, war, life-threatening situation, etc.
- Nightmares or flashbacks (of the traumatic event)
- Avoidance of the intense feelings of the event through emotional numbing

Obsessive-Compulsive
- Fear of unwanted and intrusive thoughts (obsessions)
- Repeated ritualistic actions or thoughts (compulsions) designed to neutralize the unwanted thoughts: e.g., Richard's attempts to suppress "dangerous" thoughts about sex, aggression, and religion with compulsive washing and cleaning rituals

CHAPTER 5

Somatoform and Dissociative Disorders

Student Learning Outcomes*

Use the concepts, language, and major theories of the discipline to account for psychological phenomena.	❯ Describe behavior and mental processes empirically, including operational definitions *(see textbook pages 166–168, 170–171, 172–176, 178–181, 183–189)*
Identify appropriate applications of psychology in solving problems, such as:	❯ Origin and treatment of abnormal behavior *(see textbook pages 168–169, 171–172, 176–177, 181–182, 189–193)*

*Portions of this chapter cover learning outcomes suggested by the American Psychological Association (2007) in their guidelines for the undergraduate psychology major. Chapter coverage of these outcomes is identified by APA Goal and APA Suggested Learning Outcome (SLO).

Many people continually run to the doctor even though there is nothing really wrong with them. This is usually a harmless tendency that may even be worth some good-natured jokes. But for a few individuals, the preoccupation with their health or appearance becomes so great that it dominates their lives. Their problems fall under the general heading of **somatoform disorders**. *Soma* means body, and the problems preoccupying these people seem, initially, to be physical disorders. What the somatoform disorders have in common is that there is usually no identifiable medical condition causing the physical complaints. Thus, these disorders are grouped under the shorthand label of "medically unexplained physical symptoms" (olde Hartman et al., 2009; Woolfolk & Allen, 2011).

Have you ever felt "detached" from yourself or your surroundings? ("This isn't really me," or "That doesn't really look like my hand," or "There's something unreal about this place.") During these experiences, some people feel as if they are dreaming. These mild sensations that most people experience occasionally are slight alterations, or detachments, in consciousness or identity, and they are known as *dissociation* or *dissociative experiences*. For a few people, these experiences are so intense and extreme that they lose their identity entirely and assume a new one or they lose their memory or sense of reality and are unable to function. We discuss several types of **dissociative disorders** in the second half of this chapter.

Somatoform and dissociative disorders are strongly linked historically, and evidence indicates they share common features (Kihlstrom, Glisky, & Anguilo, 1994; Prelior, Yutzy, Dean, & Wetzel, 1993). They used to be categorized under one general heading: "hysterical neurosis." You may remember (from Chapter 1) that the term *hysteria* suggests that the cause of these disorders, which were thought to occur primarily in women, can be traced to a "wandering uterus." But the term *hysterical* came to refer more generally to physical symptoms without known organic cause or to dramatic or "histrionic" behavior thought to be characteristic of women. Sigmund Freud (1894–1962) suggested that in a condition called *conversion hysteria* unexplained physical symptoms indicated the conversion of unconscious emotional conflicts into a more acceptable form. The historical term *conversion* remains with us (without the theoretical implications); however, the prejudicial and stigmatizing terms *hysteria* and *hysterical* are no longer used.

The term *neurosis,* as defined in psychoanalytic theory, suggested a specific cause for certain disorders. Specifically, neurotic disorders resulted from underlying unconscious conflicts, anxiety that resulted from those conflicts, and the implementation of ego defense mechanisms. *Neurosis* was eliminated from the diagnostic system in 1980 because it was too vague, applying to almost all nonpsychotic disorders, and because it implied a specific but unproven cause for these disorders.

Somatoform and dissociative disorders are not well understood, but they have intrigued psychopathologists and the public for centuries. A fuller understanding provides a rich perspective on the extent to which normal, everyday traits found in all of us can evolve into distorted, strange, and incapacitating disorders.

somatoform disorder Pathological concern of individuals with the appearance or functioning of their bodies, usually in the absence of any identifiable medical condition.
dissociative disorder Disorder in which individuals feel detached from themselves or their surroundings and feel reality, experience, and identity may disintegrate.

Somatoform Disorders

> **What are the defining features of somatoform disorders?**

> **What treatments have been developed for somatoform disorders?**

The *Diagnostic and Statistical Manual of Mental Disorders*, 4th edition, Text Revision *(DSM-IV-TR)* lists five basic somatoform disorders: hypochondriasis, somatization disorder, pain disorder, conversion disorder, and body dysmorphic disorder. In each, individuals are pathologically concerned with the appearance or functioning of their bodies. The first three disorders covered in this section—hypochodriasis, somatization disorder, and pain disorder—overlap considerably, and the proposal for *DSM-5* is to combine these three disorders into a new category called complex somatic symptom disorder (American Psychiatric Association, 2010f).

Hypochondriasis

Like many terms in psychopathology, **hypochondriasis** has ancient roots. To the Greeks, the *hypochondria* was the region below the ribs, and the organs in this region affected mental state. For example, ulcers and other gastric disorders were once considered part of the hypochondriac syndrome. As the actual physical causes of such disorders were discovered they were no longer considered a mental disorder, but physical complaints without a clear cause continued to be labeled *hypochondriasis* (Barsky, Wyshak, & Klerman, 1986; Taylor & Asmundson, 2009; Woolfolk & Allen, in press). In hypochondriasis, as we know it today, severe anxiety is focused on the possibility of having a serious disease. The threat seems so real that reassurance from physicians does not seem to help. Consider the case of Gail.

tions were quickly elaborated into the possibility of AIDS or cancer. Gail was afraid to go to sleep at night for fear that she would stop breathing. She avoided exercise, drinking, and even laughing because the resulting sensations upset her.

The major trigger of uncontrollable anxiety and fear was the news in the newspaper and on television. Each time an article or show appeared on the "disease of the month," Gail found herself irresistibly drawn into it, intently noting symptoms that were part of the disease. For days afterward she was vigilant, looking for the symptoms in herself and others. She even watched her dog closely to see whether he was coming down with the dreaded disease. Only with great effort could she dismiss these thoughts after several days. Real illness in a friend or relative would incapacitate her for days at a time.

Gail's fears developed during the first year of her marriage, around the time she learned of her husband's affair. At first, she spent a great deal of time and more money than they could afford going to doctors. Over the years, she heard the same thing during each visit: "There's nothing wrong with you. You're perfectly healthy." Finally, she stopped going, as she became convinced her concerns were excessive, but her fears did not go away and she was chronically miserable.

Gail · Invisibly Ill

Gail was married at 21 and looked forward to a new life. As one of many children in a lower-middle-class household, she felt weak and somewhat neglected and suffered from low self-esteem, but she believed that marriage would solve everything; she was finally someone special. Unfortunately, it didn't work out that way. She soon discovered her husband was continuing an affair with an old girlfriend.

Three years after her wedding, Gail came to our clinic. Although she complained initially of anxiety and stress, it soon became clear that her major concerns were about her health. Any time she experienced minor physical symptoms such as breathlessness or a headache, she was afraid she had a serious illness. A headache indicated a brain tumor. Breathlessness was an impending heart attack. Other sensa-

Clinical Description

Gail's problems are fairly typical of hypochondriasis. Research indicates that hypochondriasis shares many features with the anxiety and mood disorders, particularly panic disorder (Craske et al., 1996; Creed & Barsky, 2004), including similar age of onset, personality characteristics, and patterns of familial aggregation (running in families). Indeed, anxiety and mood disorders are often comorbid with hypochondriasis——that is, if individuals with a hypochondriacal disorder have additional diagnoses, these most likely are anxiety or mood disorders (Côté et al., 1996; Creed & Barsky, 2004; Rief, Hiller, & Margraf, 1998; Simon, Gureje, & Fullerton, 2001). The *DSM-5* committee is even considering the possibility that many individuals with hypochondriasis might be better considered to have an anxiety disorder, a position that receives wide support (Taylor & Asmundson, 2009).

Hypochondriasis is characterized by anxiety or fear that one has a serious disease. Therefore, the essential problem is anxiety, but its expression is different from that of the other anxiety disorders. In hypochondriasis, the individual is preoccupied with bodily symptoms, misinterpreting them as indicative of illness or disease. Almost any physical sensation may become the basis for concern for individuals with hypochondriasis. Some may focus on normal bodily functions such as heart rate or perspiration, and others may focus on minor physical abnormalities such as a cough. Some individuals complain of vague symptoms, such as aches or fatigue. Because a key feature of this disorder is preoccupation with physical symptoms, individuals with hypochondriasis almost always go initially to family physicians. They come to the attention of mental health professionals only after family physicians have ruled out realistic medical conditions as a cause of the patient's symptoms.

▲ In hypochondriasis, normal experiences and sensations are often transformed into life-threatening illnesses.

Another important feature of hypochondriasis is that reassurances from numerous doctors that all is well and the individual is healthy have, at best, only a short-term effect. It isn't long before patients like Gail are back in the office of another doctor on the assumption that the previous doctors have missed something. This is because many of these individuals mistakenly believe they have a disease, a difficult to shake belief sometimes referred to as "disease conviction" (Côté et al., 1996; Haenen, de Jong, Schmidt, Stevens, & Visser, 2000). Therefore, along with anxiety focused on the possibility of disease or illness, disease conviction is a core feature of hypochondriasis (Benedetti et al., 1997; Kellner, 1986; Woolfolk & Allen, in press).

Minor, seemingly hypochondriacal concerns are common in young children, who often complain of abdominal aches and pains that do not seem to have a physical basis. In most cases, these complaints are passing responses to stress and do not develop into a full-blown chronic hypochondriacal syndrome.

Statistics

Prevalence of hypochondriasis in the general population is estimated to be from 1% to 5% (APA, 2000). A review of five studies in primary care settings suggests that the median prevalence rate for hypochondriasis in these settings is 6.7% (Creed & Barsky, 2004). Although historically considered one of the "hysterical" disorders unique to women, the sex ratio is actually closer to 50:50 (Creed & Barsky, 2004; Kellner, 1986; Kirmayer & Robbins, 1991; Kirmayer, Looper, & Taillefer, 2003). It was thought for a long time that hypochondriasis was more prevalent in elderly populations, but this does not seem to be true (Barsky, Frank, Cleary, Wyshak, & Klerman, 1991). In fact, hypochondriasis is spread fairly evenly across various phases of adulthood. Naturally, more older adults go to see physicians, making the *total number* of patients with hypochondriasis in this age group somewhat higher than in the younger population, but the proportion of all those seeing a doctor who have hypochondriasis

is about the same. Hypochondriasis may emerge at any time of life, with the peak age periods found in adolescence, middle age (40s and 50s), and after age 60 (Kellner, 1986). As with most anxiety and mood disorders, hypochondriasis is chronic (Taylor & Asmundson, 2009).

As with anxiety disorders, culture-specific syndromes seem to fit comfortably with hypochondriasis (Kirmayer & Sartorius, 2007). Among these is the disorder of *koro*, in which there is the belief, accompanied by severe anxiety and sometimes panic, that the genitals are retracting into the abdomen. Most victims of this disorder are Chinese males, although it is also reported in females; there are few reports of the problem in Western cultures. Why does *koro* occur in Chinese cultures? Rubin (1982) points to the central importance of sexual functioning among Chinese males. He notes that typical sufferers are guilty about excessive masturbation, unsatisfactory intercourse, or promiscuity. These kinds of events may predispose men to focus their attention on their sexual organs, which could exacerbate anxiety and emotional arousal, much as it does in the anxiety disorders.

Another culture-specific disorder, prevalent in India, is an anxious concern about losing semen, something that obviously occurs during sexual activity. The disorder, called *dhat*, is associated with a vague mix of physical symptoms, including dizziness, weakness, and fatigue. These low-grade depressive or anxious symptoms are simply attributed to a physical factor, semen loss (Ranjith & Mohan, 2004). Other specific culture-bound somatic symptoms associated with emotional factors would include hot sensations in the head or a sensation of something crawling in the head, specific to African patients (Ebigno, 1986), and a sensation of burning in the hands and feet in Pakistani or Indian patients (Kirmayer & Weiss, 1993).

Medically unexplained physical symptoms may be among the more challenging manifestations of psychopathology.

hypochondriasis Somatoform disorder involving severe anxiety over belief in having a disease process without any evident physical cause.

First, a physician must rule out a physical cause for the somatic complaints before referring the patient to a mental health professional. Second, the mental health professional must determine the nature of the somatic complaints to know whether they are associated with a specific somatoform disorder or are part of some other psychopathological syndrome, such as a panic attack. Third, the clinician must be acutely aware of the specific culture or subculture of the patient, which often requires consultation with experts in cross-cultural presentations of psychopathology.

Causes

Investigators with otherwise differing points of view agree on psychopathological processes ongoing in hypochondriasis. Faulty interpretation of physical signs and sensations

as evidence of physical illness is central, so almost everyone agrees that hypochondriasis is basically a disorder of cognition or perception with strong emotional contributions (Adler, Côte, Barlow, & Hillhouse, 1994; Barsky & Wyshak, 1990; Kellner, 1985; olde Hartman et al., 2009; Rief et al., 1998; Salkovskis & Clark, 1993; Taylor & Asmundson, 2004, 2009).

Individuals with hypochondriasis experience physical sensations common to all of us, but they quickly focus their attention on these sensations. Remember that the very act of focusing on yourself increases arousal and makes the physical sensations seem more intense than they are (see Chapter 4). If you also tend to misinterpret these as symptoms of illness, your anxiety will increase further. Increased anxiety produces additional physical symptoms and becomes a vicious cycle (■ Figure 5.1) (Salkovskis, Warwick, & Deale, 2003; Warwick & Salkovskis, 1990).

Using procedures from cognitive science such as the Stroop test (see Chapter 2), a number of investigators (Hitchcock & Mathews, 1992; Pauli & Alpers, 2002) have confirmed that participants with hypochondriasis show enhanced perceptual sensitivity to illness cues. They also tend to interpret ambiguous stimuli as threatening (Haenen et al., 2000). Thus, they quickly become aware (and frightened) of any sign of possible illness or disease. A minor headache, for example, might be interpreted as a sure sign of a brain tumor. Smeets, de Jong, and Mayer (2000) demonstrated that individuals with hypochondriasis, compared to "normals," take a "better safe than sorry" approach to dealing with even minor physical symptoms by getting them checked out as soon as possible. More fundamentally, they have a restrictive concept of health as being symptom free (Rief et al., 1998).

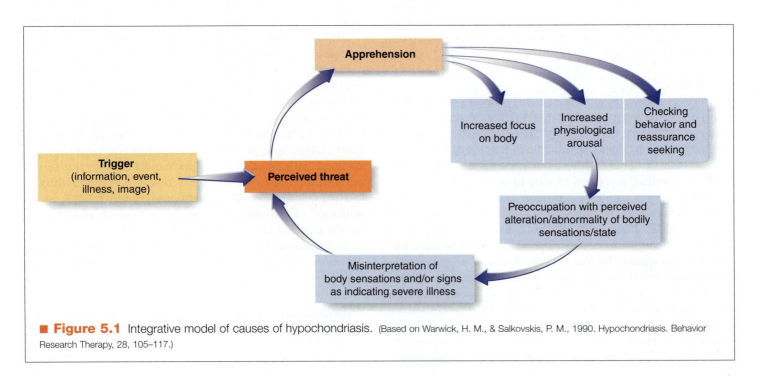

■ **Figure 5.1** Integrative model of causes of hypochondriasis. (Based on Warwick, H. M., & Salkovskis, P. M., 1990. Hypochondriasis. Behavior Research Therapy, 28, 105–117.)

What causes individuals to develop this pattern of somatic sensitivity and distorted beliefs? Although it is not certain, the cause is unlikely to be found in isolated biological or psychological factors. There is every reason to believe the fundamental causes of hypochondriasis are similar to those implicated in the anxiety disorders (Barlow, 2002; Suárez et al., 2009). For example, evidence shows that hypochondriasis runs in families (Kellner, 1985) and that there is a modest genetic contribution (Taylor, Thordarson, Jang, & Asmundson, 2006). But this contribution may be nonspecific, such as a tendency to overrespond to stress, and thus may be indistinguishable from the nonspecific genetic contribution to anxiety disorders. Hyperresponsivity might combine with a tendency to view negative life events as unpredictable and uncontrollable and, therefore, to be guarded against at all times (Noyes et al., 2004; Suárez et al., 2009). As we noted in Chapter 4, these factors would constitute biological and psychological vulnerabilities to anxiety.

Why does this anxiety focus on physical sensations and illness? We know that children with hypochondriacal concerns often report the same kinds of symptoms that other family members may have reported at one time (Kellner, 1985; Kirmayer et al., 2003; Pilowsky, 1970). It is therefore quite possible, as in panic disorder, that individuals who develop hypochondriasis have *learned* from family members to focus their anxiety on specific physical conditions and illness.

Three other factors may contribute to this etiological process (Côté et al., 1996; Kellner, 1985). First, hypochondriasis seems to develop in the context of a stressful life event, as do many disorders, including anxiety disorders. Such events often involve death or illness (Noyes et al., 2004; Sandin, Chorot, Santed, & Valiente, 2004). (Gail's traumatic first year of marriage seemed to coincide with the beginning of her disorder.) Second, people who develop hypochondriasis tend to have had a disproportionate incidence of disease in their family when they were children. Thus, even if they did not develop hypochondriasis until adulthood, they carry strong memories of illness that could easily become the focus of anxiety. Third, an important social and interpersonal influence may be operating (Noyes et al., 2003; Suárez et al., 2009). Some people who come from families where illness is a major issue seem to have learned that an ill person often gets a lot of attention. The "benefits" of being sick might contribute to the development of the disorder in some people. A "sick person" who receives increased attention for being ill and is able to avoid work or other responsibilities is described as adopting a "sick role."

Treatment

Unfortunately, relatively little is known about treating hypochondriasis. Clinical reports indicate that reassurance and education seems to be effective in some cases (Haenen et al., 2000; Kellner, 1992)—which is surprising because, by definition, patients with hypochondriasis are not supposed to benefit from reassurance about their health. However, reassurance is usually given only briefly by family doctors who have little time to provide the ongoing support and reassurance that might be necessary. Mental health professionals may be able to offer reassurance in a more effective and sensitive manner, devote sufficient time to all concerns the patient may have, and attend to the "meaning" of the symptoms (for example, their relation to the patient's life stress). Fava, Grandi, Rafanelli, Fabbri, and Cazzaro (2000) tested this idea by assigning 20 patients who met diagnostic criteria for hypochondriasis to two groups. One received "explanatory therapy" in which the clinician went over the source and origins of their symptoms in some detail. These patients were assessed immediately after the therapy and again at a 6-month follow-up. The other group was a wait-list control group that did not receive the explanatory therapy until after their 6 months of waiting. All patients received usual medical care from their physicians. In both groups, taking the time to explain in some detail the nature of the patient's disorder in an educational framework was associated with a significant reduction in hypochondriacal fears and beliefs and a decrease in health-care usage, and these gains were maintained at the follow-up. For the wait-list group, treatment gains did not occur until they received explanatory therapy, suggesting this treatment is effective.

Evaluations of more robust treatments have now appeared (Clark et al., 1998; Kroenke, 2007; Thomson & Page, 2007). For example, in the best study to date, Barsky and Ahern (2005) randomly assigned 187 patients with hypochondriasis to receive either six sessions of cognitive-behavioral treatment (CBT) from trained therapists or treatment as usual from primary care physicians. CBT focused on identifying and challenging illness-related misinterpretations of physical sensations and on showing patients how to create "symptoms" by focusing attention on certain body areas. Bringing on their own symptoms persuaded many patients that such events were under their control. Patients were also coached to seek less reassurance regarding their concerns. CBT was more effective after treatment and at each follow-up point for both symptoms of hypochondriasis and overall changes in functioning and quality of life. But results were still "modest," and many eligible patients refused to enter treatment because they were convinced their problems were medical rather than psychological.

A few recent reports suggest that drugs may help some people with hypochondriasis (Fallon et al., 2003; Kjernisted, Enns, & Lander, 2002; Kroenke, 2007; Taylor et al., 2005). Not surprisingly, these same types of drugs (antidepressants) are useful for anxiety and depression. In one study, CBT and the drug paroxetine (Paxil), a serotonin-specific reuptake inhibitor (SSRI), were both effective, but only CBT was significantly different from a placebo condition. Specifically, 45% in the CBT group, 30% in the Paxil group, and 14% in the placebo group responded to treatment among all patients who entered the study (Greeven et al., 2007).

Somatization Disorder

In 1859, Pierre Briquet, a French physician, described patients who came to see him with seemingly endless lists of somatic complaints for which he could find no medical basis (American Psychiatric Association, 1980). Despite his negative findings, patients returned shortly with either the same complaints or new lists containing slight variations. For many years, this disorder was called *Briquet's syndrome* before being changed in 1980 to **somatization disorder**. Consider the case of Linda.

Linda ❖ Full-Time Patient

Linda, an intelligent woman in her 30s, came to our clinic looking distressed and pained. As she sat down she noted that coming into the office was difficult for her because she had trouble breathing and considerable swelling in the joints of her legs and arms. She was also in some pain from chronic urinary tract infections and might have to leave at any moment to go to the restroom, but she was extremely happy she had kept the appointment. She said she knew we would have to go through a detailed initial interview, but she had something that might save time. At this point, she pulled out several sheets of paper and handed them over. One section, some five pages long, described her contacts with the health-care system for *major difficulties only*. Times, dates, potential diagnoses, and days hospitalized were noted. The second section, one-and-a-half single-spaced pages, consisted of a list of all medications she had taken for various complaints.

Linda felt she had any one of a number of chronic infections that nobody could properly diagnose. She had begun to have these problems in her teenage years. She often discussed her symptoms and fears with doctors and clergy. Drawn to hospitals and medical clinics, she had entered nursing school after high school. However, during hospital training, she noticed her physical condition deteriorating rapidly: She seemed to pick up the diseases she was learning about. A series of stressful emotional events resulted in her leaving nursing school.

After developing unexplained paralysis in her legs, Linda was admitted to a psychiatric hospital, and after a year she regained her ability to walk. On discharge she obtained disability status, which freed her from having to work full time, and she volunteered at the local hospital. With her chronic but fluctuating incapacitation, on some days she could go in and on some days she could not. She was currently seeing a family practitioner and six specialists, who monitored various aspects of her physical condition. She was also seeing two ministers for pastoral counseling.

Clinical Description

Do you notice any differences between Linda, who presented with somatization disorder, and Gail, who presented with hypochondriacal disorder? Linda was more severely impaired and had suffered in the past from symptoms of paralysis. Also, Linda did not seem as *afraid* as Gail that she had a disease. Linda was concerned with the symptoms themselves, not with what they might mean. Individuals with hypochondriasis most often take immediate action on noticing a symptom by calling the doctor or taking medication. People with somatization, however, do not feel the urgency to take action but continually feel weak and ill, and they avoid exercising, thinking it will make them worse (Rief et al., 1998).

Furthermore, Linda's entire life revolved around her symptoms. She once told her therapist that her symptoms were her identity— without them she would not know who she was. By this she meant that she would not know how to relate to people except in the context of discussing her symptoms much as other people might talk about their day at the office or their kids' accomplishments at school. Her few friends who were not health-care professionals had the patience to relate to her sympathetically, through the veil of her symptoms, and she thought of them as friends because they "understood" her suffering. Linda's case is an extreme example of adopting the "sick role" described earlier.

Statistics

Somatization disorder is rare. *DSM-III-R* criteria required 13 or more symptoms from a list of 35, making diagnosis difficult. The criteria were greatly simplified for *DSM-IV*,

---

DSM Disorder Criteria Summary
Somatization Disorder

Features of somatization disorder include the following:

❯ A history of many physical complaints beginning before the age of 30, which occur over several years and result in treatment being sought, or significant impairment in important areas of functioning

❯ Each of the following: (1) four pain symptoms; (2) two gastrointestinal symptoms other than pain (e.g., nausea, diarrhea, bloating); (3) one sexual symptom (e.g., excessive menstrual bleeding, erectile dysfunction); (4) one pseudo-neurological symptom (e.g., double vision, impaired coordination or balance, difficulty swallowing)

❯ Physical symptoms cannot be fully explained by a known general medical condition or the effects of a substance (for example, a drug of abuse or a medication) *or* where there is a related general medical condition, the physical complaints or impairment are in excess of what would be expected

❯ Complaints or impairment are not intentionally produced or feigned

Source: Based on *DSM-IV-TR.* Reprinted with permission from *Diagnostic and Statistical Manual of Mental Disorders* (4th ed., text revision). © 2000 American Psychiatric Association.

with only eight symptoms required (Cloninger, 1996). Katon and colleagues (1991) demonstrated that somatization disorder occurs on a continuum: People with only a few medically unexplained physical symptoms may experience sufficient distress and impairment of functioning to be considered to have a disorder that is called *undifferentiated somatoform disorder*. But this disorder is just somatization disorder with fewer than eight symptoms, and for that reason the label is likely to be eliminated in *DSM-5*. Using between four and six symptoms as criteria, Escobar and Canino (1989) found a prevalence of somatization disorder of 4.4% in one large city. The median prevalence in six samples of a large number of patients in a primary care setting meeting these criteria was 16.6% (Creed & Barsky, 2004).

Linda's disorder developed during adolescence, which is the typical age of onset. A number of studies have demonstrated that individuals with somatization disorder tend to be women, unmarried, and from lower socioeconomic groups (see, for example, Creed & Barsky, 2004; Lieb et al., 2002; Swartz, Blazer, George, & Landerman, 1986). For instance, 68% of the patients in a large sample studied by Kirmayer and Robbins (1991) were female. In addition to a variety of somatic complaints, individuals may have psychological complaints, usually anxiety or mood disorders (Adler et al., 1994; Kirmayer & Robbins, 1991; Lieb et al., 2002; Rief et al., 1998). Obviously, individuals with somatization disorder overuse and misuse the health-care system, with medical bills as much as 9 times more than the average patient (Barsky, Orav, & Bates, 2005; Hiller, Fichter, & Rief, 2003; Woolfolk & Allen, in press). In one study, 19% of people with this disorder were on disability (Allen, Woolfolk, Escobar, Gara, & Hamer, 2006). Although symptoms may come and go, somatization disorder and the accompanying sick role behavior are chronic, often continuing into old age.

The rates are relatively uniform around the world for medically unexplained physical symptoms, as is the sex ratio (Gureje, Simon, Ustun, & Goldberg, 1997). When the problem is severe enough to meet criteria for disorder, the sex ratio is approximately 2:1 female to male.

Causes

Somatization disorder shares some features with hypochondriasis, including a history of family illness or injury during childhood. But this history is a minor factor at best because countless families experience chronic illness or injuries without passing on severe anxiety of being ill or the sick role to children. Something else contributes strongly to somatization disorder.

Given the past difficulty in making a diagnosis, few studies of causes of somatization disorder have been done. Early studies of possible genetic contributions had mixed results. For example, in a sophisticated twin study, Torgersen (1986) found no increased prevalence of somatization disorder in monozygotic (identical) pairs, but most studies find substantial evidence that the disorder runs in families and

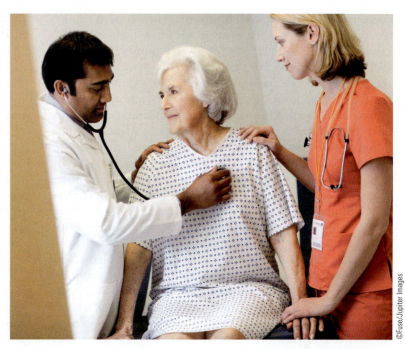

▲ In somatization disorder, primary relationships are often with medical caregivers; one's symptoms are one's identity.

may have a heritable basis (Bell, 1994; Guze, Cloninger, Martin, & Clayton, 1986; Katon, 1993). A more startling finding emerged from these studies, however. Somatization disorder is strongly linked in family and genetic studies to *antisocial personality disorder (ASPD)* (see Chapter 11), which is characterized by vandalism, persistent lying, theft, irresponsibility with finances and at work, and outright physical aggression. Individuals with ASPD seem insensitive to signals of punishment and to the negative consequences of their often impulsive behavior, and they apparently experience little anxiety or guilt.

ASPD occurs primarily in males and somatization disorder in females, but they share a number of features. Both begin early in life; typically run a chronic course; predominate among lower socioeconomic classes; are difficult to treat; and are associated with marital discord, drug and alcohol abuse, and suicide attempts, among other complications (Cloninger, 1978; Goodwin & Guze, 1984; Lilienfeld, 1992; Mai, 2004). Both family and adoption studies suggest that ASPD and somatization disorder tend to run in families and may well have a heritable component (see, for example, Bohman, Cloninger, von Knorring, & Sigvardsson, 1984; Cadoret, 1978), although it is also possible that the behavioral patterns could be learned in a maladaptive family setting.

Yet, the aggressiveness, impulsiveness, and lack of emotion characteristic of ASPD seem to be at the other end of the spectrum from somatization disorder. What could

somatization disorder Somatoform disorder involving extreme and long-lasting focus on multiple physical symptoms for which no medical cause is evident.

these two disorders possibly have in common? Although we don't yet have the answers, Scott Lilienfeld (1992; Lilienfeld & Hess, 2001) has reviewed a number of hypotheses; although they are speculative, we look at some of them here because they are a fascinating example of integrative biopsychosocial thinking about psychopathology.

One model with some support suggests that somatization disorder and ASPD share a neurobiologically based disinhibition syndrome characterized by impulsive behavior (see, for example, Cloninger, 1987; Gorenstein & Newman, 1980). Evidence indicates that impulsiveness is common in ASPD (see, for example, Newman, Widom, & Nathan, 1985). How does this apply to people with somatization disorder? Many of the behaviors and traits associated with somatization disorder also seem to reflect the impulsive characteristic of short-term gain at the expense of long-term problems. The continual development of new somatic symptoms gains immediate sympathy and attention (for a while) but eventually leads to social isolation (Goodwin & Guze, 1984). One study confirmed that patients with somatization disorder are more impulsive and pleasure seeking than patients with other disorders such as anxiety disorders (Battaglia, Bertella, Bajo, Politi, & Bellodi, 1998).

If individuals with ASPD and somatization disorder share the same underlying neurophysiological vulnerability, why do they behave so differently? The explanation is that social and cultural factors exert a strong effect. Both Cathy Spatz Widom (1984) and Robert Cloninger (1987) have pointed out that the major difference between the disorders is their degree of dependence. Aggression is strongly associated with males in most mammalian species, including rodents (Gray & Buffery, 1971). Dependence and lack of aggression are strongly associated with females. Thus, both aggression and ASPD are strongly associated with males, and dependence and somatization disorder are strongly associated with females. In support of this idea, Lilienfeld and Hess (2001), working with college students, found tendencies for females with antisocial and aggressive traits to report more somatic symptoms. Gender roles are among the strongest components of identity. It is possible that gender socialization accounts almost entirely for the profound differences in the expression of the same biological vulnerability among men and women.

Might these assumptions apply to Linda or her family? Linda's sister had been married briefly and had two children. She had been in therapy for most of her adult life. Occasionally, Linda's sister visited doctors with various somatic complaints, but her primary difficulty was unexplained periods of recurring amnesia that might last several days; these spells alternated with blackout periods during which she was rushed to the hospital.

There were signs of sexual impulsivity and ASPD in Linda and her family. The sister's older daughter, after a stormy adolescence characterized by truancy and delinquency, was sentenced to jail for violations involving drugs and assault. Amid one session with us, Linda noted that she had kept a list of people with whom she had had sexual intercourse. Linda's list numbered well over 20, and most of the sexual episodes occurred in the offices of mental health professionals or clergy!

This development in Linda's relationship with caregivers was important because she saw it as the ultimate sign that the caregivers were concerned about her as a person and she was important to them. But the relationships almost always ended tragically. Several of the caregivers' marriages disintegrated, and at least one mental health professional committed suicide. Linda herself was never satisfied or fulfilled by the relationships but was greatly hurt when they inevitably ended. The American Psychological Association has decreed that it is *always* unethical to have *any* sexual contact with a patient at any time during treatment. Violations of this ethical canon have nearly always had tragic consequences.

Treatment

Somatization disorder is exceedingly difficult to treat. Although there are treatments with proven effectiveness, mostly cognitive-behavioral ones (Woolfolk & Allen, in press), the effectiveness is somewhat lower than for other disorders such as anxiety and mood disorders. In our clinic, we concentrate on initially providing reassurance, reducing stress, and, in particular, reducing the frequency of help-seeking behaviors. One of the most common patterns is the person's tendency to visit numerous medical specialists to address the symptom of the week. There is an extensive medical and physical workup with every visit to a new physician (or to one who has not been seen for a while) at an extraordinary cost to the health-care system (Barsky et al., 2005; Hiller et al., 2003). In treatment, to limit these visits, a gatekeeper physician is assigned each patient to screen all physical complaints. Subsequent visits to specialists must be specifically authorized by this gatekeeper. In the context of a positive therapeutic relationship, most patients are amenable to this arrangement.

Additional therapeutic attention is directed at reducing the supportive consequences of relating to significant others on the basis of physical symptoms alone. More appropriate methods of interacting with others are encouraged, along with additional procedures to promote healthy social and personal adjustment without relying on being "sick." In this context, CBT may then be the most helpful (Allen et al., 2006; Mai, 2004; Woolfolk & Allen, in press). Because Linda, like many patients with this disorder, was receiving disability payments from the state, additional goals involved encouraging at least part-time employment, with the ultimate goal of discontinuing disability.

Pain Disorder

A related somatoform disorder about which little is known is **pain disorder**. Pain disorder refers to pain in one or more sites in the body that is associated with significant distress or impairment. In pain disorder, there may have been clear physical reasons for pain, at least initially, but psychological factors play a major role in maintaining it, particularly anxiety focused on the experience of pain (Asmundson &

Carleton, 2009). In *DSM-5,* the proposal is to make this condition part of a larger category called "complex somatic symptom disorder," as described in the beginning of the chapter. But the clinician could still specify complaints of chronic pain (and associated anxiety) as the principal focus. The three subtypes of pain disorder in *DSM-IV-TR* run the gamut from pain judged to result primarily from psychological factors to pain judged to result primarily from a general medical condition. Several studies suggest that this is a fairly common condition, with 5% to 12% of the population meeting criteria for pain disorder (Asmundson & Carleton, 2009; Frohlich, Jacobi, & Wittchen, 2006; Grabe et al., 2003).

An important feature of pain disorder is that the pain is real and it hurts, regardless of the causes (Aigner & Bach, 1999; King & Strain, 1991). Consider the two cases described here.

The Medical Student ┆ Temporary Pain

During her first clinical rotation, a 25-year-old third-year medical student in excellent health was seen at her student health service for intermittent abdominal pain of several weeks' duration. The student claimed no past history of similar pain. Physical examination revealed no physical problems, but she told the physician that she had recently separated from her husband. The student was referred to the health service psychiatrist. No other psychiatric problems were found. She was taught relaxation techniques and given supportive therapy to help her cope with her current stressful situation. The student's pain subsequently disappeared, and she successfully completed medical school.

DSM Disorder Criteria Summary
Pain Disorder

Features of pain disorder include the following:

> Prevalence of serious pain in one or more anatomical sites
> Pain causes clinically significant distress or impairment in functioning
> Psychological factors are judged to play a primary role in the onset, severity, exacerbation, or maintenance of the pain
> Pain is not feigned or intentionally produced

Source: Based on *DSM-IV-TR.* Reprinted with permission from *Diagnostic and Statistical Manual of Mental Disorders* (4th ed., text revision). © 2000 American Psychiatric Association.

The Woman with Cancer ┆ Managing Pain

A 56-year-old woman with metastatic breast cancer who appeared to be coping appropriately with her disease had severe pain in her right thigh for a

month. She initially obtained relief from a combination of drugs and subsequently received hypnotherapy and group therapy. These treatment modalities provided additional pain relief and enabled the patient to decrease her narcotic intake with no increase in pain.

The medical student's pain was seen as purely psychological. In the case of the second woman, the pain was probably related to cancer. But we now know that whatever its cause, pain has a strong psychological component. If medical treatments for existing physical conditions are in place and pain remains, or if the pain seems clearly related to psychological factors, psychological interventions are appropriate. Because of the complexity of pain itself and the variety of narcotics and other medications prescribed for it, multidisciplinary pain clinics are part of most large hospitals. (In Chapter 7, we delve more deeply into types of pain disorders, their causes, and treatment.)

Conversion Disorder

The term *conversion* has been used off and on since the Middle Ages (Mace, 1992) but was popularized by Freud, who believed the anxiety resulting from unconscious conflicts somehow was "converted" into physical symptoms to find expression. This allowed the individual to discharge some anxiety without actually experiencing it.

Clinical Description

Conversion disorders generally have to do with physical malfunctioning, such as paralysis, blindness, or difficulty speaking (aphonia), without any physical or organic pathology to account for the malfunction. Most conversion symptoms suggest that some kind of neurological disease is affecting sensory–motor systems, although conversion symptoms can mimic the full range of physical malfunctioning. For this reason, and because the term "conversion" implies a specific etiology for which there is limited evidence, the proposal for *DSM-5* is to change the name to "functional neurological disorder" (with "functional" referring to a symptom without organic cause) (Stone, LaFrance, Levenson, & Sharpe, 2010).

Conversion disorders provide some of the most intriguing, sometimes astounding, examples of psychopathology. What could possibly account for somebody going blind when all visual processes are normal or experiencing paralysis of the arms or legs when there is no neurological damage? Consider the case of Eloise.

pain disorder Somatoform disorder featuring true pain but for which psychological factors play an important role in onset, severity, or maintenance.
conversion disorder Physical malfunctioning, such as blindness or paralysis, suggesting neurological impairment but with no organic pathology to account for it.

Eloise ⚕ Unlearning Walking

Eloise sat on a chair with her legs under her, refusing to put her feet on the floor. Her mother sat close by, ready to assist her if she needed to move or get up. Her mother had made the appointment and, with the help of a friend, had all but carried Eloise into the office. Eloise was a 20-year-old woman of borderline intelligence who was friendly and personable during the initial interview.

Eloise's difficulty walking developed over 5 years. Her right leg had given way and she began falling. Gradually, the condition worsened to the point that 6 months before her admission to the hospital Eloise could move around only by crawling on the floor. Physical examinations revealed no physical problems.

Eloise presented with a classic case of conversion disorder. Although she was not paralyzed, her specific symptoms included weakness in her legs and difficulty keeping her balance, with the result that she fell often.

Eloise lived with her mother, who ran a gift shop in the front of her house in a small rural town. Eloise had been schooled through special education programs until she was about 15; after this, no further programs were available. When Eloise began staying home, her walking began to deteriorate.

In addition to blindness, paralysis, and aphonia, conversion symptoms may include total mutism and the loss of the sense of touch. Some people have seizures, which may be psychological in origin, because no significant electroencephalogram (EEG) changes can be documented. Another relatively common symptom is *globus hystericus,* the sensation of a lump in the throat that makes it difficult to swallow, eat, or sometimes talk (Finkenbine & Miele, 2004).

DSM Disorder Criteria Summary
Conversion Disorder

Features of conversion disorder include the following:

> One or more conditions affecting voluntary motor or sensory function that suggest a neurological or general medical condition

> Psychological factors are judged to be associated with the condition because of preceding conflicts or other stressors

> The condition cannot otherwise be explained by a general medical condition, effects of a substance, or as a culturally sanctioned behavior or experience

> The condition causes clinically significant distress or impairment

Source: Based on DSM-IV-TR. Reprinted with permission from *Diagnostic and Statistical Manual of Mental Disorders* (4th ed., text revision). © 2000 American Psychiatric Association.

Closely Related Disorders Distinguishing among conversion reactions, real physical disorders, and outright **malingering** (faking) is sometimes difficult. Several factors can help. Conversion symptoms are often precipitated by marked stress. C. V. Ford (1985) noted that the incidence of marked stress preceding a conversion symptom occurred in 52% to 93% of the studied patients. Often this stress takes the form of a physical injury. In one large survey, 324 out of 869 patients (37%) reported prior physical injury (Stone, Carson, Aditya, et al., 2009). Thus, if the clinician cannot identify a stressful event preceding the onset of the conversion symptom, the clinician might more carefully consider the presence of a true physical condition. In addition, although people with conversion symptoms can usually function normally, they seem truly unaware either of this ability or of sensory input. For example, individuals with the conversion symptom of blindness can usually avoid objects in their visual field, but they will tell you they can't see the objects. Similarly, individuals with conversion symptoms of paralysis of the legs might suddenly get up and run in an emergency and then be astounded they were able to do this. It is possible that at least some people who experience miraculous cures during religious ceremonies may have been suffering from conversion reactions. These factors may help in distinguishing between conversion and organically based physical disorders, but clinicians sometimes make mistakes, although it is not common with modern diagnostic techniques. In any case, ruling out medical causes for the symptoms is crucial to making a diagnosis of conversion and, given advances in medical screening procedures, will become the principal diagnostic criterion in *DSM-5* (APA, 2010; Stone et al., 2010).

It can also be difficult to distinguish between individuals who are truly experiencing conversion symptoms in a seemingly involuntary way and malingerers who are good at faking symptoms. Once malingerers are exposed, their motivation is clear: They are either trying to get out of something, such as work or legal difficulties, or they are attempting to gain something, such as a financial settlement. Malingerers are fully aware of what they are doing and are clearly attempting to manipulate others to gain a desired end.

More puzzling is a set of conditions called **factitious disorders**, which fall somewhere between malingering and conversion disorders. The symptoms are under voluntary control, as with malingering, but there is *no obvious reason* for voluntarily producing the symptoms except, possibly, to assume the sick role and receive increased attention. Tragically, this disorder may extend to other members of the family. An adult, almost always a mother, may purposely make her child sick, evidently for the attention and pity given to her as the mother of a sick child. When an individual deliberately makes someone else sick, the condition is called *factitious disorder by proxy* or, sometimes, *Munchausen syndrome by proxy,* but it is really an atypical form of child abuse (Check, 1998). Table 5.1 presents differences between typical child abuse and Munchausen syndrome by proxy.

The offending parent may resort to extreme tactics to create the appearance of illness in the child. For example, one mother stirred a vaginal tampon obtained during men-

Table 5.1 Child Abuse Associated with Munchausen Syndrome by Proxy versus Typical Child Abuse

	Typical Child Abuse	Atypical Child Abuse (Munchausen Syndrome by Proxy)
Physical presentation of the child	Results from direct physical contact with the child; signs often detected on physical examination	Misrepresentation of an acute or accidental medical or surgical illness not usually obvious on physical examination
Obtaining the diagnosis	The perpetrator does not invite the discovery of the manifestation of the abuse	The perpetrator usually presents the manifestations of the abuse to the health-care system
Victims	Children are either the objects of frustration and anger or are receiving undue or inappropriate punishment	Children serve as the vector in gaining the attention the mother desires; anger is not the primary causal factor
Awareness of abuse	Usually present	Not usually present

Source: Reprinted, with permission, from Check, J. R. "Munchausen Syndrome by Proxy: An Atypical Form of Child Abuse." *Journal of Practical Psychiatry and Behavioral Health,* 1998, p. 341, Table 6.2. Copyright © 1998 Lippincott Williams & Wilkins.

struation in her child's urine specimen. Another mother mixed feces into her child's vomit (Check, 1998). Because the mother typically establishes a positive relationship with a medical staff, the true nature of the illness is most often unsuspected and the staff members perceive the parent as remarkably caring, cooperative, and involved in providing for her child's well-being. Therefore, the mother is often successful at eluding suspicion.

Helpful procedures to assess the possibility of Munchausen syndrome by proxy include a trial separation of the mother and the child or video surveillance of the child while in the hospital. An important study has appeared validating the utility of surveillance in hospital rooms of children with suspected Munchausen syndrome by proxy. In this study, 41 patients presenting with chronic, difficult-to-diagnose physical problems were monitored by video during their hospital stay. In 23 of these cases, the diagnoses turned out to be Munchausen syndrome by proxy, where the parent was responsible for the child's symptoms, and in more than half of these 23 cases, video surveillance was the method used to establish the diagnosis. In the other patients, laboratory tests or "catching" the mother in the act of inducing illness in her child confirmed the diagnosis.

Unconscious Mental Processes Unconscious cognitive processes seem to play a role in much of psychopathology (although not necessarily as Freud envisioned it), but nowhere is this phenomenon more readily and dramatically apparent than when we attempt to distinguish between conversion disorders and related conditions. Information reviewed in Chapter 2 on unconscious cognitive processes becomes important in this context. We are all capable of receiving and processing information in a number of sensory channels (such as vision and hearing) without being aware of it. Remember the phenomenon of blind sight or unconscious vision? Weiskrantz (1980) and others discovered that people with small, localized damage to certain parts of their brains could identify objects in their field of vision but that they had no awareness whatsoever that they could see. Could this happen to people without brain damage? Consider the case of Celia.

DSM Disorder Criteria Summary
Factitious Disorders

Features of factitious disorders include the following:

> Intentional production or feigning of physical or psychological problems

> Behavior motivated by desire to assume the sick role

> Absence of external incentives (such as economic gain, avoiding legal responsibility)

Source: Based on *DSM-IV-TR.* Reprinted with permission from *Diagnostic and Statistical Manual of Mental Disorders* (4th ed., text revision). © 2000 American Psychiatric Association.

Celia · Seeing through Blindness

A 15-year-old girl named Celia suddenly was unable to see. Shortly thereafter, she regained some of her sight, but her vision was so severely blurred that she could not read. When she was brought to a clinic for testing, psychologists arranged a series of sophisticated vision tests that did not require her to report when she could or could not see. One of the tasks required her to examine three triangles displayed on

malingering Deliberate faking of a physical or psychological disorder motivated by gain.
factitious disorder Nonexistent physical or psychological disorder deliberately faked for no apparent gain except, possibly, sympathy and attention.

three separate screens and to press a button under the screen containing an upright triangle. Celia performed perfectly on this test without being aware that she could see anything (Grosz & Zimmerman, 1970). Was Celia faking? Evidently not, or she would have purposely made a mistake.

Sackeim, Nordlie, and Gur (1979) evaluated the potential difference between real unconscious process and faking by hypnotizing two participants and giving each a suggestion of total blindness. One participant was also told it was extremely important that she appear to everyone to be blind. The second participant was not given further instructions. The first participant, evidently following instructions to appear blind at all costs, performed far below chance on a visual discrimination task similar to the upright triangle task. On almost every trial, she chose the wrong answer. The second participant, with the hypnotic suggestion of blindness but no instructions to "appear" blind at all costs, performed perfectly on the visual discrimination tasks—although she reported she could not see anything.

How is this relevant to identifying malingering? In an earlier case, Grosz and Zimmerman (1965) evaluated a male who seemed to have conversion symptoms of blindness. They discovered that he performed much more poorly than chance on a visual discrimination task. Subsequent information from other sources confirmed that he was almost certainly malingering. To review these distinctions, someone who is truly blind would perform at a chance level on visual discrimination tasks. People with conversion symptoms, however, can see objects in their visual field and therefore would perform well on these tasks, but this experience is dissociated from their awareness of sight. Malingerers and, perhaps, individuals with factitious disorders simply do everything possible to pretend they can't see.

Statistics

We have already seen that conversion disorder may occur with other disorders, particularly somatization disorder, as in the case of Linda. Linda's paralysis passed after several months and did not return, although on occasion she would report "feeling as if" it were returning. Comorbid anxiety and mood disorders are also common (Pehlivanturk & Unal, 2002; Rowe, 2010; Stone, Carson, Duncan, et al., 2009). Conversion disorders are relatively rare in mental health settings, but remember that people who seek help for this condition are more likely to consult neurologists or other specialists. The prevalence estimate in neurological settings is high, averaging about 30% (Allin, Streeruwitz, & Curtis, 2005; Rowe, 2010; Stone, Carson, Duncan, et al., 2009). One study estimated that 10% to 20% of all patients referred to epilepsy centers have psychogenic, nonepileptic seizures (Benbadis & Allen-Hauser, 2000).

Like somatization disorder, conversion disorders are found primarily in women (Deveci et al., 2007; Folks, Ford, & Regan, 1984; Rosenbaum, 2000) and typically develop during adolescence or slightly thereafter. However, they occur relatively often in males at times of extreme stress (Chodoff, 1974). Conversion reactions are not uncommon in soldiers exposed to combat (Mucha & Reinhardt, 1970). The conversion symptoms often disappear after a time, only to return later in the same or similar form when a new stressor occurs. In other cultures, some conversion symptoms are common aspects of religious or healing rituals. Seizures, paralysis, and trances are common in some rural fundamentalist religious groups in the United States (Griffith, English, & Mayfield, 1980), and they are often seen as evidence of contact with God. Individuals who exhibit such symptoms are thus held in high esteem by their peers. These symptoms do not meet criteria for a "disorder" unless they persist and interfere with an individual's functioning.

Causes

Freud described four basic processes in the development of conversion disorder. First, the individual experiences a traumatic event—in Freud's view, an unacceptable, unconscious conflict. Second, because the conflict and the resulting anxiety are unacceptable, the person represses the conflict, making it unconscious. Third, the anxiety continues to increase and threatens to emerge into consciousness, and the person "converts" it into physical symptoms, thereby relieving the pressure of having to deal directly with the conflict. This reduction of anxiety is considered to be the *primary gain* or reinforcing event that maintains the conversion symptom. Fourth, the individual receives greatly increased attention and sympathy from loved ones and may also be allowed to avoid a difficult situation or task. Freud considered such attention or avoidance to be the *secondary gain*, the secondarily reinforcing set of events.

We believe Freud was basically correct on at least three counts but probably not on the fourth, although firm evidence supporting any of these ideas is sparse and Freud's views were far more complex than represented here. Most often, individuals with conversion disorder have experienced a traumatic event that must be escaped at all costs (Stone, Carson, Aditya, et al., 2009). This might be combat, where death is imminent, or an impossible interpersonal situation. Because simply running away is unacceptable in most cases, the socially acceptable alternative of getting sick is substituted; but getting sick on purpose is also unacceptable, so this motivation is detached from the person's consciousness. Finally, because the escape behavior (the conversion symptoms) is successful to an extent in obliterating the traumatic situation, the behavior continues until the underlying problem is resolved. One study confirms these hypotheses, at least partially (Wyllie, Glazer, Benbadis, Kotagal, & Wolgamuth, 1999). In this study, 34 child and adolescent patients, 25 of them girls, were evaluated after receiving a diagnosis of psychologi-

▲ The seizures and trances that may be symptomatic of conversion disorder are also common in some rural fundamentalist religious groups in the United States.

cally based pseudo-seizures (psychogenic nonepileptic seizures). Many of these children and adolescents presented with additional psychological disorders, including 32% with mood disorders and 24% with separation anxiety and school refusal. Other anxiety disorders were present in some additional patients.

When the extent of psychological stress in the lives of these children was examined, it was found that most of the patients had substantial stress, including a history of sexual abuse, recent parental divorce or death of a close family member, and physical abuse. The authors concluded that major mood disorders and severe environmental stress, especially sexual abuse, are common among children and adolescents with the conversion disorder of pseudo-seizures, as have other studies (Roelofs et al., 2002).

The one step in Freud's progression of events about which some questions remain is the issue of primary gain. The notion of primary gain accounts for the feature of *la belle indifférence* (cited previously), where individuals seem not the least bit distressed about their symptoms. In other words, Freud thought that because symptoms reflected an unconscious attempt to resolve a conflict, the patient would not be upset by them. But formal tests of this feature provide little support for Freud's claim. For example, Stone and colleagues (2006) in the study described earlier on "indifference" to conversion symptoms found no difference in distress over symptoms among patients with conversion disorder compared to patients with organic disease.

Social and cultural influences also contribute to conversion disorder, which, like somatization disorder, tends to occur in less educated, lower socioeconomic groups where knowledge about disease and medical illness is not well developed (Binzer, Andersen, & Kullgren, 1997; Kirmayer, Looper, & Taillefer, 2003; Woolfolk & Allen, in press). For example, Binzer and colleagues (1997) noted that 13% of their group of 30 adult patients with motor disabilities re-

sulting from conversion disorder had attended high school compared to 67% in a control group of patients with motor symptoms because of a physical cause. Prior experience with real physical problems, usually among other family members, tends to influence the later choice of specific conversion symptoms—that is, patients tend to adopt symptoms with which they are familiar (see, for example, Brady & Lind, 1961). Furthermore, the incidence of these disorders has decreased over the decades (Kirmayer et al., 2003). The most likely explanation is that increased knowledge of the real causes of physical problems by both patients and loved ones eliminates much of the possibility of secondary gain so important in these disorders.

Finally, many conversion symptoms seem to be part of a larger constellation of psychopathology. Linda had broadranging somatization disorder, as well as the severe conversion symptoms, that resulted in her hospitalization. In similar cases, individuals may have a marked biological vulnerability to develop conversion disorder when under stress, with biological processes like those discussed in the context of somatization disorder. Neuroscientists are increasingly finding a strong connectivity between the conversion symptom and parts of the brain regulating emotion, such as the amygdala, using brain-imaging procedures (Rowe, 2010; Voon et al., 2010).

For countless other cases, however, biological contributory factors seem to be less important than the overriding influence of interpersonal factors (the actions of Eloise's mother, for example), as we will discuss in the next section.

Treatment

Because conversion disorder has much in common with somatization disorder, many of the treatment principles are similar.

A principal strategy in treating conversion disorder is to identify and attend to the traumatic or stressful life event, if it is still present (either in real life or in memory). As in the case of Anna O., therapeutic assistance in reexperiencing or "reliving" the event (catharsis) is a reasonable first step.

The therapist must also work hard to reduce any reinforcing or supportive consequences of the conversion symptoms (secondary gain). For example, it was quite clear that Eloise's mother found it convenient if Eloise stayed in one place most of the day while her mother attended to the store in the front of the house. Eloise's immobility was thus strongly reinforced by motherly attention and concern. Any unnecessary mobility was punished. The therapist must collaborate with both the patient and the family to eliminate such self-defeating behaviors.

Body Dysmorphic Disorder

Some people think they are so ugly they refuse to interact with others or otherwise function normally for fear that people will laugh at their ugliness. This curious affliction is called **body dysmorphic disorder (BDD)**, and at its center is a preoccupation with some imagined defect in appearance by someone who actually looks reasonably normal. The disorder has been referred to as "imagined ugliness" (Phillips, 1991). Consider the case of Jim.

DSM Disorder Criteria Summary
Body Dysmorphic Disorder

Features of body dysmorphic disorder include the following:

› Preoccupation with an imagined defect in appearance, or gross exaggeration of a slight physical anomaly

› Preoccupation causes significant distress or impairment in functioning

› Preoccupation is not better accounted for by another mental disorder (e.g., anorexia nervosa)

Source: Based on *DSM-IV-TR.* Reprinted with permission from *Diagnostic and Statistical Manual of Mental Disorders* (4th ed., text revision). © 2000 American Psychiatric Association.

Jim • Ashamed to Be Seen

In his mid-20s, Jim was diagnosed with suspected social phobia. He had just finished rabbinical school and had been offered a position at a synagogue in a nearby city. However, he found himself unable to accept because of marked social difficulties. Lately he had given up leaving his small apartment for fear of running into people he knew and being forced to stop and interact with them.

Jim was a good-looking young man with dark hair and eyes and of about average height. Although he was somewhat depressed, a mental status exam and a brief interview focusing on current functioning and past history did not reveal any remarkable problems. There was no sign of a psychotic process (he was not out of touch with reality). We then focused on Jim's social difficulties. We expected the usual kinds of anxiety about interacting with people or "doing something" (performing) in front of them. But this was not Jim's concern. Rather, he was convinced that everyone, even his good friends, was staring at a part of his body that he found grotesque. He reported that strangers would never mention his deformity and his friends felt too sorry for him to mention it. Jim thought his head was square! Like the Beast in *Beauty and the Beast* who could not imagine people reacting to him with anything less than revulsion, Jim could not imagine people getting past his square head. To hide his condition as well as he could, Jim wore soft floppy hats and was most comfortable in winter, when he could all but completely cover his head with a large stocking cap. To us, Jim looked normal.

Clinical Description To give you a better idea of the types of concerns people with BDD present to health professionals, the locations of imagined defects in 200 patients are shown in Table 5.2. The average number of body areas of concern to these individuals was five to seven (Phillips, Menard, Fay, & Weisberg, 2005). A variety of checking or compensating rituals are common in people with BDD in attempts to alleviate their concerns. For example, excessive tanning is common, with 25% of one group of 200 patients tanning themselves in an attempt to hide skin defects (Phillips, Menard, Fay, & Weisberg, 2005). Many people with this disorder become fixated on mirrors (Veale & Riley, 2001). They often check their presumed ugly feature to see whether any change has taken place. Others avoid mirrors to an almost phobic extent. Quite understandably, suicidal ideation, suicide attempts, and suicide itself are typical consequences of this disorder (Phillips, Menard, Fay, & Weisberg, 2005; Zimmerman & Mattia, 1998). People with BDD also have "ideas of reference," which means they think everything that goes on in their world somehow is related to them—in this case, to their imagined defect. This disorder can cause considerable disruption in the patient's life. Many patients with severe cases become housebound for fear of showing themselves to other people.

Table 5.2 Location of Imagined Defects in 200 Patients with Body Dysmorphic Disorder*

Location	%	Location	%
Skin	80	Overall appearance of face	19
Hair	58	Small body build	18
Nose	39	Legs	18
Stomach	32	Face size or shape	16
Teeth	30	Chin	15
Weight	29	Lips	14.5
Breasts	26	Arms or wrists	14
Buttocks	22	Hips	13
Eyes	22	Cheeks	11
Thighs	20	Ears	11
Eyebrows	20		

Adapted from Phillips, K. A., Menard, B. A., Fay, C., & Weisberg, R., (2005). Demographic characteristics, phenomenology, comorbidity, and family history in 200 individuals with body dysmorphic disorder. *Psychosomatics, 46*(4), 317–325. © 2005 The Academy of Psychosomatic Medicine.

If this disorder seems strange to you, you are not alone. For decades, this condition, previously known as *dysmorphophobia* (literally, fear of ugliness), was thought to represent a psychotic delusional state because the affected individuals were unable to realize, even for a fleeting moment, that their ideas were irrational. Whether this is true is still debated.

Abnormal Psychology Inside Out, produced by Ira Wohl, Only Child Motion Pictures

Body Dysmorphic Disorder: Doug

"I didn't want to talk to anybody. . . . I was afraid because what I saw on my face . . . they saw. . . . If I could see it, they could see it. And I thought there was like an arrow pointing at it. And I was very self-conscious. And I felt like the only time I felt comfortable was at night because it was dark time.

Go to Psychology CourseMate at www.cengagebrain.com to watch this video.

For example, in 200 cases examined by Phillips, Menard, Fay, and Weisberg (2005) and in 50 cases reported by Veale, Boocock, and colleagues (1996), between 33% and 50% of participants were convinced their imagined bodily defect was real and a reasonable source of concern. Is this delusional? The *DSM-IV* task force wrestled long and hard with this issue and decided that individuals with BDD whose beliefs are so firmly held that they could be called delusional should receive a second diagnosis of delusional disorder, somatic type (see Chapter 12) in addition to BDD. Phillips, Menard, Pagano, Fay, and Stout (2006) looked closely at differences that may exist between delusional and nondelusional types and found nothing significant, beyond the fact that the delusional type was more severe and found in less educated patients. Other studies have supported this lack of meaningful differences between these two groups (Mancuso, Knoesen, & Castle, in press; Phillips et al., 2010). It is also the case that these two groups both respond equally well to treatments for BDD and that the "delusional" group does not respond to drug treatments for psychotic disorders (Phillips et al., in press). Thus, in *DSM-5*, the proposal is that patients would receive just a BDD diagnosis, whether they are "delusional" or not, and the practice of giving them a second diagnosis of delusional disorder (a psychotic disorder) should be dropped (Phillips et al., in press).

Statistics

The prevalence of BDD is hard to estimate because by its very nature it tends to be kept secret. However, the best estimates are that it is far more common than we had previously thought. Without some sort of treatment, it tends to run a lifelong course (Phillips, 1991; Veale, Boocock, et al., 1996). One of the patients with BDD reported by Phillips and colleagues (1993) had suffered from her condition for 71 years, since the age of 9. If you think a college friend seems to have at least a mild version of BDD, you're probably correct. Studies suggest that as many as 70% of college students report at least some dissatisfaction with their bodies, with 4% to 28% of these appearing to meet all the criteria for the disorder (Fitts, Gibson, Redding, & Deiter, 1989; Phillips, 2005). However, this study was done by questionnaire and may well have reflected the large percentage of students who are concerned simply with weight.

Another study investigated the prevalence of BDD specifically in an ethnically diverse sample of 566 adolescents be-

tween the ages of 14 and 19. The overall prevalence of BDD in this group was 2.2%, with adolescent girls more dissatisfied with their bodies than boys and African Americans of both genders less dissatisfied with their bodies than Caucasians, Asians, and Hispanics (Mayville, Katz, Gipson, & Cabral, 1999; Roberts, Cash, Feingold, & Johnson, 2006). Overall, about 1% to 2% of individuals in community samples and from 2% to 13% of student samples meet criteria for BDD (Koran, Abujaoude, Large, & Serpe, 2008; Phillips, Menard, Fay, & Weisberg, 2005; Woolfolk & Allen, in press). A somewhat higher proportion of individuals with BDD are interested in art or design compared to individuals without BDD, reflecting, perhaps, a strong interest in aesthetics or appearance (Veale, Ennis, & Lambrou, 2002).

In mental health clinics, the disorder is also uncommon because most people with BDD seek other types of health professionals, such as plastic surgeons and dermatologists. BDD is seen equally in men and women. In the larger series of 200 individuals reported by Phillips, Menard, Fay, and Weisberg (2005), 68.5% were female, but 62% of a large number of individuals with BDD in Japan were males. Generally, there are more similarities than differences between men and women with BDD, but some differences have been noted (Phillips, Menard, & Fay, 2006). Men tend to focus on body build, genitals, and thinning hair and tend to be more severe. A focus on muscle defects and body building is nearly unique to men with the disorder (Pope et al., 2005). Women focus on more varied body areas and are more likely to also have an eating disorder.

As you might suspect, few people with this disorder get married. Age of onset ranges from early adolescence through the 20s, peaking at the age of 16 or 17 (Phillips, Menard, Fay, & Weisberg, 2005; Veale, Boocock, et al., 1996; Zimmerman & Mattia, 1998). Individuals are somewhat reluctant to seek treatment. In many cases, a relative will force the issue, demanding the individual get help; this insistence may reflect the disruptiveness of the disorder for family members. One study of 62 consecutive outpatients

body dysmorphic disorder (BDD) Somatoform disorder featuring a disruptive preoccupation with some imagined defect in appearance ("imagined ugliness").

What is beauty? How would you describe the perfect body? Your perception of beauty and body image has no doubt been influenced by the social and cultural environment in which you have grown up. Such perceptions vary widely across different cultures and can often lead to behaviors aimed at enhancing one's beauty that may seem strange or even pathological to those from a different culture. For instance, having freckles or a birthmark on one's face is considered by many to be an attractive trait in the United States (such as among popular models and actresses like Cindy Crawford and Lindsay Lohan). However, over the centuries, freckles generally have not been very popular, and in many cultures chemical solutions were used to remove them, sometimes leading to significant damage to layers of one's skin (Liggett, 1974).

In many other cultures, devices are worn during infancy, childhood, or even adulthood that are intended to reshape a person's bone structure—such as by reshaping the head or nose of newborns in order to make them more attractive (e.g., Fallon, 1990; Liggett, 1974). Perhaps one of the best known examples of such a practice is the binding of girls' feet in China in order to prevent them from growing. This binding, which occurred from the 10th to the 20th century, forced women to walk in a way thought seductive by men in that culture. Although this may seem to some to be a foreign concept, can you think of anything similar done in the U.S. culture in an attempt to enhance one's beauty? Although less extreme than foot binding, many women in the United States wear tight-fitting shoes with high heels and have bags of chemicals implanted under their skin to enhance the size of their breasts or even buttocks (some celebrities in the United States voluntarily choose to undergo multiple cosmetic surgeries at one time; reality television star Heidi Montag reportedly had 10 such procedures performed in one day)—all in an effort to appear more attractive. Of course, men also do things to enhance their appearance, such as wearing hair-pieces or getting hair plugs and removing fat via liposuction. Men and women alike will go as far as to knowingly risk their health for what they believe will be increased beauty. In fact, roughly 20% of adults aged 18 to 29 years in the United States reported using indoor tanning in the past year (Heckman, Coups, & Manne, 2008), essentially accepting the health risks (i.e., melanoma and squamos cell cancer) associated with tanning lamps in exchange for darker skin; indoor tanning is widely available in the United States (Hoerster et al., 2009). Such behavior leads one to question the costs associated with beauty. More extreme examples of body modification also exist in the United States, such as skin-piercing and tattooing, which have been quite rare historically in this country but have increased significantly over the past several decades (Laumann & Derick, 2006). All of these practices are quite commonplace in our culture, but each may seem strange to those in other parts of the world.

---

with BDD found that the degree of psychological stress, quality of life, and impairment were generally worse than comparable indices in patients with depression, diabetes, or a recent myocardial infarction (heart attack) on several questionnaire measures (Phillips, Dufresne, Wilkel, & Vittorio, 2000). Similar results were reported on a larger sample of 176 patients (Phillips, Menard, Fay, & Pagano, 2005). Thus, BDD is among the more serious of psychological disorders, and depression and substance abuse are common consequences of BDD (Gustad & Phillips, 2003; Phillips et al., in press).

Further reflecting the intense suffering that accompanies this disorder, Veale (2000) collected information on 25 patients with BDD who had sought cosmetic surgery in the past. Of these, nine patients who could not afford surgery, or were turned down for other reasons, had attempted by their own hand to alter their appearance dramatically, often with tragic results. One example was a man preoccupied by his skin, who believed it was too "loose." He used a staple gun on both sides of his face to try to keep his skin taut. The staples fell out after 10 minutes and he narrowly missed damaging his facial nerve. In a second example, a woman was preoccupied by her skin and the shape of her face. She filed down her teeth to alter the appearance of her jawline. Yet another woman who was preoccupied by what she perceived as the ugliness of multiple areas of her body and desired liposuction, but could not afford it, used a knife to cut her thighs and attempted to squeeze out the fat. BDD is also stubbornly chronic. In a recent prospective study of 183 patients, only 21% were somewhat improved over the course of a year, and 15% of that group relapsed during that year (Phillips, Pagano, Menard, & Stout, 2006).

Individuals with BDD react to what they think is a horrible or grotesque feature. Thus, the psychopathology lies in their reacting to a "deformity" that others cannot perceive. Social and cultural determinants of beauty and body image largely define what is "deformed." (Nowhere is this more evident than in the greatly varying cultural standards for body weight and shape, factors that play a major role in eating disorders, as you will see in Chapter 8.)

For example, concerns with the width of the face, so common in BDD, can be culturally determined. Until recently, in some areas of France, Africa, Greenland, and Peru, the head of a newborn infant was reshaped, either by hand or by tight caps secured by strings. Sometimes the face was elongated; other times it was widened. Similarly, attempts were made to flatten the noses of newborn infants, usually by hand (Fallon, 1990; Liggett, 1974).

Also, many are aware of the old practice in China of binding girls' feet, often preventing the foot from growing to more than one-third of its normal size. Women's bound feet forced them to walk in a way that was thought seductive, as mentioned earlier. As Brownmiller (1984) points out, the myth that an unnaturally small foot signifies extraordinary beauty and grace is still with us. Can you think of the fairy tale where a small foot becomes the identifying feature of the beautiful heroine?

What can we learn about BDD from such practices? The behavior of individuals with BDD seems remarkably strange because they go *against* current cultural practices that put less emphasis on altering facial features. In other words, people who simply conform to the expectations of their culture do not have a disorder (as noted in Chapter 1). Nevertheless, aesthetic plastic surgery, particularly for the nose and lips, is still widely accepted and, because it is most often undertaken by the wealthy, carries an aura of elevated status. In this light, BDD may not be so strange. As with most psychopathology, its characteristic attitudes and behavior may simply be an exaggeration of normal culturally sanctioned behavior.

Causes and Treatment

We know little about either the etiology or the treatment of BDD. What little evidence we do have on etiology comes from a weak source: the pattern of comorbidity of BDD with other disorders. BDD is a somatoform disorder because its central feature is a psychological preoccupation with somatic (physical) issues. For example, in hypochondriasis the focus is on physical sensations, and in BDD the focus is on physical appearance. We have already seen that many of the somatoform disorders tend to co-occur. Linda presented with somatization disorder but also had a history of conversion disorder. However, BDD does not tend to co-occur with the other somatoform disorders, nor does it occur in family members of patients with other somatoform disorders.

▲ In various cultures, a child's head or face is manipulated to produce desirable features, as in the addition of rings to lengthen the neck of this Burmese girl.

A disorder that does often co-occur with BDD and is found among other family members is obsessive-compulsive disorder (OCD) (Chosak et al., 2008; Gustad & Phillips, 2003; Phillips et al., in press; Phillips & Stout, 2006; Tynes, White, & Steketee, 1990; Zimmerman & Mattia, 1998). Is BDD a variant of OCD? There are a lot of similarities. People with BDD complain of persistent, intrusive, and horrible thoughts about their appearance, and they engage in such compulsive behaviors as repeatedly looking in mirrors to check their physical features. BDD and OCD also have approximately the same age of onset and run the same course. One recent brain-imaging study demonstrated similar abnormal brain functioning between patients with BDD and patients with OCD (Rauch et al., 2003).

Perhaps most significantly, there are two, and only two, treatments for BDD with any evidence of effectiveness. First, drugs that block the reuptake of serotonin, such as clomipramine (Anafranil) and fluvoxamine (Luvox), provide relief to at least some people (Hadley, Kim, Priday, & Hollander, 2006). One controlled study of the effects of drugs on BDD demonstrated that clomipramine was significantly more effective than desipramine, a drug that does not specifically block reuptake of serotonin, for the treatment of BDD, even BDD of the delusional type (Hollander et al., 1999). A second controlled study reported similar findings for fluoxetine (Prozac), with 53% showing a good response compared to 18% on placebo after 3 months (Phillips, Albertini, & Rasmussen, 2002). Intriguingly, these are the same drugs that have the strongest effect in OCD.

Second, exposure and response prevention, the type of cognitive-behavioral therapy effective with OCD, has also been successful with BDD (McKay et al., 1997; Rosen, Reiter, & Orosan, 1995; Veale, Gournay, et al., 1996; Wilhelm, Otto, Lohr, & Deckersbach, 1999). In the Rosen and colleagues (1995) study, 82% of patients treated with this approach responded, although these patients may have been somewhat less severely affected by the disorder than in other studies (Wilhelm et al., 1999; Williams, Hadjistavropoulos, & Sharpe, 2006). Another interesting lead on causes of BDD comes from cross-cultural explorations of similar disorders. You may remember the Japanese variant of social phobia, *taijin kyofusho* (see Chapter 4), in which individuals may believe they have horrendous bad breath or body odor and thus avoid social interaction. But people with *taijin kyofusho* also have all the other characteristics of social phobia. Patients who would be diagnosed with BDD in our culture might simply be considered to have severe social phobia in Japan and Korea. Possibly, then, social anxiety is fundamentally related to BDD, a connection that would give us further hints on the nature of the disorder. Studies of comorbidity indicate that social phobia, along with OCD, is also commonly found in people with BDD (Phillips & Stout, 2006). For all of these reasons, a major proposal for *DSM-5* is to include BDD with the anxiety disorders, perhaps as a variant of OCD (Phillips et al., in press).

Plastic Surgery and Other Medical Treatments Patients with BDD believe they are physically deformed in some way and go to medical doctors to attempt to correct their deficits (Woolfolk & Allen, in press). Phillips, Grant, Siniscalchi, and Albertini (2001) studied the treatments sought by 289 patients with BDD, including 39 children or adolescents, and found that fully 76.4% had sought this type of treatment and 66% were receiving it. Dermatology (skin) treatment was the most often received (45.2%), followed by plastic surgery (23.2%). Looking at it another way, in one study of 268 patients seeking care from a dermatologist, 11.9% met criteria for BDD (Phillips, Dufresne, Wilkel, & Vittorio, 2000).

Because the concerns of people with BDD involve mostly the face or head, it is not surprising that the disorder is big business for the plastic surgery profession—but it's bad business. These patients do not benefit from surgery and may return for additional surgery or, on occasion, file malpractice lawsuits. Investigators estimate that as many as 8% to 25% of all patients who request plastic surgery may have BDD (Barnard, 2000; Crerand et al., 2004). The most common procedures are rhinoplasties (nose jobs), face-lifts, eyebrow elevations, liposuction, breast augmentation, and surgery to alter the jawline. Between 2000 and 2009, according to the American Society of Plastic Surgeons, the total number of cosmetic procedures increased 69%. In 2009, there were 203,000 eyelid surgeries and 289,000 breast enlargement surgeries. The problem is that surgery on the proportion of these people with BDD seldom produces the desired results. These individuals return for additional surgery on the same defect or concentrate on some new defect. Phillips, Menard, Fay, and Pagano (2005) report that 81% of 50 individuals seeking surgery or similar medical consults were dissatisfied with the result. In 88% of a large group of people with BDD seeking medical rather than psychological treatment, the severity of the disorder and accompanying distress either did not change or *increased* after surgery. Similar discouraging or negative results are evident from other forms of medical treatment, such as skin treatments (Phillips et al., 2001). It is important that plastic surgeons screen out these patients; many do so by collaborating with medically trained psychologists (Pruzinsky, 1988).

▲ The world-famous pop singer Michael Jackson as a child and as an adult. Many people alter their features through surgery. However, people with body dysmorphic disorder are seldom satisfied with the results.

Concept Check 5.1

Diagnose the somatoform disorders described here by choosing one of the following: (a) pain disorder, (b) hypochondriasis, (c) somatization disorder, (d) conversion disorder, and (e) body dysmorphic disorder.

1. Emily constantly worries about her health. She has been to numerous doctors for her concerns about cancer and other serious diseases, only to be reassured of her well-being. Emily's anxiousness is exacerbated by each small ailment (for example, headaches or stomach pains) that she considers to be indications of a major illness. _____

2. D. J. arrived at Dr. Blake's office with a folder crammed full of medical records, symptom documentation, and lists of prescribed treatments and drugs. Several doctors are monitoring him for his complaints, ranging from chest pain to difficulty swallowing. D. J. recently lost his job because he was using too many sick days. _____

3. Sixteen-year-old Chad suddenly lost the use of his arms with no medical cause. The complete paralysis slowly improved to the point that he could slightly raise them. However, Chad cannot drive, pick up objects, or perform most tasks necessary for day-to-day life. _____

4. Loretta is 32 and has been preoccupied with the size and shape of her nose for 2 years. She has been saving money for plastic surgery, after which, she is sure, her career will improve. The trouble is that three honest plastic surgeons have told her that her nose is fine as it is. _____

5. Betty had considerable pain when she broke her arm. A year after it healed and all medical tests indicate her arm is fine she still complains of the pain. It seems to intensify when she fights with her husband. _____

Dissociative Disorders

> What are the five types of dissociative disorders?
> What factors influence the etiology and treatment of dissociative disorders?

At the beginning of the chapter, we said that when individuals feel detached from themselves or their surroundings, almost as if they are dreaming or living in slow motion, they are having dissociative experiences. Morton Prince, the founder of the *Journal of Abnormal Psychology*, noted more than 100 years ago that many people experience something like dissociation occasionally (Prince, 1906–1907). It might be likely to happen after an extremely stressful event, such as an accident (Spiegel, 2010). It also is more likely to happen when you're tired or sleep deprived from staying up all night cramming for an exam (Giesbrecht, Smeets, Leppink, Jelicic, & Merckelbach, 2007). Perhaps because you knew the cause, the dissociation may not have bothered you much (Barlow, 2002; Noyes, Hoenk, Kuperman, & Slymen, 1977). However, it may have been extremely frightening. Transient experiences of dissociation will occur in about half of the general population at some point in their lives, and studies suggest that if a person experiences a traumatic event, between 31% and 66% will have this feeling at that time (Hunter, Sierra, & David, 2004; Keane, Marx, Sloan, & DePrince, 2011). Because it's hard to measure dissociation, the connection between trauma and dissociation is controversial (Giesbrecht, Lynn, Lilienfeld, & Merckelbach, 2008).

These kinds of experiences can be divided into two types. During an episode of *depersonalization,* your perception alters so that you temporarily lose the sense of your own reality, as if you were in a dream and you were watching yourself. During an episode of **derealization**, your sense of the reality of the external world is lost. Things may seem to change shape or size; people may seem dead or mechanical. These sensations of unreality are characteristic of the dissociative disorders because, in a sense, they are a psychological mechanism whereby one "dissociates" from reality. Depersonalization is often part of a serious set of conditions in which reality, experience, and even identity seem to disintegrate.

As we go about our day-to-day lives, we ordinarily have an excellent sense of who we are and a general knowledge of the identity of other people. We are also aware of events around us, of where we are, and of why we are there. Finally, except for occasional small lapses, our memories remain intact so that events leading up to the current moment are clear in our minds. But what happens if we can't remember why we are in a certain place or even who we are? What happens if we lose our sense that our surroundings are real? Finally, what happens if we not only forget who we are, but also begin thinking we are somebody else—somebody who has a different personality, different memories, and even different physical reactions, such as allergies we never had? These are examples of disintegrated experience (Cardeña & Gleaves, 2003; Dell & O'Neil, 2009; Spiegel & Cardeña, 1991;

Spiegel, in press; van der Hart & Nijenhuis, 2009). In each case, there are alterations in our relationship to the self, to the world, or to memory processes.

Although we have much to learn about these disorders, we briefly describe four of them—depersonalization disorder, dissociative amnesia, dissociative fugue, and dissociative trance disorder—before examining the fascinating condition of dissociative identity disorder. As you will see, the influence of social and cultural factors is strong in dissociative disorders. Even in severe cases, the expression of the pathology does not stray far from socially and culturally sanctioned forms (Giesbrecht et al., 2008; Kihlstrom, 2005).

Depersonalization Disorder

When feelings of unreality are so severe and frightening that they dominate an individual's life and prevent normal functioning, clinicians may diagnose the rare **depersonalization disorder**. Consider the case of Bonnie.

Bonnie : Dancing Away from Herself

Bonnie, a dance teacher in her late 20s, was accompanied by her husband when she first visited the clinic and complained of "flipping out." When asked what she meant, she said, "It's the most scary thing in the world. It often happens when I'm teaching my modern dance class. I'll be up in front and I will feel focused on. Then, as I'm demonstrating the steps, I just feel like it's not really me and that I don't really have control of my legs. Sometimes I feel like I'm standing in back of myself just watching. Also I get tunnel vision. It seems like I can only see in a narrow space right in front of me and I just get totally separated from what's going on around me. Then I begin to panic and perspire and shake." It turns out that Bonnie's problems began after she smoked marijuana for the first time about 10 years before. She had the same feeling then and found it scary, but with the help of friends she got through it. Lately the feeling recurred more often and more severely, particularly when she was teaching dance class.

derealization Situation in which the individual loses a sense of the reality of the external world.
depersonalization disorder Dissociative disorder in which feelings of depersonalization are so severe they dominate the individual's life and prevent normal functioning.

You may remember from Chapter 4 that during an intense panic attack many people (approximately 50%) experience feelings of unreality. People undergoing intense stress or experiencing a traumatic event may also experience these symptoms, which characterize the newly defined *acute stress disorder*. Feelings of depersonalization and derealization are part of several disorders (Boon & Draijer, 1991; Giesbrecht et al., 2008). But when severe depersonalization and derealization are the primary problem, the individual meets criteria for depersonalization disorder (APA, 2010; Steinberg, 1991). Surveys suggest that this disorder exists in approximately 0.8% of the population (Johnson, Cohen, Kasen, & Brook, 2006). Simeon, Knutelska, Nelson, & Guralnik (2003) described 117 cases approximately equally split between men and women. Mean age of onset was 16 years, and the course tended to be chronic. All patients were substantially impaired. Anxiety, mood, and personality disorders are also commonly found in these individuals (Simeon et al., 2003; Johnson et al., 2006). Among the 117 patients described, 73% suffered from additional mood disorders and 64% from anxiety disorders at some point in their lives.

Two studies (Guralnik, Schmeidler, & Simeon, 2000; Guralnik, Giesbrecht, Knutelska, Sirroff, & Simeon, 2007) have compared patients with depersonalization disorder to matched normal-comparison participants on a comprehensive neuropsychological test battery that assessed cognitive function. Although both groups were of equal intelligence, the participants with depersonalization disorder showed a distinct cognitive profile, reflecting some specific cognitive deficits on measures of attention, processing of information, short-term memory, and spatial reasoning. Basically, these patients were easily distracted and were slow to perceive and process new information. It is not clear how these cognitive and perceptual deficits develop, but they seem to correspond with reports of "tunnel vision" (perceptual distortions) and "mind emptiness" (difficulty absorbing new information) that characterize these patients.

Specific aspects of brain functioning are also associated with depersonalization (see, for example, Sierra & Berrios,

1998; Simeon, 2009; Simeon et al., 2000). Brain-imaging studies confirm deficits in perception (Simeon, 2009; Simeon et al., 2000) and emotion regulation (Phillips et al., 2001). Other studies note dysregulation in the hypothalamic–pituitary–adrenocortical (HPA) axis among these patients, compared to normal controls (Simeon, Guralnik, Knutelska, Hollander, & Schmeidler, 2001), suggesting, again, deficits in emotional responding.

Dissociative Amnesia

Perhaps the easiest to understand of the severe dissociative disorders is one called **dissociative amnesia**, which includes several patterns. People who are unable to remember anything, including who they are, are said to suffer from **generalized amnesia**. Generalized amnesia may be lifelong or may extend from a period in the more recent past, such as 6 months or a year previously. Consider the case study described here.

The Woman Who Lost Her Memory

Several years ago a woman in her early 50s brought her daughter to one of our clinics because of the girl's refusal to attend school and other severely disruptive behavior. The father, who refused to come to the session, was quarrelsome, a heavy drinker, and abusive on occasion. The girl's brother, now in his mid-20s, lived at home and was a burden on the family. Several times a week a major battle erupted, complete with shouting, pushing, and shoving, as each member of the family blamed the others for all their problems.

The mother, a strong woman, was clearly the peacemaker responsible for holding the family together. Approximately every 6 months, usually after a family battle, the mother lost her memory and the family had her admitted to the hospital. After a few days away from the turmoil, the mother regained her memory and went home, only to repeat the cycle in the coming months. Although we did not treat this family (they lived too far away), the situation resolved itself when the children moved away and the stress decreased.

Far more common than general amnesia is **localized or selective amnesia**, a failure to recall specific events, usually traumatic, that occur during a specific period. Dissociative amnesia is common during war (Cardeña & Gleaves, 2003; Loewenstein, 1991; Spiegel & Cardeña, 1991). Sackeim and Devanand (1991) describe the interesting case of a woman whose father had deserted her when she was young. She had also been forced to have an abortion at the age of 14. Years later, she came for treatment for frequent headaches. In therapy she reported early events (for example, the abortion) matter-of-factly, but under hypnosis she would relive, with intense emotion, the early abortion and remember that

---

DSM | **Disorder Criteria Summary**
Depersonalization Disorder

Features of depersonalization disorder include the following:

> Persistent or recurrent feelings of being detached from one's body or mental processes (e.g., feeling like one is in a dream)

> Reality testing remains intact during the depersonalization experience

> Depersonalization causes clinically significant distress or impairment in functioning

> The condition does not occur exclusively as part of another mental disorder, such as schizophrenia, panic disorder, or acute stress disorder

Source: Based on *DSM-IV-TR*. Reprinted with permission from *Diagnostic and Statistical Manual of Mental Disorders* (4th ed., text revision). © 2000 American Psychiatric Association.

subsequently she was raped by the abortionist. She also had images of her father attending a funeral for her aunt, one of the few times she ever saw him. Upon awakening from the hypnotic state, she had no memory of emotionally reexperiencing these events, and she wondered why she had been crying. In this case, the woman did not have amnesia for the *events themselves* but rather for her intense *emotional reactions to the events*. Absence of the subjective experience of emotion that is often present in depersonalization disorder and confirmed by brain-imaging studies (Phillips et al., 2001) becomes prominent here. In most cases of dissociative amnesia, the forgetting is selective for traumatic events or memories rather than generalized.

DSM Disorder Criteria Summary
Dissociative Amnesia

Features of dissociative amnesia include the following:

> One or more episodes of inability to recall important personal information, usually of a traumatic or stressful nature, that is too extensive to be explained by ordinary forgetfulness

> Episodes are not related to a medical condition, physiological effects of a substance (e.g., a drug of abuse), or a separate psychological disorder

> Inability to recall causes clinically significant distress or impairment in functioning

Source: Based on *DSM-IV-TR.* Reprinted with permission from *Diagnostic and Statistical Manual of Mental Disorders* (4th ed., text revision). © 2000 American Psychiatric Association.

Dissociative Fugue

A closely related disorder that will almost certainly become a subtype of dissociative amnesia in *DSM-5* (APA, 2010; Ross, 2009) is referred to as **dissociative fugue**, with *fugue* literally meaning "flight" (*fugitive* is from the same root). In these curious cases, memory loss revolves around a specific incident—an unexpected trip (or trips). In most cases, individuals just take off and later find themselves in a new place, unable to remember why or how they got there. Usually they have left behind an intolerable situation. During these trips, a person sometimes assumes a new identity or at least becomes confused about the old identity. Consider the case of Jeffrey Ingram, a 40-year-old male from Washington state, who found himself unexpectedly in Denver.

Jeffrey | A Troubled Trip

An amnesia sufferer who had been searching for his identity for more than a month was back in Washington state with his fiancée on Tuesday, but he still doesn't remember his past life or what happened, his mother said.

Jeffrey Alan Ingram, 40, was diagnosed in Denver with dissociative fugue, a type of amnesia.

He has had similar bouts of amnesia in the past, likely triggered by stress, once disappearing for 9 months. When he went missing this time, on September 6, he had been on his way to Canada to visit a friend who was dying of cancer, said his fiancée, Penny Hansen.

"I think that the stress, the sadness, the grief of facing a best friend dying was enough, and leaving me was enough to send him into an amnesia state," Hansen told KCNC-TV.

When Ingram found himself in Denver on September 10, he didn't know who he was. He said he walked around for about 6 hours asking people for help, then ended up at a hospital, where police spokeswoman Virginia Quinones said Ingram was diagnosed with a type of amnesia known as dissociative fugue.

Searched for his identity. Ingram's identity came to light last weekend after he appeared on several news shows asking the public for help: "If anybody recognizes me, knows who I am, please let somebody know."

"Penny's brother called her right away and told her 'Did you watch this newscast?' and 'I think that's Jeff that they're showing on television,'" said Marilyn Meehan, a spokeswoman for Hansen.

Hansen had filed a missing person report after Ingram failed to show up at her mother's home in Bellingham, Washington, on his way to Canada, but officials searching for him had turned up nothing.

On Monday night, two Denver police detectives accompanied Ingram on a flight to Seattle, where he was reunited with his fiancée.

His mother, Doreen Tompkins of Slave Lake, Alberta, was in tears as she talked about the struggle her son and the family still face.

"It's going to be very difficult again, but you know what, I can do it," she told CTV news of Edmonton, Alberta. "I did it before, I can do it again. I'll do it as many times as I have to just so I can have my son."

Memory never fully regained. Ingram had experienced an episode of amnesia in 1995 when he disappeared during a trip to a grocery store. Nine months later, he was found in a Seattle hospital, according to Thurston County, Washington, officials. His mother said he never fully regained his memory.

---

dissociative amnesia Dissociative disorder featuring the inability to recall personal information; usually of a stressful or traumatic nature.
generalized amnesia Loss of memory of all personal information, including identity.
localized or selective amnesia Memory loss limited to specific times and events, particularly traumatic events.
dissociative fugue Dissociative disorder featuring sudden, unexpected travel away from home, along with an inability to recall the past, sometimes with assumption of a new identity.

Dissociative amnesia and fugue states seldom appear before adolescence and usually occur in adulthood. It is rare for these states to appear for the first time after an individual reaches the age of 50 (Sackeim & Devanand, 1991). However, once they do appear, they may continue well into old age.

DSM   Disorder Criteria Summary
Dissociative Fugue

Features of dissociative fugue include the following:

> Sudden, unexpected travel from home or customary place of work, with inability to recall one's past

> Confusion about personal identity or assumption of new identity (partial or complete)

> The disturbance does not occur exclusively during the course of dissociative identity disorder and is not caused by a substance or a general medical condition

> The disturbance causes clinically significant distress or impairment of functioning

Source: Based on *DSM-IV-TR.* Reprinted with permission from *Diagnostic and Statistical Manual of Mental Disorders* (4th ed., text revision). © 2000 American Psychiatric Association.

▲ Jeffrey Alan Ingram found himself in Denver not knowing who he was or why he was there after having gone missing a month earlier from Washington state.

Fugue states usually end rather abruptly, and the individual returns home, recalling most, if not all, of what happened. In this disorder, the disintegrated experience is more than memory loss, involving at least some disintegration of identity, if not the complete adoption of a new one.

An apparently distinct dissociative disorder not found in Western cultures is called *amok* (as in "running amok"). Most people with this disorder are males. Amok has attracted attention because individuals in this trancelike state often brutally assault and sometimes kill people or animals; sometimes the person in this state is killed. Those with the disorder probably will not remember an episode occurring. Running amok is only one of a number of "running" syndromes in which an individual enters a trancelike state and suddenly, imbued with a mysterious source of energy, runs or flees for a long time. Except for amok, the prevalence of running disorders is somewhat greater in women, as with most dissociative disorders. Among native peoples of the Arctic, running disorder is termed *pivloktoq.* Among the Navajo tribe, it is called *frenzy witchcraft.* Despite their different culturally determined expression, running disorders seem to meet criteria for dissociative fugue, with the possible exception of amok.

Dissociative Trance Disorder

Dissociative disorders differ in important ways across cultures. In many areas of the world, dissociative phenomena may occur as a trance or possession. The usual sorts of dissociative symptoms, such as sudden changes in personality, are attributed to possession by a spirit important in the particular culture. Often this spirit demands and receives gifts or favors from the family and friends of the victim. Like other dissociative states, trance disorder seems to be most common in women and is often associated with stress or trauma, which, as in dissociative amnesia and fugue states, is current rather than in the past.

Trance and possession are common parts of some traditional religious and cultural practices and are not considered abnormal in that context. Dissociative trances commonly occur in India, Nigeria (where they are called *vinvusa*), Thailand *(phii pob),* and other Asian and African countries (Mezzich et al., 1992; Saxena & Prasad, 1989; van Duijil, Cardeña, & de Jong, 2005). In the United States, culturally accepted dissociation commonly occurs during African American prayer meetings (Griffith et al., 1980), Native American rituals (Jilek, 1982), and Puerto Rican spiritist sessions (Comas-Diaz, 1981). Among Bahamians and African Americans from the South, trance syndromes are often referred to colloquially as "falling out." The personality profiles of 58 cases of dissociative trance disorder in Singapore, derived from objective testing, revealed that these individuals tended to be nervous, excitable, and emotionally unstable relative to "normals" in Singapore (Ng, Yap, Su, Lim, & Ong, 2002). Although trance and possession are almost never seen in Western cultures, they are among the most common forms of dissociative disorders elsewhere. When the state is *undesirable* and considered pathological by members of the culture, particularly if the trance involves a perception of being possessed by an evil spirit or another person (described next), the proposal for *DSM-5* is to diagnose **dissociative trance disorder (DTD)** as a subtype of dissociative identity disorder (APA, 2010; Spiegel, in press).

Dissociative Identity Disorder

People with **dissociative identity disorder (DID)** may adopt as many as 100 new identities, all simultaneously coexisting, although the average number is closer to 15. In some cases, the identities are complete, each with its own behavior, tone of voice, and physical gestures. But in many cases, only a few characteristics are distinct because the identities are only partially independent. Therefore, the name of the disorder was changed in *DSM-IV* from multiple personality disorder to DID. Consider the case of Jonah, originally reported by Ludwig, Brandsma, Wilbur, Bendfeldt, and Jameson (1972).

Jonah ⁝ Bewildering Blackouts

Jonah, 27 years old and black, suffered from severe headaches that were unbearably painful and lasted for increasingly longer periods. Furthermore, he couldn't remember things that happened while he had a headache, except that sometimes a great deal of time passed. Finally, after a particularly bad night, when he could stand it no longer, he arranged for admission to the local hospital. What prompted Jonah to come to the hospital, however, was that other people told him what he did during his severe headaches. For example, he was told that the night before he had a violent fight with another man and attempted to stab him. He fled the scene and was shot at during a high-speed chase by the police. His wife told him that during a previous headache he chased her and his 3-year-old daughter out of the house, threatening them with a butcher knife. During his headaches, and while he was violent, he called himself "Usoffa Abdulla, son of Omega." Once he attempted to drown a man in a river. The man survived, and Jonah escaped by swimming a quarter of a mile upstream. He woke up the next morning in his own bed, soaking wet, with no memory of the incident.

Clinical Description

During Jonah's hospitalization, the staff was able to observe his behavior directly, both when he had headaches and during other periods that he did not remember. He claimed other names at these times, acted differently, and generally seemed to be another person entirely. The staff distinguished three separate identities, or **alters**, in addition to Jonah. (*Alters* is the shorthand term for the different identities or personalities in DID.) The first alter was named Sammy. Sammy seemed rational, calm, and in control. The second alter, King Young, seemed to be in charge of all sexual activity and was particularly interested in having as many heterosexual interactions as possible. The third alter was the violent and dangerous Usoffa Abdulla. Characteristically, Jonah knew nothing of the three alters. Sammy was most aware of the other personalities. King Young and Usoffa Abdulla knew a little bit about the others but only indirectly.

In the hospital, psychologists determined that Sammy first appeared when Jonah was about 6, immediately after Jonah saw his mother stab his father. Jonah's mother sometimes dressed him as a girl in private. On one of these occasions, shortly after Sammy emerged, King Young appeared. When Jonah was 9 or 10, he was brutally attacked by a group of white youths. At this point, Usoffa Abdulla emerged, announcing that his sole reason for existence was to protect Jonah.

DSM-IV-TR criteria for DID include amnesia, as in dissociative amnesia and dissociative fugue. It is proposed that this symptom be given even more prominence in *DSM-5* (Spiegel, in press). In DID, however, identity has also fragmented. How many personalities live inside one body is relatively unimportant, whether there are 3, 4, or even 100 of them. Again, the defining feature of this disorder is that certain aspects of the person's identity are dissociated, accounting for the change in the name of this disorder in *DSM-IV-TR* from multiple personality disorder to DID. This change also corrects the notion that multiple people somehow live inside one body.

Characteristics The person who becomes the patient and asks for treatment is usually a "host" identity. Host personalities usually attempt to hold various fragments of identity together but end up being overwhelmed. The first personality to seek treatment is seldom the original personality of the person. Usually, the host personality develops later (Putnam, 1992). Many patients have at least one impulsive alter who handles sexuality and generates income, sometimes by acting as a prostitute. In other cases, all alters may abstain from sex. Cross-gendered alters are not uncommon. For example, a small agile woman might have a strong powerful male alter who serves as a protector.

---

dissociative trance disorder (DTD) Altered state of consciousness in which people firmly believe they are possessed by spirits; considered a disorder only where there is distress and dysfunction.
dissociative identity disorder (DID) Disorder in which as many as 100 personalities or fragments of personalities coexist within one body and mind. Formerly known as *multiple personality disorder*.
alters Shorthand term for *alter ego*, one of the different personalities or identities in dissociative identity disorder.

The transition from one personality to another is called a *switch*. Usually, the switch is instantaneous (although in movies and on television it is often drawn out for dramatic effect). Physical transformations may occur during switches. Posture, facial expressions, patterns of facial wrinkling, and even physical disabilities may emerge. In one study, changes in handedness occurred in 37% of the cases (Putnam, Guroff, Silberman, Barban, & Post, 1986).

Can DID Be Faked? Are the fragmented identities "real," or is the person faking them to avoid responsibility or stress? As with conversion disorders, it is difficult to answer this question for several reasons (Kluft, 1999). First, evidence indicates that individuals with DID are suggestible (Bliss, 1984; Giesbrecht et al., 2008; Kihlstrom, 2005). It is possible that alters are created in response to leading questions from therapists, either during psychotherapy or while the person is in a hypnotic state.

Kenneth ✦ The Hillside Strangler

During the late 1970s, Kenneth Bianchi brutally raped and murdered 10 young women in the Los Angeles area and left their bodies naked and in full view on the sides of various hills. Despite overwhelming evidence that Bianchi was the "Hillside Strangler," he continued to assert his innocence, prompting some professionals to think he might have DID. His lawyer brought in a clinical psychologist, who hypnotized him and asked whether there were another part of Ken with whom he could speak. Guess what? Somebody called "Steve" answered and said he had done all the killing. Steve also said that Ken knew nothing about the murders. With this evidence, the lawyer entered a plea of not guilty by reason of insanity.

The prosecution called on the late Martin Orne, a distinguished clinical psychologist and psychiatrist

who was one of the world's leading experts on hypnosis and dissociative disorders (Orne, Dinges, & Orne, 1984). Orne used procedures similar to those we described in the context of conversion blindness to determine whether Bianchi was simulating DID or had a true psychological disorder. For example, Orne suggested during an in-depth interview with Bianchi that a true multiple personality disorder included at least three personalities. Bianchi soon produced a third personality. By interviewing Bianchi's friends and relatives, Orne established that there was no independent corroboration of different personalities before Bianchi's arrest. Psychological tests also failed to show significant differences among the personalities; true fragmented identities often score differently on personality tests. Orne concluded that Bianchi responded like someone simulating hypnosis, not someone deeply hypnotized.

Some investigators have studied the ability of individuals to fake dissociative experiences. Spanos, Weeks, and Bertrand (1985) demonstrated in an experiment that a college student could simulate an alter if it was suggested that faking was plausible, as in the interview with Bianchi. All the students in the group were told to play the role of an accused murderer claiming his innocence. The participants received exactly the same interview as Orne administered to Bianchi, word for word. More than 80% simulated an alternate personality to avoid conviction. Groups given vaguer instructions, and no direct suggestion an alternate personality might exist, were much less likely to use one in their defense.

Objective assessment of memory, particularly implicit (unconscious) memory, reveals that the memory processes in patients with DID do not differ from "normals" when the methodologies of cognitive science are used (Allen & Movius, 2000; Huntjens et al., 2002; Huntjens, Postma, Peters, Woertman, & van der Hart, 2003). Huntjens and colleagues (2006) showed that patients with DID acted more like simulators concerning other identities, about which they profess no memory (interidentity amnesia), suggesting the possibility of faking. This is in contrast to reports from interviews with patients with DID that suggest that memories are different from one alter to the next. Furthermore, Kong, Allen, and Glisky (2008) found that, much as with normal participants, patients with DID who memorized words as one identity could remember the words just as well after switching to another identity, contrary to their self-report of interidentity amnesia.

These findings on faking and the effect of hypnosis led Spanos (1996) to suggest that the symptoms of DID could mostly be accounted for by therapists who inadvertently suggested the existence of alters to suggestible individuals, a model known as the "sociocognitive model" because the possibility of identity fragments and early trauma is so-

▲ Chris Sizemore's history of dissociative identity disorder was dramatized in *The Three Faces of Eve*.

cially reinforced by a therapist (Kihlstrom, 2005; Lilienfeld et al., 1999). A survey of American psychiatrists showed little consensus on the scientific validity of DID, with only one-third in the sample believing that the diagnosis should have been included without reservation in *DSM-IV* (Pope, Oliva, Hudson, Bodkin, & Gruber, 1999). (We return to this point of view when we discuss false memories.)

However, some objective tests suggest that many people with fragmented identities are not consciously and voluntarily simulating (Kluft, 1991, 1999). Condon, Ogston, and Pacoe (1969) examined a film about Chris Sizemore, the real-life subject of the book and movie *The Three Faces of Eve*. They determined that one of the personalities (Eve Black) showed a transient microstrabismus (difference in joined lateral eye movements) that was not observed in the other personalities. These optical differences have been confirmed by S. D. Miller (1989), who demonstrated that DID patients had 4.5 times the average number of changes in optical functioning in their alter identities than control patients who simulated alter personalities. Miller concludes that optical changes, including measures of visual acuity, manifest refraction, and eye muscle balance, would be difficult to fake. Ludwig and colleagues (1972) found that Jonah's various identities had different physiological responses to emotionally laden words, including electrodermal activity, a measure of otherwise imperceptible sweat gland activity, and EEG brain waves.

Using functional magnetic resonance imaging (fMRI) procedures, changes in brain function were observed in one patient while switching from one personality to another. Specifically, this patient showed changes in hippocampal and medial temporal activity after the switch (Tsai, Condie, Wu, & Chang, 1999). A number of subsequent studies confirm that various alters have unique psychophysiological profiles (Cardeña & Gleaves, 2003; Putnam, 1997). Kluft (1999) suggests a number of additional clinical strategies to distinguish malingerers from patients with DID, including the observations that malingerers are usu-

ally eager to demonstrate their symptoms and do so in a fluid fashion. Patients with DID, on the other hand, are more likely to attempt to hide symptoms.

Statistics

Jonah had 4 identities, but the average number of alter personalities is reported by clinicians as closer to 15 (Ross, 1997; Sackeim & Devanand, 1991). Of people with DID, the ratio of females to males is as high as 9:1, although these data are based on accumulated case studies rather than survey research (Maldonado, Butler, & Spiegel, 1998). The onset is almost always in childhood, often as young as 4 years of age, although it is usually approximately 7 years after the appearance of symptoms before the disorder is identified (Maldonado et al., 1998; Putnam et al., 1986). Once established, the disorder tends to last a lifetime in the absence of treatment. The form DID takes does not seem to vary substantially over the person's life span, although some evidence indicates the frequency of switching decreases with age (Sackeim & Devanand, 1991). Different personalities may emerge in response to new life situations, as was the case with Jonah.

There are not good epidemiological studies on the prevalence of the disorder in the population at large, although investigators now think it is more common than previously estimated (Kluft, 1991; Ross, 1997). For example, semistructured interviews of large numbers of severely disturbed inpatients found prevalence rates of DID of between 3% and 6% in North America (Ross, 1997; Ross, Anderson, Fleisher, & Norton, 1991; Saxe et al., 1993) and approximately 2% in Holland (Friedl & Draijer, 2000). In the best survey to date in a nonclinical (community) setting, a prevalence of 1.5% was found during the previous year (Johnson et al., 2006).

A large percentage of DID patients have simultaneous psychological disorders that may include anxiety, substance abuse, depression, and personality disorders (Giesbrecht et al., 2008; Johnson et al., 2006; Kluft, 1999; Ross et al., 1990).

Causes

Life circumstances that encourage the development of DID seem clear in at least one respect. Almost every patient presenting with this disorder reports being horribly, often unspeakably, abused as a child.

Sybil ♦ Continual Abuse

You may have seen the movie that was based on Sybil's biography (Schreiber, 1973). Sybil's mother had schizophrenia, and her father refused or was unable to intervene in the mother's brutality. Day after day throughout her childhood, Sybil was sexually tortured and occasionally nearly murdered. Before she was 1 year old, her mother began tying her up in various ways and, on occasion, suspending her from the ceiling. Many mornings, her mother placed Sybil on the kitchen table and forcefully inserted various objects into her vagina. Sybil's mother reasoned, psychotically, that she was preparing her daughter for adult sex. In fact, she so brutally tore the child's vaginal canal that scars were evident during adult gynecological exams. Sybil was also given strong laxatives but prohibited from using the bathroom. Because of her father's detachment and the normal appearance of the family, the abuse continued without interruption throughout Sybil's childhood.

Imagine you are a child in a situation like this. What can you do? You're too young to run away. You're too young to call the authorities. Although the pain may be unbearable, you have no way of knowing it is unusual or wrong. But you can do one thing. You can escape into a fantasy world; you can be somebody else. If the escape blunts the physical and emotional pain just for a minute or makes the next hour bearable, chances are you'll escape again. Your mind learns there is no limit to the identities that can be created as needed. You do whatever it takes to get through life. Not all the trauma is caused by abuse. Putnam (1992) describes a young girl in a war zone who saw both her parents blown to bits in a minefield. In a heart-wrenching response, she tried to piece the bodies back together, bit by bit.

Such observations have led to wide-ranging agreement that DID is rooted in a natural tendency to escape or "dissociate" from the unremitting negative affect associated with severe abuse (Kluft, 1984, 1991). A lack of social support during or after the abuse also seems implicated. A study of 428 adolescent twins demonstrated that a surprisingly major portion of the cause of dissociative experience could be attributed to a chaotic, nonsupportive family environment. Individual experience and personality factors also contributed to dissociative experiences (Waller & Ross, 1997).

The behavior and emotions that make up dissociative disorders seem related to otherwise normal tendencies present in all of us to some extent. It is quite common for otherwise normal individuals to escape in some way from emotional or physical pain (Butler, Duran, Jasiukaitis, Koopman, & Spiegel, 1996; Spiegel & Cardeña, 1991). Noyes and Kletti (1977) surveyed more than 100 survivors of various life-threatening situations and found that most had experienced some type of dissociation, such as feelings of unreality, a blunting of emotional and physical pain, and even separation from their bodies. Dissociative amnesia and fugue states are clearly reactions to severe life stress. But the life stress or trauma is in the present rather than the past, as in the case of the overwrought mother who suffered from dissociative amnesia. Many patients are escaping from legal difficulties or severe stress at home or on the job (Sackeim & Devanand, 1991). But sophisticated statistical analyses indicate that "normal" dissociative reactions

differ substantially from the pathological experiences we've described (Waller, Putnam, & Carlson, 1996; Waller & Ross, 1997) and that at least some people do not develop severe pathological dissociative experiences, no matter how extreme the stress. These findings are consistent with our diathesis–stress model in that only with the appropriate vulnerabilities (the diathesis) will someone react to stress with pathological dissociation.

You may have noticed that DID seems similar in its etiology to posttraumatic stress disorder (PTSD).

One perspective suggests that DID is an extreme subtype of PTSD, with a much greater emphasis on the process of dissociation than on symptoms of anxiety, although both are present in each disorder (Butler et al., 1996). Some evidence also shows that the "developmental window" of vulnerability to the abuse that leads to DID closes at approximately 9 years of age (Putnam, 1997). After that, DID is unlikely to develop, although severe PTSD might. If true, this is a particularly good example of the role of development in the etiology of psychopathology.

We also must remember that we know relatively little about DID. Our conclusions are based on retrospective case studies or correlations rather than on the prospective examination of people who may have undergone the severe trauma that seems to lead to DID (Kihlstrom, 2005; Kihlstrom, Glisky, & Anguilo, 1994). Therefore, it is hard to say what psychological or biological factors might contribute, but there are hints concerning individual differences that might play a role.

Suggestibility Suggestibility is a personality trait distributed normally across the population, much like weight and height. Some people are more suggestible than others; some are relatively immune to suggestibility; and the majority fall in the midrange.

Did you ever have an imaginary childhood playmate? Many people did, and it is one sign of the ability to lead a rich fantasy life, which can be helpful and adaptive. But it also seems to correlate with being suggestible or easily hypnotized (some people equate the terms *suggestibility* and *hypnotizability*). A hypnotic trance is also similar to dissociation (Bliss, 1986; Butler et al., 1996; Carlson & Putnam, 1989). People in a trance tend to be focused on one aspect of their world, and they become vulnerable to suggestions by the hypnotist. There is also the phenomenon of self-hypnosis, in which individuals can dissociate from most of the world around them and "suggest" to themselves that, for example, they won't feel pain in one of their hands.

According to the *autohypnotic model*, people who are suggestible may be able to use dissociation as a defense against extreme trauma (Putnam, 1991). As many as 50% of DID patients clearly remember imaginary playmates in childhood (Ross et al., 1990); whether they were created before or after the trauma is not entirely clear. According to this view, when the trauma becomes unbearable, the person's very identity splits into multiple dissociated identities. Children's ability to distinguish clearly between real-

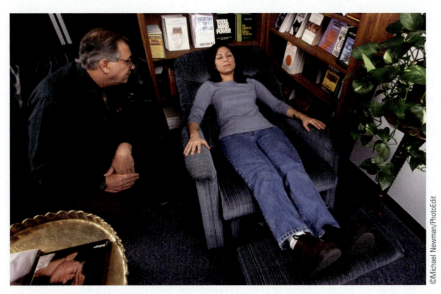

▲ A person in a hypnotic trance is suggestible and may become absorbed in a particular experience.

ity and fantasy as they grow older may be what closes the developmental window for developing DID at approximately age 9. People who are less suggestible may develop a severe posttraumatic stress reaction but not a dissociative reaction.

Biological Contributions As in PTSD, where the evidence is more solid, there is almost certainly a biological vulnerability to DID, but it is difficult to pinpoint. For example, in the large twin study mentioned earlier (Waller & Ross, 1997), none of the variance or identifiable causal factors was attributable to heredity: All of it was environmental. As with anxiety disorders, more basic heritable traits, such as tension and responsiveness to stress, may increase vulnerability. However, much as in PTSD, there is some evidence of smaller hippocampal and amygdala volume in patients with DID compared to "normals" (Vermetten, Schmahl, Lindner, Loewenstein, & Bremner, 2006).

Head injury and resulting brain damage may induce amnesia or other types of dissociative experience. But these conditions are usually easily diagnosed because they are generalized and irreversible and are associated with an identifiable head trauma (Butler et al., 1996). Finally, strong evidence exists that sleep deprivation produces dissociative symptoms such as marked hallucinatory activity (Giesbrecht et al., 2007).

Real and False Memories One of the most controversial issues in the field of abnormal psychology today concerns the extent to which memories of early trauma, particularly sexual abuse, are accurate. Some suggest that many such memories are simply the result of strong suggestions by careless therapists who assume people with this condition have been abused. The stakes in this controversy are enormous, with considerable opportunity for harm to innocent people on each side of the controversy.

On the one hand, if early sexual abuse did occur but is not remembered because of dissociative amnesia, it is crucially important to reexperience aspects of the trauma under the direction of a skilled therapist to relieve current suffering. Without therapy, the patient is likely to suffer from PTSD or a dissociative disorder indefinitely. It is also important that perpetrators are held accountable for their actions because abuse of this type is a crime and prevention is an important goal.

On the other hand, if memories of early trauma are inadvertently created in response to suggestions by a careless therapist but seem real to the patient, false accusations against loved ones could lead to irreversible family breakup and, perhaps, unjust prison sentences for those falsely accused as perpetrators. In recent years, allegedly inaccurate accusations based on false memories have led to substantial lawsuits against therapists resulting in awards of millions of dollars in damages. As with most issues that reach this level of contention and disagreement, it is clear that the final answer will not involve an all-or-none resolution. There is irrefutable evidence that false memories *can* be created by reasonably well-understood psychological processes (Bernstein & Loftus, 2009; Ceci, 2003; Geraerts et al., 2009; Lilienfeld et al., 1999; Loftus, 2003; Loftus & Davis, 2006; McNally, 2001, 2003; Schacter, 1995). But there is also good evidence that early traumatic experiences can cause selective dissociative amnesia, with substantial implications for psychological functioning (Gleaves, 1996; Gleaves, Smith, Butler, & Spiegel, 2004; Kluft, 1999; Spiegel, 1995).

Evidence supporting the existence of distorted or illusory memories comes from experiments like one by the distinguished cognitive psychologist Elizabeth Loftus and her colleagues (Loftus, 2003; Loftus & Davis, 2006). Loftus, Coan, and Pickrell (1996) successfully convinced a number of individuals that they had been lost for an extended period when they were approximately 5 years old, which was not true. A trusted companion was recruited to "plant" the memory. In one case, a 14-year-old boy was told by his older brother that he had been lost in a nearby shopping mall when he was 5 years old, rescued by an older man, and reunited with his mother and brother. Several days after receiving this suggestion, the boy reported remembering the event and even that he felt frightened when he was lost. As time went by, the boy remembered more and more details of the event, beyond those described in the "plant," including an exact description of the older man. When he was finally told the incident never happened, the boy was surprised, and he continued to describe details of the event as if they were true. More recently, Bernstein & Loftus (2009) reviewed a series of experiments demonstrating that, for example, creating a false memory of becoming ill after eating egg salad led to eating less egg salad and reporting a distaste for egg salad up to 4 months later during a test in which the participants didn't know they were being tested for food preferences.

Young children are quite unreliable in reporting accurate details of events (Bruck, Ceci, Francouer, & Renick, 1995), particularly emotional events (Howe, 2007). In one study (Bruck et al., 1995), 35 girls who were 3 years old were given a genital exam as part of their routine medical checkup; another 35 girls were not (the control group). Shortly after the exam, with her mother present, each girl was asked to describe where the doctor had touched her. She was then presented with an anatomically correct doll and asked again to point out where the doctor had touched her. The findings indicated that the children were inaccurate in reporting what happened. Approximately 60% of those who were touched in the genital region refused to indicate this, whether the dolls were used or not. Of the children in the control group, however, approximately 60% indicated genital insertions or other intrusive acts by the doctor, even though nothing of the sort had occurred.

In another set of studies (Ceci, 2003) preschool children were asked to think about actual events that they had experienced, such as an accident, and about fictitious events, such as having to go to the hospital to get their fingers removed from a mousetrap. Each week for 10 consecutive weeks an interviewer asked each child to choose one of the scenes and to "think very hard and tell me if this ever happened to you." The child thus experienced thinking hard and visualizing both real and fictitious scenes over an extended period. After 10 weeks, the children were examined by a new interviewer who had not participated in the experiment (Ceci, 1995, 2003).

In one of Ceci's studies, 58% of the preschool children described the fictitious event as if it had happened. Another 25% of the children described the fictitious events as real a majority of the time. Furthermore, the children's narratives were detailed, coherent, and embellished in ways that were not suggested originally. More telling was that in one study 27% of the children, when told their memory was false, claimed that they really did remember the event.

But there is also plenty of evidence that therapists need to be sensitive to signs of trauma that may not be fully remembered in patients presenting with symptoms of dissociative disorder or PTSD. Even if patients are unable to report or remember early trauma, it can sometimes be confirmed through corroborating evidence (Coons, 1994). In one study, Williams (1994) interviewed 129 women with previously documented histories, such as hospital records, of having been sexually abused as children. Thirty-eight percent did not recall the incidents that had been reported to authorities at least 17 years earlier, even with extensive probing of their abuse histories. This lack of recall was more extensive if the victim had been young and knew the abuser. But Goodman and colleagues (2003) interviewed 175 individuals with documented child sexual abuse histories and found that most participants (81%) remembered and reported the abuse. Older age when the abuse ended and emotional support following initial disclosure of the abuses were associated with higher rates of disclosures.

McNally and Geraerts (2009) also present evidence suggesting that some people, after many years, simply forget these early experiences and recall them after encountering some reminders outside of therapy. In this group, then, it's not necessary to invoke the concepts of repression, trauma, or false memory. It is simple forgetting. In summary, among those individuals reporting memories of sexual abuse, some may have experienced it and remembered it all along, some people may have false memories, some may have recovered memories in therapy of "repressed" sexual abuse, and some may have simply forgotten the incident but remember later.

As Brewin, Andrews, and Gotlib (1993) also point out, the available data from cognitive science would suggest that an extreme reconstructive model of (false) memory induced by careless therapists would be rare because most individuals can recall important details of their childhood, particularly if they are unique and unexpected.

How will this controversy be resolved? Because false memories can be created through strong repeated suggestions by an authority figure, therapists must be fully aware of the conditions under which this is likely to occur, particularly when dealing with young children. This requires extensive knowledge of the workings of memory and other aspects of psychological functioning and illustrates, again, the dangers of dealing with inexperienced or inadequately trained psychotherapists. Elaborate tales of satanic abuse of children under the care of elderly women in day care centers are most likely cases of memories implanted by aggressive and careless therapists or law enforcement officials (Lilienfeld et al., 1999; Loftus & Davis, 2006; McNally, 2003). In some cases, elderly caregivers have been sentenced to life in prison.

However, many people with dissociative disorder and PTSD have suffered documented extreme abuse and trauma, which could then become dissociated from awareness. It may be that future research will find that the severity of dissociative amnesia is directly related to the severity of the trauma in vulnerable individuals, and this type of severe dissociative reaction is also likely to be proved as qualitatively different from "normal" dissociative experiences we all have occasionally, such as feeling unreal or not here for a moment or two. (See, for example, Kluft, 1999; Waller et al., 1996.) Advocates on both sides of this issue agree that clinical science must proceed as quickly as possible to specify the processes under which the implantation of false memories is likely and to define the presenting features that indicate a real but dissociated traumatic experience (Gleaves et al., 2004; Kihlstrom, 1997, 2005; Lilienfeld et al., 1999; Pope, 1996, 1997). Until then, mental health professionals must be extremely careful not to prolong unnecessary suffering among both victims of actual abuse and victims falsely accused as abusers.

Treatment

Individuals who experience dissociative amnesia or a fugue state usually get better on their own and remember what they have forgotten. The episodes are so clearly related to current life stress that prevention of future episodes usually involves therapeutic resolution of the distressing situations and increasing the strength of personal coping mechanisms. When necessary, therapy focuses on recalling what happened during the amnesic or fugue states, often with the help of friends or family who know what happened, so that patients can confront the information and integrate it into their conscious experience. For more difficult cases, hypnosis or benzodiazepines (minor tranquilizers) have been used, with suggestions from the therapist that it is okay to remember the events (Maldonado et al., 1998).

For DID, however, the process is not so easy. With the person's very identity shattered into many elements, reintegrating the personality might seem hopeless. Fortunately, this is not always the case. Although no controlled research has been reported on the effects of treatment, there are some documented successes of attempts to reintegrate identities through long-term psychotherapy (Brand et al., 2009; Ellason & Ross, 1997; Kluft, 2009; Putnam, 1989; Ross, 1997). Nevertheless, the prognosis for most people remains guarded. Coons (1986) found that only 5 of 20 patients achieved a full integration of their identities. Ellason and Ross (1997) reported that 12 of 54 (22.2%) patients had achieved integration 2 years after presenting for treatment, which in most cases had been continuous. These results could be attributed to other factors than therapy because no experimental comparison was present (Powell & Howell, 1998).

The strategies that therapists use today in treating DID are based on accumulated clinical wisdom, as well as on procedures that have been successful with PTSD (Gold & Seibel, 2009; Keane, Marx, & Sloan, in press; Maldonado et al., 1998; see Chapter 4). The fundamental goal is to identify cues or triggers that provoke memories of trauma, dissociation, or both and to neutralize them. More important, the patient must confront and relive the early trauma and gain control over the horrible events, at least as they recur in the patient's mind (Kluft, 1996, 1999, 2009; Ross, 1997). To instill this sense of control, the therapist must skillfully, and slowly, help the patient visualize and relive aspects of the trauma until it is simply a terrible memory instead of a current event. Because the memory is unconscious, aspects of the experience are often not known to either the patient or the therapist until they emerge during treatment. Hypnosis is often used to access unconscious memories and bring various alters into awareness. Because the process of dissociation may be similar to the process of hypnosis, the latter may be a particularly efficient way to access traumatic memories (Maldonado et al., 1998). (There is as yet no evidence that hypnosis is a *necessary* part of treatment.) DID seems to run a chronic course and seldom improves spontaneously, which confirms that current treatments, primitive as they are, have some effectiveness.

It is possible that reemerging memories of trauma may trigger further dissociation. The therapist must be on guard against this happening. Trust is important to any therapeutic relationship, but it is essential in the treatment of DID. Occasionally, medication is combined with therapy, but there is little indication that it helps much. What little clinical evidence there is indicates that antidepressant drugs might be appropriate in some cases (Coons, 1986; Kluft, 1996; Putnam & Loewenstein, 1993).

Concept Check 5.2

Diagnose the dissociative disorders described here by choosing one of the following: (a) dissociative fugue, (b) depersonalization disorder, (c) generalized amnesia, (d) dissociative identity disorder, and (e) localized amnesia.

1. Ann was found wandering the streets, unable to recall any important personal information. After searching her purse and finding an address, doctors were able to contact her mother. They learned that Ann had just been in a terrible accident and was the only survivor. Ann could not remember her mother nor any details of the accident. She was distressed. _____

2. Karl was brought to a clinic by his mother. She was concerned because at times his behavior was strange. His speech and his way of relating to people and situations would change dramatically, almost as if he were a different person. What bothered her and Karl most was that he could not recall anything he did during these periods.

   _____

3. Terry complained about feeling out of control. She said she sometimes felt as if she were floating under the ceiling and just watching things happen to her. She also experienced tunnel vision and felt uninvolved in the things that went on in the room around her. This always caused her to panic and perspire. _____

4. Henry is 64 and recently arrived in town. He does not know where he is from or how he got here. His driver's license proves his name, but he is unconvinced it is his. He is in good health and not taking any medication. _____

5. Rosita cannot remember what happened last weekend. On Monday she was admitted to a hospital, suffering from cuts, bruises, and contusions. It also appeared that she had been sexually assaulted. _____

The grouping of somatoform disorders under the heading of "somatoform" is based largely on the assumption that "somatization" is a common process in which a mental disorder manifests itself in the form of physical symptoms. The specific disorders, then, simply reflect the different ways in which symptoms can be expressed physically. Recently, major questions have arisen concerning the classification of somatoform disorders, and a proposal now exists that would radically revise the classification of these disorders in *DSM-5* (APA, 2010; Noyes, Stuart, & Watson, 2008; Voigt et al., 2010).

Specifically, somatization disorder, hypochondriasis, undifferentiated somatoform disorder, and pain disorder all share presentations of somatic symptoms accompanied by cognitive distortions in the form of misattributions of or excessive preoccupation with symptoms. These cognitive distortions may include excessive anxiety about health or physical symptoms, a tendency to think the worst or "catastrophize" about these symptoms, and very strong beliefs that physical symptoms might be more serious than health-care professionals have recognized. Also, people presenting with these disorders often make health concerns a very central part of their lives; in other words, they adopt the "sick role." For this reason, *DSM-5* may focus on the severity and number of physical symptoms, and the severity of anxiety focused on the symptoms, and group them into a new category entitled "complex somatic symptom disorder" (CSSD). Preliminary explorations of the validity and utility of this strategy indicate that this new dimensional approach, reflecting both physical and psychological symptom severity, would be helpful to clinicians (Noyes et al., 2008; Voigt et al., 2010).

Another advantage of this approach is that there would be less burden on physicians to make tricky determinations on whether the symptoms have physical causes. Rather, the combination of chronic physical symptoms accompanied by the psychological factors of misattributing the meaning of the symptoms and excessive concern would be sufficient to make the diagnosis. The *DSM-5* proposal also suggests that the name of the larger category should be changed from "somatoform disorders" to "somatic symptom disorders"; the new category would include not only the *DSM-IV* somatoform disorders, but also psychological factors affecting medical conditions (see Chapter 7) and the factitious disorders because all involve the presentation of physical symptoms and/or concern about medical illness.

Summary

Somatoform Disorders

What are the defining features of somatoform disorders?

> Individuals with somatoform disorders are pathologically concerned with the appearance or functioning of their bodies and bring these concerns to the attention of health professionals, who usually find no identifiable medical basis for the physical complaints.

> There are several types of somatoform disorders. Hypochondriasis is a condition in which individuals believe they are seriously ill and become anxious over this possibility. Somatization disorder is characterized by a seemingly unceasing and wide-ranging pattern of physical complaints that dominate the individual's life and interpersonal relationships. In conversion disorder, there is physical malfunctioning, such as paralysis, without any apparent physical problems. In pain disorder, psychological factors are judged to play a major role in maintaining physical suffering. In body dysmorphic disorder (BDD), a person who looks normal is obsessively preoccupied with some imagined defect in appearance (imagined ugliness).

> Distinguishing among conversion reactions, real physical disorders, and outright malingering (or faking) is sometimes difficult. Even more puzzling can be factitious disorder, in which the person's symptoms are feigned and under voluntary control, as with malingering, but for no apparent reason.

> The causes of somatoform disorders are not well understood, but some, including hypochondriasis and BDD, seem closely related to anxiety disorders.

What treatments have been developed for somatoform disorders?

> Treatment of somatoform disorders ranges from basic techniques of reassurance and social support to those meant to reduce stress and remove any secondary gain for the behavior. Recently, specifically tailored cognitive-behavioral therapy has proved successful with hypochondriasis. Patients suffering from BDD often turn to plastic surgery or other medical interventions, which more often than not increase their preoccupation and distress.

Dissociative Disorders

What are the five types of dissociative disorders?

> Dissociative disorders are characterized by alterations in perceptions: a sense of detachment from one's own self, from the world, or from memories.

> Dissociative disorders include depersonalization disorder, in which the individual's sense of personal reality is temporarily lost (depersonalization), as is the reality of the external world (derealization). In dissociative amnesia, the individual may be unable to remember important personal information. In generalized amnesia, the individual is unable to remember anything; more commonly, the individual is unable to recall specific events that occur during a specific period (localized or selective amnesia). In dissociative fugue, memory loss is combined with an unexpected trip (or trips). In the extreme, new identities, or alters, may be formed, as in dissociative identity disorder (DID). Finally, the newly defined dissociative trance disorder is considered to cover dissociations that may be culturally determined.

What factors influence the etiology and treatment of dissociative disorders?

> The causes of dissociative disorders are not well understood but often seem related to the tendency to escape psychologically from memories of traumatic events.
> Treatment of dissociative disorders involves helping the patient reexperience the traumatic events in a controlled therapeutic manner to develop better coping skills. In the case of DID, therapy is often long term and may include antidepressant drugs. Particularly essential with this disorder is a sense of trust between therapist and patient.

Key Terms

somatoform disorder, 165
dissociative disorder, 165
hypochondriasis, 166
somatization disorder, 170
pain disorder, 172
conversion disorder, 173
malingering, 174

factitious disorder, 174
body dysmorphic disorder (BDD), 178
derealization, 183
depersonalization disorder, 183
dissociative amnesia, 184
generalized amnesia, 184

localized or selective amnesia, 184
dissociative fugue, 185
dissociative trance disorder (DTD), 187
dissociative identity disorder (DID), 187
alters, 187

Answers to Concept Checks

5.1

1. b; 2. c; 3. d; 4. e; 5. a

5.2

1. c; 2. d; 3. b; 4. a; 5. e

Media Resources

Log in to CengageBrain to access the resources your instructor requires. For this book, you can access:

CourseMate brings course concepts to life with interactive learning, study, and exam preparation tools that support the printed textbook. A textbook-specific website, Psychology CourseMate includes an integrated interactive eBook and other interactive learning tools including quizzes, flashcards, videos, and more.

Abnormal Psychology Videos

> *Rachel, an Example of Dissociative Identity Disorder:* These three clips explore her multiple personalities, how she copes with them, and how they emerge in response to threats within the environment.

> *Doug, an Example of Body Dysmorphic Disorder:* This interview by Katharine Phillips, an authority on this disorder, shows how it cripples this man's life until he seeks treatment for it.

CENGAGENOW CengageNow is an easy-to-use online resource that helps you study in less time to get the grade you want—NOW. Take a pre-test for this chapter and receive a personalized study plan based on your results that will identify the topics you need to review and direct you to online resources to help you master those topics. Then take a post-test to help you determine the concepts you have mastered and what you will need to work on. If your textbook does not include an access code card, go to CengageBrain.com to gain access.

aplia If your professor has assigned Aplia homework:
1. Sign in to your account.
2. Complete the corresponding homework exercises as required by your professor.
3. When finished, click "Grade It Now" to see which areas you have mastered, which need more work, and for detailed explanations of every answer.

Video Concept Reviews

CengageNOW also contains Mark Durand's *Video Concept Reviews* on these challenging topics.
> Somatoform Disorders
> Hypochondriasis
> Concept Check: Hypochondriasis versus Other Disorders
> Conversion Disorder
> Body Dysmorphic Disorder
> Dissociative Disorders
> Depersonalization Disorder
> Dissociative Amnesia
> Dissociative Fugue
> Dissociative Trance Disorder
> Dissociative Identity Disorder
> False and Recovered Memories, Malingering

Chapter Quiz

1. The primary symptom of hypochondriasis is:
   a. fear of developing a disease
   b. fear of spreading a disease
   c. fear of contact with diseased individuals
   d. fear of currently having a disease

2. Someone who presents with the following symptoms might have hypochondriasis.
   a. interpreting momentary flutters in the stomach as a sign of illness
   b. reluctance to visit the doctor for fear of having a panic attack
   c. enjoyment of the immediate attention received when visiting a doctor
   d. realization that the presence of an illness could qualify the individual for full-time disability benefits

3. Choose the scenario that best demonstrates a somatization disorder.
   a. Lisa reports that she has continuous nausea and is unable to work, but a medical exam finds no sign of illness. Lisa claims she only feels better when her husband stays home to nurse her.
   b. Eddie visits 11 different physicians in 6 months but is frustrated that no doctor seems able to make an adequate diagnosis.
   c. Sherry has physical complaints that have lasted at least 10 years. Her symptoms include pain in her feet, hands, and neck; alternating diarrhea and constipation; and difficulty walking. Sherry's physician cannot find any illness to account for these complaints.
   d. Pedro stops working because he thinks that his ears are twice the size they should be and that he looks like a freak. His therapist observes, however, that Pedro's ears are a normal size.

4. Hypochondriasis is related to _____, whereas somatization disorder is linked to _____.
   a. obsessive-compulsive disorder; schizotypal personality disorder
   b. dissociative disorder; obsessive-compulsive disorder
   c. psychotic disorders; anxiety disorders
   d. anxiety disorder; antisocial personality disorder

5. In factitious disorder:
   a. the individual is faking symptoms for personal gain
   b. the individual is voluntarily producing the symptoms without any obvious financial or other external incentives
   c. the individual is not in control of the symptoms but there is no physical explanation
   d. the symptoms are caused by a yet-to-be-identified virus

6. Jorge, a 19-year-old male, was hospitalized after his legs collapsed under him while walking to class. He could not regain his stance and has been unable to walk since, although he desperately wants to walk again. A neurological exam revealed no medical problem. Jorge's behavior is consistent with:
   a. somatization disorder
   b. conversion disorder
   c. malingering
   d. body dysmorphic disorder

7. Mrs. Thompson brought her 4-year-old daughter, Carmen, to the emergency room, stating that the child had been vomiting nonstop throughout the morning. Carmen's condition improved over the course of several days. On the day of her discharge from the hospital, a nurse walked in as Mrs. Thompson was giving Carmen a drink of floor cleaner. Mrs. Thompson's behavior is consistent with:

a. parental hypochondriasis

b. Munchausen syndrome by proxy

c. conversion syndrome by proxy

d. parental somatization

8. _____ describes the experience of losing a sense of your own reality, whereas _____ describes losing your sense of reality of the external world.

a. Depersonalization; derealization

b. Derealization; somatization

c. Derealization; depersonalization

d. Somatization; derealization

9. Michael's wife, Jennifer, reported him missing to the police in 1998. Two years later she saw Michael in an airport. He lived two states away from Jennifer, was married to another woman, and had two children with her. Michael told Jennifer that his name was Danny, not Michael, and that he had never met her before. Michael's presentation is consistent with:

a. multiple personality disorder

b. dissociative trance disorder

c. dissociative identity disorder

d. dissociative fugue

10. The different identities or personalities in dissociative identity disorder are called _____, whereas the change from one personality to another is called a _____.

a. masks; transition

b. faces; switch

c. façades; transition

d. alters; switch

(See Appendix A for answers.)

Exploring Somatoform and Dissociative Disorders

These two sets of disorders share some common features and are strongly linked historically as "hysterical neuroses." Both are relatively rare and not yet well understood.

SOMATOFORM DISORDERS
Characterized by a pathological concern with physical functioning or appearance

Hypochondriasis

Causes

Additional physical symptoms → Faulty interpretation of physical sensations → Intensified focus on symptoms → Increased anxiety → (cycle)

Characteristics

- Severe anxiety over physical problems that are medically undetectable
- Affects women and men equally
- May emerge at any age
- Evident in diverse cultures

Treatment

- Psychotherapy to challenge illness perceptions
- Counseling and/or support groups to provide reassurance

Somatization Disorder

Causes

Eventual social isolation → Continual development of new symptoms → Immediate sympathy and attention → (cycle)

Characteristics

- Reports of multiple physical symptoms without a medical basis
- Runs in families; probably heritable basis
- Rare—most prevalent among unmarried women in low socioeconomic groups
- Onset usually in adolescence; often persists into old age

Treatment

- Hard to treat
- Cognitive-behavioral therapy (CBT) to provide reassurance, reduce stress, and minimize help-seeking behaviors
- Therapy to broaden basis for relating to others

Conversion Disorder

Causes

Social influences (symptoms learned from observing real illness or injury) → Life stresses or psychological conflict → Reduced by incapacitating symptoms → (cycle)

Characteristics

- Severe physical dysfunctioning (e.g., paralysis and blindness) without corresponding physical pathology
- Affected people are genuinely unaware that they can function normally
- May coincide with other problems, especially somatization disorder
- Most prevalent in low socioeconomic groups, women, and men under extreme stress (e.g., soldiers)

Treatment

- Same as for somatization disorder, with emphasis on resolving life stress or conflict and reducing help-seeking behaviors

Body Dysmorphic Disorder (BDD)

Causes

Pathological attempts to "fix" the problem that prevents a more reality-based appraisal of the "defect" → Intrusive, anxiety-provoking idea that individual has a physical defect apparent to everyone → Intensified focus on imagined defects accompanied by extreme self-consciousness → Increased anxiety → (cycle)

Characteristics

- Socially disabling preoccupation with a normal physical feature that is believed to be hideous ("imagined ugliness")
- Prevalence is not known; affects men and women equally
- Associated with obsessive-compulsive disorder

Treatment

- CBT treatments seem most effective
- Drug treatments can provide relief for some sufferers
- Without treatment, BDD lasts a lifetime

DISSOCIATIVE DISORDERS
Characterized by detachment from the self (depersonalization) and objective reality (derealization)

Causes

Severe abuse during childhood
- Fantasy life is the only "escape"
- Practice becomes automatic and then involuntary

Similar etiology to posttraumatic stress disorder

Biological vulnerability likely

High suggestibility a possible trait

Photodisc/Getty Images

Controversy

The scientific community is divided over the question of whether multiple identities are a genuine experience or faked. Studies have shown that "false memories" can be created ("implanted") by therapists. Other tests confirm that various alters are physiologically distinct.

Disorder	Characteristics	Treatment
Dissociative Identity Disorder (DID)	• Affected person adopts new identities, or alters, that coexist simultaneously; the alters may be complete and distinct personalities or only partly independent • Average number of alters is 15 • Childhood onset; affects more women than men • Patients often suffer from other psychological disorders simultaneously • Rare outside of Western cultures	• Long-term psychotherapy may reintegrate separate personalities in 25% of patients • Treatment of associated trauma similar to posttraumatic stress disorder; lifelong condition without treatment
Depersonalization	• Severe and frightening feelings of detachment dominate the person's life • Affected person feels like an outside observer of his or her own mental or body processes • Causes significant distress or impairment in functioning, especially emotional expression and deficits in perception • Some symptoms are similar to those of panic disorder • Rare; onset usually in adolescence	• Psychological treatments similar to those for panic disorder may be helpful • Stresses associated with onset of disorder should be addressed • Tends to be lifelong
Dissociative Fugue	• Memory loss accompanies an unplanned journey • Person sometimes assumes a new identity or becomes confused about an old identity • Usually associated with an intolerable situation • Fugue states usually end abruptly • Typically adult onset	• Usually self-correcting when current life stress is resolved • If needed, therapy focuses on retrieving lost information
Dissociative Amnesia	• Generalized: Inability to remember anything, including identity; comparatively rare • Localized: Inability to remember specific events (usually traumatic); frequently occurs in war • More common than general amnesia • Usually adult onset for both types	• Usually self-correcting when current life stress is resolved • If needed, therapy focuses on retrieving lost information
Dissociative Trance	• Sudden changes in personality accompany a trance or "possession" • Causes significant distress and/or impairment in functioning • Often associated with stress or trauma • Prevalent worldwide, usually in a religious context; rarely seen in Western cultures • More common in women than in men	• Little is known

Photodisc/Getty Images

CHAPTER 6

Mood Disorders and Suicide

Demonstrate knowledge and understanding representing appropriate breadth and depth in selected content areas of psychology.	› Biological bases of behavior and mental processes, including physiology, sensation, perception, comparative, motivation, and emotion (APA SLO 1.2.a [3]) *(see textbook pages 215–217)*
	› Variability and continuity of behavior and mental processes within and across species (APA SLO 1.2.d [2]) *(see textbook pages 211–214, 236–238)*
Use the concepts, language, and major theories of the discipline to account for psychological phenomena.	› Describe behavior and mental processes empirically, including operational definitions (APA SLO 1.3.a) *(see textbook pages 202–210)*
	› Integrate theoretical perspectives to produce comprehensive and multifaceted explanations (APA SLO 1.3.e) *(see textbook pages 224–226, 238–240)*
Identify appropriate applications of psychology in solving problems, such as:	› Origin and treatment of abnormal behavior (APA SLO 4.2.b) *(see textbook pages 227–235, 241–243)*

*Portions of this chapter cover learning outcomes suggested by the American Psychological Association (2007) in their guidelines for the undergraduate psychology major. Chapter coverage of these outcomes is identified by APA Goal and APA Suggested Learning Outcome (SLO).

Understanding and Defining Mood Disorders

> **What is the difference between a depressive episode and a manic or hypomanic episode?**
> **What are the clinical symptoms of major depressive disorder, dysthymic disorder, and bipolar disorder?**

Think back over the past month of your life. It may seem normal in most respects; you studied during the week, socialized on the weekend, and thought about the future once in a while. Perhaps you were anticipating with some pleasure the next school break or seeing an old friend. But maybe sometime during the past month you also felt kind of down because you got a lower mark than you expected on a test after studying hard or broke up with your boyfriend or girlfriend or, worse yet, one of your grandparents died. Think about your feelings during this period. Were you sad? Perhaps you remember crying. Maybe you felt listless, and you couldn't seem to get up the energy to study or go out with your friends. It may be that you feel this way once in a while for no good reason you can think of and your friends think you're moody.

If you are like most people, you know your mood will pass. You will be back to your old self in a few days or a week. If you never felt down and always saw only what was good in a situation, it would be more unusual (and would also seem so to your friends) than if you were depressed once in a while. Feelings of depression (and joy) are universal, which makes it all the more difficult to understand disorders of mood, disorders that can be so incapacitating that violent suicide may seem by far a better option than living. Consider the case of Katie.

Katie | Weathering Depression

Katie was an attractive but shy 16-year-old girl who came to our clinic with her parents. For several years, Katie seldom interacted with anybody outside her family because of her considerable social anxiety. Going to school was difficult, and as her social contacts decreased her days became empty and dull. By the time she was 16, a deep, all-encompassing depression blocked the sun from her life. Here is how she described it later:

The experience of depression is like falling into a deep, dark hole that you cannot climb out of. You scream as you fall, but it seems like no one hears you. Some days you float upward without even trying; on other days, you wish that you would hit bottom so that you would never fall again. Depression affects the way you interpret events. It influences the way you see yourself and the way you see other people. I remember looking in the mirror and thinking that I was the ugliest creature in the world. Later in life, when some of these ideas would come back, I learned to remind myself that I did not have those thoughts yesterday and chances were that I would not have them tomorrow or the next day. It is a little like waiting for a change in the weather.

But at 16, in the depths of her despair, Katie had no such perspective. She often cried for hours at the end of the day. She had begun drinking alcohol the year before, with the blessing of her parents, strangely enough, because the pills prescribed by her family doctor did no good. A glass of wine at dinner had a temporary soothing effect on Katie, and both she and her parents, in their desperation, were willing to try anything that might make her a more functional person. But one glass was not enough. She drank increasingly more often. She began drinking herself to sleep. It was a means of escaping what she felt: "I had very little hope of positive change. I do not think that anyone close to me was hopeful, either. I was angry, cynical, and in a great deal of emotional pain."

For several years, Katie had thought about suicide as a solution to her unhappiness. At 13, in the presence of her parents, she reported these thoughts to a psychologist. Her parents wept, and the sight of their tears deeply affected Katie. From that point on, she never expressed her suicidal thoughts again, but they remained with her. By the time she was 16, her preoccupation with her own death had increased.

I think this was just exhaustion. I was tired of dealing with the anxiety and depression day in and day out. Soon I found myself trying to sever the few interpersonal connections that I did have, with my closest friends, with my mother, and my oldest brother. I was almost impossible to talk to. I was angry and frustrated all the time. One day I went over the edge. My mother and I had a disagreement about some unimportant little thing. I went to my bedroom where I kept a bottle of whiskey or vodka or whatever I was drinking at the time. I drank as much as I could until I could pinch myself as hard as I could and feel nothing. Then I got out a very sharp knife that I had been saving and slashed my wrist deeply. I did not feel anything but the warmth of the blood running from my wrist.

The blood poured out onto the floor next to the bed that I was lying on. The sudden thought hit me that I had failed, that this was not enough to cause my death. I got up from the bed and began to laugh. I tried to stop the bleeding with some tissues. I stayed calm and frighteningly pleasant. I walked to the kitchen and called my mother. I cannot imagine how she felt when she saw my shirt and pants covered in blood. She was amazingly calm. She asked to see the cut and said that it was not going to stop bleeding on its own and that I needed to go to the doctor immedi-

ately. I remember as the doctor shot novocaine into the cut he remarked that I must have used an anesthetic before cutting myself. I never felt the shot or the stitches.

After that, thoughts of suicide became more frequent and more real. My father asked me to promise that I would never do it again and I said I would not, but that promise meant nothing to me. I knew it was to ease his pains and fears and not mine, and my preoccupation with death continued.

Clearly, Katie's depression was outside the boundaries of normal experience because of its intensity and duration. In addition, her severe or "clinical" depression interfered substantially with her ability to function. Finally, a number of associated psychological and physical symptoms accompany clinical depression.

Because of their sometimes tragic consequences, we need to develop as full an understanding as possible of **mood disorders**. In the following sections, we describe how various emotional experiences and symptoms interrelate to produce specific mood disorders. We offer detailed descriptions of different mood disorders and examine the many criteria that define them. We discuss the relationship of anxiety and depression and the causes and treatment of mood disorders. We conclude with a discussion of suicide.

An Overview of Depression and Mania

The fundamental experiences of depression and mania contribute, either singly or together, to all the mood disorders. The most commonly diagnosed and most severe depression is called a **major depressive episode**. The *Diagnostic and Statistical Manual of Mental Disorders* (4th ed., text revision; *DSM-IV-TR)* criteria indicate an extremely depressed mood state that lasts at least 2 weeks and includes cognitive symptoms (such as feelings of worthlessness and indecisiveness) and disturbed physical functions (such as altered sleeping patterns, significant changes in appetite and weight, or a notable loss of energy) to the point that even the slightest activity or movement requires an overwhelming effort. The episode is typically accompanied by a general loss of interest in things and an inability to experience any pleasure from life, including interactions with family or friends or accomplishments at work or at school. Although all symptoms are important, evidence suggests that the most central indicators of a full major depressive episode are the physical changes (sometimes called *somatic* or *vegetative* symptoms) (Bech, 2009; Buchwald & Rudick-Davis, 1993; Keller et al., 1995; Kessler & Wang, 2009), along with the behavioral and emotional "shutdown," as reflected by low scores on behavioral activation scales (Kasch, Rottenberg, Arnow, & Gotlib, 2002; Rottenberg, Gross, & Gotlib, 2005). *Anhedonia* (loss of energy and inability to engage in pleasurable activities or have any "fun") is more characteristic of these severe episodes of depression than are, for example, reports of sadness or distress (Kasch et al., 2002) or the tendency to cry, which occurs equally in depressed and nondepressed individuals (mostly women in both cases) (Rottenberg, Gross, Wilhelm, Najmi, & Gotlib, 2002). This anhedonia reflects that these episodes represent a state of low positive affect and not just high negative affect (Brown & Barlow, 2009; Kasch et al., 2002). The duration of a major depressive episode, if untreated, is approximately 4 to 9 months (Hasin, Goodwin, Stinson, & Grant, 2005; Kessler & Wang, 2009).

DSM Disorder Criteria Summary
Major Depressive Episode

Features of a major depressive episode include the following:

> Depressed mood for most of the day (or irritable mood in children or adolescents)

> Markedly diminished interest or pleasure in most daily activities

> Significant weight loss when not dieting or weight gain, or significant decrease or increase in appetite

> Ongoing insomnia or hypersomnia

> Psychomotor agitation or retardation

> Fatigue or loss of energy

> Feelings of worthlessness or excessive guilt

> Diminished ability to think or concentrate

> Recurrent thoughts of death, suicide ideation, or suicide attempt

> Clinically significant distress or impairment

> Not associated with bereavement

> Persistence for longer than 2 months

Source: Based on *DSM-IV-TR*. Reprinted with permission from *Diagnostic and Statistical Manual of Mental Disorders* (4th ed., text revision). © 2000 American Psychiatric Association.

The second fundamental state in mood disorders is abnormally exaggerated elation, joy, or euphoria. In **mania**, individuals find extreme pleasure in every activity; some patients compare their daily experience of mania to a continuous sexual orgasm. They become extraordinarily active (hyperactive), require little sleep, and may develop grandiose plans with the belief that they can accomplish anything they desire. A proposal for *DSM-5* is to highlight this feature by adding "persistently increased activity or energy" to the "A" criteria. Speech is typically rapid and may become incoherent because the individual is attempting to express so many exciting ideas at once; this feature is typically referred to as *flight of ideas*.

DSM-IV-TR also defines a **hypomanic episode**, a less severe version of a manic episode that does not cause marked impairment in social or occupational functioning and need only last 4 days rather than a full week. (*Hypo* means "below"; thus the episode is below the level of a manic episode.) A hypomanic episode is not in itself necessarily problematic, but its presence does contribute to the definition of several mood disorders.

The Structure of Mood Disorders

Individuals who experience either depression or mania are said to have a *unipolar mood disorder* because their mood remains at one "pole" of the usual depression–mania continuum. Mania by itself (unipolar mania) does occur (Bech, 2009; Solomon et al., 2003) but is rare because most people with a unipolar mood disorder go on to develop depression eventually. Someone who alternates between depression and mania is said to have a bipolar mood disorder traveling from one "pole" of the depression–elation continuum to the other and back again. However, this label is somewhat misleading because depression and elation may not be at exactly opposite ends of the same mood state; although related, they are often relatively independent. An individual can experience manic symptoms but feel depressed or anxious at the same time. This combination is called a **dysphoric manic episode** or a **mixed manic episode** (Angst, 2009; Angst & Sellaro, 2000; Cassidy, Forest, Murry, & Carroll, 1998; Hantouche, Akiskal, Azorin, Chatenet-Duchene, & Lancrenon, 2006). The patient usually experiences the symptoms of mania as being out of control or dangerous and becomes anxious or depressed about this uncontrollability. Research suggests that manic episodes are characterized by dysphoric (anxious or depressive) features more commonly than was thought, and dysphoria can be severe (Cassidy et al., 1998). In one study, 30% of 1,090 patients hospitalized for acute mania had mixed episodes (Hantouche et al., 2006). In a more recent, carefully constructed study of more than 4,000 patients, as many as two thirds of patients with bipolar depressed episodes also had manic symptoms, most often racing thoughts (flight of ideas), distractibility, and agitation. These patients were also more severely impaired (Goldberg et al., 2009) than those without concurrent depression and manic symptoms. The rare individual who suffers from manic episodes alone also meets criteria for bipolar mood disorder because experience shows that

---

mood disorders One of a group of disorders involving severe and enduring disturbances in emotionality ranging from elation to severe depression.

major depressive episode Most common and severe experience of depression, including feelings of worthlessness, disturbances in bodily activities such as sleep, loss of interest, and inability to experience pleasure, persisting at least 2 weeks.

mania Period of abnormally excessive elation or euphoria associated with some mood disorders.

hypomanic episode Less severe and less disruptive version of a manic episode that is one of the criteria for several mood disorders.

mixed manic episode or dysphoric manic episode Condition in which the individual experiences both elation and depression or anxiety at the same time. Also known as *dysphoric manic episode*.

Major Depressive Disorder: Barbara

"I've been sad, depressed most of my life. . . . I had a headache in high school for a year and a half. . . . There have been different periods in my life when I wanted to end it all. . . . I hate me, I really hate me. I hate the way I look, I hate the way I feel. I hate the way I talk to people. . . . I do everything wrong. . . . I feel really hopeless."

Go to Psychology CourseMate at www.cengagebrain.com to watch this video.

Abnormal Psychology Inside Out. produced by Ira Wohl, Only Child Motion Pictures

most of these individuals can be expected to become depressed at a later time (Goodwin & Jamison, 2007; Miklowitz & Johnson, 2006). It is likely that in *DSM-5* the term "mixed episode" will be eliminated in favor of specifying whether a predominantly manic or predominantly depressive episode is present and then noting "with mixed features" to be more precise (American Psychiatric Association, 2010b).

Depressive Disorders

DSM-IV-TR describes several types of depressive disorders. These disorders differ from one another in the frequency with which depressive symptoms occur and the severity of the symptoms.

Clinical Descriptions

The most easily recognized mood disorder is **major depressive disorder**, **single episode**, defined by the absence of manic or hypomanic episodes before or during the dis-

order. An occurrence of just one isolated depressive episode in a lifetime is now known to be relatively rare (Angst, 2009; Eaton et al., 2008; Judd, 1997, 2000; Kessler & Wang, 2009).

If two or more major depressive episodes occurred and were separated by at least 2 months during which the individual was not depressed, **major depressive disorder**, **recurrent**, is diagnosed. Otherwise, the criteria for major depressive disorder, single episode are the same. Recurrence is important in predicting the future course of the disorder and in choosing appropriate treatments. From 35% to 85% of people with single-episode occurrences of major depressive disorder later experience a second episode and thus meet criteria for major depressive disorder, recurrent (Angst, 2009; Eaton et al., 2008; Judd, 1997, 2000), based on follow-ups as long as 23 years (Eaton et al., 2008). In the first year following an episode, the risk of recurrence is 20%, but it increases as high as 40% in the second year (Boland & Keller, 2009). Because of this finding and others reviewed later, clinical scientists have recently concluded that unipolar depression is often a chronic condition that waxes and wanes over time but seldom disappears. The median lifetime number of major depressive episodes is 4 to 7; in one large sample, 25% experienced six or more episodes (Angst, 1988, 2009; Angst & Preizig, 1996; Kessler & Wang, 2009). The median duration of recurrent major depressive episodes is 4 to 5 months (Boland & Keller, 2009; Kessler et al., 2003), somewhat shorter than the average length of the first episode.

On the basis of these criteria, how would you diagnose Katie? Katie suffered from severely depressed mood, feelings of worthlessness, difficulty concentrating, recurrent thoughts of death, sleep difficulties, and loss of energy. She clearly met the criteria for major depressive disorder, recurrent. Katie's depressive episodes were severe when they occurred, but she tended to cycle in and out of them.

Dysthymic disorder shares many of the symptoms of major depressive disorder but differs in its course. The symptoms are somewhat milder but remain relatively unchanged over long periods, sometimes 20 or 30 years or more (Angst, 2009; Klein, 2008; Klein, Schwartz, Rose, & Leader, 2000; Klein, Shankman, & Rose, 2006).

Dysthymic disorder is defined as a persistently depressed mood that continues at least 2 years, during which the patient cannot be symptom free for more than 2 months at a time. Dysthymic disorder differs from a major depressive episode only in the severity, chronicity, and number of its symptoms, which are milder and fewer but last longer. In a 10-year prospective follow-up study described later, 22% of people suffering from dysthymia eventually experienced a major depressive episode (Klein et al., 2006).

DSM Disorder Criteria Summary
Manic Episode

Features of a manic episode include the following:

› A distinct period of abnormally and persistently elevated, expansive, or irritable mood lasting at least 1 week

› Significant degree of at least three of the following: inflated self-esteem, decreased need for sleep, excessive talkativeness, flight of ideas or sense that thoughts are racing, easy distractibility, increase in goal-directed activity or psychomotor agitation, excessive involvement in pleasurable but risky behaviors

› Mood disturbance is severe enough to cause impairment in normal functioning or requires hospitalization, or there are psychotic features

› Symptoms are not caused by the direct physiological effects of a substance or a general medical condition

Source: Based on *DSM-IV-TR.* Reprinted with permission from *Diagnostic and Statistical Manual of Mental Disorders* (4th ed., text revision). © 2000 American Psychiatric Association.

Double Depression

Recently, individuals have been studied who suffer from both major depressive episodes and dysthymic disorder and who are therefore said to have **double depression**. Typically, dysthymic disorder develops first, perhaps at an early age, and then one or more major depressive episodes occur later (Boland & Keller, 2009; Klein et al., 2006). Identifying this particular pattern is important because it is associated with severe psychopathology and a problematic future course (Boland & Keller, 2009; Klein et al., 2006). For example, Keller, Lavori, Endicott, Coryell, and Klerman (1983) found that 61% of patients with double depression had not recovered from the underlying dysthymic disorder 2 years after follow-up. The investigators also found that patients who had recovered from the superimposed major depressive episode experienced high rates of relapse and recurrence. Consider the case of Jack.

Jack · A Life Kept Down

Jack was a 49-year-old divorced white man who lived at his mother's home with his 10-year-old son. He complained of chronic depression, saying he finally realized he needed help. Jack reported that he had been a pessimist and a worrier for much of his adult life. He consistently felt kind of down and depressed and did not have much fun. He had difficulty making decisions, was generally pessimistic about the future,

---

DSM Disorder Criteria Summary
Dysthymic Disorder

Features of dysthymic disorder include the following:

> Depressed mood for most of the day, on most days, for at least 2 years (or at least 1 year in children and adolescents)

> The presence, while depressed, of at least two of the following: poor appetite or overeating, insomnia or hypersomnia, low energy or fatigue, low self-esteem, poor concentration or difficulty making decisions, feelings of hopelessness

> During the 2 years or more of disturbance, the person has not been without the symptoms for more than 2 months at a time

> No major depressive episode has been present during this period

> No manic episode has occurred, and criteria have not been met for cyclothymic disorder

> The symptoms are not caused by the direct physiological effects of a substance or a medical condition

> Clinically significant distress or impairment of functioning

Source: Based on *DSM-IV-TR*. Reprinted with permission from *Diagnostic and Statistical Manual of Mental Disorders* (4th ed., text revision). © 2000 American Psychiatric Association.

and thought little of himself. During the past 20 years, the longest period he could remember in which his mood was "normal" or less depressed lasted only 4 or 5 days.

Despite his difficulties, Jack had finished college and obtained a master's degree in public administration. People told him his future was bright and he would be highly valued in state government. Jack did not think so. He took a job as a low-level clerk in a state agency, thinking he could always work his way up. He never did, remaining at the same desk for 20 years.

Jack's wife, fed up with his continued pessimism, lack of self-confidence, and relative inability to enjoy day-to-day events, became discouraged and divorced him. Jack moved in with his mother so that she could help care for his son and share expenses.

About 5 years before coming to the clinic, Jack had experienced a bout of depression worse than anything he had previously known. His self-esteem went from low to nonexistent. From indecisiveness, he became unable to decide anything. He was exhausted all the time and felt as if lead had filled his arms and legs, making it difficult even to move. He became unable to complete projects or to meet deadlines. Seeing no hope, he began to consider suicide. After tolerating a listless performance for years from someone they had expected to rise through the ranks, Jack's employers finally fired him.

After about 6 months, the major depressive episode resolved and Jack returned to his chronic but milder state of depression. He could get out of bed and accomplish some things, although he still doubted his own abilities. However, he was unable to obtain another job. After several years of waiting for something to turn up, he realized he was unable to solve his own problems and that without help his depression would continue. After a thorough assessment, we determined that Jack suffered from a classic case of double depression.

---

major depressive disorder, single or recurrent episode Mood disorder involving one major depressive episode; mood disorder involving multiple (separated by at least 2 months without depression) major depressive episodes.

dysthymic disorder Mood disorder involving persistently depressed mood, with low self-esteem, withdrawal, pessimism, or despair, present for at least 2 years, with no absence of symptoms for more than 2 months.

double depression Severe mood disorder typified by major depressive episodes superimposed over a background of dysthymic disorder.

Onset and Duration

Generally the risk for developing major depression is fairly low until the early teens, when it begins to rise in a steady (linear) fashion. The mean age of onset for major depressive disorder is 30 years, based on a large (43,000) and representative sample of the population of the United States, but 10% of all people who develop major depression are 55 or older when they have their first episode (Hasin et al., 2005). An alarming finding is that the incidence of depression and consequent suicide seem to be steadily increasing. Kessler and colleagues (2003) compared four age groups and found that fully 25% of people 18 to 29 years had already experienced major depression, a rate far higher than the rate for older groups when they were that age. Recent evidence suggests that this trend is beginning to level off (Hasin et al., 2005).

As we noted previously, the length of depressive episodes is variable, with some lasting as little as 2 weeks; in more severe cases, an episode might last for several years, with the typical duration of the first episode being 4 to 9 months if untreated (Angst, 2009; Boland & Keller, 2009; Hasin et al., 2005; Kessler et al., 2003). Although 9 months is a long time to suffer with a severe depressive episode, evidence indicates that even in the most severe cases, the probability of remission of the episode within 1 year approaches 90% (Kessler & Wang, 2009). Even in those severe cases in which the episode lasts 5 years or longer, 38% can be expected to eventually recover (Mueller et al., 1996). Occasionally, however, episodes may not entirely clear up, leaving some residual symptoms. In this case, the likelihood of a subsequent episode with another incomplete recovery is much higher (Boland & Keller, 2009). Knowing this is important to treatment planning because treatment should be continued much longer in these cases.

Recent evidence also identifies important subtypes of dysthymic disorder, mostly based on when symptoms began. Although the typical age of onset has been estimated to be in the early 20s, Klein, Taylor, Dickstein, and Harding (1988) found that onset before 21 years of age, and often much earlier, is associated with three characteristics: (1) greater chronicity (it lasts longer), (2) relatively poor prognosis (response to treatment), and (3) stronger likelihood of the disorder running in the family of the affected individual. These findings have been replicated (Akiskal & Cassano, 1997). A greater prevalence of concurrent personality disorders has been found in patients with early-onset dysthymia than in patients with major depressive disorder (Klein, 2008; Pepper et al., 1995). These findings may account for the insidiousness of the psychopathology in early-onset dysthymia. Investigators have found a lower (0.07%) prevalence of dysthymic disorder in children compared to adults (3%–6%) (Klein et al., 2000), but symptoms tend to be stable throughout childhood (Garber, Gallerani, & Frankel, 2009). Kovacs, Akiskal, Gatsonis, and Parrone (1994) found that 76% of a sample of children with dysthymia later developed major depressive disorder.

Dysthymic disorder may last 20 to 30 years or more, although studies have reported a median duration of approximately 5 years in adults (Klein et al., 2006) and 4 years in children (Kovacs et al., 1994). Klein and colleagues (2006), in the study mentioned earlier, conducted a 10-year follow-up of 97 adults with dysthymic disorder and found that 74% had recovered at some point but 71% of those had relapsed. The whole sample of 97 patients spent approximately 60% of the 10-year follow-up period meeting full criteria for a mood disorder. This compares to 21% of a group of patients with nonchronic major depressive disorder also followed for 10 years. These findings demonstrate the chronicity of dysthymia. Even worse, patients with dysthymia were more likely to attempt suicide than a comparison group with episodes of major depressive disorder during a 5-year period. It is relatively common for major depressive episodes and dysthymic disorder to co-occur (double depression) (Boland & Keller, 2009; McCullough et al., 2000). Among those who have had dysthymia, as many as 79% have also had a major depressive episode at some point in their lives.

▲ Queen Victoria remained in such deep mourning for her husband, Prince Albert, that she was unable to perform as monarch for several years after his death. Singer Alicia Keys has spoken of her struggles with depression.

From Grief to Depression

If someone you love has died—particularly if the death was unexpected and the person was a member of your immediate family—you may, after your initial reaction to the trauma, have experienced most of the symptoms of a major depressive episode: anxiety, emotional numbness, and denial (Kendler, Myers, & Zisook, 2008). The frequency of severe depression following the death of a loved one is so high (approximately 62%) that mental health professionals at present do not consider it a disorder unless severe symptoms appear, such as psychotic features or suicidal ideation, or the less alarming symptoms last longer than 6 months (Maciejewski, Zhang, Block, & Prigerson, 2007). Some grieving individuals require immediate treatment because they are so incapacitated by their symptoms (for example, severe weight loss or no energy) that they cannot function.

We must confront death and process it emotionally. All religions and cultures have rituals, such as funerals and burial ceremonies, to help us work through our losses with the support and love of our relatives and friends (Bonanno & Kaltman, 1999; Shear, 2006). Usually the natural grieving process has peaked within the first 6 months, although some people grieve for a year or longer (Clayton & Darvish, 1979; Currier, Neimeyer, & Berman, 2008; Maciejewski et al., 2007). Grief often recurs at significant anniversaries, such as the birthday of the loved one, holidays, and other meaningful occasions, including the anniversary of the death. Mental health professionals are concerned when someone does not grieve after a death because grieving is our natural way of confronting and handling loss. When grief lasts beyond typical time, mental health professionals again become concerned (Neimeyer & Currier, 2009). After a year or so, the chance of recovering from severe grief without treatment is considerably reduced, and for approximately 10% to 20% of bereaved individuals (Bonanno, 2006; Jacobs, 1993; Middleton, Burnett, Raphael, & Martinek, 1996), a normal process becomes a disorder. At this stage, suicidal thoughts increase substantially (Stroebe, Stroebe, & Abakoumkin, 2005).

Many of the psychological and social factors related to mood disorders in general, including a history of past depressive episodes (Horowitz et al., 1997; Jacobs et al., 1989), also predict the development of a typical grief response into a **pathological or impacted grief reaction**, although this reaction can develop without a preexisting depressed state (Bonanno, Wortman, & Nesse, 2004). In children and young adults, the sudden loss of a parent makes them particularly vulnerable to severe depression beyond the normal time for grieving, suggesting the need for immediate intervention (Brent, Melhem, Donohoe, & Walker, 2009). Particularly prominent symptoms include intrusive memories and distressingly strong yearnings for the loved one and avoiding people or places that are reminders of the loved one (Horowitz et al., 1997; Lichtenthal, Cruess, & Prigerson, 2004; Shear, 2006). Although a recent analysis suggests that the similarities to major depression outweigh the differences (Kendler et al., 2008), brain-imaging studies indicate that areas of the brain associated with close relationships and attachment are active in grieving people, in addition to areas of the brain associated with more general emotional responding (Gündel, O'Connor, Littrell, Fort, & Lane, 2003).

In cases of long-lasting grief, the rituals intended to help us face and accept death were ineffective. As with victims suffering from posttraumatic stress, one therapeutic approach is to help grieving individuals reexperience the trauma under close supervision. Usually, the grieving person is encouraged to talk about the loved one, the death, and the meaning of the loss while experiencing all the associated emotions, until that person can come to terms with reality. This would include incorporating positive emotions associated with memories of the relationship into the intense negative emotions connected with the loss and arriving at the position that it is possible to cope with the pain and life will go on (Bonanno & Kaltman, 1999; Currier et al., 2008). Several studies have demonstrated that this approach is successful compared with alternative psychological treatments that also focus on grief and loss (Neimeyer & Currier, 2009; Shear, Frank, Houck, & Reynolds, 2005).

Bipolar Disorders

The key identifying feature of bipolar disorders is the tendency of manic episodes to alternate with major depressive episodes in an unending roller-coaster ride from the peaks of elation to the depths of despair. Beyond that, bipolar disorders are parallel in many ways to depressive disorders. For example, a manic episode might occur only once or repeatedly. Consider the case of Jane.

Jane • Funny, Smart, and Desperate

Jane was the wife of a well-known surgeon and the loving mother of three children. They lived in an old country house on the edge of town with plenty of room for the family and pets. Jane was nearly 50 years old. The older children had moved out; the youngest son, 16-year-old Mike, was having substantial

hallucinations Psychotic symptom of perceptual disturbance in which something is seen, heard, or otherwise sensed although it is not actually present.
delusions Psychotic symptom involving disorder of thought content and presence of strong beliefs that are misrepresentations of reality.
catalepsy Motor movement disturbance seen in people with some psychoses and mood disorders in which body postures can be "sculpted" to remain fixed for long periods.
seasonal affective disorder (SAD) Mood disorder involving a cycling of episodes corresponding to the seasons of the year, typically with depression occurring during the winter.
pathological or impacted grief reaction Extreme reaction to the death of a loved one that involves psychotic features, suicidal ideation, or severe loss of weight or energy or that persists more than 2 months. Also known as an *impacted grief reaction*.

academic difficulties in school and seemed anxious. Jane brought Mike to the clinic to find out why he was having problems.

As they entered the office, I observed that Jane was well-dressed, neat, vivacious, and personable; she had a bounce to her step. She began talking about her wonderful and successful family before she and Mike even reached their seats. Mike, by contrast, was quiet and reserved. He seemed resigned and perhaps relieved that he would have to say little during the session. By the time Jane sat down, she had mentioned the personal virtues and material achievement of her husband, and the brilliance and beauty of one of her older children, and she was proceeding to describe the second child. But before she finished she noticed a book on anxiety disorders and, having read voraciously on the subject, began a litany of various anxiety-related problems that might be troubling Mike.

In the meantime, Mike sat in the corner with a small smile on his lips that seemed to be masking considerable distress and uncertainty over what his mother might do next. It became clear as the interview progressed that Mike suffered from obsessive-compulsive disorder, which disturbed his concentration both in and out of school. He was failing all his courses.

It also became clear that Jane herself was in the midst of a hypomanic episode, evident in her unbridled enthusiasm, grandiose perceptions, "uninterruptable" speech, and report that she needed little sleep these days. She was also easily distracted, as when she quickly switched from describing her children to the book on the table. When asked about her own psychological state, Jane readily admitted that she was a "manic depressive" (the old name for bipolar disorder) and that she alternated rather rapidly between feeling on top of the world and feeling depressed; she was taking medication for her condition. I immediately wondered if Mike's obsessions had anything to do with his mother's condition.

Mike was treated intensively for his obsessions and compulsions but made little progress. He said that life at home was difficult when his mother was depressed. She sometimes went to bed and stayed there for 3 weeks. During this time, she seemed be in a depressive stupor, essentially unable to move for days. It was up to the children to care for themselves and their mother, who they fed by hand. Because the older children had now left home, much of the burden had fallen on Mike. Jane's profound depressive episodes would remit after about 3 weeks, and she would immediately enter a hypomanic episode that might last several months or more. During hypomania, Jane was mostly funny, entertaining, and a delight to be with—if you could get a word in edgewise. Consultation with her therapist, an expert in the area, revealed that he had prescribed a number of medications but was so far unable to bring her mood swings under control.

Jane suffered from **bipolar II disorder**, in which major depressive episodes alternate with hypomanic episodes rather than full manic episodes. As we noted earlier, hypomanic episodes are less severe. Although she was noticeably "up," Jane functioned pretty well while in this mood state. The criteria for **bipolar I disorder** are the same, except the individual experiences a full manic episode. As in the criteria set for depressive disorder, for the manic episodes to be considered separate, there must be a symptom-free period of at least 2 months between them. Otherwise, one episode is seen as a continuation of the last.

The case of Billy illustrates a full manic episode. This individual was first encountered when he was admitted to a hospital.

DSM Disorder Criteria Summary

Bipolar II Disorder

Features of bipolar II disorder include the following:

› Presence (or history) of one or more major depressive episodes

› Presence (or history) of at least one hypomanic episode

› No history of a full manic episode or a mixed episode

› Mood symptoms are not better accounted for by schizoaffective disorder or superimposed on another disorder such as schizophrenia

› Clinically significant distress or impairment of functioning

Source: Based on *DSM-IV-TR.* Reprinted with permission from *Diagnostic and Statistical Manual of Mental Disorders* (4th ed., text revision). © 2000 American Psychiatric Association.

Billy | The World's Best at Everything

Before Billy reached the ward, you could hear him laughing and carrying on in a deep voice; it sounded like he was having a wonderful time. As the nurse brought Billy down the hall to introduce him to the staff, he spied the Ping-Pong table. Loudly, he exclaimed, "Ping-Pong! I love Ping-Pong! I have only played twice but that is what I am going to do while I am here; I am going to become the world's greatest Ping-Pong player! And that table is gorgeous! I am going to start work on that table immediately and make it the finest Ping-Pong table in the world. I am going to sand it down, take it apart, and rebuild it until it gleams and every angle is perfect!" Billy soon went on to something else that absorbed his attention.

The previous week, Billy had emptied his bank account, taken his credit cards and those of his elderly parents with whom he was living, and bought every piece of fancy stereo equipment he could find. He thought that he would set up the best sound studio in the city and make millions of dollars by renting it to people who would come from far and wide. This episode had precipitated his admission to the hospital.

During manic or hypomanic phases, patients often deny they have a problem, which was characteristic of Billy. Even after spending inordinate amounts of money or making foolish business decisions, these individuals, particularly if they are in the midst of a full manic episode, are so wrapped up in their enthusiasm and expansiveness that their behavior seems reasonable to them. The high during a manic state is so pleasurable that people may stop taking their medication during periods of distress or discouragement in an attempt to bring on a manic state again.

Returning to the case of Jane, we continued to treat Jane's son Mike for several months. We made little progress before the school year ended. Because Mike was doing so poorly, the school administrators informed his parents that he would not be accepted back the next year. Mike and his parents wisely decided it might be a good idea if he got away from the house and did something different for a while, and he began working and living at a ski and tennis resort. Several months later, his father called to tell us that Mike's obsessions and compulsions had completely lifted since he'd been away from home. The father thought Mike should continue living at the resort, where he had entered school and was doing better academically. He now agreed with our previous assessment that Mike's condition might be related to his relationship with his mother. Several years later, we heard that Jane, in a depressive stupor, had killed herself, an all-too-tragic outcome in bipolar disorder.

A milder but more chronic version of bipolar disorder called **cyclothymic disorder** is similar in many ways to dysthymic disorder (Akiskal, 2009). Like dysthymic disorder, cyclothymic disorder is a chronic alternation of mood elevation and depression that does not reach the severity of manic or major depressive episodes. Individuals with cyclothymic disorder tend to be in one mood state or the other for years with relatively few periods of neutral (or euthymic) mood. This pattern must last for at least 2 years (1 year for children and adolescents) to meet criteria for the disorder. Individuals with cyclothymic disorder alternate between the kinds of mild depressive symptoms Jack experienced during his dysthymic states and the sorts of hypomanic episodes Jane experienced. In neither case was the behavior severe enough to require hospitalization or immediate intervention. Much of the time, such individuals are just considered moody. However, the chronically fluctuating mood states are, by definition, substantial enough to interfere with functioning. Furthermore, people with cyclothymia should be treated because of their increased risk to develop the more severe bipolar I or bipolar II disorder (Akiskal, 2009; Akiskal & Pinto, 1999; Alloy

Bipolar Disorder: Mary

"Whoo, whoo, whoo—on top of the world! . . . It's going to be one great day! . . . I'm incognito for the Lord God Almighty. I'm working for him. I have been for years. I'm a spy. My mission is to fight for the American way . . . the Statue of Liberty. . . . I can bring up the wind, I can bring the rain, I can bring the sunshine, I can do lots of things. . . . I love the outdoors."

Abnormal Psychology Inside Out. produced by Ira Wohl, Only Child Motion Pictures

Go to Psychology CourseMate at www.cengagebrain.com to watch this video.

& Abramson, 2001; Goodwin & Jamison, 2007; Otto & Applebaum, 2011).

Onset and Duration

The average age of onset for bipolar I disorder is from 15 to 18 and for bipolar II disorder from 19 and 22, although cases of both can begin in childhood (Angst, 2009; Judd et al., 2003; Merikangas & Pato, 2009). This is somewhat younger than the average age of onset for major depressive disorder, and bipolar disorders begin more acutely—that is, they develop more suddenly (Angst & Sellaro, 2000; Johnson, Cuellar, & Miller, 2009). About one third of the cases of bipolar disorder begin in adolescence, and the onset is often preceded by minor oscillations in mood or mild cyclothymic mood swings (Goodwin & Ghaemi, 1998; Goodwin & Jamison, 2007; Merikangas et al., 2007). The illness of between 10% and 25% of people with bipolar II disorder will progress to full bipolar I disorder (Birmaher et al., 2009; Coryell et al., 1995).

Although unipolar and bipolar disorder have been thought distinct disorders, Angst and Sellaro (2000), in reviewing some older studies, estimated the rate of depressed individuals later experiencing a full manic episode at closer to 25%. And Cassano and colleagues (2004), along with Akiskal (2006), found that as many as 67.5% of patients with unipolar depression experienced some manic symptoms. These studies raise questions about the true distinction between unipolar depression and bipolar disorder and suggest they may be on a continuum (called a "spectrum" in psychopathology) (Johnson et al., 2009; Merikangas & Pato, 2009).

bipolar II disorder Alternation of major depressive episodes with hypomanic episodes (not full manic episodes).
bipolar I disorder Alternation of major depressive episodes with full manic episodes.
cyclothymic disorder Chronic (at least 2 years) mood disorder characterized by alternating mood elevation and depression levels that are not as severe as manic or major depressive episodes.

It is relatively rare for someone to develop bipolar disorder after the age of 40. Once it does appear, the course is chronic—that is, mania and depression alternate indefinitely. Therapy usually involves managing the disorder with ongoing drug regimens that prevent recurrence of episodes. Suicide is an all-too-common consequence of bipolar disorder, almost always occurring during depressive episodes, as it did in the case of Jane (Angst, 2009; Valtonen et al., 2007). Estimates of suicide attempts in bipolar disorder range from 12% to as high as 48% over a lifetime, and this rate is approximately 20 times higher than for individuals without bipolar disorder (Goodwin & Jamison, 2007). Rates of completed suicide are 4 times higher in people with bipolar disorder than for people with recurrent major depression (Brown, Beck, Steer, & Grisham, 2000; Miklowitz & Johnson, 2006). Even with treatment, patients with bipolar disorder tend to do poorly, with one study showing 60% of a large group experiencing poor adjustment during the first 5 years after treatment (Goldberg, Harrow, & Grossman, 1995; Goodwin et al., 2003). A more comprehensive and longer follow-up of 219 patients reported that only 16% recovered; 52% suffered from recurrent episodes, 16% had become chronically disabled, and in one study 8% had committed suicide (Angst & Sellaro, 2000); in another study with a lengthy, 40-year follow-up, 11% had committed suicide (Angst, Angst, Gerber-Werder, & Gamma, 2005).

In typical cases, cyclothymia is chronic and lifelong. In about one third to one half of patients, cyclothymic mood swings develop into full-blown bipolar disorder (Kochman et al., 2005). In one sample of cyclothymic patients, 60% were female and the age of onset was often during the teenage years or before, with some data suggesting the most common age of onset to be 12 to 14 years (Goodwin & Jamison, 2007). The disorder is often not recognized, and sufferers are thought to be high-strung, explosive, moody, or hyperactive (Akiskal, 2009; Biederman et al., 2000; Goodwin & Jamison, 2007). One subtype of cyclothymia is based on the predominance of mild depressive symptoms, one on the predominance of hypomanic symptoms, and another on an equal distribution of both.

Concept Check 6.1

Match each description or case by choosing its corresponding disorder: (a) mania, (b) double depression, (c) dysthymic disorder, (d) major depressive episode, and (e) bipolar I disorder.

1. Last week, as he does about every 3 months, Ryan went out with his friends, buying rounds of drinks, socializing until early morning, and feeling on top of the world. Today Ryan will not even get out of bed to go to work, see his friends, or even turn on the lights. _____

2. Feeling certain he would win the lottery, Charles went on an all-night shopping spree, maxing out all his credit cards without a worry. We know he's done this several times, feeling abnormally extreme elation, joy, and euphoria. _____

3. Ayana has had some mood disorder problems in the past, although some days she's better than others. Many days it seems like she has fallen into a rut. Although she manages to get by, she has trouble making decisions because she doesn't trust herself. _____

4. For the past few weeks, Jennifer has been sleeping a lot. She feels worthless, can't get up the energy to leave the house, and has lost a lot of weight. Her problem is the most common and extreme mood disorder. _____

5. Sanchez is always down and a bit blue, but occasionally he becomes so depressed that nothing pleases him. _____

DSM Disorder Criteria Summary
Cyclothymic Disorder

Features of cyclothymic disorder include the following:

> For at least 2 years, numerous periods with hypomanic symptoms and numerous periods with depressive symptoms that do not meet the criteria for a major depressive episode

> Since onset, the person has not been without the symptoms for more than 2 months at a time

> No major depressive episode, manic episode, or mixed episode has been present during the first 2 years of the disturbance

> Mood symptoms are not better accounted for by schizoaffective disorder or superimposed on another disorder such as schizophrenia

> The symptoms are not caused by the physiological effects of a substance or a general medical condition

> Clinically significant distress or impairment of functioning

Source: Based on *DSM-IV-TR.* Reprinted with permission from *Diagnostic and Statistical Manual of Mental Disorders* (4th ed., text revision). © 2000 American Psychiatric Association.

> How does the prevalence of mood disorders vary across a life span?

Several large epidemiological studies estimating the prevalence of mood disorder have been carried out in recent years (Kessler et al., 1994; Kessler & Wang, 2009; Merikangas & Pato, 2009; Weissman et al., 1991). The best estimates of the worldwide prevalence of mood disorders suggest that approximately 16% of the population experience major depressive disorder over a lifetime and approximately 6% have experienced a major depressive disorder in the past year (Hasin et al., 2005; Kessler et al., 2003, 2005). For dysthymia the prevalence rates are approximately 3.5%, both for lifetime and in the past year (Kessler & Wang, 2009; Wittchen, Knäuper, & Kessler, 1994). And for bipolar disorder the estimates are 1% lifetime prevalence and 0.8% during the past year (Merikangas & Pato, 2009). The similarity of the lifetime and past-year rates for dysthymia and bipolar disorders reflects the fact that these disorders are chronic conditions that last much of one's life. Studies indicate that women are twice as likely to have mood disorders as men (Kessler, 2006; Kessler & Wang, 2009), but the imbalance in prevalence between males and females is accounted for solely by major depressive disorder and dysthymia because bipolar disorders are distributed approximately equally across gender (Merikangas & Pato, 2009). Although equally prevalent, there are some sex-based differences in bipolar disorder. As noted previously, women are more likely than men to experience rapid cycling, but also to be anxious, and to be in a depressive phase rather than a manic phase (Altshuler et al., 2010).

It is interesting that the prevalence of major depressive disorder and dysthymia is significantly lower among blacks than among whites (Hasin et al., 2005; Kessler et al., 1994; Weissman et al., 1991), although, again, no differences appear in bipolar disorders. One study of major depressive disorder in a community sample of African Americans found a prevalence of 3.1% during the previous year (Brown, Ahmed, Gary, & Milburn, 1995) and another found a prevalence of 4.52% during the previous year (Hasin et al., 2005), compared with 5.53% among whites. Fair or poor health status was the major predictor of depression in African Americans. Few of these individuals received appropriate treatment, with only 11% coming in contact with a mental health professional (Brown et al., 1995). Native Americans, however, present with a significantly higher prevalence of depression (Hasin et al., 2005), although difficulties in translating the concept of depression to Native American cultures suggest this finding needs more study (Beals et al., 2005; Kleinman, 2004).

Prevalence in Children, Adolescents, and Older Adults

Estimates on the prevalence of mood disorders in children and adolescents vary widely, although more sophisticated studies are beginning to appear. The general conclusion is that depressive disorders occur less often in prepubertal children than in adults but rise dramatically in adolescence (Brent & Birmaher, 2009; Costello, Foley, & Angold, 2006; Garber & Carter, 2006; Garber et al., 2009; Rudolph, 2009). Among very young children ages 2 to 5, rates of major depression are about 1.5% and a bit lower later in childhood (Garber et al., 2009), but as many as 20% to 50% of children experience some depressive symptoms that are not frequent or severe enough to meet diagnostic criteria but are nevertheless impairing (Kessler, Avenevoli, & Reis Merikangas, 2001; Rudolph, 2009). Adolescents experience major depressive disorder about as often as adults (Rudolph, 2009). In children, the sex ratio for depressive disorders is approximately 50:50, but this changes dramatically in adolescence. Major depressive disorder in adolescents is largely a female disorder, as it is in adults, with puberty seemingly triggering this sex imbalance (Garber & Carter, 2006; Garber et al., 2009; Nolen-Hoeksema & Hilt, 2009). Of note, this sex imbalance is not evident for more mild depression.

▲ Among adolescents, severe major depressive disorder occurs mostly in girls.

The overall prevalence of major depressive disorder for individuals older than age 65 is about half that of the general population (Blazer & Hybels, 2009; Byers, Yaffe, Covinsky, Friedman, & Bruce, 2010; Fiske, Wetherell, & Gatz, 2009; Hasin et al., 2005; Kessler et al., 2003), perhaps because stressful life events that trigger major depressive episodes decrease with age. But milder symptoms that do not meet criteria for major depressive disorder seem to be more common among the elderly (Beekman et al., 2002; Ernst & Angst, 1995; Gotlib & Nolan, 2001) and may be associated with illness and infirmity (Delano-Wood & Abeles, 2005; Roberts, Kaplan, Shema, & Strawbridge, 1997).

Bipolar disorder seems to occur at about the same rate (1%) in childhood and adolescence as in adults (Brent & Birmaher, 2009; Merikangas & Pato, 2009). However, the rates of diagnosis of bipolar disorder in clinics has increased substantially as a result of greater interest and a controversial tendency to broaden the diagnostic criteria in children to accommodate what might be developmental variations in how bipolar disorder appears, as discussed further later in this chapter (Leibenluft & Rich, 2008; Youngstrom, Youngstrom, & Starr, 2005).

Considering the chronicity and seriousness of mood disorders (Gotlib & Hammen, 2009), the prevalence in all age groups is high indeed, demonstrating a substantial impact not only on the affected individuals and their families, but also on society.

Life Span Developmental Influences on Mood Disorders

You might assume that depression requires some experience with life, that an accumulation of negative events or disappointments might create pessimism, which then leads to depression. Like many reasonable assumptions in psychopathology, this one is not uniformly correct. There is some evidence that 3-month-old babies can become depressed. Infants of depressed mothers display marked depressive behaviors (sad faces, slow movement, lack of responsiveness) even when interacting with a nondepressed adult (Garber et al., 2009; Guedeney, 2007). Whether this behavior or temperament is caused by a genetic tendency inherited from the mother, the result of early interaction patterns with a depressed mother or primary caregiver, or a combination is not yet clear.

Most investigators agree that mood disorders are fundamentally similar in children and in adults (Brent & Birmaher, 2009; Garber et al., 2009; Weiss & Garber, 2003). Therefore, no "childhood" mood disorders in *DSM-IV-TR* are specific to a developmental stage, unlike anxiety disorders. However, it also seems clear that the "look" of depression changes with age. For example, children younger than age 3 might manifest depression by sad facial expressions, irritability, fatigue, fussiness, and tantrums and by problems with eating and sleeping. In children between the ages of 9 and 12 many of these features would not occur. Also, for preschool children (6 years old and under), Luby

and colleagues (2003) report the necessity of setting aside the strict 2-week duration requirement for major depression because it is normal for mood to fluctuate at this young age. Furthermore, if these children clearly have the core symptoms of sadness or irritability and anhedonia (loss of pleasure), then a total of four symptoms rather than five seems sufficient. But even these core symptoms of anhedonia, hopelessness, and excessive sleep and social withdrawal seem to change with age, typically becoming more severe (Garber & Carter, 2006; Weiss & Garber, 2003).

Looking at mania, children younger than age 9 seem to present with more irritability and emotional swings rather than classic manic states, particularly irritability (Fields & Fristad, 2009; Leibenluft & Rich, 2008), but it is also important to recognize that irritability alone is insufficient to diagnose mania because it is associated with many different types of problems in childhood (it is nonspecific to mania). "Emotional swing" or oscillating manic states that are less distinct than in adults may also be characteristic of children, as are brief or rapid-cycling manic episodes lasting only part of a day (Youngstrom, 2009).

One developmental difference between children and adolescents compared with adults concerns patterns of comorbidity. For example, children, especially boys, tend to become aggressive and even destructive during depressive or manic episodes. Therefore, childhood depression (and mania) is often associated with and sometimes misdiagnosed as attention deficit hyperactivity disorder (ADHD) or, more often, conduct disorder in which aggression and even destructive behavior are common (Fields & Fristad, 2009; Garber et al., 2009). Often conduct disorder and depression co-occur in bipolar disorder. In patients with bipolar disorder, between 60% and 90% of children and adolescents also meet criteria for ADHD (Biederman et al., 2000; Singh, DelBello, Kowatch, & Strakowski, 2006; Youngstrom, 2009). In any case, successful treatment of the underlying depression (or spontaneous recovery) may resolve the associated ADHD or conduct disorder in these patients. Adolescents with bipolar disorder may also become aggressive, impulsive, sexually provocative, and accident prone (Carlson, 1990; Keller & Wunder, 1990).

Is Bipolar Disorder in Youth Overdiagnosed?

Children and adolescents are being diagnosed with bipolar disorder at greatly increasing rates over the past several years. In fact, the rates of bipolar diagnoses in youth have doubled in outpatient clinical settings (up to 6%) and have quadrupled in U.S. community hospitals (up to 40%) (Youngstrom et al., 2005; Leibenluft & Rich, 2008). Why the increase? Many clinicians are now using much broader diagnostic criteria that would not correspond to current definitions of bipolar I or bipolar II disorder but rather fall under the relatively vague category of bipolar disorder not otherwise specified (NOS) and include children with chronic irritability, anger, aggression, hyperarousal, and frequent temper tantrums. Although these broader definitions of symptoms do display some similarities with more classic bipolar disorder symptoms and might respond to current treatments for bipolar disorder (Biederman et al., 2005; Biederman et al., 2000), the danger is that these children are being misdiagnosed when they might better meet criteria for more classic diagnostic categories such as ADHD or conduct disorder (see Chapter 13). In that case, the very potent drug treatments for bipolar disorder with substantial side effects would pose more risks for these children than they would benefits.

Based on the large multisite study Course and Outcome of Bipolar Youth (COBY; Axelson et al., 2006; Birmaher et al., 2006), which followed 263 youths with bipolar disorder for 2 years, the American Academy of Child and Adolescent Psychiatry has made the recommendation that most children meeting these broader criteria should not be diagnosed with bipolar disorder unless they also meet more classic definitions that involve clearly defined episodes of fluctuating and extreme moods (depression or mania) (Leibenluft & Rich, 2008; McClellan, Kowatch, & Findling, 2007). Thus, youths who have clear manic episodes that nevertheless might be too short to meet current *DSM* criteria (either elevated or irritable mood that may last only 4 hours but reoccurs a number of times) could be included in the bipolar spectrum, but youths who present with chronic, severe, impairing irritability and anger that is unremitting and not episodic, and is accompanied by symptoms of hyperarousal, temper tantrums, and/or aggression could be better described as having severe mood dysregulation (SMD), rather than bipolar disorder. Instead of receiving inappropriately strong medications, this group might benefit more from the more usual treatments for ADHD and/or depression and anxiety including psychological treatments. A proposal to make changes along these lines has been made for *DSM-5*.

Whatever the presentation, mood disorders in children and adolescents are serious because of their likely consequences (Garber et al., 2009). Fergusson and Woodward (2002), in a large prospective study, identified 13% of a group of 1,265 adolescents who developed major depressive disorder between 14 and 16 years of age. Later, between ages 16 and 21, this group was significantly at risk for occurrence of major depression, anxiety disorders, nicotine dependence, suicide attempts, drug and alcohol abuse, educational underachievement, and early parenting compared with adolescents who were not depressed. Weissman and colleagues (1999) identified a group of 83 children with an onset of major depressive disorder before puberty and followed them for 10 to 15 years. Generally, there was also a poor adult outcome in this group, with high rates of suicide attempts and social impairment compared with children without major depressive disorder. Of note, these prepubertal children were more likely to develop substance abuse or other disorders as adults rather than continue with their depression, unlike adolescents with major depressive disorder. Fergusson, Horwood, Ridder, and Beautrais (2005) found that extent and severity of depressive symptoms as an adolescent predicted extent of depression and suicidal behaviors as an adult. Clearly,

▲ Depression among the elderly is a serious problem that can be difficult to diagnose because the symptoms are often similar to those of physical illness or dementia.

becoming depressed as a child or adolescent is a dangerous, threatening event to be treated immediately or prevented if possible.

Age-Based Influences on Older Adults

Only recently have we seriously considered the problem of depression in the elderly. Some studies estimate that 14% to 42% of nursing home residents may experience major depressive episodes (Djernes, 2006; Fiske et al., 2009). In one large study, depressed elderly patients between 56 and 85 years of age were followed for 6 years; approximately 80% did not remit but continued to be depressed (or cycled in and out of depression) even if their depressive symptoms were not severe enough to meet diagnostic criteria for a disorder (Beekman et al., 2002). Late-onset depressions are associated with marked sleep difficulties, hypochondriasis (anxiety focused on possibly being sick or injured in some way), and agitation (Baldwin, 2009). It can be difficult to diagnose depression in older adults because elderly people who become physically ill or begin to show signs of dementia might become depressed about it, but the signs of depression or mood disorder would be attributed to the illness or dementia and thus missed (see, for example, Blazer & Hybels, 2009; Delano-Wood & Abeles, 2005). As many as 50% of patients with Alzheimer's disease suffer from comorbid depression, which also makes life more difficult for their families (Lyketsos & Olin, 2002).

Anxiety disorders accompany depression in from one third to one half of elderly patients, particularly generalized anxiety disorder and panic disorder (Fiske et al., 2009; Lenze et al., 2000), and when they do, patients are more severely depressed. One third will also suffer from comorbid alcohol abuse (Devanand, 2002). Several studies have shown that entering menopause also increases rates of depression among women who have never previously been depressed (Cohen, Soares, Vitonis, Otto, & Harlow, 2006; Freeman, Sammel, Lin, & Nelson, 2006). This may be because of biological factors, such as hormonal changes, or the experience of distressing physical symptoms or other life events occurring during this period. Depression can also contribute to physical disease and death in the elderly (Blazer & Hybels, 2009). Being depressed doubles the risk of death in elderly patients who have suffered a heart attack or stroke (Schulz, Drayer, & Rollman, 2002).

Wallace and O'Hara (1992), in a longitudinal study, found that elderly citizens became increasingly depressed over a 3-year period. They suggest, with some evidence, that this trend is related to increasing illness and reduced social support; in other words, as we become frailer and more alone, the psychological result is depression, which increases the probability that we will become even frailer and have even less social support. Bruce (2002) confirmed that death of a spouse, caregiving burden for an ill spouse, and loss of independence because of medical illness are among the strongest risk factors for depression in this age group. This vicious cycle is deadly because suicide rates are higher in older adults than in any other age group (Conwell, Duberstein, & Caine, 2002), although rates have been decreasing lately (Blazer & Hybels, 2009).

The earlier gender imbalance in depression reduces considerably after the age of 65. In early childhood, boys are more likely to be depressed than girls, but an overwhelming surge of depression in adolescent girls produces an imbalance in the sex ratio that is maintained until old age, when just as many women are depressed but increasing numbers of men are also affected (Fiske et al., 2009). From the perspective of the life span, this is the first time since early childhood that the sex ratio for depression is more closely balanced.

Across Cultures

We noted the strong tendency of anxiety to take somatic (physical) forms in some cultures; instead of talking about fear, panic, or general anxiety, many people describe stomachaches, chest pains or heart distress, and headaches. Much the same tendency exists across cultures for mood disorders, which is not surprising given the close relationship of anxiety and depression. Feelings of weakness or tiredness particularly characterize depression that is accompanied by mental or physical slowing or retardation (Kleinman, 2004; Ryder et al., 2008). Some cultures have their own idioms for depression; for instance, the Hopi, a Native American tribe, say they are "heartbroken" (Manson & Good, 1993).

Although somatic symptoms that characterize mood disorders seem roughly equivalent across cultures, it is difficult to compare subjective feelings. The way people think of depression may be influenced by the cultural view of the individual and the role of the individual in society (Jenkins, Kleinman, & Good, 1990; Kleinman, 2004; Ryder et al., 2008). For example, in societies that focus on the *individual* instead of the *group*, it is common to hear statements such as "I feel blue" or "I am depressed." However, in cultures where the individual is tightly integrated into the larger group, someone might say, "Our life has lost its meaning," referring to the group in which the individual resides (Manson & Good, 1993).

Weissman and colleagues (1991) looked at the lifetime prevalence of mood disorders in African American and Hispanic American ethnic groups. For each disorder, the figures are similar in the two groups (although, as noted earlier, it is somewhat lower for African Americans in major depressive disorder and dysthymia), indicating no particular difference across subcultures. However, these figures were collected on a carefully constructed sample meant to represent the whole country.

In specific locations, results can differ dramatically. Kinzie, Leung, Boehnlein, and Matsunaga (1992) used a structured interview to determine the percentage of adult members of a Native American village who met criteria for mood disorders. The lifetime prevalence for any mood disorder was 19.4% in men, 36.7% in women, and 28% overall, approximately 4 times higher than in the general population. Examined by disorder, almost all the increase is accounted for by greatly elevated rates of major depression. Findings in the same village for substance abuse are similar to the results for major depressive disorder (see Chapter 10). Hasin and colleagues (2005) found a somewhat lower overall percentage of 19.17% in a different village, which was still 1.5 times higher than the percentage found in Caucasians, a significant difference. Beals and colleagues (2005), however, reported a considerably lower prevalence in two tribes they studied, perhaps because of differences in interviewing methods or because conditions and culture can differ greatly from tribe to tribe. Still, appalling social and economic conditions on many reservations fulfill all requirements for chronic major life stress, which is so strongly related to the onset of mood disorders, particularly major depressive disorder.

Concept Check 6.2

Identify each of the following statements related to prevalence of mood disorders as either true (T) or false (F).

1. _____ Women are approximately twice as likely as men to be diagnosed with a mood disorder.

2. _____ Depression requires some life experience, indicating that babies and young children cannot experience the disorder.

3. _____ It's often difficult to diagnose depression in the elderly because its symptoms are similar to those of medical ailments or dementia.

4. _____ Somatic symptoms characterizing mood disorders are nearly equivalent across cultures.

> **What biological, psychological, and sociocultural factors contribute to the development of mood disorders?**

Psychopathologists are identifying biological, psychological, and social factors that seem strongly implicated in the etiology of mood disorders, whatever the precipitating factor. An integrative theory of the etiology of mood disorders considers the interaction of biological, psychological, and social dimensions and notes the strong relationship of anxiety and depression. Before describing these interactions, we review evidence pertaining to each contributing factor.

Biological Dimensions

Studies that would allow us to determine the genetic contribution to a particular disorder or class of disorders are complex and difficult to do. But several strategies—such as family studies and twin studies—can help us estimate this contribution.

Familial and Genetic Influences

In *family studies,* we look at the prevalence of a given disorder in the first-degree relatives of an individual known to have the disorder (the *proband*). We have found that, despite wide variability, the rate in relatives of probands with mood disorders is consistently about 2 to 3 times greater than in relatives of controls who don't have mood disorders (Gershon, 1990; Klein, Lewinsohn, Rohde, Seeley, & Durbin, 2002; Levinson, 2009). Increasing severity, recurrence of major depression, and earlier age of onset in the proband is associated with the highest rates of depression in relatives (Kendler, Gatz, Gardner, & Pedersen, 2007; Klein et al., 2002; Weissman et al., 2005).

The best evidence that genes have something to do with mood disorders comes from *twin studies,* in which we examine the frequency with which identical twins (with identical genes) have the disorder, compared to fraternal twins who share only 50% of their genes (as do all first-degree relatives). If a genetic contribution exists, the disorder should be present in identical twins to a much greater extent than in fraternal twins. A number of twin studies suggest that mood disorders are heritable (see, for example, Kendler, Neale, Kessler, Heath, & Eaves, 1993; McGuffin et al., 2003). One of the strongest studies demonstrates that an identical twin is 2 to 3 times more likely to present with a mood disorder than a fraternal twin if the first twin has a mood disorder (66.7% of identical twins compared to 18.9% of fraternal twins if the first twin has bipolar disorder; 45.6% versus 20.2% if the first twin has unipolar disorder) (McGuffin et al., 2003). But if one twin has unipolar disorder the chances of a co-twin having bipolar disorder are slim to none.

Two reports have appeared suggesting sex differences in genetic vulnerability to depression. Bierut and colleagues (1999) studied 2,662 twin pairs in the Australian twin registry and found the characteristically higher rate of depressive disorders in women. Estimates of heritability in women ranged from 36% to 44%, consistent with other studies. But estimates for men were lower and ranged from 18% to 24%. These results mostly agree with an important study of men in the United States by Lyons and colleagues (1998). The authors conclude that environmental events play a larger role in causing depression in men than in women.

Note from the studies just described that bipolar disorder confers an increased risk of developing some mood disorder in close relatives—but not necessarily bipolar disorder. This conclusion supports an assumption noted previously that bipolar disorder may simply be a more severe variant of mood disorders rather than a fundamentally different disorder. Then again, of identical twins both having (concordant for) a mood disorder, 80% are also concordant for polarity. In other words, if one identical twin is unipolar, there is an 80% chance the other twin is unipolar as opposed to bipolar. This finding suggests these disorders may be inherited separately and therefore be separate disorders after all (Nurnberger & Gershon, 1992).

McGuffin and colleagues (2003) conclude that both points are partially correct. Basically, they found that the genetic contributions to depression in both disorders are the same or similar but that the genetics of mania are distinct from depression. Thus, individuals with bipolar disorder are genetically susceptible to depression and independently genetically susceptible to mania. This hypothesis still requires further confirmation.

Although these findings do raise continuing questions about the relative contributions of psychosocial and genetic factors to mood disorders, overwhelming evidence suggests that such disorders are familial and almost certainly reflect an underlying genetic vulnerability, particularly for women. As described in some detail in Chapter 2 (see p. 15), studies are now beginning to identify a small group of genes that may confer this vulnerability, at least for some types of depression (Bradley et al., 2008; Caspi et al., 2003; Garlow, Boone, Li, Owens, & Nemeroff, 2005; Levinson, 2009). In this complex field, it is likely that many additional patterns of gene combinations will be found to contribute to varieties of depression.

In conclusion, the best estimates of genetic contributions to depression fall in the range of approximately 40% for women but seem to be significantly less for men (around 20%). Genetic contributions to bipolar disorder seem to be somewhat higher. This means that from 60% to 80% of the causes of depression can be attributed to environmental factors. Also, recent findings underscore the enormous heterogeneity of genetic associations with any mental disorder. So these percentages (40% for women, 20% for men) may not reflect any one pattern of genetic contribution associated with specific groups of genes, but perhaps many different patterns from different groups of genes (McClellan & King, 2010). As we noted in Chapter 3, behavioral geneticists break down environmental factors into events shared by twins (experiencing the same upbringing in the same house and, perhaps, experiencing the same stressful events) and events not shared. What part of our experience causes depression? There is wide agreement that it is the unique nonshared events rather than the shared ones that interact with biological vulnerability to cause depression (Bierut et al., 1999; Plomin, DeFries, McClearn, & Rutter, 1997).

Depression and Anxiety: Same Genes?

Evidence supports the assumption of a close relationship among depression, anxiety, and panic (and other emotional disorders). For example, data from family studies indicate that the more signs and symptoms of anxiety and depression there are in a given patient, the greater the rate of anxiety, depression, or both in first-degree relatives and children (Hudson et al., 2003; Leyfer & Brown, 2011). In several important reports from a major set of data on more than 2,000 female twins, Ken Kendler and his colleagues (Kendler, Heath, Martin, & Eaves, 1987; Kendler, Neale, Kessler, Heath, & Eaves, 1992b; Kendler et al., 1995) found that the same genetic factors contribute to both anxiety and depression. Social and psychological explanations seemed to account for the factors that differentiate anxiety from depression rather than genes. These findings again suggest that, with the possible exception of mania, the biological vulnerability for mood disorders may not be specific to that disorder but may reflect a more general predisposition to anxiety or mood disorders. The specific form of the disorder would be determined by unique psychological, social, or additional biological factors (Kilpatrick et al., 2007; Rutter, 2010).

Neurotransmitter Systems

In Chapter 2, we observed that we now know that neurotransmitter systems have many subtypes and interact in many complex ways with one another and with neuromodulators (products of the endocrine system). Research implicates low levels of serotonin in the causes of mood disorders, but only in relation to other neurotransmitters, including norepinephrine and dopamine (see, for example, Spoont, 1992; Thase, 2005, 2009). Remember that the apparent primary function of serotonin is to regulate our emotional reactions. For example, we are more impulsive, and our moods swing more widely, when our levels of serotonin are low. This may be because one of the functions of serotonin is to regulate systems involving norepinephrine and dopamine. According to the "permissive" hypothesis, when serotonin levels are low, other neurotransmitters are "permitted" to range more widely, become dysregulated, and contribute to mood irregularities, in-

cluding depression. A drop in norepinephrine would be one of the consequences. Mann and colleagues (1996) used sophisticated brain-imaging procedures (PET scans) to confirm impaired serotonergic transmission in patients with depression, but subsequent research suggested that this relationship holds only for more severe patients with suicidal tendencies (Mann, Brent, & Arango, 2001; Thase, 2009). Current thinking is that the balance of the various neurotransmitters and their interaction with systems of self regulation are more important than the absolute level of any one neurotransmitter (Carver, Johnson, & Joormann, 2009).

In the context of this delicate balance, there is continued interest in the role of dopamine, particularly in relationship to manic episodes, atypical depression, or depression with psychotic features (Dunlop & Nemeroff, 2007; Garlow & Nemeroff, 2003; Thase, 2009). For example, the dopamine agonist L-dopa seems to produce hypomania in bipolar patients (see, for instance, Van Praag & Korf, 1975), along with other dopamine agonists (Silverstone, 1985). Chronic stress also reduces dopamine levels and produces depressive-like behavior (Thase, 2009). But, as with other research in this area, it is difficult to pin down any relationships with certainty.

The Endocrine System

During the past several years, most attention has shifted to the endocrine system and the "stress hypothesis" of the etiology of depression (Nemeroff, 2004). This hypothesis focuses on overactivity in the hypothalamic–pituitary–adrenocortical (HPA) axis (discussed later), which produces stress hormones. Again, notice the similarity with the description of the neurobiology of anxiety in Chapter 4 (see, for example, Britton & Rauch, 2009; Charney & Drevets, 2002). Investigators became interested in the endocrine system when they noticed that patients with diseases affecting this system sometimes became depressed. For example, hypothyroidism, or Cushing's disease, which affects the adrenal cortex, leads to excessive secretion of cortisol and often to depression (and anxiety).

In Chapter 2, and again in Chapter 4, we discussed the brain circuit called the HPA axis, beginning in the hypothalamus and running through the pituitary gland, which coordinates the endocrine system (see Figure 2.10). Investigators have also discovered that neurotransmitter activity in the hypothalamus regulates the release of hormones that affect the HPA axis. These **neurohormones** are an increasingly important focus of study in psychopathology (see, for example, Garlow & Nemeroff, 2003; Nemeroff, 2004; Thase, 2009). There are thousands of neurohormones. Sorting out their relationship to antecedent neurotransmitter systems (and determining their independent effects on the central nervous system) is likely to be a complex task indeed. One of the glands influenced by the pituitary is the cortical section of the adrenal gland, which produces the stress hormone cortisol that completes the HPA axis. Cortisol is called a *stress hormone* because it is elevated during stressful life events. (We discuss this system in more detail in Chapter 7.) For now, it is enough to know that cortisol levels are elevated in depressed patients, a finding that makes sense considering the relationship between depression and severe life stress (Bradley et al., 2008; Thase, 2009).

Recognizing that stress hormones are elevated in patients with depression (and anxiety), researchers have begun to focus on the consequences of these elevations. Preliminary findings indicate that these hormones can be harmful to neurons in that they decrease a key ingredient that keeps neurons healthy and growing. You saw in Chapter 4 on anxiety disorders that individuals experiencing heightened levels of stress hormones over a long period undergo some shrinkage of a brain structure called the *hippocampus*. The hippocampus, among other things, is responsible for keeping stress hormones in check and serves important functions in facilitating cognitive processes such as short-term memory. But the new finding, at least in animals, is that long-term overproduction of stress hormones makes the organism unable to develop new neurons (neurogenesis). Thus, some theorists suspect that the connection between high stress hormones and depression is the suppression of neurogenesis in the hippocampus (Heim, Plotsky, & Nemeroff, 2004; McEwen, 1999; Thase, 2009). Now, new evidence reveals that healthy girls at risk for developing depression because their mothers suffer from recurrent depression have reduced hippocampal volume compared to girls with nondepressed mothers (Chen, Hamilton, & Gotlib, 2010). This finding suggests that low hippocampal volume may precede and perhaps contribute to the onset of depression. Scientists have already observed that successful treatments for depression, including electroconvulsive therapy, seem to produce neurogenesis in the hippocampus, thereby reversing this process (Duman, 2004; Santarelli et al., 2003; Sapolsky, 2004).

Sleep and Circadian Rhythms

We have known for several years that sleep disturbances are a hallmark of most mood disorders. Most important, in people who are depressed, there is a significantly shorter period after falling asleep before *rapid eye movement (REM) sleep* begins. As you may remember from your introductory psychology or biology course, there are two major stages of sleep: REM sleep and non-REM sleep. When we first fall asleep, we go through several substages of progressively deeper sleep during which we achieve most of our rest. After about 90 minutes, we begin to experience REM sleep, when the brain arouses, and we begin to dream. Our eyes move rapidly back and forth under our eyelids, hence the name *rapid eye movement* sleep. As the night goes on, we have increasing amounts of REM sleep. (We discuss the process of sleep in more detail in Chapter 8.) In addition to entering REM sleep more quickly, depressed patients experience REM activity that is more intense, and the stages of deepest sleep, called *slow wave sleep,* don't occur until later if at all (Jindal et al., 2002; Kupfer, 1995; Thase, 2009). It seems that some sleep characteristics occur only while we are depressed and not at other times (Riemann, Berger, & Voderholzer, 2001; Rush et al., 1986). But other evidence suggests that, at least in more severe cases with recurrent depression, disturbances in sleep continuity,, and reduction of deep sleep, may be present even when the individual is not depressed (Kupfer, 1995; Thase, 2009).

Sleep pattern disturbances in depressed children are less pronounced than in adults, perhaps because children are very deep sleepers, illustrating once again the importance of developmental stage to psychopathology (Brent & Birmaher, 2009; Garber et al., 2009). But sleep disturbances are even more severe among depressed older adults. In fact, insomnia, frequently experienced by older adults, is a risk factor for both the onset and persistence of depression (Fiske et al., 2009; Perlis et al., 2006). In an interesting new study, researchers found that treating insomnia directly in those patients who have both insomnia and depression may enhance the effects of treatment for depression (Manber et al., 2008). Sleep disturbances also occur in bipolar patients, where they are particularly severe and are characterized not only by decreased REM latency, but also by severe insomnia and hypersomnia (excessive sleep) (Goodwin & Jamison, 2007; Harvey, 2008; Harvey, Talbot, & Gershon, 2009).

Another interesting finding is that depriving depressed patients of sleep, particularly during the second half of the night, causes temporary improvement in their condition (Giedke & Schwarzler, 2002; Thase, 2009), particularly for patients with bipolar disorder in a depressive state (Johnson et al., 2009; Harvey, 2008), although the depression returns when the patients start sleeping normally again. In any case, because sleep patterns reflect a biological rhythm, there may be a relationship among seasonal affective disorder (SAD), sleep disturbances in depressed patients, and a more general disturbance in biological rhythms (Soreca, Frank, & Kupfer, 2009). This would not be surprising if it were true, because most mammals are exquisitely sensitive to day length at the latitudes at which they live and this "biological clock" controls eating, sleeping, and weight changes. Thus, substantial disruption in circadian rhythm might be particularly problematic for some vulnerable individuals (Moore, 1999; Sohn & Lam, 2005; Soreca et al., 2009).

Psychological Dimensions

Thus far we have reviewed genetic and biological factors including findings from studies of neurotransmitters, the endocrine system, sleep and circadian rhythms, and relative activity in certain areas of the brain associated with depression. But these factors are all inextricably linked to psychological and social dimensions where scientists are

---

neurohormones Hormone that affects the brain and is increasingly the focus of study in psychopathology.

also discovering strong associations with depression. We now review some of these findings.

Stressful Life Events

Stress and trauma are among the most striking unique contributions to the etiology of all psychological disorders. This is reflected throughout psychopathology and is evident in the wide adoption of the diathesis–stress model of psychopathology presented in Chapter 2 (and referred to throughout this book), which describes possible genetic and psychological vulnerabilities. But in seeking what activates this vulnerability (diathesis), we usually look for a stressful or traumatic life event.

Stress and Depression. You would think it would be sufficient to ask people whether anything major had happened in their lives before they developed depression or some other psychological disorder. Most people who develop depression report losing a job, getting divorced, having a child, or graduating from school and starting a career as a possible precipitating factor. But, as with most issues in the study of psychopathology, the significance of a major event is not easily discovered (Kessler, 1997; Monroe & Reid, 2009; Monroe, Slavich, & Georgiades, 2009), so most investigators have stopped simply asking patients whether something bad (or good) happened and have begun to look at the context of the event and the meaning it has for the individual.

For example, losing a job is stressful for most people, but it is far more difficult for some than others. A few people might even see it as a blessing. If you were laid off as a manager in a large corporation because of a restructuring but your wife is the president of another corporation and makes more than enough money to support the family, it might not be so bad. Furthermore, if you are an aspiring writer or artist who has not had time to pursue your art, becoming jobless might be the opportunity you have been waiting for.

Now consider losing your job if you are a single mother of two young children and living from paycheck to paycheck and, on account of a recent doctor's bill, you have to choose between paying the electric bill or buying food. The stressful life event is the same, but the context is different and transforms the significance of the event substantially. To complicate the scenario further, think for a minute about how various women in this situation might react to losing their job. One woman might decide she is a total failure and thus becomes unable to carry on and provide for her children. Another woman might realize the job loss was not her fault and take advantage of a job training program while scraping by somehow. Thus, both the context of the life event and its meaning are important. This approach to studying life events, developed by George W. Brown (1989b) and associates in England, is represented in ■ Figure 6.1.

Brown's study of life events is difficult to carry out, and the methodology is still evolving. Psychologists such as Scott Monroe and Constance Hammen (Hammen, 2005; Monroe et al., 2009; Monroe, Rohde, Seeley, & Lewinsohn, 1999; Dohrenwend & Dohrenwend, 1981) have developed

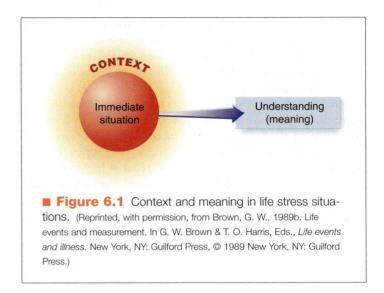

■ **Figure 6.1** Context and meaning in life stress situations. (Reprinted, with permission, from Brown, G. W., 1989b. Life events and measurement. In G. W. Brown & T. O. Harris, Eds., *Life events and illness.* New York, NY: Guilford Press, © 1989 New York, NY: Guilford Press.)

new methods. One crucial issue is the bias inherent in remembering events. If you ask people who are currently depressed what happened when they first became depressed more than 5 years ago, you will probably get different answers from those they would give if they were not currently depressed. Because current moods distort memories, many investigators have concluded that the only useful way to study stressful life events is to follow people *prospectively* to determine more accurately the precise nature of events and their relation to subsequent psychopathology.

In any case, in summarizing a large amount of research, it is clear that stressful life events are strongly related to the onset of mood disorders (Grant, Compas, Thurm, McMahon, & Gipson, 2004; Hammen, 2005; Kendler, Karkowski, & Prescott, 1999b; Kessler, 1997; Mazure, 1998; Monroe et al., 2009; Monroe & Reid, 2009). Measuring the context of events and their impact in a random sample of the population, a number of studies have found a marked relationship between severe and, in some cases, traumatic life events and the onset of depression (Brown, 1989a; Brown, Harris, & Hepworth, 1994; Kendler et al., 1999b; Mazure, 1998). Severe events precede all types of depression except, perhaps, for a small group of patients with melancholic or psychotic features who are experiencing subsequent episodes where depression emerges in the absence of life events (Brown et al., 1994). Major life stress is a somewhat stronger predictor for initial episodes of depression compared to recurrent episodes (Lewinsohn, Allen, Seeley, & Gotlib, 1999). In addition, for people with recurrent depression, the clear occurrence of a severe life stress before or early in the latest episode predicts a poorer response to treatment and a longer time before remission (Monroe et al., 2009; Monroe, Kupfer, & Frank, 1992) and a greater likelihood of recurrence (Monroe et al., 2009; Monroe, Roberts, Kupfer, & Frank, 1996).

Although the context and meaning are often more important than the exact nature of the event itself, some events are particularly likely to lead to depression. One of them is the breakup of a relationship, which is difficult for both adolescents (Monroe, Rohde, Seeley, & Lewinsohn, 1999) and adults (Kendler, Hettema, Butera, Gardner, & Prescott, 2003). Kendler and colleagues (2003) demonstrated in an elegant twin study that if one twin experienced a loss, such as the death of a loved one, that twin was 10 times more likely to become depressed than the twin who didn't experience the loss. But if one twin is also humiliated by the loss, as when, for example, a boyfriend or husband leaves the twin for a best friend and the twin still sees them all the time, then that twin would be 20 times more likely to get depressed than a twin with the same genes who didn't experience the event. Scientists have confirmed that humiliation, loss, and social rejection are the most potent stressful life events likely to lead to depression (Monroe et al., 2009).

Clearly there is a strong relationship between stress and depression, and scientists are discovering that the cause-and-effect connection between the two might go both ways. Remember in Chapter 2 where we noted that our genetic endowment might increase the probability that we will experience stressful life events? We referred to this as the *reciprocal gene–environment model* (Saudino, Pedersen, Lichenstein, McClearn, & Plomin, 1997). One example would be people who tend to seek difficult relationships because of genetically based personality characteristics that then lead to depression. Kendler and colleagues (1999a) report that about one third of the association between stressful life events and depression is not the usual arrangement where stress triggers depression but rather individuals vulnerable to depression who are placing themselves in high-risk stressful environments, such as difficult relationships or other risky situations where bad outcomes are common. What is important about the reciprocal model is that it can happen both ways in the same individual; stress triggers depression, and depressed individuals create or seek stressful events. It is interesting that, if you ask mothers, they tend to say their depressed adolescents created the problem, but adolescents blame the stressful event itself (Carter, Garber, Cielsa, & Cole, 2006). According to the reciprocal model, the truth lies somewhere between these two views.

Stress and Bipolar Disorder. The relationship of stressful events to the onset of episodes in bipolar disorder is also strong (Alloy & Abramson, 2010; Ellicott, 1988; Goodwin & Jamison, 2007; Johnson, Gruber, & Eisner, 2007; Johnson et al., 2008; Reilly-Harrington, Alloy, Fresco, & Whitehouse, 1999). However, several issues may be particularly relevant to the causes of bipolar disorders (Goodwin & Ghaemi, 1998). First, typically negative stressful life events trigger depression, but a somewhat different more positive set of stressful life events seems to trigger mania (Johnson et al., 2008). Experience associated with striving to achieve important goals, such as getting accepted into graduate school, obtaining a new job or promotion, or getting married, trigger mania in vulnerable individuals. Second, stress seems to initially trigger mania and depression, but as the disorder progresses, these epi-

sodes seem to develop a life of their own. In other words, once the cycle begins, a psychological or pathophysiological process takes over and ensures the disorder will continue (see, for example, Post, 1992; Post et al., 1989). Third, some precipitants of manic episodes seem related to loss of sleep, as in the postpartum period (Goodwin & Jamison, 2007; Harvey, 2008; Soreca et al., 2009) or as a result of jet lag—that is, disturbed circadian rhythms. In most cases of bipolar disorder, nevertheless, stressful life events are substantially indicated not only in provoking relapse, but also in preventing recovery (Alloy, Abramson, Urosevic, Bender, & Wagner, 2009; Johnson & Miller, 1997).

Finally, although almost everyone who develops a mood disorder has experienced a significant stressful event, most people who experience such events do not develop mood disorders. Although the data are not yet as precise as we would like, somewhere between 20% and 50% of individuals who experience severe events develop mood disorders. Thus, between 50% and 80% of individuals do *not* develop mood disorders or, presumably, any other psychological disorder. Again, data strongly support the interaction of stressful life events with some kind of vulnerability: genetic; psychological; or, more likely, a combination of the two influences (Barlow, 2002; Hankin & Abramson, 2001; Kendler, Kuhn, Vittum, Prescott, & Riley, 2005; Thase, 2009).

Given a genetic vulnerability (diathesis) and a severe life event (stress), what happens then? Research has isolated a number of psychological and biological processes. To illustrate one, let's return to Katie. Her stressful life event was attending a new school. Katie's feeling of loss of control leads to another important psychological factor in depression: learned helplessness.

Katie ┆ No Easy Transitions

I was a serious and sensitive 11 year old at the edge of puberty and at the edge of an adventure that many teens and preteens embark on—the transition from elementary to junior high school. A new school, new people, new responsibilities, new pressures. Academically, I was a good student up to this point but I didn't feel good about myself and generally lacked self-confidence.

Katie began to experience severe anxiety reactions. Then she became quite ill with the flu. After recovering and attempting to return to school, Katie discovered that her anxieties were worse than ever. More important, she began to feel she was losing control.

As I look back I can identify events that precipitated my anxieties and fears, but then everything seemed to happen suddenly and without cause. I was reacting emotionally and physically in a way that I didn't understand. I felt out of control of my emotions and body. Day after day I wished, as a child does, that whatever was happening to me would magically end.

Learned Helplessness

To review our discussion in Chapter 2, Martin Seligman discovered that dogs and rats have an interesting emotional reaction to events over which they have no control. If rats receive occasional shocks, they can function reasonably well as long as they can cope with the shocks by doing something to avoid them, such as pressing a lever. But if they learn that nothing they do helps them avoid the shocks, they eventually become helpless, give up, and manifest an animal equivalent of depression (Seligman, 1975).

Do humans react the same way? Seligman suggests we seem to but only under one important condition: People become anxious and depressed when they decide that they have no control over the stress in their lives (Abramson, Seligman, & Teasdale, 1978; Miller & Norman, 1979). These findings evolved into an important model called the **learned helplessness theory of depression**. Often overlooked is Seligman's point that anxiety is the first response to a stressful situation. Depression may follow marked hopelessness about coping with the difficult life events (Barlow, 1988, 2002). The depressive attributional style is (1) *internal*, in that the individual attributes negative events to personal failings ("it is all my fault"); (2) *stable*, in that, even after a particular negative event passes, the attribution that "additional bad things will always be my fault" remains; and (3) *global*, in that the attributions extend across a variety of issues. Research continues on this interesting concept, but you can see how it applies to Katie. Early in her difficulties with attending school, she began to believe events were out of her control and that she was unable even to begin to cope. More important, in her eyes the bad situation was all her fault: "I blamed myself for my lack of control." A downward spiral into a major depressive episode followed.

But a major question remains: Is learned helplessness a cause of depression or a correlated side effect of becoming depressed? If it were a cause, learned helplessness would have to exist *before* the depressive episode. Results from a 5-year longitudinal study in children shed some light on this issue. Nolen-Hoeksema, Girgus, and Seligman (1992) reported that negative attributional style did not predict later symptoms of depression in young children; rather, stressful life events seemed to be the major precipitant of symptoms. However, as they grew older, children under stress tended to develop more negative cognitive styles, which did tend to predict symptoms of depression in reaction to additional negative events. Nolen-Hoeksema and colleagues speculate that meaningful negative events early in childhood may lead to negative attributional styles, making these children more vulnerable to future depressive episodes when stressful events occur. Indeed, most studies support the finding that negative cognitive styles precede and are a risk factor for depression (Alloy & Abramson, 2006; Garber & Carter, 2006; Garber et al., 2009).

This thinking recalls the types of psychological vulnerabilities theorized to contribute to the development of anxiety disorders (Barlow, 1988, 2002; Suárez, Bennett, Goldstein, & Barlow, 2009)—that is, in a person who has a nonspecific genetic vulnerability to either anxiety or depression, stressful life events activate a psychological sense that life events are uncontrollable (Barlow, 2002; Chorpita & Barlow, 1998). Evidence suggests that negative attributional styles are not specific to depression but also characterize people with anxiety (Barlow, 2002; Hankin & Abramson, 2001; Suárez et al., 2009). This may indicate that a psychological (cognitive) vulnerability is no more specific for mood disorders than a genetic vulnerability. Both types of vulnerabilities may underlie numerous disorders.

Abramson, Metalsky, and Alloy (1989) revised the learned helplessness theory to deemphasize the influence of negative attributions and highlight the development of a sense of hopelessness as a crucial cause of many forms of depression. Attributions are important only to the extent that they contribute to a sense of hopelessness. This fits well with recent thinking on crucial differences between anxiety and depression. Both anxious and depressed individuals feel helpless and believe they lack control, but only in depression do they give up and become hopeless about ever regaining control (Alloy & Abramson, 2006; Barlow, 1991, 2002; Chorpita & Barlow, 1998).

Negative Cognitive Styles

In 1967, Aaron T. Beck (1967, 1976) suggested that depression may result from a tendency to interpret everyday events in a negative way. According to Beck, people with depression make the worst of everything; for them, the

▲ According to the learned helplessness theory of depression, people become depressed when they believe they have no control over the stress in their lives.

©Benelux/Cusp/PhotoLibrary

smallest setbacks are major catastrophes. In his extensive clinical work, Beck observed that all of his depressed patients thought this way, and he began classifying the types of "cognitive errors" that characterized this style. From the long list he compiled, two representative examples are *arbitrary inference* and *overgeneralization*. Arbitrary inference is evident when a depressed individual emphasizes the negative rather than the positive aspects of a situation. A high school teacher may assume he is a terrible instructor because two students in his class fell asleep. He fails to consider other reasons they might be sleeping (up all night partying, perhaps) and "infers" that his teaching style is at fault. As an example of overgeneralization, when your professor makes one critical remark on your paper, you then assume you will fail the class despite a long string of positive comments and good grades on other papers. You are overgeneralizing from one small remark. According to Beck, people who are depressed think like this all the time. They make cognitive errors in thinking negatively about themselves, their immediate world, and their future, three areas that together are called the **depressive cognitive triad** (■ Figure 6.2).

In addition, Beck theorized, after a series of negative events in childhood, individuals may develop a deep-seated *negative schema*, an enduring negative cognitive belief system about some aspect of life (Beck, Epstein, & Harrison, 1983; Gotlib & Krasnoperova, 1998; Gotlib, Kurtzman, &

Blehar, 1997; Gotlib & MacLeod, 1997; Young, Rygh, Weinberger, & Beck, 2008). In a self-blame schema, individuals feel personally responsible for every bad thing that happens. With a negative self-evaluation schema, they believe they can never do anything correctly. In Beck's view, these cognitive errors and schemas are automatic—that is, not necessarily conscious. Indeed, an individual might not even be aware of thinking negatively and illogically. Thus, minor negative events can lead to a major depressive episode.

A variety of evidence supports a cognitive theory of emotional disorders in general and depression in particular (Goodman & Gotlib, 1999; Ingram, Miranda, & Segal, 2006; Mazure, Bruce, Maciejewski, & Jacobs, 2000; Reilly-Harrington et al., 1999). The thinking of depressed individuals is consistently more negative than that of nondepressed individuals (Gotlib & Abramson, 1999; Hollon, Kendall, & Lumry, 1986; Joormann, 2009) in each dimension of the cognitive triad—the self, the world, and the future (see, for example, Garber & Carter, 2006; Joormann, 2009). Depressive cognitions seem to emerge from distorted and probably automatic methods of processing information. People prone to depression are more likely to recall negative events when they are depressed than when they are not depressed or than are nondepressed individuals (Gotlib, Roberts, & Gilboa, 1996; Joormann, 2009; Lewinsohn & Rosenbaum, 1987).

The implications of this theory are important. By recognizing cognitive errors and the underlying schemas, we can correct them and alleviate depression and related emotional disorders. In developing ways to do this, Beck became the father of cognitive therapy, one of the most important developments in psychotherapy in the past 50 years (see p. 230). Individuals with bipolar disorder also exhibit negative cognitive styles—but with a twist. Cognitive styles in these individuals are characterized by ambitious striving for goals, perfectionism, and self-criticism in addition to the more usual depressive cognitive styles (Alloy & Abramson, 2010; Johnson et al., 2008).

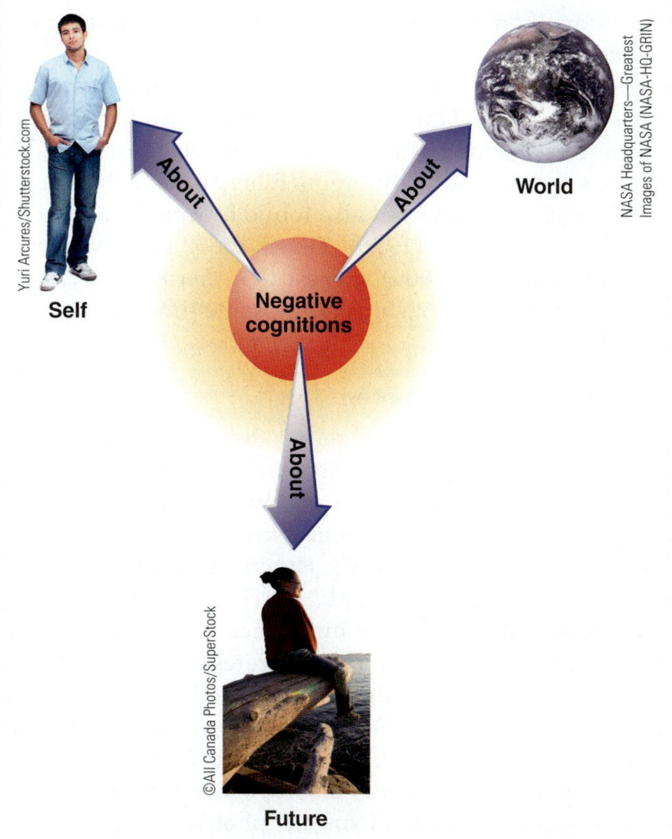

Cognitive Vulnerability for Depression: An Integration

Seligman and Beck developed their theories independently, and good evidence indicates their models are independent in that some people may have a negative outlook (dysfunctional attitudes), whereas others may explain things negatively (hopeless attributes) (Joiner & Rudd, 1996; Spangler, Simons, Monroe, & Thase, 1997). Nevertheless, the basic

Yuri Arcures/Shutterstock.com

Self

About

Negative cognitions

About

World

NASA Headquarters—Greatest Images of NASA (NASA-HQ-GRIN)

About

©All Canada Photos/SuperStock

Future

■ **Figure 6.2** Beck's cognitive triad for depression.

learned helplessness theory of depression Martin Seligman's theory that people become anxious and depressed when they make an attribution that they have no control over the stress in their lives (whether or not they actually have control).

depressive cognitive triad Thinking errors by depressed people negatively focused in three areas: themselves, their immediate world, and their future.

premises overlap a great deal and considerable evidence suggests depression is always associated with pessimistic explanatory style and negative cognitions. Evidence also exists that cognitive vulnerabilities predispose some people to view events in a negative way, putting them at risk for depression (see, for example, Ingram, Miranda, & Segal, 2006; Mazure, Bruce, Maciejewski, & Jacobs, 2000; Reilly-Harrington et al., 1999).

Good evidence supporting this conclusion comes from the Temple-Wisconsin study of cognitive vulnerability to depression conducted by Lauren Alloy and Lyn Abramson (Alloy & Abramson, 2006; Alloy, Abramson, Safford, & Gibb, 2006). University freshmen who were not depressed at the time of the initial assessment were assessed every several months for up to 5 years to determine whether they experienced any stressful life events or diagnosable episodes of depression or other psychopathology. At the first assessment, the investigators determined whether the students were cognitively vulnerable to developing depression or not on the basis of their scores on questionnaires that measure dysfunctional attitudes and hopelessness attributions. Results indicated students at high risk because of dysfunctional attitudes reported higher rates of depression in the past compared to the low-risk group. But the really important results come from the prospective portion of the study. Negative cognitive styles do indicate a vulnerability to later depression. Even if participants had never suffered from depression before in their lives, high-risk participants (who scored high on the measures of cognitive vulnerability) were 6–12 times more likely than low-risk participants to experience a major depressive episode. In addition, 16% of the high-risk participants versus only 2.7% of the low-risk participants experienced major depressive episodes, and 46% versus 14% experienced minor depressive symptoms (Alloy & Abramson, 2006). In another important study, Abela and Skitch (2007) demonstrated that children at high risk for depression because of a depressed mother showed depressive cognitive styles when under minor stress, unlike children not at risk. The data are suggestive that cognitive vulnerabilities to developing depression do exist and, when combined with biological vulnerabilities, create a slippery path to depression.

Social and Cultural Dimensions

A number of social and cultural factors contribute to the onset or maintenance of depression. Among these, marital relationships, gender, and social support are most prominent.

Marital Relations

Marital dissatisfaction and depression including bipolar disorder are strongly related, as suggested earlier when it was noted that disruptions in relationships often lead to depression (Davila, Stroud, & Starr, 2009). Bruce and Kim (1992) collected data on 695 women and 530 men and then reinterviewed them up to 1 year later. During this period, a number of participants separated from or divorced their spouses, although the majority reported stable marriages. Approximately 21% of the women who reported a marital split during the study experienced severe depression, a rate 3 times higher than that for women who remained married. Nearly 17% of the men who reported a marital split developed severe depression, a rate 9 *times* higher than that for men who remained married. However, when the researchers considered only those participants with no history of severe depression, 14% of the men who separated or divorced during the period experienced severe depression, as did approximately 5% of the women. In other words, *only the men* faced a heightened risk of developing a mood disorder for the first time immediately following a marital split.

Another finding with considerable support is that depression including bipolar disorder, particularly if it continues, may lead to substantial deterioration in marital relationships (Beach, Jones, & Franklin, 2009; Beach, Sandeen, & O'Leary, 1990; Davila et al., 2009; Gotlib & Beach, 1995; Paykel & Weissman, 1973; Uebelacker & Whisman, 2006). It is not hard to figure out why. Being around someone who is continually negative, ill tempered, and pessimistic becomes tiring after a while. Because emotions are contagious, the spouse probably begins to feel bad also. These kinds of interactions precipitate arguments or, worse, make the nondepressed spouse want to leave (Joiner & Timmons, 2009; Whisman, Weinstock, & Tolejko, 2006).

But conflict within a marriage seems to have different effects on men and women. Depression seems to cause men to withdraw or otherwise disrupt the relationship. For women, however, problems in the relationship most often cause depression. Thus, for both men and women, depression and problems in marital relations are associated, but the causal direction is different (Fincham, Beach, Harold, & Osborne, 1997), a result also found by Spangler, Simons, Monroe, and Thase (1996). Given these factors, Beach, Jones, & Franklin (2009) suggest that therapists treat disturbed marital relationships at the same time as the mood disorder.

Mood Disorders in Women

Data on the prevalence of mood disorders indicate dramatic gender imbalances. Although bipolar disorder is evenly divided between men and women, almost 70% of the individuals with major depressive disorder and dysthymia are women (Bland, 1997; Hankin & Abramson, 2001; Kessler, 2006; Weissman et al., 1991). What is particularly striking is that this gender imbalance is constant around the world, even though overall rates of disorder may vary from country to country (Kessler, 2006; Weissman & Olfson, 1995; ■ Figure 6.3). Often overlooked is the similar ratio for most anxiety disorders, particularly panic disorder and generalized anxiety disorder. Women represent an even greater proportion of specific phobias, as we noted in Chapter 2. What could account for this?

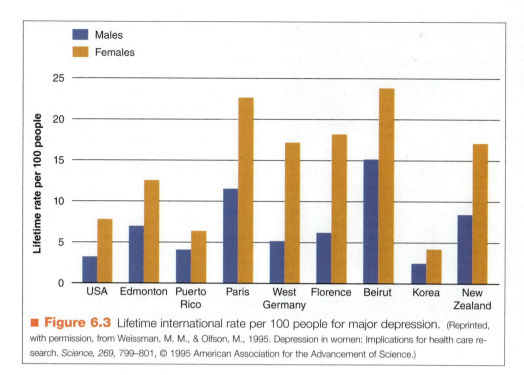

Figure 6.3 Lifetime international rate per 100 people for major depression. (Reprinted, with permission, from Weissman, M. M., & Olfson, M., 1995. Depression in women: Implications for health care research. *Science, 269*, 799–801, © 1995 American Association for the Advancement of Science.)

It may be that gender differences in the development of emotional disorders are strongly influenced by perceptions of uncontrollability (Barlow, 1988, 2002). If you feel a sense of mastery over your life and the difficult events we all encounter, you might experience occasional stress but you will not feel the helplessness central to anxiety and mood disorders. The source of these differences is cultural, in the sex roles assigned to men and women in our society. Males are strongly encouraged to be independent, masterful, and assertive; females, by contrast, are expected to be more passive, sensitive to other people, and (perhaps) to rely on others more than males do (needs for affiliation) (Cyranowski, Frank, Young, & Shear, 2000; Hankin & Abramson, 2001). Although these stereotypes are slowly changing, they still describe current sex roles to a large extent. But this culturally induced dependence and passivity may put women at heightened risk for emotional disorders by increasing their feelings of uncontrollability and helplessness.

Evidence has accumulated that parenting styles encouraging stereotypic gender roles are implicated in the development of early psychological vulnerability to later depression or anxiety (Chorpita & Barlow, 1998; Suárez et al., 2009), specifically, a smothering, overprotective style that prevents the child from developing initiative. Also interesting is the "sudden surge" in depression among girls mentioned earlier that occurs during puberty. Many thought this might be biologically based. However, Kessler (2006) notes that low self-esteem emerges quickly in girls in seventh grade if the school system has a seventh- through ninth-grade middle school, but low self-esteem among girls does not emerge until ninth grade when the school has a kindergarten through eighth-grade primary school and a 4-year high school (Simmons & Blyth, 1987). These results suggest that the younger girls just entering a new school, whether it is seventh, ninth, or some other grade, find it stressful. Also, girls who mature physically early have more distress and depression than girls who don't (Ge, Conger, & Elder, 1996).

Women tend to place greater value on intimate relationships than men, which can be protective if social networks are strong, but it may also put them at risk. Disruptions in such relationships, combined with an inability to cope with the disruptions, seem to be far more damaging to women than to men (Nolen-Hoeksema & Hilt, 2009; Rudolph & Conley, 2005). Cyranowski and associates (2000) note that the tendency for adolescent girls to express aggression by rejecting other girls, combined with a greater sensitivity to rejection, may precipitate more depressive episodes in these adolescent girls compared to boys. Kendler, Myers, and Prescott (2005) also observed that women tend to have larger and more intimate social networks than men and that emotionally supportive groups of friends protect against depression. However, data from Bruce and Kim (1992), reviewed earlier, suggest that if the disruption in a marital relationship reaches the stage of divorce, men who had previously been functioning well are at greater risk for depression.

Another potentially important gender difference has been suggested by Susan Nolen-Hoeksema (1990, 2000; Nolen-Hoeksema, Larson, & Grayson, 1999; Nolen-Hoeksema, Wisco, & Lyubomirsky, 2008). Women tend to ruminate more than men about their situation and blame themselves for being depressed. Men tend to ignore their feelings, perhaps engaging in activity to take their minds off them (Addis, 2008). This male behavior may be therapeutic because "activating" people (getting them busy doing something) is a common element of successful therapy for depression (Dimidjian, Martell, Addis, & Herman-Dunn, 2008; Jacobson, Martell, & Dimidjian, 2001).

As Strickland (1992) pointed out, women are at a disadvantage in our society: They experience more discrimination, poverty, sexual harassment, and abuse than do men. They also earn less respect and accumulate less power. Three fourths of the people living in poverty in the United States are women and children. Women, particularly single mothers, have a difficult time entering the workplace. Of note, married women employed full time outside the home report levels of depression no greater than those of employed married men. Single, divorced, and widowed women experience significantly more depression than men

▲ Of the impoverished people in the United States, three-fourths are women and children.

the onset of depressive symptoms at a later time (see, for instance, Joiner, 1997; Kendler, Kuhn et al., 2005; Lin & Ensel, 1984; Monroe, Imhoff, Wise, & Harris, 1983; Monroe et al., 2009; Phifer & Murrell, 1986). The importance of social support in preventing depression holds true in China (Wang, Wang, & Shen, 2006) and every other country in which it has been studied. Other studies have established the importance of social support in speeding recovery from depressive episodes (Keitner et al., 1995; McLeod, Kessler, & Landis, 1992; Sherbourne, Hays, & Wells, 1995). In an interesting twist, several studies examined the effects of social support in speeding recovery from both manic and depressive episodes in patients with bipolar disorder, and they came up with a surprising finding. A socially supportive network of friends and family helped speed recovery from depressive episodes but not from manic episodes (Johnson, Winett, Meyer, Greenhouse, & Miller, 1999; Johnson et al., 2008, 2009). This finding highlights the uniquely different quality of manic episodes (McGuffin et al., 2003). In any case, these and related findings on the importance of social support have led to an exciting new psychological therapeutic approach for emotional disorders called interpersonal psychotherapy, which we discuss later in this chapter.

Let's return again to Katie. In reflecting on her turbulent times and the days when death seemed more rewarding than life, one thing sticks out clearly in her mind:

> My parents are the true heroes of these early years. I will always admire their strength, their love, and their commitment. My father is a high school graduate and my mother has an eighth-grade education. They dealt with complicated legal, medical, and psychological issues. They had little support from friends or professionals, yet they continued to do what they believed best. In my eyes there is no greater demonstration of courage and love.

Katie's parents did not have the social support that might have helped them through these difficult years, but they gave it to Katie. We return to her case later.

An Integrative Theory

How do we put all this together? Basically, depression and anxiety may often share a common, genetically determined biological vulnerability (Barlow, 2002; Barlow, Chorpita, & Turovsky, 1996; Suárez et al., 2009) that can be described as an overactive neurobiological response to stressful life events. Again, this vulnerability is simply a general tendency to develop depression (or anxiety) rather than a specific vulnerability for depression or anxiety itself. But

in the same categories (Davila et al., 2009; Weissman & Klerman, 1977). This does not necessarily mean that anyone should get a job to avoid becoming depressed. Indeed, for a man or woman, feeling mastery, control, and value in the strongly socially supported role of homemaker and parent should be associated with low rates of depression.

Finally, other disorders may reflect gender role stereotypes, but in the opposite direction. Disorders associated with aggressiveness, overactivity, and substance abuse occur far more often in men than in women (Barlow, 1988, 2002). Identifying the reasons for gender imbalances across the full range of psychopathological disorders may prove important in discovering causes of disorders.

Social Support

In Chapter 2, we examined the powerful effect of social influences on our psychological and biological functioning. We cited several examples of how social influences seem to contribute to early death, such as the evil eye or lack of social support in old age. In general, the greater the number and frequency of your social relationships and contacts, the longer you are likely to live (see, for instance, House, Landis, & Umberson, 1988). It is not surprising, then, that social factors influence whether we become depressed (Beach et al., 2009).

In an early landmark study, Brown and Harris (1978) first suggested the important role of social support in the onset of depression. In a study of a large number of women who had experienced a serious life stress, they discovered that only 10% of the women who had a friend in whom they could confide became depressed, compared to 37% of the women who did not have a close supportive relationship. Later prospective studies have also confirmed the importance of social support (or lack of it) in predicting only between 20% and 40% of the causes of depression can be attributed to genes. For the remainder, we look at life experience.

People who develop mood disorders also possess a psychological vulnerability experienced as feelings of inadequacy for coping with the difficulties confronting them and depressive cognitive styles. As with anxiety, we may develop this sense of control in childhood (Barlow, 2002; Chorpita & Barlow, 1998). It may range on a continuum from total confidence to a complete inability to cope. When vulnerabilities are triggered, the pessimistic "giving up" process seems crucial to the development of depression (Alloy, Kelly, Mineka, & Clements, 1990; Alloy et al., 2000; Alloy & Abramson, 2006).

These two vulnerabilities of inadequate coping and depressive cognitive style in combination comprise the temperament of neuroticism or negative affect. You will remember from Chapter 4 that neuroticism is associated with biochemical markers of stress and depression (see, for example, Nemeroff, 2004; Thase, 2009) and different levels of arousal in different hemispheres in the brain (hemispheric lateral asymmetry) (Davidson, 1993; Heller & Nitschke, 1997), and activation of specific brain circuits (Davidson et al., 2009; Elliott, Rubinsztein, Sahakian, & Dolan, 2002; Liotti, Mayberg, McGinnis, Brannan, & Jerabek, 2002). There is also good evidence that stressful life events trigger the onset of depression in most cases in these vulnerable individuals, particularly initial episodes. How do these factors interact? Current thinking is that stressful life events activate stress hormones, which, in turn, have wide-ranging effects on neurotransmitter systems, particularly those involving serotonin, norepinephrine, and the corticotropin-releasing factor system. Booij and Van der Does (2007) have illustrated how neurotransmitter function and negative cognitive styles interact. They collaborated with 39 patients who had suffered an episode of major depression but had recovered. These patients participated in two biological test or "challenge" procedures called acute tryptophan depletion (ATD) that had the effect of temporarily lowering levels of serotonin. This is accomplished fairly easily by altering diet for 1 day by restricting intake of tryptophan (a precursor to serotonergic functioning) and increasing a mixture of essential amino acids. Participants in the experiment, of course, were fully informed of these effects and collaborated willingly.

What Booij and Van der Does (2007) found was that this biological challenge was, as usual, effective in temporarily inducing a variety of depressive symptoms in some of these individuals, but that these symptoms were more pronounced in those who also had evidence of the cognitive vulnerability marker. That is, cognitive vulnerability assessed before the biological challenge clearly predicted a depressive response. Interestingly, a challenge with ATD causes no significant changes in mood in healthy samples; rather, it is limited to those individuals who are vulnerable to depression.

What we have so far is a possible mechanism for the diathesis–stress model. Finally, it seems clear that factors such as interpersonal relationships or cognitive style may protect us from the effects of stress and therefore from developing mood disorders. Alternatively, these factors may at least determine whether we quickly recover from these disorders or not. But remember that bipolar disorder, and particularly activation of manic episodes, seems to have a somewhat different genetic basis and a different response to social support. Scientists are beginning to theorize that individuals with bipolar disorder, in addition to factors outlined so far, are also highly sensitive to the experience of life events connected with striving to reach important goals, perhaps because of an overactive brain circuit called the behavioral approach system (BAS) (Alloy & Abramson, 2010; Gruber, Johnson, Oveis, & Keltner, 2008). In these cases, stressful life events that are more positive but still stressful, such as starting a new job, or pulling all-nighters to finish an important term paper, might precipitate a manic episode in vulnerable individuals instead of a depressive episode. Individuals with bipolar disorder are also highly sensitive to disruptions in circadian rhythm. So individuals with bipolar disorder might possess brain circuits that predispose them to both depression and mania. Research of this hypothesis is just commencing.

In summary, biological, psychological, and social factors all influence the development of mood disorders, as depicted in ■ Figure 6.4. This model does not fully account for the varied presentation of mood disorders—seasonal, bipolar, and so on—although mania in bipolar disorder seems to be associated with unique genetic contributions and is triggered by relatively unique life events as noted above. But why would someone with an underlying genetic vulnerability who experiences a stressful life event develop a mood disorder rather than an anxiety or somatoform disorder? As with the anxiety disorders and other stress disorders, specific psychosocial circumstances, such as early learning experiences, may interact with specific genetic vulnerabilities and personality characteristics to produce the rich variety of emotional disorders.

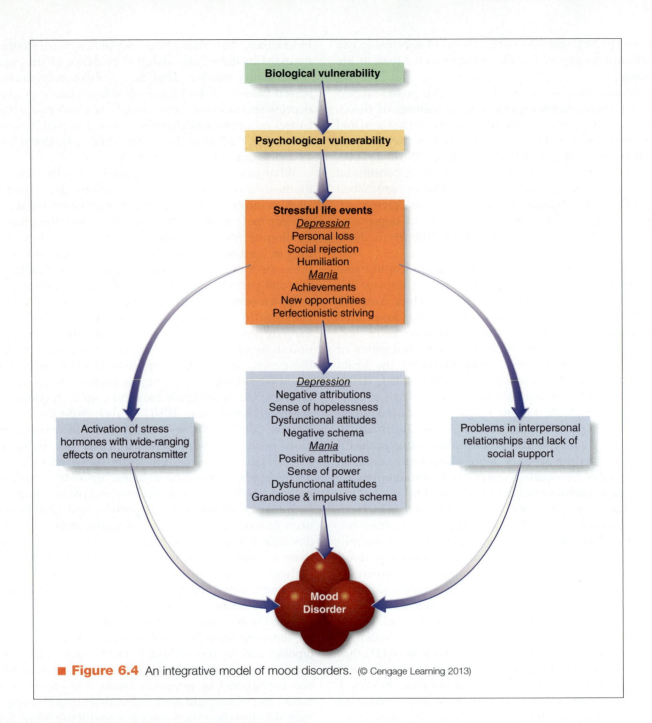

Biological vulnerability

Psychological vulnerability

Stressful life events
Depression
Personal loss
Social rejection
Humiliation
Mania
Achievements
New opportunities
Perfectionistic striving

Activation of stress hormones with wide-ranging effects on neurotransmitter

Depression
Negative attributions
Sense of hopelessness
Dysfunctional attitudes
Negative schema
Mania
Positive attributions
Sense of power
Dysfunctional attitudes
Grandiose & impulsive schema

Problems in interpersonal relationships and lack of social support

Mood Disorder

■ **Figure 6.4** An integrative model of mood disorders. (© Cengage Learning 2013)

Concept Check 6.3

Answer these questions about the various causes of mood disorders.

1. List five biological sources that can contribute to mood disorders. _____ _____ _____ _____ _____

2. What psychological factors can have an impact on mood disorders? _____ _____ _____ _____

3. Name several social and cultural dimensions that contribute to mood disorders. _____ _____ _____

> **What medical and psychological treatments have been successful in treating mood disorders?**

Researchers have learned a great deal about the neurobiology of mood disorders during the past several years. Findings on the complex interplay of neurochemicals are beginning to shed light on the nature of mood disorders. As we have noted, the principal effect of medications is to alter levels of these neurotransmitters and other related neurochemicals. Other biological treatments, such as electroconvulsive therapy, dramatically affect brain chemistry. A more interesting development alluded to throughout this book, however, is that powerful psychological treatments also alter brain chemistry. Despite these advances, most cases of depression go untreated because neither health care professionals nor patients recognize and correctly identify or diagnose depression. Similarly, many professionals and patients are unaware of the existence of effective and successful treatments (Delano-Wood & Abeles, 2005; Hirschfeld et al., 1997).

Medications

A number of medications are effective treatments for depression. New information often becomes available on new medications or the latest estimates of effectiveness of older medications.

Antidepressants

Four basic types of antidepressant medications are used to treat depressive disorders: selective serotonin reuptake inhibitors (SSRIs), mixed reuptake inhibitors, tricyclic antidepressants, and monoamine oxidase (MAO) inhibitors. It is important to note at the outset that there are few, if any, differences in effectiveness among the different antidepressants; approximately 50% of patients receive some benefit, with about half of the 50% coming very close to normal functioning (remission). If dropouts are excluded and only those who complete treatment are counted, the percentage of patients receiving at least some benefit increases to between 60% and 70%.

The class of drugs currently considered the first choice in drug treatment for depression seems to have a specific effect on the serotonin neurotransmitter system (although such drugs affect other systems to some extent). These *selective-*serotonin reuptake inhibitors specifically block the presynaptic reuptake of serotonin. This temporarily increases levels of serotonin at the receptor site, but again the precise long-term mechanism of action is unknown, although levels of serotonin are eventually increased (Gitlin, 2009; Thase & Denko, 2008). Perhaps the best-known drug in this class is *fluoxetine* (Prozac). Like many other medications, Prozac was initially hailed as a breakthrough drug; it even made the cover of *Newsweek* (Cowley & Springen, 1990). Then reports

began to appear that it might lead to suicidal preoccupation; paranoid reactions; and, occasionally, violence (see, for example, Mandalos & Szarek, 1990; Teicher, Glod, & Cole, 1990). Prozac went from being a wonder drug in the eyes of the press to a potential menace to modern society. Neither conclusion was true. Findings indicated that the risks of suicide with this drug for the general population were no greater than with any other antidepressant (Fava & Rosenbaum, 1991), and the effectiveness is about the same as that of other antidepressants.

Recently, concerns about suicidal risks (increased thoughts, and so on) have surfaced again, particularly among adolescents, and this time it looks like the concerns are justified, at least for adolescents (Baldessarini, Pompili, & Tondo, 2006; Berman, 2009; Fergusson, Doucette, et al., 2005; Hammad, Laughren, & Racoosin, 2006; Olfson, Marcus, & Schaffer, 2006). These findings have led to warnings from the Food and Drug Administration (FDA) and other regulatory agencies around the world about these drugs. However, Gibbons, Hur, Bhaumik, and Mann (2006) found that actual suicide rates were lower in sections of the United States where prescriptions for SSRIs were higher. In addition, the SSRIs were also associated with a small but statistically significant *decrease* in actual suicides among adolescents compared to depressed adolescents not taking these drugs based on a large community survey (Olfson, Shaffer, Marcus & Greenberg, 2003). These findings are *correlational,* meaning we can't conclude that increased prescriptions for SSRIs caused lower suicide rates. Research will continue on this important question. One possible conclusion is that SSRIs cause increased thoughts about suicide in the first few weeks in some adolescents but, once they start working after a month or more, may prevent the depression from leading to suicide (Berman, 2009; Simon, 2006). Prozac and other SSRIs have their own set of side effects, the most prominent of which are physical agitation, sexual dysfunction, low sexual desire (which is prevalent, occurring in 50% to 75% of cases), insomnia, and gastrointestinal upset. But these side effects, on the whole, seem to bother most patients less than the side effects associated with tricyclic antidepressants, with the possible exception of the sexual dysfunction. Studies suggest similar effectiveness of SSRIs and tricyclics with dysthymia (Lapierre, 1994).

Two newer antidepressants (sometimes termed *mixed reuptake inhibitors*) seem to have somewhat different mechanisms of neurobiological action. Venlafaxine (Effexor) is related to tricyclic antidepressants, but acts in a slightly different manner, blocking reuptake of norepinephrine and serotonin. Some side effects associated with the SSRIs are reduced with venlafaxine, as is the risk of damage to the cardiovascular system. Other typical side effects remain, including nausea and sexual dysfunction.

Nefazodone (Serzone) is closely related to the SSRIs but seems to improve sleep efficiency instead of disrupting sleep. Both drugs are roughly comparable in effectiveness to older antidepressants (American Psychiatric Association, 2000; Nemeroff, 2006; Preskorn, 1995; Thase & Kupfer, 1996), but nefazodone has now been withdrawn because of the risk of liver damage (Gitlin, 2009).

MAO inhibitors work differently. As their name suggests, they block the enzyme MAO that breaks down such neurotransmitters as norepinephrine and serotonin. The result is roughly equivalent to the effect of the tricyclics. Because they are not broken down, the neurotransmitters pool in the synapse, leading to a down-regulation. The MAO inhibitors seem to be as effective as or slightly more effective than the tricyclics (American Psychiatric Association, 2000; Depression Guideline Panel, 1993), with somewhat fewer side effects. Some evidence suggests they are relatively more effective for depression with atypical features (Thase & Kupfer, 1996). But MAO inhibitors are used far less often because of two potentially serious consequences: Eating and drinking foods and beverages containing tyramine, such as cheese, red wine, or beer, can lead to severe hypertensive episodes and, occasionally, death. In addition, many other drugs that people take daily, such as cold medications, are dangerous and even fatal in interaction with an MAO inhibitor. Therefore, MAO inhibitors are usually prescribed only when other antidepressants are not effective.

Tricyclic antidepressants were the most widely used treatments for depression before the introduction of SSRIs, but are now used less commonly (Gitlin, 2009; Thase & Denko, 2008). The best-known variants are probably imipramine (Tofranil) and amitriptyline (Elavil). It is not yet clear how these drugs work, but initially, at least, they block the reuptake of certain neurotransmitters, allowing them to pool in the synapse and, as the theory goes, desensitize or down-regulate the transmission of that particular neurotransmitter (so less of the neurochemical is transmitted). Tricyclic antidepressants seem to have their greatest effect by down-regulating norepinephrine, although other neurotransmitter systems, particularly serotonin, are also affected. This process then has a complex effect on both presynaptic and postsynaptic regulation of neurotransmitter activity, eventually restoring appropriate balance. Side effects include blurred vision, dry mouth, constipation, difficulty urinating, drowsiness, weight gain (at least 13 pounds on average), and, sometimes, sexual dysfunction. Therefore, as many as 40% of these patients may stop taking the drug, thinking the cure is worse than the disease. Nevertheless, with careful management, many side effects disappear over time. Another issue clinicians must consider is that tricyclics are *lethal* if taken in excessive doses; therefore, they must be prescribed with great caution to patients with suicidal tendencies.

Because the SSRI and other drugs relieve symptoms of depression to some extent in about 50% of all patients treated but eliminate depression or come close to it in only 25% to 30% of all patients treated (termed *remission*) (Trivedi et al., 2006), the question remains: What do clinicians do when depression does not respond adequately to drug treatment, often called treatment-resistant depression? A large study called the Sequenced Treatment Alternatives to Relieve Depression (STAR*D) examined whether offering those individuals who did not achieve remission the alternatives of either adding a second drug or switching to a second drug is useful. Among those who were willing, approximately 20% (for switching) to approximately 30% (for adding a second drug) achieved remission. When repeating this with a third drug among those who had failed to achieve remission with the first two drugs, the results weren't as good (between 10% and 20% achieved remission) (Insel, 2006; Menza, 2006; Rush, 2007), and very few clinicians would go to a third drug in the same class after failing on the first two (Gitlin, 2009). The conclusion is that it's worth being persistent as long as individuals with depression are still willing to try a second drug because some people who don't improve with the first drug could improve with a different drug. Later, we report on combining psychological treatments with drugs. In summary, all antidepressant medications work about the same in large clinical trials, but sometimes a patient will not do well on one drug and respond better to another.

Current studies indicate that drug treatments effective with adults are not necessarily effective with children (American Psychiatric Association, 2000; Geller et al., 1992; Kaslow, Davis, & Smith, 2009; Ryan, 1992). Sudden deaths of children younger than age 14 who were taking tricyclic antidepressants have been reported, particularly during exercise, as in routine school athletic competition (Tingelstad, 1991). The causes imply cardiac side effects. But evidence indicates that at least one of the SSRIs, fluoxetine (Prozac), is safe and has some evidence for efficacy with adolescents both initially (Kaslow et al., 2009; Treatment for Adolescents with Depression Study [TADS] Team, 2004), and at follow-up (TADS Team, 2009), particularly if combined with cognitive behavioral therapy (CBT) (March & Vitiello, 2009). Traditional antidepressant drug treatments are usually effective with the elderly, but administering them takes considerable skill because older people may suffer from a variety of side effects not experienced by younger adults, including memory impairment and physical agitation (Blazer & Hybels, 2009; Delano-Wood & Abeles, 2005; Deptula & Pomara, 1990; Fiske et al., 2009; Marcopulos & Graves, 1990). Use of a depression care manager to deliver care to depressed elderly patients right in the office of their primary medical care doctor including encouraging compliance with drug taking, monitoring side effects unique to older adults, and delivering a bit of psychotherapy was more effective than usual care (Alexopoulos et al., 2005; Unutzer et al., 2002).

Clinicians and researchers have concluded that recovery from depression, although important, may not be the most important therapeutic outcome (Frank et al., 1990; Thase, 2009). Most people eventually recover from a major depressive episode, some rather quickly. A more important goal is often to delay the next depressive episode or even prevent it entirely (National Institute of Mental Health, 2003; Prien & Potter, 1993; Thase, 2009; Thase & Kupfer, 1996). This is particularly important for patients who retain some symptoms of depression or have a past history of chronic depression or multiple depressive episodes. Because all these factors put people at risk for relapse, it is recommended that drug treatment go well beyond the termination of a depressive episode, continuing perhaps 6 to 12 months after the episode is over, or even longer (American Psychiatric Association, 2000; Insel, 2006). The drug is then gradually withdrawn over weeks or months. Long-term administration of antidepressants has not been studied extensively, and there is even some evidence that long-term treatment lasting several years may worsen the course of depression (Fava, 2003).

Antidepressant medications have relieved severe depression and undoubtedly prevented suicide in tens of thousands of patients around the world. Although these medications are readily available, many people refuse them or are not eligible to take them. Some are wary of long-term side effects. Women of childbearing age must protect themselves against the possibility of conceiving while taking antidepressants because of possible damage to the fetus, although the best evidence suggests that preterm birth, but not damage, is the most likely outcome (Wisner et al., 2009). In addition, approximately 30% to 40% of patients who take a full course of treatment do not respond adequately to these drugs, and a substantial number of the remainder are left with residual symptoms.

Lithium

Another type of antidepressant drug, *lithium carbonate*, is a common salt widely available in the natural environment (Nemeroff, 2006). It is found in our drinking water in amounts too small to have any effect. However, the side effects of therapeutic doses of lithium are potentially more serious than those of other antidepressants. Dosage has to be carefully regulated to prevent toxicity (poisoning) and lowered thyroid functioning, which might intensify the lack of energy associated with depression. Substantial weight gain is also common. Lithium, however, has one major advantage that distinguishes it from other antidepressants: It is also often effective in preventing and treating manic episodes. Therefore, it is most often referred to as a **mood-stabilizing drug**. Antidepressants can induce manic episodes, even in individuals without preexisting bipolar disorder (Goodwin & Ghaemi, 1998; Goodwin & Jamison, 2007; Prien et al., 1984), and lithium remains the gold standard for treatment of bipolar disorder (Thase & Denko, 2008).

Results indicate that 50% of bipolar patients respond well to lithium initially, meaning at least a 50% reduction in manic symptoms (Goodwin & Jamison, 2007). Thus, although effective, lithium provides many people with inadequate therapeutic benefit. Patients who don't respond to lithium can take other drugs with antimanic properties,

including anticonvulsants such as carbamazepine and valproate (Divalproex) and calcium channel blockers such as verapamil (Keck & McElroy, 2002; Sachs & Rush, 2003; Thase & Denko, 2008). Valproate has recently overtaken lithium as the most commonly prescribed mood stabilizer for bipolar disorder (Goodwin et al., 2003; Keck & McElroy, 2002; Thase & Denko, 2008) and is equally effective, even for patients with rapid-cycling symptoms (Calabrese et al., 2005). But newer studies

▲ Kay Redfield Jamison, an internationally respected authority on bipolar disorder, has suffered from the disease since adolescence.

show that these drugs have one distinct disadvantage: They are less effective than lithium in preventing suicide (Thase & Denko, 2008; Thies-Flechtner, Muller-Oerlinghausen, Seibert, Walther, & Greil, 1996; Tondo, Jamison, & Baldessarini, 1997). Goodwin and colleagues (2003) reviewed records of more than 20,000 patients taking either lithium or valproate and found the rate of completed suicides was 2.7 times higher in people taking valproate than in people taking lithium. Thus, lithium remains the preferred drug for bipolar disorder (Goodwin & Ghaemi, 1998; Goodwin & Jamison, 2007). This finding was confirmed in a large trial demonstrating no advantage to adding a traditional antidepressant drug such as an SSRI to a mood stabilizer such as lithium (Sachs et al., 2007).

For those patients who do respond to lithium, studies following patients for up to 5 years report that approximately 70% relapse, even if they continue to take the lithium (Frank et al., 1999; Gitlin, Swendsen, Heller, & Hammen, 1995; Peselow, Fieve, Difiglia, & Sanfilipo, 1994). Nevertheless, for almost anyone with recurrent manic episodes, maintenance on lithium or a related drug is recommended to prevent relapse (Yatham et al., 2006). Another problem with drug treatment of bipolar disorder is that people usually like the euphoric or high feeling that mania produces and they often stop taking lithium to maintain or regain the state; that is, they do not comply with the medication regimen. Because the evidence now clearly indicates that individuals who stop their medication are at considerable risk for relapse, other treatment methods, usually psychological in nature, are used to increase compliance.

mood-stabilizing drug A medication used in the treatment of mood disorders, particularly bipolar disorder, that is effective in preventing and treating pathological shifts in mood.

Electroconvulsive Therapy and Transcranial Magnetic Stimulation

When someone does not respond to medication (or in an extremely severe case), clinicians may consider a more dramatic treatment, **electroconvulsive therapy (ECT)**, the most controversial treatment for psychological disorders after psychosurgery. In Chapter 1, we described how ECT was used in the early 20th century. Despite many unfortunate abuses along the way, ECT is considerably changed today. It is now a safe and reasonably effective treatment for severe depression that has not improved with other treatments (American Psychiatric Association, 2000; Gitlin, 2009; National Institute of Mental Health, 2003; Nemeroff, 2006).

In current administrations, patients are anesthetized to reduce discomfort and given muscle-relaxing drugs to prevent bone breakage from convulsions during seizures. Electric shock is administered directly through the brain for less than a second, producing a seizure and a series of brief convulsions that usually lasts for several minutes. In current practice, treatments are administered once every other day for a total of 6 to 10 treatments (fewer if the patient's mood returns to normal). Side effects are generally limited to short-term memory loss and confusion that disappear after a week or two, although some patients may have long-term memory problems. For severely depressed inpatients with psychotic features, controlled studies indicate that approximately 50% of those *not responding* to medication will benefit. Continued treatment with medication or psychotherapy is then necessary because the relapse rate approaches 60% or higher (American Psychiatric Association Practice Guideline, 2000; Depression Guideline Panel, 1993; Fernandez, Levy, Lachar, & Small, 1995; Gitlin, 2009). For example, Sackeim and colleagues (2001) treated 84 patients with ECT and then randomly assigned them to follow-up placebo or one of several antidepressant drug treatments. All patients assigned to placebo relapsed within 6 months compared to 40% to 60% on medication. Thus, follow-up treatment with antidepressant drugs or psychological treatments is necessary, but relapse is still high. Nevertheless, it may not be in the best interest of psychotically depressed and acutely suicidal inpatients to wait 3 to 6 weeks to determine whether a drug or psychological treatment is working; in these cases, immediate ECT may be appropriate.

Recently, another method for altering electrical activity in the brain by setting up a strong magnetic field has been introduced. This procedure is called *transcranial magnetic stimulation (TMS)*, and it works by placing a magnetic coil over the individual's head to generate a precisely localized electromagnetic pulse. Anesthesia is not required, and side effects are usually limited to headaches. Initial reports, as with most new procedures, showed promise in treating depression (Fitzgerald et al., 2003, 2006; George, Lisanby, & Sackheim, 1999), and recent reviews have confirmed that TMS can be effective (Schutter, 2009). But results from several important clinical trials with severe or treatment-resistant psychotic depression reported ECT to be clearly more effective than TMS (Eranti et al., 2007). It

may be that TMS is more comparable to antidepressant medication than to ECT (Gitlin, 2009).

Several other nondrug approaches for treatment-resistant depression are in development. Vagus nerve stimulation involves implanting a pacemaker-like device that generates pulses to the vagus nerve in the neck, which, in turn, is thought to influence neurotransmitter production in the brain stem and limbic system (Gitlin, 2009; Marangell et al., 2002). Sufficient evidence has accumulated so that the FDA has approved this procedure, but results are generally weak and it has been little used. Deep brain stimulation has been used with a few severely depressed patients. In this procedure, electrodes are surgically implanted in the limbic system (the emotional brain). These electrodes are also connected to a pacemaker-like device (Mayberg et al., 2005). Time will tell if this is a useful treatment.

Psychological Treatments

Of the effective psychological treatments now available for depressive disorders, two major approaches have the most evidence supporting their efficacy. The first is a cognitive-behavioral approach; Aaron T. Beck, the founder of cognitive therapy, is most closely associated with this approach. The second approach, interpersonal psychotherapy, was developed by Myrna Weissman and Gerald Klerman.

Cognitive-Behavioral Therapy

Beck's **cognitive therapy** grew directly out of his observations of the role of deep-seated negative thinking in generating depression (Beck, 1967, 1976; Beck & Young, 1985; Young et al., 2008). Clients are taught to examine carefully their thought processes while they are depressed and to recognize "depressive" errors in thinking. This task is not always easy because many thoughts are automatic and beyond clients' awareness. Clients are taught that errors in thinking can directly cause depression. Treatment involves correcting cognitive errors and substituting less depressing and (perhaps) more realistic thoughts and appraisals. Later in therapy, underlying negative cognitive schemas (characteristic ways of viewing the world) that trigger specific cognitive errors are targeted, not only in the office but also as part of the client's day-to-day life. The therapist purposefully takes a Socratic approach (teaching by asking questions—see the following dialogue), making it clear that therapist and client are working as a team to uncover faulty thinking patterns and the underlying schemas from which they are generated. Therapists must be skillful and highly trained. Following is an example of an actual interaction between Beck and a depressed client named Irene.

Beck and Irene ✦ A Dialogue

Because an intake interview had already been completed by another therapist, Beck did not spend time reviewing Irene's symptoms in detail or taking a history. Irene began by describing her "sad states." Beck almost immediately started to elicit her automatic thoughts during these periods.

THERAPIST: What kind of thoughts go through your mind when you've had these sad feelings this past week?

PATIENT: Well . . . I guess I'm thinking what's the point of all this. My life is over. It's just not the same. . . . I have thoughts like, "What am I going to do? . . . Sometimes I feel mad at him, you know my husband. How could he leave me? Isn't that terrible of me? What's wrong with me? How can I be mad at him? He didn't want to die a horrible death. . . . I should have done more. I should have made him go to the doctor when he first started getting headaches. . . . Oh, what's the use. . . ."

T: It sounds like you are feeling quite bad right now. Is that right?

P: Yes.

T: Keep telling me what's going through your mind right now.

P: I can't change anything. . . . It's over. . . . I don't know. . . . It all seems so bleak and hopeless. . . . What do I have to look forward to . . . sickness and then death. . . .

T: So one of the thoughts is that you can't change things and that it's not going to get any better?

P: Yes.

T: And sometimes you believe that completely?

P: Yeah, I believe it, sometimes.

T: Right now do you believe it?

P: I believe it—yes.

T: Right now you believe that you can't change things and it's not going to get better?

P: Well, there is a glimmer of hope but it's mostly. . . .

T: Is there anything in your life that you kind of look forward to in terms of your own life from here on?

P: Well, what I look forward to—I enjoy seeing my kids but they are so busy right now. My son is a lawyer and my daughter is in medical school. . . . So, they are very busy. . . . They don't have time to spend with me.

By inquiring about Irene's automatic thoughts, the therapist began to understand her perspective—that she would go on forever, mostly alone. This illustrates the hopelessness about the future that is characteristic of most depressed patients. A second advantage to this line of inquiry is that the therapist introduced Irene to the idea of looking at her own thoughts, which is central to cognitive therapy (Young et al., 2008).

Between sessions, clients are instructed to *monitor and log* their thought processes carefully, particularly in situations where they might feel depressed. They also attempt to change their behavior by carrying out specific activities assigned as homework, such as tasks in which clients can test their faulty thinking. For example, a client who has to participate in an upcoming meeting might think, "If I go to that meeting, I'll just make a fool of myself and all my colleagues will think I'm stupid." The therapist might instruct the client to go to the meeting, predict ahead of time the reaction of the colleagues, and then see what really happens. This part of treatment is called *hypothesis testing* because the client makes a hypothesis about what's going to happen (usually a depressing outcome) and then, most often, discovers it is incorrect ("My colleagues congratulated me on my presentation"). The therapist typically schedules other activities to *reactivate* depressed patients who have given up most activities, helping them put some fun back into their lives. Cognitive therapy typically takes from 10 to 20 sessions, scheduled weekly.

The late Neil Jacobson and colleagues have shown that increased activities alone can improve self-concept and lift depression (Dimidjian, Martell, Addis, & Herman-Dunn, 2008; Jacobson et al., 1996). This more behavioral treatment has been reformulated because initial evaluation suggests it is as effective as, or more effective than, cognitive approaches (Jacobson, Martell, & Dimidjian, 2001). The new focus of this approach is on preventing avoidance of social and environmental cues that produce negative affect or depression and result in avoidance and inactivity. Rather, the individual is helped to face the cues or triggers and work through them and the depression they produce, with the therapist, by developing better coping skills. Similarly, programmed exercise over the course of weeks or months is surprisingly effective in treating depression (Stathopoulou, Powers, Berry, Smits, & Otto, 2006). Babyak and colleagues (2000) demonstrated that programmed aerobic exercise 3 times a week was as effective as treatment with antidepressive medication (Zoloft) or the combination of exercise and Zoloft after 4 months. More important, exercise was *better* at preventing relapse in the 6 months following treatment compared to the drug or combination treatment, particularly if the patients continued exercising. This general approach of focusing on activities is consistent with findings about the most powerful methods to change dysregulated emotions (see the "On the

electroconvulsive therapy (ECT) Biological treatment for severe, chronic depression involving the application of electrical impulses through the brain to produce seizures. The reasons for its effectiveness are unknown.

cognitive therapy Treatment approach that involves identifying and altering negative thinking styles related to psychological disorders such as depression and anxiety and replacing them with more positive beliefs and attitudes—and, ultimately, more adaptive behavior and coping styles.

Spectrum" box later in this chapter) (Barlow, Allen, & Choate, 2004; Campbell-Sills & Barlow, 2007), and we are likely to see more research on this approach in the near future.

Interpersonal Psychotherapy

We have seen that major disruptions in our interpersonal relationships are an important category of stresses that can trigger mood disorders (Joiner & Timmons, 2009; Kendler et al., 2003). In addition, people with few, if any, important social relationships seem at risk for developing and sustaining mood disorders (Beach et al., 2009; Sherbourne et al., 1995). **Interpersonal psychotherapy (IPT)** (Bleiberg & Markowitz, 2008; Klerman, Weissman, Rounsaville, & Chevron, 1984; Weissman, 1995) focuses on resolving problems in existing relationships and learning to form important new interpersonal relationships.

Like cognitive-behavioral approaches, IPT is highly structured and seldom takes longer than 15 to 20 sessions, usually scheduled once a week. After identifying life stressors that seem to precipitate the depression, the therapist and patient work collaboratively on the patient's current interpersonal problems. Typically, these include one or more of four interpersonal issues: *dealing with interpersonal role disputes,* such as marital conflict; *adjusting to the loss of a relationship,* such as grief over the death of a loved one; *acquiring new relationships,* such as getting married or establishing professional relationships; and *identifying and correcting deficits in social skills* that prevent the person from initiating or maintaining important relationships.

To take a common example, the therapist's first job is to identify and define an interpersonal dispute (Bleiberg & Markowitz, 2008; Weissman, 1995), perhaps with a wife who expects her spouse to support her but has had to take an outside job to help pay bills. The husband might expect the wife to share equally in generating income. If this dispute seems to be associated with the onset of depressive symptoms and to result in a continuing series of arguments and disagreements without resolution, it would become the focus for IPT.

After helping identify the dispute, the next step is to bring it to a resolution. First, the therapist helps the patient determine the stage of the dispute.

1. *Negotiation stage.* Both partners are aware it is a dispute, and they are trying to renegotiate it.
2. *Impasse stage.* The dispute smolders beneath the surface and results in low-level resentment, but no attempts are made to resolve it.
3. *Resolution stage.* The partners are taking some action, such as divorce, separation, or recommitting to the marriage.

The therapist works with the patient to define the dispute clearly for both parties and develop specific strategies for resolving it. Studies comparing the results of cognitive therapy and IPT to those of antidepressant drugs and other control conditions have found that psychological approaches and medication are equally effective immediately following

treatment, and all treatments are more effective than placebo conditions, brief psychodynamic treatments, or other appropriate control conditions for both major depressive disorder and dysthymia (Beck, Hollon, Young, Bedrosian, & Budenz, 1985; Blackburn & Moore, 1997; Hollon et al., 1992; Hollon & Dimidjian, 2009; Miller, Norman, & Keitner, 1989; Paykel & Scott, 2009; Schulberg et al., 1996; Shapiro et al., 1995). Depending on how "success" is defined, approximately 50% or more of people benefit from treatment to a significant extent, compared to approximately 30% in placebo or control conditions (Craighead, Hart, Craighead, & Ilardi, 2002; Hollon & Dimidjian, 2009).

Similar results have been reported in depressed children and adolescents (Kaslow et al., 2009). In one notable clinical trial, Brent et al. (2008) demonstrated that, in over 300 severely depressed adolescents who had failed to respond to an SSRI antidepressant, CBT was significantly more effective than switching to another antidepressant. Kennard et al. (2009) showed that this was particularly true if the adolescents received at least nine sessions of the CBT.

Furthermore, studies have not found differences in treatment effectiveness based on severity of depression (Hollon et al., 1992; Hollon, Stewart, & Strunk, 2006; McLean & Taylor, 1992). For example, DeRubeis, Gelfand, Tang, and Simons (1999) carefully evaluated the effects of cognitive therapy versus medication in severely depressed patients only, across four studies, and found no advantage for one treatment or the other. O'Hara, Stuart, Gorman, and Wenzel (2000) reported positive effects for IPT in a group of women with postpartum depression, demonstrating that this approach is a worthwhile strategy in patients with postpartum depression who are reluctant to go on medication because, for example, they are breastfeeding. In an important related study, Spinelli and Endicott (2003) compared IPT to an alternative psychological approach in 50 depressed pregnant women unable to take drugs because of potential harm to the fetus. Fully 60% of these women recovered, leading the authors to recommend that IPT should be the first choice for pregnant depressed women, although it is likely that CBT would produce similar results. IPT has also been successfully administered to depressed adolescents by school-based clinicians trained to deliver IPT right in the school setting (Mufson et al., 2004). This practical approach shows good promise of reaching a larger number of depressed adolescents.

Prevention

In view of the seriousness of mood disorders in children and adolescents, work has begun on preventing these disorders in these age groups (Horowitz & Garber, 2006; Muñoz, 1993; Muñoz, Le, Clarke, Barrera, & Torres, 2009). The Institute of Medicine (IOM) delineated three types of programs: *universal* programs, which are applied to everyone; *selected* interventions, which target individuals at risk for depression because of factors such as divorce, family alcoholism, and so on; and *indicated* interventions, where the individual is already showing mild symptoms of depression (Muñoz et al., 2009). As an example of selected interventions, Gillham, Reivich, Jaycox, and Seligman (1995) taught cognitive and social problem-solving techniques to 69 fifth- and sixth-grade children who were at risk for depression because of negative thinking styles. Compared to children in a matched no-treatment control group, the prevention group reported fewer depressive symptoms during the 2 years they were followed. More important, moderate to severe symptoms were reduced by half, and the positive effects of this program increased during the period of follow-up.

Now, results from a major clinical trial which combined "selected" and "indicated" approaches have been reported on adolescents at risk for depression (Garber et al., 2009). Three hundred sixteen adolescent offspring of parents with current or prior depressive disorders were entered into the trial and randomized to a CBT prevention program or to usual care. To be included, adolescents had to have either a past history of depression, or current depressive symptoms that would not be severe enough to meet criteria for a disorder, or both. The adolescents in the CBT prevention group received eight weekly group sessions and six monthly continuation sessions. The usual care group included a fairly active use of mental health or other health care services that, however, did not include any of the procedures used in the CBT group. The results indicated that the CBT prevention program was significantly more effective than usual care in preventing future episodes of depression but only for those adolescents whose parents were not currently in a depressive episode themselves. If the parents were in a depressive episode while the adolescents were receiving care, the adolescents became somewhat less depressed based on their own report but did not have significantly fewer depressive episodes during the follow-up period. These results are important because they show the potential power of preventive programs and that living with a depressed parent reduces the power of this preventive program to some degree (Hammen, 2009). The results also suggest that to prevent future depressive episodes it is necessary to treat depression in the whole family in a coordinated manner.

Another recent study also demonstrated that meeting in an integrated fashion with families that included parents who had a history of depression and their 9- to 15-year-old children (who were at risk because of their parents' depression) was successful in preventing depression in these families during a follow-up period (Compas et al., 2009). Additional studies have indicated that preventing depression is possible in older adults in primary care settings (van't Veer-Tazelaar et al., 2009) and also in poststroke patients, a particularly high-risk group (Reynolds, 2009; Robinson et al., 2008).

Combined Treatments

One important question is whether combining psychosocial treatments with medication is more effective than either treatment alone in treating depression or preventing relapse. In a large study reported by Keller and colleagues (2000) on the treatment of chronic major depression, 681 patients at 12 clinics around the country were assigned to receive antidepressant medication (nefazodone), a CBT constructed specifically for chronically depressed patients (CBASP, discussed earlier) (McCullough, 2000), or the combination of two treatments. Researchers found that 48% of patients receiving each of the individual treatments went into remission or responded in a clinically satisfactory way compared to 73% of the patients receiving combined treatment. Because this study was conducted with only a subset of depressed patients, those with chronic depression, the findings would need to be replicated before researchers could say combined treatment was useful for depression generally. In addition, because the study did not include a fifth condition in which the CBT was combined with placebo, we cannot rule out that the enhanced effectiveness of the combined treatment was the result of placebo factors. Nevertheless, a meta-analysis summarizing all studies conducted to date concludes that combined treatment does provide some advantage (Pampallona, Bollini, Tibaldi, Kupelnick, & Munizza, 2004). Notice how this conclusion differs from the conclusion in Chapter 4 on anxiety disorders, where no advantage of combining treatments was apparent. Combining two treatments is also expensive, however, so many experts think that a sequential strategy makes more sense, where you start with one treatment first (maybe the one the patient prefers or the one that's available) and then switch to the other only if the first choice was not entirely satisfactory (see, for example, Schatzberg et al., 2005).

Preventing Relapse

Given the high rate of recurrence in depression, it is not surprising that more than 50% of patients on antidepressant medication relapse if their medication is stopped within 4 months after their last depressive episode (Hollon, Shelton, & Loosen, 1991; Thase, 1990). Therefore, one important question has to do with **maintenance treatment** to prevent relapse or recurrence over the long term. In a number of studies, cognitive therapy reduced rates of subsequent relapse in depressed patients by more than 50% over groups treated with antidepressant medication (see, for example, Evans et al., 1992; Hollon et al., 2005, 2006; Kovacs, Rush, Beck, & Hollon, 1981; Simons, Murphy, Levine, & Wetzel, 1986; Teasdale et al., 2000).

interpersonal psychotherapy (IPT) Brief treatment approach that emphasizes resolution of interpersonal problems and stressors, such as role disputes in marital conflict, forming relationships in marriage, or a new job. It has demonstrated effectiveness for such problems as depression.

maintenance treatment Combination of continued psychosocial treatment, medication, or both designed to prevent relapse following therapy.

In one of the most impressive studies to date, patients were treated with either antidepressant medication or cognitive therapy compared to placebo (see DeRubeis et al., 2005), then the study began (Hollon et al., 2005; Hollon, Stewart, & Strunk, 2006). All patients who had responded well to treatment were followed for 2 years. During the first year, one group of patients who were originally treated with antidepressant medication continued on the medication but then stopped for the second year. A second group of patients originally receiving cognitive therapy were given up to three additional (booster) sessions during that first year but none after that. A third group was also originally treated with antidepressant medication but then switched to placebo.

Outcomes during the first year, patients who were withdrawn from medication and placed onto pill placebo were considerably more likely to relapse over the ensuing 12-month interval than were patients continued on medication (23.8% did not relapse on placebo versus 52.8% on medication). In comparison, 69.2% of patients with a history of cognitive therapy did not relapse. At this point, there was no statistically significant difference in relapse rates among patients who had received cognitive therapy versus those who continued on antidepressant medication. This suggests that prior cognitive therapy has an enduring effect that is at least as large in magnitude as keeping the patients on medications. In the second year, when all treatments had stopped, patients who had continued to receive medications during the first year were more likely to experience a recurrence (56.3%) than patients who had originally received cognitive therapy (17.5%). These studies would seem to confirm that psychological treatments for depression are most notable for their enduring ability to prevent relapse or recurrence.

Psychological Treatments for Bipolar Disorder

Although medication, particularly lithium, seems a necessary treatment for bipolar disorder, most clinicians emphasize the need for psychological interventions to manage interpersonal and practical problems (for example, marital and job difficulties that result from the disorder) (Otto & Applebaum, 2011). Until recently, the principal objective of psychological intervention was to increase compliance with medication regimens such as lithium. We noted before that the "pleasures" of a manic state make refusal to take lithium a major therapeutic obstacle. Giving up drugs between episodes or skipping dosages during an episode significantly undermines treatment. Therefore, increasing compliance with drug treatments is important (Goodwin & Jamison, 2007; Scott, 1995). For example, Clarkin, Carpenter, Hull, Wilner, and Glick (1998) evaluated the advantages of adding a psychological treatment to medication for inpatients and found it improved adherence to medication for all patients and resulted in better overall outcomes for the most severe cases compared to medication alone.

More recently, psychological treatments have also been directed at psychosocial aspects of bipolar disorder. In a new approach, Ellen Frank and her colleagues are testing a psychological treatment that regulates circadian rhythms by helping patients regulate their eating and sleep cycles and other daily schedules and cope more effectively with stressful life events, particularly interpersonal issues (Frank et al., 2005; Frank et al., 1997; Frank et al., 1999). In an evaluation of this approach, called *interpersonal and social rhythm therapy* (IPSRT), patients receiving IPSRT survived longer without a new manic or depressive episode compared to patients undergoing standard, intensive clinical management. Initial results with adolescents are also promising (Hlastala, Kotler, McClellan, & McCauley, 2010).

David Miklowitz and his colleagues found that family tension is associated with relapse in bipolar disorder. Preliminary studies indicate that treatments directed at helping families understand symptoms and develop new coping skills and communication styles do change communication styles (Simoneau, Miklowitz, Richards, Saleem, & George, 1999) and prevent relapse (Miklowitz, 2008; Miklowitz & Goldstein, 1997). Miklowitz, George, Richards, Simoneau, and Suddath (2003) demonstrated that their family-focused treatment combined with medication results in significantly less relapse 1 year following initiation of treatment than occurs in patients receiving crisis management and medication over the same period. Specifically, only 35% of patients receiving family therapy plus medication relapsed compared to 54% in the comparison group. Similarly, family therapy patients averaged over a year and a half (73.5 weeks) before relapsing, significantly longer than the comparison group. Rea, Tompson, and Miklowitz (2003) compared this approach to an individualized psychotherapy in which patients received the same number of sessions over the same period and continued to find an advantage for the family therapy after 2 years. In another important study, Lam et al. (2003) and Lam, Hayward, Watkins, Wright, and Sham (2005) showed that patients with bipolar disorders treated with cognitive therapy plus medication relapsed significantly less over both a 1-year follow-up and a 2-year follow-up compared to a control group receiving just medication. Reilly-Harrington et al. (2007) found some evidence that CBT is effective for bipolar patients with the rapid-cycling feature. In view of the relative ineffectiveness of antidepressant medication for the depressive stage of bipolar disorder reviewed earlier, Miklowitz et al. (2007) reported an important study showing that up to 30 sessions of an intensive psychological treatment was significantly more effective than usual and customary best treatment in promoting recovery from bipolar depression and remaining well. The specificity of this effect on bipolar depression, which is the most common stage of bipolar disorder, combined with the lack of effectiveness of antidepressants, suggest that these procedures will provide an important contribution to the comprehensive treatment of bipolar disorder. Otto et al. (2008a, 2008b) have synthesized these evidence-based psychological treatment procedures for bipolar disorder into a new treatment protocol.

Let us now return to Katie, who, you will remember, had made a serious suicide attempt amid a major depressive episode.

Katie • The Triumph of the Self

Like the overwhelming majority of people with serious psychological disorders, Katie had never received an adequate course of treatment, although she was evaluated occasionally by various mental health professionals. She lived in a rural area where competent professional help was not readily available. Her life ebbed and flowed with her struggle to subdue anxiety and depression. When she could manage her emotions sufficiently, she took an occasional course in the high school independent study program. Katie discovered that she was fascinated by learning. She enrolled in a local community college at the age of 19 and did extremely well, even though she had not progressed beyond her freshman year in high school. At the college, she earned a high school equivalency degree. She went to work in a local factory. She continued to drink heavily and to take Valium, however; occasionally, anxiety and depression would return and disrupt her life.

Finally, Katie left home, attended college full time, and fell in love. But the romance was one-sided, and she was rejected.

One night after a phone conversation with him, I nearly drank myself to death. I lived in a single room alone in the dorm. I drank as much vodka as quickly as I could. I fell asleep. When I awoke, I was covered in vomit and couldn't recall falling asleep or being sick. I was drunk for much of the next day. When I awoke the following morning, I realized I could have killed myself by choking on my own vomit. More importantly, I wasn't sure if I fully wanted to die. That was the last of my drinking.

Katie decided to make some changes. Taking advantage of what she had learned in the little treatment she had received, she began looking at life and herself differently. Instead of dwelling on how inadequate and evil she was, she began to pay attention to her strengths. "But I now realized that I needed to accept myself as is, and work with any stumbling blocks that I faced. I needed to get myself through the world as happily and as comfortably as I could. I had a right to that." Other lessons learned in treatment now

became valuable, and Katie became more aware of her mood swings:

I learned to objectify periods of depression as [simply] periods of "feeling." They are a part of who I am, but not the whole. I recognize when I feel that way, and I check my perceptions with someone that I trust when I feel uncertain of them. I try to hold on to the belief that these periods are only temporary.

Katie developed other strategies for coping successfully with life:

I try to stay focused on my goals and what is important to me. I have learned that if one strategy to achieve some goal doesn't work there are other strategies that probably will. My endurance is one of my blessings. Patience, dedication, and discipline are also important. None of the changes that I have been through occurred instantly or automatically. Most of what I have achieved has required time, effort, and persistence.

Katie dreamed that if she worked hard enough she could help other people who had problems similar to her own. Katie pursued that dream and earned her PhD in psychology.

Concept Check 6.4

Indicate which type of treatment for mood disorders is being described in each statement.

1. The controversial but somewhat successful treatment involving the production of seizures through electrical current to the brain. _____

2. This teaches clients to carefully examine their thought process and recognize "depressive" styles in thinking. _____

3. These come in three main types (tricyclics, MAO inhibitors, and SSRIs) and are often prescribed but have numerous side effects. _____

4. This antidepressant must be carefully regulated to avoid illness but has the advantage of affecting manic episodes. _____

5. This therapy focuses on resolving problems in existing relationships and learning to form new interpersonal relationships. _____

6. This is an effort to prevent relapse or recurrence over the long run. _____

> **What is the relationship between suicide and mood disorders?**

Most days we are confronted with news about the war on cancer or the frantic race to find a cure for AIDS. We also hear never-ending admonitions to improve our diet and to exercise more to prevent heart disease. But another cause of death ranks right up there with the most frightening and dangerous medical conditions. This is the inexplicable decision to kill themselves made by approximately 40,000 people a year in the United States alone.

Statistics

Suicide is officially the 11th leading cause of death in the United States (Nock, Borges, Bromet, Cha, et al., 2008), and most epidemiologists agree that the actual number of suicides may be 2 to 3 times higher than what is reported. Many of these unreported suicides occur when people deliberately drive into a bridge or off a cliff (Blumenthal, 1990). Around the world, suicide causes more deaths per year than homicide or HIV/AIDS (Nock, Borges, Bromet, Cha, et al., 2008).

Suicide is overwhelmingly a white phenomenon. Most minority groups, including African Americans and Hispanics, seldom resort to this desperate alternative, as is evident in ■ Figure 6.5. As you might expect from the incidence of depression in Native Americans, however, their suicide rate is extremely high, far outstripping the rates in other ethnic groups (Beals et al., 2005; Hasin et al., 2005; Nock, Borges, Bromet, Cha, et al., 2008); although there is great variability across tribes (Berlin, 1987). Even more alarming is the dramatic increase in death by suicide beginning in adolescence. In the United States, rates of death by suicide per 100,000 people rise from 1.29 in the 10–14 age group to 12.35 in the 20–24 age group (Centers for Disease Control and Prevention [CDC], 2010b; Nock, Cha, & Dour, 2011). For teenagers, suicide was the *third* leading cause of death behind unintentional injury such as motor vehicle accidents and homicide in 2007 (CDC, 2010b; Minino et al., 2002; Ventura, Peters, Martin, & Maurer, 1997). Prevalence differs greatly depending on ethnic group, as is evident in Figure 6.5. This fact underscores the importance of attending to cultural considerations in the prevention and treatment of adolescent suicide (Goldston et al., 2008).

Note also the dramatic increase in suicide rates among the elderly compared to the rates for younger age groups shown in ■ Figure 6.6. This rise has been connected to the growing incidence of medical illness in our oldest citizens and to their increasing loss of social support (Conwell, Duberstein, & Caine, 2002), and resulting depression (Fiske et al., 2009). As we have noted, a strong relationship exists between illness or infirmity and hopelessness or depression.

Regardless of age, in every country around the world except China males are 4 times more likely to *commit* suicide than females (CDC, 2010b; Nock et al., 2011; World Health Organization, 2010). This startling fact seems to be related partly to gender differences in the types of suicide *attempts*. Males generally choose far more violent methods, such as guns and hanging; females tend to rely on less violent options, such as drug overdose (Gallagher-Thompson & Osgood, 1997; Nock et al., 2011). More men commit suicide during old age and more women during middle age, partly because most attempts by older women are unsuccessful (Berman, 2009; Kuo, Gallo, & Tien, 2001).

Uniquely in China more women commit suicide than men, particularly in rural settings (Murray, 1996; Murray & Lopez, 1996; Nock, Borges, Bromet, Cha, et al., 2008; Phillips, Li, & Zhang, 2002). What accounts for this culturally determined reversal? Chinese scientists agree that China's suicide rates, probably the highest in the world, are the

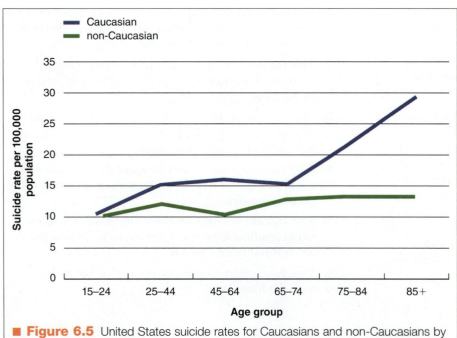

■ **Figure 6.5** United States suicide rates for Caucasians and non-Caucasians by age group, sexes combined (data from the National Center for Health Statistics, Vital Statistics of the United States, 2001). (From Centers for Disease Control and Prevention, 2003. Deaths: Final data for 2001. *National Vital Statistics Reports*, 52(3). Hyattsville, MD: National Center for Health Statistics.)

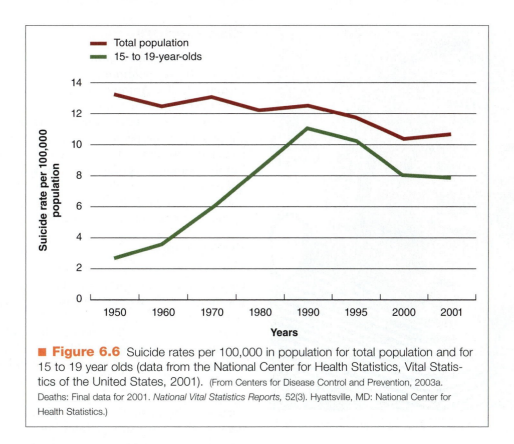

■ **Figure 6.6** Suicide rates per 100,000 in population for total population and for 15 to 19 year olds (data from the National Center for Health Statistics, Vital Statistics of the United States, 2001). (From Centers for Disease Control and Prevention, 2003a. Deaths: Final data for 2001. *National Vital Statistics Reports*, 52(3). Hyattsville, MD: National Center for Health Statistics.)

result of an absence of stigma. Suicide, particularly among women, is often portrayed in classical Chinese literature as a reasonable solution to problems. A rural Chinese woman's family is her entire world, and suicide is an honorable solution if the family collapses. Furthermore, highly toxic farm pesticides are readily available and it is possible that many women who did not necessarily intend to kill themselves die after accidentally swallowing poison.

In addition to completed suicides, three other important indices of suicidal behavior are **suicidal ideation** (thinking seriously about suicide), **suicidal plans** (the formulation of a specific method for killing oneself), and **suicidal attempts** (the person survives) (Kessler, Berglund, Borges, Nock, & Wang, 2005; Nock et al., 2011). Also, Nock and Kessler (2006) distinguish "attempters" (self-injurers with the intent to die) from "gesturers" (self-injurers who intend not to die but to influence or manipulate somebody or communicate a cry for help). In a carefully done cross-national study using consistent definitions, the prevalence of suicide ideation has been estimated at 9.2%; 3.1% reported a suicide plan and 2.7% attempted suicide during their lifetime (Nock, Borges, Bromet, Alonso et al., 2008). Although males *commit* suicide more often than females in most of the world, females *attempt* suicide at least 3 times as often (Berman & Jobes, 1991; Kuo et al., 2001). And the overall rate of nonlethal suicidal thoughts, plans, and (unsuccessful) attempts is 40% to 60% higher in women than in men (Nock et al., 2011). This high incidence may reflect that more women than men are depressed and that depression is strongly related to suicide attempts (Berman,

2009). It is also interesting that despite the much higher rate of completed suicides among whites, there are no significant ethnic or racial differences in rates of suicide ideation, plans, or attempts (Kessler et al., 2005). Among adolescents the ratio of *thoughts* about suicide to *attempts* is also between 3:1 and 6:1. In other words, between 16% and 30% of adolescents who think about killing themselves actually attempt it (Kovacs, Goldston, & Gatsonis, 1993; Nock, Borges, Bromet, Cha, et al., 2008). "Thoughts" in this context do not refer to a fleeting philosophical type of consideration but rather to a serious contemplation of the act. The first step down the dangerous road to suicide is thinking about it.

In a study of college students (among whom suicide is the second leading cause of death), approximately 10% to 25% had thoughts about suicide during the past 12 months (Brener, Hassan, & Barrios, 1999; Meehan, Lamb, Saltzman, & O'Carroll, 1992; Schwartz & Whitaker, 1990). Only a minority of these college students with thoughts of suicide (perhaps around 15%) attempt to kill themselves, and only a few succeed (Kovacs et al., 1993). Nevertheless, given the enormity of the problem, suicidal thoughts are taken seriously by mental health professionals.

suicidal ideation Serious thoughts about committing suicide.
suicidal plans The formulation of a specific method of killing oneself.
suicidal attempts Effort made to kill oneself.

▲ Men often choose violent means of suicide. Nirvana's Kurt Cobain shot himself.

Causes

The great sociologist Emile Durkheim (1951) defined a number of suicide types based on the social or cultural conditions in which they occurred. One type is "formalized" suicides that were approved of, such as the ancient custom of *harakiri* in Japan, in which an individual who brought dishonor to himself or his family was expected to impale himself on a sword. Durkheim referred to this as *altruistic suicide*. Durkheim also recognized the loss of social supports as an important provocation for suicide; he called this *egoistic suicide*. (Older adults who kill themselves after losing touch with their friends or family fit into this category.) Magne-Ingvar, Ojehagen, and Traskman-Bendz (1992) found that only 13% of 75 individuals who had seriously attempted suicide had an adequate social network of friends and relationships. *Anomic suicides* are the result of marked disruptions, such as the sudden loss of a high-prestige job. (*Anomie* is feeling lost and confused.) Finally, *fatalistic suicides* result from a loss of control over one's own destiny. The mass suicide of 39 Heaven's Gate cult members in 1997 is an example of this type. Durkheim's work was important in alerting us to the social contribution to suicide. Sigmund Freud (1917/1957) believed that suicide (and depression, to some extent) indicated unconscious hostility directed inward to the self rather than outward to the person or situation causing the anger. Indeed, suicide victims often seem to be psychologically "punishing" others who may have rejected them or caused some other personal hurt. Current thinking considers social and psychological factors but also highlights the potential importance of biological contributions.

Risk Factors

Edward Shneidman pioneered the study of risk factors for suicide (Shneidman, 1989; Shneidman, Farberow, & Litman, 1970). Among the methods he and others have used to study those conditions and events that make a person vulnerable is **psychological autopsy**. The psychological profile of the person who committed suicide is reconstructed through extensive interviews with friends and family members who are likely to know what the individual was thinking and doing in the period before death. This and other methods have allowed researchers to identify a number of risk factors for suicide.

Family History

If a family member committed suicide, there is an increased risk that someone else in the family will also (Berman, 2009; Kety, 1990; Mann, Waternaux, Haas, & Malone, 1999; Mann et al., 2005; Nock et al., 2011). Brent and colleagues (2002) noted that offspring of family members who had attempted suicide had 6 times the risk of suicide attempts compared to offspring of nonattempters. If a sibling was also a suicide attempter, the risk increased even more (Brent et al., 2003). This may not be surprising because so many people who kill themselves are depressed or have some related mental disorder, and these disorders run in families (Nock et al., 2011). Nevertheless, the question remains: Are people who kill themselves simply adopting a familiar solution that they've witnessed in family members, or does an inherited trait, such as impulsivity, account for increased suicidal behavior in families? It seems both factors may contribute. If individuals have an early onset of their mood disorder, and aggressive or impulsive traits, then their families are at a greater risk for suicidal behavior (Mann et al., 2005). The possibility that something is inherited is also supported by several adoption studies. One found an increased rate of suicide in the biological relatives of adopted individuals who had committed suicide compared to a control group of adoptees who had not committed suicide (Nock et al., 2011; Schulsinger, Kety, & Rosenthal, 1979; Wender et al., 1986). This suggests some biological (genetic) contribution to suicide, even if it is relatively small, although it may not be independent of genetic contribution to depression or associated disorders.

Neurobiology

A variety of evidence suggests that low levels of serotonin may be associated with suicide and with violent suicide attempts (Asberg, Nordstrom, & Traskman-Bendz, 1986; Cremniter et al., 1999; Winchel, Stanley, & Stanley, 1990). As we have noted, extremely low levels of serotonin are associated with impulsivity, instability, and the tendency to overreact to situations. It is possible then that low levels of serotonin may contribute to creating a vulnerability to act impulsively. This may include killing oneself, which is sometimes an impulsive act. The studies by Brent and colleagues (2002) and Mann and colleagues (2005) suggest

Suicide is one of the leading causes of death worldwide, responsible for approximately 1 million deaths per year and 1 death every 40 seconds (Nock, Borges, Bromet, Cha, et al., 2008). Although suicide is a leading cause of death, it is difficult to predict and prevent, partly because the person who dies by suicide obviously can no longer provide information about the factors leading up to the death. In addition, many people who die by suicide leave behind few clues about the factors that influenced their decision to end their life. In an effort to better understand and predict suicide, researchers now often study people who have experienced suicidal thoughts and have made nonlethal suicide attempts. The results of such studies have provided interesting information about suicidal behaviors around the world.

Data from a recent survey of people in 17 countries indicate that approximately 9% of all adults report that they have seriously considered suicide at some point in their life, 3% have made an actual suicide plan, and just under 3% have made a suicide attempt (Nock, Borges, Bromet, Alonso, et al., 2008). However, the rate of suicidal thoughts and attempts varies significantly across countries. For instance, only 3% of people in Italy have had suicidal thoughts, compared to 16% of people in New Zealand. Researchers are still trying to understand why these rates are so dissimilar across countries. Of note, once people report that they have had suicidal thoughts or made a suicide attempt, the characteristics look quite similar across countries. For instance, in every country examined, the rate of suicidal thoughts sharply increases during adolescence, approximately one third of those with suicidal thoughts go on to make a suicide attempt, and more than 60% of those who do attempt suicide do so within the first year after they initially had suicidal thoughts. In addition, risk factors for suicidal thoughts and attempts are quite consistent cross-nationally and include being female, younger, less educated, and unmarried and having a mental disorder (Nock, Borges, Bromet, Alonso, et al., 2008). Unfortunately, although an increasing number of risk factors for suicidal behaviors have been identified, to date no theories of suicide have been able to tie them together into a clear model that allows us to accurately predict who is most at risk and how to prevent them from engaging in suicidal behavior.

that transmission of vulnerabilities for a mood disorder, including the trait of impulsivity, may mediate family transmission of suicide attempts.

Existing Psychological Disorders and Other Psychological Risk Factors

More than 80% of people who kill themselves suffer from a psychological disorder, usually mood, substance use, or impulse control disorders (Berman, 2009; Brent & Kolko, 1990; Conwell et al., 1996; Joe, Baser, Breeden, Neighbors, & Jackson, 2006; Nock, Hwang, Sampson, & Kessler, 2009). Suicide is often associated with mood disorders— and for good reason. As many as 60% of suicides (75% of adolescent suicides) are associated with an existing mood disorder (Berman, 2009; Brent & Kolko, 1990; Oquendo et al., 2004). Many people with mood disorders do not attempt suicide, however, and, conversely, many people who attempt suicide do not have mood disorders. Therefore, depression and suicide, although strongly related, are still independent. Looking more closely at the relationship of mood disorder and suicide, some investigators have isolated hopelessness, a specific component of depression, as strongly predicting suicide (Beck, 1986; Beck, Steer, Kovacs, & Garrison, 1985; Goldston, Reboussin, & Daniel, 2006). A recent important theoretical account of suicide termed the "interpersonal theory of suicide" cites a perception of oneself as a burden on others and a diminished sense of belonging as powerful predictors of hopelessness and subsequently suicide (van Orden et al., 2010).

Alcohol use and abuse are associated with approximately 25% to 50% of suicides and are particularly evident in adolescent suicides (Berman, 2009; Brener et al., 1999; Conwell et al., 1996; Hawton, Houston, Haw, Townsend, & Harriss, 2003; Woods et al., 1997). Brent and colleagues (1988) found that about one third of adolescents who commit suicide were intoxicated when they died and that many more might have been under the influence of drugs. Combinations of disorders, such as substance abuse and mood disorders in adults or mood disorders and conduct disorder in children and adolescents, seem to create a stronger vulnerability than any one disorder alone (Conwell et al., 1996; Nock et al., 2009; Woods et al., 1997). For example, Nock and colleagues (2009) noticed that depression alone did not predict suicidal ideation or attempts, but depression combined with impulse control problems and anxiety/agitation did. For adolescents, Woods and colleagues (1997) also found that substance abuse with other risk-taking behaviors, such as getting into fights, carrying a gun, or smoking, were predictive of teenage suicide, possibly reflecting impulsivity in these troubled adolescents. Esposito and Clum (2003) also noted that the presence of anxiety and mood disorders predicted suicide attempts in adolescents. Past suicide attempts are another strong risk factor and must be taken seriously (Berman, 2009). Cooper and colleagues (2005) followed almost 8,000 individuals who were treated in the emergency room for deliberate self-harm for up to 4 years. Sixty of these people had killed themselves, which is 30 times the risk compared to population statistics.

psychological autopsy Postmortem psychological profile of a suicide victim constructed from interviews with people who knew the person before death.

A disorder characterized more by impulsivity than depression is borderline personality disorder (see Chapter 11). Individuals with this disorder, known for making manipulative and impulsive suicidal gestures without necessarily wanting to destroy themselves, sometimes kill themselves by mistake in as many as 10% of the cases. The combination of borderline personality disorder and depression is particularly deadly (Soloff, Lynch, Kelly, Malone, & Mann, 2000).

The association of suicide with severe psychological disorders, especially depression, belies the myth that it is a response to disappointment in people who are otherwise healthy.

Stressful Life Events

Perhaps the most important risk factor for suicide is a severe, stressful event experienced as shameful or humiliating, such as a failure (real or imagined) in school or at work, an unexpected arrest, or rejection by a loved one (Blumenthal, 1990; Conwell et al., 2002; Joiner & Rudd, 2000). Physical and sexual abuse are also important sources of stress (Wagner, 1997). Evidence confirms that the stress and disruption of natural disasters increase the likelihood of suicide (Krug et al., 1998). Based on data from 337 countries experiencing natural disasters in the 1980s, the authors concluded that the rates of suicide increased 13.8% in the 4 years after severe floods, 31% in the 2 years after hurricanes, and 62.9% in the first year after an earthquake. Given preexisting vulnerabilities—including psychological disorders, traits of impulsiveness, and lack of social support—a stressful event can often put a person over the edge. An integrated model of the causes of suicidal behavior is presented in ■ Figure 6.7.

Is Suicide Contagious?

Most people react to hearing the news of a suicide with sadness and curiosity. Some people react by attempting suicide themselves, often by the same method they have just heard about. Gould (1990) reported an increase in suicides during a 9-day period after widespread publicity about a suicide. Clusters of suicides (several people copying one person) seem to predominate among teenagers, with as many as 5% of all teenage suicides reflecting an imitation (Gould, 1990; Gould, Greenberg, Velting, & Shaffer, 2003).

Why would anyone want to copy a suicide? First, suicides are often romanticized in the media: An attractive young person under unbearable pressure commits suicide and becomes a martyr to friends and peers by getting even with the (adult) world for creating such a difficult situation. Also, media accounts often describe in detail the methods used in the suicide, thereby providing a guide to potential victims. Little is reported about the paralysis, brain damage, and other tragic consequences of the incomplete or failed suicide or about how suicide is almost always associated with a severe psychological disorder. More important, even less is said about the futility of this method of solving problems (Gould, 1990, 2001; O'Carroll, 1990). To prevent these tragedies, mental health professionals must intervene immediately in schools and other locations with people who might be depressed or otherwise vulnerable to the contagion of suicide. But it isn't clear that suicide is "contagious" in the infectious disease sense. Rather, the stress of a friend's suicide or some other major stress may affect several individuals who are vulnerable because of existing psychological disorders (Joiner, 1999).

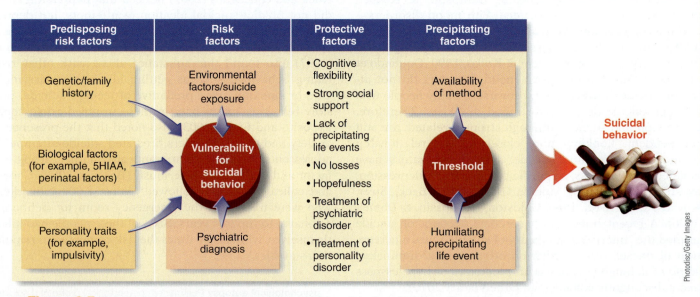

■ **Figure 6.7** Threshold model for suicidal behavior. 5HIAA = 5-hydroxyindoleacetic acid. (Reprinted, with permission, from Blumenthal, S. J., & Kupfer, D. J., 1988. Clinical assessment and treatment of youth suicide. *Journal of Youth and Adolescence, 17*, 1–24, © 1988 by Plenum Publishing.)

Treatment

Despite the identification of important risk factors, predicting suicide is still an uncertain art. Individuals with few precipitating factors unexpectedly kill themselves, and many who live with seemingly insurmountable stress and illness and have little social support or guidance somehow survive and overcome their difficulties.

Mental health professionals are thoroughly trained in assessing for possible suicidal ideation (Joiner et al., 2007). Others might be reluctant to ask leading questions for fear of putting the idea in someone's head. However, we know it is far more important to check for these "secrets" than to do nothing because the risk of inspiring suicidal thoughts is small to nonexistent and the risk of leaving them undiscovered is enormous (Berman, 2009). Gould and colleagues (2005) found that more than 1,000 high school students who were asked about suicidal thoughts or behaviors during a screening program showed no risk of increased suicidal thoughts compared to a second group of 1,000 students who had the screening program without the questions about suicide. Therefore, if there is any indication that someone is suicidal, the mental health professional will inquire, "Has there been any time recently when you've thought that life wasn't worth living or had some thoughts about hurting yourself or possibly killing yourself?"

One difficulty with this approach is that sometimes these thoughts are implicit or out of awareness. Now Cha, Najmi, Park, Finn, and Nock (2010) have developed measures of implicit (unconscious) cognition, adapted from the labs of cognitive psychology, to assess implicit suicidal ideation. In this assessment using the Stroop test described in Chapter 2, people who demonstrated an implicit association between the words *death/suicide* and *self*, even if they weren't aware of it, were 6 times more likely to make a suicide attempt in the next 6 months than those without this specific association; thus, this assessment is a better predictor of suicide attempts than both patients' own predictions and clinicians' predictions (Nock et al., 2010). The mental health professional will also check for possible recent humiliations and determine whether any of the factors are present that might indicate a high probability of suicide. For example, does a person who is thinking of suicide have a detailed plan or just a vague fantasy? If a plan is discovered that includes a specific time, place, and method, the risk is high. Does the detailed plan include putting all personal affairs in order, giving away possessions, and other final acts? If so, the risk is higher still. What specific method is the person considering? Generally, the more lethal and violent the method (guns, hanging, poison, and so on), the greater the risk it will be used. Does the person understand what might actually happen? Many people do not understand the effects of the pills on which they might overdose. Finally, has the person taken any precautions against being discovered? If so, the risk is extreme (American Psychiatric Association, 2003).

If a risk is present, clinicians attempt to get the individual to agree to or even sign a no-suicide contract. Usually this includes a promise not to do anything remotely connected with suicide without contacting the mental health professional first. If the person at risk refuses a contract (or the clinician has serious doubts about the patient's sincerity) and the suicidal risk is judged to be high, immediate hospitalization is indicated, even against the will of the patient. Whether the person is hospitalized or not, treatment aimed at resolving underlying life stressors and treating existing psychological disorders should be initiated immediately.

In view of the public health consequences of suicide, a number of programs have been implemented to reduce the rates of suicide. Most research indicates that such curriculum-based programs targeting the general population (universal programs) in schools or organizations on how to handle life stress or increase social support are not effective (Berman, 2009; Garfield & Zigler, 1993; Shaffer, Garland, Vieland, Underwood, & Busner, 1991). More helpful are programs targeted to at-risk individuals, including adolescents in schools where a student has committed suicide. The Institute of Medicine (2002) recommends making services available immediately to friends and relatives of victims. An important step is limiting access to lethal weapons for anyone at risk for suicide. A recent analysis suggests that this may be the most powerful part of a suicide prevention program (Mann et al., 2005). Telephone hotlines and other crisis intervention services also seem to be useful. Nevertheless, as Garfield and Zigler (1993) point out, hotline volunteers must be backed up by competent mental health professionals who can identify potentially serious risks. One large health maintenance organization carefully screened all of its 200,000 members who came in for services for suicide risk and then intervened if any risk was noted. Suicides were greatly reduced in the very promising program (Hampton, 2010).

Specific treatments for people at risk have also been developed. For example, Salkovskis, Atha, and Storer (1990) treated 20 patients at high risk for repeated suicide attempts with a cognitive-behavioral problem-solving approach. Results indicated that they were significantly less likely to attempt suicide in the 6 months following treatment. Marsha Linehan and colleagues developed a noteworthy treatment for the type of impulsive suicidal behavior associated with borderline personality disorder (see Chapter 11). David Rudd and colleagues developed a brief psychological treatment targeting young adults who were at risk for suicide because of the presence of suicidal ideation accompanied by previous suicidal attempts, mood or substance use disorders, or both (Rudd et al., 1996). They randomly assigned 264 young people either to this new treatment or to treatment as usual in the community. Patients undergoing the new treatment spent approximately 9 hours each day for 2 weeks at a hospital treatment facility. Treatment consisted of problem solving, developing social competence, coping more adaptively with life's problems, and recognizing emotional and life experiences that may have precipitated the suicide attempt or ideation. Patients were assessed up to 2 years following treatment, and results indicated reductions in suicidal ideation and behavior, and marked improvement in problem-solving ability. Furthermore, the brief experimental treatment was significantly more effective at retaining the highest-risk young adults in the program. This program has been expanded into a psychological treatment for suicidal behavior with empirical support for its efficacy (Rudd, Joiner, & Rajab, 2001). One of the more important studies to date has demonstrated that 10 sessions of cognitive therapy for recent suicide attempters cuts the risk of additional attempts by 50% over the next 18 months (Brown et al., 2005). Specifically 24% of those in the cognitive therapy group made a repeat attempt compared to 42% in the care-as-usual group. Because cognitive therapy is relatively widely available, this is an important development in suicide prevention.

Concept Check 6.5

Match each of the following summaries with the correct suicide type, choosing from (a) altruistic, (b) egoistic, (c) anomic, and (d) fatalistic.

1. Ralph's wife left him and took the children. He is a well-known television personality, but, because of a conflict with the new station owners, he was recently fired. If Ralph kills himself, his suicide would be considered _____.

2. Sam killed himself while a prisoner of war in Vietnam. _____

3. Sheiba lives in a remote village in Africa. She was recently caught in an adulterous affair with a man in a nearby village. Her husband wants to kill her but won't have to because of a tribal custom that requires her to kill herself. She leaps from the nearby "sinful woman's cliff." _____

4. Mabel lived in a nursing home for many years. At first, her family and friends visited her often; now they come only at Christmas. Her two closest friends in the nursing home died recently. She has no hobbies or other interests. Mabel's suicide would be identified as what type? _____

On the Spectrum A New Unified Transdiagnostic Treatment for Emotional Disorders

The mood disorders discussed in this chapter and the anxiety disorders discussed in Chapter 4 are often lumped together under the term "emotional disorders." This is because these disorders have many common features, including difficulty in managing intense emotional experiences. This difficulty is often referred to as "emotion dysregulation." It is also the case that these groups of disorders share common risk factors including the same set of genetic risk factors (described earlier). They are also highly comorbid—that is, many people with an anxiety disorder also have, or have had, depressive disorders, and most people with depression either have, or have had, an anxiety disorder. The presence of significant anxiety is associated with more severe forms of depression and bipolar disorders and a longer course and poorer outcomes from treatment (Coryell et al., 2009; Fava et al., 2008). Individuals with both anxiety and mood disorders experience more frequent and intense negative moods than healthy individuals and view

these experiences as much more aversive. They also experience similar negative cognitive processes.

Psychological treatments for the mood and anxiety disorders differ from disorder to disorder, but all share common components. These include changing negative attitudes, cognitive styles, and attributions; preventing avoidance of situations or experiences that might provoke intense emotions such as anxiety or depression; and encouraging therapeutic activities and exposure to experiences that trigger strong emotions. Recognizing these advances, we have developed a new unified transdiagnostic psychological treatment in one of our clinics that is designed to be applicable to anyone suffering from emotional disorders even if they have more than one emotional disorder (comorbidity), unusual variations of an anxiety or mood disorder, or for some reason don't quite meet the criteria for one of the diagnostic categories of anxiety and mood disorders (Barlow et al., 2011a, 2011b). The term "unified" is used because it integrates

principles that are relevant to all emotional disorders. The new treatment, called the unified protocol (UP) for *Transdiagnostic Treatment of Emotional Disorders* (Barlow et al., 2011a, 2011b), consists of five core modules: (1) increasing awareness of emotional experiences (because people with emotional disorders are uncomfortable with their emotions and often try to suppress or ignore them); (2) encouraging greater flexibility in appraisals and attributions concerning emotional situations (because people with anxiety and mood disorders usually just think the worst when they are experiencing intense emotions); (3) identifying and preventing tendencies to avoid certain situations and intense emotions (because patients are often unaware of many of their avoidant tendencies such as trying to distract themselves when they are feeling anxiety); (4) engaging patients in exercises designed to evoke physical sensations analogous to those typically associated with their anxiety and distress; and (5) encouraging patients to increase their tolerance of intense or uncomfortable emotions through exposure to both the situational cues or triggers as well as their own internal physical cues associated with intense emotions. Preliminary results show that this treatment is effective across a broad range of disorders (Ellard, Fairholme, Boisseau, Farchione, & Barlow, 2010). If these results hold up upon further testing, then the UP should eliminate the necessity for applying a different treatment to every single variation of an emotional disorder and, perhaps, be more effective across a broad range of emotional disorders.

Other recent research is making the idea of transdiagnostic treatment more interesting. Researchers have found that the most important function of antidepressant drugs may not be changes in neurotransmitter activity, although this obviously occurs, but rather changes in the neuropsychological process of regulating emotional reactions that seem to occur very soon after beginning antidepressant drugs and before full therapeutic effect is noted (Harmer, 2010). If this is the case, the fundamental mechanism of action of transdiagnostic psychological treatments, and antidepressant drugs (which work equally well in anxiety disorders) may be more similar than different in that they both target emotion dysregulation.

Summary

Understanding and Defining Mood Disorders

What is the difference between a depressive episode and a manic or hypermanic episode?

> Mood disorders are among the most common psychological disorders, and the risk of developing them is increasing worldwide, particularly in younger people.

> Two fundamental experiences can contribute either singly or in combination to all specific mood disorders: a major depressive episode and mania. A less severe episode of mania that does not cause impairment in social or occupational functioning is known as a hypomanic episode. An episode of mania coupled with anxiety or depression is known as a dysphoric manic or mixed episode.

> An individual who suffers from episodes of depression only is said to have a unipolar disorder. An individual who alternates between depression and mania has a bipolar disorder.

What are the clinical symptoms of major depressive disorder, dysthymic disorder, and bipolar disorder?

> Major depressive disorder may be a single episode or recurrent, but it is always time limited; in another form of depression, dysthymic disorder, the symptoms are somewhat milder but remain relatively unchanged over long periods. In cases of double depression, an individual experiences both depressive episodes and dysthymic disorder.

> Approximately 20% of bereaved individuals may experience a pathological, complicated grief reaction in which the normal grief response develops into a full-blown mood disorder.

> The key identifying feature of bipolar disorders is an alternation of manic episodes and major depressive episodes. Cyclothymic disorder is a milder but more chronic version of bipolar disorder.

> Patterns of additional features that sometimes accompany mood disorders, called specifiers, may predict the course or patient response to treatment, as does the temporal patterning or course of mood disorders. One pattern, seasonal affective disorder, most often occurs in winter.

Prevalence of Mood Disorders

How does the prevalence of mood disorders vary across a life span?

> Mood disorders in children are fundamentally similar to mood disorders in adults.

> Symptoms of depression are increasing dramatically in our elderly population.

> The experience of anxiety across cultures varies, and it can be difficult to make comparisons, especially, for example, when we attempt to compare subjective feelings of depression.

Causes of Mood Disorders

What biological, psychological, and sociocultural factors contribute to the development of mood disorders?

> The causes of mood disorders lie in a complex interaction of biological, psychological, and social factors. From a biological perspective, researchers are particularly interested in the stress hypothesis and the role of neurohormones. Psychological theories of depression focus on learned helplessness, the depressive cognitive schemas, and interpersonal disruptions.

Treatment of Mood Disorders

What medical and psychological treatments have been successful in treating mood disorders?

> A variety of treatments, both biological and psychological, have proved effective for the mood disorders, at least in the short term. For those individuals who do not respond to antidepressant drugs or psychosocial treatments, a more dramatic physical treatment, electroconvulsive therapy, is sometimes used. Two psychosocial treatments—cognitive therapy and interpersonal therapy—seem effective in treating depressive disorders.

> Relapse and recurrence of mood disorders are common in the long term, and treatment efforts must focus on maintenance treatment—that is, on preventing relapse or recurrence.

Suicide

What is the relationship between suicide and mood disorders?

› Suicide is often associated with mood disorders but can occur in their absence or in the presence of other disorders. It is the 11th leading cause of death, but among adolescents, it is the 3rd leading cause of death.

› In understanding suicidal behavior, three indices are important: suicidal ideation (serious thoughts about committing suicide), suicidal plans (a detailed method for killing oneself), and suicidal attempts (that are not successful). Important, too, in learning about risk factors for suicides is the psychological autopsy, in which the psychological profile of an individual who has committed suicide is reconstructed and examined for clues.

Key Terms

mood disorders, 202
major depressive episode, 202
mania, 203
hypomanic episode, 203
mixed manic episode or dysphoric manic episode, 203
major depressive disorder, single or recurrent episode, 204
dysthymic disorder, 204
double depression, 205
hallucinations, 207

delusions, 207
catalepsy, 207
seasonal affective disorder (SAD), 207
pathological or impacted grief reaction, 207
bipolar II disorder, 208
bipolar I disorder, 208
cyclothymic disorder, 209
neurohormones, 216
learned helplessness theory of depression, 220

depressive cognitive triad, 221
mood-stabilizing drug, 229
electroconvulsive therapy (ECT), 230
cognitive therapy, 230
interpersonal psychotherapy (IPT), 232
maintenance treatment, 233
suicidal ideation, 237
suicidal plans, 237
suicidal attempts, 237
psychological autopsy, 238

Answers to Concept Checks

6.1

1. e; 2. a; 3. c; 4. d; 5. b

6.2

1. T; 2. F (it does not require life experience); 3. T; 4. T

6.3

1. genetics, neurotransmitter system abnormalities, endocrine system, circadian or sleep rhythms, neurohormones
2. stressful life events, learned helplessness, depressive cognitive triad, a sense of uncontrollability
3. marital dissatisfaction, gender, few social supports

6.4

1. electroconvulsive therapy; 2. cognitive therapy; 3. antidepressants; 4. lithium; 5. interpersonal psychotherapy; 6. maintenance treatment

6.5

1. c; 2. d; 3. a; 4. b

Media Resources

Log in to CengageBrain to access the resources your instructor requires. For this book, you can access:

CourseMate brings course concepts to life with interactive learning, study, and exam preparation tools that support the printed textbook. A textbook-specific website, Psychology CourseMate includes an integrated interactive eBook and other interactive learning tools including quizzes, flashcards, videos, and more.

Abnormal Psychology Videos

› *Barbara, a Client with Major Depressive Disorder:* Barbara has a major depressive disorder that's rather severe and long-lasting.
› *Evelyn, a Patient with Major Depressive Disorder:* Evelyn has a major depressive disorder that gives a more positive view of long-term prospects for change.
› *Mary, a Client with Bipolar Disorder:* Mary is shown in both a manic and depressive phase of her illness. You

may notice the similarity of the delusions in both phases of her illness.

CENGAGENOW CengageNow is an easy-to-use online resource that helps you study in less time to get the grade you want—NOW. Take a pre-test for this chapter and receive a personalized study plan based on your results that will identify the topics you need to review and direct you to online resources to help you master those topics. Then take a post-test to help you determine the concepts you have mastered and what you will need to work on. If your textbook does not include an access code card, go to CengageBrain.com to gain access.

aplia If your professor has assigned Aplia homework:
1. Sign in to your account.
2. Complete the corresponding homework exercises as required by your professor.

3. When finished, click "Grade It Now" to see which areas you have mastered, which need more work, and for detailed explanations of every answer.

Video Concept Reviews

CengageNOW also contains Mark Durand's *Video Concept Reviews* on these challenging topics.

› Overview of Moods
› Overview of Mood Disorders
› Major Depressive Disorder

› Major Depression: Single or Recurrent Episode
› Dysthymia
› Double Depression
› Bipolar I Disorder
› Bipolar II Disorder
› Cyclothymic Disorder
› Concept Check: Dysthymia Versus Major Depression
› Mood Disorders: Course Specifiers
› Learned Helplessness
› Electroconvulsive Therapy (ECT)
› Suicide

Chapter Quiz

1. An individual who is experiencing an elevated mood, a decreased need for sleep, and distractibility is most likely experiencing:
   a. panic disorder
   b. mania
   c. depersonalization
   d. hallucinations

2. What is the general agreement among mental health professionals about the relationship between bereavement and depression?
   a. Bereavement is less severe than depression in all cases.
   b. Depression can lead to bereavement in many cases.
   c. Bereavement can lead to depression in many cases.
   d. Symptoms of bereavement and depression rarely overlap.

3. Bipolar I disorder is characterized by _____, whereas bipolar II is characterized by _____.
   a. full manic episodes; hypomanic episodes
   b. hypomanic episodes; full manic episodes
   c. both depressive and manic episodes; full manic episodes
   d. full manic episodes; both depressive and manic episodes

4. Treatment for bereavement often includes:
   a. finding meaning in the loss
   b. replacing the lost person with someone else
   c. finding humor in the tragedy
   d. replacing sad thoughts about the lost person with more happy thoughts

5. Which statement best characterizes the relationship between anxiety and depression?
   a. Anxiety usually precedes the development of depression.
   b. Depression usually precedes the development of anxiety.
   c. Almost all depressed patients are anxious, but not all anxious patients are depressed.
   d. Almost all anxious patients are depressed, but not all depressed patients are anxious.

6. Which theory suggests that depression occurs when individuals believe that they have no control over the circumstances in their lives?
   a. attribution theory
   b. learned helplessness
   c. social learning theory
   d. theory of equifinality

7. In treating depressed clients, a psychologist helps them think more positively about themselves, about their place in the world, and about the prospects for the future. This psychologist is basing her techniques on whose model of depression?
   a. Sigmund Freud
   b. Carl Rogers
   c. Rollo May
   d. Aaron Beck

8. Maintenance treatment for depression can be important because it can prevent:
   a. transmission
   b. bereavement
   c. incidence
   d. relapse

9. Which of the following explains why some people refuse to take medications to treat their depression or take those medications and then stop?
   a. The medications are in short supply and are unavailable.
   b. The medications don't work for most people.
   c. For some people the medications cause serious side effects.
   d. The medications work in the short term but not the long term.

10. Which of the following is a risk factor for suicide?
    a. having a relative who committed suicide
    b. playing aggressive, full-contact sports
    c. a history of multiple marriages
    d. an abstract, philosophical cognitive style
    (See Appendix A for answers.)

Exploring Mood Disorders

People with mood disorders experience one or both of the following:

> **Mania:** A frantic "high" with extreme overconfidence and energy, often leading to reckless behavior

> **Depression:** A devastating "low" with extreme lack of energy, interest, confidence, and enjoyment of life

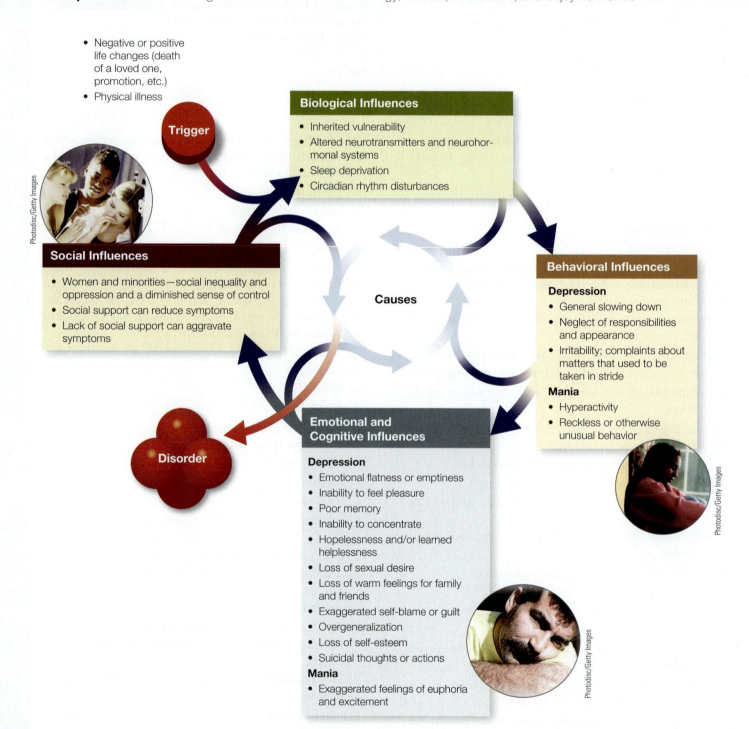

- Negative or positive life changes (death of a loved one, promotion, etc.)
- Physical illness

Photodisc/Getty Images

Trigger

Biological Influences

- Inherited vulnerability
- Altered neurotransmitters and neurohormonal systems
- Sleep deprivation
- Circadian rhythm disturbances

Social Influences

- Women and minorities—social inequality and oppression and a diminished sense of control
- Social support can reduce symptoms
- Lack of social support can aggravate symptoms

Causes

Behavioral Influences

Depression
- General slowing down
- Neglect of responsibilities and appearance
- Irritability; complaints about matters that used to be taken in stride

Mania
- Hyperactivity
- Reckless or otherwise unusual behavior

Photodisc/Getty Images

Disorder

Emotional and Cognitive Influences

Depression
- Emotional flatness or emptiness
- Inability to feel pleasure
- Poor memory
- Inability to concentrate
- Hopelessness and/or learned helplessness
- Loss of sexual desire
- Loss of warm feelings for family and friends
- Exaggerated self-blame or guilt
- Overgeneralization
- Loss of self-esteem
- Suicidal thoughts or actions

Mania
- Exaggerated feelings of euphoria and excitement

Photodisc/Getty Images

TYPES OF MOOD DISORDERS

Depressive

Major Depressive Disorder
Symptoms of major depressive disorder:
• begin suddenly, often triggered by a crisis, change, or loss
• are extremely severe, interfering with normal functioning
• can be long term, lasting months or years if untreated
Some people have only one episode, but the pattern usually involves repeated episodes or lasting symptoms.

Dysthymia
Long-term unchanging symptoms of mild depression, sometimes lasting 20 to 30 years if untreated. Daily functioning not as severely affected, but over time impairment is cumulative.

Double Depression
Alternating periods of major depression and dysthymia

Photodisc/Getty Images

Bipolar

People who have a bipolar disorder live on an unending emotional roller coaster.

Types of Bipolar Disorders
• **Bipolar I:** major depression and full mania
• **Bipolar II:** major depression and mild mania
• **Cyclothymia:** mild depression with mild mania, chronic and long term

During the **Depressive Phase**, the person may:
• lose all interest in pleasurable activities and friends
• feel worthless, helpless, and hopeless
• have trouble concentrating
• lose or gain weight without trying
• have trouble sleeping or sleep more than usual
• feel tired all the time
• feel physical aches and pains that have no medical cause
• think about death or attempt suicide

During the **Manic Phase**, the person may:
• feel extreme pleasure and joy from every activity
• be extraordinarily active, planning excessive daily activities
• sleep little without getting tired
• develop grandiose plans leading to reckless behavior: unrestrained buying sprees, sexual indiscretions, foolish business investments, etc.
• have "racing thoughts" and talk on and on
• be easily irritated and distracted

TREATMENT OF MOOD DISORDERS
Treatment for mood disorders is most effective and easiest when it's started early. Most people are treated with a combination of these methods.

Treatment

Medication
Antidepressants can help to control symptoms and restore neurotransmitter functioning.
Common types of antidepressants:

• Tricyclics (Tofranil, Elavil)
• Monamine oxidase inhibitors (MAOIs): (Nardil, Parnate); MAOIs can have severe side effects, especially when combined with certain foods or over-the-counter medications
• Selective-serotonin reuptake inhibitors or SSRIs (Prozac, Zoloft) are newer and cause fewer side effects than tricyclics or MAOIs
• Lithium is the preferred drug for bipolar disorder; side effects can be serious; and dosage must be carefully regulated

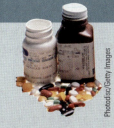

Photodisc/Getty Images

Cognitive-Behavioral Therapy
Helps depressed people:

• learn to replace negative depressive thoughts and attributions with more positive ones
• develop more effective coping behaviors and skills

Interpersonal Psychotherapy
Helps depressed people:

• focus on the social and interpersonal triggers for their depression (such as the loss of a loved one)
• develop skills to resolve interpersonal conflicts and build new relationships

Electroconvulsive Therapy (ECT)

• For severe depression, ECT is used when other treatments have been ineffective. It usually has temporary side effects, such as memory loss and lethargy. In some patients, certain intellectual and/or memory functions may be permanently lost.

Light Therapy

• For seasonal affective disorder

Photodisc/Getty Images

CHAPTER 7

Physical Disorders and Health Psychology

Demonstrate knowledge and understanding representing appropriate breadth and depth in selected content areas of psychology:	› Biological bases of behavior and mental processes, including physiology, sensation, perception, comparative, motivation, and emotion (APA SLO 1.2.a (3)) *(see textbook pages 251–257)*
Use the concepts, language, and major theories of the discipline to account for psychological phenomena:	› Identify antecedents and consequences of behavior and mental processes (APA SLO 1.3.b) *(see textbook pages 257–270)*
Identify appropriate applications of psychology in solving problems, such as:	› Origin and treatment of abnormal behavior (APA SLO 4.2.b) *(see textbook pages 270–278)*

*Portions of this chapter cover learning outcomes suggested by the American Psychological Association (2007) in their guidelines for the undergraduate psychology major. Chapter coverage of these outcomes is identified by APA Goal and APA Suggested Learning Outcome (SLO).

Psychological and Social Factors That Influence Health

> **What is the difference between behavioral medicine and health psychology?**
> **How are immune system function, stress, and physical disorders related?**

At the beginning of the 20th century the leading causes of death were from infectious diseases such as influenza, pneumonia, diphtheria, tuberculosis, typhoid fever, measles, and gastrointestinal infections. Since then, the percentage of yearly total deaths from these diseases has been reduced greatly, from 38.9% to 5.5% (Table 7.1). This reduction represents the first revolution in public health that eliminated many infectious diseases and mastered many more. But the enormous success of our health-care system in reducing mortality from disease has revealed a more complex and challenging problem: At present, some major contributing factors to illness and death in this country are *psychological and behavioral.*

In Chapter 2, we described the profound effects of psychological and social factors on brain structure and function. These factors seem to influence neurotransmitter activity, the secretion of neurohormones in the endocrine system, and, at a more fundamental level, gene expression. We have repeatedly looked at the complex interplay of biological, psychological, and social factors in the production and maintenance of psychological disorders. But psychological and social factors are important to a number of additional disorders, including endocrinological disorders such as diabetes, cardiovascular disorders, and disorders of the immune system such as acquired immune deficiency syndrome (AIDS). These and the other disorders discussed in this chapter are clearly *physical disorders.* They have known (or strongly inferred) physical causes and mostly observable physical pathology (for example, genital herpes, damaged heart muscle, malignant tumors, or measurable hypertension). Contrast this with the somatoform disorders discussed in Chapter 5: In conversion disorders, for example, clients complain of physical damage or disease but show no physical pathology. In the fourth edition, text revision, of the *Diagnostic and Statistical Manual (DSM-IV-TR),* physical disorders such as hypertension and diabetes are coded separately on Axis III. However, there is a provision for recognizing "psychological factors affecting medical condition."

The study of how psychological and social factors affect physical disorders used to be distinct and somewhat separate from the remainder of psychopathology. Early on, the field was called *psychosomatic medicine* (Alexander, 1950), which meant that *psychological* factors affected *somatic* (physical) function. The label *psychophysiological disorders* was used to communicate a similar idea. Such terms are less often used today because they are misleading. Describing as psychosomatic a disorder with an obvious physical component gave the impression that psychological (mental) disorders of mood and anxiety did not have a strong biological component. As we now know, this assumption is not viable. Biological, psychological, and social factors are implicated in the cause and maintenance of every disorder, both mental and physical.

The contribution of psychosocial factors to the etiology and treatment of physical disorders is widely studied.

Table 7.1 The 10 Leading Causes of Death in the United States in 1900 and in 2007 (Percentage of Total Deaths)

1900	Percentage	2007	Percentage
1. Pneumonia and influenza	11.8	1. Coronary heart disease	25.4
2. Tuberculosis	11.3	2. Malignant neoplasms (cancer)	23.2
3. Diarrhea, enteritis, and ulceration of the intestines	8.3	3. Stroke and other cerebrovascular diseases	5.6
4. Diseases of the heart	8.0	4. Chronic lower respiratory diseases	5.3
5. Intracranial lesions of vascular origin	6.2	5. Accidents (unintentional injury)	5.1
6. Nephritis (kidney disease)	5.2	6. Alzheimer's disease	3.1
7. Accidents (unintentional injury)	4.2	7. Diabetes mellitus	2.9
8. Cancer and other malignant tumors	3.7	8. Influenza and pneumonia	2.2
9. Senility	2.9	9. Nephritis (kidney disease)	1.9
10. Diphtheria	2.3	10. Septicemia	1.4
Other*	36.1	Other*	23.9

*Includes hemophilia, blood transfusion, perinatal exposure, transmission within health-care settings, and risk not reported or identified.

Source: Figures for the world adapted from UNAIDS (2009, November), *AIDS epidemic update.* Figures for the U.S. adapted from Centers for Disease Control and Prevention (2010), *Diagnosis of HIV infection and AIDS in the U.S. and dependent areas, 2008* (HIV Surveillance Report, Volume 20).

Some of the discoveries are among the more exciting findings in all of psychology and biology. For example, we described briefly in Chapter 2 that lowering stress levels and having a rich social network of family and friends is associated with better heath, living longer, and less cognitive decline as one ages (Cohen & Janicki-Deverts, 2009). Remember, too, the tragic physical and mental deterioration among elderly people who are removed from social networks of family and friends (Hawkley & Capioppo, 2007).

Health and Health-Related Behavior

The shift in focus from infectious disease to psychological factors has been called the second revolution in public health. Two closely related new fields of study have developed. In the first, **behavioral medicine** (Agras, 1982; Meyers, 1991), knowledge derived from behavioral science is applied to the prevention, diagnosis, and treatment of medical problems. This is an interdisciplinary field in which psychologists, physicians, and other health professionals work closely together to develop new treatments and preventive strategies (Schwartz & Weiss, 1978). A second field, **health psychology**, is not interdisciplinary, and it is usually considered a subfield of behavioral medicine. Practitioners study psychological factors that are important to the promotion and maintenance of health; they also analyze and recommend improvements in health-care systems and health policy formation within the discipline of psychology (Feuerstein, Labbe, & Kuczmierczyk, 1986; Stone, 1987; Taylor, 2009).

Psychological and social factors influence health and physical problems in *two* distinct ways (■ Figure 7.1). First, they can affect the basic biological processes that lead to illness and disease. Second, long-standing behavior patterns may put people at risk to develop certain physical disorders. Sometimes both these avenues contribute to the etiology or maintenance of disease (Kiecolt-Glaser & Newton, 2001; Miller & Blackwell, 2006; Schneiderman, 2004; Taylor, Repetti, & Seeman, 1997; Williams, Barefoot, & Schneiderman, 2003). Consider the example of *genital herpes.* There's a chance that someone you know has genital herpes and hasn't told you about it. It's not difficult to understand why: Genital herpes is an incurable sexually transmitted disease. Estimates indicate that more than 50 million Americans—about 20% of the entire population—have been infected by the herpes simplex virus affecting either oral or genital areas (Brentjens, Yeung-Yue, Lee, & Tyring, 2003). Because the disease is concentrated in young adults, the percentage in that group is much higher. The virus remains dormant until it is reactivated periodically. When it recurs in the genital region, infected individuals usually experience any of a number of symptoms, including pain, itching, vaginal or urethral discharge, and, most commonly, ulcerative lesions (open sores) in the genital area. Lesions recur approximately four times each year but can appear more often. Cases of genital herpes have increased dramatically in recent years, for reasons that are as much psychological and behavioral as biological. Although genital herpes is a biological disease, it spreads rapidly because people choose not to change their behavior by simply using a condom.

① Psychosocial factors (such as negative emotions and stress) disrupt basic biological processes, which may lead to physical disorders and disease.

Stress

Lack of control

Terry Vine/Blend Images/JupiterImages

② "Risky" behaviors cause or contribute to a variety of physical disorders and disease.

Smoking
Drinking
Poor eating habits
No exercise

©vario images GmbH & Co.KG/Alamy

■ **Figure 7.1** Psychosocial factors directly affect physical health in two ways.

Stress also plays a role in triggering herpes recurrences (Chida & Mao, 2009; Goldmeier, Garvey, & Barton, 2008; Pereira et al., 2003). Stress-control procedures, particularly relaxation, seems to decrease recurrences of genital herpes, and the duration of each episode, most likely through the positive effects of such practices on the immune system (Burnette, Koehn, Kenyon-Jump, Huttun, & Stark, 1991; Pereira et al., 2003).

Consider also the tragic example of AIDS. AIDS is a disease of the immune system that is directly affected by stress (Cohen & Herbert, 1996; Kennedy, 2000), so stress may promote the deadly progression of AIDS. This is an example of how psychological factors may directly influence biological processes. We also know that a variety of things we may choose to do put us at risk for AIDS—for example, having unprotected sex or sharing dirty needles. Because there is no medical cure for AIDS yet, our best weapon is large-scale behavior modification to *prevent acquisition* of the disease.

Other behavioral patterns contribute to disease. Fully 50% of deaths from the 10 leading causes of death in the United States can be traced to behaviors common to certain lifestyles (Centers for Disease Control and Prevention [CDC],

2003b; Taylor, 2009). Smoking is the leading preventable cause of death in the United States and has been estimated to cause 20% of all deaths (CDC, 2007). Other unhealthy behaviors include poor eating habits, lack of exercise, and insufficient injury control (not wearing seat belts, for example). These behaviors are grouped under the label *lifestyle* because they are mostly enduring habits that are an integral part of a person's daily living pattern (Lewis, Statt, & Marcus, 2011; Oyama & Andrasik, 1992). Available evidence suggests that the same kinds of causal factors active in psychological disorders—social, psychological, and biological—play a role in some physical disorders (Mostofsky & Barlow, 2000; Uchino, 2009). But the factor attracting the most attention is *stress*, particularly the neurobiological components of the stress response.

©Bettmann/Corbis

▲ Hans Selye suggested in 1936 that stress contributes to certain physical problems.

The Nature of Stress

In 1936, a young scientist in Montreal, Canada, named Hans Selye noticed that one group of rats he injected with a certain chemical extract developed ulcers and other physiological problems, including atrophy of immune system tissues. But a control group of rats who received a daily saline (salty water) injection that should not have had any effect developed the *same* physical problems. Selye pursued this unexpected finding and discovered that the daily injections themselves seemed to be the culprit rather than the injected substance. Furthermore, many types of environmental changes produced the same results. Borrowing a term from engineering, he decided the cause of this nonspecific reaction was *stress*. As so often happens in science, an accidental or serendipitous observation led to a new area of study, in this case, *stress physiology* (Selye, 1936).

Selye theorized that the body goes through several stages in response to *sustained stress*. The first phase is a type of *alarm* response to immediate danger or threat. With continuing stress, we seem to pass into a stage of *resistance*, in which we mobilize various coping mechanisms to respond to the stress. Finally, if the stress is too intense or lasts too long, we may enter a stage of *exhaustion*, in which

behavioral medicine Interdisciplinary approach applying behavioral science to the prevention, diagnosis, and treatment of medical problems. Also known as *psychosomatic medicine*.
health psychology Subfield of behavioral medicine that studies psychological factors important in health promotion and maintenance.

our bodies suffer permanent damage or death (Selye, 1936, 1950). Selye called this sequence the **general adaptation syndrome (GAS)**.

The word *stress* means many things in modern life. In engineering, stress is the strain on a bridge when a heavy truck drives across it; stress is the *response* of the bridge to the truck's weight. But stress is also a *stimulus*. The truck is a "stressor" for the bridge, just as being fired from a job or facing a difficult final exam is a stimulus or stressor for a person. These varied meanings can create some confusion, but we concentrate on **stress** as the physiological response of the individual to a stressor.

The Physiology of Stress

In Chapter 2, we described the physiological effects of the early stages of stress, noting in particular its activating effect on the sympathetic nervous system, which mobilizes our resources during times of threat or danger by activating internal organs to prepare the body for immediate action, either fight or flight. These changes increase our strength and mental activity. We also noted in Chapter 2 that the activity of the endocrine system increases when we are stressed, primarily through activation of the hypothalamic–pituitary–adrenocortical (HPA) axis (see p. 46 in Chapter 2). Although a variety of neurotransmitters begin flowing in the nervous system, much attention has focused on the endocrine system's neuromodulators or neuropeptides, hormones affecting the nervous system that are secreted by the glands directly into the bloodstream (Chaouloff & Groc, 2010; Owens, Mulchahey, Stout, & Plotsky 1997; Taylor, Maloney, Dearborn & Weiss, 2009). These neuromodulating hormones act much like neurotransmitters in carrying the brain's messages to various parts of the body. One of the neurohormones, *corticotropin-releasing factor (CRF)*, is secreted by the hypothalamus and stimulates the pituitary gland. Farther down the chain of the HPA axis, the pituitary gland (along with the autonomic nervous system) activates the adrenal gland, which secretes, among other things, the hormone *cortisol*. Because of their close relationship to the stress response, cortisol and other related hormones are known as the *stress hormones*.

Remember that the HPA axis is closely related to the limbic system. The hypothalamus, at the top of the brain stem, is right next to the limbic system, which contains the hippocampus and seems to control our emotional memories. The hippocampus is responsive to cortisol. When stimulated by this hormone during HPA axis activity, the hippocampus helps to *turn off* the stress response, com-pleting a feedback loop between the limbic system and the various parts of the HPA axis.

This loop may be important for a number of reasons. Working with primates, Robert Sapolsky and his colleagues (see, for example, Sapolsky & Meaney, 1986; Sapolsky, 2000a, 2000b, 2007) showed that increased levels of cortisol in response to chronic stress may kill nerve cells in the hippocampus. If hippocampal activity is thus compromised, excessive cortisol is secreted and, over time, the ability to turn off the stress response decreases, which leads to further aging of the hippocampus. These findings indicate that chronic stress leading to chronic secretion of cortisol may have long-lasting effects on physical function, including brain damage. Cell death may, in turn, lead to deficient problem-solving abilities among the aged and, ultimately, dementia. This physiological process may also affect susceptibility to infectious disease and recovery from it in other pathophysiological systems. Sapolsky's work is important because we now know that hippocampal cell death associated with chronic stress and anxiety occurs in humans with, for example, posttraumatic stress disorder (see Chapter 4) and depression (see Chapter 6). The long-term effects of this cell death are not yet known.

Contributions to the Stress Response

Stress physiology is profoundly influenced by psychological and social factors (Kemeny, 2003; Taylor et al., 2009). This

▲ Baboons at the top of the social hierarchy have a sense of predictability and control that allows them to cope with problems and maintain physical health; baboons at the bottom of the hierarchy suffer the symptoms of stress because they have little control over access to food, resting places, and mates.

link has been demonstrated by Sapolsky (1990, 2000a, 2000b, 2007). He studied baboons living freely in a national reserve in Kenya because their primary sources of stress, like those of humans, are psychological rather than physical. As with many species, baboons arrange themselves in a social hierarchy with dominant members at the top and submissive members at the bottom. And life is tough at the bottom! The lives of subordinate animals are made difficult (Sapolsky calls it "stressful") by continual bullying from the dominant animals, and they have less access to food, preferred resting places, and sexual partners. Particularly interesting are Sapolsky's findings on levels of cortisol in the baboons as a function of their social rank in a dominance hierarchy.

Remember from our description of the HPA axis that the secretion of cortisol from the adrenal glands is the final step in a cascade of hormone secretion that originates in the limbic system in the brain during periods of stress. The secretion of cortisol contributes to our arousal and mobilization in the short run but, if produced chronically, it can damage the hippocampus. In addition, muscles atrophy, fertility is affected by declining testosterone, hypertension develops in the cardiovascular system, and the immune response is impaired. Sapolsky discovered that dominant males in the baboon hierarchy ordinarily had *lower* resting levels of cortisol than subordinate males. When an emergency occurred, however, cortisol levels rose more quickly in the dominant males than in the subordinate males.

Sapolsky and his colleagues sought the causes of these differences by working backward up the HPA axis. They found an excess secretion of CRF by the hypothalamus in subordinate animals, combined with a diminished sensitivity of the pituitary gland (which is stimulated by CRF). Therefore, subordinate animals, unlike dominant animals, continually secrete cortisol, probably because their lives are so stressful. In addition, their HPA system is less sensitive to the effects of cortisol and therefore less efficient in turning off the stress response.

Sapolsky also discovered that subordinate males have fewer circulating lymphocytes (white blood cells) than dominant males, a sign of immune system suppression. In addition, subordinate males evidence less circulating high-density lipoprotein cholesterol, which puts them at higher risk for atherosclerosis and coronary heart disease, a subject we discuss later in this chapter.

What is it about being on top that produces positive effects? Sapolsky concluded that it is primarily the psychological benefits of having *predictability* and *controllability* concerning events in one's life. Parts of his data were gathered during years in which a number of male baboons were at the top of the hierarchy, with no clear "winner." Although these males dominated the rest of the animals in the group, they constantly attacked one another. Under these conditions, they displayed hormonal profiles more like those of subordinate males. Thus, dominance combined with stability produced optimal stress hormone profiles. But the most important factor in regulating stress physiology seems to be a sense of control (Sapolsky & Ray, 1989), a finding strongly confirmed in subsequent research

(Kemeny, 2003; Sapolsky, 2007). Control of social situations and the ability to cope with any tension that arises go a long way toward blunting the long-term effects of stress.

Stress, Anxiety, Depression, and Excitement

If you have read the chapters on anxiety, mood, and related psychological disorders, you might conclude, correctly, that stressful life events combined with psychological vulnerabilities such as an inadequate sense of control are a factor in both psychological and physical disorders. Is there any relationship between psychological and physical disorders? There seems to be a strong one. In a classic study, George Vaillant (1979) studied more than 200 Harvard University sophomore men between 1942 and 1944 who were mentally and physically healthy. He followed these men closely for more than 30 years. Those who developed psychological disorders or who were highly stressed became chronically ill or died at a significantly higher rate than men who remained well adjusted and free from psychological disorders, a finding that has been repeatedly confirmed (see, for example, Katon, 2003; Robles et al., 2005). This suggests that the same types of stress-related psychological factors that contribute to psychological disorders may contribute to the later development of physical disorders and that stress, anxiety, and depression are closely related. Can you tell the difference among feelings of stress, anxiety, depression, and excitement? You might say, "No problem," but these four states have a lot in common. Which one you experience may depend on your *sense of control* at the moment or how well you think you can cope with the threat or challenge you are facing (Barlow, 2002; Barlow, Chorpita, & Turovsky, 1996; Suárez, Bennett, Goldstein, & Barlow, 2009). This continuum of feelings from excitement to stress to anxiety to depression is shown in ■ Figure 7.2.

Consider how you feel when you are excited. You might experience a rapid heartbeat, a sudden burst of energy, or a jumpy stomach. But if you're well prepared for the challenge—for example, if you're an athlete, up for the game and confident in your abilities, or a musician, sure you are going to give an outstanding performance—these feelings of *excitement* can be pleasurable.

Sometimes when you face a challenging task, you feel you could handle it if you only had the time or help you need, but because you don't have these resources, you feel pressured. In response, you may work harder to do better and be perfect, even though you think you will be all right in the end. If you are under too much pressure, you may

general adaptation syndrome (GAS) Sequence of reactions to sustained stress described by Hans Selye. These stages are alarm, resistance, and exhaustion, which may lead to death.

stress Body's physiological response to a stressor, which is any event or change that requires adaptation.

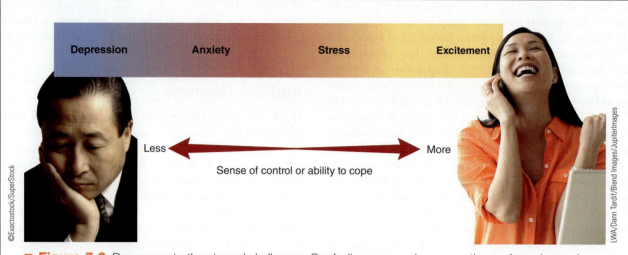

Figure 7.2 Responses to threats and challenges. Our feelings range along a continuum from depression to anxiety to stress to excitement, depending partly on our sense of control and ability to cope. (Adapted, with permission, from Barlow, D. H., Rapee, R. M., & Reisner, L. C., 2001. *Mastering stress 2001: A lifestyle approach.* Dallas, TX: American Health, © 2001 American Health Publishing.)

become tense and irritable or develop a headache or an upset stomach. This is what *stress* feels like. If something really is threatening and you believe there is little you can do about it, you may feel *anxiety*. The threatening situation could be anything from a physical attack to making a fool of yourself in front of someone. As your body prepares for the challenge, you worry about it incessantly. Your sense of control is considerably less than if you were stressed. In some cases, there may not be a difficult situation. Sometimes we are anxious for no reason except that we feel certain aspects of our lives are out of control. Finally, individuals who always perceive life as threatening may lose hope about ever having control and slip into a state of *depression*, no longer trying to cope.

To sum up, the underlying physiology of these particular emotional states seems relatively similar in some basic ways. This is why we refer to a similar pattern of sympathetic arousal and activation of specific neurotransmitters and neurohormones in discussing anxiety, depression, and stress-related physical disorders. However, there seem to be some differences. Blood pressure may increase when the challenges seem to overwhelm coping resources, resulting in a low sense of control (anxiety, depression), but blood pressure will be unchanged during excitement or marked stress (Blascovich & Tomaka, 1996). Nevertheless, it is psychological factors—specifically a sense of control and confidence that we can cope with stress or challenges, called **self-efficacy** by Bandura (1986)—that differ most markedly among these emotions, leading to different feelings (Taylor et al., 1997).

Stress and the Immune Response

Have you had a cold during the past several months? How did you pick it up? Did you spend the day with someone else who had a cold? Did someone sneeze nearby while you were sitting in class? Exposure to cold viruses is a necessary factor in developing a cold, but, as mentioned briefly in Chapter 2, the level of stress you are experiencing at the time seems to play a major role in whether the exposure results in a cold. Sheldon Cohen and his associates (Cohen, 1996; Cohen, Doyle, & Skoner, 1999; Cohen, Tyrrell, & Smith, 1991, 1993) exposed volunteer participants to a specific dosage of a cold virus and followed them closely. They found that the chance a participant would get sick was directly related to how much stress the person had experienced during the past year. Cohen and colleagues (1995) also linked the intensity of stress and negative affect at the time of exposure to the later *severity* of the cold, as measured by mucus production. In an interesting twist, Cohen, Doyle, Turner, Alper, and Skoner (2003) have demonstrated that how sociable you are—that is, the quantity and quality of your social relationships—affects whether you come down with a cold when exposed to the virus, perhaps because socializing with friends relieves stress (Cohen & Janicki-Devarts, 2009).

Almost certainly, the effect of stress on susceptibility to infections is mediated through the **immune system**, which protects the body from any foreign materials that may enter it. Humans under stress show clearly increased rates of infectious diseases, including colds, herpes, and mononucleosis (Cohen & Herbert, 1996; Taylor, 2009). Direct evidence links a number of stressful situations to lowered immune system functioning, including marital discord or relationship difficulties (Kiecolt-Glaser et al., 2005; Kiecolt-Glaser & Newton, 2001; Uchino, 2009), job loss, and the death of a loved one (Hawkley & Cacioppo, 2007; Morris, Cook, & Shaper, 1994; Pavalko, Elder, & Clipp, 1993).

We have already noted that psychological disorders seem to make us more susceptible to developing physical disorders (Katon, 2003; Robles et al., 2005; Vaillant, 1979). In fact, direct evidence indicates that depression lowers immune system functioning (Herbert & Cohen, 1993;

Miller & Blackwell, 2006; Stone, 2000; Weisse, 1992), particularly in older adults (Herbert & Cohen, 1993). It may be that the level of depression—and, more importantly, the underlying sense of uncontrollability that accompanies most depressions—is the crucial mechanism in lowering immune system functioning, a mechanism present during most negative stressful life events, such as job loss (Miller & Blackwell, 2006; Robles et al., 2005; Weisse, 1992). Depression can also lead to poor self-care and a tendency to engage in riskier behaviors. Like Sapolsky's baboons, for humans the ability to retain a sense of control over events in our lives may be one of the most important psychological contributions to good health.

Most studies concerning stress and the immune system have examined a sudden or acute stressor. But *chronic stress* may be more problematic because the effects, by definition, last longer (Schneiderman, 2004). For example, lowered immune system functioning has been reported for people who care for chronically ill family members, such as Alzheimer's disease patients (Holland & Gallagher-Thompson, 2011; Mills et al., 2004).

To understand how the immune system protects us, we must first understand how it works. We take a brief tour of the immune system next, using ■ Figure 7.3 as a visual guide, and then we examine psychological contributions to the biology of two diseases strongly related to immune system functioning: AIDS and cancer.

How the Immune System Works

The immune system identifies and eliminates foreign materials, called **antigens**, in the body. Antigens can be any of a number of substances, usually bacteria, viruses, or parasites. But the immune system also targets the body's own cells that have become aberrant or damaged in some way, perhaps as part of a malignant tumor. Donated organs are foreign, so the immune system attacks them after surgical transplant; consequently, it is necessary to suppress the immune system temporarily after surgery.

The immune system has two main parts: the humoral and the cellular. Specific types of cells function as agents of both. White blood cells, called *leukocytes*, do most of the work. There are several types of leukocytes. *Macrophages* might be considered one of the body's first lines of defense: They surround identifiable antigens and destroy them. They also signal *lymphocytes*, which consist of two groups, B cells and T cells.

The *B cells* operate within the humoral part of the immune system, releasing molecules that seek antigens in blood and other bodily fluids with the purpose of neutralizing them. The B cells produce highly specific molecules called *immunoglobulins* that act as *antibodies,* which combine with the antigens to neutralize them. After the antigens are neutralized, a subgroup called *memory B cells* are cre-

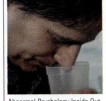

Abnormal Psychology Inside Out. Produced by Ira Wohl, Only Child Motion Pictures

Studying the Effects of Emotions on Physical Health

People with the lowest level of sociability are most likely to get a cold, whereas people with the highest level of sociability are least likely to develop a cold.

Go to Psychology CourseMate at www.cengagebrain.com to watch this video.

ated so that the next time that antigen is encountered, the immune system response will be even faster. This action accounts for the success of inoculations, or vaccinations, you may have received for mumps or measles as a child. An inoculation contains small amounts of the targeted organism but not enough to make you sick. Your immune system then "remembers" this antigen and prevents you from coming down with the full disease when you are exposed to it.

Members of the second group of lymphocytes, called *T cells,* operate in the cellular branch of the immune system. These cells don't produce antibodies. Instead, one subgroup, *killer T cells,* directly destroys viral infections and cancerous processes (Dustin & Long, 2010; Wan, 2010). When the process is complete, *memory T cells* are created to speed future responses to the same antigen. Other subgroups of T cells help regulate the immune system. For example, *T4 cells* are called *helper T cells* because they enhance the immune system response by signaling B cells to produce antibodies and telling other T cells to destroy the antigen. *Suppressor T cells* suppress the production of antibodies by B cells when they are no longer needed.

We should have twice as many T4 (helper) cells as suppressor T cells. With too many T4 cells, the immune system is overreactive and may attack the body's normal cells rather than antigens. When this happens, we have what is called an **autoimmune disease**, such as **rheumatoid arthritis**. With too many suppressor T cells, the body is subject to invasion by a number of antigens. The human immunodeficiency virus (HIV) directly attacks the helper T cells, lymphocytes that are crucial to both humoral and cellular immunity, thereby severely weakening the immune system and causing AIDS.

self-efficacy Perception of having the ability to cope with stress or challenges.

immune system Body's means of identifying and eliminating any foreign materials (for example, bacteria, parasites, and even transplanted organs) that enter.

antigens Foreign material that enters the body, including bacteria and parasites.

autoimmune disease Condition in which the body's immune system attacks healthy tissue rather than antigens.

rheumatoid arthritis Painful, degenerative disease in which the immune system essentially attacks itself, resulting in stiffness, swelling, and even destruction of the joints. Cognitive–behavioral treatments can help relieve pain and stiffness.

Psychological and Social Factors That Influence Health

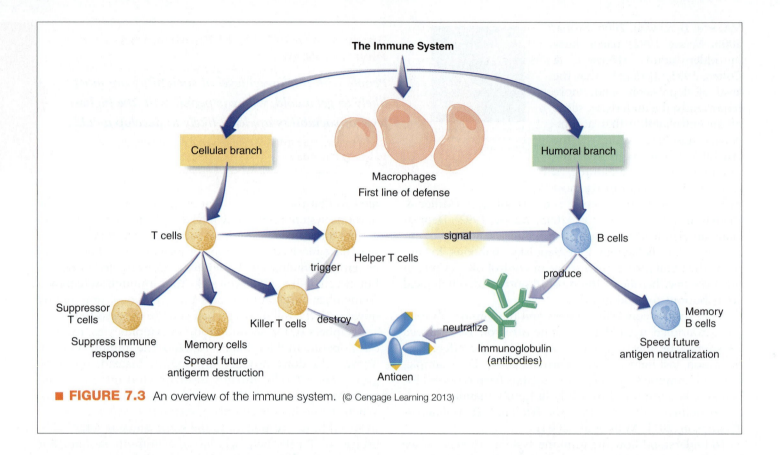

The Immune System

Cellular branch

Macrophages
First line of defense

Humoral branch

T cells

Helper T cells

signal

B cells

trigger

produce

Suppressor
T cells

Killer T cells

destroy

neutralize

Memory
B cells

Suppress immune
response

Memory cells

Immunoglobulin
(antibodies)

Speed future
antigen neutralization

Spread future
antigerm destruction

Antigen

■ **FIGURE 7.3** An overview of the immune system. (© Cengage Learning 2013)

Until the mid-1970s most scientists believed the brain and the immune system operated independently of each other. However, in 1974, Robert Ader and his colleagues (see, for example, Ader & Cohen, 1975, 1993) made a startling discovery. Working with a classical conditioning paradigm, they gave sugar-flavored water to rats, together with a drug that suppresses the immune system. Ader and Cohen then demonstrated that giving the same rats only the sweet-tasting water produced similar changes in the immune system. In other words, the rats had "learned" (through classical conditioning) to respond to the water by suppressing their immune systems. We now know there are many connections between the nervous system and the immune system. These findings have generated a field of study known as **psychoneuroimmunology**, or **PNI** (Ader & Cohen, 1993), which simply means the object of study is *psycho*logical influences on the *neuro*logical responding implicated in our *immune* response.

Researchers have learned a great deal recently about pathways through which psychological and social factors may influence immune system functioning. Direct connections among the brain (central nervous system), the HPA axis (hormonal), and the immune system have already been described. Behavioral changes in response to stressful events, such as increased smoking or poor eating habits, may also suppress the immune system (Cohen & Herbert, 1996; ■ Figure 7.4). Now scientists have uncovered a chain of molecules that connects stress to the onset of disease by turning on certain genes (Cole et al., 2010). Basically, stress seems to activate certain molecules in cells that activate genes (called

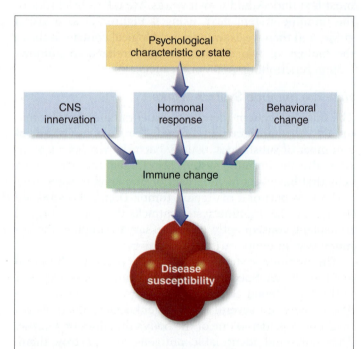

■ **Figure 7.4** Pathways through which psychological factors might influence onset and progression of immune system–mediated disease. For simplicity, arrows are drawn in only one direction, from psychological characteristics to disease. No lack of alternative paths is implied. CNS = central nervous system. (From Cohen, S., & Herbert, T. B., 1996. Health psychology: Psychological factors and physical disease from the perspective of human psychoneuroimmunology. *Annual Review of Psychology, 47,* 113–142.)

a transcription factor), in this case the GABA-1 transcription factor that activates the interleukin-6 gene. This gene makes a protein that turns on the inflammatory response, which brings infection-fighting cells of the immune system to the area. This is great if you've cut yourself, but very damaging if it occurs over a long period. It is this chronic inflammatory response that exacerbates cancer, heart disease, and diabetes and shortens life. Of course, other genes, such as the serotonin transporter gene mentioned in Chapter 2, are also implicated in making one vulnerable to certain types of stressors (Way & Taylor, 2010). Undoubtedly many more groups of genes and integrative psychobiological paths implicated in the effects of the stress response will be discovered (Segerstrom & Sephton, 2010).

Concept Check 7.1

Assess your knowledge of the immune system by matching components of the immune system with their function in the body: (a) macrophages, (b) B cells, (c) immunoglobins, (d) killer T cells, (e) suppressor T cells, and (f) memory B cells.

1. This subgroup targets viral infections within the cells by directly destroying the antigens. _____

2. A type of leukocyte that surrounds identifiable antigens and destroys them. _____

3. Highly specific molecules that act as antibodies. They combine with antigens to neutralize them. _____

4. Lymphocytes that operate within the humoral part of the system and circulate in the blood and bodily fluids. _____

5. These are created so that when a specific antigen is encountered in the future, the immune response will be faster. _____

6. These T cells stop the production of antibodies by B cells when they are no longer needed. _____

Psychosocial Effects on Physical Disorders

> How is stress related to AIDS, cancer, and cardiovascular disease?
> What are the potential causes of acute and chronic pain, and how do the two types of pain differ?

With an enhanced understanding of the effects of emotional and behavioral factors on the immune system, we can now examine how these factors influence specific physical disorders. We begin with AIDS.

AIDS

The ravages of the AIDS epidemic have made this disease the highest priority of public health systems around the world. The number of people worldwide living with HIV continues to grow, reaching an estimated 33.4 million in 2008, which is 20% higher than in 2000 (UNAIDS, 2009). Only in 2004 did adult and child deaths begin to level off with aggressive treatment and prevention efforts in some parts of the world (Bongaarts & Over, 2010). Despite this modest success, 2.7 million new HIV infections occurred worldwide in 2008, and 2 million people died of AIDS (Grabbe & Bunnell, 2010; UNAIDS, 2009). An estimated 430,000 new infections occurred among children under the age of 15 in 2008, with most new infections stemming from transmission in utero, during delivery, or as a result of breast feeding (UNAIDS, 2009). In the hardest hit regions in southern Africa, between 20% and 40% of the adult population are believed to be HIV positive, comprising two thirds of cases worldwide, with approximately 18 million children orphaned by the disease (Klimas, Koneru, & Fletcher, 2008). AIDS is also spreading rapidly to the densely populated regions of India and China (Normile, 2009), and in Latin America, rates are projected to increase from 2 million in 2006 to 3.5 million by 2015 (Cohen, 2006).

Once a person is infected with HIV, the course of the disease is variable. After several months to several years with no symptoms, patients may develop minor health problems such as weight loss, fever, and night sweats, symptoms that make up the condition known as **AIDS-related complex (ARC)**. A diagnosis of AIDS itself is not made until one of several serious diseases appears, such as pneumocystis pneumonia, cancer, dementia, or a wasting syndrome in which the body literally withers away. The median time from initial infection to the development of full-blown AIDS has been estimated to range from 7.3 to

psychoneuroimmunology (PNI) Study of psychological influences on the neurological responding involved in the body's immune response.
AIDS-related complex (ARC) Group of minor health problems such as weight loss, fever, and night sweats that appears after HIV infection but before development of full-blown AIDS.

10 years or more (Pantaleo, Graziosi, & Fauci, 1993). Clinical scientists have developed powerful new combinations of drugs referred to as highly active antiretroviral therapy (HAART) that suppress the virus in those infected with HIV, even in advanced cases (Hammer et al., 2006; Thompson et al., 2010). This has been a very positive development that has slowed disease progression and decreased mortality. For example, most people with AIDS die within 1 year of diagnosis without treatment, as is the case in many developing countries (Zwahlen & Egger, 2006). But the proportion of people who receive treatment surviving with AIDS 2 years or longer increased to 85% by 2005, and the death rate from AIDS declined 80% since 1990 (Knoll, Lassmann & Temesgen, 2007).

Nevertheless, HAART does not seem to be a cure because the most recent evidence suggests the virus is seldom eliminated but rather lies dormant in reduced numbers; thus, infected patients face a lifetime of taking multiple medications (Buscher & Giordano, 2010; Cohen, 2002; Hammer et al., 2006). Also, the percentage who stop using HAART because of severe side effects, such as nausea and diarrhea, is high—61% in one study (O'Brien, Clark, Besch, Myers, & Kissinger, 2003). For this reason, earlier recommendations were to postpone treatment until those infected are in imminent danger of developing symptomatic disease (Cohen, 2002; Hammer et al., 2006), but in view of the success of this treatment regimen with cases of newly acquired HIV, current recommendations are to start as early as possible after detecting infection and to work closely with patients to increase adherence to the schedule for the medication (Thompson et al., 2010). Unfortunately, drug-resistant strains of HIV are now being transmitted.

Because AIDS is a relatively new disease and takes at least several years to develop, we are still learning about the factors, including possible psychological factors, that extend survival (Klimas et al., 2008; Taylor, 2009). Investigators identified a group of people who have been exposed repeatedly to the AIDS virus but have not contracted the disease. A major distinction of these people is that their immune systems, particularly the cellular branch, are robust and strong (Ezzel, 1993), most likely because of genetic factors (Kaiser, 2006). Therefore, efforts to boost the immune system may contribute to the prevention of AIDS.

Because psychological factors affect immune system functioning, investigators have begun to examine whether these psychological factors influence the progression of HIV. For example, high levels of stress and depression and low levels of social support have been associated with a faster progression to disease (Leserman, 2008; Leserman et al., 2000). But an even more intriguing question is whether psychological interventions can slow the progression of the disease, even among those who are symptomatic (Cole, 2008; Gore-Felton & Koopman, 2008). In fact, several important studies suggest that cognitive-behavioral stress-management (CBSM) programs may have positive effects on the immune systems of individuals who are already symptomatic (Antoni et al., 2000; Carrico & Antoni, 2008; Lutgendorf et al., 1997). Specifically, Lutgendorf and colleagues (1997) used an intervention program that significantly decreased depression and

anxiety compared to a control group that did not receive the treatment. More important, there was a significant reduction in antibodies to the herpes simplex virus II in the treatment group compared to the control group, which reflects the greater ability of the cellular component of the immune system to control the virus.

In a study by Antoni and colleagues (2000), 73 gay or bisexual men already infected with HIV and symptomatic with the disease were assigned to a CBSM program or a control group receiving usual care without the program. As in previous studies, men receiving the stress-management treatment showed significantly lower posttreatment levels of anxiety, anger, and perceived stress than those in the control group, indicating the treatment was effective. More important, as long as a year after the intervention had ended, men who had received the treatment evidenced better immune system functioning as indicated by higher levels of T cells.

Similarly, Goodkin and colleagues (2001) reported that a 10-week psychological treatment significantly buffered against an increase in HIV viral load, which is a powerful and reliable predictor of progression to full-blown AIDS, when compared to a control group. Antoni and colleagues (2006) took their important line of research a step further. HIV-positive men on HAART drug regimens received 10 weeks of training in how to take their medication properly by taking the exact amount prescribed as closely as possible to the assigned times. Half of this group also received the investigators' CBSM program. Men receiving CBSM actually showed a decrease in viral load 15 months later compared to those with medication training only, who showed no change. This reduction in viral load was primarily the result of decreases in depression, which, in turn, reduced the stress hormone cortisol. Thus, even in progressed, symptomatic HIV disease, psychological interventions may not only enhance psychological adjustment, but also influence immune system functioning, and this effect may be long lasting.

It is too early to tell whether these results will be strong or persistent enough to translate into increased survival time for AIDS patients, although results from Antoni and colleagues (2000, 2006) suggest they might. If stress and related variables *are* clinically significant to immune response, functioning, and disease progression in HIV-infected patients, as suggested by a number of studies (Cole, 2008; Leserman, 2008), then psychosocial interventions to bolster the immune system might increase survival rates and, in the most optimistic scenario, prevent the slow deterioration of the immune system (Carrico & Antoni, 2008; Kennedy, 2000). Of course, the most effective interventions focus on changing behavior to prevent acquiring HIV in the first place, such as reducing risky behavior and promoting safe sexual practices (Temoshok, Wald, Synowki, & Garzino-Demo, 2008).

Cancer

Among the more mind-boggling developments in the study of illness and disease is the discovery that the development and course of different varieties of **cancer** are subject to psychosocial influences (Emery, Anderson, & Andersen, 2011;

Williams & Schneiderman, 2002). This has resulted in a new field of study called **psycho-oncology** (Andersen, 1992; Antoni & Lutgendorf, 2007; Helgeson, 2005; Lutgendorf, Costanzo, & Siegel, 2007). *Oncology* means the study of cancer. In a widely noted study, David Spiegel, a psychiatrist at Stanford University, and his colleagues (Spiegel, Bloom, Kramer, & Gotheil, 1989) studied 86 women with advanced breast cancer that had metastasized to other areas of their bodies and was expected to kill them within 2 years. Clearly, the prognosis was poor indeed. Although Spiegel and his colleagues had little hope of affecting the disease itself, they thought that by treating these people in group psychotherapy at least they could relieve some of their anxiety, depression, and pain.

All patients had routine medical care for their cancer. In addition, 50 patients (of the 86) met with their therapist for psychotherapy once a week in small groups. Much to everyone's surprise, including Spiegel's, the therapy group's survival time was significantly longer than that of the control group who did not receive psychotherapy but otherwise benefited from the best care available. The group receiving therapy lived twice as long on average (approximately 3 years) as the controls (approximately 18 months). Four years after the study began, one third of the therapy patients were still alive and all the patients receiving the best medical care available *without* therapy had died. Subsequently, a careful reanalysis of medical treatment received by each group revealed no differences that could account for the effects of psychological treatment (Kogon, Biswas, Pearl, Carlson, & Spiegel, 1997). These findings do not mean that psychological interventions cured advanced cancer. At 10 years, only three patients in the therapy group still survived.

Subsequent studies seemed to support these findings on increased survival and reduced recurrence with different types of cancer (Fawzy, Cousins, et al., 1990; Fawzy, Kemeny, et al., 1990). But other studies did not replicate the finding that psychological treatments prolong life (Coyne, Stefanek, & Palmer, 2007). One such study confirmed that psychological treatments reduced depression and pain and increased well-being, but did not find the survival-enhancing effects of treatment (Goodwin et al., 2001).

However, recently in an important study, Andersen et al. (2008) randomly assigned 227 patients who had been surgically treated for breast cancer to a psychological intervention plus assessment, or to an assessment-only condition. The intervention included strategies to reduce stress, improve mood, alter important health behaviors (reducing smoking, increasing exercise, etc.), and maintain adherence to cancer treatment and care. The treatment was successful in reducing stress and increasing positive mood and healthy behavior (Andersen et al., 2007). More important, after a median of 11 years follow-up, patients receiving the psychological intervention reduced their risk of dying by breast cancer by 56% and their risk of breast cancer recurrence by 45%, supporting once again the survival-enhancing potential of psychological treatments.

As a result of these studies, psychosocial treatment for various cancers to reduce stress, improve quality of life, and perhaps even to increase survival and reduce recurrence are now more readily available (Manne & Ostroff, 2008; Penedo, Antoni, & Schneiderman, 2008). The initial success of these psychological treatments on length of survival in at least some studies generated a great deal of interest in exactly

Abnormal Psychology Inside Out. Produced by Ira Wohl, Only Child Motion Pictures

Breast Cancer Support and Education

Women who had low self-esteem, low body image, feelings of low control, low optimism, and a lack of support at home were even more likely to benefit from an education intervention.

Go to Psychology CourseMate at www.cengagebrain.com to watch this video.

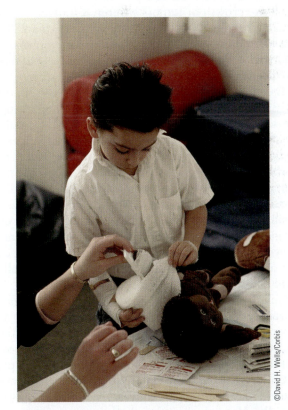
©David H. Wells/Corbis

▲ Psychological preparation reduces suffering and facilitates recovery in children who undergo surgery.

cancer Category of often-fatal medical conditions involving abnormal cell growth and malignancy.
psycho-oncology Study of psychological factors involved in the course and treatment of cancer.

how they might work, if they do work (Antoni et al., 2009; Antoni & Lutgendorf, 2007; Emery et al., 2011; Helgeson, 2005). Possibilities include better health habits, closer adherence to medical treatment, and improved endocrine functioning and response to stress, all of which may improve immune function (Antoni et al., 2006, 2009; Classen, Diamond, & Spiegel, 1998; Emery et al., 2011; Foley, Baillie, Huxter, Price, & Sinclair, 2010; Nezu et al., 1999).

Anything that promotes closer, more supportive relationships in cancer patients also is very important because it slows disease progression (Antoni et al., 2006; Foley, Baillie, Huxter, Price, & Sinclair, 2010; Nezu, et al., 1999; Weighs, Enright, & Simmens, 2008). There is even preliminary evidence that psychological factors may contribute not only to the *course* but also to the *development* of cancer and other diseases (Antoni & Lutgendorf, 2007; Lutgendorf et al., 2007). Perceived lack of control, inadequate coping responses, overwhelmingly stressful life events, or the use of inappropriate coping responses (such as denial) may all contribute to the development of cancer, probably through changes in immune function, but also through regulating the activity of cancer-causing viruses, deoxyribonucleic acid (DNA) repair processes, and the expression of genes that control the growth of tumors (Antoni & Lutgendorf, 2007; Lutgendorf et al., 2007; Williams & Schneiderman, 2002).

These studies have also led to a renewed emphasis on an overlooked result of cancer—that is, some people discover some positive consequences. For example, many patients with breast cancer experience an enhanced sense of purpose, deepening spirituality, closer ties to others, and changes in life priorities (Lechner & Antoni, 2004; Park, Edmondson, Fenster, & Blank, 2008; Yanez et al., 2009). These experiences have been called "benefit finding" and may reflect the types of traits, such as coping skills, a sense of control, and optimism, that underlie resiliency and reduce the harmful effect of stress (Bower, Moskowitz, & Epel, 2009). It is these traits and skills that are among the most important goals of psychological treatment. Antoni and colleagues (2006) targeted these goals in 199 women with nonmetastatic breast cancer using a CBSM program, and they found substantially improved quality of life in the year following treatment.

Psychological factors are also prominent in treatment and recovery from cancer in children (Koocher, 1996). Many types of cancer require invasive and painful medical procedures; the suffering can be difficult to bear, not only for children, but also for parents and health-care providers. Children usually struggle and cry hysterically, so to complete many of the procedures, they must be physically restrained. Not only does their behavior interfere with successful completion, but also the stress and anxiety associated with repeated painful procedures may have their own detrimental effect on the disease process. Psychological procedures designed to reduce pain and stress in these children include breathing exercises, watching films of exactly what happens to take the uncertainty out of the procedure, and rehearsal of the procedure with dolls, all of which make the interventions more tolerable and therefore more successful for young patients (Brewer, Gleditsch,

Syblik, Tietjens, & Vacik, 2006; Hubert, Jay, Saltoun, & Hayes, 1988; Jay, Elliott, Ozolins, Olson, & Pruitt, 1985). Much of this work is based on the pioneering efforts of Barbara Melamed and her colleagues, who demonstrated the importance of incorporating psychological procedures into children's medical care, particularly children about to undergo surgery (see, for example, Melamed & Siegel, 1975). In any case, pediatric psychologists are making more routine use of these procedures.

Reducing stress in parents who could then provide more supportive care is important because almost all parents develop posttraumatic stress symptoms after hearing that their children have cancer (Kazak, Boeving, Alderfer, Hwang, & Reilly, 2005). Sahler and colleagues (2005) treated mothers of children with newly diagnosed cancer with a cognitive-behavioral problem-solving intervention and compared the results to the usual care available to these mothers. Mothers in the problem-solving group became less negative, less stressed, and better problem solvers, certainly a positive outcome in parents who have to deal with the tragedy of cancer in their own children.

Cardiovascular Problems

The *cardiovascular system* comprises the heart, blood vessels, and complex control mechanisms for regulating their function. Many things can go wrong with this system and lead to **cardiovascular disease**. For example, many individuals, particularly older individuals, suffer **strokes**, also called **cerebral vascular accidents (CVAs)**, which are temporary blockages of blood vessels leading to the brain or a rupture of blood vessels in the brain that results in temporary or permanent brain damage and loss of functioning. People with Raynaud's disease lose circulation to peripheral parts of their bodies such as their fingers and toes, suffering some pain and continual sensations of cold in their hands and feet. The cardiovascular problems receiving the most attention these days are hypertension and coronary heart disease, and we look at both. First, let's consider the case of John.

John ‖ The Human Volcano

John is a 55-year-old business executive who is married with two teenage children. For most of his adult life, John has smoked about a pack of cigarettes each day. Although he maintains a busy and active schedule, John is mildly obese, partly from regular meals with business partners and colleagues. He has been taking several medications for high blood pressure since age 42. John's doctor has warned him repeatedly to cut down on his smoking and to exercise more often, especially because John's father died of a heart attack. Although John has episodes of chest pain, he continues his busy and stressful lifestyle. It is difficult for John to slow down because his business has been doing extremely well during the past 10 years.

There is a great deal of evidence on the value of stress-reduction procedures in preventing future heart attacks (Emery et al., 2011; Williams & Schneiderman, 2002). In one report summarizing results from 37 studies and using analytic procedures that combine the results from these studies (meta-analysis), the effects of stress-reduction programs on CHD were apparent. Specifically, as a group, these studies yielded a 34% reduction in death from heart attacks; a 29% reduction in the recurrence of heart attacks; and a significant positive effect on blood pressure, cholesterol levels, body weight, and other risk factors for CHD (Dusseldorp, van Elderen, Maes, Meulman, & Kraaij, 1999). Another major clinical study confirmed the benefits of stress reduction and exercise in reducing emotional distress and improving heart function and risk for future attacks in a group of individuals with established heart disease (Blumenthal et al., 2005). This brings us to an important question: Can we identify, before an attack, people who are under a great deal of stress that might make them susceptible to a first heart attack? The answer seems to be yes, but the answer is more complex than we first thought.

Clinical investigators reported several decades ago that certain groups of people engage in a cluster of behaviors in stressful situations that seem to put them at considerable risk for CHD. These behaviors include excessive competitive drive, a sense of always being pressured for time, impatience, incredible amounts of energy that may show up in accelerated speech and motor activity, and angry outbursts. This set of behaviors, which came to be called the **type A behavior pattern**, was first identified by two cardiologists, Meyer Friedman and Ray Rosenman (1959, 1974). The **type B behavior pattern**, also described by these clinicians, applies to people who basically do not have type A attributes. In other words, the type B individual is more relaxed, less concerned about deadlines, and seldom feels the pressure or perhaps the excitement of challenges or overriding ambition.

The concept of the type A personality or behavior pattern is widely accepted in our hard-driving, goal-oriented culture. Indeed, some early studies supported the concept of type A behavior as putting people at risk for CHD (Friedman & Rosenman, 1974). But the most convincing evidence came from two large prospective studies that followed thousands of patients over a long period to determine the relationship of their behavior to heart disease. The first study was the Western Collaborative Group Study (WCGS). In this project, 3,154 healthy men, age 39 to 59, were interviewed at the beginning of the study to determine their typical behavioral patterns. They were then followed for 8 years. The basic finding was that the men who displayed a type A behavior pattern at the beginning of the study were at least twice as likely to develop CHD as the men with a type B behavior pattern. When the investigators analyzed the data for the younger men in the study (age 39 to 49), the results were even more striking, with CHD developing approximately 6 times more often in the type A group than in the type B group (Rosenman et al., 1975).

A second major study is the Framingham Heart Study that has been ongoing for more than 40 years (Haynes, Feinleib, & Kannel, 1980) and has taught us much of what we know about the development and course of CHD. In this study, 1,674 healthy men and women were categorized by a type A or type B behavior pattern and followed for 8 years. Again, both men and women with a type A pattern were more than twice as likely to develop CHD as their type B counterparts (in men, the risk was nearly 3 times as great). For women with type A behavior pattern, the likelihood of developing CHD was highest for those with a low level of education (Eaker, Pinsky, & Castelli, 1992).

Population-based studies in Europe essentially replicated these results (De Backer, Kittel, Kornitzer, & Dramaix, 1983; French-Belgian Collaborative Group, 1982). It is interesting that a large study of Japanese men conducted in Hawaii did *not* replicate these findings (Cohen & Reed, 1985). The prevalence of type A behavior among Japanese men is much lower than among men in the United States (18.7% versus approximately 50%). Similarly, the prevalence of CHD is equally low in Japanese men (4%, compared to 13% in American men in the Framingham study) (Haynes & Matthews, 1988). In a study that illustrates the effects of culture more dramatically, 3,809 Japanese Americans were classified into groups according to how "traditionally Japanese" they were (in other words, they spoke Japanese at home, retained traditional Japanese values and behaviors, and so on). Japanese Americans who were the "most Japanese" had the lowest incidence of CHD, not significantly different from Japanese men in Japan. In contrast, the group that was the "least Japanese" had a 3 to 5 times greater incidence of CHD levels (Marmot & Syme, 1976; Matsumoto, 1996). Clearly, sociocultural differences are important.

Despite these straightforward results, at least in Western cultures, the type A concept has proved more complex and elusive than scientists had hoped. First, it is difficult to determine whether someone is type A from structured interviews, questionnaires, or other measures of this construct, because the measures often do not agree with one another. Many people have *some* characteristics of type A but not all of them, and others present with a mixture of types A and B. The notion that we can divide the world into two types of people—an assumption underlying the early work in this area—has long since been discarded. As a result, subsequent studies did not necessarily support the relationship of type A behavior to CHD (Dembroski & Costa, 1987; Hollis, Connett, Stevens, & Greenlick, 1990).

coronary heart disease (CHD) Blockage of the arteries supplying blood to the heart muscle; a major cause of death in Western culture, with social and psychological factors involved.

type A behavior pattern Cluster of behaviors including excessive competitiveness, time-pressured impatience, accelerated speech, and anger, originally thought to promote high risk for heart disease.

type B behavior pattern Cluster of behaviors including a relaxed attitude, indifference to time pressure, and less forceful ambition; originally thought to promote low risk for heart disease.

The Role of Chronic Negative Emotions

At this point, investigators decided that something might be wrong with the type A construct itself (Matthews, 1988; Rodin & Salovey, 1989). A consensus developed that some—but not all—behaviors and emotions representative of the type A personality might be important in the development of CHD. One factor that seems to be responsible for much of the type A–CHD relationship is anger (Miller et al., 1996), which will come as no surprise if you read the Ironson study in Chapter 2 and the previous section on hypertension. As you may remember, Ironson and colleagues (1992) compared increased heart rate when they instructed individuals with heart disease to imagine situations or events in their own lives that made them angry with heart rates when they imagined other situations, such as exercise. They found that anger impaired the pumping efficiency of the heart, putting these individuals at risk for dangerous disturbances in heart rhythm (arrhythmias). This study confirms earlier findings relating the frequent experience of anger to later CHD (Dembroski, MacDougall, Costa, & Grandits, 1989; Houston, Chesney, Black, Cates, & Hecker, 1992; Smith, 1992). Results from an important study strengthen this conclusion. Iribarren and colleagues (2000) evaluated 374 young, healthy adults, both white and African American, over a period of 10 years. Those with high hostility and anger showed evidence of coronary artery calcification, an early sign of CHD.

Is type A irrelevant to the development of heart disease? Most investigators conclude that some components of the type A construct are important determinants of CHD, particularly a chronically high level of negative affect (such as anger) and the time urgency or impatience factor (Matthews, 2005; Thoresen & Powell, 1992; Williams, Barefoot, & Schneiderman, 2003; Winters & Schneiderman, 2000). Recall again the case of John, who had all the type A behaviors, including time urgency, but also had frequent angry outbursts. But what about people who experience closely related varieties of negative affect on a chronic basis? Look back to Figure 7.2 and notice the close relationship among stress, anxiety, and depression. Some evidence indicates that the physiological components of these emotions and their effects on the cardiovascular system may be identical or at least similar (Suls & Bunde, 2005). We also know that the emotion of anger, so commonly associated with stress, is closely related to the emotion of fear, as evidenced in flight or fight response. Fight is the typical behavioral action tendency associated with anger, and flight or escape is associated with fear. But our bodily alarm response, activated by an immediate danger or threat, is associated with both emotions.

Some investigators, after reviewing the literature, have concluded that anxiety and depression are as important as anger in the development of CHD (Albert, Chae, Rexrode, Manson, & Kawachi, 2005; Barlow, 1988; Frasure-Smith & Lesperance, 2005; Strike & Steptoe, 2005; Suls & Bunde, 2005), even anxious and depressive features noticeable at an early age (Grossardt, Bower, Geda, Colligan, & Rocca, 2009). In a study of 896 people who had suffered heart attacks, Frasure-Smith and colleagues (Frasure-Smith, Les-

perance, Juneau, Talajic, & Bourassa, 1999) found that patients who were depressed were 3 times more likely to die in the year following their heart attacks than those who were not depressed, regardless of how severe their initial heart disease was. In a study of 1,017 patients with CHD, Whooley and colleagues (2008) found a 31% higher rate of cardiovascular events such as heart attacks or arrhythmias in patients with depressive symptoms compared to those without depressive symptoms. Severe depression, as in major depressive episodes, is particularly implicated in cardiovascular damage (Agatisa et al., 2005; Emery et al., 2011). Thus, it may be that the chronic experience of the negative emotions of stress (anger), anxiety (fear), and depression (ongoing) and the neurobiological activation that accompanies these emotions provide the most important psychosocial contributions to CHD, and perhaps to other physical disorders.

Investigators are also learning more about the process through which negative emotions contribute to CHD. Once again, the inflammatory processes associated with the stress response (and with all negative emotions) play a major role because inflammation directly contributes to atherosclerosis and heart failure (Matthews et al., 2007; Taylor, 2009). Gallo and Matthews (2003; Matthews, 2005) provide a model of the contribution of psychosocial factors to CHD (see ■ Figure 7.5). Lower socioeconomic status and relatively few resources or low prestige is in the first box. Stressful life events are in the second. Coping skills and social support contribute to a reserve capacity that may buffer the effects of stress, as represented in the third box. Both negative emotions and negative cognitive styles then constitute a major risk factor. Positive emotions and an optimistic style, on the other hand, reduce the risk of CHD (Giltay, Geleijnse, Zitman, Hoekstra, & Schouten, 2004) and may turn out to be just as important as negative emotions in their effects on CHD. Both negative and positive emotions are in the fourth box. This model summarizes nicely what we know about the influence of psychosocial factors on CHD.

Chronic Pain

Pain is not in itself a disorder, yet for most of us it is the fundamental signal of injury, illness, or disease. If we can't relieve the pain ourselves or we are not sure of its cause, we usually seek medical help. The National Institutes of Health has identified chronic pain as the costliest medical problem in America, affecting nearly 100 million individuals (Byrne & Hochwarter, 2006; Otis & Pincus, 2008). Overall the total cost of chronic pain, including treatments and indirect costs such as loss of productivity at work, have been estimated between $100 billion and $260 billion annually (Byrne & Hochwarter, 2006; Edwards, Campbell, Jamison, & Wiech, 2009). Americans spend at least $125 billion annually on treatment for chronic pain, including over-the-counter medication to reduce temporary pain from headaches, colds, and other minor disorders (Gatchel, 2005; Taylor, 2009). Pain is the cause of 80% of all visits to physicians (Gatchel, Peng, Peters, Fuchs, & Turk, 2007;

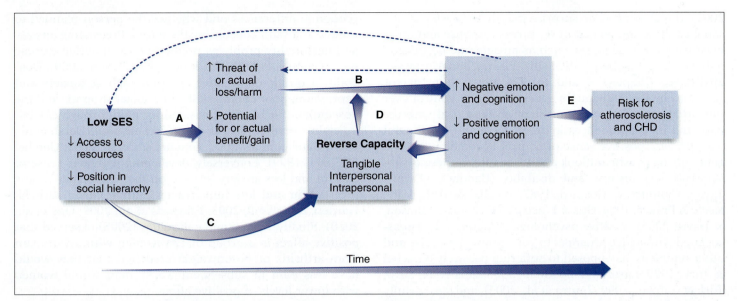

■ **Figure 7.5** The reserve capacity model for associations among environments of low socioeconomic status (SES), stressful experiences, psychosocial resources, and emotions and cognitions, which represent pathways to increased risk for CHD. Note: Arrow A depicts the direct influence of SES on exposure to stressful experiences. Arrow B indicates the direct impact of stress experiences on emotion and cognition. Arrow C shows that SES conditions and shapes the bank of resources (that is, the reserve capacity) available to manage stress. Arrow D shows that reserve capacity represents a potential moderator of the association between stress and emotional–cognitive factors. Arrow E indicates the direct effects of emotional–cognitive factors on intermediate pathways and risk for atherosclerosis and CHD. The dashed lines note the possible reverse influences. (Adapted from Gallo, L. C., & Matthews, K. A. (2003). Understanding the association between socioeconomic status and physical health: Do negative emotions play a role?" *Psychological Bulletin, 129,* 34 (Figure 1), © 2003 American Psychological Association. Reprinted, with permission, from Matthews, K. A. (2005). Psychological perspectives on the development of coronary heart disease. *American Psychologist, 60*(8), 791 (Figure 2), © 2005 American Psychological Association.)

Turk & Gatchel, 2002), making it by far the most common reason to see a primary care physician (Otis, MacDonald, & Dobscha, 2006). Yet most researchers now agree that the cause of chronic pain and the resulting enormous drain on our health-care system *are substantially psychological and social* (Dersh, Polatin, & Gatchel, 2002; Gatchel et al., 2007; Taylor, 2009; Turk & Monarch, 2002).

There are two kinds of clinical pain: acute and chronic. **Acute pain** typically follows an injury and disappears once the injury heals or is effectively treated, often within a month. **Chronic pain**, by contrast, may begin with an acute episode but *does not decrease* over time, even when the injury has healed or effective treatments have been administered. Typically, chronic pain is in the muscles, joints, or tendons, particularly in the lower back. Vascular pain because of enlarged blood vessels may be chronic, as may headaches. Pain caused by the slow degeneration of tissue, as in some terminal diseases, and pain caused by the growth of cancerous tumors that impinge on pain receptors also may be chronic (Melzack & Wall, 1982; Otis & Pincus, 2008; Taylor, 2009).

To better understand the experience of pain, clinicians and researchers generally make a clear distinction between the subjective experience termed *pain*, reported by the patient, and the overt manifestations of this experience, termed *pain behaviors*. Pain behaviors include changing the way one sits or walks, continually complaining about pain to others, grimacing, and, most important, avoiding various activities, particularly those involving work or leisure. Finally, an

emotional component of pain called *suffering* sometimes accompanies pain and sometimes does not (Fordyce, 1988; Liebeskind, 1991). Because they are so important, we first review psychological and social contributions to pain.

Psychological and Social Aspects of Pain

In mild forms, chronic pain can be an annoyance that eventually wears you down and takes the pleasure out of your life. Severe chronic pain may cause you to lose your job, withdraw from your family, give up the fun in your life, and focus your entire awareness on seeking relief. What is interesting for our purposes is that the *severity* of the pain does not seem to predict the *reaction* to it. Some individuals experience intense pain frequently yet continue to work productively, rarely seek medical services, and lead reasonably normal lives; others become invalids. These differences appear to be primarily the result of psychological factors (Dersh et al., 2002; Gatchel, 2005; Gatchel & Turk, 1999; Keefe, Dunsmore, & Burnett, 1992; Turk & Monarch,

acute pain Pain that typically follows an injury and disappears once the injury heals or is effectively treated.
chronic pain Enduring pain that does not decrease over time; may occur in muscles, joints, and the lower back; and may be caused by enlarged blood vessels or degenerating or cancerous tissue. Other significant factors are social and psychological.

2002). It will come as no surprise that these factors are the same as those implicated in the stress response and other negative emotional states, such as anxiety and depression (Ohayon & Schatzberg, 2003; Otis, Pincus, and Murawski, 2010) (see Chapters 4 and 6). The determining factor seems to be the individual's general sense of control over the situation: whether or not he or she can deal with the pain and its consequences in an effective and meaningful way. When a positive sense of control is combined with a generally optimistic outlook about the future, there is substantially less distress and disability (Bandura, O'Leary, Taylor, Gauthier, & Gossard, 1987; Gatchel & Turk, 1999; Keefe & France, 1999; Otis & Pincus, 2008; Zautra, Johnson, & Davis, 2005). Positive psychological factors are also associated with active attempts to cope, such as exercise and other regimens, as opposed to suffering passively (Gatchel & Turk, 1999; Lazarus & Folkman, 1984; Otis et al., 2010; Turk & Gatchel, 1999; Zautra et al., 2005), and successfully treating depression diminishes the experience of chronic pain (Teh, Zaslavsky, Reyolds, & Cleary, 2009).

To take one example, Philips and Grant (1991) studied 117 patients who suffered from back and neck pain after an injury. Almost all were expected to recover quickly, but fully 40% of them still reported substantial pain at 6 months, thereby qualifying for "chronic pain" status. Of the 60% who reported no pain at the 6-month point, most had been pain free since approximately 1 month after the accident. Furthermore, Philips and Grant report that the relationship between the experience of pain and the subsequent disability was not as strongly related to the intensity of the pain as other factors, such as personality and socio-economic differences and whether the person planned to initiate a lawsuit concerning the injury. Preexisting anxiety and personality problems predict who will suffer chronic pain (Gatchel, Polatin, & Kinney, 1995; Taylor, 2009). Generally, a profile of negative emotion such as anxiety and depression, poor coping skills, low social support, and the possibility of being compensated for pain through disability claims predict most types of chronic pain (Dersh et al., 2002; Gatchel et al., 2007; Gatchel & Dersh, 2002; Gatchel & Epker, 1999). Conversely, developing a greater sense of control and less anxiety focused on the pain results in less severe pain and less impairment (Burns, Glenn, Bruehl, Harden, & Lofland, 2003; Edwards et al., 2009; Otis et al., 2010). Finally, Zautra and colleagues (2005) observed that positive affect in a group of 124 women with severe pain from arthritis or fibromyalgia predicted that they would have less pain in subsequent weeks than would women with lower levels of positive affect.

Examples of psychological influences on pain are encountered every day. Athletes with significant tissue damage often continue to perform and report relatively little pain. In an important study, 65% of war veterans wounded in combat reported feeling no pain when they were injured. Presumably, their attention was focused externally on what they had to do to survive rather than internally on the experience of pain (Melzack & Wall, 1982).

Social factors also influence how we experience pain (Fordyce, 1976, 1988). For example, family members who were formerly critical and demanding may become caring and sympathetic (Kerns, Rosenberg, & Otis, 2002; Otis & Pincus, 2008; Romano, Jensen, Turner, Good, & Hops, 2000).

▲ It is not uncommon for people to feel specific pain in limbs that are no longer part of them.

▲ Some people with chronic pain or disability cope extremely well and become high achievers.

This phenomenon is referred to as *operant* control of pain behavior because the behavior clearly seems under the control of social consequences. But these consequences have an uncertain relation to the amount of pain being experienced.

By contrast, a strong network of social support may reduce pain. Jamison and Virts (1990) studied 521 chronic pain patients (with back, abdominal, and chest conditions) and discovered that those who lacked social support from their families reported more pain sites and showed more pain behavior, such as staying in bed. These patients also exhibited more emotional distress *without* rating their pain as any more intense than participants with strong socially supportive families. The participants with strong support returned to work earlier, showed less reliance on medications, and increased their activity levels more quickly than the others. Even having just a photo of a loved one to look at reduces the experience of pain (Master et al., 2009).

Although these results may seem to contradict studies on the operant control of pain, different mechanisms may be at work. General social support may reduce the stress associated with pain and injury and promote more adaptive coping procedures and control. However, specifically reinforcing pain behaviors, particularly in the absence of social supports, may powerfully increase such behavior. These complex issues have not yet been entirely sorted out.

Biological Aspects of Pain

No one thinks pain is entirely psychological, just as no one thinks it is entirely physical. As with other disorders, we must consider how psychological and physical factors interact.

Mechanisms of Pain Experience and Pain Control. The *gate control theory of pain* (Melzack & Wall, 1965, 1982) accommodates both psychological and physical factors. According to this theory, nerve impulses from painful stimuli make their way to the spinal column and from there to the brain. An area called the *dorsal horns of the spinal column* acts as a "gate" and may open and transmit sensations of pain if the stimulation is sufficiently intense. Specific nerve fibers referred to as *small fibers* (A-delta and C fibers) and *large fibers* (A-beta fibers) determine the pattern, and the intensity, of the stimulation. Small fibers tend to open the gate, thereby increasing the transmission of painful stimuli, whereas large fibers tend to close the gate.

Most important for our purpose is that the brain sends signals back down the spinal cord that may affect the gating mechanism. For example, a person with negative emotions such as fear or anxiety may experience pain more intensely because the basic message from the brain is to be vigilant against possible danger or threat. Then again, in a person whose emotions are more positive or who is absorbed in an activity (such as a runner intent on finishing a long race), the brain sends down an inhibitory signal that closes the gate. Although many think that the gate control theory is overly simplistic (and it has recently been updated; see Melzack, 1999, 2005), research findings continue to support its basic elements, particularly as it describes the complex interaction of psychological and biological factors in the experience of pain (Edwards et al., 2009; Gatchel et al., 2007; Gatchel & Turk, 1999; Otis & Pincus, 2008; Turk & Monarch, 2002).

Endogenous Opioids. The neurochemical means by which the brain inhibits pain is an important discovery (Taylor, 2009). Drugs such as heroin and morphine are manufactured from opioid substances. It now turns out that **endogenous** (natural) **opioids** exist within the body. Called *endorphins* or *enkephalins,* they act much like neurotransmitters. The brain uses them to shut down pain, even in the presence of marked tissue damage or injury. Because endogenous opioids are distributed widely throughout the body, they may be implicated in a variety of psychopathological conditions, including eating disorders and, more commonly, the "runner's high" that accompanies the release of endogenous opioids after intense (and sometimes painful) physical activity. Bandura and colleagues (1987) found that people with a greater sense of self-efficacy and control had a higher tolerance for pain than individuals with low self-efficacy and that they increased their production of endogenous opioids when they were confronted with a painful stimulus. Most recently, Edwards et al. (2009) have articulated the neurobiological processes underlying the effectiveness of psychological coping procedures that successfully alter the experience of pain. Certain procedures, such as reappraising the significance of the pain instead of catastrophizing or thinking the worst about it, activate a variety of brain circuits that modulate or diminish pain experience and allow for more normal functioning.

Gender Differences in Pain

Men and women seem to experience different types of pain. On the one hand, in addition to menstrual cramps and labor pains, women suffer more often than men from migraine headaches, arthritis, carpal tunnel syndrome, and temporomandibular joint (TMJ) pain in the jaw (Lipchik, Holroyd, & Nash, 2002; Miaskowski, 1999). Men, on the other hand, have more cardiac pain and backache. Both males and females have endogenous opioid systems, although in males it may be more powerful. But women seem to have additional pain-regulating mechanisms that may be different. The female neurochemistry may be based on an estrogen-dependent neuronal system that may have evolved to cope with the pain associated with reproductive activity (Mogil, Sternberg, Kest, Marek, & Liebeskind, 1993). It is an "extra" pain-regulating pathway in females that, if taken away by removing hormones, has no implications for the remaining pathways, which continue to work. One implica-

endogenous opioids Substance occurring naturally throughout the body that functions like a neurotransmitter to shut down pain sensation even in the presence of marked tissue damage. These opioids may contribute to psychological problems such as eating disorders. Also known as an *endorphin* or *enkephalin.*

tion of this finding is that males and females may benefit from different kinds of drugs, different kinds of psychological interventions, or unique combinations of these treatments to best manage and control pain.

Chronic Fatigue Syndrome

Chronic fatigue syndrome (CFS) is prevalent throughout the Western world (Jason, Fennell, & Taylor, 2006; Prins, van der Meer, & Bleijenberg, 2006). The symptoms of CFS, listed in Table 7.2, have been attributed to various causes including viral infection—specifically the Epstein-Barr virus (Straus et al., 1985) or, most recently, XMRV, a retrovirus with some similarities to HIV (Kean, 2010)—and immune system dysfunction (Strauss, 1988), exposure to toxins, or clinical depression (Chalder, Cleare, & Wessely, 2000; Costa e Silva & De Girolamo, 1990). Although promising leads appear on occasion, no evidence has yet to support any of these hypothetical physical causes (Chalder et al., 2000; Jason et al., 2003; Kean, 2010; Prins et al., 2006). Jason and colleagues (1999) conducted a sophisticated study of the prevalence of CFS in the community and reported that 0.4% of their sample was determined to have CFS, with higher rates in Latino and African American respondents com-

Table 7.2 Definition of Chronic Fatigue Syndrome

Inclusion Criteria
1. Clinically evaluated, medically unexplained fatigue of at least 6 months duration that is
   - of new onset (not lifelong)
   - not resulting from ongoing exertion
   - not substantially alleviated by rest
   - a substantial reduction in previous level of activities
2. The occurrence of four or more of the following symptoms:
   - Subjective memory impairment
   - Sore throat
   - Tender lymph nodes
   - Muscle pain
   - Joint pain
   - Headache
   - Unrefreshing sleep
   - Postexertional malaise lasting more than 24 hours

Source: Adapted from Fukuda, K., Straus, S. E., Hickie, I., Sharpe, M. B., Dobbins, J. G., & Komaroff, A. L. (1994). Chronic fatigue syndrome: A comprehensive approach to its diagnosis and management. *Annals of Internal Medicine, 121,* 953–959.

Discussing Diversity — The Influence of Culture on Individual Health and Development: Female Reproduction around the World

The study of Psychology and the many different mental states and possible disorders experienced by individuals requires a high degree of sensitivity to the fact that people are inexorably intertwined with the cultural values and experiences in which they are raised. A fascinating example of varying cultural influences, and the psychological and physical effects of such experiences, can be seen through an examination of female reproduction around the world. It turns out that even this most basic of aspect of human biology is heavily influenced by cultural, environmental, and resulting psychological components. Women's ability to reproduce begins during a process called menarche, which refers to a girl's first menstrual bleeding that signals the beginning of fertility. Women generally are able to reproduce throughout adulthood until they reach menopause, which refers to the cessation of the menstrual cycle and signals the end of fertility. Although all women experience the events of menarche and menopause, the experience can be quite different de-

pending on the cultural, environmental, and resulting psychological context in which these processes occur.

The timing of menarche can be influenced by cultural and environmental factors. For instance, differences in nutrition during the past several decades may have contributed to an earlier age of menarche, and such differences may help explain differences in the age of onset of menarche seen in different parts of the world (Euling et al., 2008). In addition, girls in more stressful home environments and in father-absent homes experience menarche earlier, perhaps because from an evolutionary perspective these events signal the need to leave the home and start one's own family (Weisfeld & Woodward, 2004).

There also are significant cross-cultural differences in the psychological and social experience of menopause, with some cultures celebrating each transition and others considering these issues taboo or cause for shame. For instance, in some cultures the loss of the ability to repro-

duce may be associated with diminished health or social standing (such as in Italy), whereas in other cultures (such as in China and India) menopause confers a higher and more prestigious place in society (Fu, Anderson & Courtney, 2003; Gifford, 1994). Interestingly, these different perceptions of menopause not only influence how different cultures react to menopausal women but also can affect the occurrence of menopausal symptoms, with those for whom menopause is seen as a positive life transition experiencing fewer or no negative symptoms (Fu et al., 2003). All of these findings point out how sensitive clinicians must be to the various cultural differences clients bring with them to therapy and how culture might influence how clients experience and describe their current problems (e.g., Ryder et al., 2008). Can you think of some ways in which disorders such as Major Depression and Bipolar may be influenced by culture and experienced and expressed differently by those with different backgrounds?

pared to whites. CFS occurs in up to 3% of patients in a primary care clinic, predominantly in women, and usually begins in early adulthood (Afari & Buchwald, 2003), but it can occur in children as young as 7 years (Sankey, Hill, Brown, Quinn, & Fletcher, 2006). A study of 4,591 twins yielded a 2.7% prevalence rate (Furberg et al., 2005), and a prospective study of a larger birth cohort revealed that by age 53, 1.1% reported a diagnosis of CFS (Harvey, Wadsworth, Wessely, & Hotopf, 2008). To get a better idea of prevalence, large-scale population studies need to be done.

People with CFS suffer considerably and often must give up their careers because the disorder runs a chronic course (Taylor et al., 2003). In a group of 100 patients followed for 18 months, chronic fatigue symptoms did not decrease significantly in fully 79% of cases. Better mental health to begin with, and less use of sedating medications and a more "psychological" as opposed to medical attribution for causes, led to better outcomes (Schmaling, Fiedelak, Katon, Bader, & Buchwald, 2003). Fortunately, CFS patients do not seem to be at risk for increased mortality (death) through disease or suicide compared to the general population (Smith, Noonan, & Buchwald, 2006). As Abbey and Garfinkel (1991) and Sharpe (1997) point out, both neurasthenia in the 19th century and CFS in the 20th century through the present have been attributed to an extremely stressful environment, the changing role of women, and the rapid dissemination of new technology and information. Both disorders are most common in women. It is possible that a virus or a specific immune system dysfunction will be found to account for CFS. Another possibility suggested by Abbey and Garfinkel (1991) is that the condition represents a rather nonspecific response to stress, and Heim and colleagues (2006) found a higher level of adverse early stressful events in people with CFS compared to nonfatigued controls, reminiscent of Sapolsky's monkeys (discussed earlier in the chapter). Furthermore, a recent large study looking at personality factors that may contribute to CFS found preexisting stress and emotional instability to be important factors (Kato, Sullivan, Evengard, & Pederson, 2006). But it is not clear why certain individuals respond with chronic fatigue instead of some other psychological or physical disorder.

Michael Sharpe (1997) has developed one of the first models of the causes of CFS that accounts for all of its features (■ Figure 7.6). Sharpe theorizes that individuals with particularly achievement-oriented lifestyles (driven, perhaps, by a basic sense of inadequacy) undergo a period of extreme stress or acute illness. They misinterpret the lingering symptoms of fatigue, pain, and inability to function at their usual high levels as a continuing disease that is worsened by activity and improved by rest. This results in behavioral avoidance, helplessness, depression, and frustration. They think they should be able to conquer the problem and cope with its symptoms. Chronic inactivity leads to lack of stamina, weakness, and increased feelings of depression and helplessness that in turn result in episodic bursts of long activity followed by further fatigue. Certainly genetic factors probably influence the impact of

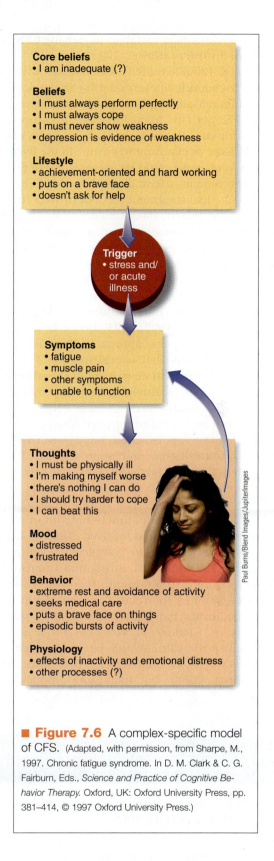

■ **Figure 7.6** A complex-specific model of CFS. (Adapted, with permission, from Sharpe, M., 1997. Chronic fatigue syndrome. In D. M. Clark & C. G. Fairburn, Eds., *Science and Practice of Cognitive Behavior Therapy.* Oxford, UK: Oxford University Press, pp. 381–414, © 1997 Oxford University Press.)

chronic fatigue syndrome (CFS) Incapacitating exhaustion following only minimal exertion, accompanied by fever, headaches, muscle and joint pain, depression, and anxiety.

stress and psychological variables in causing CFS, as is the case with all disorders (Kaiser, 2006).

Harvey et al. (2008) studied 34 individuals with CFS and found very high levels of exercise prior to the development of CFS and increased long bursts of exercise even after the onset of CFS, perhaps as an attempt to compensate for feelings of fatigue. Because no evidence emerged for increased illnesses or exposure to viruses in the lives of these individuals, one cause could be overexercise in these hard-driving, achievement-oriented people.

Pharmacological treatment has not proved effective for CFS (Afari & Buchwald, 2003; Chalder et al., 2000; Sharpe, 1992), but Sharpe has developed a cognitive-behavioral program that includes procedures to increase activity, regulate periods of rest, and direct cognitive therapy at the cognitions specified in Figure 7.7. This treatment also includes relaxation, breathing exercises, and general stress-reduction procedures, interventions we describe in the next section (Sharpe, 1992, 1993, 1997). In an early controlled trial evaluating this approach, 60 patients were assigned to the cognitive-behavioral treatment or to treatment as usual. Seventy-three percent of the patients in the cognitive-behavioral treatment group improved on measures of fatigue, disability, and illness belief, a result far superior to that in the control group (Sharpe et al., 1996). In a second, more sophisticated, large-scale evaluation of a similar cognitive-behavioral approach to CFS (Deale, Chalder, Marks, & Wessely, 1997), 60 patients with CFS were randomly assigned to cognitive-behavioral therapy or relaxation exercises alone. The results indicated that fatigue diminished and overall functioning improved significantly more in the group that received cognitive-behavioral therapy. Of individuals who completed cognitive-behavioral therapy, 70% achieved substantial improvement in physical functioning at a 6-month follow-up compared to only 19% of those in the relaxation-only group. A 5-year follow-up indicates the gains were largely maintained (Deale, Husain, Chalder, & Wessely, 2001). Subsequent studies confirm the value of this basic approach (Knoop, Prins, Moss-Morris, & Bleijenberg, 2010; Price, Mitchell, Tidy, & Hunot, 2008), but increasing emphasis is now placed on preventing bursts of overexercise (e.g., Harvey & Wessely, 2009; Jason et al., 2010). This is because increasing exercise and activity does not seem to facilitate beneficial change. Rather, other ingredients in treatment, such as cognitive reappraisal of the meaning of fatigue in one's life, and increased self-efficacy seem more important (Friedberg & Sohl, 2009).

Concept Check 7.2

Answer the following questions about the psychosocial effects on physical disorders.

1. Which of the following is not considered part of the experience of pain?
   a. The subjective impression of pain as reported by the patient
   b. Pain behaviors or overt manifestations of pain
   c. Cuts, bruises, and other injuries
   d. An emotional component called suffering

2. Some evidence shows that psychological factors may contribute to both the course and the _____ of cancer, AIDS, and other diseases and treatment and recovery.

3. Psychosocial and biological factors contribute to the development of _____, a potentially deadly condition of high blood pressure, and to the development of _____, the blockage of arteries supplying blood to the heart muscle.

4. Psychologists identified two types of behavior patterns that they alleged to contribute to the development of disease. What types were developed? _____ and _____

5. No confirmed evidence exists to show that there is a physical cause for the disease of _____ that often causes individuals to give up their careers and suffer considerably.

Psychosocial Treatment of Physical Disorders

› **What procedures and strategies are used in stress management and in prevention and intervention programs?**

Certain experiments suggest that pain not only is bad for you, but also may kill you. Several years ago, John Liebeskind and his colleagues (Page, Ben-Eliyahu, Yirmiya, & Liebeskind, 1993) demonstrated that postsurgical pain in rats doubles the rate at which a certain cancer metastasizes (spreads) to the lungs. Rats undergoing abdominal surgery *without* morphine developed twice the number of lung metastases as rats who were given morphine for the same surgery. The rats undergoing surgery with the pain-killing drug had even lower rates of metastases than rats that did not have surgery.

This effect may result from the interaction of pain with the immune system. Pain may reduce the number of natural killer cells in the immune system, perhaps because of the general stress reaction to the pain. Thus, if a rat is in *extreme* pain, the associated stress may further enhance the pain, completing a vicious circle. Because this finding also seems to apply to humans (Taylor, 2009), it is important because the consensus is that we are reluctant to use pain-killing medication in chronic diseases such as cancer. Some estimates suggest that fewer than half of all cancer patients in the United States receive sufficient pain relief. Direct evidence is available on the benefits of early pain relief in patients undergoing surgery (Coderre, Katz, Vaccarino, & Melzack, 1993; Keefe & France, 1999; Taylor, 2009). Patients receiving pain medication before surgery reported less pain after surgery and requested less pain medication. Adequate pain-management procedures, either medical or psychological, are an essential part of the management of chronic disease.

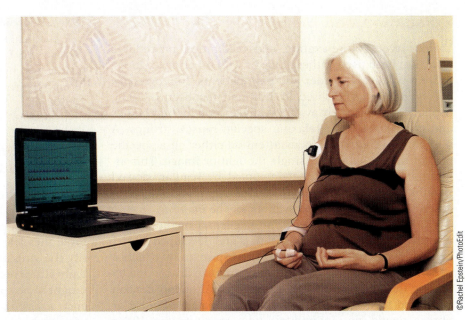

▲ In biofeedback, the patient learns to control physiological responses that are visible on a screen.

A variety of psychological treatments have been developed for physical disorders and pain, including biofeedback, relaxation procedures, and hypnosis (Gatchel, 2005; Linden & Moseley, 2006; Otis & Pincus, 2008; Otis et al., 2010; Turk & Monarch, 2002). Because of the overriding role of stress in the cause and maintenance of many physical disorders, however, comprehensive stress-management programs are increasingly incorporated into medical centers where such disorders are treated. We briefly review specific psychosocial approaches to physical disorders and describe a typical comprehensive stress-management program.

Biofeedback

Biofeedback is a process of making patients aware of specific physiological functions that, ordinarily, they would not notice consciously, such as heart rate, blood pressure, muscle tension in specific areas of the body, electroencephalogram rhythms (brain waves), and patterns of blood flow (Andrasik, 2000; Schwartz & Andrasik, 2003).

Clinicians use physiological monitoring equipment to make the response, such as heart rate, visible or audible to the patient. The patient then works with the therapist to learn to control the response. A successful response produces some type of signal. For example, if the patient is successful in lowering her blood pressure by a certain amount, the pressure reading will be visible on a gauge and a tone will sound. It wasn't long before researchers discovered that humans could discriminate changes in autonomic nervous system activity with a high degree of accuracy (Blanchard & Epstein, 1977).

One goal of biofeedback has been to reduce tension in the muscles of the head and scalp, thereby relieving headaches. Pioneers such as Ed Blanchard, Ken Holroyd, and Frank Andrasik found that biofeedback was successful in this area (Holroyd, Andrasik, & Noble, 1980), although no

more successful than deep muscle relaxation procedures (Andrasik, 2000; Blanchard & Andrasik, 1982; Blanchard, Andrasik, Ahles, Teders, & O'Keefe, 1980; Holroyd & Penzien, 1986). Because of these results, some have thought that biofeedback might achieve its effects with tension headaches by simply teaching people to relax. However, Holroyd and colleagues (1984) concluded instead that the success of biofeedback, at least for headaches, may depend not on the reduction of tension but on the extent to which the procedures instill a sense of *control* over the pain. (How do you think this relates to the study of stress in baboons described in the beginning of the chapter?)

Whatever the mechanism, biofeedback and relaxation are more effective treatments than, for example, placebo medication interventions, and the results of these two treatments are not altogether interchangeable, in that some people benefit more from biofeedback and others benefit from relaxation procedures. Therefore, applying both treatments is a safe strategy (Andrasik, 2000; Schwartz & Andrasik, 2003). Several reviews have found that 38% to 63% of patients undergoing relaxation or biofeedback achieve significant reductions in headaches compared to approximately 35% who receive placebo medication (Blanchard, 1992; Blanchard et al., 1980; Holroyd & Penzien, 1986). Furthermore, the effects of biofeedback and relaxation seem to be long lasting (Andrasik, 2000; Blanchard, 1987; Lisspers & Öst, 1990).

biofeedback Use of physiological monitoring equipment to make individuals aware of their own bodily functions, such as blood pressure or brain waves, that they cannot normally access, with the purpose of controlling these functions.

Relaxation and Meditation

Various types of relaxation and meditation procedures have also been used, either alone or with other procedures, to treat physical disorder and pain patients. In *progressive muscle relaxation,* devised by Edmund Jacobson in 1938, people become acutely aware of any tension in their bodies and counteract it by relaxing specific muscle groups. A number of procedures focus attention either on a specific part of the body or on a single thought or image. This attentional focus is often accompanied by regular, slowed breathing. In *transcendental meditation,* attention is focused solely on a repeated syllable, or the *mantra.*

Herbert Benson stripped transcendental meditation of what he considered its nonessentials and developed a brief procedure he calls the **relaxation response**, in which a person silently repeats a mantra to minimize distraction by closing the mind to intruding thoughts. Although Benson suggested focusing on the word *one,* any neutral word or phrase would do. Individuals who meditate for 10 or 20 minutes a day report feeling calmer or more relaxed throughout the day. These brief, simple procedures can be powerful in reducing the flow of certain neurotransmitters and stress hormones, an effect that may be mediated by an increased sense of control and mastery (Benson, 1975,

1984). Benson's ideas are popular and are taught in 60% of U.S. medical schools and offered by many major hospitals (Roush, 1997). Relaxation has generally positive effects on headaches, hypertension, and acute and chronic pain, although the results are sometimes relatively modest (Taylor, 2009).

A Comprehensive Stress- and Pain-Reduction Program

In our own stress-management program (Barlow, Rapee, & Reisner, 2001), individuals practice a variety of stress-management procedures presented to them in a workbook. First, they learn to monitor their stress closely and to identify the stressful events in their daily lives. (A sample of a daily stress record is in ■ Figure 7.7.) Note that clients are taught to be specific about recording the times they experience stress, the intensity of the stress, and what seems to trigger the stress. They also note the somatic symptoms and thoughts that occur when they are stressed. All this monitoring becomes important in carrying through with the program, but it can be helpful in itself because it reveals precise patterns and causes of stress and helps clients learn what changes to make to cope better.

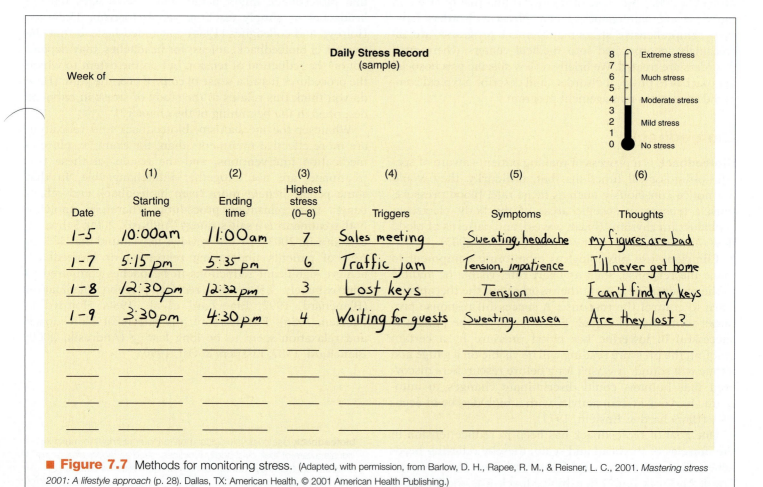

■ **Figure 7.7** Methods for monitoring stress. (Adapted, with permission, from Barlow, D. H., Rapee, R. M., & Reisner, L. C., 2001. *Mastering stress 2001: A lifestyle approach* (p. 28). Dallas, TX: American Health, © 2001 American Health Publishing.)

After learning to monitor stress, clients are taught deep muscle relaxation, which first involves tensing various muscles to identify the location of different muscle groups. (Instructions for tensing specific muscle groups are included in Table 7.3.) Clients are then systematically taught to relax the muscle groups beyond the point of inactivity—that is, to actively let go of the muscle so that no tension remains in it.

Appraisals and attitudes are an important part of stress, and clients learn how they exaggerate the negative impact of events in their day-to-day lives. In the program, therapist and client use cognitive therapy to develop more realistic appraisals and attitudes, as exemplified in the case of Sally.

Sally • Improving Her Perception

(Sally is a 45-year-old real estate agent.)

PATIENT: My mother is always calling just when I'm in the middle of doing something important and it makes me so angry, I find that I get short with her.

THERAPIST: Let's try and look at what you just said in another way. When you say that she *always* phones in the middle of something, it implies 100% of the time. Is that true? How likely is it that she will call when you are doing something important?

P: Well, I suppose that when I think back over the last 10 times she's called, most of the times I was just watching TV or reading. There was once when I was making dinner and it burned because she interrupted me. Another time, I was busy with some work I had brought home from the office, and she called. I guess that makes it 20% of the time.

T: OK, great. Now let's go a bit further. So what if she calls at an inconvenient time?

P: Well, I know that one of my first thoughts is that she doesn't think anything I do is important. But before you say anything, I know that is a major overestimation since she obviously doesn't know what I'm doing when she calls. However, I suppose I also think that it's a major interruption and inconvenience to have to stop at that point.

T: Go on. What is the chance that it is a major inconvenience?

P: When I was doing my work, I forgot what I was up to and it took me 10 minutes to work it out again. I guess that's not so bad—it's only 10 minutes. And when the dinner burned, it was really not too bad, just a little burned. Part of that was my fault anyway because I could have turned the stove down before I went to the phone.

T: So, it sounds like quite a small chance that it would be a major inconvenience, even if your mother does interrupt you.

Table 7.3 Suggestions for Tensing Muscles

Large Muscle Groups	Suggestions for Tensing Muscles
Lower arm	Make fist, palm down, and pull wrist toward upper arm.
Upper arm	Tense biceps; with arms by side, pull upper arm toward side without touching. (Try not to tense lower arm while doing this; let lower arm hang loosely.)
Lower leg and foot	Point toes upward to knees.
Thighs	Push feet hard against floor.
Abdomen	Pull in stomach toward back.
Chest and breathing	Take deep breath and hold it about 10 seconds, then release.
Shoulders and lower neck	Shrug shoulders, bring shoulders up until they almost touch ears.
Back of neck	Put head back and press against back of chair.
Lips	Press lips together; don't clench teeth or jaw.
Eyes	Close eyes tightly but don't close too hard (be careful if you have contacts).
Lower forehead	Pull eyebrows down and in (try to get them to meet).
Upper forehead	Raise eyebrows and wrinkle forehead.

Source: Adapted, with permission, from Barlow, D. H., Rapee, R. M., & Reisner, L. C. (2001). *Mastering stress 2001: A lifestyle approach.* Dallas, TX: American Health, pp. 113–114, © 2001 American Health Publishing.

P: True. And I know what you are going to say next. Even if it is a major inconvenience, it's not the end of the world. I have handled plenty of bigger problems than this at work.

In this program, individuals work hard to identify unrealistic negative thoughts and to develop new appraisals and attitudes almost instantaneously when negative thoughts occur. Such assessment is often the most difficult part of the program. After the session just related, Sally

relaxation response Active components of meditation methods, including repetitive thoughts of a sound to reduce distracting thoughts and closing the mind to other intruding thoughts, that decrease the flow of stress hormones and neurotransmitters and cause a feeling of calm.

began using what she had learned in cognitive therapy to reappraise stressful situations. Finally, clients in stress-reduction programs develop new coping strategies, such as time management and assertiveness training. During *time-management training*, patients are taught to prioritize their activities and pay less attention to nonessential demands. During *assertiveness training*, they learn to stand up for themselves in an appropriate way. Clients also learn other procedures for managing everyday problems.

A number of studies have evaluated some version of this comprehensive program. The results suggest that it is generally more effective than individual components alone, such as relaxation or biofeedback, for chronic pain (Keefe et al., 1992; Otis & Pincus, 2008; Turk & Monarch, 2002), CFS (Deale et al., 1997), tension headaches (Blanchard et al., 1990; Lipchik et al., 2002), hypertension (Ward, Swan, & Chesney, 1987), temporomandibular joint (jaw) pain (Turner, Mancl, & Aaron, 2006), and cancer pain (Andersen et al., 2007; Crichton & Morey, 2003).

Drugs and Stress-Reduction Programs

Some evidence suggests that chronic reliance on over-the-counter analgesic (pain reliever) medications lessens the efficacy of comprehensive programs in the treatment of headache and may make headaches worse because patients experience *increased* headache pain every time the medication wears off or is stopped (rebound headaches) (Capobianco, Swanson, & Dodick, 2001).

Holroyd, Nash, Pingel, Cordingley, and Jerome (1991) compared a comprehensive cognitive-behavioral treatment to an antidepressant drug, amitriptyline, in the treatment of tension headache. The psychological treatment produced at least a 50% reduction in headache activity in 56% of the patients, whereas the drug produced a comparable reduction in only 27% of users. Grazzi and colleagues (2002) treated 61 patients with migraine headaches and analgesic overuse by withdrawing the patients from analgesics and then starting them on a more comprehensive but nonaddicting medication regimen, either with biofeedback and relaxation or without these (drugs only). After 3 years, significantly more individuals in the medication-only condition had relapsed by resuming analgesic use and were experiencing more headache pain. It is important that psychological treatment also seems to reduce drug consumption fairly consistently (Radnitz, Appelbaum, Blanchard, Elliott, & Andrasik, 1988), as it did in the study by Grazzi and colleagues (2002), not only for headaches but also for severe hypertension.

Denial as a Means of Coping

We have emphasized the importance of confronting and working through our feelings, particularly after stressful or traumatic events. Beginning with Sigmund Freud, mental health professionals have recognized the importance of reliving or processing intense emotional experiences to put them behind us and to develop better coping responses.

For example, individuals undergoing coronary artery bypass surgery who were optimistic recovered more quickly, returned to normal activities more rapidly, and reported a stronger quality of life 6 months after surgery than those who were not optimistic (Scheier et al., 1989). Scheier and colleagues also discovered that optimistic people are less likely to use denial as a means of coping with a severe stressor such as surgery. Most mental health professionals work to eliminate denial because it has many negative effects. For example, people who deny the severe pain connected with disease may not notice meaningful variations in their symptoms, and they typically avoid treatment regimens or rehabilitation programs.

But is denial always harmful? The well-known health psychologist Shelley Taylor (2009) points out that most individuals who are functioning well deny the implications of a potentially serious condition, at least initially. A common reaction is to assume that what they have is not serious or will go away quickly. Most people with serious diseases react this way, including those with cancer (Meyerowitz, 1983) and CHD (Krantz & Deckel, 1983). Several groups of investigators (see, for example, Hackett & Cassem, 1973; Meyerowitz, 1983) have found that during that extremely stressful period when a person is first diagnosed, denial may help patients endure the shock more easily. They are then better able to develop coping responses later. The value of denial as a coping mechanism may depend more on timing than on anything else. In the long run, however, all evidence indicates that at some point we must face the situation, process our emotions, and come to terms with what is happening (Compas et al., 2006).

Modifying Behaviors to Promote Health

As early as 1991, the director of the National Institutes of Health said that "many common diseases can be prevented and others can be postponed or controlled simply by making possible lifestyle changes" (Department of Health and Human Services, 1991). Unhealthy eating habits, lack of exercise, and smoking are three of the most common behaviors that put us at risk in the long term for a number of physical disorders (Lewis et al., 2011). Other high-risk behaviors and conditions include unprotected sex, failure to take precautions to avoid injuries, excessive use of alcohol, and excessive exposure to the sun, just to name a few. Many of these behaviors contribute to diseases and physical disorders that are among the leading causes of death, including not only CHD and cancer but also accidents of various kinds (related to consumption of alcohol and the nonuse of safety restraints), cirrhosis of the liver (related to excessive consumption of alcohol), and a variety of respiratory diseases, including influenza and pneumonia (related to smoking and stress) (Lewis et al., 2011). Even now, fully 21% of adults in the United States are regular smokers (CDC, 2007), and smoking is the leading preventable cause of death, killing approximately 443,000 people each year (CDC, 2008). According to a recent survey from the American Cancer Society (ACS), 8.6 million people had at least one chronic disease related to a history or prevalence of smoking (ACS, 2007).

Considerable work is ongoing to develop effective behavior modification procedures that improve diet, increase adherence to drug and medical treatment programs, and develop optimal exercise programs. Here we review briefly three areas of interest: injury control, the prevention of AIDS, and a major community intervention known as the Stanford Three Community Study.

Injury Prevention

Accidents are the leading cause of death for people age 1 to 45 and the fifth leading cause of death among all causes in the United States (see Table 7.1). Furthermore, the loss of productivity to the individual and society, and years of life lost from injuries, is far greater than from the other four leading causes of death: heart disease, cancer, stroke, and respiratory disease (Institute of Medicine, 1999). Therefore, the U.S. government has become interested in methods for reducing injury (Scheidt, Overpeck, Trifiletti, & Cheng, 2000). Spielberger and Frank (1992) point out that psychological variables are crucial in leading to virtually all factors that lead to injury. A good example is the work of the late Lizette Peterson and her colleagues (see, for example, Peterson & Roberts, 1992). Peterson was particularly interested in preventing accidents in children. Injuries kill more children than the next six causes of childhood death combined (Scheidt et al., 1995; Taylor, 2009), and nearly half of all cases of poisoning each year occur in children younger than age 6 (CDC, 2006). Yet most people, including parents, don't think too much about prevention, even in their own children, because they usually consider injuries to be fated and, therefore, out of their hands (Peterson, Farmer, & Kashani, 1990; Peterson & Roberts, 1992).

However, a variety of programs focusing on behavior change have proved effective for preventing injuries in children (Sleet, Hammond, Jones, Thomas, & Whitt, 2003; Taylor, 2009). For example, children have been systematically and successfully taught to escape fires (Jones & Haney, 1984), identify and report emergencies (Jones & Ollendick, 2002; Jones & Kazdin, 1980), safely cross streets (Yeaton & Bailey, 1978), ride bicycles safely, and deal with injuries such as serious cuts (Peterson & Thiele, 1988). In many of these programs, the participating children maintained the safety skills they had learned for months after the intervention—as long as assessments were continued, in most cases. Because little evidence indicates that repeated warnings are effective in preventing injuries, programmatic efforts to change behavior are important. Such programs, however, are nonexistent in most communities.

AIDS Prevention

Earlier we documented the horrifying spread of AIDS, particularly in developing countries. Table 7.4 illustrates modes of transmission of AIDS in the United States and the world as they existed through 2008 and 2009. In developing countries, such as Africa, for instance, AIDS is almost exclusively linked to heterosexual intercourse with an infected partner. There is no vaccine for the disease. *Changing high-risk behavior is the only effective prevention strategy* (Catania et al., 2000).

Comprehensive programs are particularly important because testing alone to learn whether one is HIV positive or HIV negative does little to change behavior (see, for example, Landis, Earp, & Koch, 1992). Even educating at-risk individuals is generally ineffective in changing high-risk behavior (Helweg-Larsen & Collins, 1997). One of the most successful behavior-change programs was carried out in San Francisco several years ago. Table 7.5 shows what behaviors were specifically targeted and what methods were used to achieve behavior change in various groups. Before this program was introduced, frequent unprotected sex was reported by 37.4% of one sample of gay men and 33.9% of another sample (Stall, McKusick, Wiley, Coates, & Ostrow, 1986). At a follow-up point in 1988, the incidence had dropped to 1.7% and 4.2%, respectively, in the same two samples (Ekstrand & Coates, 1990). These changes did not occur in comparable groups where a program of this type had not been instituted. In a similar, large, community-based program in eight small cities, Kelly and colleagues (1997) trained popular and well-liked members of the gay community to provide information and education. Risky sexual practices were substantially reduced in the four cities where the program occurred, compared to four cities where only educational pamphlets were distributed.

It is crucial that these programs be extended to minorities and women, who often do not consider themselves at risk, probably because most media coverage in the United States until recently has focused on gay white males (Mays & Cochran, 1988). In 2003, women accounted for 50% of new AIDS cases (World Health Organization, 2003). Furthermore, the age of highest risk for women is between 15 and 25 years; the peak risk for men is during their late 20s and early 30s. In view of the different circumstances in

Table 7.4 AIDS Cases by Mode of Transmission (World, 2009; U.S., 2008) Percentage Estimates of Total Cases

Transmission Category	World (%)	United States (%)*
Male-to-male sexual contact	5–10	50
Injection drug use	10	17
Male-to-male sexual contact and injection drug use	—	5
Heterosexual contact	59–69	32
Other**	16–21	1

*Because totals were calculated independently from the subpopulations, the percentages may not sum exactly to 100%. **Includes hemophilia, blood transfusion, perinatal exposure, transmission within healthcare settings, and risk not reported or identified.

which women put themselves at risk for HIV infection—for example, prostitution in response to economic deprivation—effective behavior-change programs for them must be different from those developed for men (World Health Organization, 2000).

In Africa, where the primary mode of transmission of HIV is heterosexual, a greater focus on the interpersonal and social system of the individual at risk has also begun. One important new initiative is to focus prevention techniques on couples rather than individuals (Grabbe & Bunnell, 2010). This is important, because studies demonstrate that only 22% of adults age 15–49 years know their HIV status in Africa and condom use within regular partnerships is very low because the assumption is that their partner is "safe" and they are at low risk. Because 55% to 93% of new HIV infections occur within cohabiting relationships, this means that most transmissions occur within couples who are unaware of their HIV status. The success-ful initiation of couples counseling and testing has occurred in Rwanda, Uganda, and Kenya. Couples counseling for HIV prevention also provides opportunities for delivering and providing more comprehensive maternal and child health services.

The Stanford Three Community Study

One of the best-known and most successful efforts to reduce risk factors for disease in the community is the Stanford Three Community Study (Meyer, Nash, McAlister, Maccoby, & Farquhar, 1980). Although it was conducted a number of years ago, it remains a model program. Rather than assemble three groups of people, these investigators studied three entire communities in central California that were reasonably alike in size and type of residents between 1972 and 1975. The target was reduction of risk factors for CHD. The positive behaviors that were introduced focused on smoking, high blood pressure, diet, and weight reduc-

Table 7.5 The San Francisco Model: Coordinated Community-Level Program to Reduce New HIV Infection

Information	Skills
Intervention: Media Educate about how HIV is and is not transmitted. ***Health-Care Establishments and Providers*** Provide educational materials and classes about HIV transmission. ***Schools*** Distribute materials about HIV transmission and prevention. ***Worksites*** Distribute materials about HIV transmission and prevention. ***STD, Family Planning, and Drug Abuse Treatment Centers*** Distribute materials and video models about HIV transmission ***Community Organizations (Churches, Clubs)*** Make guest speakers, materials, and videos available. ***Antibody Testing Centers*** Distribute materials and instruction about HIV transmission. **Motivation** Provide examples of different kinds of individuals who have become HIV infected. Ask all patients about risk factors for HIV transmission. Advise high-risk patients to be tested for HIV antibodies. Provide models of teens who became infected with HIV. Provide examples of co-workers who became infected with HIV. Make detailed assessment of HIV risk. Advise about testing for antibodies to HIV. Provide examples that HIV-infected individuals are similar to club or organization membership.	Model how to clean needles and use condoms and spermicides. Model skills for safe sex and needle negotiation. Provide classes and videos to demonstrate safe-sex skills. Provide classes and models for safe-sex and drug injection skills. Instruct and rehearse safe-sex and drug injection skills during medical and counseling encounters. Provide classes and videos for AIDS risk-reduction skills. ***Norms*** Publicize the low prevalence of high-risk behaviors. Publicize public desirability of safe-sex classes and condom advertisements. Advise patients about prevalent community norms. Create a climate of acceptance for HIV-infected students and teachers. Publicize student perceptions about desirability of safe sex. Create a climate of acceptance for HIV-infected people. Provide classes and videos for AIDS risk-reduction skills. ***Policy and Legislation*** Generate concern and action about policy. Advocate policies and laws that will prevent spread of HIV. Mobilize students and faculty to work to allow sex education to take place in the schools. Install condom machines in public bathrooms. Allow HIV-infected people to work. Mobilize clients to request additional treatment slots and facilities. Advocate beneficial laws and policies. Advocate confidentiality and nondiscrimination. Advocate confidentiality and nondiscrimination.

STD = sexually transmitted disease

Source: Reprinted, with permission, from Coates, T. J. (1990). Strategies for modifying sexual behavior for primary and secondary prevention of HIV disease. *Journal of Consulting and Clinical Psychology, 58*(1), 57–69, © 1990 American Psychological Association.

tion. In Tracy, the first community, no interventions were conducted, but detailed information was collected from a random sample of adults to assess any increases in their knowledge of risk factors, as well as any changes in risk factors over time. In addition, participants in Tracy received a medical assessment of their cardiovascular factors. The residents of Gilroy and part of Watsonville were subjected to a media blitz on the dangers of behavioral risk factors for CHD, the importance of reducing these factors, and helpful hints for doing so. Most residents of Watsonville, the third community, also had a face-to-face intervention in which behavioral counselors worked with the townspeople judged to be at particularly high risk for CHD. Participants in all three communities were surveyed once a year for a 3-year period following the intervention. Results indicate that the interventions were markedly successful at reducing risk factors for CHD in these communities (■ Figure 7.8). Furthermore, for the residents of Watsonville who also received individual counseling, risk factors were substantially lower than for people in Tracy or even for those in Gilroy and people in the part of Watsonville that received only the media blitz, and their knowledge of risk factors was substantially higher.

Interventions such as the Stanford study cost money, although in many communities the media are willing to donate time to such a worthy effort. Results show that mounting an effort like this is worthwhile to individuals, to the community, and to public health officials because many lives will be saved and disability leave will be decreased to an extent that will more than cover the original cost of the program. Unfortunately, implementation of this type of program is still not widespread.

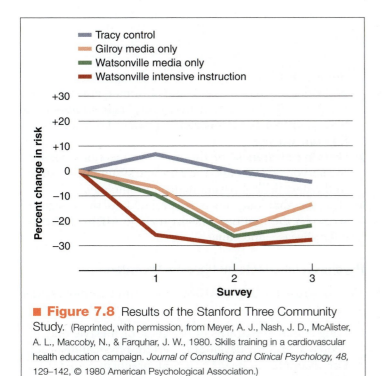

■ **Figure 7.8** Results of the Stanford Three Community Study. (Reprinted, with permission, from Meyer, A. J., Nash, J. D., McAlister, A. L., Maccoby, N., & Farquhar, J. W., 1980. Skills training in a cardiovascular health education campaign. *Journal of Consulting and Clinical Psychology, 48,* 129–142, © 1980 American Psychological Association.)

Concept Check 7.3

Check your understanding of psychosocial treatment by matching the treatments to the correct scenarios or statements: (a) biofeedback, (b) meditation and relaxation, (c) cognitive coping procedures, (d) denial, (e) modify behaviors to promote health, and (f) Stanford Three Community Study.

1. Mary is often upset by stupid things other people are always doing. Her doctor wants her to realize her exaggeration of these events and suggests _____.

2. Tyrone can't seem to focus on anything at work. He feels too stressed. He needs _____, a way of minimizing intruding thoughts that he can do at work in a short amount of time.

3. Harry's blood pressure soars when he feels stressed. His doctor showed him how to become aware of his body process to control them better by using _____.

4. At a world conference, leaders met to discuss how to reduce the risk of childhood injuries, AIDS risks, and the number of smoking-related diseases. Professionals suggested programs involving teaching individuals how to _____.

5. Initially, strong _____ can help a patient endure the shock of bad news; however, later it can inhibit or prevent the healing process.

6. The _____ is one of the best-known efforts to reduce community disease risk factors.

In this chapter and earlier chapters we have described the profound influence of psychological factors on brain function and structure, showing how, for example, psychological interventions may affect physical illnesses such as CHD and AIDS. The fascinating study of the placebo response adds another layer to the discussion. To take one example, do "phony" placebo pills really decrease pain—or is it just that individuals think or report that they are feeling less pain? This is one of the major controversies in the study of placebo responses—not only for pain, but also for conditions such as depression.

With the help of the latest brain-imaging technology, several experiments have demonstrated that when pain is induced in some volunteers (for example, by injecting salt water in their jaws) after they are given a placebo, their brains operate in such a way that they actually feel less pain as opposed to simply thinking they feel less pain or reporting that they feel less pain (Wager, 2005; Zubieta et al., 2005). Specifically, broad areas of the brain are affected, but the most important system that is activated may be the endogenous opioid system (or endorphins),

which, among other functions, suppresses pain. Increased endorphin activity across broad areas of the brain was associated with lower ratings of pain intensity and reductions in the sensations of pain and emotional reactions to it. Thus, the studies show that the placebo effect is certainly not "all in your head." "Phony" pills really do spur chemical changes in the brain that reduce pain.

But does it also work the other way? Do medical treatments, such as drugs, affect what are clearly psychological processes, and if they do, are drugs affecting different regions in the brain compared to purely psychological interventions to achieve the same end? For example, we know that drugs can relieve anxiety and depression, but the presumption is that these medications are having their effects in different areas of the brain compared to psychological treatments. Now, an interesting study has demonstrated that physical pain (such as that caused by physical injury) and social pain (such as hurt feelings caused by social rejection) may rely on some of the same behavioral and neural mechanisms (DeWall et al., 2010). In

one experiment, participants took a drug commonly used for physical pain, acetaminophen (Tylenol), while another group took a placebo. They then recorded on a form their pain feelings every day for 3 weeks. Subjects taking the acetaminophen reported substantially fewer feelings of pain than the placebo group. In a second experiment, the investigators found that the acetaminophen reduced neural responses to social rejection in brain regions known to be associated with both social pain and physical pain (the dorsal anterior cingulate cortex and the anterior insula). These findings indicate substantial overlap between social and physical pain (Wager, 2005). They also illustrate again the theme of this book: You cannot easily separate brain function induced biochemically from brain function induced by psychological factors, including expectancies and appraisals. The body and the mind are indeed inseparable, and only a multidimensional integrative approach focusing on the full spectrum of responding will produce a complete understanding of behavior, either normal or pathological.

Summary

Psychological and Social Factors that Influence Health

What is the difference between behavioral medicine and health psychology?

> Psychological and social factors play a major role in developing and maintaining a number of physical disorders.

> Two fields of study have emerged as a result of a growing interest in psychological factors contributing to illness. Behavioral medicine involves the application of behavioral science techniques to prevent, diagnose, and treat medical problems. Health psychology is a subfield that focuses on psychological factors involved in the promotion of health and well-being.

How are immune system function, stress, and physical disorders related?

> Psychological and social factors may contribute directly to illness and disease through the psychological effects of stress on the immune system and other physical func-

tioning. If the immune system is compromised, it may no longer be able to attack and eliminate antigens from the body effectively, or it may even begin to attack the body's normal tissue instead, a process known as autoimmune disease.

> Growing awareness of the many connections between the nervous system and the immune system has resulted in the new field of psychoneuroimmunology.

> Diseases that may be partly related to the effects of stress on the immune system include AIDS, cardiovascular disease, and cancer.

Psychosocial Effects on Physical Disorders

How is stress related to AIDS, cancer, and cardiovascular disease?

> Long-standing patterns of behavior or lifestyle may put people at risk for developing certain physical disorders. For example, unhealthy sexual practices can lead to AIDS and other sexually transmitted diseases, and un-

healthy behavioral patterns, such as poor eating habits, lack of exercise, or type A behavior pattern, may contribute to cardiovascular diseases such as stroke, hypertension, and coronary heart disease.

Of the 10 leading causes of death in the United States, fully 50% of deaths can be traced to lifestyle behaviors.

> What are the potential causes of acute and chronic pain, and how do the two types of pain differ?

Psychological and social factors also contribute to chronic pain. The brain inhibits pain through naturally occurring endogenous opioids, which may also be implicated in a variety of psychological disorders.

Chronic fatigue syndrome is a relatively new disorder that is attributed at least partly to stress but may also have a viral or immune system dysfunction component.

Psychosocial Treatment of Physical Disorders

What procedures and strategies are used in stress management and in prevention and intervention programs?

> A variety of psychosocial treatments have been developed with the goal of either treating or preventing physical disorders. Among these are biofeedback and the relaxation response.
> Comprehensive stress- and pain-reduction programs include not only relaxation and related techniques but also new methods to encourage effective coping, including stress management, realistic appraisals, and improved attitudes through cognitive therapy.
> Comprehensive programs are generally more effective than individual components delivered singly.
> Other interventions aim to modify such behaviors as unsafe sexual practices, smoking, and unhealthy dietary habits. Such efforts have been made in a variety of areas, including injury control, AIDS prevention, smoking cessation campaigns, and programs to reduce risk factors for diseases such as CHD.

Key Terms

behavioral medicine, 250
health psychology, 250
general adaptation syndrome (GAS), 252
stress, 252
self-efficacy, 254
immune system, 254
antigens, 255
autoimmune disease, 255
rheumatoid arthritis, 255

psychoneuroimmunology (PNI), 256
AIDS-related complex (ARC), 257
cancer, 258
psycho-oncology, 259
cardiovascular disease, 260
stroke/cerebral vascular accident (CVA), 260
hypertension, 261
essential hypertension, 261
coronary heart disease (CHD), 263

type A behavior pattern, 264
type B behavior pattern, 264
acute pain, 265
chronic pain, 265
endogenous opioids, 267
chronic fatigue syndrome (CFS), 268
biofeedback, 271
relaxation response, 272

Answers to Concept Checks

7.1

1. d; 2. a; 3. c; 4. b; 5. f; 6. e

7.2

1. c; 2. development; 3. hypertension, coronary heart disease; 4. type A (hard-driving, impatient), type B (relaxed, less concerned); 5. chronic fatigue syndrome

7.3

1. c; 2. b; 3. a; 4. e; 5. d; 6. f

Media Resources

Log in to CengageBrain to access the resources your instructor requires. For this book, you can access:

CourseMate brings course concepts to life with interactive learning, study, and exam preparation tools that support the printed textbook. A textbook-specific website, Psychology CourseMate includes an integrated interactive eBook and other interactive learning tools including quizzes, flashcards, videos, and more.

Abnormal Psychology Videos

> *Orel, Social Support and HIV:* This African American client demonstrates the power of strong social support from family and friends and pursuing personal interests such as art, to deal with the ongoing struggles of being an HIV/AIDS patient.

> *The Immune System, Effects of Stress and Emotion:* This video illustrates recent findings on how emotional experiences—such as stress, loneliness, and sociability—affect physical health.

> *Cancer, Education and Support Groups:* This clip investigates whether providing group support or group education is more helpful to women facing breast cancer.

CENGAGENOW CengageNow is an easy-to-use online resource that helps you study in less time to get the grade you want—NOW. Take a pre-test for this chapter and receive a personalized study plan based on your results that will identify the topics you need to review and direct you to online resources to help you master those topics. Then take a post-test to help you determine the concepts you have mastered and what you will need to work on. If your textbook does not include an access code card, go to CengageBrain.com to gain access.

> Visit www.cengagebrain.com to access your account and purchase materials.

aplia If your professor has assigned Aplia homework:
1. Sign in to your account.

2. Complete the corresponding homework exercises as required by your professor.
3. When finished, click "Grade It Now" to see which areas you have mastered, which need more work, and for detailed explanations of every answer.

Video Concept Reviews

CengageNOW also contains Mark Durand's *Video Concept Reviews* on these challenging topics.

> Behavioral Medicine
> Health Psychology
> Stress
> General Adaptation Syndrome (GAS)
> HPA-Stress Response Cycle
> AIDS-Related Complex (ARC)
> Cancer and Psycho-oncology
> Hypertension
> Acute and Chronic Pain
> Concept Check: Integrative Process with Physical Disorders
> Chronic Fatigue Syndrome
> Biofeedback and Relaxation Techniques

Chapter Quiz

1. Which of the following is an interdisciplinary field that applies knowledge about human thoughts, emotions, and activities to prevent, diagnose, and treat medical problems?
   a. behavioral medicine
   b. endogenous medicine
   c. health psychology
   d. medical psychology

2. The general adaptation syndrome describes several stages people experience in response to sustained stress. These stages occur in which order?
   a. alarm, resistance, exhaustion
   b. resistance, alarm, exhaustion
   c. resistance, exhaustion, alarm
   d. exhaustion, alarm, resistance

3. Cortisol is:
   a. a neurotransmitter that reduces anxiety
   b. a neurohormone whose chronic secretion enhances hippocampal and immune functioning
   c. a portion of the brain that stimulates the HPA axis in response to stress
   d. a hormone that stimulates the hippocampus to turn off the stress response

4. Next month Shanti has to take an important college entrance exam. Which factor is most likely to influence whether her response to the exam is positive or negative?
   a. the genetic vulnerability to stress that Shanti has inherited from her parents
   b. whether Shanti will be taking the exam in a room by herself or with other students
   c. Shanti's beliefs about how much control she has over the situation
   d. how much time Shanti has to study before the exam

5. Joan has been living with HIV for 3 years and has just started participating in a stress-management support group. Based on previous research, what might Joan expect from her participation?
   a. an increase in the activity of T helper and natural killer cells
   b. an increase in the amount of antigens in her system
   c. an increase in depression as she discusses her illness
   d. an increase in immune functioning, but only for the first few weeks of the group

6. The study of how psychosocial factors influence cancer is known as:
   a. psychopathology
   b. psychopharmacology
   c. psycho-oncology
   d. oncosociology

7. Which of the following is a risk factor for coronary heart disease?
   a. anger that is part of the type A behavior pattern
   b. belligerence that is part of the type B behavior pattern
   c. competitive drive that is part of the type B behavior pattern
   d. carefree disregard for deadlines that is part of the type A behavior pattern

8. Biofeedback can be used to teach people how to:
   a. reduce their competitive drive and sense of urgency
   b. consciously control physiological functions that are outside awareness
   c. develop more supportive social support networks
   d. control their facial expressions to control their mood

9. Which of the following accurately characterizes the effects of denial as a coping strategy?
   a. Individuals who undergo coronary artery bypass surgery return to normal activities more rapidly if they deny their pain.
   b. Denial may have damaging short-term consequences in terms of the stress response, but it seems to be helpful to rehabilitation in the long term.
   c. People who deny their disease may not notice meaningful variations in their symptoms.
   d. Denial appears to have exclusively negative consequences on health and adaptation.

10. Which three behaviors, all of which can be modified, put people at the most risk for physical problems?
    a. unhealthy diet, lack of exercise, smoking
    b. pollution, unhealthy diet, lack of exercise
    c. lack of exercise, smoking, reckless driving
    d. smoking, alcohol use, "road rage"
    (See Appendix A for answers.)

Exploring Physical Disorders and Health Psychology

Psychological and behavioral factors are major contributors to illness and death.

❯ Behavioral medicine applies behavioral science to medical problems.

❯ Health psychology focuses on psychological influences on health and improving health care.

PSYCHOLOGICAL AND SOCIAL FACTORS INFLUENCE BIOLOGY

Stress

Anxiety

Causes

Depression

Weakened immune system/ compromised nervous system

Responses to threats and challenges may predict the effect of stress on the immune system.

Depression **Anxiety** **Stress** **Excitement**

Sense of control or ability to cope

Less control

More control

Photodisc/Getty Images

ILLNESS

©PhotoDisc/Getty Images

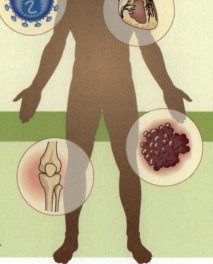

AIDS (Acquired Immune Deficiency Syndrome)

- The human immunodeficiency virus (HIV) attacks the immune system and opportunistic infections develop uncontrollably.
- Psychological treatments focus on strengthening the immune system and gaining a sense of control.
- Although drug therapy may control the virus, there is so far no biological means of prevention and the disease is still always fatal.

Cardiovascular Problems

- The heart and blood vessels can be damaged by
  - *Stroke:* Blockage or rupture of blood vessels in the brain
  - *Hypertension:* Constriction of blood vessels at organs and extremities puts extra pressure on the heart, which eventually weakens
  - *Coronary heart disease:* Blockage of arteries supplying blood to the heart
- Biological, psychological, and social factors contribute to all these conditions and are addressed in treatment.

Chronic Pain

- May begin with an acute episode but does not diminish when injury heals.
- Typically involves joints, muscles, and tendons; may result from enlarged blood vessels, tissue degeneration, or cancerous tumors.
- Psychological and social influences may cause and maintain chronic pain to a significant degree.

Cancer

- Abnormal cell growth produces malignant tumors.
- Psychosocial treatments may prolong life, alleviate symptoms, and reduce depression and pain.
- Different cancers have different rates of recovery and mortality.
- Psychoncology is the study of psychosocial factors involved in the course and treatment of cancer.

PSYCHOSOCIAL TREATMENTS FOR PHYSICAL DISORDERS

The stress reaction associated with pain may reduce the number of natural killer cells in the immune system:

Disease or Injury;
Enhanced Disease
or Injury

Extreme
Pain

Causes

Stress

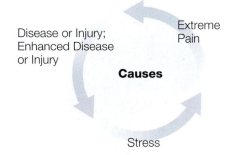

Biofeedback

- Electronic monitors make physiological responses such as heartbeat visible on a computer screen.
- Patient learns to increase or decrease the response, thereby improving functioning (decreasing tension).
  – Developing a sense of control may be therapeutic.

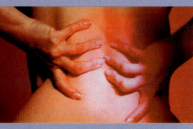

Suza Scalora/Photodisc/Getty Images

Relaxation and Meditation

- ***Progressive muscle relaxation:*** Person learns to locate physical tension and to counteract it by relaxing a specific muscle group.
- ***Meditation:*** Focusing attention on a specific body part or process or on an affirming thought or image; in some forms, focusing on a single silently repeated syllable (mantra) "empties" the mind. Meditation is accompanied by slow, regular breathing.
  – Meditating daily for at least 10 to 20 minutes imparts calm and relaxation by reducing certain neurotransmitters and stress hormones and increasing a sense of control.

Ryan McVay/Photodisc/Getty Images

BEHAVIOR MODIFICATION TO PROMOTE HEALTH

Many injuries and diseases can be prevented or controlled through lifestyle changes involving diet, substance use, exercise, and safety precautions.

Injury Control

- Injuries are the leading cause of death for people age 1 to 45, especially children.
- Most people consider injuries to be out of their control and therefore do not change high-risk behaviors.
- In children, prevention focuses on
  – escaping fires
  – crossing streets
  – using car seats, seat belts, and bicycle helmets
  – first aid.

Karl Weatherly/Photodisc/Getty Images

AIDS Prevention

- Changing high-risk behavior through individual and community education is the only effective strategy.
  – Eliminate unsafe sexual practices through cognitive-behavioral self-management training and social support networks.
  – Show drug abusers how to clean needles and make safe injections.
- Target minorities and women, groups that do not perceive themselves to be at risk.
  – Media coverage focuses on gay white males.
  – More women are infected through heterosexual interactions than through intravenous drug use.

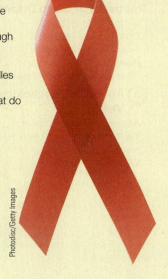

Photodisc/Getty Images

CHAPTER

8

Eating and Sleep Disorders

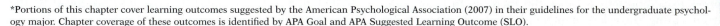

| Use the concepts, language, and other major theories of the discipline to account for psychological phenomena: | ❭ Describe behavior and mental processes empirically, including operational definitions *(see textbook pages 285–293, 309–317)* |
| Identify appropriate applications of psychology in solving problems, such as: | ❭ Origin and treatment of abnormal behavior *(see textbook pages 294–304, 306–308, 318–322)* |

*Portions of this chapter cover learning outcomes suggested by the American Psychological Association (2007) in their guidelines for the undergraduate psychology major. Chapter coverage of these outcomes is identified by APA Goal and APA Suggested Learning Outcome (SLO).

Most of us take our bodies for granted. We wake up in the morning assuming we will be alert enough to handle our required daily activities; we eat two or three meals a day and perhaps a number of snacks; we may engage in some vigorous exercise and, on some days, in sexual activity. We don't focus on our functioning to any great degree unless it is disrupted by illness or disease. Yet psychological and social factors can significantly disrupt these "activities of survival."

In this chapter we talk about psychological disruptions of two of our relatively automatic behaviors, eating and sleeping, that substantially affect the rest of our behavior.

Major Types of Eating Disorders

> ❭ **What are the defining features of bulimia nervosa and anorexia nervosa?**
> ❭ **How does binge-eating disorder differ from bulimia?**

Although some disorders we discuss in this chapter can be deadly, many of us are not aware they are widespread among us. They began to increase during the 1950s or early 1960s and have spread insidiously over the ensuing decades. In **bulimia nervosa**, out-of-control eating episodes, or **binges**, are followed by self-induced vomiting, excessive use of laxatives, or other attempts to purge (get rid of) the food. In **anorexia nervosa**, the person eats nothing beyond minimal amounts of food, so body weight sometimes drops dangerously. In **binge-eating disorder**, individuals may binge repeatedly and find it distressing but do not attempt to purge the food. The chief characteristic of these related disorders is an overwhelming, all-encompassing drive to be thin. Of the people with anorexia nervosa who are followed over a sufficient period, up to 20% die as a result of their disorder, with slightly more than 5% dying within 10 years (see, for example, Keel et al., 2003; Millar et al., 2005; Papadopoulos, Ekbom, Brandt, & Ekselius, 2009; Theander, 1985; Zipfel, Lowe, Deter, & Herzog, 2000).

As many as 30% of anorexia-related deaths are suicides, which is 50 times higher than the risk of death from suicide in the general population (Agras, 2001; Chavez & Insel 2007; Keel et al., 2003; Thompson & Kinder, 2003).

A growing number of studies in different countries indicate that eating disorders are widespread and increased dramatically in Western countries from about 1960 to 1995, according to the most recent data we have (Bulik et al., 2006; Hoek, 2002). For example, Eagles and colleagues (1995) documented a steady increase of more than 5% per year in Scotland.

Even more dramatic are the data for bulimia nervosa. Garner and Fairburn (1988) reviewed rates of referral to a major eating disorder center in Canada. Between 1975 and 1986, the referral rates for anorexia rose slowly but the

---

bulimia nervosa An eating disorder involving recurrent episodes of uncontrolled excessive (binge) eating followed by compensatory actions to remove the food (for example, deliberate vomiting, laxative abuse, and excessive exercise).

binge A relatively brief episode of uncontrolled, excessive consumption, usually of food or alcohol.

anorexia nervosa An eating disorder characterized by recurrent food refusal, leading to dangerously low body weight.

binge-eating disorder (BED) A pattern of eating involving distress-inducing binges not followed by purging behaviors; being considered as a new DSM diagnostic category.

Yuri Arcurs/Shutterstock.com

rates for bulimia rose dramatically—from virtually none to more than 140 per year. Similar findings have been reported from other parts of the world (Hay & Hall, 1991; Lacey, 1992), although more recent surveys suggest that rates for bulimia are leveling off or even beginning to drop from highs reached in the 1990s (Keel, Heatherton, Dorer, Joiner, & Zalta, 2006). The figures on mortality mentioned previously represent 6 times the increase in death rates from eating disorders compared to death rates in the normal population (Crisp, Callender, Halek, & Hsu, 1992; Papadopoulos et al., 2009). Eating disorders were included for the first time as a separate group of disorders in the fourth edition of the *Diagnostic and Statistical Manual (DSM-IV)*, published in 2000.

The increases in eating disorders during the last half of the 20th century would be puzzling enough if they occurred across the population. What makes them even more intriguing is that they tend to be culturally specific. Until recently, eating disorders were not found in developing countries, where access to sufficient food is so often a daily struggle; only in the West, where food is generally plentiful, have they been rampant. Now this is changing; evidence suggests that eating disorders are going global. Unsystematic interviews with health professionals in Asia (Efon, 1997), and more formal studies (Lee, 1993), show estimates of prevalence in those countries, particularly Japan and Hong Kong, are approaching those in the United States and other Western countries.

Not everyone in the world is at risk. Eating disorders tend to occur in a relatively small segment of the population. More than 90% of the severe cases are young females, mostly in families with upper-middle-class and upper-class socioeconomic status, who live in a socially competitive environment. Increasingly, this group of girls and young women with eating disorders seek one another out on the Internet through "pro-ana" (anorexia) and "pro-mia" (bulimia) websites and social networks, where they find support and, in some cases, inspiration (Peng, 2008; pro-ana-nation, 2010).

The very specificity of these disorders in terms of sex, age, and social class is unparalleled and makes the search for causes all the more interesting. In these disorders, unlike most others, the strongest contributions to etiology seem to be sociocultural rather than psychological or biological factors.

Obesity is not considered an official disorder in the *DSM*, but we consider it here because it is thought to be one of the most dangerous epidemics confronting public health authorities around the world today. The latest surveys indicate that close to 70% of adults in the United States are overweight, and more than 30% meet criteria for obesity (Flegal, Carroll, Ogden, & Curtin, 2010). These rates have been increasing for decades, although they may now be leveling off (Flegal et al., 2010; Ogden et al., 2006). Definitions of underweight, overweight, and obesity will be discussed further later, but they are based on body mass index (BMI), which is highly correlated with body fat. The more overweight someone is at a given height, the greater the risks to health. These risks are widespread and involve greatly increased prevalence of cardiovascular disease, diabetes, hypertension, stroke, gallbladder disease, respiratory disease, muscular skeletal problems, and hormone-related cancers (Flegal, Graubard, Williamson, & Gail, 2005; Henderson & Brownell, 2004; Must et al., 1999; Williams, Wake, Hesketh, Maher, & Waters, 2005). Obesity is included in this chapter because it is produced by the consumption of a greater number of calories than are expended in energy. The behavior that produces this distorted energy equation contradicts a common assumption—namely, that people who are obese do not necessarily eat more or exercise less than their lean counterparts. They do. Although the tendency to overeat and exercise too little unquestionably has a genetic component, as described later, the excessive eating at the core of the problem is the reason that obesity could be considered a disorder of eating.

Bulimia Nervosa

You are probably familiar with bulimia nervosa from your own experience or a friend's. It is one of the most common psychological disorders on college campuses. Consider the case of Phoebe.

Phoebe ❖ Apparently Perfect

Phoebe was a classic all-American girl: popular, attractive, intelligent, and talented. By the time she was a senior in high school, she had accomplished a great deal. She was a class officer throughout high school, homecoming princess her sophomore year, and junior prom queen. She dated the captain of the football team. Phoebe had many talents, among them a beautiful singing voice and marked ability in ballet. She played on several school athletic teams. Phoebe maintained an A-minus average, was considered a model student, and was headed for a top-ranked university.

But Phoebe had a secret: She was haunted by her belief that she was fat and ugly. Every single bite of food that she put in her mouth was, in her mind, another step down the inexorable path that led to the end of her success and popularity. Phoebe had been concerned about her weight since she was 11. Ever the perfectionist, she began regulating her eating in junior high school. She would skip breakfast (over the protestations of her mother), eat a small bowl of pretzels at noon, and allow herself one half of whatever she was served for dinner.

This behavior continued into high school, but as Phoebe struggled to restrict her eating, occasionally she would binge on junk food. Sometimes she stuck her fingers down her throat after a binge (she even tried a toothbrush once), but this tactic was unsuccessful—she did not vomit. By the time she was a senior, Phoebe was obsessed with what she would eat and when. She used every bit of her willpower attempting to restrict her eating, but occasionally she failed. One day during the fall of her senior year, she came home after school and, alone in front of the television, she ate two big boxes of candy. Depressed, guilty, and desperate, she went to the bathroom and stuck her fingers farther down her throat than she had ever before dared. She vomited. And she kept vomiting. Although so physically exhausted that she had to lie down for half an hour, Phoebe had never in her life felt such an overwhelming sense of relief from the anxiety, guilt, and tension that always accompanied her binges. She realized that she had gotten to eat all that candy and now her stomach was empty. It was the perfect solution to her problems.

Phoebe learned quickly what foods she could easily vomit. And she always drank lots of water. She began to restrict her eating even more. She ate almost nothing until after school, but then the results of her dreaming and scheming and planning all morning would be realized. She might pick up a dozen doughnuts and a box of cookies. When she got home, she might make a bowl of popcorn.

And then she ate and ate, forcing down the doughnuts, cookies, and popcorn until her stomach hurt. Finally, with a mixture of revulsion and relief, she purged, forcing herself to vomit. When she was done, she stepped on the scale to make sure she had not gained any weight and then collapsed into bed and slept for about half an hour.

This routine went on for about 6 months, until April of her senior year in high school. By this time, Phoebe had lost much of her energy, and her schoolwork was deteriorating. Her teachers noticed this and saw that she looked bad. She was continually tired, her skin was broken out, and her face puffed up, particularly around her mouth. Her teachers and mother suspected that she might have an eating problem. When they confronted her, she was relieved her problem was finally out in the open.

In an effort to eliminate opportunities to binge and purge, her mother rearranged her schedule to be home in the afternoon when Phoebe got there; in general, her parents minimized the occasions when Phoebe was left alone, particularly after eating. This tactic worked for about a month. Mortally afraid of gaining weight and losing her popularity, Phoebe resumed her pattern, but she was now much better at hiding it. For 6 months Phoebe binged and purged approximately 15 times a week.

When Phoebe went away to college that fall, things became more difficult. Now she had a roommate to contend with, and she was more determined than ever to keep her problem a secret. Although the student health service offered workshops and seminars on eating disorders for the freshman women, Phoebe knew that she could not break her cycle without the risk of gaining weight. To avoid the communal bathroom, she went to a deserted place behind a nearby building to vomit. Social life at college often involved drinking beer and eating fattening foods, so she vomited more often. Nevertheless, she gained 10 pounds. Gaining weight was common among freshmen, but her mother commented without thinking one day that Phoebe seemed to be putting on weight. This remark was devastating to Phoebe.

She kept her secret until the beginning of her sophomore year, when her world fell apart. One night, after drinking a lot of beer at a party, Phoebe and her friends went to Kentucky Fried Chicken. Although Phoebe did not truly binge because she was with friends, she did eat a lot of fried chicken, the most forbidden food on her list. Her guilt, anxiety, and tension increased to new heights. Her stomach throbbed with pain, but when she tried to vomit, her gag reflex seemed to be gone. Breaking into hysterics, she called her boyfriend and told him she was ready to kill herself. Her loud sobbing and crying attracted the attention of her friends in her dormitory, who attempted to comfort her. At this point, Phoebe realized that her life was out of control and that she needed professional help.

Clinical Description

The hallmark of bulimia nervosa is eating a larger amount of food—typically, more junk food than fruits and vegetables—than most people would eat under similar circumstances (Fairburn & Cooper, 1993; Fairburn, Cooper, Shafran, & Wilson, 2008). Patients with bulimia readily identify with this description even though the actual caloric intake for binges varies significantly from person to person (Franko, Wonderlich, Little, & Herzog, 2004). Just as important as the *amount* of food eaten is that the eating is experienced as *out of control* (Fairburn, Cooper, & Cooper, 1986; Sysko & Wilson, 2011), a criterion that is an integral part of the definition of binge eating.

Another important criterion is that the individual attempts to *compensate* for the binge eating and potential weight gain, almost always by **purging techniques**. Techniques include self-induced vomiting immediately after eating, as in the case of Phoebe, and using laxatives (drugs that relieve constipation) and diuretics (drugs that result in

obesity An excess of body fat resulting in a body mass index (a ratio of weight to height) of 30 or more.
purging techniques In the eating disorder bulimia nervosa, the self-induced vomiting or laxative abuse used to compensate for excessive food ingestion.

loss of fluids through greatly increased frequency of urination). Some people use both methods; others attempt to compensate in other ways. Some exercise excessively (although rigorous exercising is more usually a characteristic of anorexia nervosa; Davis et al. [1997] found that 57% of a group of patients with bulimia nervosa exercised excessively but fully 81% of a group with anorexia did). Others fast for long periods between binges. Bulimia nervosa is subtyped in *DSM-IV-TR* into *purging type* (e.g., vomiting, laxatives, or diuretics) or *nonpurging type* (e.g., exercise and/or fasting). But the nonpurging type has turned out to be rare, accounting for only 6% to 8% of patients with bulimia (Hay & Fairburn, 1998; Striegel-Moore et al., 2001).

DSM Disorder Criteria Summary
Bulimia Nervosa

Features of bulimia nervosa include the following:

> Recurrent episodes of binge eating, characterized by an abnormally large intake of food within a 2-hour period, combined with a sense of lack of control over eating during these episodes

> Recurrent, inappropriate compensatory behavior to prevent weight gain, such as self-induced vomiting, misuse of laxatives, fasting, or excessive exercising

> On average, bingeing and inappropriate compensatory behaviors occur at least twice a week for at least 3 months

> Excessive preoccupation with body shape and weight

Source: Based on *DSM-IV-TR*. Reprinted with permission from *Diagnostic and Statistical Manual of Mental Disorders* (4th ed., text revision). © 2000 American Psychiatric Association.

Purging is not a particularly efficient method of reducing caloric intake. Vomiting reduces approximately 50% of the calories just consumed, less if it is delayed (Kaye, Weltzin, Hsu, McConaha, & Bolton, 1993); laxatives and related procedures have little effect, acting, as they do, so long after the binge.

One of the more important additions to the *DSM-IV* criteria is the specification of a psychological characteristic clearly present in Phoebe. Despite her accomplishments and success, she felt her continuing popularity and self-esteem would largely be determined by the weight and shape of her body. Garfinkel (1992) noted that, of 107 women seeking treatment for bulimia nervosa, only 3% did not share this attitude. Recent investigations confirm that the major features of the disorder (bingeing, purging, overconcern with body shape, and so on) "cluster together" in someone with this problem, which strongly supports the validity of the diagnostic category (Bulik, Sullivan, & Kendler, 2000; Fairburn, Cooper, Shafran, & Wilson, 2008; Fairburn, Stice, et al., 2003; Franko et al., 2004; Gleaves, Lowe, Snow, Green, & Murphy-Eberenz, 2000; Keel, Mitchell, Miller, Davis, & Crow, 2000). One problem with the *DSM-IV* criteria is that the "nonpurging" subtype has

proved difficult to define and may not be necessary in *DSM-5* (van Hoeken, Veling, Sinke, Mitchell, & Hoek, 2009).

Medical Consequences

Chronic bulimia with purging has a number of medical consequences (Mehler, Birmingham, Crow, & Jahraus, 2010; Pomeroy, 2004). One is salivary gland enlargement caused by repeated vomiting, which gives the face a chubby appearance. This was noticeable with Phoebe. Repeated vomiting also may erode the dental enamel on the inner surface of the front teeth and tear the esophagus. More important, continued vomiting may upset the chemical balance of bodily fluids, including sodium and potassium levels. This condition, called an *electrolyte imbalance*, can result in serious medical complications if unattended, including cardiac arrhythmia (disrupted heartbeat), seizures, and renal (kidney) failure, all of which can be fatal. Young women with bulimia also develop more body fat than age- and weight-matched healthy controls (Ludescher et al., 2009), the very effect they are trying to avoid. Normalization of eating habits will quickly reverse the imbalance. Intestinal problems resulting from laxative abuse are also potentially serious; they can include severe constipation or permanent colon damage. Finally, some individuals with bulimia have marked calluses on their fingers or the backs of their hands caused by the friction of contact with the teeth and throat when repeatedly sticking their fingers down their throat to stimulate the gag reflex.

Associated Psychological Disorders

An individual with bulimia usually presents with additional psychological disorders, particularly anxiety and mood disorders (Sysko & Wilson, 2011). We compared 20 patients with bulimia nervosa to 20 individuals with panic disorder and another 20 with social phobia (Schwalberg, Barlow, Alger, & Howard, 1992). The most striking finding was that 75% of the patients with bulimia also presented with an anxiety disorder such as social phobia or generalized anxiety disorder. This finding was close to the results from the recent definitive national survey on the prevalence of eating disorders and associated psychological disorders, where 80.6% of individuals with bulimia had an anxiety disorder at some point during their lives (Hudson et al., 2007). Patients with anxiety disorders in the study by Schwalberg and colleagues (1992), however, did not necessarily have an elevated rate of eating disorders. Mood disorders, particularly depression, also commonly co-occur with bulimia, with about 20% of bulimic patients meeting criteria for a mood disorder when interviewed and between 50% and 70% meeting criteria at some point during the course of their disorder (Agras, 2001; Hudson et al., 2007; Sysko & Wilson, 2011).

For a number of years, one prominent theory suggested that eating disorders are simply a way of expressing depression. But most evidence indicates that depression *follows* bulimia and may be a reaction to it (Brownell & Fairburn, 1995; Hsu, 1990). Finally, substance abuse commonly accompanies bulimia nervosa. For example, Kendler and colleagues (1991) surveyed more than 2,000 twins who were not necessarily seeking treatment and found an elevated rate of alcoholism (15.5%) in participants with bulimia. Keel and colleagues (2003) reported that 33% of their combined sample of individuals with bulimia, anorexia, or both also met criteria for substance abuse, including both alcohol and drugs. In summary, bulimia seems strongly related to anxiety disorders and somewhat less so to mood and substance use disorders. Underlying traits of emotional instability and novelty seeking in these individuals may account for these patterns of comorbidity.

Anorexia Nervosa

The overwhelming majority of individuals with bulimia are within 10% of their normal weight (Hsu, 1990). In contrast, individuals with anorexia nervosa (which literally means a "nervous loss of appetite," an incorrect definition because appetite often remains healthy) differ in one important way from individuals with bulimia. They are so successful at losing weight that they put their lives in considerable danger. Both anorexia and bulimia are characterized by a morbid fear of gaining weight and losing control over eating. The major difference seems to be whether the individual is successful at losing weight. People with anorexia are proud of both their diets and their extraordinary control. People with bulimia are ashamed of both their eating issues and their lack of control (Brownell & Fairburn, 1995). Consider the case of Julie.

Julie ⚫ The Thinner, the Better

Julie was 17 years old when she first came for help. She looked emaciated and unwell. Eighteen months earlier she had been overweight, weighing 140 pounds at 5 feet 1 inch. Her mother, a well-meaning but overbearing and demanding woman, nagged Julie incessantly about her appearance. Her friends were kinder but no less relentless. Julie, who had never had a date, was told by a friend she was cute and would have no trouble getting dates if she lost some weight. So she did! After many previous unsuccessful attempts, she was determined to succeed this time.

After several weeks on a strict diet, Julie noticed she was losing weight. She felt a control and mastery that she had never known before. It wasn't long before she received positive comments, not only from her friends, but also from her mother. Julie began to feel good about herself. The difficulty was that she was losing weight too fast. She stopped menstruating. But now nothing could stop her from dieting. By the time she reached our clinic, she weighed 75 pounds. Her parents had just begun to worry about her. Julie did not initially seek treatment for her eating behavior. Rather, she had developed a numbness in her left

lower leg and a left foot drop—an inability to lift up the front part of the foot—that a neurologist determined was caused by peritoneal nerve paralysis believed to be related to inadequate nutrition. The neurologist referred her to our clinic.

Like most people with anorexia, Julie said she probably should put on a little weight, but she didn't mean it. She thought she looked fine, but she had "lost all taste for food," a report that may not have been true because most people with anorexia crave food at least some of the time but control their cravings. Nevertheless, she was participating in most of her usual activities and continued to do extremely well in school and in her extracurricular pursuits. Her parents were happy to buy her most of the workout videotapes available, and she began doing one every day—and then two. When her parents suggested she was exercising enough, and perhaps too much, she worked out when no one was around. After every meal, she exercised with a workout tape until, in her mind, she burned up all the calories she had just taken in.

The tragic consequences of anorexia among young celebrities and within the modeling world have been well publicized in the media. In November 2006, 21-year-old Brazilian model Ana Carolina Reston died; she weighed 88 pounds. At 5 feet 8 inches, she had a BMI of 13.4 (16 is considered starvation). Around the same time, first Spain, then Italy, Brazil, and India instituted bans on models with BMIs less than 18 from their top fashion shows (30% of models in Spain were turned away). It is not clear yet whether the bans have affected popular perception of ideal body size in these countries.

Clinical Description

Anorexia nervosa is less common than bulimia, but there is a great deal of overlap. For example, many individuals with bulimia have a history of anorexia—that is, they once used fasting to reduce their body weight below desirable levels (Fairburn, Cooper, Shafran, & Wilson, 2008; Fairburn, Welch, et al., 1997).

Although decreased body weight is the most notable feature of anorexia nervosa, it is not the core of the disorder. Many people lose weight because of a medical condition, but people with anorexia have an intense fear of obesity and relentlessly pursue thinness (Fairburn, Cooper, Shafran, & Wilson, 2008; Hsu, 1990; Schlundt & Johnson, 1990; Stice, Cameron, Killen, Hayward, & Taylor, 1999). As with Julie, the disorder most commonly begins in an adolescent who is overweight or who perceives herself to be. She then starts a diet that escalates into an obsessive preoccupation with being thin. Severe, almost punishing exercise is common (Davis et al., 1997). Dramatic weight loss is achieved through severe caloric restriction or by combining caloric restriction and purging.

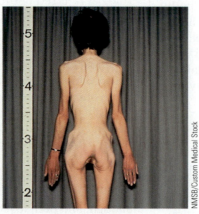

▲ These women are at different stages of anorexia.

DSM Disorder Criteria Summary
Anorexia Nervosa

Features of anorexia nervosa include the following:

> Refusal to maintain body weight at or above a minimally normal level

> Intense fear of gaining weight

> Inappropriate evaluation of one's weight or shape or denial of the seriousness of the current low body weight

> Amenorrhea

Source: Based on DSM-IV-TR. Reprinted with permission from Diagnostic and Statistical Manual of Mental Disorders (4th ed., text revision). © 2000 American Psychiatric Association.

DSM-IV specifies two subtypes of anorexia nervosa. In the *restricting type*, individuals diet to limit calorie intake; in the *binge-eating–purging type*, they rely on purging. Unlike individuals with bulimia, binge-eating–purging anorexics binge on relatively small amounts of food and purge more consistently, in some cases each time they eat. Approximately half the individuals who meet criteria for anorexia engage in binge eating and purging (Agras, 1987; Fairburn, Cooper, Shafran, & Wilson, 2008; Garfinkel, Moldofsky, & Garner, 1979). Prospective data collected over 8 years on 136 individuals with anorexia reveal few differences between these two subtypes on severity of symptoms or personality (Eddy et al., 2002). At that time, 62% of the restricting subtype had begun bingeing or purging. Thus, subtyping may not be useful in predicting the future course of the disorder but rather may reflect a certain phase or stage of anorexia, a finding confirmed in a more recent study (Eddy et al., 2008). For this reason, a proposal likely to be adopted in *DSM-5* specifies that subtyping refer only to the past 3 months (Peat, Mitchell, Hoek, & Wonderlich, 2009).

Individuals with anorexia are never satisfied with their weight loss. Staying the same weight from one day to the next or gaining any weight is likely to cause intense panic, anxiety, and depression. Only continued weight loss every day for weeks on end is satisfactory. Although *DSM-IV* criteria specify body weight 15% below that expected, the average is approximately 25% to 30% below normal by the time treatment is sought (Hsu, 1990). Another key criterion of anorexia is a marked disturbance in body image. When Julie looked at herself in the mirror, she saw something different from what others saw. They saw an emaciated, sickly, frail girl in the throes of semistarvation. Julie saw a girl who still needed to lose at least a few pounds from some parts of her body. For Julie, her face and buttocks were the problems. Other girls might focus on other parts, such as the arms or legs or stomach.

After seeing numerous doctors, people like Julie become good at mouthing what others expect to hear. They may agree they are underweight and need to gain a few pounds—but they don't believe it. Question further and they will tell you the girl in the mirror is fat. Therefore, individuals with anorexia seldom seek treatment on their own. Usually pressure from somebody in the family leads to the initial visit, as in Julie's case (Agras, 1987; Fairburn, Cooper, Shafran, & Wilson, 2008). Perhaps as a demonstration of absolute control over their eating, some individuals with anorexia show increased interest in cooking and food. Some have become expert chefs, preparing all the food for the family. Others hoard food in their rooms, looking at it occasionally.

Medical Consequences

One common medical complication of anorexia nervosa is cessation of menstruation (amenorrhea), which also occurs relatively often in bulimia (Crow, Thuras, Keel, & Mitchell, 2002). This feature can be an objective physical index of the degree of food restriction but is inconsistent because it does not occur in all cases (Franko et al., 2004). Because of this inconsistency, amenorrhea is likely to be dropped as a diagnostic criteria in *DSM-5* (Attia & Roberto, 2009; Fairburn, Cooper, Shafran, & Wilson, 2008; Mitchell, Cook-Myers, & Wonderlich, 2005). Other medical signs and symptoms of anorexia include dry skin, brittle hair or nails, and sensitivity to or intolerance of cold temperatures. Also, it is relatively common to see *lanugo*, downy hair on the limbs and cheeks. Cardiovascular problems, such as chronically low blood pressure and heart rate, can also result. If vomiting is part of the anorexia, electrolyte imbalance and resulting cardiac and kidney problems can result, as in bulimia (Mehler et al., 2010).

Associated Psychological Disorders

As with bulimia nervosa, anxiety disorders and mood disorders are often present in individuals with anorexia (Agras, 2001; Kaye et al., 1993; Sysko & Wilson, 2011;

Vitiello & Lederhendler, 2000), with rates of depression occurring at some point during their lives in as many as 71% of cases (Godart et al., 2007). Of interest, one anxiety disorder that seems to co-occur often with anorexia is obsessive-compulsive disorder (OCD) (see Chapter 4; Keel et al., 2004). In anorexia, unpleasant thoughts are focused on gaining weight, and individuals engage in a variety of behaviors, some of them ritualistic, to rid themselves of such thoughts. Substance abuse is also common in individuals with anorexia nervosa (Keel et al., 2003; Root et al., 2010), and, in conjunction with anorexia, is a strong predictor of mortality, particularly by suicide.

Binge-Eating Disorder

Beginning in the 1990s, research focused on a group of individuals who experience marked distress because of binge eating but do *not* engage in extreme compensatory behaviors and therefore cannot be diagnosed with bulimia (Castonguay, Eldredge, & Agras, 1995; Fairburn et al., 1998; Spitzer et al., 1991). These individuals have binge-eating disorder (BED). Currently, BED is in the appendix of *DSM-IV-TR* as a potential new disorder requiring further study, but it will almost certainly be included as a disorder in its own category in *DSM-5* (Wonderlich, Gordon, Mitchell, Crosby, & Engel, 2009). Evidence that supports this distinction includes somewhat different patterns of heritability compared to other eating disorders (Bulik et al., 2000) and a greater likelihood of occurring in males and a later age of onset. There is also a greater likelihood of remission and a better response to treatment in BED compared to other eating disorders (Striegel-Moore & Franko, 2008; Wonderlich et al., 2009).

Individuals who meet preliminary criteria for BED are often found in weight-control programs. For example, Brody, Walsh, and Devlin (1994) studied mildly obese participants in a weight-control program and identified 18.8% who met criteria for BED. In other programs, with participants ranging in degree of obesity, close to 30% met criteria (see, for example, Spitzer et al., 1993). But Hudson and colleagues (2006) concluded that BED is a disorder caused by a separate set of factors from obesity without BED and is associated with more severe obesity. The general consensus is that about 20% of obese individuals in weight-loss programs engage in binge eating, with the number rising to approximately 50% among candidates for bariatric surgery (surgery to correct severe or morbid obesity). Fairburn, Cooper, Doll, Norman, and O'Connor (2000) identified 48 individuals with BED and were able to prospectively follow 40 of them for 5 years. The prognosis was relatively good for this group, with only 18% retaining the full diagnostic criteria for BED at a 5-year follow-up. The percentage of this group who were obese, however, increased from 21% to 39% at the 5-year mark.

About half of individuals with BED try dieting before bingeing, and half start with bingeing and then attempt to diet (Abbott et al., 1998); those who begin bingeing first become more severely affected by BED and are more likely to have additional disorders (Spurrell, Wilfley, Tanofsky, & Brownell, 1997). It's also increasingly clear that individuals with BED have some of the same concerns about shape and weight as people with anorexia and bulimia, which distinguishes them from individuals who are obese without BED (Fairburn, Cooper, Shafran, & Wilson, 2008; Goldschmidt et al., 2010; Grilo, Masheb, & White, 2010; Hrabosky, Masheb, White, & Grilo, 2007). It seems that approximately 33% of those with BED binge to alleviate "bad moods" or negative affect (see, for example, Grilo, Masheb, & Wilson, 2001; Stice, Akutagawa, Gaggar, & Agras, 2000; Stice et al., 2001). These individuals are more psychologically disturbed than the 67% who do not use bingeing to regulate mood (Grilo et al., 2001).

Statistics

Clear cases of bulimia have been described for thousands of years (Parry-Jones & Parry-Jones, 2002), but bulimia nervosa was recognized as a distinct psychological disorder only in the 1970s (Boskind-Lodahl, 1976; Russell, 1979). Therefore, information on prevalence has been acquired relatively recently.

Among those who present for treatment, the overwhelming majority (90% to 95%) of individuals with bulimia are women; most are white and middle to upper-middle class. Males with bulimia have a slightly later age of onset, and a large minority are predominantly gay males or bisexual (Rothblum, 2002). For example, Carlat, Camargo, and Herzog (1997) accumulated information on 135 male patients with eating disorders who were seen over 13 years and found that 42% were either gay or bisexual, a far higher rate of eating disorders than found in heterosexual males (Feldman & Meyer, 2007). Male athletes in sports that require weight regulation, such as wrestling, are another large group of males with eating disorders (Ricciardelli & McCabe, 2004). Among women, adolescent girls are most at risk. A recent prospective 8-year survey of 496 adolescent girls reported that more than 12% experienced some form of eating disorder by the time they were 20 (Stice, Marti, Shaw, & Jaconis, 2009). In another elegant prospective study, eating-related problems of 1,498 freshmen women at a large university were studied over the 4-year college experience. Only 28% to 34% had no eating-related concerns. But 29% to 34% consistently attempted to limit their food intake because of weight/shape concerns; 14% to 18% engaged in overeating and binge eating; another 14% to 17% combined attempts to limit intake with binge eating; and 6% to 7% had pervasive bulimic-like concerns. And these tendencies were stable for the most part throughout their 4 years of college (Cain, Epler, Steinley, & Sher, 2010).

A somewhat different view of the prevalence of bulimia comes from studies of the population rather than of specific groups of adolescents, with the most definitive study appearing in 2007 (Hudson et al., 2007). These results from the national comorbidity survey reflect lifetime and 12-month prevalence, not only for the three major eating disorders described here, but also for "subthreshold" BED, where binge eating occurred at a high-enough frequency but some additional criteria, such as "marked distress" regarding the binge eating, were not met. Therefore, the disorder did not meet the diagnostic "threshold" for BED. In addition, only a 3-month duration was required for BED (or subthreshold BED), as is proposed for *DSM-5*, rather than the 6 months required in *DSM-IV-TR*. Thus, the prevalence of BED reported in this survey may be slightly higher than if the *DSM-IV* 6-month criteria were used. Finally, if binge eating occurred at least twice a week for 3 months, even if it was just a symptom of the four other disorders in Table 8.1 rather than a separate condition, the case was listed under "Any binge eating." This latter category provides an overall picture of the prevalence of binge eating. These data are all presented in Table 8.1. As you can see, lifetime prevalence was consistently 2 to 3 times greater for females, with the exception of subthreshold BED. This sex ratio reflects a somewhat higher proportion of males than found in other samples, but because there are so few males in any study of eating disorders, these results tend to be unstable. No 12-month cases of anorexia were found in this sample, but a large study in Finland based on a telephone survey found a higher lifetime prevalence of anorexia of 2.2%, and half those cases had not been detected in the health-care system (Keski-Rahkonen et al., 2007). So it is possible that the prevalence of anorexia is underrepresented in some surveys.

The median age of onset for all eating-related disorders occurred in a narrow range of 18 to 21 years (Hudson et al., 2007). For anorexia, this age of onset was fairly consistent, with younger cases tending to begin at age 15, but it was more common for cases of bulimia to begin as early as age 10, as it did for Phoebe.

Once bulimia develops, it tends to be chronic if untreated (Fairburn et al., 2000; Fairburn, Stice, et al., 2003; Hudson et al., 2007; Keel & Mitchell, 1997); one study shows the "drive for thinness" and accompanying symptoms still present in a group of women 10 years after diagnosis (Joiner, Heatherton, & Keel, 1997). In an important study of the course of bulimia, referred to earlier, Fairburn and colleagues (2000) identified a group of 102 females with bulimia nervosa and followed 92 of them prospectively for 5 years. About a third improved to the point where they no longer met diagnostic criteria each year, but another third who had improved previously relapsed. Between 50% and 67% exhibited serious eating disorder symptoms at the end of each year of the 5-year study, indicating this disorder has a relatively poor prognosis. In a follow-up study, Fairburn, Stice, and colleagues (2003) reported that the strongest predictors of persistent bulimia were a history of childhood obesity and a continuing overemphasis on the importance of being thin. Similarly, once anorexia develops, its course seems chronic—although not so chronic as bulimia, based on data from Hudson and colleagues (2007), particularly if it is caught early and treated. But individuals with anorexia tend to maintain a low BMI over a long period, along with distorted perceptions of

Table 8.1 Lifetime and 12-Month Prevalence Estimates of *DSM-IV-TR* Eating Disorders and Related Problems

	Male	Female	Total
	%	%	%
I. Lifetime prevalence Anorexia nervosa	0.3	0.9	0.6
Bulimia nervosa	0.5	1.5	1.0
Binge-eating disorder	2.0	3.5	2.8
Subthreshold binge-eating disorder	1.9	0.6	1.2
Any binge eating	4.0	4.9	4.5
II. 12-month prevalence* Bulimia nervosa	0.1	0.5	0.3
Binge-eating disorder	0.8	1.6	1.2
Subthreshold binge-eating disorder	0.8	0.4	0.6
Any binge eating	1.7	2.5	2.1
(n) Number of participants	(1,220)	(1,760)	(2,980)

*None of the respondents met criteria for 12-month anorexia nervosa.
Source: From Hudson et al. (2007). The prevalence and correlates of eating disorders in the national comorbidity survey replication. *Biological Psychiatry,* 61, 348–358. © Society for Biological Psychiatry.

shape and weight, indicating that even if they no longer meet criteria for anorexia they continue to restrict their eating (Fairburn, Cooper, Shafran, & Wilson, 2008). Perhaps for this reason, anorexia is thought to be more resistant to treatment than bulimia, based on clinical studies (Herzog et al., 1999; Vitiello & Lederhendler, 2000). In one 7-year study following individuals who had received treatment, 33% of those with anorexia versus 66% of those with bulimia reached full remission at some point during the follow-up (Eddy et al., 2008).

Cross-Cultural Considerations

We have already discussed the highly culturally specific nature of anorexia and bulimia. A particularly striking finding is that these disorders develop in immigrants who have recently moved to Western countries (Anderson-Fye, 2009). One of the more interesting studies is Nasser's 1986 survey of 50 Egyptian women in London universities and 60 Egyptian women in Cairo universities (Nasser, 1988). There were no instances of eating disorders in Cairo, but 12% of the Egyptian women in England had developed eating disorders.

The prevalence of eating disorders varies among most North American minority populations, including African Americans, Hispanics, Native Americans, and Asians. Compared to Caucasians, the prevalence of eating disorders is lower among African American and Asian American females, equally common among Hispanic females, and

▲ Anorexia seldom occurs among North American black women.

more common among Native Americans (Crago, Shisslak, & Estes, 1997). Generally, surveys reveal that African American adolescent girls have less body dissatisfaction, fewer weight concerns, and a more positive self-image and perceive themselves to be thinner than they are compared to Caucasian adolescent girls (Celio, Zabinski, & Wilfley, 2002). Greenberg and LaPorte (1996) observed in an experiment that young white males preferred somewhat thinner figures in women than African American males, which may contribute to the somewhat lower incidence of eating disorders in African American women.

There is a relatively high incidence of purging behavior in some minority groups. In most cases, the purging seems to be associated with obesity. Rosen and colleagues (1988) found widespread purging and related behaviors in a group of American Indian Chippewa women. Among this group, 74% had dieted and 55% had used harmful weight-loss techniques such as fasting or purging; 12% had vomited and 6% reported use of laxatives or diuretics.

In Japan, the prevalence of anorexia nervosa among teenage girls is still lower than the rate in North America, but, as mentioned previously, it seems to be increasing. The need to be thin or the fear of becoming overweight has not been as important in Japanese culture as it is in North America, although this may be changing as cultures around the world become more Westernized (Kawamura, 2002).

In conclusion, anorexia and bulimia are relatively homogeneous and, until recently, were overwhelmingly associated with Western cultures. In addition, the frequency and pattern of occurrence among minority Western cultures differs somewhat but is associated with closer identification with Caucasian middle-class and upper-class values.

Developmental Considerations

Because the overwhelming majority of cases begin in adolescence, it is clear that anorexia and bulimia are strongly related to development (Smith, Simmons, Flory, Annus, & Hill, 2007). As pointed out by Striegel-Moore, Silberstein, and Rodin (1986) and Attie and Brooks-Gunn (1995), differential patterns of physical development in girls and boys interact with cultural influences to create eating disorders. After puberty, girls gain weight primarily in fat tissue, whereas boys develop muscle and lean tissue. As the ideal look in Western countries is tall and muscular for men and thin and prepubertal for women, physical development brings boys closer to the ideal and takes girls further away.

Eating disorders, particularly anorexia nervosa, occasionally occur in children younger than age 11 (Walsh, 2010). Negative attitude toward being overweight emerges as early as 3 years of age, and more than half of girls age 6–8 would like to be thinner (Striegel-Moore & Franko, 2002). By 9 years of age, 20% of girls reported trying to lose weight, and by 14, 40% were trying to lose weight (Field et al., 1999).

Both bulimia and anorexia can occur in later years, particularly after the age of 55. Hsu and Zimmer (1988) reported that most of these individuals had had an eating disorder for decades with little change in their behavior. However, in a few cases onset did not occur until later years, and it is not yet clear what factors were involved. Generally, concerns about body image decrease with age (Tiggemann & Lynch, 2001; Whitbourne & Skultety, 2002).

Concept Check 8.1

Check your understanding of eating disorders by identifying the proper disorder in the following scenarios: (a) bulimia nervosa, (b) anorexia nervosa, and (c) binge-eating disorder.

1. Manny has been having episodes lately when he eats prodigious amounts of food. He's been putting on a lot of weight because of it. _____

2. I noticed Elena eating a whole pie, a cake, and two bags of potato chips the other day when she didn't know I was there. She ran to the bathroom when she was finished and it sounded like she was vomiting. This disorder can lead to an electrolyte imbalance, resulting in serious medical problems.

_____

3. Joo-Yeon eats large quantities of food in a short time. She then takes laxatives and exercises for long periods to prevent weight gain. She has been doing this almost daily for several months and feels she will become worthless and ugly if she gains even an ounce. _____

4. Kirsten has lost several pounds and now weighs less than 90 pounds. She eats only a small portion of the food her mother serves her and fears that intake above her current 500 calories daily will make her fat. Since losing the weight, Kirsten has stopped having periods. She sees a fat person in the mirror. _____

We all eat. However, what we eat and how much of it we consume is strongly influenced by the culture in which we live. As mentioned earlier, cultural influences contribute to differences in the rates of eating disorders, such as anorexia nervosa and bulimia nervosa, across sexes, ethnicities, and geographic regions. Eating disorders are much more prevalent among women than men and occur significantly more often among European American women than African American women (Striegel-Moore et al., 2003).

How is it that culture influences eating in way that makes eating disorders more prevalent among these groups? A leading possibility is the beliefs held in different cultures about the ideal body shape. The more a culture values thinness, the greater the desire of people within that culture to attain a lower weight and thinner body shape. Interestingly, studies have shown that as the ideal body shape for women to have has become ever thinner (as shown, for example, in the shrinking measurements of *Playboy* centerfolds and Miss America Pageant contestants over the past several decades), the rates of eating disorders among young girls in Western cultures have increased (Keel & Klump, 2003).

Evidence of the influence of cultural factors—and not some genetic or other biological factor operating within Western cultures—comes from several interesting studies that investigate how a change in culture can influence the rate of eating disorders. Such studies have shown that women from Eastern and Middle Eastern cultures who attend Western universities have much higher rates of eating disorders while in the Western culture compared with women from their home country (Mumford, Whitehouse, & Platts, 1991; Nasser, 1988). One could argue that something about the women who decided to study in the West influenced the occurrence of the eating disorders in that group. However, further evidence of the influence of aspects of Western culture, such as the thin ideal for women, comes from an interesting study on the development of eating problems among girls on the island of Fiji after the introduction of television on Fiji in 1995. Within 1 month of seeing television for the first time, 7.9% of Fijian girls reported binge eating, and the rate of self-induced vomiting increased from 0% to 11% over the next 3 years (Becker, Burwell, Gilman, Herzog, & Hamburg, 2002). Interviews with Fijian girls revealed that they had begun to model themselves after the girls observed on television, providing evidence for the influence of Western culture on their eating behavior. Overall, although there appears to be a genetic basis for eating disorders, these studies highlight the strong influence that culture can have on a person's self-image, eating habits, and likelihood of developing an eating disorder.

Causes of Eating Disorders

> **What social, psychological, and neurobiological factors might cause eating disorders?**

As with all disorders discussed in this book, biological, psychological, and social factors contribute to the development of these serious eating disorders. However, the evidence is increasingly clear that the most dramatic factors are social and cultural.

Social Dimensions

Remember that anorexia and bulimia are the most culturally specific psychological disorders yet identified. What drives so many young people into a punishing and life-threatening routine of semistarvation or purging? For many young Western women, looking good is more important than being healthy. For young females in middle- to upper-class competitive environments, self-worth, happiness, and success are largely determined by body measurements and percentage of body fat—factors that have little or no correlation with personal happiness and success in the long run. The cultural imperative for thinness directly results in dieting, the first dangerous step down the slippery slope to anorexia and bulimia.

Levine and Smolak (1996) refer to "the glorification of slenderness" in magazines and on television, where most females are thinner than average American women. Because overweight men are 2 to 5 times more common as television characters than overweight women, the message from the media to be thin is clearly aimed at women, and the message gets through loud and clear. Grabe, Ward, and Hyde (2008), reviewing 77 studies, demonstrated a strong relationship between exposure to media images depicting the thin-ideal body and body image concerns in women. An analysis of prime-time television situation comedies revealed that 12% of female characters were dieting and many were making disparaging comments about their body image (Tiggemann, 2002). Finally, Thompson and Stice (2001) found that risk for developing eating disorders was directly related to the extent to which women internalize or "buy in" to the media messages and images glorifying thinness, a finding also confirmed by Cafri, Yamamiya, Brannick, and Thompson (2005).

The problem with today's standards is that they are increasingly difficult to achieve because the size and weight of the average woman has increased over the years with improved nutrition; there is also a general increase in size throughout history (Brownell, 1991; Brownell & Rodin, 1994). Whatever the cause, the collision between our culture and our physiology (Brownell, 1991; Brownell & Fairburn, 1995) has had some negative effects, one of which is that women became dissatisfied with their bodies.

Fallon and Rozin (1985), studying male and female undergraduates, found that men rated their current size, their ideal size, and the size they figured would be most attractive to the opposite sex as approximately equal; indeed, they rated their ideal body weight as *heavier* than the weight females thought most attractive in men (■ Figure 8.1). Women, however, rated their current figures as much heavier than what they judged the most attractive, which in turn, was rated as heavier than what they thought was ideal. This conflict between reality and fashion seems most closely related to the current epidemic of eating disorders.

Other researchers have presented interesting data that support Fallon and Rozin's findings that men have different body image perceptions than women. Pope and colleagues (2000) confirmed that men generally desire to be heavier and more muscular than they are. The authors measured the height, weight, and body fat of college-age men in three countries—Austria, France, and the United States. They asked the men to choose the body image that they felt represented (1) their own body, (2) the body they ideally would like to have, (3) the body of an average man of their age, and (4) the male body they believed was preferred by women. In all three countries, men chose an ideal body weight that was approximately 28 pounds more muscular than their current one. They also estimated that women would prefer a male body about 30 pounds more muscular than their current one. In contradiction to the impression, Pope and colleagues (2000) demonstrated, in a pilot study, that most women preferred an ordinary male body without the added muscle. Men who abuse anabolic–androgenic steroids to increase muscle mass and "bulk up" possess these distorted attitudes toward muscles, weight,

and the "ideal man" to a greater degree than men who don't use steroids (Kanayama, Barry, & Pope, 2006).

We have some specific information on how these attitudes are socially transmitted in adolescent girls. Paxton, Schutz, Wertheim, and Muir (1999) explored the influence of close friendship groups on attitudes concerning body image, dietary restraint, and extreme weight-loss behaviors. In a clever experiment, the authors identified 79 different friendship cliques in a group of 523 adolescent girls. They found that these friendship cliques tended to share the same attitudes toward body image, dietary restraint, and the importance of attempts to lose weight. It was also clear from the study that these friendship cliques contributed significantly to the formation of individual body image concerns and eating behaviors. In other words, if your friends tend to use extreme dieting or other weight-loss techniques, there is a greater chance that you will, too (Field et al., 2001; Vander Wal & Thelen, 2000).

The abhorrence of fat can have tragic consequences. In one study, toddlers with affluent parents appeared at hospitals with "failure to thrive" syndrome, in which growth and development are severely retarded because of inadequate nutrition. In each case, the parents had put their young, healthy, but somewhat chubby toddlers on diets in the hope of preventing obesity at a later date (Pugliese, Weyman-Daun, Moses, & Lifshitz, 1987).

Most people who diet don't develop eating disorders, but Patton, Johnson-Sabine, Wood, Mann, and Wakeling (1990) determined in a prospective study that adolescent girls who dieted were 8 times more likely to develop an eating disorder 1 year later than those who weren't dieting. And Telch and Agras (1993) noted marked increases in bingeing during and after rigorous dieting in 201 obese women.

Stice and colleagues (1999) demonstrated that one of the reasons attempts to lose weight may lead to eating disorders is that weight-reduction efforts in adolescent girls are more likely to result in weight *gain* than weight

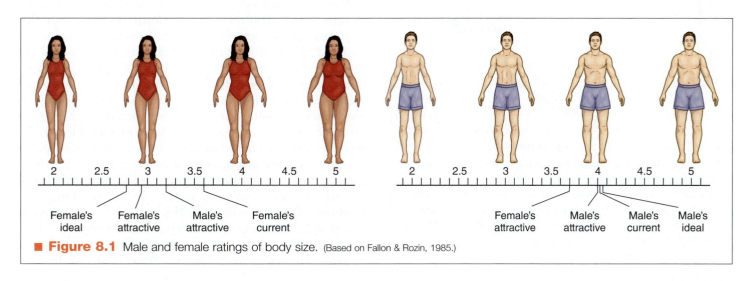

■ **Figure 8.1** Male and female ratings of body size. (Based on Fallon & Rozin, 1985.)

Peter Will/SuperStock

Michael Bush/UPI/Landov

▲ Changing concepts of ideal weight are evident in a 17th-century painting by Peter Paul Rubens and in a photograph of a current fashion model.

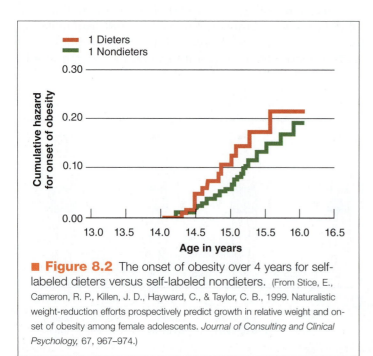

■ **Figure 8.2** The onset of obesity over 4 years for self-labeled dieters versus self-labeled nondieters. (From Stice, E., Cameron, R. P., Killen, J. D., Hayward, C., & Taylor, C. B., 1999. Naturalistic weight-reduction efforts prospectively predict growth in relative weight and onset of obesity among female adolescents. *Journal of Consulting and Clinical Psychology, 67,* 967–974.)

loss. To establish this finding, 692 girls, initially the same weight, were followed for 4 years. Girls who attempted dieting faced more than 300% greater risk of obesity than those who did not diet. Results are presented in ■ Figure 8.2.

It is not yet entirely clear why dieting leads to bingeing in only some people (Polivy & Herman, 1993), but the relationship is strong. In one study, Urbszat, Herman, and Polivy (2002) told 46 undergraduates that they would either be dieting for a week (Group 1) or not (Group 2) and then presented them with food under the pretext of giving them a taste test. But investigators were really looking at how much they ate during the test, not their ratings of taste. People who expected to go on a diet ate more than the group that didn't—but *only* if they were "restrained eaters" who were continually attempting to restrict their intake of food, particularly fattening food. Thus, attempts to restrict intake may put people at risk for bingeing. Fairburn, Cooper, Doll, and Davies (2005) examined a group of 2,992 young women who were dieting and identified 104 who developed an eating disorder over the next 2 years. Among all of these dieters, several risk factors were identified. Those most at risk for developing an eating disorder were already binge eating and purging, were eating in secret, expressed a desire to have an empty stomach, were preoccupied with food, and were afraid of losing control over eating.

Distortions of body image in some males can also have tragic consequences. Olivardia, Pope, and Hudson (2000) have described a syndrome in men, particularly male weight lifters, that they initially termed "reverse anorexia nervosa." Men with this syndrome reported they were extremely concerned about looking small, even though they were muscular. Many of these men avoided beaches, locker rooms, and other places where their bodies might be seen. These men also were prone to using anabolic–androgenic steroids to bulk up, risking both the medical and the psychological consequences of taking steroids. The conflict over body image would be bad enough if size were infinitely malleable, but it is not. Increasing evidence indicates a strong genetic contribution to body size; that is, some of us are born to be heavier than others, and we are all shaped differently. Although most of us can be physically fit, few can achieve the levels of fitness and shape so highly valued today. Biologically, it is nearly impossible (Brownell, 1991; Brownell & Fairburn, 2002). Nevertheless, many young people in our society fight biology to the point of starvation. In adolescence, cultural standards are often experienced as peer pressure and are more influential than reason and fact. The high number of males who are homosexual among the relatively small numbers of males with eating disorders has also been attributed to pressures among gay men to be physically trim (Carlat et al., 1997; Feldman & Meyer, 2007). Conversely, pressure to appear more fit and muscular is also apparent for a substantial proportion of men (Pope et al., 2000).

Dietary Restraint

If cultural pressures to be thin are as important as they seem to be in triggering eating disorders, then such disorders would be expected to occur where these pressures are particularly severe, which is just what happens to ballet dancers, who are under extraordinary pressures to be thin. Garner, Garfinkel, Rockert, and Olmsted (1987) followed a group of 11- to 14-year-old female students in ballet school. The conservative estimate was that at least 25% of these girls developed eating disorders during the 2 years of the study. Similar results are apparent among athletes (such as gymnasts), particularly females. What goes on in ballet classes that has such a devastating effect on girls? Consider the case of Phoebe again.

Abnormal Psychology Inside Out. Produced by Ira Wohl, Only Child Motion Pictures

Anorexia Nervosa: Susan

"Basically . . . I don't want to eat because it seems like, as soon as I eat, I just gain weight, get fat. . . . There are some times when I can't stop it, I just have to, and then, once I eat, there is a strong urge to either purge or take a laxative. . . . It never stops. . . . It becomes very obsessive, where you're getting on the scales 10 times a day. . . . I weigh 96 pounds now."

Go to Psychology CourseMate at www.cengagebrain.com to watch this video.

Phoebe • Dancing to Destruction

Phoebe remembered clearly that during her early years in ballet the older girls talked incessantly about their weight. Phoebe performed well and looked forward to the rare compliment. The ballet mistress seemed to comment more on weight than on dance technique, often remarking, "You'd dance better if you lost weight." If one little girl lost a few pounds through heroic dieting, the instructor always pointed it out: "You've done well working on your weight. The rest of you had better follow this example." One day, without warning, the instructor said to Phoebe, "You need to lose 5 pounds before the next class." At that time, Phoebe was 5 feet 2 inches and weighed 98 pounds. The next class was in 2 days. After one of these admonitions and several days of restrictive eating, Phoebe experienced her first uncontrollable binge.

Early in high school, Phoebe gave up the rigors of ballet to pursue a variety of other interests. She did not forget the glory of her starring roles as a young dancer or how to perform the steps. She still danced occasionally by herself and retained the grace that serious dancers effortlessly display. But in college, as she stuck her head in the toilet bowl, vomiting her guts out for perhaps the third time that day, she realized there was one lesson she had learned in ballet class more deeply and thoroughly than any other—the life-or-death importance of being thin at all costs.

Thus, dieting is one factor that can contribute to eating disorders (Polivy & Herman, 2002), and, along with dissatisfaction with one's body, is a primary risk factor for later eating disorders (Stice, Ng, & Shaw, 2010).

Family Influences

Much has been made of the possible significance of family interaction patterns in cases of eating disorders. A number of investigators (see, for example, Attie & Brooks-Gunn,

1995; Bruch, 1985; Humphrey, 1986, 1988, 1989; Minuchin, Rosman, & Baker, 1978) have found that the "typical" family of someone with anorexia is successful, hard-driving, concerned about external appearances, and eager to maintain harmony. To accomplish these goals, family members often deny or ignore conflicts or negative feelings and tend to attribute their problems to other people at the expense of frank communication among themselves (Fairburn, Shafran, & Cooper, 1999; Hsu, 1990).

Pike and Rodin (1991) confirmed the differences in interactions within the families of girls with disordered eating in comparison with control families. Basically, mothers of girls with disordered eating seemed to act as "society's messengers" in wanting their daughters to be thin (Steinberg & Phares, 2001). They were likely to be dieting themselves and, generally, were more perfectionistic than comparison mothers in that they were less satisfied with their families and family cohesion (Fairburn, Cooper, et al., 1999; Fairburn, Welch, et al., 1997).

Whatever the preexisting relationships, after the onset of an eating disorder, particularly anorexia, family relationships can deteriorate quickly. Educated and knowledgeable parents, including psychologists and psychiatrists with full understanding of the disorder, have reported resorting to physical violence (for example, hitting or slapping) in moments of extreme frustration, in a vain attempt to get their daughters to put some food, however little, in their mouths. The parents' guilt and anguish was considerable.

Biological Dimensions

Like most psychological disorders, eating disorders run in families and thus seem to have a genetic component (Strober, 2002). Although completed studies are only preliminary, they suggest that relatives of patients with eating disorders are 4 to 5 times more likely than the general population to develop eating disorders themselves, with the risks for female relatives of patients with anorexia a bit higher (see, for example, Hudson, Pope, Jonas, & Yurgelun-Todd, 1983; Strober, Freeman, Lampert, Diamond, & Kaye, 2000; Strober & Humphrey, 1987). In important twin studies of bulimia by Kendler and colleagues (1991) and of anorexia by Walters and Kendler (1995), researchers used structured interviews to ascertain the prevalence of the disorders among 2,163 female twins. In 23% of identical twin pairs, both twins had bulimia, as compared to 9% of fraternal twins. Because no adoption studies have yet been reported, strong sociocultural influences cannot be ruled out, and other studies have produced inconsistent results (Fairburn, Cowen, & Harrison, 1999). For anorexia, numbers were too small for precise estimates, but the disorder in one twin did seem to confer a significant risk for both anorexia and bulimia in the co-twin.

An emerging consensus is that genetic makeup is about half of the equation among causes of anorexia and bulimia

(Klump, Kaye, & Strober, 2001; Strober, 2002; Wade, Bulik, Neale, & Kendler, 2000). Again, there is no clear agreement on just *what* is inherited (Fairburn, Cowen, et al., 1999). Hsu (1990) speculates that nonspecific personality traits such as emotional instability and, perhaps, poor impulse control might be inherited. In other words, a person might inherit a tendency to be emotionally responsive to stressful life events and, as one consequence, might eat impulsively in an attempt to relieve stress and anxiety (Kaye, 2008; Strober, 2002). Klump and colleagues (2001) mention perfectionist traits, along with negative affect. This biological vulnerability might then interact with social and psychological factors to produce an eating disorder. Wade and colleagues (2008) found support for this idea in a study of 1,002 same-sex twins in which anorexia was associated with, and maybe a reflection of, a trait of perfectionism and a need for order that runs in families.

Biological processes are quite active in the regulation of eating and thus of eating disorders, and substantial evidence points to the hypothalamus as playing an important role. Investigators have studied the hypothalamus and the major neurotransmitter systems—including norepinephrine, dopamine, and, particularly, serotonin—that pass through it to determine whether something is malfunctioning when eating disorders occur (Kaye, 2008; Vitiello & Lederhendler, 2000). Low levels of serotonergic activity are associated with impulsivity generally and binge eating specifically (see Chapter 2). Thus, most drugs under study as treatments for bulimia target the serotonin system (see, for example, de Zwaan, Roerig, & Mitchell, 2004; Kaye, 2008; Kaye et al., 1998; Walsh et al., 1997).

If investigators do find a strong association between neurobiological functions and eating disorders, the question of cause or effect remains. At present, the consensus is that some neurobiological abnormalities do exist in people with eating disorders but that they are a *result* of semistarvation or a binge–purge cycle rather than a cause, although they may well contribute to the *maintenance* of the disorder once it is established.

Psychological Dimensions

Clinical observations indicate that many young women with eating disorders have a diminished sense of personal control and confidence in their own abilities and talents (Bruch, 1973, 1985; Striegel-Moore, Silberstein, & Rodin, 1993; Walters & Kendler, 1995). This may manifest as strikingly low self-esteem (Fairburn, Cooper, & Shafran, 2003). They also display more perfectionistic attitudes, perhaps learned or inherited from their families, which may reflect attempts to exert control over important events in their lives (Fairburn, Cooper, et al., 1999; Fairburn, Welch, et al., 1997; Joiner et al., 1997). Shafran, Lee, Payne, and Fairburn (2006) artificially raised perfectionistic standards in otherwise normal women by instructing them to pursue the highest possible standards in everything they do for the next 24 hours. These instructions caused them to eat fewer high-calorie foods, to restrict their eating, and to have more regret after eating than women told to just do the minimum for 24 hours. This occurred even though eating was not specifically mentioned as part of pursuing the "highest standards."

Perfectionism alone, however, is only weakly associated with the development of an eating disorder because individuals must consider themselves overweight and manifest low self-esteem before the trait of perfectionism makes a contribution (Vohs, Bardone, Joiner, Abramson, & Heatherton, 1999). But when perfectionism is directed to distorted perception of body image, a powerful engine to drive eating disorder behavior is in place (Lilenfeld, Wonderlich, Riso, Crosby, & Mitchell, 2006; Shafran, Cooper, & Fairburn, 2002). Women with eating disorders are intensely preoccupied with how they appear to others (Fairburn, Stice, et al., 2003; Smith et al., 2007). They also perceive themselves as frauds, considering false any impressions they make of being adequate, self-sufficient, or worthwhile. In this sense, they feel like impostors in their social groups and experience heightened levels of social anxiety (Smolak & Levine, 1996). Striegel-Moore and colleagues (1993) suggest these social self-deficits are likely to increase as a consequence of the eating disorder, further isolating the woman from the social world.

Specific distortions in perception of body shape change often, depending on day-to-day experience. McKenzie, Williamson, and Cubic (1993) found that women with bulimia judged that their bodies were larger after they ate a candy bar and soft drink, whereas the judgments of women in control groups were unaffected by snacks. Thus, rather minor events related to eating may activate fear of gaining weight, further distortions in body image, and corrective schemes such as purging.

Rosen and Leitenberg (1985) observed substantial anxiety before and during snacks, which they theorized is *relieved* by purging. They suggested the state of relief strongly reinforces the purging, in that we tend to repeat behavior that gives us pleasure or relief from anxiety. This seemed to be true for Phoebe. However, other evidence suggests that in treating bulimia, reducing the anxiety associated with eating is less important than countering the tendency to overly restrict food intake and the associated negative attitudes about body image that lead to bingeing and purging (see, for example, Agras, Schneider, Arnow, Raeburn, & Telch, 1989; Fairburn, Agras, & Wilson, 1992; Fairburn, Cooper, Shafran, & Wilson, 2008).

Another important observation is that at least a subgroup of these patients has difficulty tolerating any negative emotion (mood intolerance) and may binge or engage in other behaviors, such as self-induced vomiting or intense exercise, in an attempt to regulate their mood (Paul, Schroeter, Dahme, & Nutzinger, 2002).

An Integrative Model

Although the three major eating disorders are identifiable by their unique characteristics, and the specific diagnoses have some validity, it is becoming increasingly clear that all eating disorders have much in common in terms of causal factors. It may be more useful to lump the eating disorders into one diagnostic category, simply noting which specific features occur, such as dietary restraint, bingeing, or purging.

In putting together what we know about eating disorders, it is important to remember, again, that no one factor seems sufficient to cause them (see ■ Figure 8.3). Individuals with eating disorders may have some of the same biological vulnerabilities (such as being highly responsive to stressful life events) as individuals with anxiety disorders (Kendler et al., 1995; Rojo, Conesa, Bermudez, & Livianos, 2006). Anxiety and mood disorders are also common in the families of individuals with eating disorders (Schwalberg et al., 1992), and negative emotions, along with "mood intolerance," seem to trigger binge eating in many patients. In addition, as you will see, drug and psychological treatments with proven effectiveness for anxiety disorders are also the treatments of choice for eating disorders. Indeed, we could conceptualize eating disorders as anxiety disorders focused exclusively on a fear of becoming overweight.

In any case, it is clear that social and cultural pressures to be thin motivate significant restriction of eating, usually through severe dieting. Remember, however, that many people go on strict diets, including adolescent females, but only a small minority develop eating disorders, so dieting alone does not account for the disorders. It is also important to note that the social interactions in high-income, high-achieving families may well be a factor. An emphasis in these families on looks and achievement, and perfectionistic tendencies, may help establish strong attitudes about the overriding importance of physical appearance to popularity and success. These attitudes result in an exaggerated focus on body shape and weight.

Finally, there is the question of why a small minority of individuals with eating disorders can successfully control their intake through dietary restraint, resulting in alarming weight loss (anorexia), whereas the majority are unsuccessful at losing weight and compensate in a cycle of bingeing and purging (bulimia), although most individuals with anorexia do go on to bingeing and purging at some point (Eddy et al., 2002; Eddy et al., 2008). These differences, at least initially, may be determined by biology or physiology, such as a genetically determined disposition to be somewhat thinner initially. Then again, perhaps preexisting personality characteristics, such as a tendency to be overcontrolling, are important determinants of which disorder an individual develops.

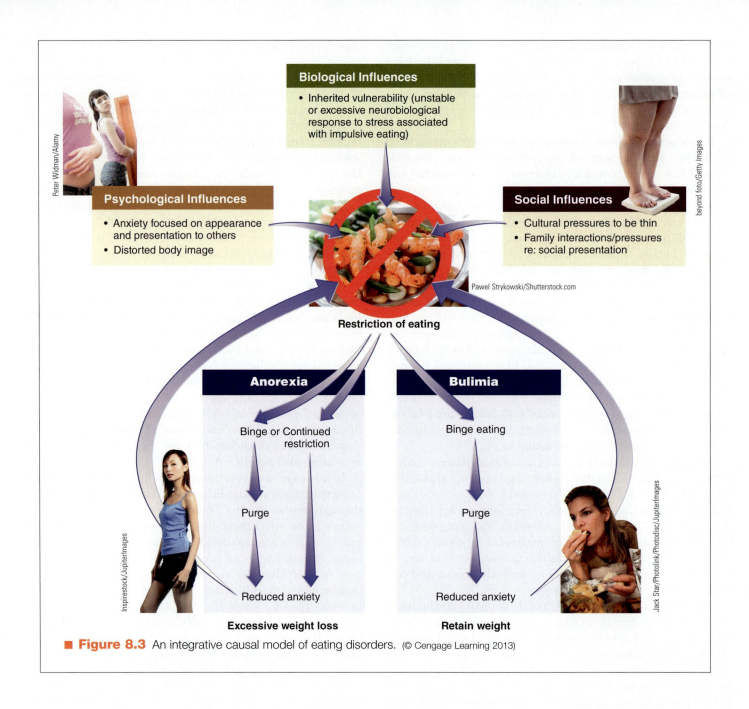

Figure 8.3 An integrative causal model of eating disorders. (© Cengage Learning 2013)

Labels within the figure:

Biological Influences
- Inherited vulnerability (unstable or excessive neurobiological response to stress associated with impulsive eating)

Psychological Influences
- Anxiety focused on appearance and presentation to others
- Distorted body image

Social Influences
- Cultural pressures to be thin
- Family interactions/pressures re: social presentation

Restriction of eating

Pawel Strykowski/Shutterstock.com

Anorexia
Binge or Continued restriction
Purge
Reduced anxiety
Excessive weight loss

Bulimia
Binge eating
Purge
Reduced anxiety
Retain weight

Peter Widman/Alamy

beyond foto/Getty Images

Inspirestock/JupiterImages

Jack Star/Photolink/Photodisc/JupiterImages

Treatment of Eating Disorders

> **How does the use of medications compare with psychological therapies for the treatment of eating disorders?**

Only since the 1980s have there been treatments for bulimia; treatments for anorexia have been around much longer but were not well developed. Rapidly accumulating evidence indicates that at least one, and possibly two, psychological treatments are effective, particularly for bulimia nervosa. Certain drugs may also help, although the evidence is not so strong.

Drug Treatments

At present, drug treatments have not been found to be effective in the treatment of anorexia nervosa (see, for example, Attia, Haiman, Walsh, & Flater, 1998; Crow, Mitchell, Roerig, & Steffen, 2009; de Zwaan et al., 2004; Vitiello & Lederhendler, 2000; Wilson & Fairburn, 2002).

For example, a recent definitive study reported that fluoxetine (Prozac) had no benefit in preventing relapse in patients with anorexia after weight has been restored (Walsh et al., 2006).

However, there is some evidence that drugs may be useful for some people with bulimia. The drugs generally considered the most effective for bulimia are the same antidepressant medications that proved effective for mood disorders and anxiety disorders (Broft, Berner, & Walsh, 2010; Shapiro et al., 2007; Wilson & Fairburn, 2002). The Food and Drug Administration (FDA) in 1996 approved Prozac as effective for eating disorders. Effectiveness is usually measured by reductions in the frequency of binge eating, and by the percentage of patients who stop binge eating and purging altogether, at least for a while. In two studies, one of several tricyclic antidepressant drugs and the other of Prozac, researchers found the average *reduction* in binge eating and purging was, respectively, 47% and 65% (Walsh, 1991; Walsh, Hadigan, Devlin, Gladis, & Roose, 1991). However, although antidepressants are more effective than placebo in the short term and they may enhance the effects of psychological treatment somewhat (Whittal, Agras, & Gould, 1999; Wilson et al., 1999), the available evidence suggests that antidepressant drugs alone do not have substantial long-lasting effects on bulimia nervosa (Walsh, 1995; Wilson & Fairburn, 2002).

Psychological Treatments

Short-term cognitive-behavioral treatments target problem eating behavior and associated attitudes about the overriding importance and significance of body weight and shape, and these strategies have become the treatment of choice for bulimia (Pike, Devlin, & Loeb, 2004; Sysko & Wilson, 2011; Wilson, Grilo, & Vitousek, 2007).

Bulimia Nervosa

In the cognitive-behavioral treatment approach pioneered by Fairburn (1985), the first stage is teaching the patient the physical consequences of binge eating and purging and the ineffectiveness of vomiting and laxative abuse for weight control. The adverse effects of dieting are also described, and patients are scheduled to eat small, manageable amounts of food 5 or 6 times per day with no more than a 3-hour interval between any planned meals and snacks, which eliminates the alternating periods of overeating and dietary restriction that are hallmarks of bulimia. In later stages of treatment, cognitive therapy focuses on altering dysfunctional thoughts and attitudes about body shape, weight, and eating. Coping strategies for resisting the impulse to binge and purge are also developed, including arranging activities so that the individual will not spend time alone after eating during the early stages of treatment (Fairburn, Marcus, & Wilson, 1993; Fairburn, Cooper, Shafran, & Wilson, 2008).

Evaluations of short-term (approximately 3 months) cognitive-behavioral treatments for bulimia have been good, showing superior efficacy to credible alternative psychological treatments not only for bingeing and purging but also for distorted attitudes and accompanying depression. Furthermore, these results seem to last (Fairburn, Jones, Peveler, Hope, & O'Connor, 1993; Pike, Walsh, Vitousek, Wilson, & Bauer, 2003; Thompson-Brenner, Glass, & Westen, 2003; Whittal et al., 1999), although there are, of course, a number of patients who improve only modestly or do not benefit. One study is worth examining more closely.

Agras, Walsh, Fairburn, Wilson, and Kraemer (2000) randomly assigned 220 patients meeting diagnostic criteria for bulimia nervosa to 19 sessions of either cognitive-behavioral therapy (CBT) or interpersonal psychotherapy (IPT) focused on improving interpersonal functioning. The investigators found that, for those who completed treatment, CBT was significantly superior to IPT at the end of treatment, with 45% recovered in the CBT group versus 8% in the IPT group. The percentage who remitted (no longer met diagnostic criteria for an eating disorder but still had some problems) was 67% in the CBT group versus 40% in the IPT group. However, after 1 year, these differences again were no longer significant, as patients in the IPT group tended to "catch up" to patients in the CBT group. The results for both recovered and remitted patients indicate that approximately the same percentage of patients (40%) remained recovered in the CBT group but 27% of those receiving IPT had now recovered. The results are similar for the less stringent criteria of remission. In a subsequent analysis, Agras and colleagues (2000) were able to demonstrate that substantial improvement in the first six sessions was the best predictor of who would recover by the end of treatment.

Phoebe | Taking Control

During her sophomore year in college, Phoebe entered a short-term CBT program similar to the program discussed here. She made good progress during the first several months and worked carefully to eat regularly and gain control over her eating. She also made sure that she was with somebody during her high-risk times and planned alternative activities that would reduce her temptation to purge if she felt she had eaten too much at a restaurant or drunk too much beer at a party. During the first 2 months, Phoebe had three slips, and she and her therapist discussed what led to her temporary relapse. Much to Phoebe's surprise, she did not gain weight on this program, even though she did not have time to increase her exercise. Nevertheless, she still was preoccupied with food, was concerned about her weight and appearance, and had strong urges to vomit if she thought she had overeaten the slightest amount.

During the 9 months following treatment, Phoebe reported that her urges seemed to decrease somewhat, although she had one major slip after eating a big pizza and drinking a lot of beer. She reported that she was thoroughly disgusted with herself for purging and was careful to return to her program after this episode. Two years after finishing treatment, Phoebe reported that her urges to vomit had disappeared, a report confirmed by her parents.

Short-term treatments for bulimia, although effective for many, may not provide a lasting solution. Indeed, some people do not benefit from short-term CBT. Evidence now suggests that combining drugs with psychosocial treatments might boost the overall outcome, at least in the short term (Whittal et al., 1999; Wilson et al., 1999). In the largest study to date (Walsh et al., 1997), CBT was significantly superior to supportive psychotherapy (in which the therapist is understanding and sympathetic and encourages patients to achieve their goals) in the treatment of bulimia nervosa; adding two antidepressant medications to CBT, including a serotonin-specific reuptake inhibitor (SSRI), modestly increased the benefit of CBT. But CBT remains the preferred treatment for bulimia and is superior to medication alone (Sysko & Wilson, 2011). There is also evidence that people who do not respond to CBT might benefit from interpersonal psychotherapy (Fairburn, Jones, et al., 1993; Klerman, Weissman, Rounsaville, & Chevron, 1984) or from antidepressant medication (Walsh et al., 2000).

Binge-Eating Disorder

Smith, Marcus, and Kaye (1992) adapted CBT for bulimia to obese binge eaters and demonstrated that the frequency of binge eating was reduced by an average of 81%, with 50% of the participants abstinent from bingeing by the end of treatment. Agras, Telch, Arnow, Eldredge, and Marnell (1997) followed 93 obese individuals with BED for 1 year and found that immediately after treatment with CBT, 41% of the participants abstained from bingeing and 72% binged less frequently. After 1 year, binge eating was reduced by 64%, and 33% of the group refrained from bingeing altogether. Importantly, those who had stopped binge eating during CBT maintained a weight loss of approximately 9 pounds over this 1-year follow-up period; those who continued to binge gained approximately 8 pounds. Thus, stopping binge eating is critical to sustaining weight loss in obese patients, a finding consistent with other studies of weight-loss procedures (Marcus, Wing, & Hopkins, 1988; Marcus et al., 1990; Telch, Agras, & Rossiter, 1988).

In contrast to results with bulimia, it appears that IPT is every bit as effective as CBT for binge eating. Wilfley and colleagues (2002) treated 162 overweight or obese men and women with BED with either CBT or IPT and found comparable results from each treatment. Fully 60% refrained from bingeing at a 1-year follow-up. In an important comparative study of treatments for binge eating, Grilo, Masheb, and Wilson (2004) compared Prozac, placebo,

CBT and Prozac, and CBT and placebo. Prozac showed no effect on BED compared to placebo, and both CBT treatments (with Prozac or placebo) were superior with no difference between them. Fully 73% of the CBT and placebo patients completing treatment did not binge for a month, which was the definition of remission. Thus, Prozac did not add anything to CBT, at least right after treatment terminated. If individuals began to respond rapidly to CBT treatment (by the 4th week), the response was particularly good, both short term and long term (Grilo, Masheb, & Wilson, 2006). Fortunately, it appears that self-help procedures may be useful in the treatment of BED. In one of the best studies of this approach, Carter and Fairburn (1998) randomly assigned 72 females with BED to either a pure self-help group, in which participants were simply mailed their manual; guided self-help, in which therapists would meet with the patients periodically as they read the manual; or a wait-list control group. Fifty percent of the guided self-help group and 43% of the pure self-help group eliminated binge eating versus 8% of the wait-list control group. These improvements were maintained at a 6-month follow-up.

More recently, CBT delivered as guided self-help was demonstrated to be more effective than a standard behavioral weight-loss program for BED both after treatment and at a 2-year follow-up (Wilson, Wilfley, Agras, & Bryson, 2010), and this same program is effective when delivered out of a doctor's office in a primary care setting (Striegel-Moore et al., 2010). In view of these results, it would seem a self-help approach should probably be the first treatment offered before engaging in more expensive and time-consuming therapist-led treatments. Much as with bulimia, however, more severe cases may need the more intensive treatment delivered by a therapist, particularly cases with multiple (comorbid) disorders in addition to BED, as well as and low self-esteem (Wilson et al., 2010). It is also important to emphasize again that if an obese person is bingeing, standard weight-loss procedures will be ineffective without treatment directed at bingeing.

Anorexia Nervosa

In anorexia, the most important initial goal is to restore the patient's weight to a point that is at least within the low-normal range (American Psychiatric Association, 2010). If body weight is below 85% of the average healthy body weight for a given individual or if weight has been lost rapidly and the individual continues to refuse food, inpatient treatment is recommended (American Psychiatric Association, 2010; Casper, 1982) because severe medical complications, particularly acute cardiac failure, could occur if weight is not restored immediately. If the weight loss has been more gradual and seems to have stabilized, weight restoration can be accomplished on an outpatient basis.

Restoring weight is probably the easiest part of treatment. Clinicians who treat patients in different settings, as reported in a variety of studies, find that at least 85% will be able to gain weight. The gain is often as much as a half-pound to a pound a day until weight is within the normal range. Knowing they can leave the hospital when their weight gain is adequate is often sufficient to motivate individuals with anorexia (Agras, Barlow, Chapin, Abel, & Leitenberg, 1974). Julie gained about 18 pounds during her 5-week hospital stay.

Then the difficult stage begins. As Hsu (1988) and others have demonstrated, initial weight gain is a poor predictor of long-term outcome in anorexia. Without attention to the patient's underlying dysfunctional attitudes about body shape and interpersonal disruptions in her life, she will almost always relapse. For restricting anorexics, the focus of treatment must shift to their marked anxiety over becoming obese and losing control of eating and to their undue emphasis on thinness as a determinant of self-worth, happiness, and success. In this regard, effective treatments for restricting anorexics are similar to those for patients with bulimia nervosa (Fairburn, Cooper, Shafran, & Wilson, 2008; Pike, Loeb, & Vitousek, 1996; Vitousek, Watson, & Wilson, 1998). In one well done study (Pike, Walsh, Vitousek, Wilson, & Bauer, 2003), extended (1-year) outpatient CBT was found to be significantly better than continued nutritional counseling in preventing relapse after weight restoration, with only 22% failing (relapsing or dropping out) with CBT versus 73% failing with nutritional counseling. More recently, Carter et al. (2009) reported similar findings and both studies demonstrate the ineffectiveness of nutritional counseling alone.

In addition, every effort is made to include the family to accomplish two goals. First, the negative and dysfunctional communication in the family regarding food and eating must be eliminated and meals must be made more structured and reinforcing. Second, attitudes toward body shape and image distortion are discussed at some length in family sessions. Unless the therapist attends to these attitudes, individuals with anorexia are likely to face a lifetime preoccupation with weight and body shape, struggle to maintain marginal weight and social adjustment, and be subject to repeated hospitalization. Family therapy directed at the goals mentioned here seems effective, particularly with young girls (younger than 19 years of age) with a short history of the disorder (Eisler et al., 1997; Eisler et al., 2000; Lock, le Grange, Agras, & Dare, 2001). Nevertheless, the long-term results of treatment for anorexia are more discouraging than for bulimia, with substantially lower rates of full recovery than for bulimia over a 7.5-year period (Eddy et al., 2008; Herzog et al., 1999). A recent proposal to focus treatment more directly on the extreme anxiety over gaining weight using therapeutic principles successful in anxiety disorders is promising (Steinglass et al., 2010).

Preventing Eating Disorders

Attempts are being made to prevent the development of eating disorders (Stice, Shaw, & Marti, 2007). If successful methods are confirmed, they will be important because many cases of eating disorders are resistant to treatment and most individuals who do not receive treatment suffer for years, in some cases all of their lives (Eddy et al., 2008; Herzog et al., 1999; Keel, Mitchell, Miller, Davis, & Crow, 1999). The development of eating disorders during adolescence is a risk factor for a variety of additional disorders during adulthood, including cardiovascular symptoms, chronic fatigue and infectious diseases, and anxiety and mood disorders (Johnson, Cohen, Kasen, & Brook, 2002). Before implementing a prevention program, however, it is necessary to target specific behaviors to change. Killen and colleagues (1994) conducted a prospective analysis on a sample of 887 young adolescent girls. Over a 3-year interval, 32 girls, or 3.6% of the sample, developed symptoms of eating disorders.

Early concern about being overweight was the most powerful predictive factor of later symptoms. The instrument used to measure weight concerns is presented in Table 8.2. Girls who scored high on this scale (an average score of 58) were at substantial risk for developing serious symptoms compared to girls who scored lower (an average score of 33). Killen and colleagues (1996) then evaluated a prevention program on 967 sixth- and seventh-grade girls from 11 to 13 years of age. This is the universal approach described in Chapter 7, where the program is applied to everyone. Half the girls were put on the intervention program, and the other half were not. The program emphasized that female weight gain after puberty is normal and that excessive caloric restriction could cause increased gain. The interesting results were that the intervention had relatively little effect on the treatment group compared to the control group. But for those girls at high risk for developing eating disorders (as reflected by a high score on the scale in Table 8.2), the program significantly reduced weight concerns (Killen, 1996; Killen et al., 1994). The authors conclude from this preliminary study that the most cost-effective preventive approach would be to carefully screen girls who are at high risk for developing eating disorders and to apply the program selectively to them (Killen, 1996). Could these preventive programs be delivered over the Internet? It seems they can! Winzelberg and colleagues (2000) studied a group of university women who did not have eating disorders at the time of the study but were concerned about their body image and the possibility of being overweight. College women in general are a high-risk group, and sorority women in particular are at higher risk than nonsorority women (Becker, Smith, & Ciao, 2005). The investigators developed the "student bodies program" (Winzelberg et al., 1998), a structured, interactive health education program designed to improve body image satisfaction and delivered through the Internet. The interactive software featured text, audio, and video components and online self-monitoring journals and behavior change assignments. The program continued for 8 weeks with various assignments administered each week. In addition, participants were expected to post a message to a discussion group related to the themes under consideration that week. If participants missed their assignments, they were contacted by e-mail and encouraged to get back

Table 8.2 Weight Concerns*

1. How much *more* or *less* do you feel you worry about your weight and body shape than other girls your age?
   a. I worry a lot less than other girls (4)
   b. I worry a little less than other girls (8)
   c. I worry about the same as other girls (12)
   d. I worry a little more than other girls (16)
   e. I worry a lot more than other girls (20)

2. How afraid are you of gaining 3 pounds?
   a. Not afraid of gaining (4)
   b. Slightly afraid of gaining (8)
   c. Moderately afraid of gaining (12)
   d. Very afraid of gaining (16)
   e. Terrified of gaining (20)

3. When was the last time you went on a diet?
   a. I've never been on a diet (3)
   b. I was on a diet about 1 year ago (6)
   c. I was on a diet about 6 months ago (9)
   d. I was on a diet about 3 months ago (12)
   e. I was on a diet about 1 month ago (15)
   f. I was on a diet less than 1 month ago (18)
   g. I'm now on a diet (21)

4. How important is your weight to you?
   a. My weight is not important compared to other things in my life (5)
   b. My weight is a little more important than some other things (10)
   c. My weight is more important than most, but not all, things in my life (15)
   d. My weight is the most important thing in my life (20)

5. Do you ever feel fat?
   a. Never (4)
   b. Rarely (8)
   c. Sometimes (12)
   d. Often (16)
   e. Always (20)

*Value assigned to each answer is in parentheses. Thus, if you chose an answer worth 12 in questions 1, 2, 3, and 5 and an answer worth 10 in question 4, your score would be 58. (Remember that the prediction from this scale worked for girls age 11–13 but hasn't been evaluated in college students.)
Source: Killen, J. D. (1996). Development and evaluation of a school-based eating disorder symptoms prevention program. In L. Smolak, M. P. Levine, & R. Striegel-Moore (Eds.), *The developmental psychopathology of eating disorders: Implications for research, prevention, and treatment* (pp. 313–339). Mahwah, NJ: Erlbaum.

on track. The results indicated this program was markedly successful because participants, compared to controls, reported a significant improvement in body image and a decrease in drive for thinness. Subsequently, these investigators developed innovations to improve compliance with this program to levels of 85% (Celio, Winzelberg, Dev, & Taylor, 2002).

Concept Check 8.2

Mark the following statements about the causes and treatment of eating disorders as either true (T) or false (F).

1. ___Many young women with eating disorders have a diminished sense of personal control and confidence in their own abilities and talents, are perfectionists, and/or are intensely preoccupied with how they appear to others.

2. ___Biological limitations, and the societal pressure to use diet and exercise to achieve nearly impossible weight goals, contribute to the high numbers of people with anorexia nervosa and bulimia nervosa.

3. ___One study showed that males consider a smaller female body size to be more attractive than women do.

4. ___Antidepressants help individuals overcome anorexia nervosa but have no effect on bulimia nervosa.

5. ___Cognitive-behavioral treatment (CBT) and interpersonal psychotherapy (IPT) are both successful treatments for bulimia nervosa, although CBT is the preferred method.

6. ___Attention must be focused on dysfunctional attitudes about body shape in anorexia or relapse will most likely occur after treatment.

Obesity

> **What are some possible causes of obesity?**
> **What treatments are available?**

As noted at the beginning of the chapter, obesity is not formally considered an eating disorder in the *DSM*. But, in the year 2000, the number of adults with excess weight worldwide surpassed the number of those who were underweight (Caballero, 2007). Indeed, the prevalence of obesity is so high that one might consider it statistically "normal" if it weren't for the serious implications for health and social and psychological functioning.

Statistics

The prevalence of obesity (BMI 30 or greater) among adults in the United States in 2000 was 30.5% of the population, increasing to 30.6% in 2002, 32.2% in 2004, and 33.8% in 2008 (Flegal, Carroll, Ogden, & Curtin, 2010; Ogden et al., 2006). What is particularly disturbing is that this prevalence of obesity represents close to a tripling from 12% of adults in 1991. Medical costs for obesity and overweight are estimated at $147 billion or 9.1% of U.S. health-care expenditures (Brownell et al., 2009). This condition accounted for more than 164,000 deaths in the United States in 2000 (Flegal et al., 2005). The direct relationship between obesity and mortality (dying prematurely) is shown in ■ Figure 8.4. At a BMI of 30, risk of mortality increases by 30%, and at a BMI of 40 or more, risk of mortality is 100% or more (Manson et al., 1995; Wadden, Brownell, & Foster, 2002). Because 5.7% of the adult population has a BMI over 40 (Flegal et al., 2010), a substantial number of people, perhaps 10 million or more in the United States alone, are in serious danger.

For children and adolescents, the numbers are even worse, with the number of overweight youngsters tripling in the past 25 years (Critser, 2003). In the past decade, the obesity rates for children ages 2–19 (defined as above the 95th percentile for sex-specific BMI for that age) have increased from 13.9% in 2000 to 17.1% in 2004 (Ogden et al., 2006), but now may be leveling off with a 16.9% rate in 2008 (Ogden, Carroll, Curtin, Lamb, & Flegal, 2010). If one looks at children and adolescents either overweight (above the 85th percentile in BMI) or obese, the rate is 31.7%. The stigma of obesity has a major impact on quality of life

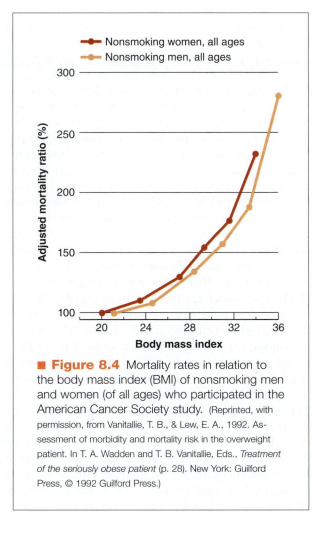

■ **Figure 8.4** Mortality rates in relation to the body mass index (BMI) of nonsmoking men and women (of all ages) who participated in the American Cancer Society study. (Reprinted, with permission, from Vanitallie, T. B., & Lew, E. A., 1992. Assessment of morbidity and mortality risk in the overweight patient. In T. A. Wadden and T. B. Vanitallie, Eds., *Treatment of the seriously obese patient* (p. 28). New York: Guilford Press, © 1992 Guilford Press.)

(Neumark-Sztainer & Haines, 2004). For example, most overweight individuals are subjected to prejudice and discrimination in college, at work, and in housing (Henderson and Brownell, 2004). Obesity is not limited to North America. Rates of obesity in eastern and southern European nations are as high as 50% (Berghöfer et al., 2008; Bjorntorp, 1997), and the rate is greatly increasing in developing nations. In Japan, obesity in men has doubled since 1992 and has nearly doubled in young women. Although less extreme, increases in obesity are also occurring in China (Henderson & Brownell, 2004; World Health Organization, 1998), where the proportion of Chinese who are overweight increased from 6% to 8% in a 7-year period (Holden, 2005). Obesity is also the main driver of type 2 diabetes, which has reached epidemic status. Ethnicity also is a factor in rates of obesity. In the United States, 50% of African American women and 43% of Hispanic American women are obese compared to 33% of Caucasian women (Flegal et al., 2010). Rates among minority adolescents are even more concerning. First Lady Michelle Obama has made lowering rates of childhood obesity her top priority.

Disordered Eating Patterns in Cases of Obesity

There are two forms of maladaptive eating patterns in people who are obese. The first is binge eating, and the second is **night eating syndrome** (Striegel-Moore, Franko, & Garcia, 2009). We discussed BED earlier in the chapter, but it is important to note that only a minority of patients with obesity, between 7% and 19%, present with patterns of binge eating. When they do, treatment for binge eating reviewed earlier should be integrated into weight-loss programs.

More interesting is the pattern of night eating syndrome that occurs in between 6% and 16% of obese individuals seeking weight-loss treatment but in as many as 42% of those with extreme obesity seeking bariatric surgery (discussed later) (Lamberg, 2003; Sarwer, Foster, & Wadden, 2004; Stunkard, Allison, & Lundgren, 2008). Individuals with night eating syndrome consume a third or more of their daily intake after their evening meal and get out of bed at least once during the night to have a high-calorie snack. In the morning, however, they are not hungry and do not usually eat breakfast. These individuals do not binge during their night eating and seldom purge. Occasionally, nonobese individuals will engage in night eating, but the behavior is overwhelmingly associated with being overweight or obese (Lundgren et al., 2006; Striegel-Moore et al., 2010).

Notice that this condition is not the same as the nocturnal eating syndrome described later in the chapter in the

night eating syndrome Consuming a third or more of daily food intake after the evening meal and getting out of bed at least once during the night to have a high-calorie snack. In the morning, individuals with night eating syndrome are not hungry and do not usually eat breakfast. These individuals do not binge during their night eating and seldom purge.

section about sleep disorders. In that condition, individuals get up during the night and raid the refrigerator but never wake up. They also may eat uncooked or other dangerous foods while asleep. On the contrary, in night eating syndrome, the individuals are awake as they go about their nightly eating patterns. Night eating syndrome is an important target for treatment in any obesity program to reregulate patterns of eating so that individuals eat more during the day, when their energy expenditure is highest.

Causes

Henderson and Brownell (2004) make a point that this obesity epidemic is clearly related to the spread of modernization. In other words, as we advance technologically, we are getting fatter. The promotion of an inactive, sedentary lifestyle and the consumption of a high-fat, energy-dense diet is the largest single contributor to the obesity epidemic (Caballero, 2007; Levine et al., 2005). Kelly Brownell (2002, 2003; Brownell et al., 2010) notes that in our modern society, individuals are continually exposed to heavily advertised, inexpensive fatty foods that have low nutritional value. When consumption of these is combined with an increasingly inactive lifestyle, it is not surprising that the prevalence of obesity is increasing. Brownell has referred to this as the "toxic environment" (Schwartz & Brownell, 2007). He notes that the best example of this phenomenon comes from a study of the Pima Indians from Mexico. A portion of this tribe of Indians migrated to Arizona relatively recently. Examining the result of this migration, Ravussin, Valencia, Esparza, Bennett, and Schulz (1994) determined that Arizona Pima women consumed 41% of their total calories in fat on the average and weighed 44 pounds on average more than Pima women who stayed in Mexico, who consumed 23% of their calories from fat. Because this relatively small tribe retains a strong genetic similarity, it is likely that the "toxic environment" in the more modern United States has contributed to the obesity epidemic among the Arizona Pima women.

Not everyone exposed to the modernized environment such as that in the United States becomes obese, and this is where genetics, physiology, and personality come in. On average, genetic contributions may constitute a smaller portion of the cause of obesity than cultural factors, but it helps explain why some people become obese and some don't when exposed to the same environment. For example, genes influence the number of fat cells an individual has, the likelihood of fat storage, and, most likely, activity levels (Cope, Fernandez, & Allison, 2004; Hetherington & Cecil, 2010). Generally, genes are thought to account for about 30% of the equation in causation of obesity (Bouchard, 2002), but this is misleading because it takes a "toxic" environment to turn on these genes. Physiological processes, particularly hormonal regulation of appetite, play a large role in the initiation and maintenance of eating and vary considerably from individual to individual (Friedman, 2009; Smith & Gibbs, 2002). Psychological processes of emotional regulation (for example, eating to try

to cheer yourself up when you're feeling down), impulse control, attitudes and motivation toward eating, and responsiveness to the consequences of eating are also important (Blundell, 2002; Stice, Presnell, Shaw, & Rohde, 2005).

Many of these attitudes and eating habits are strongly influenced by family and close friends. In an important study, Christakis and Fowler (2007) studied the social networks (close friends and neighbors) of more than 12,000 people for more than 30 years. They found that a person's chance of becoming obese increased from 37% to 57% if a spouse, sibling, or even a close friend was obese, but it did not if a neighbor or coworker with whom the person did not socialize was obese. Thus, it seems that obesity spreads through social networks. Although the etiology of obesity is extraordinarily complex, as with most disorders, an interaction of biological and psychological factors with a notably strong environmental and cultural contribution provides the most complete account.

Treatment

The treatment of obesity is only moderately successful at the individual level (Svetkey et al., 2008), with somewhat greater long-term evidence for effectiveness in children and adolescents compared to adults (Sarwer et al., 2004). Treatment is usually organized in a series of steps from least intrusive to most intrusive depending on the extent of obesity. One plan is presented in ■ Figure 8.5. As you can see, the first step is usually a self-directed weight-loss program in individuals who buy a popular diet book. The most usual result is that some individuals may lose some weight in the short term but almost always regain that weight. Furthermore, these books do little to change lifelong eating and exercise habits (Freedman, King, & Kennedy, 2001) and few individuals successfully achieve long-term results on these diets, one of the reasons the latest one is always on the best-seller list. Similarly there is little evidence that physician counseling results in any changes. Nevertheless, physicians can play an important role by providing specific treatment recommendations, including referral to professionals (Sarwer et al., 2004).

The next step is commercial self-help programs such as Weight Watchers, Jenny Craig, and similar programs. Weight Watchers reports that more than 1.4 million people attend more than 50,000 meetings weekly around the world (Weight Watchers International, 2010). These programs stand a better chance of achieving some success, at least compared to self-directed programs (Heshka et al., 2003). Among members who successfully lost weight initially and kept their weight off for at least 6 weeks after completing the program, between 19% and 37% weighed within 5 pounds of their goal weight at least 5 years after treatment (Lowe, Miller-Kovach, Frie, & Phelan, 1999; Sarwer et al., 2004). This means that up to 80% of individuals, even if they are initially successful, are not successful in the long run. The most successful programs are professionally directed behavior modification programs, particularly if patients attend group maintenance sessions periodically in the year following initial weight reduction

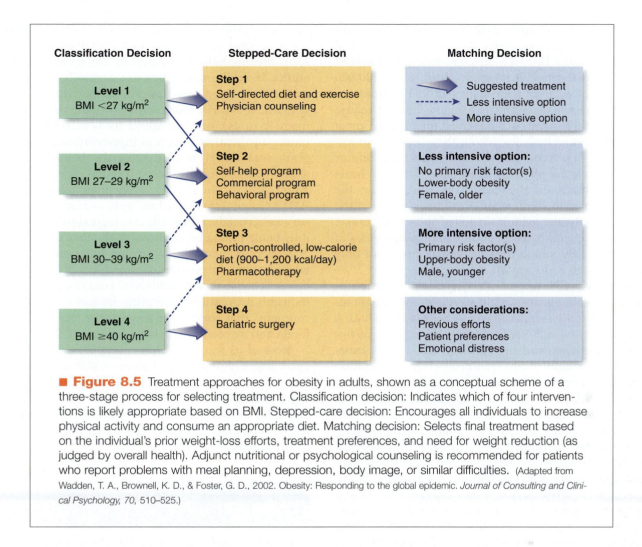

Figure 8.5 Treatment approaches for obesity in adults, shown as a conceptual scheme of a three-stage process for selecting treatment. Classification decision: Indicates which of four interventions is likely appropriate based on BMI. Stepped-care decision: Encourages all individuals to increase physical activity and consume an appropriate diet. Matching decision: Selects final treatment based on the individual's prior weight-loss efforts, treatment preferences, and need for weight reduction (as judged by overall health). Adjunct nutritional or psychological counseling is recommended for patients who report problems with meal planning, depression, body image, or similar difficulties. (Adapted from Wadden, T. A., Brownell, K. D., & Foster, G. D., 2002. Obesity: Responding to the global epidemic. *Journal of Consulting and Clinical Psychology, 70,* 510–525.)

(Perri et al., 2001). In a major study, Svetkey et al. (2008) randomly assigned 1,032 overweight or obese adults who had lost at least 10 pounds (4 kilograms) during a 6-month behavior modification program to one of three weight-loss maintenance conditions for 30 months: (1) once-a-month contact with a counselor to help them maintain their program, (2) a website they could log on to when they wanted to maintain their program (interactive technology group), and (3) a control comparison where they were on their own. Overall, 71% remained below their entry weights, which was a very good result, but the group with once-a-month contact gained back less weight than the interactive technology and the control comparison groups. Nevertheless, even these programs do not produce impressive results. For those individuals who have become more dangerously obese, very-low-calorie diets and possibly drugs, combined with behavior modification programs, are recommended. Patients lose as much as 20% of their weight on very-low-calorie diets, which typically consist of 4–6 liquid meal replacement products, or "shakes," a day. At the end of 3 or 4 months, they are then placed on a low-calorie balanced diet. As with all weight-loss programs, patients typically regain up to 50% of their lost weight in the year following treatment (Wadden & Osei, 2002). But

more than half of them are able to maintain a weight loss of at least 5%, which is important in these very obese people (Sarwer et al., 2004). Similarly, drug treatments that reduce internal cues signaling hunger may be effective, particularly if combined with a behavioral approach targeting lifestyle change. Currently the FDA has approved two drugs for this purpose, sibutramine (Meridia) and orlistat (Xenical). For patients who remain on medication for more than 1 year, weight loss of 7% to 8% has been observed on average, but just recently warnings have been issued that adverse cardiovascular functioning can be a major side effect of sibutramine (Kuehn, 2010). Thus, there is promise for these combination treatments in maintaining some weight loss (Wadden et al., 2005). However, medications produce a number of side effects and are not well tolerated by some.

Finally, the surgical approach to extreme obesity—called **bariatric surgery**—is an increasingly popular ap-

bariatric surgery The surgical approach to extreme obesity, usually accomplished by stapling the stomach to create a small stomach pouch or bypassing the stomach through gastric bypass surgery.

proach for individuals with a BMI of at least 40 (Omalu et al., 2007; Wolfe & Morton, 2005). As noted earlier, 5.7% of the population in the United States now falls into this BMI of 40 or above category (Flegal et al., 2010). Up to 220,000 individuals received bariatric surgery in 2009 (American Society for Metabolic & Bariatric Surgery, 2009). Because the surgery is permanent, it is reserved only for the most severely obese individuals for whom the obesity is an imminent health risk. Typically, patients must have one or more obesity-related physical conditions, such as heart disease or diabetes. In the most common surgery, the stomach is stapled to create a small stomach pouch at the base of the esophagus, which severely limits food intake. Alternatively, a gastric bypass operation creates a bypass of the stomach, as the name implies, which limits not only food intake but also absorption of calories.

Approximately 15% of patients who have bariatric surgery fail to lose significant weight or regain lost weight after surgery (Latfi, Kellum, DeMaria, & Sugarman, 2002). A small percentage of individuals, from 0.1% to 0.5%, do not survive the operation, and an additional 15% to 20% experience severe complications requiring rehospitalization and additional surgery within the first year after surgery and in each of the next 2 years after that (O'Brien et al., 2010; Zingmond, McGory, & Ko, 2005). Therefore, surgeons typically require patients to exhaust all other treatment options and to undergo a thorough psychological assessment to ascertain whether they can adapt to the radically changed eating patterns required postsurgery (Kral, 2002; Livingston, 2010; Sarwer et al., 2004).

New psychological programs have been designed specifically to prepare patients for this surgery and help them adapt following surgery (Apple, Lock, & Peebles, 2006). In contrast to adults, the treatment of obesity in children and adolescents has achieved better outcome both short term and long term (Cooperberg & Faith, 2004; Epstein, Myers, Raynor, & Saelens, 1998). A number of studies report that behavior modification programs, particularly those that include parents, may produce a 20% reduction in overweight, a change maintained for at least several years after the end of the study. Again, these behavior modification programs include a number of strategies to change dietary habits, particularly decreasing high-calorie, high-fat snacks. These programs also target reduction of sedentary habits in children and adolescents, such as viewing television, playing video games, and sitting in front of a computer. These programs may be more successful than with

adults because parents are typically fully engaged in the program and provide constant and continuing support. Also, dietary habits in children are less engrained than adults. In addition, children are generally more physically active if provided with appropriate activities (Cooperberg & Faith, 2004). For more seriously obese adolescents (BMI from 32 to 44), one important study confirmed that combining medication with a comprehensive behavioral program was more effective than the behavioral program alone (Berkowitz, Wadden, Tershakovec, & Cronquist, 2003). And for the most severely obese adolescents with a BMI greater than 35, a less intrusive and safer bariatric surgical procedure than the one typically done on adults is now being evaluated (O'Brien et al., 2010).

Society is increasingly turning its attention to ways in which we might prevent continuation of the obesity epidemic. The greatest benefits may come from strategies that focus on prevention by altering factors in the "toxic environment" that strongly encourage the intake of unhealthy foods and a sedentary lifestyle (Brownell, 2002).

Most of us recognize that eating is essential to our survival. Equally important is sleep, a still relatively mysterious process crucial to everyday functioning and strongly implicated in many psychological disorders. We turn our attention to this additional survival activity in an effort to understand better how and why we can be harmed by sleep disturbances.

Concept Check 8.3

Mark the following statements about obesity as either true (T) or false (F).

1. ___Obesity is the single most expensive health problem in the United States, surpassing both smoking and alcohol abuse.

2. ___Individuals with night eating syndrome consume at least half their daily intake after their evening meal.

3. ___Fatty foods and technology are not to blame for the obesity epidemic in the United States.

4. ___Professionally directed behavior modification programs represent the most successful treatment for obesity.

> ❯ What are the critical diagnostic features of the major sleep disorders?
> ❯ What medical and psychological treatments are used for the treatment of sleep disorders?
> ❯ How are rapid eye movement and nonrapid eye movement sleep related to the parasomnias?

We spend about one third of our lives asleep. That means most of us sleep nearly 3,000 hours per *year*. For many of us, sleep is energizing, both mentally and physically. Unfortunately, most people do not get enough sleep, and 20% of Americans report getting less than 6 hours of sleep per night, up from 12% who reported this lack of sleep in 1998 (National Sleep Foundation, 2009). Most of us know what it's like to have a bad night's sleep. The next day we're a little groggy, and as the day wears on we may become irritable. Research tells us that even minor sleep deprivation over only a few days impedes our ability to think clearly (Buysse, Strollo, Black, Zee, & Winkelman, 2008). Lack of sleep also affects you physically. People who do not get enough sleep are more susceptible to illnesses such as the common cold (Cohen, Doyle, Alper, Janicki-Deverts, & Turner, 2009), perhaps because immune system functioning is reduced with the loss of even a few hours of sleep (Imeri & Opp, 2009).

Here you might ask yourself how sleep disorders fit into a textbook on abnormal psychology. Different variations of disturbed sleep clearly have physiological bases and therefore could be considered purely medical concerns. However, like other physical disorders, sleep problems interact in important ways with psychological factors.

An Overview of Sleep Disorders

The study of sleep has long influenced concepts of abnormal psychology. Moral treatment, used in the 19th century for people with severe mental illness, included encouraging patients to get adequate amounts of sleep as part of therapy (Charland, 2008). Researchers who prevented people from sleeping for prolonged periods found that chronic sleep deprivation often had profound effects. A number of the disorders covered in this book are often associated with sleep complaints, including schizophrenia, major depression, bipolar disorder, and anxiety-related disorders. You may think at first that a sleep problem is the result of a psychological disorder. For example, how often have you been anxious about a future event (an upcoming exam, perhaps) and not been able to fall asleep? However, the relationship between sleep disturbances and mental health is more complex. Sleep problems may cause the difficulties people experience in everyday life (Buysse et al., 2008), or they may result from some disturbance common to a psychological disorder.

In Chapter 4 we explained how a brain circuit in the limbic system may be involved with anxiety. We know that this region of the brain is also involved with our dream sleep, which is called **rapid eye movement (REM) sleep** (Steiger, 2008). This mutual neurobiological connection suggests that anxiety and sleep may be interrelated in important ways, although the exact nature of the relationship is still unknown. Similarly, REM sleep seems related to depression, as noted in Chapter 7 (Joska & Stein, 2008). Sleep abnormalities are preceding signs of serious clinical depression, which may suggest that sleep problems can help predict who is at risk for later mood disorders (Terman & Terman, 2006). In an intriguing study, researchers found that CBT improved symptoms among a group of depressed men and normalized REM sleep patterns (Nofzinger et al., 1994). Furthermore, sleep deprivation has temporary antidepressant effects on some people (Benedetti et al., 2003), although in people who are not already depressed sleep deprivation may bring on a depressed mood (Perlis et al., 2006). We do not fully understand how psychological disorders are related to sleep, yet accumulating research points to the importance of understanding sleep if we are to complete the broader picture of abnormal behavior.

Sleep disorders are divided into two major categories: **dyssomnias** and **parasomnias** (Table 8.3). Dyssomnias involve difficulties in getting enough sleep, problems with sleeping when you want to (not being able to fall asleep until 2 A.M. when you have a 9 A.M. class), and complaints about the quality of sleep, such as not feeling refreshed even though you have slept the whole night. Parasomnias are characterized by abnormal behavioral or physiological events that occur during sleep, such as nightmares and sleepwalking.

The clearest and most comprehensive picture of your sleep habits can be determined only by a **polysomnographic (PSG) evaluation** (Savard, Savard, & Morin, 2010). The patient spends one or more nights sleeping in a sleep laboratory being monitored on a number of measures, including respiration and oxygen desaturation

---

rapid eye movement (REM) sleep The periodic intervals of sleep during which the eyes move rapidly from side to side, and dreams occur, but the body is inactive.

dyssomnias A problem in getting to sleep or in obtaining sleep of sufficient quality.

parasomnias An abnormal behavior such as a nightmare or sleepwalking that occurs during sleep.

polysomnographic (PSG) evaluation An assessment of sleep disorders in which a client sleeping in the lab is monitored for heart, muscle, respiration, brain wave, and other functions.

Table 8.3 Summary of *DSM* Sleep Disorders

Sleep Disorder	Description
Dyssomnias	(Disturbances in the amount, timing, or quality of sleep)
Primary insomnia	Difficulty initiating or maintaining sleep or sleep that is not restorative (person not feeling rested even after normal amounts of sleep)
Primary hypersomnia	Complaint of excessive sleepiness that is displayed as either prolonged sleep episodes or daytime sleep episodes
Narcolepsy	Irresistible attacks of refreshing sleep occurring daily, accompanied by episodes of brief loss of muscle tone (cataplexy)
Breathing-related sleep disorder	Sleep disruption leading to excessive sleepiness or insomnia that is caused by sleep-related breathing difficulties
Circadian rhythm sleep disorder (sleep–wake schedule disorder)	Persistent or recurrent sleep disruption leading to excessive sleepiness or insomnia that is due to a mismatch between the sleep–wake schedule required by a person's environment and his or her circadian sleep–wake pattern
Parasomnias	(Disturbances in arousal and sleep stage transition that intrude into the sleep process)
Nightmare disorder (dream anxiety disorder)	Repeated awakenings with detailed recall of extended and extremely frightening dreams, usually involving threats to survival, security, or self-esteem; the awakenings generally occur during the second half of the sleep period
Sleep terror disorder	Recurrent episodes of abrupt awakening from sleep, usually occurring during the first third of the major sleep episode and beginning with a panicky scream
Sleepwalking disorder	Repeated episodes of arising from bed during sleep and walking about, usually occurring during the first third of the major sleep episode

Source: Reprinted, with permission, from American Psychiatric Association. (2000). *Diagnostic and statistical manual of mental disorders* (4th ed., text revision). Washington, DC: Author, © 2000 American Psychiatric Association.

(a measure of airflow); leg movements; brain wave activity, measured by an *electroencephalogram;* eye movements, measured by an *electrooculogram;* muscle movements, measured by an *electromyogram;* and heart activity, measured by an *electrocardiogram.* Daytime behavior and typical sleep patterns are also noted—for example, whether the person uses drugs or alcohol, is anxious about work or interpersonal problems, takes afternoon naps, or has a psychological disorder. Collecting all these data can be both time consuming and costly, but it is important to ensure an accurate diagnosis and treatment plan. One alternative to the comprehensive assessment of sleep is to use a wristwatch-size device called an **actigraph**. This instrument records the number of arm movements, and the data can be downloaded into a computer to determine the length and quality of sleep. Several studies have now tested the usefulness of this type of device in measuring the sleep of astronauts aboard the space shuttle, and they find it can reliably detect when they fall asleep, when they wake up, and how restful their in-space sleep is (e.g., Barger, Wright, & Czeisler, 2008).

In addition, clinicians and researchers find it helpful to know the average number of hours the individual sleeps each day, taking into account **sleep efficiency (SE)**, the percentage of time actually

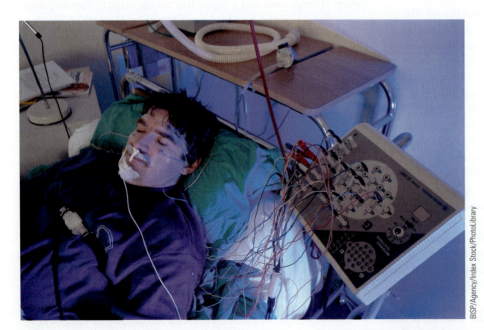

▲ This participant is undergoing a polysomnograph, an overnight electronic evaluation of sleep patterns.

BISP/Agency/Index Stock/PhotoLibrary

spent asleep, not just lying in bed trying to sleep. SE is calculated by dividing the amount of time sleeping by the amount of time in bed. An SE of 100% would mean you fall asleep as soon as your head hits the pillow and do not wake up during the night. In contrast, an SE of 50% would mean half your time in bed is spent trying to fall asleep; that is, you are awake half the time. Such measurements help the clinician determine objectively how well you sleep.

One way to determine whether a person has a problem with sleep is to observe his daytime sequelae, or behavior while awake. For example, if it takes you 90 minutes to fall asleep at night but this doesn't bother you and you feel rested during the day, then you do not have a problem. A friend who also takes 90 minutes to fall asleep but finds this delay anxiety provoking and is fatigued the next day might be considered to have a sleep problem. It is to some degree a subjective decision, partly depending on how the person perceives the situation and reacts to it.

Primary Insomnia

Insomnia is one of the most common sleep disorders. You may picture someone with insomnia as being awake all the time. However, it isn't possible to go completely without sleep. For example, after being awake for about 40 hours, a person begins having **microsleeps** that last several seconds or longer (Mendelson, 2005). In the rare occurrences of fatal familial insomnia (a degenerative brain disorder), total lack of sleep eventually leads to death (Minagar, Alekseeva, Shapshak, & Fernandez, 2009). Despite the common use of the term *insomnia* to mean "not sleeping," it actually applies to a number of complaints. People are considered to have insomnia if they have trouble falling asleep at night (difficulty initiating sleep), if they wake up frequently or too early and can't go back to sleep (difficulty maintaining sleep), or even if they sleep a reasonable number of hours but are still not rested the next day (nonrestorative sleep). Consider the case of Sonja.

Sonja • School on Her Mind

Sonja was a 23-year-old law student with a history of sleep problems. She reported that she never really slept well, both having trouble falling asleep at night and usually awakening again in the early morning. Since she started law school last year, her sleep problems had grown even worse. She would lie in bed awake until the early morning hours thinking about school, getting only 3–4 hours of sleep on a typical night. In the morning, she had a great deal of difficulty getting out of bed and was frequently late for her early-morning class.

Sonja's sleep problems and their interference with her schoolwork were causing her to experience increasingly severe depression. In addition, she recently reported having a severe anxiety attack that woke her in the middle of the night. All of these difficulties caused her to be increasingly isolated from family and friends, who finally convinced her to seek help.

We return to Sonja later in this chapter.

Clinical Description

Sonja's symptoms meet the *DSM-IV-TR* criteria for **primary insomnia**, with *primary* indicating that the complaint is not related to other medical or psychiatric problems. Looking at sleep disorders as primary recalls the overlap of sleep problems with psychological disorders such as anxiety and depression. Because not sleeping makes you anxious and anxiety further interrupts your sleep, which makes you more anxious, and so on, it is uncommon to find a person with a simple sleep disorder and no related problems.

Sonja's is a typical case of insomnia. She had trouble both initiating and maintaining sleep. Other people sleep all night but still feel as if they've been awake for hours. Although most people can carry out necessary day-to-day activities, their inability to concentrate can have serious consequences, such as debilitating accidents when they attempt to drive long distances (like bus drivers) or handle dangerous material (like electricians). Students with insomnia like Sonja's may do poorly in school because of difficulty concentrating.

Statistics

Almost a third of the population reports some symptoms of insomnia during any given year (National Sleep Foundation, 2009). For many of these individuals, sleep difficulties are a lifetime affliction (Mendelson, 2005). Approximately 35% of older adults report excessive daytime sleepiness, with older black men reporting the most problems (Green, Ndao-Brumblay, & Hart-Johnson, 2009).

A number of psychological disorders are associated with insomnia. Total sleep time often decreases with depression, substance use disorders, anxiety disorders, and dementia of the Alzheimer's type. The interrelationship between alcohol use and sleep disorders can be particularly troubling. Alcohol is often used to initiate sleep (Schuckit, 2009). In small amounts, it helps make people drowsy, but it also interrupts ongoing sleep. Interrupted sleep causes anxiety, which often leads to repeated alcohol use and an obviously vicious cycle.

actigraph A small electronic device that is worn on the wrist like a watch and records body movements. This device can be used to record sleep–wake cycles.
sleep efficiency (SE) The percentage of time actually spent sleeping of the total time spent in bed.
microsleeps The short, seconds-long periods of sleep that occurs when someone has been deprived of sleep.
primary insomnia A difficulty in initiating, maintaining, or gaining from sleep; not related to other medical or psychological problems.

Women report insomnia twice as often as men. Does this mean that men sleep better than women? Not necessarily. Remember, a sleep problem is considered a disorder *only if you experience discomfort* about it. Women may be more often diagnosed as having insomnia because they more often report the problem, not necessarily because their sleep is disrupted more. Just as people's needs concerning normal sleep change over time, complaints of insomnia differ in frequency among people of different ages. Children who have difficulty falling asleep usually throw a tantrum at bedtime or do not want to go to bed. Many children cry when they wake in the middle of the night. Estimates of insomnia among young children range from 25% to more than 40% (Owens, Rosen, & Mindell, 2003). Growing evidence points to both biological and cultural explanations for poor sleep among adolescents. As children move into adolescence, their biologically determined sleep schedules shift toward a later bedtime (Mindell & Owens, 2009). However, at least in the United States, children are still expected to rise early for school, causing chronic sleep deprivation. This problem is not observed among all adolescents, with ethnocultural differences reported among youth from different backgrounds. One study, for example, found that Chinese American youth reported the least problems with insomnia, and Mexican American adolescents reported the most difficulty sleeping (Roberts, Roberts, & Chen, 2000).

The percentage of individuals who complain of sleep problems increases as they become older adults. This higher rate in reports of sleeping problems among older people makes sense when you remember that the number of hours we sleep decreases as we age. It is not uncommon for someone older than age 65 to sleep fewer than 6 hours and wake up several times each night.

Causes

Insomnia accompanies many medical and psychological disorders, including pain and physical discomfort, physical inactivity during the day, and respiratory problems. Sometimes insomnia is related to problems with the biological clock and its control of temperature. Some people who can't fall asleep at night may have a delayed temperature rhythm: Their body temperature doesn't drop and they don't become drowsy until later at night. As a group, people with insomnia seem to have higher body temperatures than good sleepers, and their body temperatures seem to vary less; this lack of fluctuation may interfere with sleep (Lack, Gradisar, Van Someren, Wright, & Lushington, 2008).

Among the other factors that can interfere with sleeping are drug use and a variety of environmental influences such as changes in light, noise, or temperature. People admitted to hospitals often have difficulty sleeping because the noises and routines differ from those at home. Other sleep disorders, such as *sleep apnea* (a disorder that involves obstructed nighttime breathing) or *periodic limb movement disorder* (excessive jerky leg movements), can cause interrupted sleep and may seem similar to insomnia.

Finally, various psychological stresses can also disrupt your sleep. For example, one study looked at how medical and dental school students were affected by a particularly stressful event—in this case, participating in cadaver dissection (Snelling, Sahai, & Ellis, 2003). Among the effects reported by the students was a decrease in their ability to sleep.

People with insomnia may have unrealistic expectations about how much sleep they need ("I need a full 8 hours") and about how disruptive disturbed sleep will be ("I won't be able to think or do my job if I sleep for only 5 hours") (Sidani et al., 2009). The actual amount of sleep each person needs varies, and is assessed by how it affects you during the day. It is important to recognize the role of cognition in insomnia; our thoughts alone may disrupt our sleep.

Is poor sleeping a learned behavior? It is generally accepted that people suffering from sleep problems associate the bedroom and bed with the frustration and anxiety that go with insomnia. Eventually, the arrival of bedtime itself may cause anxiety (Ebben & Spielman, 2009). Interactions associated with sleep may contribute to children's sleep problems. For example, one study found that when a parent was present when the child fell asleep, the child was more likely to wake during the night (Adair, Bauchner, Philipp, Levenson, & Zuckerman, 1991). Researchers think that some children learn to fall asleep only with a parent present; if they wake up at night, they are frightened at finding themselves alone and their sleep is disrupted. Cross-cultural sleep research has focused primarily on children. In the predominant culture in the United States, infants are expected to sleep on their own, in a separate bed, and, if possible, in a separate room. However, in many other cultures as diverse as rural Guatemala and Korea and urban Japan, the child spends the first few years of life in the same room and sometimes the same bed as the mother (Mosko, Richard, & McKenna, 1997). In many cultures, mothers report that they do not ignore the cries of their children (K. Lee, 1992;

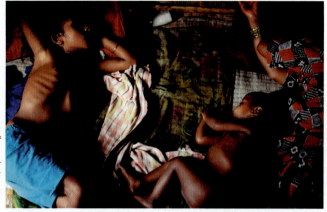

▲ In the United States, children usually sleep alone *(left)*. In many cultures, all family members share the same bed *(right)*.

Morelli, Rogoff, Oppenheim, & Goldsmith, 1992), in stark contrast to the United States, where many pediatricians recommend that parents ignore the cries of their infants over a certain age at night (Ferber, 1985). One conclusion from this research is that sleep can be affected by cultural norms. Unmet demands can result in stress that negatively affects the ultimate sleep outcome for children (Durand, 2008).

An Integrative Model

An integrative view of sleep disorders includes several assumptions. The first is that, at some level, both biological and psychological factors are present in most cases. A second assumption is that these multiple factors are reciprocally related. This can be seen in the study we noted earlier, in which Adair and colleagues (1991) observed that children who woke frequently at night often fell asleep in the presence of parents. However, they also noted that child temperament (or personality) may have played a role in this arrangement because these children had comparatively difficult temperaments and their parents were presumably present to attend to sleep initiation difficulties. In other words, personality characteristics, sleep difficulties, and parental reaction interact in a reciprocal manner to produce and maintain sleep problems.

People may be biologically vulnerable to disturbed sleep. This vulnerability differs from person to person and can range from mild to more severe disturbances. For example, a person may be a light sleeper (easily aroused at night) or have a family history of insomnia, narcolepsy, or obstructed breathing. All these factors can lead to eventual sleeping problems. Such influences have been referred to as *predisposing conditions* (Spielman & Glovinsky, 1991); they may not, by themselves, always cause problems, but they may combine with other factors to interfere with sleep (■ Figure 8.6).

Biological vulnerability may, in turn, interact with *sleep stress* (Durand, 2008), which includes a number of events that can negatively affect sleep. For example, poor bedtime habits (such as having too much alcohol or caffeine) can interfere with falling asleep (Stepanski, 2006). Note that biological vulnerability and sleep stress influence each other (see Figure 8.6). Although we may intuitively assume that biological factors come first, extrinsic influences such

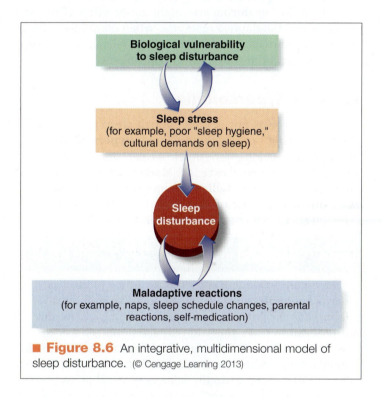

■ **Figure 8.6** An integrative, multidimensional model of sleep disturbance. (© Cengage Learning 2013)

as poor sleep hygiene (the daily activities that affect how we sleep) can affect the physiological activity of sleep. One of the most striking examples of this phenomenon is jet lag, in which people's sleep patterns are disrupted, sometimes seriously, when they fly across several time zones. Whether disturbances continue or become more severe may depend on how they are managed. For example, many people react to disrupted sleep by taking over-the-counter sleeping pills. Unfortunately, most people are not aware that **rebound insomnia**—where sleep problems reappear,

rebound insomnia In a person with insomnia, the worsened sleep problems that can occur when medications are used to treat insomnia and then withdrawn.

sometimes worse—may occur when the medication is withdrawn. This rebound leads people to think they still have a sleep problem, readminister the medicine, and go through the cycle repeatedly. In other words, taking sleep aids can perpetuate sleep problems.

Other ways of reacting to poor sleep can also prolong problems. It seems reasonable that a person who hasn't had enough sleep can make up for this loss by napping during the day. Unfortunately, naps that alleviate fatigue during the day can also disrupt sleep that night. Anxiety can also extend the problem. Lying in bed worrying about school, family problems, or even about not being able to sleep will interfere with sleep (Uhde, Cortese, & Vedeniapin, 2009). The behavior of parents can also help maintain these problems in children. Children who receive a great deal of positive attention at night when they wake up may wake up during the night more often (Durand, 2008). Such maladaptive reactions, when combined with a biological predisposition to sleep problems and sleep stress, may account for continuing problems.

Primary Hypersomnia

Insomnia involves not getting enough sleep (the prefix *in* means "lacking" or "without"), and **hypersomnia** is a problem of sleeping too much (*hyper* means "in great amount" or "abnormal excess"). Many people who sleep all night find themselves falling asleep several times the next day. Consider the case of Ann.

Ann ⦚ Sleeping in Public

Ann, a college student, came to my office to discuss her progress in class. We talked about several questions that she got wrong on the last exam, and as she was about to leave she said that she never fell asleep during my class. This seemed like faint praise, but I thanked her for the feedback. "No," she said, "you don't understand. I usually fall asleep in *all* of my classes, but not in yours." Again, I didn't quite understand what she was trying to tell me and joked that she must pick her professors more carefully. She laughed. "That's probably true. But I also have this problem with sleeping too much."

As we talked more seriously, Ann told me that excessive sleeping had been a problem since her teenage years. In situations that were monotonous or boring, or when she couldn't be active, she fell asleep. This could happen several times a day, depending on what she was doing. Recently, large lecture classes had become a problem unless the lecturer was particularly interesting or animated. Watching television and driving long distances were also problematic.

Ann reported that her father had a similar problem. He had recently been diagnosed with narcolepsy (which we discuss next) and was now getting help at

a clinic. Both she and her brother had been diagnosed with hypersomnia. Ann had been prescribed Ritalin (a stimulant medication) about 4 years ago and said that it was only somewhat effective in keeping her awake during the day. She said the drug helped reduce the sleep attacks but did not eliminate them altogether.

The *DSM-IV-TR* diagnostic criteria for hypersomnia include not only the excessive sleepiness that Ann described but also the subjective impression of this problem (American Psychiatric Association, 2000). Remember that whether insomnia is a problem depends on how it affects each person. Ann found her disorder disruptive because it interfered with driving and paying attention in class. Hypersomnia caused her to be less successful academically and upset her personally, both of which are defining features of this disorder. She slept approximately 8 hours each night, so her daytime sleepiness couldn't be attributed to insufficient sleep.

DSM Disorder Criteria Summary
Primary Hypersomnia

Features of primary hypersomnia include the following:

> Excessive sleepiness for at least 1 month (or less if recurrent) as evidenced by either prolonged sleep episodes or daytime sleep episodes that occur almost daily

> The excessive sleepiness causes clinically significant distress or impairment in functioning

> The excessive sleepiness is not better accounted for by insomnia, does not occur exclusively during the course of another sleep disorder, and cannot be accounted for by an inadequate amount of sleep

> The disturbance does not occur exclusively during the course of another mental disorder

> The disturbance is not due to the direct physiological effects of a substance or a general medical condition

Source: Based on *DSM-IV-TR.* Reprinted with permission from *Diagnostic and Statistical Manual of Mental Disorders* (4th ed., text revision). © 2000 American Psychiatric Association.

Several factors that can cause excessive sleepiness would not be considered hypersomnia. For example, people with insomnia (who get inadequate amounts of sleep) often report being tired during the day. In contrast, people with hypersomnia sleep through the night and appear rested upon awakening but still complain of being excessively tired throughout the day. Another sleep problem that can cause a similar excessive sleepiness is a breathing-related sleep disorder called **sleep apnea**. People with this problem have difficulty breathing at night. They often snore loudly, pause between breaths, and wake in the morning with a dry mouth and headache. In identifying hypersomnia, the clinician needs to rule out insomnia, sleep apnea, or other reasons for sleepiness during the day (American Psychiatric Association, 2000).

We are just beginning to understand the nature of hypersomnia, so relatively little research has been done on its causes. Genetic influences seem to be involved in a portion of cases, with individuals having an increased likelihood of having certain gene factors (HLA-Cw2 and HLA-DR11) (Buysse et al., 2008). A significant subgroup of people diagnosed with hypersomnia previously were exposed to a viral infection such as mononucleosis, hepatitis, and viral pneumonia, which suggests there may be more than one cause (Hirshkowitz, Seplowitz, & Sharafkhaneh, 2009).

▲ Excessive sleepiness can be disruptive.

Monkey Business Images/Shutterstock.com

Narcolepsy

Ann described her father as having **narcolepsy**, a different form of the sleeping problem she and her brother shared (Buysse et al., 2008). In addition to daytime sleepiness, people with narcolepsy experience *cataplexy,* a sudden loss of muscle tone. Cataplexy occurs while the person is awake and can range from slight weakness in the facial muscles to complete physical collapse. Cataplexy lasts from several seconds to several minutes; it is usually preceded by strong emotion such as anger or happiness. Imagine that while cheering for your favorite team, you suddenly fall asleep; while arguing with a friend, you collapse to the floor in a sound sleep. You can imagine how disruptive this disorder can be!

Cataplexy appears to result from a sudden onset of REM sleep. Instead of falling asleep normally and going through the four nonrapid eye movement (NREM) stages that typically precede REM sleep, people with narcolepsy periodically progress right to this dream-sleep stage almost directly from the state of being awake. One outcome of REM sleep is the inhibition of input to the muscles, and this seems to be the process that leads to cataplexy.

Two other characteristics distinguish people who have narcolepsy (Buysse et al., 2008). They commonly report *sleep paralysis,* a brief period after awakening when they can't move or speak that is often frightening to those who go through it. The last characteristic of narcolepsy is *hypnagogic hallucinations,* vivid and often terrifying experiences that begin at the start of sleep and are said to be unbelievably realistic because they include not only visual aspects, but also touch, hearing, and even the sensation of body movement. Examples of hypnagogic hallucinations, which, like sleep paralysis, can be terrifying, include the vivid illusion of being caught in a fire or flying through the air. Narcolepsy is relatively rare, occurring in 0.03% to 0.16% of the population, with the numbers approximately equal among males and females. Although some cases have been reported in young children, the problems associated with narcolepsy usually are first seen during the teenage years. Excessive sleepiness usually occurs first, with cataplexy appearing either at the same time or with a delay of up to 30 years. Fortunately, the cataplexy, hypnagogic hallucinations, and sleep paralysis often decrease in frequency over time, although sleepiness during the day does not seem to diminish with age.

DSM Disorder Criteria Summary
Narcolepsy

Features of narcolepsy include the following:

› Irresistible attacks of refreshing sleep that occur daily over at least 3 months

› The presence of one or both of the following: (1) cataplexy (i.e., brief episodes of sudden bilateral loss of muscle tone, most often in association with intense emotion), (2) recurrent intrusions of elements of rapid eye movement (REM) sleep into the transition between sleep and wakefulness, as manifested by either hypnopompic or hypnagogic hallucinations or sleep paralysis at the beginning or end of sleep episodes

› The disturbance is not due to the direct physiological effects of a substance or another general medical condition

Source: Based on *DSM-IV-TR.* Reprinted with permission from *Diagnostic and Statistical Manual of Mental Disorders* (4th ed., text revision). © 2000 American Psychiatric Association.

hypersomnia Abnormally excessive sleep. A person with this condition falls asleep several times a day.
sleep apnea A disorder involving brief periods when breathing ceases during sleep.
narcolepsy The sleep disorder involving sudden and irresistible sleep attacks.

Specific genetic models of narcolepsy are now being developed (Tafti, 2009). Previous research with Doberman pinschers and Labrador retrievers, which also inherit this disorder, suggests that narcolepsy is associated with a cluster of genes on chromosome 6, and it may be an autosomal recessive trait. Advances in understanding the etiology and treatment of such disorders can be credited to the help of "man's best friend."

Breathing-Related Sleep Disorders

For some people, sleepiness during the day or disrupted sleep at night has a physical origin—namely, problems with breathing while asleep. In *DSM-IV-TR*, these problems are diagnosed as **breathing-related sleep disorders**. People whose breathing is interrupted during their sleep experience numerous brief arousals throughout the night and do not feel rested even after 8 or 9 hours asleep (Hirshkowitz et al., 2009). For all of us, the muscles in the upper airway relax during sleep, constricting the passageway somewhat and making breathing a little more difficult. For some, unfortunately, breathing is constricted a great deal and may be labored *(hypoventilation)* or, in the extreme, there may be short periods (10 to 30 seconds) when they stop breathing altogether, called *sleep apnea*. Often the affected person is only minimally aware of breathing difficulties and doesn't attribute the sleep problems to the breathing. However, a bed partner usually notices loud snoring (which is one sign of this problem) or will have noticed frightening episodes of interrupted breathing. Other signs that a person has breathing difficulties are heavy sweating during the night, morning headaches, and episodes of falling asleep during the day *(sleep attacks)* with no resulting feeling of being rested (Hirshkowitz et al., 2009).

There are three types of apnea, each with different causes, daytime complaints, and treatment: obstructive, central, and mixed sleep apnea. *Obstructive sleep apnea* occurs when airflow stops despite continued activity by the respiratory system (Abad & Guilleminault, 2009). In some people, the airway is too narrow; in others, some abnormality or damage interferes with the ongoing effort to breathe. Everyone in a group of people with obstructive sleep apnea reported snoring at night (Guilleminault, 1989). Obesity is sometimes associated with this problem, as is increasing age. Some work now suggests that the use of MDMA (ecstasy) can lead to obstructive apnea even in young and otherwise healthy adults (McCann, Sgambati, Schwartz, & Ricaurte, 2009). Obstructive sleep apnea is most common in males and is thought to occur in 10% to 20% of the population (Jennum & Riha, 2009).

The second type of apnea, *central sleep apnea*, involves the complete cessation of respiratory activity for brief periods and is often associated with certain central nervous system disorders, such as cerebral vascular disease, head trauma, and degenerative disorders (Buysse et al., 2008). Unlike people with obstructive sleep apnea, those with central sleep apnea wake up frequently during the night but they tend not to report excessive daytime sleepiness

and often are not aware of having a serious breathing problem. Because of the lack of daytime symptoms, people tend not to seek treatment, so we know relatively little about this disorder's prevalence or course.

The third breathing disorder, *mixed sleep apnea*, is a combination of both obstructive and central sleep apneas. All these breathing difficulties interrupt sleep and result in symptoms similar to those of insomnia.

DSM Disorder Criteria Summary
Breathing-Related Sleep Disorders

Features of breathing-related sleep disorders include the following:

> Sleep disruption, leading to excessive sleepiness or insomnia, that is judged to be due to a sleep-related breathing condition (e.g., obstructive or central sleep apnea syndrome, central alveolar hypoventilation syndrome)

> The disruption is not better accounted for by another mental disorder and is not due to the direct physiological effects of a substance or another general medical condition

Source: Based on *DSM-IV-TR*. Reprinted with permission from *Diagnostic and Statistical Manual of Mental Disorders* (4th ed., text revision). © 2000 American Psychiatric Association.

DSM Disorder Criteria Summary
Circadian Rhythm Sleep Disorders (Formerly Sleep–Wake Schedule Disorders)

Features of circadian rhythm sleep disorders include the following:

> A persistent or recurrent pattern of sleep disruption leading to excessive sleepiness or insomnia that is due to a mismatch between the sleep–wake schedule required by a person's environment and his or her circadian sleep–wake pattern

> The sleep disturbance causes clinically significant distress or impairment in functioning

> The disturbance does not occur exclusively during the course of another sleep disorder or other mental disorder

> The disturbance is not due to the direct physiological effects of a substance or a general medical condition

Source: Based on *DSM-IV-TR*. Reprinted with permission from *Diagnostic and Statistical Manual of Mental Disorders* (4th ed., text revision). © 2000 American Psychiatric Association.

Circadian Rhythm Sleep Disorders

"Spring ahead; fall back": People in most of the United States use this mnemonic device to remind themselves to turn the clocks ahead 1 hour in the spring and back again 1 hour in the fall. Most of us are surprised to see how disruptive this time change can be. For at least a day or two, we may be sleepy during the day and have difficulty falling asleep at night, almost as if we had jet lag. The reason for this disruption is not just that we gain or lose 1 hour of sleep; our bodies adjust to this fairly easily. The difficulty has to do with how our biological clocks adjust to this change in time. Convention says to go to sleep at this new time while our brains are saying something different. If the struggle continues for any length of time, you may have what is called a **circadian rhythm sleep disorder**. This disorder is characterized by disturbed sleep (either insomnia or excessive sleepiness during the day) brought on by the brain's inability to synchronize its sleep patterns with the current patterns of day and night.

In the 1960s, German and French scientists identified several bodily rhythms that seem to persist without cues from the environment, rhythms that are self-regulated (Aschoff & Wever, 1962; Siffre, 1964). Because these rhythms don't exactly match our 24-hour day, they are called circadian (from *circa* meaning "about" and *dian* meaning "day"). If our circadian rhythms don't match the 24-hour day, why isn't our sleep completely disrupted over time?

Fortunately, our brains have a mechanism that keeps us in sync with the outside world. Our biological clock is in the *suprachiasmatic nucleus* in the hypothalamus. Connected to the suprachiasmatic nucleus is a pathway that comes from our eyes. The light we see in the morning and the decreasing light at night signal the brain to reset the biological clock each day. Unfortunately, some people have trouble sleeping when they want to because of problems with their circadian rhythms. The causes may be outside the person (for example, crossing several time zones in a short amount of time) or internal.

There are several types of circadian rhythm sleep disorders. *Jet lag type* is, as its name implies, caused by rapidly crossing multiple time zones (Buysse et al., 2008). People with jet lag usually report difficulty going to sleep at the proper time and feeling fatigued during the day. Older people, introverts (loners), and early risers (morning people) are most likely to be negatively affected by these time zone changes (Gillin, 1993). Research with mice suggests that the effects of jet lag can be serious—at least among older adults. When older mice were exposed to repeated artificial jet lag, a significant number of them lived shorter lives (Davidson et al., 2006). *Shift work type* sleep problems are associated with work schedules (Åkerstedt & Wright Jr., 2009). Many people, such as hospital employees, police, or emergency personnel, work at night or must work irregular hours; as a result, they may have problems sleeping or experience excessive sleepiness during waking hours. Unfortunately, the problems of working (and thus staying awake) at unusual times can go beyond sleep and may contribute to cardiovascular disease, ulcers, and breast cancer in women (Richardson, 2006). Research suggests that people with circadian rhythm disorders are at greater risk of having one or more personality disorders (Dagan, Dela, Omer, Hallis, & Dar, 1996). Almost two thirds of all workers on rotating shifts complain of poor sleep (Neylan, Reynolds, & Kupfer, 2003).

In contrast with jet lag and shift work sleep-related problems, which have external causes such as long-distance travel and job selection, several circadian rhythm sleep disorders seem to arise from within the person experiencing the problems. Extreme night owls, people who stay up late and sleep late, may have a problem known as *delayed sleep phase type*. Sleep is delayed or later than normal bedtime. At the other extreme, people with an *advanced sleep phase type* of circadian rhythm disorder are "early to bed and early to rise." Here, sleep is advanced or earlier than normal bedtime. Partly because of our general lack of knowledge about them, *DSM-IV-TR* does not include these sleep phases as circadian rhythm sleep disorders.

Research on why our sleep rhythms are disrupted is advancing at a great pace, and we are beginning to understand the circadian rhythm process. Scientists believe the hormone *melatonin* contributes to the setting of our biological clocks that tell us when to sleep. This hormone is produced by the pineal gland, in the center of the brain. Melatonin (don't confuse this with *melanin*, the chemical that determines skin color) has been nicknamed the "Dracula hormone" because its production is stimulated by darkness and ceases in daylight. When our eyes see that it is nighttime, this information is passed on to the pineal gland, which, in turn, begins producing melatonin. Researchers believe that both light and melatonin help set the biological clock.

Concept Check 8.4

Match the following descriptions of sleeping problems with the correct term: (a) cataplexy, (b) primary hypersomnia, (c) primary insomnia, (d) sleep apnea, (e) sleep paralysis, (f) narcolepsy, (g) circadian rhythm sleep disorder, and (h) breathing-related sleep disorder.

1. Timothy wakes up frequently every night because he feels he is about to hyperventilate. He can't seem to get enough air, and many times his wife will wake him to tell him to quit snoring. He is suffering from a _____.

2. Sonia has problems staying awake throughout the day. Even while talking on the phone or riding the bus, she unexpectedly loses muscle tone and falls asleep for a while. This is due to _____.

3. Jaime sometimes awakens and cannot move or speak. This is a particularly frightening experience known as _____.

---

breathing-related sleep disorders A sleep disruption leading to excessive sleepiness or insomnia, caused by a breathing problem such as interrupted (sleep apnea) or labored (hypoventilation) breathing.
circadian rhythm sleep disorders A sleep disturbance resulting in sleepiness or insomnia, caused by the body's inability to synchronize its sleep patterns with the current pattern of day and night.

4. Brett has started a new job that requires him to change shifts monthly. He sometimes has day shifts and at other times has night shifts. Since then he has had considerable trouble sleeping. _____

5. Rama is extremely overweight. His wife suspects he may be suffering from _____ because he snores every night and often wakes up exhausted as though he never slept.

6. Melinda sleeps all night and still finds herself falling asleep throughout the next day. This happens even when she goes to bed early and gets up as late as possible. _____

Treatment of Sleep Disorders

> What medical treatments are available for chronic sleep problems?
> What are the limitations of those treatments?

When we can't fall asleep or we awaken frequently, or when sleep does not restore our energy and vitality, we need help. A number of biological and psychological interventions have been designed and evaluated to help people regain the benefits of normal sleep.

Medical Treatments

People who complain of insomnia to a medical professional are likely prescribed one of several benzodiazepine or related medications, which include short-acting drugs such as triazolam (Halcion), zaleplon (Sonata), and zolpidem (Ambien) and long-acting drugs such as flurazepam (Dalmane). Short-acting drugs (those that cause only brief drowsiness) are preferred because the long-acting drugs sometimes do not stop working by morning and people report more daytime sleepiness. The long-acting medications are sometimes preferred when negative effects such as daytime anxiety are observed in people taking the short-acting drugs (Neubauer, 2009). Newer medications, such as those that work directly with the melatonin system (e.g., ramelteon [Rozerem]), are also being developed to help people fall and stay asleep. People older than age 65 are most likely to use medication to help them sleep, although people of all ages, including young children (Durand, 2008), have been prescribed medications for insomnia.

There are several drawbacks to medical treatments for insomnia (Pagel, 2006). First, benzodiazepine medications can cause excessive sleepiness. Second, people can easily become dependent on them and rather easily misuse them, deliberately or not. Third, these medications are meant for short-term treatment and are not recommended for use longer than 4 weeks. Longer use can cause dependence and rebound insomnia. A newer concern for some medications (e.g., Ambien) is that they may increase the likelihood of sleepwalking-related problems, such as sleep-related eating disorder (Morgenthaler & Silber, 2002). Therefore, although medications may be helpful for sleep problems that will correct themselves in a short period (e.g., insomnia because of anxiety related to hospitalization), they are not intended for long-term chronic problems.

To help people with hypersomnia or narcolepsy, physicians usually prescribe a stimulant such as methylphenidate (Ritalin, the medication Ann was taking) or modafinil (Nevsimalova, 2009). Cataplexy, or loss of muscle tone, can be treated with antidepressant medication, not because people with narcolepsy are depressed but because antidepressants suppress REM (or dream) sleep. Also, gamma-hydroxybutyrate (GHB) is the first medication specifically approved to treat cataplexy. Cataplexy seems to be related to the sudden onset of REM sleep; therefore, the antidepressant medication can be helpful in reducing these attacks.

Treatment of breathing-related sleep disorders focuses on helping the person breathe better during sleep. For some, this means recommending weight loss. In some people who are obese, the neck's soft tissue compresses the airways. Unfortunately, as we have seen earlier in this chapter, voluntary weight loss is rarely successful in the long term; as a result, this treatment has not proved successful for breathing-related sleep disorders (Sanders & Givelber, 2006).

The gold standard for the treatment of obstructive sleep apnea involves the use of a mechanical device—called the continuous positive air pressure (CPAP) machine—that improves breathing. Patients wear a mask that provides slightly pressurized air during sleep and it helps them breathe more normally throughout the night. Unfortunately, many peo-

▲ William C. Dement is a pioneering sleep researcher and director of the Sleep Disorders Center at Stanford University.

ple have difficulty using the device because of issues of comfort and some even experience a form of claustrophobia. To assist these individuals, a variety of strategies are tried, including the use of psychological interventions including desensitization for claustrophobia, patient and partner education, and attendance of support groups (Abad & Guilleminault, 2009). Severe breathing problems may require surgery to help remove blockages in parts of the airways.

Environmental Treatments

Because medication as a primary treatment isn't usually recommended, other ways of getting people back in step with their sleep rhythms are usually tried. One general principle for treating circadian rhythm disorders is that *phase delays* (moving bedtime later) are easier than *phase advances* (moving bedtime earlier). In other words, it is easier to stay up several hours later than usual than to force yourself to go to sleep several hours earlier. Scheduling shift changes in a clockwise direction (going from day to evening schedule) seems to help workers adjust better. People can best readjust their sleep patterns by going to bed several hours later each night until bedtime is at the desired hour (Buysse et al., 2008). A drawback of this approach is that it requires the person to sleep during the day for several days, which is difficult for people with regularly scheduled responsibilities.

Another strategy to help people with sleep problems involves using bright light to trick the brain into readjusting the biological clock. Research indicates that bright light (also referred to as *phototherapy*) may help people with circadian rhythm problems readjust their sleep patterns (Bjorvatn & Pallesen, 2009). People typically sit in front of a bank of fluorescent lamps that generate light greater than 2,000 lux, an amount significantly different from normal indoor light (250 lux). Several hours of exposure to this bright light have successfully reset the circadian rhythms of many individuals. This type of treatment provides some hope for people with schedule-related sleep problems.

Psychological Treatments

As you can imagine, the limitations of using medication to help people sleep better has led to the development of psychological treatments. Table 8.4 briefly describes some psychological approaches to insomnia. Different treatments help people with different kinds of sleep problems. For example, relaxation treatments reduce the physical tension that seems to prevent some people from falling asleep at night. Some people report that their anxiety about work, relationships, or other situations prevents them from sleeping or wakes them up in the middle of the night. To address this problem, cognitive treatments are used.

Research shows that some psychological treatments for insomnia may be more effective than others. For adult sleep problems, stimulus control may be recommended. People are instructed to use the bedroom only for sleeping and for sex and *not* for work or other anxiety-provoking activities (for example, watching the news on television). Progressive relaxation or sleep hygiene (changing daily habits that may interfere with sleep) alone may not be as effective as stimulus control alone for some people (Means & Edinger, 2006). Because sleep problems are so widespread, there is a growing interest in developing Internet-based treatments to determine if certain sufferers can help themselves with appropriate guidance. One study, for example, randomly assigned adults to a control group or an Internet-based education group (Ritterband et al., 2009). The Internet group received online instruction on the proper use of several of the psychological treatments (e.g.,

Table 8.4 Psychological Treatments for Insomnia

Sleep Treatment	Description
Cognitive	This approach focuses on changing the sleepers' unrealistic expectations and beliefs about sleep ("I must have 8 hours of sleep each night"; "If I get less than 8 hours of sleep, it will make me ill"). The therapist attempts to alter beliefs and attitudes about sleeping by providing information on topics such as normal amounts of sleep and a person's ability to compensate for lost sleep.
Guided imagery relaxation	Because some people become anxious when they have difficulty sleeping, this approach uses meditation or imagery to help with relaxation at bedtime or after a night waking.
Graduated extinction	Used for children who have tantrums at bedtime or wake up crying at night, this treatment instructs the parent to check on the child after progressively longer periods until the child falls asleep on his or her own.
Paradoxical intention	This technique involves instructing individuals in the opposite behavior from the desired outcome. Telling poor sleepers to lie in bed and try to stay awake as long as they can is used to try to relieve the performance anxiety surrounding efforts to try to fall asleep.
Progressive relaxation	This technique involves relaxing the muscles of the body in an effort to introduce drowsiness.

sleep restriction, stimulus control, sleep hygiene, cognitive restructuring, and relapse prevention). The findings were striking, suggesting that not only could the treatment be delivered over the Internet, but also that sleep improved in this group even 6 months later. Under certain circumstances people are able to use *evidence-based instruction* (education on the use of a treatment that has empirical support) to improve a variety of psychological problems.

Sonja—the law student we profiled in the beginning of this section—was helped with her sleep problems using several techniques. She was instructed to limit her time in bed to about 4 hours of sleep time (sleep restriction), about the amount of time she slept each night. The period was lengthened when she began to sleep through the night. Sonja was also asked not to do any schoolwork while in bed and to get out of bed if she couldn't fall asleep within 15 minutes (stimulus control). Finally, therapy involved confronting her unrealistic expectations about how much sleep was enough for a person of her age (cognitive therapy). Within about 3 weeks of treatment, Sonja was sleeping longer (6 to 7 hours per night as opposed to 4 to 5 hours previously) and had fewer interruptions in her sleep. Also, she felt more refreshed in the morning and had more energy during the day. Sonja's results mirror those of studies that find combined treatments to be effective in older adults with insomnia (Petit, Azad, Byszewski, Sarazan, & Power, 2003). One important study, using a randomized placebo-control design, found that cognitive-behavioral therapy (CBT) may be more successful treating sleep disorders in older adults than a medical (drug) intervention (Sivertsen et al., 2006).

For young children, some cognitive treatments may not be possible. Instead, treatment often includes setting up bedtime routines such as a bath, followed by a parent's reading a story, to help children go to sleep at night. Graduated extinction (described in Table 8.5) has been used with some success for bedtime problems and for waking up at night (Durand, 2008).

Preventing Sleep Disorders

Sleep professionals generally agree that a significant portion of the sleep problems people experience daily can be prevented by following a few steps during the day. Referred to as *sleep hygiene*, these changes in lifestyle can be relatively simple to follow and can help avoid problems such as insomnia for some people (Gellis & Lichstein, 2009). Some sleep hygiene recommendations rely on allowing the brain's normal drive for sleep to take over, replacing the restrictions we place on our activities that interfere with sleep. For example, setting a regular time to go to sleep and awaken each day can help make falling asleep at night easier. Avoiding the use of caffeine and nicotine—which are both stimulants—can also help prevent problems such as nighttime awakening. Table 8.5 illustrates a number of the sleep hygiene steps recommended for preventing sleep problems.

Table 8.5 Good Sleep Habits

- Establish a set bedtime routine.
- Develop a regular bedtime and a regular time to awaken.
- Eliminate all foods and drinks that contain caffeine 6 hours before bedtime.
- Limit any use of alcohol or tobacco.
- Drink milk before bedtime.
- Eat a balanced diet, limiting fat.
- Go to bed only when sleepy and get out of bed if you are unable to fall asleep or back to sleep after 15 minutes.
- Do not exercise or participate in vigorous activities in the hours before bedtime.
- Do include a weekly program of exercise during the day.
- Restrict activities in bed to those that help induce sleep.
- Reduce noise and light in the bedroom.
- Increase exposure to natural and bright light during the day.
- Avoid extreme temperature changes in the bedroom (that is, too hot or too cold).

Source: Adapted, with permission, from Durand, V. M. (1998). *Sleep better: A guide to improving sleep for children with special needs* (p. 60). Baltimore: Paul H. Brookes.

A few studies have investigated the value of educating parents about the sleep of their young children in an effort to prevent later difficulties. Adachi and colleagues (2009), for example, provided 10 minutes of group guidance and a simple educational booklet to the parents of 4-month-old children. They followed up on these children 3 months later and found that, compared to a randomly selected control group of children, the ones whose parents received education about sleep experienced fewer sleep problems. Because so many children display disruptive sleep problems, this type of preventive effort could significantly improve the lives of many families.

Parasomnias and Their Treatment

Parasomnias are not problems with sleep itself but abnormal events that occur either during sleep or during that twilight time between sleeping and waking. Some events associated with parasomnia are not unusual if they happen while you are awake (e.g., walking to the kitchen to look into the refrigerator) but can be distressing if they take place while you are sleeping.

Parasomnias are of two types: those that occur during REM sleep, and those that occur during NREM sleep. As you might have guessed, **nightmares** occur during REM or dream sleep (Blanes, Burgess, Marks, & Gill, 2009). About 10% to 50% of children and about 1% of adults experience them regularly (Hirshkowitz et al., 2009). To qualify as a nightmare disorder, according to *DSM-IV-TR* criteria, these experiences must be so distressful that they impair a person's ability to carry on normal activities (such as making a person too anxious to try to sleep at night). Some researchers distinguish nightmares from bad dreams by whether or not you wake up as a result. Nightmares are defined as disturbing dreams that awaken the sleeper; bad

▲ A nightmare is distressing for both child and parent.

DSM Disorder Criteria Summary
Nightmare Disorder

Features of nightmare disorder include the following:

> Repeated awakenings from the major sleep period or naps with detailed recall of extended and extremely frightening dreams, generally during the second half of the sleep period

> On awakening from the frightening dreams, the person rapidly becomes oriented and alert

> The dream experience, or the sleep disturbance resulting from the awakening, causes significant distress or impairment in functioning

> Nightmares do not occur exclusively during the course of another mental disorder and are not due to the direct physiological effects of a substance or a general medical condition

Source: Based on *DSM-IV-TR.* Reprinted with permission from *Diagnostic and Statistical Manual of Mental Disorders* (4th ed., text revision). © 2000 American Psychiatric Association.

dreams are those that do not awaken the person experiencing them. Using this definition, college students report an average of 30 bad dreams and 10 nightmares per year (Zadra & Donderi, 2000). Because nightmares are so common, you would expect that a great deal of research would have focused on their causes and treatment. Unfortunately, this is not so, and we still know little about why people have nightmares and how to treat them. Fortunately, they tend to decrease with age.

Sleep terrors, which most commonly afflict children, usually begin with a piercing scream. The child is extremely upset, often sweating, and frequently has a rapid heartbeat. On the surface, sleep terrors appear to resemble nightmares—the child cries and appears frightened—but they occur during NREM sleep and therefore are not caused by frightening dreams. During sleep terrors, children cannot be easily awakened and comforted, as they can during a nightmare. Children do not remember sleep terrors, despite their often dramatic effect on the observer (Durand, 2008). Approximately 5% of children (more boys than girls) may experience sleep terrors; for adults, the prevalence rate is less than 1% (Buysse, Reynolds, & Kupfer, 1993). As with nightmares, we know relatively little about sleep terrors, although several theories have been proposed, including the possibility of a genetic component because the disorder tends to occur in families (Durand, 2008). Treatment for sleep terrors usually begins with a recommendation to wait and see if they disappear on their own.

One approach to reducing chronic sleep terrors is the use of *scheduled awakenings*. In the first controlled study of its kind, Durand and Mindell (1999) instructed parents of children who were experiencing almost nightly sleep terrors to awaken their child briefly approximately 30 minutes before a typical episode (these usually occur around the same time each evening). This simple technique, which was faded out over several weeks, was successful in almost eliminating these disturbing events.

It might surprise you to learn that **sleepwalking** (also called **somnambulism**) occurs during NREM sleep (Shatkin & Ivanenko, 2009). This means that when people walk in their sleep, they are probably not acting out a dream. This parasomnia typically occurs during the first few hours while a person is in the deep stages of sleep. The *DSM-IV-TR* criteria for sleepwalking require that the person leave the bed, although less active episodes can involve small motor behaviors, such as sitting up in bed and picking at the blanket or gesturing. Because sleepwalking occurs during the deepest stages of sleep, waking someone during an episode is difficult; if the person is wakened, she typically will not remember what has happened. It is not true, however, that waking a sleepwalker is somehow dangerous.

nightmare A frightening and anxiety-provoking dream occurring during rapid eye movement sleep. The individual recalls the bad dream and recovers alertness and orientation quickly.

sleep terror An episode of apparent awakening from sleep, accompanied by signs of panic and followed by disorientation and amnesia for the incident. Sleep terrors occur during nonrapid eye movement sleep and so do not involve frightening dreams.

sleepwalking (somnambulism) Parasomnia that involves leaving the bed during nonrapid eye movement sleep. See also somnambulism.

Sleepwalking is primarily a problem during childhood, although a small proportion of adults are affected. A relatively large number of children—from 15% to 30%—have at least one episode of sleepwalking, with about 2% reported to have multiple incidents (Neylan et al., 2003). In most cases, the course of sleepwalking is short, and few people older than age 15 continue to exhibit this parasomnia.

We do not yet clearly understand why some people sleepwalk, although factors such as extreme fatigue, previous sleep deprivation, the use of sedative or hypnotic drugs,

and stress have been implicated (Shatkin & Ivanenko, 2009). On occasion, sleepwalking episodes have been associated with violent behavior, including homicide and suicide (Cartwright, 2006). In one case, a man drove to his in-laws' house, succeeded in killing his mother-in-law, and attempted to kill his father-in-law. He was acquitted of the charges of murder, using sleepwalking as his legal defense (Broughton, Billings, & Cartwright, 1994). These cases are still controversial, although there is evidence for the legitimacy of some violent behavior coinciding with sleepwalking episodes.

There also seems to be a genetic component to sleepwalking, with a higher incidence observed among identical twins and within families (Broughton, 2000). A related disorder, *nocturnal eating syndrome,* is when individuals rise from their beds and eat although they are still asleep (Striegel-Moore et al., 2010). This problem, which is different than the *night eating syndrome* discussed earlier in the chapter in the eating disorders section, may be more frequent than previously thought; it was found in almost 6% of individuals in one study who were referred because of insomnia complaints (Manni, Ratti, & Tartara, 1997; Winkelman, 2006).

There is an increasing awareness that sleep is important for both our mental and our physical well-being. Sleep problems are also comorbid with many other disorders and therefore can compound the difficulties of people with significant psychological difficulties. Researchers are coming closer to understanding the basic nature of sleep and its disorders, and we anticipate significant treatment advances in the years to come.

Concept Check 8.5

Part A

Diagnose the sleep problems of the cases here using one of the following: (a) nocturnal eating syndrome, (b) sleep terrors, and (c) nightmares.

1. Jaclyn's dad is sometimes awakened by his daughter's screams. He runs to Jaclyn's room to comfort her and is eventually able to calm her down. Jaclyn usually explains that she was being chased by a big, one-eyed, purple monster. The events typically happen after watching scary movies with friends. _____

2. Sho-jen's parents hear her piercing screams on many nights and rush to comfort her, but she does not respond. During these episodes, her heart rate is elevated and her pajamas are soaked in sweat. However, when she gets up the next day she has no memory of the experience. _____

3. Jack has made a serious commitment to his diet for more than a month but continues to gain weight. He has no memory of eating but

noticed that food is always missing from the refrigerator. _____

Part B

Fill in the blanks to make the following statements correct about the treatment of sleep disorders.

4. Karen wakes up screaming every night, disregarding her parents' efforts to comfort her. Her heart rate is elevated in these episodes, and her pajamas are soaked in sweat. The next day, she has no memory of the experience. To help reduce these night terrors, Karen's pediatrician used _____.

5. After George's wife died at the age of 68, he could not sleep. To help him through the hardest first week, Dr. Brown prescribed _____ for his insomnia.

6. Carl's doctor suggested some relatively simple lifestyle changes, otherwise known as good _____, when he expressed concern about developing a sleep disorder.

 On the Spectrum A Transdiagnostic Treatment of Eating Disorders

In *DSM-IV*, eating disorders for the most part are considered to be mutually exclusive. For example, according to *DSM-IV* guidelines a person cannot meet criteria for both anorexia and bulimia. But investigators working in this area have discovered that features of the various eating disorders overlap considerably (Fairburn, Cooper, Shafran, & Wilson, 2008). Furthermore, a large portion of patients, perhaps as many as 50% or more, who meet criteria for a clinically severe eating disorder do not meet criteria for anorexia or bulimia and are diagnosed with "eating disorder not otherwise specified" (eating disorder NOS) (Fairburn & Bohn, 2005). As described earlier in the chapter, some of these patients would now meet criteria for "binge eating disorder," which is likely to be included as a full-fledged diagnostic category in *DSM-5*. A schematic representation of the relationship of anorexia, bulimia, and eating disorder NOS is presented in ■ Figure 8.7. The figure's two inner circles, representing anorexia and bulimia, overlap; this overlapping area would include those people who would meet criteria for both disorders, if *DSM-IV* allowed such overlap.

As noted in Figure 8.3, these eating disorders have very similar causal influences including similar inherited biological vulnerabilities, similar social influences (primarily cultural influences glorifying thinness), and a strong family influence toward perfectionism in all things. Finally, all eating disorders seem to share anxiety focused on one's appearance and presentation to others and distorted body image. Now, Christopher Fairburn and associates have proposed a transdiagnostic treatment protocol designed to be applicable across several eating disorder diagnoses (Fairburn, Cooper, Shafran, & Wilson, 2008; Fairburn, Cooper, Doll, et al., 2009). In this treatment protocol, the essential components of cognitive-behavioral therapy (CBT) directed at causal factors common to all eating disorders are targeted in an integrated way. (Individuals with anorexia and a very low weight—BMI of 17.5 or less—who would need inpatient treatment would be excluded until their weight was restored to an adequate level when they could then benefit from the program.) Thus, the principal foci of this protocol are on the distorted evaluation of body shape and weight; maladaptive attempts to control weight in the form of strict dieting, possibly accompanied by binge eating; and methods to compensate for overeating such as purging, laxative misuse, etc.

Because additional psychological problems including difficulty tolerating negative moods, tendencies to perfectionism, accompanying low self-esteem, and interpersonal difficulties commonly accompany eating disorders, Fairburn and colleagues developed what they called an "enhanced treatment" (CBT-E) that also addresses

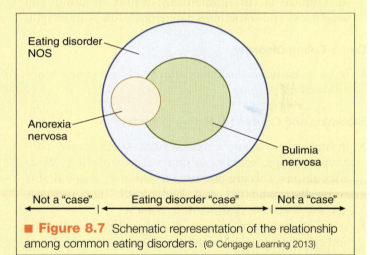

■ **Figure 8.7** Schematic representation of the relationship among common eating disorders. (© Cengage Learning 2013)

these factors (Fairburn, Cooper, Shafran, Bohn, et al., 2008). In a landmark study (Fairburn, Cooper, Doll, et al., 2009), this CBT-E protocol was evaluated against a more focused transdiagnostic protocol dealing only with features specific to the eating disorders. Findings indicated that indeed the enhanced protocol was more effective than the focused protocol in treating eating disorders and accompanying complex psychopathology including perfectionism and interpersonal difficulties, whereas the focused protocol was all that was required for any of the eating disorders without complex psychopathology. This transdiagnostic protocol has already been adopted widely in eating disorder clinics around the world and represents yet another example of the trend away from dealing with discrete, narrowly defined diagnostic categories in favor of more broad-based dimensions of psychopathology within a spectra of related disorders.

Summary

What are the defining features of bulimia nervosa and anorexia nervosa?

> The prevalence of eating disorders has increased rapidly over the past half century. As a result, they were included for the first time as a separate group of disorders in *DSM-IV.*

Bulimia Nervosa and Anorexia Nervosa

How does binge-eating disorder differ from bulimia?

> There are two prevalent eating disorders. In bulimia nervosa, dieting results in out-of-control binge-eating episodes that are often followed by purging the food through vomiting or other means. Anorexia nervosa, in which food intake is cut dramatically, results in substantial weight loss and sometimes dangerously low body weight.

Binge-Eating Disorder

> In binge-eating disorder, a pattern of binge eating is *not* followed by purging.

Statistics and Course for Eating Disorders

> Bulimia nervosa and anorexia nervosa are largely confined to young, middle- to upper-class women in Western cultures who are pursuing a thin body shape that is culturally mandated and biologically inappropriate, making it extremely difficult to achieve.
> Without treatment, eating disorders become chronic and can, on occasion, result in death.

Causes of Eating Disorders

What social, psychological, and neurobiological factors might cause eating disorders?

> In addition to sociocultural pressures, causal factors include possible biological and genetic vulnerabilities (the disorders tend to run in families), psychological factors (low self-esteem), social anxiety (fears of rejection), and distorted body image (relatively normal-weight individuals view themselves as fat and ugly).

Treatment of Eating Disorders

How does the use of medications compare with psychological therapies for the treatment of eating disorders?

> Several psychosocial treatments are effective, including cognitive-behavioral approaches combined with family therapy and interpersonal psychotherapy. Drug treatments are less effective at the current time.

Obesity

What are some possible causes of obesity?

> Obesity is not a disorder in *DSM* but is one of the more dangerous epidemics confronting the world today. Cultural norms that encourage eating high-fat foods combine with genetic and other factors to cause obesity, which is difficult to treat.

What treatments are available?

> Professionally directed behavior modification programs, possibly combined with drugs, are moderately successful, but prevention efforts in the form of changes in government policy on nutrition seem the most promising.

Sleep Disorders

What are the critical diagnostic features of the major sleep disorders?

> Sleep disorders are highly prevalent in the general population and are of two types: dyssomnias (disturbances of sleep) and parasomnias (abnormal events such as nightmares and sleepwalking that occur during sleep).
> Of the dyssomnias, the most common disorder, primary insomnia, involves the inability to initiate sleep, problems maintaining sleep, or failure to feel refreshed after a full night's sleep. Other dyssomnias include primary hypersomnia (excessive sleep), narcolepsy (sudden and irresistible sleep attacks), circadian rhythm sleep disorders (sleepiness or insomnia caused by the body's inability to synchronize its sleep patterns with day and night), and breathing-related sleep disorders (disruptions that have a physical origin, such as sleep apnea, that lead to excessive sleepiness or insomnia).
> The formal assessment of sleep disorders, a polysomnographic evaluation, is typically done by monitoring the heart, muscles, respiration, brain waves, and other functions of a sleeping client in the lab. In addition to such monitoring, it is helpful to determine the individual's sleep efficiency, a percentage based on the time the individual actually sleeps as opposed to time spent in bed trying to sleep.

What medical and psychological treatments are used for the treatment of sleep disorders?

> Benzodiazepine medications have been helpful for short-term treatment of many of the dyssomnias, but they must be used carefully or they might cause rebound insomnia, a withdrawal experience that can cause worse sleep problems after the medication is stopped. Any long-term treatment of sleep problems should include psychological interventions such as stimulus control and sleep hygiene.

How are rapid eye movement and nonrapid eye movement sleep related to the parasomnias?

> Parasomnias such as nightmares occur during rapid eye movement (or dream) sleep, and sleep terrors and sleepwalking occur during nonrapid eye movement sleep.

Key Terms

bulimia nervosa, 285
binge, 285
anorexia nervosa, 285
binge-eating disorder (BED), 285
obesity, 287
purging techniques, 287
night eating syndrome, 305
bariatric surgery, 307
rapid eye movement (REM) sleep, 309

dyssomnias, 309
parasomnias, 309
polysomnographic (PSG) evaluation, 309
actigraph, 311
sleep efficiency (SE), 311
microsleeps, 311
primary insomnia, 311
rebound insomnia, 313
hypersomnia, 315

sleep apnea, 315
narcolepsy, 315
breathing-related sleep disorders, 317
circadian rhythm sleep disorders, 317
nightmares, 321
sleep terrors, 321
sleepwalking (somnambulism), 321

Answers to Concept Checks

8.1

1. c; 2. a; 3. a; 4. b

8.2

1. T; 2. T; 3. F (females find a smaller size more attractive than do men); 4. F (they help with bulimia nervosa, not anorexia); 5. T; 6. T

8.3

1. T; 2. F (it's only one third or more); 3. F; 4. T

8.4

1. h; 2. f; 3. e; 4. g; 5. d; 6. b

8.5

Part A

1. c; 2. b; 3. a

Part B

4. scheduled awakenings; 5. benzodiazepines; 6. sleep hygiene

Media Resources

Log in to CengageBrain to access the resources your instructor requires. For this book, you can access:

CourseMate brings course concepts to life with interactive learning, study, and exam preparation tools that support the printed textbook. A textbook-specific website, Psychology CourseMate includes an integrated interactive eBook and other interactive learning tools including quizzes, flashcards, videos, and more.

Abnormal Psychology Videos

› *Susan, a Client with Anorexia Nervosa:* Susan talks about her fears of not being "skinny enough."
› *Weight Control:* Consider how researchers are helping people deal with the obesity epidemic.
› *Sleep Cycle:* This clip describes the normal cycle of REM and NREM sleep throughout the night—a cycle that may be altered in sleep disorders.

CENGAGENOW CengageNow is an easy-to-use online resource that helps you study in less time to get the grade you want—NOW. Take a pre-test for this chapter and receive a personalized study plan based on your results that will identify the topics you need to review and direct you to online resources to help you master those topics. Then take a post-test to help you determine the concepts you have mastered and what you will need to work on. If your textbook does not include an access code card, go to CengageBrain.com to gain access.

Visit www.cengagebrain.com to access your account and purchase materials.

aplia If your professor has assigned Aplia homework:

1. Sign in to your account.
2. Complete the corresponding homework exercises as required by your professor.
3. When finished, click "Grade It Now" to see which areas you have mastered, which need more work, and for detailed explanations of every answer.

Chapter Quiz

1. It is estimated that _____ of individuals with eating disorders die as a result of the disorder, with as many as 50% of those deaths coming from _____.
   a. 20%; homicide
   b. 20%; suicide
   c. 50%; homicide
   d. 50%; suicide

2. Dr. Thompson sees a patient with a chubby face, calluses on her fingers, and small scars on the back of her hand. Tests indicate that the patient weighs slightly more than her expected weight and that she has an electrolyte imbalance. The patient reports that she is having persistent constipation and that she feels as if her heart has been skipping beats. These symptoms are consistent with:
   a. depression
   b. anxiety
   c. anorexia nervosa
   d. bulimia nervosa

3. Research on bulimia nervosa suggests that it most often co-occurs with:
   a. anxiety disorders
   b. mood disorders
   c. psychotic disorders
   d. substance use disorders

4. The typical age of onset for anorexia nervosa and bulimia nervosa is _____, with younger cases of anorexia tending to begin at _____ and younger cases of bulimia tending to begin at _____.
   a. 30; 25; 20
   b. 20; 15; 10
   c. 15; 10; 5
   d. 15; 13; 12

5. In a study by Fallon and Rozin, female undergraduates:
   a. rated their current body size the same as the ideal body size
   b. rated the ideal body size smaller than the attractive body size
   c. rated the ideal body size heavier than the attractive body size
   d. rated their current body size smaller than the ideal body size

6. Which of the following statements is true of cognitive–behavioral therapy (CBT) and interpersonal therapy (IPT) in the treatment of bulimia?
   a. CBT appears to work faster than IPT, but they both seem to have the same positive effect at a 1-year follow-up.
   b. CBT and IPT appear to have the same impact in both the short term and the long term.
   c. IPT appears to work faster than CBT, but they both seem to have the same positive effect at a 1-year follow-up.
   d. Neither CBT nor IPT appears to be effective in the treatment of bulimia.

7. Which of the following is used to measure arm movements as an indicator of sleep activity and sleep quality?
   a. electrocardiogram
   b. electromyograph
   c. electroencephalograph
   d. actigraph

8. While sleeping, Michael, a 55-year-old overweight male, experiences a cessation in his breathing for short periods. Michael's wife reports that he snores continuously and never feels rested. Michael's symptoms are consistent with:

a. narcolepsy

b. sleep apnea

c. sleep–wake schedule disorder

d. cataplexy

9. Mr. Dunn has been experiencing insomnia for several weeks. His doctor recommends that he only lie in bed for 3 hours, the amount of time that he actually sleeps each night. The amount of time Mr. Dunn lies in bed is then increased as he begins to sleep more. This treatment is known as:

a. sleep hygiene

b. sleep restriction

c. phase delay

d. progressive relaxation

10. The primary difference between sleep terrors and nightmares is:

a. sleep terrors usually begin with a scream

b. children do not remember nightmares

c. sleep terrors occur during NREM sleep

d. sleep terrors are more prevalent in the population

(See Appendix A for answers.)

Exploring Eating Disorders

Individuals with eating disorders:

› Feel a relentless, all-encompassing drive to be thin
› Are overwhelmingly young females from middle- to upper-class families, who live in socially competitive environments
› Lived only in Western countries until recently

Psychological—Diminished sense of personal control and self-confidence, causing low self-esteem. Distorted body image.

Social—Cultural and social emphasis on slender ideal, leading to body dissatisfaction and pre-occupation with food and eating.

Causes

Biological—Possible genetic tendency to poor impulse control, emotional instability, and perfectionistic traits

EATING DISORDERS

Disorder	Characteristics	Treatment
Bulimia Nervosa	• Out-of-control consumption of excessive amounts of mostly non-nutritious food within a short time • Elimination of food through self-induced vomiting and/or abuse of laxatives or diuretics • To compensate for binges, some bulimics exercise excessively or fast between binges • Vomiting may enlarge salivary glands (causing a chubby face), erode dental enamel, and cause electrolyte imbalance resulting in cardiac failure or kidney problems • Weight usually within 10% of normal • Age of onset is typically 16 to 19 years of age	• Drug treatment, such as antidepressants • Short-term cognitive-behavioral therapy (CBT) to address behavior and attitudes on eating and body shape • Interpersonal psychotherapy (IPT) to improve interpersonal functioning • Tends to be chronic if left untreated
Anorexia Nervosa	• Intense fear of obesity and persistent pursuit of thinness; perpetual dissatisfaction with weight loss • Severe caloric restriction, often with excessive exercise and sometimes with purging, to the point of semi-starvation • Severely limiting caloric intake may cause cessation of menstruation, downy hair on limbs and cheeks, dry skin, brittle hair or nails, sensitivity to cold, and danger of acute cardiac or kidney failure • Weight at least 15% below normal • Average age of onset is about 13 years of age	• Hospitalization (at 70% below normal weight) • Outpatient treatment to restore weight and correct dysfunctional attitudes on eating and body shape • Family therapy • Tends to be chronic if left untreated; more resistant to treatment than bulimia
Binge-Eating	• Similar to bulimia with out-of-control food binges, but no attempt to purge the food (vomiting, laxatives, diuretics) or compensate for excessive intake • Marked physical and emotional stress; some sufferers binge to alleviate bad moods • Binge eaters share some concerns about weight and body shape as individuals with anorexia and bulimia • Tends to affect more older people than either bulimia or anorexia	• Short-term CBT to address behavior and attitudes on eating and body shape • IPT to improve interpersonal functioning • Drug treatments that reduce feelings of hunger • Self-help approaches

Photodisc/Getty Images

Disorder	Characteristics	Treatment
Obesity	• Up to 65% of U.S. adults are overweight, and over 30% are obese • Worldwide problem; increased risk in urban rather than rural settings • Two forms of maladaptive eating patterns associated with obesity-binge eating and night eating syndrome • Increases risk of cardiovascular disease, diabetes, hypertension, stroke, and other physical problems	• Self-directed weight loss programs • Commercial self-help programs, such as Weight Watchers • Professionally directed behavior modification programs, which are the most effective treatment • Surgery, as a last resort

Stockbyte/Getty Images

Psychological—Affects impulse control, attitudes, and motivation towards eating, and responsiveness to the consequences of eating.

Social—Advancing technology promotes sedentary lifestyle and consumption of high fat foods.

Causes

Biological—Genes influence an individual's number of fat cells, tendency toward fat storage, and activity levels.

Exploring Sleep Disorders

Characterized by extreme disruption in the everyday lives of affected individuals, and are an important factor in many psychological disorders.

SLEEP DISORDERS

Diagnosing Sleep Disorders

A polysomnographic (PSG) evaluation assesses an individual's sleep habits with various electronic tests to measure airflow, brain activity, eye movements, muscle movements, and heart activity. Results are weighed with a measure of sleep efficiency (SE), the percentage of time spent asleep.

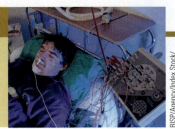

BISP/Agency/Index Stock/PhotoLibrary

Dyssomnias
Disturbances in the timing, amount, or quality of sleep

Disorder	Characteristics	Causes	Treatment
Primary Insomnia	• Characteristics include difficulty initiating sleep, difficulty maintaining sleep, or nonrestorative sleep	• Causes include pain, insufficient exercise, drug use, environmental influences, anxiety, respiratory problems, and biological vulnerability.	• Treatment may be medical (benzodiazepines) or psychological (anxiety reduction, improved sleep hygiene); combined approach is usually most effective.
Narcolepsy	• Characteristics include sudden daytime onset of REM sleep combined with cataplexy, a rapid loss of muscle tone that can be quite mild or result in complete collapse. Often accompanied by sleep paralysis and/or hypnagogic hallucinations.	• Causes are likely to be genetic.	• Treatment is medical (stimulant drugs).
Primary Hypersomnia	• Characteristics include abnormally excessive sleep and sleepiness, and involuntary daytime sleeping. Classified as a disorder only when it's subjectively perceived as disruptive.	• Causes may involve genetic link and/or excess serotonin.	• Treatment is usually medical (stimulant drugs).
Breathing-Related Sleep Disorder	• Characteristics include disturbed sleep and daytime fatigue resulting from hypoventilation (labored breathing) or sleep apnea (suspended breathing).	• Causes may include narrow or obstructed airway, obesity, and increasing age.	• Treatments to improve breathing are medical or mechanical.
Circadian Rhythm Sleep Disorder	• Characteristics include sleepiness or insomnia.	• Caused by inability to synchronize sleep patterns with current pattern of day and night due to jet lag, shift work, delayed sleep, or advanced sleep (going to bed earlier than normal bedtime).	• Treatment includes phase delays to adjust bedtime and bright light to readjust biological clock.

Parasomnias
Abnormal behaviors that occur during sleep.

Image Source/Getty Images

Nightmares

Frightening REM dreams that awaken the sleeper. Nightmares qualify as nightmare disorder when they are stressful enough to impair normal functioning. Causes are unknown, but they tend to decrease with age.

Sleep Terrors

Occur during non-REM (nondreaming) sleep and most commonly afflict children. Sleeping child screams, cries, sweats, sometimes walks, has rapid heartbeat, and cannot easily be awakened or comforted. More common in boys than girls, and possible genetic link since tend to run in families. May subside with time.

Sleepwalking

Occurs at least once during non-REM sleep in 15% to 30% of children under age 15. Causes may include extreme fatigue, sleep deprivation, sedative or hypnotic drugs, and stress. Adult sleepwalking is usually associated with other psychological disorders. May have a genetic link.

CHAPTER 9

Sexual and Gender Identity Disorders

Demonstrate knowledge and understanding representing appropriate breadth and depth in selected content areas of psychology:	› Biological bases of behavior and mental processes, including physiology, sensation, perception, comparative, motivation, and emotion (APA SLO 1.2.a (3)) *(see textbook pages 348–351)*
Use the concepts, language, and major theories of the discipline to account for psychological phenomena.	› Describe behavior and mental processes empirically, including operational definitions (APA SLO 1.3.a) *(see textbook pages 335–347, 355–359)*
Identify appropriate applications of psychology in solving problems, such as:	› Origin and treatment of abnormal behavior (APA SLO 4.2.b) *(see textbook pages 336–340, 347–354, 359–363)*
	› Psychological tests and measurements (APA SLO 4.2.c) *(see textbook pages 347–348)*

*Portions of this chapter cover learning outcomes suggested by the American Psychological Association (2007) in their guidelines for the undergraduate psychology major. Chapter coverage of these outcomes is identified by APA Goal and APA Suggested Learning Outcome (SLO).

What Is Normal Sexuality?

> **How do sociocultural factors influence what are considered "normal" sexual behaviors?**

You have all read magazine surveys reporting sensational information on sexual practices. According to one, men can reach orgasm 15 or more times a day (in reality, such ability is rare) and women fantasize about being raped. (Women do have idealized fantasies of submission in the context of being desired, but these fantasies are far from imagining an actual rape [Critelli & Bivona, 2008].) Surveys like this fail us on two counts: First, they claim to reveal sexual norms but they are reporting mostly distorted half-truths. Second, the facts they present typically are not based on any scientific methodology that would make them reliable, although they do sell magazines.

What is normal sexual behavior? As you will see, it depends. More to the point, when is sexual behavior that is somewhat different from the norm a disorder? Again, it depends. Current views tend to be quite tolerant of a variety of sexual expressions, even if they are unusual, unless the behavior is associated with a substantial impairment in functioning or involves nonconsenting individuals such as children. Three kinds of sexual behavior meet this definition. In *gender identity disorder,* there is psychological dissatisfaction with one's biological sex. The disorder is not specifically sexual but rather a disturbance in the person's sense of identity as a male or a female. But these disorders are often grouped with sexual disorders. Individuals with *sexual dysfunction* find it difficult to function adequately while having sex; for example, they may not become aroused or achieve orgasm. And *paraphilia,* the relatively new term for sexual deviation, includes disorders in which sexual arousal occurs primarily in the context of inappropriate objects or individuals. *Philia* refers to a strong attraction or liking, and *para* indicates the attraction is abnormal. Paraphilic arousal patterns tend to be focused rather narrowly, often precluding mutually consenting adult partners, even if desired. Before describing these three types of disorders, we return to our initial question,

"What is normal sexual behavior?" to gain an important perspective.

Determining the prevalence of sexual practices accurately requires careful surveys that randomly sample the population. In a scientifically sound survey, Billy, Tanfer, Grady, and Klepinger (1993) reported data from 3,321 men in the United States age 20 to 39. The participants were interviewed, which is more reliable than having them fill out a questionnaire, and the responses were analyzed in detail. The purpose of this survey was to ascertain risk factors for sexually transmitted diseases, including AIDS. Some of the data are presented in ■ Figure 9.1. The most recent survey from the National Health and Nutrition Examination Survey sponsored by the Centers for Disease Control and Prevention (CDC) was reported in June 2007 (Fryar et al., 2007). More than 6,000 men and women participated in this study, which provides some updated data, although the areas of sexual behavior sampled were more limited.

Virtually all men studied by Billy and colleagues and in the CDC study were sexually experienced, with vaginal intercourse a nearly universal experience, even for those who had never been married. Three fourths of the men in the study by Billy and colleagues also engaged in oral sex, but only one fifth had ever engaged in anal sex, a particularly high-risk behavior for AIDS transmission, and half of these had not had anal sex in the previous year and a half. Slightly more troublesome is the finding that 23.3% had had sex with 20 or more partners, another high-risk behavior. Then again, more than 70% had had only one sexual partner during the previous year, and fewer than 10% had had four or more partners during the same period. The CDC study reports similar figures, with 29% of men having sex with 15 or more partners during their lifetime (compared to 9% of women).

A surprising finding from Billy and colleagues is that the overwhelming majority of the men had engaged exclu-

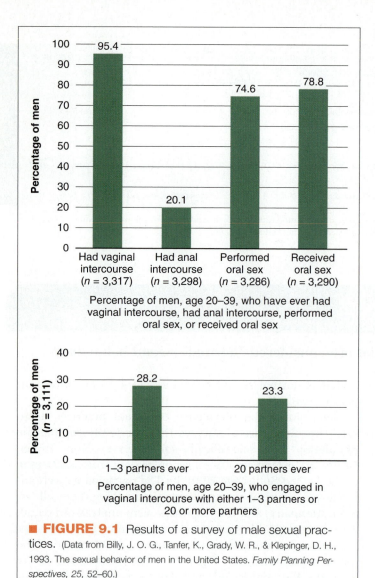

■ FIGURE 9.1 Results of a survey of male sexual practices. (Data from Billy, J. O. G., Tanfer, K., Grady, W. R., & Klepinger, D. H., 1993. The sexual behavior of men in the United States. *Family Planning Perspectives, 25,* 52–60.)

sively in **heterosexual behavior** (sex with the opposite sex). Only 2.3% had also engaged in **homosexual behavior** (sex with the same sex), and only 1.1% engaged exclusively in homosexual activity. But if same-sex attractions are included in addition to behavior, another sophisticated survey found that nearly 9% of women and 10% of men reported some homosexual attractions or behavior. For adolescents, 5% of male teenagers and 11% of female teenagers report some homosexual behavior (Diamond, Butterworth, & Savin-Williams, 2011; Mosher, Chandra, & Jones, 2005). But this is mostly in addition to heterosexual behavior, and most of these teenagers identify as heterosexual (Diamond et al., 2011).

One study from Britain (Johnson, Wadsworth, Wellings, Bradshaw, & Field, 1992) and one from France (Spira et al., 1992) surveyed sexual behavior and practices among more than 20,000 men and women in each country. The results were surprisingly similar to those reported for American men. More than 70% of the respondents from all age groups in the British and French studies reported no more than one sexual partner during the past year. Women

were somewhat more likely than men to have had fewer than two partners. Only 4.1% of French men and 3.6% of British men reported ever having had a male sexual partner, and this figure drops to 1.5% for British men if we consider only the last 5 years. Almost certainly, the percentage of males engaging exclusively in homosexual behavior would be considerably lower. The consistency of these data across three countries suggests strongly that the results represent something close to the norm, at least for Western countries. Also interesting is that sexual practices and the determinants of sexual satisfaction are now remarkably similar around the world, as recently demonstrated in a large survey of Chinese urban adults (Parish et al., 2007).

Another interesting set of data counters the many views we have of sexuality among older adults. Sexual behavior can continue well into old age, even past 80 for some people. Notably, 50% of men and 36% of women age 75 to 79 were sexually active. Reasons for the discrepancy between men and women are not clear, although given the earlier mortality of men, many older women lack a suitable partner; it is also possible that some women are married to men in an older age bracket. The sample of individuals older than age 80 is too small to allow meaningful conclusions, although many remained sexually active. Decreases in sexual activity are mostly correlated with decreases in general mobility and various disease processes and consequent medication, which may reduce arousal. Furthermore, the speed and intensity of various vasocongestive responses decrease with age.

Gender Differences

Although both men and women tend toward a monogamous (one partner) pattern of sexual relationships, gender differences in sexual behavior do exist, and some of them are dramatic. Most recently, Petersen and Hyde (2010) reported a sophisticated analysis summarizing results from hundreds of studies examining gender differences in sexual attitudes and behaviors. One common finding among sexual surveys is a much higher percentage of men than women report that they masturbate (self-stimulate to orgasm) (Oliver & Hyde, 1993; Peplau, 2003; Petersen & Hyde, 2010). When Leitenberg, Detzer, and Srebnik (1993) surveyed 280 university students, they also found this discrepancy (81% of men versus only 45% of women reported ever masturbating) even though for 25 years prior women had been encouraged to take more responsibility for their own sexual fulfillment and to engage in more sexual self-exploration.

Among those who did masturbate, the frequency was about 3 times greater for men than for women and had been throughout adolescence. Masturbation was not related to later sexual functioning—that is, whether individuals masturbated or not during adolescence had no influence on whether they had experienced intercourse, the frequency of intercourse, the number of partners, or other factors reflecting sexual adjustment.

▲ Sexual behavior often continues well into old age.

another popular term among college students for casual sex but in the context of an ongoing relationship (Bisson & Levine, 2009).

By contrast, results from a large number of studies suggest that *no* gender differences are currently apparent in attitudes about homosexuality (generally acceptable), the experience of sexual satisfaction (important for both), or attitudes toward masturbation (generally accepting). Small to moderate gender differences were evident in attitudes toward premarital intercourse when the couple was engaged or in a committed relationship (with men more approving than women) and in attitudes toward extramarital sex (sex outside of the marital relationship, which men also approved of more than women). As in the British and French studies, the number of sexual partners and the frequency of intercourse were slightly greater for men, and men were slightly younger at age of first sexual intercourse. Examining trends from 1943 to 1999, we find that almost all existing gender differences became smaller over time, especially in regard to attitudes toward premarital sex. Specifically, only 12% of young women approved of premarital sex in 1943 compared to 73% in 1999. The figures for men were 40% in 1943 and 79% in 1999 (Wells & Twenge, 2005). More recently, in the late 1990s and after 2000, investigators have noted a *decrease* in number of sexual partners and a tendency to delay sexual intercourse among adolescent boys, perhaps because of a fear of AIDS. Few changes over this time period were noted for adolescent girls (Petersen & Hyde, 2010).

Although they are decreasing, differences still exist between men and women in sexual behavior and attitudes toward sexuality (Peplau, 2003; Petersen & Hyde, 2010). For example, differences seem to exist in patterns of sexual arousal (Chivers, Rieger, Latty, & Bailey, 2004). Men are more specific and narrow in their patterns of arousal—that is, heterosexual men are aroused by female sexual stimuli but not male sexual stimuli. For gay men, it's the opposite. Men with gender identity disorder (discussed later) who had surgery to become female retained this specificity (attracted to males but not females). Females, however, whether heterosexual or lesbian, experience arousal to both male and female sexual stimuli, demonstrating a broader, more general pattern of arousal.

In an impressive series of studies, Barbara Andersen and her colleagues have assessed gender differences in basic or core beliefs about sexual aspects of one's self. These core beliefs about sexuality are referred to as "sexual self-schemas." Specifically, in a series of studies (Andersen & Cyranowski, 1994; Andersen, Cyranowski, & Espindle, 1999; Cyranowski, Aarestad, & Andersen, 1999), Andersen

Why women masturbate less frequently than men puzzles sex researchers, particularly when other long-standing gender differences in sexual behavior, such as the probability of engaging in premarital intercourse, have virtually disappeared (Clement, 1990; Petersen & Hyde, 2010). One traditional view accounting for differences in masturbatory behavior is that women have been taught to associate sex with romance and emotional intimacy, whereas men are more interested in physical gratification. But the discrepancy continues despite decreases in gender-specific attitudes toward sexuality. A more likely reason is anatomical. Because of the nature of the erectile response in men and their relative ease in providing sufficient stimulation to reach orgasm, masturbation may simply be more convenient for men than for women. This may explain why gender differences in masturbation are also evident in primates and other animals (Ford & Beach, 1951). In any case, incidence of masturbation continues to be the largest gender difference in sexuality.

Another continuing gender difference is reflected in the incidence of casual sex, attitudes toward casual premarital sex, and pornography use, with men expressing more permissive attitudes and behaviors than women. The most current term for casual sex, particularly among college students, is "hooking up," which refers specifically to a range of physically intimate behavior outside of a committed relationship (Owen, Rhoades, Stanley, & Fincham, 2010). Studies of "hooking up" demonstrate similar findings to older studies of casual sex, in that it is often precipitated by alcohol and women are less likely to consider it a positive experience than men. "Friends with benefits" is

heterosexual behavior Sexual activity with members of the opposite gender.
homosexual behavior Sexual activity with members of the same gender.

and colleagues demonstrated that women tend to report the experience of passionate and romantic feelings as an integral part of their sexuality and an openness to sexual experience. However, a substantial number of women also hold an embarrassed, conservative, or self-conscious schema that sometimes conflicts with more positive aspects of their sexual attitudes. Men, however, show a strong component of feeling powerful, independent, and aggressive as part of their sexuality, in addition to being passionate, loving, and open to experience. Also, men do not generally possess negative core beliefs reflecting self-consciousness, embarrassment, or feeling behaviorally inhibited.

Peplau (2003) summarizes research to date on gender differences in human sexuality as highlighting four themes: (1) men show more sexual desire and arousal than women; (2) women emphasize committed relationships as a context for sex more than men; (3) men's sexual self-concept, unlike women's, is characterized partly by power, independence, and aggression; and (4) women's sexual beliefs are more "plastic" in that they are more easily shaped by cultural, social, and situational factors. For example, women are more likely to change sexual orientation over time (Diamond, 2007; Diamond et al., 2011) or may be more variable in frequency of sex, alternating periods of high frequency with low frequency if a sexual partner leaves.

What happened to the sexual revolution? Where are the effects of the "anything goes" attitude toward sexual expression and fulfillment that supposedly began in the 1960s and 1970s? Clearly there has been some change. The double standard has disappeared, in that most women no longer feel constrained by a stricter and more conservative social standard of sexual conduct. The sexes are definitely drawing together in their attitudes and behavior, although some differences in attitudes, core beliefs, and behavior remain. Regardless, the overwhelming majority of individuals engage in heterosexual, vaginal intercourse in the context of a relationship with one partner. Based on these data, the sexual revolution may be largely a creation of the media, focusing as it does on extreme or sensational cases. In fact, what appeals to us sexually seems to have strong evolutionary roots that foster propagation of the species. For example, men with "attractive" (to women) faces have higher sperm quality. Women with "attractive" (to men) bodies are more fertile; and both men and women with "attractive" voices lose their virginity sooner (Gallup & Frederick, 2010). Thus sexual attraction (and behavior) is closely tied to evolutionary mandates reflecting the importance of this behavior for the species.

Cultural Differences

What is normal in Western countries may not necessarily be normal in other parts of the world (McGoldrick, Loonan, & Wohlsifer, 2007). The Sambia in Papua New Guinea believe semen is an essential substance for growth and development in young boys of the tribe. They also believe semen is *not* produced naturally—that is, the body is incapable of

producing it spontaneously. Therefore, all young boys in the tribe, beginning at approximately age 7, become semen recipients by engaging exclusively in homosexual oral sex with teenage boys. Only oral sexual practices are permitted; masturbation is forbidden and absent. Early in adolescence, the boys switch roles and become semen providers to younger boys. Heterosexual relations and even contact with the opposite sex are prohibited until the boys become teenagers. Late in adolescence, the boys are expected to marry and begin exclusive heterosexual activity. And they do, with no exceptions (Herdt, 1987; Herdt & Stoller, 1989). By contrast, the Munda of northeast India require adolescents and children to live together. But in this group, both male and female children live in the same setting, and the sexual activity, consisting mostly of petting and mutual masturbation, is all heterosexual (Bancroft, 1989).

In about half of more than 100 societies surveyed worldwide, premarital sexual behavior is culturally accepted and encouraged; in the remaining half, premarital sex is unacceptable and discouraged (Bancroft, 1989; Broude & Greene, 1980). Thus, what is normal sexual behavior in one culture is not necessarily normal in another, and the range of sexual expression must be considered in diagnosing the presence of a disorder.

The Development of Sexual Orientation

Reports suggest that homosexuality runs in families (Bailey & Benishay, 1993), and concordance for homosexuality is more common among identical twins than among fraternal twins or natural siblings. In two well-done twin studies, homosexual orientation was shared in approximately 50% of identical twins, compared with 16% to 22% of fraternal twins. Approximately the same or a slightly lower percentage of nontwin brothers or sisters were gay (Bailey & Pillard, 1991; Bailey, Pillard, Neale, & Agyei, 1993; Whitnam, Diamond, & Martin, 1993). Sophisticated studies on the causes of homosexual behavior reveal that in men, genetic effects explain from 34% to 39% of the cause, and in women 18% to 19%, with the remainder accounted for by environmental influences (Långström, Rahman, Carlström, & Lichtenstein, 2010). Remember from Chapter 2 that environmental influences might include unique biological experiences—for example, differential hormone exposure in utero (before birth). Other reports indicate that homosexuality and also gender atypical behavior during childhood is associated with differential exposure to hormones, particularly atypical androgen levels in utero (Auyeng et al., 2009; Ehrhardt et al., 1985; Gladue, Green, & Hellman, 1984; Hershberger & Segal, 2004) and that the actual structure of the brain might be different in individuals with homosexual as compared to heterosexual arousal patterns (Allen & Gorski, 1992; Byne et al., 2000; LeVay, 1991).

Several findings lend some support to the theory of differential hormone exposure in utero. One is the observation that individuals with homosexual orientations have a 39% greater chance of being non–right handed (left handed or mixed handed) than those with heterosexual orientations (Lalumière, Blanchard, & Zucker, 2000), although these findings were not replicated in a later study (Mustanski, Bailey, & Kaspar, 2002). There is also the finding that gay/bisexual men are significantly shorter and lighter than heterosexual men, though no differences were found for women (Bogart, 2010). Another is the intriguing findings that heterosexual males and masculine ("butch") lesbians tend to have a longer fourth ("ring") finger than index finger but that heterosexual females and gay males show less of a difference or even have a longer second finger than fourth finger (Brown, Finn, Cooke, & Breedlove, 2002; Hall & Love, 2003), although this finding seems to be influenced by ethnic group membership (Loehlin, McFadden, Medland, & Martin, 2006; McFadden et al., 2005). Yet another report had suggested a possible gene (or genes) for homosexuality on the X chromosome (Hamer, Hu, Magnuson, Hu, & Pattatucci, 1993).

The principal conclusion drawn in the media is that sexual orientation has a biological cause. Gay rights activists are decidedly split on the significance of these findings. Some are pleased with the biological interpretation because people can no longer assume gays have made a morally depraved choice of supposedly deviant arousal patterns. Others, however, note how quickly the public has pounced on the implication that something is biologically wrong with individuals with homosexual arousal patterns, assuming that someday the abnormality will be detected in the fetus and prevented, perhaps through genetic engineering.

Do such arguments over biological causes sound familiar? Think back to studies described in Chapter 2 that attempted to link complex behavior to particular genes. In almost every case, these studies could not be replicated and investigators fell back on a model in which genetic contributions to behavioral traits and psychological disorders come from many genes, each making a relatively small contribution to a *vulnerability*. This generalized biological vulnerability then interacts in a complex way with various environmental conditions, personality traits, and other contributors to determine behavioral patterns. We also discussed reciprocal gene–environment interactions

in which certain learning experiences and environmental events may affect brain structure and function and genetic expression.

The same thing is now happening with sexual orientation. For example, neither Bailey and colleagues (1999) nor Rice, Anderson, Risch, and Ebers (1999) in later studies could replicate the report suggesting a specific gene for homosexuality (Hamer et al., 1993). Most theoretical models outlining these complex interactions for sexual orientation imply that there may be many pathways to the development of heterosexuality or homosexuality and that no one factor— biological or psychological—can predict the outcome (Bancroft, 1994; Byne & Parsons, 1993). It is likely, too, that different types of homosexuality (and, perhaps, heterosexuality), with different patterns of cause, may be discovered (Diamond et al., 2011; Savin-Williams, 2006).

One of the more intriguing findings from the twin studies of Bailey and his colleagues is that approximately 50% of the identical twins with exactly the same genetic structure and the same environment (growing up in the same house) *did not* have the same sexual orientation (Bailey & Pillard, 1991). Also intriguing is the finding in a study of 302 gay males that those growing up with older brothers are more likely to be gay, whereas having older sisters, or younger brothers or sisters, is not correlated with later sexual orientation. This study found that each additional older brother increased the odds of being gay by one third. This finding, which has been replicated several times and is referred to as the "fraternal birth order hypothesis," may suggest the importance of environmental influences, although the mechanism has not been identified (Blanchard, 2008; Blanchard & Bogaert, 1996, 1998; Cantor, Blanchard, Paterson, & Bogaert, 2002).

In any case, the simple one-dimensional claims that homosexuality is caused by a gene or that heterosexuality is caused by healthy early developmental experiences will continue to appeal to the general population. Neither explanation is likely to be proved correct. Almost certainly, biology sets certain limits within which social and psychological factors affect development (Diamond, 1995; Diamond et al., 2011; Långström et al., 2010).

Gender Identity Disorder

> **What are the defining clinical features, causes, and treatments of gender identity disorder?**

What is it that makes you think you are a man? Or a woman? Clearly, it's more than your sexual arousal patterns or your anatomy. It's also more than the reactions and experiences of your family and society. The essence of your masculinity or femininity is a deep-seated personal sense called gender identity. **Gender identity disorder** is present if a person's physical gender is not consistent with the person's sense of identity. People with this disorder feel

trapped in a body of the wrong sex. Consider the case of Joe.

gender identity disorder A psychological dissatisfaction with biological gender, or a disturbance in the sense of identity as a male or female. The primary goal is not sexual arousal but rather to live the life of the opposite gender.

Joe | Trapped in the Wrong Body

Joe was a 17-year-old male and the last of five children. Although his mother had wanted a girl, he became her favorite child. His father worked long hours and had little contact with the boy. For as long as Joe could remember, he had thought of himself as a girl. He began dressing in girls' clothes of his own accord before he was 5 years old and continued cross-dressing into junior high school. He developed interests in cooking, knitting, crocheting, and embroidering, skills he acquired by reading an encyclopedia.

Joe associated mostly with girls during this period, although he remembered being strongly attached to a boy in the first grade. In his sexual fantasies, which developed around 12 years of age, he pictured himself as a female having intercourse with a male. His extremely effeminate behavior made him the object of scorn and ridicule when he entered high school at age 15. Usually passive and unassertive, he ran away from home and attempted suicide. Unable to continue in high school, he attended secretarial school, where he was the only boy in his class. During his first interview with a therapist, he reported, "I am a woman trapped in a man's body and I would like to have surgery to become a woman."

Defining Gender Identity Disorder

Gender identity disorder (or *transsexualism,* as it used to be called) must be distinguished from transvestic fetishism, a paraphilic disorder (discussed later) in which individuals, usually males, are sexually aroused by wearing articles of clothing associated with the opposite sex. There is an occasional preference on the part of the male with transvestite patterns of sexual arousal for the female role, but the primary purpose of cross-dressing is sexual gratification. In the case of gender identity disorder, the primary goal is not sexual gratification but rather the desire to live life openly in a manner consistent with that of the other gender.

Gender identity disorder must also be distinguished from *intersex individuals (hermaphrodites),* who are born with ambiguous genitalia associated with documented hormonal or other physical abnormalities. Depending on their particular mix of characteristics, hermaphrodites are usually "assigned" to a specific sex at birth, sometimes undergoing surgery and hormonal treatments, to alter their sexual anatomy. Individuals with gender identity disorder, by contrast, have no demonstrated physical abnormalities. Finally, gender identity disorder must be distinguished from the same-sex arousal patterns of a male who sometimes behaves effeminately or a woman with same-sex arousal patterns and masculine mannerisms. Such an individual does not feel like a woman trapped in a man's body or have any desire to be a woman, or vice versa. Note also,

as the *DSM-IV-TR* criteria do, that gender identity is independent of sexual arousal patterns (Savin-Williams, 2006). For example, a male-to-female transsexual (a biological male with a feminine gender identity) may be sexually attracted to females. Similarly, Eli Coleman and his associates (Coleman, Bockting, & Gooren, 1993) reported on nine female-to-male cases in which the individuals were sexually attracted to men. Thus, heterosexual women before surgery were gay men after surgery. Chivers and Bailey (2000) compared a group of female-to-male individuals who were attracted to men (a rare occurrence) to a group of female-to-male individuals who were attracted to women (the usual pattern) both before and after surgery. They found the groups did not differ in the strength of their gender identity (as males), although the latter group was more sexually assertive and, understandably, more interested in surgery to create an artificial penis.

Gender identity disorder is relatively rare. The estimated incidence based on studies in Sweden, Australia, and the Netherlands is 1 in 37,000 in Sweden, 1 in 24,000 in Australia, and 1 in 11,000 in the Netherlands for biological males, compared to 1 in 103,000 in Sweden, 1 in 150,000 in Australia, and 1 in 30,000 in the Netherlands for biological females (Baker, van Kesteren, Gooren, & Bezemer, 1993; Ross, Walinder, Lundstrom, & Thuwe, 1981; Sohn & Bosinski, 2007). These numbers reflect the fact that gender identity disorder occurs approximately 3 times more frequently in males than in females (American Psychological Association Task Force on Gender Identity and Gender Variance, 2008). Many countries now require a series of legal steps to change gender identity. In Germany, between 2.1 and 2.4 per 100,000 in the population took at least the first legal step of changing their first names in the 1990s; in that country, the male:female ratio of people with gender identity disorder is 2.3:1 (Weitze & Osburg, 1996). In some cultures, individuals with mistaken gender identity are often accorded the status of "shaman" or "seer" and treated as wisdom figures. A shaman is almost always a male adopting a female role (see, for example, Coleman, Colgan, & Gooren, 1992). Stoller (1976) reported on two contemporary feminized Native American men who were not only accepted, but also esteemed by their tribes for their expertise in healing rituals. Contrary to the respect accorded these individuals in some cultures, social tolerance for them is relatively low in Western cultures, where they are the objects of curiosity at best and derision at worst.

Causes

Research has yet to uncover any specific biological contributions to gender identity disorder, although it seems likely that a biological predisposition will be discovered. Coolidge, Thede, and Young (2002) estimated that genetics contributed about 62% to creating a vulnerability to experience gender identity disorder in their twin sample. Thirty-eight percent of the vulnerability came from nonshared (unique) environmental events. A recent study from the

Lesbian, gay, bisexual, and transgender (LGBT) issues have come to the forefront of discussion in the United States in response to recent events including suicides in response to school bullying and debate over gay marriage rights. Although the "L," "G," and "B" are more often included, the "T" is sometimes left out of the conversation, perhaps because of a lack of understanding or confusion over this group. Transgender is an umbrella term for someone with unconventional gender expression (i.e., not identifying with their physical sex at birth). Such individuals are recognized differently across cultures.

In Western culture it is believed that people are firmly male or female. Therefore, transgendered individuals are considered to have gender identity disorder and are required to fully assert their identity with their non-birth gender before being approved for sex reassignment surgery. Interestingly, in many cultures around the world, gender is not fixed as only male or female, but a mix or alternative gender expression is accepted. Take for instance "hijras" in India or "kathoey" or "ladyboys" in Thailand. In both of these groups, the biological male dresses in women's clothing and identifies with femininity; such individuals are accepted by their society as a third gender. For instance, the hijras, who are considered "neither man, nor woman" (Nanda, 1999), may have actually had castration surgery, receive religious and cultural legitimacy through Hindu mythology (e.g., travestism existed before the conception of mankind), and are believed by some to have divine power (Bakshi, 2004). In fact, hijras serve a special function within their culture, performing at weddings and birth rituals, and their behavior is considered to be natural. Similarly kathoey, biological males with what the Thai refer to as a "female heart," are recognized as a third gender. In some places, these individuals even have been given their own restroom with a symbol on the door of a human divided in half with a blue side wearing pants and a red side dressed in a skirt (Beech, 2008). Whereas those within Western cultures believe that people are fully male or female and places such as India and Thailand accept hijras and kathoeys as a third sex, other cultures completely fail to accept transgendered individuals. For example, in Iran being transsexual can result in death, as was the case with a 24-year-old transsexual woman (born a male and underwent sex reassignment surgery) who was found strangled to death by her own brothers. The brothers confessed to killing their sister due to "opposing her immorality." This form of murder, known as an "honor killing" is performed in defense of family "dishonor." Iranian laws currently concede to this behavior, and the brothers in this case will serve only 1 to 3 years in jail for murder (Littauer, 2010).

Although the understanding and treatment of transgendered individuals varies across cultures, LGBT individuals receive international support through recognition events such as "National Coming Out Day" (NCOD; Human Rights Campaign). NCOD, October 11th, is a civil awareness day for discussion and pride in "coming out" for gays, lesbians, bisexuals, and transgendered individuals in the United States, Australia, Canada, Croatia, Germany, New Zealand, and the United Kingdom (celebrated on Oct. 12 in the United Kingdom).

Netherlands twin registry suggested that 70% of the vulnerability for cross-gender behavior (behaving in a manner consistent with the opposite biological sex) was genetic as opposed to environmental, but this behavior is not the same as gender identity, which was not measured (as explained later) (van Beijsterveldt, Hudziak, & Boomsma, 2006). Gomez-Gil et al. (2010) found a somewhat higher prevalence of gender identity disorder than would be expected by chance in nontwin siblings of a larger group (995) of individuals with gender identity disorder. Segal (2006), however, found two monozygotic (identical) female twin pairs in which one twin had gender identity disorder and the other did not; no unusual medical or life history factors were identified to account for this difference. Nevertheless, genetic contributions are clearly part of the picture.

Early research suggested that, as with sexual orientation, slightly higher levels of testosterone or estrogen at certain critical periods of development might masculinize a female fetus or feminize a male fetus (see, for example, Gladue et al., 1984; Keefe, 2002). Variations in hormonal levels could occur naturally or because of medication that a pregnant mother is taking. Scientists have studied girls

age 5 to 12 with an intersex condition known as congenital adrenal hyperplasia (CAH). In CAH the brains of these chromosomal females are flooded with male hormones (androgens), which, among other results, produce mostly

DSM Disorder Criteria Summary
Gender Identity Disorder

A. A strong and persistent cross-gender identification (not merely a desire for any perceived cultural advantages of being the other sex).

B. Persistent discomfort with his or her sex or sense of inappropriateness in the gender role of that sex.

C. The disturbance is not concurrent with a physical intersex condition.

D. The disturbance causes clinically significant distress or impairment in social, occupational, or other important areas of functioning.

Source: Reprinted with permission from *Diagnostic and Statistical Manual of Mental Disorders* (4th ed., text revision). © 2000 American Psychiatric Association.

masculine external genitalia, although internal organs (ovaries and so on) remain female. Meyer-Bahlburg and colleagues (2004) studied 15 girls with CAH who had been correctly identified as female at birth and raised as girls and looked at their development. Compared to groups of girls and boys without CAH, the CAH girls were masculine in their behavior, but there were no differences in gender identity. Thus, scientists have yet to establish a link between prenatal hormonal influence and later gender identity, although it is still possible that one exists. At least some evidence suggests that gender identity firms up between 18 months and 3 years of age (Ehrhardt & Meyer-Bahlburg, 1981; Money & Ehrhardt, 1972) and is relatively fixed after that. But newer studies suggest that possible preexisting biological factors have already had their impact. One interesting case illustrating this phenomenon was originally reported by Green and Money (1969), who described the sequence of events that occurred in the case of Bruce/Brenda. There do seem to be other case studies of children whose gender was reassigned at birth who adapted successfully (see, for example, Gearhart, 1989), but it certainly seems that biology expressed itself in Bruce's case.

Bruce/Brenda | Gender vs. Biology

A set of male identical twins was born into a well-adjusted family. Several months later, an unfortunate accident occurred. Although circumcision went routinely for one of the boys, the physician's hand slipped so that the electric current in the device burned off the penis of the second baby. After working through their hostility toward the physician, the parents consulted specialists in children with intersexual problems and were faced with a choice. The specialists pointed out that the easiest solution would be to reassign their son Bruce as a girl, and the parents agreed. At the age of several months, Bruce became "Brenda." The parents purchased a new wardrobe and treated the child in every way possible as a girl. These twins were followed through childhood and, upon reaching puberty, the young girl was given hormonal replacement therapy. After 6 years, the doctors lost track of the case but assumed the child had adjusted well. However, Brenda endured almost intolerable inner turmoil. We know this because two clinical scientists found this individual and reported a long-term follow-up (Diamond & Sigmundson, 1997). Brenda never adjusted to her assigned gender. As a child, she preferred rough-and-tumble play and resisted wearing girls' clothes. In public bathrooms, she often insisted on urinating while standing up, which usually made a mess. By early adolescence, Brenda was pretty sure she was a boy, but her doctors pressed her to act more feminine. When she was 14 she confronted her parents, telling them she was so miserable she was considering suicide. At that point

they told her the true story and the muddy waters of her mind began to clear. Shortly thereafter, Brenda had additional surgery changing her back to Bruce, who married and became the father of three adopted children. But the turmoil of his early life never fully resolved. Perhaps because of this, perhaps because his twin brother had recently died and he had lost his job and was divorcing, or perhaps because of a combination of these factors, David Reimer (his real name) committed suicide at age 38 in 2004.

Fred Greenslade/©Reuters/Corbis

▲ After gender reassignment as a baby and subsequently being raised as a girl, David Reimer reclaimed his male gender identity in his teens and lived his life as a man. He spoke out against infant gender reassignment until his death in 2004.

Richard Green, a pioneering researcher in this area, has studied boys who behave in feminine ways and girls who behave in masculine ways, investigating what makes them that way and following what happens to them (Green, 1987). This set of behaviors and attitudes is referred to as **gender nonconformity** (see, for example, Skidmore, Linsenmeier, & Bailey, 2006). Green discovered that when most young boys spontaneously display "feminine" interests and behaviors, they are typically discouraged by most families and these behaviors usually cease. However, boys who consistently display these behaviors are not discouraged and are sometimes encouraged.

Other factors, such as excessive attention and physical contact on the part of the mother, may also play some role, as may a lack of male playmates during the early years of socialization. These are just some factors identified by Green as characteristic of gender-nonconforming boys. Remember that as-yet-undiscovered biological factors may also contribute to the spontaneous display of cross-gender behaviors and interests. For example, one recent study found that exposure to higher levels of fetal testosterone was associated with more masculine play behavior in both boys and girls during childhood (Auyeng et al., 2009). However, in following up these boys, Green discovered that few seem to develop the "wrong" gender identity. The most likely outcome is the development of homosexual preferences, but even this particular sexual arousal pattern seems to occur exclusively in only approximately 40% of the gender-nonconforming boys. Another 32% show some degree of *bisexuality*, sexual attraction to both their own and the opposite sex. Looking at it from the other side, 60% were functioning heterosexually.

These results were replicated in subsequent prospective studies of boys (Zucker, 2005). Girls with gender-nonconforming behavior are seldom studied because their behavior attracts much less attention in Western societies. But one recent study followed 25 girls prospectively, beginning at approximately 9 years of age, whose behavior was extreme enough that they were referred to a gender identity clinic. Most of these girls met criteria for childhood gender identity disorder or came very close to it. At a follow-up when these girls (now women) averaged 25 years of age, only three met criteria for gender identity disorder. Another six reported bisexual/homosexual behavior; eight more would have homosexual fantasies but not behavior. The remaining eight women were heterosexual (Drummond, Bradley, Peterson-Badali, & Zucker, 2008).

This finding of only a very loose relationship between gender-nonconforming behavior and later sexual development is not unique to American culture. For example, similar relationships between early gender-nonconforming behavior and later development exist among the Fa'afafine, a group of males with homosexual orientation in the Pacific Islands country of Samoa (Bartlett & Vasey, 2006). And even in strict Muslim societies where any hint of gender-nonconforming behavior is severely discouraged, gender-nonconforming behavior, gender identity disorder, or both may develop (Dogăn & Dogăn, 2006). We can safely say that the causes of mistaken gender identity are still something of a mystery.

Treatment

Treatment is available for gender identity disorder in a few specialty clinics around the world, although much controversy surrounds treatment (Carroll, 2007). At present, the most common decision is to alter the anatomy physically to be consistent with the identity through **sex reassignment surgery**. Recently, psychosocial treatments to directly alter gender identity to match physical anatomy itself have been attempted in a few cases.

Sex Reassignment Surgery

To qualify for surgery at a reputable clinic, individuals must live in the opposite-sex role for 1 to 2 years so that they can be sure they want to change sex. They also must be stable psychologically, financially, and socially. In male-to-female candidates, hormones are administered to promote *gynecomastia* (the growth of breasts) and the development of other secondary sex characteristics. Facial hair is typically removed through electrolysis. If the individual is satisfied with the events of the trial period, the genitals are removed and a vagina is constructed.

For female-to-male transsexuals, an artificial penis is typically constructed through plastic surgery, using sections of skin and muscle from elsewhere in the body, such as the thigh. Breasts are surgically removed. Genital surgery is more difficult and complex in biological females. Estimates of transsexuals' satisfaction with surgery indicate predominantly successful adjustment (approximately 75% improved) among those who could be reached for follow-ups, with people who undergo female-to-male conversions generally adjusting better than those who make male-to-female transitions (Bancroft, 1989; Blanchard & Steiner, 1992; Bodlund & Kullgren, 1996; Carroll, 2007; Green & Fleming, 1990; Kuiper & Cohen-Kettenis, 1988). Approximately 7% of individuals who have sex reassignment surgery later regret having the surgery (Bancroft, 1989; Lundstrom, Pauly, & Walinder, 1984). This is unfortunate because the surgery is irreversible. Also, as many as 2% attempt suicide after surgery, a rate much higher than the rate for the general population. Nevertheless, surgery has made life worth living for some people who suffered the effects of existing in what they felt to be the wrong body.

Treatment of Intersexuality

As we noted, surgery and hormonal replacement therapy has been standard treatment for many intersex individuals (hermaphrodites) who may be born with physical characteristics of both sexes. This group of individuals has been the subject of more careful evaluation, resulting in some new ideas and new approaches to treatment (Fausto-Sterling, 2000a, 2000b). Specifically, Anne Fausto-Sterling had suggested previously that there are actually five sexes: males; females; "herms," who are named after true hermaphrodites, or people born with both testes and ovaries; "merms," who are anatomically more male than female but possess some aspect of female genitalia; and "ferms," who have ovaries but possess some aspect of male genitalia. She estimates, based on the best evidence available, that for every 1,000 children born, 17, or 1.7%, may be intersexual in some form. What Fausto-Sterling (2000b) and others have noted is that individuals in this group are often dissatisfied with surgery, much as Bruce was in the case we described.

gender nonconformity Individuals expressing behavior and attitudes consistently characteristic of the opposite sex.

sex reassignment surgery A surgical procedure to alter a person's physical anatomy to conform to that person's psychological gender identity.

▲ Chaz Bono, the son of Cher and Sonny Bono, is a female-to-male transgender writer, musician, actor, and activist, who first came out as a homosexual female (left) and later chose sex reassignment surgery (right).

▶ Physician Renee Richards played competitive tennis when she was a man, Richard Raskin, and after sex reassignment surgery.

Fausto-Sterling suggests that an increasing number of pediatric endocrinologists, urologists, and psychologists are examining the wisdom of early genital surgery that results in an irreversible gender assignment. Instead, health professionals may want to examine closely the precise nature of the intersex condition and consider surgery only as a last resort and only when they are sure the particular condition will lead to a specific psychological gender identity. Otherwise, psychological treatments to help individuals adapt to their particular sexual anatomy, or their emerging gender identity, might be more appropriate.

Concept Check 9.1

Answer the following questions about normal sexuality and gender identity disorder.

1. Name some gender differences that exist in sexual attitudes and sexual behavior. _____

2. Which sexual preference or preferences are normal, and how are they developed? _____

3. Charlie always felt out of place with the boys. At a young age he preferred to play with girls and insisted that his parents call him "Charlene." He later claimed that he felt like a woman trapped in a man's body. What disorder could Charlie have? _____

4. What could be the cause(s) of Charlie's disorder? _____

5. What treatments could be given to Charlie? _____

An Overview of Sexual Dysfunctions

> How do psychologists define sexual dysfunction?
> How is sexual dysfunction related to the sexual response cycle?

Before we describe **sexual dysfunction**, it's important to note that the problems that arise in the context of sexual interactions may occur in both heterosexual and homosexual relationships. Inability to become aroused or reach orgasm seems to be as common in homosexual as in heterosexual relationships, but we discuss them in the context of heterosexual relationships, which are the majority of cases we see in our clinic. The three stages of the sexual response cycle—desire, arousal, and orgasm (■ Figure 9.2)—are each associated with specific sexual dysfunctions. In addition, pain can become associated with sexual functioning, which leads to additional dysfunctions.

An overview of the *DSM-IV-TR* categories of the sexual dysfunctions we examine is in Table 9.1. As you can see,

both males and females can experience parallel versions of most disorders, which take on specific forms determined by anatomy and other gender-specific characteristics. However, two disorders are sex specific: Premature ejaculation occurs only in males, and vaginismus—painful contractions or spasms of the vagina during attempted penetration—appears only in females. Sexual dysfunctions can be either lifelong or acquired. *Lifelong* refers to a chronic condition that is present during a person's entire sexual life; *acquired* refers to a disorder that begins after sexual activity has been relatively normal. In addition, disorders can either be *generalized*, occurring every time the individual attempts sex, or they can be *situational*, occurring with some partners or at certain times but not with

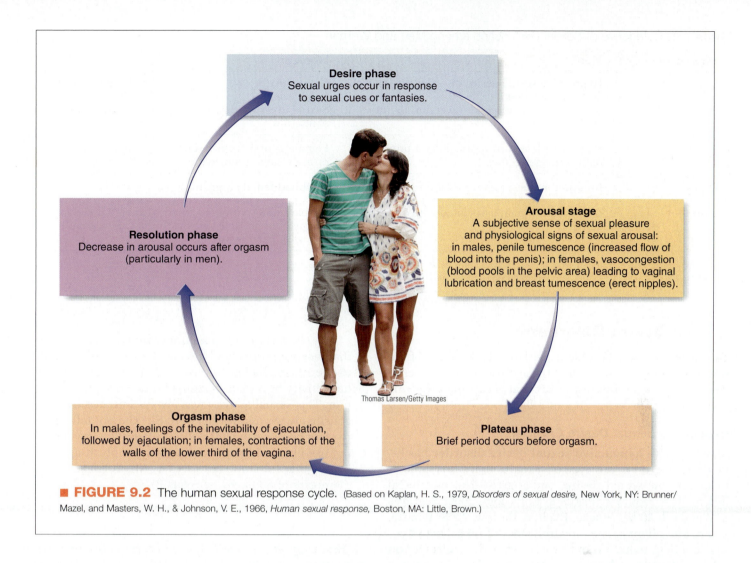

Desire phase
Sexual urges occur in response to sexual cues or fantasies.

Arousal stage
A subjective sense of sexual pleasure and physiological signs of sexual arousal: in males, penile tumescence (increased flow of blood into the penis); in females, vasocongestion (blood pools in the pelvic area) leading to vaginal lubrication and breast tumescence (erect nipples).

Resolution phase
Decrease in arousal occurs after orgasm (particularly in men).

Plateau phase
Brief period occurs before orgasm.

Orgasm phase
In males, feelings of the inevitability of ejaculation, followed by ejaculation; in females, contractions of the walls of the lower third of the vagina.

Thomas Larsen/Getty Images

■ **FIGURE 9.2** The human sexual response cycle. (Based on Kaplan, H. S., 1979, *Disorders of sexual desire,* New York, NY: Brunner/ Mazel, and Masters, W. H., & Johnson, V. E., 1966, *Human sexual response,* Boston, MA: Little, Brown.)

other partners or at other times. Finally, sexual dysfunctions are further specified as (1) resulting from psychological factors or (2) resulting from psychological factors combined with a general medical condition. The latter specification occurs when there is a demonstrable vascular, hormonal, or associated physical condition known to contribute to the sexual dysfunction.

Before we describe the prevalence of specific sexual dysfunctions, we need to note a classic study by Ellen Frank and her colleagues (1978), who carefully interviewed 100 well-educated, happily married couples who were not seeking treatment. More than 80% of these couples reported that their marital and sexual relations were happy and satisfying. Surprisingly, 40% of the men reported occasional erectile and ejaculatory difficulties and 63% of the women reported occasional dysfunctions of arousal or orgasm. But the crucial finding was that these dysfunctions did not detract from the respondents' overall sexual satisfaction. In another study, only 45% of women experiencing difficulties with orgasm reported the issue as problematic (Fugl-Meyer & Sjogren Fugl-Meyer, 1999).

Bancroft, Loftus, and Long (2003) extended this analysis in a survey of close to 1,000 women in the United States involved in a heterosexual relationship for at least 6 months.

The interesting results indicate that, although 44.3% met objective criteria for one of the disorders in Table 9.1, only 24.4% of these individuals were distressed about it. Many of these women just did not consider the issue to be a problem. Indeed, the best predictor of sexual distress among these women were deficits in general emotional well-being or emotional relationships with the partner during sexual relations, not lack of lubrication or orgasm. These studies indicate that sexual satisfaction and occasional sexual dysfunction are not mutually exclusive categories (Bradford & Meston, 2011; Graham, 2010). In the context of a healthy relationship, occasional or partial sexual dysfunctions are easily accommodated. But this does raise problems for diagnosing sexual dysfunctions. Should a sexual problem be identified as a diagnosis when dysfunction is clearly present but the person is not distressed about it? This is one debate that has occurred during discussions about possible revisions for *DSM-5* (Balon, Segraves, & Clayton, 2007; Zucker, 2010).

sexual dysfunction A sexual disorder in which the client finds it difficult to function adequately while having sex.

Table 9.1 Categories of Sexual Dysfunction among Men and Women

Type of Disorder	Men	Women
Desire	Hypoactive sexual desire disorder (little or no desire to have sex) Sexual aversion disorder (aversion to and avoidance of sex)	Hypoactive sexual desire disorder (little or no desire to have sex) Sexual aversion disorder (aversion to and avoidance of sex)
Arousal	Male erectile disorder (difficulty attaining or maintaining erections)	Female sexual arousal disorder (difficulty attaining or maintaining lubrication or swelling response)
Orgasm	Inhibited male orgasm; premature ejaculation	Inhibited female orgasm
Pain	Dyspareunia (pain associated with sexual activity)	Dyspareunia (pain associated with sexual activity); vaginismus (muscle spasms in the vagina that interfere with penetration)

Source: Reprinted, with permission, from Wincze, J. P., & Carey, M. P. (2001). *Sexual dysfunction: A guide for assessment and treatment.* New York, NY: Guilford Press, © 1991 Guilford Press.

Sexual Desire Disorders

Two disorders reflect problems with the desire phase of the sexual response cycle. Each of these disorders is characterized by little or no interest in sex that is causing problems in a relationship.

Hypoactive Sexual Desire Disorder

A person with **hypoactive sexual desire disorder** has little or no interest in any type of sexual activity. It is difficult to assess low sexual desire, and a great deal of clinical judgment is required (Pridal & LoPiccolo, 2000; Segraves & Woodard, 2006; Wincze, Bach, & Barlow, 2008; Wincze, 2009). You might gauge it by frequency of sexual activity— say, less than twice a month for a married couple. Or you might determine whether someone ever thinks about sex or has sexual fantasies. Then there is the person who has sex twice a week but really doesn't want to and thinks about it only because his wife is on his case to live up to his end of the marriage and have sex more often. This individual might have no desire, despite having frequent sex. Consider the case of Mr. and Mrs. C.

Mr. and Mrs. C. | Getting Started

Mrs. C., a 31-year-old successful businesswoman, was married to a 32-year-old lawyer. They had two children, ages 2 and 5, and had been married 8 years when they entered therapy. The presenting problem was Mrs. C.'s lack of sexual desire. Mr. and Mrs. C. were interviewed separately during the initial assessment, and both professed attraction to and love for their partner. Mrs. C. reported that she could enjoy sex once she got involved and almost always was orgasmic. The problem was her lack of desire to get involved. She avoided her husband's sexual advances and looked on his affection and romanticism with great skepticism and, usually, anger and tears.

Mrs. C. was raised in an upper-middle-class family that was supportive and loving. However, from age 6 to age 12, she had been repeatedly pressured into sexual activity by a male cousin who was 5 years her senior. This sexual activity was always initiated by the cousin, always against her will. She did not tell her parents because she felt guilty because the boy did not use physical force to make her comply. It appeared that romantic advances by Mr. C. triggered memories of abuse by her cousin.

Best estimates suggest that more than 50% of patients who come to sexuality clinics for help complain of hypoactive sexual desire (Kaplan, 1979; Pridal & LoPiccolo, 2000). In many clinics, it is the most common presenting complaint of women; men present more often with erectile dysfunction (Hawton, 1995). The U.S. survey confirmed that 22% of women and 5% of men suffer from hypoactive sexual disorder. But in a larger international survey, as many as 43% of women reported this problem (Laumann et al., 2005). For men, the prevalence increases with age; for women, it decreases with age (DeLamater & Sill, 2005; Laumann, Paik, & Rosen, 1999). Schreiner-Engel and Schiavi (1986) noted that patients with this disorder rarely have sexual fantasies, seldom masturbate (35% of the women and 52% of the men never masturbated, and most of the rest in their sample masturbated no more than once a month), and attempt intercourse once a month or less. Suggested revisions for *DSM-5* would recognize that one of the reasons for low desire is that these individuals experience little sexual arousal, leading to a new label of "sexual interest/arousal disorder" (Brotto, 2010a).

Sexual Aversion Disorder

On a continuum with hypoactive sexual desire disorder is **sexual aversion disorder**, in which even the thought of sex or a brief casual touch may evoke fear, panic, or disgust

DSM Disorder Criteria Summary
Hypoactive Sexual Desire Disorder

A. Persistently or recurrently deficient (or absent) sexual fantasies and desire for sexual activity. The judgment of deficiency or absence is made by the clinician, taking into account factors that affect sexual functioning, such as age and the context of the person's life.

B. The disturbance causes marked distress or interpersonal difficulty.

C. The sexual dysfunction is not better accounted for by another Axis I disorder (except another Sexual Dysfunction) and is not due exclusively to the direct physiological effects of a substance (e.g., a drug of abuse, a medication) or a general medical condition.

Source: Reprinted with permission from *Diagnostic and Statistical Manual of Mental Disorders* (4th ed., text revision). © 2000 American Psychiatric Association.

(Kaplan, 1987). In some cases, the principal problem might be panic disorder (see Chapter 4), in which the fear or alarm response is associated with the physical sensations of sex. In other cases, sexual acts and fantasies may trigger traumatic images or memories similar to but perhaps not as severe as those experienced by people with posttraumatic stress disorder (see Chapter 4). There are few data on prevalence, but the majority of those presenting to clinics with sexual aversion disorder seem to be women (Brotto, 2010b; Wincze et al., 2008). Consider the case of Lisa from one of our clinics.

Lisa ⊹ The Terror of Sex

Lisa was 36, had been married for 3 years, and was a full-time student working on an associate's degree. She had been married once before. Lisa reported that sexual problems had begun 9 months earlier. She complained of poor lubrication during intercourse and of having "anxiety attacks" during sex. She had not attempted intercourse in 2 months and had tried only intermittently during the past 9 months. Despite their sexual difficulties, Lisa had a loving and close relationship with her husband. She could not remember precisely what happened 9 months ago except that she had been under a great deal of stress and experienced an anxiety attack during sex. Even her husband's touch was becoming increasingly intolerable because she was afraid it might bring on the scary feelings again. Her primary fear was of having a heart attack and dying during sex.

Among male patients presenting for sexual aversion disorder, 10% experienced panic attacks during attempted sexual activity. Kaplan (1987) reports that 25% of 106 patients presenting with sexual aversion disorder also met criteria for panic disorder. In such cases, treating the panic disorder may be a necessary first step. Because sexual aver-

sion disorder is basically anxiety or panic focused on sexual activity, one proposal for the *DSM-5* is to move it to the anxiety disorder category (Brotto, 2010b).

Sexual Arousal Disorders

Disorders of arousal are called **male erectile disorder** and **female sexual arousal disorder**. The problem here is not desire. Many individuals with arousal disorders have frequent sexual urges and fantasies and a strong desire to have sex. Their problem is in becoming physically aroused: A male has difficulty achieving or maintaining an erection, and a female cannot achieve or maintain adequate lubrication (Basson, 2007; Rosen, 2007; Segraves & Althof, 1998; Wincze, 2009; Wincze et al., 2008). Consider the case of Bill.

Bill ⊹ Long Marriage, New Problem

Bill, a 58-year-old white man, was referred to our clinic by his urologist. He was a retired accountant who had been married for 29 years to his 57-year-old wife, a retired nutritionist. They had no children. For the past several years, Bill had had difficulties obtaining and maintaining an erection. He reported a rather rigid routine he and his wife had developed to deal with the problem. They scheduled sex for Sunday mornings. However, Bill had to do a number of chores first, including letting the dog out, washing the dishes, and shaving. The couple's current behavior consisted of mutual hand stimulation. Bill was "not allowed" to attempt insertion until after his wife had climaxed. Bill's wife was adamant that she was not going to change her sexual behavior and "become a whore," as she put it. This included refusing to try K-Y jelly as a lubricant appropriate to her postmenopausal decrease in lubrication.

Bill and his wife agreed that despite marital problems over the years they had always maintained a good sexual relationship until the onset of the current problem. Useful information was obtained in separate interviews. Bill masturbated on Saturday night in an attempt to control his erection the following morning; his wife was unaware of this. In addition, he quickly and easily achieved a full erection when viewing erot-

hypoactive sexual desire disorder An apparent lack of interest in sexual activity or fantasy that would not be expected considering the person's age and life situation.

sexual aversion disorder An extreme and persistent dislike of sexual contact or similar activities.

male erectile disorder The recurring inability in some men to attain or maintain adequate penile erection until completion of sexual activity.

female sexual arousal disorder The recurrent inability in some women to attain or maintain adequate lubrication and sexual excitement swelling responses until completion of sexual activity.

ica in the privacy of the sexuality clinic laboratory (surprising the assessor). Bill's wife privately acknowledged being angry at her husband for an affair that he had had 20 years earlier.

At the final session, three specific recommendations were made: for Bill to cease masturbating the evening before sex, for the couple to use a lubricant, and for them to delay the morning routine until after they had had sexual relations. The couple called back 1 month later to report that their sexual activity was much improved.

The old and somewhat derogatory terms for male erectile disorder and female arousal disorder are *impotence* and *frigidity,* but these are imprecise labels that do not identify the specific phase of the sexual response in which the problems are localized. A man typically feels more impaired by his problem than a woman does by hers. Inability to achieve and maintain an erection makes intercourse difficult or impossible. Women who are unable to achieve vaginal lubrication, however, may be able to compensate by using a commercial lubricant (Schover & Jensen, 1988; Wincze, 2009). In women, arousal and lubrication may decrease at any time but, as in men, such problems tend to accompany aging (Bartlik & Goldberg, 2000; Basson, 2007; DeLamater & Sill, 2005; Laumann et al., 1999; Morokoff, 1993; Rosen, 2000). It is unusual for a man to be completely unable to achieve an erection. More typical is a situation like Bill's, where full erections are possible during masturbation and partial erections occur during attempted intercourse but with insufficient rigidity to allow penetration.

The prevalence of erectile dysfunction is startlingly high and increases with age. Although data from the U.S. survey indicate that 5% of men between 18 and 59 fully meet a stringent set of criteria for erectile dysfunction (Laumann et al., 1999), this figure certainly underestimates the prevalence because erectile dysfunction increases rapidly in men after age 60. Rosen, Wing, Schneider, and Gendrano (2005) reviewed evidence from around the world and found that 60% of men 60 and older suffered from erectile dysfunction. Data from another study (shown in ■ Figure 9.3) suggest that at least some impairment is present in approximately 40% of men in their 40s and 70% of men in their 70s (Feldman, Goldstein, Hatzichristou, Krane, & McKunlay, 1994; Kim & Lipshultz, 1997; Rosen, 2007). Male erectile disorder is easily the most common problem for which men seek help, accounting for 50% or more of the men referred to specialists for sexual problems (Hawton, 1995).

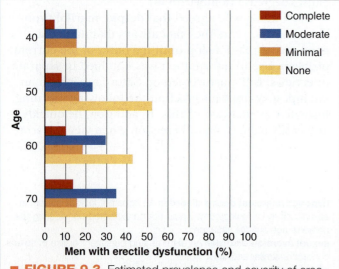

■ **FIGURE 9.3** Estimated prevalence and severity of erectile dysfunction in a sample of 1,290 men between 40 and 70 years of age. (Reprinted, with permission, from Feldman et al., 1994. Impotence and its medical and psychosocial correlates: Results of the Massachusetts male aging study. *Journal of Urology, 51,* 54–61.

The prevalence of female arousal disorders is somewhat more difficult to estimate because many women still do not consider absence of arousal to be a problem, let alone a disorder. The U.S. survey reports a prevalence of 14% of females experiencing an arousal disorder (Laumann et al., 1999). Because disorders of desire, arousal, and orgasm often overlap, it is difficult to estimate precisely how many women with specific arousal disorders present to sex clinics (Basson, 2007; Segraves & Althof, 1998; Wincze & Carey, 2001).

Orgasm Disorders

The orgasm phase of the sexual response cycle can also become disrupted in one of several ways. As a result, either the orgasm occurs at an inappropriate time or it does not occur.

Inhibited Orgasm

An inability to achieve an orgasm despite adequate sexual desire and arousal is commonly seen in women (Stock, 1993; Wincze, 2009), but **inhibited orgasm** is relatively rare in men. Consider the case of Greta and Will.

Greta and Will • Loving Disunion

Greta, a teacher, and Will, an engineer, were an attractive couple who came together to the first interview and entered the office clearly showing affection for each other. They had been married for 5 years and were in their late 20s. When asked about the problems that had brought them to the office, Greta quickly reported that she didn't think she had ever had an orgasm—"didn't think" because she wasn't really sure what an orgasm was.

Will certainly didn't think Greta was reaching orgasm. In any case, he reported, they were clearly going in "different directions" sexually, in that Greta's interest was decreasing. She had progressed from initiating sex occasionally early in their marriage to almost never doing so, except for an occasional spurt every 6 months or so. But Greta noted that it was the physical closeness she wanted most during these times rather than sexual pleasure. Further inquiry revealed that she did become sexually aroused occasionally but had never reached orgasm, even during several attempts at masturbation mostly before her marriage.

Greta had been brought up in a strict but loving and supportive Catholic family that more or less ignored sexuality. The parents were always careful not to display their affection in front of Greta, and when her mother caught Greta touching her genital area, she was cautioned rather severely to avoid that kind of activity.

An inability to reach orgasm is the most common complaint among women who seek therapy for sexual problems. Although the U.S. survey did not estimate the prevalence of **female orgasmic disorder** specifically, approximately 25% of women report significant difficulty reaching orgasm (Heiman, 2000; Laumann et al., 1999), although estimates vary widely (Graham, 2010). The problem is equally present in different age groups, and unmarried women were 1.5 times more likely than married women to experience orgasm disorder. In diagnosing this problem, it is necessary to determine that the women "never or almost never" reach orgasm (Wincze & Carey, 2001). This distinction is important because only approximately 20% of all women reliably experience regular orgasms during sexual intercourse (Graham, 2010; Lloyd, 2005). Therefore, approximately 80% do not achieve orgasm with every sexual encounter, unlike most men, who tend to experience orgasm more consistently. Thus, the "never or almost never" inquiry is important, along with establishing the extent of the couple's distress, in diagnosing orgasmic dysfunction.

In the U.S. survey, approximately 8% of men report having delayed orgasms or none during sexual interactions (Laumann et al., 1999). Men seldom seek treatment for this condition. It is possible that in many cases some men reach climax through alternative forms of stimulation and that **male orgasmic disorder** is accommodated by the couple (Apfelbaum, 2000).

Some men who are unable to ejaculate with their partners can obtain an erection and ejaculate during masturbation. In the most usual pattern, ejaculation is delayed; this is called *retarded ejaculation*. Occasionally men suffer from *retrograde ejaculation*, in which ejaculatory fluids travel backward into the bladder rather than forward. This phenomenon is almost always caused by the effects of certain drugs or a coexisting medical condition and should not be confused with male orgasmic disorder.

DSM — Disorder Criteria Summary
Orgasmic Disorders

DSM-IV TR Criteria for Female Orgasmic Disorder (formerly Inhibited Female Orgasm)

A. Persistent or recurrent delay in, or absence of, orgasm following a normal sexual excitement phase. Women exhibit wide variability in the type or intensity of stiulation that triggers orgasm. The diagnosis of Female Orgasmic Disorder should be based on the clinician's judgment that the woman's orgasmic capacity is less than would be reasonable for her age, sexual experience, and the adequacy of sexual stimulation she receives.

DSM-IV TR Criteria for Male Orgasmic Disorder (formerly Inhibited Male Orgasm)

A. Persistent or recurrent delay in, or absence of, orgasm following a normal sexual excitement phase during sexual activity that the clinician, taking into account the person's age, judges to be adequate in focus, intensity, and duration.

Note: both disorders share the following criteria:

B. The disturbance causes marked distress or interpersonal difficulty.

C. The orgasmic dysfunction is not better accounted for by another Axis I disorder (except another Sexual Dysfunction) and is not due exclusively to the direct physiological effects of a substance (e.g., a drug of abuse, a medication) or a general medical condition.

Source: Reprinted with permission from *Diagnostic and Statistical Manual of Mental Disorders* (4th ed., text revision). © 2000 American Psychiatric Association.

---

inhibited orgasm An inability to achieve orgasm despite adequate sexual desire and arousal; commonly seen in women but relatively rare in men.

female orgasmic disorder The recurring delay or absence of orgasm in some women following a normal sexual excitement phase, relative to their prior experience and current stimulation. Also known as inhibited orgasm (female).

male orgasmic disorder The recurring delay in or absence of orgasm in some men following a normal sexual excitement phase, relative to age and current stimulation. Also known as inhibited orgasm (male).

Premature Ejaculation

A far more common male orgasmic disorder is **premature ejaculation**, ejaculation that occurs well before the man and his partner wish it to (Althof, 2006; Polonsky, 2000; Wincze, 2009). Consider the rather typical case of Gary.

The frequency of premature ejaculation seems to be quite high. In the U.S. survey, 21% of all men met criteria for premature ejaculation, making it the most common male sexual dysfunction (Laumann et al., 1999). In one clinic, premature ejaculation was the principal complaint of 16% of men seeking treatment (Hawton, 1995).

It is difficult to define "premature." An adequate length of time before ejaculation varies from individual to individual. Patrick and colleagues (2005) found that men who complain of premature ejaculation ejaculated 1.8 minutes after penetration, compared with 7.3 minutes in individuals without this complaint. A perceived lack of control over orgasm, however, may be the more important psychological determinant of premature ejaculation (Wincze et al., 2008). Although occasional early ejaculation is normal, consistent premature ejaculation appears to occur primarily in inexperienced men with less education about sex (Laumann et al., 1999).

Sexual Pain Disorders

In the **sexual pain disorders**, intercourse is associated with marked pain. For some men and women, sexual desire is present, and arousal and orgasm are easily attained, but the pain of intercourse is so severe that sexual behavior is disrupted. This subtype is named **dyspareunia**. Dyspareunia is diagnosed only if no medical reasons for pain can be found. It can be tricky to make this assessment (Binik, 2010; Binik, Bergeron, & Khalifé, 2000; Payne et al., 2005). Several years ago, a patient of ours described having sharp pains in his head, like a migraine headache, which began during ejaculation and lasted for several minutes. This man, in his 50s at the time, had had a healthy sexual relationship with his wife until a severe fall approximately 2 years earlier that left him partially disabled and with a severe limp. The pain during ejaculation developed shortly thereafter. Extensive medical examination from a number of specialists revealed no physical reason for the pain. Thus, he met the criteria for dyspareunia, and psychological interventions were administered—in this case without benefit. He subsequently engaged in manual stimulation of his wife and, occasionally, intercourse, but he avoided ejaculation.

Dyspareunia is rarely seen in clinics, with estimates of those affected ranging from 1% to 5% of men (Bancroft, 1989; Spector & Carey, 1990) and a more substantial 10% to 15% of women (Hawton, 1995; Rosen & Leiblum, 1995).

DSM **Disorder Criteria Summary**
Sexual Pain Disorders

DSM-IV TR Criteria for Dyspareunia (Not Due to a General Medical Condition)

A. Recurrent or persistent genital pain associated with sexual intercourse in either a male or a female.

B. The disturbance causes marked distress or interpersonal difficulty.

C. The disturbance is not caused exclusively by Vaginismus or lack of lubrication, is not better accounted for by another Axis I disorder (except another Sexual Dysfunction), and is not due exclusively to the direct physiological effects of substance (e.g., a drug of abuse, a medication) or a general medical condition.

DSM-IV TR Criteria for Vaginismus (Not Due to a General Medical Condition)

A. Recurrent or persistent involuntary spasm of the musculature of the outer third of the vagina that interferes with sexual intercourse.

B. The disturbance causes marked distress or interpersonal difficulty.

C. The disturbance is not better accounted for by another Axis I disorder (e.g., Somatization Disorder) and is not due exclusively to the direct physiological effects of a general medical condition.

Source: Reprinted with permission from *Diagnostic and Statistical Manual of Mental Disorders* (4th ed., text revision). © 2000 American Psychiatric Association.

Binik (2005; Binik, Bergeron, & Khalifé, 2007) does not think that dyspareunia should be classified as a sexual disorder but rather as a "urogenital pain disorder." He believes that this would focus therapy on pain control.

A more common problem is **vaginismus**, in which the pelvic muscles in the outer third of the vagina undergo involuntary spasms when intercourse is attempted (Bancroft, 1997; Binik et al., 2007). The spasm reaction of vaginismus may occur during any attempted penetration, including a gynecological exam or insertion of a tampon (Beck, 1993; Bradford & Meston, 2011). Women report sensations of "ripping, burning, or tearing during attempted intercourse" (Beck, 1993, p. 384). Consider the case of Jill.

Jill · Sex and Spasms

Jill was referred to our clinic by another therapist because she had not consummated her marriage of 1 year. At 23 years of age, she was an attractive and loving wife who managed a motel while her husband worked as an accountant. Despite numerous attempts in a variety of positions to engage in intercourse, Jill's severe vaginal spasms prevented penetration of any kind. Jill was also unable to use tampons. With great reluctance, she submitted to gynecological exams at infrequent intervals. Jill, an anxious young woman, came from a family in which sexual matters were seldom discussed and sexual contact between the parents had ceased some years before. Although she enjoyed petting, Jill's general attitude was that intercourse was disgusting. Furthermore, she expressed some fears of becoming pregnant despite taking adequate contraceptive measures. She also thought that she would perform poorly when she did engage in intercourse, therefore embarrassing herself with her new husband.

Although there are no data on the prevalence of vaginismus in community samples, best estimates are that it affects 6% of women (Bradford & Meston, 2011). Crowley, Richardson, and Goldmeir (2006) found that 25% of women who report suffering from some sexual dysfunction experience vaginismus. The prevalence of this condition in cultures with conservative views of sexuality, such as Ireland, may be higher—as high as 42% to 55% in at least two clinic samples (Barnes, Bowman, & Cullen, 1984; O'Sullivan, 1979). (Results from any one clinic may not be applicable even to other clinics, let alone to the population of Ireland.) Because vaginismus and dyspareunia both involve pain and overlap quite a bit in women, current proposals suggest combining these two problems in a single pain-related category (Binik, 2005; Binik et al., 2010; Payne et al., 2005). Results from the U.S. survey indicate that approximately 7% of women suffer from one or the other type of sexual pain disorder, with higher proportions of younger and less educated women reporting this problem (Laumann et al., 1999).

Assessing Sexual Behavior

There are three major aspects to the assessment of sexual behavior (Wiegel, Wincze, & Barlow, 2002):

1. *Interviews,* usually supported by numerous questionnaires because patients may provide more information on paper than in a verbal interview
2. A *thorough medical evaluation,* to rule out the variety of medical conditions that can contribute to sexual problems
3. A *psychophysiological assessment,* to directly measure the physiological aspects of sexual arousal

Many clinicians assess the ability of individuals to become sexually aroused under a variety of conditions by taking psychophysiological measurements while the patient is either awake or asleep. In men, penile erection is measured directly, using, for example, a *penile strain gauge* developed in our clinic (Barlow, Becker, Leitenberg, & Agras, 1970). As the penis expands, the strain gauge picks up the changes and records them on a polygraph. Note that participants are often not aware of these more objective measures of their arousal—that is, their self-report of how aroused they are differs from the objective measure—and this discrepancy increases or decreases as a function of the type of sexual problem they have. Penile rigidity is also important to measure in cases of erectile dysfunction because large erections with insufficient rigidity will not be adequate for intercourse (Wiegel et al., 2002).

The comparable device for women is a *vaginal photoplethysmograph,* developed by James Geer and his associates (Geer, Morokoff, & Greenwood, 1974; Prause & Janssen, 2006; Rosen & Beck, 1988). This device, which is smaller than a tampon, is inserted by the woman into her vagina. A light source at the tip of the instrument and two light-sensitive photoreceptors on the sides of the instrument measure the amount of light reflected back from the vaginal walls. Because blood flows to the vaginal walls during arousal, the amount of light passing through them decreases with increasing arousal.

Typically in our clinic, individuals undergoing physiological assessment view an erotic videotape for 2 to 5 minutes or, occasionally, listen to an erotic audiotape (see, for example, Bach, Brown, & Barlow, 1999; Weisburg, Brown, Wincze, & Barlow, 2001). The patient's sexual responsivity

premature ejaculation A recurring ejaculation before the person wishes it, with minimal sexual stimulation.
sexual pain disorders (dyspareunia) A recurring genital pain in either males or females before, during, or after sexual intercourse. Also known as *dyspareunia.*
vaginismus A recurring involuntary muscle spasms in the outer third of the vagina that interfere with sexual intercourse.

during this time is assessed psychophysiologically using the strain gauge or photoplethysmograph just described. Patients also report subjectively on the amount of sexual arousal they experience. This assessment allows the clinician to carefully observe the conditions under which arousal is possible for the patient. For example, many individuals with psychologically based sexual dysfunctions may achieve strong arousal in a laboratory but be unable to become aroused with a partner (Bancroft, 1997; Sakheim, Barlow, Abrahamson, & Beck, 1987).

Concept Check 9.2

Diagnose the following sexual dysfunctions.

1. Juanita is in a serious sexual relationship and is content. Lately, however, the thought of her boyfriend's touch disgusts her. Juanita has no idea what is causing this. She could be suffering from (a) panic disorder, (b) sexual arousal disorder, (c) sexual aversion disorder, or (d) both a and b.

2. After Bob was injured playing football, he started having pain in his arm during sex. All medical reasons for the pain have been ruled out. Bob is probably displaying (a) dyspareunia, (b) vaginismus, (c) penile strain gauge, or (d) male orgasmic disorder.

3. Kelly has no real desire for sex. She has sex only because she feels that otherwise her husband may leave her. Kelly suffers from (a) sexual aversion disorder, (b) hypoactive sexual desire disorder, (c) boredom, or (d) female sexual arousal disorder.

4. Aadarsh lacks the ability to control ejaculation. The majority of the time he ejaculates within seconds of penetration. He suffers from (a) male erectile disorder, (b) stress, (c) premature ejaculation, or (d) both a and b.

5. Samantha came into the office because she is unable to reach orgasm. She loves her husband but stopped initiating sex. She is most likely suffering from (a) female orgasmic disorder, (b) female sexual arousal disorder, (c) vaginismus, or (d) dislike for her husband.

Causes and Treatment of Sexual Dysfunction

> What are the defining features and known causes of sexual dysfunction?
> What psychosocial and medical treatments are available, and are they effective?

As with most disorders, biological, psychological, and social factors contribute to the development of sexual dysfunction. And these problems can be treated either psychologically or medically.

Causes of Sexual Dysfunction

Individual sexual dysfunctions seldom occur in isolation. Usually, a patient referred to a sexuality clinic complains of a wide assortment of sexual problems, although one may be of most concern (Rosen, 2007; Wincze, 2009). A 45-year-old man recently referred to our clinic had been free of problems until 10 years earlier, when he was under a great deal of pressure at work and was preparing to take a major career-related licensing examination. He began experiencing erectile dysfunction about 50% of the time, a condition that had progressed to approximately 80% of the time. In addition, he reported that he had no control over ejaculation, often ejaculating before penetration with only a semierect penis. Over the past 5 years, he had lost most interest in sex and was coming to treatment only at his wife's insistence. Thus, this man suffered simultaneously from erectile dysfunction, premature ejaculation, and low sexual desire.

Because of the frequency of such combinations, we discuss the causes of various sexual dysfunctions together, reviewing briefly the biological, psychological, and social contributions and specifying causal factors thought to be associated exclusively and specifically with one or another dysfunction.

Biological Contributions

A number of physical and medical conditions contribute to sexual dysfunction (Basson, 2007; Rosen, 2007; Wiegel et al., 2002; Wincze & Carey, 2001; Wincze et al., 2008). Neurological diseases and other conditions that affect the nervous system, such as diabetes and kidney disease, may directly interfere with sexual functioning by reducing sensitivity in the genital area, and they are a common cause of erectile dysfunction in males (Rosen, 2007; Wincze, 2009). Feldman and colleagues (1994) reported that 28% of men with diabetes experienced complete erectile failure. Vascular disease is a major cause of sexual dysfunction because erections in men and vaginal engorgement in women depend on adequate blood flow. The two relevant vascular problems in men are arterial insufficiency (constricted arteries), which makes it difficult for blood to reach the penis, and venous leakage (blood flows out too quickly for an erection to be maintained) (Wincze & Carey, 2001).

Chronic illness can also indirectly affect sexual functioning. For example, it is not uncommon for individuals who have had heart attacks to be wary of the physical exercise involved in sexual activity to the point of preoccupation. They often become unable to achieve arousal despite being assured by their physicians that sexual activity is safe for them (Cooper, 1988). Also, coronary artery disease and sexual dysfunction commonly coexist, and it is now recommended that men presenting with erectile dysfunction should be screened for cardiovascular disease (Jackson, Rosen, Kloner, & Kostis, 2006).

A major physical cause of sexual dysfunction is prescription medication. Drug treatments for high blood pressure, called *antihypertensive medications*, in the class known as beta-blockers, including propranolol, may contribute to sexual dysfunction. Serotonin-specific reuptake inhibitor (SSRI) antidepressant medications and other antidepressant and antianxiety drugs may also interfere with sexual desire and arousal in both men and women (Balon, 2006; Segraves & Althof, 1998). Sexual dysfunction—specifically low sexual desire and arousal difficulties—is the most widespread side effect of the antidepressant SSRIs, such as Prozac (see Chapter 6). Some people are aware that alcohol suppresses sexual arousal, but they may not know that most other drugs of abuse, such as cocaine and heroin, also produce widespread sexual dysfunction in frequent users and abusers, both male and female. There is also the misconception that alcohol facilitates sexual arousal and behavior. What actually happens is that alcohol at low and moderate levels reduces social inhibitions so that people feel more like having sex (and perhaps are more willing to request it) (Crowe & George, 1989; Wiegel, Scepkowski, & Barlow, 2006). Physically, alcohol is a central nervous system suppressant, and for men to achieve erection and women to achieve lubrication is more difficult when the central nervous system is suppressed (Schiavi, 1990). Chronic alcohol abuse may cause permanent neurological damage and may virtually eliminate the sexual response cycle. Such abuse may lead to liver and testicular damage, resulting in decreased testosterone levels and related decreases in sexual desire and arousal. This dual effect of alcohol (social disinhibition and physical suppression) has been recognized since the time of Shakespeare: "It provokes the desire, but it takes away the performance" (*Macbeth*, II, iii, 29).

Many people report that cocaine or marijuana enhances sexual pleasure. Although little is known about the effects of marijuana across the range of use, it is unlikely that

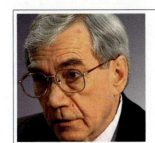

Abnormal Psychology Inside Out. Produced by Ira Wohl, Only Child Motion Pictures

Erectile Dysfunction: Clark

"In the process of becoming aroused, all of a sudden it would be over. And I didn't understand that at all. So then everything is coupled with a bunch of depressing thoughts, like fear of failure. And so I begin to say, is this happening to me because I'm afraid I'm going to fail, and I don't want to be embarrassed by that? It's really very difficult to deal with emotionally . . . The worse I feel about myself, the slower I am sexually, and sometimes I describe it as the fear of losing masculinity."

Go to Psychology CourseMate at www.cengagebrain.com to watch this video.

chemical effects increase pleasure. Rather, in those individuals who report some enhancement of sexual pleasure (and many don't), the effect may be psychological in that their attention is focused more completely and fully on sensory stimulation (Buffum, 1982), a factor that seems to be an important part of healthy sexual functioning. If so, imagery and attentional focus can be enhanced with nondrug procedures such as meditation, in which a person practices concentrating on something with as few distractions as possible. Finally, one report from Mannino, Klevens, and Flanders (1994), studying more than 4,000 male army veterans, found that cigarette smoking alone was associated with increased erectile dysfunction after controlling for other factors, such as alcohol use and vascular disease (Wincze et al., 2008).

Psychological Contributions

How do we account for sexual dysfunction from a psychological perspective? Basically, we have to break the concept of performance anxiety into several components. One component is arousal, another is cognitive processes, and the third is negative affect (Wiegel et al., 2006; Wincze et al., 2008).

When confronted with the possibility of having sexual relations, individuals who are dysfunctional tend to expect the worst and find the situation to be relatively negative and unpleasant (Weisburg et al., 2001). As far as possible, they avoid becoming aware of any sexual cues (and therefore are not aware of how aroused they are physically, thus underreporting their arousal). They also may distract themselves with negative thoughts, such as, "I'm going to make a fool of myself" or "I'll never be able to get aroused and she [or he] will think I'm stupid." We know that as arousal increases, a person's attention focuses more intently and consistently. But the person who is focusing on negative thoughts will find it impossible to become sexually aroused.

People with normal sexual functioning react to a sexual situation positively. They focus their attention on the erotic cues and do not become distracted. When they become aroused, they focus even more strongly on the sexual and erotic cues, allowing themselves to become increasingly sexually aroused. The model presented in ■ Figure 9.4 illustrates both functional and dysfunctional sexual arousal (Barlow, 1986, 2002). These experiments demonstrate that sexual arousal is strongly determined by psychological factors, particularly cognitive and emotional factors, that are powerful enough to determine whether blood flows to the appropriate areas of the body, such as the genitals, confirming again the strong interaction of psychological and biological factors in most of our functioning.

In summary, normally functioning individuals show increased sexual arousal during "performance demand" conditions, experience positive affect, are distracted by nonsexual stimuli, and have a good idea of how aroused they are. Individuals with sexual problems, such as erectile dysfunction in males, show decreased arousal during performance demand, experience negative affect, are not distracted by nonsexual stimuli, and do not have an accurate sense of how aroused they are. This process seems to apply to most sexual dysfunctions, which, you will remember, tend to occur together, but it is particularly applicable to sexual arousal disorders (Wiegel et al., 2006).

Although little is known about the psychological (or biological) factors associated with premature ejaculation (Althof, 2007; Bradford & Meston, 2011; Weiner, 1996), the condition is most prevalent in young men and excessive physiological arousal in the sympathetic nervous system may lead to rapid ejaculation. These observations suggest some men may have a naturally lower threshold for ejaculation—that is, they require less stimulation and arousal to ejaculate. Unfortunately, the psychological factor of anxiety also increases sympathetic arousal. Thus, when a man becomes anxious about ejaculating too quickly, his concern only makes the problem worse.

Social and Cultural Contributions

The model of sexual dysfunction displayed in Figure 9.4 helps explain why some individuals may be dysfunctional *at the present time* but it does not explain how they *became* that way. Although it is not known for sure why some people develop problems, many people learn early that sexuality can be negative and somewhat threatening, and the responses they develop reflect this belief. Donn Byrne and his colleagues call this negative cognitive set *erotopho-*

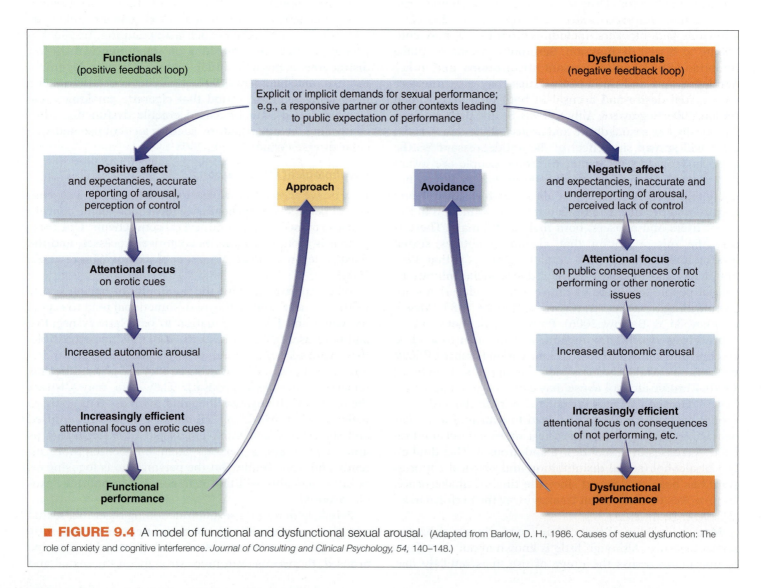

■ **FIGURE 9.4** A model of functional and dysfunctional sexual arousal. (Adapted from Barlow, D. H., 1986. Causes of sexual dysfunction: The role of anxiety and cognitive interference. *Journal of Consulting and Clinical Psychology, 54,* 140–148.)

bia. They have demonstrated that erotophobia, presumably learned early in childhood from families, religious authorities, or others, seems to predict sexual difficulties later in life (Byrne & Schulte, 1990). Thus, for some individuals, sexual cues become associated early with negative affect. In other cases, both men and women may experience specific negative or traumatic events after a period of relatively well-adjusted sexuality. These negative events might include sudden failure to become aroused or actual sexual trauma such as rape and early sexual abuse.

Laumann and colleagues (1999), in the U.S. sex survey, found a substantial impact of early traumatic sexual events on later sexual functioning, particularly in women. For example, if women were sexually victimized by an adult before puberty or were forced to have sexual contact of some kind, they were approximately twice as likely to have orgasmic dysfunction as women who had not been touched before puberty or forced to have sex at any time. For male victims of adult–child contact, the probability of experiencing erectile dysfunction is more than 3 times greater than if they had not had the contact. It is interesting that men who admitted sexually assaulting women are 3.5 times as likely to report erectile dysfunction as those who did not. Thus, traumatic sexual acts of all kinds have long-lasting effects on subsequent sexual functioning, in both men and women, sometimes lasting decades beyond the occurrence of the original event (Hall, 2007). Such stressful events may initiate negative affect, in which individuals experience a loss of control over their sexual response cycle, throwing them into the kind of dysfunctional pattern depicted in Figure 9.4. It is common for people who experience erectile failure during a particularly stressful time to continue sexual dysfunction long after the stressful situation has ended.

In addition to generally negative attitudes or experiences associated with sexual interactions, a number of other factors may contribute to sexual dysfunction. Among these, the most common is a marked deterioration in close interpersonal relationships (Wincze, Bach, & Barlow, 2008). It is difficult to have a satisfactory sexual relationship in the context of growing dislike for a partner. Occasionally, the partner may no longer seem physically attractive. Finally, it is also important to feel attractive yourself. Koch, Mansfield, Thurau, and Carey (2005) found that the more a woman perceived herself as less attractive than before, the more likely she was to have sexual problems. Poor sexual skills might also lead to frequent sexual failure and, ultimately, lack of desire. For example, men with erectile dysfunction report a greatly restricted range of sexual behaviors compared to men without these problems (Wincze et al., 2008).

Thus, social and cultural factors seem to affect later sexual functioning. John Gagnon has studied this phenomenon and constructed an important concept called *script theory* of sexual functioning, according to which we all operate by following "scripts" that reflect social and cultural expectations and guide our behavior (Gagnon, 1990; Laumann, Gagnon, Michael, & Michaels, 1994). Discover-

ing these scripts, both in individuals and across cultures, will tell us much about sexual functioning. For example, a person who learns that sexuality is potentially dangerous, dirty, or forbidden is more vulnerable to developing sexual dysfunction later in life. This pattern is most evident in cultures with restrictive attitudes toward sex (McGoldrick et al., 2007). For example, vaginismus is relatively rare in North America but is considerably more prevalent in Ireland and Turkey (Doğan, 2009; McGoldrick et al., 2007). Even in our own culture, certain socially communicated expectations and attitudes may stay with us despite our relatively enlightened and permissive attitude toward sex. Barbara Andersen and her colleagues (see, for example, Cyranowski et al., 1999) have demonstrated that being emotional and self-conscious about sex (having a negative sexual self-schema, described earlier in the chapter) may later lead to sexual difficulties under stressful situations. Zilbergeld (1999), one of the foremost authorities on male sexuality, has described a number of myths about sex believed by many men, and Baker and DeSilva (1988) converted an earlier version of Zilbergeld's male myths into a questionnaire and presented it to groups of sexually functional and dysfunctional men. They found that men with dysfunctions showed significantly greater belief in the myths than did men who were sexually functional.

Interaction of Psychological and Physical Factors

Having reviewed the various causes, we must now say that seldom is any sexual dysfunction associated exclusively with either psychological or physical factors (Bancroft, 1997; Rosen, 2007; Wiegel et al., 2006). More often, there is a subtle combination of factors. To take a typical example, a young man, vulnerable to developing anxiety and holding to a certain number of sexual myths (the social contribution), may experience erectile failure unexpectedly after using drugs or alcohol, as many men do (the biological contribution). He will anticipate the next sexual encounter with anxiety, wondering if the failure might happen again. This combination of experience and apprehension activates the psychological sequence depicted in Figure 9.4, regardless of whether he's had a few drinks.

In summary, socially transmitted negative attitudes about sex may interact with a person's relationship difficulties and predispositions to develop performance anxiety and, ultimately, lead to sexual dysfunction. From a psychological point of view, it is not clear why some individuals develop one dysfunction and not another, although it is common for several dysfunctions to occur in the same patient. Possibly an individual's specific biological predispositions interact with psychological factors to produce a specific sexual dysfunction.

Treatment of Sexual Dysfunction

Unlike most other disorders discussed in this book, one surprisingly simple treatment is effective for a large number of individuals who experience sexual dysfunction: education. Ignorance of the most basic aspects of the sexual response cycle and intercourse often leads to long-lasting dysfunctions (Bach, Wincze, & Barlow, 2001; Wincze et al., 2008; Wincze & Carey, 2001). Consider the case of Carl, who recently came to our sexuality clinic.

Carl • Never Too Late

Carl, a 55-year-old white man, was referred to our clinic by his urologist because he had difficulty maintaining an erection. Although he had never been married, he was involved in an intimate relationship with a 50-year-old woman. This was only his second sexual relationship. A careful interview revealed that Carl engaged in sex twice a week, but requests by the clinician for a step-by-step description of his sexual activities revealed an unusual pattern: Carl skipped foreplay and immediately proceeded to intercourse. Unfortunately, because his partner was not aroused and lubricated, he was unable to penetrate her. His valiant efforts sometimes resulted in painful abrasions for both of them. Two sessions of extensive sex education, including specific step-by-step instructions for carrying out foreplay, provided Carl with a new outlook on sex. For the first time he had successful, satisfying intercourse, much to his delight and his partner's.

In the case of hypoactive sexual desire disorder, a marked difference within a couple often leads to one partner being labeled as having low desire. For example, if one partner is quite happy with sexual relations once a week but the other partner desires sex every day, the latter partner may accuse the former of having low desire and, unfortunately, the former partner might agree. Facilitating better conditions often resolves these misunderstandings. Fortunately for people with this and more complex sexual dysfunctions, treatments are now available, both psychosocial and medical. Advances in medical treatments, particularly for erectile dysfunction, have been dramatic in just the past few years. We look first at psychosocial treatments, then we examine the latest medical procedures.

Psychosocial Treatments

Among the many advances in our knowledge of sexual behavior, none was more dramatic than the publication in 1970 by William Masters and Virginia Johnson of *Human Sexual Inadequacy*. The procedures outlined in this book literally revolutionized sex therapy by providing a brief, direct, and reasonably successful therapeutic program for sexual dysfunctions. Underscoring again the common basis of most sexual dysfunctions, a similar approach to therapy is taken with all patients, male and female, with slight variations depending on the specific sexual problem (for example, premature ejaculation or orgasmic disorder).

This intensive program involves a male and a female therapist to facilitate communication between the dysfunctional partners. (Masters and Johnson were the original male and female therapists.) Therapy is conducted daily over a 2-week period.

The actual program is straightforward. In addition to providing basic education about sexual functioning, altering deep-seated myths, and increasing communication, the clinicians' primary goal is to eliminate psychologically based performance anxiety (refer back to Figure 9.4). To accomplish this, Masters and Johnson introduced *sensate focus* and *nondemand pleasuring*. In this exercise, couples are instructed to refrain from intercourse or genital caressing and simply to explore and enjoy each other's body through touching, kissing, hugging, massaging, or similar kinds of behavior. In the first phase, nongenital pleasuring, breasts and genitals are excluded from the exercises. After successfully accomplishing this phase, the couple moves to genital pleasuring but with a ban on orgasm and intercourse and clear instructions to the man that achieving an erection is not the goal.

At this point, arousal should be reestablished and the couple should be ready to attempt intercourse. So as not to proceed too quickly, this stage is also broken down into parts. For example, a couple might be instructed to attempt the beginnings of penetration—that is, the depth of penetration and the time it lasts are only gradually built up—and both genital and nongenital pleasuring continue. Eventually, full intercourse and thrusting are accomplished. After this 2-week intensive program, recovery was reported by Masters and Johnson for the vast majority of more than 790 sexually dysfunctional patients, with some differences in the rate of recovery depending on the disorder. Close to 100% of individuals with premature ejaculation recovered, whereas the rate for more difficult cases of lifelong generalized erectile dysfunction was closer to 60%.

Sex therapists have expanded on and modified these procedures over the years to take advantage of recent advances in knowledge (see, for example, Bancroft, 1997; Rosen, 2007; Wincze, 2009; Wincze et al., 2008). Results with sex therapy for erectile dysfunction indicate that as many as 60% to 70% of the cases show a positive treatment outcome for at least several years, although there may be some slipping after that (Rosen, 2007; Sarwer & Durlak, 1997; Segraves & Althof, 1998). For better treatment of specific sexual dysfunctions, sex therapists integrate specific procedures into the context of general sex therapy. For example, to treat premature ejaculation, most sex therapists use a procedure developed by Semans (1956), sometimes called the *squeeze* technique, in which the penis is stimulated, usually by the partner, to nearly full erection. At this point, the partner firmly squeezes the penis near the top where the head of the penis joins the shaft, which quickly reduces arousal. These steps are repeated until (for heterosexual partners) eventually the penis is briefly inserted in the vagina without thrusting. If arousal occurs too quickly, the penis is withdrawn and the squeeze technique is used again. In this way, the man develops a sense of control over arousal and ejaculation. Reports of success with this approach over the past 20 years suggest that 60% to 90% of men benefit, but the success rates drop to about 25% after 3 years or more of follow-up (Althof, 2007; Polonsky, 2000). Gary, the 31-year-old salesman, was treated with this method, and his wife was cooperative during the procedures. Brief marital therapy also persuaded Gary that his insecurity over his perception that his wife no longer found him attractive was unfounded. After treatment, he reduced his work hours somewhat, and the couple's marital and sexual relations improved.

Lifelong female orgasmic disorder may be treated with explicit training in masturbatory procedures. For example, Greta was still unable to achieve orgasm with manual stimulation by her husband, even after proceeding through the basic steps of sex therapy. At this point,

▲ A therapist usually treats a dysfunction in one partner by seeing the couple together.

following certain standardized treatment programs for this problem (see, for example, Heiman, 2000; Heiman & LoPiccolo, 1988), Greta and Will purchased a vibrator and Greta was taught to let go of her inhibitions by talking out loud about how she felt during sexual arousal, even shouting or screaming if she wanted to. In the context of appropriate genital pleasuring and disinhibition exercises, the vibrator brought on Greta's first orgasm. With practice and good communication, the couple eventually learned how to bring on Greta's orgasm without the vibrator. Summaries of results from a number of studies suggest 70% to 90% of women will benefit from treatment, and these gains are stable and even improve further over time (Heiman, 2007; Heiman & Meston, 1997; Segraves & Althof, 1998).

To treat vaginismus, the woman and, eventually, the partner gradually insert increasingly larger dilators at the woman's pace. After the woman (and then the partner) can insert the largest dilator, in a heterosexual couple, the woman gradually inserts the man's penis. These exercises are carried out in the context of genital and nongenital pleasuring so as to retain arousal. Close attention must be accorded to any increased fear and anxiety that may be associated with the process, which may trigger memories of early sexual abuse that may have contributed to the onset of the condition. These procedures are highly successful, with a large majority of women (80% to 100%) overcoming vaginismus in a relatively short period (Beck, 1993; Binik et al., 2007; Leiblum & Rosen, 2000; Segraves & Althof, 1998; ter Kuile et al., 2007).

A variety of treatment procedures have also been developed for low sexual desire (see, for example, Pridal & LoPiccolo, 2000; Wincze, 2009; Wincze & Carey, 2001). At the heart of these treatments are the standard reeducation and communication phases of traditional sex therapy with,

possibly, the addition of masturbatory training and exposure to erotic material. Each case may require individual strategies. Remember Mrs. C., who was sexually abused by her cousin? Therapy involved helping the couple understand the impact of the repeated, unwanted sexual experiences in Mrs. C.'s past and to approach sex so that Mrs. C. was more comfortable with foreplay. She gradually lost the idea that once sex was started she had no control. She and her husband worked on starting and stopping sexual encounters. Cognitive restructuring was used to help Mrs. C. interpret her husband's amorousness in a positive rather than a skeptical light. In general, approximately 50% to 70% of individuals with low sexual desire benefit from sex therapy, at least initially (Basson, 2007; Brotto, 2006; Hawton, 1995; Segraves & Althof, 1998).

Medical Treatments

A variety of pharmacological and surgical techniques have been developed in recent years to treat sexual dysfunction, almost all focusing on male erectile disorder. The drug Viagra, introduced in 1998, and similar drugs such as Levitra and Cialis, introduced subsequently, are the best known. We look at the four most popular procedures: oral medication, injection of vasoactive substances directly into the penis, surgery, and vacuum device therapy. Before we begin, note that it is important to combine any medical treatment with a comprehensive educational and sex therapy program to ensure maximum benefit.

In 1998, the drug sildenafil (trade name Viagra) was introduced for erectile dysfunction. Approval from the Food and Drug Administration occurred early in 1998, and results from several clinical trials suggested that between 50% and 80% of a large number of men benefit from this treatment (Conti, Pepine, & Sweeney, 1999; Goldstein et al., 1998) in that erections become sufficient for intercourse, compared to approximately 30% who benefit from placebo. Results are similar with Cialis and Levitra (Carrier et al., 2005).

However, as many as 30% of men may suffer severe headaches as a side effect, particularly at higher doses (Rosen, 2000, 2007; Virag, 1999), and reports of sexual satisfaction are not optimal. Also, the large majority of men stop using the drug after a trial of several months or a year, indicating less than satisfactory long-term results (Rosen, 2007). To address this issue Bach, Barlow, and Wincze (2004) evaluated the addition of cognitive-behavioral treatment (CBT) to treatment with Viagra. Results were encouraging because couples reported greater satisfaction and increased sexual activity after combined drug therapy and CBT compared to a period when only the drug was used.

There was also some hope that Viagra would be useful for dysfunction in postmenopausal women, but results were disappointing (Kaplan et al., 1999). Berman and colleagues (2003) reported some improvement from Viagra in postmenopausal women with female sexual arousal disorder but only in those women without diminished sexual desire.

For some time, testosterone (Schiavi, White, Mandeli, & Levine, 1997) has been used to treat erectile dysfunction. But although it is safe and has relatively few side effects, only negligible effects on erectile dysfunction have been reported (Mann et al., 1996). Some urologists teach patients to inject vasodilating drugs such as *papaverine* or *prostaglandin* directly into the penis when they want to have sexual intercourse. These drugs dilate the blood vessels, allowing blood to flow to the penis and thereby producing an erection within 15 minutes that can last from 1 to 4 hours (Kim & Lipshultz, 1997; Rosen, 2007; Segraves & Althof, 1998). Because this procedure is a bit painful (although not as much as you might think), a substantial number of men, usually 50% to 60%, stop using it after a short time. In one study, 50 of 100 patients discontinued papaverine for various reasons (Lakin, Montague, Vanderbrug Medendorp, Tesar, & Schover, 1990; Segraves & Althof, 1998). A soft capsule that contains papaverine (called MUSE) can be inserted directly into the urethra, but this is somewhat painful, is less effective than injections, and remains awkward and artificial enough to preclude wide acceptance (Delizonna, Wincze, Litz, Brown, & Barlow, 2001). However, Heiman and colleagues (2006) recently demonstrated that topical application of papaverine externally to women's genitalia produced vasocongestion and arousal in postmenopausal women compared to placebo in the laboratory. Studies must now determine whether this drug treatment is effective outside of the laboratory.

Insertion of *penile prostheses* or implants has been a surgical option for almost 100 years; only recently have they become good enough to approximate normal sexual functioning. One procedure involves implanting a semi-rigid silicone rod that can be bent by the male into correct position for intercourse and maneuvered out of the way at other times. In a more popular procedure, the male squeezes a small pump that is surgically implanted into the scrotum, forcing fluid into an inflatable cylinder and thus producing an erection. A newer penile prosthetic device is an inflatable rod that contains the pumping device, which is more convenient than having the pump outside the rod. However, surgical implants fall short of restoring presurgical sexual functioning or assuring satisfaction in most patients (Gregoire, 1992; Kim & Lipshultz, 1997); they are now generally used only if other approaches don't work. However, this procedure has proved useful for men who must have a cancerous prostate removed because this surgery often causes erectile dysfunction, although newer "nerve-sparing" surgeries reduce the effect to some extent (Ramsawh, Morgentaler, Covino, Barlow, & DeWolf, 2005).

▲ An inflatable penile implant may be used for men with inadequate sexual functioning.

Another approach is *vacuum device therapy*, which works by creating a vacuum in a cylinder placed over the penis. The vacuum draws blood into the penis, which is then trapped by a specially designed ring placed around the base of the penis. Although using the vacuum device is rather awkward, between 70% and 100% of users report satisfactory erections, particularly if psychological sex therapy is ineffective (Segraves & Althof, 1998; Witherington, 1988). The procedure is also less intrusive than surgery or injections, but it remains awkward and artificial enough to preclude wide acceptance (Delizonna et al., 2001).

Summary

Treatment programs, both psychosocial and medical, offer hope to most people who suffer from sexual dysfunctions. Unfortunately, such programs are not readily available in many locations because few health and mental health professionals are trained to apply them, although the availability of drugs for male erectile dysfunction is widespread. Psychological treatment of sexual arousal disorders requires further improvement, and treatments for low sexual desire are largely untested. New medical developments appear yearly, but most are still intrusive and clumsy, although drugs such as Viagra and Levitra exhibit some success for erectile dysfunction and many more such drugs are in development.

Unfortunately, most health professionals tend to ignore the issue of sexuality in older adults. Along with the usual emphasis on communication, education, and sensate focus, appropriate lubricants for women and a discussion of methods to maximize the erectile response in men should be a part of any sexual counseling for older couples. More important, even with reduced physical capabilities, continued sexual relations, not necessarily including intercourse, should be an enjoyable and important part of an aging couple's relationship.

Paraphilia: Clinical Descriptions

> ❭ What are the clinical features of the major paraphilias?
> ❭ What is known about the causes of paraphilias?

If you are like most people, your sexual interest is directed to other physically mature adults (or late adolescents), all of whom are capable of freely offering or withholding their consent. But what if you are sexually attracted to something or somebody other than another adult, such as animals (particularly horses and dogs) (Williams & Weinberg, 2003) or a vacuum cleaner? (Yes, it does happen!) Or what if your only means of obtaining sexual satisfaction is to commit a brutal murder? Such patterns of sexual arousal and countless others exist in a large number of individuals, causing untold human suffering both for them and, if their behavior involves other people, for their victims. As noted in the beginning of the chapter, these disorders of sexual arousal are called **paraphilias**.

Over the years, we have assessed and treated a large number of these individuals, ranging from the slightly eccentric and sometimes pitiful case to some of the most dangerous killer–rapists encountered anywhere. Many of our patients may present with two, three, or more patterns, although one is usually dominant (Abel et al., 1987; Abel, Becker, Cunningham-Rathner, Mittelman, & Rouleau, 1988; Brownell, Hayes, & Barlow, 1977). Furthermore, it is not uncommon for individuals with paraphilia to also suffer from comorbid mood, anxiety, and substance abuse disorders (Kafka & Hennen, 2003; Raymond, Coleman, Ohlerking, Christenson, & Miner, 1999). Although paraphilias are not widely prevalent and estimates of their frequency are hard to come by, some disorders, such as transvestic fetishism (cross-dressing, discussed later), seem relatively common (Bancroft, 1989; Mason, 1997). You may have been the victim of **frotteurism** in a large city, typically on a crowded subway or bus. (We mean really crowded, with people packed in like sardines.) In this situation, women have been known to experience more than the usual jostling and pushing from behind. What they

discover, much to their horror, is a male with a frotteuristic arousal pattern rubbing against them until he is stimulated to the point of ejaculation. Because the victims cannot escape easily, the frotteuristic act is usually successful (Lussier & Piché, 2008).

Fetishism

In **fetishism**, a person is sexually attracted to nonliving objects. There are almost as many types of fetishes as there are objects, although women's undergarments and shoes are popular (Darcangelo, 2008). Fetishistic arousal is associated with two classes of objects or activities: (1) an inanimate object or (2) a source of specific tactile stimulation, such as rubber, particularly clothing made out of rubber. Shiny black plastic is also used (Bancroft, 1989; Junginger, 1997). Most of the person's sexual fantasies, urges, and desires focus on this object. A third source of attraction (sometimes called *partialism*) is a part of the body, such as the foot, buttocks, or hair, but this attraction is no longer technically classified as a fetish because distinguishing it from more normal patterns of arousal is often difficult.

---

paraphilias A sexual disorder or deviation in which sexual arousal occurs almost exclusively in the context of inappropriate objects or individuals.

frotteurism Paraphilia in which the person gains sexual gratification by rubbing against unwilling victims in crowds from which they cannot escape.

fetishism Long-term, recurring, intense sexually arousing urges, fantasies, or behavior involving the use of nonliving, unusual objects, which cause distress or impairment in life functioning.

Voyeurism and Exhibitionism

Voyeurism is the practice of observing, to become aroused, an unsuspecting individual undressing or naked. **Exhibitionism**, by contrast, is achieving sexual arousal and gratification by exposing genitals to unsuspecting strangers. Consider the case of Robert.

Robert ⚬ Outside the Curtains

Robert, a 31-year-old, married, blue-collar worker, reported that he first started "peeping" into windows when he was 14. He rode around the neighborhood on his bike at night, and when he spotted a female through a window he stopped and stared. During one of these episodes, he felt the first pangs of sexual arousal. Eventually he began masturbating while watching, thereby exposing his genitals, although out of sight. When he was older, he drove around until he spotted some prepubescent girls. He parked his car near them, unzipped his fly, called them over, and attempted to carry on a nonsexual conversation. Later he was sometimes able to talk a girl into mutual masturbation and *fellatio*, or oral stimulation of the penis. Although he was arrested several times, paradoxically, the threat of arrest increased his arousal (Barlow & Wincze, 1980).

DSM Disorder Criteria Summary
Fetishism

A. Over a period of at least 6 months, recurrent, intense sexually arousing fantasies, sexual urges, or behaviors involving the use of nonliving objects (e.g., female undergarments).

B. The fantasies, sexual urges, or behaviors cause clinically significant distress or impairment in social, occupational, or other important areas of functioning.

C. The fetish objects are not limited to articles of female clothing used in cross-dressing (as in Transvestic Fetishism) or devices designed for the purpose of tactile genital stimulation (e.g., a vibrator).

Source: Reprinted with permission from *Diagnostic and Statistical Manual of Mental Disorders* (4th ed., text revision). © 2000 American Psychiatric Association.

Remember that anxiety actually increases arousal under some circumstances. Many voyeurs just don't get the same satisfaction from attending readily available strip shows at a local bar.

The Lawyer Who Needed the Bus

Several years ago, a distinguished lawyer reported that he needed help and that his career was on the line. An intelligent, good-looking single man, he noted without bragging that he could have sex with any number of beautiful women in the course of his law practice. However, the only way he could become aroused was to leave his office, go down to the bus stop, ride around the city until a reasonably attractive young woman got on, expose himself just before the next stop, and then run off the bus, often with people chasing after him. To achieve maximal arousal, the bus could not be full or empty; there had to be just a few people sitting on the bus, and the woman getting on had to be the right age. Sometimes hours would pass before these circumstances lined up correctly. The lawyer observed that if he was not fired for exhibitionism he would be fired for all the time he was missing from work. On several occasions he had requested a girlfriend to role-play sitting on a bus in his apartment. Although he exposed himself to her, he could not achieve sexual arousal and gratification because the activity just wasn't exciting.

Although prevalence is unknown (Murphy & Page, 2008), in a random sample of 2,450 adults in Sweden, 31% reported at least one incident of being sexually aroused by exposing their genitals to a stranger and 7.7% reported at least one incident of being sexually aroused by spying on others having sex (Långström & Seto, 2006). To meet diagnosis for exhibitionism, the behavior must occur repeatedly and be compulsive or out of control.

DSM Disorder Criteria Summary
Voyeurism and Exhibitionism

DSM-IV TR Criteria for Voyeurism

A. Over a period of at least 6 months, recurrent, intense sexually arousing fantasies, sexual urges, or behaviors involving the act of observing an unsuspecting person who is naked, in the process of disrobing, or engaging in sexual activity.

DSM-IV TR Criteria for Exhibitionism

A. Over a period of at least 6 months, recurrent, intense sexually arousing fantasies, sexual urges, or behaviors involving the exposure of one's genitals to an unsuspecting stranger.

Note: both disorders share the following criteria:

B. The person has acted on these sexual urges, or the sexual urges or fantasies cause marked distress or interpersonal difficulty.

Source: Reprinted with permission from *Diagnostic and Statistical Manual of Mental Disorders* (4th ed., text revision). © 2000 American Psychiatric Association.

Transvestic Fetishism

In **transvestic fetishism**, sexual arousal is strongly associated with the act of dressing in clothes of the opposite sex, or cross-dressing (Wheeler, Newring, & Draper, 2008). Consider the case of Mr. M.

Mr. M. ⦿ Strong Man in a Dress

Mr. M., a 31-year-old married police officer, came to our clinic seeking treatment for uncontrollable urges to dress in women's clothing and appear in public. He had been doing this for 16 years and had been discharged from the Marine Corps for cross-dressing. Since then he had risked public disclosure on several occasions. Mr. M.'s wife had threatened to divorce him because of the cross-dressing, yet she often purchased women's clothing for him and was "compassionate" while he wore them.

Note that Mr. M. was in the Marine Corps before he joined the police force. It is not unusual for males who are strongly inclined to dress in female clothes to compensate by associating with so-called macho organizations. Nevertheless, most individuals with this disorder do not seem to display any compensatory behaviors. The same survey in Sweden mentioned earlier found 2.8% of men and 0.4% of women reported at least one episode of transvestic fetishism (Långström & Zucker, 2005).

Of note, the wives of many men who cross-dress have accepted their husbands' behavior and can be supportive if it is a private matter between them. Docter and Prince (1997) reported that 60% of more than 1,000 men with transvestic fetishism were married at the time of the survey. Some people, both married and single, join cross-dressing clubs that meet periodically or subscribe to newsletters devoted to the topic.

Sexual Sadism and Sexual Masochism

Both **sexual sadism** and **sexual masochism** are associated with either inflicting pain or humiliation (sadism) or suffering pain or humiliation (masochism) (Hucker, 2008; Yates, Hucker, & Kingston, 2008). Although Mr. M. was extremely concerned about his cross-dressing, he was also disturbed by another problem. To maximize his sexual pleasure during intercourse with his wife, he had her wear a collar and leash, tied her to the bed, and handcuffed her. He sometimes tied himself with ropes, chains, handcuffs, and wires, all while he was cross-dressed. Mr. M. was concerned he might injure himself seriously. In many such cases, something goes wrong and the individual accidentally hangs himself, an event that should be distinguished from the closely related condition called *hypoxiphilia*, which involves self-strangulation to reduce the flow of oxygen to the brain and enhance the sensation of orgasm. It may seem paradoxical that someone has to either inflict or receive pain to become sexually aroused, but these types of cases are not uncommon. On many occasions, the behaviors themselves are mild and harmless (Krueger, 2010), but they can become dangerous and costly.

DSM Disorder Criteria Summary
Sexual Sadism and Sexual Masochism

DSM-IV TR Criteria for Sexual Sadism

A. Over a period of at least 6 months, recurrent, intense sexually arousing fantasies, sexual urges, or behaviors involving acts (real, not simulated) in which the psychological or physical suffering (including humiliation) of the victim is sexually exciting to the person.

B. The person has acted on these sexual urges with a nonconsenting person, or the sexual urges or fantasies cause marked distress or interpersonal difficulty.

DSM-IV TR Criteria for Sexual Masochism

A. Over a period of at least 6 months, recurrent, intense sexually arousing fantasies, sexual urges, or behaviors involving the act (real, not simulated) of being humiliated, beaten, bound, or otherwise made to suffer.

B. The fantasies, sexual urges, or behaviors cause clinically significant distress or impairment in social, occupational, or other important areas of functioning.

Source: Reprinted with permission from *Diagnostic and Statistical Manual of Mental Disorders* (4th ed., text revision). © 2000 American Psychiatric Association.

Sadistic Rape

After murder, rape is the most devastating assault one person can make on another. It is not classified as a paraphilia because most instances of rape are better characterized as an assault by a male (or, rarely, a female) whose patterns of sexual arousal are not paraphilic. Instead, many rapists meet criteria for antisocial personality disorder (see Chapter 11) and may engage in a variety of antisocial and aggressive acts (Bradford & Meston, 2011; McCabe & Wauchope, 2005; Quinsey, 2010). Many rapes could be described as opportunistic, in that an aggressive or antisocial individual with a marked lack of empathy and disregard for inflicting pain on others (Bernat, Calhoun, & Adams, 1999) spontaneously took advantage of a vulnerable and unsuspecting woman. These unplanned assaults often occur during robberies or other criminal events. Rapes can also be motivated by anger and vindictiveness against specific women and may have been planned in advance (Hucker, 1997; Knight & Prentky, 1990; McCabe & Wauchope, 2005; Quinsey, 2010).

voyeurism Paraphilia in which sexual arousal is derived from observing unsuspecting individuals undressing or naked.

exhibitionism A sexual gratification attained by exposing genitals to unsuspecting strangers.

transvestic fetishism Paraphilia in which individuals, usually males, are sexually aroused or receive gratification by wearing clothing of the opposite sex.

sexual sadism Paraphilia in which sexual arousal is associated with inflicting pain or humiliation.

sexual masochism Paraphilia in which sexual arousal is associated with experiencing pain or humiliation.

A number of years ago we determined in our sexuality clinic that certain rapists do fit definitions of paraphilia closely and could probably better be described as sadists, a finding that has since been confirmed (McCabe & Wauchope, 2005; Quinsey, 2010). We constructed two audiotapes on which were described (1) mutually enjoyable sexual intercourse and (2) sexual intercourse involving force on the part of the male (rape). The nonrapists became sexually aroused to descriptions of mutually consenting intercourse but not to those involving force. Rapists, however, became aroused by both types of descriptions.

Pedophilia and Incest

Perhaps the most tragic sexual deviance is a sexual attraction to children (or young adolescents), called **pedophilia** (Blanchard, 2010; Seto, 2009). People around the world have become more aware of this problem following the well-publicized scandal in the Catholic Church, where priests, many of whom undoubtedly met criteria for pedophilia, abused children repeatedly, only to be transferred to another church where they would do it again. Individuals with this pattern of arousal may be attracted to male children, female children, or both. In one survey, as many as 12% of men and 17% of women reported being touched inappropriately by adults when they were children; another survey estimated that the number of sexually abused children rose 125% in the 1990s to more than 330,000 children in the United States (Fagan, Wise, Schmidt, & Berlin, 2002). Approximately 90% of abusers are male, and 10% are female (Fagan et al., 2002; Seto, 2009). Much as with adult rape, as many as 40% to 50% of sexual offenders do not have pedophilic arousal patterns and do not meet criteria for pedophilia. Rather, their offenses are associated with brutal antisocial and aggressive opportunistic acts (Blanchard, 2010; Seto, 2009). Child pornography investigations have made much news lately, and individuals convicted of downloading child pornography often defend themselves by pointing out that they were "just looking" and are not pedophiles. But now an important study indicates that being charged with a child pornography offense is one of the best diagnostic indications of pedophilia (Seto, Cantor, & Blanchard, 2006).

If the children are the person's relatives, the pedophilia takes the form of **incest**. Although pedophilia and incest have much in common, victims of pedophilia tend to be young children and victims of incest tend to be girls beginning to mature physically (Rice & Harris, 2002). Marshall, Barbaree, and Christophe (1986) and Marshall (1997) demonstrated by using penile strain gauge measures that incestuous males are, in general, more aroused by adult women than are males with pedophilia, who tend to focus exclusively on children. Thus, incestuous relations may have more to do with availability and interpersonal issues ongoing in the family than pedophilia, as in the case of Tony.

▲ Murderer Jeffrey Dahmer obtained sexual gratification from acts of sadism and cannibalism. (In prison, he was killed by fellow inmates.)

Allen Fredrickson/©Reuters/Corbis

Tony ✦ More and Less a Father

Tony, a 52-year-old married television repairman, came in depressed. About 10 years earlier he had begun sexual activity with his 12-year-old daughter. Light kissing and some fondling gradually escalated to heavy petting and, finally, mutual masturbation. When his daughter was 16 years old, his wife discovered the ongoing incestuous relationship. She separated from her husband and eventually divorced him, taking her daughter with her. Soon, Tony remarried. Just before his initial visit to our clinic, Tony visited his daughter, then 22 years old, who was living alone in a different city. They had not seen each other for 5 years. A second visit, shortly after the first, led to a recurrence of the incestuous behavior. At this point, Tony became extremely depressed and told his new wife the whole story. She contacted our clinic with his full cooperation while his daughter sought treatment in her own city.

DSM Disorder Criteria Summary
Pedophilia

A. Over a period of at least 6 months, recurrent, intense sexually arousing fantasies, sexual urges, or behaviors involving sexual activity with a prepubescent child or children (generally age 13 years or younger).

B. The person has acted on these sexual urges, or the sexual urges or fantasies cause marked distress or interpersonal difficulty.

C. The person is at least age 16 years and at least 5 years older than the child or children in Criterion A.

Source: Reprinted with permission from *Diagnostic and Statistical Manual of Mental Disorders* (4th ed., text revision). © 2000 American Psychiatric Association.

We return to the case of Tony later, but several features are worth noting. First, Tony loved his daughter and was bitterly disappointed and depressed over his behavior. Occasionally, a child molester is abusive and aggressive, sometimes killing the victims; in these cases, the disorder is often both sexual sadism and pedophilia. But most child molesters are *not* physically abusive. Rarely is a child physically forced or injured. From the molester's perspective, no harm is done because there is no physical force or threats. Child molesters often rationalize their behavior as "loving" the child or teaching the child useful lessons about sexuality. The child molester almost never considers the psychological damage the victim suffers, yet these interactions often destroy the child's trust and ability to share intimacy. Child molesters rarely gauge their power over the children, who may participate in the molestation without protest yet be frightened and unwilling. Often children feel responsible for the abuse because no outward force or threat was used by the adult, and only after the abused children grow up are they able to understand they were powerless to protect themselves and not responsible for what was done to them.

Paraphilia in Women

Estimates suggest that approximately 5% to 10% of all sexual offenders are women (Logan, 2009; Wiegel, 2008). For example, Federoff, Fishell, and Federoff (1999) have reported 12 cases of women with paraphilia seen in their clinic. One heterosexual woman was convicted of sexually molesting an unrelated 9-year-old boy while she was babysitting. It seems she had touched the boy's penis and asked him to masturbate in front of her while she watched religious programs on television. It is not unusual for individuals with paraphilia to rationalize their behavior by engaging in some other practices that they consider to be morally correct or uplifting at the same time. Yet another woman came to treatment because of her "uncontrollable" rituals of undressing in front of her apartment window and masturbating approximately five times a month. In addition she would, occasionally, drive her truck through the neighborhood, where she would attempt to befriend cats and dogs by offering them food. She would then place honey or other food substances on her genital area so that the animals would lick her. As with most people with paraphilias, the woman was horrified by this activity and was seeking treatment to eliminate it, although she found it highly sexually arousing.

Causes of Paraphilia

Although no substitute for scientific inquiry, case histories often provide hypotheses that can then be tested by controlled scientific observations. Let's return to the cases of Robert and Tony to see if their histories contain any clues.

Robert | Revenge on Repression

Robert (who sought help for exhibitionism) was raised by a stern authoritarian father and a passive mother in a small Texas town. His father, who was a firm believer in old-time religion, often preached the evils of sexual intercourse to his family. Robert learned little about sex from his father except that it

was bad, so he suppressed any emerging heterosexual urges and fantasies and as an adolescent felt uneasy around girls his own age. By accident, he discovered a private source of sexual gratification: staring at attractive and unsuspecting females through the window. This led to his first masturbatory experience.

Robert reported in retrospect that being arrested was not so bad because it disgraced his father, which was his only way of getting back at him. The courts treated him lightly (which is not unusual), and his father was publicly humiliated, forcing the family to move from their small Texas town (Barlow & Wincze, 1980).

Tony | Trained Too Young

Tony, who sought help because of an incestuous relationship with his daughter, was brought up in a reasonably loving and outwardly normal Catholic family, but he had an uncle who did not fit the family pattern. When he was 9 or 10, Tony was encouraged by his uncle to observe a game of strip poker that the uncle was playing with a neighbor's wife. During this period, he also observed his uncle fondling a waitress at a drive-in restaurant and shortly thereafter was instructed by his uncle to fondle his young female cousin. Thus, he had an early model for mutual fondling and masturbation and obtained some pleasure from interacting in this way with young girls. Although the uncle never touched Tony, his behavior was clearly abusive. When Tony was about 13, he engaged in mutual manipulation with a sister and her girlfriend, which he remembers as pleasurable. Later, when Tony was 18, a brother-in-law took him to a prostitute and he first experienced sexual intercourse. He remembered this visit as unsatisfactory because, on that and subsequent visits to prostitutes, he ejaculated prematurely—a sharp contrast to his early experience with young girls. Other experiences with adult women were also unsatisfactory. When he joined the service and was sent overseas, he sought out prostitutes who were often as young as 12.

pedophilia Paraphilia involving strong sexual attraction toward children.
incest A deviant sexual attraction (pedophilia) directed toward a family member; often the attraction of a father toward a daughter who is maturing physically.

These cases remind us that deviant patterns of sexual arousal often occur in the context of other sexual and social problems. Undesired kinds of arousal may be associated with deficiencies in levels of "desired" arousal with consensual adults; this was certainly true for both Tony and Robert, whose sexual relationships with adults were incomplete. In many cases, an inability to develop adequate social relations with the appropriate people for sexual relationships seems to be associated with a developing of inappropriate sexual outlets (Barlow & Wincze, 1980; Marshall, 1997). Indeed, integrated theories of the causes of paraphilias all note the presence of disordered relationships during childhood and adolescence with resulting deficits in healthy sexual development (Marshall & Barbaree, 1990; Ward & Beech, 2008). However, many people with deficient sexual and social skills do not develop deviant patterns of arousal.

Early experience seems to have an effect that may be accidental. Tony's early sexual experiences just happened to be of the type he later found sexually arousing. Many pedophiles also report being abused themselves as children, which turns out to be a strong predictor of later sexual abuse by the victim (Fagan et al., 2002). Robert's first erotic experience occurred while he was "peeping." But many of us do not find our early experiences reflected in our sexual patterns.

Another factor may be the nature of the person's early sexual fantasies. For example, Rachman and Hodgson (1968; see also Bancroft, 1989) demonstrated that sexual arousal could become associated with a neutral object—a boot, for example—if the boot was repeatedly presented while the individual was sexually aroused. One of the most powerful engines for developing unwanted arousal may be early sexual fantasies that are repeatedly reinforced through the strong sexual pleasure associated with masturbation (Bradford & Meston, 2011). Before a pedophile or sadist ever acts on his behavior, he may fantasize about it thousands of times while masturbating. Expressed as a clinical or operant-conditioning paradigm, this is another example of a learning process in which a behavior (sexual arousal to a specific object or activity) is repeatedly reinforced through association with a pleasurable consequence (orgasm). This mechanism may explain why paraphilias are almost exclusively male disorders. The basic differences in frequency of masturbation between men and women that exist across cultures may contribute to the differential development of paraphilias. However, if early experiences contribute strongly to later sexual arousal patterns, then what about the Sambia males who practice exclusive homosexual behavior during childhood and early adolescence and yet are exclusively heterosexual as adults? In such cohesive societies, the social demands or "scripts" for sexual interactions are stronger and more rigid than in our culture and thus may override the effects of early experiences (Baldwin & Baldwin, 1989).

In addition, therapists and sex researchers who work with paraphilics have observed what seems to be an incredibly strong sex drive. It is not uncommon for some paraphilics to masturbate three or four times a day. In one case seen in our clinic, a sadistic rapist masturbated approximately every half hour all day long, just as often as it was physiologically possible. We have speculated elsewhere that activity this consuming may be related to the obsessional processes of obsessive-compulsive disorder (Barlow, 2002). In both instances, the very act of trying to suppress unwanted, emotionally charged thoughts and fantasies seems to have the paradoxical effect of *increasing* their frequency and intensity (see Chapter 4). This process is also ongoing in people with eating disorders and addictions, when attempts to restrict strong addictive cravings lead to uncontrollable increases in the undesired behaviors.

Psychopathologists are also becoming interested in the phenomenon of weak inhibitory control across these paraphilic disorders, which may indicate a weak biologically based behavioral inhibition system (BIS) in the brain (Fowles, 1993; Kafka, 1997; Ward & Beech, 2008) that might repress serotonergic functioning. The model shown in ■ Figure 9.5 incorporates the factors thought to contribute to the development of paraphilia. Nevertheless, all speculations, including the hypotheses we have described, have little scientific support at this time. For example, this model does not include the biological dimension. Excess arousal in paraphilics could be biologically based. Before we can make any steadfast conclusions here, more research is needed.

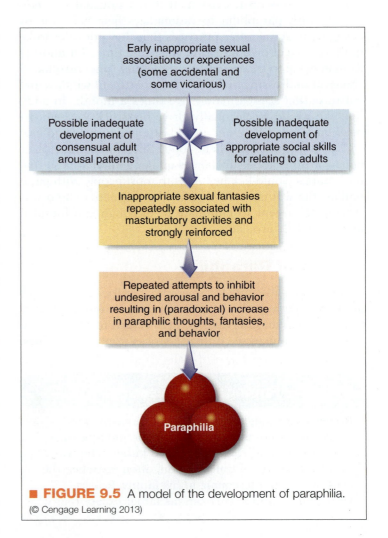

■ **FIGURE 9.5** A model of the development of paraphilia.
(© Cengage Learning 2013)

> What psychosocial and drug treatments are available for paraphilias, and how effective are they?

In recent years, researchers have developed sophisticated methods for assessing specific patterns of sexual arousal (Maletzky, 1998; Wincze, 2009). This development is important in studying paraphilia because sometimes even the individual presenting with the problem is not fully aware of what caused arousal.

Using the model of paraphilia described previously, we assess each patient not only for the presence of deviant arousal, but also for levels of appropriate arousal to adults, for social skills, and for the ability to form relationships. Tony had no problems with social skills: He was 52 years old, reasonably happily married, and generally compatible with his second wife. His major difficulty was his continuing strong, incestuous attraction to his daughter. Nevertheless, he loved his daughter and wished strongly to interact in a normal fatherly way with her.

Psychological Treatment

A number of treatment procedures are available for decreasing unwanted arousal. Most are behavior therapy procedures directed at changing the associations and context from arousing and pleasurable to neutral. One procedure, carried out entirely in the imagination of the patient, called **covert sensitization**, was first described by Joseph Cautela (1967; see also Barlow, 1993). In this treatment, patients associate sexually arousing images in their imagination with some reasons why the behavior is harmful or dangerous. Before treatment, the patient knows about these reasons, but the immediate pleasure and strong reinforcement the sexual activity provides is enough to overcome any thoughts of possible harm or danger that might arise in the future.

In imagination, harmful or dangerous consequences can be associated directly with the unwanted behavior and arousal in a powerful and emotionally meaningful way. One of the most powerful negative aspects of Tony's behavior was his embarrassment over the thought of being discovered by his current wife; other family members; or, most important, the family priest. Therefore, he was guided through the fantasy described here.

Tony ❘ Imagining the Worst

You are alone with your daughter in your trailer. You realize that you want to caress her breasts. So you put your arm around her, slip your hand inside her blouse, and begin to caress her breasts. Unexpectedly the door to the trailer opens and in walks your wife with Father X. Your daughter immediately jumps up and runs out the door. Your wife follows her. You are left alone with Father X. He is looking at you as if waiting for an explanation of what he has just seen. Seconds pass, but they seem like hours. You know what Father X must be thinking as he stands there staring at you. You are embarrassed and want to say something, but you can't seem to find the right words. You realize that Father X can no longer respect you as he once did. Father X finally says, "I don't understand this; this is not like you." You both begin to cry. You realize that you may have lost the love and respect of both Father X and your wife, who are important to you. Father X asks, "Do you realize what this has done to your daughter?" You think about this and you hear your daughter crying; she is hysterical. You want to run, but you can't. You are miserable and disgusted with yourself. You don't know if you will ever regain the love and respect of your wife and Father X.

(Reproduced, with permission of the authors and publisher, from Harbert, T. L., Barlow, D. H., Hersen, M., & Austin, J. B., 1974. Measurement and modification of incestuous behavior: A case study. *Psychological Reports, 34*, 79–86, © 1974 Psychological Reports.)

During six or eight sessions, the therapist narrates such scenes dramatically, and the patient is then instructed to imagine them daily until all arousal disappears. The results of Tony's treatment are presented in Figure 9.6. "Card-sort scores" are a measure of how much Tony wanted sexual interactions with his daughter in comparison with his wish for nonsexual fatherly interactions. His incestuous arousal was largely eliminated after 3 to 4 weeks, but the treatment did not affect his desire to interact with his daughter in a healthier manner. These results were confirmed by psychophysiological measurement of his arousal response. A return of some arousal at a 3-month follow-up prompted us to ask Tony if anything unusual was happening in his life. He confessed that his marriage had taken a turn for the worse and sexual relations with his wife had all but ceased. A period of marital therapy restored the therapeutic gains (see ■ Figure 9.6). Several years later, after his daughter's

covert sensitization A cognitive–behavioral intervention to reduce unwanted behaviors by having clients imagine the extremely aversive consequences of the behaviors and establish negative rather than positive associations with them.

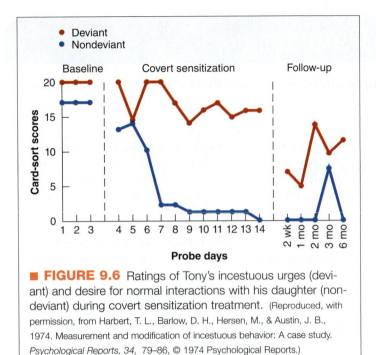

■ **FIGURE 9.6** Ratings of Tony's incestuous urges (deviant) and desire for normal interactions with his daughter (nondeviant) during covert sensitization treatment. (Reproduced, with permission, from Harbert, T. L., Barlow, D. H., Hersen, M., & Austin, J. B., 1974. Measurement and modification of incestuous behavior: A case study. *Psychological Reports, 34,* 79–86, © 1974 Psychological Reports.)

therapist decided she was ready, she and Tony resumed a nonsexual relationship, which they both wanted.

Two major areas in Tony's life needed treatment: deviant (incestuous) sexual arousal and marital problems. Most individuals with paraphilic arousal patterns need a great deal of attention to family functioning or other interpersonal systems in which they operate (Barbaree & Seto, 1997; Fagan et al., 2002; Rice & Harris, 2002). In addition, many require intervention to help strengthen appropriate patterns of arousal. In **orgasmic reconditioning**, patients are instructed to masturbate to their usual fantasies but to substitute more socially acceptable ones just before ejaculation. With repeated practice, patients should be able to begin the desired fantasy earlier in the masturbatory process and still retain their arousal. This technique, first described by Gerald Davison (1968), has been used with some success in a variety of settings (Brownell et al., 1977; Maletzky, 2002). Finally, as with most strongly pleasurable but undesirable behaviors (including addiction), care must be taken to provide the patient with coping skills to prevent slips or relapses. *Relapse prevention* treatment created for addictions (Laws, 1989; Laws & O'Donohue, 1997) does just that. Patients are taught to recognize the early signs of temptation and to institute a variety of self-control procedures before their urges become too strong.

Evidence on the effects of psychological treatments for sexual offenders is decidedly mixed at this time. For sexual offenders who have come into contact with the legal system, including those who are incarcerated (obviously a very severe group), the results are modest at best in terms of preventing later occurrences of offending (termed recidivism). Reviews of large numbers of studies with these populations are hampered because of the substantially different methods and procedures in accessing recidivism

rates. But several large surveys following up sexual offenders for a period of 4 to 5 years indicate reductions in sexual recidivism (that is, reoffending) of up to 11% to 20% over what would be expected with the usual and customary treatment, with cognitive-behavioral programs proving to be the most effective in reducing recidivism (Hanson et al., 2002; Lösel & Schmucker, 2005). However, a large study from the state of California with participants who were incarcerated for their sexual offense showed very little effect of any intervention in rates of sexual or violent offending over an 8-year follow-up period after these individuals were released (Marques, Wederanders, Day, Nelson, & van Ommeren, 2005).

For outpatients, however, there is at least some evidence for success when treatment is carried out by an experienced professional. For example, Barry Maletzky, a psychiatrist at the University of Oregon Medical School, and his staff reported on the treatment of more than 8,000 sexual offenders of numerous types over 20 years (Maletzky, 2002). A variety of procedures were used in a program of 3 to 4 months in a clinic devoted exclusively to this type of treatment. What makes the report notable is that Maletzky collected objective physiological outcome measures using the penile strain gauge described earlier with almost every participant in the program, in addition to patients' reports of progress. In many cases, he also obtained corroborating information from families and legal authorities.

In his follow-up of these patients, Maletzky defined a treatment as successful when someone had (1) completed all treatment sessions, (2) demonstrated no deviant sexual arousal on objective physiological testing at any annual follow-up testing session, (3) reported no deviant arousal or behavior at any time since treatment ended, and (4) had no legal record of any charges of deviant sexual activity, even if unsubstantiated. He defined as a treatment failure anyone who was not a success. Any offender who did not complete treatment for any reason was counted as a failure, even though some may have benefited from the partial treatment and gone on to recover. Using this criteria, from 75% to 95% of individuals, depending on the type of sexual offense (such as pedophilia, rape, or voyeurism), had a successful outcome. However, Maletzky's results were not derived from a scientifically controlled clinical trial.

Men who rape had the lowest success rate among all offenders with a single diagnosis (75%) and individuals with multiple paraphilias had the lowest success rate of any group. Maletzky also examined factors associated with failure. Among the strongest predictors were a history of unstable social relationships, an unstable employment history, strong denial the problem exists, a history of multiple victims, and a situation in which the offender continues to live with a victim (as might be typical in cases of incest). Many of these problems characterize the presumably more severe incarcerated population mentioned above.

Nevertheless, other groups using similar treatment procedures have achieved comparable success rates (Abel, 1989; Becker, 1990; Fagan et al., 2002; Pithers, Martin, & Cumming, 1989). Therapist knowledge and expertise seems to be important in successfully carrying out these treatments to prevent future sexual offenses among patients.

Drug Treatments

The most popular drug used to treat paraphilics is an antiandrogen called *cyproterone acetate* (Bradford, 1997; Seto, 2009). This "chemical castration" drug eliminates sexual desire and fantasy by reducing testosterone levels dramatically, but fantasies and arousal return as soon as the drug is removed. A second drug is *medroxyprogesterone* (Depo-Provera is the injectable form), a hormonal agent that reduces testosterone (Fagan et al., 2002). These drugs may be useful for dangerous sexual offenders who do not respond to alternative treatments or to temporarily suppress sexual arousal in patients who require it, but it is not always successful.

Summary

Based on evidence from a number of settings, evidence for the psychosocial treatment of paraphilia is mixed, with more success reported in outpatient settings with presumably less severe, more stable patients. But most results are uncontrolled observations from a small number of clinical research centers, and results may not be as good in other clinics and offices. In any case, as with treatment for sexual dysfunctions, psychosocial approaches to paraphilia are not readily available outside of specialized treatment centers. In the meantime, the outlook for most individuals with these disorders is bleak because paraphilias run a chronic course and recurrence is common.

Concept Check 9.4

Check your understanding of sexual paraphilias by matching the scenarios with the correct label: (a) exhibitionism, (b) voyeurism, (c) fetishism, or (d) sexual masochism.

1. Mae enjoys being slapped with leather whips during foreplay. Without such stimulation, she is unable to achieve orgasm during sex. _____

2. Kai has a collection of women's panties that arouse him. He loves to look at, collect, and wear them. _____

3. Sam finds arousal in walking up to strangers in the park and showing them his genitals. _____

4. Peeping Tom loves to look through Susie's bedroom window and watch her undress. He gets extremely excited as she disrobes. He is practicing _____.

5. What Peeping Tom does not realize is that Susie knows that he is watching. She is aroused by slowly undressing while others are watching, and she fantasizes about what they are thinking. Susie's behavior is called _____.

6. What Peeping Tom will be shocked to find out is that "Susie" is actually Scott, a man who can become aroused only if he wears feminine clothing. Scott's behavior is _____.

orgasmic reconditioning The learning procedure to help clients strengthen appropriate patterns of sexual arousal by pairing appropriate stimuli with the pleasurable sensations of masturbation.

On the Spectrum
Gender Nonconformity in Children and Gender Variation in Adults

Earlier in this chapter, we discussed the findings on what is now called gender nonconformity in children and noted that long-term prospective follow-up studies indicate a complex relationship between gender nonconformity as a child and the development of gender identity, sexual orientation, or both as an adult. Briefly, findings indicate that a higher proportion of gender-nonconforming children develop a homosexual orientation as adults compared to those who are gender conforming. But most individuals with homosexual orientations as adults conform to their biological sex as children (boys act like boys and girls act like girls). It is also

clear that a small minority of gender-nonconforming children are expressing a gender identity disorder in which their gender is different from their biological sex. These children will consistently identify with the opposite sex, thereby meeting diagnostic criteria for gender identity disorder in adulthood. We also reviewed research by Fausto-Sterling (2000b)—on intersexed individuals who may have some physical characteristics of the opposite sex—who surmises that both physical sex and gender identity may occur on a continuum.

A question under debate is whether to refer gender-nonconforming children for interventions early on that would bring their

behavior and interests more into line with their biological sex. On the one hand, some segments of society, particularly in more traditionally tolerant areas of the country such as San Francisco and New York, are becoming more open to gender variations in both children and adults. In 2006, New York City decided to let people alter the sex listed on their birth certificates, which is certainly helpful to intersexed individuals who decide to live as the gender consistent with their current identity but not the identity assigned at birth. In some schools, children are being allowed and even encouraged to dress and appear in gender-nonconforming ways on the assumption that this gives freer rein to who they "really are" (Brown, 2006). However, Skidmore and colleagues (2006) examined whether gender nonconformity was related to psychological distress in a community-based sample of gay men and lesbians. Gender nonconformity was measured by self-reports of childhood gender nonconformity and ratings of current behavior. The researchers found that gender nonconformity was related to psychological distress (depression, anxiety) but only for gay men and not for lesbians.

Although only a minority of gay men report gender nonconformity as boys, research indicates that many of these gender-nonconforming boys defeminize as they reach adulthood, probably because of persistent social pressure from their family and peers. Also, interventions exist to alter gender-nonconforming behavior in young children to avoid the ostracism and scorn these children encounter in most school settings (Rekers, Kilgus, & Rosen, 1990).

Thus, society is faced with a dilemma that requires more research. Should the free expression of gender nonconformity be encouraged knowing that, in most parts of the world, gender nonconformity will make for difficult social adaptation leading to substantial psychological distress for decades to come? Or will psychological adjustment be more positive if gender nonconformity is allowed and facilitated? And for intersexed individuals, rather than surgery to make individuals more physically consistent with one sex or the other, should society encourage expression along a dimension ranging from male to female, and will that be "healthier" for these individuals? If research confirms that adjustment is more positive if individuals find their own place on a gender continuum, then large-scale campaigns to alter social norms may occur along the lines of the successful campaigns of the last several decades for gay

rights, after a consensus developed in the 1990s that homosexuality was not a disorder. Research will continue on this important and interesting topic.

JIM WILSON/The New York Times/Redux Pictures

Summary

What Is Normal Sexuality?

How do sociocultural factors influence what are considered "normal" sexual behaviors?

> Patterns of sexual behavior, both heterosexual and homosexual, vary around the world in terms of both behavior and risks. Approximately 20% of individuals who have been surveyed engage in sex with numerous partners, which puts them at risk for sexually transmitted diseases such as AIDS. Recent surveys also suggest that as many as 60% of American college females practice unsafe sex by not using condoms.

> Three types of disorders are associated with sexual functioning and gender identity: gender identity disorder, sexual dysfunctions, and paraphilias.

Gender Identity Disorder

What are the defining clinical features, causes, and treatments of gender identity disorder?

> Gender identify disorder is a dissatisfaction with one's biological sex and the sense that one is really the opposite gender (for example, a woman trapped in a man's body). A person develops gender identity between 18 months and 3 years of age, and it seems that both

appropriate gender identity and mistaken gender identity have biological roots influenced by learning.

> Treatment for adults may include sex reassignment surgery integrated with psychological approaches.

Overview of Sexual Dysfunctions

How do psychologists define sexual dysfunction?

> Sexual dysfunction includes a variety of disorders in which people find it difficult to function adequately during sexual relations.

How is sexual dysfunction related to the sexual response cycle?

> Specific sexual dysfunctions include disorders of sexual desire (hypoactive sexual desire disorder and sexual aversion disorder) in which interest in sexual relations is extremely low or nonexistent; disorders of sexual arousal (male erectile disorder and female sexual arousal disorder) in which achieving or maintaining adequate penile erection or vaginal lubrication is problematic; and orgasmic disorders (female orgasmic disorder and male orgasmic disorder) in which orgasm occurs too quickly or not at all. The most common disorder in this

category is premature ejaculation, which occurs in males; inhibited orgasm is commonly seen in females.

> Sexual pain disorders, in which unbearable pain is associated with sexual relations, include dyspareunia and vaginismus.

> The three components of assessment are interviews, a complete medical evaluation, and psychophysiological assessment.

Causes and Treatment of Sexual Dysfunction

What are the defining features and known causes of sexual dysfunction?

> Sexual dysfunction is associated with socially transmitted negative attitudes about sex, current relationship difficulties, and anxiety focused on sexual activity.

What psychosocial and medical treatments are available, and are they effective?

> Psychosocial treatment of sexual dysfunctions is generally successful but not readily available. In recent years, various medical approaches have become available, including the drug Viagra. These treatments focus mostly on male erectile dysfunction and are promising.

Paraphilia: Clinical Descriptions

What are the clinical features of the major paraphilias?

> Paraphilia is sexual attraction to inappropriate people, such as children, or to inappropriate objects, such as articles of clothing.

> The paraphilias include fetishism, in which sexual arousal occurs almost exclusively in the context of inappropriate objects or individuals; exhibitionism, in which sexual gratification is attained by exposing one's genitals to unsuspecting strangers; voyeurism, in which sexual arousal is derived from observing unsuspecting individuals undressing or naked; transvestic fetishism, in which individuals are sexually aroused by wearing clothing of the opposite sex; sexual sadism, in which sexual arousal is associated with inflicting pain or humiliation; sexual masochism, in which sexual arousal is associated with experiencing pain or humiliation; and pedophilia, in which there is a strong sexual attraction toward children. Incest is a type of pedophilia in which the victim is related, often a son or daughter.

What is known about the causes of paraphilias?

> The development of paraphilia is associated with deficiencies in consensual adult sexual arousal, deficiencies in consensual adult social skills, deviant sexual fantasies that may develop before or during puberty, and attempts by the individual to suppress thoughts associated with these arousal patterns.

Assessing and Treating Paraphilia

What psychosocial and drug treatments are available for paraphilias, and how effective are they?

> Psychosocial treatments of paraphilia are only modestly effective at best among individuals who are incarcerated, but they are somewhat more successful in less severe outpatients.

Key Terms

Answers to Concept Checks

9.1

1. More men masturbate and do it more often, men are more permissive about casual sex, women want more intimacy from sex, and so on.
2. Both heterosexuality and homosexuality are normal; genetics appear to play some role in the development of sexual preference.
3. Gender identity disorder

4. Abnormal hormone levels during development, social or parental influences
5. Sex reassignment surgery, psychosocial treatment to adjust to either gender

9.2

1. c; 2. a; 3. b; 4. c; 5. a

9.3

1. T; 2. F (sometimes increases arousal); 3. T; 4. T; 5. F (nondemand pleasuring, squeeze technique, and so on); 6. T

9.4

1. d; 2. c; 3. a; 4. b; 5. a; 6. c

Media Resources

Log in to CengageBrain to access the resources your instructor requires. For this book, you can access:

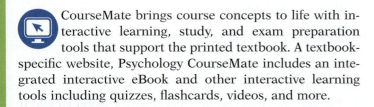 CourseMate brings course concepts to life with interactive learning, study, and exam preparation tools that support the printed textbook. A textbook-specific website, Psychology CourseMate includes an integrated interactive eBook and other interactive learning tools including quizzes, flashcards, videos, and more.

Abnormal Psychology Videos

> *Clark, a Man with Erectile Dysfunction:* This illustrates a complicated case in which depression, physical symptoms, and cultural expectations all seem to play a role in Clark's problem.
> *Jessica, Changing Over:* Jessica discusses her life as a transsexual, both before and after her sex reassignment surgery.

CENGAGENOW CengageNow is an easy-to-use online resource that helps you study in less time to get the grade you want—NOW. Take a pre-test for this chapter and receive a personalized study plan based on your results that will identify the topics you need to review and direct you to online resources to help you master those topics. Then take a post-test to help you determine the concepts you have mastered and what you will need to work on. If your textbook does not include an access code card, go to CengageBrain.com to gain access.

Visit www.cengagebrain.com to access your account and purchase materials.

 aplia If your professor has assigned Aplia homework:

1. Sign in to your account.
2. Complete the corresponding homework exercises as required by your professor.
3. When finished, click "Grade It Now" to see which areas you have mastered, which need more work, and for detailed explanations of every answer.

Video Concept Reviews

CengageNOW also contains Mark Durand's *Video Concept Reviews* on these challenging topics.

> Normal versus Abnormal Sexual Behavior
> Sexual Orientation
> Sexual and Gender Identity Disorders
> Gender Identity Disorders
> Concept Check: Gender Identity Disorder, Transvestic Fetishism, and Transgendered
> Sexual Reassignment Surgery
> Human Sexual Response Cycle
> Hypoactive Sexual Desire Disorder
> Sexual Aversion Disorder
> Male Erectile Disorder and Female Sexual Arousal Disorder
> Inhibited Orgasm
> Premature Ejaculation
> Sexual Pain Disorders (Dyspareunia)
> Vaginismus
> Paraphilias

Chapter Quiz

1. Statistics about sexual activity have suggested that:
   a. more people engage in oral intercourse than vaginal intercourse
   b. the majority of people engage in heterosexual, vaginal intercourse in the context of a relationship with one partner
   c. 10% to 15% of the population has exclusively homosexual sex
   d. in the 1990s, people were more likely to be having sex with multiple partners than they were to be in a monogamous sexual relationship

2. Research evidence on the origins of homosexuality has suggested a possible role for all of the following EXCEPT:
   a. genetic or chromosomal influences
   b. emotionally distant fathers
   c. size or function of brain structures
   d. exposure to hormones

3. The most common form of treatment for gender identity disorder is:
   a. exposure therapy
   b. antidepressant medication
   c. cognitive–behavioral therapy
   d. sexual reassignment surgery

4. In which phase of the sexual response cycle can men experience difficulty attaining or maintaining erections?
   a. resolution
   b. orgasm
   c. arousal
   d. plateau

5. Simone and her partner have sexual intercourse about once a month. Simone says she wants to have sex but can't seem to achieve adequate lubrication to make sex enjoyable. Simone's symptoms are most consistent with:
   a. impotence
   b. sexual aversion disorder
   c. sexual arousal disorder
   d. vaginismus

6. Which component is essential to the diagnosis of female orgasmic disorder?
   a. orgasms occur less frequently than desired
   b. a 20% to 30% reduction in the frequency of orgasms in the last 6 months
   c. a 70% to 80% reduction in the frequency of orgasms in the last year
   d. orgasm never or almost never occurs

7. The overarching goal of Masters and Johnson's psychosocial treatment for sexual dysfunction was:
   a. reducing or eliminating psychologically based performance anxiety
   b. helping couples to increase the frequency of their sexual encounters to normalize sexual experiences
   c. encouraging couples to be more willing to try medical treatments, despite their potential side effects
   d. helping both individuals in a couple to understand past parental influences on contemporary sexual relations within the couple

8. A disorder in which an inappropriate, inanimate object is the source of sexual arousal is known as a:
   a. parapathology   c. paraphilia
   b. paranormality   d. paraphasia

9. Which of the following statements is an accurate characterization of pedophilia?
   a. It involves an attraction to male children more often than female children.
   b. It is most commonly directed at girls who are beginning to mature physically.
   c. It is often rationalized by the perpetrator as an acceptable way to teach children about sexuality.
   d. It involves the use of physical force to get a child to perform sexual acts.

10. Shane is being treated for a paraphilia by imagining harmful consequences occurring in response to his unwanted behavior and arousal. Shane is receiving what kind of treatment?
    a. covert sensitization
    b. marital therapy
    c. relapse prevention
    d. orgasmic reconditioning
    (See Appendix A for answers.)

Exploring Sexual and Gender Identity Disorders

> Sexual behavior is considered normal in our culture unless it is associated with one of three kinds of impaired functioning—gender identity disorder, sexual dysfunction, or paraphilia.

> Sexual orientation probably has a strong biological basis that is influenced by environmental and social factors.

GENDER IDENTITY DISORDERS

Present when a person feels trapped in a body that is the "wrong" sex, that does not match his or her innate sense of personal identity. (Gender identity is independent of sexual arousal patterns.) Relatively rare.

Causes

Biological Influences

- Not yet confirmed, although likely to involve prenatal exposure to hormones
  - Hormonal variations may be natural or result from medication

Psychological Influences

- Gender identity develops between 1½ and 3 years of age
  - "Masculine" behaviors in girls and "feminine" behaviors in boys evoke different responses in different families

©Thinkstock/Getty Images

Treatment

- Sex reassignment surgery: removal of breasts or penis; genital reconstruction
  - Requires rigorous psychological preparation and financial and social stability
- Psychosocial intervention to change gender identity
  - Usually unsuccessful except as temporary relief until surgery

PARAPHILIAS

Sexual arousal occurs almost exclusively in the context of inappropriate objects or individuals.

Types

- *Fetishism:* Sexual attraction to nonliving objects
- *Voyeurism:* Sexual arousal achieved by viewing unsuspecting person undressing or naked
- *Exhibitionism:* Sexual gratification from exposing one's genitals to unsuspecting strangers
- *Transvestite fetishism:* Sexual arousal from wearing opposite-sex clothing (cross-dressing)
- *Sexual sadism:* Sexual arousal associated with inflicting pain or humiliation
- *Sexual masochism:* Sexual arousal associated with experiencing pain or humiliation
- *Pedophilia:* Strong sexual attraction to children
- *Incest:* Sexual attraction to family member

Causes

- Preexisting deficiencies
  - In levels of arousal with consensual adults
  - In consensual adult social skills
- Treatment received from adults during childhood
- Early sexual fantasies reinforced by masturbation
- Extremely strong sex drive combined with uncontrollable thought processes

Treatment

- *Covert sensitization:* Repeated mental reviewing of aversive consequences to establish negative associations with behavior
- *Relapse prevention:* Therapeutic preparation for coping with future situations
- *Orgasmic reconditioning:* Pairing appropriate stimuli with masturbation to create positive arousal patterns
- *Medical:* Drugs that reduce testosterone to suppress sexual desire; fantasies and arousal return when drugs are stopped

©PhotoDisc/Getty Images

©Thinkstock/Getty Images

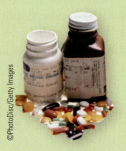
©PhotoDisc/Getty Images

SEXUAL DYSFUNCTIONS

Sexual dysfunctions can be
- *Lifelong:* Present during entire sexual history
- *Acquired:* Interrupts normal sexual pattern
- *Generalized:* Present in every encounter
- *Situational:* Present only with certain partners or at certain times

The Human Sexual Response Cycle
A dysfunction is an impairment in one of the sexual response stages.

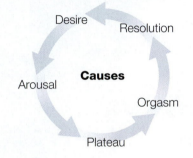

Desire
Resolution
Causes
Arousal
Orgasm
Plateau

Types of Sexual Dysfunctions

Sexual Desire Disorders
- *Hypoactive sexual desire disorder:* Apparent lack of interest in sexual activity or fantasy
- *Sexual aversion disorder:* Extreme persistent dislike of sexual contact

Sexual Arousal Disorders
- *Male erectile disorder:* Recurring inability to achieve or maintain adequate erection
- *Female sexual arousal disorder:* Recurring inability to achieve or maintain adequate lubrication

Orgasm Disorders
- *Inhibited orgasm:* Inability to achieve orgasm despite adequate desire and arousal
- *Premature ejaculation:* Ejaculation before it is desired, with minimal stimulation

Sexual Pain Disorders
- *Dyspareunia:* Marked pain associated with intercourse for which there is no medical cause; occurs in males and females
- *Vaginismus:* Involuntary muscle spasms in the front of the vagina that prevent or interfere with intercourse

Psychological Contributions
- Distraction
- Underestimates of arousal
- Negative thought processes

Psychological and Physical Interactions
- A combination of influences is almost always present
  - Specific biological predisposition *and* psychological factors may produce a particular disorder

Causes

Sociocultural Contributions
- Erotophobia, caused by formative experiences of sexual cues as alarming
- Negative experiences, such as rape
- Deterioration of relationship

Biological Contributions
- Neurological or other nervous system problems
- Vascular disease
- Chronic illness
- Prescription medication
- Drugs of abuse, including alcohol

Treatment

- *Psychosocial:* Therapeutic program to facilitate communication, improve sexual education, and eliminate anxiety. Both partners participate fully.
- *Medical:* Almost all interventions focus on male erectile disorder, including drugs, prostheses, and surgery. Medical treatment is combined with sexual education and therapy to achieve maximum benefit.

Romilly Lockyer/Brand X Pictures/
PictureQuest/JupiterImages

Substance-Related and Impulse-Control Disorders

Demonstrate knowledge and understanding representing appropriate breadth and depth in selected content areas of psychology.	› Biological bases of behavior and mental processes, including physiology, sensation, perception, comparative, motivation, and emotion (APA SLO 1.2.a (3)) *(see textbook pages 375–379, 391–395, 398–399)*
Use the concepts, language, and major theories of the discipline to account for psychological phenomena.	› Describe behavior and mental processes empirically, including operational definitions (APA SLO 1.3.a) *(see textbook pages 372–392, 403–405)*
Identify appropriate applications of psychology in solving problems, such as:	› Origin and treatment of abnormal behavior (APA SLO 4.2.b) *(see textbook pages 392–403)*

*Portions of this chapter cover learning outcomes suggested by the American Psychological Association (2007) in their guidelines for the undergraduate psychology major. Chapter coverage of these outcomes is identified by APA Goal and APA Suggested Learning Outcome (SLO).

In this chapter, we explore **substance-related disorders**, which are associated with the abuse of drugs such as alcohol, cocaine, and heroin and with a variety of other substances people take to alter the way they think, feel, and behave. These disorders represent a problem that has cursed us for centuries and continues to affect how we live, work, and play.

Equally disruptive to the people affected, **impulse-control disorders** represent a number of related problems that involve the inability to resist acting on a drive or temptation. Included in this group are those who cannot resist aggressive impulses or the impulse to steal, to set fires, to gamble, or to pull out their own hair. Controversy surrounds both substance-related and impulse-control disorders because our society sometimes believes that these problems result simply from a lack of "will." If you wanted to stop drinking, using cocaine, or gambling, well, you would just stop. We first examine those individuals who are being harmed by their use of a variety of chemical substances (substance-related disorders) and then turn our attention to the puzzling array of disorders that are under the heading of impulse-control disorders.

Perspectives on Substance-Related Disorders

› **What are substance-related disorders?**

The cost in lives, money, and emotional turmoil has made the issue of drug abuse a major concern worldwide. Currently, more than 8% of the general population is believed to use illegal drugs (Substance Abuse and Mental Health Services Administration, 2009). Many U.S. presidential administrations have declared various "wars on drugs," but the problem remains. The Roman Catholic Church issued a universal catechism in 1992 that officially declared drug abuse and drunk driving to be sins (Riding, 1992). Yet from the drug-related deaths of rock stars Jimi Hendrix and Janis Joplin in 1970 to contemporary celebrities such as Michael Jackson and Heath Ledger, drug use continues to negatively affect the lives of many.

Consider the case of Danny, who has the disturbing but common habit of **polysubstance use**, using multiple substances.

Danny ∤ Multiple Dependencies

At the age of 43, Danny was in jail, awaiting trial on vehicular manslaughter charges stemming from a DWI accident that left one woman dead. Danny grew up in the suburban United States, the youngest of three children. He was well liked in school and an average student. Like many of his friends, he smoked cigarettes in his early teens and drank beer with his friends at night behind his high school. Unlike most of his friends, however, Danny almost always drank until he was obviously drunk; he also experimented with many other drugs, including cocaine, heroin, "speed" (amphetamines), and "downers" (barbiturates).

substance-related disorder One of a range of problems associated with the use and abuse of drugs such as alcohol, cocaine, heroin, and other substances people use to alter the way they think, feel, and behave. These are extremely costly in human and financial terms.
impulse-control disorders A disorder in which a person acts on an irresistible, but potentially harmful, impulse.
polysubstance use The use of multiple mind- and behavior-altering substances, such as drugs.

pidjoe/Vetta/Getty Images

After high school, Danny attended a local community college for one semester, but he dropped out after failing most of his courses. His dismal performance in school seemed to be related to his missing most classes rather than to an inability to learn and understand the material. He had difficulty getting up for classes after partying most of the night, which he did with increasing frequency. His moods were highly variable, and he was often unpleasant. Danny's family knew he occasionally drank too much, but they didn't know (or didn't want to know) about his other drug use. He had for years forbidden anyone to go into his room after his mother found little packets of white powder (probably cocaine) in his sock drawer. He said he was keeping them for a friend and that he would return them immediately. He was furious that his family might suspect him of using drugs. Money was sometimes missing from the house, and once some stereo equipment "disappeared," but if his family members suspected Danny, they never admitted it.

Danny held a series of low-paying jobs, and when he was working his family reassured themselves that he was back on track and things would be fine. Unfortunately, he rarely held a job for more than a few months. Because he continued to live at home, Danny could survive despite frequent periods of unemployment. When he was in his late 20s, Danny seemed to have a personal revelation. He announced that he needed help and planned to check into an alcohol rehabilitation center; he still would not admit to using other drugs. His family's joy and relief were overwhelming, and no one questioned his request for several thousand dollars to help pay for the private program he said he wanted to attend. Danny disappeared for several weeks, presumably because he was in the rehabilitation program. However, a call from the local police station put an end to this fantasy: Danny had been found high and living in an abandoned building. Danny's deceptiveness and financial irresponsibility greatly strained his relationship with his family. He was allowed to continue living at home, but his parents and siblings excluded him from their emotional lives. Danny seemed to straighten out, and he held a job at a gas station for almost 2 years. He became friendly with the station owner and his son, and he often went hunting with them during the season. However, without any obvious warning, Danny resumed drinking and using drugs and was arrested for robbing the very place that had kept him employed for many months.

Why did Danny become dependent on drugs when many of his friends and siblings did not? Why did he steal from his family and friends? What ultimately became of him? We return to Danny's frustrating story later when we look at the causes and treatment of substance-related disorders.

▲ Model Kate Moss was photographed in 2005 preparing and snorting cocaine. There is an increasing concern that celebrity use of illegal drugs glamorizes their use without showing their negative effects.

Levels of Involvement

Although each drug described in this chapter has unique effects, there are similarities in the ways they are used and how people who abuse them are treated. We first survey some concepts that apply to substance-related disorders in general.

Can you use drugs and not abuse them? Can you abuse drugs and not become addicted to them? To answer these important questions, we first need to outline what we mean by *substance use, substance intoxication, substance abuse,* and *dependence.* The term *substance* refers to chemical compounds that are ingested to alter mood or behavior. Although you might first think of drugs such as cocaine and heroin, this definition also includes more commonplace legal drugs such as alcohol, the nicotine found in tobacco, and the caffeine in coffee, soft drinks, and chocolate. As you will see, these so-called safe drugs also affect mood and behavior, they can be addictive, and they account for more health problems and a greater mortality rate than all illegal drugs combined. To understand substance-related disorders, we must first know what it means to ingest **psychoactive substances**—which alter mood, behavior, or both—to become intoxicated or high, to

▲ Substance use.

abuse these substances, and to become dependent on or addicted to them.

Substance Use

Substance use is the ingestion of psychoactive substances in moderate amounts that does not significantly interfere with social, educational, or occupational functioning. Most of you reading this chapter probably use some sort of psychoactive substance occasionally. Drinking a cup of coffee in the morning to wake up or smoking a cigarette and having a drink with a friend to relax are examples of substance use, as is the occasional ingestion of illegal drugs such as marijuana, cocaine, amphetamines, or barbiturates.

Intoxication

Our physiological reaction to ingested substances—drunkenness or getting high—is referred to as **substance intoxication**. For a person to become intoxicated depends on which drug is taken, how much is ingested, and the person's individual biological reaction. For many of the substances we discuss here, intoxication is experienced as impaired judgment, mood changes, and lowered motor ability (for example, problems walking or talking).

Substance Abuse

Defining **substance abuse** by how much of a substance is ingested is problematic. For example, is drinking two glasses of wine in an hour abuse? Three glasses? Six? Is taking one injection of heroin considered abuse? The text revision of the fourth edition of the *Diagnostic and Statistical Manual (DSM-IV-TR)* defines substance abuse in terms of how significantly it interferes with the user's life. If substances disrupt your education, job, or relationships with others, and put you in physically dangerous situations (for example, while driving), and if you have related legal problems, you would be considered a drug abuser. Some evidence suggests that high school drug use can predict later job outcomes. In one study, researchers controlled for factors such as educational interests and other problem behavior, and still found that repeated hard drug use (using one or more of the following: amphetamines, barbiturates, crack, cocaine, PCP, LSD, other psychedelics, crystal meth, inhalants, heroin, or other narcotics) predicted poor job outcomes at age 29 (Ringel, Ellickson, & Collins, 2007).

Danny seems to fit this definition of abuse. His inability to complete a semester of community college was a direct result of drug use. Danny often drove while drunk or under the influence of other drugs, and he had already been arrested twice. Danny's use of multiple substances was so relentless and pervasive that he would probably be diagnosed as drug dependent, which indicates a severe form of the disorder.

DSM Disorder Criteria Summary
Substance Intoxication

A. The development of a reversible substance-specific syndrome due to recent ingestion of (or exposure to) a substance. **Note:** Different substances may produce similar or identical syndromes.

B. Clinically significant maladaptive behavioral or psychological changes that are due to the effect of the substance on the central nervous system (e.g., belligerence, mood lability, cognitive impairment, impaired judgment, impaired social or occupational functioning) and develop during or shortly after use of the substance.

C. The symptoms are not due to a general medical condition and are not better accounted for by another mental disorder.

Source: Reprinted with permission from Diagnostic and Statistical Manual of Mental Disorders (4th ed., text revision). © 2000 American Psychiatric Association.

---

psychoactive substances Substances, such as a drugs, that alter mood or behavior.

substance intoxication A physiological reaction, such as impaired judgment and motor ability, as well as mood change, resulting from the ingestion of a psychoactive substance.

substance abuse A pattern of psychoactive substance use leading to significant distress or impairment in social and occupational roles and in hazardous situations.

DSM Disorder Criteria Summary
Substance Abuse

A. A maladaptive pattern of substance use leading to clinically significant impairment or distress, as manifested by one (or more) of the following, occurring within a 12-month period:

(1) recurrent substance use resulting in a failure to fulfill major role obligations at work, school, or home (e.g., repeated absences or poor work performance related to substance use; substance-related absences, suspensions, or expulsions from school; neglect of children or household); (2) recurrent substance use in situations in which it is physically hazardous (e.g., driving an automobile or operating a machine when impaired by substance use); (3) recurrent substance-related legal problems (e.g., arrests for substance-related disorderly conduct); (4) continued substance use despite having persistent or recurrent social or interpersonal problems caused or exacerbated by the effects of the substance (e.g., arguments with spouse about consequences of intoxication, physical fights)

B. The symptoms have never met the criteria for Substance Dependence for this class of substance.

Source: Reprinted with permission from *Diagnostic and Statistical Manual of Mental Disorders* (4th ed., text revision). © 2000 American Psychiatric Association.

DSM Disorder Criteria Summary
Substance Dependence

A maladaptive pattern of substance use, leading to clinically significant impairment or distress, as manifested by three (or more) of the following, occurring at any time in the same 12-month period:

(1) tolerance, as defined by either of the following:

(a) a need for markedly increased amounts of the substance to achieve intoxication or desired effect

(b) markedly diminished effect with continued use of the same amount of the substance

(2) withdrawal, as manifested by either of the following:

(a) the characteristic withdrawal syndrome for the substance (refer to Criteria A and B of the criteria sets for Withdrawal from the specific substances)

(b) the same (or a closely related) substance is taken to relieve or avoid withdrawal symptoms

(3) the substance is often taken in larger amounts or over a longer period than was intended

(4) there is a persistent desire or unsuccessful efforts to cut down or control substance use

(5) a great deal of time is spent in activities necessary to obtain the substance (e.g., visiting multiple doctors or driving long distances), use the substance (e.g., chainsmoking), or recover from its effects

(6) important social, occupational, or recreational activities are given up or reduced because of substance use

(7) the substance use is continued despite knowledge of having a persistent or recurrent physical or psychological problem that is likely to have been caused or exacerbated by the substance (e.g., current cocaine use despite recognition of cocaine-induced depression, or continued drinking despite recognition that an ulcer was made worse by alcohol consumption)

Specify if:

With Physiological Dependence: evidence of tolerance or withdrawal (i.e., either Item 1 or 2 is present)

Without Physiological Dependence: no evidence of tolerance or withdrawal (i.e., neither Item 1 nor 2 is present)

Source: Reprinted with permission from *Diagnostic and Statistical Manual of Mental Disorders* (4th ed., text revision). © 2000 American Psychiatric Association.

Substance Dependence

Drug dependence is usually described as addiction. Although we use the term *addiction* routinely when we describe people who seem to be under the control of drugs, there is some disagreement about how to define addiction, or **substance dependence** (Strain, 2009). In one definition, the person is physiologically dependent on the drug or drugs, requires increasingly greater amounts of the drug to experience the same effect (**tolerance**), and will respond physically in a negative way when the substance is no longer ingested (**withdrawal**) (American Psychiatric Association, 2007). Tolerance and withdrawal are physiological reactions to the chemicals being ingested. How many of you have experienced headaches when you didn't get your morning coffee? You were probably going through caffeine withdrawal. In a more extreme example, withdrawal from alcohol can cause alcohol withdrawal delirium, in which a person can

experience frightening hallucinations and body tremors. Withdrawal from many substances can bring on chills, fever, diarrhea, nausea and vomiting, and aches and pains. However, not all substances are physiologically addicting. For example, you do not go through severe physical withdrawal when you stop taking LSD. Cocaine withdrawal has a pattern that includes anxiety, lack of motivation, and boredom (Leamon, Wright, & Myrick, 2008), and withdrawal from marijuana includes such symptoms as nervousness, appetite change, and sleep disturbance (Ehlers et al., 2010). In fact, although previously believed not to be a problem, marijuana (cannabis) withdrawal is now being considered for inclusion in *DSM-5* (Martin, Chung, & Langenbucher, 2008).

Another view of substance dependence uses the "drug-seeking behaviors" themselves as a measure of dependence. The repeated use of a drug, a desperate need to ingest more of the substance (stealing money to buy drugs, standing outside in the cold to smoke), and the likelihood that use will resume after a period of abstinence are behaviors that define the extent of drug dependence. Such behavioral reac-

▲ Intoxication.

Andrew Hobbs/Stone/Getty Images

▲ Substance abuse.

tions are different from the physiological responses to drugs we described before and are sometimes referred to in terms of psychological dependence. The *DSM-IV-TR* definition of substance dependence combines the physiological aspects of tolerance and withdrawal with their behavioral and psychological aspects (American Psychiatric Association Practice Guideline, 2000a).

This definition of dependence must be seen as a "work in progress." By these criteria, many people can be considered dependent on such activities as sex, work, or even eating chocolate. What most people consider serious addiction to drugs is qualitatively different from dependence on shopping or television. The physiological and behavioral patterns may need to be further refined before we can separate the truly serious phenomenon of substance dependence from less debilitating so-called addictions.

Let's go back to the questions we started with: "Can you use drugs and not abuse them?" and "Can you abuse drugs and not become addicted to or dependent on them?" The answer to the first question is yes. Some people drink wine or beer regularly without drinking to excess. Although it is not commonly believed, some people use drugs such as heroin, cocaine, or crack (a form of cocaine) occasionally

(for instance, several times a year) without abusing them (Goldman & Rather, 1993). What is disturbing is that we do not know ahead of time who might be likely to lose control and abuse these drugs and who is likely to become dependent with even a passing use of a substance.

It may seem counterintuitive, but dependence can be present without abuse. For example, cancer patients who take morphine for pain may become dependent on the drug—build up a tolerance and go through withdrawal if it is stopped—without abusing it (Portenoy & Mathur, 2009). Later in this chapter, we discuss biological and psychosocial theories of the causes of substance-related disorders and of why we have individualized reactions to these substances.

Experts in the substance use field were asked about the relative "addictiveness" of various drugs (Franklin, 1990). The survey results are shown in ■ Figure 10.1. You may be surprised to see nicotine placed just ahead of methamphetamine and crack cocaine as the most addictive of drugs. Although this is only a subjective rating by these experts, it shows that our society sanctions or forbids drugs based on factors other than their addictiveness.

Diagnostic Issues

In early editions of the *DSM*, alcoholism and drug abuse weren't treated as separate disorders. Instead, they were categorized as "sociopathic personality disturbances" (a forerunner of the current *antisocial personality disorder*, which we discuss in Chapter 11) because substance use was seen as a symptom of other problems. It was considered a sign of moral weakness, and the influence of genetics and biology was hardly acknowledged. A separate category was created for substance abuse disorders in *DSM-III* in 1980, and since then we have acknowledged the complex biological and psychological nature of the problem.

The *DSM-IV-TR* term *substance-related disorders* indicates several subtypes of diagnoses for each substance, including dependence, abuse, intoxication, withdrawal, or a combination of these. These distinctions help clarify the problem and focus treatment on the appropriate aspect of the disorder. Danny received the diagnosis "cocaine dependence" because of the tolerance he showed for the drug, his use of larger amounts than he intended, his unsuccessful attempts to stop using it, and the activities he gave up to buy it. His pattern of use was more pervasive than simple

substance dependence A maladaptive pattern of substance use characterized by the need for increased amounts to achieve the desired effect, negative physical effects when the substance is withdrawn, unsuccessful efforts to control its use, and substantial effort expended to seek it or recover from its effects. Also known as *addiction*.
tolerance The need for increased amounts of a substance to achieve the desired effect, and a diminished effect with continued use of the same amount.
withdrawal A severely negative physiological reaction to removal of a psychoactive substance, which can be alleviated by the same or a similar substance.

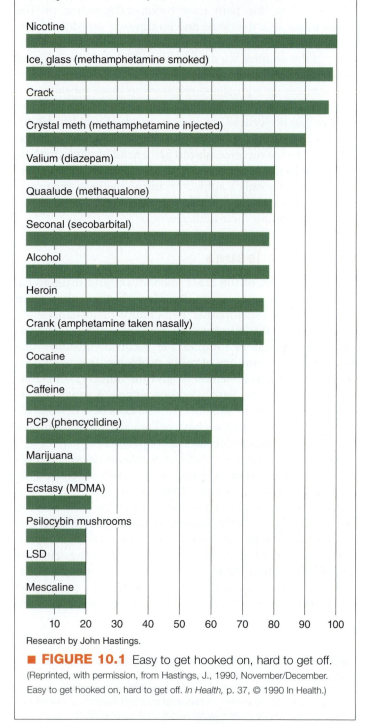

Nicotine

Ice, glass (methamphetamine smoked)

Crack

Crystal meth (methamphetamine injected)

Valium (diazepam)

Quaalude (methaqualone)

Seconal (secobarbital)

Alcohol

Heroin

Crank (amphetamine taken nasally)

Cocaine

Caffeine

PCP (phencyclidine)

Marijuana

Ecstasy (MDMA)

Psilocybin mushrooms

LSD

Mescaline

10 20 30 40 50 60 70 80 90 100

Research by John Hastings.

■ **FIGURE 10.1** Easy to get hooked on, hard to get off.

(Reprinted, with permission, from Hastings, J., 1990, November/December. Easy to get hooked on, hard to get off. *In Health*, p. 37, © 1990 In Health.)

does drug use and its consequences (for example, loss of friends, job) create depression? Researchers estimate that almost three quarters of the people in addiction treatment centers have an additional psychiatric disorder, with mood disorders (such as major depression) observed in more than 40% and anxiety disorders and posttraumatic stress disorder seen in more than 25% of the cases (McGovern, Xie, Segal, Siembab, & Drake, 2006).

Substance use might occur concurrently with other disorders for several reasons (Strain, 2009). Substance-related disorders and anxiety and mood disorders are highly prevalent in our society and may occur together so often just by chance. Drug intoxication and withdrawal can cause symptoms of anxiety, depression, and psychosis. Disorders such as schizophrenia and antisocial personality disorder are highly likely to include a secondary problem of substance use.

Because substance-related disorders can be so complicated, *DSM-IV-TR* tries to define when a symptom is a result of substance use and when it is not. Basically, if symptoms seen in schizophrenia or in extreme states of anxiety appear during intoxication or within 6 weeks after withdrawal from drugs, they aren't considered signs of a separate psychiatric disorder. So, for example, individuals who show signs of severe depression just after they have stopped taking heavy doses of stimulants would not be diagnosed with a major mood disorder. However, individuals who were severely depressed before they used stimulants and those whose symptoms persist more than 6 weeks after they stop might have a separate disorder (Leamon et al., 2008).

We now turn to the individual substances themselves, their effects on our brains and bodies, and how they are used in our society. We have grouped the substances into five general categories.

> **Depressants**: These substances result in behavioral sedation and can induce relaxation. They include alcohol (ethyl alcohol) and the sedative, hypnotic, and anxiolytic drugs in the families of barbiturates (for example, Seconal) and benzodiazepines (for example, Valium, Xanax).
> **Stimulants**: These substances cause us to be more active and alert and can elevate mood. Included in this group are amphetamines, cocaine, nicotine, and caffeine.
> **Opiates**: The major effect of these substances is to produce analgesia temporarily (reduce pain) and euphoria. Heroin, opium, codeine, and morphine are included in this group.
> **Hallucinogens**: These substances alter sensory perception and can produce delusions, paranoia, and hallucinations. Marijuana and LSD are included in this category.
> **Other Drugs of Abuse**: Other substances that are abused but do not fit neatly into one of the categories here include inhalants (for example, airplane glue), anabolic steroids, and other over-the-counter and prescription medications (for example, nitrous oxide). These substances produce a variety of psychoactive effects that are characteristic of the substances described in the previous categories.

abuse, and the diagnosis of dependence provided a clear picture of his need for help.

Symptoms of other disorders can complicate the substance abuse picture significantly. For example, do some people take drugs to excess because they are depressed, or

> **What are the physiological and psychological effects of alcohol?**

Depressants primarily *decrease* central nervous system activity. Their principal effect is to reduce our levels of physiological arousal and help us relax. Included in this group are alcohol and the sedative, hypnotic, and anxiolytic drugs, such as those prescribed for insomnia (see Chapter 8). These substances are among those most likely to produce symptoms of physical dependence, tolerance, and withdrawal. We first look at the most commonly used of these substances—alcohol—and the **alcohol use disorders** that can result.

Alcohol Use Disorders

DSM Disorder Criteria Summary
Alcohol Intoxication

A. Recent ingestion of alcohol.

B. Clinically significant maladaptive behavioral or psychological changes (e.g., inappropriate sexual or aggressive behavior, mood lability, impaired judgment, impaired social or occupational functioning) that developed during, or shortly after, alcohol ingestion.

C. One (or more) of the following signs, developing during, or shortly after, alcohol use: (1) slurred speech; (2) incoordination; (3) unsteady gait; (4) nystagmus; (5) impairment in attention or memory; (6) stupor or coma

D. The symptoms are not due to a general medical condition and are not better accounted for by another mental disorder.

Source: Reprinted with permission from *Diagnostic and Statistical Manual of Mental Disorders* (4th ed., text revision). © 2000 American Psychiatric Association.

Clinical Description

Although alcohol is a depressant, its initial effect is an apparent stimulation. We generally experience a feeling of well-being, our inhibitions are reduced, and we become more outgoing. This is because what are initially depressed—or slowed—are the inhibitory centers in the brain. With continued drinking, however, alcohol depresses more areas of the brain, which impedes the ability to function properly. Motor coordination is impaired (staggering, slurred speech), reaction time is slowed, we become confused, our ability to make judgments is reduced, and even vision and hearing can be negatively affected, all of which help explain why driving while intoxicated is clearly dangerous.

Effects

Alcohol affects many parts of the body (■ Figure 10.2). After it is ingested, it passes through the esophagus (1 in Figure 10.2) and into the stomach (2), where small amounts are absorbed. From there, most of it travels to the small intestine (3), where it is easily absorbed into the bloodstream. The circulatory system distributes the alcohol throughout the body, where it contacts every major organ,

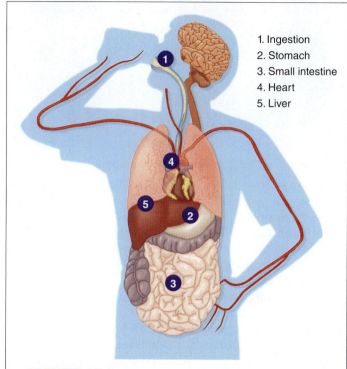

1. Ingestion
2. Stomach
3. Small intestine
4. Heart
5. Liver

■ **FIGURE 10.2** The path traveled by alcohol throughout the body (see text for complete description). (© Cengage Learning 2013)

including the heart (4). Some of the alcohol goes to the lungs, where it vaporizes and is exhaled, a phenomenon that is the basis for the *breathalyzer test* that measures levels of intoxication. As alcohol passes through the liver (5), it is broken down or metabolized into carbon dioxide and water by enzymes (Maher, 1997).

Most substances we describe in this chapter, including marijuana, opiates, and tranquilizers, interact with specific receptors in the brain cells. The effects of alcohol, however, are more complex. Alcohol influences a number of neuro-

depressant A psychoactive substance that results in behavioral sedation; such substances include alcohol and the sedative, hypnotic, and anxiolytic drugs.

stimulant A psychoactive substance that elevates mood, activity, and alertness; such substances include amphetamines, caffeine, cocaine, and nicotine.

opiate An addictive psychoactive substance such as heroin, opium, or morphine that causes temporary euphoria and analgesia (pain reduction).

hallucinogen Any psychoactive substance, such as LSD or marijuana, that can produce delusions, hallucinations, paranoia, and altered sensory perception.

alcohol use disorders A cognitive, biological, behavioral, and social problem associated with alcohol use and abuse.

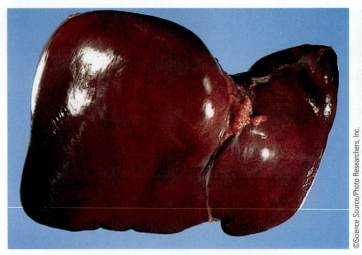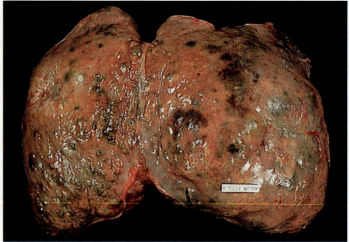

▲ A healthy liver *(left)*, and a cirrhotic liver scarred by years of alcohol abuse *(right)*.

receptor systems, which makes it difficult to study. For example, the *gamma-aminobutyric acid (GABA)* system, which we discussed in Chapters 2 and 4, seems to be particularly sensitive to alcohol. GABA, as you will recall, is an inhibitory neurotransmitter. Its major role is to interfere with the firing of the neuron it attaches to. When GABA attaches to its receptor, chloride ions enter the cell and make it less sensitive to the effects of other neurotransmitters. Alcohol seems to reinforce the movement of these chloride ions; as a result, the neurons have difficulty firing. In other words, although alcohol seems to loosen our tongues and makes us more sociable, it makes it difficult for neurons to communicate with one another (Strain, 2009). Because the GABA system seems to act on our feelings of anxiety, alcohol's antianxiety properties may result from its interaction with the GABA system.

The *glutamate system* is under study for its role in the effects of alcohol. In contrast to the GABA system, the glutamate system is excitatory, helping neurons fire. It is suspected to involve learning and memory, and it may be the avenue through which alcohol affects our cognitive abilities. Blackouts, the loss of memory for what happens during intoxication, may result from the interaction of alcohol with the glutamate system. The serotonin system also appears to be sensitive to alcohol. This neurotransmitter system affects mood, sleep, and eating behavior and is thought to be responsible for alcohol cravings (Strain, 2009). Because alcohol affects so many neurotransmitter systems, we should not be surprised that it has such widespread and complex effects.

The long-term effects of heavy drinking are often severe. Withdrawal from chronic alcohol use typically includes hand tremors and, within several hours, nausea or vomiting, anxiety, transient hallucinations, agitation, insomnia, and, at its most extreme, **withdrawal delirium** (or **delirium tremens**—the **DTs**), a condition that can produce frightening hallucinations and body tremors. The devastating experience of delirium tremens can be reduced with adequate medical treatment (Schuckit, 2009b).

Whether alcohol will cause organic damage depends on genetic vulnerability, the frequency of use, the length of drinking binges, the blood alcohol levels attained during the drinking periods, and whether the body is given time to recover between binges. Consequences of long-term excessive drinking include liver disease, pancreatitis, cardiovascular disorders, and brain damage.

Part of the folklore concerning alcohol is that it permanently kills brain cells (neurons). As you will see later, this

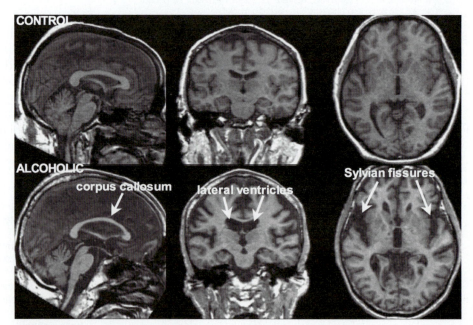

▲ MRI scans from a 53-year-old control man *(upper)* and a 53-year-old man with alcoholism *(lower)*. Note the enlargement of the lateral ventricles and sulci, reduced cortical tissue, and skinnier corpus callosum in the man with a long history of alcohol abuse compared with the control. (Adapted from Rosenbloom MJ, Pfefferbaum A (2008): Alcohol Res Health 31:362–376)

may not be true. Some evidence for brain damage comes from the experiences of people who are alcohol dependent and experience blackouts, seizures, and hallucinations. Memory and the ability to perform certain tasks may also be impaired. More seriously, two types of organic brain syndromes may result from long-term heavy alcohol use: dementia and Wernicke-Korsakoff syndrome. *Dementia,* which we discuss more fully in Chapter 13, involves the general loss of intellectual abilities and can be a direct result of neurotoxicity or "poisoning of the brain" by excessive amounts of alcohol (Leamon et al., 2008). *Wernicke-Korsakoff syndrome* results in confusion, loss of muscle coordination, and unintelligible speech (Schuckit, 2009b); it is believed to be caused by a deficiency of thiamine, a vitamin metabolized poorly by heavy drinkers. The dementia caused by this disease does not go away once the brain is damaged.

The effects of alcohol abuse extend beyond the health and well-being of the drinker. **Fetal alcohol syndrome (FAS)** is now generally recognized as a combination of problems that can occur in a child whose mother drank while she was pregnant. These problems include fetal growth retardation, cognitive deficits, behavior problems, and learning difficulties (Gray, Mukherjee, & Rutter, 2009). In addition, children with FAS often have characteristic facial features.

Statistics on Use and Abuse

Most adults in the United States characterize themselves as light drinkers or abstainers. However, about half of all Americans over the age of 12 report being current drinkers

Abnormal Psychology Inside Out. Produced by Ira Wohl, Only Child Motion Pictures

Substance Use Disorder: Tim

"When I drink, I don't care about anything, as long as I'm drinking. Nothing bothers me. The world doesn't bother me. So when I'm not drinking, the problems come back, so you drink again. The problems will always be there. You just don't realize it when you're drinking. That's why people tend to drink a lot."

Go to Psychology CourseMate at www.cengagebrain.com to watch this video.

of alcohol, and there are considerable differences among people from different racial and ethnic backgrounds (■ Figure 10.3; Substance Abuse and Mental Health Services Administration, 2009). Whites report the highest frequency of drinking (56.5%); drinking is lowest among Native Hawaiians (37.3%).

About 58 million Americans (23%) report binge drinking (five or more drinks on the same occasion) in the past month—an alarming statistic (Substance Abuse and Mental Health Services Administration, 2009). Again, there are racial differences, with Asians reporting the lowest level of binge drinking (11.9%) and American Indians (24.4%) and Hispanics (25.6%) reporting the highest. In a large survey among college-age men and women, about 42% of respondents said they had gone on a binge of heavy drinking once in the preceding 2 weeks (Presley & Meilman, 1992). Men, however, were more likely to report several binges in the 2-week period. The same survey found that students with a grade point average of A had no more than 3 drinks per week, whereas D and F students averaged 11 alcoholic drinks per week (Presley & Meilman, 1992).

Statistics on Dependence

Our everyday experience tells us that not everyone who drinks becomes dependent on alcohol or abuses it. However, researchers estimate that more than 3 million adults are alcohol dependent (Substance Abuse and Mental Health Services Administration, 2009).

Outside the United States, rates of alcohol abuse and dependence vary widely. The prevalence of alcohol dependence in Peru is about 35%; in South Korea, it is approximately 22%; it is about 3.5% in Taipei and as low as 0.45% in Shanghai (Helzer & Canino, 1992; Yamamoto, Silva, Sasao, Wang, & Nguyen, 1993). Such cultural differences can be accounted for by different attitudes toward drink-

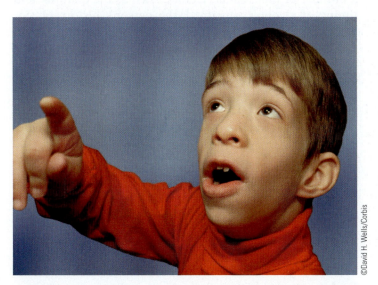

©David H. Wells/Corbis

▲ Physical characteristics of fetal alcohol syndrome (FAS) include skin folds at the corners of the eyes, low nasal bridge, short nose, groove between nose and upper lip, small head circumference, small eye opening, small midface, and thin upper lip.

withdrawal delirium (delirium tremens/DTs) The frightening hallucinations and body tremors that result when a heavy drinker withdraws from alcohol. Also known as *delirium tremens (DT)*.

fetal alcohol syndrome (FAS) A pattern of problems, including learning difficulties, behavior deficits, and characteristic physical flaws, resulting from heavy drinking by the victim's mother when she was pregnant with the victim.

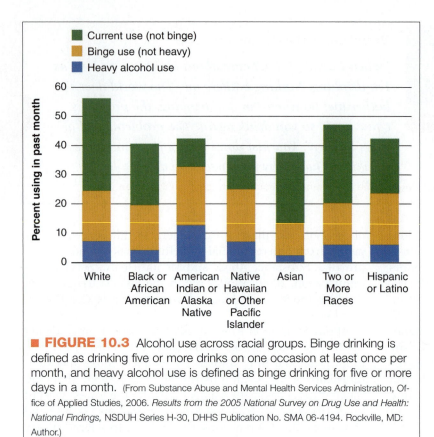

■ FIGURE 10.3 Alcohol use across racial groups. Binge drinking is defined as drinking five or more drinks on one occasion at least once per month, and heavy alcohol use is defined as binge drinking for five or more days in a month. (From Substance Abuse and Mental Health Services Administration, Office of Applied Studies, 2006. *Results from the 2005 National Survey on Drug Use and Health: National Findings*, NSDUH Series H-30, DHHS Publication No. SMA 06-4194. Rockville, MD: Author.)

ing, the availability of alcohol, physiological reactions, and family norms and patterns.

Progression

Remember that Danny went through periods of heavy alcohol and drug use but also had times when he was relatively "straight" and did not use drugs. Similarly, many people who abuse alcohol or are dependent on it fluctuate between drinking heavily, drinking "socially" without negative effects, and being abstinent (not drinking) (Schuckit, 2009a). It seems that about 20% of people with severe alcohol dependence have a spontaneous remission (they are able to stop drinking on their own) and do not reexperience problems with drinking.

It used to be thought that once problems arose with drinking they would become steadily worse, following a predictable downward pattern as long as the person kept drinking (Sobell & Sobell, 1993). In other words, like a disease that isn't treated properly, alcoholism will get progressively worse if left unchecked. First championed by Jellinek more than 50 years ago, this view continues to influence the way people view and treat the disorder (Jellinek, 1946, 1952, 1960). Unfortunately, Jellinek based his model of the progression of alcohol use on a now famous but faulty study (Jellinek, 1946).

It appears instead that the course of alcohol dependence may be progressive for most people, whereas the course of alcohol abuse may be more variable. For example, early use of alcohol may predict later abuse. A study of almost 6,000 lifetime drinkers found that drinking at an early age—from ages 11 to 14—was predictive of later alcohol use disorders (DeWitt, Adlaf, Offord, & Ogborne, 2000). A second study followed 636 male inpatients in an alcohol rehabilitation center (Schuckit et al., 1993). Among these chronically alcohol-dependent men, a general progression of alcohol-related life problems did emerge, although not in the specific pattern proposed by Jellinek. Three quarters of the men reported moderate consequences of their drinking, such as demotions at work, in their 20s. During their 30s, the men had more serious problems, such as regular blackouts and signs of alcohol withdrawal. By their late 30s and early 40s, these men demonstrated long-term serious consequences of their drinking, which included hallucinations, withdrawal convulsions, and hepatitis or pancreatitis. This study suggests a common pattern among people with chronic alcohol abuse and dependence, one with increasingly severe consequences. This progressive pattern is not inevitable for everyone who abuses alcohol, although we do not as yet understand what distinguishes those who are and those who are not susceptible (Schuckit, 2009a).

Finally, statistics often link alcohol with violent behavior (Bye, 2007). Numerous studies have found that many people who commit such violent acts as murder, rape, and assault are intoxicated at the time of the crime (Murdoch, Pihl, & Ross, 1990). We hope you are skeptical of this type of correlation. Just because drunkenness and violence overlap does not mean that alcohol will necessarily make you violent. Laboratory studies show that alcohol does make participants more aggressive (Bushman, 1993). However, whether a person behaves aggressively outside the laboratory probably involves a number of interrelated factors, such as the quantity and timing of alcohol consumed, the person's history of violence, expectations about drinking, and what happens to the individual while intoxicated. Alcohol does not *cause* aggression, but it may increase a person's likelihood of engaging in impulsive acts and it may impair the ability to consider the consequences of acting impulsively (Bye, 2007). Given the right circumstances, such impaired rational thinking may increase a person's risk of behaving aggressively.

Sedative, Hypnotic, or Anxiolytic Substance Use Disorders

The general group of depressants also includes sedative (calming), hypnotic (sleep-inducing), and anxiolytic (anxiety-reducing) drugs (Ciraulo & Sarid-Segal, 2009). These drugs include barbiturates and benzodiazepines. **Barbiturates** (which include Amytal, Seconal, and Nembutal) are a family of sedative drugs first synthesized in Germany in 1882 (Cozanitis, 2004). They were prescribed to help people sleep and replaced such drugs as alcohol

People use alcohol and drugs all over the world. However, the rates of use differ significantly across countries and cultures, due in part to availability and social norms. A recent survey of people from 17 countries around the world revealed that approximately 85% to 95% of people report using alcohol at some point in their lifetime (the U.S. rate is 92%), although the rates in Africa and the Middle East are significantly lower (40%–58%) (Degenhardt et al., 2008). The use of other drugs such as tobacco, cannabis, and cocaine are significantly lower across all countries; however, the rates in the United States are significantly higher for each of these drugs than in virtually all other countries studied. For instance, the rate of cannabis use is 0% to 19% in most countries, but is 42% in the United States (and New Zealand). The rate of cocaine use is 0% to 4% in every country except the United States, in which 16% of people report using cocaine at some point in their life. The exact reason for these higher rates of use in the United States are not known, but

drug use is significantly associated with higher income, and so availability of drugs and the accumulation of wealth in the United States may play a strong role.

Although the rate of alcohol and drug use varies across countries, some interesting similarities in use are found across many different countries. Young people use alcohol and drugs more than older people, and although men have historically been shown to use alcohol and drugs at much higher rates than women, women appear to be catching up. This is true for both alcohol use (Grucza, Bucholz, Rice, & Bierut, 2008; Grucza, Norberg, Bucholz, & Bierut, 2008) and for drug use more generally (Degenhardt et al., 2008). Many possible explanations exist for the observed change in rates of female alcohol and drug use, with the majority focusing on the fact that over the past several decades, women have achieved greater economic, social, and political status. More specifically, explanations included the following: (1) changes in occupational options for women (e.g.,

women are more likely to be employed and may adopt the traditional male notion of alcohol as a reasonable reward for a day of hard work, or may be more exposed to opportunities/occasions for drinking), (2) changes in social roles for women (e.g., cohabitation is becoming more prevalent and has been associated with higher rates of drinking), and (3) changes in adherence to gender stereotypes (e.g., women no longer conform to meeting traditional roles put on them of being nurturing, caring, and emotional) (for additional explanations see the review by Plant et al., 2008). Although it seems to be more socially and culturally accepted for women to engage in such drinking (and drug use) behaviors, women still experience greater barriers to treatment and stigma than men with similar dependence. Studies are needed to better understand exactly why this change has occurred and to develop better methods for preventing such high rates of abuse and dependence in the United States and around the globe.

and opium. Barbiturates were widely prescribed by physicians during the 1930s and 1940s, before their addictive properties were fully understood. By the 1950s, they were among the drugs most abused by adults in the United States (Franklin & Frances, 1999).

Benzodiazepines (which today include Valium, Xanax, Rohypnol, and Halcion) have been used since the 1960s, primarily to reduce anxiety. These drugs were originally touted as a miracle cure for the anxieties of living in our highly pressured technological society. Although in 1980 the U.S. Food and Drug Administration ruled that they are not appropriate for reducing the tension and anxiety resulting from everyday stresses and strains, an estimated 74 million prescriptions are written for benzodiazepines in the United States each year (Ciraulo & Sarid-Segal, 2009). In general, benzodiazepines are considered much safer than barbiturates, with less risk of abuse and dependence. Reports on the misuse of Rohypnol, however, show how dangerous even these benzodiazepine drugs can be. Rohypnol (otherwise known as "forget-me-pill," "roofenol," "roofies," or "ruffies") gained a following among teenagers in the 1990s because it has the same effect as alcohol without the telltale odor. However, there have been numerous incidents of men giving the drug to women without their knowledge, making it easier for them to engage in date rape (Nicoletti, 2009).

Clinical Description

At low doses, barbiturates relax the muscles and can produce a mild feeling of well-being. However, larger doses can have results similar to those of heavy drinking: slurred speech and problems walking, concentrating, and working. At extremely high doses, the diaphragm muscles can relax so much that they cause death by suffocation. Overdosing on barbiturates is a common means of suicide.

Like the barbiturates, benzodiazepines are used to calm an individual and induce sleep. In addition, drugs in this class are prescribed as muscle relaxants and anticonvulsants (antiseizure medications) (Ciraulo & Sarid-Segal, 2009). People who use them for nonmedical reasons report first feeling a

alcohol dehydrogenase (ADH) An enzyme that helps humans metabolize alcohol. Different levels of its subtypes many account for different susceptibilities to disorders such as fetal alcohol syndrome.
barbiturates A sedative (and addictive) drug such as Amytal, Seconal, or Nembutal that is used as a sleep aid.
benzodiazepines An antianxiety drug such as Valium, Xanax, Dalmane, or Halcion also used to treat insomnia. Effective against anxiety (and, at high potency, panic disorder), benzodiazepines show some side effects, such as some cognitive and motor impairment, and may result in substance dependence. Relapse rates are extremely high when such a drug is discontinued.

▲ Intoxication is often involved in cases of domestic violence.

pleasant high and a reduction of inhibition, similar to the effects of drinking alcohol. However, with continued use, tolerance and dependence can develop. Users who try to stop taking the drug experience symptoms like those of alcohol withdrawal (anxiety, insomnia, tremors, and delirium).

The *DSM-IV* criteria for sedative, hypnotic, and anxiolytic drug use disorders do not differ substantially from those for alcohol disorders. Both include maladaptive behavioral changes such as inappropriate sexual or aggressive behavior, variable moods, impaired judgment, impaired social or occupational functioning, slurred speech, motor coordination problems, and unsteady gait.

Like alcohol, sedative, hypnotic, and anxiolytic drugs affect the brain by influencing the GABA neurotransmitter system (Ciraulo & Sarid-Segal, 2009), although by slightly different mechanisms; as a result, when people use alcohol with any of these drugs or combine multiple types there can be synergistic effects. In other words, if you drink alcohol after taking a benzodiazepine or barbiturate or combine these drugs, the total effects can reach dangerous levels. Actor Heath Ledger's death in 2008 was attributed to the combined effects of oxycodone and a variety of other barbiturates and benzodiazepines.

Statistics

Barbiturate use has declined and benzodiazepine use has increased since 1960 (Substance Abuse and Mental Health Services Administration, 2009). Of those seeking treatment for substance-related problems, less than 1% present problems with benzodiazepines compared to other drugs of abuse. Those who do seek help with these drugs tend to be female, Caucasian, and over the age of 35 (Substance Abuse and Mental Health Services Administration, 2009).

DSM | Disorder Criteria Summary
Sedative, Hypnotic, or Anxiolytic Intoxication

A. Recent use of a sedative, hypnotic, or anxiolytic.

B. Clinically significant maladaptive behavioral or psychological changes (e.g., inappropriate sexual or aggressive behavior, mood lability, impaired judgment, impaired social or occupational functioning) that developed during, or shortly after, sedative, hypnotic, or anxiolytic use.

C. One (or more) of the following signs, developing during, or shortly after, sedative, hypnotic, or anxiolytic use:
(1) slurred speech; (2) incoordination; (3) unsteady gait; (4) nystagmus; (5) impairment in attention or memory; (6) stupor or coma

D. The symptoms are not due to a general medical condition and are not better accounted for by another mental disorder.

Source: Reprinted with permission from *Diagnostic and Statistical Manual of Mental Disorders* (4th ed., text revision). © 2000 American Psychiatric Association.

Concept Check 10.1

Part A

Check your understanding of substance-related definitions by stating whether the following case summaries describe (a) use, (b) intoxication, (c) abuse, or (d) dependence.

1. Giya started a new job 5 weeks ago and is about to be fired. This is her third job for the year. She has been absent from work at least once a week for the past 5 weeks. She was reprimanded in the past after being seen at a local pub in a drunken state during regular office hours although she called in sick. At her previous job, she was fired after she came to work unable to conduct herself appropriately and with alcohol on her breath. When confronted about her problems, Giya went to the nearest bar and drank some more to forget the situation. _____

2. Brennan scored the winning goal for his high school soccer team and his friends take him out to celebrate. He doesn't smoke, but he doesn't mind drinking alcohol occasionally. Because Brennan had such a good game, he decides to have a few drinks. Despite his great performance in the game, he is easily irritated, laughing one minute and yelling the next. The more Brennan rambles on about his game-winning goal, the more difficult it is to understand him. _____

3. Marti is a 24-year-old college student who started drinking heavily when he was 15. Marti drinks a moderate amount every night, unlike his schoolmates who get drunk at weekend parties only. In high school, he would become drunk after about four beers; now his tolerance has more than doubled. Marti claims alcohol relieves the pressures of college life. He once attempted to quit drinking, but he had chills, fever, diarrhea, nausea and vomiting, and body aches and pains. _____

4. Over the past year Henry picked up a habit of having a cigarette every day after lunch. Instead of sitting in the lounge with his friends he goes to his favorite spot in the courtyard and has his cigarette. If for some reason he is unable to have his cigarette after lunch, he is not dependent on it and can still function normally. _____

Part B

Match the following disorders with their corresponding effects: (a) substance-related disorder, (b) dementia, (c) impulse-control disorder, (d) alcohol use disorder, and (e) Wernicke-Korsakoff syndrome.

5. Disorder that deprives a person of the ability to resist acting on a drive or temptation. _____

6. Disorder in which the effects of the drug impede the ability to function properly by affecting vision, motor control, reaction time, memory, and hearing. _____

7. The decline of intellectual abilities through, for example, excess consumption of alcohol. _____

8. A class of disorders that affects the way people think, feel, and behave. _____

Stimulants

> **What are the physiological and psychological effects of stimulants?**

Of all the psychoactive drugs used in the United States, the most commonly consumed are stimulants. Included in this group are caffeine (in coffee, chocolate, and many soft drinks), nicotine (in tobacco products such as cigarettes), amphetamines, and cocaine. You probably used caffeine when you got up this morning. In contrast to the depressant drugs, stimulants—as their name suggests—make you more alert and energetic. They have a long history of use. Chinese physicians, for example, prescribed an amphetamine compound called ma-huang *(Ephedra sinica)* for more than 5,000 years for illnesses such as headaches, asthma, and the common cold (Fushimi, Wang, Ebisui, Cai, & Mikage, 2008). We describe several stimulants and their effects on behavior, mood, and cognition.

Amphetamine Use Disorders

At low doses, amphetamines can induce feelings of elation and vigor and can reduce fatigue. You literally feel "up." However, after a period of elevation, you come back down and "crash," feeling depressed or tired. In sufficient quantities, stimulants can lead to **amphetamine use disorders**.

Amphetamines are manufactured in the laboratory; they were first synthesized in 1887 and later used as a treatment for asthma and as a nasal decongestant (McCann & Ricaurte, 2009). Because amphetamines also reduce appetite, some people take them to lose weight. Adolph Hitler, partly because of his other physical maladies, became addicted to amphetamines (Judge & Rusyniak, 2009). Long-haul truck drivers, pilots, and some college students trying to "pull all-nighters" use amphetamines to get that extra energy boost and stay awake. Some of these drugs (Ritalin) are even given to children with *attention deficit hyperactivity disorder (ADHD)* (discussed in Chapter 13), although these too are being abused for their psychostimulant effects. One study found that as many as 1 in 10 students at one college reported using prescription stimulants illegally (Carroll, McLaughlin, & Blake, 2006).

DSM-IV-TR diagnostic criteria for amphetamine intoxication include significant behavioral symptoms, such as euphoria or affective blunting (a lack of emotional expression), changes in sociability, interpersonal sensitivity, anxiety, tension, anger, stereotyped behaviors, impaired judg-

ment, and impaired social or occupational functioning. In addition, physiological symptoms occur during or shortly after amphetamine or related substances are ingested and can include heart rate or blood pressure changes, perspiration or chills, nausea or vomiting, weight loss, muscular weakness, respiratory depression, chest pain, seizures, or coma. Severe intoxication or overdose can cause hallucinations, panic, agitation, and paranoid delusions (Leamon et al., 2008). Amphetamine tolerance builds quickly, making it

DSM Disorder Criteria Summary
Amphetamine Intoxication

A. Recent use of amphetamine or a related substance (e.g., methylphenidate).

B. Clinically significant maladaptive behavioral or psychological changes (e.g., euphoria or affective blunting; changes in sociability; hypervigilance; interpersonal sensitivity; anxiety, tension, or anger; stereotyped behaviors; impaired judgment; or impaired social or occupational functioning) that developed during, or shortly after, use of amphetamine or a related substance.

C. Two (or more) of the following, developing during, or shortly after, use of amphetamine or a related substance: (1) tachycardia or bradycardia; (2) pupillary dilation; (3) elevated or lowered blood pressure; (4) perspiration or chills; (5) nausea or vomiting; (6) evidence of weight loss; (7) psychomotor agitation or retardation; (8) muscular weakness, respiratory depression, chest pain, or cardiac arrhythmias; (9) confusion, seizures, dyskinesias, dystonias, or coma

D. The symptoms are not due to a general medical condition and are not better accounted for by another mental disorder.

Specify if:

With Perceptual Disturbances: This specifier may be noted when hallucinations with intact reality testing or auditory, visual, or tactile illusions occur in the absence of a delirium. Intact reality testing means that the person knows that the hallucinations are induced by the substance and do not represent external reality. When hallucinations occur in the absence of intact reality testing, a diagnosis of Substance-Induced Psychotic Disorder, With Hallucinations, should be considered.

Source: Reprinted with permission from *Diagnostic and Statistical Manual of Mental Disorders* (4th ed., text revision). © 2000 American Psychiatric Association.

amphetamine use disorders Psychological, biological, behavioral, and social problems associated with amphetamine use and abuse.

doubly dangerous. Withdrawal often results in apathy, prolonged periods of sleep, irritability, and depression.

Periodically, certain "designer drugs" appear in local miniepidemics. An amphetamine called methylenedioxymethamphetamine (MDMA), first synthesized in 1912 in Germany, was used as an appetite suppressant (McCann & Ricaurte, 2009). Recreational use of this drug, now commonly called Ecstasy, rose sharply in the late 1980s. After methamphetamine, MDMA is the club drug most often bringing people to emergency rooms, and it has passed LSD in frequency of use (Substance Abuse and Mental Health Services Administration, 2009). Its effects are described by users in a variety of ways: Ecstasy makes you "feel happy" and "love everyone and everything"; "music feels better" and "it's more fun to dance"; "You can say what is on your mind without worrying what others will think" (Levy, O'Grady, Wish, & Arria, 2005, p. 1431). A purified, crystallized form of amphetamine, called methamphetamine (commonly referred to as "crystal meth" or "ice"), is ingested through smoking. This drug causes marked aggressive tendencies and stays in the system longer than cocaine, making it particularly dangerous. This drug gained popularity in the gay community, although its use has now spread to others (Parsons, Kelly, & Weiser, 2007). However enjoyable these various amphetamines may be in the short term, the potential for users to become dependent on them is extremely high, with great risk for long-term difficulties.

Amphetamines stimulate the central nervous system by enhancing the activity of norepinephrine and dopamine. Specifically, amphetamines help the release of these neurotransmitters and block their reuptake, thereby making more of them available throughout the system (McCann & Ricaurte, 2009). Too much amphetamine—and therefore too much dopamine and norepinephrine—can lead to hallucinations and delusions. As we see in Chapter 12, this effect has stimulated theories on the causes of schizophrenia, which can also include hallucinations and delusions.

Cocaine Use Disorders

Clinical Description

Like the amphetamines, in small amounts cocaine increases alertness, produces euphoria, increases blood pressure and pulse, and causes insomnia and loss of appetite. Remember that Danny snorted (inhaled) cocaine when he partied through the night with his friends. He later said the drug made him feel powerful and invincible—the only way he really felt self-confident. The effects of cocaine are short lived; for Danny they lasted less than an hour, and he had to snort repeatedly to keep himself up. During these binges, he often became paranoid, experiencing exaggerated fears that he would be caught or that someone would steal his cocaine. Such paranoia—referred to as *cocaine-induced paranoia*—is common among cocaine abusers, occurring in two thirds or more (Kalayasiri et al., 2006). Cocaine also makes the heart beat more rapidly and irregularly, and it can have fatal consequences, depending on a person's physical condition and

the amount of the drug ingested. Billy Mays, the TV salesman for products such as OxiClean, died of heart disease in 2009 with cocaine listed as a contributory cause of death.

Statistics

In the United States, more than 1.9 million people report using cocaine each year, more than any other drug besides marijuana (Substance Abuse and Mental Health Services Administration, 2009). White males account for about a third of all admissions to emergency rooms for cocaine-related problems (29%) followed by black males (23%), white females (18%), and black females (12%) (Substance Abuse and Mental Health Services Administration, 2002). Approximately 17% of cocaine users have also used crack cocaine (a crystallized form of cocaine that is smoked) (Closser, 1992). One estimate is that about 0.2% of Americans have tried crack and that an increasing proportion of the abusers seeking treatment are young, unemployed adults living in urban areas (Substance Abuse and Mental Health Services Administration, 2009).

Cocaine is in the same group of stimulants as amphetamines because it has similar effects on the brain. The "up" seems to come primarily from the effect of cocaine on the dopamine system. Look at ■ Figure 10.4 to see how this action occurs. Cocaine enters the bloodstream and is carried to the brain. There the cocaine molecules block the reuptake of dopamine. As you know, neurotransmitters released at the synapse stimulate the next neuron and then are recycled back to the original neuron. Cocaine seems to bind to places where dopamine neurotransmitters reenter their home neuron, blocking their reuptake. The dopamine that cannot be taken in by the neuron remains in the synapse, causing repeated stimulation of the next neuron. This stimulation of

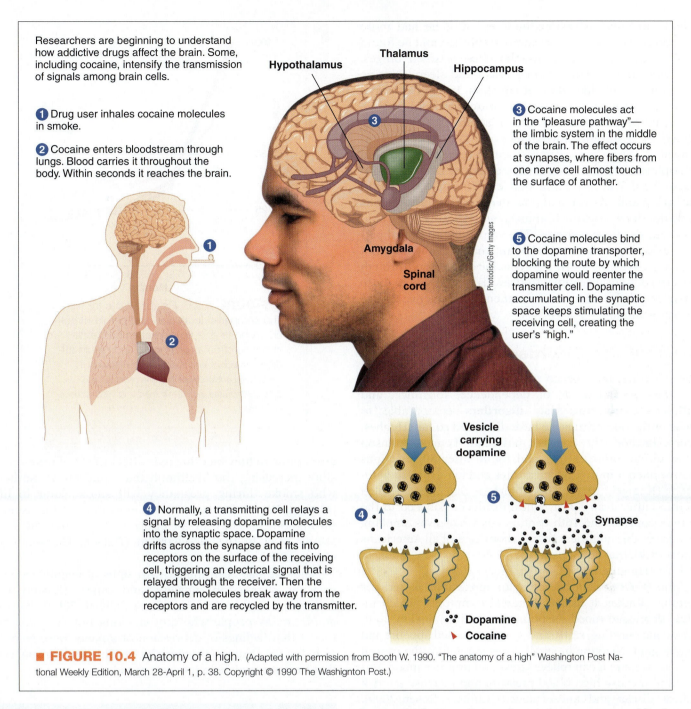

Researchers are beginning to understand how addictive drugs affect the brain. Some, including cocaine, intensify the transmission of signals among brain cells.

1 Drug user inhales cocaine molecules in smoke.

2 Cocaine enters bloodstream through lungs. Blood carries it throughout the body. Within seconds it reaches the brain.

Hypothalamus

Thalamus

Hippocampus

3 Cocaine molecules act in the "pleasure pathway"— the limbic system in the middle of the brain. The effect occurs at synapses, where fibers from one nerve cell almost touch the surface of another.

Amygdala

Spinal cord

Photodisc/Getty Images

5 Cocaine molecules bind to the dopamine transporter, blocking the route by which dopamine would reenter the transmitter cell. Dopamine accumulating in the synaptic space keeps stimulating the receiving cell, creating the user's "high."

Vesicle carrying dopamine

Synapse

4 Normally, a transmitting cell relays a signal by releasing dopamine molecules into the synaptic space. Dopamine drifts across the synapse and fits into receptors on the surface of the receiving cell, triggering an electrical signal that is relayed through the receiver. Then the dopamine molecules break away from the receptors and are recycled by the transmitter.

• **Dopamine**

▶ **Cocaine**

■ **FIGURE 10.4** Anatomy of a high. (Adapted with permission from Booth W. 1990. "The anatomy of a high" Washington Post National Weekly Edition, March 28-April 1, p. 38. Copyright © 1990 The Washignton Post.)

the dopamine neurons in the "pleasure pathway" (the site in the brain that seems to be involved in the experience of pleasure) causes the high associated with cocaine use.

As late as the 1980s, many felt cocaine was a wonder drug that produced feelings of euphoria without being addictive (Weiss & Iannucci, 2009). Such a conservative source as the *Comprehensive Textbook of Psychiatry* in 1980 indicated that "taken no more than two or three times per week, cocaine creates no serious problems" (Grinspoon & Bakalar, 1980). Just imagine—a drug that gives you extra energy, helps you think clearly and more creatively, and lets you accomplish more throughout the day, all without any negative side effects! In our highly competitive and complex technological society, this would be a dream come true. But, as you probably realize, such temporary benefits

have a high cost. Dependence does not resemble that of many other drugs early on; typically, people find only that they have a growing inability to resist taking more (Weiss & Iannucci, 2009). Few negative effects are noted at first; however, with continued use, sleep is disrupted, increased tolerance causes a need for higher doses, paranoia and other negative symptoms set in, and the cocaine user gradually becomes socially isolated.

Again, Danny's case illustrates this pattern. He was a social user for a number of years, using cocaine only with

cocaine use disorders Cognitive, biological, behavioral, and social problems associated with the use and abuse of cocaine.

friends and only occasionally. Eventually, he had more frequent episodes of excessive use or binges, and he found himself increasingly craving the drug between binges. After the binges, Danny would crash and sleep. Cocaine withdrawal isn't like that of alcohol. Instead of rapid heartbeat, tremors, or nausea, withdrawal from cocaine produces pronounced feelings of apathy and boredom. Think for a minute how dangerous this type of withdrawal is. First, you're bored with everything and find little pleasure from the everyday activities of work or relationships. The one thing that can "bring you back to life" is cocaine. As you can imagine, a particularly vicious cycle develops: Cocaine is abused, withdrawal causes apathy, cocaine abuse resumes. The atypical withdrawal pattern misled people into believing that cocaine was not addictive. We now know that cocaine abusers go through patterns of tolerance and withdrawal comparable to those experienced by abusers of other psychoactive drugs (Weiss & Iannucci, 2009).

Nicotine Use Disorders

The nicotine in tobacco is a psychoactive substance that produces patterns of dependence, tolerance, and withdrawal—**nicotine use disorders**—comparable to those of the other drugs we have discussed so far (Hughes, 2009). In 1942 the Scottish physician Lennox Johnson "shot up" nicotine extract and found after 80 injections that he liked it more than cigarettes and felt deprived without it (Kanigel, 1988). This colorless, oily liquid—called nicotine after Jean Nicot, who introduced tobacco to the French court in the 16th century—is what gives smoking its pleasurable qualities. Today, about 21% of all Americans smoke, which is down from the 42.4% who were smokers in 1965 (Hughes, 2009).

DSM-IV-TR does not describe an intoxication pattern for nicotine. Rather, it lists withdrawal symptoms, which include depressed mood, insomnia, irritability, anxiety, difficulty concentrating, restlessness, and increased appetite and weight gain. Nicotine in small doses stimulates the central nervous system; it can relieve stress and improve mood. But it can also cause high blood pressure and increase the risk of heart disease and cancer (Stewart, Cutler, & Rosen, 2009). High doses can blur your vision, cause confusion, lead to convulsions, and sometimes even cause death. Once smokers are dependent on nicotine, going without it causes withdrawal symptoms. If you doubt the addictive power of nicotine, consider that the rate of relapse among people trying to give up drugs is equivalent among those using alcohol, heroin, and cigarettes (■ Figure 10.5)

Nicotine is inhaled into the lungs, where it enters the bloodstream. Only 7 to 19 seconds after a person inhales the smoke, the nicotine reaches the brain. Nicotine appears to stimulate specific receptors—nicotinic acetylcholine receptors (nAChRs)—in the midbrain reticular formation and the limbic system, the site of the brain's pleasure pathway (the dopamine system responsible for feelings of euphoria) (Benowitz, 2008). Some evidence

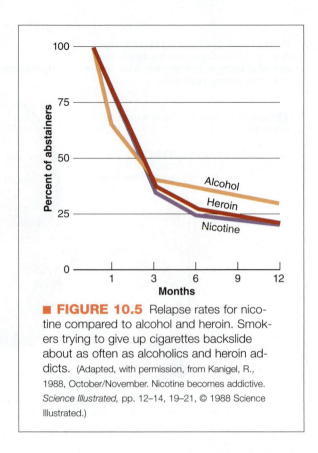

■ **FIGURE 10.5** Relapse rates for nicotine compared to alcohol and heroin. Smokers trying to give up cigarettes backslide about as often as alcoholics and heroin addicts. (Adapted, with permission, from Kanigel, R., 1988, October/November. Nicotine becomes addictive. *Science Illustrated*, pp. 12–14, 19–21, © 1988 Science Illustrated.)

also points to how nicotine may affect the fetal brain, possibly increasing the likelihood that children of mothers who smoke during pregnancy will smoke later in life (Kandel, Wu, & Davies, 1994). Smokers dose themselves throughout the day in an effort to keep nicotine at a steady level in the bloodstream (Dalack, Glassman, & Covey, 1993).

Smoking has been linked with signs of negative affect, such as depression, anxiety, and anger (Rasmusson, Anderson, Krishnan-Sarin, Wu, & Paliwal, 2006). For example, many people who quit smoking but later resume report that feelings of depression or anxiety were responsible for the relapse (Hughes, 2009). This finding suggests that nicotine may help improve mood.

DSM Disorder Criteria Summary
Nicotine Withdrawal

A. Daily use of nicotine for at least several weeks.

B. Abrupt cessation of nicotine use, or reduction in the amount of nicotine used, followed within 24 hours by four (or more) of the following signs: (1) dysphoric or depressed mood; (2) insomnia; (3) irritability, frustration, or anger; (4) anxiety; (5) difficulty concentrating; (6) restlessness; (7) decreased heart rate; (8) increased appetite or weight gain

C. The symptoms in Criterion B cause clinically significant distress or impairment in social, occupational, or other important areas of functioning.

D. The symptoms are not due to a general medical condition and are not better accounted for by another mental disorder.

Source: Reprinted with permission from *Diagnostic and Statistical Manual of Mental Disorders* (4th ed., text revision). © 2000 American Psychiatric Association.

Caffeine Use Disorders

Caffeine is the most common of the psychoactive substances, used regularly by almost 90% of all Americans (Juliano & Griffiths, 2009). Called the "gentle stimulant" because it is thought to be the least harmful of all addictive drugs, caffeine can still lead to **caffeine use disorders**. This drug is found in tea, coffee, many cola drinks sold today, and cocoa products. High levels of caffeine are added to the "energy drinks" that are widely consumed in the United States today but are banned in some European countries (including France, Denmark, and Norway) because of health concerns.

As most of you have experienced firsthand, caffeine in small doses can elevate your mood and decrease fatigue. In larger doses, it can make you feel jittery and can cause insomnia. Because caffeine takes a relatively long time to leave our bodies (about 6 hours), sleep can be disturbed if the caffeine is ingested in the hours close to bedtime. This effect is especially pronounced among those already suffering from insomnia (Saln-Pascual, Castao, Shiromani, Valencia-Flores, & Campos, 2006). As with the other psychoactive drugs, people react variously to caffeine; some are sensitive to it, and others can consume relatively large amounts with little effect. Research suggests that moderate use of caffeine (a cup of coffee per day) by pregnant women does not harm the developing fetus (CARE Study Group, 2008).

As with other stimulants, regular caffeine use can result in tolerance and dependence on the drug. Those of you who have experienced headaches, drowsiness, and a generally unpleasant mood when denied your morning coffee have had the withdrawal symptoms characteristic of this drug (Juliano & Griffiths, 2009). Caffeine's effect on the brain seems to involve the neuromodulator *adenosine* and, to a lesser extent, the neurotransmitter *dopamine* (Herrick, Shecterle, & St. Cyr, 2009). Caffeine seems to block adenosine reuptake. However, we do not yet know the role of adenosine in brain function or whether the interruption of the adenosine system is responsible for the elation and increased energy that come with caffeine use.

Opioids

› **What are the psychological and physiological effects of opiates?**

The word *opiate* refers to the natural chemicals in the opium poppy that have a narcotic effect (they relieve pain and induce sleep). In some circumstances, they can cause **opioid use disorders**. The broader term *opioids* refers to the family of substances that includes natural opiates, synthetic variations (heroin, methadone, hydrocodone, oxycodone), and the comparable substances that occur naturally in the brain (enkephalins, beta-endorphins, and dynorphins). References to the use of opium as a medicine date back more than 3,500 years (Strain, Lofwall, & Jaffe, 2009). In *The Wizard of Oz*, the Wicked Witch of the West puts Dorothy, Toto, and their companions to sleep by making them walk through a field of poppies, a literary allusion to the opium poppies used to produce morphine, codeine, and heroin.

Just as the poppies lull the Tin Man, the Scarecrow, Dorothy, the Cowardly Lion, and Toto, opiates induce euphoria, drowsiness, and slowed breathing. High doses can lead to death if respiration is completely depressed. Opiates are also analgesics, substances that help relieve pain. People are sometimes given morphine before and after surgery to calm them and help block pain.

Withdrawal from opioids can be so unpleasant that people may continue to use these drugs despite a sincere desire to stop. However, barbiturate and alcohol withdrawal can be even more distressing. Even so, people who cease or reduce their opioid intake begin to experience symptoms within 6 to 12 hours; these include excessive yawning, nausea and vomiting, chills, muscle aches, diarrhea, and insomnia—temporarily disrupting work, school, and social relationships. The symptoms can persist for 1 to 3 days, and the withdrawal process is completed in about a week.

nicotine use disorders Cognitive, biological, behavioral, and social problems associated with the use and abuse of nicotine.
caffeine use disorders Cognitive, biological, behavioral, and social problems associated with the use and abuse of caffeine.
opioid use disorders Cognitive, biological, behavioral, and social problems associated with the use and abuse of opiates and their synthetic variants.

Nicotine Dependence

"You can't simply focus on nicotine itself. Many medications do that—they focus on replacing the nicotine, such as nicotine gum or the patch—and that's valuable, but you really have to focus on all the triggers, the cues, and the environment."

Abnormal Psychology Inside Out. Produced by Ira Wohl, Only Child Motion Pictures

Go to Psychology CourseMate at www.cengagebrain.com to watch this video.

Abuse of and dependence on heroin—the most commonly abused opiate—are reported in about a quarter million people in the United States (Substance Abuse and Mental Health Services Administration, 2009). Illicit use of opioid-containing prescription medicines has risen in recent years; one survey found that 9.3% of high school seniors reported using hydrocodone without a prescription and 5% used oxycodone (Johnston, Bachman, & Schulenberg, 2005). People who use opiates face risks beyond addiction and the threat of overdose. Because these drugs are usually injected intravenously, users are at increased risk for HIV infection and therefore AIDS.

The life of an opiate addict can be bleak. Results from a 33-year follow-up study of more than 80 addicts in an English town highlight a pessimistic view of many of their lives (Rathod, Addenbrooke, & Rosenbach, 2005). At the follow-up, 22% of addicts had died, about twice the national rate of about 12%. More than half the deaths were the result of drug overdose, and several took their own lives. The good news from this study was that of those who survived, 80% were no longer using opioids and the remaining 20% were being treated with methadone.

The high or "rush" experienced by users comes from activation of the body's natural opioid system. In other words, the brain already has its own opioids—called enkephalins and endorphins—that provide narcotic effects (Strain et al., 2009). Heroin, opium, morphine, and other opiates activate this system. The discovery of the natural opioid system was a major breakthrough in the field of psychopharmacology: Not only does it allow us to study the effects of addictive drugs on the brain, but it also has led to important discoveries that may help us treat people dependent on these drugs.

Dan Gair/JupiterImages

▲ Opium poppies.

DSM | Disorder Criteria Summary
Opioid Intoxication

A. Recent use of an opioid.

B. Clinically significant maladaptive behavioral or psychological changes (e.g., initial euphoria followed by apathy, dysphoria, psychomotor agitation or retardation, impaired judgment, or impaired social or occupational functioning) that developed during, or shortly after, opioid use.

C. Pupillary constriction (or pupillary dilation due to anoxia from severe overdose) and one (or more) of the following signs, developing during, or shortly after, opioid use: (1) drowsiness or coma; (2) slurred speech; (3) impairment in attention or memory

D. The symptoms are not due to a general medical condition and are not better accounted for by another mental disorder.

Specify if:

With Perceptual Disturbances: This specifier may be noted in the rare instance in which hallucinations with intact reality testing or auditory, visual, or tactile illusions occur in the absence of a delirium. Intact reality testing means that the person knows that the hallucinations are induced by the substance and do not represent external reality. When hallucinations occur in the absence of intact reality testing, a diagnosis of Substance-Induced Psychotic Disorder, With Hallucinations, should be considered.

Source: Reprinted with permission from *Diagnostic and Statistical Manual of Mental Disorders* (4th ed., text revision). © 2000 American Psychiatric Association.

Hallucinogens

› **How do opioids differ from hallucinogens?**

The substances we have examined so far affect people by making them feel "up," if they are stimulants such as cocaine, caffeine, and nicotine, or "down," if they are depressants such as alcohol and the barbiturates. Next, we explore the substances that can lead to **hallucinogen use disorder**. They essentially change the way the user perceives the world. Sight, sound, feelings, taste, and even smell are distorted, sometimes in dramatic ways, when a person is under the influence of drugs such as marijuana and LSD.

Marijuana

Marijuana is the most routinely used illegal substance, with 15.2 million Americans reporting they used the drug in the past month (Substance Abuse and Mental Health Services Administration, 2009). **Marijuana** is the name given to the dried parts of the cannabis or hemp plant (its full scientific name is *Cannabis sativa*) (Hall & Degenhardt, 2009). Cannabis grows wild throughout the tropical and temperate regions of the world, which accounts for one of its nicknames: "weed."

Reactions to marijuana usually include mood swings. Otherwise-normal experiences seem extremely funny, or the person might enter a dreamlike state in which time seems to stand still. Users often report heightened sensory experiences, seeing vivid colors, or appreciating the subtleties of music. Perhaps more than any other drug, however, marijuana can produce different reactions in people. It is not uncommon for someone to report having no reaction to the first use of the drug; it also appears that people can "turn off" the high if they are sufficiently motivated (Hall & Degenhardt, 2009). The feelings of well-being produced by small doses can change to paranoia, hallucinations, and dizziness when larger doses are taken. High school–age marijuana smokers get lower grades and are less likely to graduate (Lynskey & Hall, 2000). Research on frequent marijuana users suggests that impairments of memory, concentration, relationships with others, and employment may be negative outcomes of long-term use,

although some researchers suggest that some psychological problems precede usage—increasing the likelihood that someone will use marijuana (Macleod et al., 2004).

The evidence for marijuana tolerance is contradictory. Chronic and heavy users report tolerance, especially to the euphoric high (Mennes, Ben Abdallah, & Cottler, 2009); they are unable to reach the levels of pleasure they experienced earlier. However, evidence also indicates "reverse tolerance," when regular users experience more pleasure from the drug after repeated use. Major signs of withdrawal do not usually occur with marijuana. Chronic users who stop taking the drug report a period of irritability, restlessness, appetite loss, nausea, and difficulty sleeping (National Institute on Drug Abuse, 2005).

Controversy surrounds the use of marijuana for medicinal purposes. However, there appears to be an increasing database documenting the successful use of marijuana and its by-products for the symptoms of certain diseases. In Canada, for example, four cannabis products are available for medical use, including an herbal cannabis extract (Sativex—delivered in a nasal spray), dronabinol (Marinol), nabilone (Cesamet), and the herbal form of cannabis that is typically smoked (Wang, Collet, Shapiro, & Ware, 2008). These cannabis-derived products are prescribed for chemotherapy-induced nausea and vomiting, HIV-associated anorexia, neuropathic pain in multiple sclerosis, and cancer pain. Unfortunately, marijuana smoke may contain as many carcinogens as tobacco smoke, and long-term use of the smoked form of the drug may contribute to diseases such as lung cancer. Most marijuana users inhale the drug by smoking the dried leaves in marijuana cigarettes; others use preparations such as hashish, which is the dried form of the resin in the leaves of the female plant. Marijuana contains more than 80 varieties of the chemicals called *cannabinoids,* which are believed to alter mood and behavior. The most common of these chemicals includes the *tetrahydrocannabinols,* otherwise known as *THC.* An exciting finding in the area of marijuana research is that the brain makes its own version of THC, a neurochemical called *anandamide* after the Sanskrit word *ananda,* which means "bliss" (Sedlak & Kaplin, 2009). Scientists are only beginning to explore how this neurochemical affects the brain and behavior.

LSD and Other Hallucinogens

LSD (*d*-lysergic acid diethylamide), sometimes referred to as "acid," is the most common hallucinogenic drug. It is produced synthetically in laboratories, although naturally

▲ Marijuana.

©WILDLIFE GmbH/Alamy

occurring derivatives of this grain fungus (ergot) have been found historically. In Europe during the Middle Ages, an outbreak of illnesses occurred as a result of people's eating grain that was infected with the fungus. One version of this illness—later called *ergotism*—constricted the flow of blood to the arms or legs and eventually resulted in gangrene and the loss of limbs. Another type of illness resulted in convulsions, delirium, and hallucinations. Years later, scientists connected ergot with the illnesses and began studying versions of this fungus for possible benefits. LSD remained in the laboratory until the 1960s, when it was first produced illegally for recreational use. The mind-altering effects of the drug suited the social effort to reject established culture and enhanced the search for enlightenment that characterized the mood and behavior of many people during that decade. The late Timothy Leary, at the time a Harvard University research professor, first used LSD in 1961 and immediately began a movement to have every child and adult try the drug and "turn on, tune in, and drop out."

There are a number of other hallucinogens, some occurring naturally in a variety of plants: *psilocybin* (found in certain species of mushrooms); *lysergic acid amide* (found in the seeds of the morning glory plant); *dimethyltryptamine (DMT)* (found in the bark of the Virola tree, which grows in South and Central America); and *mescaline* (found in the peyote cactus plant).

The *DSM-IV-TR* diagnostic criteria for hallucinogen intoxication are similar to those for marijuana: perceptual changes such as the subjective intensification of perceptions, depersonalization, and hallucinations. Physical symptoms include pupillary dilation, rapid heartbeat, sweating, and blurred vision (American Psychiatric Association, 2000). Many users have written about hallucinogens, and they describe a variety of experiences. In one well-designed placebo-controlled study of hallucinogens, researchers at Johns Hopkins School of Medicine gave volunteers either the hallucinogen psilocybin or a control drug (the ADHD medication Ritalin) and assessed their reactions (Griffiths, Richards, McCann, & Jesse, 2006). Psilocybin ingestion resulted in individualized reactions including perceptual changes (for example, mild visual hallucinations) and mood changes (for example, joy or happiness, anxiety, or fearfulness). Interestingly, the drug increased reports of mystical experiences (for example, deeply felt positive mood), and 2 months later many rated the experience as having a spiritual significance. More research is needed to explore how these types of drugs work, and this research may also tell us how our brains process experiences such as personal meaning and spirituality (Griffiths, Richards, Johnson, McCann, & Jesse, 2008).

Tolerance develops quickly to a number of hallucinogens, including LSD, psilocybin, and mescaline (Jones, 2009). If taken repeatedly over a period of days, these drugs lose their effectiveness. However, sensitivity returns after about a week of abstinence. For most hallucinogens, no withdrawal symptoms are reported. Even so, a number of concerns have been expressed about their use. One is the possibility of psychotic reactions. Stories in the popular press about people who jumped out of windows because they believed they could fly or who stepped into moving traffic with the mistaken idea that they couldn't be hurt have provided for sensational reading, but little evidence suggests that using hallucinogens produces a greater risk than being drunk or under the influence of any other drug. People do report having "bad trips"; these are the sort of frightening episodes in which clouds turn into threatening monsters or deep feelings of paranoia take over. Usually someone on a bad trip can be "talked down" by supportive people who provide constant reassurance that the experience is the temporary effect of the drug and it will wear off in a few hours.

We still do not fully understand how LSD and the other hallucinogens affect the brain. Most of these drugs bear some resemblance to neurotransmitters; LSD, psilocybin, lysergic acid amide, and DMT are chemically similar to serotonin; mescaline resembles norepinephrine; and a number of other hallucinogens we have not discussed are similar to acetylcholine. However, the mechanisms responsible for the hallucinations and other perceptual changes that users experience remain unknown.

Other Drugs of Abuse

A number of other substances are used by individuals to alter sensory experiences. We briefly describe inhalants, steroids, and a group of drugs commonly referred to as designer drugs.

Inhalants include a variety of substances found in volatile solvents—making them available to breathe into the lungs directly. Some common inhalants that are used abusively include spray paint, hair spray, paint thinner, gasoline, amyl nitrate, nitrous oxide ("laughing gas"), nail polish remover, felt-tipped markers, airplane glue, contact cement, dry-cleaning fluid, and spot remover (Sakai & Crowley, 2009). A typical person who engages in inhalant use tends to be male, Caucasian, live in rural or small towns, have higher levels of anxiety and depression, and show more impulsive and fearless temperaments (Perron & Howard, 2009). These drugs are rapidly absorbed into the bloodstream through the lungs by inhaling them from containers or on a cloth held up to the mouth and nose. The high associated with the use of inhalants resembles that of alcohol intoxication and usually includes dizziness, slurred speech, incoordination, euphoria, and lethargy (American Psychiatric Association, 2000). Users build up a tolerance to the drugs, and withdrawal—which involves sleep disturbance, tremors, irritability, and nausea—can last from 2 to 5 days. Unfortunately, use can also increase aggressive and antisocial behavior, and long-term use can damage bone marrow, kidneys, liver, and the brain (Sakai & Crowley, 2009).

Anabolic–androgenic steroids (more commonly referred to as steroids or "roids" or "juice") are derived from or are a synthesized form of the hormone testosterone (Pope & Brower, 2009). The legitimate medical uses of these drugs focus on people with asthma, anemia, breast cancer, and males with inadequate sexual development. However, the anabolic action of these drugs (that can produce increased body mass) has resulted in their illicit use by those wishing to bulk up and improve their physical abilities. Steroids can be taken orally or through injection, and some estimates suggest that approximately 2% of males will use the drug illegally at some point in their lives (Kanayama, Brower, Wood, Hudson, & Pope Jr., 2010). Users sometimes administer the drug on a schedule of several weeks or months followed by a break from its use—called "cycling"—or combine several types of steroids—called "stacking." Steroid use differs from other drug use because the substance does not produce a desirable high but instead is used to enhance performance and body size. Dependence on the substance therefore seems to involve the desire to maintain the performance gains obtained rather than a need to reexperience an altered emotional or physical

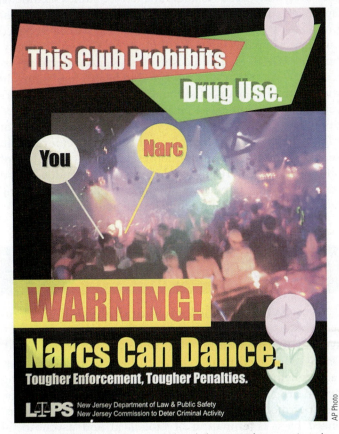

▲ The proliferation of new recreational drugs such as ecstasy inspires ever more vigilance on the part of the legal system.

state. Research on the long-term effects of steroid use seems to suggest that mood disturbances are common (for example, depression, anxiety, and panic attacks) (Pope & Brower, 2009), and there is a concern that more serious physical consequences may result from regular use.

Another class of drugs—dissociative anesthetics—causes drowsiness, pain relief, and the feeling of being out of one's body (Javitt & Zukin, 2009). Sometimes referred to as designer drugs, this growing group of drugs was originally developed by pharmaceutical companies to target specific diseases and disorders. It was only a matter of time before some began using the developing technology to design "recreational drugs." We have already described one of the more common illicit designer drugs—MDMA, or ecstasy—in the section on stimulants. This amphetamine is one of a small but feared growing list of related substances that includes 3,4-methelenedioxyethamphetamine (MDEA, or eve), and 2-(4-bromo-2,5-dimethoxy-phenyl)-ethylamine (BDMPEA, or Nexus) (Wu et al., 2009). Their ability to heighten a person's auditory and visual perception, and the senses of taste and touch, has been incorporated into the activities of those who attend nightclubs, all-night dance parties (raves), or large social gatherings of primarily gay men (called "circuit parties").

Phencyclidine (or PCP) is snorted, smoked, or injected intravenously, and it causes impulsivity and aggressiveness. A drug related to phencyclidine and associated with the "drug club" scene is ketamine (street names include K, Special K, and cat valium), a dissociative anesthetic that produces a sense of detachment, along with a reduced awareness of pain (Javitt & Zukin, 2009). Gamma-hydroxybutyrate (GHB, or liquid ecstasy) is a central nervous system depressant that was marketed in health food stores in the 1980s as a means of stimulating muscle growth. Users report that, at low doses, it can produce a state of relaxation and increased tendency to verbalize but that at higher doses or with alcohol or other drugs it can result in seizures, severe respiratory depression, and coma. Use of all these drugs can result in tolerance and dependence, and their increasing popularity among adolescents and young adults raises significant public health concerns.

Concept Check 10.2

Determine whether the following statements about stimulants are true (T) or false (F).

1. __ Use of crack cocaine by a pregnant woman always adversely affects the developing fetus.

2. __ Regular use of stimulants can result in tolerance and dependence on the drugs.

3. __ Amphetamines have been used as appetite suppressants.

4. __ Compared to all other drugs, caffeine can produce the most variable reactions in people.

5. __ Amphetamines are naturally occurring drugs that induce feelings of elation and vigor and can reduce fatigue.

6. __ Stimulants are produced only in a laboratory.

Causes of Substance-Related Disorders

> **What psychological and physiological processes lead to substance dependence?**

We saw that despite his clear potential as an individual, Danny continued to use drugs to his detriment. Various factors help explain why people like Danny persist in using drugs. Drug abuse and dependence, once thought to be the result of moral weakness, are now understood to be influenced by a combination of biological and psychosocial factors.

Why do some people use psychoactive drugs without abusing or becoming dependent on them? Why do some people stop using these drugs or use them in moderate amounts after being dependent on them and others continue a lifelong pattern of dependence despite their efforts to stop? These questions continue to occupy the time and attention of numerous researchers throughout the world.

Biological Dimensions

In 2007, when American model and television personality Anna Nicole Smith died from an apparently accidental overdose of at least nine prescription medications—including methadone, Valium, and the sedative chloral hydrate—the unfortunate news created a media sensation. The tragedy was compounded by the fact that, just months before, her only son Daniel had died, also from an apparent drug overdose. Did the son inherit a vulnerability to addiction from his mother? Did he pick up Anna Nicole's habits from living with her over the years? Is it just a coincidence that both mother and son were so involved with drugs?

Familial and Genetic Influences

As you already have seen throughout this book, many psychological disorders are influenced in important ways by genetics. Mounting evidence indicates that drug abuse follows this pattern. A great deal of animal research confirms the importance of genetic influences on substance abuse. In work with humans, researchers conducting twin, family, and adoption studies have found that certain people are genetically vulnerable to drug abuse (Strain, 2009). Twin studies of smoking, for example, indicate a moderate genetic influence (e.g., Hardie, Moss, & Lynch, 2006; McCaffery, Papandonatos, Stanton, Lloyd-Richardson, & Niaura, 2008). However, most genetic data on substance abuse come from research on alcoholism, which is widely studied because alcohol use is legal and many people are dependent on it. Research in general suggests that genetic risk factors cut across all mood-altering drugs (Strain, 2009).

In a major twin study, the role of the environment, and the role of genetics, was examined in substance use, abuse, and dependence. Researchers studied more than 1,000 pairs of male twins and questioned them about their use of marijuana, cocaine, hallucinogens, sedatives, stimulants, and opiates (Kendler, Jacobson, Prescott, & Neale, 2003). The findings suggest that there are common genetic influences on the use of all of these drugs. However, the *use* of illegal drugs was primarily influenced by environmental factors, whereas *abuse and dependence* may be influenced primarily by genetic factors. Therefore, whether or not you use drugs such as cocaine or heroin may be a factor of whom and what you are exposed to, but whether you will become addicted is largely a function of your biology. As the search for the genes influencing substance use, abuse, and dependence continues, the next obvious question is how these genes function when it comes to addiction—a field of research called *functional genomics* (Khokhar, Ferguson, Zhu, & Tyndale, 2010).

Genetic research to date tells us that substance abuse in general is affected by our genes but no one gene causes substance abuse or dependence. Genetic factors may affect how people experience certain drugs, which in turn may partly determine who will or will not become abusers. Just to illustrate how complex these relationships can be, research has found that certain genes are associated with a greater likelihood of heroin addiction in Hispanic and African American populations (Nielsen et al., 2008).

Neurobiological Influences

In general, the pleasurable experiences reported by people who use psychoactive substances partly explain why people continue to use them (Strain, 2009). In behavioral terms, people are positively reinforced for using drugs. But what mechanism is responsible for such experiences? Complex and fascinating studies indicate the brain appears to have a natural "pleasure pathway" that mediates our experience of reward. All abused substances seem to affect this internal reward center. In other words, what psychoactive drugs may have in common is their ability to activate this reward center and provide the user with a pleasurable experience, at least for a time.

The pleasure center was discovered more than 50 years ago by James Olds, who studied the effects of electrical stimulation on rat brains (Olds, 1956; Olds & Milner, 1954). If certain areas were stimulated with small amounts of electricity, the rats behaved as if they had received something pleasant, such as food. The exact location of the area in the human brain is still subject to debate, although it is believed to include the *dopaminergic system* and its *opioid-releasing neurons*, which begin in the midbrain *ventral tegmental area* and then work their way forward through the *nucleus accumbens* and on to the frontal cortex (Strain, 2009).

How do different drugs that affect different neurotransmitter systems all converge to activate the pleasure pathway, which is primarily made up of dopamine-sensitive neurons? Researchers are only beginning to sort out the answers to this question, but some surprising findings have emerged in recent years. For example, we know that amphetamines and cocaine act directly on the dopamine system. Other drugs, however, appear to increase the availability of dopamine in more roundabout and intricate ways. For example, the neurons in the brain's ventral tegmental area are kept from continuous firing by GABA neurons. One thing that keeps us from being on an unending high is the presence of these GABA neurons, which act as the "brain police," or superegos of the reward neurotransmitter system. Opiates (opium, morphine, heroin) inhibit GABA, which in turn stops the GABA neurons from inhibiting dopamine, which makes more dopamine available in the brain's pleasure pathway. Drugs that stimulate the reward center directly or indirectly include not only amphetamine, cocaine, and opiates but also nicotine and alcohol (Strain, 2009).

This complicated picture is far from complete. We now understand that other neurotransmitters in addition to dopamine—including serotonin and norepinephrine—are also involved in the brain's reward system (Khokhar et al., 2010). The coming years should yield interesting insights into the interaction of drugs and the brain. One aspect that awaits explanation is how drugs not only provide pleasurable experiences (positive reinforcement) but also help remove unpleasant experiences such as pain, feelings of illness, or anxiety (negative reinforcement). Aspirin is a negative reinforcer: We take it not because it makes us feel good but because it stops us from feeling bad. In much the same way, one property of the psychoactive drugs is that they stop people from feeling bad, an effect as powerful as making them feel good.

With several drugs, negative reinforcement is related to the anxiolytic effect, the ability to reduce anxiety (discussed briefly in the section on the sedative, hypnotic, and anxiolytic drugs). Alcohol has an anxiolytic effect. The neurobiology of how these drugs reduce anxiety seems to involve the septal–hippocampal system (Gray, 1987), which includes a large number of GABA-sensitive neurons. Certain drugs may reduce anxiety by enhancing the activity of GABA in this region, thereby inhibiting the brain's normal reaction (anxiety or fear) to anxiety-producing situations (Gordis, 2000; Pihl, Peterson, & Lau, 1993). Researchers have identified individual differences in the way people respond to alcohol. Understanding these response differences is important because they may help explain why some people continue to use drugs until they acquire a dependence on them, whereas others stop before this happens. A number of studies compare individuals with and without a family history of alcoholism (Gordis, 2000). They concluded that, compared to the sons of nonalcoholics, the sons of alcoholics may be more sensitive to alcohol when it is first ingested and then become less sensitive to its effects as the hours pass after drinking. This finding is significant because the euphoric effects of alcohol occur just after drinking but the experience after several hours is often sadness and depression. People who are at risk for developing alcoholism (in this case, the sons of alcoholics) may be better able to appreciate the initial highs of drinking and be less sensitive to the lows that come later, making them ideal candidates for continued drinking. In support of this observation, follow-up research over a 10-year period found that those men who tended to be less sensitive to alcohol also tended to drink more heavily and more often (Schuckit, 1994, 1998).

Psychological Dimensions

We have shown that the substances people use to alter mood and behavior have unique effects. The high from heroin differs substantially from the experience of smoking a cigarette, which in turn differs from the effects of amphetamines or LSD. Nevertheless, it is important to point out the similarities in the way people mentally react to most of these substances.

Positive Reinforcement

The feelings that result from using psychoactive substances are pleasurable in some way, and people will continue to take the drugs to recapture the pleasure. Research shows quite clearly that many drugs used and abused by humans also seem to be pleasurable to animals (Young & Herling, 1986). Laboratory animals will work to have their bodies injected with drugs such as cocaine, amphetamines, opiates, sedatives, and alcohol, which demonstrates that even without social and cultural influences these drugs are pleasurable.

Human research also indicates that to some extent all psychoactive drugs provide a pleasurable experience (Strain, 2009). In addition, the social contexts for drug taking may encourage its use, even when the use alone is not the desired outcome. One study found that among volunteers who preferred not to take Valium, pairing money with pill taking caused participants to switch from a placebo to Valium (Alessi, Roll, Reilly, & Johanson, 2002). Positive reinforcement in the use and the situations surrounding the use of drugs contributes to whether or not people decide to try to continue using drugs.

Negative Reinforcement

Most researchers have looked at how drugs help reduce unpleasant feelings through negative reinforcement. Many people are likely to initiate and continue drug use to escape from unpleasantness in their lives. In addition to the initial euphoria, many drugs provide escape from physical pain (opiates), from stress (alcohol), or from panic and anxiety (benzodiazepines). This phenomenon has been explored under a number of different names, including *tension reduction, negative affect,* and *self-medication,* each of which has a somewhat different focus (Strain, 2009).

Basic to many views of abuse and dependence is the premise that substance use becomes a way for users to cope with the unpleasant feelings that go along with life circumstances. For example, one study of 1,252 U.S. Army soldiers returning home from Operation Iraqi Freedom found that those exposed to violent combat and human trauma and those having direct responsibility for taking the life of another person were at increased risk for risk-taking and for more frequent and greater alcohol use (Killgore et al., 2008). People who experience other types of trauma such as sexual abuse are also more likely to abuse alcohol (Ullman, Najdowski, & Filipas, 2009). These observations emphasize the important role played by each aspect of abuse and dependence—biological, psychological, social, and cultural—in determining who will and who will not have difficulties with these substances.

In a study that examined substance use among adolescents as a way to reduce stress (Chassin, Pillow, Curran, Molina, & Barrera, 1993), researchers compared a group of adolescents with alcoholic parents with a group whose parents did not have drinking problems. The average age of the adolescents was 12.7 years. The researchers found that just having a parent with alcohol dependence was a major factor in predicting who would use alcohol and other drugs. However, they also found that adolescents who reported negative affect, such as feeling lonely, crying a lot, or being tense, were more likely than others to use drugs. The researchers further determined that the adolescents from both groups tended to use drugs as a way to cope with unpleasant feelings. This study and others (see, for example, Pardini, Lochman, & Wells, 2004) suggest that one contributing factor to adolescent drug use is the desire to escape from unpleasantness. It also suggests that to prevent people from using drugs we may need to address influences such as stress and anxiety, a strategy we discuss in our section on treatment.

Many people who use psychoactive substances experience a crash after being high. If people reliably crash, why don't they just stop taking drugs? One explanation is given by Solomon and Corbit in an interesting integration of both the positive and the negative reinforcement processes (Solomon, 1980; Solomon & Corbit, 1974). The *opponent-process theory* holds that an increase in positive feelings will be followed shortly by an increase in negative feelings. Similarly, an increase in negative feelings will be followed by a period of positive feelings (Skinner & Aubin, 2010). Athletes often report feeling depressed after finally attaining a long-sought goal. The opponent-process theory claims that this mechanism is strengthened with use and weakened by disuse. So a person who has been using a drug for some time will need more of it to achieve the same results (tolerance). At the same time, the negative feelings that follow drug use tend to intensify. For many people, this is the point at which the motivation for drug taking shifts from desiring the euphoric high to alleviating the increasingly unpleasant crash. Unfortunately, the best remedy is more of the same drug. People who are hung over after drinking too much alcohol are often advised to have "the hair of the dog that bit you" (that is, have another drink). The sad irony here is that the very drug that can make you feel so bad is also the one thing that can take away your pain. You can see why people can become enslaved by this insidious cycle.

Researchers have also looked at substance abuse as a way of self-medicating for other problems. If people have difficulties with anxiety, for example, they may be attracted to barbiturates or alcohol because of their anxiety-reducing qualities. In one study, researchers were successful in treating a group of cocaine addicts who had ADHD with methylphenidate (Ritalin) (Levin, Evans, Brooks, & Garawi, 2007). They had hypothesized that these individuals used cocaine to help focus their attention. Once their ability to concentrate improved with the methylphenidate, the users reduced their use of cocaine.

Cognitive Factors

What people expect to experience when they use drugs influences how they react to them. A person who expects to be less inhibited when she drinks alcohol will act less inhibited whether she actually drinks alcohol or a placebo she thinks is alcohol (Moss & Albery, 2009). This observation about the influence of how we think about drug use has been labeled an *expectancy effect* and has received considerable research attention.

Expectancies develop before people actually use drugs, perhaps as a result of parents' and peers' drug use, advertising, and media figures who model drug use (Campbell & Oei, 2010). In one study, a large group of seventh- and eighth-graders were given questionnaires that focused on their expectations about drinking. The researchers reexamined the students 1 year later to see how their expectancies predicted their later drinking (Christiansen, Smith, Roehling, & Goldman, 1989). One surprising finding was the marked increase in drinking among the students only 1 year later. When researchers first questioned them, about 10% of the students reported getting drunk 2 to 4 times per year. This number had risen to 25% by the next year. The students' expectations of drinking did predict who would later have drinking problems. Students who thought that drinking would improve their social behavior and their cognitive and motor abilities (despite all evidence to the contrary) were more likely to have drinking problems 1 year later. These results suggest that adolescents may begin drinking partly because they believe drinking will have positive effects.

Expectations appear to change as people have more experience with drugs, although their expectations are similar for alcohol, nicotine, marijuana, and cocaine (Simons, Dvorak, & Lau-Barraco, 2009). Some evidence points to positive expectancies—believing you will feel good if you take a drug—as an indirect influence on drug problems. In other words, what these beliefs may do is increase the likelihood you will take certain drugs, which in turn will increase the likelihood that problems will arise.

Once people stop taking drugs after prolonged or repeated use, powerful urges called "cravings" can interfere with efforts to remain off these drugs (Epstein, Marrone, Heishman, Schmittner, & Preston, 2010). If you've ever tried to give up ice cream and then found yourself compelled to have some, you have a limited idea of what it might be like to crave a drug. These urges seem to be triggered by factors such as the availability of the drug, contact with things associated with drug taking (for example, sitting in a bar), specific moods (for example, being depressed), or having a small dose of the drug. For example, one study used a virtual reality apparatus to simulate visual, auditory, and olfactory (an alcohol-dipped tissue) cues (Lee et al., 2009) for alcohol-dependent adults. The participants could choose among kinds of alcoholic beverages (e.g., beer, whiskey, or wine), snacks, and drinking environments (beer garden, restaurant, and pub). The researchers found significant increases in cravings for alcohol under these conditions (Lee et al., 2009). This type of technology may make it easier for clinicians to assess potential problem areas for clients, which can then be targeted to help keep them from relapsing. Research is under way to determine how cravings may work in the brain and if certain medications can be used to reduce these urges and help supplement treatment (Skinner & Aubin, 2010).

Social Dimensions

Previously, we pointed out the importance of exposure to psychoactive substances as a necessary prerequisite to their use and possible abuse. You could probably list a number of ways people are exposed to these substances—through friends, through the media, and so on. For example, research on the consequences of cigarette advertising suggests the effects of media exposure may be more influential than peer pressure in determining whether teens smoke (Jackson, Brown, & L'Engle, 2007).

Research suggests that drug-addicted parents spend less time monitoring their children than parents without drug problems (Dishion, Patterson, & Reid, 1988) and that this is an important contribution to early adolescent substance use (Barnes, Hoffman, Welte, Farrell, & Dintcheff, 2006). When parents did not provide appropriate supervision, their children tended to develop friendships with peers who supported drug use. Children influenced by drug use at home may be exposed to peers who use drugs as well. A self-perpetuating pattern seems to be associated with drug use that extends beyond the genetic influences we discussed previously.

How does our society view people who are dependent on drugs? This issue is of tremendous importance because it affects efforts to legislate the sale, manufacture, possession, and use of these substances. It also dictates how drug-dependent individuals are treated. Two views of substance abuse and dependence characterize contemporary thought: the moral weakness and the disease models of dependence. According to the *moral weakness model of chemical dependence,* drug use is seen as a failure of self-control in the face of temptation; this is a psychosocial perspective. Proponents of this model see drug users as lacking the character or moral fiber to resist the lure of drugs. The *disease model of dependence,* in contrast, assumes that drug dependence is caused by an underlying physiological disorder; this is a biological perspective. Those who ascribe to this model think that just as diabetes or asthma can't be blamed on the afflicted individuals, neither should drug dependence. AA and similar organizations see drug dependence as an incurable disease over which the addict has no control (Kelly, Stout, Magill, Tonigan, & Pagano, 2010).

Neither perspective does justice to the complex interrelationship between the psychosocial and biological influences that affect substance disorders. Viewing drug use as moral weakness leads to punishing those afflicted with the disorder, whereas a disease model includes seeking treatment for a medical problem. Messages that the disorder is out of their control can at times be counterproductive. A comprehensive view of substance-related disorders that includes both psychosocial and biological influences is needed for this important societal concern to be addressed adequately.

Cultural Dimensions

When we examine a behavior as it appears in different cultures, it is necessary to reexamine what is considered abnormal (Kohn, Wintrob, & Alarcon, 2009). Each culture has its own preferences for acceptable psychoactive drugs and its own prohibitions for substances it finds unacceptable. Keep in mind that in addition to defining what is or is not acceptable, cultural norms affect the rates of substance abuse and dependence in important ways. For example, poor economic conditions in certain parts of the world limit the availability of drugs, which appears partly to account for the relatively low prevalence of substance abuse in Mexico and Brazil (de Almeidia-Filho, Santana, Pinto, & de Carvalho-Neto, 1991; Ortiz & Medicna-Mora, 1988).

However, in certain cultures, including Korea, people are expected to drink alcohol heavily on certain social occasions (C. K. Lee, 1992). As we have seen before, exposure to these substances, in addition to social pressure for heavy and frequent use, may facilitate their abuse, and this may explain the high alcohol abuse rates in countries like Korea. This cultural influence provides an interesting natural experiment when exploring gene–environment interactions. People of Asian descent are more likely to have the ALDH2 gene, which produces a severe "flushing" effect (reddening and burning of the face) after drinking alcohol. This flushing effect was thought to be responsible for a relatively low rate of drinking in the population. However, between 1979 and 1992—when increased drinking became socially expected—there was an increase in alcohol abuse (Higuchi et al., 1994). The protective value of having the ALDH2 gene was diminished by the change in cultural norms (Rutter, Moffit, & Caspi, 2006).

Cultural factors not only influence the rates of substance abuse but also determine how it is manifest. Research indicates that alcohol consumption in Poland and Finland is relatively low, yet conflicts related to drinking and arrests for drunkenness in those countries are high compared to those in the Netherlands, which has about the same rate of alcohol consumption (Osterberg, 1986). Our discussion of expectancies may provide some insight into how the same amount of drinking can have different behavioral outcomes. Expectancies about the effects of alcohol use differ across cultures (for example, "Drinking makes me more aggressive" versus "Drinking makes me more withdrawn"); these differing expectancies may partially account for the variations in the consequences of drinking in Poland, Finland, and the Netherlands. Whether substance use is considered a harmful dysfunction often depends on the assumptions of the cultural group.

An Integrative Model

Any explanation of substance use, abuse, and dependence must account for the basic issue raised earlier in this chapter: Why do some people use drugs but not abuse them or become dependent? ■ Figure 10.6 illustrates how the multiple influences we have discussed may interact to account for this process. Access to a drug is a necessary but not a sufficient condition for abuse or dependence. Exposure has many sources, including the media, parents, peers, and, indirectly, lack of supervision. Whether people use a drug depends also on social and cultural expectations, some encouraging and some discouraging, such as laws against possession or sale of the drug.

The path from drug use to abuse and dependence is more complicated (see Figure 11.9). As major stressors aggravate many disorders we have discussed, so do they increase the risk of abuse and dependence on psychoactive substances. Genetic influences may be of several types. Some individuals may inherit a greater sensitivity to the effects of certain drugs; others may inherit an ability to metabolize substances more quickly and are thereby able to tolerate higher (and more dangerous) levels. Other psychiatric conditions may indirectly put someone at risk for substance abuse. Antisocial personality disorder, characterized by the frequent violation of social norms (see Chapter 11), is thought to include a lowered rate of arousal; this may account for the increased prevalence of substance abuse in this group. People with mood disorders or anxiety disorders may self-medicate by using drugs to relieve the negative symptoms of their disorder, and this may account for the high rates of substance abuse in this group.

We know also that continued use of certain substances changes the way our brains work through a process called *neuroplasticity*. With the continued use of substances such as alcohol, cocaine, or the other drugs we explore in this chapter, the brain reorganizes itself to adapt. Un-

▲ In many cultures, alcohol is used ceremonially.

©W. Perry Conway/Corbis

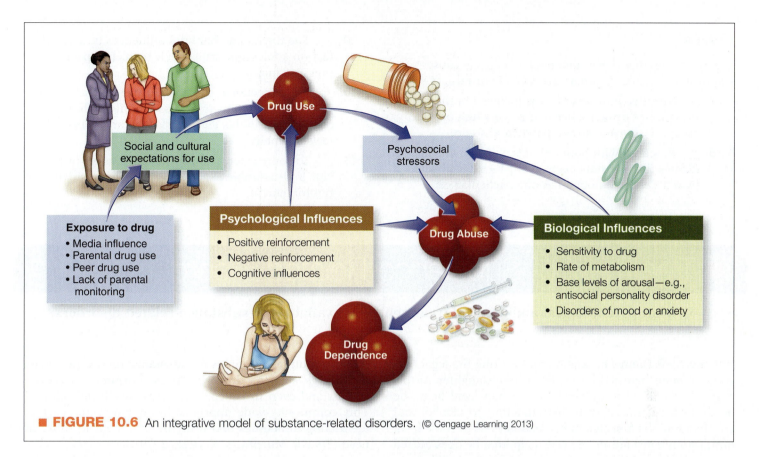

■ FIGURE 10.6 An integrative model of substance-related disorders. (© Cengage Learning 2013)

fortunately, this change in the brain increases the drive to obtain the drug and decreases the desire for other nondrug experiences—both of which contribute to continued use and relapse (Russo, Mazei-Robison, Ables, & Nestler, 2009).

It is clear that abuse and dependence cannot be predicted from one factor, be it genetic, neurobiological, psychological, or cultural. For example, *some* people with the genes common to many with substance abuse problems do not become abusers. Many people who experience the most crushing stressors, such as abject poverty or bigotry and violence, cope without resorting to drug use. There are different pathways to abuse, and we are only now beginning to identify their basic outlines.

Once a drug has been used repeatedly, biology and cognition conspire to create dependence. Continual use of most drugs causes tolerance, which requires the user to ingest more of the drug to produce the same effect. Conditioning is also a factor. If pleasurable drug experiences are associated with certain settings, a return to such a setting will later cause urges to develop, even if the drugs themselves are not available.

Concept Check 10.3

Part A

Match the following descriptions with their corresponding stimulants: (a) opioids, (b) amphetamines,
(c) cocaine, (d) hallucinogens, (e) nicotine, and (f) caffeine.

1. This is the most common psychoactive substance because it is legal, elevates mood, and decreases fatigue. It's readily available in many beverages. _____

2. This substance causes euphoria, appetite loss, and increased alertness. Dependence appears after years of use. Mothers addicted to this have the potential to give birth to irritable babies. _____

3. These drugs, including LSD, influence perception, distortion of feelings, sights, sounds, and smells. _____

4. These lead to euphoria, drowsiness, and slowed breathing. These substances are analgesics, relieving pain. Users tend to be secretive, preventing a great deal of research in this area. _____

5. This substance stimulates the nervous system and relieves stress. The *DSM-IV-TR* describes withdrawal symptoms instead of an intoxication pattern. _____

6. These create feelings of elation and vigor and reduce fatigue. They are prescribed to people with narcolepsy and ADHD. _____

Indicate whether these statements about the causes of substance-related disorders are true (T) or false (F).

7. ___ Negative reinforcement is involved in the continuance of drug use because drugs often provide escape from pain, stress, panic, and so on.

8. ___ Research with both animals and humans indicates that substance abuse in general is affected by our genes, although not one particular gene.

9. ___ The media and parental influences have no effect on adolescent drug use; it is solely a peer pressure factor.

10. ___ The expectancy effect is illustrated when a person who expects to be less inhibited when drinking alcohol is given a placebo and acts or feels normally.

11. ___ To some extent, all psychoactive drugs provide a pleasurable experience, creating positive reinforcement.

⟲ Treatment of Substance-Related Disorders

> **What psychological and medical treatments are available for substance-related disorders?**

When we left Danny, he was in jail awaiting the legal outcome of being arrested for vehicular manslaughter. At this point in his life, Danny needs more than legal help—he needs to free himself from his addiction to alcohol and cocaine. And the first step in his recovery has to come from him. Danny must admit he needs help, that he does indeed have a problem with drugs, and that he needs others to help him overcome his chronic dependence. The personal motivation to work on a drug problem appears to be essential in the treatment of substance abuse (Miller, 2009). Unfortunately, although Danny's arrest seemed to shock him into realizing how serious his problems had become, he was not ready to confront them head-on.

Treating people who have substance-related disorders is a difficult task. Perhaps because of the combination of influences that often work together to keep people hooked, the outlook for those who are dependent on drugs is often not positive. You will see in the case of heroin dependence, for example, that a best-case scenario is often just trading one addiction (heroin) for another (methadone). And even people who successfully cease taking drugs may feel the urge to resume drug use all their lives.

Treatment for substance-related disorders focuses on multiple areas. Sometimes the first step is to help someone through the withdrawal process; typically, the ultimate goal is abstinence. In other situations, the goal is to get a person to maintain a certain level of drug use without escalating its intake, and sometimes it is geared toward preventing exposure to drugs. Because substance abuse arises from so many influences, it should not be surprising that treating people with substance-related disorders is not a simple matter of finding just the right drug or the best way to change thoughts or behavior.

Importantly, it is estimated that fewer than 25% of the people who have significant problems with substance use seek treatment for their problems (Dawson et al., 2005). To reach out to these individuals, efforts are under way to put in place routine screenings for substance-related problems in settings such as doctor's offices, hospital emergency rooms, and even in college and university health clinics. This community-wide approach is an important part of identifying difficulties and bringing treatment to those in need (Tucker, Murphy, & Kertesz, 2010).

We discuss the treatment of substance-related disorders as a group because treatments have so much in common. For example, many programs that treat people for dependence on a variety of substances also teach skills for coping with life stressors. Some biological treatments focus on how to cancel out the effects of the ingested substances. We discuss the obvious differences among substances as they arise.

Biological Treatments

There have been a variety of biologically based approaches designed primarily to change the way substances are experienced. In other words, scientists are trying to find ways to prevent people from experiencing the pleasant highs associated with drug use or to find alternative substances that have some of the positive effects (for example, reducing anxiety) without their addictive properties.

Agonist Substitution

Increased knowledge about how psychoactive drugs work on the brain has led researchers to explore ways of changing how they are experienced by people who are dependent on them. One method, **agonist substitution**, involves providing the person with a safe drug that has a chemical makeup similar to the addictive drug (therefore the name *agonist*). *Methadone* is an opiate agonist that is often given as a heroin substitute (e.g., Schwartz et al., 2009). However, when users develop a tolerance for methadone it loses its analgesic and sedative qualities. Because heroin and methadone have *cross-tolerance*, meaning they act on the same neurotransmitter receptors, a heroin addict who takes methadone may become addicted to the methadone instead, but this is not always the case (Maremmani et al., 2009). Research suggests that when addicts combine methadone with counseling, many reduce their use of heroin and engage in less criminal activity (Schwartz et al., 2009). A newer agonist—buprenorphine—blocks the effects of opiates and seems to encourage better compliance than would a nonopiate or opiate antagonist (Strain et al., 2009).

Addiction to cigarette smoking is also treated by a substitution process. The drug—nicotine—is provided to smokers in the form of gum, patch, inhaler, or nasal spray, which lack the carcinogens included in cigarette smoke; the dose is later tapered off to lessen withdrawal from the drug. In general, these replacement strategies successfully help people stop smoking, although they work best with supportive psychological therapy (Hughes, 2009). People must be taught how to use the gum properly, and a portion of the people who successfully quit smoking become dependent on the gum itself (Etter, 2009). The nicotine patch, which requires less effort and provides a steadier nicotine replacement, may be somewhat more effective in helping people quit smoking (Hughes, 2009). Another medical treatment for smoking—bupropion (Zyban)—is also commonly prescribed, under the trade name Wellbutrin, as an antidepressant. This drug curbs the cravings without being an agonist for nicotine (rather than helping smokers trying to quit by making them less depressed).

Antagonist Treatments

We described how many psychoactive drugs produce euphoric effects through their interaction with the neurotransmitter systems in the brain. What would happen if the effects of these drugs were blocked so that the drugs no longer produced the pleasant results? Would people stop using the drugs? **Antagonist drugs** block or counteract the effects of psychoactive drugs, and a variety of drugs that seem to cancel out the effects of opiates have been used with people dependent on a variety of substances. The most often prescribed opiate-antagonist drug, *naltrexone*, has had only limited success with individuals who are not simultaneously participating in a structured treatment program (Krupitsky & Blokhina, 2010). When it is given to a person who is dependent on opiates, it produces immediate withdrawal symptoms, an extremely unpleasant effect. A person must be free from these withdrawal symptoms completely before starting naltrexone, and because it removes the euphoric effects of opiates, the user must be highly motivated to continue treatment. *Acamprosate* also seems to decrease cravings in people dependent on alcohol, and it works best with highly motivated people who are also participating in psychosocial interventions (Kennedy et al., 2010). The brain mechanisms for the effects of this drug are not well understood (Oslin & Klaus, 2009).

Overall, naltrexone or the other drugs being explored are not the magic bullets that would shut off the addict's response to psychoactive drugs and put an end to dependence. They do appear to help some drug abusers handle withdrawal symptoms and the cravings that accompany attempts to abstain from drug use; antagonists may therefore be a useful addition to other therapeutic efforts.

Aversive Treatment

In addition to looking for ways to block the euphoric effects of psychoactive drugs, clinicians in this area may prescribe drugs that make ingesting the abused substances extremely unpleasant. The expectation is that a person who associates the drug with feelings of illness will avoid using the drug. The most commonly known aversive treatment uses *disulfiram (Antabuse)* with people who are alcohol dependent (Ivanov, 2009). Antabuse prevents the breakdown of acetaldehyde, a by-product of alcohol, and the resulting buildup of acetaldehyde causes feelings of illness. People who drink alcohol after taking Antabuse experience nausea, vomiting, and elevated heart rate and respiration. Ideally, Antabuse is taken each morning, before the desire to drink arises. Unfortunately, noncompliance is a major concern, and a person who skips the Antabuse for a few days is able to resume drinking.

Efforts to make smoking aversive have included the use of *silver nitrate* in lozenges or gum. This chemical combines with the saliva of a smoker to produce a bad taste in the mouth. Research has not shown it to be particularly effective (Jensen, Schmidt, Pedersen, & Dahl, 1991). Both Antabuse for alcohol abuse and silver nitrate for cigarette smoking have generally been less than successful as treatment strategies on their own, primarily because they require that people be extremely motivated to continue taking them outside the supervision of a mental health professional.

Other Biological Approaches

Medication is often prescribed to help people deal with the often-disturbing symptoms of withdrawal. *Clonidine*, developed to treat hypertension, has been given to people withdrawing from opiates. Because withdrawal from certain prescribed medications such as sedative drugs can cause cardiac arrest or seizures, these drugs are gradually tapered off to minimize dangerous reactions. In addition, sedative drugs (benzodiazepines) are often prescribed to help minimize discomfort for people withdrawing from other drugs, such as alcohol (Sher, Martinez, & Littlefield, 2011).

Psychosocial Treatments

Most biological treatments for substance abuse show some promise with people who are trying to eliminate their drug habit. However, not one of these treatments alone is suc-

agonist substitution A replacement of a drug on which a person is dependent with one that has a similar chemical makeup, an agonist. Used as a treatment for substance dependence.
antagonist drug The medication that blocks or counteracts the effects of a psychoactive drug.

cessful for most people (Schuckit, 2009b). Most research indicates a need for social support or therapeutic intervention. Because so many people need help to overcome their substance disorder, a number of models and programs have been developed. Unfortunately, in no other area of psychology have unvalidated and untested methods of treatment been so widely accepted. A reminder: A program that has not been subject to the scrutiny of research *may* work, but the sheer number of people receiving services of unknown value is still cause for concern. We next review several therapeutic approaches that *have* been evaluated.

Inpatient Facilities

The first specialized facility for people with substance abuse problems was established in 1935, when the first federal narcotic "farm" was built in Lexington, Kentucky. Now mostly privately run, such facilities are designed to help people get through the initial withdrawal period and to provide supportive therapy so that they can go back to their communities (Morgan, 1981). Inpatient care can be extremely expensive (Bender, 2004). The question arises, then, as to how effective this type of care is compared to outpatient therapy that can cost 90% less. Research suggests there may be no difference between intensive residential setting programs and quality outpatient care in the outcomes for alcoholic patients (Miller & Hester, 1986) or for drug treatment in general (Guydish, Sorensen, Chan, Werdegar, & Acampora, 1999; Smith, Kraemer, Miller, DeBusk, & Taylor, 1999).

Alcoholics Anonymous and Its Variations

Without question, the most popular model for the treatment of substance abuse is a variation of the Twelve Steps program first developed by Alcoholics Anonymous (AA). Established in 1935 by two alcoholic professionals, William "Bill W." Wilson and Robert "Dr. Bob" Holbrook Smith, the foundation of AA is the notion that alcoholism is a disease and alcoholics must acknowledge their addiction to alcohol and its destructive power over them. The addiction is seen as more powerful than any individual; therefore, they must look to a higher power to help them overcome their shortcomings. Central to the design of AA is its independence from the established medical community and the freedom it offers from the stigmatization of alcoholism (Denzin, 1987; Robertson, 1988). An important component is the social support it provides through group meetings.

Since 1935, AA has steadily expanded to include almost 106,000 groups in more than 100 countries (White & Kurtz, 2008). In one survey, 9% of the adult population in the United States reported they had at one time attended an AA meeting (Room & Greenfield, 2006). The Twelve Steps of AA are the basis of its philosophy (see Table 10.1). In them, you can see the reliance on prayer and a belief in God.

Reaction is rarely neutral to AA and similar organizations, such as Cocaine Anonymous and Narcotics Anonymous (Miller, Gold, & Pottash, 1989). Many people credit the approach with saving their lives, whereas others object

Table 10.1 Twelve Suggested Steps of Alcoholics Anonymous

1. We admitted we were powerless over alcohol—that our lives had become unmanageable.
2. We came to believe that a power greater than ourselves could restore us to sanity.
3. We made a decision to turn our will and our lives over to the care of God as we understood Him.
4. We made a searching and fearless moral inventory of ourselves.
5. We admitted to God, to ourselves, and to another human being the exact nature of our wrongs.
6. We were entirely ready to have God remove all these defects of character.
7. We humbly asked Him to remove our shortcomings.
8. We made a list of all persons we had harmed and became willing to make amends to them all.
9. We made direct amends to such people wherever possible, except when to do so would injure them or others.
10. We continued to take personal inventory and, when we were wrong, promptly admitted it.
11. We sought through prayer and meditation to improve our conscious contact with God as we understood Him, praying only for knowledge of His will for us and the power to carry that out.
12. Having had a spiritual awakening as the result of these steps, we tried to carry this message to alcoholics and to practice these principles in all our affairs.

Source: The Twelve Steps are reprinted with permission of Alcoholics Anonymous World Services (AAWS). Permission to reprint the Twelve Steps does not mean that AAWS has reviewed or approved the contents of the publication or that AAWS necessarily agrees with the views expressed herein. AA is a program of recovery from alcoholism only—use of the Twelve Steps in connection with programs and activities which are patterned after AA, but which address other problems, or in any other non-AA context, does not imply otherwise.

that its reliance on spirituality and its adoption of a disease model fosters dependence. Although there are not enough data to show what percentage of people abstain from using alcohol as a result of participating in AA, research finds that those people who regularly participate in AA activities—or other similar supportive approaches—and follow its guidelines carefully are more likely to have a positive outcome (Moos & Moos, 2007). AA can be an effective treatment for highly motivated people with alcohol dependence. We do not yet know, however, who is likely to succeed and who is likely to fail in AA. Other groups now exist (e.g., Rational Recovery, Moderation Management, Women for Sobriety, SMART Recovery) for individuals who benefit from the social support of others but who may not want the abstinence-oriented twelve-step program offered by groups modeled after AA (Tucker et al., 2010).

Controlled Use

One of the tenets of AA is total abstinence; recovering alcoholics who have just one sip of alcohol are believed to have "slipped" until they again achieve abstinence. However, some researchers question this assumption and believe at least a portion of abusers of several substances (notably alcohol and nicotine) may be capable of becoming social users without resuming their abuse of these drugs.

In the alcoholism treatment field, the notion of teaching people **controlled drinking** is extremely controversial, partly because of a classic study showing partial success in teaching severe abusers to drink in a limited way (Sobell & Sobell, 1978). The participants were 40 male alcoholics in an alcoholism treatment program at a state hospital who were thought to have a good prognosis. The men were assigned either to a program that taught them how to drink in moderation (experimental group) or to a group that was abstinence oriented (control group). The researchers, Mark and Linda Sobell, followed the men for more than 2 years, maintaining contact with 98% of them. During the second year after treatment, those who participated in the controlled drinking group were functioning well 85% of the time, whereas the men in the abstinence group were reported to be doing well only 42% of the time. Although results in the two groups differed significantly, some men in both groups suffered serious relapses and required rehospitalization and some were incarcerated. The results of this study suggest that controlled drinking may be a viable alternative to abstinence for some alcohol abusers, although it clearly isn't a cure.

The controversy over this study began with a paper published in the prestigious journal *Science* (Pendery, Maltzman, & West, 1982). The authors reported they had contacted the men in the Sobell study after 10 years and found that only 1 of the 20 men in the experimental group maintained a pattern of controlled drinking. Although this reevaluation made headlines and was the subject of a segment on the *60 Minutes* television show, it had a number of flaws (Marlatt, Larimer, Baer, & Quigley, 1993). Most serious was the lack of data on the abstinence group over the same 10-year follow-up period. Because no treatment study on substance abuse pretends to help everyone who participates, control groups are added to compare progress. In this case, we need to know how well the controlled drinking group fared compared to the abstinence group.

The controversy over the Sobell study still has a chilling effect on controlled drinking as a treatment of alcohol abuse in the United States. In contrast, controlled drinking is widely accepted as a treatment for alcoholism in the United Kingdom. Despite opposition, research on this approach has been conducted in the ensuing years (e.g., Orford & Keddie, 2006), and the results seem to show that controlled drinking is at least as effective as abstinence but that neither treatment is successful for 70% to 80% of patients over the long term—a rather bleak outlook for people with alcohol dependence problems.

Component Treatment

Most comprehensive treatment programs aimed at helping people with substance abuse and dependence problems have a number of components thought to boost the effectiveness of the "treatment package." We saw in our review of biological treatments that their effectiveness is increased when psychologically based therapy is added. In aversion therapy, which uses a conditioning model, substance use is paired with something extremely unpleasant, such as a brief electric shock or feelings of nausea. For example, a person might be offered a drink of alcohol and receive a painful shock when the glass reaches his lips. The goal is to counteract the positive associations with substance use with negative associations. The negative associations can also be made by imagining unpleasant scenes in a technique called *covert sensitization* (Cautela, 1966); the person might picture herself beginning to snort cocaine and be interrupted with visions of herself becoming violently ill (Kearney, 2006).

One component that seems to be a valuable part of therapy for substance use is *contingency management* (Higgins, Sigmon, & Heil, 2008). Here, the clinician and the client together select the behaviors that the client needs to change and decide on the reinforcers that will reward reaching certain goals, perhaps money or small retail items like CDs. In a study of cocaine abusers, clients received cash vouchers (up to almost $2,000) for having cocaine-negative urine specimens (Higgins et al., 2006). This study found greater abstinence rates among cocaine-dependent users with the contingency management approach and other skills training than among users in a more traditional counseling program that included a twelve-step approach to treatment.

Another package of treatments is the *community reinforcement approach* (Higgins et al., 2008). In keeping with the multiple influences that affect substance use, several facets of the drug problem are addressed to help identify and correct aspects of the person's life that might contribute to substance use or interfere with efforts to abstain. First, a spouse, friend, or relative who is not a substance user is recruited to participate in relationship therapy to help the abuser improve relationships with other important people. Second, clients are taught how to identify the antecedents and consequences that influence their drug taking. For example, if they are likely to use cocaine with certain friends, clients are taught to recognize the relationships and encouraged to avoid the associations. Third, clients are given assistance with employment, education, finances, or other social service areas that may help reduce their stress. Fourth, new recreational options help the person replace substance use with new activities. There is now strong empirical support for the effectiveness of this approach with alcohol and cocaine abusers (Higgins et al., 2008).

Obstacles to successful treatment for substance use and dependence include a lack of personal awareness that one has a problem and an unwillingness to change. An increas-

controlled drinking An extremely controversial treatment approach to alcohol dependence, in which severe abusers are taught to drink in moderation.

ingly common intervention approach that directly addresses these needs is referred to as *motivational interviewing* (Miller, 2009). Motivational interviewing (MI) is based on the work of Miller and Rollnick (2002), who proposed that behavior change in adults is more likely with empathetic and optimistic counseling (the therapist understands the client's perspective and believes that he or she can change) and a focus on a personal connection with the client's core values (for example, drinking and its consequences interferes with spending more time with family). By reminding the client about what he or she cherishes most, MI intends to improve the individual's belief that any changes made (e.g., drinking less) will have positive outcomes (e.g., more family time) and the individual is therefore more likely to make the recommended changes. Motivational interviewing has been used to assist individuals with a variety of substance use problems, and it appears to be a useful component to add to psychological treatment (Lundahl, Kunz, Brownell, Tollefson, & Burke, 2010).

Cognitive-behavioral therapy (CBT) is an effective treatment approach for many psychological disorders (see Chapter 4, for example) and it is also one of the most well designed and studied approaches for treating substance dependence (Carroll, 2008; Sher et al., 2011). This treatment addresses multiple aspects of the disorder, including a person's reactions to cues that lead to substance use (for example, being among certain friends) (Ferguson & Shiffman, 2009) and thoughts and behaviors to resist use (Wiers et al., 2008). Another target of CBT addresses the problem of relapse. Marlatt and Gordon's (1985) **relapse prevention** treatment model looks at the learned aspects of dependence and sees relapse as a failure of cognitive and behavioral coping skills (Witkiewitz & Marlatt, 2004). Therapy involves helping people remove any ambivalence about stopping their drug use by examining their beliefs about the positive aspects of the drug ("There's nothing like a cocaine high") and confronting the negative consequences of its use ("I fight with my wife when I'm high"). High-risk situations are identified ("having extra money in my pocket"), and strategies are developed to deal with potentially problematic situations and with the craving that arises from abstinence. Incidents of relapse are dealt with as occurrences from which the person can recover; instead of looking on these episodes as inevitably leading to more drug use, people in treatment are encouraged to see them as episodes brought on by temporary stress or a situation that can be changed. Research on this technique suggests that it may be particularly effective for alcohol problems (Irvin, Bowers, Dunn, & Wang, 1999), and in treating a variety of other substance use disorders (see, for example, Burleson & Kaminer, 2005).

Prevention

Over the past few years, the strategies for preventing substance abuse and dependence have shifted from education-based approaches (for example, teaching schoolchildren that drugs can be harmful) to more wide-ranging approaches, including changes in the laws regarding drug possession and use and community-based interventions (Sher et al., 2011). Many states, for example, have implemented education-based programs in schools to try to deter students from using drugs. The widely used Drug Abuse Resistance Education (DARE) program encourages a "no drug use" message through fear of consequences, rewards for commitments not to use drugs, and strategies for refusing offers of drugs. Unfortunately, several extensive evaluations suggest that this type of program may not have its intended effects (Pentz, 1999).

Fortunately, more comprehensive programs that involve skills training to avoid or resist social pressures (such as peers) and environmental pressures (such as media portrayals of drug use) can be effective in preventing drug abuse among some. For example, one large-scale longitudinal study used a community-based intervention strategy to reduce binge drinking and alcohol-related injuries (for example, car crashes and assaults) (Holder et al., 2000). Three communities were mobilized to encourage responsible beverage service (that is, not serving too much alcohol to bar patrons), limit alcohol access to underage drinkers, and increase local enforcement of drinking and driving laws to limit access to alcohol. People's self-reports of drinking too much and drinking and driving were fewer after the intervention, as were alcohol-related car accidents and assaults.

It may be that our most powerful preventive strategy involves cultural change. Over the past 25 years or so, we have gone from a "turn on, tune in, drop out," "if it feels good, do it," and "I get high with a little help from my friends" society to one that champions statements like "Just say no to drugs." The social unacceptability of excessive drinking, smoking, and other drug use is probably responsible for this change.

Implementing this sort of intervention is beyond the scope of one research investigator or even a consortium of researchers collaborating across many sites. It requires the cooperation of governmental, educational, and even religious institutions. We may need to rethink our approach to preventing drug use and abuse (Cook, 1993, p. 1750).

Concept Check 10.4

Determine whether you understand how treatments for substance-related disorders work by matching the examples with the following terms: (a) dependent, (b) cross-tolerant, (c) agonist substitution, (d) antagonist, (e) relapse prevention, (f) controlled drinking, (g) aversion therapy, (h) covert sensitization, (i) contingency management, and (j) anonymous.

1. _____ is a controversial treatment for alcohol abuse because of a negative but flawed experimental finding but also because it conflicts with the belief in total abstinence.

2. Methadone is used to help heroin addicts kick their habit in a method called _____.

3. _____ drugs block or counteract the effects of psychoactive drugs and are sometimes effective in treating addicts.

4. In _____, the clinician and the client work together to decide which behaviors the client needs to change and which reinforcers will be used as rewards for reaching set goals.

5. It has been difficult to evaluate rigorously the effectiveness of Alcoholics Anonymous because the participants are _____.

6. In _____, substance use is paired with something extremely unpleasant (like alcohol and vomiting with Antabuse).

7. Heroin and methadone are _____, which means they affect the same neurotransmitter receptors.

8. The _____ model involves therapy that helps individuals remove ambivalence about stopping their drug use by examining their beliefs about the positive and negative aspects of drug use.

9. By imagining unpleasant scenes, the _____ technique helps the person associate the negative effects of the drug with drug use.

10. Unfortunately, the heroin addict may become permanently _____ on methadone.

Impulse-Control Disorders

> **What conditions are listed in *DSM-IV-TR* as impulse-control disorders?**

A number of the disorders we describe in this book start with an irresistible impulse—usually one that will ultimately be harmful to the person affected. Typically, the person experiences increasing tension leading up to the act and, sometimes, pleasurable anticipation of acting on the impulse. For example, paraphilias such as pedophilia (sexual attraction to children), eating disorders, and the substance-related disorders in this chapter often commence with temptations or desires that are destructive but difficult to resist. *DSM-IV-TR* includes five additional impulse-control disorders (labeled "impulse-control disorders not elsewhere classified") that are not included under other categories—intermittent explosive disorder, kleptomania, pyromania, pathological gambling, and trichotillomania (Moeller, 2009; Nock, Cha, & Dour, 2011).

Intermittent Explosive Disorder

People with **intermittent explosive disorder** have episodes in which they act on aggressive impulses that result in serious assaults or destruction of property (Coccaro & McCloskey, 2010). Although it is common, unfortunately, among the general population to observe aggressive outbursts, when you rule out the influence of other disorders (for example, antisocial personality disorder, borderline personality disorder, a psychotic disorder, and Alzheimer's disease) or substance use, this disorder is not often diagnosed. In a rare but important large study of more than 9,000 people, researchers found that the lifetime prevalence of this disorder was 7.3% (Kessler et al., 2006).

This diagnosis is controversial and has been debated throughout the development of the *DSM*. One concern, among others, is that by validating a general category that covers aggressive behavior it may be used as a legal defense—insanity—for all violent crimes (Coccaro & McCloskey, 2010).

Research is at the beginning stages for intermittent explosive disorder and focuses on the influence of neurotransmitters such as serotonin and norepinephrine and testosterone levels, along with their interaction with psychosocial influences (stress, disrupted family life, and parenting styles). These and other influences are being examined to explain the origins of this disorder (Moeller, 2009). Cognitive-behavioral interventions (for example, helping the person identify and avoid "triggers" for aggressive outbursts) and approaches modeled after drug treatments appear the most effective for these individuals, although few controlled studies yet exist (McCloskey, Noblett, Deffenbacher, Gollan, & Coccaro, 2008).

Kleptomania

The story of wealthy actress Winona Ryder stealing $5,500 worth of merchandise from Saks Fifth Avenue in Beverly Hills, California in December 2001, was as puzzling as it was

relapse prevention The extending therapeutic progress by teaching the client how to cope with future troubling situations.
intermittent explosive disorder The episodes during which a person acts on aggressive impulses that result in serious assaults or destruction of property.

titillating. Why risk a multimillion-dollar career over some clothes that she could easily afford? Was hers a case of **kleptomania**—a recurrent failure to resist urges to steal things that are not needed for personal use or their monetary value? This disorder appears to be rare, but it is not well studied, partly because of the stigma associated with identifying oneself as acting out this illegal behavior. The patterns described by those with this disorder are strikingly similar—the person begins to feel a sense of tension just before stealing, which is followed by feelings of pleasure or relief while the theft is committed (Nock et al., 2011). People with kleptomania score high on assessments of impulsivity, reflecting their inability to judge the immediate gratification of stealing compared to the long-term negative consequences (for example, arrest, embarrassment) (Grant & Kim, 2002). Patients with kleptomania often report having no memory (amnesia) about the act of shoplifting (Hollander, Berlin, & Stein, 2009). Brain-imaging research supports these observations, with one study finding damage in areas of the brain associated with poor decision making (inferior frontal regions) (Grant, Correia, & Brennan-Krohn, 2006).

There appears to be high comorbidity between kleptomania and mood disorders and to a lesser extent with substance abuse and dependence (Baylé, Caci, Millet, Richa, & Olié, 2003). Some refer to kleptomania as an "antidepressant" behavior, or a reaction on the part of some to relieve unpleasant feelings through stealing (Fishbain,

1987). To date, only case study reports of treatment exist, and these involve either behavioral interventions or use of antidepressant medication.

Pyromania

Just as we know that someone who steals does not necessarily have kleptomania, it is also true that not everyone who sets fires is considered to have **pyromania**—an impulse-control disorder that involves having an irresistible urge to set fires. Again, the pattern parallels that of kleptomania, where the person feels a tension or arousal before setting a fire and a sense of gratification or relief while the fire burns. These individuals will also be preoccupied with fires and the associated equipment involved in setting and putting out these fires (Lejoyeux, McLoughlin, & Ades, 2006). Also rare, pyromania is diagnosed in less than 4% of arsonists (Scott, Hilty, & Brook, 2003) because arsonists can include people who set fires for monetary gain or revenge rather than to satisfy a physical or psychological urge. Because so few people are diagnosed with this disorder, research on etiology and treatment is almost nonexistent. Research that has been conducted follows the general group of arsonists (of which only a small percentage have pyromania) and examines the role of a family history of fire setting along with comorbid impulse disorders (antisocial personality disorder and alcoholism). Treatment is generally cognitive-behavioral and involves helping the person identify the signals that initiate the urges and teaching coping strategies to resist the temptation to start fires (Bumpass, Fagelman, & Brix, 1983; McGrath, Marshall, & Prior, 1979).

Pathological Gambling

Gambling has a long history—for example, dice have been found in Egyptian tombs (Greenberg, 2005). It is growing in popularity in this country, and in many places it is a legal and acceptable form of entertainment. Perhaps as a result, and unlike the other impulse-control disorders, which are relatively rare, **pathological gambling** affects an increasing number of people, estimated between 3% and 5% of adult Americans (Greenberg, 2005). It is estimated that among pathological gamblers, 14% have lost at least one job, 19% have declared bankruptcy, 32% have been arrested, and 21% have been incarcerated (Gerstein et al., 1999). The *DSM-IV* criteria for pathological gambling set forth the associated behaviors that characterize people who are problem gamblers. These include the same pattern of urges we observe in the other impulse-control disorders. Note too the parallels with substance dependence, with the need to gamble increasing amounts of money over time and the "withdrawal symptoms" such as restlessness and irritability when attempting to stop. In fact, these parallels to substance abuse have led to discussions about recategorizing pathological gambling in *DSM-5;* some believe that this disorder should be moved from the group of disorders called "impulse-control disorders not elsewhere classified" to the "substance-related disorders" category and that this "substance-related

REUTERS/Lee Celano/Pool/Landov

▲ In 2002, actress Winona Ryder was found guilty of shoplifting items worth several thousand dollars from a Beverly Hills department store.

disorders" category should be renamed "addiction and related disorders" (Moeller, 2009).

There is a growing body of research on the nature and treatment of pathological gambling. For example, work is under way to explore the biological origins of the urge to gamble among pathological gamblers. In one study, brain-imaging technology (echoplanar functional magnetic resonance imaging) was used to observe brain function while gamblers observed videotapes of other people gambling (Potenza et al., 2003). A decreased level of activity was observed in those regions of the brain that are involved in impulse regulation when compared to controls, suggesting an interaction between the environmental cues to gamble and the brain's response (which may be to decrease the ability to resist these cues). Abnormalities in the dopamine system (which may account for the pleasurable consequences of gambling) and the serotonin system (involved in impulsive behavior) have been found in some studies of pathological gamblers (Moeller, 2009).

Treatment of gambling problems is difficult. Those with pathological gambling exhibit a combination of characteristics—including denial of the problem, impulsivity, and continuing optimism ("One big win will cover my losses!")—that interfere with effective treatment. Pathological gamblers often experience cravings similar to those who are substance dependent (Wulfert, Franco, Williams, Roland, & Maxson, 2008; Wulfert, Maxson, & Jardin, 2009). Treatment is often similar to substance dependence treatment, and there is a parallel Gambler's Anonymous that incorporates the same twelve-step program we discussed previously. However, the evidence of effectiveness for Gambler's Anonymous suggests that 70% to 90% drop out of these programs and that the desire to quit must be present before intervention (McElroy & Arnold, 2001). Cognitive-behavioral interventions are also being studied, with one study including a variety of components—setting financial limits, planning alternative activities, preventing relapse, and imaginal desensitization. This preliminary research provides a more optimistic view of potential outcomes (Dowling, Smith, & Thomas, 2007).

Trichotillomania

The urge to pull out one's own hair from anywhere on the body, including the scalp, eyebrows, and arms, is referred to as **trichotillomania**. This behavior results in noticeable hair loss, distress, and significant social impairments. This disorder can often have severe social consequences, and, as a result, those affected can go to great lengths to conceal their behavior. Compulsive hair pulling is more common than once believed and is observed in between 1% and 5% of college students, with females reporting the problem more than males (Scott et al., 2003). There may be some genetic influence on trichotillomania, with one study finding a unique genetic mutation in a small number of people (Zuchner et al., 2006). Stress also seems to be involved, and there is an increased overlap with posttraumatic stress disorder (Chamberlain, Menzies, Sahakian, & Fineberg,

2007). There is considerable controversy over just how this problem should be classified, and there is a proposal to reclassify it from "impulse control disorders not elsewhere classified" to "anxiety and obsessive-compulsive spectrum disorders" in *DSM-5* (Nock et al., 2011). Research using serotonin-specific reuptake inhibitors holds some promise for treatment, as do cognitive-behavioral interventions, although rigorous research trials have yet to be conducted (Chamberlain et al., 2007).

In addition to these five impulse-control disorders, other impulsive behaviors may occasionally rise to the level of these difficulties. Some individuals show the same irresistible urges to engage in compulsive buying or shopping (oniomania), self-mutilation, skin picking (psychogenic excoriation), severe nail biting (onychophagia), and excessive computer use ("Internet addiction") (McElroy & Arnold, 2001). There is a limited but growing literature that will help us understand and ultimately treat these impulse-control problems.

Concept Check 10.5

Match the following disorders with their corresponding symptoms: (a) pathological gambling, (b) trichotillomania, (c) intermittent explosive disorder, (d) kleptomania, and (e) pyromania.

1. This rarely diagnosed disorder is characterized by episodes of aggressive impulses and can sometimes be treated with cognitive-behavioral interventions, drug treatments, or both. _____

2. This disorder begins with the person feeling a sense of tension that is released and followed with pleasure after they have committed a robbery. _____

3. This disorder affects somewhere between 3% and 5% of the adult American population and is characterized by the need to gamble. _____

4. This disorder refers to compulsive hair pulling and is more common in females than males. _____

5. Individuals with this disorder are preoccupied with fires and the equipment involved in setting and putting out fires. _____

---

kleptomania A recurrent failure to resist urges to steal things not needed for personal use or their monetary value.
pyromania An impulse-control disorder that involves having an irresistible urge to set fires.
pathological gambling A persistent and recurrent maladaptive gambling behavior.
trichotillomania People's urge to pull out their own hair from anywhere on the body, including the scalp, eyebrows, and arm.

Research on a spectrum of disorders that covers the substance-related disorders or the impulse-control disorders is in its infancy. One of the difficulties in researching these disorders is their complexity. The problems that fall under disorders of substance use or impulse control are multifaceted and overlap a great deal with other disorders (comorbidity). For example, people with disorders as wide ranging as antisocial personality disorder (see Chapter 11) (Copeland, Shanahan, Costello, & Angold, 2009), anxiety disorders (see Chapter 4) (Hofmann, Richey, Kashdan, & McKnight, 2009), schizophrenia (see Chapter 12) (Horsfall, Cleary, Hunt, & Walter, 2009), bipolar disorder (see Chapter 6) (Joshi & Wilens, 2009), and depression (see Chapter 6) (Rao, Hammen, & Poland, 2009) all have an increased risk of also meeting criteria for a substance-related disorder. At the same time, there are other mental health concerns that resemble the pattern of use, dependence, and withdrawal of the substance-related disorders but do not involve the use of mood-altering substances. For example, as we have seen, discussion is under way to include pathological gambling as part of a new category of disorders, "addiction and related disorders," in *DSM-5*—which would then expand the "addictions" beyond just mood-altering substances (Moeller, 2009). Other problems that cause real dysfunction among some people, including "Internet addiction" (Block, 2008) and even "tanning addiction" (Poorsattar & Hornung, 2010), are being taken seriously as similar types of problems.

One contender for a spectrum of disorders that is currently being researched is referred to as the *externalizing spectrum* (Krueger, Markon, Patrick, & Iacono, 2005; Sher et al., 2011). This categorization includes the substance-related disorders along with antisocial behavior (a personality disorder characterized by the violation of social norms with a disregard for the rights and feelings of others; see Chapter 11) and personality traits such as aggression and impulsivity, all of which often oc-

cur together (Krueger et al., 2005). If we return to the case of Danny, we can see that he displayed many if not all of the characteristics of this spectrum of disorders. Recall that in addition to his substance abuse problems he would steal from his family and his employers, he lied frequently to everyone, and yet he never expressed any true remorse for how his behavior affected others—all characteristics of antisocial personality disorder. In fact, even awaiting trial in jail for his DWI-related traffic fatality, he was talking to as many people as he could to try to blame the medication he was on at the time for his difficulty and never admitted any guilt or expressed any concern for the family of the woman he killed. This collection of difficulties, which have at their core a variety of characteristics including novelty seeking and sensation seeking, is now being explored in a variety of research paradigms (including genetic research) as a possible unifying spectrum that may lead to a deeper understanding of these troubling problems (e.g., Dick et al., 2008).

Summary

Perspectives on Substance-Related Disorders

What are substance-related disorders?

> In *DSM-IV-TR*, substance-related disorders are divided into depressants (alcohol, barbiturates, and benzodiazepines), stimulants (amphetamine, cocaine, nicotine, and caffeine), opiates (heroin, codeine, and morphine), and hallucinogens (marijuana and LSD).

> Specific diagnoses are further categorized as substance dependence, substance abuse, substance intoxication, and substance withdrawal.

> Nonmedical drug use in the United States has declined in recent times, although it continues to cost billions of dollars and seriously impairs the lives of millions of people each year.

Depressants, Stimulants, Opioids, and Hallucinogens

What are the physiological and psychological effects of depressants?

> Depressants are a group of drugs that decrease central nervous system activity. The primary effect is to reduce our levels of physiological arousal and help us relax. Included in this group are alcohol and sedative, hypnotic, and anxiolytic drugs, such as those prescribed for insomnia.

What are the physiological and psychological effects of stimulants?

> Stimulants, the most commonly consumed psychoactive drugs, include caffeine (in coffee, chocolate, and many soft drinks), nicotine (in tobacco products such as cigarettes), amphetamines, and cocaine. In contrast to the depressant drugs, stimulants make us more alert and energetic.

What are the psychological and physiological effects of opiates?

> Opiates include opium, morphine, codeine, and heroin; they have a narcotic effect—relieving pain and inducing sleep. The broader term *opioids* is used to refer to the family of substances that includes these opiates and synthetic variations created by chemists (e.g., methadone) and the similarly acting substances that occur naturally in our brains (enkephalins, beta-endorphins, and dynorphins).

How do opioids differ from hallucinogens?

› Hallucinogens essentially change the way the user perceives the world. Sight, sound, feelings, and even smell are distorted, sometimes in dramatic ways, in a person under the influence of drugs such as marijuana and LSD.

Causes and Treatment of Substance-Related Disorders

What psychological and physiological processes lead to substance dependence?

› Most psychotropic drugs seem to produce positive effects by acting directly or indirectly on the dopaminergic mesolimbic system (the pleasure pathway). In addition, psychosocial factors such as expectations, stress, and cultural practices interact with the biological factors to influence drug use.

What psychological and medical treatments are available for substance-related disorders?

› Substance dependence is treated successfully only in a minority of those affected, and the best results reflect the motivation of the drug user and a combination of biological and psychosocial treatments.

› Programs aimed at preventing drug use may have the greatest chance of significantly affecting the drug problem.

Impulse-Control Disorders

What conditions are listed in *DSM-IV-TR* as impulse-control disorders?

› In *DSM-IV-TR*, impulse-control disorders include five separate disorders: intermittent explosive disorder, kleptomania, pyromania, pathological gambling, and trichotillomania.

Key Terms

substance-related disorders, 371
impulse-control disorders, 371
polysubstance use, 371
psychoactive substances, 372
substance intoxication, 373
substance abuse, 373
substance dependence, 374
tolerance, 374
withdrawal, 374
depressants, 376
stimulants, 376
opiates, 376
hallucinogen, 376

alcohol use disorders, 377
withdrawal delirium (delirium tremens/DTs), 378
fetal alcohol syndrome (FAS), 379
barbiturates, 380
alcohol dehydrogenase (ADH), 381
benzodiazepines, 381
amphetamine use disorders, 383
cocaine use disorders, 384
nicotine use disorders, 386
caffeine use disorders, 387
opioid use disorders, 387
hallucinogen use disorders, 388

marijuana *(Cannabis sativa)*, 389
LSD (*d*-lysergic acid diethylamide), 389
agonist substitution, 398
antagonist drugs, 399
controlled drinking, 401
relapse prevention, 402
intermittent explosive disorder, 403
kleptomania, 404
pyromania, 404
pathological gambling, 404
trichotillomania, 405

Answers to Concept Checks

10.1

Part A

1. c; 2. b; 3. d; 4. a

Part B

5. c; 6. d; 7. b; 8. A

10.2

1. False (the use of crack by pregnant mothers adversely affects only some babies); 2. True; 3. True; 4. False (marijuana produces the most variable reactions in people); 5. False

(amphetamines are produced in the lab); 6. False (stimulants occur naturally)

10.3

Part A

1. f; 2. c; 3. d; 4. a; 5. e; 6. b

Part B

7. T; 8. T; 9. F (all have an effect); 10. F (they would still act uninhibited); 11. T

10.4

1. f; 2. c; 3. d; 4. i; 5. j; 6. g; 7. b; 8. e; 9. h; 10. a

10.5

1. c; 2. d; 3. a; 4. b; 5. e

Media Resources

Log in to CengageBrain to access the resources your instructor requires. For this book, you can access:

CourseMate brings course concepts to life with interactive learning, study, and exam preparation tools that support the printed textbook. A textbook-specific website, Psychology CourseMate includes an integrated interactive eBook and other interactive learning tools including quizzes, flashcards, videos, and more.

Abnormal Psychology Videos

> *Tim, an Example of Substance Use Disorder:* Tim describes the key criteria and shows how the disorder has had an impact on his life.
> *Nicotine Dependence:* Learn how nicotine increases the power of cues associated with smoking and how this research might help in the design of more effective programs to help people quit tobacco.

CENGAGENOW CengageNow is an easy-to-use online resource that helps you study in less time to get the grade you want—NOW. Take a pre-test for this chapter and receive a personalized study plan based on your results that will identify the topics you need to review and direct you to online resources to help you master those topics. Then take a post-test to help you determine the concepts you have mastered and what you will need to work on. If your textbook does not include an access code card, go to CengageBrain.com to gain access.
Visit www.cengagebrain.com to access your account and purchase materials.

 aplia If your professor has assigned Aplia homework:
1. Sign in to your account.
2. Complete the corresponding homework exercises as required by your professor.
3. When finished, click "Grade It Now" to see which areas you have mastered, which need more work, and for detailed explanations of every answer.

Video Concept Reviews

CengageNOW also contains Mark Durand's *Video Concept Reviews* on these challenging topics.
> Substance Intoxication, Abuse and Dependence
> Tolerance and Withdrawal
> Alcohol Use Disorders
> Sedative, Hypnotic, and Anxiolytic Substances
> Stimulants
> Amphetamine Use Disorders
> Cocaine Use Disorders
> Nicotine Use Disorders
> Caffeine Use Disorders
> Opioid Use Disorders
> Hallucinogen Use Disorders
> Marijuana
> LSD and Other Hallucinogens
> Inhalants
> Anabolic Steroids
> Designer Drugs
> Drug Use: Psychological Perspective
> Concept Check: Impulse Control Disorders Versus Substance Use

Chapter Quiz

1. The definition of substance abuse according to the *DSM-IV-TR* is based on:
   a. how much of the substance is consumed per day
   b. how much of the substance is consumed per week
   c. how significantly the substance interferes with the user's life
   d. the type of substance used

2. _____ is the need for greater amounts of a drug to experience the same effect, whereas _____ is the negative physical response that occurs when a drug is not taken.
   a. Tolerance; withdrawal
   b. Delirium; withdrawal
   c. Dependence; tolerance
   d. Accommodation; abuse

3. Which of the following statements most accurately describes the relationship between gender and alcohol consumption?
   a. Women are more likely to use alcohol, but men are more likely to be heavy drinkers.
   b. Men are more likely to use alcohol, but women are more likely to be heavy drinkers.
   c. Women are more likely to use alcohol and be heavy drinkers.
   d. Men are more likely to use alcohol and be heavy drinkers.

4. Dr. Myers prescribes medication to help control a patient's seizures. The patient reports that the medication also makes her feel calm and helps her sleep. Dr. Myers most likely prescribed a(n):
   a. hallucinogen
   b. opiate
   c. benzodiazepine
   d. amphetamine

5. The primary neurotransmitter affected by cocaine is _____, whereas the primary neurotransmitter affected by opiates is _____.
   a. GABA; norepinephrine
   b. acetylcholine; GABA
   c. norepinephrine; dopamine
   d. dopamine; GABA

6. For marijuana users, "reverse tolerance" occurs when:
   a. chronic use renders the user unable to feel high
   b. a first-time user does not feel high
   c. more pleasure from the drug is reported after repeated use
   d. a chronic user experiences withdrawal symptoms

7. Gino is a recovering alcoholic. To help with his treatment, Gino's physician prescribed a drug that causes Gino to experience shortness of breath and severe vomiting if he drinks. What drug has the physician prescribed?
   a. Antabuse
   b. MDMA
   c. amyl nitrate
   d. PCP

8. One psychological component of addiction may involve taking a drug to avoid negative feelings associated with coming down from a high. What theory describes this use of substances to avoid worsening lows?
   a. tolerance theory
   b. substance cycle theory
   c. opponent-process theory
   d. polydependence theory

9. Research shows that the way individuals think about a drug influences the way they act when using the drug. This phenomenon is known as the:
   a. tolerance paradigm
   b. expectancy effect
   c. dependency model
   d. opponent-process theory

10. Carlos's psychiatrist treats him for cocaine abuse by delivering a shock when Carlos attempts to use cocaine, a treatment known as _____. In contrast, Lisa's therapist has her imagine having painful seizures at the same time that Lisa is thinking about using cocaine, a treatment known as _____.
    a. aversion therapy; covert sensitization
    b. contingency management; relapse prevention
    c. narcotics anonymous; controlled use
    d. agonist substitution; aversive treatment
    (See Appendix A for answers.)

Exploring Substance-Related Disorders

❯ Many kinds of problems can develop when people use and abuse substances that alter the way they think, feel, and behave.

❯ Once seen as due to personal weakness, drug abuse and dependence are now thought influenced by both biological and psychosocial factors.

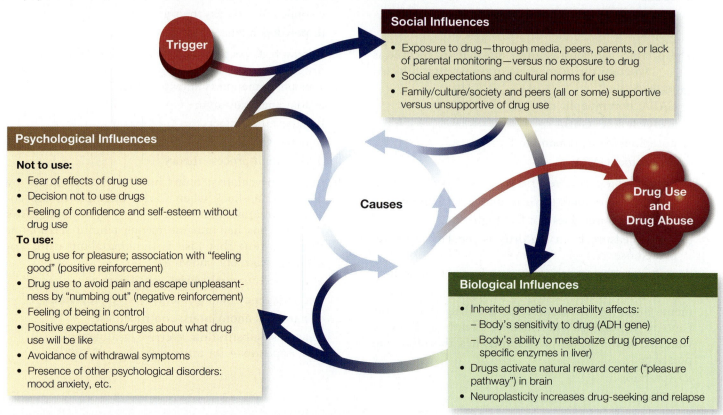

Trigger

Social Influences

- Exposure to drug—through media, peers, parents, or lack of parental monitoring—versus no exposure to drug
- Social expectations and cultural norms for use
- Family/culture/society and peers (all or some) supportive versus unsupportive of drug use

Causes

Drug Use and Drug Abuse

Psychological Influences

Not to use:
- Fear of effects of drug use
- Decision not to use drugs
- Feeling of confidence and self-esteem without drug use

To use:
- Drug use for pleasure; association with "feeling good" (positive reinforcement)
- Drug use to avoid pain and escape unpleasantness by "numbing out" (negative reinforcement)
- Feeling of being in control
- Positive expectations/urges about what drug use will be like
- Avoidance of withdrawal symptoms
- Presence of other psychological disorders: mood anxiety, etc.

Biological Influences

- Inherited genetic vulnerability affects:
  - Body's sensitivity to drug (ADH gene)
  - Body's ability to metabolize drug (presence of specific enzymes in liver)
- Drugs activate natural reward center ("pleasure pathway") in brain
- Neuroplasticity increases drug-seeking and relapse

TREATMENT: BEST TO USE MULTIPLE APPROACHES

Psychosocial Treatments

- Aversion therapy—to create negative associations with drug use (shocks with drinking, imagining nausea with cocaine use)
- Contingency management to change behaviors by rewarding chosen behaviors
- Alcoholics Anonymous and its variations
- Inpatient hospital treatment (can be expensive)
- Controlled use
- Community reinforcement
- Relapse prevention

Biological Treatments

- Agonist substitution
  - Replacing one drug with a similar one (methadone for heroin, nicotine gum and patches for cigarettes)
- Antagonist substitution
  - Blocking one drug's effect with another drug (naltrexone for opiates and alcohol)
- Aversive treatments
  - Making taking drug very unpleasant (using Antabuse, which causes nausea and vomiting when mixed with alcohol, to treat alcoholism)
- Drugs to help recovering person deal with withdrawal symptoms (clonidine for opiate withdrawal, sedatives for alcohol, etc.)

TYPES OF DRUGS

	Examples	Effects
Depressants	Alcohol, barbiturates (sedatives: Amytal, Seconal, Nembutal), benzodiazepines (antianxiety: Valium, Xanax, Halcion)	• Decreased central nervous system activity • Reduced levels of body arousal • Relaxation
Stimulants	Amphetamines, cocaine, nicotine, caffeine	• Increased physical arousal • User feels more alert and energetic
Opiates	Heroin, morphine, codeine	• Narcotic—reduce pain and induce sleep and euphoria by mirroring opiates in the brain (endorphins, etc.)
Hallucinogens	Marijuana, LSD, Ecstasy	• Altered mental and emotional perception • Distortion (sometimes dramatic) of sensory perceptions

Exploring Impulse-Control Disorders

Characterized by inability to resist acting on a drive or temptation. Sufferers often perceived by society as having a problem simply due to a lack of "will."

TYPES OF IMPULSE-CONTROL DISORDERS

Disorder		Characteristics	Treatment
Intermittent Explosive	Tom Morrison/Stone/Getty Images	• Acting on aggressive impulses that result in assaults or destruction of property • Current research is focused on how neurotransmitters and testosterone levels interact with psychosocial influences (stress, parenting styles)	Cognitive-behavioral interventions (helping person identify and avoid triggers for aggressive outbursts) and approaches modeled after drug treatments appear most effective
Kleptomania	Mauro Speziale/Photonica/Getty Images	• Recurring failure to resist urges to steal unneeded items • Feeling tense just before stealing, followed by feelings of pleasure or relief when committing the theft • High comorbidity with mood disorders and, to a lesser degree, with substance abuse/dependence	Behavioral interventions or antidepressant medication
Pathological Gambling	Tom and Steve/Flickr/Getty Images	• Preoccupation with gambling/with need to gamble increasing amounts of money to feel the same excitement • "Withdrawal symptoms" of restlessness and irritability when attempting to stop • May have a biological component involving brain activity (decreased activity in brain region controlling impulse regulation, abnormalities in dopamine and serotonin systems)	Gamblers Anonymous; similar to substance-dependence treatment
Trichotillomania	©Wedgworth/Custom Medical Stock Photo (CMSP)	• Urge to pull out one's own hair from anywhere on the body • Sufferers go to great lengths to conceal behavior • Relatively common (seen 1%–5% of college students)	SSRIs may help; cognitive-behavior interventions hold promise
Pyromania	Joel Sartore/National Geographic/Getty Images	• Irresistible urge to set fires • Feeling aroused prior to setting fire then a sense of gratification or relief while the fire burns • Rare; diagnosed in less than 4% of arsonists	Cognitive-behavioral interventions (helping person identify signals triggering urges, and teaching coping strategies to resist setting fires)

11 Personality Disorders

Demonstrate knowledge and understanding representing appropriate breadth and depth in selected content areas of psychology:	› Biological bases of behavior and mental processes, including physiology, sensation, perception, comparative, motivation, and emotion (APA SLO 1.2.a (3)) *(see textbook pages 429–431)*
Use the concepts, language, and major theories of the discipline to account for psychological phenomena.	› Describe behavior and mental processes empirically, including operational definitions (APA SLO 1.3.a) *(see textbook pages 413–443)*
Identify appropriate applications of psychology in solving problems, such as:	› Origin and treatment of abnormal behavior (APA SLO 4.2.b) *(see textbook pages 420–424, 428–432, 434–443)*

*Portions of this chapter cover learning outcomes suggested by the American Psychological Association (2007) in their guidelines for the undergraduate psychology major. Chapter coverage of these outcomes is identified by APA Goal and APA Suggested Learning Outcome (SLO).

An Overview of Personality Disorders

› **What are the essential features of personality disorders, and why are they listed on Axis II in the text revision of the fourth edition of the *Diagnostic and Statistical Manual (DSM-IV-TR)*?**

We all think we know what a personality is. It's all the characteristic ways a person behaves and thinks: "Michael tends to be shy;" "Mindy likes to be dramatic;" "Juan is always suspicious of others;" "Annette is outgoing;" "Bruce seems to be sensitive and gets upset easily over minor things;" "Sean has the personality of an eggplant!" We tend to type people as behaving in one way in many situations. For example, like Michael, many of us are shy with people we don't know, but we won't be shy around our friends. A truly shy person is shy even among people he has known for some time. The shyness is part of the way the person behaves in most situations. We also have all probably behaved in all the other ways noted here (dramatic, suspicious, outgoing, easily upset). However, we usually consider a way of behaving part of a person's personality only if it occurs in many times and places. In this chapter, we look at characteristic ways of behaving in relation to personality disorders. First we examine how we conceptualize personality disorders and the issues related to them; then we describe the disorders themselves.

Aspects of Personality Disorders

What if a person's characteristic ways of thinking and behaving cause significant distress to themselves or others? What if the person can't change this way of relating to the world and is unhappy? We might consider this person to have a **personality disorder**. The *DSM-IV-TR* definition notes that these personality characteristics are "inflexible and maladaptive and cause significant functional impairment or subjective distress." Unlike many of the disorders we have already discussed, personality disorders are chronic; they do not come and go but originate in childhood and continue throughout adulthood. Because they affect personality, these chronic problems pervade every aspect of a person's life. For example, if a woman is overly suspicious (a sign of a possible paranoid personality disorder), this trait will affect almost everything she does, including her employment (she may have to change jobs often if she believes coworkers conspire against her), her relationships (she may not be able to sustain a lasting relationship if she can't trust anyone), and even where she lives (she may have to move often if she suspects her landlord is out to get her).

However, individuals with personality disorders may not feel any subjective distress; indeed, it may be others who acutely feel distress because of the actions of the person with the disorder. This is particularly common with antisocial personality disorder because the individual may show a blatant disregard for the rights of others yet exhibit no remorse (Patrick, 2006). In certain cases, someone other than the person with the personality disorder must decide whether the disorder is causing significant functional impairment because the affected person often cannot make such a judgment.

DSM-IV-TR lists 10 specific personality disorders and several others that are being studied for future consideration; we review them all. Although the prospects for treatment success for people who have personality disorders may be more optimistic than previously thought (see, for example, Svartberg, Stiles, & Seltzer, 2004), unfortunately, as you will see later, many people who have personality disorders in addition to other psychological problems (for

personality disorder An enduring maladaptive pattern for relating to the environment and self, exhibited in a range of contexts that cause significant functional impairment or subjective distress.

example, major depression) tend to do poorly in treatment. Most disorders we discuss in this book are in Axis I of *DSM-IV-TR*, which includes the standard traditional disorders. The personality disorders are included in a separate axis, Axis II, because as a group they are distinct. The characteristic traits are more ingrained and inflexible in people who have personality disorders, and the disorders themselves are less likely to be successfully modified.

Because personality disorders are on a separate axis, clinicians are required to consider symptom by symptom whether the person has a personality disorder. In the axis system, a patient can receive a diagnosis on only Axis I, only Axis II, or on both axes. A diagnosis on both Axis I and Axis II indicates that a person has both a current disorder (Axis I) and a more chronic problem (for example, personality disorder). As you will see, it is not unusual for one person to be diagnosed on both axes.

Categorical and Dimensional Models

Most of us are sometimes suspicious of others and a little paranoid, overly dramatic, too self-involved, or reclusive. Fortunately, these characteristics have not lasted long or been overly intense, and they haven't significantly impaired how we live and work. People with personality disorders, however, display problem characteristics over extended periods and in many situations, which can cause great emotional pain for themselves, others, or both (Ferguson, 2010b). Their difficulty, then, can be seen as one of *degree* rather than *kind;* in other words, the problems of people with personality disorders may just be extreme versions of the problems many of us experience temporarily, such as being shy or suspicious (South, Oltmanns, & Krueger, 2011).

The distinction between problems of degree and problems of kind is usually described in terms of *dimensions* instead of *categories*. The issue that continues to be debated in the field is whether personality disorders are extreme versions of otherwise normal personality variations (dimensions) or ways of relating that are different from psychologically healthy behavior (categories) (Widiger & Trull, 2007). You can see the difference between dimensions and categories in everyday life. For example, we tend to look at gender categorically. Our society views us as being in one category—"female"—or the other—"male." Yet we could also look at gender in terms of dimensions. For example, we know that "maleness" and "femaleness" are partly determined by hormones. We could identify people along testosterone, estrogen, or both dimensions and rate them on a continuum of maleness and femaleness rather than in the absolute categories of male or female. Many researchers and clinicians in this field see personality disorders as extremes on one or more personality dimensions. Yet because of the way people are diagnosed with the *DSM*, the personality disorders—like most other disorders—end up being viewed in categories. You have two choices—either you do ("yes") or you do not ("no") have a disorder. For example, either you have antisocial personality disor-

der or you don't. The *DSM* doesn't rate how dependent you are; if you meet the criteria, you are labeled as having dependent personality disorder. There is no "somewhat" when it comes to personality disorders.

There are advantages to using categorical models of behavior, the most important being their convenience. With simplification, however, comes problems. One is that the mere act of using categories leads clinicians to reify them—that is, to view disorders as real "things," comparable to the realness of an infection or a broken arm. Some argue that personality disorders are not things that exist but points at which society decides a particular way of relating to the world has become a problem. There is the important unresolved issue again: Are personality disorders just an extreme variant of normal personality, or are they distinctly different disorders?

Some have proposed that the *DSM-IV-TR* personality disorders section be replaced or at least supplemented by a dimensional model (South et al., 2011; Widiger & Trull, 2007) in which individuals would not only be given categorical diagnoses but also would be rated on a series of personality dimensions. Although no general consensus exists about what the basic personality dimensions might be, there are several contenders (South et al., 2011). One of the more widely accepted is called the *five-factor model*, or the "Big Five," and is taken from work on normal personality (McCrae & Costa, 2008). In this model, people can be rated on a series of personality dimensions and the combination of five components describes why people are so different. The five factors or dimensions are *extroversion* (talkative, assertive, and active versus silent, passive, and reserved); *agreeableness* (kind, trusting, and warm versus hostile, selfish, and mistrustful); *conscientiousness* (organized, thorough, and reliable versus careless, negligent, and unreliable); *neuroticism* (even-tempered versus nervous, moody, and temperamental); and *openness to experience* (imaginative, curious, and creative versus shallow and imperceptive) (McCrae & Costa, 2008). On each dimension, people are rated high, low, or somewhere between.

Cross-cultural research establishes the universal nature of the five dimensions—although there are individual differences across cultures (Hofstede & McCrae, 2004). For example, one study found in general that Austrian, Swiss, and Dutch samples scored the highest on openness to experience, whereas the Danes, Malaysians, and Telugu Indians (India) scored the lowest on this factor (McCrae, 2002). A number of researchers are trying to determine whether people with personality disorders can also be rated in a meaningful way along these dimensions and whether the system will help us better understand these disorders (Skodol et al., 2005).

Personality Disorder Clusters

DSM-IV-TR divides the personality disorders into three groups, or clusters (see Table 11.1) (American Psychiatric Association, 2000). The cluster division is based on resemblance. Cluster A is called the odd or eccentric cluster; it

Table 11.1 Personality Disorders

Personality Disorder	Description
Cluster A—Odd or Eccentric Disorders	
Paranoid personality disorder	The strong tendency to mistrust the motives of others, leading to a high degree of suspiciousness.
Schizoid personality disorder	Characterized by social detachment and a lack of emotional expression not due to social anxiety.
Schizotypal personality disorder	Social and interpersonal difficulties that are due to social anxiety but also involves distorted views of the world and unusual behavior.
Cluster B—Dramatic, Emotional, or Erratic Disorders	
Antisocial personality disorder	Characterized by behavior that shows limited regard for other people.
Borderline personality disorder	Characterized by a high level of unstable relationships and emotional outbursts, poor self-image, and a difficulty controlling impulses.
Histrionic personality disorder	The tendency to display flamboyant emotions with the goal of seeking attention.
Narcissistic personality disorder	Pervasive belief that the individual is better than everyone else, which leads to attention-seeking and a lack of concern for others.
Cluster C—Anxious or Fearful Disorders	
Avoidant personality disorder	Characterized by strong feelings of being inadequate, which can result in inhibition in social situations and sensitivity to any negative feedback.
Dependent personality disorder	A strong need to be cared for by others, including patterns of submissiveness and fear of separation.
Obsessive-compulsive personality disorder	Characterized by a desire for being perfect both mentally and interpersonally, a need for orderliness, and reduced flexibility and openness.

© Cengage Learning 2013

includes paranoid, schizoid, and schizotypal personality disorders. Cluster B is the dramatic, emotional, or erratic cluster; it consists of antisocial, borderline, histrionic, and narcissistic personality disorders. Cluster C is the anxious or fearful cluster; it includes avoidant, dependent, and obsessive-compulsive personality disorders. We follow this order in our review.

Statistics and Development

Personality disorders are found in 0.5% to 2.5% of the general population, 10% to 30% of all individuals served in inpatient settings, and 2% to 10% of those individuals in outpatient settings (American Psychiatric Association, 2000). However, an important population survey suggests that as many as 1 in 10 adults in the United States may have a diagnosable personality disorder (Lenzenweger, Lane, Loranger, & Kessler, 2007b), which makes them relatively common (Table 11.2). Numbers vary somewhat across countries, but worldwide about 6% of adults may have at least one personality disorder (Huang et al., 2009). Differences in prevalence estimates may be the result of

surveying people in clinical settings versus surveying the general population—even those not seeking assistance. Similarly, gender differences in the disorders—for example, more women diagnosed with borderline personality disorder and more men identified with antisocial personality disorder—are not apparent when surveying the general population.

Personality disorders are thought to originate in childhood and continue into the adult years (Cloninger & Svakic, 2009); they are also thought to be so ingrained that an onset is difficult to pinpoint. Maladaptive personality characteristics develop over time into the maladaptive behavior patterns that create distress for the affected person and draw the attention of others. Our relative lack of information about such important features of personality disorders as their developmental course is a repeating theme. The gaps in our knowledge of the course of about half these disorders are visible in Table 11.2. One reason for this dearth of research is that many individuals do not seek treatment in the early developmental phases of their disorder but only after years of distress. This makes it difficult to study people with personality disorders from the begin-

Table 11.2 Statistics and Development of Personality Disorders

Disorder	Prevalence*	Gender Differences[†]	Course
Paranoid personality disorder	In the clinical population: 4.2% In the general population: 2.3%–2.4%	In the clinical population: More common in males In the general population: No difference	Insufficient information
Schizoid personality disorder	In the clinical population: 1.4% In the general population: 1.7%–4.9%	In the clinical population: More common in males In the general population: No difference	Insufficient information
Schizotypal personality disorder	In the clinical population: 0.6% In the general population: 0.6%–3.3%	In the clinical population: More common in males In the general population: No difference	Chronic; some go on to develop schizophrenia
Antisocial personality disorder	In the clinical population: 3.6% In the general population: 0.7%–1%	In the clinical population: More common in males In the general population: No difference	Dissipates after age 40 (Hare, McPherson, & Forth, 1988)
Borderline personality disorder	In the clinical population: 9.3% In the general population: 0.7%–1.6%	In the clinical population: More common in females In the general population: No difference	Symptoms gradually improve if individuals survive into their 30s (Zanarini et al., 2006); approximately 6% die by suicide (Perry, 1993)
Histrionic personality disorder	In the clinical population: 1.0% In the general population: .1%–2.0%	In the clinical population: No difference In the general population: No difference	Chronic
Narcissistic personality disorder	In the clinical population: 2.3% In the general population: .1%	In the clinical population: More common in males In the general population: No difference	May improve over time (Cooper & Ronningstam, 1992; Gunderson, Ronningstam, & Smith, 1991)
Avoidant personality disorder	In the clinical population: 14.7% In the general population: 5.0%–5.2%	In the clinical population: No difference In the general population: No difference	Insufficient information
Dependent personality disorder	In the clinical population: 1.4% In the general population: 0.6%–1.5%	In the clinical population: No difference In the general population: No difference	Insufficient information
Obsessive-compulsive personality disorder	In the clinical population: 8.7% In the general population: 2.0%–2.4%	In the clinical population: More common in males In the general population: No difference	Insufficient information

*Clinical population data reported in Zimmerman, Rothschild, and Chelminski (2005). General population data reported from two community samples: Lenzenweger et al. (2007b) and Torgersen, Kringlen, and Cramer (2001).
[†]Clinical population data reported in *DSM-IV-TR* (American Psychiatric Association, 2000) and general population data from Lenzenweger et al. (2007b).

ning, although a few research studies have helped us understand the development of several disorders.

People with borderline personality disorder are characterized by their volatile and unstable relationships; they tend to have persistent problems in early adulthood, with frequent hospitalizations, unstable personal relationships, severe depression, and suicidal gestures. Almost 10% attempt suicide, and approximately 6% succeed in their at-

tempts (Skodol & Gunderson, 2008). On the bright side, their symptoms gradually improve if they survive into their 30s (Zanarini, Frankenburg, Hennen, Reich, & Silk, 2006), although elderly individuals with borderline personality disorder may have difficulty making plans and may be disruptive in nursing homes (Hunt, 2007). People with antisocial personality disorder display a characteristic disregard for the rights and feelings of others; they tend to continue their destructive behaviors of lying and manipulation through adulthood. Fortunately, some tend to "burn out" after the age of about 40 and engage in fewer criminal activities (Douglas, Vincent, & Edens, 2006). As a group, however, the problems of people with personality disorders continue, as shown when researchers follow their progress over the years (Ferguson, 2010b).

Gender Differences

Borderline personality disorder is diagnosed more often in females (although as you will see next, this may be the result of diagnostic bias), who make up about 75% of the identified cases (Cloninger & Svakic, 2009) (see Table 11.2). Historically, histrionic and dependent personality disorders were identified by clinicians more often in women (Dulit, Marin, & Frances, 1993; Stone, 1993), but according to more recent studies of their prevalence in the general population, equal numbers of males and females may have histrionic and dependent personality disorders (see Table 11.2). If this observation holds up in future studies, why have these disorders been predominantly diagnosed among females in general clinical practice and in other studies?

Do the disparities indicate differences between men and women in certain basic experiences that are genetic, sociocultural, or both, or do they represent biases on the part of the clinicians who make the diagnoses? Take, for example, a classic study by Maureen Ford and Thomas Widiger (1989), who sent fictitious case histories to clinical psychologists for diagnosis. One case described a person with *antisocial personality disorder*, which is characterized by irresponsible and reckless behavior and usually diagnosed in males; the other case described a person with *histrionic personality disorder*, which is characterized by excessive emotionality and attention seeking and more often diagnosed in females. The subject was identified as male in some versions of each case and as female in others, although everything else was identical. As the graph in ■ Figure 11.1 shows, when the antisocial personality disorder case was labeled male, most psychologists gave the correct diagnosis. However, when the same case of antisocial personality disorder was labeled female, most psychologists diagnosed it as histrionic personality disorder rather than antisocial personality disorder. In the case of histrionic personality disorder, being labeled a woman increased the likelihood of that diagnosis. Ford and Widiger (1989) concluded that the psychologists incorrectly diagnosed more women as having histrionic personality disorder.

This gender difference in diagnosis has also been criticized by other authors (see, for example, Kaplan, 1983) on the grounds that histrionic personality disorder, like several of the other personality disorders, is biased against

▲ Personality disorders tend to begin in childhood.

females. As Kaplan (1983) points out, many of the features of histrionic personality disorder, such as overdramatization, vanity, seductiveness, and overconcern with physical appearance, are characteristic of the Western "stereotypical female." This disorder may simply be the embodiment of extremely "feminine" traits (Chodoff, 1982); branding such an individual mentally ill, according to Kaplan, reflects society's inherent bias against females.

The issue of gender bias in diagnosing personality disorder remains highly controversial. Remember, however, that just because certain disorders are observed more in men or women doesn't necessarily indicate bias (Lilienfeld, Van-Valkenburg, Larntz, & Akiskal, 1986). When it is present, bias can occur at different stages of the diagnostic process. Widiger and Spitzer (1991) point out that the criteria for the disorder may themselves be biased *(criterion gender bias)* or the assessment measures and the way they are used may be biased *(assessment gender bias)*. In general, the criteria themselves do not appear to have strong gender bias (Jane, Oltmanns, South, & Turkheimer, 2007), although there may be some tendency for clinicians to use their own bias when using the criteria and therefore diagnose males and females differently (Morey, Alexander, & Boggs, 2005)

Comorbidity

Looking at Table 11.2 and adding up the prevalence rates across the personality disorders, you might conclude that up to 25% of all people are affected. In fact, the percentage of people in the population with a personality disorder is likely closer to 10% (Huang et al., 2009; Lenzenweger et al., 2007b). What accounts for this discrepancy? A major concern with the personality disorders is that people tend to be diagnosed with more than one. The term *comorbidity* historically describes the condition in which a person has

Hill Street Studios/Blend Images/Getty Images

▲ Gender bias may affect the diagnosis of clinicians who associate certain behavioral characteristics with one sex or the other.

multiple diseases (Caron & Rutter, 1991). A fair amount of disagreement is ongoing about whether the term should be used with psychological disorders because of the frequent overlap of different disorders (Skodol, 2005). In just one example, Zimmerman, Rothschild, and Chelminski (2005) conducted a study of 859 psychiatric outpatients and assessed how many had one or more personality disorders. Table 11.3 shows the odds that a person with a particular personality disorder would also meet the criteria for other disorders. For example, a person identified with borderline personality disorder is also likely to receive diagnoses of paranoid, schizotypal, antisocial, narcissistic, avoidant, and dependent personality disorders.

Do people really tend to have more than one personality disorder? Are the ways we define these disorders inaccurate, and do we need to improve our definitions so that they do not overlap? Or did we divide the disorders in the wrong way, and do we need to rethink the categories? Such questions about comorbidity are just a few of the important issues faced by researchers who study personality disorders.

Personality Disorders under Study

Other personality disorders have been studied for inclusion in the *DSM*—for example, sadistic personality disorder, which includes people who receive pleasure by inflicting pain on others (Morey, Hopwood, & Klein, 2007), and self-defeating personality disorder, which includes people who are overly passive and accept the pain and suffering imposed by others (Skodol, 2005). However, few studies support the existence of these disorders, so they were not included in the *DSM-IV-TR* (Cloninger & Svakic, 2009).

Two new personality disorders are under study for inclusion in *DSM-5*. *Depressive personality disorder* includes self-criticism, dejection, a judgmental stance toward others, and a tendency to feel guilt. Some evidence indicates this may indeed be a personality disorder distinct from dysthymic disorder (the mood disorder described in Chapter 6 that involves a persistently depressed mood lasting at least 2 years); research is continuing in this area (Orstavik, Kendler, Czajkowski, Tambs, & Reichborn-Kjennerud, 2007; Vachon, Sellbom, Ryder, Miller, & Bagby, 2009). *Passive-aggressive (negativistic) personality disorder* is characterized by passive aggression in which people adopt a negativistic attitude to resist routine demands and expectations. This category is an expansion of a previous *DSM-III-R* category, *passive-aggressive personality disorder*, and may be a subtype of a narcissistic personality disorder (Hopwood et al., 2009).

We now review the personality disorders currently in *DSM-IV-TR*, 10 in all. Then we look briefly at a few categories being considered for inclusion in *DSM-5*.

■ **FIGURE 11.1** Gender bias in diagnosing personality disorders (P.D.). Data are shown for the percentage of cases clinicians rated as antisocial personality disorder or histrionic personality disorder, depending on whether the case was described as a male or a female. (From Ford, M. R., & Widiger, T. A., 1989. Sex bias in the diagnosis of histrionic and antisocial personality disorders. *Journal of Consulting and Clinical Psychology, 57*, 301–305.)

Table 11.3 Diagnostic Overlap of Personality Disorders

Odds Ratio† of People Qualifying for Other Personality Disorder Diagnoses

Diagnosis	Paranoid	Schizoid	Schizotypal	Antisocial	Borderline	Histrionic	Narcissistic	Avoidant	Dependent	Obsessive-Compulsive
Paranoid		2.1	37.3*	2.6	12.3*	0.9	8.7*	4.0*	0.9	5.2*
Schizoid	2.1		19.2	1.1	2.0	3.9	1.7	12.3*	2.9	5.5*
Schizotypal	37.3*	19.2		2.7	15.2*	9.4	11.0	3.9*	7.0	7.1
Antisocial	2.6	1.1	2.7		9.5*	8.1*	14.0*	0.9	5.6	0.2
Borderline	12.3*	2.0	15.2*	9.5*		2.8	7.1*	2.5*	7.3*	2.0
Histrionic	0.9	3.9	9.4	8.1*	2.8		13.2*	0.3	9.5	1.3
Narcissistic	8.7*	1.7	11.0	14.0*	7.1*	13.2*		0.3	4.0	3.7*
Avoidant	4.0*	12.3*	3.9*	0.9	2.5*	0.3	0.3		2.0	2.7
Dependent	0.9	2.9	7.0	5.6	7.3*	9.5	4.0	2.0		0.9
Obsessive-compulsive	5.2*	5.5*	7.1	0.2	2.0	1.3	2.0	2.7	0.9	

†The "odds ratio" indicates how likely it is that a person would have both disorders. The odds ratios with an asterisk (*) indicate that, statistically, people are likely to be diagnosed with both disorders—with a higher number meaning people are more likely to have both. Some higher odds ratios are not statistically significant because the number of people with the disorder in this study was relatively small.
Source: Reprinted, with permission, from Zimmerman, M., Rothschild, L., & Chelminski, I., 2005. The prevalence of DSM-IV personality disorders in psychiatric outpatients. *American Journal of Psychiatry, 162,* 1911–1918, © 2005 American Psychiatric Association.

Concept Check 11.1

Fill in the blanks to complete the following statements about personality disorders.

1. Personality disorders as a group are distinct and therefore placed on a separate axis, _____.

2. _____ refers to a condition where people with personality disorders are diagnosed with other disorders.

3. The personality disorders are divided into three clusters or groups: _____ contains the odd or eccentric disorders; _____ contains the dramatic, emotional, and erratic disorders; and contains _____ the anxious and fearful disorders.

4. It's debated whether personality disorders are extreme versions of otherwise normal personality variations (therefore classified as dimensions) or ways of relating that are different from psychologically healthy behavior (classified as _____).

5. Personality disorders are described as _____ because unlike many disorders, they originate in childhood and continue throughout adulthood.

6. Although gender differences are evident in the research of personality disorders, some differences in the findings may be the result of _____.

Cluster A Personality Disorders

> **What are the nature, etiology, and treatment of each of the odd or eccentric personality disorders?**

Three personality disorders—paranoid, schizoid, and schizotypal—share common features that resemble some of the psychotic symptoms seen in schizophrenia. These odd or eccentric personality disorders are described next.

Paranoid Personality Disorder

Although it is probably adaptive to be a little wary of other people and their motives, being too distrustful can interfere with making friends, working with others, and getting through daily interactions in a functional way. People with **paranoid personality disorder** are excessively mistrustful and suspicious of others, without any justification. They assume other people are out to harm or trick them; therefore, they tend not to confide in others. Consider the case of Jake.

Clinical Description

The defining characteristic of people with paranoid personality disorder is a pervasive unjustified distrust (Edens, Marcus, & Morey, 2009). Certainly, there may be times when someone is deceitful and "out to get you"; however, people with paranoid personality disorder are suspicious in situations in which most other people would agree their suspicions are unfounded. Even events that have nothing to do with them are interpreted as personal attacks (Bernstein & Useda, 2007). These people would view a neighbor's barking dog or a delayed airline flight as a deliberate attempt to annoy them. Unfortunately, such mistrust often

extends to people close to them and makes meaningful relationships difficult.

Suspicion and mistrust can show themselves in a number of ways. People with paranoid personality disorder may be argumentative, may complain, or may be quiet. This style of interaction is communicated, sometimes nonverbally, to others, often resulting in discomfort among those who come in contact with them because of this volatility. They often appear tense and are "ready to pounce" when they think they've been slighted by someone. These individuals are sensitive to criticism and have an excessive need for autonomy (Bernstein & Useda, 2007).

Causes

Evidence for biological contributions to paranoid personality disorder is limited. Some research suggests the disorder may be slightly more common among the relatives of people who have schizophrenia, although the association does not seem to be strong (Tienari et al., 2003). As you will see later with the other odd or eccentric personality disorders in Cluster A, there seems to be some relationship with schizophrenia, although its exact nature is not yet clear. In general, however, there appears to be a strong role for genetics in paranoid personality disorder (Kendler et al., 2006).

Psychological contributions to this disorder are even less certain, although some interesting speculations have been made. Some psychologists point directly to the thoughts of people with paranoid personality disorder as a way of explaining their behavior. One view is that people with this disorder have the following basic mistaken assumptions about others: "People are malevolent and deceptive," "They'll attack you if they get the chance," and "You can be okay only if you stay on your toes" (Freeman, Pretzer, Fleming, & Simon, 1990). This is a maladaptive way to view the world, yet it seems to pervade every aspect of the lives of these individuals. Although we don't know why they develop these perceptions, some speculation is that the roots are in their early upbringing. Their parents may teach them to be careful about making mistakes and may impress on them that they are different from other people. This vigilance causes them to see signs that other people are deceptive and malicious (Carroll, 2009).

Cultural factors have also been implicated in paranoid personality disorder. Certain groups of people, such as prisoners, refugees, people with hearing impairments, and older adults, are thought to be particularly susceptible because of their unique experiences (Rogler, 2007). Imagine how you might view other people if you were an immigrant who had difficulty with the language and the customs of your new culture. Such innocuous things as other people laughing or talking quietly might be interpreted as somehow directed at you. You have seen how someone could misinterpret ambiguous situations as malevolent. Therefore, cognitive and cultural factors may interact to produce the suspiciousness observed in some people with paranoid personality disorder.

Treatment

Because people with paranoid personality disorder are mistrustful of everyone, they are unlikely to seek professional help when they need it and they have difficulty developing the trusting relationships necessary for successful therapy (Skodol & Gunderson, 2008). When these individuals finally do seek therapy, the trigger is usually a crisis in their lives—such as Jake's threats to harm strangers—or other problems such as anxiety or depression, not necessarily their personality disorder (Kelly, Casey, Dunn, Ayuso-Mateos, & Dowrick, 2007).

Therapists try to provide an atmosphere conducive to developing a sense of trust (Bender, 2005). They often use cognitive therapy to counter the person's mistaken assumptions about others, focusing on changing the person's beliefs that all people are malevolent and most people cannot be trusted (Skodol & Gunderson, 2008). However, a survey of mental health professionals indicated that only 11% of therapists who treat paranoid personality disorder thought these individuals would continue in therapy long enough to be helped (Quality Assurance Project, 1990).

Schizoid Personality Disorder

Do you know someone who is a "loner"? Someone who would choose a solitary walk over an invitation to a party? A person who comes to class alone, sits alone, and leaves alone? Now, magnify this preference for isolation many times over and you can begin to grasp the impact of **schizoid personality disorder** (Cloninger & Svakic, 2009). People with this personality disorder show a pattern of detachment from social relationships and a limited range of emotions in interpersonal situations. They seem aloof, cold, and indifferent to other people. The term *schizoid* is relatively old, having been used by Bleuler (1924) to describe people who have a tendency to turn inward and away from the outside world. These people were said to lack emotional expressiveness and pursued vague interests. Consider the case of Mr. Z.

©Michael Newman/Photo Edit

▲ People with paranoid personality disorder often believe that impersonal situations exist specifically to annoy or otherwise disturb them.

paranoid personality disorder A cluster A (odd or eccentric) personality disorder involving pervasive distrust and suspiciousness of others such that their motives are interpreted as malevolent.
schizoid personality disorder A cluster A (odd or eccentric) personality disorder featuring a pervasive pattern of detachment from social relationships and a restricted range of expression of emotions.

A 39-year-old scientist was referred after his return from a tour of duty in Antarctica where he had stopped cooperating with others, withdrawn to his room, and begun drinking on his own. Mr. Z. was orphaned at age 4 years, raised by an aunt until age 9, and subsequently looked after by an aloof housekeeper. At university he excelled at physics, but chess was his only contact with others. Throughout his subsequent life he made no close friends and engaged primarily in solitary activities. Until the tour of duty in Antarctica, he had been quite successful in his research work in physics. He was now, some months after his return, drinking at least a bottle of schnapps each day, and his work had continued to deteriorate. He presented as self-contained and unobtrusive and was difficult to engage effectively. He was at a loss to explain his colleagues' anger at his aloofness in Antarctica and appeared indifferent to their opinion of him. He did not appear to require any interpersonal relations, although he did complain of some tedium in his life and at one point during the interview became sad, expressing longing to see his uncle in Germany, his only living relation.

(Cases and excerpts reprinted, with permission of the Royal Australian and New Zealand College of Psychiatrists, from Quality Assurance Project, 1990. Treatment outlines for paranoid, schizotypal and schizoid personality disorders. *Australian and New Zealand Journal of Psychiatry, 24*, 339–350.)

Clinical Description

Individuals with schizoid personality disorder seem neither to desire nor to enjoy closeness with others, including romantic or sexual relationships. As a result they appear cold and detached and do not seem affected by praise or criticism. Some, however, are sensitive to the opinions of others but are unwilling or unable to express this emotion. For them, social isolation may be extremely painful. Unfortunately, homelessness appears to be prevalent among people with this personality disorder, perhaps as a result of their lack of close friendships and lack of dissatisfaction about not having a sexual relationship with another person (Rouff, 2000).

The social deficiencies of people with schizoid personality disorder are similar to those of people with paranoid personality disorder, although they are more extreme. As Beck and Freeman (1990, p. 125) put it, they "consider themselves to be observers rather than participants in the world around them." They do not seem to have the unusual thought processes that characterize the other disorders in Cluster A (Cloninger & Svakic, 2009) (Table 11.4). For example, people with paranoid and schizotypal personality disorders often have *ideas of reference*, mistaken beliefs that meaningless events relate just to them. In contrast, those with schizoid personality disorder share the social

Table 11.4 Grouping Schema for Cluster A Disorders

Cluster A Personality Disorder	Psychotic-Like Symptoms	
	Positive (for example, Ideas of Reference, Magical Thinking, and Perceptual Distortions)	Negative (for example, Social Isolation, Poor Rapport, and Constricted Affect)
Paranoid	Yes	Yes
Schizoid	No	Yes
Schizotypal	Yes	No

Source: Adapted from Siever, L. J., 1992. Schizophrenia spectrum personality disorders. In A. Tasman & M. B. Riba (Eds.), *Review of psychiatry* (Vol. 11, pp. 25–42). Washington, DC: American Psychiatric Press, © 1992 American Psychiatric Press.

isolation, poor rapport, and constricted affect (showing neither positive nor negative emotion) seen in people with paranoid personality disorder. You will see in Chapter 12 that this distinction among psychotic-like symptoms is important to understanding people with schizophrenia, some of whom show the "positive" symptoms (actively unusual behaviors such as ideas of reference) and others only the "negative" symptoms (the more passive manifestations of social isolation or poor rapport with others).

DSM Disorder Criteria Summary
Schizoid Personality Disorder

A. A pervasive pattern of detachment from social relationships and a restricted range of expression of emotions in interpersonal settings, beginning by early adulthood and present in a variety of contexts, as indicated by four (or more) of the following: (1) neither desires nor enjoys close relationships, including being part of a family; (2) almost always chooses solitary activities; (3) has little, if any, interest in having sexual experiences with another person; (4) takes pleasure in few, if any, activities; (5) lacks close friends or confidants other than first-degree relatives; (6) appears indifferent to the praise or criticism of others; (7) shows emotional coldness, detachment, or flattened affectivity

B. Does not occur exclusively during the course of Schizophrenia, a Mood Disorder With Psychotic Features, another Psychotic Disorder, or a Pervasive Developmental Disorder and is not due to the direct physiological effects of a general medical condition.

Note: If criteria are met prior to the onset of Schizophrenia, add Premorbid," e.g., "Schizoid Personality Disorder (Premorbid)."

Source: Reprinted with permission from *Diagnostic and Statistical Manual of Mental Disorders* (4th ed., text revision). © 2000 American Psychiatric Association.

Causes and Treatment

Childhood shyness is reported as a precursor to later adult schizoid personality disorder. It may be that this personality trait is inherited and serves as an important determinant in the development of this disorder. Abuse and neglect in child-hood are also reported among individuals with this disorder (Johnson, Bromley, & McGeoch, 2005). Research over the past several decades points to biological causes of autism (a disorder we discuss in more detail in Chapter 13), and parents of children with autism are more likely to have schizoid personality disorder (Constantino et al., 2009). It is possible that a biological dysfunction found in both autism and schizoid personality disorder combines with early learning or early problems with interpersonal relationships to produce the social deficits that define schizoid personality disorder.

It is rare for a person with this disorder to request treatment except in response to a crisis such as extreme depression or losing a job (Kelly et al., 2007). Therapists often begin treatment by pointing out the value in social relationships. The person with the disorder may even need to be taught the emotions felt by others to learn empathy (Skodol & Gunderson, 2008). Because their social skills were never established or have atrophied through lack of use, people with schizoid personality disorder often receive social skills training. The therapist takes the part of a friend or significant other in a technique known as role-playing and helps the patient practice establishing and maintaining social relationships (Skodol & Gunderson, 2008). This type of social skills training is helped by identifying a social network—a person or people who will be supportive (Bender, 2005).

Schizotypal Personality Disorder

People with **schizotypal personality disorder** are typically socially isolated, like those with schizoid personality disorder. In addition, they also behave in ways that would seem unusual to many of us, and they tend to be suspicious and have odd beliefs (Cloninger & Svakic, 2009). Schizotypal personality disorder is considered by some to be on a continuum (that is, on the same spectrum) with schizophrenia—the severe disorder we discuss in the next chapter—but without some of the more debilitating symptoms, such as hallucinations and delusions. Consider the case of Mr. S.

Mr. S ⦚ Man with a Mission

Mr. S. was a 35-year-old chronically unemployed man who had been referred by a physician because of a vitamin deficiency. This was thought to have eventuated because Mr. S. avoided any foods that "could have been contaminated by machine." He had begun to develop alternative ideas about diet in his 20s and soon left his family and began to study an Eastern religion. "It opened my third eye—corruption is all about," he said.

He now lived by himself on a small farm, attempting to grow his own food and bartering for items he could not grow himself. He spent his days and evenings researching the origins and mechanisms of food contamination and, because of this knowledge, had developed a small band who followed his ideas. He had never married and maintained little contact with his family: "I've never been close to my father. I'm a vegetarian."

He said he intended to do an herbalism course to improve his diet before returning to his life on the farm. He had refused medication from the physician and became uneasy when the facts of his deficiency were discussed with him.

(Cases and excerpts reprinted, with permission of the Royal Australian and New Zealand College of Psychiatrists, from Quality Assurance Project, 1990. Treatment outlines for paranoid, schizotypal and schizoid personality disorders. *Australian and New Zealand Journal of Psychiatry, 24,* 339–350.)

Clinical Description

People given a diagnosis of schizotypal personality disorder have psychotic-like (but not psychotic) symptoms (such as believing everything relates to them personally), social deficits, and sometimes cognitive impairments or paranoia (Cloninger & Svakic, 2009). These individuals are often considered odd or bizarre because of how they relate to other people, how they think and behave, and even how they dress. They have *ideas of reference*, which means they think insignificant events relate directly to them. For example, they may believe that somehow everyone on a passing city bus is talking about them, yet they may be able to acknowledge this is unlikely. Again, as you will see in Chapter 12, some people with schizophrenia also have ideas of reference, but they are usually not able to "test reality" or see the illogic of their ideas.

Individuals with schizotypal personality disorder also have odd beliefs or engage in "magical thinking," believing, for example, that they are clairvoyant or telepathic. In addition, they report unusual perceptual experiences, including such illusions as feeling the presence of another person when they are alone. Notice the subtle but important difference between *feeling* as if someone else is in the room and the more extreme perceptual distortion in people with schizophrenia who might report there *is* someone else in the room when there isn't. Unlike people who simply have unusual interests or beliefs, those with schizotypal personality disorder tend to be suspicious and have paranoid thoughts, express little emotion, and may dress or behave in unusual ways (for example, wear many layers of clothing in the summertime or mumble to themselves) (Cloninger & Svakic, 2009). Prospective research on children who later develop schizotypal personality disorder found that they tend to be passive and unengaged and are hypersensitive to criticism (Olin et al., 1997).

schizotypal personality disorder A cluster A (odd or eccentric) personality disorder involving a pervasive pattern of interpersonal deficits featuring acute discomfort with, and reduced capacity for, close relationships, as well as cognitive or perceptual distortions and eccentricities of behavior.

Clinicians must be aware that different cultural beliefs or practices may lead to a mistaken diagnosis of schizotypal personality disorder. For example, some people who practice certain religious rituals—such as speaking in tongues, practicing voodoo, or mind reading—may do so with such obsessiveness as to make them seem extremely unusual, thus leading to a misdiagnosis (American Psychiatric Association, 2000). Mental health workers have to be particularly sensitive to cultural practices that may differ from their own and can distort their view of certain seemingly unusual behaviors.

Causes

Historically, the word *schizotype* was used to describe people who were predisposed to develop schizophrenia (Meehl, 1962; Rado, 1962). Schizotypal personality disorder is viewed by some to be one phenotype of a schizophrenia genotype. Recall that a *phenotype* is one way a person's genetics is expressed. A *genotype* is the gene or genes that make up a particular disorder. However, depending on a variety of other influences, the way you turn out—your phenotype—may vary from other people with a similar genetic makeup. Some people are thought to have "schizophrenia genes" (the genotype) yet, because of the relative lack of biological influences (for example, prenatal illnesses) or environmental stresses (for example, poverty), some will have the less severe schizotypal personality disorder (the phenotype).

The idea of a relationship between schizotypal personality disorder and schizophrenia arises partly from the way people with the disorders behave. Many characteristics of schizotypal personality disorder, including ideas of reference, illusions, and paranoid thinking, are similar but milder forms of behaviors observed among people with schizophrenia. Genetic research also seems to support a relationship. Family, twin, and adoption studies have shown an increased prevalence of schizotypal personality disorder among relatives of people with schizophrenia who do not also have schizophrenia themselves (Siever & Davis, 2004). However, these studies also tell us that the environment can strongly influence schizotypal personality disorder. Some research suggests that schizotypal symptoms are strongly associated with childhood maltreatment among men and this childhood maltreatment seems to result in posttraumatic stress disorder (PTSD) symptoms (see Chapter 4) among women (Berenbaum, Thompson, Milanak, Boden, & Bredemeier, 2008). Cognitive assessment of people with this disorder points to mild to moderate decrements in their ability to perform on tests involving memory and learning, suggesting some damage in the left hemisphere (Siever & Davis, 2004). Other research, using magnetic resonance imaging, points to generalized brain abnormalities in those with schizotypal personality disorder (Modinos et al., 2009).

Treatment

Some estimate that between 30% and 50% of the people with schizotypal personality disorder who request clinical help also meet the criteria for major depressive disorder. Treatment includes some of the medical and psychological treatments for depression (Cloninger & Svakic, 2009; Mulder, Frampton, Luty, & Joyce, 2009).

Controlled studies of attempts to treat groups of people with schizotypal personality disorder are few. However, there is now growing interest in treating this disorder because it is being viewed as a precursor to schizophrenia (McClure et al., 2010). One study used a combination of approaches, including antipsychotic medication, community treatment (a team of support professionals providing therapeutic services), and social skills training, to treat the symptoms experienced by individuals with this disorder. Researchers found that this combination of approaches either reduced their symptoms or postponed the onset of later schizophrenia (Nordentoft et al., 2006).

Concept Check 11.2

Which personality disorders are described here?

1. Heidi trusts no one and wrongly believes other people want to harm her or cheat her out of her life earnings. She is sure her husband is secretly planning to leave her and take their three boys, although she has no proof. She no longer confides in

friends or divulges any information to coworkers for fear that it will be used in a plot against her. She is usually tense and ready to argue about harmless comments made by family members. _____

2. Rebecca lives alone out in the country with her birds and has little contact with relatives or any other individuals in the nearby town. She is extremely concerned with pollution, fearing that harmful chemicals are in the air and water around her. She has developed her own water purification system and makes her own clothes. If it is necessary for her to go outside, she covers her body with excessive clothing and wears a face mask to avoid the contaminated air. _____

3. Doug is a college student who has no close friends. He comes to class every day and sits in a corner and is sometimes seen having lunch alone on the park bench. Most students find him difficult to engage and complain about his lack of involvement in class activities, but he appears indifferent to what others say. He has never had a girlfriend and expresses no desire to have sex. He is meeting with a therapist only because his family tricked him into going. _____

Cluster B Personality Disorders

> **What are the essential characteristics of dramatic, emotional, or erratic personality disorders?**

People diagnosed with the Cluster B personality disorders—antisocial, borderline, histrionic, and narcissistic—all have behaviors that have been described as dramatic, emotional, or erratic. These personality disorders are described next.

Antisocial Personality Disorder

People with **antisocial personality disorder** are among the most puzzling of the individuals a clinician will see in a practice and are characterized as having a history of failing to comply with social norms. They perform actions most of us would find unacceptable, such as stealing from friends and family. They also tend to be irresponsible, impulsive, and deceitful (De Brito & Hodgins, 2009). Robert Hare, a pioneer in the study of people with this disorder, describes people with antisocial personality disorder as "social predators who charm, manipulate, and ruthlessly plow their way through life, leaving a broad trail of broken hearts, shattered expectations, and empty wallets. Completely lacking in conscience and empathy, they selfishly take what they want and do as they please, violating social norms and expectations without the slightest sense of guilt or regret" (Hare, 1993, p. xi). Consider the case of Ryan.

Ryan | The Thrill Seeker

I first met Ryan on his 17th birthday. Unfortunately, he was celebrating the event in a psychiatric hospital. He had been truant from school for several months and had gotten into some trouble; the local judge who heard his case had recommended psychiatric evaluation.

My first impression was that Ryan was cooperative and pleasant. He pointed out a tattoo on his arm that he had made himself, saying that it was a "stupid" thing to have done and that he now regretted it. He regretted many things and was looking forward to moving on with his life. I later found out that he was never truly remorseful for anything.

Our second interview was quite different. In the 48 hours since our first interview, Ryan had done a number of things that showed why he needed a great deal of help. The most serious incident involved a 15-year-old girl named Ann who attended class with Ryan in the hospital school. Ryan had told her that he was going to get himself discharged, get in trouble, and be sent to the same prison Ann's father was in, where he would rape her father. Ryan's threat so upset Ann that she hit her teacher and several of the staff. When I spoke to Ryan about this, he smiled slightly and said he was bored and that it was fun to upset Ann. When I asked whether it bothered him that his behavior might extend her stay in the hospital, he looked puzzled and said, "Why should it bother me? She's the one who'll have to stay in this hellhole!"

antisocial personality disorder A cluster B (dramatic, emotional, or erratic) personality disorder involving a pervasive pattern of disregard for and violation of the rights of others. Similar to the non-*DSM-IV-TR* label psychopathy but with greater emphasis on overt behavior than on personality traits.

Just before Ryan's admittance, a teenager in his town was murdered. A group of teens went to the local cemetery at night to perform satanic rituals, and a young man was stabbed to death, apparently over a drug purchase. Ryan was in the group, although he did not stab the boy. He told me that they occasionally dug up graves to get skulls for their parties—not because they really believed in the devil but because it was fun and it scared the younger kids. I asked, "What if this was the grave of someone you knew, a relative or a friend? Would it bother you that strangers were digging up the remains?" He shook his head. "They're dead, man. They don't care. Why should I?"

Ryan told me he loved PCP, or "angel dust," and that he would rather be dusted than anything else. He routinely made the 2-hour trip to New York City to buy drugs in a particularly dangerous neighborhood. He denied that he was ever nervous. This wasn't machismo; he really seemed unconcerned.

Ryan made little progress. I discussed his future in family therapy sessions and we talked about his pattern of showing supposed regret and remorse and then stealing money from his parents and going back onto the street. Most of our discussions centered on trying to give his parents the courage to say no to him and not to believe his lies.

Ryan was eventually discharged to a drug rehabilitation program. Within 4 weeks, he had convinced his parents to take him home, and within 2 days he had stolen all their cash and disappeared; he apparently went back to his friends and to drugs.

When he was in his 20s, after one of his many arrests for theft, he was diagnosed as having antisocial personality disorder. His parents never summoned the courage to turn him out or refuse him money, and he continues to con them into providing him with a means of buying more drugs.

Clinical Description

Individuals with antisocial personality disorder tend to have long histories of violating the rights of others (De Brito & Hodgins, 2009). They are often described as being aggressive because they take what they want, indifferent to the concerns of other people. Lying and cheating seem to be second nature to them, and often they appear unable to tell the difference between the truth and the lies they make up to further their own goals. They show no remorse or concern over the sometimes-devastating effects of their actions. Substance abuse is common, occurring in 60% of people with antisocial personality disorder, and appears to be a lifelong pattern among these individuals (Taylor & Lang, 2006). The long-term outcome for people with antisocial personality disorder is usually poor, regardless of gender (Colman et al., 2009). One classic study, for example, followed 1,000 delinquent and nondelinquent boys over a 50-year period (Laub & Vaillant, 2000). Many of the delinquent boys would today receive a diagnosis of conduct disorder, which you will see later may be a precursor to antisocial personality disorder in adults. The delinquent boys were more than twice as likely to die an unnatural death (for example, accident, suicide, or homicide) as their nondelinquent peers, which may be attributed to factors such as alcohol abuse and poor self-care (for example, reckless behavior and infections).

Antisocial personality disorder has had a number of names over the years. Philippe Pinel (1801/1962) identified what he called *manie sans délire* (mania without delirium) to describe people with unusual emotional responses and impulsive rages but no deficits in reasoning ability (Charland, 2010). Other labels have included moral insanity, egopathy, sociopathy, and psychopathy. A great deal has been written about these labels; we focus on the two that have figured most prominently in psychological research: **psychopathy** and *DSM-IV-TR*'s antisocial personality disorder. As you will see, there are important differences between the two.

Defining Criteria. Hervey Cleckley (1941/1982), a psychiatrist who spent much of his career working with the "psychopathic personality," identified a constellation of 16 major characteristics, most of which are personality traits and are sometimes referred to as the "Cleckley criteria." Hare and his colleagues, building on the descriptive work of Cleckley, researched the nature of psychopathy (see, for example, Hare, 1970; Harpur, Hare, & Hakstian, 1989) and developed a 20-item checklist that serves as an assessment tool. Six of the criteria that Hare includes in his Revised Psychopathy Checklist (PCL-R) are as follows:

1. Glibness/superficial charm
2. Grandiose sense of self-worth
3. Proneness to boredom/need for stimulation
4. Pathological lying
5. Conning/manipulative
6. Lack of remorse

(Neumann, Hare, & Newman, 2007: pg., 103)

With some training, clinicians are able to gather information from interviews with a person, along with material from significant others or institutional files (for example, prison records), and assign the person scores on the checklist, with high scores indicating psychopathy (Hare & Neumann, 2006).

The *DSM-IV-TR* criteria for antisocial personality focus almost entirely on observable *behaviors* (for example, "impulsively and repeatedly changes employment, residence, or sexual partners"). In contrast, the Cleckley/Hare criteria focus primarily on underlying *personality traits* (for example, being self-centered or manipulative). *DSM-IV-TR* and previous versions chose to use only observable behaviors so that clinicians could reliably agree on a diagnosis.

Antisocial Personality Disorder

A. There is a pervasive pattern of disregard for and violation of the rights of others occurring since age 15 years, as indicated by three (or more) of the following:
(1) failure to conform to social norms with respect to lawful behaviors as indicated by repeatedly performing acts that are grounds for arrest; (2) deceitfulness, as indicated by repeated lying, use of aliases, or conning others for personal profit or pleasure; (3) impulsivity or failure to plan ahead; (4) irritability and aggressiveness, as indicated by repeated physical fights or assaults; (5) reckless disregard for safety of self or others; (6) consistent irresponsibility, as indicated by repeated failure to sustain consistent work behavior or honor financial obligations; (7) lack of remorse, as indicated by being indifferent to or rationalizing having hurt, mistreated, or stolen from another

B. The individual is at least age 18 years.

C. There is evidence of Conduct Disorder with onset before age 15 years.

D. The occurrence of antisocial behavior is not exclusively during the course of Schizophrenia or a Manic Episode.

Source: Reprinted with permission from *Diagnostic and Statistical Manual of Mental Disorders* (4th ed., text revision). © 2000 American Psychiatric Association.

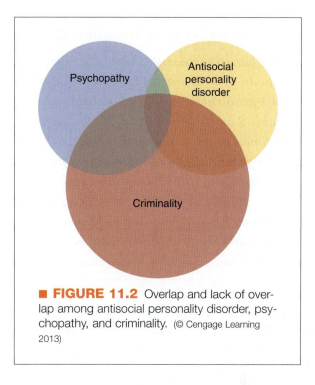

■ **FIGURE 11.2** Overlap and lack of overlap among antisocial personality disorder, psychopathy, and criminality. (© Cengage Learning 2013)

Antisocial Personality, Psychopathy, and Criminality. Although Cleckley did not deny that many psychopaths are at greatly elevated risk for criminal and antisocial behaviors, he did emphasize that some have few or no legal or interpersonal difficulties. In other words, some psychopaths are not criminals and some do not display the aggressiveness that is a *DSM-IV-TR* criterion for antisocial personality disorder. Although the relationship between psychopathic personality and antisocial personality disorder is uncertain, the two syndromes clearly do not overlap perfectly (De Brito & Hodgins, 2009). ■ Figure 11.2 illustrates the relative overlap among the characteristics of psychopathy as described by Cleckley and Hare; antisocial personality disorder as outlined in *DSM-IV-TR;* and criminality, which includes all people who get into trouble with the law.

As you can see in the diagram, not everyone who has psychopathy or antisocial personality disorder becomes involved with the legal system. What separates many in this group from those who get into trouble with the law may be their intelligence quotient (IQ). In a classic prospective, longitudinal study, White, Moffitt, and Silva (1989) followed almost 1,000 children, beginning at age 5, to see what predicted antisocial behavior at age 15. They found that, of the 5 year olds determined to be at high risk for later delinquent behavior, 16% did indeed have run-ins with the law by the age of 15 and 84% did not. What distinguished these two groups? In general, the at-risk children with lower IQs were the ones who got in trouble. This suggests that having a higher IQ may help protect some people from developing more serious problems or may at least prevent them from getting caught.

Some psychopaths function quite successfully in certain segments of society (for example, politics, business, and entertainment). Because of the difficulty in identifying these people, such "successful" or "subclinical" psychopaths (who meet some of the criteria for psychopathy) have not been the focus of much research. In a clever exception, Widom (1977; pg., 677) recruited a sample of subclinical psychopaths through advertisements in underground newspapers that invited many of the major personality characteristics of psychopathy. For example, one of the advertisements reads as follows:

> Wanted: charming, aggressive, carefree people who are impulsively irresponsible but are good at handling people and at looking after number one.

Widom found that her sample appeared to possess many of the same characteristics as imprisoned psychopaths; for example, a large percentage of them received low scores on questionnaire measures of empathy and socialization and their parents tended to have higher rates of psychopathology, including alcoholism. But many of these individuals had stable occupations and had managed to stay out of prison. Widom's study, although lacking a control group, shows that at least some individuals with psychopathic personality traits avoid repeated contact with the legal system and may even function successfully in society.

psychopathy A non-*DSM-IV-TR* category similar to antisocial personality disorder but with less emphasis on overt behavior. Indicators include superficial charm, lack of remorse, and other personality characteristics.

Identifying psychopaths among the criminal population seems to have important implications for predicting their future criminal behavior. As you can imagine, having personality characteristics such as a lack of remorse and impulsivity can lead to difficulty staying out of trouble with the legal system. In general, people who score high on measures of psychopathy commit crimes at a higher rate than those with lower scores and are at greater risk for more violent crimes and recidivism (repeating offenses) (Widiger, 2006).

Conduct Disorder. Before we discuss causal factors, it is important to note the developmental nature of antisocial behavior. *DSM-IV-TR* provides a separate diagnosis for children who engage in behaviors that violate society's norms: *conduct disorder.* Many children with conduct disorder—most often diagnosed in boys—become juvenile offenders and tend to become involved with drugs (Durand, 2011). Ryan fit into this category. More important, the lifelong pattern of antisocial behavior is evident because young children who display antisocial behavior are likely to continue these behaviors as they grow older (Soderstrom, Sjodin, Carlstedt, & Forsman, 2004). Data from long-term follow-up research indicate that many adults with antisocial personality disorder or psychopathy had conduct disorder as children (Robins, 1978; Salekin, 2006); the likelihood of an adult having antisocial personality disorder increases if, as a child, he or she had both conduct disorder and attention deficit/hyperactivity disorder (Biederman, Mick, Faraone, & Burback, 2001; Moffitt, Caspi, Rutter, & Silva, 2001). In many cases, the types of norm violations that an adult would engage in—irresponsibility regarding work or family—appear as younger versions in conduct disorder, such as truancy from school or running away from home. A major difference is that lack of remorse is included under antisocial personality disorder but not in the conduct disorder criteria—that is, unlike those with antisocial personality disorder, some children with conduct disorder do feel remorseful about their behavior.

Genetic Influences

Family, twin, and adoption studies all suggest a genetic influence on both antisocial personality disorder and criminality (Ferguson, 2010a). For example in a classic study, Crowe (1974) examined children whose mothers were felons and who were later adopted by other families and compared them with adopted children of normal mothers. All were separated from their mothers as newborns, minimizing the possibility that environmental factors from their biological families were responsible for the results. Crowe found that the adopted offspring of felons had significantly higher rates of arrests, conviction, and antisocial personality than did the adopted offspring of normal mothers, which suggests at least some genetic influence on criminality and antisocial behavior.

However, Crowe found something else interesting: The adopted children of felons who themselves later became criminals had spent more time in interim orphanages than either the adopted children of felons who did not become criminals or the adopted children of normal mothers. As Crowe points out, this suggests a gene–environment interaction; in other words, genetic factors may be important only in the presence of certain environmental influences (alternatively, certain environmental influences are important only in the presence of certain genetic predispositions). Genetic factors may present a vulnerability, but actual development of criminality may require environmental factors, such as a deficit in early, high-quality contact with parents or parent surrogates.

This gene–environment interaction was demonstrated most clearly by Cadoret, Yates, Troughton, Woodworth, and Stewart (1995), who studied adopted children and their likelihood of developing conduct problems. If the children's biological parents had a history of antisocial personality disorder and their adoptive families exposed them to chronic stress through marital, legal, or psychiatric problems, the children were at greater risk for conduct problems. Again, research shows that genetic influence does not necessarily mean certain disorders are inevitable. Large-scale research on twins with conduct disorder supports the role of genetic and environmental influences on this disorder as well (Thomas, 2009).

If you remember back to Chapter 3, we introduced the concept of an *endophenotype*—underlying aspects of a disorder that might be more directly influenced by genes. In the case of antisocial personality disorder, gene researchers are looking for genetic differences that may influence factors such as serotonin and dopamine levels or the relative lack of anxiety or fear seen in these individuals (which we discuss next) (van Goozen, Fairchild, Snoek, & Harold,

A. A repetitive and persistent pattern of behavior in which the basic rights of others or major age-appropriate societal norms or rules are violated, as manifested by the presence of three (or more) of the following criteria in the past 12 months, with at least one criterion present in the past 6 months:

Aggression to people and animals

(1) often bullies, threatens, or intimidates others

(2) often initiates physical fights

(3) has used a weapon that can cause serious physical harm to others (e.g., a bat, brick, broken bottle, knife, gun)

(4) has been physically cruel to people

(5) has been physically cruel to animals

(6) has stolen while confronting a victim (e.g., mugging, purse snatching, extortion, armed robbery)

(7) has forced someone into sexual activity

Destruction of property

(8) has deliberately engaged in fire setting with the intention of causing serious damage

(9) has deliberately destroyed others' property (other than by fire setting)

Deceitfulness or theft

(10) has broken into someone else's house, building, or car

(11) often lies to obtain goods or favors or to avoid obligations (i.e., "cons" others)

(12) has stolen items of nontrivial value without confronting a victim (e.g., shoplifting, but without breaking and entering; forgery)

Serious violations of rules

(13) often stays out at night despite parental prohibitions, beginning before age 13 years

(14) has run away from home overnight at least twice while living in parental or parental surrogate home (or once without returning for a lengthy period)

(15) is often truant from school, beginning before age 13 years

B. The disturbance in behavior causes clinically significant impairment in social, academic, or occupational functioning.

C. If the individual is age 18 years or older, criteria are not met for Antisocial Personality Disorder.

Source: Reprinted with permission from *Diagnostic and Statistical Manual of Mental Disorders* (4th ed., text revision). © 2000 American Psychiatric Association.

2007; Waldman & Rhee, 2006). Although at its early stages, this research is refining the search for genes—not for ones that "cause" antisocial personality disorder but for genes that create the unusual aspects of an antisocial personality, such as fearlessness, aggressiveness, impulsivity, and lack of remorse.

Neurobiological Influences

A great deal of research has focused on neurobiological influences that may be specific to antisocial personality disorder. One thing seems clear: General brain damage does not explain why some people become psychopaths or criminals; these individuals appear to score as well on neuropsychological tests as the rest of us (Hart, Forth, & Hare, 1990). However, such tests are designed to detect significant damage in the brain and will not pick up subtle changes in chemistry or structure that could affect behavior.

Arousal Theories. The fearlessness, seeming insensitivity to punishment, and thrill-seeking behaviors characteristic of those with antisocial personality disorder (especially those with psychopathy) sparked interest in what neurobiological processes might contribute to these unusual reactions. Early theoretical work on people with antisocial personality disorder emphasized two hypotheses: the underarousal hypothesis and the fearlessness hypothesis. According to the *underarousal hypothesis,* psychopaths have abnormally low levels of cortical arousal (Sylvers, Ryan, Alden, & Brennan, 2009). There appears to be an inverted U-shaped relation between arousal and performance. The *Yerkes-Dodson curve* suggests that people with either high or low levels of arousal tend to experience negative affect and perform poorly in many situations, whereas individuals with intermediate levels of arousal tend to be relatively content and perform satisfactorily in most situations.

According to the underarousal hypothesis, the abnormally low levels of cortical arousal characteristic of psychopaths are the primary cause of their antisocial and risk-taking behaviors; they seek stimulation to boost their chronically low levels of arousal. This means that Ryan lied, took drugs, and dug up graves to achieve the same level of arousal we might get from talking on the phone with a good friend or watching television. Several researchers have examined childhood and adolescent psychophysiological predictors of adult antisocial behavior and criminality. Raine, Venables, and Williams (1990), for example, assessed a sample of 15 year olds on a variety of autonomic and central nervous system variables. They found that future criminals had lower skin conductance activity, lower heart rate during rest periods, and more slow-frequency brain-wave activity, all indicative of low arousal.

According to the fearlessness hypothesis, psychopaths possess a higher threshold for experiencing fear than most other individuals (Lykken, 1957, 1982). In other words, things that greatly frighten the rest of us have little effect on the psychopath. Remember that Ryan was unafraid of going alone to dangerous neighborhoods to buy drugs. According to proponents of this hypothesis, the fearlessness of the psychopath gives rise to all the other major features of the syndrome.

Theorists have tried to connect what we know about the workings of the brain with clinical observations of people with antisocial personality disorder, especially those with psychopathy. Several theorists have applied Jeffrey Gray's (1987) model of brain functioning to this population (Fowles, 1988; Quay, 1993). According to Gray, three major brain systems influence learning and emotional behavior: the behavioral inhibition system (BIS), the reward system,

▲ Many prisons allow visits between inmates and their children, partly to help reduce later problems in those children.

and the fight/flight system. Two of these systems, the BIS and the reward system, have been used to explain the behavior of people with psychopathy. The BIS is responsible for our ability to stop or slow down when we are faced with impending punishment, nonreward, or novel situations; activation of this system leads to anxiety and frustration. The BIS is thought to be located in the septohippocampal system and involves the noradrenergic and serotonergic neurotransmitter systems. The reward system is responsible for how we behave—in particular, our approach to positive rewards—and is associated with hope and relief. This system probably involves the dopaminergic system in the mesolimbic area of the brain, which we previously noted as the "pleasure pathway" for its role in substance use and abuse (see Chapter 10).

If you think about the behavior of psychopaths, the possible malfunctioning of these systems is clear. An imbalance between the BIS and the reward system may make the fear and anxiety produced by the BIS less apparent and the positive feelings associated with the reward system more prominent (Levenston, Patrick, Bradley, & Lang, 2000; Quay, 1993). Theorists have proposed that this type of neurobiological dysfunction may explain why psychopaths aren't anxious about committing the antisocial acts that characterize their disorder.

Researchers continue to explore how differences in neurotransmitter function (for example, serotonin) and neurohormone function (for example, androgens such as testosterone and the stress neurohormone cortisol) in the brains of these individuals can explain the callousness, superficial charm, lack of remorse, and impulsivity that characterize people with psychopathy. Integrative theories that link these differences to both genetic and environmental influences are just now beginning to be outlined (van Goozen et al., 2007) and may lead to better understanding and treatments for this debilitating disorder.

Psychological and Social Dimensions

What goes on in the mind of a psychopath? In one of several studies of how psychopaths process reward and punishment, Newman, Patterson, and Kosson (1987) set up a card-playing task on a computer; they provided five-cent rewards and fines for correct and incorrect answers to psychopathic and nonpsychopathic criminal offenders. The game was constructed so that at first players were rewarded about 90% of the time and fined only about 10% of

the time. Gradually, the odds changed until the probability of getting a reward was 0%. Despite feedback that reward was no longer forthcoming, the psychopaths continued to play and lose, whereas those without psychopathy stopped playing. As a result of this and other studies, the researchers hypothesized that once psychopaths set their sights on a reward goal, they are less likely than nonpsychopaths to be deterred despite signs the goal is no longer achievable (Dvorak-Bertscha, Curtin, Rubinstein, & Newman, 2009). Again, considering the reckless and daring behavior of some psychopaths (robbing banks without a mask and getting caught immediately), failure to abandon an unattainable goal fits the overall picture.

Interesting research suggests that this pattern of persisting in the face of failure may not be true for psychopaths from different racial groups. In replicating the type of research just described across samples of Caucasian and African American offenders, Newman and Schmitt (1998) found that the African American offenders did not make the same types of errors as their Caucasian counterparts. One explanation for this difference may be that because African American males are incarcerated at a higher rate than people from other groups, the population in prison may have a lower rate of psychopathy and therefore less likely to commit such errors (Newman & Schmitt, 1998).

Gerald Patterson's influential work suggests that aggression in children with antisocial personality disorder may escalate, partly as a result of their interactions with their parents (Granic & Patterson, 2006; Patterson, 1982). He found that the parents often give in to the problem behaviors displayed by their children. For example, a boy's parents ask him to make his bed and he refuses. One parent yells at the boy. The boy yells back and becomes abusive. At some point, his interchange becomes so aversive that the parent stops fighting and walks away, thereby ending the fight but also letting the son not make his bed. Giving in to these problems results in short-term gains for both the parent (calm is restored in the house) and the child (he gets what he wants), but it results in continuing problems. The child has learned to continue fighting and not give up, and the parent learns that the only way to "win" is to withdraw all demands. This "coercive family process" combines with other factors, such as parental depression, poor monitoring of their child's activities, and less parental involvement, to help maintain the aggressive behaviors (Chronis et al., 2007; Patterson, DeBaryshe, & Ramsey, 1989).

Although little is known about which environmental factors play a direct role in causing antisocial personality disorder and psychopathy (as opposed to childhood conduct disorders), evidence from adoption studies strongly suggests that shared environmental factors—that tend to make family members similar—are important to the etiology of criminality and perhaps antisocial personality disorder. For example, in the adoption study by Sigvardsson, Cloninger, Bohman, and von-Knorring (1982), low social status of the adoptive parents increased the risk of nonviolent criminality among females. Like children with conduct disorders, individuals with antisocial personality disorder come from homes with inconsistent parental discipline (see, for example, Robins, 1966). It is not known for certain, however, whether inconsistent discipline directly causes antisocial personality disorder; it is conceivable, for example, that parents have a genetic vulnerability to antisocial personality disorder that they pass on to their children but that also causes them to be inadequate parents.

Developmental Influences

The forms that antisocial behaviors take change as children move into adulthood, from truancy and stealing from friends to extortion, assaults, armed robbery, or other crimes. Fortunately, clinical lore, as well as scattered empirical reports (Robins, 1966), suggest that rates of antisocial behavior begin to decline rather markedly around the age of 40. In their classic study, Hare, McPherson, and Forth (1988) provided empirical support for this phenomenon. They examined the conviction rates of male psychopaths and male nonpsychopaths who had been incarcerated for a variety of crimes. The researchers found that between the ages of 16 and 45 the conviction rates of nonpsychopaths remained relatively constant. In contrast, the conviction rates of psychopaths remained relatively constant up until about 40, at which time they decreased markedly (■ Figure 11.3). Why antisocial behavior often declines around middle age remains unanswered.

An Integrative Model

How can we put all this information together to get a better understanding of people with antisocial personality disorder? Remember that the research just discussed sometimes involved people labeled as having antisocial personality disorder but at other times included people labeled as psychopathic or even criminals. Whatever the label, it appears these people have a genetic vulnerability to antisocial behaviors and personality traits.

One potential gene–environment interaction may be seen in the role of fear conditioning in children. If you remember back to Chapters 1 and 4, we discussed how we learn to fear things that can harm us (for example, a hot stove) through the pairing of an unconditioned stimulus (e.g., heat from burner) and a conditioned stimulus (e.g., parent's warning to stay away), resulting in avoidance of the conditioned stimulus. But what if this conditioning is somehow impaired and you do not learn to avoid things that can harm you?

An important study looked at whether abnormal responses to fear conditioning as a young child could be responsible for later antisocial behavior in adults (Gao, Raine, Venables, Dawson, & Mednick, 2010). This large 20-year study assessed fear conditioning in a group of 1,795 children at age 3 and then looked to see who had a criminal record at age 23. They found that offenders showed significantly reduced fear conditioning at age 3 compared to matched comparison participants, with many of these children showing no fear conditioning at all. Deficits in

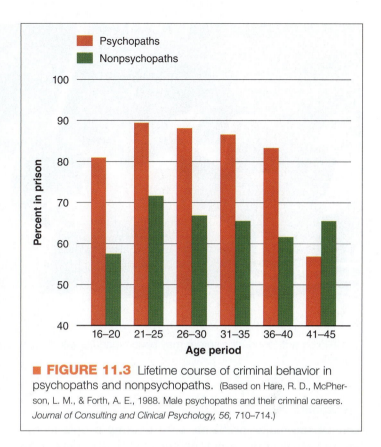

■ **FIGURE 11.3** Lifetime course of criminal behavior in psychopaths and nonpsychopaths. (Based on Hare, R. D., McPherson, L. M., & Forth, A. E., 1988. Male psychopaths and their criminal careers. *Journal of Consulting and Clinical Psychology, 56*, 710–714.)

amygdala functioning is thought to make individuals unable to recognize cues that signal threat, making them relatively fearless, which suggests that these children had problems in this area of the brain (Sterzer, 2010). If these findings are replicated, it may point to a mechanism by which genetic influences (leading to damage in the amygdala) interact with environmental influences (learning to fear threats) to produce adults who are relatively fearless and therefore engage in behaviors that cause harm to themselves and others.

Biological influences further interact with other environmental experiences such as early childhood adversity. In a family that may already be under stress because of divorce or substance abuse, there may be an interaction style that encourages antisocial behavior on the part of the child (Thomas, 2009). The child's antisocial and impulsive behavior—partly caused by the child's difficult temperament and impulsivity (Chronis et al., 2007; Kochanska, Aksan, & Joy, 2007)—alienates other children who might be good role models and attracts others who encourage antisocial behavior. These behaviors may also result in the child dropping out of school and a poor occupational history in adulthood, which help create increasingly frustrating life circumstances that further incite acts against society (Thomas, 2009).

This is, admittedly, an abbreviated version of a complex scenario. The important element is that in this integrative model of antisocial behavior, biological, psychological, and cultural factors combine in intricate ways to create someone like Ryan.

▲ Children with conduct disorder may become adults with antisocial personality disorder.

Treatment

One of the major problems with treating people in this group is typical of numerous personality disorders: They rarely identify themselves as needing treatment. Because of this, and because they can be manipulative even with their therapists, most clinicians are pessimistic about the outcome of treatment for adults who have antisocial personality disorder, and there are few documented success stories (National Collaborating Centre for Mental Health, 2010). In general, therapists agree with incarcerating these people to deter future antisocial acts. Clinicians encourage identification of high-risk children so that treatment can be attempted before they become adults (National Collaborating Centre for Mental Health, 2010; Thomas, 2009).

The most common treatment strategy for children involves parent training (Patterson, 1986; Sanders, 1992). Parents are taught how to recognize behavior problems early and how to use praise and privileges to reduce problem behavior and encourage prosocial behaviors. Treatment studies typically show that these types of programs can significantly improve the behaviors of many children who display antisocial behaviors (Conduct Problems Prevention Research Group, 2010). A number of factors, however, put families at risk either for not succeeding in treatment or for dropping out early; these include cases with a high degree of family dysfunction, socioeconomic disadvantage, high family stress, a parent's history of antisocial behavior, and severe conduct disorder on the part of the child (Kaminski, Valle, Filene, & Boyle, 2008).

Prevention

The aggressive behavior of young children is remarkably stable, meaning that children who hit, insult, and threaten others are likely to continue as they grow older. Unfortunately, these behaviors become more serious over time and are the early signs of the homicides and assaults seen among some adults (Eron & Huesmann, 1990; Singer & Flannery, 2000).

Approaches to change this aggressive course are being implemented mainly in school and preschool settings and emphasize behavioral supports for good behavior and skills training to improve social competence (Reddy, Newman, De Thomas, & Chun, 2009). Research using parent training for young children (toddlers from 1½ to 2½ years) suggests that early intervention may be particularly helpful (Shaw, Dishion, Supplee, Gardner, & Arnds, 2006). Aggression can be reduced and social competence (for example, making friends and sharing) can be improved among young children, and these results generally are maintained over a few years (Conduct Problems Prevention Research, 2010; Reddy et al., 2009). It is too soon to assess the success of such programs in preventing adult antisocial behaviors typically observed among people with this personality disorder. However, given the ineffectiveness of treatment for adults, prevention may be the best approach to this problem.

Borderline Personality Disorder

People with **borderline personality disorder** lead tumultuous lives. Their moods and relationships are unstable and usually they have a poor self-image. These people often feel empty and are at great risk of dying by their own hands. Consider the case of Claire.

Claire • A Stranger among Us

I have known Claire for more than 40 years and have watched her through the good but mostly bad times of her often shaky and erratic life as a person with borderline personality disorder. Claire and I went to school together from the eighth grade through high school, and we've kept in touch periodically. My earliest memory of her is of her hair, which was cut short rather unevenly. She told me that when things were not going well she cut her own hair severely, which helped to "fill the void." I later found out that the long sleeves she usually wore hid scars and cuts that she had made herself.

Claire was the first of our friends to smoke. What was unusual about this and her later drug use was not that they occurred or that they began early; it was that she didn't seem to use them to get attention, like everyone else. Claire was also one of the first whose parents divorced, and both of them seemed to abandon her emotionally. She later told me that her father was an alcoholic who had regularly beaten her and her mother. She did poorly in school and had a low opinion of herself. She often said she was stupid and ugly, yet she was neither.

Throughout our school years, Claire left town periodically, without any explanation. I learned many years later that she was in psychiatric facilities to get help with her suicidal depression. She often threatened to kill herself, although we didn't guess that she was serious.

In our later teens, we all drifted away from Claire. She had become increasingly unpredictable, sometimes berating us for a perceived slight ("You're walking too fast. You don't want to be seen with me!") and at other times desperate to be around us. We were confused by her behavior. With some people, emotional outbursts can bring you closer together. Unfortunately for Claire, these incidents and her overall demeanor made us feel that we didn't know her. As we all grew older, the "void" she described in herself became overwhelming and eventually shut us all out.

Claire married twice and both times had passionate but stormy relationships interrupted by hospitalizations. She tried to stab her first husband during a particularly violent rage. She tried a number of drugs but mainly used alcohol to "deaden the pain."

Now, in her mid-50s, things have calmed down some, although she says she is rarely happy. Claire does feel a little better about herself and is doing well as a travel agent. Although she is seeing someone, she is reluctant to become involved because of her personal history. Claire was ultimately diagnosed with depression and borderline personality disorder.

Clinical Description

Borderline personality disorder is one of the most common personality disorders observed in clinical settings; it is observed in every culture and is seen in about 1% to 2% of the general population (Cloninger & Svakic, 2009). Claire's life illustrates the instability characteristic of people with borderline personality disorder. They tend to have turbulent relationships, fearing abandonment but lacking control over their emotions (Linehan & Dexter-Mazza, 2008). They often engage in behaviors that are suicidal, self-mutilative, or both, cutting, burning, or punching themselves. Claire sometimes used her cigarette to burn her palm or forearm, and she carved her initials in her arm. A significant proportion—about 6%—succeed at suicide (McGirr, Paris, Lesage, Renaud, & Turecki, 2009). On the positive side, the long-term outcome for people with borderline personality disorder is encouraging, with up to 88% achieving remission more than 10 years after initial treatment (Zanarini et al., 2006).

People with this personality disorder are often intense, going from anger to deep depression in a short time. Dysfunction in the area of emotion is sometimes considered one of the core features of borderline personality disorder (Linehan & Dexter-Mazza, 2008) and is one of the best predictors of suicide in this group (McGirr et al., 2009).

These individuals also are characterized by impulsivity, which can be seen in their drug abuse and self-mutilation. Although not so obvious as to why, the self-injurious behaviors such as cutting sometimes are described as tension reducing by people who engage in these behaviors (Nock, Cha, & Dour, 2011). Claire's empty feeling is also common; these people are sometimes described as chronically bored and have difficulties with their own identities (Linehan & Dexter-Mazza, 2008). The mood disorders we discussed in Chapter 6 are common among people with borderline personality disorder, with about 20% having major depression and about 40% having bipolar disorder (Grant et al., 2008). Eating disorders are also common, particularly bulimia (see Chapter 8). Almost 25% of people with bulimia also have borderline personality disorder (Zanarini, Reichman, Frankenburg, Reich, & Fitzmaurice, 2010). Up to 67% of the people with borderline personality disorder are also diagnosed with at least one substance use disorder (Grant et al., 2008). As with antisocial personality disorder, people with borderline personality disorder tend to improve during their 30s and 40s, although they may continue to have difficulties into old age (National Collaborating Centre for Mental Health, 2009).

Dr. P. Marazzi/Photo Researchers, Inc.

▲ Borderline personality disorder is often accompanied by self-mutilation.

borderline personality disorder A cluster B (dramatic, emotional, or erratic) personality disorder involving a pervasive pattern of instability of interpersonal relationships, self-image, affect, and control over impulses.

How would you describe a woman who regularly exhibits unstable relationships (e.g., falls in and out of love quickly), problems with her self-identity (e.g., frequently changes her career goals), and impulsive decision making (e.g., goes on reckless shopping sprees)? Are these just "normal" behaviors, expressions, and decisions for a woman or do they indicate the presence of a psychological disorder? The *Diagnostic and Statistical Manual of Mental Disorders* (*DSM-IV;* American Psychological Association, 2000) states that "a pervasive pattern of instability of interpersonal relationships, self-image, and affects, and marked impulsivity that begins by early adulthood and is present in a variety of contexts" is the primary feature of borderline personality disorder (BPD) (APA, 2000, p. 706). With this *DSM-IV* understanding, the woman described here might be diagnosed with BPD—a disorder that is predominately (75% of the time) found in women. This differential sex prevalence rate, and several of the criteria for BPD,

have led to wide debate over the possibility of gender bias in the diagnosis of BPD.

From a socialization perspective, it has been argued that women are trained from a young age to be what our society calls "dependent" and can be more sensitive to criticism or rejection from others (e.g., girls are taught to place high emphasis on things such as relatedness and tend to view themselves through the appraisals of others) (Becker, 1997). Additionally, in attempting to understand how a BPD diagnosis affects women, feminist literature has argued that "the diagnosis of BPD is the latest manifestation of historical attempts to explain away the strategies which some women use to survive and resist oppression and abuse, by describing these strategies as symptomatic of a disturbed personality/pathology" (Shaw & Proctor, 2005, p. 484). Both of these perspectives suggest that BPD is an unfair diagnosis: either pathologizing socialized expressions of gender or devaluing the experiences and expressions of women. However, diagnos-

ing and treating such extreme behaviors may be the appropriate action. What do you think? Is it the case that extremes in socialized gender expression unfairly lead to labels of personality disorder and devaluation, or do such extreme expressions suggest unhealthiness and call for diagnosis and treatment?

In terms of gender bias in personality disorders, the *DSM-IV* states that two personality disorders occur more frequently in women (including dependent and histrionic) and six personality disorders occur more often in men (including antisocial, narcissistic, obsessive-compulsive, paranoid, schizotypal, and schizoid). Therefore, just as women are more likely to be diagnosed with BPD, men are more than three times more likely to be diagnosed with antisocial personality disorder (Kessler et al., 1994), and similar socialization and various gender biases in the *DSM-IV* may play a part. How do you view the potential gender bias in the other personality disorders listed here?

DSM | Disorder Criteria Summary
Borderline Personality Disorder

A pervasive pattern of instability of interpersonal relationships, self-image, and affects, and marked impulsivity beginning by early adulthood and present in a variety of contexts, as indicated by five (or more) of the following:

(1) frantic efforts to avoid real or imagined abandonment. **Note:** Do not include suicidal or self-mutilating behavior covered in Criterion 5.

(2) a pattern of unstable and intense interpersonal relationships characterized by alternating between extremes of idealization and devaluation

(3) identity disturbance: markedly and persistently unstable self image or sense of self

(4) impulsivity in at least two areas that are potentially self-damaging (e.g., spending, sex, substance abuse, reckless driving, binge eating). **Note:** Do not include suicidal or self-mutilating behavior covered in Criterion 5.

(5) recurrent suicidal behavior, gestures, or threats, or self-mutilating behavior

(6) affective instability due to a marked reactivity of mood (e.g., intense episodic dysphoria, irritability, or anxiety usually lasting a few hours and only rarely more than a few days)

(7) chronic feelings of emptiness

(8) inappropriate, intense anger or difficulty controlling anger (e.g., frequent displays of temper, constant anger, recurrent physical fights)

(9) transient, stress-related paranoid ideation or severe dissociative symptoms

Source: Reprinted with permission from *Diagnostic and Statistical Manual of Mental Disorders* (4th ed., text revision). © 2000 American Psychiatric Association.

Causes

The results from numerous family studies suggest that borderline personality disorder is more prevalent in families with the disorder and somehow linked with mood disorders (Distel, Trull, & Boomsma, 2009). Studies of monozygotic (identical) and dizygotic (fraternal) twins indicated a higher concordance rate among monozygotic twins, further supporting the role of genetics in the expression of borderline personality disorder (for example, Reichborn-Kjennerud et al., 2009).

The emotional reactivity that is a central aspect of borderline personality disorder has led researchers to look at this personality trait for clues about inherited influences (endophenotypes). Important genetic studies are investigating genes associated with the neurochemical serotonin because dysfunction in this system has been linked to the emotional instability, suicidal behaviors, and impulsivity seen in people with this disorder (Distel et al., 2009). This research is in its early stages and there are as yet no solid answers for how genetic differences lead to the symptoms of borderline personality disorder.

Neuroimaging studies, designed to locate areas in the brain contributing to borderline personality disorder, point to the limbic network (Nunes et al., 2009). Significantly, this area in the brain is involved in emotion regulation and dysfunctional serotonin neurotransmission, linking these findings with genetic research.

Cognitive factors in borderline personality disorder are just beginning to be explored. Here, the questions are, just how do people with this disorder process information, and does this contribute to their difficulties? One study that looked at the thought processes of these individuals asked people with and without borderline personality disorder to look at words projected on a computer screen and try to remember some of the words and try to forget others (Korfine & Hooley, 2000). When the words were not related to the symptoms of borderline personality disorder—for example, "celebrate," "charming," and "collect"—both groups performed equally well. However, when they were presented with words that might be relevant to the disorder—for example, "abandon," "suicidal," and "emptiness"—individuals with borderline personality disorder remembered more of these words despite being instructed to forget them. This preliminary evidence for a memory bias may hold clues to the nature of this disorder and may someday be helpful in designing more effective treatment (Geraerts & McNally, 2008).

An important environmental risk factor in a gene–environment interaction explanation for borderline personality disorder is the possible contribution of early trauma, especially sexual and physical abuse. Numerous studies show that people with this disorder are more likely to report abuse than are healthy individuals or those with other psychiatric conditions (see, for example, Bandelow et al., 2005; Goldman, D'Angelo, DeMaso, & Mezzacappa, 1992; Ogata et al., 1990). Unfortunately, these types of studies (based on recollection and a correlation between the two phenomena) do not tell us directly whether abuse and neglect cause later borderline personality disorder. In an important study, researchers followed 500 children who had documented cases of childhood physical and sexual abuse and neglect and compared them in adulthood with a control group (no history of reported abuse or neglect) (Widom, Czaja, & Paris, 2009). Significantly more abused and neglected children went on to develop borderline personality disorder compared to controls. This finding is particularly significant for girls and women because girls are two or three times more likely to be sexually abused than boys (Bebbington et al., 2009).

It is clear that a majority of people who receive the diagnosis of borderline personality disorder have suffered terrible abuse or neglect from both parents, sexual abuse, physical abuse by others, or a combination of these (Ball & Links, 2009). For those who have not reported such histories, some workers are examining just how they could develop borderline personality disorder. For example, factors such as temperament (emotional nature, such as being impulsive, irritable, or hypersensitive) or neurological impairments (being exposed prenatally to alcohol or drugs) and how they interact with parental styles may account for some cases of borderline personality disorder (Graybar & Boutilier, 2002).

Borderline personality disorder has been observed among people who have gone through rapid cultural changes. The problems of identity, emptiness, fears of abandonment, and low anxiety threshold have been found in child and adult immigrants (Laxenaire, Ganne-Vevonec, & Streiff, 1982; Skhiri, Annabi, Bi, & Allani, 1982). These observations further support the possibility that prior trauma may, in some individuals, lead to borderline personality disorder.

Remember, however, that a history of childhood trauma, including sexual and physical abuse, occurs in people with other disorders, such as schizoid personality disorder, somatoform disorder (see Chapter 5), panic disorder (see Chapter 4), and dissociative identity disorder (see Chapter 5). In addition, a portion of individuals with borderline personality disorder have no apparent history of such abuse (Cloninger & Svakic, 2009). Although childhood sexual and physical abuse seems to play an important role in the etiology of borderline personality disorder, neither appears to be necessary or sufficient to produce the syndrome.

An Integrative Model

Although there is no currently accepted integrative model for this disorder, it is tempting to borrow from the work on anxiety disorders to outline a possible view. In Chapter 4, we described the "triple vulnerability" theory (Barlow, 2002; Suárez, Bennett, Goldstein, & Barlow, 2008). The first vulnerability (or diathesis) is a generalized biological vulnerability. We can see the genetic vulnerability to emotional reactivity in people with borderline personality disorder and how this affects specific brain function. The second vulnerability is a generalized psychological vulnerability. In the case of people with this personality disorder, they tend to view the world as threatening and to react strongly to real and perceived threats. The third vulnerability is a specific psychological vulnerability, learned from early environmental experiences; this is where early trauma, abuse, or both may advance this sensitivity to threats. When stressed, a person's biological tendency to be overly reactive interacts with the psychological tendency to feel threatened. This may result in the outbursts and suicidal behaviors commonly observed in this group. This preliminary model awaits validation and further research.

Treatment

In stark contrast to individuals with antisocial personality disorder who rarely acknowledge requiring help, those with borderline personality disorder appear quite distressed and are more likely to seek treatment even than people with anxiety and mood disorders (Ansell, Sanislow, McGlashan, & Grilo, 2007). Reviews of research on the use of medical treatment for people with this disorder suggest that anticonvulsants (such as drugs used for people with epilepsy) and newer antipsychotics may be effective for treating some of the core symptoms of borderline personality disorder, but that antidepressants have limited usefulness (Citrome et al., 2010). Efforts to provide successful treatment are complicated by problems with drug abuse, compliance with treatment, and suicide attempts. As a result, many clinicians are reluctant to work with people who have borderline personality disorder.

One of the most thoroughly researched psychosocial treatments was developed by Marsha Linehan (Linehan et al., 2006; Linehan et al., 1999; Linehan & Dexter-Mazza, 2008). This approach—called **dialectical behavior therapy (DBT)**—involves helping people cope with the stressors that seem to trigger suicidal behaviors. Priority in treatment is first given to those behaviors that may result in harm (suicidal behaviors), then those behaviors that interfere with therapy, and, finally, those that interfere with the patient's quality of life. Weekly individual sessions provide support, and patients are taught how to identify and regulate their emotions. Problem solving is emphasized so that patients can handle difficulties more effectively. In addition, they receive treatment similar to that used for people with PTSD, in which prior traumatic events are reexperienced to help extinguish the fear associated with them (see Chapter 4). In the final stage of therapy, clients learn to trust their own responses rather than depend on the validation of others, sometimes by visualizing themselves not reacting to criticism.

Results from a number of studies suggest that DBT may help reduce suicide attempts, dropouts from treatment, and hospitalizations (Linehan & Dexter-Mazza, 2008; Stanley & Brodsky, 2009). A follow-up of 39 women who received either dialectical behavior therapy or general therapeutic support (called "treatment as usual") for 1 year showed that, during the first 6 months of follow-up, the women in the DBT group were less suicidal, less angry, and better adjusted socially (Linehan & Kehrer, 1993). Another study examined how treating these individuals with DBT in an inpatient setting (a psychiatric hospital) for approximately 5 days would improve their outcomes (Yen, Johnson, Costello, & Simpson, 2009). The participants improved in a number of areas, such as with a reduction in depression, hopelessness, anger expression, and dissociation. A growing body of evidence is now available to document the effectiveness of this approach to aid many individuals with this debilitating disorder (Stanley & Brodsky, 2005).

Probably some of the most intriguing research we describe in this book involves using the techniques in brain imaging to see how psychological treatments influence brain function. One pilot study examined emotional reactions to upsetting photos (for example, pictures of women being attacked) in controls and in women with borderline personality disorder (Schnell & Herpertz, 2007). This study found that among the women who benefited from treatment, arousal (in the amygdala and hippocampus) to the upsetting photos improved over time as a function of treatment. No changes occurred in controls or in women who did not have positive treatment experiences. This type of integrative research holds enormous promise for our understanding of borderline personality disorder and the mechanisms underlying successful treatment.

Histrionic Personality Disorder

Individuals with **histrionic personality disorder** tend to be overly dramatic and often seem almost to be acting, which is why the term *histrionic,* which means theatrical in manner, is used. Consider the case of Pat.

Pat • Always Onstage

When we first met, Pat seemed to radiate enjoyment of life. She was single, in her mid-30s, and was going to night school for her master's degree. She often dressed flamboyantly. During the day she taught children with disabilities, and when she didn't have class she was often out late on a date. When I first spoke with her, she enthusiastically told me how impressed she was with my work in the field of developmental disabilities and that she had been extremely successful in using some of my techniques with her students. She was clearly overdoing the praise, but who wouldn't appreciate such flattering comments?

Because some of our research included children in her classroom, I saw Pat often. Over a period of weeks, however, our interactions grew strained. She often complained of various illnesses and injuries (falling in the parking lot, twisting her neck looking out a window) that interfered with her work. She was disorganized, often leaving to the last minute tasks that required considerable planning. Pat made promises to other people that were impossible to keep but seemed to be aimed at winning their approval; when she broke the promise, she usually made up a story designed to elicit sympathy and compassion.

Pat often interrupted meetings about research to talk about her latest boyfriend. The boyfriends changed almost weekly, but her enthusiasm ("Like no other man I have ever met!") and optimism about the future ("He's the guy I want to spend the rest of my life with!") remained high for each of them. Wedding plans were seriously discussed with almost every one, despite their brief acquaintance. Pat was ingratiating, especially to the male teachers, who often helped her out of trouble she got into because of her disorganization.

When it became clear that she would probably lose her teaching job because of her poor performance, Pat managed to manipulate several of the male teachers and the assistant principal into recommending her for a new job in a nearby school district. A year later, she was still at the new school but had been moved twice to different classrooms. According to teachers she worked with, Pat still lacked close interpersonal relationships, although she described her current romantic relationship as "deeply involved." After a rather long period of depression, Pat sought help from a psychologist, who diagnosed her as also having histrionic personality disorder.

Clinical Description

People with histrionic personality disorder are inclined to express their emotions in an exaggerated fashion, for example, hugging someone they have just met or crying uncontrollably during a sad movie (Skodol & Gunderson, 2008). They also tend to be vain, self-centered, and uncomfortable when they are not in the limelight. They are often seductive in appearance and behavior, and they are typically concerned about their looks. (Pat, for example, spent a great deal of money on unusual jewelry and was sure to point it out to anyone who would listen.) In addition, they seek reassurance and approval constantly and may become upset or angry when others do not attend to them or praise them. People with histrionic personality disorder also tend to be impulsive and have great difficulty delaying gratification.

The cognitive style associated with histrionic personality disorder is impressionistic (Beck, Freeman, & Davis, 2007), characterized by a tendency to view situations in global, black-and-white terms. Speech is often vague, lacking in detail, and characterized by exaggeration (Nestadt et al., 2009). For example, when Pat was asked about a date she had had the night before, she might say it was "way cool" but fail to provide more detailed information.

The high rate of this diagnosis among women versus men raises questions about the nature of the disorder and its diagnostic criteria. As we first discussed in the beginning of this chapter, there is some thought that the features of histrionic personality disorder, such as overdramatization, vanity, seductiveness, and overconcern with physical appearance, are characteristic of the Western "stereotypical female" and may lead to an overdiagnosis among women. Sprock (2000) examined this important question and found some evidence for a bias among psychologists and psychiatrists to associate the diagnosis with women rather than men.

Radius Images/JupiterImages

▲ People with histrionic personality disorder tend to be vain, extravagant, and seductive.

Causes

Despite its long history, little research has been done on the causes or treatment of histrionic personality disorder. One hypothesis involves a possible relationship with antisocial personality disorder. Evidence suggests that histrionic personality and antisocial personality co-occur more often than chance would account for. Lilienfeld and colleagues (1986), for example, found that roughly two thirds of people with a histrionic personality also met criteria for antisocial personality disorder. The evidence for this association has led to the suggestion (see, for example, Cloninger, 1978; Lilienfeld, 1992) that histrionic personality and antisocial personality may be sex-typed alternative expressions of the same unidentified underlying condition. Females with the underlying condition may be predisposed to exhibit a predominantly histrionic pattern, whereas males with the underlying condition may be predisposed to exhibit a predominantly antisocial pattern. Whether this association exists remains a controversial issue, however, and further research on this potential relationship is needed (Dolan & Völlm, 2009; Salekin, Rogers, & Sewell, 1997). The overlap of histrionic personality disorder with other personality disorders (for example, borderline, narcissistic, and dependent personality disorders) has caused some to question whether histrionic personality disorder should be reclassified in *DSM-5* to be included under an-

---

---

dialectical behavior therapy (DBT) A promising treatment for borderline personality disorder that involves exposing the client to stressors in a controlled situation, as well as helping the client regulate emotions and cope with stressors that might trigger suicidal behavior.

histrionic personality disorder A cluster B (dramatic, emotional, or erratic) personality disorder involving a pervasive pattern of excessive emotionality and attention seeking.

other personality disorder (such as narcissistic personality disorder) (Bakkevig & Karterud, 2010).

Treatment

Although a great deal has been written about ways of helping people with histrionic personality disorder, little research demonstrates success (Cloninger & Svakic, 2009). Some therapists have tried to modify the attention-getting behavior. Kass, Silvers, and Abrams (1972) worked with five women, four of whom had been hospitalized for suicide attempts and all of whom were later diagnosed with histrionic personality disorder. The women were rewarded for appropriate interactions and fined for attention-getting behavior. The therapists noted improvement after an 18-month follow-up, but they did not collect scientific data to confirm their observation.

A large part of therapy for these individuals usually focuses on the problematic interpersonal relationships. They often manipulate others through emotional crises, using charm, sex, seduction, or complaining (Beck et al., 2007). People with histrionic personality disorder often need to be shown how the short-term gains derived from this interactional style result in long-term costs, and they need to be taught more appropriate ways of negotiating their wants and needs.

Narcissistic Personality Disorder

We all know people who think highly of themselves—perhaps exaggerating their real abilities. They consider themselves somehow different from others and deserving of special treatment. In **narcissistic personality disorder**, this tendency is taken to its extreme. In Greek mythology, Narcissus was a youth who spurned the love of Echo, so enamored was he of his own beauty. He spent his days admiring his own image reflected in a pool of water. Psychoanalysts, including Freud, used the term *narcissistic* to describe people who show an exaggerated sense of self-importance and are preoccupied with receiving attention (Cloninger & Svakic, 2009). Consider the case of Willie.

Willie • It's All about Me

Willie was an office assistant in a small attorney's office. Now in his early 30s, Willie had an extremely poor job history. He never stayed employed at the same place for more than 2 years, and he spent considerable time working through temporary employment agencies. Your first encounter, however, would make you believe that he was extremely competent and that he ran the office. If you entered the waiting room you were greeted by Willie, even though he wasn't the receptionist. He would be extremely solicitous, asking how he could be of assistance, offer you coffee, and ask you to make yourself comfortable in "his" reception area. Willie liked to talk, and any conversation was quickly redirected in a way that kept him the center of attention.

This type of ingratiating manner was welcomed at first but soon annoyed other staff. This was especially true when he referred to the other workers in the office as his staff, even though he was not responsible for supervising any of them. The conversations with visitors and staff often consumed a great deal of his time and the time of other staff, and this was becoming a problem.

He quickly became controlling in his job—a pattern revealed in his other positions also—eagerly taking charge of duties assigned to others. Unfortunately, he did not complete these tasks well, and this created a great deal of friction.

When confronted with any of these difficulties, Willie would first blame others. Ultimately, however, it would become clear that Willie's self-centeredness and controlling nature were at the root of many of the office inefficiencies. During a disciplinary meeting with all of the law firm's partners, an unusual step, Willie became explosively abusive and blamed them for being out to get him. He insisted that his performance was exceptional at all of his previous positions—something contradicted by his previous employers—and that they were at fault. After calming down, he revealed a previous drinking problem, a history of depression, and multiple family problems, all of which he believed contributed to any difficulties he experienced.

The firm recommended he be seen at a university clinic as a condition of his continued employment, where he was diagnosed with major depression and narcissistic personality disorder. Ultimately, his behavior—including lateness and incomplete work—resulted in his termination. In a revealing turn of events, Willie reapplied for another position at the same firm 2 years later. A mix-up in records failed to reveal his previous termination, but he lasted only 3 days—showing up late to work on his second and third days. He was convinced he could be successful, yet he could not change his behavior to conform to even the minimal standards needed to be successful at work.

Clinical Description

People with narcissistic personality disorder have an unreasonable sense of self-importance and are so preoccupied with themselves that they lack sensitivity and compassion for other people (Miller, Campbell, & Pilkonis, 2007). Their exaggerated feelings and their fantasies of greatness, called *grandiosity*, create a number of negative attributes. They require and expect a great deal of special attention—the best table in the restaurant, the illegal parking space in front of the movie theater. They also tend to use or exploit others for their own interests and show little empathy. When confronted with successful people, they can be extremely envious and arrogant. And because they often fail to live up to their own expectations, they are often depressed.

Causes and Treatment

We start out as infants being self-centered and demanding, which is part of our struggle for survival. However, part of the socialization process involves teaching children empathy and altruism. Some writers, including Kohut (1971, 1977), believe that narcissistic personality disorder arises largely from a profound failure by the parents of modeling empathy early in a child's development. As a consequence, the child remains fixated at a self-centered, grandiose stage of development. In addition, the child (and later the adult) becomes involved in an essentially endless and fruitless search for the ideal person who will meet her unfulfilled empathic needs.

DSM Disorder Criteria Summary
Narcissistic Personality Disorder

A pervasive pattern of grandiosity (in fantasy or behavior), need for admiration, and lack of empathy, beginning by early adulthood and present in a variety of contexts, as indicated by five (or more) of the following:

(1) has a grandiose sense of self-importance (e.g., exaggerates achievements and talents, expects to be recognized as superior without commensurate achievements)

(2) is preoccupied with fantasies of unlimited success, power, brilliance, beauty, or ideal love

(3) believes that he or she is "special" and unique and can only be understood by, or should associate with, other special or high-status people (or institutions)

(4) requires excessive admiration

(5) has a sense of entitlement, i.e., unreasonable expectations of especially favorable treatment or automatic compliance with his or her expectations

(6) is interpersonally exploitative, i.e., takes advantage of others to achieve his or her own ends

(7) lacks empathy: is unwilling to recognize or identify with the feelings and needs of others

(8) is often envious of others or believes that others are envious of him or her

(9) shows arrogant, haughty behaviors or attitudes

Source: Reprinted with permission from Diagnostic and Statistical Manual of Mental Disorders (4th ed., text revision). © 2000 American Psychiatric Association.

Research on treatment options is extremely limited in both number of studies and reports of success (Cloninger & Svakic, 2009; Dhawan, Kunik, Oldham, & Coverdale, 2010). When therapy is attempted with these individuals, it often focuses on their grandiosity, their hypersensitivity to evaluation, and their lack of empathy toward others (Beck et al., 2007). Cognitive therapy strives to replace their fantasies with a focus on the day-to-day pleasurable experiences that are truly attainable. Coping strategies such as relaxation training are used to help them face and accept criticism. Helping them focus on the feelings of others is also a goal. Because individuals with this disorder are vulnerable to severe depressive episodes, particularly in middle age, treatment is often initiated for the depression. However, it is impossible to draw any conclusions about the impact of such treatment on the actual narcissistic personality disorder.

Concept Check 11.3

Correctly identify the type of personality disorder described here.

1. Elaine has low self-esteem and usually feels empty unless she does dangerous and exciting things. She takes illegal drugs and has casual sexual encounters, even with strangers. She threatens to commit suicide if her boyfriend suggests getting help or if he talks about leaving her. She alternates between passionately loving him and hating him, sometimes going from one extreme to the next in a short time. _____

2. Lance is 17 and has been in trouble with the law for the past 2 years. He lies to his parents, vandalizes buildings in the community, and often fights with others. He shows no remorse for whom he injures or the grief that he causes his ailing parents. _____

3. Nancy thinks she is the best at everything. She thinks her performance is always excellent and is extremely critical of anyone else's success. She constantly looks for admiration and reassurance from others. _____

4. Samantha is known for being overly dramatic. She cries uncontrollably during sad movies and we sometimes think that she is acting. She is vain and self-centered, interrupting many of our class conversations to discuss her personal life. _____

narcissistic personality disorder A cluster B (dramatic, emotional, or erratic) personality disorder involving a pervasive pattern of grandiosity in fantasy or behavior, need for admiration, and lack of empathy.

Cluster C Personality Disorders

> ### What are the essential characteristics of anxious or fearful personality disorders?

People diagnosed with the next three personality disorders we highlight—avoidant, dependent, and obsessive-compulsive—share common features with people who have anxiety disorders. These anxious or fearful personality disorders are described next.

Avoidant Personality Disorder

As the name suggests, people with **avoidant personality disorder** are extremely sensitive to the opinions of others and therefore avoid most relationships. Their extremely low self-esteem, coupled with a fear of rejection, causes them to be limited in their friendships and dependent on those they feel comfortable with. Consider the case of Jane.

Jane ⦁ Not Worth Noticing

Jane was raised by an alcoholic mother who had borderline personality disorder and who abused her verbally and physically. As a child, she made sense of her mother's abusive treatment by believing that she (Jane) must be an intrinsically unworthy person to be treated so badly. As an adult in her late 20s, Jane still expected to be rejected when others found out that she was inherently unworthy and bad.

Jane was highly self-critical and predicted that she would not be accepted. She thought that people would not like her, that they would see she was a loser, and that she would not have anything to say. She became upset if she perceived that someone in even the most fleeting encounter was reacting negatively or neutrally. If a newspaper vendor failed to smile at her, or a sales clerk was slightly curt, Jane automatically thought it must be because she (Jane) was somehow unworthy or unlikable. She then felt sad. Even when she was receiving positive feedback from a friend, she discounted it. As a result, Jane had few friends and certainly no close ones.

(Case and excerpt reprinted, with permission, from Beck, A. T., & Freeman, A., 1990. *Cognitive therapy of personality disorders.* New York: Guilford Press. © 1990 Guilford Press.)

Clinical Description

Theodore Millon (1981), who initially proposed this diagnosis, notes that it is important to distinguish between individuals who are asocial because they are apathetic, affectively flat, and relatively uninterested in interpersonal relationships (comparable to what *DSM-IV-TR* terms *schizoid personality disorder*) and individuals who are asocial because they are interpersonally anxious and fearful of rejection. It is the latter who fit the criteria of avoidant personality disorder (Millon & Martinez, 1995). These individuals feel chronically rejected by others and are pessimistic about their future.

Causes

Some evidence has found that avoidant personality disorder is related to other subschizophrenia-related disorders—occurring more often in relatives of people who have schizophrenia (Fogelson et al., 2007). A number of theories have been proposed that integrate biological and psychosocial influences as the cause of avoidant personality disorder. Millon (1981), for example, suggests that these individuals may be born with a difficult temperament or personality characteristics. As a result, their parents may reject them, or at least not provide them with enough early, uncritical love. This rejection, in turn, may result in low self-esteem and social alienation, conditions that persist into adulthood. Limited support does exist for psychosocial influences in the cause of avoidant personality disorder. For example, Stravynski, Elie, and Franche (1989) questioned a group of people with avoidant personality disorder and a group of control participants about their early treatment by their parents. Those with the disorder remembered their parents as more rejecting, more guilt

---

DSM Disorder Criteria Summary
Avoidant Personality Disorder

A pervasive pattern of social inhibition, feelings of inadequacy, and hypersensitivity to negative evaluation, beginning by early adulthood and present in a variety of contexts, as indicated by four (or more) of the following:

(1) avoids occupational activities that involve significant interpersonal contact, because of fears of criticism, disapproval, or rejection

(2) is unwilling to get involved with people unless certain of being liked

(3) shows restraint within intimate relationships because of the fear of being shamed or ridiculed

(4) is preoccupied with being criticized or rejected in social situations

(5) is inhibited in new interpersonal situations because of feelings of inadequacy

(6) views self as socially inept, personally unappealing, or inferior to others

(7) is unusually reluctant to take personal risks or to engage in any new activities because they may prove embarrassing

Source: Reprinted with permission from *Diagnostic and Statistical Manual of Mental Disorders* (4th ed., text revision). © 2000 American Psychiatric Association.

engendering, and less affectionate than the control group, suggesting parenting may contribute to the development of this disorder. Similarly, Meyer and Carver (2000) found that these individuals were more likely to report childhood experiences of isolation, rejection, and conflict with others.

Treatment

In contrast to the scarcity of research into most other personality disorders, there are a number of well-controlled studies on approaches to therapy for people with avoidant personality disorder (Beck et al., 2007). Behavioral intervention techniques for anxiety and social skills problems have had some success (for example, Borge et al., 2010). Because the problems experienced by people with avoidant personality disorder resemble those of people with social phobia, many of the same treatments are used for both groups (see Chapter 4). Therapeutic alliance—the collaborative connection between therapist and client—appears to be an important predictor for treatment success in this group (Strauss et al., 2006).

Dependent Personality Disorder

We all know what it means to be dependent on another person. People with **dependent personality disorder**, however, rely on others to make ordinary decisions and important ones, which results in an unreasonable fear of abandonment. Consider the case of Karen.

Karen • Whatever You Say

Karen was a 45-year-old married woman who was referred for treatment by her physician for problems with panic attacks. During the evaluation, she appeared to be worried, sensitive, and naive. She was easily overcome with emotion and cried on and off throughout the session. She was self-critical at every opportunity throughout the evaluation. For example, when asked how she got along with other people, she reported, "Others think I'm dumb and inadequate," although she could give no evidence as to what made her think that. She reported that she didn't like school because "I was dumb" and that she always felt that she was not good enough.

Karen described staying in her first marriage for 10 years, even though "[i]t was hell." Her husband had affairs with many other women and was verbally abusive. She tried to leave him many times but gave in to his repeated requests to return. She was finally able to divorce him, and shortly afterward she met and married her current husband, who she described as kind, sensitive, and supportive. Karen stated that she preferred to have others make important decisions and agreed with other people to avoid conflict. She worried about being left alone without anyone to

take care of her and reported feeling lost without other people's reassurance. She also reported that her feelings were easily hurt, so she worked hard not to do anything that might lead to criticism.

(Case and excerpt reprinted, with permission, from Beck, A. T., & Freeman, A., 1990. *Cognitive therapy of personality disorders.* New York: Guilford Press, © 1990 by Guilford Press.)

Clinical Description

Individuals with dependent personality disorder sometimes agree with other people when their own opinion differs so as not to be rejected (Cloninger & Svakic, 2009). Their desire to obtain and maintain supportive and nurturant relationships may lead to their other behavioral characteristics, including submissiveness, timidity, and passivity. People with this disorder are similar to those with avoidant personality disorder in their feelings of inadequacy, sensitivity to criticism, and need for reassurance. However, people with avoidant personality disorder respond to these feelings by avoiding relationships, whereas those with dependent personality disorder respond by clinging to relationships (Cloninger & Svakic, 2009).

Causes and Treatment

We are all born dependent on other people for food, physical protection, and nurturance. Part of the socialization process involves helping us live independently (Bornstein, 1992). It is thought that such disruptions as the early death of a parent or neglect or rejection by caregivers may cause people to grow up fearing abandonment (Stone, 1993). This view comes from work in child development on "attachment," or how children learn to bond with their parents and other people who are important in their lives (Bowlby, 1977). If early bonding is interrupted, individuals may be constantly anxious that they will lose people close to them.

The treatment literature for this disorder is mostly descriptive; little research exists to show whether a particular treatment is effective (Borge et al., 2010; Paris, 2008). On the surface, because of their attentiveness and eagerness to give responsibility for their problems to the therapist, people with dependent personality disorder can appear to be ideal patients. However, their submissiveness negates one of the major goals of therapy, which is to make the person more independent and personally responsible. Therapy therefore progresses gradually as the patient de-

avoidant personality disorder A cluster C (anxious or fearful) personality disorder featuring a pervasive pattern of social inhibition, feelings of inadequacy, and hypersensitivity to criticism.
dependent personality disorder A cluster C (anxious or fearful) personality disorder characterized by a person's pervasive and excessive need to be taken care of, a condition that leads to submissive and clinging behavior and fears of separation.

A pervasive and excessive need to be taken care of that leads to submissive and clinging behavior and fears of separation, beginning by early adulthood and present in a variety of contexts, as indicated by five (or more) of the following:

(1) has difficulty making everyday decisions without an excessive amount of advice and reassurance from others

(2) needs others to assume responsibility for most major areas of his or her life

(3) has difficulty expressing disagreement with others because of fear of loss of support or approval. Note: Do not include realistic fears of retribution.

(4) has difficulty initiating projects or doing things on his or her own (because of a lack of self-confidence in judgment or abilities rather than a lack of motivation or energy)

(5) goes to excessive lengths to obtain nurturance and support from others, to the point of volunteering to do things that are unpleasant

(6) feels uncomfortable or helpless when alone because of exaggerated fears of being unable to care for himself or herself

(7) urgently seeks another relationship as a source of care and support when a close relationship ends

(8) is unrealistically preoccupied with fears of being left to take care of himself or herself

Source: Reprinted with permission from *Diagnostic and Statistical Manual of Mental Disorders* (4th ed., text revision). © 2000 American Psychiatric Association.

velops confidence in his ability to make decisions independently (Beck et al., 2007). There is a particular need for care that the patient does not become overly dependent on the therapist.

Obsessive-Compulsive Personality Disorder

People who have **obsessive-compulsive personality disorder** are characterized by a fixation on things being done "the right way." Although many might envy their persistence and dedication, this preoccupation with details prevents them from completing much of anything. Consider the case of Daniel.

Daniel ❖ Getting It Exactly Right

Each day at exactly 8 A.M., Daniel arrived at his office at the university where he was a graduate student in psychology. On his way, he always stopped at the 7-Eleven for coffee and the *New York Times*. From 8 A.M. to 9:15 A.M., he drank his coffee and read the paper. At 9:15 A.M., he reorganized the files that held the hundreds of papers related to his doctoral dissertation, now several years overdue. From 10 A.M. until noon, he read one of these papers, highlighting relevant passages. Then he took the paper bag that held

his lunch (always a peanut butter and jelly sandwich and an apple) and went to the cafeteria to purchase a soda and eat by himself. From 1 P.M. until 5 P.M., he held meetings, organized his desk, made lists of things to do, and entered his references into a new database program on his computer. At home, Daniel had dinner with his wife, then worked on his dissertation until after 11 P.M., although much of the time was spent trying out new features of his home computer.

Daniel was no closer to completing his dissertation than he had been 4.5 years ago. His wife was threatening to leave him because he was equally rigid about everything at home and she didn't want to remain in this limbo of graduate school forever. When Daniel eventually sought help from a therapist for his anxiety over his deteriorating marriage, he was diagnosed as having obsessive-compulsive personality disorder.

Clinical Description

Like many with this personality disorder, Daniel is work oriented, spending little time going to movies or parties or doing anything that isn't related to his graduate studies. Because of their general rigidity, these people tend to have poor interpersonal relationships (Cloninger & Svakic, 2009).

A pervasive pattern of preoccupation with orderliness, perfectionism, and mental and interpersonal control, at the expense of flexibility, openness, and efficiency, beginning by early adulthood and present in a variety of contexts, as indicated by four (or more) of the following:

(1) is preoccupied with details, rules, lists, order, organization, or schedules to the extent that the major point of the activity is lost

(2) shows perfectionism that interferes with task completion (e.g., is unable to complete a project because his or her own overly strict standards are not met)

(3) is excessively devoted to work and productivity to the exclusion of leisure activities and friendships (not accounted for by obvious economic necessity)

(4) is overconscientious, scrupulous, and inflexible about matters of morality, ethics, or values (not accounted for by cultural or religious identification)

(5) is unable to discard worn-out or worthless objects even when they have no sentimental value

(6) is reluctant to delegate tasks or to work with others unless they submit to exactly his or her way of doing things

(7) adopts a miserly spending style toward both self and others; money is viewed as something to be hoarded for future catastrophes

(8) shows rigidity and stubbornness

Source: Reprinted with permission from *Diagnostic and Statistical Manual of Mental Disorders* (4th ed., text revision). © 2000 American Psychiatric Association.

This personality disorder seems to be only distantly related to obsessive-compulsive disorder, one of the anxiety disorders we described in Chapter 4. People like Daniel tend not to have the obsessive thoughts and the compulsive behaviors seen in the like-named obsessive-compulsive disorder. Although people with the anxiety disorder sometimes show characteristics of the personality disorder, they show the characteristics of other personality disorders also (for example, avoidant, histrionic, or dependent) (Eisen, Mancebo, Chiappone, Pinto, & Rasmussen, 2008).

An intriguing theory suggests that the psychological profiles of many serial killers point to the role of obsessive-compulsive personality disorder. Ferreira (2000) notes that these individuals do not often fit the definition of someone with a severe mental illness—such as schizophrenia—but are "masters of control" in manipulating their victims. Their need to control all aspects of the crime fits the pattern of people with obsessive-compulsive personality disorder, and some combination of this disorder and unfortunate childhood experiences may lead to this disturbing behavior pattern. Obsessive-compulsive personality disorder may also play a role among some sex offenders—in particular, pedophiles. Brain-imaging research on pedophiles suggests that brain functioning in these individuals is similar to those with obsessive-compulsive personality disorder (Schiffer et al., 2007). At the other end of the behavioral spectrum, it is also common to find obsessive-compulsive personality disorder among gifted children, whose quest for perfectionism can be quite debilitating (Nugent, 2000).

Causes and Treatment

There seems to be a weak genetic contribution to obsessive-compulsive personality disorder (Cloninger & Svakic, 2009). Some people may be predisposed to favor structure in their lives, but to reach the level it did in Daniel may require parental reinforcement of conformity and neatness.

Therapy often attacks the fears that seem to underlie the need for orderliness. These individuals are often afraid that what they do will be inadequate, so they procrastinate and excessively ruminate about important issues and minor details alike. Therapists help the individual relax or use distraction techniques to redirect the compulsive thoughts. This form of cognitive-behavioral therapy appears to be effective for people with this personality disorder (Svartberg et al., 2004).

▲ People with obsessive-compulsive personality disorder are preoccupied with doing things "the right way."

Manchan/Digital Vision/Getty Images

Concept Check 11.4

Match the following scenarios with the correct personality disorder.

1. During a therapy session John gets up for a glass of water. Ten minutes later John still is not back. He first had to clean the fountain area and neatly arrange the glasses before pouring his glass of water. _____

2. Whitney is self-critical and claims she is unintelligent and has no skills. She is also afraid to be alone and seeks constant reassurance from her family and friends. She says and does nothing about her cheating husband because she thinks that if she shows any resolve or initiative she will be abandoned and will have to take care of herself. _____

3. Mike has no social life because of his great fear of rejection. He disregards compliments and reacts excessively to criticism, which only feeds his pervasive feelings of inadequacy. Mike takes everything personally. _____

obsessive-compulsive personality disorder A cluster C (anxious or fearful) personality disorder featuring a pervasive pattern of preoccupation with orderliness, perfectionism, and mental and interpersonal control at the expense of flexibility, openness, and efficiency.

On the Spectrum Emerging Views of Personality Disorders

We opened the chapter discussing the controversies surrounding the classification of the personality disorders. The great degree of overlap (comorbidity) of the disorders—for example, some people are diagnosed with three or more personality disorders—and the use of categories as opposed to dimensions continue to concern the researchers who study these disorders and the clinicians who care for these individuals (South et al., 2011). For example, the organization that we use in the chapter (the three clusters of A, B, and C) is also used by *DSM-IV* but is nothing more than a convenient way for clinicians to remember the disorders and

is not based on any scientific evidence (Widiger, 2007). Perhaps the most anticipated change in this field is a radical redefinition of the disorders using dimensions, and we expect that the next version of the *DSM*—*DSM-5*—will introduce this new approach and perhaps make us rethink how we view many of the other disorders we cover in this book (Krueger, Skodol, Livesley, Shrout, & Huang, 2008; Lopez, Compton, Grant, & Breiling, 2008; Widiger & Trull, 2007).

One way to introduce dimensions that is currently being discussed is to rate clients on six broad personality trait domains (negative emotionality, introversion, antago-

nism, disinhibition, compulsivity, and schizotypy) (American Psychiatric Association, 2010b). Each of these domains would include more specific "trait facets." For example, under the domain of "compulsivity" would be the facets of perfectionism, perseveration, rigidity, orderliness, and risk aversion. Clinicians would rate clients on a four-point scale as to the extent that these traits are present (from "very little or not at all" to "extremely descriptive"), therefore providing some indication of the dimensional quality of their difficulties. If and how this classification scheme will ultimately be incorporated into mainstream clinical work remains to be resolved.

Summary

An Overview of Personality Disorders

What are the essential features of personality disorders, and why are they listed on Axis II in *DSM-IV-TR*?

› The personality disorders represent long-standing and ingrained ways of thinking, feeling, and behaving that can cause significant distress. Because people may display two or more of these maladaptive ways of interacting with the world, considerable disagreement remains over how to categorize the personality disorders.

› *DSM-IV-TR* includes 10 personality disorders that are divided into three clusters: Cluster A (odd or eccentric) includes paranoid, schizoid, and schizotypal personality disorders; Cluster B (dramatic, emotional, or erratic) includes antisocial, borderline, histrionic, and narcissistic personality disorders; and Cluster C (anxious or fearful) includes avoidant, dependent, and obsessive-compulsive personality disorders.

Cluster A Personality Disorders

What are the nature, etiology, and treatment of each of the odd or eccentric personality disorders?

› People with paranoid personality disorder are excessively mistrustful and suspicious of other people without any justification. They tend not to confide in others and expect other people to do them harm.

› People with schizoid personality disorder show a pattern of detachment from social relationships and a limited range of emotions in interpersonal situations. They seem aloof, cold, and indifferent to other people.

› People with schizotypal personality disorder are typically socially isolated and behave in ways that would seem unusual to most of us. In addition, they tend to be suspicious and have odd beliefs about the world.

Cluster B Personality Disorders

What are the essential characteristics of dramatic, emotional, or erratic personality disorders?

› People with antisocial personality disorder have a history of failing to comply with social norms. They perform actions most of us would find unacceptable, such as stealing from friends and family. They also tend to be irresponsible, impulsive, and deceitful.

› In contrast to the *DSM-IV-TR* criteria for antisocial personality, which focus almost entirely on observable behaviors (for example, impulsively and repeatedly changing employment, residence, or sexual partners), the related concept of psychopathy primarily reflects underlying personality traits (for example, self-centeredness or being manipulative).

› People with borderline personality disorder lack stability in their moods and in their relationships with other people, and they usually have poor self-esteem. These individuals often feel empty and are at great risk of suicide.

› Individuals with histrionic personality disorder tend to be overly dramatic and often appear to be acting.

› People with narcissistic personality disorder think highly of themselves—beyond their real abilities. They consider themselves somehow different from others and deserving of special treatment.

Cluster C Personality Disorders

What are the essential characteristics of anxious or fearful personality disorders?

› People with avoidant personality disorder are extremely sensitive to the opinions of others and therefore avoid social relationships. Their extremely low self-esteem, coupled with a fear of rejection, causes them to reject the attention of others.

› Individuals with dependent personality disorder rely on others to the extent of letting them make everyday decisions and major ones; this results in an unreasonable fear of being abandoned.

› People who have obsessive-compulsive personality disorder are characterized by a fixation on things being done "the right way." This preoccupation with details prevents them from completing much of anything.

› Treating people with personality disorders is often difficult because they usually do not see that their difficulties are a result of the way they relate to others.

› Personality disorders are important for the clinician to consider because they may interfere with efforts to treat more specific problems such as anxiety, depression, or substance abuse. Unfortunately, the presence of one or more personality disorders is associated with a poor treatment outcome and a generally negative prognosis.

Key Terms

Answers to Concept Checks

11.1

1. Axis II; 2. comorbidity; 3. Cluster A, Cluster B, Cluster C; 4. categories; 5. chronic; 6. bias

11.2

1. paranoid; 2. schizotypal; 3. schizoid

11.3

1. borderline; 2. antisocial; 3. narcissistic; 4. histrionic

11.4

1. obsessive-compulsive; 2. dependent; 3. avoidant

Media Resources

Log in to CengageBrain to access the resources your instructor requires. For this book, you can access:

CourseMate brings course concepts to life with interactive learning, study, and exam preparation tools that support the printed textbook. A textbook-specific website, Psychology CourseMate includes an integrated interactive eBook and other interactive learning tools including quizzes, flashcards, videos, and more.

Abnormal Psychology Videos

› *George, an Example of Antisocial Personality Disorder:* George describes his long history of violating people's rights.

CENGAGENOW CengageNow is an easy-to-use online resource that helps you study in less time to get the grade you want—NOW. Take a pre-test for this chapter and re-

ceive a personalized study plan based on your results that will identify the topics you need to review and direct you to online resources to help you master those topics. Then take a post-test to help you determine the concepts you have mastered and what you will need to work on. If your textbook does not include an access code card, go to CengageBrain.com to gain access.

› Visit www.cengagebrain.com to access your account and purchase materials.

 aplia If your professor has assigned Aplia homework:

1. Sign in to your account.
2. Complete the corresponding homework exercises as required by your professor.
3. When finished, click "Grade It Now" to see which areas you have mastered, which need more work, and for detailed explanations of every answer.

CHAPTER QUIZ

1. The dimensional versus categorical debate over the nature of personality disorders can also be described as a debate between _____ and _____.
   a. diagnosis; prognosis
   b. state; trait
   c. degree; kind
   d. qualitative; quantitative

2. Some personality disorders are diagnosed more frequently in men than in women. One explanation for this difference is as follows:
   a. Symptoms are interpreted by clinicians in different ways depending on the gender of the person with the symptoms.
   b. Men are more likely to seek help from mental health professionals than women.
   c. Most clinicians are men, and they tend to see psychopathology more often in patients of the same gender as themselves.
   d. Because of hormonal differences, women are more likely to have acute disorders and men are more likely to have chronic personality disorders.

3. Genetic research and an overlap in symptoms suggest a common relationship between schizophrenia and:
   a. borderline personality disorder
   b. schizotypal personality disorder
   c. schizoid personality disorder
   d. antisocial personality disorder

4. Criteria for psychopathy emphasize _____, and criteria for antisocial personality disorder emphasize _____.
   a. behavior; personality
   b. personality; behavior
   c. criminal conduct; social isolation
   d. social isolation; criminal conduct

5. Which symptom is characteristic of persons with borderline personality disorder?
   a. impulsivity
   b. aloofness
   c. mania
   d. grandiosity

6. Which theory suggests psychopaths may engage in antisocial and risk-taking behavior to stimulate their cortical system?
   a. equifinality hypothesis
   b. transcortical magnetic stimulation hypothesis
   c. underarousal hypothesis
   d. equipotential hypothesis

7. Greeting a new acquaintance with effusive familiarity, crying uncontrollably during a movie, and trying to be the center of attention at a party are typical behaviors of someone with:
   a. borderline personality disorder
   b. narcissistic personality disorder
   c. histrionic personality disorder
   d. paranoid personality disorder

8. Which of the following statements is most true about borderline personality disorder?

    a. Childhood abuse is rare in people with borderline personality disorder.

    b. Borderline personality disorder is more frequently diagnosed in men than in women.

    c. Behaviors in borderline personality disorder overlap those seen in posttraumatic stress disorder.

    d. Borderline personality disorder is seldom accompanied by self-mutilation.

9. People with which personality disorder often exhibit childlike, egocentric behaviors?

    a. paranoid

    b. antisocial

    c. schizotypal

    d. narcissistic

10. An individual who is preoccupied with details, rules, organization, and scheduling to the extent that it interferes with daily functioning may have:

    a. obsessive-compulsive personality disorder

    b. narcissistic personality disorder

    c. antisocial personality disorder

    d. schizoid personality disorder

(See Appendix A for answers.)

Exploring Personality Disorders

› People with personality disorders think and behave in ways that cause distress to themselves and/or the people who care about them.

› There are three main groups, or clusters, of personality disorders, which usually begin in childhood.

CLUSTER A

Odd or Eccentric

©Gazelle Technologies/RF

Schizoid
social isolation

Psychological Influences
- Very limited range of emotions
- Apparently cold and unconnected
- Unaffected by praise or criticism

Causes

Biological Influences
- May be associated with lower density of dopamine receptors

Treatment
- Learning value of social relationships
- Social skills training with role playing

Social/Cultural Influences
- Preference for social isolation
- Lack of social skills
- Lack of interest in close relationships, including romantic or sexual

Paranoid
extreme suspicion

Psychological Influences
- Thoughts that people are malicious, deceptive, and threatening
- Behavior based on mistaken assumptions about others

Biological Influences
- Possible but unclear link with schizophrenia

Causes

Social/Cultural Influences
- "Outsiders" may be susceptible because of unique experiences (e.g., prisoners, refugees, people with hearing impairments, and the elderly)
- Parents' early teaching may influence

Treatment
- Difficult because of client's mistrust and suspicion
- Cognitive work to change thoughts
- Low success rate

Schizotypal
suspicion and odd behavior

Psychological Influences
- Unusual beliefs, behavior, or dress
- Suspiciousness
- Believing insignificant events are personally relevant ("ideas of reference")
- Expressing little emotion
- Symptoms of major depressive disorder

Biological Influences
- Genetic vulnerability for schizophrenia but without the biological or environmental stresses present in that disorder

Causes

Treatment
- Teaching social skills to reduce isolation and suspicion
- Medication (haloperidol) to reduce ideas of reference, odd communication, and isolation
- Low success rate

Social/Cultural Influences
- Preference for social isolation
- Excessive social anxiety
- Lack of social skills

CLUSTER C

Anxious or Fearful

©Photodisc/Getty Images

Dependent
pervasive need to be taken care of

Psychological Influences
- Early "loss" of caretaker (death, rejection, or neglect) leads to fear of abandonment
- Timidity and passivity

Biological Influences
- Each of us born dependent for protection, food, and nurturance

Causes

Social/Cultural Influences
- Agreement for the sake of avoiding conflict
- Similar to Avoidant in
  – inadequacy
  – sensitivity to criticism
  – need for reassurance
  BUT
  for those same shared reasons
- Avoidants withdraw
- Dependents cling

Treatment
- Very little research
- Appear as ideal clients
- Submissiveness negates independence

CLUSTER B

Dramatic,
Emotional,
or Erratic

*Note: Cluster B also
includes Narcissistic
Personality Disorder.*

©Thinkstock Images/Comstock
Images/Getty Images

Antisocial
violation of
others' rights

Psychological Influences

- Difficulty learning to
  avoid punishment
- Indifferent to
  concerns of others

Causes

Biological Influences

- Genetic vulnerability
  combined with environ-
  mental influences
- Abnormally low cortical
  arousal
- High fear threshold

Histrionic
excessively emotional

Psychological Influences

- Vain and self-centered
- Easily upset if ignored
- Vague and hyperbolic
- Impulsive; difficulty delaying
  gratification

Causes

Biological Influences

- Possible link to antisocial
  disorder
  – women histrionic/men
    antisocial

Social/Cultural Influences

- Criminality
- Stress/exposure to trauma
- Inconsistent parental discipline
- Socioeconomic disadvantage

Treatment

- Seldom successful
  (incarceration
  instead)
- Parent training if
  problems are caught
  early
- Prevention through
  preschool programs

Treatment

- Little evidence of
  success
- Rewards and fines
- Focus on
  interpersonal
  relations

Social/Cultural Influences

- Overly dramatic behavior attracts
  attention
- Seductive
- Approval-seeking

Borderline
tumultuous
instability

Psychological Influences

- Suicidal
- Erratic moods
- Impulsivity

Biological Influences

- Familial link to mood disorders
- Possibly inherited tendencies
  (impulsivity or volatility)

Causes

Social/Cultural Influences

- Early trauma, especially sexual/physical abuse
- Rapid cultural changes (immigration) may
  trigger symptoms

Treatment

- Dialectical behavior
  therapy (DBT)
  Medication:
  – tricyclic antide-
    pressants
  – minor tranquilizers
  – lithium

Avoidant
inhibition

Psychological Influences

- Low self-esteem
- Fear of rejection,
  criticism leads to fear
  of attention
- Extreme sensitivity
- Resembles social
  phobia

Causes

Biological Influences

- Innate character-
  istics may cause
  rejection

Obsessive-compulsive
fixation on details

Biological Influences

- Distant relation to OCD
- Probable weak genetic role
  – predisposition to structure combined
    with parental reinforcement

Psychological Influences

- Generally rigid
- Dependent on routines
- Procrastinating

Causes

Social/Cultural Influences

- Insufficient parental affection

Social/Cultural Influences

- Very work-oriented
- Poor interpersonal relationships

Treatment

- Behavioral intervention techniques sometimes successful
  – systematic desensitization
  – behavioral rehearsal
- Improvements usually modest

Treatment

- Little information
- Therapy
  – attack fears behind need
  – relaxation or distraction
    techniques redirect
    compulsion to order

CHAPTER 12

Schizophrenia and Other Psychotic Disorders

Demonstrate knowledge and understanding representing appropriate breadth and depth in selected content areas of psychology:	❯ Biological bases of behavior and mental processes, including physiology, sensation, perception, comparative, motivation, and emotion (APA SLO 1.2.a (3)) *(see textbook pages 463–471)*
	❯ The history of psychology, including the evolution of methods of psychology, its theoretical conflicts, and its sociocultural contexts (APA SLO 1.2.b) *(see textbook pages 451–452)*
Use the concepts, language, and major theories of the discipline to account for psychological phenomena.	❯ Describe behavior and mental processes empirically, including operational definitions (APA SLO 1.3.a) *(see textbook pages 452–461)*
Identify appropriate applications of psychology in solving problems, such as:	❯ Origin and treatment of abnormal behavior (APA SLO 4.2.b) *(see textbook pages 461–477)*

*Portions of this chapter cover learning outcomes suggested by the American Psychological Association (2007) in their guidelines for the undergraduate psychology major. Chapter coverage of these outcomes is identified by APA Goal and APA Suggested Learning Outcome (SLO).

Perspectives on Schizophrenia

❯ **How is schizophrenia defined, and what symptoms are included in its diagnosis?**

A middle-aged man walks the streets of New York City with aluminum foil on the inside of his hat so Martians can't read his mind. A young woman sits in her college classroom and hears the voice of God telling her she is a vile and disgusting person. You try to strike up a conversation with the supermarket bagger, but he stares at you vacantly and will say only one or two words in a flat, toneless voice. Each of these people may have **schizophrenia**, the startling disorder characterized by a broad spectrum of cognitive and emotional dysfunctions including delusions and hallucinations, disorganized speech and behavior, and inappropriate emotions.

Schizophrenia is a complex syndrome that inevitably has a devastating effect on the lives of the person affected and on family members. Society often devalues these individuals. And despite important advances in treatment, complete recovery from schizophrenia is rare. This catastrophic disorder takes a tremendous emotional toll on everyone involved. In addition to the emotional costs, the financial drain is considerable. The annual cost of schizophrenia in the United States is estimated to exceed $60 billion when factors such as family caregiving, lost wages, and treatment are considered (Jablensky, 2009; Wu et al., 2005). Because schizophrenia is so widespread, affecting approximately 1 of every 100 people at some point in their lives, and because its consequences are so severe, research on its causes and treatment has expanded rapidly. In this chapter, we explore this intriguing disorder and review efforts to determine whether schizophrenia is distinct or a combination of disorders. The search is complicated by the presence of subtypes: different presentations and combinations of symptoms such as hallucinations; delusions; and disorders of speech, emotion, and socialization. After discussing the characteristics of people with schizophrenia, we describe research into its causes and treatment.

Early Figures in Diagnosing Schizophrenia

In *Observations on Madness and Melancholy,* published in 1809, John Haslam eloquently portrayed what he called "a form of insanity."

About the same time Haslam was writing his description in England, the French physician Philippe Pinel was writing about people we would describe as having schizophrenia (Pinel, 1801/1962, 1809). Some 50 years later, another physician, Benedict Morel, used the French term *démence* (loss of mind) *précoce* (early, premature) because the onset of the disorder is often during adolescence.

Toward the end of the 19th century, the German psychiatrist Emil Kraepelin (1899) built on the writings of Haslam, Pinel, and Morel (among others) to give us what stands today as the most enduring description and categorization of schizophrenia. Two of Kraepelin's accomplishments are especially important. First, he combined several symptoms of insanity that had usually been viewed as reflecting separate and distinct disorders: **catatonia** (alternating immobility and excited agitation), **hebephrenia** (silly and immature emotionality), and **paranoia** (delu-

---

schizophrenia A devastating psychotic disorder that may involve characteristic disturbances in thinking (delusions), perception (hallucinations), speech, emotions, and behavior.

catatonia A disorder of movement involving immobility or excited agitation.

hebephrenia A silly and immature emotionality, a characteristic of some types of schizophrenia.

paranoia People's irrational beliefs that they are especially important (delusions of grandeur) or that other people are seeking to do them harm.

iStockphoto.com/hidesy

sions of grandeur or persecution). Kraepelin thought these symptoms shared similar underlying features and included them under the Latin term **dementia praecox**. Although the clinical manifestation might differ from person to person, Kraepelin believed an early onset at the heart of each disorder develops into "mental weakness."

In a second important contribution, Kraepelin (1898) distinguished dementia praecox from manic-depressive illness (now called bipolar disorder). For people with dementia praecox, an early age of onset and a poor outcome were characteristic; in contrast, these patterns were not essential to manic depression (Lewis, Escalona, & Keith, 2009). Kraepelin also noted the numerous symptoms in people with dementia praecox, including hallucinations, delusions, negativism, and stereotyped behavior.

A second major figure in the history of schizophrenia was Kraepelin's contemporary, Eugen Bleuler (1908), a Swiss psychiatrist who introduced the term *schizophrenia* (Fusar-Poli & Politi, 2008). The label was significant because it signaled Bleuler's departure from Kraepelin on what he thought was the core problem. *Schizophrenia*, which comes from the combination of the Greek words for "split" *(skhizein)* and "mind" *(phren)*, reflected Bleuler's belief that underlying all the unusual behaviors shown by people with this disorder was an **associative splitting** of the basic functions of personality. This concept emphasized the "breaking of associative threads," or the destruction of the forces that connect one function to the next. Furthermore, Bleuler believed that a difficulty keeping a consistent train of thought characteristic of all people with this disorder led to the many and diverse symptoms they displayed. Whereas Kraepelin focused on early onset and poor outcomes, Bleuler highlighted what he believed to be the universal underlying problem. Unfortunately, the concept of "split mind" inspired the common but incorrect use of the term *schizophrenia* to mean split or multiple personality.

Identifying Symptoms

As you read about different disorders in this book, you have learned that a particular behavior, way of thinking, or emotion usually defines or is characteristic of each disorder. For example, depression always includes feelings of sadness, and panic disorder is always accompanied by intense feelings of anxiety. It may be surprising, but this isn't the case for schizophrenia. Schizophrenia is a number of behaviors or symptoms that aren't necessarily shared by all people who are given this diagnosis.

Despite these complexities, researchers have identified clusters of symptoms that make up the disorder of schizophrenia. Later we describe these dramatic symptoms, such as seeing or hearing things that others do not (hallucinations) or having beliefs that are unrealistic, bizarre, and not shared by others in the same culture (delusions). But first, consider the following case of an individual who had an intense but relatively rare short-term episode of psychotic behavior.

Arthur | Saving the Children

We first met 22-year-old Arthur at an outpatient clinic in a psychiatric hospital. Arthur's family was extremely concerned and upset by his unusual behavior and was desperately seeking help for him. They said that he was "sick" and "talking like a crazy man," and they were afraid he might harm himself.

Arthur had a normal childhood in a middle-class suburban neighborhood. His parents had been happily married until his father's death several years earlier. Arthur was an average student throughout school and had completed an associate's degree in junior college. He had worked in a series of temporary jobs, and his mother reported that he seemed satisfied with what he was doing. He lived and worked in a major city, some 15 minutes from his mother and his married brother and sister.

Arthur's family said that about 3 weeks before he came to the clinic he had started speaking strangely. He had been laid off from his job a few days before because of cutbacks and hadn't communicated with any of his family members for several days. When they next spoke with him, his behavior startled them. Although he had always been idealistic and anxious to help other people, he now talked about saving all the starving children in the world with his "secret plan." At first, his family assumed this was just an example of Arthur's sarcastic wit, but his demeanor changed to one of extreme concern and he spoke nonstop about his plans. He began carrying several spiral notebooks that he claimed contained his scheme for helping starving children; he said he would reveal it only at the right time to the right person. Suspecting that Arthur might be taking drugs, which could explain the sudden and dramatic change in his behavior, his family searched his apartment. Although they didn't find any evidence of drug use, they did find his checkbook and noticed a number of strange entries. Over the past several weeks, Arthur's handwriting had deteriorated, and he had written notes instead of the usual check information ("Start to begin now"; "This is important!"; "They must be saved"). He had also made unusual notes in several of his most prized books.

As the days went on, Arthur showed dramatic changes in emotion, often crying and acting apprehensive. He stopped wearing socks and underwear and, despite the extremely cold weather, wouldn't wear a jacket when he went outdoors. At the family's insistence, he moved into his mother's apartment. He slept little and kept the family up until the early morning. Each morning his mother would wake up with a knot in her stomach, not wanting to get out of bed because she felt so helpless to do anything to rescue Arthur from his obvious distress.

The family's sense of alarm grew as Arthur revealed more details of his plan. He said that he was going to the German embassy because that was the only place people would listen to him. He would climb the fence at night when everyone was asleep and present his plan to the German ambassador. Fearing that Arthur would be hurt trying to enter the embassy grounds, his family contacted a local psychiatric hospital, described Arthur's condition, and asked that he be admitted. Much to their surprise and disappointment, they were told that Arthur could commit himself but that they couldn't bring him in involuntarily unless he was in danger of doing harm to himself or others. His family finally talked Arthur into meeting the staff at the outpatient clinic.

In our interview, it was clear he was delusional, firmly believing in his ability to help all starving children. After some cajoling, I finally convinced him to let me see his books. He had written random thoughts (for example, "The poor, starving souls"; "The moon is the only place") and made drawings of rocket ships. Parts of his plan involved building a rocket ship that would go to the moon, where he would create a community for all malnourished children, a place where they could live and be helped. After a few brief comments on his plan, I began to ask him about his health.

"You look tired; are you getting enough sleep?"

"Sleep isn't really needed," he noted. "My plans will take me through, and then they can all rest."

"Your family is worried about you," I said. "Do you understand their concern?"

"It's important for all concerned to get together, to join together," he replied.

With that, he got up and walked out of the room and out of the building, after telling his family that he would be right back. After 5 minutes they went to look for him, but he had disappeared. He was missing for 2 days, which caused his family a great deal of concern about his health and safety. In an almost miraculous sequence of events, they found him walking the streets of the city. He acted as if nothing had happened. Gone were his notebooks and the talk of his secret plan.

We will never know exactly what happened to Arthur to make him behave so bizarrely and then recover so quickly and completely. However, research that we discuss next may shed some light on schizophrenia and potentially help other Arthurs and their families.

Clinical Description, Symptoms, and Subtypes

> **What are the distinctions among positive, negative, and disorganized symptoms of schizophrenia?**

> **What are the clinical characteristics and major types of schizophrenia and other psychotic disorders?**

The case of Arthur shows the range of problems experienced by people with schizophrenia or other psychotic disorders. The term **psychotic behavior** has been used to characterize many unusual behaviors, although in its strictest sense it usually involves delusions and/or hallucinations. Schizophrenia is one of the disorders that involves psychotic behavior; we describe others in more detail later.

Schizophrenia can affect all the functions we rely on each day. Before we describe the symptoms, it is important to look carefully at the specific characteristics of people who exhibit these behaviors, partly because we constantly see distorted images of people with schizophrenia. Evidence for violence among people with schizophrenia suggests that although they may be more likely to commit violent acts than the general population, you are more likely to see violence from people with substance abuse problems and personality disorders (antisocial or borderline personality disorders) (Douglas, Guy, & Hart, 2009). Despite this information, more than 70% of characters in prime-time television dramas with schizophrenia are portrayed as violent, with more than one fifth depicted as murderers (Wahl, 1995).

The text revision of the fourth edition of the *Diagnostic and Statistical Manual of Mental Disorders (DSM-IV-TR)* has a multiple-part process for determining whether or not someone has schizophrenia. Later we discuss the symptoms the person experiences during the disorder (active phase symptoms), the course of the disorder, and the subtypes of schizophrenia currently in use.

dementia praecox The Latin term meaning premature loss of mind; an early label for what is now called schizophrenia, emphasizing the disorder's frequent appearance during adolescence.

associative splitting A separation among basic functions of human personality (for example, cognition, emotion, and perception) seen by some as the defining characteristic of schizophrenia.

psychotic behavior A severe psychological disorder category characterized by hallucinations and loss of contact with reality.

Mental health workers typically distinguish between *positive* and *negative* symptoms of schizophrenia. A third dimension, *disorganized* symptoms, also appears to be an important aspect of the disorder (Lewis et al., 2009). There is not yet universal agreement about which symptoms should be included in these categories. Positive symptoms generally include the more active manifestations of abnormal behavior or an excess or distortion of normal behavior; these include delusions and hallucinations. Negative symptoms involve deficits in normal behavior in such areas as speech and motivation. Disorganized symptoms include rambling speech, erratic behavior, and inappropriate affect (for example, smiling when you are upset). A diagnosis of schizophrenia requires that two or more positive, negative, and/or disorganized symptoms be present for at least 1 month. A great deal of research has focused on the different symptoms of schizophrenia, each of which is described here in some detail.

DSM Disorder Criteria Summary
Schizophrenia

A. Characteristic symptoms: Two (or more) of the following, each present for a significant portion of time during a 1-month period (or less if successfully treated): (1) delusions; (2) hallucinations; (3) disorganized speech (e.g., frequent derailment or incoherence); (4) grossly disorganized or catatonic behavior; (5) negative symptoms, i.e., affective flattening, alogia, or avolition
   Note: Only one Criterion A symptom is required if delusions are bizarre or hallucinations consist of a voice keeping up a running commentary on the person's behavior or thoughts, or two or more voices conversing with each other.

B. Social/occupational dysfunction: For a significant portion of the time since the onset of the disturbance, one or more major areas of functioning such as work, interpersonal relations, or self-care are markedly below the level achieved prior to the onset (or when the onset is in childhood or adolescence, failure to achieve expected level of interpersonal, academic, or occupational achievement).

C. Duration: Continuous signs of the disturbance persist for at least 6 months. This 6-month period must include at least 1 month of symptoms (or less if successfully treated) that meet Criterion A (i.e., active-phase symptoms) and may include periods of prodromal or residual symptoms. During these prodromal or residual periods, the signs of the disturbance may be manifested by only negative symptoms or two or more symptoms listed in Criterion A present in an attenuated form (e.g., odd beliefs, unusual perceptual experiences).

D. Schizoaffective and Mood Disorder exclusion: Schizoaffective Disorder and Mood Disorder With Psychotic Features have been ruled out because either (1) no Major Depressive, Manic, or Mixed Episodes have occurred concurrently with the active-phase symptoms; or (2) if mood episodes have occurred during active-phase symptoms, their total duration has been brief relative to the duration of the active and residual periods.

E. Substance/general medical condition exclusion: The disturbance is not due to the direct physiological effects of a substance (e.g., a drug of abuse, a medication) or a general medical condition.

F. Relationship to a Pervasive Developmental Disorder: If there is a history of Autistic Disorder or another Pervasive Developmental Disorder, the additional diagnosis of Schizophrenia is made only if prominent delusions or hallucinations are also present for at least a month (or less if successfully treated).

Source: Reprinted with permission from *Diagnostic and Statistical Manual of Mental Disorders* (4th ed., text revision). © 2000 American Psychiatric Association.

Positive Symptoms

We next describe the **positive symptoms** of schizophrenia, which are the more obvious signs of psychosis. These include the disturbing experiences of delusions and hallucinations. Between 50% and 70% of people with schizophrenia experience hallucinations, delusions, or both (Lindenmayer & Khan, 2006).

Delusions

A belief that would be seen by most members of a society as a misrepresentation of reality is called a *disorder of thought content,* or a **delusion**. Because of its importance in schizophrenia, delusion has been called "the basic characteristic of madness" (Jaspers, 1963, p. 93). If, for example, you believe that squirrels are aliens sent to Earth on a reconnaissance mission, you would be considered delusional. The media often portray people with schizophrenia as believing they are famous or important people (such as Napoleon or Jesus Christ), although this is only one type of delusion. Arthur's belief that he could end starvation for all the world's children is also a *delusion of grandeur* (a mistaken belief that the person is famous or powerful).

A common delusion in people with schizophrenia is that others are "out to get them." Called *delusions of persecution,* these beliefs can be most disturbing. One of us worked with a world-class cyclist who was on her way to making the Olympic team. Tragically, however, she developed a belief that other competitors were determined to sabotage her efforts, which forced her to stop riding for years. She believed opponents would spray her bicycle with chemicals that would take her strength away, and they would slow her down by putting small pebbles in the road that only she would ride over. These thoughts created a great deal of anxiety, and she refused even to go near her bicycle for some time.

Other more unusual delusions include Capgras syndrome, in which the person believes someone he or she knows has been replaced by a double, and Cotard's syndrome, in which the person believes he is dead (Christodoulou, Margariti, Kontaxakis, & Christodoulou, 2009; Debruyne, Portzky, Van den Eynde, & Audenaert, 2009).

Why would someone come to believe such obviously improbable things (for example, a friend is replaced by a double or your vote will determine the outcome of a national election)? A number of theories exist and can be summarized into two themes—motivational or deficit theories (McKay, Langdon, & Coltheart, 2007). A *motivational view of delusions* would look at these beliefs as attempts to deal with and relieve anxiety and stress. A person develops "stories" around some issue—for example, a famous person is in love with her (erotomania)—that in a way helps the person make sense out of uncontrollable anxieties in a tumultuous world. Preoccupation with the delusion distracts the individual from the upsetting aspects of the world, such as hallucinations. In contrast, a *deficit view of delusion* sees these beliefs as resulting from brain dysfunction that creates these disordered cognitions or perceptions.

Hallucinations

Did you ever think someone called your name, only to discover that no one was there? Did you ever think you saw something move by you, yet nothing did? We all have fleeting moments when we think we see or hear something that isn't there. However, for many people with schizophrenia, these perceptions are real and occur regularly. The experience of sensory events without any input from the surrounding environment is called a **hallucination**. The case of David illustrates the phenomena of hallucinations in addition to other disorders of thought that are common among people with schizophrenia.

David | Missing Uncle Bill

David was 25 years old when I met him; he had been living in a psychiatric hospital for about 3 years. He was a little overweight and of average height; he typically dressed in a T-shirt and jeans and tended to be active. I first encountered him while I was talking to another man who lived on the same floor. David interrupted us by pulling on my shoulder. "My Uncle Bill is a good man. He treats me well." Not wanting to be impolite, I said, "I'm sure he is. Maybe after I've finished talking to Michael here, we can talk about your uncle." David persisted, "He can kill fish with a knife. Things can get awfully sharp in your mind, when you go down the river. I could kill you with my bare hands—taking things into my own hands. . . . I know you know!" He was now speaking quickly and had gained emotionality, along with speed, as he spoke. I talked to him quietly until he calmed down for the moment; later, I looked into David's file for some information about his background.

David was brought up on a farm by his Aunt Katie and Uncle Bill. His father's identity is unknown and his mother, who had mental retardation, couldn't care for him. David, too, was diagnosed as having mental retardation, although his functioning was only mildly impaired, and he attended school. The year David's Uncle Bill died, his high school teachers first reported unusual behavior. David occasionally talked to his deceased Uncle Bill in class. Later, he became increasingly agitated and verbally aggressive toward others and was diagnosed as having schizophrenia. He managed to graduate from high school but never obtained a job after that; he lived at home with his aunt for several years. Although his aunt sincerely wanted him to stay with her, his threatening behavior escalated to the point that she requested he be seen at the local psychiatric hospital.

I spoke with David again and had a chance to ask him a few questions. "Why are you here in the hospital, David?" "I really don't want to be here," he told me. "I've got other things to do. The time is right, and you know, when opportunity knocks." He continued for a few minutes until I interrupted him. "I was sorry to hear that your Uncle Bill died a few years ago. How are you feeling about him these days?" "Yes, he died. He was sick and now he's gone. He likes to fish with me, down at the river. He's going to take me hunting. I have guns. I can shoot you and you'd be dead in a minute."

David's conversational speech resembled a ball rolling down a rocky hill. Like an accelerating object, his speech gained momentum the longer he went on and, as if bouncing off obstacles, the topics almost always went in unpredictable directions. If he continued for too long, he often became agitated and spoke of harming others. David also told me that his uncle's voice spoke to him repeatedly. He heard other voices also, but he couldn't identify them or tell me what they said. We return to David's case later in this chapter when we discuss causes and treatments.

Hallucinations can involve any of the senses, although hearing things that aren't there, or *auditory hallucination*, is the most common form experienced by people with schizophrenia. David had frequent auditory hallucinations, usually of his uncle's voice. When David heard a voice that belonged to his Uncle Bill, he often couldn't understand what his uncle was saying; on other occasions, the voice was clearer. "He told me to turn off the TV. He said, 'It's too damn loud, turn it down, turn it down.'" This is consistent with recent views of hallucinations as being related to metacognition or "thinking about thinking." In other words, metacognition is a phrase to describe examining your own thoughts. Most of us have had an occasional intrusive thought that we try not to focus on. People who experience hallucinations appear to have intrusive thoughts, but they believe they are coming from somewhere or someone else. They then worry about having these thoughts and engage in meta-worry—or worrying about worrying (Ben-Zeev, Ellington, Swendsen, & Granholm, 2010).

Exciting research on hallucinations uses sophisticated brain-imaging techniques to try to localize these phenomena in the brain. Using single photon emission computed tomography (SPECT) to study the cerebral blood flow of men with schizophrenia who also had auditory hallucinations, researchers in London made a surprising discovery (McGuire, Shah, & Murray, 1993). The researchers used the brain-imaging technique while the men were experiencing hallucinations and while they were not, and they found that the part of the brain most active during halluci-

---

positive symptom A more overt symptom, such as a delusion or hallucination, displayed by some people with schizophrenia.
delusion A psychotic symptom involving disorder of thought content and presence of strong beliefs that are misrepresentations of reality.
hallucination A psychotic symptom of perceptual disturbance in which something is seen, heard, or otherwise sensed although it is not actually present.

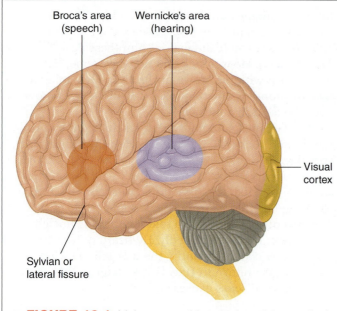

■ FIGURE 12.1 Major areas of functioning of the cerebral cortex. In most people, only the left hemisphere is specialized for language. (© Cengage Learning 2013)

nations was Broca's area (■ Figure 12.1). This is surprising because Broca's area is known to be involved in speech *production*, rather than language *comprehension*. Because auditory hallucinations usually involve understanding the "speech" of others, you might expect more activity in Wernicke's area, which involves language comprehension. However, this study supports an earlier finding by a different group of researchers who also found that Broca's area was more active than Wernicke's area during auditory hallucinations (Cleghorn et al., 1992). These observations support the metacognition theory that people who are hallucinating are *not* hearing the voices of others but are listening

▲ Negative symptoms of schizophrenia include social withdrawal and apathy.

to their own thoughts or their own voices and cannot recognize the difference (e.g., Ford et al., 2009).

Negative Symptoms

In contrast to the active presentations that characterize the positive symptoms of schizophrenia, the **negative symptoms** usually indicate the absence or insufficiency of normal behavior. They include apathy, poverty of (i.e., limited) thought or speech, and emotion and social withdrawal, and approximately 25% of people with schizophrenia display these symptoms (Lewis et al., 2009).

Avolition

Avolition is the inability to initiate and persist in activities. People with this symptom (also referred to as *apathy*) show little interest in performing even the most basic day-to-day functions, including those associated with personal hygiene.

Alogia

Alogia refers to the relative absence of speech. A person with alogia may respond to questions with brief replies that have little content and may appear uninterested in the conversation.

Such deficiency in communication is believed to reflect a negative thought disorder rather than inadequate communication skills. Some researchers, for example, suggest that people with alogia may have trouble finding the right words to formulate their thoughts (Kerns, 2009). Sometimes alogia takes the form of delayed comments or slow responses to questions. Talking with individuals who manifest this symptom can be extremely frustrating, making you feel as if you are "pulling teeth" to get them to respond.

Anhedonia

A related symptom is called **anhedonia**, the presumed lack of pleasure experienced by some people with a psychological disorder. Like some mood disorders, anhedonia signals an indifference to activities that would typically be considered pleasurable, including eating, social interactions, and sexual relations.

Affective Flattening

Imagine that people wore masks at all times: You could communicate with them verbally, but you wouldn't be able to see their emotional reactions. Approximately one fourth of the people with schizophrenia exhibit what is called **flat affect** (Lewis et al., 2009). They are similar to people wearing masks because they do not show emotions when you would normally expect them to. They may stare at you vacantly, speak in a flat and toneless manner, and seem unaffected by things going on around them. However, although they do not react openly to emotional situations, they may be responding on the inside.

Howard Berenbaum and Thomas Oltmanns (1992) compared people with schizophrenia who had flat (or "blunted") affect with those who did not. The two groups were shown clips from comedies and dramas selected to create emotional reactions in the viewer. Berenbaum and Oltmanns found that the people with flat affect showed little change in facial expression, although they reported experiencing the appropriate emotions. The authors concluded that the flat affect in schizophrenia may represent difficulty expressing emotion, not a lack of feeling. Researchers can now use computer analyses of facial expressions to more objectively assess the emotional expressiveness of people with disorders such as schizophrenia. One such study confirmed the difficulty of people with this disorder to express themselves properly with facial expressions (Alvino et al., 2007).

The expression of affect—or the lack of this expression—may be an important symptom of the development of schizophrenia. In a particularly innovative study, researchers videotaped high-risk children (those with one or more parents who had schizophrenia) eating lunch in 1972 and followed them up almost 20 years later (Schiffman et al., 2004). The researchers were able to show that children who later went on to develop schizophrenia typically displayed less positive and more negative affect than those children who did not develop the disorder. This suggests that emotional expression may be one way to identify potential schizophrenia in children.

Disorganized Symptoms

Perhaps the least studied and therefore the least understood symptoms of schizophrenia are referred to as the "disorganized symptoms." These include a variety of erratic behaviors that affect speech, motor behavior, and emotional reactions. The prevalence of these behaviors among those with schizophrenia is unclear.

Disorganized Speech

A conversation with someone who has schizophrenia can be particularly frustrating. If you want to understand what is bothering or upsetting this person, eliciting relevant information is especially difficult. For one thing, people with schizophrenia often lack *insight*, an awareness that they have a problem. In addition, they experience what Bleuler called "associative splitting" and what researcher Paul Meehl called "cognitive slippage" (Bleuler, 1908; Meehl, 1962). These phrases help describe the speech problems of people with schizophrenia: Sometimes they jump from topic to topic, and at other times they talk illogically. *DSM-IV-TR* uses the term **disorganized speech** to describe such communication problems. Let's go back to our conversation with David to demonstrate the symptom.

THERAPIST: Why are you here in the hospital, David?

DAVID: I really don't want to be here. I've got other things to do. The time is right, and you know, when opportunity knocks . . .

Abnormal Psychology Inside Out, produced by Ira Wohl, Only Child Motion

David didn't really answer the question he was asked. This type of response is called *tangentiality*—that is, going off on a tangent instead of answering a specific question. David also abruptly changed the topic of conversation to unrelated areas, a behavior that has variously been called *loose association* or *derailment* (Barrera, McKenna, & Berrios, 2009).

THERAPIST: I was sorry to hear that your Uncle Bill died a few years ago. How are you feeling about him these days?

DAVID: Yes, he died. He was sick, and now he's gone. He likes to fish with me, down at the river. He's going to take me hunting. I have guns. I can shoot you and you'd be dead in a minute.

Again, David didn't answer the question. It was unclear whether he didn't understand the question, couldn't focus his attention, or found it too difficult to talk about his uncle. You can see why people spend a great deal of time trying to interpret all the hidden meanings behind this type of conversation. Unfortunately, however, such analyses have yet to provide us with useful information about the nature of schizophrenia or its treatment.

Inappropriate Affect and Disorganized Behavior

Occasionally, people with schizophrenia display **inappropriate affect**, laughing or crying at improper times. Sometimes they exhibit bizarre behaviors such as hoarding

negative symptom A less outgoing symptom, such as flat affect or poverty of speech, displayed by some people with schizophrenia.

avolition An inability to initiate or persist in important activities. Also known as *apathy*.

alogia A deficiency in the amount or content of speech, a disturbance often seen in people with schizophrenia.

anhedonia An inability to experience pleasure, associated with some mood and schizophrenic disorders.

flat affect An apparently emotionless demeanor (including toneless speech and vacant gaze) when a reaction would be expected.

disorganized speech A style of talking often seen in people with schizophrenia, involving incoherence and a lack of typical logic patterns.

inappropriate affect An emotional display that is improper for the situation.

objects or acting in unusual ways in public. People with schizophrenia engage in a number of other "active" behaviors that are usually viewed as unusual. For example, catatonia is one of the most curious symptoms in some individuals with schizophrenia; it involves motor dysfunctions that range from wild agitation to immobility. On the active side of the continuum, some people pace excitedly or move their fingers or arms in stereotyped ways. At the other end of the extreme, people hold unusual postures, as if they were fearful of something terrible happening if they move (**catatonic immobility**). This manifestation can also involve *waxy flexibility*, or the tendency to keep their bodies and limbs in the position they are put in by someone else.

Again, to receive a diagnosis of schizophrenia, a person must display two or more positive, negative, and/or disorganized symptoms for a major portion of at least 1 month. Depending on the combination of symptoms displayed, two people could receive the same diagnosis but behave differently—for example, one having marked hallucinations and delusions and the other displaying disorganized speech and some negative symptoms. Proper treatment depends on differentiating individuals in terms of their varying symptoms.

Schizophrenia Subtypes

Three main types of schizophrenia have been identified: paranoid (delusions of grandeur or persecution), disorganized (or hebephrenic; silly and immature emotionality), and catatonic (alternate immobility and excited agitation). Although these categories continue to be used in *DSM-IV-TR*, their usefulness is in question. We will discuss in the "On the Spectrum" section at the end of the chapter that they may not be included in *DSM-5* (American Psychiatric Association, 2010). And, as research advances on the underlying biological influences (endophenotypes) of this disorder, it is not clear that they will match these subtypes. In addition, a person's diagnosis can sometimes change over the course of his or her illness, so people can move from one category to another (Lewis et al., 2009). However, we describe the schizophrenia subtypes next for their historic value and because the current diagnostic system relies on these distinctions.

Paranoid Type

People with the **paranoid type of schizophrenia** stand out because of their delusions or hallucinations; at the same time, their cognitive skills and affect are relatively intact. They generally do not have disorganized speech or flat affect, and they typically have a better prognosis than people with other forms of schizophrenia. The delusions and hallucinations usually have a theme, such as grandeur or persecution. The *DSM-IV-TR* criteria for inclusion in this subtype specify preoccupation with one or more delusions or frequent auditory hallucinations but without a marked display of disorganized speech, disorganized or catatonic behavior, or flat or inappropriate affect (American Psychiatric Association, 2000).

▲ Homeless people who suffer from paranoid schizophrenia often bear the additional burden of persecutory delusions, which interfere with outside efforts to help.

Disorganized Type

In contrast to the paranoid type of schizophrenia, people with the **disorganized type of schizophrenia** show marked disruption in their speech and behavior; they also show flat or inappropriate affect, such as laughing in a silly way at the wrong times (American Psychiatric Association, 2000). They also seem unusually self-absorbed and may spend considerable amounts of time looking at themselves in the mirror (Lewis et al., 2009). If delusions or hallucinations are present, they tend not to be organized around a central theme, as in the paranoid type, but are more fragmented. This subtype was previously called *hebephrenic*. Individuals with this diagnosis tend to show signs of difficulty early, and their problems are often chronic, lacking the remissions (improvement of symptoms) that characterize other forms of the disorder (Lindenmayer & Khan, 2006).

Catatonic Type

In addition to the unusual motor responses of remaining in fixed positions (called "waxy flexibility" because their limbs and body position can be moved by others) and engaging in excessive activity, individuals with the **catatonic type of schizophrenia** sometimes display odd mannerisms with their bodies and faces, including grimacing (American Psychiatric Association, 2000). They sometimes repeat or mimic the words of others *(echolalia)* or the movements of others *(echopraxia)*. There may be subtypes of catatonic schizophrenia, with some individuals showing primarily symptoms of labeled "negative withdrawal" (immobility, posturing, mutism), "automatic" (routine obedience, waxy flexibility), "repetitive/echo" (grimacing, perseveration, echolalia), and "agitated/resistive" (excitement, impulsivity, combativeness) (Ungvari, Goggins, Leung, & Gerevich, 2007).

Undifferentiated Type

People who do not fit neatly into these subtypes are classified as having an **undifferentiated type of schizophrenia**; they include people who have the major symptoms of schizophrenia but who do not meet the criteria for paranoid, disorganized, or catatonic types.

Residual Type

People who have had at least one episode of schizophrenia but who no longer manifest major symptoms are diagnosed as having the **residual type of schizophrenia**. Although they may not suffer from bizarre delusions or hallucinations, they may display residual or "leftover" symptoms, such as negative beliefs, or they may still have unusual ideas that are not fully delusional. Residual symptoms can include social withdrawal, bizarre thoughts, inactivity, and flat affect.

Several other disorders also characterized by psychotic behaviors such as hallucinations and delusions do not manifest in the same way as schizophrenia. In the next section, we first distinguish them from schizophrenia and then describe them in greater detail.

Other Psychotic Disorders

Schizophreniform Disorder

Some people experience the symptoms of schizophrenia for a few months only; they can usually resume normal lives. The symptoms sometimes disappear as the result of successful treatment, but they often do so for reasons unknown. The label **schizophreniform disorder** classifies these symptoms, but because relatively few studies are available on this disorder, data on important aspects of it are sparse. It appears, however, that the lifetime prevalence is approximately 0.2% (American Psychiatric Association, 2000). The *DSM-IV-TR* diagnostic criteria for schizophreniform disorder include onset of psychotic symptoms within 4 weeks of the first noticeable change in usual behavior, confusion at the height of the psychotic episode, good *premorbid* (before the psychotic episode) social and occupational functioning (functioning before the psychotic episode), and the absence of blunted or flat affect (Kendler & Walsh, 2007).

Schizoaffective Disorder

Historically, people who had symptoms of schizophrenia and who exhibited the characteristics of mood disorders (for example, depression or bipolar disorder) were lumped in the category of schizophrenia. Now, however, this mixed bag of problems is diagnosed as **schizoaffective disorder** (Sikich, 2009). The prognosis is similar to the prognosis for people with schizophrenia—that is, individuals tend not to get better on their own and are likely to continue experiencing major life difficulties for many years. *DSM-IV-TR* criteria for schizoaffective disorder require, in addition to the presence of a mood disorder, delusions or hallucinations for at least 2 weeks in the absence of prominent mood symptoms (American Psychiatric Association, 2000).

Delusional Disorder

The major feature of **delusional disorder** is a persistent belief that is contrary to reality in the absence of other characteristics of schizophrenia. For example, a woman who believes without any evidence that coworkers are tormenting her by putting poison in her food and spraying her apartment with harmful gases has a delusional disorder. This disorder is characterized by a persistent delusion that is not the result of an organic factor such as brain seizures or of any severe psychosis. Individuals with delusional disorder tend not to have flat affect, anhedonia, or other negative symptoms of schizophrenia; it is important to note, however, they may become socially isolated because they are suspicious of others. The delusions are often long-standing, sometimes persisting over several years (Suvisaari et al., 2009).

DSM | **Disorder Criteria Summary**
Schizophreniform Disorder

A. Criteria A, D, and E of Schizophrenia are met.

B. An episode of the disorder (including prodromal, active, and residual phases) lasts at least 1 month but less than 6 months. (When the diagnosis must be made without waiting for recovery, it should be qualified as "Provisional.")

Specify if:

Without Good Prognostic Features

With Good Prognostic Features: as evidenced by two (or more) of the following: (1) onset of prominent psychotic symptoms within 4 weeks of the first noticeable change in usual behavior or functioning; (2) confusion or perplexity at the height of the psychotic episode; (3) good premorbid social and occupational functioning; (4) absence of blunted or flat affect

Source: Reprinted with permission from *Diagnostic and Statistical Manual of Mental Disorders* (4th ed., text revision). © 2000 American Psychiatric Association.

---

catatonic immobility A disturbance of motor behavior in which the person remains motionless, sometimes in an awkward posture, for extended periods.

paranoid type of schizophrenia A type of schizophrenia in which symptoms primarily involve delusions and hallucinations; speech and motor and emotional behavior are relatively intact.

disorganized type of schizophrenia A type of schizophrenia featuring disrupted speech and behavior, disjointed delusions and hallucinations, and silly or flat affect.

catatonic type of schizophrenia A type of schizophrenia in which motor disturbances (rigidity, agitation, and odd mannerisms) predominate.

undifferentiated type of schizophrenia A category for individuals who meet the criteria for schizophrenia but not for one of the defined subtypes.

residual type of schizophrenia A diagnostic category for people who have experienced at least one episode of schizophrenia and who no longer display its major symptoms but still show some bizarre thoughts or social withdrawal.

schizophreniform disorder A psychotic disorder involving the symptoms of schizophrenia but lasting less than 6 months.

schizoaffective disorder A psychotic disorder featuring symptoms of both schizophrenia and major mood disorder.

delusional disorder A psychotic disorder featuring a persistent belief contrary to reality (delusion) but no other symptoms of schizophrenia.

DSM-IV-TR recognizes the following delusional subtypes: erotomanic, grandiose, jealous, persecutory, and somatic. An *erotomanic type* of delusion is the irrational belief that one is loved by another person, usually of higher status. Some individuals who stalk celebrities appear to have erotomanic delusional disorder. The *grandiose type* of delusion involves believing in one's inflated worth, power, knowledge, identity, or special relationship to a deity or famous person. A person with the *jealous type* of delusion believes the sexual partner is unfaithful. The *persecutory type* of delusion involves believing oneself (or someone close) is being malevolently treated in some way. Finally, with the *somatic delusions* the person feels afflicted by a physical defect or general medical condition. These delusions differ from the more bizarre types often found in people with schizophrenia because in delusional disorder *the imagined events could be happening but aren't* (for example, mistakenly believing you are being followed); in schizophrenia, however, *the imagined events aren't possible* (for example, believing your brain waves broadcast your thoughts to other people around the world).

Delusional disorder seems to be relatively rare, affecting 24 to 30 people out of every 100,000 in the general population (Suvisaari et al., 2009). Among those people with psychotic disorders in general, between 2% and 8% are thought to have delusional disorder (Vahia & Cohen, 2009). The onset of delusional disorder is relatively late: The average age of first admission to a psychiatric facility is between 40 and 49 (Vahia & Cohen, 2009). However, because many people with this disorder can lead relatively normal lives, they may not seek treatment until their symptoms become most disruptive. Delusional disorder seems to afflict more females than males (55% and 45%, respectively, of the affected population).

In a longitudinal study, Opjordsmoen (1989) followed 53 people with delusional disorder for an average of 30 years and found they tended to fare better in life than people with schizophrenia but not and those with some other psychotic disorders, such as schizoaffective disorder. About 80% of the 53 individuals had been married at some time, and half were employed, which demonstrates an ability to function relatively well despite delusions.

We know relatively little about either the biological or the psychosocial influences on delusional disorder (Vahia & Cohen, 2009). Research on families suggests that the characteristics of suspiciousness, jealousy, and secretiveness may occur more often among the relatives of people with delusional disorder than among the population at large, suggesting some aspect of this disorder may be inherited (Kendler & Walsh, 2007).

A number of other disorders can cause delusions, and their presence should be ruled out before diagnosing delusional disorder. For example, abuse of amphetamines, alcohol, and cocaine can cause delusions, as can brain tumors, Huntington's disease, and Alzheimer's disease (Vahia & Cohen, 2009).

Brief Psychotic Disorder

Recall the puzzling case of Arthur, who suddenly experienced the delusion that he could save the world and whose intense emotional swings lasted for only a few days. He would receive the *DSM-IV-TR* diagnosis of **brief psychotic disorder**, which is characterized by the presence of one or more positive symptoms such as delusions, hallucinations, or disorganized speech or behavior lasting 1 month or less. Individuals like Arthur regain their previous ability to function well in day-to-day activities. Brief psychotic disorder is often precipitated by extremely stressful situations.

Shared Psychotic Disorder (Folie à Deux)

Relatively little is known about **shared psychotic disorder (folie à deux)**, the condition in which an individual develops delusions simply as a result of a close relationship with a delusional individual. The content and nature of the delusion originate with the partner and can range from the relatively bizarre, such as believing enemies are sending harmful gamma rays through your house, to the fairly ordinary, such as believing you are about to receive a major promotion despite evidence to the contrary. Although it was once thought that this disorder was more common among mother–daughter or sister–sister pairs, this does not appear to be the case (Shimizu, Kubota, Toichi, & Baba, 2007).

Schizotypal personality disorder, discussed in Chapter 11, is a related psychotic disorder. As you may recall, the characteristics are similar to those experienced by people with schizophrenia but are less severe. Some evidence also suggests that schizophrenia and schizotypal personality disorder may be genetically related as part of a "schizophrenia spectrum."

Remember that although people with related psychotic disorders display many of the characteristics of schizophrenia, these disorders differ significantly.

Concept Check 12.1

Part A

Determine which subtype of schizophrenia is described in each scenario.

1. Jane has spent the past half hour staring in the mirror. As you approach her she turns away and giggles. When you ask what she's laughing at, she answers, but you're having difficulty understanding what she says. _____

2. Two years ago Drew had an episode of schizophrenia, but he no longer displays the major symptoms of the disorder. He does, however, still have some bizarre thoughts and displays flat affect on occasion. _____

3. Greg's cognitive skills and affect are relatively intact. He, however, often has delusions and hallucinations that convince him enemies are out to persecute him. _____

4. Alice usually holds an unusual posture and is sometimes seen grimacing. _____

5. Cameron suffers from a type of schizophrenia that is identified by disruption and incoherence in his speech and behavior. He also shows inappropriate affect, often laughing in a silly way in sad situations. _____

Part B

Diagnose the type of psychotic disorders described in each of the following. Choose from (a) schizophreniform disorder, (b) schizoaffective disorder, (c) delusional disorder, and (d) shared psychotic disorder.

6. Lately Dom has become more isolated because he believes his coworkers are conspiring to get him fired. He becomes agitated whenever he sees a group of employees talking and laughing because he believes that they are plotting against him. _____

7. Natalie reveals to her therapist that she hears numerous voices talking to her and giving her orders. Her doctor has just sent her to this therapist for what he believes to be a major depressive episode. She had begun to sleep all the time and contemplated suicide often. _____

8. If Shawn's schizophrenic symptoms disappeared after about 4 months and he returned to his normal life, what diagnosis might he have received? _____

9. Elias believes the government is out to get him. He thinks agents follow him daily, monitor his calls, and read his mail. His roommate, Cedric, tried to convince him otherwise. However, after a year of this, Cedric began to believe Elias was correct and the government was out to get him, too. _____

⟡ Prevalence and Causes of Schizophrenia

> › **What are the potential genetic, neurobiological, developmental, and psychosocial risk factors for schizophrenia?**

To uncover the causes of this disorder, researchers look in several areas: (1) the possible genes involved in schizophrenia, (2) the chemical action of the drugs that help many people with this disorder, and (3) abnormalities in the working of the brains of people with schizophrenia (Tamminga, 2009). We now examine the nature of schizophrenia and learn how researchers have attempted to understand and treat people who have it.

Statistics

Worldwide, the lifetime prevalence rate of schizophrenia is roughly equivalent for men and women, and it is estimated to be 0.2% to 1.5% in the general population (Mueser & Marcello, 2011), which means the disorder will affect around 1% of the population at some point. Life expectancy is slightly less than average, partly because of the higher rate of suicide and accidents among people with schizophrenia.

brief psychotic disorder A psychotic disturbance involving delusions, hallucinations, or disorganized speech or behavior but lasting less than 1 month; often occurs in reaction to a stressor.
shared psychotic disorder (folie à deux) A psychotic disturbance in which individuals develop a delusion similar to that of a person with whom they share a close relationship. Also known as *folie à deux*.
schizotypal personality disorder A cluster A (odd or eccentric) personality disorder involving a pervasive pattern of interpersonal deficits featuring acute discomfort with, and reduced capacity for, close relationships, as well as cognitive or perceptual distortions and eccentricities of behavior.

Although there is some disagreement about the distribution of schizophrenia between men and women, the difference between the sexes in age of onset is clear. For men, the likelihood of onset diminishes with age, but it can still first occur after the age of 75. The frequency of onset for women is lower than for men until age 36, when the relative risk for onset switches, with more women than men being affected later in life (Mueser & Marcello, 2011). Women appear to have more favorable outcomes than do men.

Development

The more severe symptoms of schizophrenia first occur in late adolescence or early adulthood, although we saw that there may be signs of the development of the disorder in early childhood (Murray & Bramon, 2005). Children who go on to develop schizophrenia show early clinical features such as mild physical abnormalities, poor motor coordination, and mild cognitive and social problems (Schiffman et al., 2004; Welham et al., 2008). Unfortunately, these types of early problems are not specific enough to schizophrenia—meaning they could also be signs of other problems, such as the pervasive developmental disorders we review in Chapter 13—to be able to say for sure that a particular child will later develop schizophrenia.

Up to 85% of people who later develop schizophrenia go through a *prodromal stage*—a 1- to 2-year period before the serious symptoms occur but when less severe yet unusual behaviors start to show themselves (Murray & Bramon, 2005; Yung, Phillips, Yuen, & McGorry, 2004). These behaviors (which you should recognize from Chapter 11 as symptoms seen in schizotypal personality disorders) include ideas of reference (thinking insignificant events relate directly to them), magical thinking (believing they have special abilities such as being clairvoyant or telepathic), and illusions (such as feeling the presence of another person when they are alone). In addition, other symptoms are common, such as isolation, marked impairment in functioning, and a lack of initiative, interests, or energy (Moukas, Stathopoulou, Gourzis, Beratis, & Beratis, 2010).

Once the symptoms of schizophrenia develop, it typically takes 1 to 2 years before the person is diagnosed and receives treatment (Woods et al., 2001). Part of this delay may be the result of hiding symptoms from others (sometimes because of increasing paranoia). Once treated, patients with this disorder will often improve. Unfortunately, most will also go through a pattern of relapse and recovery (Harvey & Bellack, 2009). This relapse rate is important when discussing the course of schizophrenia. For example, the data from one clas-

sic study show the course of schizophrenia among four prototypical groups (Zubin, Steinhauer, & Condray, 1992). About 22% of the group had one episode of schizophrenia and improved without lasting impairment. However, the remaining 78% experienced several episodes, with differing degrees of impairment between them. People with schizophrenia have a poorer prognosis than those with most of the other disorders we describe in this book—including a high risk of suicide—although a significant number of individuals can experience long periods of recovery (Jobe & Harrow, 2005). To illustrate this complex developmental picture, ■ Figure 12.2 graphically depicts the developmental course of schizophrenia. Life stages (from before birth to the end of life) are listed across the top of the graph, with the colored regions showing periods of decline and recovery.

Cultural Factors

Because schizophrenia is so complex, the diagnosis itself can be controversial. Some have argued that "schizophrenia" does not really exist but is a derogatory label for people who behave in ways outside the cultural norm (see, for example, Laing, 1967; Sarbin & Mancuso, 1980; Szasz, 1961). This concern takes us back to our discussions in the first chapter about the difficulty defining what is abnormal. Although the idea that schizophrenia exists only in the minds of mental health professionals is provocative, this extreme view is contradicted by experience. We have both had a great deal of contact with people who have this disorder and with their families and friends, and the tremendous amount of emotional pain resulting from schizophrenia gives definite credence to its existence. In addition, many people in extremely diverse cultures have the symptoms of schizophrenia, which supports the notion that it is a reality for many people worldwide. Schizophrenia is thus

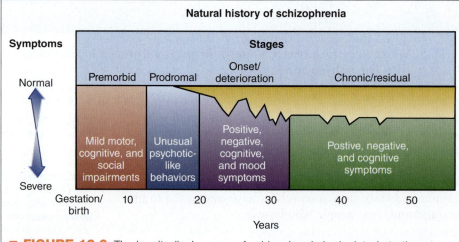

■ **FIGURE 12.2** The longitudinal course of schizophrenia is depicted starting at birth through old age. The severity of the symptoms is showing on the left axis, and the changes in symptoms across each phase (premorbid, prodromal, onset, and chronic) are labeled. (Adapted from Lieberman, J. A., Perkins, D., Belger, A., Chakos, M., Jarskog, F., Boteva, K., & Gilmore, J., 2001. The early stages of schizophrenia: Speculations on pathogenesis, pathophysiology, and therapeutic approaches. *Biological Psychiatry, 50*, p. 885.)

universal, affecting all racial and cultural groups studied so far.

However, the course and outcome of schizophrenia vary from culture to culture. For example, the stressors associated with significant political, social, and economic problems that are prevalent in many areas of Africa, Latin America, and Asia may contribute to poorer outcomes for people with schizophrenia in these countries (Burns, 2009). These differences also may be the result of cultural variations or prevalent biological influences such as immunization, but we cannot yet explain these differences in outcomes.

In the United States, proportionately more African Americans than Caucasians receive the diagnosis of schizophrenia (Schwartz & Feisthamel, 2009). Research from both England and the United States suggests that people from devalued ethnic minority groups (Afro-Caribbean in England and African Americans and Puerto Ricans in the United States) may be victims of bias and stereotyping (Jones & Gray, 1986; Lewis, Croft-Jeffreys, & Anthony, 1990); in other words, they may be more likely to receive a diagnosis of schizophrenia than members of a dominant group. One prospective study of schizophrenia among different ethnic groups in London found that, although the outcomes of schizophrenia appear similar across these groups, blacks were more likely to be detained against their will, brought to the hospital by police, and given emergency injections (Goater et al., 1999). The differing rates of schizophrenia, therefore, may be partially the result of *misdiagnosis* rather than to any real cultural distinctions. However, an additional factor contributing to this imbalance may be the levels of stress associated with factors such as stigma and isolation (Pinto, Ashworth, & Jones, 2008). There also may be genetic variants unique to certain racial groups that contribute to the development of schizophrenia (Glatt, Tampilic, Christie, DeYoung, & Freimer, 2004), a factor we explore in detail next.

Genetic Influences

We could argue that no other area of abnormal psychology so clearly illustrates the enormous complexity and intriguing mystery of genetic influences on behavior as does the phenomenon of schizophrenia (Braff, Schork, & Gottesman, 2007). Despite the possibility that schizophrenia may be several different disorders, we can safely make one generalization: *Genes are responsible for making some individuals vulnerable to schizophrenia*. We look at a range of research findings from family, twin, adoptee, offspring of twins, and linkage and association studies. We conclude by discussing the compelling reasons that no one gene is responsible for schizophrenia; rather, thousands of gene variances combine to produce vulnerability (Purcell et al., 2009; Wray & Visscher, 2010).

Family Studies

In 1938, Franz Kallmann published a major study of the families of people with schizophrenia (Kallmann, 1938). Kallmann examined family members of more than 1,000 people diagnosed with schizophrenia in a Berlin psychiatric hospital. He showed that the severity of the parent's disorder influenced the likelihood of the child's having schizophrenia: The more severe the parent's schizophrenia, the more likely the children were to develop it. Another observation was important: All forms of schizophrenia (for example, catatonic and paranoid) were seen within the families. In other words, it does not appear that you inherit a predisposition for, say, paranoid schizophrenia. Instead, you may inherit a general predisposition for schizophrenia that manifests in the same form or differently from that of your parent. More recent research confirms this observation and suggests that families that have a member with schizophrenia are at risk not just for schizophrenia alone or for all psychological disorders; instead, there appears to be some familial risk for a spectrum of psychotic disorders related to schizophrenia.

In a classic analysis, Gottesman (1991) summarized the data from about 40 studies of schizophrenia, as shown in ■ Figure 12.3. The most striking feature of this graph is its orderly demonstration that the risk of having schizophrenia varies according to how many genes an individual shares with someone who has the disorder. For example, you have the greatest chance (approximately 48%) of hav-

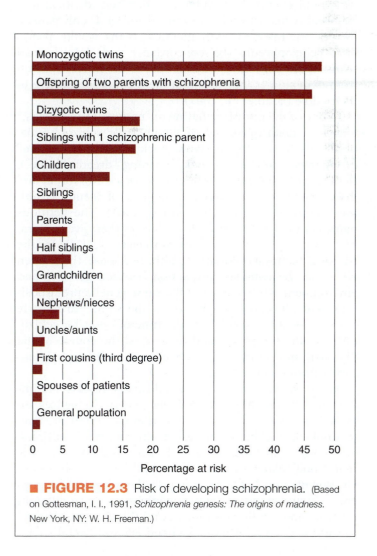

■ **FIGURE 12.3** Risk of developing schizophrenia. (Based on Gottesman, I. I., 1991, *Schizophrenia genesis: The origins of madness*. New York, NY: W. H. Freeman.)

ing schizophrenia if it has affected your identical (monozygotic) twin, a person who shares 100% of your genetic information. Your risk drops to about 17% with a fraternal (dizygotic) twin, who shares about 50% of your genetic information. And having any relative with schizophrenia makes you more likely to have the disorder than someone without such a relative (about 1% if you have no relative with schizophrenia). Because family studies can't separate genetic influence from the impact of the environment, we use twin and adoption studies to help us evaluate the role of shared experiences in the cause of schizophrenia.

Twin Studies

If they are raised together, identical twins share 100% of their genes and 100% of their environment, whereas fraternal twins share only about 50% of their genes and 100% of their environment. If the environment is solely responsible for schizophrenia, we would expect little difference between identical and fraternal twins with regard to this disorder. If only genetic factors are relevant, both identical twins would always have schizophrenia (be concordant) and the fraternal twins would both have it about 50% of the time. Research from twin studies indicates that the truth is somewhere in the middle (Braff et al., 2007).

In one of the most fascinating of "nature's experiments," identical quadruplets, all of whom have schizophrenia, have been studied extensively. Nicknamed the "Genain" quadruplets (from the Greek, meaning "dreadful gene"), these women have been followed by David Rosenthal and his colleagues at the National Institute of Mental Health for a number of years (Rosenthal, 1963). The fictitious names of the girls reported in studies of their lives—Nora, Iris, Myra, and Hester—represent the letters NIMH for the National Institute of Mental Health. In a sense, the women represent the complex interaction between genetics and environment. All four shared the same genetic predisposition, and all were brought up in the same particularly dysfunctional household; yet the time of onset for schizophrenia, the symptoms and diagnoses, the course of the disorder, and, ultimately, their outcomes differed significantly from sister to sister.

The case of the Genain quadruplets reveals an important consideration in studying genetic influences on behavior—*unshared environments* (Plomin, 1990). We tend to think that siblings, and especially identical multiples, are brought up exactly the same way. The impression is that "good" parents expose their children to favorable environments and "bad" parents give them unstable experiences. However, even identical siblings can have different prenatal and family experiences and therefore be exposed to varying degrees of biological and environmental stress.

▲ The Genain quadruplets all had schizophrenia but exhibited different symptoms over the years.

For example, Hester, one of the Genain sisters, was described by her parents as a habitual masturbator, and she had more social problems than her sisters as she grew up. Hester was the first to experience severe symptoms of schizophrenia, at age 18, but her sister Myra was not hospitalized until 6 years later. This unusual case demonstrates that even siblings who are close in every aspect of their lives can still have considerably different experiences physically and socially as they grow up, which may result in vastly different outcomes. A follow-up on the lives of these women showed the progression of their disorder stabilized and in some cases improved when they were assessed at age 66 (Mirsky et al., 2000).

Adoption Studies

Several adoption studies have distinguished the roles of the environment and genetics as they affect schizophrenia. The largest adoption study is currently being conducted in Finland (Tienari, 1991). From a sample of almost 20,000 women with schizophrenia, the researchers found 190 children who had been given up for adoption. The data from this study support the idea that schizophrenia represents a spectrum of related disorders, all of which overlap genetically. If an adopted child had a biological mother with schizophrenia, that child had about a 5% chance of having the disorder (compared to about only 1% in the general population). However, if the biological mother had schizophrenia or one of the related psychotic disorders (for example, delusional disorder or schizophreniform disorder), the risk that the adopted child would have one of these disorders rose to about 22% (Tienari et al., 2003; Tienari, Wahlberg, & Wynne, 2006). Even when raised away from their biological parents, children of parents with schizophrenia have a much higher chance of having the disorder themselves. At the same time, there appears to be a protective factor if these children are brought up in healthy supportive homes. In other words, a gene–environment interaction was observed in this study, with a good home environment reducing the risk of schizophrenia (Gilmore, 2010; Wynne et al., 2006).

The Offspring of Twins

Twin and adoption studies strongly suggest a genetic component for schizophrenia, but what about children who develop schizophrenia even though their parents do not? For example, the study by Tienari and colleagues (2003, 2006) we just discussed found that 1.7% of the children with nonschizophrenic parents developed schizophrenia. Does this mean you can develop schizophrenia without "schizophrenic genes"? Or are some people carriers, having the genes for schizophrenia but for some reason not showing the disorder themselves? An important clue to this question comes from research on the children of twins with schizophrenia.

In a study begun in 1971 by Margit Fischer and later continued by Irving Gottesman and Aksel Bertelsen, 21 identical twin pairs and 41 fraternal twin pairs with a history of schizophrenia were identified, along with their children (Fischer, 1971; Gottesman & Bertelsen, 1989). The researchers wanted to determine the relative likelihood that a child would have schizophrenia if his or her parent did and if the parent's twin had schizophrenia but the parent did not. ■ Figure 12.4 illustrates the findings from this study. For example, if your parent is an identical (monozygotic) twin with schizophrenia, you have about a 17% chance of having the disorder yourself, a figure that holds if you are the child of an unaffected identical twin whose co-twin has the disorder.

However, look at the risks for the child of a fraternal (dizygotic) twin. If your parent is the twin with schizophrenia, you have about a 17% chance of having schizophrenia yourself. However, if your parent does not have schizo-

phrenia but your parent's fraternal twin does, your risk is only about 2%. The only way to explain this finding is through genetics. The data clearly indicate that you can have genes that predispose you to schizophrenia, not show the disorder yourself, but still pass on the genes to your children. In other words, you can be a "carrier" for schizophrenia. This is some of the strongest evidence yet that people are genetically vulnerable to schizophrenia. Remember, however, there is only a 17% chance of inheritance if your parent has schizophrenia, meaning that other factors help determine who will have this disorder.

Linkage and Association Studies

Genetic linkage and association studies rely on traits such as blood types (whose exact location on the chromosome is already known) inherited in families with the disorder you are looking for—in this case, schizophrenia. Because researchers have determined the location of the genes for these traits (called *marker genes*), they can make a rough guess about the location of the disorder genes inherited with them. To date, researchers have looked at several sites for genes that may be responsible for schizophrenia. For example, regions of chromosomes 1, 2, 3, 5, 6, 8, 10, 11, 13, 20, and 22 are implicated in this disorder (Kirov & Owen, 2009).

Endophenotypes. Genetic research on schizophrenia is evolving, and the information on the findings from these sophisticated studies is now being combined with advances in our understanding of specific deficits found in people with this disorder. Remember, in complex disorders such as this, researchers are not looking for a "schizophrenia gene" or genes. Instead, researchers try to find basic processes that contribute to the behaviors or symptoms of the disorder and then find the gene or genes that cause these difficulties—a strategy called *endophenotyping* (Braff et al., 2007).

Several potential candidates for endophenotypes for schizophrenia have been studied over the years. One of the more highly researched is called *smooth-pursuit eye movement*, or eye-tracking. Keeping their head still, typical people are able to track a moving pendulum, back and forth, with their eyes. The ability to track objects smoothly across the visual field is deficient in many people who have schizophrenia (Clementz & Sweeney, 1990; Holzman & Levy, 1977; Iacono, Bassett, & Jones, 1988); it does not appear to be the result of drug treatment or institutionalization (Lieberman et al., 1993). It also seems to be a problem for relatives of those with schizophrenia (Lenzenweger, McLachlan, & Rubin, 2007a). ■ Figure 12.5 shows the decreasing likelihood of observing this abnormal eye-tracking ability the further a person is genetically from someone with schizophrenia. When all these observations are combined, they suggest an eye-tracking deficit may be an endophenotype for schizophrenia that could be used in further study.

Other such research is looking at the social, cognitive, and emotional deficits characteristic of schizophrenia. One

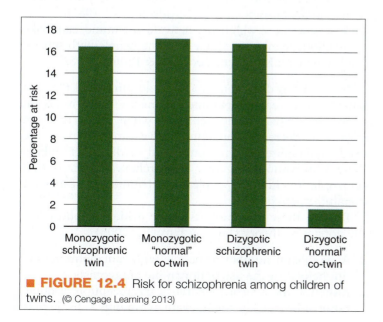

■ **FIGURE 12.4** Risk for schizophrenia among children of twins. (© Cengage Learning 2013)

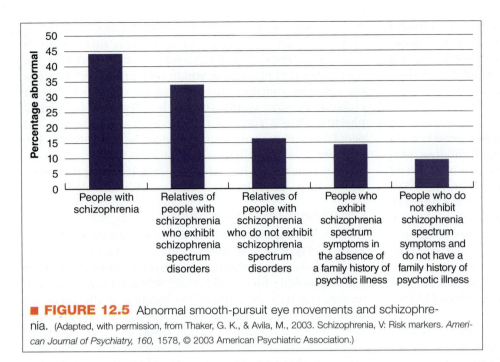

■ **FIGURE 12.5** Abnormal smooth-pursuit eye movements and schizophrenia. (Adapted, with permission, from Thaker, G. K., & Avila, M., 2003. Schizophrenia, V: Risk markers. *American Journal of Psychiatry, 160,* 1578, © 2003 American Psychiatric Association.)

study, for example, looked at multiple generations of families who had someone with schizophrenia (Gur et al., 2007). They tested them on a variety of skills for identified cognitive deficits in areas we described previously—such as emotion identification—and showed that specific problems were inherited in the same manner as schizophrenia (suggesting that these cognitive deficits might be endophenotypes for schizophrenia). Combining genetic research—in this case, a large family study—with neurocognitive assessment may bring us closer to understanding just what is inherited in this disorder (Braff et al., 2007).

Neurobiological Influences

Dopamine

One of the most enduring yet controversial theories of the cause of schizophrenia involves the neurotransmitter *dopamine* (Howes & Kapur, 2009). Before we consider the research, however, let's review briefly how neurotransmitters operate in the brain and how they are affected by neuroleptic medications, which reduce hallucinations and delusions. In Chapter 2, we discussed the sensitivity of specific neurons to specific neurotransmitters and described how they cluster throughout the brain. The top of ■ Figure 12.6 shows two neurons and the important synaptic gap that separates them. Neurotransmitters are released from the storage vessels (synaptic vesicles) at the end of the axon, cross the gap, and are taken up by receptors in the dendrite of the next axon. Chemical "messages" are transported in this way from neuron to neuron throughout the brain.

This process can be influenced in a number of ways, and the rest of Figure 12.6 illustrates some of them. The chemical messages can be increased by agonistic agents or decreased by antagonistic agents. Antagonistic effects slow or stop messages from being transmitted by preventing the release of the neurotransmitter, blocking uptake at the level of the dendrite, or causing leaks that reduce the amount of neurotransmitter released. However, agonistic effects assist with the transference of chemical messages and, if extreme, can produce too much neurotransmitter activity by increasing production or release of the neurotransmitter and by affecting more receptors at the dendrites.

What we've learned about antipsychotic medications points to the possibility that the dopamine system is too active in people with schizophrenia. The simplified picture in Figure 12.6 does not show that there are different receptor sites and that a chemical such as dopamine produces different results depending on which of those sites it affects. In schizophrenia, attention has focused on several dopamine sites, in particular those referred to simply as D_1 and D_2.

In a story that resembles a mystery plot, several pieces of "circumstantial evidence" are clues to the role of dopamine in schizophrenia:

1. Antipsychotic drugs (neuroleptics) often effective in treating people with schizophrenia are dopamine antagonists, partially blocking the brain's use of dopamine (Creese, Burt, & Snyder, 1976; Seeman, Lee, Chau Wong, & Wong, 1976).
2. These neuroleptic drugs can produce negative side effects similar to those in Parkinson's disease, a disorder known to be caused by insufficient dopamine.
3. The drug L-dopa, a dopamine agonist used to treat people with Parkinson's disease, produces schizophrenia-like symptoms in some people (Davidson et al., 1987).
4. Amphetamines, which also activate dopamine, can make psychotic symptoms worse in some people with schizophrenia (van Kammen, Docherty, & Bunney, 1982).

In other words, when drugs are administered that are known to increase dopamine (agonists), there is an increase in schizophrenic behavior; when drugs that are known to decrease dopamine activity (antagonists) are used, schizophrenic symptoms tend to diminish. Taking these observations together, researchers theorized that schizophrenia in some people was attributable to excessive dopamine activity.

Despite these observations, some evidence contradicts the dopamine theory (Javitt & Laruelle, 2006):

1. A significant number of people with schizophrenia are not helped by the use of dopamine antagonists.
2. Although the neuroleptics block the reception of dopamine quite quickly, the relevant symptoms subside only

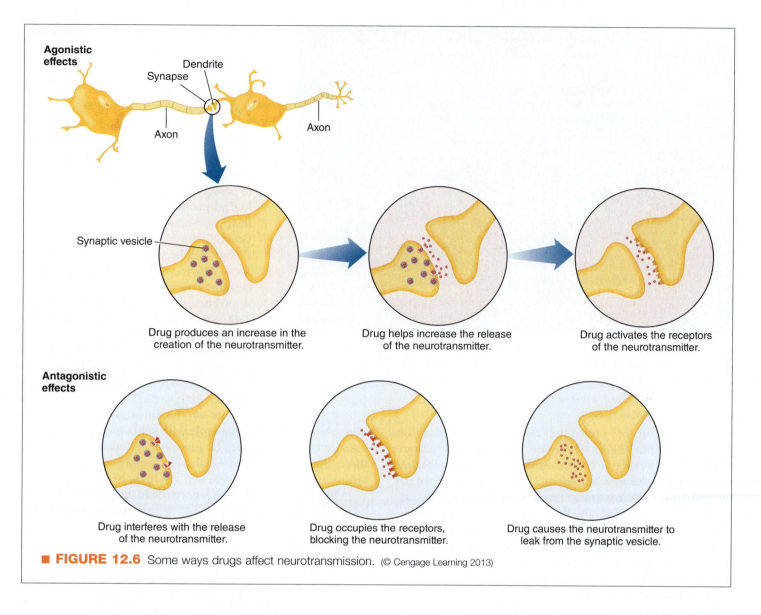

Agonistic effects

Dendrite

Synapse

Axon

Axon

Synaptic vesicle

Drug produces an increase in the creation of the neurotransmitter.

Drug helps increase the release of the neurotransmitter.

Drug activates the receptors of the neurotransmitter.

Antagonistic effects

Drug interferes with the release of the neurotransmitter.

Drug occupies the receptors, blocking the neurotransmitter.

Drug causes the neurotransmitter to leak from the synaptic vesicle.

■ **FIGURE 12.6** Some ways drugs affect neurotransmission. (© Cengage Learning 2013)

after several days or weeks, more slowly than we would expect.

3. These drugs are only partly helpful in reducing the negative symptoms (for example, flat affect or anhedonia) of schizophrenia.

In addition to these concerns, there is evidence of a "double-edged sword" with respect to schizophrenia. A medication called *olanzapine*—along with a family of similar drugs—is effective with many people who were not helped with traditional neuroleptic medications (Kane, Stroup, & Marder, 2009). That's the good news. The bad news for the dopamine theory is that olanzapine and these other new medications are weak dopamine antagonists, much less able to block the sites than other drugs (Javitt & Laruelle, 2006). Why would a medication inefficient at blocking dopamine be effective as a treatment for schizophrenia if schizophrenia is caused by excessive dopamine activity?

The answer may be that although dopamine is involved in the symptoms of schizophrenia, the relationship is more complicated than once thought (Howes & Kapur, 2009).

Current thinking—based on growing evidence from highly sophisticated research techniques—points to *at least three specific neurochemical abnormalities* simultaneously at play in the brains of people with schizophrenia.

Strong evidence now leads us to believe that schizophrenia is partially the result of excessive stimulation of striatal dopamine D_2 receptors (Javitt & Laruelle, 2006). The striatum is part of the basal ganglia found deep within the brain. These cells control movement, balance, and walking, and they rely on dopamine to function. How do we know that excessive stimulation of D_2 receptors is involved in schizophrenia? One clue is that the most effective antipsychotic drugs all share dopamine D_2 receptor antagonism—meaning they help block the stimulation of the D_2 receptors (Ginovart & Kapur, 2010). Using brain-imaging techniques such as SPECT, scientists can view the living brain of a person with schizophrenia and can observe how the newer, "second generation" antipsychotic medications work on these specific dopamine sites.

A second area of interest to scientists investigating the cause of schizophrenia is the observation of a deficiency in

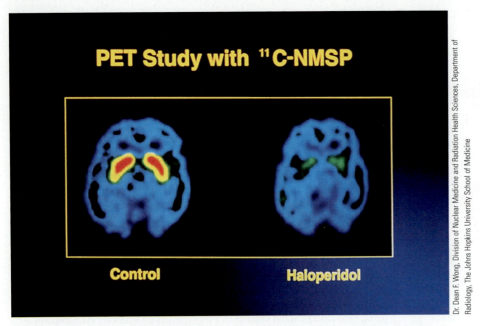

PET Study with ¹¹C-NMSP

Control   **Haloperidol**

Dr. Dean F. Wong, Division of Nuclear Medicine and Radiation Health Sciences, Department of Radiology, The Johns Hopkins University School of Medicine

▲ These PET images show the brain of a man with schizophrenia who had never been medicated *(left)* and after he received haloperidol *(right)*. The red and yellow areas indicate activity in the D₂ receptors; haloperidol evidently reduced dopamine activity.

the stimulation of prefrontal dopamine D_1 receptors (Howes & Kapur, 2009). Therefore, while some dopamine sites may be overactive (for example, striatal D_2), a second type of dopamine site in the part of the brain that we use for thinking and reasoning (prefrontal D_1 receptors) appears to be less active and may account for other symptoms common in schizophrenia. As you will see later in this chapter, people with schizophrenia display a range of deficits in the prefrontal section of the brain, and this area may be less active in people with schizophrenia.

Finally, a third area of neurochemical interest involves research on alterations in prefrontal activity involving glutamate transmission (Javitt & Laruelle, 2006). Glutamate is an excitatory neurotransmitter that is found in all areas of the brain and is only now being studied in earnest. Just as we saw with dopamine (for example, D_1 and D_2 receptors), glutamate has different types of receptors, and the ones being studied for their role in schizophrenia are the N-methyl-d-aspartate (NMDA) receptors. And, just as researchers were led to the study of dopamine by observations from the effects of dopamine-specific drugs on behavior, the effects of certain drugs that affect NMDA receptors point to clues to schizophrenia. Two recreational drugs described in Chapter 10—phencyclidine (PCP) and ketamine—can result in psychotic-like behavior in people without schizophrenia and can exacerbate psychotic symptoms in those with schizophrenia. Both PCP and ketamine are also NMDA antagonists, suggesting that a deficit in glutamate or blocking of NMDA sites may be involved in some symptoms of schizophrenia (Goff & Coyle, 2001).

Research on these two neurotransmitters and their relationship to each other is complex and awaits further clarification. However, advances in technology are leading us

closer to the clues behind this enigmatic disorder and closer still to better treatments.

Brain Structure

Evidence for neurological damage in people with schizophrenia comes from a number of observations. Many children with a parent who has the disorder, and who are therefore at risk, tend to show subtle but observable neurological problems, such as abnormal reflexes and inattentiveness (Wan, Abel, & Green, 2008). These difficulties are persistent: Adults who have schizophrenia show deficits in their ability to perform certain tasks and to attend during reaction time exercises (Cleghorn & Albert, 1990). Such findings suggest that brain damage or dysfunction may cause or accompany schizophrenia, although no one site is probably responsible for the whole range of symptoms (Belger & Dichter, 2006).

One of the most reliable observations about the brain in people with schizophrenia involves the size of the ventricles (■ Figure 12.7). As early as 1927, these liquid-filled cavities showed enlargement in some brains examined in people with schizophrenia (Jacobi & Winkler, 1927). Since then, more sophisticated techniques have been developed for observing the brain, and in the

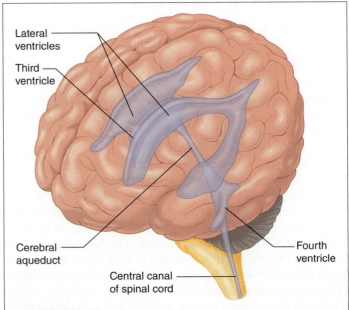

Lateral ventricles

Third ventricle

Cerebral aqueduct

Central canal of spinal cord

Fourth ventricle

■ **FIGURE 12.7** Location of the cerebrospinal fluid in the human brain. This extracellular fluid surrounds and cushions the brain and spinal cord. It also fills the four interconnected cavities (cerebral ventricles) within the brain and the central canal of the spinal cord. (© Cengage Learning 2013)

Table 12.2 Independent Living Skills Program at UCLA

Module	Skill Areas	Learning Objectives
Symptom management	Identifying warning signs of relapse	• To identify personal warning signs • To monitor personal warning signs with assistance from others
	Managing warning signs	• To obtain assistance from health-care providers in differentiating personal warning signs from persistent symptoms, medication side effects, and variations in mood; to develop an emergency plan for responding to warning signs
	Coping with persistent symptoms	• To recognize and monitor persistent personal symptoms; to obtain assistance from health-care providers in differentiating persistent symptoms from warning signs, medication side effects, and variations in mood; to use specific techniques for coping with persistent symptoms • To monitor persistent symptoms daily
	Avoiding alcohol and street drugs	• To identify adverse effects of alcohol and illicit drugs and benefits of avoiding them; to refuse offers of alcohol and street drugs; to know how to resist using these substances in coping with anxiety, low self-esteem, or depression; to discuss openly use of alcohol and drugs with health-care providers
Medication management	Obtaining information about antipsychotic medication Knowing correct self-administration and evaluation Identifying side effects of medication Negotiating medication issues with health-care providers	• To understand how these drugs work, why maintenance drug therapy is used, and the benefits of taking medication • To follow the appropriate procedures for taking medication; to evaluate responses to medication daily • To know the specific side effects that sometimes result from taking medication and what to do when these problems occur • To practice ways of obtaining assistance when problems occur with medication

Source: Reprinted, with permission, from Eckman, T. A., Wirshing, W. C., Marder, S. R., Liberman, R. P., Johnston-Cronk, K., Zimmermann, K., & Mintz, J. (1992). Techniques for training schizophrenic patients in illness self-management: A controlled trial. *American Journal of Psychiatry, 149*, 1549–1555, © 1992 American Psychiatric Association.

delusions, problems with social skills can be the most visible impairment displayed by people with schizophrenia and can prevent them from getting and keeping jobs and making friends. Clinicians attempt to reteach social skills such as basic conversation, assertiveness, and relationship building to people with schizophrenia (Mueser & Marcello, 2011).

Therapists divide complex social skills into their component parts, which they model. Then the clients do role-playing and ultimately practice their new skills in the "real world," all the while receiving feedback and encouragement at signs of progress. This isn't as easy as it may sound. For example, how would you teach someone to make a friend? Many skills are involved, such as maintaining eye contact when you talk to someone and providing the prospective friend with some (but not too much) positive feedback on her own behavior ("I really enjoy talking to you"). Such individual skills are practiced and then combined until they can be used naturally (Swartz, Lauriello, & Drake, 2006). The challenge of teaching social skills, as with all therapies, is to maintain the effects over a long period.

In addition to social skills, programs often teach a range of ways people can adapt to their disorder yet live in the community. At the Independent Living Skills Program at the University of California, Los Angeles, for example, the focus is on helping people take charge of their own care by such methods as identifying signs that warn of a relapse and learning how to manage their medication (Table 12.2) (Liberman, 2007). Preliminary evidence indicates that this type of training may help prevent relapses by people with schizophrenia, although longer-term outcome research is needed to see how long the effects last. To address some obstacles to this much-desired maintenance, such programs combine skills training with the support of a multidisciplinary team that provides services directly in the community, which seems to reduce hospitalization (Swartz et al., 2006). The more time and effort given to these services, the more likely the improvement.

In our discussion of the psychosocial influences on schizophrenia, we reviewed some work linking the person's social and emotional environments to the recurrence of schizophrenic episodes (McNab et al., 2007). It is logical to ask whether families could be helped by learning to reduce their level of expressed emotion and whether this would result in fewer relapses and better overall functioning for

token economy A social learning behavior modification system in which individuals earn items they can exchange for desired rewards by displaying appropriate behaviors.

people with schizophrenia. Several studies have addressed these issues in a variety of ways (Falloon et al., 1985; Hogarty et al., 1986, 1991), and behavioral family therapy has been used to teach the families of people with schizophrenia to be more supportive (Dixon & Lehman, 1995; Mueser, Liberman, & Glynn, 1990). Research on professionals who provide care for people who have schizophrenia, and who may display high levels of expressed emotion, is also an active area of study (Grice et al., 2009).

In contrast to traditional therapy, behavioral family therapy resembles classroom education (Lefley, 2009). Family members are informed about schizophrenia and its treatment, relieved of the myth that they caused the disorder, and taught practical facts about antipsychotic medications and their side effects. They are also helped with communication skills so that they can become more empathic listeners, and they learn constructive ways of expressing negative feelings to replace the harsh criticism that characterizes some family interactions. In addition, they learn problem-solving skills to help them resolve conflicts that arise. Like the research on social skills training, outcome research suggests that the effects of behavioral family therapy are significant during the first year but less robust 2 years after intervention (Montero, Masanet, Bellver, & Lacruz, 2006; Montero et al., 2005). This type of therapy, therefore, must be ongoing if patients and their families are to benefit from it.

Adults with schizophrenia face great obstacles to maintaining gainful employment. Their social skills deficits make reliable job performance and adequate employee relationships a struggle. To address these difficulties, some programs focus on vocational rehabilitation, such as supportive employment. Supportive employment involves providing coaches who give on-the-job training, and these efforts can help some people with schizophrenia maintain meaningful jobs (Mueser & Marcello, 2011).

Where treatment occurs, it has expanded over the years from locked wards in large mental hospitals, to family homes, to local communities. In addition, the services have expanded to include self-advocacy and self-help groups. Former patients have organized programs such as Fountain House in New York City to provide mutual support. Psychosocial clubs have differing models, but all are "person centered" and focus on obtaining positive experiences through employment opportunities, friendship, and empowerment. Many see this consumer-run self-help model as an added component to more specific interventions such as social skills training, family intervention, and medical management of symptoms. Some research indicates that participation may help reduce relapses, but as it is also possible that those who participate may be a special group of individuals, it is difficult to interpret improvements (Goering et al., 2006).

Because schizophrenia is a complex disorder that affects multiple areas of functioning, effective treatment is carried out at several levels. Table 12.3 lists six approaches to treatment that have proved effective in assisting these individuals to achieve higher quality lives. Probably the

Table 12.3 An Integrative Treatment Approach

Treatment	Description
Collaborative psychopharmacology	Using antipsychotic medications to treat the main symptoms of the disorder (hallucinations, delusions) and using other medications for secondary symptoms (for example, antidepressant medication for people with secondary depression)
Assertive community treatment	Providing support in the community, with emphasis on small caseloads for care providers, services in the community setting rather than a clinic, and 24-hour coverage
Family psychoeducation	Assisting family members, including educating them about the disorder and its management, helping them reduce stress and tension in the home, and providing social support
Supportive employment	Providing sufficient support before and during employment so that the person can find and keep a meaningful job
Illness management and recovery	Helping the individual become an active participant in treatment, including providing education about the disorder, teaching effective use of medication strategies for collaborating with clinicians, and coping with symptoms when they reoccur
Integrated dual-disorders treatment	Treating coexisting substance use

Source: © Cengage Learning 2013

most extensively studied program is the assertive community treatment (ACT) program that grew out of work by researchers in Madison, Wisconsin (Swartz et al., 2006). ACT involves using a multidisciplinary team of professionals to provide broad-ranging treatment across all domains, including medication management, psychosocial treatment, and vocational training and support. As you can see, one approach alone is not sufficient to address the many needs of people with schizophrenia and their families (Mueser & Marcello, 2011).

Treatment across Cultures

Treatment of schizophrenia and its delivery differ from one country to another and across cultures within countries. For example, the vast majority of the Xhosa people of South Africa who have schizophrenia report using traditional healers who sometimes recommend the use of oral treatments to induce vomiting, enemas, and the slaughter of cattle to appease the spirits (Koen, Niehaus, Muller, & Laurent, 2008). Hispanics may be less likely than other groups to seek help in institutional settings, relying instead on family sup-

Although people in different parts of the world who are diagnosed with schizophrenia experience many of the same symptoms, the treatment they receive differs greatly depending on the culture in which they live. Some of these differences are not specific to the diagnosis of schizophrenia but instead result from differences in the mental health services each country provides. For instance, one recent study revealed that in a given year only 2% of people in Nigeria receive mental health care compared to 18% of those in the United States and that such differences are largely explained by the amount of money each country dedicates toward mental health services (Wang et al., 2007). Cultural differences also exist within each country as related to the treatment and understanding of schizo-

phrenia specifically. Within the United States, Hispanics diagnosed with schizophrenia appear less likely than other groups to seek help from formal institutional settings and instead receive support from their families (Dassori, Miller, & Saldana, 1995). Because of this focus on the family, treatments for schizophrenia among Hispanics are more likely to include relatives in the treatment process (Kopelowicz, Liberman, & Zarate, 2006).

Differences in treatment approaches around the world also are influenced to some degree by varying perspectives about the causes of schizophrenia. For instance, people from Eastern cultures (e.g., China) hold more religious beliefs about the causes of schizophrenia than those in Western cultures (e.g., the United Kingdom), with those in the United King-

dom putting greater emphasis on biological and psychological factors (Furnham & Wong, 2007). These differences in beliefs about the causes of schizophrenia translate into differences in how schizophrenia is treated across cultures, with China relying more on alternative medicine approaches and the United Kingdom making greater use of biological and psychological treatments (Furnham & Wong, 2007). Many newer studies on the prediction and treatment of schizophrenia are being conducted across different cultures and countries (Bertelsen et al., 2008; Cannon et al., 2008). It is likely that studies taking this broader approach will lead to an enhanced understanding of the ways in which culture can influence the study, assessment, and treatment of this serious mental disorder.

port (Liberman & Kopelowicz, 2009). Adapting treatments to make them culturally relevant—in this case, adding important relatives to the social skills training of Latinos with schizophrenia—is essential for effectiveness (Kopelowicz, Mintz, Liberman, Zarate, & Gonzalez-Smith, 2004). In one interesting study, beliefs about symptoms and treatments were compared between British and Chinese populations (Furnham & Wong, 2007). Native Chinese hold more religious beliefs about both the causes and the treatments of schizophrenia than those living in England—for example, endorsing statements such as, "Schizophrenia is due to evil done in a previous life" and "Ancestor worship (burning candles and joss sticks) will help treat schizophrenia." These different beliefs translate into practice—with the British using more biological, psychological, and community treatments and the Chinese relying more on alternative medicine (Furnham & Wong, 2007). Supernatural beliefs about the cause of schizophrenia among family members in Bali lead to limited use of antipsychotic medication in treatment (Kurihara, Kato, Reverger, & Gusti Rai Tirta, 2006). In many countries in Africa, people with schizophrenia are kept in prisons, primarily because of the lack of adequate alternatives (Mustafa, 1990). In general, the movement from housing people in large institutional settings to community care is ongoing in most Western countries.

Prevention

One strategy for preventing a disorder such as schizophrenia—which typically first shows itself in early adulthood—is to identify and treat children who may be at risk for getting

the disorder later in life. In our discussion of genetics, we noted that approximately 17% of the children born to parents who have schizophrenia are likely themselves to develop the disorder. These high-risk children have been the focus of several studies.

A classic at-risk study was initiated in the 1960s by Sarnoff Mednick and Fini Schulsinger (1965, 1968). They identified 207 Danish children of mothers who had severe cases of schizophrenia and 104 control children born to mothers who had no history of the disorder. The average age of these children was about 15 when they were first identified, and the researchers followed them for 10 more years to determine whether any factors had predicted who would and would not develop schizophrenia. We have already discussed pregnancy and delivery-related complications. Mednick and Schulsinger also identified *instability of early family rearing environment*, which suggests that environmental influences may trigger the onset of schizophrenia (Cannon et al., 1991). Poor parenting may place additional strain on a vulnerable person who is already at risk.

As we await the outcomes of long-term studies, other approaches may prove valuable for reducing the rates of this disorder. For example, we have seen that factors such as birth complications and certain early illnesses (for example, viruses) may trigger the onset of schizophrenia, especially among those individuals who are genetically predisposed. Therefore, interventions such as vaccinations against viruses for women of childbearing age and interventions related to improving prenatal nutrition and care may be effective preventive measures (McGrath, 2010).

On the Spectrum Emerging Views of Schizophrenia

Although *DSM-IV-TR* does not use this language, there is a recognition in the field of schizophrenia that the group of diagnoses that we cover in this chapter (and in others) constitute *schizophrenia spectrum disorders*. In fact, Eugen Bleuler, who coined the term *schizophrenia* in his book *Dementia Praecox or the Group of Schizophrenias* (1911), identified the different variants that were all included within this spectrum (Heckers, 2009). The *DSM* has struggled with this concept in its varied presentations over the years, and, as we describe in this chapter, *DSM-IV-TR* currently lists five subtypes of schizophrenia (paranoid, disorganized, catatonic, undifferentiated, and residual) and other related psychotic disorders that

fall under this heading (schizophreniform, schizoaffective, delusional, brief psychotic, and shared psychotic disorders). In addition, a personality disorder (schizotypal personality disorder, discussed in Chapter 11) and possibly two mood disorders (psychotic bipolar disorder and psychotic depression) are also considered by some to be included under this umbrella category of schizophrenia spectrum disorders. All of these difficulties seem to share features of extreme reality distortion (for example, hallucinations, delusions).

Discussions for *DSM-5* include the possible removal of the subtypes of schizophrenia and instead adding a dimensional rating for some of the core symptoms of schizophrenia (American

Psychiatric Association, 2010). For example, one possibility being discussed is to rate the extent to which an individual has and is distressed by the following dimensions: hallucinations, delusions, disorganization, abnormal psychomotor behavior, restricted emotional expression, avolition, impaired cognition, depression, and mania. This would allow clinicians the ability to provide a richer description of the complex problems faced by an individual that often go unspecified within single labels (for example, paranoid schizophrenia) that people are assigned. What is required is a thorough study of the soundness of these types of dimensional structures and a determination of whether or not they represent valid diagnoses.

Concept Check 12.3

Read the descriptions and then match them to the following words: (a) olanzapine, (b) extrapyramidal symptoms, (c) serotonin, (d) dopamine, (e) metabolites, (f) token economy, (g) vocational rehabilitation, (h) social skills training, (i) family intervention.

1. Setting up an elaborate _____ in which patients are fined for disruptive or inappropriate behavior and rewarded for appropriate behavior is beneficial in hospitals.

2. In _____ clinicians attempt to reteach such behaviors as basic conversation, assertiveness, and relationship building to people with schizophrenia.

3. Aside from social skills training, two psychosocial treatments for schizophrenia, _____ (teach-

ing family members to be supportive) and _____ (teaching meaningful jobs), may be helpful.

4. Recent studies sometimes indicate that the relationship of the neurotransmitters _____ and _____ may explain some positive symptoms of schizophrenia.

5. Because antipsychotic medications may cause serious side effects, some patients stop taking them. One serious side effect is called _____, which may include parkinsonian symptoms.

6. Difficult cases of schizophrenia seem to improve with a serotonin and dopamine antagonist called _____.

Summary

Clinical Description, Symptoms, and Subtypes

› Schizophrenia is characterized by a broad spectrum of cognitive and emotional dysfunctions that include delusions and hallucinations, disorganized speech and behavior, and inappropriate emotions.

› The symptoms of schizophrenia can be divided into positive, negative, and disorganized. Positive symptoms are active manifestations of abnormal behavior, or an excess or distortion of normal behavior, and include delusions and hallucinations. Negative symptoms in-

volve deficits in normal behavior on such dimensions as affect, speech, and motivation. Disorganized symptoms include rambling speech, erratic behavior, and inappropriate affect.

› *DSM-IV-TR* divides schizophrenia into five subtypes. People with the paranoid type of schizophrenia have prominent delusions or hallucinations, whereas their cognitive skills and affect remain relatively intact. People with the disorganized type of schizophrenia tend to show marked disruption in their speech and behavior; they also show flat or inappropriate affect. People with the catatonic type of schizophrenia have unusual motor responses, such as remaining in fixed positions (waxy flexibility), excessive activity, and being oppositional by remaining rigid. In addition, they display odd mannerisms with their bodies and faces, including grimacing. People who do not fit neatly into these subtypes are classified as having an undifferentiated type of schizophrenia. Some people who have had at least one episode of schizophrenia but who no longer have major symptoms are diagnosed as having the residual type of schizophrenia.

> Several other disorders are characterized by psychotic behaviors, such as hallucinations and delusions; these include schizophreniform disorder (which includes people who experience the symptoms of schizophrenia for less than 6 months); schizoaffective disorder (which includes people who have symptoms of schizophrenia and who exhibit the characteristics of mood disorders, such as depression and bipolar affective disorder); delusional disorder (which includes people with a persistent belief that is contrary to reality, in the absence of the other characteristics of schizophrenia); brief psychotic disorder (which includes people with one or more positive symptoms, such as delusions, hallucinations, or disorganized speech or behavior over the course of less than a month); and shared psychotic disorder (which includes individuals who develop delu-

sions simply as a result of a close relationship with a delusional individual).

Prevalence and Causes of Schizophrenia

> A number of causative factors have been implicated for schizophrenia, including genetic influences, neurotransmitter imbalances, structural damage to the brain caused by a prenatal viral infection or birth injury, and psychological stressors.
> Relapse appears to be triggered by hostile and critical family environments characterized by high expressed emotion.

Treatment of Schizophrenia

> Successful treatment for people with schizophrenia rarely includes complete recovery. However, the quality of life for these individuals can be meaningfully affected by combining antipsychotic medications with psychosocial approaches, employment support, and community-based and family interventions.
> Treatment typically involves antipsychotic drugs that are usually administered with a variety of psychosocial treatments, with the goal of reducing relapse and improving skills in deficits and compliance in taking the medications. The effectiveness of treatment is limited because schizophrenia is typically a chronic disorder.

Key Terms

schizophrenia, 451
catatonia, 451
hebephrenia, 451
paranoia, 451
dementia praecox, 452
associative splitting, 452
psychotic behavior, 453
positive symptoms, 454
delusion, 455
hallucination, 454
negative symptoms, 456
avolition, 456

alogia, 456
anhedonia, 456
flat affect, 456
disorganized speech, 457
inappropriate affect, 457
catatonic immobility, 458
paranoid type of schizophrenia, 458
disorganized type of schizophrenia, 458
catatonic type of schizophrenia, 458
undifferentiated type of schizophrenia, 459

residual type of schizophrenia, 459
schizophreniform disorder, 459
schizoaffective disorder, 459
delusional disorder, 459
brief psychotic disorder, 460
shared psychotic disorder (folie à deux), 460
schizotypal personality disorder, 460
schizophrenogenic mother, 470
double bind communication, 470
expressed emotion (EE), 470
token economy, 474

Answers to Concept Checks

12.1

Part A

1. disorganized; 2. residual; 3. paranoid; 4. catatonic; 5. disorganized

Part B

6. c; 7. b; 8. a; 9. d

12.2

1. f, h, a; 2. a, a; 3. d, i

12.3

1. f; 2. h; 3. i, g; 4. d, c; 5. b; 6. a

Media Resources

Log in to CengageBrain to access the resources your instructor requires. For this book, you can access:

CourseMate brings course concepts to life with interactive learning, study, and exam preparation tools that support the printed textbook. A textbook-specific website, Psychology CourseMate includes an integrated interactive eBook and other interactive learning tools including quizzes, flashcards, videos, and more.

Abnormal Psychology Videos

> *Etta, a Patient with Schizophrenia:* An example of a lower-functioning patient with schizophrenia.

CENGAGENOW CengageNow is an easy-to-use online resource that helps you study in less time to get the grade you want—NOW. Take a pre-test for this chapter and receive a personalized study plan based on your results that will identify the topics you need to review and direct you to online resources to help you master those topics. Then take a post-test to help you determine the concepts you have mastered and what you will need to work on. If your textbook does not include an access code card, go to CengageBrain.com to gain access.

> Visit www.cengagebrain.com to access your account and purchase materials.

aplia If your professor has assigned Aplia homework:
1. Sign in to your account.
2. Complete the corresponding homework exercises as required by your professor.
3. When finished, click "Grade It Now" to see which areas you have mastered, which need more work, and for detailed explanations of every answer.

Video Concept Reviews

CengageNOW also contains Mark Durand's *Video Concept Reviews* on these challenging topics.
> Schizophrenia
> Positive Symptoms
> Delusions
> Hallucinations
> Negative Symptoms
> Avolition, Alogia, Anhedonia and Flat Affect
> Disorganized Symptoms
> Paranoid Type of Schizophrenia
> Catatonic Type of Schizophrenia
> Delusional Disorder
> Brief Psychotic Disorder and Shared Psychotic Disorder
> Expressed Emotion and Stress

Chapter Quiz

1. One distinction used to characterize symptoms of schizophrenia divides them into what two broad categories?
   a. paranoid and catatonic
   b. episodic and chronic
   c. psychiatric and somatic
   d. positive and negative

2. Emotional and social withdrawal, apathy, and poverty of speech and thought are examples of what type of symptoms in schizophrenia?
   a. psychotic
   b. negative
   c. disorganized
   d. positive

3. Rhonda fears that her employer is trying to poison her with gas emitted from the overhead lights in her office. Given what you know about Rhonda's thoughts, what subtype of schizophrenia is she most likely to have?

a. catatonic

b. disorganized

c. paranoid

d. undifferentiated

4. Which disorder is characterized by symptoms similar to those seen in schizophrenia but of shorter duration, often with successful remission of symptoms?

a. schizophreniform disorder

b. delusional disorder

c. schizoaffective disorder

d. bipolar disorder

5. Most people with schizophrenia:

a. have multiple episodes that get progressively worse

b. have only one episode with full recovery after it

c. have episodes of alternating positive and negative symptoms

d. have multiple episodes, with different degrees of impairment between episodes

6. Research on cultural factors and schizophrenia suggests that African Americans:

a. may have higher rates than other ethnic groups because of misdiagnosis

b. may have higher rates than other ethnic groups because they are exposed to more prejudice and bias

c. may be more vulnerable to schizophrenia because of chromosomal differences

d. with schizophrenia are more likely to experience negative symptoms than positive symptoms

7. Which sibling of an individual with schizophrenia is most likely to develop schizophrenia?

a. monozygotic twin raised in the same home

b. monozygotic twin raised in a different home

c. dizygotic twin raised in the same home

d. dizygotic twin raised in a different home

8. Which statement is true about antipsychotic medications and the treatment of schizophrenia?

a. Antipsychotic medications are not as effective as psychosocial treatments.

b. Different medications are effective with different people and to a different degree.

c. All antipsychotic medications appear to be equally effective for all patients.

d. Most patients go through a trial-and-error period to determine whether antipsychotic, antidepressant, or antianxiety medications are most effective for them.

9. Which type of psychosocial treatment has been most effective for treating the behavioral problems seen in schizophrenia?

a. psychodynamic psychotherapy

b. moral treatment

c. psychosurgery

d. token economies

10. Which two psychosocial interventions appear to be most helpful for people with schizophrenia?

a. hypnosis and psychosurgery

b. ECT and social skills training

c. psychoanalytic psychotherapy and expressed emotion management

d. family education and vocational rehabilitation

(See Appendix A for answers.)

Exploring Schizophrenia

❯ Schizophrenia disrupts perception of the world, thought, speech, movement, and almost every other aspect of daily functioning.

❯ Usually chronic with a high relapse rate; complete recovery from schizophrenia is rare.

- Stressful, traumatic life event
- High expressed emotion (family criticism, hostility, and/or intrusion)
- Sometimes no obvious trigger

Trigger

Biological Influences

- Inherited tendency (multiple genes) to develop disease
- Prenatal/birth complications—viral infection during pregnancy/birth injury affect child's brain cells
- Brain chemistry (abnormalities in the dopamine and glutamate systems)
- Brain structure (enlarged ventricles)

Social Influences

- Environment (early family experiences) can trigger onset
- Culture influences interpretation of disease/symptoms (hallucinations, delusions)

Causes

©Dynamic Graphics/Jupiter Images

Behavioral Influences

- **Positive symptoms:**
  - Active manifestations of abnormal behavior (delusions, hallucinations, disorganized speech, odd body movements, or catatonia)
- **Negative symptoms:**
  - Flat affect (lack of emotional expression)
  - Avolition (lack of initiative, apathy)
  - Alogia (relative absence in amount or content of speech)

Javier Pierini/Photodisc/Getty Images

Emotional and Cognitive Influences

- Interaction styles that are high in criticism, hostility, and emotional overinvolvement can trigger a relapse

TREATMENT OF SCHIZOPHRENIA

Treatment		
Individual, Group, and Family Therapy		• Can help patient and family understand the disease and symptom triggers. • Teaches families communication skills. • Provides resources for dealing with emotional and practical challenges.
Social Skills Training		• Can occur in hospital or community settings. • Teaches the person with schizophrenia social, self-care, and vocational skills.

Medications		• Taking neuroleptic medications may help people with schizophrenia to:
		  —Clarify thinking and perceptions of reality
		  —Reduce hallucinations and delusions
		• Drug treatment must be consistent to be effective. Inconsistent dosage may aggravate existing symptoms or create new ones.

Photos (top to bottom):
David Buffington/Photodisc/Getty Images
Duncan Smith/Photodisc/Getty Images
Photodisc/Getty Images

SYMPTOMS OF SCHIZOPHRENIA

People with schizophrenia do not all show the same kinds of symptoms. Symptoms vary from person to person and may be cyclical. Common symptoms include:

Symptoms		
Delusions	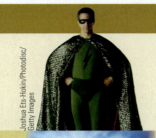 Joshua Ets-Hokin/Photodisc/Getty Images	• Unrealistic and bizarre beliefs not shared by others in the culture • May be delusions of grandeur (that you are really Mother Teresa or Napoleon) or delusions of persecution (the cyclist who believed her competitors were sabotaging her by putting pebbles in the road)
Hallucinations	 Don Farrall/Photodisc/Getty Images	• Sensory events that aren't based on any external event (hearing voices, seeing people who have died) • Many have auditory hallucinations (David hears his dead uncle talking to him)
Disorganized Speech	 ©Royalty Free/Corbis	• Jumping from topic to topic • Talking illogically (not answering direct questions, going off on tangents) • Speaking in unintelligible words and sentences
Behavioral Problems	 ©Dynamic Graphics/Jupiter Images	• Pacing excitably, wild agitation • Catatonic immobility • Waxy flexibility (keeping body parts in the same position when they are moved by someone else) • Inappropriate dress (coats in the summer, shorts in the winter) • Inappropriate affect • Ignoring personal hygiene
Withdrawal	 ©Photodisc/Getty Images	• Lack of emotional response (flat speech, little change in facial expressions) • Apathy (little interest in day-to-day activities) • Delayed and brief responses in conversation • Loss of enjoyment in pleasurable activities (eating, socializing, sex)

TYPES OF SCHIZOPHRENIA

Paranoid	Disorganized	Catatonic	Residual	Undifferentiated
• Delusions of grandeur or persecution • Hallucinations (especially auditory) • Higher level of functioning between episodes • May have stronger familial link than other types	• Disorganized speech and/or behavior • Immature emotionality (inappropriate affect) • Chronic and lacking in remissions	• Alternating immobility and excited agitation • Unusual motor responses (waxy flexibility, rigidity) • Odd facial or body mannerisms (often mimicking others) • Rare	• Has had at least one schizophrenic episode but no longer shows major symptoms • Still shows "leftover" symptoms (social withdrawal, bizarre thoughts, inactivity, flat affect)	• Symptoms of several types that taken together do not neatly fall into one specific category

CHAPTER 13

Developmental and Cognitive Disorders

Demonstrate knowledge and understanding representing appropriate breadth and depth in selected content areas of psychology:	› Biological bases of behavior and mental processes, including physiology, sensation, perception, comparative, motivation, and emotion (APA SLO 1.2.a (3)) *(see textbook pages 499–500, 506–508, 520–522)*
Use the concepts, language, and major theories of the discipline to account for psychological phenomena.	› Describe behavior and mental processes empirically, including operational definitions (APA SLO 1.3.a) *(see textbook pages 485–487, 491–493, 496–499, 502–505, 511–520)*
Identify appropriate applications of psychology in solving problems, such as:	› Origin and treatment of abnormal behavior (APA SLO 4.2.b) *(see textbook pages 488–491, 493–495, 499–502, 505–513, 520–525)*

*Portions of this chapter cover learning outcomes suggested by the American Psychological Association (2007) in their guidelines for the undergraduate psychology major. Chapter coverage of these outcomes is identified by APA Goal and APA Suggested Learning Outcome (SLO).

Common Developmental Disorders

› **What are the central defining features of attention deficit/hyperactivity disorder?**
› **What are the main types of learning disorders, and how are they typically treated?**

Almost all disorders described in this book are developmental disorders in the sense that they change over time. Most disorders originate in childhood, although the full presentation of the problem may not manifest itself until much later. Disorders that show themselves early in life often persist as the person grows older, so the term *childhood disorder* may be misleading. In this chapter, we cover those disorders that are revealed in a clinically significant way during a child's developing years and are of concern to families and educators. Remember, however, that these difficulties often persist through adulthood and are typically lifelong problems, not problems unique to children.

Again, a number of difficulties and, indeed, distinct disorders begin in childhood. In certain disorders, some children are fine except for difficulties with talking. Others have problems relating to their peers. Still other children have a combination of conditions that significantly hinder their development.

Before we discuss specific disorders, we need to address the broad topic of development in relation to disorders usually first diagnosed in infancy, childhood, or adolescence. For example, what effect do the early disruptions in skills have on a child's later life? Does it matter when in the developmental period certain problems arise? Are disruptions in development permanent, thus making any hope for treatment doubtful?

Childhood is considered particularly important because the brain changes significantly for several years after birth; this is also when critical developments occur in social, emotional, cognitive, and other important competency areas. These changes mostly follow a pattern: The child develops one skill before acquiring the next. Although this pattern of change is only one aspect of development, it is an important concept at this point because it implies that any disruption in the development of early skills will, by the very nature of this sequential process, disrupt the development of later skills. For example, some researchers believe that people with autism suffer from a disruption in early social development, which prevents them from developing important social relationships, even with their parents. From a developmental perspective, the absence of early and meaningful social relationships has serious consequences. Children whose motivation to interact with others is disrupted may have a more difficult time learning to communicate—that is, they may not want to learn to speak if other people are not important to them. Researchers don't know whether a disruption in communication skills is a direct outcome of the disorder or a by-product of disrupted early social development.

Understanding this type of developmental relationship is important for several reasons. Knowing what processes are disrupted will help us understand the disorder better and may lead to more appropriate intervention strategies. It may be important to identify children with attention deficit/hyperactivity disorder, for example, because their problems with impulsivity may interfere with their ability to create and maintain friendships, an important developmental consideration. Similarly, identifying a disorder such as autism at an early age is important for these children so that their social deficits can be addressed before they affect other skill domains, such as language and communication. Too often, people see early and pervasive disruptions in developmental skills and expect a negative prognosis, with the problems predetermined and permanent. However, remember that biological and psychosocial influences continuously interact with each other.

Therefore, even for disorders such as attention deficit/hyperactivity disorder and autism that have clear biological bases, the presentation of the disorder is different for each individual. Changes at the biological or the psychosocial level may reduce the impact of the disorder.

One note of caution is appropriate here. There is real concern in the profession, especially among developmental psychologists, that some workers in the field may view aspects of normal development as symptoms of abnormality. For example, *echolalia*, which involves repeating the speech of others, was once thought to be a sign of autism. However, when we study the development of speech in children without disorders, we find that repeating what someone else says is an intermediate step in language development. In children with autism, therefore, echolalia is just a sign of relatively delayed language skills and not a symptom of their disorder (Tager-Flusberg et al., 2009). Knowledge of development is important for understanding the nature of psychological disorders.

With that caveat in mind, we now examine several disorders usually diagnosed first in infancy, childhood, or adolescence, including *attention deficit/hyperactivity disorder*, which involves characteristics of inattention or hyperactivity and impulsivity, and *learning disorders*, which are characterized by one or more difficulties in areas such as reading and writing. We then focus on *autistic disorder*, a more severe disability in which the child shows significant impairment in social interactions and communication and has restricted patterns of behavior, interest, and activities. We also discuss the less severe Asperger's disorder. Finally, we examine *intellectual disability*, which involves considerable deficits in cognitive abilities.

Attention Deficit/Hyperactivity Disorder

Do you know people who flit from activity to activity, who start many tasks but seldom finish one, who have trouble concentrating, and who don't seem to pay attention when others speak? These people may have **attention deficit/hyperactivity disorder (ADHD)**, one of the most common reasons children are referred for mental health services in the United States (Durand, 2011; Greenhill & Hechtman, 2009). The primary characteristics of such people include a pattern of inattention, such as not paying attention to school- or work-related tasks, or of hyperactivity and impulsivity. These deficits can significantly disrupt academic efforts and social relationships. Consider the case of Danny.

Danny : The Boy Who Couldn't Sit Still

Danny, a handsome 9-year-old boy, was referred to us because of his difficulties at school and at home. Danny had a great deal of energy and loved playing most sports, especially baseball. Academically, his work was adequate, although his teacher reported

that his performance was diminishing and she believed he would do better if he paid more attention in class. Danny rarely spent more than a few minutes on a task without some interruption: He would get up out of his seat, riffle through his desk, or constantly ask questions. His peers were frustrated with him because he was equally impulsive during their interactions: He never finished a game, and in sports he tried to play all positions simultaneously.

At home, Danny was considered a handful. His room was in a constant mess because he became engaged in a game or activity only to drop it and initiate something else. Danny's parents reported that they often scolded him for not carrying out some task, although the reason seemed to be that he forgot what he was doing rather than that he deliberately tried to defy them. They also said that, out of their own frustration, they sometimes grabbed him by the shoulders and yelled, "Slow down!" because his hyperactivity drove them crazy.

Clinical Description

Danny has many characteristics of ADHD. Like Danny, people with this disorder have a great deal of difficulty sustaining their attention on a task or activity (Barkley, 2006e). As a result, their tasks are often unfinished and they often seem not to be listening when someone else is speaking. In addition to this serious disruption in attention, some people with ADHD display motor hyperactivity. Children with this disorder are often described as fidgety in school, unable to sit still for more than a few minutes. Danny's restlessness in his classroom was a considerable source of concern for his teacher and peers, who were frustrated by his impatience and excessive activity. In addition to hyperactivity and problems sustaining attention, impulsivity—acting apparently without thinking—is a common complaint made about people with ADHD. For instance, during meetings of his baseball team, Danny often shouted responses to the coach's questions even before the coach had a chance to finish his sentence.

For ADHD, the text revision of the fourth edition of the *Diagnostic and Statistical Manual of Mental Disorders (DSM-IV-TR)* differentiates three types of symptoms. The first includes problems of *inattention*. People may appear not to listen to others; they may lose necessary school assignments, books, or tools; and they may not pay enough attention to details, making careless mistakes. The second type of symptom includes *hyperactivity*, which includes fidgeting, having trouble sitting for any length of time, and always being on the go. The third general symptom is *impulsivity*, which includes blurting out answers before questions have been completed and having trouble waiting turns. Either the first (inattention) or the second and third (hyperactivity and impulsivity) symptoms must be present for someone to be diagnosed with ADHD.

ADHD is most often diagnosed among boys and among children and adolescents. This has led some to question whether this disorder looks different in girls and adults than it does in young boys or whether ADHD is simply less common in these groups. Most research to date on ADHD has used research samples made up mostly of young boys, which has made it difficult to determine frequency and symptoms of ADHD in girls and adults. Some have suggested that part of the reason for the focus on young boys is that many researchers and clinicians have paid more attention to symptoms of hyperactivity than to problems with inattention because the former are more disruptive and easily measurable than the latter and that hyperactivity is more common in boys. So has ADHD been overlooked among girls and adults because the symptoms of this disorder look different in these groups?

Several recent large-scale studies have begun to shed light on this question. In one study, researchers at the Pediatric Psychopharmacology Unit at the Massachusetts General Hospital tested whether the symptoms of ADHD differ between boys and girls (Biederman et al., 2001b). Of interest, they found that girls with ADHD are more likely than boys to have the inattentive subtype of ADHD and are less likely to have symptoms of hyperactivity, opposition, and other disruptive behaviors. A study by Fayyad and colleagues (2007) examined the occurrence of ADHD among adults in 10 countries. This study revealed that 3.4% of adults report having ADHD, with a slightly higher rate found among men (4.1%) than among women (2.7%). Perhaps more concerning than this surprisingly high prevalence rate is that adult ADHD was found to be associated with significant levels of comorbidity and impairment at work. Moreover, few of those with adult ADHD reported receiving treatment for this problem (Fayyad et al., 2007).

Studies such as these suggest that, although ADHD may look a bit different among girls and adults, it certainly does occur and is associated with significant problems in functioning and unmet need for treatment. It is hopeful that, with a new understanding of how ADHD manifests differently across sex and age groups, efforts to accurately identify and effectively treat this problem will lead to improvements in the life of those affected by ADHD.

Inattention, hyperactivity, and impulsivity often cause other problems that appear secondary to ADHD. Academic performance tends to suffer, especially as the child progresses in school. Children with **ADHD** are likely to be unpopular and rejected by their peers (Nijmeijer et al., 2008). One study found that young girls with **ADHD** in general were likely to be rejected by peers but that this likelihood was more pronounced in those with hyperactivity, impulsivity, and inattention when compared to girls who had only the inattentive type (Hinshaw, 2002).

Statistics

ADHD is estimated to occur in 3% to 7% of school-age children in the United States, and an important analysis of prevalence suggests that the disorder is found in about 5.2% of the child populations across all regions of the world (Polanczyk, de Lima, Horta, Biederman, & Rohde, 2007). Boys are 3 times more likely to be diagnosed with **ADHD** than girls, and this discrepancy increases for children being seen in clinics (Spencer, Biederman, & Mick, 2007). The reason for this gender difference is largely unknown. It may be that adults are more tolerant of hyperactivity among girls, who tend to be less active than boys with **ADHD**. Boys tend to be more aggressive, which will more likely result in attention by mental health professionals (Barkley, 2006e). Girls with **ADHD**, however, tend to display more behaviors referred to as "internalizing"—specifically, anxiety and depression (Mick et al., 2011).

Children with **ADHD** are first identified as different from their peers around age 3 or 4; their parents describe them as active, mischievous, slow to toilet train, and oppositional (Conners, March, Frances, Wells, & Ross, 2001). The symptoms of inattention, impulsivity, and hyperactivity become increasingly obvious during the school years. Despite the perception that children grow out of **ADHD**, their problems usually continue: It is estimated that about half of the children with **ADHD** have ongoing difficulties through adulthood (McGough, 2005). Over time, children with **ADHD** seem to be less impulsive, although inattention persists. During adolescence, the impulsivity manifests itself in different areas; for example, teens with **ADHD** are at greater risk for pregnancy and contracting sexually transmitted infections. They are also more likely to have driving difficulties, such as crashes; to be cited for speeding; and to have their licenses suspended (Barkley, 2006a). Several other *DSM-IV-TR* disorders, also found in children, appear to overlap significantly with this disorder. Specifically, oppositional defiant disorder (ODD), conduct disorder, and bipolar disorder all have characteristics seen in children with **ADHD**. ODD is a *DSM-IV-TR* disorder that includes symptoms such as "often loses temper," "argues with adults," "often deliberately annoys people," "touchy and easily annoyed by others," and "often spiteful and vindictive." The impulsivity and hyperactivity observed in chil-

attention deficit/hyperactivity disorder (ADHD) Developmental disorder featuring maladaptive levels of inattention, excessive activity, and impulsiveness.

dren with ADHD can manifest themselves in some of these symptoms. It's been estimated that at least half of those with ADHD could also be diagnosed with ODD (Durand, 2011). Similarly, conduct disorder—which, as you saw in Chapter 11, can be a precursor to antisocial personality disorder—is also observed in many children with ADHD (Nock, Kazdin, Hiripi, & Kessler, 2006). Bipolar disorder—one of the mood disorders—also overlaps significantly with ADHD. This overlap can complicate diagnosis in these children.

Causes

As with many other disorders, we are at a period when important information about the genetics of ADHD is beginning to be uncovered (Kebir, Tabbane, Sengupta, & Joober, 2009; Waldman & Gizer, 2006). Researchers have known for some time that ADHD is more common in families in which one person has the disorder. For example, the relatives of children with ADHD have been found to be more likely to have ADHD themselves than would be expected in the general population (Fliers et al., 2009). It is important to note that these families display an increase in psychopathology in general, including conduct disorder, mood disorders, anxiety disorders, and substance abuse (Faraone et al., 2000). This research and the comorbidity in the children themselves suggest that some shared genetic deficits may contribute to the problems experienced by individuals with these disorders (Brown, 2009).

ADHD is considered to be highly influenced by genetics, with a relatively small role played by environmental influences in the cause of the disorder when compared to many other disorders we discuss in this book. As with other disorders, researchers are finding that multiple genes are responsible for ADHD (Nikolas & Burt, 2010). Most attention to date focuses on genes associated with the neurochemical dopamine, although norepinephrine, serotonin, and gamma-aminobutyric acid (GABA) are also implicated in the cause of ADHD. More specifically, there is strong evidence that ADHD is associated with the dopamine D_4 receptor gene, the dopamine transporter gene (DAT1), and the dopamine D_5 receptor gene. DAT1 is of particular interest because methylphenidate (Ritalin)—one of the most common medical treatments for ADHD—inhibits this gene and increases the amount of dopamine available. As with several other disorders we've discussed, researchers are looking for endophenotypes, those basic deficits—such as specific attentional problems—characteristic of ADHD. The goal is to link these deficits to specific brain dysfunctions. It is not surprising that specific areas of current interest for ADHD are the brain's attention system, working memory functions, inattentiveness, and impulsivity. Researchers are now trying to tie specific genetic defects to these cognitive processes to make the link between genes and behavior.

DSM Disorder Criteria Summary

Attention Deficit/Hyperactivity Disorder (ADHD)

A. Either (1) or (2):

(1) six (or more) of the following symptoms of inattention have persisted for at least 6 months to a degree that is maladaptive and inconsistent with developmental level:

Inattention

(a) often fails to give close attention to details or makes careless mistakes in schoolwork, work, or other activities; (b) often has difficulty sustaining attention in tasks or play activities; (c) often does not seem to listen when spoken to directly; (d) often does not follow through on instructions and fails to finish schoolwork, chores, or duties in the workplace (not due to oppositional behavior or failure to understand instructions); (e) often has difficulty organizing tasks and activities; (f) often avoids, dislikes, or is reluctant to engage in tasks that require sustained mental effort (such as schoolwork or homework); (g) often loses things necessary for tasks or activities (e.g., toys, school assignments, pencils, books, or tools); (h) is often easily distracted by extraneous stimuli; (i) is often forgetful in daily activities

(2) six (or more) of the following symptoms of hyperactivity/impulsivity have persisted for at least 6 months to a degree that is maladaptive and inconsistent with developmental level:

Hyperactivity

(a) often fidgets with hands or feet or squirms in seat; (b) often leaves seat in classroom or in other situations in which remaining seated is expected; (c) often runs about or climbs excessively in situations in which it is inappropriate (in adolescents or adults, may be limited to subjective feelings of restlessness); (d) often has difficulty playing or engaging in leisure activities quietly; (e) is often "on the go" or often acts as if "driven by a motor;" (f) often talks excessively

Impulsivity

(g) often blurts out answers before questions have been completed; (h) often has difficulty awaiting turn; (i) often interrupts or intrudes on others (e.g., butts into conversations or games)

B. Some hyperactive-impulsive or inattentive symptoms that caused impairment were present before age 7 years.

C. Some impairment from the symptoms is present in two or more settings (e.g., at school [or work] and at home).

D. There must be clear evidence of clinically significant impairment in social, academic, or occupational functioning.

E. The symptoms do not occur exclusively during the course of a Pervasive Developmental Disorder, Schizophrenia, or other Psychotic Disorder and are not better accounted for by another mental disorder (e.g., Mood Disorder, Anxiety Disorder, Dissociative Disorder, or a Personality Disorder).

Source: Reprinted with permission from *Diagnostic and Statistical Manual of Mental Disorders* (4th ed., text revision). © 2000 American Psychiatric Association.

Some research indicates that poor "inhibitory control" (the ability to stop responding to a task when signaled) may be common among both children with ADHD and their unaffected family members (siblings and parents) and may be one genetic marker (an endophenotype) for this disorder (Goos, Crosbie, Payne, & Schachar, 2009).

The strong genetic influence in ADHD does not rule out any role for the environment (Ficks & Waldman, 2009). In one of a growing number of gene–environment interaction studies of ADHD, for example, researchers found that children with a specific mutation involving the dopamine system (called the DAT1 genotype) were more likely to exhibit the symptoms of ADHD if their mothers smoked during pregnancy (Kahn, Khoury, Nichols, & Lanphear, 2003). Prenatal smoking seemed to interact with this genetic predisposition to increase the risk for hyperactive and impulsive behavior. Other research is now pointing to additional environmental factors, such as low socioeconomic status and parental marital instability and discord, as involved in these gene–environment interactions (Ficks & Waldman, 2009).

For several decades, ADHD has been thought to involve brain damage, and this notion is reflected in the previous use of labels such as "minimal brain damage" or "minimal brain dysfunction" (Ross & Pelham, 1981). Researchers now know that the overall volume of the brain in those with this disorder is slightly smaller (3% to 4%) than in children without this disorder (Narr et al., 2009). A number of areas in the brains of those with ADHD appear affected (Valera, Faraone, Murray, & Seidman, 2007). In addition, more research is starting to focus on the structure and function of the brain in adults with ADHD.

A variety of such toxins as allergens and food additives have been considered as possible causes of ADHD over the years, although little evidence supports the association. The theory that food additives such as artificial colors, flavorings, and preservatives are responsible for the symptoms of ADHD has been highly controversial. Feingold (1975) presented this view along with recommendations for eliminating these substances as a treatment for ADHD. Hundreds of thousands of families have put their children on the Feingold diet, despite arguments by some that the diet has little or no effect on the symptoms of ADHD (Barkley, 1990; Kavale & Forness, 1983). However, some large-scale research now suggests that there may be a small but measurable impact of artificial food colors and additives on the behavior of young children. One study found that 3-year-old and 8- to 9-year-old children who consumed typical amounts of preservatives (sodium benzoate) and food colorings had increased levels of hyperactive behaviors (inattention, impulsivity, and overactivity) (McCann et

al., 2007). Other research now points to the possible role of the pesticides found in foods as contributing to an increased risk of ADHD (Bouchard, Bellinger, Wright, & Weisskopf, 2010).

Psychological and social dimensions of ADHD may further influence the disorder itself—especially how the child fares over time. Negative responses by parents, teachers, and peers to the affected child's impulsivity and hyperactivity may contribute to feelings of low self-esteem, especially in children who are also depressed (Anastopoulos, Sommer, & Schatz, 2009). Years of constant reminders by teachers and parents to behave, sit quietly, and pay attention may create a negative self-image in these children, which, in turn, can negatively affect their ability to make friends. Thus, the possible biological influences on impulsivity, hyperactivity, and

ADHD: Sean

"[He] would never think before he did stuff. And actually, the thing that really made me go, 'Something is desperately wrong here'—we had a little puppy. Real tiny little dog. And Sean was upstairs playing with it. And my daughter had gone upstairs, and went, 'Mom, something's wrong with the dog's paw.' And I looked and this poor little dog had a broken paw. Sean had dropped her. But—didn't say anything to anyone. Just left the poor little dog sitting there. And I thought, 'Wow. This is just not normal.'"

Go to Psychology CourseMate at www.cengagebrain.com to watch this video.

▲ A child with ADHD is likely to behave inappropriately regardless of the setting.

©Sky Bonillo/PhotoEdit

attention, combined with attempts to control these children, may lead to rejection and consequent poor self-image. An integration of the biological and psychological influences on ADHD suggests that both need to be addressed when designing effective treatments (Durand, 2011).

Treatment of ADHD

Treatment for ADHD has proceeded on two fronts: biological and psychosocial interventions. Typically, the goal of biological treatments is to reduce the children's impulsivity and hyperactivity and to improve their attentional skills. Psychosocial treatments generally focus on broader issues such as improving academic performance, decreasing disruptive behavior, and improving social skills. Although these two kinds of approaches have typically developed independently, recent efforts combine them to have a broader impact on people with ADHD.

The first types of medication used for children with ADHD were stimulants. It is estimated that more than 2.5 million children in the United States are being treated with these medications (Centers for Disease Control and Prevention, 2005). Drugs such as methylphenidate (Ritalin, Metadate, Concerta) and D-amphetamine (Dexedrine, Dextrostat) have proved helpful for more than 70% of cases in at least temporarily reducing hyperactivity and impulsivity and improving concentration on tasks (Greenhill & Hechtman, 2009). Adderall, which is a longer-acting version of these psychostimulants, reduces the need for multiple doses for children during the day but has similar positive effects (Connor, 2006).

Originally, it seemed paradoxical or contrary to expect that children would calm down after taking a stimulant. However, on the same low doses, children and adults with and without ADHD react in the same way. It appears that stimulant medications reinforce the brain's ability to focus attention during problem-solving tasks (Connor, 2006). Although the use of stimulant medications remains controversial, especially for children, most clinicians recommend them temporarily, in combination with psychosocial interventions, to help improve children's social and academic skills.

The concerns over the use of stimulant medications now include their potential for abuse. In Chapter 10, we discussed that drugs such as Ritalin are sometimes abused for their ability to create elation and reduce fatigue (Setlik, Bond, & Ho, 2009). And the widespread misperception that use of these prescription medications is harmless is also of great concern (Desantis & Hane, 2010). This is particularly worrisome for children with ADHD because they are at increased risk for later substance abuse (Wagner & Pliszka, 2009). A newer drug—atomoxetine (Strattera)—also appears effective for some children with ADHD, but it is a selective norepinephrine-reuptake inhibitor and therefore does not produce the same "highs" when used in larger doses. Research suggests that other drugs, such as some antidepressants (bupropion, imipramine) and a drug used for treating high blood pressure (clonidine), may have similar effects as Strattera on people with ADHD (Wagner & Pliszka, 2009). Not all children with ADHD have depression or high blood pressure (although depression can be a problem in some of these children), but these drugs work on the same neurotransmitter systems (norepinephrine and dopamine) involved in ADHD. All these drugs seem to improve compliance and decrease negative behaviors in many children, and their effects do not usually last when the drugs are discontinued.

Some portion of children with ADHD do not respond to medications, and most children who do respond show improvement in ability to focus their attention but do not show gains in the important areas of academics and social skills (Smith, Barkley, & Shapiro, 2006). In addition, the medications often result in unpleasant side effects, such as insomnia, drowsiness, or irritability (Kollins, 2008). Because of these findings, researchers have applied various behavioral interventions to help these children at home and in school (Ollendick & Shirk, 2011; Ramsay, 2009). In general, the programs set such goals as increasing the amount of time the child remains seated, the number of math papers completed, or appropriate play with peers. Reinforcement programs reward the child for improvements and, at times, punish misbehavior with loss of rewards. Other programs incorporate parent training to teach families how to respond constructively to their child's behaviors and how to structure the child's day to help prevent difficulties (Ollendick & Shirk, 2011). Social skills training for these children, which includes teaching them how to interact appropriately with their peers, also seems to be an important treatment component (de Boo & Prins, 2007).

For adults with ADHD, cognitive-behavioral intervention to reduce distractibility and improve organizational skills appears quite helpful. Most clinicians typically recommend a combination of approaches designed to individualize treatments for those with ADHD, targeting both short-term management issues (decreasing hyperactivity and impulsivity) and long-term concerns (preventing and reversing academic decline and improving social skills).

Helpful "Designer Drugs"

Get ready to learn a new word—*psychopharmacogenetics.*

Psychopharmacogenetics is the study of how your genetic makeup influences your response to certain drugs. The hope for this field is that medications can be matched or even "designed" for individuals to better complement their specific needs (Weinshilboum, 2003). For example, one study looked at the use of methylphenidate (Ritalin) for children and adolescents with ADHD (Polanczyk, Zeni, et al., 2007). For those who had a specific gene defect—the adrenergic alpha-2A receptor gene (ADRA2A)—methylphenidate had a strong positive effect, especially on their problems with inattention. This was not the case for those with ADHD who did not have the ADRA2A gene defect. Currently, the use of drug treatments tends to be by trial and error: A medication is attempted at a particular dose; if it is not effective, the dose is changed. If that does not work, a different medication is tried. This new study holds the promise of potentially eliminating this guesswork and tailoring the treatment to the individual.

This exciting new approach to medical treatment for mental illness brings with it some weighty concerns. Central to these concerns are issues of privacy and confidentiality. Genetic screening to identify defects is likely to identify any number of potential genetic problems in each of us. How will schools, employment sites, and insurance companies view this information if they have access? The concern is that people will be discriminated against based on this information (for example, having the genes that may or may not lead to having ADHD or another disorder). Will the desire to better target drug treatments outweigh these types of ethical concerns? Most new technical advances, like those promised with psychopharmacogenetics, also uncover new problems, and it is essential that ethical issues be part of the discussion as researchers move forward in this area.

Evaluating Treatment Approaches

To determine whether a combined approach to treatment is the most effective, a large-scale study initiated by the National Institute of Mental Health was conducted by six teams of researchers (Jensen et al., 2001). Labeled the Multimodal Treatment of Attention Deficit/Hyperactivity Disorder (MTA) study, this 14-month study included 579 children who were randomly assigned to one of four groups. One group of the children received routine care without medication or specific behavioral interventions (community care). The three treatment groups consisted of medication management (usually methylphenidate), intensive behavioral treatment, and a combination of the two treatments. Initial reports from the study suggested that the combination of behavioral treatments and medication, and medication alone, were superior to behavioral treatment alone and community intervention for ADHD symptoms. For problems that went beyond the specific symptoms of ADHD, such as social skills, academics, parent–child relations, oppositional behavior, and anxiety or depression, results suggested slight advantages of combination over single treatments (medication management, behavioral treatment) and community care.

Some controversy surrounds the interpretation of these findings—specifically, whether or not the combination of behavioral and medical treatments is superior to medication alone (Biederman, Spencer, Wilens, & Greene, 2001; Pelham, 1999). One of the concerns surrounding the study was that although medication continued to be dispensed, the behavioral treatment was faded over time, which may account for the observed differences.

Practically, if there is no difference between these two treatments, most parents and therapists would opt for simply providing medication for these children. As we mentioned previously, behavioral interventions have the added benefit of improving aspects of the child and family that are not directly affected by medication. Reinterpretations of the data from this large-scale study continue, and more research likely will be needed to clarify the combined and separate effects of these two approaches to treatment (Ollendick & Shirk, 2011). Despite these advances, however, children with ADHD continue to pose a considerable challenge to their families and to the educational system.

Learning Disorders

Because parents often invest a great deal of time, resources, and emotional energy to ensure their children's academic success, it can be extremely upsetting when a child with no obvious intellectual deficits does not achieve as expected. In this section, we describe **learning disorders** in reading, mathematics, and written expression—all characterized by performance that is substantially below what would be expected given the person's age, intelligence quotient (IQ) score, and education. We also look briefly at disorders that involve how we communicate. Consider the case of Alice.

Alice • Taking a Reading Disorder to College

Alice, a 20-year-old college student, sought help because of her difficulty in several of her classes. She reported that she had enjoyed school and had been a good student until about the sixth grade, when her grades suffered significantly. Her teacher informed her parents that she wasn't working up to her potential and she needed to be better motivated. Alice had always worked hard in school but promised to try harder. However, with each report card her mediocre grades made her feel worse about herself. She managed to graduate from high school, but by that time she felt she was not as bright as her friends.

Alice enrolled in the local community college and again found herself struggling with the work. Over the years, she had learned several tricks that seemed to help her study and at least get passing grades. She read the material in her textbooks aloud to herself; she had earlier discovered that she could recall the

learning disorders Reading, mathematics, or written expression performance substantially below the level expected relative to the person's age, intelligence quotient score, and education.

material much better this way than if she just read silently to herself. In fact, reading silently, she could barely remember any of the details just minutes later.

After her sophomore year, Alice transferred to the university, which she found even more demanding and where she failed most of her classes. After our first meeting, I suggested that she be formally assessed to identify the source of her difficulty. As suspected, Alice had a learning disability.

Scores from an IQ test placed her slightly above average, but she was assessed to have significant difficulties with reading. Her comprehension was poor, and she could not remember most of the content of what she read. We recommended that she continue with her trick of reading aloud because her comprehension for what she heard was adequate. In addition, Alice was taught how to analyze her reading—that is, how to outline and take notes. She was even encouraged to audiotape her lectures and play them back to herself as she drove around in her car. Although Alice did not become an A student, she was able to graduate from the university, and she now works with young children who themselves have learning disabilities.

Clinical Description

According to *DSM-IV-TR* criteria, Alice would be diagnosed as having a **reading disorder**, which is defined as a significant discrepancy between a person's reading achievement and what would be expected for someone of the same age—referred to by some as "unexpected underachievement" (Fletcher, Lyon, Fuchs, & Barnes, 2007). More specifically, the criteria require that the person read at a level significantly below that of a typical person of the same age, cognitive ability (as measured on an IQ test), and educational background. In addition, a diagnosis of reading disorder requires that the person's disability not be caused by a sensory difficulty, such as trouble with sight or hearing, and should not be the result of poor or absent instruction. Similarly, *DSM-IV-TR* defines a **mathematics disorder** as achievement below expected performance in mathematics and defines a **disorder of written expression** as achievement below expected performance in writing. In each of these disorders, the difficulties are sufficient to interfere with the students' academic achievement and to disrupt daily activities.

There is some controversy over using the discrepancy between IQ and achievement as part of the process of identifying children with learning disorders. Part of the criticism involves the delay between when learning problems occur and when they finally result in a large enough difference between IQ scores and achievement scores—which may not be measurable until later in a child's academic life. An alternative approach—called *response to intervention*—is now being used by many clinicians. It involves identifying a child as having a learning disorder when the response to a known effective intervention (for example, an early reading pro-

gram) is significantly inferior to the performance by peers (Jackson, Pretti-Frontczak, Harjusola-Webb, Grisham-Brown, & Romani, 2009). This provides an early warning system and focuses on providing effective instruction.

Statistics

Estimates of how prevalent learning disorders are range from 5% to 10% (Altarac & Saroha, 2007), although the frequency of this diagnosis appears to increase in wealthier regions of the country—suggesting that with better access to diagnostic services, more children are identified (■ Figure 13.1). It is currently believed that nearly 6 million children in the United States are diagnosed as having a specific learning disorder (Altarac & Saroha, 2007). There do appear to be racial differences in the diagnosis of learning disorders. Approximately 1% of white children and 2.6% of black children were receiving services for problems with learning in 2001 (Bradley, Danielson, & Hallahan, 2002). However, this research also suggests that the differences were related to the economic status of the child, not ethnic background.

Difficulties with reading are the most common of the learning disorders and occur in some form in 4% to 10% of the general population (Pennington & Bishop, 2009). Mathematics disorder appears in approximately 1% of the population (Tannock, 2009a), but there is limited information about the prevalence of disorder of written expression among children and adults. Early studies suggested that boys were more likely to have a reading disorder than girls, although more recent research indicates that boys and girls may be equally affected by this disorder (Feinstein & Phillips, 2006). Students with learning disorders are more likely to drop out of school (Vogel & Reder, 1998), more likely to be unemployed (Shapiro & Lentz, 1991), and more likely to have suicidal thoughts and attempt suicide (Daniel et al., 2006).

A group of disorders loosely identified as verbal or *communication disorders* seems closely related to learning dis-

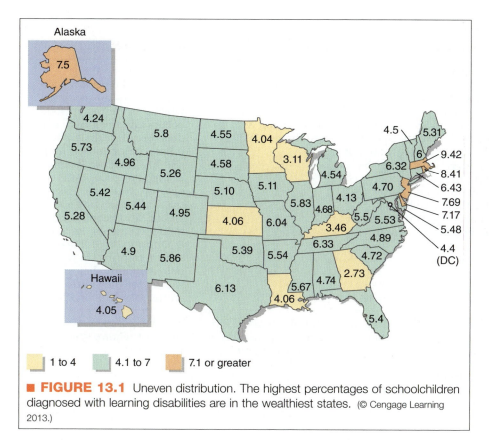

| 1 to 4 | 4.1 to 7 | 7.1 or greater |

■ FIGURE 13.1 Uneven distribution. The highest percentages of schoolchildren diagnosed with learning disabilities are in the wealthiest states. (© Cengage Learning 2013.)

orders. These disorders can appear deceptively benign, yet their presence early in life can cause wide-ranging problems later. For a brief overview of these disorders, which include **stuttering**, **expressive language disorder**, **selective mutism**, and **tic disorder**, see Table 13.1.

Causes

Theories about the causes of learning disorders include genetic, neurobiological, and environmental factors. The genetic research in this area is particularly complex. It is clear that learning disorders run in families, and sophisticated family and twin studies bear this out (Fletcher et al., 2007). Yet, analyses of the genes involved suggest that many effects are not specific—meaning that there are not different genes responsible for reading disorders and mathematics disorders. Instead, there are genes that affect learning and they may contribute to problems across domains (reading, mathematics, writing) (Plomin & Kovas, 2005).

The different problems associated with learning themselves have different origins. For example, children (and adults) often have very different problems associated with reading. Reading disorders are sometimes broken into problems with word recognition (difficulty decoding single words—sometimes called *dyslexia*), fluency (problems being able to read words and sentences smoothly and automatically), and comprehension (difficulty getting meaning from what is read) (Tannock, 2009b). Most research to date focuses on problems with word recognition, and there is evidence that some develop these problems primarily through

their genes, whereas others develop problems as a result of environmental factors (Shaywitz, Mody, & Shaywitz, 2006). Genes located on chromosomes 1, 2, 3, 6, 11, 12, 15, and 18 have all been repeatedly linked to these difficulties (Tannock, 2009b). At the same time, environmental influences such as the home reading habits of families can significantly affect outcomes—especially with skills such as word recognition—suggesting that reading to children at risk for reading disorders can reduce the impact of the genetic influence (Petrill, Deater-Deckard, Thompson, DeThorne, & Schatschneider, 2006).

Various forms of subtle brain impairment have also been thought responsible for learning disabilities; some of the earliest theories involve a neurological explanation (Hinshelwood, 1896). Research suggests structural, and functional, differences in the brains of people with learning disabilities. Specifically, three areas of the left hemisphere appear to be involved in problems with dyslexia (word recognition)—Broca's area (which affects articulation and word analysis), an area in the left parietotemporal area (which affects word analysis), and an area in the left occipitotemporal area (which affects recognizing word form) (Shaywitz et al., 2006). A different area in the left hemisphere—the intraparietal sulcus—seems to be critical for the development of a sense of numbers and is implicated in mathematics disorder (Fletcher et al., 2007). In contrast, there is no current evidence for specific deficits responsible for disorders of written expression.

reading disorder Reading performance significantly below the standard for that age level.

mathematics disorder Mathematics performance significantly below the standard for that age level.

disorder of written expression Condition in which writing performance is significantly below the standard for that age level.

stuttering Disturbance in the fluency and time patterning of speech (for example, sound and syllable repetitions or prolongations).

expressive language disorder Individual's problems in spoken communication, as measured by significantly low scores on standardized tests of expressive language relative to nonverbal intelligence test scores. Symptoms may include a markedly limited vocabulary or errors in verb tense.

selective mutism Developmental disorder characterized by the individual's consistent failure to speak in specific social situations despite speaking in other situations.

tic disorder Disruption in early development involving involuntary motor movements or vocalizations.

Table 13.1 Communication and Related Disorders

Disorder	Clinical Description	Statistics	Causes	Treatments
Stuttering	A disturbance in speech fluency—repeating syllables or words, prolonging certain sounds, making obvious pauses, or substituting words to replace ones that are difficult to articulate.	Occurs twice as often among boys as among girls. Begins most often in children younger than age 3, and 98% of cases occur before the age of 10. Approximately 80% of children who stutter before they enter school will no longer stutter after they have been in school a year or so (Kroll & Beitchman, 2009).	Multiple brain pathways appear to be involved, and genetic influences may be a factor (Kroll & Beitchman, 2009).	Regulated-breathing method—the person is instructed to stop speaking when a stuttering episode occurs and then to take a deep breath (exhale, then inhale) before proceeding (Bothe, Davidow, Bramlett, & Ingham, 2006). Altered auditory feedback (electronically changing speech feedback to people who stutter) (Lincoln, Packman, & Onslow, 2006). Forms of self-monitoring, in which people modify their own speech for the words they stutter (Venkatagiri, 2005).
Expressive language disorders	Limited speech in *all* situations. *Expressive language* (what is said) is significantly below *receptive language* (what is understood); the latter is usually average.	Occurs in 10% to 15% of children younger than 3 years of age and is almost five times as likely to affect boys as girls (Koyama, Beitchman, & Johnson, 2009).	An unfounded psychological explanation is that the children's parents may not speak to them enough. A biological theory is that middle ear infection is a contributory cause.	May be self-correcting and may not require special intervention.
Selective mutism	Persistent failure to speak in specific situations—such as school—despite the ability to do so (Kearney, 2010).	Occurs in less than 1% of children and most often between the ages of 5 and 7. More prevalent among girls than boys.	Not much is known. Anxiety is one possible cause (Bergman & Lee, 2009).	*Contingency management:* Giving children praise and reinforcers for speaking while ignoring their attempts to communicate in other ways. Reinforcing successive approximations to speaking (Bergman & Lee, 2009).
Tic disorders	Involuntary motor movements *(tics)*, such as head twitching, or vocalizations, such as grunts, that often occur in rapid succession, come on suddenly, and happen in idiosyncratic or stereotyped ways. In one type, *Tourette's disorder*, vocal tics often include the involuntary repetition of obscenities.	Of all children, up to 20% show some tics during their growing years, and 1 to 10 children out of every 1,000 have Tourette's disorder (Jummani & Coffey, 2009). Usually develops before the age of 14. High comorbidity between tics and ADHD and obsessive-compulsive disorder (Jummani & Coffey, 2009).	There are likely multiple vulnerability genes that influence the form and severity of tics (Jummani & Coffey, 2009).	*Psychological:* Self-monitoring, relaxation training, and habit reversal. *Pharmacological:* haloperidol; more recently, risperidone and ziprasidone.

© Cengage Learning 2013

You saw that Alice persisted despite the obstacles caused by her learning disorder and by the reactions of teachers and others. What helped her continue toward her goal when others choose, instead, to drop out of school? Psychological and motivational factors that have been reinforced by others seem to play an important role in the eventual outcome of people with learning disorders. Factors such as socioeconomic status, cultural expectations, parental interactions and expectations, and child management practices, together with existing neurological deficits and the types of support provided in the school, seem to determine outcome (Tannock, 2009b).

Treatment of Learning Disorders

As you will see in the case of intellectual disability, learning disorders primarily require educational intervention. Biological (drug) treatment is typically restricted to those individuals who may also have ADHD, which as we discussed involves impulsivity and an inability to sustain attention and can be helped with certain stimulant medications, such as methylphenidate (Ritalin). Educational efforts can be broadly categorized into (1) specific skills instruction, including instruction on vocabulary, finding the main idea, and finding facts in readings; and (2) strategy instruction, which includes efforts to improve cognitive skills through decision making and critical thinking (Fletcher et al., 2007).

Many programs are used to assist children with their problems related to learning. One approach that has received considerable research support is called Direct Instruction (Coyne et al., 2009). This program includes several components; among them are systematic instruction (using highly scripted lesson plans that place students together in small groups based on their progress) and teach for mastery (teaching students until they understand all concepts). In addition, children are constantly assessed and plans are modified based on progress or lack of progress. Direct Instruction and several related training

Courtesy of Laureate Learning Systems Inc.

▲ Specially designed computer games may help children with learning disorders improve their language skills.

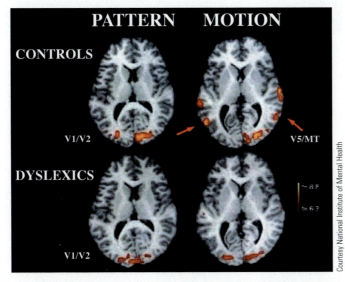

Courtesy National Institute of Mental Health

▲ These functional magnetic resonance imaging (fMRI) scans of composite data from six adults with dyslexia and eight controls show a horizontal slice through the brain, with the face at the top. Imaging shows atypical brain activity associated with dyslexia. The scans were performed while subjects tracked a pattern of moving dots on a computer screen. A brain area (V5/MT) normally active during such motion tasks did not switch on in dyslexic subjects *(right)*. Their brain activity was more similar to that of controls during a pattern recognition task *(left)*.

programs appear to significantly improve academic skills in children with learning disorders (Coyne et al., 2009).

How do these behavioral and educational approaches help children with reading difficulties? Are they just tricks or adaptations to learning, or do these treatments have a more profound effect on the way these children process information? Exciting research using brain-imaging technology is allowing us to answer these important questions. One study used functional magnetic resonance imaging scanning (fMRI) to compare how children with and without reading disorders processed simple tasks (Temple et al., 2003). The children with reading difficulties were then exposed to 8 weeks of intensive training on a computer program that helped them work on their auditory and language-processing skills. Not only did the children improve their reading skills, but also their brains started functioning in a way similar to the brains of their peers who were good readers. This and similar studies (Keller & Just, 2009) mirror results seen with other disorders—namely, that behavioral interventions can change the way the brain works and that we can use such interventions to help individuals with significant problems.

Pervasive Developmental Disorders

> How are pervasive developmental disorders defined?
> What are the three major characteristics of autistic disorder?

People with **pervasive developmental disorders** experience problems with language, socialization, and cognition (Durand, 2011). The word *pervasive* means that these problems are not relatively minor but significantly affect individuals throughout their lives. Included under the heading of pervasive developmental disorders are autistic disorder (or autism), **Asperger's disorder**, **Rett's disorder**, **childhood disintegrative disorder**, and **pervasive developmental disorder not otherwise specified**. We focus on two of the more prevalent pervasive developmental disorders—autistic disorder and Asperger's disorder; the other disorders are highlighted in Table 13.2. Note that discussions are under way to possibly reorganize these disorders under the title "autism spectrum disorders" in *DSM-5;* this spectrum of disorders would include autistic disorder (autism), Asperger's disorder, childhood disintegrative disorder, and pervasive developmental disorder not otherwise specified (American Psychiatric Association, 2010d).

Autistic Disorder

Autistic disorder (autism) is a childhood disorder characterized by significant impairment in social interactions and communication and by restricted patterns of behavior, interest, and activities (Durand, 2011). Individuals with this disorder have a puzzling array of symptoms. Consider the case of Amy.

Amy • In Her Own World

Amy, 3 years old, spends much of her day picking up pieces of lint. She drops the lint in the air and then watches intently as it falls to the floor. She also licks the back of her hands and stares at the saliva. She hasn't spoken yet and can't feed or dress herself. Several times a day she screams so loudly that the neighbors at first thought she was being abused. She doesn't seem to be interested in her mother's love and affection but will take her mother's hand to lead her to the refrigerator. Amy likes to eat butter—whole pats of it, several at a time. Her mother uses the pats of butter that you get at some restaurants to help Amy learn and to keep her well-behaved. If Amy helps with dressing herself, or if she sits quietly for several minutes, her mother gives her some butter. Amy's mother knows that the butter isn't good for her, but it is the only thing that seems to get through to the child. The family's pediatrician has been concerned about Amy's developmental delays for some time and has recently suggested that she be evaluated by specialists. The pediatrician thinks Amy may have autism and the child and her family will probably need extensive support.

Table 13.2 Additional Pervasive Developmental Disorders

Disorder	Clinical Description	Statistics	Causes	Treatments
Rett's disorder	A progressive neurological disorder that primarily affects girls. Includes constant hand-wringing, increasingly severe intellectual disability, and impaired motor skills, *after* typical development (Sigafoos et al., 2009). Motor skills deteriorate over time; social skills develop typically at first, decline between the ages of 1 and 3, and then partially improve. May be removed from *DSM-5* because it is minimally related to autism.	Rett's disorder is relatively rare, occurring in approximately 1 per 12,000 to 15,000 live female births.	A mutation of a gene on the X chromosome (MECP2) appears responsible for over 80% of cases (Toth & King, 2010).	Focuses on teaching self-help and communication skills and on efforts to reduce problem behaviors (Sigafoos et al., 2009).
Childhood disintegrative disorder	Involves severe regression in language, adaptive behavior, and motor skills after a 2- to 4-year period of normal development (Volkmar et al., 2009).	Rare, occurring in 1 of approximately every 100,000 births.	Although no specific cause has been identified, several factors suggest an accumulation of a number of rare genetic mutations (Volkmar et al., 2009).	Typically involves behavioral interventions to regain lost skills and behavioral and pharmacological treatments to help reduce behavioral problems.
Pervasive developmental disorder not otherwise specified	Severe and pervasive impairments in social interactions but without all criteria for autistic disorder. These individuals may not display the early avoidance of social interaction but still may exhibit significant social problems. Their problems may become more obvious after 3 years of age.	Little good evidence for prevalence at this time, although appears more common than autistic disorder.	Some of the same genetic influences and neurobiological impairments common in autism are likely involved in these individuals also (Volkmar et al., 2009).	Focuses on teaching socialization and communication skills and on efforts to reduce problem behaviors.

© Cengage Learning 2013

Clinical Description

Three major characteristics of autism are expressed in *DSM-IV-TR:* impairment in social interactions; impairment in communication; and restricted behavior, interests, and activities (American Psychiatric Association, 2000).

Impairment in Social Interactions. One of the defining characteristics of people with autistic disorder is that they do not develop the types of social relationships expected for their age (Volkmar, Klin, Schultz, & State, 2009). Amy never made friends among her peers and often limited her contact with adults to using them as tools—for example, taking the adult's hand to reach for something she wanted. For young children, the signs of social problems usually include a failure to engage in skills such as joint attention (Dawson et al., 2004; MacDonald et al., 2006). When sitting with a parent in front of a favorite toy, young children will typically look back and forth between the parent and the toy, smiling, in an attempt to engage the parent with the toy. However, this skill in joint attention is noticeably absent in children with autism.

Research using sophisticated eye-tracking technology shows how this social awareness problem evolves as the children grow older. In one study, scientists showed an adult man with autism scenes from some movies and compared how he looked at social scenes with how a man without

autism did so (Klin, Jones, Schultz, Volkmar, & Cohen, 2002). You can see from the photo that the man with autism (indicated by the red lines) scanned nonsocial aspects of the scene (the actors' mouth and jacket), whereas the man without autism looked at the socially meaningful sections (looking from eye to eye of the people conversing). This research suggests that people with autism—for reasons not yet fully understood—may not be interested in social situations and

pervasive developmental disorders One of several wide-ranging, significant, and long-lasting dysfunctions that appear before the age of 18.

Asperger's disorder Pervasive developmental disorder characterized by impairments in social relationships and restricted or unusual behaviors but without the language delays seen in autism.

Rett's disorder Progressive neurological developmental disorder featuring constant hand-wringing, mental retardation, and impaired motor skills.

childhood disintegrative disorder Pervasive developmental disorder involving severe regression in language, adaptive behavior, and motor skills after a 2- to 4-year period of normal development.

pervasive developmental disorder not otherwise specified Wide-ranging, significant, and long-lasting dysfunctions that appear before the age of 18.

autistic disorder (autism) Pervasive developmental disorder characterized by significant impairment in social interactions and communication and restricted patterns of behavior, interest, and activity. Also known as *autism*.

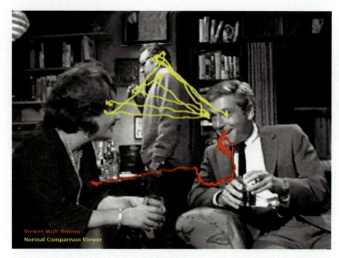

▲ Researchers are exploring how people with autism view social interactions among other people. (Reprinted with permission from the *American Journal of Psychiatry*, (Copyright 2002). American Psychiatric Association.)

therefore may not enjoy meaningful relationships with others or have the ability to develop them.

Impairment in Communication. People with autism nearly always have severe problems with communicating. About one third never acquire speech (Tager-Flusberg et al., 2009). In those with some speech, much of their communication is unusual. Some repeat the speech of others, a pattern called echolalia we referred to earlier as a sign of delayed speech development. If you say, "My name is Eileen, what's yours?" they will repeat all or part of what you said: "Eileen, what's yours?" Often, not only are your words repeated, but so is your intonation. Some people with autism who can speak are unable or unwilling to carry on conversations with others.

Restricted Behavior, Interests, and Activities. The more striking characteristics of autism include *restricted patterns of behavior, interests,* and *activities.* Amy appeared to like things to stay the same: She became extremely upset if even a small change was introduced (such as moving her toys in her room). This intense preference for the status quo has been called *maintenance of sameness.* Often, people with autism spend countless hours in *stereotyped and ritualistic behaviors,* making such stereotyped movements as spinning around in circles, waving their hands in front of their eyes with their heads cocked to one side, or biting their hands (Durand, 2011).

Statistics

Autism was once thought to be a rare disorder, although more recent estimates of its occurrence seem to show an increase in its prevalence. Previous estimates found a rate of 2 to 20 per 10,000 people, although it is now believed to be as high as 1 in every 500 births (Shattuck, 2006). The prevalence of autism spectrum disorders (which include autistic disorder, pervasive developmental disorder not otherwise specified, and Asperger's disorder) is estimated as high as 1 in every 110 births (Centers for Disease Control and Prevention, 2009). This rise in the rates may be the result of increased awareness on the part of professionals

who now distinguish the pervasive developmental disorders from intellectual disability. However, other environmental factors (such as exposure to toxic chemicals) cannot as yet be ruled out as contributing to this rise.

Gender differences for autism vary depending on the IQ level of the person affected. For people with IQs under 35, autism is more prevalent among females; in the higher IQ range, it is more prevalent among males. The reason for these differences is not known (Centers for Disease Control and Prevention, 2009). Autistic disorder appears to be a universal phenomenon, identified in every part of the world, including Sweden (Gillberg, 1984), Japan (Sugiyama & Abe, 1989), Russia (Lebedinskaya & Nikolskaya, 1993), and China (Chung, Luk, & Lee, 1990). Most people with autism develop the associated symptoms before the age of 36 months (American Psychiatric Association, 2000).

People with autism have a range of IQ scores. Earlier estimates placed the rate of intellectual disability among children with autism as high as 75%, although more recent work—using more appropriate tests for these children—indicates the range between 40% and 55% (Chakrabarti & Fombonne, 2001; Edelson, 2006). This means that 45% to 60% of people with autism have average or above-average IQs.

IQ measures are used to determine prognosis: The higher children score on IQ tests, the less likely they are to need extensive support by family members or people in the helping professions. Conversely, young children with autistic disorder who score poorly on IQ tests are more likely to be severely delayed in acquiring communication skills and to need a great deal of educational and social support as they grow older. Usually, language abilities and IQ scores are reliable predictors of how children with autistic disorder will fare later in life: The better the language skills and IQ test performance, the better the prognosis (Ben Itzchak, Lahat, Burgin, & Zachor, 2008).

Causes: Psychological and Social Dimensions

Autism is a puzzling condition, so you should not be surprised to find numerous theories of why it develops. One theory is that autistic disorder probably does not have a single cause (Durand, 2011; Volkmar et al., 2009). Instead, a number of biological contributions may combine with psychosocial influences to result in the unusual behaviors of people with autism.

Historically, autistic disorder was seen as the result of failed parenting (Bettelheim, 1967; Ferster, 1961; Tinbergen & Tinbergen, 1972). Mothers and fathers of children with autism were characterized as perfectionistic, cold, and aloof (Kanner, 1949), with relatively high socioeconomic status (Allen, DeMyer, Norton, Pontius, & Yang, 1971; Cox, Rutter, Newman, & Bartak, 1975) and higher IQs than the general population (Kanner, 1943). These views were devastating to a generation of parents, who felt guilty and responsible for their children's problems. More sophisticated research using larger samples of children and families suggests that the parents of individuals with autism may not differ substantially from parents of children without disabilities (Bhasin & Schendel, 2007).

Other theories about the origins of autism were based on the unusual speech patterns of some individuals—namely, their tendency to avoid first-person pronouns such as *I* and *me* and to use *he* and *she* instead. For example, if you ask a child with autism, "Do you want something to drink?" he might say, "He wants something to drink" (meaning "I want something to drink"). This observation led some theorists to wonder whether autism involves a lack of self-awareness (Goldfarb, 1963; Mahler, 1952). Such a debilitating view of the world was used to explain the unusual ways people with autism behaved. Theorists suggested that the withdrawal seen among people with autistic disorder reflected a lack of awareness of their own existence.

However, later research has shown that some people with autistic disorder do seem to have self-awareness (Lind & Bowler, 2009) and that it follows a developmental progression. Just like children without a disability, those with cognitive abilities below the level expected for a child of

Abnormal Psychology Inside Out, produced by Ira Wohl, Only Child Motion Pictures

Autism: Christina

"Last year she used [the communication book] a lot more in communicating with us. We have different pictures in the book. They're called picture symbols to represent what she might want, what she might need, what she's asking of us."

Go to Psychology CourseMate at www.cengagebrain.com to watch this video.

18 to 24 months show little or no self-recognition, but people with more advanced abilities do demonstrate self-awareness. Self-concept may be lacking when people with autism also have cognitive disabilities or delays, not because of autism itself.

Myths about people with autism are perpetuated when the idiosyncrasies of the disorder are highlighted. These perceptions are furthered by portrayals such as Dustin Hoffman's in *Rain Man*—his character could, for instance, instantaneously and accurately count hundreds of toothpicks falling to the floor. This type of ability—referred to as savant skills—is just not typical with autism. It is important always to separate myth from reality and to be aware that such portrayals do not accurately represent the full range of manifestations of this complex disorder.

The phenomenon of echolalia, repeating a word or phrase spoken by another person, was once believed to be an unusual characteristic of this disorder. Subsequent work in developmental psychopathology, however, has demonstrated that repeating the speech of others is part of the normally developing language skills observed in most young children (Dawson, Mottron, & Gernsbacher, 2008). Even a behavior as disturbing as the self-injurious behavior sometimes seen in people with autism is observed in milder forms, such as head banging, among typically developing infants (de Lissovoy, 1961). This type of research has helped clinicians isolate the facts from the myths about autism and clarify the role of development in the disorder. One generally accepted conclusion is that social deficiencies are the primary distinguishing characteristic of people with autism.

Causes: Biological Dimensions

To the relief of many families, it is now clear that poor parenting is not responsible for autism. Deficits in such skills as socialization and communication appear to be biological in origin.

Genetic Influences. It is now clear that autism has a genetic component (Volkmar, Klin, & Schultz, 2005). Families that have one child with autism have a 5% to 10% risk of having another child with the disorder. This rate is 50 to 200 times the risk in the general population, providing strong evidence of a genetic component in the disorder. One area that is receiving attention involves the genes responsible for the brain chemical oxytocin. Because oxytocin is shown to have a role in how we bond with others and in our social memory, researchers are looking for whether

Abnormal Psychology Inside Out, produced by Ira Wohl, Only Child Motion Pictures

genes responsible for this neurochemical are involved with the disorder. Preliminary work identifies an association between autism and an oxytocin receptor gene (Wermter et al., 2010), and researchers expect more connections will be identified in the coming years.

Neurobiological Influences. As in the area of genetics, many neurobiological influences are being studied to help explain the social and communication problems observed in autism (Volkmar et al., 2009). One intriguing theory involves research on the amygdala—the area of the brain that, as you saw in Chapter 4, is involved in emotions such as anxiety and fear. Researchers studying the brains of people with autism after they died note that adults with and without the disorder have amygdalae of about the same size but that those with autism have fewer neurons in this structure (Schumann & Amaral, 2006). Earlier research showed that young children with autism actually have a larger amygdala. The theory being proposed is that the amygdala in children with autism is enlarged early in life—causing excessive anxiety and fear (perhaps contributing to their social withdrawal). With continued stress, the release of the stress hormone cortisol damages the amygdala, causing the relative absence of these neurons in adulthood. The damaged amygdala may account for the different way people with autism respond to social situations (Lombardo, Chakrabarti, & Baron-Cohen, 2009).

An additional neurobiological influence we mentioned in the section on genetics involves the neuropeptide oxytocin. Remember that this is an important social neurochemical that influences bonding and is found to increase trust and reduce fear. Some research on children with autism found lower levels of oxytocin in their blood (Modahl et al., 1998), and giving people with autism oxytocin improved their ability to remember and process information with emotion content (such as remembering happy faces), a problem that is symptomatic of autism (Guastella et al., 2010).

▲ Temple Grandin has a PhD in animal science and a successful career designing humane equipment for handling livestock. She also has autism.

Frederick M. Brown/Getty Images

One highly controversial theory is that mercury—specifically, the mercury previously used as a preservative in childhood vaccines (thimerosol)—is responsible for the increases seen in autism over the last decade. Large epidemiological studies conducted in Denmark show that there is no increased risk of autism in children who are vaccinated (Madsen et al., 2002; Parker, Schwartz, Todd, & Pickering, 2004). Despite this and other convincing evidence, the correlation between when a child is vaccinated for measles, mumps, and rubella (12–15 months) and when the symptoms of autism first become evident (before 3 years) continues to fuel the belief by many families that there must be some connection.

Asperger's Disorder

Asperger's disorder involves a significant impairment in the ability to engage in meaningful social interaction, along with restricted and repetitive stereotyped behaviors but without the severe delays in language or other cognitive skills characteristic of people with autism (American Psychiatric Association, 2000). First described by Hans Asperger in 1944, it was Lorna Wing in the early 1980s who recommended that Asperger's disorder be reconsidered as a separate disorder from autism, with an emphasis on the unusual and limited interests (such as train schedules) displayed by these individuals (Volkmar et al., 2009).

Clinical Description

People with Asperger's disorder display impaired social relationships and restricted or unusual behaviors or activities (such as following airline schedules or memorizing

▲ Timothy plays violin and piano, and baseball. Autistic disorder occurs in all cultures and races.

Courtesy Lee-Yun Chu

ZIP codes), but unlike individuals with autism they can often be quite verbal. This tendency to be much more interested with esoteric facts than people, along with their often formal and academic style of speech, has led some to refer to the disorder as the "little professor syndrome." Individuals with Asperger's disorder show few severe cognitive impairments and usually have IQ scores within the average range (Volkmar et al., 2009). They often exhibit clumsiness and poor coordination. Some researchers think Asperger's disorder may be a milder form of autism rather than a separate disorder.

Statistics

Until recently, most diagnosticians were relatively unfamiliar with Asperger's disorder, and it is generally believed that many individuals with the disorder went undiagnosed. Current estimates of the prevalence are between 1 and 2 per 10,000, and it is believed to occur more often in boys than in girls (Volkmar et al., 2009).

Causes

Little research about the causes of Asperger's disorder exists, although a possible genetic contribution is suspected. Asperger's disorder does seem to run in families, and there appears to be a higher prevalence of both autism and Asperger's disorder in some families. Because of the social–emotional disturbances observed in people with this disorder, as you just saw with autism, researchers are looking at the amygdala for its possible role in the cause (Schultz, Romanski, & Tsatsanis, 2000), although to date there is no conclusive evidence for a specific biological or psychological model.

Treatment of Pervasive Developmental Disorders

Most treatment research has focused on children with autism, so we primarily discuss treatment research for these individuals. However, because treatment for all of the pervasive developmental disorders relies on a similar approach, this research should be relevant across disorders. One generalization that can be made about autism, and the other pervasive developmental disorders, is that no completely effective treatment exists. Attempts to eliminate the social problems experienced by these individuals have not been successful to date. Rather, like the approach to individuals with intellectual disability, most efforts at treating people with pervasive developmental disorders focus on enhancing their communication and daily living skills and on reducing problem behaviors, such as tantrums and self-injury (Durand, 2011). We describe some of these approaches next, including work on early intervention for young children with autism.

Problems with communication and language are among the defining characteristics of this disorder. People with autism often do not acquire meaningful speech; they tend either to have limited speech or to use unusual speech, such as echolalia. Teaching people to speak in a useful way is difficult. Think about how we teach languages: It mostly involves imitation. Imagine how you would teach a young girl to say the word *spaghetti*. You could wait for several days until she said a word that sounded something like *spaghetti* (maybe *confetti*) and then reinforce her. You could then spend several days or weeks trying to shape *confetti* into something closer to *spaghetti*. Or you could just prompt, "Say 'spaghetti.'" Fortunately, most children can imitate and learn to communicate efficiently. But a child who has autism can't or won't imitate.

In the mid-1960s, the late Ivar Lovaas and his colleagues took a monumental first step toward addressing the difficulty of getting children with autism to respond. They used the basic behavioral procedures of shaping and discrimination training to teach these nonspeaking children to imitate others verbally (Lovaas, Berberich, Perloff, & Schaeffer, 1966). The first skill the researchers taught the children was to imitate other people's speech. They began by reinforcing a child with food and praise for making any sound while watching the teacher. After the child mastered that step, they reinforced the child only if she made a sound after the teacher made a request—such as the phrase, "Say 'ball'" (a procedure known as *discrimination training*). Once the child reliably made some sound after the teacher's request, the teacher used *shaping* to reinforce only approximations of the requested sound, such as the sound of the letter "b." Sometimes the teacher helped the child with physical prompting—in this case, by gently holding the lips together to help the child make the sound of "b." Once the child responded successfully, a second word was introduced—such as "mama"—and the procedure was repeated. This continued until the child could correctly respond to multiple requests, demonstrating imitation by copying the words or phrases made by the teacher. Once the children could imitate, speech was easier, and progress was made in teaching some of them to use labels, plurals, sentences, and other more complex forms of language (Lovaas, 1977). Despite the success of some children in learning speech, other children do not respond to this training, and workers sometimes use alternatives to vocal speech, such as sign language and devices that have vocal output and can literally "speak" for the child (Tager-Flusberg et al., 2009).

One of the most striking features of people with autism is their unusual reactions to other people. Although social deficits are among the more obvious problems experienced by people with autism, they can also be the most difficult to teach. A number of approaches are now used to teach social skills (for example, how to carry on a conversation and ask questions of other people), including the use of peers who do not have autism as trainers, and there is evidence that those with autism can improve their socialization skills (e.g., Cotugno, 2009).

Lovaas and his colleagues at the University of California, Los Angeles, reported on their early intervention efforts with young children (Lovaas, 1987). They used intensive behavioral treatment for communication and social skills problems for 40 hours or more per week, which seemed to improve intellectual and educational functioning. Follow-up suggests that these improvements are long lasting (McEachin, Smith, & Lovaas, 1993). These studies created considerable interest and controversy. Some critics question the research on practical, and experimental, grounds, claiming that one-on-one therapy for 40 hours per week was too expensive and time consuming; they also criticized the studies for having no proper control group. Nevertheless, the findings from this important work and a number of replications around the world suggest that early intervention is promising for children with autism (Eldevik et al., 2009).

Biological Treatments

No one medical treatment has been found to cure autism. In fact, medical intervention has had little success on the core symptoms of social and language difficulties. A variety of pharmacological treatments are used to decrease agitation, and the major tranquilizers and serotonin-specific reuptake inhibitors seem helpful here (Volkmar et al., 2009).

Because autism may result from a variety of deficits, it is unlikely that one drug will work for everyone with this disorder. Much current work is focused on finding pharmacological treatments for specific behaviors or symptoms.

Integrating Treatments

The treatment of choice for people with pervasive developmental disorder—including autism and Asperger's disorder—combines various approaches to the many facets of this disorder. For children, most therapy consists of school education with special psychological supports for problems with communication and socialization. Behavioral approaches have been most clearly documented as benefiting children in this area. Pharmacological treatments can help some of them temporarily. Parents also need support because of the great demands and stressors involved in living with and caring for such children. As children with autism grow older, intervention focuses on efforts to integrate them into the community, often with supported living arrangements and work settings. Because the range of abilities of people with autism is so great,

however, these efforts differ dramatically. Some people are able to live in their own apartments with only minimal support from family members. Others, with more severe forms of cognitive impairment, require more extensive efforts to support them in their communities.

Concept Check 13.2

Determine how well you are able to diagnose the disorder in each of the following situations by labeling them (a) autistic disorder, (b) Asperger's disorder, (c) Rett's disorder, (d) childhood disintegrative disorder, or (e) pervasive developmental disorder.

1. Six-year-old Tangelique has a low IQ and enjoys sitting in the corner by herself, where she arranges her toys or spins around in circles. She is unable to communicate verbally. She throws temper tantrums when her routine is changed even in the slightest way or when her parents try to get her to do something she doesn't want to do. _____

2. At an early age, Dwight became preoccupied with geography and could name all of the state capitals. His speech development was not delayed, but he does not like to play with other children or to be touched or held. _____

3. Five-year-old Alicia has increasingly severe intellectual disability and is beginning to have trouble walking on her own. One of the characteristics of her disorder is constant hand-wringing.

   _____

4. Once Rolondo turned 5, his parents noticed that his motor skills and language abilities were beginning to regress dramatically. _____

5. Six-year-old Megan doesn't entirely avoid social interactions, but she experiences many problems in communicating and dealing with people.

   _____

Intellectual Disability

> How is intellectual disability defined, and what categories are used to classify people with intellectual disabilities?

Intellectual disability (ID) (previously referred to as mental retardation) is a disorder evident in childhood as significantly below-average intellectual and adaptive functioning (Toth & King, 2010). People with intellectual disability experience difficulties with day-to-day activities to an extent that reflects both the severity of their cognitive deficits and the type and amount of assistance they receive. Perhaps more than any other group you have studied in

this text, people with intellectual disability have throughout history received treatment that can best be described as shameful (Scheerenberger, 1983). With notable exceptions, societies throughout the ages have devalued individuals whose intellectual abilities are deemed less than adequate. Although *DSM-IV-TR* uses the term "mental retardation," we use "intellectual disability" throughout this chapter to be consistent with changes in terminology in

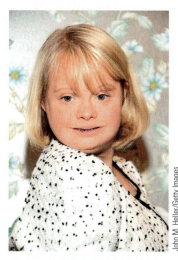

▲ Lauren Potter (an actress with Down syndrome) plays "Becky Jackson" in the popular television show *Glee*.

this field and possible changes in *DSM-5* (American Psychiatric Association, 2010b).

The manifestations of intellectual disability are varied. Some individuals function quite well, even independently, in our complex society. For example, Chris Burke (an actor with Down syndrome) was the first actor with an intellectual disability to star in a television series (*Life Goes On*) and also appeared on *Touched by an Angel*. Also, Lauren Potter (another actor with Down syndrome) played a cheerleader in the television show *Glee*. Others with intellectual disability have significant cognitive and physical impairments and require considerable assistance to carry on day-to-day activities. Consider the case of James.

James ┆ Up to the Challenge

James's mother contacted us because he was disruptive at school and at work. James was 17 and attended the local high school. He had Down syndrome and was described as likable and, at times, mischievous. He enjoyed skiing, bike riding, and many other activities common among teenage boys. His desire to participate was a source of some conflict between him and his mother: He wanted to take the driver's education course at school, which his mother felt would set him up for failure, and he had a girlfriend he wanted to date, a prospect that also caused his mother concern.

School administrators complained because James didn't participate in activities such as physical education, and at the work site that was part of his school program he was often sullen, sometimes lashing out at the supervisors. They were considering moving him to a program with more supervision and less independence.

James's family had moved often during his youth, and they experienced striking differences in the way each community responded to James and his intellectual disability. In some school districts, he was immediately placed in classes with other children his age and his teachers were provided with additional assistance and consultation. In others, it was just as quickly recommended that he be taught separately. Sometimes the school district had a special classroom

in the local school for children with intellectual disability. Other districts had programs in other towns, and James would have to travel an hour to and from school each day. Every time he was assessed in a new school, the evaluation was similar to earlier ones. He received scores on his IQ tests in the range of 40 to 50, which placed him in the moderate range of intellectual disability. Each school gave him the same diagnosis: Down syndrome with moderate intellectual disability.

In high school, James had several academic classes in a separate classroom for children with learning problems, but he participated in some classes, such as gym, with students who did not have intellectual disability. His current difficulties in gym (not participating) and at work (being oppositional) were jeopardizing his placement in both programs. When I spoke with James's mother, she expressed frustration that the work program was beneath him because he was asked to do boring, repetitive work such as folding paper. James expressed a similar frustration, saying that he was treated like a baby. He could communicate fairly well when he wanted to, although he sometimes would become confused about what he wanted to say and it was difficult to understand everything he tried to articulate. On observing him at school and at work, and after speaking with his teachers, we realized that a common paradox had developed. James resisted work he thought was too easy. His teachers interpreted his resistance to mean that the work was too hard for him, and they gave him even simpler tasks. He resisted or protested more vigorously, and they responded with even more supervision and structure.

Clinical Description

People with intellectual disability display a broad range of abilities and personalities. Individuals like James, who have mild or moderate impairments, can, with proper preparation, carry out most of the day-to-day activities expected of any of us. Those with more severe impairments may need help to eat, bathe, and dress themselves, although with proper training and support they can achieve a degree of independence. These individuals experience impairments that affect most areas of functioning. Language and communication skills are often the most obvious. James was only mildly impaired in this area, needing help with articulation. In contrast, people with more severe forms of intellectual disability may never learn to use speech as a form of communication, requiring alternatives such as sign lan-

intellectual disability A diagnosis received when one achieves a significantly below-average score on a test of intelligence and by limitations in the ability to function in areas of daily life.

A. Significantly subaverage intellectual functioning: an IQ of approximately 70 or below on an individually administered IQ test (for infants, a clinical judgment of significantly subaverage intellectual functioning).

B. Concurrent deficits or impairments in present adaptive functioning (i.e., the person's effectiveness in meeting the standards expected for his or her age by his or her cultural group) in at least two of the following areas: communication, selfcare, home living, social/interpersonal skills, use of community resources, self-direction, functional academic skills, work, leisure, health, and safety.

C. The onset is before age 18 years.

Source: Reprinted with permission from *Diagnostic and Statistical Manual of Mental Disorders* (4th ed., text revision). © 2000 American Psychiatric Association.

guage or special communication devices to express even their most basic needs. Because many cognitive processes are adversely affected, individuals with intellectual disability have difficulty learning, the level of challenge depending on how extensive the cognitive disability is.

Before examining the specific criteria for intellectual disability, note that, like the personality disorders we described in Chapter 11, intellectual disability is included on Axis II of *DSM-IV-TR*. Remember that separating disorders by axes serves two purposes: first, indicating that disorders on Axis II tend to be more chronic and less amenable to treatment, and second, reminding clinicians to consider whether these disorders, if present, are affecting an Axis I disorder. People can be diagnosed on both Axis I (for example, generalized anxiety disorder) and Axis II (for example, mild intellectual disability).

The *DSM-IV-TR* criteria for intellectual disability are in three groups. First, a person must have *significantly subaverage intellectual functioning*, a determination made with one of several IQ tests with a cutoff score set by *DSM-IV-TR* of approximately 70. Roughly 2% to 3% of the population score at 70 or below on these tests. The American Association on Intellectual and Developmental Disabilities (AAIDD), which has its own, similar definition of intellectual disability, has a cutoff score of approximately 70 to 75 (Thompson et al., 2009; Toth & King, 2010).

The second criterion of both *DSM-IV-TR* and the AAIDD definitions for intellectual disability calls for *concurrent deficits or impairments in adaptive functioning*. In other words, scoring "approximately 70 or below" on an IQ test is not sufficient for a diagnosis of intellectual disability; a person must also have significant difficulty in at least two of the following areas: communication, self-care, home living, social and interpersonal skills, use of community resources, self-direction, functional academic skills, work, leisure, health, and safety. To illustrate, although James had many strengths, such as his ability to communicate and his social and interpersonal skills (he had several good friends), he was not as proficient as other teenagers at caring for himself in areas such as home living, health, and safety or in academic areas. This aspect of the definition is important because it excludes

people who can function quite well in society but for various reasons do poorly on IQ tests. The final criterion for intellectual disability is the *age of onset*. The characteristic below-average intellectual and adaptive abilities must be evident before the person is 18. This cutoff is designed to identify affected individuals when the brain is developing and therefore when any problems should become evident. The age criterion rules out the diagnosis of intellectual disability for adults who suffer from brain trauma or forms of dementia that impair their abilities. The imprecise definition of intellectual disability brings up an important issue: Intellectual disability, perhaps more than any of the other disorders, is defined by society. The cutoff score of 70 or 75 is based on a statistical concept (two or more standard deviations from the mean), not on qualities inherent in people who supposedly have intellectual disability. There is little disagreement about the diagnosis for people with the most severe disabilities; however, the majority of people diagnosed with intellectual disability are in the mild range of cognitive impairment. They need some support and assistance, but remember that the criteria for using the label of intellectual disability are based partly on a somewhat arbitrary cutoff score for IQ that can (and does) change with changing social expectations.

People with intellectual disability differ significantly in their degree of disability. Almost all classification systems have differentiated these individuals in terms of their ability or on the cause of the intellectual disability (Toth & King, 2010). Traditionally (and still evident in *DSM-IV-TR*), classification systems have identified four levels of intellectual disability: *mild*, which is identified by an IQ score between 50–55 and 70; *moderate*, with a range of 35–40 to 50–55; *severe*, ranging from 20–25 to 35–40; and *profound*, which includes people with IQ scores below 20–25. It is difficult to categorize each level of intellectual disability according to "average" individual achievements by people at each level. A person with severe or profound intellectual disability tends to have extremely limited formal communication skills (no spoken speech or only one or two words) and may require great or even total assistance in dressing, bathing, and eating. Yet people with these diagnoses have a range of skills that depend on training and the availability of other supports. Similarly, people like James, who have mild or moderate intellectual disability, should be able to live independently or with minimal supervision; again, however, their achievement depends partly on their education and the community support available to them.

Perhaps the most controversial change being suggested in the new AAIDD definition of intellectual disability is its description of different levels of this disorder, which are based on the level of support or assistance people need: *intermittent, limited, extensive,* or *pervasive* (Thompson et al., 2009). The important difference is that the AAIDD system identifies the role of "needed supports" in determining level of functioning, whereas *DSM-IV-TR* implies that the ability of the person is the sole determining factor. The AAIDD system focuses on specific areas of assistance a person needs that can then be translated into training goals. Whereas his *DSM-IV-TR* diagnosis might be "moder-

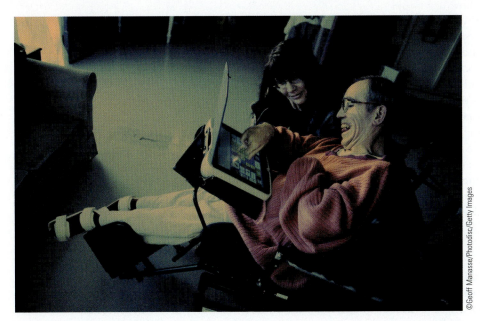

▲ Although he cannot speak, this man is learning to communicate with an eye-gaze board, pointing to or simply looking at the image that conveys his message.

the *DSM-IV-TR* system; time will tell whether the AAIDD categories will be widely adopted.

Statistics

Approximately 90% of people with intellectual disability fall under the label of mild intellectual disability (IQ of 50 to 70). When you add individuals with moderate, severe, and profound intellectual disability (IQ below 50), the total population of people with this disorder represents 1% to 3% of the general population (Toth & King, 2010).

The course of intellectual disability is chronic, meaning that people do not go through periods of remission, such as with substance use disorders or anxiety disorders. However, the prognosis for people with this disorder varies considerably. Given appropriate training and support, individuals with less severe forms of intellectual disability can live relatively independent and productive lives. People with more severe impairments require more assistance to participate in work and community life.

ate intellectual disability," James might receive the following AAIDD diagnosis: "a person with intellectual disability who needs limited supports in home living, health and safety, and in academic skills." The AAIDD definition emphasizes the types of support James and others require, and it highlights the need to identify what assistance is available when considering a person's abilities and potential. However, at this writing, the AAIDD system has not been assessed empirically to determine whether it has greater value than traditional *(DSM)* systems.

An additional method of classification has been used in the educational system to identify the abilities of students with intellectual disability. It relies on three categories: *educable intellectual disability* (based on an IQ of 50 to approximately 70–75), *trainable intellectual disability* (IQ of 30 to 50), and *severe intellectual disability* (IQ below 30) (Cipani, 1991). The assumption is that students with educable intellectual disability (comparable to mild intellectual disability) could learn basic academic skills; students with trainable intellectual disability (comparable to moderate intellectual disability) could not master academic skills but could learn rudimentary vocational skills; and students with severe intellectual disability (comparable to severe and profound intellectual disability) would not benefit from academic or vocational instruction. Built into this categorization system is the automatic negative assumption that certain individuals cannot benefit from certain types of training. This system and the potentially stigmatizing and limiting *DSM-IV-TR* categories (mild, moderate, severe, and profound intellectual disability) inspired the AAIDD categorization of needed supports. Current trends are away from the educational system of classification because it inappropriately creates negative expectations in teachers. Clinicians continue to use

Causes

There are literally hundreds of known causes of intellectual disability, including the following:

Environmental: For example, deprivation, abuse, and neglect
Prenatal: For instance, exposure to disease or drugs while still in the womb
Perinatal: Such as difficulties during labor and delivery
Postnatal: For example, infections and head injury

▲ Intellectual disability can be defined in terms of the level of support people need.

As we mentioned in Chapter 10, heavy use of alcohol among pregnant women can produce a disorder in their children called *fetal alcohol syndrome*, a condition that can lead to severe learning disabilities. Other prenatal factors that can produce intellectual disability include the pregnant woman's exposure to disease and chemicals and poor nutrition. In addition, lack of oxygen (anoxia) during birth and malnutrition and head injuries during the developmental period can lead to severe cognitive impairments. Despite the large number of known causes of intellectual disability, it's important to remember one fact: Nearly 25% of cases either cannot be attributed to any known cause or are thought to be the result of social and environmental influences (Toth & King, 2010).

Biological Dimensions

Most research on the causes of intellectual disability focuses on biological influences. We next look at biological dimensions that appear to be responsible for the more common forms of intellectual disability.

Genetic Influences. Almost 300 genes have been identified as having the potential to contribute to intellectual disability, and it is expected that there are many more (Inlow & Restifo, 2004). A portion of the people with more severe intellectual disability have identifiable single-gene disorders, involving a *dominant gene* (expresses itself when paired with a normal gene), a *recessive gene* (expresses itself only when paired with another copy of itself), or an *X-linked gene* (present on the X or sex chromosome).

Only a few dominant genes result in intellectual disability, probably because of natural selection: Someone who carries a dominant gene that results in intellectual disability is less likely to have children and thus less likely to pass the gene to offspring. Therefore, this gene becomes less likely to continue in the population. However, some people, especially those with mild intellectual disability, do marry and have children, thus passing on their genes. One example of a dominant gene disorder, *tuberous sclerosis*, is relatively rare, occurring in one of approximately every 30,000 births. About 60% of the people with this disorder have intellectual disability, and most have seizures (uncontrolled electrical discharges in the brain) and characteristic bumps on the skin that during their adolescence resemble acne (Curatolo, Bombardieri, & Jozwiak, 2008).

The next time you drink a diet soda, notice the warning, "Phenylketonurics: Contains Phenylalanine." This is a caution for people with the recessive disorder called **phenylketonuria (PKU)**, which affects one of every 14,000 newborns and is characterized by an inability to break down a chemical in our diets called phenylalanine. Until the mid-1960s, the majority of people with this disorder had intellectual disability, seizures, and behavior problems, resulting from high levels of this chemical. However, researchers developed a screening technique that identifies the existence of PKU; infants are now routinely tested at birth, and any individuals identified with PKU can be successfully treated with a special diet that avoids the chemical phenyl-alanine. This is a rare example of the successful prevention of one form of intellectual disability.

Because untreated maternal PKU can harm the developing fetus, there is concern now that women with PKU who are of childbearing age may not stick to their diets and inadvertently cause PKU-related intellectual disability in their children before birth. Many physicians recommend dietary restriction through the person's lifetime and especially during the childbearing period—thus the warnings on products with phenylalanine (Widaman, 2009).

Lesch-Nyhan syndrome, an X-linked disorder, is characterized by intellectual disability; signs of cerebral palsy (spasticity or tightening of the muscles); and self-injurious behavior, including finger and lip biting (Nyhan, 1978). Only males are affected because a recessive gene is responsible; when it is on the X chromosome in males, it does not have a normal gene to balance it because males do not have a second X chromosome. Women with this gene are carriers and do not show any of the symptoms.

As our ability to detect genetic defects improves, more disorders will be identified genetically. The hope is that our increased knowledge will be accompanied by improvements in our ability to treat or, as in the case of PKU, prevent intellectual disability and other negative outcomes.

Chromosomal Influences. It was only about 50 years ago that the number of chromosomes in human cells—46—was correctly identified (Tjio & Levan, 1956). Three years later, researchers found that people with Down syndrome (the disorder James displayed) had an additional small chromosome (Lejeune, Gauthier, & Turpin, 1959). Since that time, a number of other chromosomal aberrations that result in intellectual disability have been identified. We describe Down syndrome and fragile X syndrome in some detail, but there are hundreds of other ways in which abnormalities among the chromosomes can lead to intellectual disability.

Down syndrome, the most common chromosomal form of intellectual disability, was first identified by the British physician Langdon Down in 1866. Down had tried to develop a classification system for people with intellectual disability based on their resemblance to people of other races; he described individuals with this particular disorder as "mongoloid" because they resembled people from Mongolia (Scheerenberger, 1983). The term *mongoloidism* was used for some time but has been replaced with the term *Down syndrome*. The disorder is caused by the presence of an extra 21st chromosome and is therefore sometimes referred to as *trisomy 21*. For reasons not completely understood, during cell division two of the 21st chromosomes stick together (a condition called nondisjunction), creating one cell with one copy that dies and one cell with three copies that divide to create a person with Down syndrome.

People with Down syndrome have characteristic facial features, including folds in the corners of their upwardly slanting eyes, a flat nose, and a small mouth with a flat roof that makes the tongue protrude somewhat. Like

James, they tend to have congenital heart malformations. Tragically, adults with Down syndrome have a greatly increased risk of dementia of the Alzheimer's type, a degenerative brain disorder that causes impairments in memory and other cognitive disorders (Wiseman, Alford, Tybulewicz, & Fisher, 2009). This disorder among people with Down syndrome occurs earlier than usual (sometimes in their early 20s) and has led to the finding that at least one form of Alzheimer's disease is attributable to a gene on the 21st chromosome.

The incidence of children born with Down syndrome has been tied to maternal age: As the age of the mother increases, so does her chance of having a child with this disorder (see ■ Figure 13.2). A woman at age 20 has a one in 2,000 chance of having a child with Down syndrome, at the age of 35 this risk increases to one in 500, and at the age of 45 it increases again to one in 18 births (Girirajan, 2009). Despite these numbers, many more children with Down syndrome are born to younger mothers simply because younger mothers have more children. The reason for the rise in incidence with maternal age is not clear. Some suggest that because a woman's ova (eggs) are all produced in youth, the older ones have been exposed to toxins, radiation, and other harmful substances over longer periods. This exposure may interfere with the normal meiosis (division) of the chromosomes, creating an extra 21st chromosome (Pueschel & Goldstein, 1991). Others believe the hormonal changes that occur as women age are responsible for this error in cell division (Crowley, Hayden, & Gulati, 1982).

For some time, it has been possible to detect the presence of Down syndrome—but not the degree of intellectual disability—through **amniocentesis**, a procedure that involves removing and testing a sample of the fluid that surrounds the fetus in the amniotic sac, and through **chorionic villus sampling (CVS)**, in which a small piece of placenta tissue is removed and tested. These types of test are not always desirable because it is an invasive procedure (inserting a needle that could cause unwanted damage to the developing fetus). Fortunately, there are now more sophisticated tests of a mother's blood that can be used to detect Down syndrome as early as the first trimester of pregnancy (Schmitz, Netzer, & Henn, 2009).

Fragile X syndrome is a second common chromosomally related cause of intellectual disability (Toth & King, 2010). As its name suggests, this disorder is caused by an abnormality on the X chromosome, a mutation that makes the tip of the chromosome look as though it were hanging from a thread, giving it the appearance of fragility. As with Lesch-Nyhan syndrome, which also involves the X chromosome, fragile X primarily affects males because they do

Abnormal Psychology Inside Out, produced by Ira Wohl, Only Child Motion Pictures

Lauren: A Kindergartner with Down Syndrome

"The speech has been the most difficult . . . and communication naturally just causes tremendous behavior difficulties. . . . If there is not a way for her to communicate to us what her needs are and how she's feeling . . . it really causes a lot of actual shutdowns with Lauren. . . . She knows exactly what she wants and she is going to let you know even though she can't verbalize it.

Go to Psychology CourseMate at www.cengagebrain.com to watch this video.

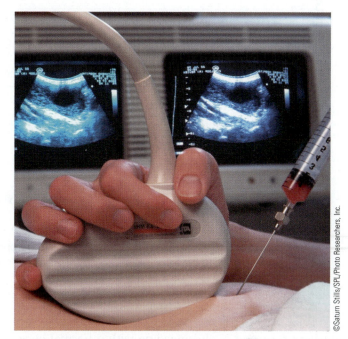

©Saturn Stills/SPL/Photo Researchers, Inc.

▲ Amniocentesis can detect the presence of Down syndrome in a fetus. Guided by an ultrasound image, the doctor withdraws amniotic fluid for analysis.

phenylketonuria (PKU) Recessive gene disorder involving the inability to break down a food chemical whose buildup causes mental retardation, seizures, and behavior problems. PKU can be detected by infant screening and prevented by a specialized diet.
Lesch-Nyhan syndrome X-linked gene disorder characterized by mental retardation, signs of cerebral palsy, and self-injurious behavior.
Down syndrome Type of mental retardation caused by a chromosomal aberration (chromosome 21) and involving characteristic physical appearance. Also known as *trisomy 21*.
amniocentesis Prenatal medical procedure that allows the detection of abnormalities (for example, Down syndrome) in the developing fetus. It involves removal and analysis of amniotic fluid from the mother.
chorionic villus sampling (CVS) A genetic test conducted during early pregnancy that samples cells found in the placenta (chorionic villi) and assesses possible genetic or chromosomal problems in the fetus.
fragile X syndrome Pattern of abnormality caused by a defect in the X chromosome resulting in mental retardation, learning problems, and unusual physical characteristics.

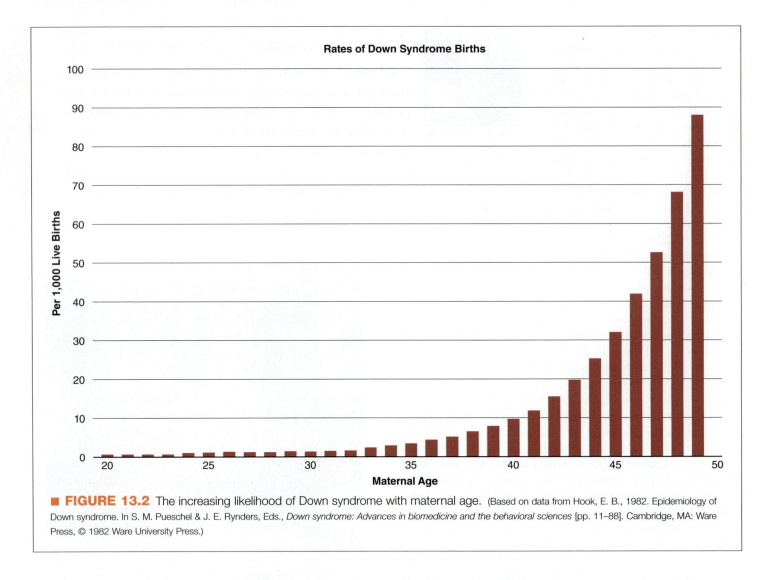

Rates of Down Syndrome Births

■ **FIGURE 13.2** The increasing likelihood of Down syndrome with maternal age. (Based on data from Hook, E. B., 1982. Epidemiology of Down syndrome. In S. M. Pueschel & J. E. Rynders, Eds., *Down syndrome: Advances in biomedicine and the behavioral sciences* [pp. 11–88]. Cambridge, MA: Ware Press, © 1982 Ware University Press.)

not have a second X chromosome with a normal gene to balance out the mutation. Unlike Lesch-Nyhan carriers, however, women who carry fragile X syndrome commonly display mild to severe learning disabilities (Koukoui & Chaudhuri, 2007). Men with the disorder display moderate to severe levels of intellectual disability and have higher rates of hyperactivity, short attention spans, gaze avoidance, and perseverative speech (repeating the same words again and again). In addition, such physical characteristics as large ears, testicles, and head circumference are common. Estimates are that one of every 4,000 males and one of every 8,000 females are born with fragile X syndrome (Toth & King, 2010).

Psychological and Social Dimensions

Up to 25% of the cases of intellectual disability fall in the mild range and are not associated with any obvious genetic or physical disorders. Sometimes referred to as **cultural–familial intellectual disability**, people with these characteristics are thought to have cognitive impairments that result from a combination of psychosocial and biological influences, although the specific mechanisms that lead to this type of intellectual disability are not yet understood.

The cultural influences that may contribute to this condition include abuse, neglect, and social deprivation.

It is sometimes useful to consider people with intellectual disability in two distinct groups: those with cultural–familial and those with biological (or "organic") forms of intellectual disability. People in the latter group have more severe forms of intellectual disability that are usually traceable to known causes such as fragile X syndrome. ■ Figure 13.3 shows that the cultural–familial group is composed primarily of individuals at the lower end of the IQ continuum (in other words, just part of the normal distribution), whereas in the organic group, genetic, chromosomal, and other factors affect intellectual performance which explains the "bump" in their numbers at that end of the distribution. The organic group increases the number of people at the lower end of the IQ continuum so that it exceeds the expected rate for a normal distribution (Toth & King, 2010).

Treatment

Biological treatment of intellectual disability is currently not a viable option. Generally, the treatment of individuals with intellectual disability parallels that of people with

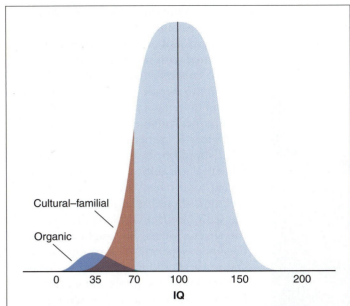

■ **FIGURE 13.3** The actual distribution of IQ scores for individuals with cultural–familial intellectual disability and organic intellectual disability. Note that the cultural–familial group represents the normal expected lower end of the continuum but the organic group is a separate and overlapping group. (Adapted, with permission, from Zigler, E., & Hodapp, R. M., 1986. *Understanding mental retardation.* Cambridge: Cambridge University Press, © 1986 Cambridge University Press.)

pervasive developmental disorders, attempting to teach them the skills they need to become more productive and independent. For individuals with mild intellectual disability, intervention is similar to that for people with learning disorders. Specific learning deficits are identified and addressed to help the student improve such skills as reading and writing. At the same time, these individuals often need additional support to live in the community. For people with more severe disabilities, the general goals are the same; however, the level of assistance they need is often more extensive. Remember that the expectation for all people with intellectual disability is that they will in some way participate in community life, attend school and later hold a job, and have the opportunity for meaningful social relationships. Advances in electronic and educational technologies have made this goal realistic even for people with profound intellectual disability.

Individuals with intellectual disability can acquire skills through the many behavioral innovations first introduced in the early 1960s to teach such basic self-care as dressing, bathing, feeding, and toileting to people with even the most severe disabilities (Durand, 2011). The skill is broken into its component parts (a procedure called a *task analysis*), and people are taught each part in succession until they can perform the whole skill. Performance on each step is encouraged by praise and by access to objects or activities the people desire (reinforcers). Success in teaching these skills is usually measured by the level of independence people can attain by using them. Typically, most in-

dividuals, regardless of their disability, can be taught to perform some skills.

Communication training is important for people with intellectual disability. Making their needs and wants known is essential for personal satisfaction and for participation in most social activities. The goals of communication training differ, depending on the existing skills. For people with mild levels of intellectual disability, the goals may be relatively minor (for example, improving articulation) or more extensive (for example, organizing a conversation) (Sigafoos, Arthur-Kelly, & Butterfield, 2006). Some, like James, have communication skills that are already adequate for day-to-day needs.

For individuals with the most severe disabilities, communication skills training can be particularly challenging because they may have multiple physical or cognitive deficits that make spoken communication difficult or impossible. Creative researchers, however, use alternative systems that may be easier for these individuals, including the sign language, used primarily by people with hearing disabilities, and *augmentative communication strategies*. Augmentative strategies may use picture books, teaching the person to make a request by pointing to a picture—for instance, pointing to a picture of a cup to request a drink (Sigafoos et al., 2009). A variety of computer-assisted devices can be programmed so that the individual presses a button to produce complete spoken sentences (for example, "Would you come here? I need your help."). People with limited communication skills can be taught to use these devices, which helps them reduce the frustration of not being able to relate their feelings and experiences to other people (Durand, in press).

Concern is often expressed by parents, teachers, and employers that some people with intellectual disability can be physically or verbally aggressive or may hurt themselves. Considerable debate has ensued over the proper way to reduce these behavior problems; the most heated discussions involve whether to use painful punishers (Repp & Singh, 1990). Alternatives to punishment that may be equally effective in reducing behavior problems such as aggression and self-injury (Durand, in press) include teaching people how to communicate their need or desire for such things as attention that they seem to be getting with their problem behaviors. Important advances are being made in significantly reducing even severe behavior problems for some people.

In addition to ensuring that people with intellectual disability are taught specific skills, caretakers focus on the important task of supporting them in their communities. "Supported employment" involves helping an individual find and participate satisfactorily in a competitive job (Hall, Butterworth, Winsor, Gilmore, & Metzel, 2007). Research

cultural–familial intellectual disability Mild form of mental retardation that may be caused largely by environmental influences.

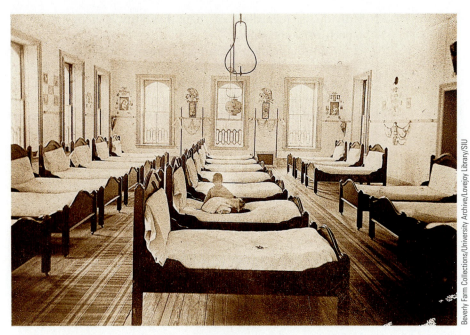

▲ The Illinois Asylum for Feeble-Minded Children, about 1880. Today, great efforts are made to keep children with intellectual disability in their homes and communities.

has shown not only that people with intellectual disability can be placed in meaningful jobs but also that, despite the costs associated with supported employment, it can be cost-effective (Sandys, 2007). The benefits to people who achieve the satisfaction of being a productive part of society are incalculable.

There is general agreement about *what* should be taught to people with intellectual disability. The controversy in recent years has been over *where* this teaching should take place. Should people with intellectual disability, especially the severe forms, be taught in specially designed separate classrooms or workshops, or should they attend their neighborhood public schools and work at local businesses? Increasingly, teaching strategies to help these students learn are being used in regular classrooms and in preparing them to work at jobs in the community (Frankel & Gold, 2007).

Prevention of Developmental Disorders

Prevention efforts for the developmental disorders outlined in this chapter are in their early stages of development. One such effort—early intervention—has been described for the pervasive developmental disorders and appears to hold considerable promise for some children. In addition, early intervention can target and assist children who, because of inadequate environments, are at risk for developing cultural–familial intellectual disability (Eldevik, Jahr, Eikeseth, Hastings, & Hughes, 2010). The national Head Start program is one such effort at early intervention; it combines educational, medical, and social supports for these children and their families. One project identified a group of children shortly after birth and provided them with an intensive preschool program, along with medical and nutritional supports. This intervention continued until the children began formal education in kindergarten (Martin, Ramey, & Ramey, 1990). The researchers of this study found that for all but one of the children in a control group who received medical and nutritional support but not the intensive educational experiences, each had IQ scores below 85 at age 3, but that 3-year-olds in the experimental group all tested above 85. Such findings are important because they show the potential for creating a lasting impact on the lives of children with developmental disorders and their families (Engle et al., 2007).

Although it appears that many children can make significant progress if interventions are initiated early in life (Eldevik et al., 2010), a number of important questions remain regarding early intervention efforts. Not all children,

for example, benefit significantly from such efforts, and future research will need to resolve a number of lingering concerns. For example, researchers need to determine how best to identify children and families who will benefit from such programs, how early in the child's development programs should begin, and how long to continue these early intervention programs to produce desirable outcomes.

Given recent advances in genetic screening and technology, it may someday be possible to detect and correct genetic and chromosomal abnormalities; related ongoing research could fundamentally change our approach to children with developmental disorders. For example, one study used mice that were genetically engineered to model fragile X syndrome found in many individuals with intellectual disability (Suvrathan, Hoeffer, Wong, Klann, & Chattarji, 2010). Researchers found that they could improve the functioning of certain glutamate receptors in the amygdala of the mice with a drug that blocks these receptors. The results were more normalized functioning between these neurons, a potential early medical intervention for children with fragile X disorder (Suvrathan et al., 2010). Someday, it may be possible for similar research to be performed prenatally on children identified as having syndromes associated with intellectual disability. For example, it may soon be possible to conduct prenatal gene therapy, where a developing fetus that has been screened for a genetic disorder may be the target of intervention before birth (Ye, Mitchell, Newman, & Batshaw, 2001).

This prospect is not without its difficulties, however (Durand, 2001). One cause of concern is the reliability of gene therapy. This technology is not sufficiently advanced to produce the intended results consistently. Currently, any such intervention may cause unwanted mutations or other complications, which in turn could be fatal to the fetus. Gene therapy will probably not be practical for those disorders that involve numerous genes, but rather may be limited to single-gene disorders such as PKU.

Concept Check 13.3

In the following situations, label each level of intellectual disability as mild, moderate, severe, or profound. Also label the corresponding levels of necessary support: intermittent, limited, extensive, or pervasive.

1. Kevin received an IQ score of 20. He needs help with all his basic needs, including dressing, bathing, and eating. _____, _____

2. Adam received an IQ score of 45. He lives in a fully staffed group home and needs a great deal of help with many tasks. He is beginning to receive training for a job in the community. _____, _____

3. Jessica received an IQ score of 30. She lives in a fully staffed group home where she is trained in basic adaptive skills and communication. She is improving over time and can communicate by pointing or using her eye-gaze board. _____, _____

4. LeBron received an IQ score of 65. He lives at home, goes to school, and is preparing to work when he is through with school. _____, _____

Cognitive Disorders

› **What are the symptoms of delirium and dementia?**
› **What are the principal causes of and treatments for amnestic disorder?**

Whereas intellectual disability and other learning disorders are believed to be present from birth, most cognitive disorders develop much later in life. In the rest of this chapter, we review three classes of cognitive disorders: *delirium,* an often temporary condition displayed as confusion and disorientation; *dementia,* a progressive condition marked by gradual deterioration of a range of cognitive abilities; and *amnestic disorders,* dysfunctions of memory resulting from a medical condition or a drug or toxin.

The label "cognitive disorders" in the *DSM-IV-TR* reflects a shift in the way these disorders are viewed (Sweet, 2009). In previous editions of the *DSM* they were labeled "organic mental disorders," along with mood, anxiety, personality, hallucinosis (an abnormal mental state involving hallucinations), and delusional disorders. The word *organic* indicated that brain damage or dysfunction was believed to be involved. Although brain dysfunction is still thought to be the primary cause of cognitive disorders, we now know that some dysfunction in the brain is involved in most disorders described in *DSM-IV-TR* (American Psychiatric Association Practice Guideline, 2000c).

Once the term *organic* was dropped, attention moved to developing a better label for delirium, dementia, and the amnestic disorders. The label "cognitive disorders" signifies that their predominant feature is the impairment of such cognitive abilities as memory, attention, perception, and thinking. Although disorders such as schizophrenia and depression also involve cognitive problems, cognitive issues are not believed to be primary characteristics. Problems still exist with this term, however, because, although the cognitive disorders usually first appear in older adults, mental retardation and learning disorders (which are apparent early) also have cognitive impairment as a predominant characteristic. Currently, discussions are under way for *DSM-5* to keep the label "delirium" but to combine the other cognitive disorders (such as dementia and amnestic disorders) and call them "neurocognitive disorders"; their dimensional quality would be specified as either the "major" or "minor" subtype (American Psychiatric Association, 2010). In part, this may be the result of the overlap of the different types of dementia (e.g., Alzheimer's disorder) and amnestic disorder found in people such that one person may actually suffer from multiple types of neurocognitive problems (Sweet, 2009).

As with certain other disorders, it may be useful to clarify why cognitive disorders are discussed in a textbook on abnormal psychology. Because they so clearly have organic causes, you could argue that they are purely medical concerns. You will see, however, that the consequences of a cognitive disorder often include profound changes in a person's behavior and personality. Intense anxiety, depression, or both are common, especially among people with dementia. In addition, paranoia is often reported, as are extreme agitation and aggression. Families and friends are also profoundly affected by such changes. Imagine your emotional distress as a loved one is transformed into a different person, often one who no longer remembers who you are or your history together. The deterioration of cognitive ability, behavior, and personality and the effects on others are major concerns for mental health professionals.

Delirium

The disorder known as **delirium** is characterized by impaired consciousness and cognition during the course of several hours or days. Delirium is one of the earliest-recognized mental disorders: Descriptions of people with these symptoms were written more than 2,400 years ago (Solai, 2009). Consider the case of Mr. J.

Mr. J. • Sudden Distress

Mr. J., an older gentleman, was brought to the hospital emergency room. He didn't know his own name, and at times he didn't seem to recognize his daughter, who was with him. Mr. J. appeared confused, disoriented, and a little agitated. He had difficulty speaking clearly and could not focus his attention to answer even the most basic questions. Mr. J.'s daughter reported that he had begun acting this way the night before, had been awake most of the time since then, was frightened, and seemed even more confused today. She told the nurse that this behavior was not normal for him and she was worried that he was becoming senile. She mentioned that his doctor had just changed his hypertension medication and wondered whether the new medication could be causing her father's distress. Mr. J. was ultimately diagnosed as having substance-induced delirium (a reaction to his new medication); once the medication was stopped, he improved significantly over the course of the next 2 days.

Clinical Description and Statistics

People with delirium appear confused, disoriented, and out of touch with their surroundings. They cannot focus and sustain their attention on even the simplest tasks. There are marked impairments in memory and language. Mr. J. had trouble speaking; he was not only confused but also couldn't remember basic facts, such as his own name. As you saw, the symptoms of delirium do not come on gradually but develop over hours or a few days, and they can vary over the course of a day.

Delirium is estimated to be present in as many as 30% of older adults who are admitted into acute care facilities such as emergency rooms (Fearing & Inouye, 2009). It is most prevalent among older adults, people undergoing medical procedures, cancer patients, and people with acquired immunodeficiency syndrome (AIDS). Delirium subsides relatively quickly. Once thought to be only a temporary problem, more recent work indicates that the effects of delirium may be more lasting (Cole, Ciampi, Belzile, &

Zhong, 2009). Some individuals continue to have problems on and off; some even lapse into a coma and may die. Many medical conditions that impair brain function have been linked to delirium, including intoxication by drugs and poisons; withdrawal from drugs such as alcohol and sedative, hypnotic, and anxiolytic drugs; infections; head injury; and various other types of brain trauma (Fearing & Inouye, 2009).

DSM Disorder Criteria Summary
Delirium

A. Disturbance of consciousness (i.e., reduced clarity of awareness of the environment) with reduced ability to focus, sustain, or shift attention.

B. A change in cognition (such as memory deficit, disorientation, language disturbance) or the development of a perceptual disturbance that is not better accounted for by a preexisting, established, or evolving dementia.

C. The disturbance develops over a short period of time (usually hours to days) and tends to fluctuate during the course of the day.

D. There is evidence from the history, physical examination, or laboratory findings that the disturbance is caused by the direct physiological consequences of a general medical condition.

Source: Reprinted with permission from *Diagnostic and Statistical Manual of Mental Disorders* (4th ed., text revision). © 2000 American Psychiatric Association.

Causes

DSM-IV-TR recognizes several causes of delirium among its subtypes. The criteria for delirium due to a general medical condition include a disturbance of consciousness (reduced awareness of the environment) and a change in cognitive abilities such as memory and language skills, occurring over a short period and brought about by a general medical condition. Other subtypes include the diagnosis received by Mr. J.—substance-induced delirium—and delirium due to multiple causes and delirium not otherwise specified. The rise in the use of drugs such as ecstasy (methylene-dioxymethamphetamine) is of particular concern because of such drugs' potential to produce delirium (Solai, 2009). The last two categories indicate the often complex nature of delirium.

That delirium can be brought on by the improper use of medication, which is a particular problem for older adults because they tend to use prescription medications more than any other age group. The risk of problems among the elderly is increased further because they tend to eliminate drugs from their systems less efficiently than younger individuals. It is not surprising, then, that adverse drug reactions resulting in hospitalization are almost 6 times higher among elderly people than in other age groups (Olivier et al., 2009). And it is believed that delirium is responsible for many of the falls that cause debilitating hip fractures in the elderly (Stenvall et al., 2006). Although there has been some improvement in the use of medication among older adults with physicians using more care with drug dosages and the use of multiple drugs, improper use continues to produce serious side effects, including symptoms of delirium (Olivier et al., 2009). Because possible combinations of illnesses and medications are so numerous, determining the cause of delirium is extremely difficult (Solai, 2009).

Delirium may be experienced by children who have high fevers or who are taking certain medications and is often mistaken for noncompliance (Smeets et al., 2010). It often occurs during the course of dementia; as many as 50% of people with dementia suffer at least one episode of delirium (Kwok, Lee, Lam, & Woo, 2008). Because many of the primary medical conditions can be treated, delirium is often reversed within a relatively short time. Yet, in about a quarter of cases, delirium can be a sign of the end of life (Wise, Hilty, & Cerda, 2001).

Factors other than medical conditions can trigger delirium. Age itself is an important factor; older adults are more susceptible to developing delirium as a result of mild infections or medication changes (Fearing & Inouye, 2009). Sleep deprivation, immobility, and excessive stress can also cause delirium (Solai, 2009).

Treatment

Delirium brought on by withdrawal from alcohol or other drugs is usually treated with haloperidol or other antipsychotic medications, which help calm the individual. Infections, brain injury, and tumors are given the necessary and appropriate medical intervention, which often then resolves the accompanying delirium. The antipsychotic drug haloperidol is also prescribed for individuals in acute delirium when the cause is unknown (Fearing & Inouye, 2009).

The recommended first line of treatment for a person experiencing delirium is psychosocial intervention. The goal of nonmedical treatment is to reassure the individual to help him or her deal with the agitation, anxiety, and hallucinations of delirium. A person in the hospital may be comforted by familiar personal belongings such as family photographs (Fearing & Inouye, 2009). Also, a patient who is included in all treatment decisions retains a sense of control (Katz, 1993). This type of psychosocial treatment can help the person manage during this disruptive period until the medical causes are identified and addressed. Some evidence suggests that this type of support can also delay institutionalization for elderly patients (Rahkonen et al., 2001).

Prevention

Preventive efforts may be most successful in assisting people who are susceptible to delirium. Proper medical care for illnesses and therapeutic drug monitoring can play significant roles in preventing delirium (Fearing & Inouye, 2009). For example, the increased number of older adults involved in managed care and patient counseling on drug use appear to have led to more appropriate use of prescription drugs among the elderly (U.S. General Accounting Office, 1995).

▲ Patients in care facilities are often comforted by having their personal belongings nearby.

©Richard Hutchings/PhotoEdit

Concept Check 13.4

Match the terms with the following descriptions of delirium: (a) memory, (b) cause, (c) counseling, (d) confused, (e) elderly, and (f) trauma.

1. Managed care and patient _____ have been successful in preventing delirium in older adults.

2. Treatment of delirium depends on the _____ of the episode and can include medications, psychosocial intervention, or both.

3. Delirium severely affects people's _____, making tasks such as recalling one's own name difficult.

4. The _____ population is at the greatest risk of experiencing delirium resulting from improper use of medications.

5. Various types of brain _____, such as head injury or infection, have been linked to delirium.

6. People who suffer from delirium appear to be _____ or out of touch with their surroundings.

delirium Rapid-onset reduced clarity of consciousness and cognition, with confusion, disorientation, and deficits in memory and language.

Dementia

Few things are more frightening than the possibility that you will one day not recognize those you love, that you will not be able to perform the most basic of tasks, and—worse yet—that you will be acutely aware of this failure of your mind. When family members show these signs, initially adult children often deny any difficulty, coming up with excuses ("I forget things, too") for their parents' failing abilities. **Dementia** is the cognitive disorder that makes these fears real: a gradual deterioration of brain functioning that affects judgment, memory, language, and other advanced cognitive processes. Dementia is caused by several medical conditions and by the abuse of drugs or alcohol that cause negative changes in cognitive functioning. Some of these conditions—for instance, infection or depression—can cause dementia, although it is often reversible through treatment of the primary condition. Some forms of the disorder, such as Alzheimer's disease, are at present irreversible. Although delirium and dementia can occur together, dementia has a gradual progression as opposed to delirium's acute onset; people with dementia are not disoriented or confused in the early stages, unlike people with delirium. Like delirium, however, dementia has many causes, including a variety of traumas to the brain such as stroke (which destroys blood vessels), the infectious diseases of syphilis and HIV, severe head injury, the introduction of certain toxic or poisonous substances, and diseases such as Parkinson's, Huntington's, and, the most common cause of dementia, Alzheimer's. Consider the personal account by Diana, a woman who poignantly writes of her experiences with this disorder (McGowin, 1993).

Diana • Humiliation and Fear

At the age of 45, Diana Friel McGowin was a successful legal assistant, wife, and mother, but she was beginning to experience "lapses." She writes about developing these problems just before a party she was planning for her family.

Nervously, I checked off the table appointments on a list retrieved from my jumpsuit pocket. Such a list had never been necessary before, but lately I noticed frequent little episodes of confusion and memory lapses.

I had decided to "cheat" on this family buffet and have the meal prepared on a carry-out basis. Cooking was also becoming increasingly difficult, due to what my children and my husband Jack teasingly referred to as my "absentmindedness." (pp. 1–2)

In addition to memory difficulties, other problems began at this time, including brief dizzy spells. Diana wrote of her family's growing awareness of the additional symptoms.

Shaun walked past me on his way to the kitchen, and paused. "Mom, what's up? You look ragged," he com-

mented sleepily. "Late night last night, plenty of excitement, and then up early to get your father off to work," I answered. Shaun laughed disconcertingly. I glanced up at him ruefully. "What is so funny?" I demanded. "You, Mom! You are talking as though you are drunk or something! You must really be tired!" (pp. 4–5)

In the early stages of her dementia, Diana tended to explain these changes in herself as temporary, with such causes as tension at work. However, the extent of her dysfunction continued to increase, and she had more frightening experiences. In one episode, she describes an attempt to drive home from a brief errand.

Suddenly, I was aware of car horns blowing. Glancing around, nothing was familiar. I was stopped at an intersection and the traffic light was green. Cars honked impatiently, so I pulled straight ahead, trying to get my bearings. I could not read the street sign, but there was another sign ahead; perhaps it would shed some light on my location. A few yards ahead, there was a park ranger building. Trembling, I wiped my eyes, and breathing deeply, tried to calm myself. Finally, feeling ready to speak, I started the car again and approached the ranger station. The guard smiled and inquired how he could assist me. "I appear to be lost," I began, making a great effort to keep my voice level, despite my emotional state. "Where do you need to go?" the guard asked politely. A cold chill enveloped me as I realized I could not remember the name of my street. Tears began to flow down my cheeks. I did not know where I wanted to go. (pp. 7–8)

Diana's difficulties continued. She sometimes forgot the names of her children, and once she astounded her nephew when she didn't recognize him. If she left home, she almost invariably got lost. She learned to introduce herself as a tourist from out of town because people would give her better directions. She felt as if there "was less of me every day than there was the day before" (p. 33).

During initial medical examinations, Diana didn't recall this type of problem in her family history. However, a look through some of her late mother's belongings revealed that she was not the first to experience symptoms of dementia.

Then I noticed the maps. After mother's death I had found mysterious hand drawn maps and bits of directions scribbled on note papers all over her home. They were in her purses, in bureau drawers, in the desks, seemingly everywhere. Too distraught at the time to figure out their purpose, I simply packed them all away with other articles in the box. Now I smoothed out each map and scrawled note, and placed them side by side. They covered the bedroom floor. There were maps to every place my mother went about town, even to my home and my brother's home. As I deciphered each note and map, I began recollecting my mother's other eccentric habits. She would not drive out of her neighborhood. She would not drive at night. She was teased by both myself and my brother about "memory goofs" and would become irate with both of her children over their loving teasing.

Then with a chill, I recalled one day when I approached my mother to tell her something, and she did not recognize me. (p. 52)

After several evaluations, which included magnetic resonance imaging (MRI) showing some damage in several parts of her brain, Diana's neurologist concluded that she had dementia. The cause could be a stroke she had had years before that damaged several small areas of her brain by breaking or blocking several blood vessels. The dementia could also indicate Alzheimer's disease. People at the same stage of decline as Diana will continue to deteriorate and eventually may die from complications of their disorder.

Clinical Description and Statistics

Depending on the individual and the cause of the disorder, the gradual progression of dementia may have somewhat different symptoms, although all aspects of cognitive functioning are eventually affected. In the initial stages, memory impairment is typically seen as an inability to register ongoing events. In other words, a person can remember how to talk and may remember events from many years ago but will have trouble remembering what happened in the past hour. For example, Diana still knew how to use the stove but couldn't remember whether she had turned it on or off.

Diana couldn't find her way home because visuospatial skills are impaired among people with dementia. **Agnosia,** the inability to recognize and name objects, is one of the most familiar symptoms. **Facial agnosia,** the inability to recognize even familiar faces, can be extremely distressing to family members. Diana failed to recognize not only her nephew but also coworkers she had seen daily for years. A general deterioration of intellectual function results from impairment in memory, planning, and abstract reasoning.

Perhaps partly because people suffering from dementia are aware that they are deteriorating mentally, emotional changes often occur also. Common side effects are delusions (irrational beliefs), depression, agitation, aggression, and apathy (Richards & Sweet, 2009). Again, it is difficult to establish the cause-and-effect relationship. It is not known how much behavioral change is caused by progressive brain deterioration directly and how much is a result of the frustration and discouragement that inevitably accompany the loss of function and the isolation of "losing" loved ones. Cognitive functioning continues to deteriorate until the person requires almost total support to carry out day-to-day activities. Ultimately, death occurs as the result of inactivity, combined with the onset of other illnesses, such as pneumonia.

Dementia can occur at almost any age, although this disorder is more frequent in older adults. Current estimates in the United States suggest a prevalence of a little more than 5% in people older than 65; this rate increases to 20% to 40% in those older than 85 (Richards & Sweet, 2009). Estimates of the increasing number of people with just one form of dementia—dementia of the Alzheimer's type—are alarming. Table 13.3 illustrates how the prevalence of dementia of the Alzheimer's type is projected to dramatically increase in older adults, partly as a result of the increase of baby boomers who will become senior citizens (Hebert, Scherr, Bienias, Bennett, & Evans, 2003). Among the eldest of adults, research on centenarians (people 100 years and older) indicates that up to 100% showed signs of dementia (Imhof et al., 2007). Dementia of the Alzheimer's type rarely occurs in people under 45 years of age.

A problem with confirming prevalence figures for dementia is that survival rates alter the outcomes. Because adults are generally living longer and therefore more are at greater risk of developing dementia, it is not surprising that dementia is more prevalent. Incidence studies, which count the number of new cases in a year, may thus be the most reliable method for assessing the frequency of dementia, especially among the elderly. Research shows that the rate for new cases doubles with every 5 years of age after age 75. Many studies find greater increases of dementia among women (Richards & Sweet, 2009), although this may be because of the tendency of women to live longer. Dementia of the Alzheimer's type may, as we discuss later, be more prevalent among women. Together, results suggest that dementia is a relatively common disorder among older adults and the chances of developing it increase rapidly after the age of 75.

In addition to the human costs of dementia, the financial costs are staggering. Estimates of the costs of caring for people with dementia of the Alzheimer's type are often quoted to be about $100 billion per year in the United

Table 13.3 Estimates of Prevalence of Alzheimer's Disease in the United States Through 2050 (in millions)

Year	Age 65–74	Age 75–84	Age 85 and Older
2000	0.3	2.4	1.8
2010	0.3	2.4	2.4
2020	0.3	2.6	2.8
2030	0.5	3.8	3.5
2040	0.4	5.0	5.6
2050	0.4	4.8	8.0

Source: Adapted from Hebert, L. E., Scherr, P. A., Bienias, J. L., Bennett, D. A., & Evans, D. A. (2003). Alzheimer disease in the U.S. population: Prevalence estimates using the 2000 Census. *Archives of Neurology, 60,* 1119–1122.

dementia Gradual-onset deterioration of brain functioning, involving memory loss, inability to recognize objects or faces, and problems in planning and abstract reasoning. These are associated with frustration and discouragement.
agnosia Inability to recognize and name objects; may be a symptom of dementia or other brain disorders.
facial agnosia Type of agnosia characterized by a person's inability to recognize even familiar faces.

▲ People with facial agnosia, a common symptom of dementia, are unable to recognize faces, even of their closest friends and relatives.

called the disorder an "atypical form of senile dementia"; thereafter, it was referred to as **Alzheimer's disease**.

The *DSM-IV-TR* diagnostic criteria for **dementia of the Alzheimer's type** include multiple cognitive deficits that develop gradually and steadily. Predominant are impairment of memory, orientation, judgment, and reasoning. The inability to integrate new information results in failure to learn new associations. Individuals with Alzheimer's disease forget important events and lose objects. Their interest in nonroutine activities narrows. They tend to lose interest in others and, as a result, become more socially isolated. As the disorder progresses, they can become agitated, confused, depressed, anxious, or even combative. Many of these difficulties become more pronounced late in the day—in a phenomenon referred to as "sundowner syndrome"—perhaps as a result of fatigue or a disturbance in the brain's biological clock (Lemay & Landreville, 2010).

People with dementia of the Alzheimer's type also display one or more other cognitive disturbances, including aphasia (difficulty with language), apraxia (impaired motor functioning), agnosia (failure to recognize objects), or difficulty with activities such as planning, organizing, sequencing, or abstracting information. These cognitive impairments have a serious negative impact on social and occupational functioning, and they represent a significant decline from previous abilities.

Research using brain scans is being conducted on people with mild cognitive impairment to see whether changes in brain structure early in the development of Alzheimer's disease can be detected, which can lead to early diagnosis. In the past, a definitive diagnosis of Alzheimer's disease could be made only after an autopsy determined that certain characteristic types of damage were present in the brain. However, there is now growing evidence that the use of sophisticated brain scans along with new chemical tracers may soon be able to help clinicians identify the presence of Alzheimer's disease before the significant declines in cognitive abilities (through a project called the Alzheimer's Disease Neuroimaging Initiative [ADNI]) or death (Weiner et al., 2010). Currently, to make a diagnosis without direct examination of the brain, a simplified version of a mental status exam is used to assess language and memory problems (see Table 13.3).

In an interesting, somewhat controversial study—referred to as the "Nun Study"—the writings of a group of Catholic nuns collected over several decades appeared to indicate early in life which women were most likely to develop Alzheimer's disease later (Snowdon et al., 1996). Researchers observed that samples from the nuns' journals over the years differed in the number of ideas each contained, which the scientists called "idea density." In other words, some sisters described events in their lives simply: "I was born in Eau

States. One estimate indicates that the total worldwide societal cost of dementia is more than $315 billion (Wimo, Winblad, & Jonsson, 2007). However, these numbers do not factor in the costs to businesses for health care in the form of insurance and for those who care for these individuals—estimated to be more than $140 billion in the United States alone (Weiner et al., 2010). Many times, family members care for an afflicted person around the clock, which is an inestimable personal and financial commitment (Richards & Sweet, 2009).

The statistics on prevalence and incidence cover dementias that arise from a variety of causes. *DSM-IV-TR* groups are based on presumed cause, but determining the cause of dementia is an inexact process. Sometimes, as with dementia of the Alzheimer's type, clinicians rely on ruling out alternative explanations—identifying all the things that are not the cause—instead of determining the precise origin.

Five classes of dementia based on etiology have been identified: (1) dementia of the Alzheimer's type; (2) vascular dementia; (3) dementia due to other general medical conditions; (4) substance-induced persisting dementia; (5) dementia due to multiple etiologies; and (6) dementia not otherwise specified, when cause cannot be determined. We emphasize dementia of the Alzheimer's type because of its prevalence (almost half of those with dementia exhibit this type) and the relatively large amount of research conducted on its etiology and treatment.

Dementia of the Alzheimer's Type

The German psychiatrist Alois Alzheimer first described the disorder that bears his name in 1907. He wrote of a 51-year-old woman who had a "strange disease of the cerebral cortex" that manifested as a progressive memory impairment and other behavioral and cognitive problems, including suspiciousness (Richards & Sweet, 2009). He

by repetitive **head trauma** that can provoke distinctive neurodegeneration (Gavett, Stern, Cantu, Nowinski, & McKee, 2010). In their effect on cognitive ability, all of these disorders are comparable to the other forms of dementia we have discussed so far.

The **human immunodeficiency virus type 1 (HIV-1)**, which causes AIDS, can also cause dementia (Rappaport & Berger, 2010). This impairment seems to be independent of the other infections that accompany HIV; in other words, the HIV infection itself seems to be responsible for the neurological impairment. The early symptoms of dementia resulting from HIV are cognitive slowness, impaired attention, and forgetfulness. Affected individuals also tend to be clumsy, to show repetitive movements such as tremors and leg weakness, and to become apathetic and socially withdrawn.

People with HIV seem particularly susceptible to impaired thinking in the later stages of HIV infection, although significant declines in cognitive abilities may occur earlier. Cognitive impairments were highly common among those infected with AIDS, but with the introduction of new medications (highly active antiretroviral therapies, or HAARTs) less than 10% of patients now experience dementia (Neugroschi et al., 2005). HIV-1 accounts for a relatively small percentage of people with dementia compared to Alzheimer's disease and vascular causes, but its presence can complicate an already-devastating set of medical conditions.

Like dementia from Parkinson's disease, Huntington's disease, and several other causes, dementia resulting from HIV is sometimes referred to as *subcortical dementia* because it affects primarily the inner areas of the brain, below the outer layer called the cortex (Bourgeois, Seaman, & Servis, 2003). The distinction between cortical (including dementia of the Alzheimer's type) and subcortical dementia is important because of the different expressions of dementia in these two categories (see Table 13.3). **Aphasia**, which involves impaired language skills, occurs among people with dementia of the Alzheimer's type but not among people with subcortical dementia. In contrast, people with subcortical dementia are more likely to experience severe depression and anxiety than those with dementia of the Alzheimer's type. In general, motor skills including speed and coordination are impaired early on among those with subcortical dementia. The differing patterns of impairment can be attributed to the different areas of the brain affected by the disorders causing the dementia.

Parkinson's disease is a degenerative brain disorder that affects about 1 in every 1,000 people worldwide (Marsh & Margolis, 2009). Movie and television star Michael J. Fox and former Attorney General Janet Reno both suffer from this progressive disorder. Motor problems are characteristic among people with Parkinson's disease, who tend to have stooped posture, slow body movements (called *bradykinesia*), tremors, and jerkiness in walking. The voice is also affected; afflicted individuals speak in a soft monotone. The changes in motor movements are the result of damage to dopamine pathways. Because dopamine is involved in complex movement, a reduction in this neurotransmitter makes affected individuals increasingly unable to control their

muscle movements, which leads to tremors and muscle weakness. The course of the disease varies widely, with some individuals functioning well with treatment.

It is estimated that about 75% of people who survive more than 10 years with Parkinson's disease develop dementia; conservative estimates place the rate at 4 to 6 times that found in the general population (Aarsland & Kurz, 2010). The pattern of impairments for these individuals fits the general pattern of subcortical dementia (see Table 13.3).

Jed Jacobsohn/Getty Images Entertainment/Getty Images

▲ Michael J. Fox provides his time and celebrity status to efforts to cure Parkinson's disease, a degenerative disease that is severely affecting his life.

Huntington's disease is a genetic disorder that initially affects motor movements, typically in the form of *chorea*, involuntary limb movements (Marsh & Margolis, 2009). People with Huntington's disease can live for 20 years after the first signs of the disease appear, although skilled nursing care is often required during the last stages. Just as with Parkinson's disease, only a portion of people with Huntington's disease go on to display dementia— somewhere between 20% and 80%—although some researchers believe that all patients with Huntington's disease would eventually display dementia if they lived long enough (Marsh & Margolis, 2009). Dementia resulting from Huntington's disease also follows the subcortical pattern.

For some time, researchers have known that the disease is inherited as an autosomal dominant disorder, meaning that approximately 50% of the offspring of an adult with Huntington's disease will develop the disease. Since 1979, behavioral scientist Nancy Wexler and a team of researchers have been studying the largest known extended family in the world afflicted by Huntington's disease, in small villages in Venezuela. The villagers have cooperated with the research, partly because Wexler herself lost her mother,

vascular dementia Progressive brain disorder involving loss of cognitive functioning, caused by blockage of blood flow to the brain, that appears concurrently with other neurological signs and symptoms.

head trauma Injury to the head and, therefore, to the brain, typically caused by accidents; can lead to cognitive impairments, including memory loss.

human immunodeficiency virus type 1 (HIV-1) Disease that causes AIDS.

aphasia Impairment or loss of language skills resulting from brain damage caused by stroke, Alzheimer's disease, or other illness or trauma.

Parkinson's disease Degenerative brain disorder principally affecting motor performance (for example, tremors and stooped posture) associated with reduction in dopamine. Dementia may be a result as well.

Huntington's disease Genetic disorder marked by involuntary limb movements and progressing to dementia.

three uncles, and her maternal grandfather to Huntington's disease, and she, too, may develop the disorder (Wexler & Rawlins, 2005). Using genetic linkage analysis techniques (see Chapter 3), these researchers first mapped the deficit to an area on chromosome 4 (Gusella et al., 1983) and then identified the elusive gene (Huntington's Disease Collaborative Research Group, 1993). Finding that one gene causes a disease is exceptional; research on other inherited mental disorders typically points to multiple gene (polygenic) influences.

Pick's disease is a rare neurological condition—occurring in about 5% of those people with dementia—that produces a cortical dementia similar to that of Alzheimer's disease. The course of this disease is believed to last from 5 to 10 years, although its cause is as yet unknown (Richards & Sweet, 2009). Like Huntington's disease, Pick's disease usually occurs relatively early in life—during a person's 40s or 50s—and is therefore considered an example of presenile dementia. An even rarer condition, **Creutzfeldt-Jakob disease**, is believed to affect only one in every million individuals (Heath et al., 2010). An alarming development in the study of Creutzfeldt-Jacob disease is the finding of 10 cases of a new variant that may be linked to bovine spongiform encephalopathy, more commonly referred to as "mad cow disease" (Neugroschi et al., 2005). This discovery led to a ban on exporting beef from the United Kingdom because the disease might be transmitted from infected cattle to humans. We do not yet have definitive information about the link between mad cow disease and the new form of Creutzfeldt-Jacob disease (Wiggins, 2009).

Substance-Induced Persisting Dementia

Prolonged drug use, especially combined with poor diet, can damage the brain and, in some circumstances, can lead to dementia. This impairment unfortunately lasts beyond the period involved in intoxication or withdrawal from these substances.

DSM-IV-TR identifies several drugs that can lead to symptoms of dementia, including alcohol, inhalants such as glue or gasoline (which some people inhale for the euphoric feeling they produce), and sedative, hypnotic, and anxiolytic drugs (see Chapter 10). These drugs pose a threat because they create dependence, making it difficult for a user to stop ingesting them. The resulting brain damage can be permanent and can cause the same symptoms as seen in dementia of the Alzheimer's type. The *DSM-IV-TR* criteria for substance-induced persisting dementia are essentially the same as those for the other forms of dementia; they include memory impairment and at least one of the following cognitive disturbances: aphasia (language disturbance), apraxia (inability to carry out motor activities despite intact motor function), agnosia (failure to recognize or identify objects despite intact sensory function), or a disturbance in executive functioning (such as planning, organizing, sequencing, and abstracting).

Causes of Dementia

A complete description of what is known about the origins of this type of brain impairment is beyond the scope of this book, but we highlight some insights available for more common forms of dementia.

Biological Influences. Cognitive abilities can be adversely compromised in many ways. As you have seen, dementia can be caused by a number of processes: Alzheimer's disease, Huntington's disease, Parkinson's disease, head trauma, substance abuse, and others. The most common cause of dementia, Alzheimer's disease, is also the most mysterious. Because of its prevalence and our relative ignorance about the factors responsible for it, Alzheimer's disease has held the attention of many researchers, who are trying to find the cause and ultimately a treatment or cure for this devastating condition.

A lesson in scientific caution comes from research that demonstrates a negative correlation between cigarette smoking and Alzheimer's disease (Brenner et al., 1993). In other words, the study found that smokers are less likely than nonsmokers to develop Alzheimer's disease. Does this mean smoking has a protective effect, shielding a person against the development of this disease? On close examination, the finding may instead be the result of the differential survival rates of those who smoke and those who do not. In general, nonsmokers tend to live longer and are thereby more likely to develop Alzheimer's disease, which appears later in life. Some even believe the relative inability of cells to repair themselves, a factor that may be more pronounced among people with Alzheimer's disease, may interact with cigarette smoking to shorten the lives of smokers who are at risk for Alzheimer's disease (Riggs, 1993). Put another way, smoking may exacerbate the degenerative process of Alzheimer's disease, causing people with the disease who also smoke to die earlier than nonsmokers who have Alzheimer's disease. These types of studies and the conclusions drawn from them should make us sensitive to the complicated nature of the disorders.

What do we know about Alzheimer's disease, the most common cause of dementia? After the death of the patient he described as having a "strange disease of the cerebral cortex," Alois Alzheimer performed an autopsy. He found that the brain contained large numbers of tangled, strandlike filaments within the brain cells (referred to as *neurofibrillary tangles*). This type of damage occurs in everyone with Alzheimer's disease. A second type of degeneration results from gummy protein deposits—called *amyloid plaques* (also referred to as *neuritic* or *senile plaques*)—that accumulate between the neurons in the brains of people with this disorder. Amyloid plaques are also found in older adults who do not have symptoms of dementia, but they have far fewer of them than do individuals with Alzheimer's disease (Richards & Sweet, 2009). Both forms of damage—neurofibrillary tangles and amyloid plaques—accumulate over the years and are believed to produce

Table 13.4 Characteristics of Dementias

Characteristic	Dementia of the Alzheimer's Type	Subcortical Dementias
Language	Aphasia (difficulties with articulating speech)	No aphasia
Memory	Both recall and recognition are impaired	Impaired recall; normal or less impaired recognition
Visuospatial skills	Impaired	Impaired
Mood	Less severe depression and anxiety	More severe depression and anxiety
Motor speed	Normal	Slowed
Coordination	Normal until late in the progression	Impaired

Source: Adapted, with permission of Oxford University Press, from Cummings, J. L. (Ed.) (1990). *Subcortical dementia.* New York, NY: Oxford University Press, © 1990 Jeffrey L. Cummings.

the characteristic cognitive disorders we have been describing.

These two types of degeneration affect extremely small areas and can be detected only by a microscopic examination of the brain. As mentioned earlier, scientists are close, however, to developing the neuroimaging technology that may soon detect the early development of these types of brain cell damage without having to rely on an autopsy (Weiner et al., 2010). In addition to having neurofibrillary tangles and amyloid plaques, over time the brains of many people with Alzheimer's disease atrophy (shrink) to a greater extent than would be expected through normal aging (Richards & Sweet, 2009). Because brain shrinkage has many causes, however, only by observing the tangles and plaques can a diagnosis of Alzheimer's disease be properly made.

Rapid advances are being made toward uncovering the genetic bases of Alzheimer's disease (e.g., Seshadri et al., 2010). As with most other behavioral disorders we have examined, multiple genes seem to be involved in the development of Alzheimer's disease. Table 13.4 illustrates what we know so far. Genes on chromosomes 21, 19, 14, 12, and 1 have all been linked to certain forms of Alzheimer's disease (Neugroschi et al., 2005). The link to chromosome 21 was discovered first, and it resulted from the unfortunate observation that individuals with Down syndrome, who have three copies of chromosome 21 instead of the usual two, developed the disease at an unusually high rate (Report of the Advisory Panel on Alzheimer's Disease, 1995). More recent work has located relevant genes on other chromosomes. These discoveries indicate that there is

more than one genetic cause of Alzheimer's disease. Some forms, including the one associated with chromosome 14, have an early onset. Diana may have an early-onset form because she started noting symptoms at the age of 45. In contrast, Alzheimer's disease associated with chromosome 19 seems to be a late-onset form of the disease that has an effect only after the age of about 60.

Some genes that are now identified are **deterministic**, meaning that if you have one of these genes you have a nearly 100% chance of developing Alzheimer's disease (Bettens, Sleegers, & Van Broeckhoven, 2010). Deterministic genes such as the precursor gene for small proteins called *amyloid beta peptides* (also referred to as beta-amyloid or Aβ) and the *Presenilin 1* and *Presenilin 2* genes will inevitably lead to Alzheimer's disease, but, fortunately, these genes are also rare in the general population. For treatment purposes, this means that even if researchers can find a way to prevent these genes from leading to Alzheimer's disease, it will only help a relatively small number of people. However, some genes—including the *apolipoprotein E4 (apo E4)* gene—are known as **susceptibility** genes. These genes only slightly increase the risk of developing Alzheimer's disease, but in contrast to the deterministic genes, these are more common in the general population (Bettens et al., 2010). If future research can find ways to interfere with the apo E4 gene, many people will be helped.

Although closing in on the genetic origins of Alzheimer's disease has not brought immediate treatment implications, researchers are nearer to understanding how the disease develops, which may result in medical interventions. Genetic research has advanced our knowledge of how the amyloid plaques develop in the brains of people with Alzheimer's disease and may hold a clue to its origins. In the core of the plaques is a solid waxy substance made up of Aβ. Just as cholesterol buildup on the walls of blood vessels chokes the blood supply, deposits of Aβ are believed by some researchers to cause the cell death associated with Alzheimer's disease (Gatz, 2007). This type of research holds the potential for better understanding the complex nature of Alzheimer's disease and may lead to important prevention strategies (such as lowering cholesterol levels and exercising regularly) (Pedersen, 2010).

For all disorders described in this book, we have identified the role of biological, psychological, or both types of

Pick's disease Rare neurological disorder that results in presenile dementia.

Creutzfeldt-Jakob disease Extremely rare condition that causes dementia.

deterministic In genetics, genes that lead to nearly a 100% chance of developing the associated disorder. These are rare in the population.

susceptibility In genetics, genes that only slightly increase the risk of developing the disorder, but in contrast to the deterministic genes, these are more common in the population.

stressors as partially responsible for the onset of the disorder. Does dementia of the Alzheimer's type—which appears to be a strictly biological event—follow the same pattern? One of the leading candidates for an external contributor to this disorder is head trauma. As we have seen, it appears that repeated blows to the head can bring on *dementia pugilistica*, named after the boxers who suffer from this type of dementia. Fighters who carry the apo E4 gene may be at greater risk for developing dementia attributed to head trauma (Jordan et al., 1997). In addition to boxers, news accounts suggest links to the trauma experienced by NFL players and the development of dementia in these former athletes (Schwarz, 2007). Because it is now known that not only boxers are affected by this type of dementia, the disorder is now termed *chronic traumatic encephalopathy (CTE)*. Head trauma may be one of the stressors that initiates the onset of dementias of varying types. Other such stressors include having diabetes, high blood pressure, or herpes simplex virus-1 (Richards & Sweet, 2009). As with each of the disorders discussed, psychological and biological stressors may interact with physiological processes to produce Alzheimer's disease.

Psychological and Social Influences. Research has mostly focused on the biological conditions that produce dementia. Although few would claim that psychosocial influences directly cause the type of brain deterioration seen in people with dementia, they may help determine onset and course. For example, a person's lifestyle may involve contact with factors that can cause dementia. You saw, for instance, that substance abuse can lead to dementia and, as we discussed previously (see Chapter 10), whether a person abuses drugs is determined by a combination of biological and psychosocial factors. In the case of vascular dementia, a person's biological vulnerability to vascular disease will influence the chances of strokes that can lead to this form of dementia. Lifestyle issues such as diet, exercise, and stress influence cardiovascular disease and therefore help determine who experiences vascular dementia.

Cultural factors may also affect this process. For example, hypertension and strokes are prevalent among African Americans and certain Asian Americans (King, Mainous Iii, & Geesey, 2007), which may explain why vascular dementia is more often observed in members of these groups. In an extreme example, exposure to a viral infection can lead to dementia similar in form to Creutzfeldt-Jakob disease through a condition known as kuru. This virus is passed on through a ritual form of cannibalism practiced in Papua New Guinea as a part of mourning (Collinge et al., 2006). Dementia caused by head trauma and malnutrition are relatively prevalent in preindustrial rural societies (Del Parigi, Panza, Capurso, & Solfrizzi, 2006). Not getting enough of vitamins B_9 and B_{12} in particular seems to lead to dementia, although the process is as yet unknown. These findings suggest that occupational safety (such as protecting workers from head injuries) and economic conditions influencing diet also affect the prevalence of certain forms of dementia.

Psychosocial factors themselves influence the course of dementia. Recall that educational attainment may affect the onset of dementia (Richards & Sweet, 2009). Having certain skills may help some people cope better than others with the early stages of dementia. As you saw earlier, Diana's mother was able to carry on her day-to-day activities by making maps and using other tricks to help compensate for her failing abilities. The early stages of confusion and memory loss may be better tolerated in cultures with lowered expectations of older adults. In certain cultures, including the Chinese, younger people are expected to take the demands of work and care from older adults after a certain age, and symptoms of dementia are viewed as a sign of normal aging (Gallagher-Thompson et al., 2006; Hinton, Guo, Hillygus, & Levkoff, 2000). Dementia may go undetected for years in these societies.

Much remains to be learned about the cause and course of most types of dementia. As you saw with Alzheimer's disease and Huntington's disease, certain genetic factors make some individuals vulnerable to progressive cognitive deterioration. In addition, brain trauma, some diseases, and exposure to certain drugs, such as alcohol, inhalants, and sedative, hypnotic, and anxiolytic drugs, can cause the characteristic decline in cognitive abilities. We also noted that psychosocial factors can help determine who is subject to these causes and how they cope with the condition. Looking at dementia from this integrative perspective should help you view treatment approaches in a more optimistic light. It may be possible to protect people from conditions that lead to dementia and to support them in dealing with the devastating consequences of having it.

Treatment

For many of the disorders discussed in other chapters, treatment prospects are fairly good. Clinicians can combine various strategies to reduce suffering significantly. Even when treatment does not bring expected improvements, mental health professionals have usually been able to stop problems from progressing. This is not the case in the treatment of dementia.

One factor preventing major advances in the treatment of dementia is the nature of the damage caused by this disorder. The brain contains billions of neurons, many more than are used. Damage to some can be compensated for by others because of plasticity. However, there is a limit to where and how many neurons can be destroyed before vital functioning is disrupted. Researchers are closing in on how to use the brain's natural process of regeneration to potentially reverse the damage caused in dementia (Khachaturian, 2007). Currently, however, with extensive brain damage, no known treatment can restore lost abilities. The goals of treatment therefore become (1) trying to prevent certain conditions, such as substance abuse, that may bring on dementia; (2) trying to delay the onset of symptoms to provide better quality of life; and (3) attempting to help these individuals and their caregivers cope with the advancing deterioration. Most efforts in treating dementia have focused on the second and third goals, with biological treatments aimed at stopping the cerebral deterioration and psychosocial treatments directed at helping patients and caregivers cope.

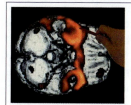

Abnormal Psychology Inside Out, produced by Ira Wohl, Only Child Motion Pictures

Computer Simulations and Senile Dementia

"Our cognitive activity arises from the neural networks in the brain. Whenever you lose an individual neuron, you're not losing an idea, you're just losing a tiny bit of the resolution, or the crispness, of that idea."

Go to Psychology CourseMate at www.cengagebrain.com to watch this video.

A troubling statistic further clouds the tragic circumstances of dementia: More than 23% of caregivers of people with dementia—usually relatives—have the symptoms characteristic of one or more anxiety disorders and 10% are clinically depressed (Katona & Livingston, 2009). Compared with the public, these caregivers use more psychotropic medications (designed to reduce symptoms of various psychological disorders) and report stress symptoms at 3 times the normal rate. Caring for people with dementia, especially in its later stages, is clearly a trying experience. In fact, there is some evidence to suggest that the stress associated with caring for a person with dementia may place the caregiver at greatly increased risk for developing dementia themselves (Norton et al., 2010). As a result, clinicians are becoming increasingly sensitive to the needs of these caregivers, and research is now exploring interventions to assist them in caring for people with dementia (Lee, Czaja, & Schulz, 2010).

Biological Treatments. Dementia resulting from known infectious diseases, nutritional deficiencies, and depression can be treated if it is caught early. Unfortunately, however, no known treatment exists for most types of dementia that are responsible for the vast majority of cases. Dementia caused by stroke, HIV, Parkinson's disease, or Huntington's disease is not currently treatable because there is no effective treatment for the primary disorder. However, exciting research in several related areas has brought us closer to helping individuals with these forms of dementia. A substance that may help preserve and perhaps restore neurons—called glial cell–derived neurotrophic factor—may someday be used to help reduce or reverse the progression of degenerative brain diseases (Zuccato & Cattaneo, 2009). Researchers are also looking into the possible benefits of transplanting stem cells (fetal brain tissue) into the brains of people with such diseases. Initial results from these studies are still preliminary but appear promising (Arenas, 2010). Dementia brought on by strokes may now be more preventable by new drugs that help prevent much of the damage inflicted by the blood clots characteristic of stroke (Richards & Sweet, 2009). Most current attention is on a treatment for dementia of the Alzheimer's type because it affects so many people. Here, too, however, success has been modest at best.

Much work has been directed at developing drugs that will enhance the cognitive abilities of people with dementia of the Alzheimer's type. Many seem to be effective initially, but long-term improvements have not been observed in placebo-controlled studies (Richards & Sweet, 2009). Several drugs (called *cholinesterase inhibitors*) have had a modest impact on cognitive abilities in some patients and include donepezil (Aricept), rivastigmine (Exelon), and galantamine (Reminyl). *Tacrine hydrochloride* (Cognex), another in this family of drugs, is rarely used today because of the potential for liver damage (Rabins, 2006). These drugs prevent the breakdown of the neurotransmitter acetylcholine (which is deficient in people with Alzheimer's disease), thus making more acetylcholine available to the brain. Research suggests that, when using these drugs, people's cognitive abilities improve to the point where they were 6 months earlier (Lyketos, 2009). But the gain is not permanent. Even people who respond positively do not stabilize but continue to experience the cognitive decline associated with Alzheimer's disease. In addition, if they stop taking the drug—as almost three-quarters of the patients do because of negative side effects such as liver damage and nausea—they lose even that 6-month gain (Lyketos, 2009). Newer drugs are now being investigated for the treatment of Alzheimer's disease. These include drugs that target the beta-amyloid (plaques) in the brain, and it is hoped that these advances will finally provide a positive prognosis for this devastating disease (Rafii & Aisen, 2009).

Several other medical approaches are being explored to slow the course of Alzheimer's disease, but initial excitement generated by these approaches has waned with the findings from researchers. For example, most of you have heard of using *Ginkgo biloba* (maidenhair) to improve memory. Initial research suggested that this herbal remedy may produce modest improvements in the memory of people with Alzheimer's disease, but other studies have not replicated this benefit (DeKosky et al., 2008). Similarly, the effects of vitamin E have been evaluated. One large study found that among individuals with moderately severe impairment, high doses of the vitamin (2,000 international units per day) delayed progression compared to a placebo (Sano et al., 1997), but it did not prevent the development of the disease. Further research, in fact, indicates that taking high doses of vitamin E may actually increase mortality and therefore this intervention is no longer recommended (Richards & Sweet, 2009). Modest slowing of the progression of the disease also may be obtained by introducing exercise to patients (Rockwood & Middleton, 2007; Teri et al., 2003). To date, however, no medical interventions are available that directly treat and therefore stop the progression of the conditions that cause the cerebral damage in Alzheimer's disease.

Medical interventions for dementia also include the use of drugs to help with some associated symptoms. A variety of antidepressants—such as serotonin-specific reuptake inhibitors—are commonly recommended to alleviate the depression and anxiety that too often accompany the cognitive decline. Antipsychotic medication is sometimes used for those who become unusually agitated (Richards & Sweet, 2009).

Psychosocial Treatments. Psychosocial treatments are now receiving a great deal of attention for their ability to delay the onset of severe cognitive decline. These efforts focus on enhancing the lives of people with dementia and those of their families. People with dementia can be taught skills to compensate for their lost abilities. Recall that Diana's mother learned on her own to make maps to help her get from place to place. Diana herself began making lists so that she would not forget important things. Some researchers have evaluated more formal adaptations to help people in the early stages of dementia. Michelle Bourgeois (2007) created "memory wallets" to help people with dementia carry on conversations. On white index cards inserted into a plastic wallet are printed declarative statements such as, "My husband John and I have 3 children," or "I was born on January 6, 1921, in Pittsburgh." In one of her studies, Bourgeois (1992) found that adults with dementia could, with minimal training, use this memory aid to improve their conversations with others. Adaptations such as these help people communicate with others,

Power™ Cognitive Fitness System: Kara Kenna photographer.
www.dakim.com

▲ A resident of an assistive living facility practices cognitive stimulation using one of several computer-based systems (the Dakim™ Power Brain Fitness System).

help them remain aware of their surroundings, and can reduce the frustration that comes with the awareness of their own decline.

Cognitive stimulation—encouraging people with dementia to practice learning and memory skills—seems to be an effective method for delaying the onset of the more severe cognitive effects of this disorder (Knowles, 2010). These activities include word games, tests of memory of famous and familiar faces, and practice with numbers (for example, how much change back you would receive from a purchase). These types of skill-building exercises can maintain cognitive activity and improve the quality of life in those patients when compared to controls.

Individuals with advanced dementia are not able to feed, bathe, or dress themselves. They cannot communicate with or recognize even familiar family members. They may wander away from home and become lost. Because they are no longer aware of social stigma, they may engage in public displays of sexual behavior, such as masturbation. They may be frequently agitated or even physically violent. To help both the person with dementia and the caregiver, researchers have explored interventions for dealing with these consequences of the disorder (Richards & Sweet, 2009). For example, some research indicates that a combination of exercise for patients and instruction for caregivers on how to handle behavior problems can improve the overall health and the depression in people with Alzheimer's disease (Logsdon, McCurry, Pike, & Teri, 2009; Teri et al., 2003).

Of great concern is the tendency of people with dementia to wander. Sometimes they wind up in places or situations that may be dangerous (for example, stairwells or the street). Often, the person is tied to a chair or bed, or sedated, to prevent roaming. Unfortunately, physical and medical restraint has its own risks, including additional medical complications; it also adds greatly to the loss of control and independence that already plague the person with dementia. Psychological treatment as an alternative to restraint sometimes involves providing cues for people to help them safely navigate around their home or other areas. New innovations in surveillance technology—creating a "smart home" that can monitor the location of the patient and warn caregivers—may provide more peace of mind for those who care for these patients. At the same time, ethical concerns are being raised about the use of this technology because of its ability to invade privacy (Bharucha et al., 2009; Mahoney et al., 2007).

Someone with dementia can become agitated and sometimes verbally and physically aggressive. This behavior is understandably stressful for people trying to provide care. In these situations, medical intervention is often used, although many times with only modest results (Testad, Ballard, Brønnick, & Aarsland, 2010). Caregivers are often given assertiveness training to help them deal with hostile behaviors (Table 13.5). Otherwise, caregivers may either passively accept all criticism inflicted by the person with dementia, which increases stress, or become angry and aggressive in return. This last response is of particular concern because of the potential for elder abuse. Withholding food or medication or inflicting physical abuse is most common among caregivers of elderly people who have cognitive deficits (Post, Page, Conner, & Prokhorov, 2010). It is important to teach caregivers how to handle stressful circumstances so that they do not escalate into abusive situations. Not a great deal of objective evidence supports the usefulness of assertiveness training for reducing caregiver stress, and more research is needed to guide future efforts.

In general, families of people with dementia can benefit from supportive counseling to help them cope with the frustration, depression, guilt, and loss that take a heavy emotional toll. However, clinicians must first recognize that the ability to adapt to stressors differs among people. One study, for example, found cultural differences in the coping styles of caregivers. In one area of rural Alabama, white caregivers used acceptance and humor as coping strategies, and black caregivers used religion and denial (Kosberg, Kaufman, Burgio, Leeper, & Sun, 2007). Another large-scale study of 555 principal caregivers over a 3-year period identified a number of steps that can be taken to support caregivers through this difficult time (Aneshensel, Pearlin, Mullan, Zarit, & Whitlatch, 1995). However, despite numerous studies aimed at supporting caregivers, the results to date remain weak and additional work is needed to determine how best to support these individuals (Schoenmakers, Buntinx, & DeLepeleire, 2010).

Overall, the outlook for slowing (but not stopping) the cognitive decline characteristic of dementia is optimistic. The best available medications provide some recovery of function, but they do not stop the progressive deterioration. Psychological interventions may help people cope more effectively with the loss of cognitive abilities, especially in the earlier stages of this disorder. In addition, emphasis is placed on helping caregivers—the other victims of dementia—as the person they care for continues to decline.

Prevention

Without treatment, we need to rely even more heavily on prevention strategies for dementia. You can imagine that it is difficult to study prevention efforts for dementia because of the need to follow individuals for long periods to see whether the efforts are effective. One major study conducted in Sweden—where socialized medicine provides complete medical histories of all residents—looked at many of the risk factors (those factors that increase the chance of having dementia) and protective factors (those that decrease the risk) under study today (Fratiglioni, Winblad, & von Strauss, 2007). They looked at the medical records of 1,810 participants who were older than 75 at the time and followed them for about 13 years. Through interviews and medical histories, they came to two major conclusions: Control your blood pressure, and lead an active physical and social life. These two recommendations came out as the major factors that individuals can change—because you cannot change your genetics, for example—that will decrease the chances of developing dementia. Additional prevention research is ongoing, and there may be other potentially fruitful research areas that can lead to the successful prevention of this devastating disorder.

DSM Disorder Criteria Summary
Alzheimer's Disease

Features of dementia of the Alzheimer's type include the following:

> Multiple cognitive deficits, including memory impairment, and at least one of the following disturbances: aphasia, apraxia, agnosia, or disturbance in executive functioning (e.g., planning, sequencing)

> Significant impairment in functioning involving a decline from the previous level

> Gradual onset and continuing cognitive decline

Source: Based on *DSM-IV-TR*. Reprinted with permission from *Diagnostic and Statistical Manual of Mental Disorders* (4th ed., text revision). © 2000 American Psychiatric Association.

Table 13.5 Genetic Factors in Alzheimer's Disease

Gene	Chromosome	Age of Onset (years)
APP	21	43 to 59
Presenilin 1	14	33 to 60
Presenilin 2	1	50 to 90
apo E4	19	60
A2M	12	70

A2M = alpha-2-macroglobulin; AAP = amyloid precursor protein; apo E4 = apolipoprotein E4.

Concept Check 13.5

Part A

Identify the following symptoms of dementia from the descriptions: (a) facial agnosia, (b) agnosia, and (c) aphasia.

1. Timmy's elderly grandmother does not recognize her own home any more. _____

2. She can no longer form complete, coherent sentences. _____

3. She no longer recognizes Timmy when he visits, even though he is her only grandchild.

_____

Part B

Identify the cognitive disorders described.

4. Julian is a recovering alcoholic. When asked about his wild adventures as a young man, his stories usually end quickly because he can't remember the whole tale. He even has to write down things he has to do in a notebook; otherwise, he's likely to forget. _____

5. Mr. Brown has suffered from a number of strokes but can still care for himself. However, his ability to remember important things has been declining steadily for the past few years. _____

6. A decline in cognitive functioning that is gradual and continuous and has been associated with neurofibrillary tangles and amyloid plaques is called _____.

Amnestic Disorder

Say these three words to yourself: _apple, bird, roof._ Try to remember them, and then count backward from 100 by 3s. After about 15 seconds of counting, can you still recall the three words? Probably so. However, people with **amnestic disorder** will not remember them, even after such a short period (Bourgeois, Seaman, & Servis, 2008). The loss of this type of memory, which we described as a primary characteristic of dementia, can occur without the loss of other high-level cognitive functions. The main deficit of amnestic disorder appears to be the inability to transfer information like the list we just described into long-term memory, which can cover minutes, hours, or years. This disturbance in memory is caused by either the physiological effects of a medical condition, such as head trauma, or the long-term effects of a drug. Consider the case of S. T.

S. T. | Remembering Fragments

S. T., a 67-year-old white woman, suddenly fell but did not lose consciousness. She appeared bewildered and anxious but oriented to person and place. Language functioning was normal, yet she was not ori-

ented to time. She was unable to recall her birthplace, the ages of her children, or any recent presidents of the United States. She could not remember three objects for 1 minute, nor recall what she had eaten for her last meal. She could not name the color of any object shown to her but could correctly name the color related to certain words—for example, _grass_ and _sky._ Object naming was normal. Examined 1 year later, she could repeat five digits forward and backward but could not recall her wedding day, the cause of her husband's death, or her children's ages. She did not know her current address or phone number and remembered none of three objects after 5 minutes. Although she was described by her family as extremely hard-working before her illness, after hospitalization she spent most of her time sitting and watching television. She was fully oriented, displayed normal language function, and performed simple calculations without error (Cole, Winkelman, Morris, Simon, & Boyd, 1992, pp. 63–64).

The _DSM-IV-TR_ criteria for amnestic disorder describe the inability to learn new information or to recall previously learned information. As with all cognitive disorders, memory disturbance causes significant impairment in social and occupational functioning. The woman just described was diagnosed with a type of amnestic disorder called _Wernicke-Korsakoff syndrome,_ which is caused by damage to the thalamus, a small region deep inside the brain that acts as a relay station for information from many other parts of the brain. In her case, the damage to the thalamus was believed to be the result of a stroke that caused vascular damage. Another common cause of Wernicke-Korsakoff syndrome is chronic heavy alcohol use.

As you saw with the other cognitive impairments, a range of traumas to the brain can cause permanent amnestic disorders. Research has focused on attempting to prevent the damage associated with Wernicke-Korsakoff syndrome. Specifically, a deficiency in thiamine (vitamin B_1) resulting from alcohol abuse in people developing Wernicke-Korsakoff syndrome is leading researchers to try supplementing this vitamin, especially for heavy drinkers (Sechi & Serra, 2007). To date, however, there is little research pointing to successful long-term assistance in treating people with amnestic disorders (Bourgeois et al., 2008).

On the Spectrum Emerging Views of Developmental Disorders

The developmental disorders described in this chapter represent a broad range of problems first evident in childhood (Durand, 2011). Some of the disorders discussed may be considered part of a spectrum of disorders. For instance, some of the pervasive developmental disorders are being studied under the category of "autism spectrum disorders" and this change is being discussed for possible inclusion in *DSM-5*. Autistic disorder and Asperger's disorder are thought to be related in the spectrum, although re-

search continues on the co-occurrence of childhood disintegrative disorder and pervasive developmental disorder not otherwise specified (PDD-NOS) (Swedo, Thorsen, & Pine, 2008).

Two other major disorders—conduct disorder (CD) and oppositional defiant disorder (ODD)—may be part of a spectrum of "disruptive behavior disorders," although this research is in a beginning stage (Shaffer, Leibenluft, Rohde, Sirovatka, & Regier, 2009). There is also considerable

comorbidity among attention deficit disorder, CD, and ODD, although any conclusion about their being part of a spectrum of disorders is premature (Shaffer, Leibenluft, Rohde, Sirovatka, & Regier, 2009). To move this research ahead in the coming years, researchers are examining the complex genetics of CD and ODD to see if there are meaningful ways to view these childhood problems and their apparent overlap (some children have some symptoms of both disorders).

Summary

Common Developmental Disorders

> What are the central defining features of attention deficit/hyperactivity disorder?

Developmental psychopathology is the study of how disorders arise and change with time. These changes usually follow a pattern, with the child mastering one skill before acquiring the next. This aspect of development is important because it implies that any disruption in the acquisition of early skills will, by the very nature of the developmental process, also disrupt the development of later skills.

The primary characteristics of people with attention deficit/hyperactivity disorder are a pattern of inattention (such as not paying attention to school- or work-related tasks), hyperactivity/impulsivity, or both. These deficits can significantly disrupt academic efforts and social relationships.

> What are the main types of learning disorders, and how are they typically treated?

DSM-IV-TR groups the learning disorders as reading disorder, mathematics disorder, and disorder of written expression. All are defined by performance that falls far short of expectations based on intelligence and school preparation.

Verbal or communication disorders seem closely related to learning disorders. They include stuttering, a disturbance in speech fluency; expressive language disorder, limited speech in all situations but without the types of cognitive deficits that lead to language problems in people with intellectual disability or one of the pervasive developmental disorders; selective mutism, refusal to speak despite having the ability to do so; and tic disorders, which include involuntary motor movements such as head twitching and vocalizations

such as grunts that occur suddenly, in rapid succession, and in idiosyncratic or stereotyped ways.

Pervasive Developmental Disorders

> How are pervasive developmental disorders defined?

People with pervasive developmental disorders all experience trouble progressing in language, socialization, and cognition. The use of the word *pervasive* means these are not relatively minor problems (like learning disabilities) but are conditions that significantly affect how individuals live. Included in this group are autistic disorder, Rett's disorder, Asperger's disorder, and childhood disintegrative disorder.

> What are the three major characteristics of autistic disorder?

Autistic disorder, or autism, is a childhood disorder characterized by significant impairment in social interactions, gross and significant impairment in communication, and restricted patterns of behavior, interest, and activities. It probably does not have a single cause; instead, a number of biological conditions may contribute, and these, in combination with psychosocial influences, result in the unusual behaviors displayed by people with autism.

Asperger's disorder is characterized by impairments in social relationships and restricted or unusual behaviors or activities, but people with Asperger's disorder do not have the language delays observed in people with autism.

amnestic disorder Deterioration in the ability to transfer information from short- to long-term memory, in the absence of other dementia symptoms, as a result of head trauma or drug abuse.

Rett's disorder, almost exclusively observed in females, is a progressive neurological disorder characterized by constant hand-wringing, intellectual disability, and impaired motor skills.

Childhood disintegrative disorder involves severe regression in language, adaptive behavior, and motor skills after a period of normal development for 2 to 4 years.

Pervasive developmental disorder not otherwise specified is a childhood disorder characterized by significant impairment in social interactions; gross and significant impairment in communication; and restricted patterns of behavior, interest, and activities. Children who have this disorder are similar to those with autism but may not meet the age criterion for autism or may not meet the criteria for some symptoms of autism.

Intellectual Disability

> How is intellectual disability defined, and what categories are used to classify people with intellectual disabilities?

The definition of intellectual disability has three parts: significantly subaverage intellectual functioning, concurrent deficits or impairments in present adaptive functioning, and onset before the age of 18.

Down syndrome is a type of intellectual disability caused by the presence of an extra 21st chromosome. It is possible to detect the presence of Down syndrome in a fetus through a process known as amniocentesis.

Two other types of intellectual disability are common: fragile X syndrome, which is caused by a chromosomal abnormality of the tip of the X chromosome, and cultural–familial intellectual disability, the presumed cause, possibly by a combination of psychosocial and biological factors, of up to 75% of intellectual disability.

Cognitive Disorders

> What are the symptoms of delirium and dementia?

Delirium is a temporary state of confusion and disorientation that can be caused by brain trauma, intoxication by drugs or poisons, surgery, and a variety of other stressful conditions, especially among older adults.

Dementia is a progressive and degenerative condition marked by gradual deterioration of a range of cognitive abilities including memory, language, and planning, organizing, sequencing, and abstracting information.

Alzheimer's disease is the leading cause of dementia, affecting approximately 4 million Americans; there is currently no known cause or cure.

To date, there is no effective treatment for the irreversible dementias caused by Alzheimer's disease, Parkinson's disease, Huntington's disease, and various less common conditions that produce this progressive cognitive impairment. Treatment often focuses on helping patients cope with the continuing loss of cognitive skills and helping caregivers deal with the stress of caring for affected individuals.

Amnestic Disorder

> What are the principal causes of and treatments for amnestic disorder?

Amnestic disorders involve a dysfunction in the ability to recall recent and past events. The most common is Wernicke-Korsakoff syndrome, a memory disorder usually associated with chronic alcohol abuse.

Key Terms

attention deficit/hyperactivity disorder (ADHD), 486
learning disorders, 491
reading disorder, 492
mathematics disorder, 492
disorder of written expression, 492
stuttering, 493
expressive language disorder, 493
selective mutism, 493
tic disorder, 493
pervasive developmental disorders, 496
Asperger's disorder, 496
Rett's disorder, 496
childhood disintegrative disorder, 496

pervasive developmental disorder not otherwise specified, 496
autistic disorder (autism), 496
intellectual disability, 506
phenylketonuria (PKU), 506
Lesch-Nyhan syndrome, 506
Down syndrome, 506
amniocentesis, 507
chorionic villus sampling (CVS), 507
fragile X syndrome, 507
cultural–familial intellectual disability, 508
delirium, 512
dementia, 514
agnosia, 515
facial agnosia, 515
Alzheimer's disease, 516

dementia of the Alzheimer's type, 516
vascular dementia, 518
head trauma, 519
human immunodeficiency virus type 1 (HIV-1), 519
aphasia, 519
Parkinson's disease, 519
Huntington's disease, 519
Pick's disease, 520
Creutzfeldt-Jakob disease, 520
deterministic, 521
susceptibility, 521
amnestic disorder, 526

Answers to Concept Checks

13.1

1. b; 2. c; 3. b; 4. d; 5. e; 6. a

13.2

1. a; 2. b; 3. d; 4. e; 5. c

13.3

1. profound, pervasive support;
2. moderate, limited support;

3. severe, extensive support;
4. mild, intermittent support

13.4

1. c; 2. b; 3. a; 4. e; 5. f; 6. d

13.5

Part A

1. b; 2. c; 3. a

Part B

4. substance-induced persisting dementia; 5. vascular dementia; 6. dementia of Alzheimer's type

13.6

1. T; 2. F; 3. T; 4. T

Media Resources

Log in to CengageBrain to access the resources your instructor requires. For this book, you can access:

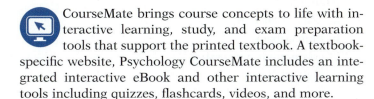 CourseMate brings course concepts to life with interactive learning, study, and exam preparation tools that support the printed textbook. A textbook-specific website, Psychology CourseMate includes an integrated interactive eBook and other interactive learning tools including quizzes, flashcards, videos, and more.

Abnormal Psychology Videos

> *Nature of the Disorder—Autism:* Mark Durand's research program deals with the motivation behind problem behaviors and how communication training can be used to reduce such behaviors.
> *Christina, a Student with Autism:* This clip shows Christina's school, where you see how she spends a typical day in a mainstreamed classroom. There are interviews with her teacher's aide and a background interview with Mark Durand to describe functional communication issues and other cutting-edge research trends in autism.
> *Rebecca, an Autistic Child:* This segment shows an autistic child in a mainstreamed first-grade classroom and interviews her teachers about what strategies work best in helping Rebecca learn and control her behavior.
> *Lauren, a Child with Down Syndrome:* The teacher and mother of a kindergartner with Down syndrome are interviewed to discuss strategies for teaching her new skills and managing her behavior difficulties.
> *Tom, a Patient with Alzheimer's Disease:* This is a rather moving clip in which Tom's family talks about him and you see a surprising example of memory that still works.
> *Mike, an Amnestic Patient:* Following an accident, Mike struggles with memory problems that affect his employment, his relationship, and his sense of self. You'll notice how he expresses himself both in his language and in the flatness of his emotion.
> *Neural Networks: Cognition and Dementia:* In this clip, James McClelland proposes that computer simulations of the brain's neural networks can reveal how human cognition works—and even how cognition fails in dementia.

CENGAGENOW CengageNow is an easy-to-use online resource that helps you study in less time to get the grade you want—NOW. Take a pre-test for this chapter and receive a personalized study plan based on your results that will identify the topics you need to review and direct you to online resources to help you master those topics. Then take a post-test to help you determine the concepts you have mastered and what you will need to work on. If your textbook does not include an access code card, go to CengageBrain.com to gain access.

> Visit www.cengagebrain.com to access your account and purchase materials.

aplia If your professor has assigned Aplia homework:
1. Sign in to your account.
2. Complete the corresponding homework exercises as required by your professor.
3. When finished, click "Grade It Now" to see which areas you have mastered, which need more work, and for detailed explanations of every answer.

Video Concept Reviews

CengageNOW also contains Mark Durand's *Video Concept Reviews* on these challenging topics.

> Attention Deficit/Hyperactivity Disorder (ADHD)
> Reading Disorder
> Mathematics Disorder
> Pervasive Developmental Disorders
> Autistic Disorder (Autism)
> Asperger's Disorder
> Intellectual Disability

CHAPTER QUIZ

1. According to the *DSM-IV-TR,* the two symptoms that are characteristic of ADHD are:
   a. inattention and hyperactivity
   b. echolalia and impulsivity
   c. hallucinations and delusions
   d. obsessions and compulsions

2. Echolalia is characterized by which of the following behaviors?
   a. continuously reading the same sentence or words
   b. repeating the speech of others
   c. mimicking the movements of others
   d. staring ahead without blinking for long periods

3. Behavioral techniques are often used to address communication problems that occur with autism. _____ involves rewarding the child for progressive approximations of speech, and _____ involves rewarding the child for making sounds that the teacher requests.
   a. Shaping; discrimination training
   b. Modeling; syntax training
   c. Imitating; expression training
   d. Processing; academic training

4. Research has shown that ADHD in children is associated with:
   a. chronic neglect
   b. having an alcoholic father
   c. maternal smoking during pregnancy
   d. death of a parent in early childhood

5. The regulated breathing method, a behavioral technique used to reduce _____, involves taking a deep breath when an episode occurs before continuing.
   a. motor tics
   b. stuttering
   c. mutism
   d. impulsivity

6. _____ is a form of intellectual disability caused by the presence of an extra 21st chromosome.
   a. Down syndrome
   b. Fragile X syndrome
   c. PKU syndrome
   d. Fetal alcohol syndrome

7. Joe has a mild intellectual disability. His therapist is teaching him a skill by breaking it down into its component parts. Joe's therapist is implementing what technique?
   a. skills treatment
   b. biofeedback
   c. component processing
   d. task analysis

8. _____ is characterized by acute confusion and disorientation; whereas _____ is marked by deterioration in a broad range of cognitive abilities.
   a. Delirium; amnesia
   b. Amnesia; delirium
   c. Dementia; delirium
   d. Delirium; dementia

9. Which disorder can be diagnosed definitively only at autopsy by the presence of large numbers of amyloid plaques and neurofibrillary tangles?

a. vascular dementia

b. dementia of the Alzheimer's type

c. delirium

d. Parkinson's disease

10. Psychological and social influences are important to consider when studying dementia because they:

a. can accelerate the type of brain damage seen in this disease

b. provide a rationale for psychopharmacological intervention

c. may help determine the time of onset and course of dementia

d. can be used to reverse the progression of Alzheimer's disease

(See Appendix A for answers.)

Exploring Developmental Disorders

Disorders that appear early in life disrupt the normal course of development.

❯ Interrupting or preventing the development of one skill impedes mastery of the skill that is normally acquired next.

❯ Knowing what skills are disrupted by a particular disorder is essential to developing appropriate intervention strategies.

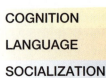

COGNITION

LANGUAGE

SOCIALIZATION

Infancy   **Childhood**   **Adolescence**

TYPES OF DEVELOPMENTAL DISORDERS

		Description	Causes	Treatment

Attention Deficit/ Hyperactivity Disorder (ADHD)	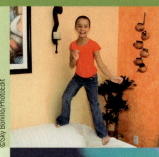	• Inattentive, overactive, and impulsive behavior
		• Disrupted schooling and relationships
		• Symptoms may change with maturity, but problems persist.
		• More prevalent in boys than girls
			• Research suggests hereditary factor
			• Abnormal neurology
			• Possible link with maternal smoking
			• Negative responses by others create low self-esteem.
				• Biological (medication)
				  – improves compliance
				  – decreases negative behaviors
				  – effects not long term
				• Psychological (behavioral)
				  – goal setting and reinforcement

Learning Disorders		• Reading, math, and written expression fall behind IQ, age, and education.
		• May also be accompanied by ADHD
			• Theories assume genetic, neurobiological, and environmental factors.	• Education intervention
				  – basic processing
				  – cognitive and behavioral skills

		Types	Description	Treatment
Communication Disorders Closely related to learning disorders, but comparatively benign. Early appearance, wide range of problems later in life.		Stuttering	Disturbance in speech fluency (repeating words, prolonging sounds, extended pauses)	• Psychological • Pharmacological
		Expressive Language Disorders	Limited speech in all situations	• May be self-correcting
		Selective Mutism	Failure to speak in specific situations (e.g., school)	• Contingency management
		Tic Disorders	Involuntary motor movements (tics), such as physical twitches or vocalizations	• Psychological • Pharmacological

PERVASIVE DEVELOPMENTAL DISORDERS

	Description	Causes	Treatment

Autistic Disorder	• Severely impaired socialization and communication
	• Restricted behavior, interests, and activities
	  – echolalia
	  – maintenance of sameness
	  – stereotyped, ritualistic behaviors
	• Symptoms almost always develop before 36 months of age.
		• Little conclusive data
		• Numerous biological factors
		  – clear genetic component
		  – evidence of brain damage (cognitive deficits) combined with psychosocial influences
			• Behavioral focus
			  – communication
			  – socialization
			  – living skills
			• Inclusive schooling
			• Temporary benefits from medication

Asperger's Disorder	Impaired socialization and restricted/unusual behaviors, but without language delays • Few cognitive impairments (average IQ) • May be mild autism, not separate disorder		
Rett's Disorder	Progressive neurological disorder after apparently normal early development • Primarily affects girls • Mental retardation • Deteriorating motor skills • Constant hand-wringing		
Childhood Disintegrative Disorder	Severe regression after 2–4 years normal development • Affects language, adaptive behavior, and motor skills • Evidence of neurological origin		

Nicola Sutton/Life File/Getty Images

©moodboard/Corbis

©Paul Conklin/PhotoEdit

INTELLECTUAL DISABILITY

Photodisc/Getty Images

Description	Causes	Treatment

• Adaptive and intellectual functioning significantly below average
  – language and communication impairments
• Wide range of impairment—from mild to profound—in daily activities (90% of affected individuals have mild impairments)
	• Hundreds of identified factors
	  – genetic
	  – prenatal
	  – perinatal
	  – postnatal
	  – environmental
	• Nearly 75% of cases cannot be attributed to any known cause.
		• No biological intervention
		• Behavioral focus similar to that for autism
		• Prevention
		  – genetic counseling
		  – biological screening
		  – maternal care

Exploring Cognitive Disorders

> When the brain is damaged, the effects are irreversible, accumulating until learning, memory, or consciousness are obviously impaired.

> Cognitive disorders develop much later than intellectual disability and other learning disorders, which are believed to be present at birth.

TYPES OF COGNITIVE DISORDERS

Todd Pearson/Digital Vision/Getty Images

Delirium

Description	Causes (subtypes)	Treatment
• Impaired consciousness and cognition for several hours or days – confusion, disorientation, inability to focus • Most prevalent among older adults, people with AIDS, and patients on medication	• Delirium due to a general medical condition • Substance-induced delirium • Delirium due to multiple etiologies • Delirium not otherwise specified	• Pharmacological – benzodiazepines – antipsychotics • Psychosocial – reassurance – presence of personal objects – inclusion in treatment decisions

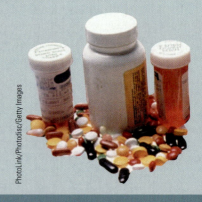

PhotoLink/Photodisc/Getty Images

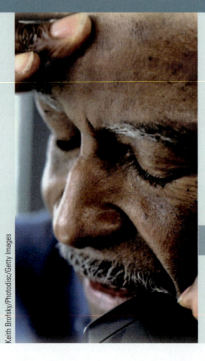

Keith Brofsky/Photodisc/Getty Images

Amnestic Disorder

Description	Causes	Treatment
• Permanent short-term memory loss without impairment of other cognitive functions – inability to learn new information or recall previously learned information – significant impairment in social and occupational functioning	• Medical condition such as head trauma • Lasting effects of a drug, even after the substance is no longer ingested	• Prevention: proper medical care and drug monitoring • No long-term success at combating damage

Subtype

Wernicke/Korsakoff Syndrome

Caused by damage to the thalamus from injury (stroke) or chronic heavy alcohol use (thiamine depletion)

Dementia

> Gradual deterioration of brain functioning that affects judgment, memory, language, and other advanced cognitive processes
> Caused by medical condition or drug abuse
> Some forms are irreversible, some are resolved by treatment of primary condition.

TYPES OF DEMENTIA

		Description	Causes	Treatment
Dementia of the Alzheimer's Type	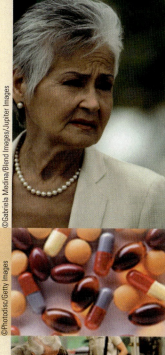 ©Gabriela Medina/Blend Images/Jupiter Images	• Increasing memory impairment and other multiple behavioral and cognitive deficits, affecting language, motor function-ing, ability to recognize people or things, and/or planning • Most prevalent dementia • Subject of most research	• Progressive brain damage, evident in neurofibrillary tangles and neuritic plaque, confirmed by autopsy but assessed by simplified mental status exam • Involves multiple genes	• No cure so far, but hope lies in genetic research and amyloid protein in neurine plaques. • Management may include lists, maps, and notes to help maintain orientation. • New medications that prevent acetylcholine breakdown and vitamin therapy show promise.
Substance-induced Persisting Dementia	 ©Photodisc/Getty Images	• Caused by brain damage due to prolonged drug use, especially in combination with poor diet, as in alcohol dependency; other substances may include inhalants, and the sedative, hypnotic, and anxiolytic drugs • Treatment focuses on prevention.		
Vascular Dementia	 Stockbyte/Getty Images	• Permanent deterioration due to blocked or damaged blood vessels in the brain (stroke) • Symptoms identical to Alzheimer's and may also include problems with walking and weakness of limbs • Treatment focuses on coping.		
Dementia Due to Other General Medical Conditions	 ©Harmut Schwarzbach/Peter Arnold/PhotoLibrary	• Similar in effect to other cognitive disorders, but caused by: – head trauma – HIV, Parkinson's, Huntington's, Pick's, or Creutzfeldt-Jakob disease – hydrocephalus, hypothyroidism, brain tumor, and vitamin B12 deficiency • Treatment of primary condition is sometimes possible.		

CHAPTER

14

Mental Health Services: Legal and Ethical Issues

©John Neubauer/PhotoEdit

Identify appropriate applications of psychology in solving problems, such as:	❯ Psychology-based interventions in clinical, counseling, educational, industrial/organizational, community, and other settings and their empirical evaluation (APA SLO 4.2.d) *(see textbook pages 537–540, 548–553)*
Articulate how psychological principles can be used to explain social issues and inform public policy.	❯ Use psychological principles to explain social issues and inform public policy (APA SLO 4.3) *(see textbook pages 540–548)*

*Portions of this chapter cover learning outcomes suggested by the American Psychological Association (2007) in their guidelines for the undergraduate psychology major. Chapter coverage of these outcomes is identified by APA Goal and APA Suggested Learning Outcome (SLO).

We begin this chapter with a return to Arthur, who we described in Chapter 12 as having psychotic symptoms.

Arthur ◆ A Family's Dilemma

As you may remember, Arthur was brought to our clinic by family members because he was speaking and acting strangely. He talked incessantly about his "secret plan" to save all the starving children in the world. His family's concern intensified when Arthur said he was planning to break into the German embassy and present his plan to the German ambassador. Alarmed by his increasingly inappropriate behavior and fearing he would be hurt, the family was astounded to learn they could not force him into a psychiatric hospital. Arthur could admit himself—which was not likely, given his belief that nothing was wrong with him—but they had no power to admit him involuntarily unless he was in danger of doing harm to himself or others. Even if they sincerely believed some harm might be forthcoming, this wasn't sufficient reason to admit him involuntarily. The family coped with this emergency as best they could for several weeks until the worst of Arthur's behaviors began to diminish.

Why wouldn't the mental health facility admit Arthur, who was clearly out of touch with reality and in need of help? Why couldn't his own family authorize the mental health facility to act? What would have happened if Arthur had entered the German embassy and hurt or even killed someone? Would he have gone to jail, or would he have finally received help from the mental health community? Would Arthur have been held responsible if he hurt other people while he was delusional? These are just a few of the many issues that surface when we try to balance the rights of people who have psychological disorders with the responsibilities of society to provide care.

Mental health professionals face such questions daily. They must both diagnose and treat people and consider individual and societal rights and responsibilities. As we describe how systems of ethics and legal concepts have developed, remember they change with time and with shifting societal and political perspectives on mental illness. How we treat people with psychological disorders is partly a function of how society views these people. For example, do people with mental illness need help and protection, or does society need protection from them? As public opinion about people with mental illness changes, so do the relevant laws, and legal and ethical issues affect both research and practice. As you will see, the issues affecting research and practice are often complementary. For example, confidentiality is required to protect the identity of a participant in a research study and of a patient seeking help for a psychological disorder. Because people who receive mental health services often simultaneously participate in research studies, we must consider the concerns of both constituencies.

⊙ Civil Commitment

> How does the legal concept of mental illness differ from a clinically diagnosed psychological disorder?
> What is the relationship between dangerousness and mental illness?
> What are the interactions among mental illness, deinstitutionalization, and homelessness?

Laws have been designed to protect people who display abnormal behavior and to protect society. Often, achieving this protection is a delicate balancing act, with the scales sometimes thought to be tipped in favor of the rights of individuals and at other times in favor of society. For example, each state has **civil commitment laws** that detail when a person can be legally declared to have a mental illness and be placed in a hospital for treatment (Simon & Shuman, 2009). When Arthur's family tried to have him involuntarily committed to a mental health facility, hospital officials decided that because he was not in imminent danger of hurting himself or others he could not be committed against his will. In this case, the laws protected Arthur from involuntary commitment, but they also put him and others at potential risk by not compelling him to get help.

Civil commitment laws in the United States date back to the late 19th century. Before this time, almost all people with severe mental illness were cared for by family members or the community or were left to care for themselves. With the development of a large public hospital system devoted to treating such individuals came an alarming trend: involuntary commitment of people for reasons unrelated to mental illness (Simon & Shuman, 2009). There were even instances in which women were committed to psychiatric hospitals by their husbands simply for holding differing personal or political views. In the 1800s, Mrs. E. P. W. Packard crusaded for better civil commitment laws after being involuntarily confined to a psychiatric hospital for 3 years (Grob, 2009).

Criteria for Civil Commitment

Historically, states have permitted commitment when several conditions have been met: (1) The person has a "mental illness" and is in need of treatment, (2) the person is dangerous to himself or herself or others, or (3) the person is unable to care for himself, a situation considered a "grave disability." How these conditions are interpreted has varied over the years and has always been controversial. It is important to see that the government justifies its right to act against the wishes of an individual—in this case, to commit someone to a mental health facility—under two types of authority: police power and *parens patriae* ("state or country as the parent") power. Under police power, the government takes responsibility for protecting the public health, safety, and welfare and can create laws and regulations to ensure this protection. Criminal offenders are held in custody if they are a threat to society. The state applies *parens patriae* power when citizens are not likely to act in their own best interest—for example, to assume custody of children who have no living parents. Similarly, it is used to commit individuals with severe mental illness to mental health facilities when it is believed that they might be harmed because they are unable to secure the basic ne-

cessities of life, such as food and shelter (grave disability) or because they do not recognize their need for treatment (Simon & Shuman, 2008). Under *parens patriae* power, the state acts as a surrogate parent, presumably in the best interests of a person who needs help.

A person in need of help can always voluntarily request admission to a mental health facility; after an evaluation by a mental health professional, a patient may be accepted for treatment. However, when an individual does not voluntarily seek help but others feel that treatment or protection is necessary, the formal process of civil commitment can be initiated. The specifics of this process differ from state to state, but it usually begins with a petition by a relative or mental health professional to a judge. The court may then request an examination to assess psychological status, ability for self-care, need for treatment, and potential for harm. The judge considers this information and decides whether commitment is appropriate. This process is similar to other legal proceedings, and the person under question has all the rights and protections provided by the law. In most states, the person can even request that a jury hear the evidence and make a determination. In all cases, the person must be notified that the civil commitment proceedings are taking place, must be present during the trial, must have representation by an attorney, and can examine the witnesses and request an independent evalu-

▲ The government can exert *parens patriae* to protect people from hurting themselves.

ation. These safeguards are built into the civil commitment process to guarantee the rights of the person being examined and to ensure that no one is involuntarily committed to a psychiatric facility for other than legitimate reasons.

In emergency situations, when there is clearly immediate danger, a short-term commitment can be made without the formal proceedings required of a civil commitment. Family members or sometimes police officers certify that the person presents a "clear and present danger" to herself or to others (Simon & Shuman, 2009). Arthur's family was unsuccessful in having him admitted on an emergency basis because it was not clear that anyone was in immediate danger, only that someone might be hurt. Again, deciding what is a clear and present danger sometimes requires a great deal of subjective judgment from the court and from mental health professionals.

Defining Mental Illness

The concept of mental illness figures prominently in civil commitment, and it is important to understand how it is defined. **Mental illness** is a legal concept, typically meaning severe emotional or thought disturbances that negatively affect an individual's health and safety. Each state has its own definition. For example, in New York "'[m]ental illness' means an affliction with a mental disease or mental condition which is manifested by a disorder or disturbance in behavior, feeling, thinking, or judgment to such an extent that the person afflicted requires care, treatment and rehabilitation" (*New York Mental Hygiene Law*, 1992). In contrast, in Connecticut "'[m]entally ill person' means a person who has a mental or emotional condition that has substantial adverse effects on his or her ability to function and who requires care and treatment, and specifically excludes a person who is an alcohol-dependent person or a drug-dependent person" (Conn. Gen. Stat. Ann., 1992). Many states exclude cognitive disability or substance-related disorders from the definition of mental illness.

Mental illness is *not* synonymous with psychological disorder; in other words, receiving a diagnosis according to the text revision of the fourth edition of the *Diagnostic and Statistical Manual of Mental Disorders (DSM-IV-TR)* does not necessarily mean that a person's condition fits the legal definition of mental illness. Although the *DSM* is quite specific about criteria that must be met for diagnosis, there is considerable ambiguity about what constitutes a "mental condition" or what are "adverse effects on his or her ability to function." This allows flexibility in making decisions individually, but it also maintains the possibility of subjective impression and bias as influences on these decisions.

Dangerousness

Assessing whether someone is a danger to self or others is a critical determinant of the civil commitment process. **Dangerousness** is a particularly controversial concept to describe people with mental illness: Popular opinion tends to be that people who are mentally ill are more dangerous than those who are not. Although this conclusion is questionable, it is still widespread, partly because of sensational media reports.

There is a widespread popular belief that mental illness causes a person to be violent (Kobau, DiIorio, Chapman, & Delvecchio, 2010). The results of research on dangerousness and mental illness are often mixed, but evidence points to a moderately increased rate of violence among people with mental illness (Elbogen & Johnson, 2009). Closer examination of this kind of research reveals that although having a mental illness generally does increase the likelihood of future violence, specific symptoms (such as hallucinations, delusions, or having a comorbid personality disorder) appear to be associated with people at increased risk of violence (Lurigio & Harris, 2009). Even previously violent individuals with mental illness are not necessarily going to commit violent crimes after they are released, although the presence of certain symptoms may increase the risk.

Unfortunately, the widely held misperception that people with mental illness are more dangerous may differentially affect ethnic minorities (Vinkers, de Vries, van Baars, & Mulder, 2010). Black males are often perceived as dangerous, even when they don't exhibit any violent behavior, which may partly explain why blacks are overrepresented among those who are involuntarily committed to state psychiatric institutions (Lindsey, Joe, Muroff, & Ford, 2010).

To return to the general issue, how do you determine whether a person is dangerous to others? How accurate are mental health professionals at predicting who will and who will not later be violent? The answers bear directly on the process of civil commitment and on protection for society. If we can't accurately predict dangerousness, how can we justify involuntary commitment?

Clinicians are better at assessing the relative risk required of the legal system than determining dangerousness case by case (Scott, Quanbeck, & Resnick, 2008). Stated in another way, mental health professionals can identify groups of people who are at greater risk than the general population for being violent—such as having a previous history of both violence and drug or alcohol dependence—and can so advise the court. What clinicians cannot yet do is predict with certainty whether a particular person will or will not become violent.

---

civil commitment laws Legal proceeding that determines a person is mentally disordered and may be hospitalized, even involuntarily.

mental illness Term formerly used to mean psychological disorder but less preferred because it implies that the causes of the disorder can be found in a medical disease process.

dangerousness Tendency to violence that, contrary to popular opinion, is not more likely among mental patients.

Changes Affecting Civil Commitment

Clearly, there are significant problems with the process of civil commitment. In particular, deciding whether a person has a mental illness or is dangerous requires considerable subjective judgment, and, because of varying legal language, this determination can differ from state to state. These problems have resulted in a number of significant legal developments.

▲ Larry Hogue was involuntarily committed to a psychiatric hospital because, homeless and under the influence of drugs *(left)*, he terrorized residents of a New York City neighborhood for years. Once off drugs *(right)*, Hogue was able to control himself.

The Supreme Court and Civil Commitment

In 1957, the parents of Kenneth Donaldson had him committed to the Florida State Hospital for treatment of paranoid schizophrenia. Donaldson was not considered dangerous, yet, despite repeated offers of placement in a halfway house or with a friend, Dr. O'Connor, the superintendent of the hospital, refused to release him for almost 15 years, during which Donaldson received virtually no treatment (Donaldson, 1976). Donaldson successfully sued Dr. O'Connor for damages, winning $48,500. In deciding the case, the Supreme Court found that "a State cannot constitutionally confine . . . a non-dangerous individual who is capable of surviving safely in freedom by himself or with the help of willing and responsible family and friends" (*O'Connor v. Donaldson*, 1975).

Here, and in a subsequent decision known as *Addington v. Texas* (1979), the Supreme Court said that more than just a promise of improving quality of life is required to commit someone involuntarily. If nondangerous people can survive in the community with the help of others, they should not be detained against their will. Needing treatment or having a grave disability was not sufficient to commit someone involuntarily with a mental illness. The effect of this decision was to limit substantially the government's ability to commit individuals unless they were dangerous (Simon & Shuman, 2008).

Criminalization

Because of the tightened restrictions on involuntary commitment that prevailed in the 1960s and 1970s, many people who would normally have been committed to mental health facilities for treatment were instead being handled by the criminal justice system. In other words, people with severe mental illness were now living in the community, but many were not receiving the mental health services they needed and would eventually run afoul of the legal system because of their behavior. This "criminalization" of the mentally ill was of great concern because the criminal justice system was not prepared to care for these individuals (Lamb, 2009; Lamb & Weinberger, 2009). Family members were increasingly frustrated that they couldn't obtain treatment for their loved ones, who were instead languishing in jail without help.

Deinstitutionalization and Homelessness

In addition to criminalization, two other trends emerged at this time, starting in the 1980s: an increase in the number of people who were homeless and **deinstitutionalization**, the movement of people with severe mental illness out of institutions. Remember that homelessness is not exclusively a problem of the mentally ill. Approximately 2 million to 3 million people will experience a night of homelessness in the United States each year, and estimates place the numbers of homeless people at up to 800,000 on any given night (Hudson & Vissing, 2010). Best estimates suggest that diagnoses of severe mental illness (for example, schizophrenia and bipolar disorder) among homeless persons range from 3% to 42%, depression from 4% to 41%, and personality disorders from 3% to 71% (Fazel, Khosla, Doll, & Geddes, 2008). For reasons not yet fully understood, ethnicity may also play a part in who among people with mental illness becomes homeless. In a large study in San Diego County, for example, Latinos and Asian Americans with mental illness were less likely to become homeless, but African Americans were more likely to be homeless (Folsom et al., 2005).

Information on the characteristics of people who are homeless is important because it provides us with clues about why people become homeless, and it dispels the notion that all homeless people have mental health problems. For a time, homelessness was blamed on strict civil commitment criteria and deinstitutionalization (Colp, 2009)—that is, policies to severely limit who can be involuntarily committed, the limits placed on the hospital stays of people with severe mental illness, and the concurrent closing of large psychiatric hospitals were held responsible for the substantial increase in homelessness during the 1980s. Although a sizable percentage of homeless people have mental illness, the rise in homelessness is also the result of such

▲ People become homeless because of many factors, including economic conditions, mental health status, and drug use.

for society's rights and by the belief that people with mental illness were not properly served by being forced into treatment. Others, however, especially relatives of afflicted people, felt that by not coercing some individuals into treatment, the system was sanctioning their mental decline and placing them at grave risk of harm. The culmination of a number of factors—such as the lack of success with deinstitutionalization, the rise in homelessness, and the criminalization of people with severe mental illness—gave rise to a backlash against their perceived causes, including the strict civil commitment laws. The case of Joyce Brown captures this clash of concerns between individual freedoms for people with mental illness and society's responsibility to treat them.

economic factors as increased unemployment and a shortage of low-income housing (Wright, 2009). Yet the perception that civil commitment restrictions and deinstitutionalization caused homelessness resulted in movements to change commitment procedures.

Reforms in civil commitment that made it more difficult to commit someone involuntarily occurred at the same time the policy of deinstitutionalization was closing large psychiatric hospitals (Lamb & Weinberger, 2009). Deinstitutionalization had two goals: (1) to close the large state mental hospitals and (2) to create a network of community mental health centers where the released individuals could be treated. Although the first goal appears to have been substantially accomplished, with about a 75% decrease in the number of hospitalized patients (Kiesler & Sibulkin, 1987), the essential goal of providing alternative community care appears not to have been attained. Instead, there was **transinstitutionalization**, or the movement of people with severe mental illness from large psychiatric hospitals to nursing homes or other group residences, including jails and prisons, many of which provide only marginal services (Lamb & Weinberger, 2009). Because of the deterioration in care for many people who had previously been served by the mental hospital system, deinstitutionalization is largely considered a failure. Although many praise the ideal of providing community care for people with severe mental illness, the support needed to provide this type of care has been severely deficient.

Reactions to Strict Commitment Procedures

Arthur's psychotic reaction and his family's travails in trying to get help occurred during the mid-1970s, a time characterized by greater concern for individual freedom than

---

Joyce Brown | Homeless but Not Helpless

During a 1988 winter emergency in New York City, Mayor Ed Koch ordered that all homeless people who appeared to be mentally ill should be involuntarily committed to a mental health facility for their protection. He used the legal principle of *parens patriae* to justify this action, citing the need to protect these individuals from the cold and from themselves. One of the people who was taken off the streets, 40-year-old Joyce Brown, was picked up against her will and admitted to Bellevue Hospital, where she received a diagnosis of paranoid schizophrenia. She had been homeless for some time, swearing at people as they walked by; at one point, she adopted the name Billie Boggs after a New York television personality with whom she fantasized a relationship. Supported by the New York Civil Liberties Union, Brown contested her commitment and was released after 3 months (Tushnet, 2008).

This case is important because it illustrates the conflicting interests over civil commitment. Brown's family had for some time been concerned about her well-being and had tried unsuccessfully to have her involuntarily committed. Although she had never hurt anyone or tried to commit sui-

deinstitutionalization Systematic removal of people with severe mental illness or mental retardation from institutions like psychiatric hospitals.
transinstitutionalization Movement of people with severe mental illness from large psychiatric hospitals to smaller group residences.

cide, they felt that living on the streets of New York City was too hazardous, and they feared for her welfare. City officials expressed concern for Brown and others like her, especially during the dangerously cold winter, although some suspected that this was an excuse to remove people with disturbing behavior from the streets of affluent sections (Kasindorf, 1988). Brown chose not to seek treatment and resisted efforts to place her in alternative settings. At times, she could be articulate in making a case for her freedom of choice. Only weeks after she was released from the hospital, she was again living on the streets. Rulings such as *O'Connor v. Donaldson* and *Addington v. Texas* had argued that mental illness and dangerousness should be criteria for involuntary commitment. However, because of cases like Brown's and concerns about homelessness and criminalization, a movement emerged calling for a return to broader civil procedures that would permit commitment not only of those who showed dangerousness to self or others, but also of individuals who were not dangerous but were in need of treatment and of those with grave disability. Groups including the National Alliance on Mental Illness, a coalition of family members of people with mental illness, argued for legal reform to make involuntary commitment easier—an emotional response to the failure to protect and treat people with mental illness. Several states in the late 1970s and early 1980s changed their civil commitment laws in an attempt to address these concerns. For example, the state of Washington revised its laws in 1979 to allow commitment of people who were judged to be in need of treatment, which produced a 91% increase in the number of involuntary commitments in the first year it was in effect (Durham & La Fond, 1985). There was essentially no change in the size of the hospital population at this time, only in the status under which patients were committed (La Fond & Durham, 1992). Whereas people were previously detained because of violence, they were now admitted under *parens patriae* powers; also, whereas most admissions had been voluntary, they were now involuntary. Hospitals began to fill up because of longer stays and repeated admissions and they accepted only involuntary admissions; therefore, the result of easing the procedure for involuntarily committing people with mental illness was only to change the authority under which they were admitted.

The special case of sex offenders has attracted public attention in recent years, and the issue of how to treat repeat offenders is at the heart of the concerns over civil commitment. In the years between 1930 and 1960, some states passed "sexual psychopath laws" that provided hospitalization instead of incarceration but for an indefinite period (Saleh, Malin, Grudzinskas Jr., & Vitacco, 2010). Sex offenders (rapists and pedophiles) could be civilly committed until they demonstrated that treatment was effective. However, because treatment is often unsuccessful when attempted with uncooperative clients (see Chapter 9) and because public opinion moved from a priority to treat to a priority to punish, these laws were repealed or went unused. Recent efforts have focused on incarcerating sex offenders for their crimes and, if they are judged still dangerous at the end of their sentences, civilly committing

▲ A significant number of the homeless are individuals with mental disorders, many of whom live with their children in shelters or on the streets.

them. Such "sexual predator" laws were first enacted in 1990, and the Kansas version was upheld as constitutional by the U.S. Supreme Court (*Kansas v. Hendricks*, 1997). Confinement of this type was viewed by the court as acceptable because it was seen as treatment, even though the justices conceded that such treatment is often ineffective (Zonana & Buchanan, 2009). Some are greatly concerned that these types of laws give the government too much latitude in using civil commitment (as opposed to incarceration) just to keep certain individuals away from others in society (La Fond, 2005).

An Overview of Civil Commitment

What should the criteria be for involuntarily committing someone with severe mental illness to a mental health facility? Should imminent danger to self or others be the only justification, or should society act as a parent and coerce people who appear to be in distress and in need of asylum or safety? How do we address the concerns of families like Arthur's who see their loved ones overcome by psychological problems? And what of our need not to be harassed by people like Brown? When do these rights take precedence over the rights of an individual to be free from unwanted incarceration? It is tempting to conclude that the legal system has failed to address these issues and reacts only to the political whims of the times.

However, from another point of view, the periodic change in laws is a sign of a healthy system that responds to the limitations of previous decisions. The reactions by the Supreme Court in the 1970s to the coercive and arbitrary nature of civil commitment were as understandable as more recent attempts to make it easier to commit people in obvious need of help. As the consequences of these changes become apparent, the system responds to correct injustices. Although improvements may seem excruciat-

Mental disorders are associated with significant psychological distress and impairment but also can have a huge negative impact on people's ability to earn a living and carry out their day-to-day activities. For instance, several recent studies have shown that serious forms of mental illness, such as depressive disorders (such as both unipolar and bipolar depression) are associated with significantly decreased work performance (Kessler et al., 2006) and reduced earnings (Kessler et al., 2008). It is estimated that mental disorders cost U.S. society approximately $193.2 billion per year, with 75% of this because of lost earnings among those with serious mental illness and 25% because of not being employed as a result of having a mental illness (Kessler et al., 2008).

Of note, some negative effects of mental disorders seem to hit some groups harder than others. One recent study of 10,340 residents of San Diego,

California, found that 15% of patients receiving treatment for a serious mental illness (such as schizophrenia, bipolar disorder, and major depression) had an episode of homelessness in the past year and, more importantly, that African American patients were at significantly higher risk of homelessness than all other patients (Folsom et al., 2005). Also, Latino and Asian American patients were at significantly lower risk of homelessness relative to Caucasian and African American patients. These differences remained even after controlling for differences in the rates of psychiatric disorders, substance abuse, medical benefits, and overall level of functioning (Folsom et al., 2005), which suggests that some other factors are needed to explain the differences in rates of homelessness among these different ethnic groups. The researchers suggest that this difference may be the result not of ethnicity but of cultural differences in

the availability of social and community resources for each group—with Latinos and Asian Americans offering higher levels of support and resources than Caucasian and African Americans.

Another potential explanation is that differences exist in the treatments provided to these groups and that these differences could influence patients' ability to find housing and regular employment. In support of this view, a recent study by Kuno and Rothbard (2002) revealed that African American Medicaid recipients are significantly less likely than Caucasian recipients to receive newer and more effective antipsychotic treatments. Although the exact reasons for these differences are not currently known, these studies make it clear that gaining greater clarity about the interactions of mental illness, occupational function, homeless, and culture must be a top priority for mental health researchers and clinicians.

ingly slow and may not always correctly address the issues in need of reform, the fact that laws can be changed should make us optimistic that the needs of individuals and of society can ultimately be addressed through the courts.

Concept Check 14.1

Check your understanding of civil commitment by filling in the blanks.
Several conditions must be met before the state is permitted to commit a person involuntarily: The person has a(n) (1) _____ and is in need of treatment, the person is considered (2) _____ to herself or others, and the person is unable to care for himself or herself, also known as (3) _____. Mental illness is a(n) (4) _____ concept, typically meaning severe emotional or thought disturbances that negatively affect an individual's health and safety, although this definition differs from state to state. When the laws about civil commitment emerged, (5) _____ (movement of disabled individuals out of mental institutions) and (6) _____ (movement of disabled individuals to a lesser facility) also occurred.

Criminal Commitment

> **What are the legal standards for invoking the insanity defense and determining competency to stand trial?**

What would have happened if Arthur had been arrested for trespassing on embassy grounds or, worse yet, if he had hurt or killed someone in his effort to present his plan for saving the world? Would he have been held responsible for his actions, given his obvious disturbed mental state? How would a jury have responded to him when he seemed fine

just several days later? If he was not responsible for his behavior then, why does he seem so normal now?

These questions are of enormous importance as we debate whether people should be held responsible for their criminal behavior despite the possible presence of mental illness. Cases such as that of Andrea Yates, who was first convicted and sentenced to life in prison for drowning her five children in a bathtub in 2001 but later found not guilty by reason of insanity (NGRI), cause some to wonder whether the laws have gone too far. **Criminal commitment** is the process by which people are held because (1) they have been accused of committing a crime and are detained in a mental health facility until they can be assessed as fit or unfit to participate in legal proceedings against them or (2) they have been found not guilty of a crime by reason of insanity.

The Insanity Defense

The purpose of our criminal justice system is to protect our lives, our liberty, and our pursuit of happiness, but not all people are punished for criminal behavior. The law recognizes that, under certain circumstances, people are not responsible for their behavior and it would be unfair and perhaps ineffective to punish them. Current views originate from a case recorded more than 150 years ago in England. Daniel M'Naghten today might receive the diagnosis of paranoid schizophrenia. He held the delusion that the English Tory party was persecuting him, and he set out to kill the British prime minister. He mistook the man's secretary for the prime minister and killed the secretary instead. In what has become known as the M'Naghten rule, the English court decreed that people are not responsible for their criminal behavior if they do not know what they are doing or if they don't know that what they are doing is

wrong. This ruling was, in essence, the beginning of the *insanity defense* (see summary in Table 14.1). For more than 100 years, this rule was used to determine culpability when a person's mental state was in question.

In the intervening years, other standards have been introduced to modify the M'Naghten rule because many critics felt that simply relying on an accused person's knowledge of right or wrong was too limiting and a broader definition was needed (Simon & Shuman, 2009). Mental illness alters not only a person's cognitive abilities, but also that person's emotional functioning, and mental health professionals believed the entire range of functioning should be taken into account when a person's responsibility was determined. One influential decision, known as the Durham rule, was initiated in 1954 by Judge David Bazelon of the Federal Circuit Court of Appeals for the District of Columbia and based on the case *Durham v. United States* (1954). The Durham rule broadened the criteria for responsibility from knowledge of right or wrong to include the presence of a "mental disease or defect" (see Table 14.1). This decision was initially hailed by mental health professionals because it allowed them to present to a judge or jury a complete picture of the person with mental illness. Unfortunately, it was soon apparent that mental health professionals did not have the expertise to assess reliably whether a person's mental illness caused the criminal behavior in question and therefore that decisions were being based on unscientific opinions (Simon & Shuman, 2009). Although the Durham rule is no longer used, it

Table 14.1 Important Factors in the Evolution of the Insanity Defense

Factor	Date	Quotation
M'Naghten rule	1843	[I]t must be clearly proved that at the time of committing the act, the party accused was labouring under such a defect of reason, from disease of the mind, as not to know the nature and quality of the act he was doing; or if he did know it, that he did not know he was doing what was wrong. (101 Cl. & F. 200, 8 Eng. Rep. 718, H.L. 1843)
Durham rule	1954	An accused is not criminally responsible if his unlawful act was the product of mental disease or mental defect. (*Durham v. United States*, 1954)
American Law Institute (ALI) rule	1962	1. A person is not responsible for criminal conduct if at the time of such conduct as a result of mental disease or defect he lacks substantial capacity either to appreciate the criminality (wrongfulness) of his conduct or to conform his conduct to the requirements of law. 2. As used in the Article, the terms "mental disease or defect" do not include an abnormality manifested only by repeated criminal or otherwise antisocial conduct. (American Law Institute, 1962)
Diminished capacity	1978	Evidence of abnormal mental condition would be admissible to affect the degree of crime for which an accused could be convicted. Specifically, those offenses requiring intent or knowledge could be reduced to lesser included offenses requiring only reckless or criminal neglect. (New York State Department of Mental Hygiene, 1978)
Insanity Defense Reform Act	1984	A person charged with a criminal offense should be found not guilty by reason of insanity if it is shown that, as a result of mental disease or mental retardation, he was unable to appreciate the wrongfulness of his conduct at the time of his offense. (American Psychiatric Association, 1983, p. 685)

Source: Reprinted, with permission, from Silver, E., Cirincione, C., & Steadman, H. J. (1994). Demythologizing inaccurate perceptions of the insanity defense. *Law and Human Behavior, 18,* 63–70, © 1994 Plenum Press.

caused a reexamination of the criteria used in the insanity defense.

An influential study of this question was conducted around the same time as the Durham decision by a group of attorneys, judges, and law scholars who belonged to the American Law Institute (ALI). Their challenge was to develop criteria for determining whether a person's mental competence makes him answerable for criminal behavior. The ALI first reaffirmed the importance of distinguishing the behavior of people with mental illness from that of people without mental disorders. Its members pointed out that the threat of punishment was unlikely to deter someone who had severe mental illness; the group's position was that these individuals should instead be treated until they improve and should then be released. (The ALI concluded that people are not responsible for their criminal behavior if, because of their mental illness, they cannot recognize the inappropriateness of their behavior or control it (ALI, 1962). The criteria shown in Table 14.1, known as the ALI test, stipulate that a person must either be unable to distinguish right from wrong—as set forth in the M'Naghten rule—or be incapable of self-control to be shielded from legal consequences.

The ALI also included provisions for the concept of **diminished capacity**, which holds that people's ability to understand the nature of their behavior and therefore their criminal intent can be diminished by their mental illness. The theory of criminal intent—otherwise called *mens rea*, or having a "guilty mind"—is important legally because to convict someone of a crime, there must be proof of the physical act *(actus rea)* and the mental state *(mens rea)* of the person committing the act (Simon & Shuman, 2009). For example, if a woman accidentally hits someone who steps in front of her car and the person subsequently dies, the woman would not be held criminally responsible; although a person was killed, there was no criminal intent— the driver didn't deliberately hit the person and attempt murder. The diminished capacity concept proposes that a person with mental illness who commits a criminal offense may not, because of the illness, have criminal intent and therefore cannot be held responsible.

Reactions to the Insanity Defense

Judicial rulings through the 1960s and 1970s regarding criminal responsibility parallel the course of civil commitment. An effort was made to focus on the needs of people with mental illness who also broke the law, providing mental health treatment instead of punishment. However, the successful use of concepts such as *insanity* or *diminished capacity* in criminal cases alarmed large segments of the population. For instance, in 1979 a man successfully pleaded NGRI after being arrested for writing bad checks. His case was based on the testimony of an expert witness who said he suffered from pathological gambling disorder and he therefore could not distinguish right from wrong (*State v. Campanaro*, 1980). Other successful defenses were based on disorders in the *DSM*, such as posttraumatic

stress disorder and kleptomania (Novak, 2010), and on disorders not covered in the *DSM*, including battered wife syndrome (Cookson, 2009).

Without question, the case that prompted the strongest outrage against the insanity defense and the most calls for its abolition is that of John W. Hinckley, Jr. (Zapf, Zottoli, & Pirelli, 2009). On March 31, 1981, as President Ronald Reagan walked out of the Washington Hilton Hotel, Hinckley fired several shots, hitting and seriously wounding the president, a Secret Service agent, and James Brady, the president's press secretary. In an instant, Secret Service agents tackled and disarmed Hinckley. Hinckley was obsessed with actress Jodie Foster; he claimed he tried to kill the president to impress her. Hinckley was judged by a jury to be NGRI, using the ALI standard. The verdict sent shock waves throughout the country and legal community (Zapf et al., 2009). Although the insanity defense had already been criticized, about 75% of the U.S. states substantially changed their insanity defense rules after Hinckley's verdict, making it more difficult to use this defense (Simon & Shuman, 2008). As you have seen before, such impulses often are based more on emotion than on fact. Highly publicized cases such as those of Hinckley, Charles Manson, Jeffrey Dahmer, and Ted Kaczynski, with the media characterization of people with mental illness as excessively violent, have created an unfavorable public perception of the insanity defense. One telephone survey study found that 91% of people who responded agreed with the statement, "[J]udges and juries have a hard time telling whether the defendants are really sane or insane" (Hans, 1986). Almost 90% agreed the "insanity plea is a loophole that allows too many guilty people to go free."

Is there hard evidence that the insanity defense is used too often? A study of the public's impression of the insanity defense compared it to the actual use of the defense and its outcomes (Silver, Cirincione, & Steadman, 1994). As Table 14.2 shows, the public's perception that this defense is used in 37% of all felony cases is a gross overestimate; the actual figure is less than 1%. The public also overestimates how often the defense is successful and how often people judged NGRI are set free. People tend to underestimate the length of hospitalization of those who are acquitted. This last issue is important: In contrast to public perceptions, the length of time a person is confined to a hospital after being judged NGRI may exceed the time the person would have spent in jail had that person been convicted of the crime (Simon & Shuman, 2008). Hinckley, for example, has been a patient in St. Elizabeth's Hospital for more than

criminal commitment Legal procedure by which a person found not guilty of a crime by reason of insanity must be confined in a psychiatric hospital.

diminished capacity Evidence of an abnormal mental condition in people that causes criminal charges against them requiring intent or knowledge to be reduced to lesser offenses requiring only reckless or criminal neglect.

Table 14.2 Comparison of Public Perceptions with the Actual Occurrence of the Insanity Defense

	Public Perception (%)	Actual Occurrence (%)
Use of Insanity Defense		
Felony indictments resulting in an insanity plea	37.0	0.9
Insanity pleas resulting in acquittal	44.0	26.0
Disposition of Insanity Acquittees		
Insanity acquittees sent to a mental hospital	50.6	84.7
Insanity acquittees set free	25.6	15.3
—Conditional release		11.6
—Outpatient		2.6
—Release		1.1
Length of Confinement of Insanity Acquittees (in months)		
All crimes	21.8	32.5
—Murder		76.4

Source: Reprinted, with permission, from Silver, E., Cirincione, C., & Steadman, H. J. (1994). Demythologizing inaccurate perceptions of the insanity defense. *Law and Human Behavior, 18,* 63–70, © 1994 Plenum Press.

of guilty but mentally ill (GBMI) (Torry & Billick, 2010). Although there are several versions of the GBMI verdict, the shared premise is that the consequences for a person ruled GBMI are different from those for a person who is NGRI. People found to be NGRI are not sent to prison but are evaluated at a psychiatric facility until such time as they are judged ready for release. A person determined to be no longer mentally ill must be released. If Arthur had committed a crime and was found NGRI, because his brief psychotic disorder was quickly resolved, he would probably have been released immediately. In contrast, one version of the GBMI verdict in theory allows the system both to treat and to punish the individual. The person found guilty is given a prison term just as if there were no question of mental illness. Whether the person is incarcerated in prison or in a mental health facility is decided by legal authorities. If the person recovers from mental illness before the sentence has passed, that person can be confined in prison for the maximum length of the term. If Arthur were found GBMI under this system, he could serve a full prison sentence, even though his mental illness was resolved. This version of GBMI has been adopted by a number of states (Simon & Shuman, 2008).

The second version of GBMI is even harsher for the mentally ill offender. Convicted individuals are imprisoned, and prison authorities may provide mental health services if they are available. The verdict itself is simply a declaration by the jury that the person was mentally ill at the time the crime was committed and does not result in differential treatment for the perpetrator. Idaho, Montana, and Utah have abandoned the insanity defense altogether and have adopted this version of GBMI ("The Evolving Insanity Defense," 2006).

As noted, the GBMI verdict was a reaction to the perceived loophole provided by the insanity defense. It has been

30 years. Other research shows that individuals with mental illness who are found guilty of *nonviolent* crimes can be committed more than 8 times as long as those people without mental illness placed in prison (Perlin, 2000). In contrast to public perception, people with mental illness apparently do not often "beat the rap" as a result of being judged NGRI.

Despite sound evidence that it is not used excessively and does not result in widespread early release of dangerous individuals, major changes were made in the criteria for the insanity defense after the Hinckley verdict. Both the American Psychiatric Association (1983) and the American Bar Association (1984) recommended modifications, moving back toward M'Naghten-like definitions. Shortly afterward, Congress passed the Insanity Defense Reform Act of 1984, which incorporated these suggestions and made successful use of the insanity defense more difficult.

Another attempt at reforming the insanity plea has been to replace the NGRI verdict with a verdict

 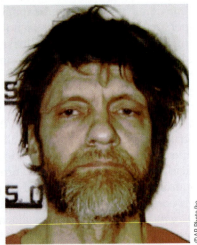

▲ Theodore Kaczynski, once a promising mathematician *(left),* became a notorious terrorist who killed three people and injured 23 more with handmade bombs sent through the mail. Awaiting trial as the Unabomber *(right),* Kaczynski refused to cooperate with his lawyers, who fought to have him declared mentally ill to save his life. Ironically, the prosecution, in pressing for the death penalty, supported his claim of sanity. (In the end, Kaczynski pleaded guilty and accepted a life sentence.)

used in several states for more than 15 years, and its effects have been investigated by researchers. Two studies have shown that people who receive the GBMI verdict are more likely to be imprisoned and to receive longer sentences than people pleading NGRI (Callahan, McGreevy, Cirincione, & Steadman, 1992; Keilitz, 1987). Research also indicates that individuals receiving GBMI verdicts are no more likely to receive treatment than other prisoners who have mental illness (Keilitz, 1987; Smith & Hall, 1982). Currently, the type of verdicts available (NGRI versus GBMI) depends on the laws of the particular state where the crimes were committed.

Overall, some estimate that there are more than 3 times the number of people with severe mental illness in jails than in hospitals, pointing to the consequences of these changes in mental health laws (Torrey, Eslinger, Lamb, & Pavle, 2010). Figure 14.1 illustrates how people with severe mental illness are increasingly being placed in prisons rather than in special mental health facilities. The percentage of placements in prisons is approaching rates comparable to that of those more than 150 years ago, before adequate services were available.

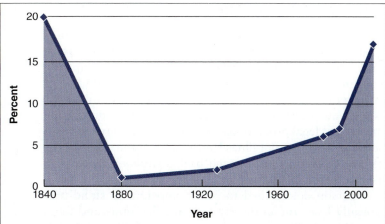

■ **Figure 14.1** The percentage of jail and prison inmates with serious mental illness. The graph shows the increasing trend over the past few decades to incarcerate people with severe mental illness rather than to provide treatment. (From Torrey, E., Eslinger, S., Lamb, R., & Pavle, J. [2010]. *More mentally ill persons are in jails and prisons than hospitals: A survey of the states* [p. 13]. Arlington, VA: Treatment Advocacy Center.)

Therapeutic Jurisprudence

There is a built-in tension between the judicial system and the mental health system. The legal system is, by design, adversarial. In other words, it was created with prosecutors and defendants, winners and losers. In contrast, the mental health system is set up to find solutions to important psychological problems without placing blame on any parties. The goal is for both sides to "win." Fortunately, there is an increasing recognition in the legal system that a strict adversarial approach to dealing with people with mental health problems may be harmful to everyone. As a result of this change in thinking, when individuals with psychological disorders break the law, they may now find themselves in one of a variety of "problem-solving courts" (King & Wexler, 2010). These new courts are designed to address the unique needs of people with specific problems. For example, today in many states you can find drug treatment courts, domestic violence courts, and mental health courts, among others. It is interesting that models of problem-solving courts have their roots in the legal systems of tribal societies in the United States, Canada, Australia, and New Zealand (King & Wexler, 2010).

These problem-solving courts are based on the concept of therapeutic jurisprudence—in essence, using what we know about behavior change to help people in trouble with the law. In drug treatment court, for example, a judge might be assigned to all criminal cases involving drug-addicted defendants. The judge would have the leeway to delay sentencing under the condition that the accused obtained and held a job for 6 months, received drug treatment during that time, and remained drug free. Similarly, a defendant in a mental health court might be helped by referrals to existing programs in the community and involvement of family members. Rather than simply trying to decide between prison and freedom, the court can serve as an instrument of social change. This evolving concept may provide effective alternatives in the criminal justice system for people with severe mental illness.

Society has long recognized the need to identify criminals who may not be in control of their behavior and who may not benefit from simple incarceration. The challenge is in trying to do what may be impossible: determining whether the person knew what she was doing, knew right from wrong, and could control her behavior. Mental health professionals cannot assess mental health retrospectively. An additional dilemma is the desire, on the one hand, to provide care to people with mental illness and, on the other, to treat them as responsible individuals. Finally, we must resolve the simultaneous and conflicting interests of wanting to assist people with mental illness and wanting to be protected from them. The recent trend of using problem-solving courts may be one way to address these concerns. We must reach a national consensus about the basic value of people with mental illness to decide how they should be dealt with legally.

Competence to Stand Trial

Before people can be tried for a criminal offense, they must be able to understand the charges against them and to assist with their own defense, criteria outlined by the Supreme Court in *Dusky v. United States* (1960). Thus, in addition to interpreting a person's state of mind during the criminal act, experts must also anticipate his state of mind during the subsequent legal proceedings. A person could be ruled NGRI because of his mental illness at the time of the criminal act yet still be competent to stand trial, a situation that would have occurred in Arthur's case had he committed a crime.

A person determined to be incompetent to stand trial typically loses the authority to make decisions and faces commitment. Because a trial requires a determination of **competence**, most people with obvious and severe impairments who commit crimes are never tried. Some observers estimate that for every person who receives a verdict of NGRI, 45 others are committed to a mental health facility with a diagnosis of severe mental illness (Butler, 2006). The length of stay is the time it takes the committed person to regain competence. Because this period can be drawn out, the courts have ruled it cannot be indefinite and that, after a reasonable amount of time, the person must be found competent, set free, or committed under civil law (*Jackson v. Indiana,* 1972). Laws are often not precise in their language, and the phrase "reasonable amount of time" is open to a great deal of interpretation.

A final issue relates to the legal concept of burden of proof, the weight of evidence needed to win a case. In decisions of competence to stand trial, an important ruling placed responsibility on the defendant to provide the burden of proof—in this case, that she is incompetent to stand trial (*Medina v. California,* 1992). Again, public concern that dangerous individuals with mental illness are routinely acquitted and let loose on society after committing multiple violent offenses flies in the face of the facts. More realistically, a person with mental illness commits a nonviolent crime and receives treatment through legal actions, such as the competence proceedings.

Duty to Warn

What are the responsibilities of professionals who suspect that someone with whom they are working may hurt or even kill another person? Must they contact the appropriate authority or the person who may be harmed, or are they forbidden to discuss information disclosed during therapy sessions?

These issues were the subject of a tragic case known as *Tarasoff v. Regents of the University of California* (1974, 1976). In 1969, Prosenjit Poddar, a graduate student at the University of Califor-

nia, killed a fellow student, Tatiana Tarasoff, who had previously rejected his romantic advances. At the time of the murder, he was being seen by two therapists at the University Health Center and had received a diagnosis of paranoid schizophrenia. At his last session, Poddar hinted that he was going to kill Tarasoff. His therapist believed this threat was serious and contacted the campus police, who investigated the allegation and received assurances from Poddar that he would leave Tarasoff alone. Weeks later, after repeated attempts to contact her, Poddar shot and stabbed Tarasoff until she died.

After learning of the therapists' role in the case, Tarasoff's family sued the university, the therapists, and the university police, saying they should have warned Tarasoff that she was in danger. The court agreed, and the Tarasoff case has been used ever since as a standard for therapists concerning their **duty to warn** a client's potential victims. Related cases have further defined the role of the therapist in warning others (Masona, Worsleyb, & Coylea, 2010). Courts have generally ruled that the threats must be specific. In *Thompson v. County of Alameda* (1980), the California Supreme Court ruled that a therapist does not have a duty to warn when a person makes nonspecific threats against nonspecific people. It is difficult for therapists to know their exact responsibilities for protecting third parties from their clients. Good clinical practice dictates that any time they are in doubt they should consult with colleagues.

Mental Health Professionals as Expert Witnesses

Judges and juries often have to rely on **expert witnesses**, individuals who have specialized knowledge, to assist them in making decisions (Mullen, 2010). We have alluded

▲ Elizabeth Loftus, a psychologist at the University of Washington in Seattle and an expert in human memory, testifies during the pretrial hearing of former White House official Lewis "Scooter" Libby.

to several instances in which mental health professionals serve in such a capacity, providing information about a person's dangerousness or ability to understand and participate in the defense. The public's perception of expert witnesses is characterized by ambivalence. On one hand, they see the value of persuasive expert testimony in educating a jury; on the other, they see expert witnesses as "hired guns" whose opinions suit the side that pays their bills (Simon & Shuman, 2009). How reliable are the judgments of mental health professionals who act as expert witnesses?

To take one example, in deciding whether someone should be civilly committed, the assessor must determine the person's potential for future violence. Research suggests that mental health professionals can make reliable predictions of dangerousness over the short term, for 2 to 20 days after the evaluation (Scott et al., 2008). However, they have not been able to make reliable predictions of violence after longer periods (Tardiff, 2003). A second area in which mental health professionals are often asked to provide consultation is in assigning a diagnosis. In Chapter 3, we discussed the development of systems to ensure the reliability of diagnoses. Recent revisions of diagnostic criteria, most notably *DSM-III-R* and the current *DSM-IV-TR*, have addressed this issue directly, thus helping clinicians make diagnoses that are generally reliable. Remember, however, that the legal definition of mental illness is not matched by a comparable disorder in *DSM-IV-TR*. Therefore, statements about whether someone has a "mental illness" reflect determinations made by the court, not by mental health professionals.

Mental health professionals appear to have expertise in identifying *malingering* and in assessing competence. Remember that to malinger is to fake or grossly exaggerate symptoms, usually to be absolved from blame. For example, a person might claim to have been actively hallucinating at the time of the crime and therefore not responsible. Research indicates that the Minnesota Multiphasic Personality Inventory test is extremely accurate in revealing malingering in people claiming to have serious mental illness. The examiners look for true symptoms but ones people with mental illness rarely report. Malingerers, in their rush to fake their illness, will often overreport these problems, perhaps to convince others they are mentally ill (Gassen, Pietz, Spray, & Denney, 2007). Mental health professionals also appear capable of providing reliable information about a person's competence, or ability to understand and assist with a defense (Shulman, Cohen, Kirsh, Hull, & Champine, 2007). Overall, mental health professionals can provide judges and juries with reliable and useful information in certain areas (Scott et al., 2008).

The research described here does not indicate how accurate expert testimony is under everyday conditions. In other words, under the right circumstances, experts can make accurate determinations of the short-term risks that a person will commit an act of violence, is faking certain symptoms, or is competent to stand trial and of what diagnosis should be made. Still, other factors conspire to influence expert testimony. Personal and professional opinions that exceed the competence of the expert witness can influence what information is or is not presented and how it is relayed to the court (Simon & Shuman, 2009). For instance, if the expert witness believes generally that people should not be involuntarily committed to mental health facilities, this opinion will likely influence how the witness presents clinical information in civil commitment court proceedings.

Concept Check 14.2

Check your understanding of criminal commitment by identifying the following concepts: (a) competence to stand trial, (b) diminished capacity, (c) American Law Institute rule, (d) Durham rule, (e) M'Naghten rule, (f) malingering, (g) expert witness, and (h) duty to warn.

1. The defendant does not go to trial because she is unable to understand the proceedings and assist in the defense. _____

2. The person could not distinguish between right and wrong at the time of the crime. _____

3. The person is not responsible for the crime if he is not able to appreciate the wrongfulness of behavior caused by mental disease or defect.

   _____

4. One of my clients threatened his mother's life during his session today. Now I must decide whether I have a(n) _____.

5. A mental disorder could reduce a person's ability to understand criminal behavior and to form criminal intent. _____

6. Dr. Z testified in court that the defendant was faking and exaggerating symptoms to evade responsibility. Dr. Z is acting as a(n) _____, and the defendant is _____.

7. The person is not criminally responsible if the crime was the result of "mental disease or mental defect." _____

---

competence Ability of legal defendants to participate in their own defense and understand the charges and the roles of the trial participants.
duty to warn Mental health professional's responsibility to break confidentiality and notify the potential victim whom a client has specifically threatened.
expert witness Person who because of special training and experience is allowed to offer opinion testimony in legal trials.

> **What are the key rights of patients in the mental health system?**

Until about 30 years ago, people in mental health facilities were accorded few rights. What treatment they received and whether they could make phone calls, send and receive mail, or have visitors were typically decided by hospital personnel who rarely consulted with the patient. However, abuses of this authority led to legal action and subsequent rulings by the courts concerning the rights of people in these facilities.

The Right to Treatment

One of the most fundamental rights of people in mental health facilities is the right to treatment. For too many people and for too long, conditions were poor and treatment was lacking in numerous large mental health facilities. Starting in the early 1970s, a series of class-action lawsuits (filed on behalf of many individuals) helped establish the rights of people with mental illness and mental retardation. A landmark case, *Wyatt v. Stickney* (1972), grew out of a lawsuit filed by the employees of large institutions in Alabama who were fired because of funding difficulties and established for the first time the minimum standards that facilities had to meet in relation to the people who were hospitalized. Among the standards set by *Wyatt v. Stickney* were minimum staff–patient ratios and physical requirements, such as a certain number of showers and toilets for a given number of residents. The case also mandated that facilities make positive efforts to attain treatment goals for their patients.

Wyatt v. Stickney went further and expanded on a concept called the "least restrictive alternative," indicating that, wherever possible, people should be provided with care and treatment in the least confining and limiting environment possible. For example, the court noted the following for those with mental retardation:

> Residents shall have a right to the least restrictive conditions necessary to achieve the purpose of habilitation. To this end the institution shall make every attempt to move residents from (1) more to less structured living; (2) large to smaller facilities; (3) large to smaller living units; (4) group to individual residences; (5) segregated from the community to integrated into the community; (6) dependent living to independent living. (*Wyatt v. Stickney*, 1972)

Despite this movement to secure treatment for people in mental health facilities, a gap was left as to what constituted proper treatment. The case of *Youngberg v. Romeo* (1982) reaffirmed the need to treat people in nonrestrictive settings but essentially left to professionals the decision about the type of treatment to be provided. This concerned patient advocates because, historically, leaving treatment to professional judgment has not always resulted in the intended end for the people in need of help. In 1986, Congress provided a number of safeguards by passage of the Protection and Advocacy for Mentally Ill Individuals Act (Woodside & Legg, 1990), which established a series of protection and advocacy agencies in each state to investigate allegations of abuse and neglect and to act as legal advocates.

The Right to Refuse Treatment

One of the most controversial issues in mental health today is the right of people, especially those with severe mental illness, to refuse treatment (Simon & Shuman, 2009). In recent times, the argument has centered on the use of antipsychotic medications. On one side of the issue are the mental health professionals who believe that, under certain circumstances, people with severe mental illness are not capable of making a decision in their own best interest and that the clinician is therefore responsible for providing treatment, despite the protestations of the affected people. On the other side, patients and their advocates argue that all people have a fundamental right to make decisions about their own treatment, even if doing so is not in their own best medical interests.

Although this controversy is not yet resolved, one court case has responded to a related question: Can people be "forced" to become competent to stand trial? This is an interesting dilemma: If people facing criminal charges are delusional or have such frequent severe hallucinations that they cannot fully participate in the legal proceedings, can they be forced against their will to take medication to reduce these symptoms, thereby making them competent to stand trial? A Supreme Court ruling, *Riggins v. Nevada* (1992), stated that, because of the potential for negative side effects (such as the involuntary motor movements associated with tardive dyskinesia), people cannot be forced to take antipsychotic medication. Although this decision does not settle the issue of refusing treatment, it does indicate the high court's wish to honor individual choice (Simon & Shuman, 2008).

Research Participants' Rights

Throughout this text we have described research conducted worldwide with people who have psychological disorders. We also touched briefly on the issue of the rights of these individuals. In general, people who participate in psychological research have the following rights (American Psychological Association, 2010a, 2010b):

1. The right to be informed about the purpose of the research study
2. The right to privacy
3. The right to be treated with respect and dignity
4. The right to be protected from physical and mental harm

5. The right to choose to participate or to refuse to participate without prejudice or reprisals
6. The right to anonymity in the reporting of results
7. The right to the safeguarding of their records

These rights are particularly important for people with psychological disorders who may not be able to understand them fully. One of the most important concepts in research is that those who participate must be fully informed about the risks and benefits of the study. Simple consent is not sufficient; it must be *informed consent,* or formal agreement by the subject to participate after being fully apprised of all important aspects of the study, including any possibility of harm. An important case underlines the significance of informed consent and the sometimes-gray areas that exist in applied research.

▲ Greg Aller (*right,* with his parents) participated in a drug study at UCLA and suffered a severe relapse of psychotic symptoms when medication was withdrawn. He and his family subsequently raised the issue of informed consent for such research.

Greg Aller • Concerned about Rights

In 1988, 23-year-old Greg Aller signed a consent form agreeing to participate in a treatment study at the University of California at Los Angeles (UCLA) Neuropsychiatric Institute (Willwerth, 1993). Since the previous year, Greg had experienced vivid and frightening hallucinations and delusions about space aliens. His parents had contacted UCLA for assistance. They learned that the university was initiating a new study to evaluate people in the early stages of schizophrenia and to assess the effects of the withdrawal of medication. If Greg participated, he could receive extremely expensive drug therapy and counseling free. After taking the drug Prolixin for 3 months as part of the study, he improved dramatically; the hallucinations and delusions were gone.

Although overjoyed with the results, Greg's parents were concerned about the second phase of the study, which involved taking him off the medication. They were reassured by the researchers that this was an important and normal part of treatment for people with schizophrenia and that the potential for negative side effects of taking the drug for too long was great. They were also told the researchers would put Greg back on the medication if he grew considerably worse without it.

Toward the end of 1989, Greg was slowly taken off the drug, and he soon started having delusions about then-President Ronald Reagan and space aliens. Although his deterioration was obvious to his parents, Greg did not indicate to the researchers that he needed the medication or tell them of his now-continuous hallucinations and delusions. Greg continued to deteriorate, at one point threatening to kill his parents. After several more months, Greg's parents persuaded him to ask for more medication. Although better than he was earlier, Greg has still not returned to the much-improved state he achieved following his first round of medication.

This case highlights the conflicts that can arise when researchers attempt to study important questions in psychopathology. Administrators at the National Institutes of Health reported that the UCLA researchers did not give Greg and his family all the information about the risks of treatment and the possibility of other approaches (Aller & Aller, 1997). Critics claim that informed consent in this and similar situations is too often not fully met and that information is often colored to ensure participation. However, the UCLA researchers note that what they did was no different from what would have happened outside the research study: They attempted to remove Greg from potentially dangerous antipsychotic medication. The controversy emerging from this case should be an added warning to researchers about their responsibilities to people who participate in their studies and their obligation to design added safeguards to protect the welfare of their study subjects. Some are now exploring methods to assess formally whether participants with mental illness fully understand the risks and benefits associated with these studies (e.g., Jeste et al., 2009).

Evidence-Based Practice and Clinical Practice Guidelines

Governments and health-care policy makers are increasingly promoting evidence-based practice (EBP)—health-care practices supported by research findings demonstrating that they are effective. EBP is one of those ideas that comes along occasionally and takes the world by storm. Although some tenets of EBP have been around for decades, it is only in the past 15 years that EBP has been formally identified as a systematic method of delivering clinical care (Institute of Medicine, 2001; Sackett, Strauss, Richardson, Rosenberg, & Haynes, 2000). The American Psychological Association Presidential Task Force in 2006 adopted as policy a report describing EBP in psychology and encouraging wide adoption of the notion of basing principles of psychological practice on evidence (American Psychological Association, 2006).

As described throughout this book, evidence has accumulated on the effectiveness of psychological treatments for specific disorders both in research clinics and in clinics that serve the public directly. When this evidence is put in the form of recommendations on how to treat a particular problem, these recommendations are called clinical practice guidelines. In 1989, legislation established a new branch of the federal government called the Agency for Health Care Policy and Research. In 1999, this agency was reauthorized by Congress and renamed the Agency for Healthcare Research and Quality. The purpose of this agency is to establish uniformity in the delivery of effective health and mental health care and to communicate to practitioners, policy makers, and patients alike throughout the country the latest developments in treating certain disorders effectively. The agency is also responsible for research into improving systems for the delivery of health and mental health services. Now with the passage in 2010 of legislation to provide a form of national health insurance in the United States (the Patient Protection and Affordable Care Act), making health care more efficient and effective is more important than ever.

The government hopes not only to reduce costs by eliminating unnecessary or ineffective treatments but also to facilitate the utilization of effective interventions based on the latest research evidence. In recent years, governments have allocated billions of dollars to facilitate dissemination and implementation of evidence-based psychological treatments in various health-care systems such as the Veterans Health Administration in the United States and the National Health Service in the United Kingdom (McHugh & Barlow, 2010). Treating people effectively—alleviating their pain and distress—is the most important way to reduce health-care costs because these individuals will no longer request one treatment after another in an unending search for relief. To this end, the new legislation creates the Patient-Centered Outcomes Research Institute to facilitate research on which treatments for what conditions are most effective, and to disseminate this information widely (Dickersin, 2010).

Anticipating the importance of this trend and the necessity that clinical practice guidelines be sound and valid, a task force of the American Psychological Association composed a template, or set, of principles for constructing and evaluating guidelines for clinical interventions for both psychological disorders and psychosocial aspects of physical disorders. These principles were published in 1995 and revised in 2002 with relatively few changes (American Psychological Association, 2002a and b).

The task force decided that clinical practice guidelines for specific disorders should be constructed on the basis of two simultaneous considerations, or axes: the clinical efficacy axis and the clinical utility axis. The **clinical efficacy axis** is a thorough consideration of the scientific evidence to determine whether the intervention in question is effective. This evidence would answer the question, Is the treatment effective when compared to an alternative treatment or to no treatment in a controlled clinical research context?

In Chapter 3, we reviewed the various research strategies used to determine whether an intervention is effective. As you will remember, for many reasons, a treatment might seem effective when it is not. For instance, if patients improve on their own while being treated simply because of the passage of time or the natural healing process, the treatment had little to do with the improvement. It is possible that nonspecific effects of the treatment—perhaps just meeting with a caring health professional—are enough to make someone feel better without any contribution from the particular treatment technique. To determine clinical efficacy, experiments called clinical trials must establish whether the intervention in question is better than no therapy, better than a nonspecific therapy, or better than an alternative therapy. Clinicians might also rely on information collected from various clinics where a large number of practitioners are treating the disorder in question. If these clinicians collect systematic data on the outcomes of their patients, they can ascertain how many are "cured," how many improve somewhat without recovering, and how many fail to respond to the intervention. Such data are referred to as *quantified clinical observations* or *clinical replication series*. Finally, a *clinical consensus* of leading experts is also a valuable source of information, although not as valuable as data from quantified clinical observations or randomized controlled trials (in which individuals are assigned randomly to a treatment or a control condition to evaluate the efficacy of the treatment).

The **clinical utility axis** is concerned with the effectiveness of the intervention in the practice setting in which it is to be applied, regardless of research evidence on its efficacy; in other words, will an intervention with proven efficacy in a research setting also be effective in the various clinical settings where the interventions are most often applied? Also, is application of the intervention in the settings where it is needed feasible and cost-effective? This axis is concerned with external validity, the extent to which an internally valid intervention is effective in different settings or under different circumstances from those where it was tested, and how easily it can be disseminated and implemented in those settings.

The first major issue to consider on the clinical utility axis is feasibility. Will patients accept the intervention and comply with its requirements, and is it relatively easy to administer? As noted in Chapter 6, electroconvulsive therapy is an effective treatment for severe depression in many

Table 14.3 Overview of Template for Constructing Psychological Intervention Guidelines

Clinical Efficacy (Internal Validity)	Clinical Utility (External Validity)

A. Better than alternative therapy (randomized controlled trials, or RCTs)
B. Better than nonspecific therapy (RCTs)
C. Better than no therapy (RCTs)
D. Quantified clinical observations
E. Clinical consensus
  1. Strongly positive
  2. Mixed
  3. Strongly negative
  4. Contradictory evidence
	A. Feasibility
	  1. Patient acceptability (cost, pain, duration, side effects, and so on)
	  2. Patient choice in face of relatively equal efficacy
	  3. Probability of compliance
	  4. Ease of dissemination (number of practitioners with competence, requirements for training, opportunities for training, need for costly technologies or additional support personnel, and so on)
	B. Generalizability
	  1. Patient characteristics
	    a. Cultural background issues
	    b. Gender issues
	    c. Developmental level issues
	    d. Other relevant patient characteristics
	  2. Therapist characteristics
	  3. Issues of robustness when applied in practice settings with different time frames, and so on
	  4. Contextual factors regarding setting in which treatment is delivered
	C. Costs and benefits
	  1. Costs of delivering intervention to individual and society
	  2. Costs to individual and society of withholding intervention

Note: Confidence in treatment efficacy is based on both (a) absolute and relative efficacy of treatment and (b) quality and replicability of studies in which this judgment is made.

Note: Confidence in clinical utility as reflected on these three dimensions should be based on systematic and objective methods and strategies for assessing these characteristics of treatment as they are applied in actual practice. In some cases, randomized controlled trials will exist. More often, data will be in the form of quantified clinical observations (clinical replication series) or other strategies, such as health economic calculations.

Source: Reprinted, with permission, from American Psychological Association Board of Professional Affairs Task Force on Psychological Intervention Guidelines. (1995). *Template for developing guidelines: Interventions for mental disorders and psychosocial aspects of physical disorders.* Approved by APA Council of Representatives, February 1995. Washington, D.C.: American Psychological Association, © 1995 American Psychological Association.

cases, but it is extremely frightening to patients, many of whom refuse it. The treatment also requires sophisticated procedures and close supervision by medical personnel, usually in a hospital setting. Therefore, it is not particularly feasible and is used only as a last resort.

A second issue on the clinical utility axis is generalizability, which refers to the extent to which an intervention is effective with patients of differing backgrounds (ethnicity, age, or sex) and in different settings (inpatient, outpatient, or community) or with different therapists. Again, an intervention could be effective in a research setting with one group of patients but generalize poorly across different ethnic groups. In summary, a treatment can be highly effective as determined by the clinical efficacy axis, but unless the treatment is widely generalizable, feasible, and cost-effective, it is unlikely to be disseminated or implemented. For a summary of these two axes, see Table 14.3.

In 2010, the American Psychological Association decided to develop its own set of clinical practice guidelines on providing the best evidence-based psychological care for people with psychological disorders.

In Chapter 1, we reviewed various activities that make up the role of scientist-practitioners in the mental health professions, who take a scientific approach to their clinical work to provide the most effective assessment procedures and interventions. Changes in the delivery of mental health services are likely to be accompanied by considerable disruption because this is a major system that affects millions of people. But the change will also bring opportunities. Scientist-practitioners will contribute to the process of guidelines development in several ways. For example, as attempts are made to assess the clinical utility or external validity of interventions, the collected experience of thousands of mental health professionals will be immensely valuable. Most information relevant to clinical utility or external validity will be collected by these clinicians in the course of their practice.

clinical efficacy axis One of a proposed set of guidelines for evaluating clinical interventions on the evidence of their effectiveness (compare with clinical utility axis).

clinical utility axis One of a proposed set of guidelines for evaluating clinical interventions by whether they can be applied effectively and cost effectively in real clinical settings (compare with clinical efficacy axis).

Summary

Civil Commitment

How does the legal concept of mental illness differ from a clinically diagnosed psychological disorder?

What is the relationship between dangerousness and mental illness?

What are the interactions among mental illness, deinstitutionalization, and homelessness?

> Civil commitment laws determine the conditions under which a person may be certified legally to have a mental illness and therefore to be placed in a hospital, sometimes in conflict with the person's own wishes.

> Historically, states have permitted commitment when several conditions have been met: (1) the person has a mental illness and is in need of treatment, (2) the person is dangerous to himself or to others, or (3) the person is unable to care for himself.

> *Mental illness* as used in legal system language is not synonymous with *psychological disorder;* each state has its own definition of mental illness, usually meant to include people with severe disturbances that negatively affect their health and safety.

> Having a mental illness does not seem to increase the likelihood of dangerousness, that is, that a person will commit violent acts in the future, although having symptoms of hallucinations and delusions does seem to indicate more risk for behaving violently.

> The combination of the lack of success with deinstitutionalization, which has resulted instead in transinstitutionalization; the rise in homelessness; and the criminalization of people with severe mental illness led to a backlash against the perceived causes of these factors, including the strict civil commitment laws.

Criminal Commitment

What are the legal standards for invoking the insanity defense and determining competency to stand trial?

> Criminal commitment is the process by which people are held for one of two reasons: (1) They have been accused of committing a crime and are detained in a mental health facility until they can be determined fit or unfit to participate in legal proceedings against them, or (2) they have been found not guilty of a crime by reason of insanity.

> The insanity defense is defined by a number of legal rulings: The M'Naghten rule states that people are not responsible for criminal behavior if they do not know what they are doing, or if they do know and they don't know it is wrong. The Durham rule broadened the criteria for responsibility from knowledge of right or wrong to the presence of a "mental disease or defect." The American Law Institute criteria concluded that people were not responsible for their criminal behavior if, because of their mental illness, they lacked either the cognitive ability to recognize the inappropriateness of their behavior or the ability to control their behavior.

> The concept of diminished capacity holds that people's ability to understand the nature of their behavior and therefore their criminal intent could be lessened by their mental illness.

> A determination of competence must be made before an individual can be tried for a criminal offense: To stand trial, people must be competent—able to understand the charges against them and to assist with their own defense.

> Duty to warn is a standard that sets forth the responsibility of the therapist to warn potential victims that a client may attempt to hurt or kill them.

> Individuals who have specialized knowledge and who assist judges and juries in making decisions, especially about such issues as competence and malingering, are called expert witnesses.

Patients' Rights and Clinical Practice Guidelines

What are the key rights of patients in the mental health system?

> One of the more fundamental rights of patients in mental health facilities is their right to treatment—that is, they have a legal right to some sort of ongoing effort to both define and strive toward treatment goals. By contrast, a great deal of controversy exists over whether all patients are capable of making a decision to refuse treatment. This is an especially difficult dilemma in the case of antipsychotic medications that may improve

patients' symptoms but bring with them severe negative side effects.

> Subjects who participate in any research study must be fully informed of the risks and benefits and formally give their informed consent to indicate they have been fully informed.

> Clinical practice guidelines can play a major role in providing information about types of interventions that are likely to be effective for a specific disorder, thereby setting the stage for evidence-based practice. Critical to such a determination are measures of clinical efficacy (internal validity) and clinical utility (external validity); in other words, the former is a measure of whether a treatment works, and the latter is a measure of whether the treatment is effective in a variety of settings and can be implemented in those settings.

Key Terms

civil commitment laws, 538
mental illness, 539
dangerousness, 539
deinstitutionalization, 540

transinstitutionalization, 541
criminal commitment, 544
diminished capacity, 545
competence, 548

duty to warn, 548
expert witness, 548
clinical efficacy axis, 552
clinical utility axis, 552

Answers to Concept Checks

14.1

1. mental disorder; 2. dangerous;
3. grave disability; 4. legal;
5. deinstitutionalization;
6. transinstitutionalization

14.2

1. a; 2. e; 3. c; 4. h; 5. b; 6. g, f; 7. d

14.3

1. d; 2. c; 3. a; 4. e; 5. b

Media Resources

Log in to CengageBrain to access the resources your instructor requires. For this book, you can access:

CourseMate brings course concepts to life with interactive learning, study, and exam preparation tools that support the printed textbook. A textbook-specific website, Psychology CourseMate includes an integrated interactive eBook and other interactive learning tools including quizzes, flashcards, videos, and more.

Abnormal Psychology Videos

> *False Memory Research:* This clip of Elizabeth Loftus raises a host of questions about the use of therapy-related testimony in trials related to child abuse.

CENGAGENOW CengageNow is an easy-to-use online resource that helps you study in less time to get the grade you want—NOW. Take a pre-test for this chapter and re-

ceive a personalized study plan based on your results that will identify the topics you need to review and direct you to online resources to help you master those topics. Then take a post-test to help you determine the concepts you have mastered and what you will need to work on. If your textbook does not include an access code card, go to CengageBrain.com to gain access.

> Visit www.cengagebrain.com to access your account and purchase materials.

 aplia If your professor has assigned Aplia homework:

1. Sign in to your account.
2. Complete the corresponding homework exercises as required by your professor.
3. When finished, click "Grade It Now" to see which areas you have mastered, which need more work, and for detailed explanations of every answer.

CHAPTER QUIZ

1. According to a recent review by La Fond and Durham, since the 1960s mental health law in the United States has followed what pattern?
   a. A commitment to protecting society, followed by a shift in emphasis to protecting the individual.
   b. A commitment to protecting the individual, followed by a shift in emphasis to protecting society.
   c. A consistent protection of the individual above protection of society.
   d. A consistent protection of society above protection of the individual.

2. Sally has stopped eating because of her delusional belief that extraterrestrial aliens are trying to poison her. Because of her symptoms, Sally is placed in a psychiatric hospital involuntarily based on what civil authority?
   a. malingering
   b. uninformed consent
   c. police power
   d. *parens patriae*

3. Which statement is true regarding the relationship between mental illness and dangerousness?
   a. Men with mental illness who are Hispanic are more likely to be dangerous than men with mental illness from other ethnic groups.
   b. People with mental illness are more likely to be dangerous if they have been committed to a mental health facility against their will.
   c. Women with mental illness are more likely to be dangerous than women without mental illness.
   d. Most studies suggest that people with mental illness are no more likely to be dangerous than people without mental illness.

4. One goal of taking people out of mental health facilities (deinstitutionalization) was to:
   a. create mental health centers in the community that could provide a network of supportive treatments
   b. reduce the need for civil commitments, which had become too ethically complex
   c. allow families to provide more intensive care in more familiar environments
   d. test the effectiveness of new antipsychotic medications that had just been developed

5. The M'Naghten rule incorporated what criterion to determine whether a person's mental state influenced guilt or innocence?
   a. whether the act was within the individual's control
   b. whether an "average citizen" would excuse the act
   c. whether the individual knew that the act committed was wrong
   d. whether the individual felt remorse for the act

6. "Diminished capacity" is a legal concept that proposes that when people with mental illness commit a crime they may lack:
   a. intent
   b. guilt
   c. remorse
   d. memory

7. Research regarding use of the not guilty by reason of insanity (NGRI) defense has found that:
   a. the public underestimates how often people use the defense in felony cases
   b. the public overestimates how often people use this defense successfully
   c. the public underestimates how often people who use the defense are set free
   d. the public overestimates how long people who are judged NGRI are confined to a hospital

8. The guilty but mentally ill (GBMI) verdict is different from the NGRI verdict in that:
   a. only in GBMI are people assumed to have no knowledge that what they did was wrong
   b. people convicted of GBMI can be treated successfully for their mental illness yet still serve a full term in prison
   c. people convicted of GBMI can be taken to prison, but they must receive treatment for their mental illness
   d. people convicted of GBMI are detained in psychiatric hospitals, not prisons

9. An individual who commits a crime but is judged to be incompetent to stand trial may be:

a. immediately released

b. sent to prison without a trial

c. committed to a mental health facility until he is competent

d. committed to a mental health facility indefinitely

10. According to the Tarasoff verdict, a therapist can release confidential information about a client when:

a. the therapist suspects the client may be dangerous, even though a threat has not been made

b. the client has made a nonspecific threat but the client has a history of violent behavior

c. the client poses a threat to the safety of a specific individual

d. the client has made any threat of violence, even a nonspecific threat

(See Appendix A for answers.)

APPENDIX A: ANSWERS TO CHAPTER QUIZZES

Chapter 1 (page 26)

1. b   2. c   3. d   4. a   5. d   6. b   7. b
8. c   9. d   10. c

Chapter 2 (page 68)

1. b   2. b   3. d   4. d   5. b   6. b   7. c
8. c   9. d   10. c

Chapter 3 (page 114)

1. c   2. b   3. a   4. d   5. a   6. d   7. b
8. c   9. a   10. c

Chapter 4 (page 160)

1. c   2. a   3. b   4. d   5. d   6. a   7. c
8. a   9. a   10. d

Chapter 5 (page 196)

1. d   2. a   3. c   4. d   5. b   6. b   7. b
8. a   9. d   10. d

Chapter 6 (page 245)

1. b   2. c   3. a   4. a   5. c   6. b   7. b
8. d   9. c   10. a

Chapter 7 (page 280)

1. a   2. a   3. d   4. c   5. a   6. c   7. a
8. b   9. c   10. a

Chapter 8 (page 326)

1. b   2. d   3. a   4. b   5. b   6. a   7. d
8. b   9. b   10. c

Chapter 9 (page 367)

1. b   2. b   3. d   4. c   5. c   6. d   7. a
8. c   9. c   10. a

Chapter 10 (page 408)

1. c   2. a   3. d   4. c   5. d   6. c   7. a
8. c   9. b   10. a

Chapter 11 (page 446)

1. c   2. a   3. b   4. b   5. a   6. c   7. c
8. c   9. d   10. a

Chapter 12 (page 480)

1. d   2. b   3. c   4. a   5. d   6. a   7. a
8. b   9. d   10. d

Chapter 13 (page 530)

1. a   2. b   3. a   4. c   5. b   6. a   7. d
8. d   9. b   10. c

Chapter 14 (page 556)

1. b   2. d   3. d   4. a   5. c   6. a   7. b
8. b   9. c   10. c

GLOSSARY

abnormal behavior Actions that are unexpected and often evaluated negatively because they differ from typical or usual behavior.

acetylcholine Neurotransmitter, pervasive throughout the nervous system, that contributes to movement, attention, arousal, and memory. A deficiency of acetylcholine is found in people with **Alzheimer's disease**.

actigraph Small electronic device that is worn on the wrist like a watch and records body movements. This device can be used to record sleep–wake cycles.

acute onset Sudden beginning of a disease or disorder (contrast with **insidious onset**).

acute pain Pain that typically follows an injury and disappears once the injury heals or is effectively treated.

acute PTSD Posttraumatic stress disorder diagnosed 1 to 3 months following the traumatic event.

acute stress disorder Severe reaction immediately following a terrifying event, often including amnesia about the event, emotional numbing, and **derealization**. Many victims later develop **posttraumatic stress disorder**.

addiction Informal term for **substance dependence**.

adoption studies In genetics research, the study of first-degree relatives reared in different families and environments. If they share common characteristics, such as a disorder, this finding suggests that those characteristics have a genetic component.

advanced sleep phase type of circadian rhythm sleep disorder Type of circadian rhythm problem, not a *DSM-IV-TR* disorder, involving a persistent pattern of early sleep onset and awakening times.

affect Conscious, subjective aspect of an **emotion** that accompanies an action at a given time.

age of onset Person's age when developing or exhibiting symptoms of a disease or condition.

agnosia Inability to recognize and name objects; may be a symptom of **dementia** or other brain disorders.

agonist In **neuroscience**, a chemical substance that effectively increases the activity of a **neurotransmitter** by imitating its effects.

agonist substitution A replacement of a drug on which a person is dependent with one that has a similar chemical makeup, an **agonist**. Used as a treatment for **substance dependence**.

agoraphobia **Anxiety** about being in places or situations from which escape might be difficult.

agreeableness One of the dimensions of the five-factor model of personality and individual differences, involving being warm,

kind, and trusting as opposed to hostile, selfish, and mistrustful.

AIDS-related complex (ARC) Group of minor health problems such as weight loss, fever, and night sweats that appears after HIV infection but before development of full-blown AIDS.

akinesia **Extrapyramidal symptom** involving slow motor activity, an expressionless face, and emotionless speech.

alcohol By-product of the fermentation of yeasts, sugar, and water; the most commonly used and abused **depressant** substance.

alcohol dehydrogenase (ADH) An enzyme that helps humans metabolize **alcohol**. Different levels of its subtypes may account for different susceptibilities to disorders such as **fetal alcohol syndrome**.

alcohol use disorders A cognitive, biological, behavioral, and social problem associated with **alcohol** use and abuse.

alogia A deficiency in the amount or content of speech, a disturbance often seen in people with **schizophrenia**.

alpha wave Regular pattern of brain-wave voltage changes typical of calm relaxation.

alpha-adrenergic receptor Nervous system **receptor** stimulated by the **neurotransmitter norepinephrine**.

alters Shorthand term for *alter ego*, one of the different personalities or identities in **dissociative identity disorder**.

altruistic suicide Formalized suicide approved of and even expected by some cultures.

Alzheimer's disease Disease of the cerebral cortex that causes an atypical form of senile dementia, discovered in 1906 by German **psychiatrist** Alois Alzheimer.

amnestic disorder Deterioration in the ability to transfer information from short- to long-term memory, in the absence of other **dementia** symptoms, as a result of **head trauma** or drug abuse.

amniocentesis Prenatal medical procedure that allows the detection of abnormalities (for example, **Down syndrome**) in the developing fetus. It involves removal and analysis of amniotic fluid from the mother.

amok One of several running disorders seen in non-Western cultures—as in "running amok"—in which individuals enter a trance-like state and may commit violent acts. Later, they have amnesia about the episode.

amphetamine **Stimulant** medication used to treat **hypersomnia** by keeping the person awake during the day and to treat **narcolepsy**, including sudden-onset episodes, by suppressing **rapid eye movement sleep**.

amphetamine use disorders Psychological, biological, behavioral, and social problems associated with **amphetamine** use and abuse.

amygdala Part of the brain's limbic system that regulates **emotions** and the ability to learn and control impulses; figures prominently in some **psychopathology**.

amyloid plaque Clusters of dead **neurons** found during autopsy in the brains of people with **Alzheimer's disease**. Also known as *neuritic plaque*.

amyloid beta peptide Large protein, controlled by a **gene** on chromosome 21, that breaks down to contribute to the **amyloid plaque** characteristic of people with **Alzheimer's disease**. Also known as *beta-amyloid* or *A*(b).

amyloid protein Solid, waxy substance forming the core of the **amyloid plaque** characteristic of people with **Alzheimer's disease**.

analgesic rebound headache Headache, more severe than the original one, that occurs after the medication used to treat headache pain has "worn off."

analog model Approach to research that employs subjects who are similar to clinical clients, allowing replication of a clinical problem under controlled conditions.

anandamide Neurochemical that seems to be a naturally occurring version of the active chemical in **marijuana**.

angina pectoris Chest pain caused by partial blockage of the arteries that supply blood to the heart.

anhedonia An inability to experience pleasure, associated with some **mood** and schizophrenic disorders.

animal phobia Unreasonable, enduring **fear** of animals or insects that usually develops early in life.

anomic suicide Suicide motivated by loss and confusion caused by a major life disruption.

anorexia nervosa An eating disorder characterized by recurrent food refusal, leading to dangerously low body weight.

antagonist In **neuroscience**, a chemical substance that decreases or blocks the effects of a **neurotransmitter**.

antagonist drug The medication that blocks or counteracts the effects of a psychoactive drug.

antibody Highly specific molecule, called an immunoglobulin, produced by a **B cell** to combine with and neutralize an **antigen**.

antigens Foreign material that enters the body, including bacteria and parasites.

antisocial personality disorder A cluster B (dramatic, emotional, or erratic) **personality disorder** involving a pervasive pattern of disregard for and violation of the rights of others. Similar to the non-*DSM-IV-TR* label **psychopathy** but with greater emphasis on overt behavior than on personality traits.

anxiety **Mood** state characterized by marked **negative affect** and bodily symptoms of tension in which a person apprehensively anticipates future danger or misfortune. Anxiety may involve feelings, behaviors, and physiological responses.

apathy See **avolition**.

aphasia Impairment or loss of language skills resulting from brain damage caused by **stroke**, **Alzheimer's disease**, or other illness or trauma.

apolipoprotein E4 (apo E4) Protein involved in the transport of cholesterol. High concentration of one subtype, controlled by a **gene** on chromosome 19, is associated with **Alzheimer's disease**.

arrhythmia Irregular heartbeat.

Asperger's disorder Pervasive developmental disorder characterized by impairments in social relationships and restricted or unusual behaviors but without the language delays seen in **autism**.

assertiveness training Instruction in which individuals learn to cope with **stress** by rehearsing ways to protect their time and personal rights in appropriate ways to avoid being exploited and feeling used. For example, caregivers of people with **Alzheimer's disease** learn assertiveness to prevent them from resorting to abuse in frustration.

assessment gender bias Possibility that gender differences in the reported prevalence or **diagnosis** of certain diagnostic categories may be the result of prejudice in the assessment measures or the ways in which they are used.

association studies Research strategy for comparing **genetic markers** in groups of people with and without a particular disorder.

associative splitting A separation among basic functions of human personality (for example, cognition, **emotion**, and perception) seen by some as the defining characteristic of **schizophrenia**.

asylum Safe refuge; specifically, an institution to house mentally disordered people.

atherosclerosis Process by which a fatty substance or plaque builds up inside arteries to form obstructions.

attention deficit/hyperactivity disorder (ADHD) Developmental disorder featuring maladaptive levels of inattention, excessive activity, and impulsiveness.

atypical depressive episode Depressive episode characterized by some ability to experience interest and pleasure, increased **anxiety**, overeating, and oversleeping.

auditory hallucination Psychotic disturbance in perception in which a person hears a sound or a voice although it is not real or actually present. The voice is often critical, accusatory, or demanding.

augmentative communication strategy Picture or computer aid to assist people with communication deficits so that they can communicate.

autism See **autistic disorder**.

autistic disorder Pervasive developmental disorder characterized by significant impairment in social interactions and communication and restricted patterns of behavior, interest, and activity. Also known as *autism*.

autoimmune disease Condition in which the body's **immune system** attacks healthy tissue rather than **antigens**.

autonomic nervous system Part of the **peripheral nervous system** that regulates cardiovascular (heart and blood vessel), endocrine (**hormone**), and digestive functions. Includes the **sympathetic** and **parasympathetic nervous systems**.

autonomic restrictor Term for someone with **generalized anxiety disorder** because such people show lower heart rate, blood pressure, skin conductance, and respiration rate activity than do people with other anxiety disorders.

avoidant personality disorder A cluster C (anxious or fearful) **personality disorder** featuring a pervasive pattern of social inhibition, feelings of inadequacy, and hypersensitivity to criticism.

avolition An inability to initiate or persist in important activities. Also known as *apathy*.

axis One of several dimensions for which information is provided in *DSM-IV-TR* **diagnosis** protocols—for example, clinical disorders and medical conditions.

axon Nerve cell branch that transmits outgoing electrochemical impulses to other **neurons**.

B cell Special type of white blood cell produced in bone marrow. B cells release into the humoral branch of the **immune system** molecules that circulate in the blood to seek, identify, and neutralize **antigens**.

barbiturates A sedative (and addictive) drug such as Amytal, Seconal, or Nembutal that is used as a sleep aid.

bariatric surgery Surgical approach to extreme **obesity**, usually accomplished by stapling the stomach to create a small stomach pouch or bypassing the stomach through gastric bypass surgery.

basal ganglia Brain area at the base of the **forebrain** that seems to control motor behavior and to be involved in **obsessive-compulsive disorder**.

baseline Measured rate of a behavior before introduction of an intervention that allows comparison and assessment of the effects of the intervention.

behavior rating scale Structured assessment instrument used before and during treatment to evaluate the frequency and severity of a specific behavior.

behavior therapy Array of therapeutic methods based on the principles of behavioral and **cognitive science**, as well as principles of learning as applied to clinical problems. It considers specific behaviors rather than inferred conflicts as legitimate targets for change.

behavioral assessment Measuring, observing, and systematically evaluating (rather than inferring) the client's thoughts, feelings, and behavior in the actual problem situation or context.

behavioral inhibition system (BIS) Brain circuit in the **limbic system** that responds to threat signals by inhibiting activity and causing **anxiety**.

behavioral medicine Interdisciplinary approach applying behavioral science to the prevention, **diagnosis**, and treatment of medical problems. Also known as *psychosomatic medicine*.

behavioral model Explanation of human behavior, including dysfunction, based on principles of learning and adaptation derived from experimental psychology.

behaviorism Explanation of human behavior, including dysfunction, based on principles of learning and adaptation derived from experimental psychology.

Bender Visual–Motor Gestalt Test Neuropsychological test for children in which they copy a variety of lines and shapes.

benzodiazepines An antianxiety drug such as Valium, Xanax, Dalmane, or Halcion also used to treat insomnia. Effective against **anxiety** (and, at high potency, **panic disorder**), benzodiazepines show some side effects, such as some cognitive and motor impairment, and may result in **substance dependence**. **Relapse** rates are extremely high when such a drug is discontinued.

beta-adrenergic receptor Nervous system **receptor** stimulated by the **neurotransmitter norepinephrine** to increase blood pressure and heart rate. Drugs called beta-blockers act at this level to control high blood pressure.

beta-amyloid See **beta peptide**.

binge A relatively brief episode of uncontrolled, excessive consumption, usually of food or **alcohol**.

binge-eating disorder (BED) A pattern of eating involving distress-inducing **binges** not followed by purging behaviors; being considered as a new *DSM* diagnostic category.

biofeedback Use of physiological monitoring equipment to make individuals aware of their own bodily functions, such as blood pressure or brain waves, that they cannot normally access, with the purpose of controlling these functions.

biological model Explanation of psychological dysfunction that primarily emphasizes brain disorder or illness as the cause.

bipolar I disorder Alternation of **major depressive episodes** with full **manic episodes**.

bipolar II disorder Alternation of **major depressive episodes** with hypomanic episodes (not full **manic episodes**).

bisexuality Attraction to both same- and opposite-sex sexual partners.

blindsight Phenomenon in which a person is able to perform visual functions while having no awareness or memory of these abilities. Also called *unconscious vision*.

blood–injury–injection phobia Unreasonable **fear** and avoidance of exposure to blood, injury, or the possibility of an injection. Victims experience fainting and a drop in blood pressure.

body dysmorphic disorder (BDD) Somatoform disorder featuring a disruptive preoccupation with some imagined defect in appearance ("imagined ugliness").

borderline personality disorder A cluster B (dramatic, emotional, or erratic) **personality disorder** involving a pervasive pattern of instability of interpersonal relationships, self-image, affect, and control over impulses.

bradykinesia Slowed body movements, as occur in **Parkinson's disease**.

brain circuits Neurotransmitter current or neural pathway in the brain.

brain stem Ancient lower part of the brain responsible for many life-sustaining automatic functions, such as breathing and coordinated movement.

breathalyzer test Measure of **alcohol** intoxication that uses a breath sample because some consumed alcohol is vaporized in the lungs and exhaled.

breathing-related sleep disorders A sleep disruption leading to excessive sleepiness or insomnia, caused by a breathing problem such as interrupted **(sleep apnea)** or labored **(hypoventilation)** breathing.

Brief Psychiatric Rating Scale Behavior rating scale used to assess the severity of patient problem areas, such as guilt feelings and preoccupation with health.

brief psychotic disorder A psychotic disturbance involving **delusions**, **hallucinations**, or **disorganized speech** or behavior but lasting less than 1 month; often occurs in reaction to a stressor.

Briquet's syndrome Obsolete term for **somatization disorder**.

bulimia nervosa An eating disorder involving recurrent episodes of uncontrolled excessive **(binge)** eating followed by compensatory actions to remove the food (for example, deliberate vomiting, laxative abuse, and excessive exercise).

caffeine use disorders Cognitive, biological, behavioral, and social problems associated with the use and abuse of caffeine.

cancer Category of often-fatal medical conditions involving abnormal cell growth and malignancy.

cannabinoid Member of a family of chemicals in **marijuana** believed to be responsible for its mood- and behavior-altering ability.

cardiovascular disease Afflictions in the mechanisms, including the heart, blood vessels, and their controllers, responsible for transporting blood to the body's tissues and organs. Psychological factors may play important roles in such diseases and their treatments.

cardiovascular system Heart, blood vessels, and their controlling mechanisms, all of which transport blood and nutrients to the tissues of the body.

case study method Research procedure in which a single person or small group is studied in detail. The method does not allow conclusions about cause-and-effect relationships, and findings can be generalized only with great caution (contrast with **single-case experimental design**).

castration anxiety In **psychoanalysis**, the **fear** in young boys that they will be mutilated genitally because of their lust for their mothers.

catalepsy Motor movement disturbance seen in people with some psychoses and **mood disorders** in which body postures can be "sculpted" to remain fixed for long periods.

cataplexy Sudden loss of muscle tone that accompanies **narcolepsy**.

catatonia A disorder of movement involving immobility or excited agitation.

catatonic immobility A disturbance of motor behavior in which the person remains motionless, sometimes in an awkward posture, for extended periods.

catatonic type of schizophrenia A type of **schizophrenia** in which motor disturbances (rigidity, agitation, and odd mannerisms) predominate.

catecholamine Outdated, simplistic theory of the **etiology** of **mood disorders** stating that **norepinephrine** (a catecholamine) excess causes **mania**, and that low levels of it cause some forms of depression.

catharsis Rapid or sudden release of emotional tension thought to be an important factor in psychoanalytic therapy.

caudate nucleus Brain structure, part of the **basal ganglia**, that controls motor behavior and is implicated in **obsessive-compulsive disorder**.

cellular branch Branch of the **immune system** using specialized cells to protect the body cells against viral and parasite infections.

central nervous system Brain and spinal cord.

central sleep apnea Brief periods of cessation in respiratory activity during sleep that may be associated with **central nervous system** disorders. Most clients awaken often as a result but do not report sleepiness and may be unaware of any problem.

cerebellum Part of the **hindbrain** in the **brain stem** that controls motor coordination and may be involved in **autism**.

cerebral cortex Largest part of the **forebrain**, divided into two hemispheres; responsible for human functions such as perceiving, reasoning, planning, creating, and remembering.

cerebral vascular accident (CVA) See **stroke**.

childhood disintegrative disorder **Pervasive developmental disorder** involving severe regression in language, adaptive behavior, and motor skills after a 2- to 4-year period of normal development.

chemical imbalance Relative excess or deficit in brain chemicals, such as **neurotransmitters**, that may be implicated in some **psychological disorders**.

choking phobia **Fear** and avoidance of swallowing pills, foods, and fluids, which may lead to significant weight loss.

chorea Motor problems characterized by involuntary limb movements.

chorionic villus sampling (CVS) A genetic test conducted during early pregnancy that samples cells found in the placenta (chorionic villi) and assesses possible genetic or chromosomal problems in the villus.

chronic fatigue syndrome (CFS) Incapacitating exhaustion following only minimal exertion, accompanied by fever, headaches, muscle and joint pain, depression, and **anxiety**.

chronic pain Enduring pain that does not decrease over time; may occur in muscles, joints, and the lower back; and may be caused by enlarged blood vessels or degenerating or cancerous tissue. Other significant factors are social and psychological.

chronic PTSD **Posttraumatic stress disorder** that endures longer than 3 months and is associated with greater avoidance and a higher likelihood of **comorbidity** with additional disorders.

chronological age Person's age in calendar years.

circadian rhythm sleep disorder A sleep disturbance resulting in sleepiness or insomnia, caused by the body's inability to synchronize its sleep patterns with the current pattern of day and night.

civil commitment laws Legal proceeding that determines a person is mentally disordered and may be hospitalized, even involuntarily.

classical categorical approach Classification method founded on the assumption of clear-cut differences among disorders, each with a different known cause. Also known as *pure categorical approach*.

classical conditioning Fundamental learning process first described by Ivan Pavlov. An event that automatically elicits a response is paired with another stimulus event that does not (a neutral stimulus). After repeated pairings, the neutral stimulus becomes a **conditioned stimulus** that by itself can elicit the desired response.

classification Assignment of objects or people to categories on the basis of shared characteristics.

clinical assessment Systematic evaluation and measurement of psychological, biological, and social factors in a person presenting with a possible **psychological disorder**.

clinical description Details of the combination of behaviors, thoughts, and feelings of an individual that make up a particular disorder.

clinical efficacy axis One of a proposed set of guidelines for evaluating clinical interventions on the evidence of their effectiveness (compare with **clinical utility axis**).

clinical psychologist Person who has earned a Ph.D. or related degree (for example, Psy.D.) in psychology and is trained to conduct research into the causes and treatment of severe **psychological disorders**, as well as to diagnose, assess, and treat them.

clinical significance Degree to which research findings have useful and meaningful applications to real problems.

clinical utility axis One of a proposed set of guidelines for evaluating clinical interventions by whether they can be applied effectively and cost effectively in real clinical settings (compare with **clinical efficacy axis**).

clonidine Medical treatment for **hypertension** that is often used to reduce the **negative symptoms** of **withdrawal** from **opiates**.

cocaine Derivative of coca leaves used medically as a local anesthetic and narcotic; often a substance of abuse.

cocaine use disorders Cognitive, biological, behavioral, and social problems associated with the use and abuse of **cocaine**.

cognitive restructuring Cognitive therapy procedure used to change negative or unrealistic thoughts or attributions.

cognitive science Field of study that examines how humans and other animals acquire, process, store, and retrieve information.

cognitive therapy Treatment approach that involves identifying and altering negative thinking styles related to **psychological disorders** such as depression and **anxiety** and replacing them with more positive beliefs and attitudes—and, ultimately, more adaptive behavior and coping styles.

cognitive–behavioral treatment (CBT) Group of treatment procedures aimed at identifying and modifying faulty thought processes, attitudes and attributions, and problem behaviors; often used synonymously with **cognitive therapy**.

cohort Participants in each age group of a study with a **cross-sectional design**.

cohort effect Observation that people of different age groups differ in their values and experiences.

collective unconscious Accumulated wisdom of a culture collected and remembered across generations, a psychodynamic concept introduced by Carl Jung.

communication disorder Problem in transmitting or conveying information, including **stuttering**, **selective mutism**, and **expressive language disorder**.

community intervention Approach to treating and preventing disorders by directing action at the organizational, agency, and community levels rather than at individuals.

comorbidity Presence of two or more disorders in an individual at the same time.

comparative treatment research Outcome research that contrasts two or more treatment methods to determine which is most effective.

competence Ability of legal defendants to participate in their own defense and understand the charges and the roles of the trial participants.

Comprehensive System Standardized system of administering and scoring the **Rorschach inkblot test** that seeks to improve its **reliability** and **validity**.

compulsions Repetitive, ritualistic, time-consuming behavior or mental act a person feels driven to perform.

computerized axial tomography (CAT) scan Noninvasive imaging procedure useful in identifying abnormalities in the structure or shape of the brain. Also known as a *CT scan*.

concurrent validity Condition of testing in which the results from one test correspond to the results of other measures of the same phenomenon. Also known as *descriptive validity*.

conditioned response (CR) Learned reaction, similar to the **unconditioned response**, elicited by a **conditioned stimulus** following **classical conditioning**.

conditioned stimulus (CS) Environmental event that acquires the ability to elicit a learned response as a result of **classical conditioning** associated with an **unconditioned stimulus**.

conditioning Process by which behaviors can be learned or modified through interaction with the environment. See **classical conditioning** and **operant conditioning**.

confound Any factor occurring in a study that makes the results uninterpretable because its effects cannot be separated from those of the variables being studied.

confounding variable Variable in a research study that was not part of the intended design and that may contribute to changes in the **dependent variable**.

conscientiousness One of the dimensions of the five-factor model of personality and individual differences involving being organized, thorough, and reliable as opposed to careless, negligent, and unreliable.

construct validity Degree to which signs and symbols used to categorize a disorder relate to one another while differing from those for other disorders.

content validity Degree to which the characteristics of a disorder are a true sample of the phenomenon in question.

contingency management Encouragement of those reinforcers that promote and maintain desired behaviors and removal of those reinforcers that maintain undesired behaviors.

control group Group of individuals in a study who are similar to the experimental subjects in every way but are not exposed to the treatment received by the experimen-

tal group. Their presence allows for a comparison of the differential effects of the treatment.

controlled drinking An extremely controversial treatment approach to **alcohol** dependence, in which severe abusers are taught to drink in moderation.

conversion disorder Physical malfunctioning, such as blindness or paralysis, suggesting neurological impairment but with no organic pathology to account for it.

conversion hysteria Obsolete term for **conversion disorder** derived from the Freudian notion that physical symptoms represented a conversion of **unconscious** conflicts into a more acceptable form.

coronary heart disease (CHD) Blockage of the arteries supplying blood to the heart muscle; a major cause of death in Western culture, with social and psychological factors involved.

correlation Degree to which two variables are associated. In a **positive correlation**, the two variables increase or decrease together. In a **negative correlation**, one variable decreases as the other increases.

correlation coefficient Computed statistic reflecting the strength and direction of any association between two variables. It can range from 21.00 through 0.00 (indicating no association) to 11.00, with the absolute value indicating the strength and the sign reflecting the direction.

correlational study Research procedure in which variables are measured and compared to detect any association but are not manipulated. Conclusions about cause-and-effect relationships are not permissible.

corticotropin-releasing factor (CRF) Neuromodulator hormone secreted into the blood by the **hypothalamus**. It stimulates the pituitary gland as part of a reaction chain called the **stress** response. It may be implicated in **mood disorders**, as well as physical problems.

cortisol **Stress** hormone secreted by the cortex of the adrenal glands as part of the **stress** response.

counseling psychologist Person who has earned a Ph.D. or related degree in psychology and is trained to study and treat adjustment and vocational issues in relatively healthy people.

course Pattern of development and change of a disorder over time.

covert sensitization A cognitive–behavioral intervention to reduce unwanted behaviors by having clients imagine the extremely aversive consequences of the behaviors and establish negative rather than positive associations with them.

crack Cocaine in a highly potent, solid, rocklike form.

Creutzfeldt-Jakob disease Extremely rare condition that causes **dementia**.

criminal commitment Legal procedure by which a person found not guilty of a crime by reason of **insanity** must be confined in a psychiatric hospital.

criterion gender bias Possibility that gender differences in the reported prevalence or **diagnosis** of certain diagnostic categories may be the result of prejudice in the defining criteria for the disorder or the ways in which they are used.

criterion validity Extent to which categorization accurately predicts the future **course**

of a disorder, whether treated or untreated. See also **predictive validity**.

cross-generational effect Limit on the **generalizability** of longitudinal research because the group under study may differ from others in culture and experience.

cross-sectional design Methodology to examine a characteristic by comparing individuals of different ages (contrast with **longitudinal design**).

cross-tolerant Condition in which a person may replace **addiction** to one drug with addiction to another when the two drugs have similar chemical makeup and act on the same **neurotransmitter receptors**.

CT scan See **computerized axialtomography (CAT) scan**.

cultural–familial intellectual disability Mild form of **intellectual disability** that may be caused largely by environmental influences.

cyclothymic disorder Chronic (at least 2 years) **mood disorder** characterized by alternating **mood** elevation and depression levels that are not as severe as **manic** or **major depressive episodes**.

dangerousness Tendency to violence that, contrary to popular opinion, is not more likely among mental patients.

defense mechanism Common pattern of behavior, often an adaptive coping style when it occurs in moderation, observed in response to a particular situation. Psychoanalytic theory suggests that defense mechanisms are **unconscious** processes originating in the **ego**.

deinstitutionalization Systematic removal of people with severe **mental illness** or **intellectual disability** from institutions like psychiatric hospitals.

delayed sleep phase type of circadian rhythm sleep disorder Persistent pattern of late sleep onset and awakening time.

delayed-onset PTSD Posttraumatic stress disorder with onset more than 6 months after the traumatic event.

delirium Rapid-onset reduced clarity of consciousness and cognition, with confusion, disorientation, and deficits in memory and language.

delirium tremens (DT) See **withdrawal delirium**.

delta wave Relatively slow and irregular pattern of brain waves typical of the deepest, most relaxed stage of sleep. This is the time when sleeping **panic attacks** may occur. Delta activity during wakefulness may indicate brain dysfunction. Also known as *slow wave sleep*.

delusions A psychotic symptom involving disorder of thought content and presence of strong beliefs that are misrepresentations of reality.

delusion of grandeur Psychotic symptom; people's unfounded belief that they are more famous or important than is true.

delusion of persecution People's unfounded belief that others seek to harm them.

delusional disorder A psychotic disorder featuring a persistent belief contrary to reality (**delusion**) but no other symptoms of **schizophrenia**.

dementia Gradual-onset deterioration of brain functioning, involving memory loss, inability to recognize objects or faces, and problems in planning and abstract reasoning. These are associated with frustration and discouragement.

dementia of the Alzheimer's type Gradual onset of cognitive deficits caused by **Alzheimer's disease,** principally identified by a person's inability to recall newly or previously learned material. The most common form of **dementia.**

dementia praecox The Latin term meaning premature loss of mind; an early label for what is now called **schizophrenia**, emphasizing the disorder's frequent appearance during adolescence.

dendrite Nerve cell branches that receive incoming electrochemical information for transmission along the **neuron.**

dependent personality disorder A cluster C (anxious or fearful) **personality disorder** characterized by a person's pervasive and excessive need to be taken care of, a condition that leads to submissive and clinging behavior and fears of separation.

dependent variable In an experimental study, the phenomenon that is measured and expected to be influenced (compare with **independent variable**).

depersonalization Altering of perception that causes people to temporarily lose a sense of their own reality; most prevalent in people with the **dissociative disorders**. There is often a feeling of being outside observers of their own behavior.

depersonalization disorder Dissociative disorder in which feelings of **depersonalization** are so severe they dominate the individual's life and prevent normal functioning.

depressant A **psychoactive substance** that results in behavioral sedation; such substances include **alcohol** and the sedative, hypnotic, and anxiolytic drugs.

depressive cognitive triad Thinking errors by depressed people negatively focused in three areas: themselves, their immediate world, and their future.

depressive personality disorder Pervasive pattern dominated by dejection, self-criticism, and a judgmental stance toward other people; under consideration as a future *DSM* category.

depressive stupor Rare but severe depressive episode experienced by someone with a **mood disorder**, featuring, usually, substantial reduction in spontaneous motor movement or, occasionally, agitation or odd mannerisms.

derailment See **loose association**.

derealization Situation in which the individual loses a sense of the reality of the external world.

descriptive validity See **concurrent validity**.

deterministic In genetics, **genes** that lead to nearly a 100% chance of developing the associated disorder. These are rare in the population.

developmental psychology Study of changes in behavior that occur over time.

developmental psychopathology Study of changes in **abnormal behavior** that occur over time.

deviation IQ Intelligence test score that estimates how much a child's school performance is likely to deviate from the average performance of others of the same age.

diagnosis Process of determining whether a **presenting problem** meets the established criteria for a specific **psychological disorder**.

Diagnostic and Statistical Manual, Fourth Edition, Text Revision (DSM-IV-TR) Current version of the official **classification** system for **psychological disorders**, published by the American Psychiatric Association.

dialectical behavioral therapy A promising treatment for **borderline personality disorder** that involves exposing the client to stressors in a controlled situation, as well as helping the client regulate **emotions** and cope with stressors that might trigger suicidal behavior.

diastolic blood pressure Blood pressure level when the heart is at rest or between heartbeats.

diathesis–stress model Hypothesis that both an inherited tendency (a **vulnerability**) and specific stressful conditions are required to produce a disorder.

dimensional approach Method of categorizing characteristics on a continuum rather than on a binary, either-or, or all-or-none basis.

dimethyltryptamine (DMT) Natural **hallucinogen** from the bark of trees that grow in Central and South America.

diminished capacity Evidence of an abnormal mental condition in people that causes criminal charges against them requiring intent or knowledge to be reduced to lesser offenses requiring only reckless or criminal neglect.

directionality Possibility that when two variables, A and B, are correlated variable A causes variable B or variable B causes variable A.

discrimination training Arrangement of experiences in which the person or animal learns to respond under certain conditions and not to respond under other conditions.

disease conviction Core feature of **hypochondriasis**; people's firm belief that they currently have a disease, based on the misinterpretation of their own symptoms and sensations.

disease model of chemical dependence View that drug dependence is caused by a physiological disorder. This implies the user is a blameless victim of an illness.

disorder of written expression Condition in which writing performance is significantly below the standard for that age level.

disorganized speech A style of talking often seen in people with **schizophrenia**, involving incoherence and a lack of typical logic patterns.

disorganized type of schizophrenia A type of **schizophrenia** featuring disrupted speech and behavior, disjointed **delusions** and **hallucinations**, and silly or **flat affect**.

displacement Defense mechanism in which a person directs a problem impulse toward a safe substitute.

dissociation Detachment or loss of integration between identity or reality and consciousness.

dissociative amnesia Dissociative disorder featuring the inability to recall personal information; usually of a stressful or traumatic nature.

dissociative disorder Disorder in which individuals feel detached from themselves or their surroundings and feel reality, experience, and identity may disintegrate.

dissociative fugue Dissociative disorder featuring sudden, unexpected travel away from home, along with an inability to recall the past, sometimes with assumption of a new identity.

dissociative identity disorder (DID) Disorder in which as many as 100 personalities or fragments of personalities coexist within one body and mind. Formerly known as *multiple personality disorder*.

dissociative trance disorder (DTD) Altered state of consciousness in which people firmly believe they are possessed by spirits; considered a disorder only where there is distress and dysfunction.

disulfiram Chemical (trade name Antabuse) used as an aversion treatment for heavy drinking because it causes a buildup in the body of an **alcohol** by-product, making the person vomit after drinking. Clients must continue taking it for the chemical to remain effective.

dominant gene One **gene** of any pair of genes that determines a particular trait.

dopamine Neurotransmitter whose generalized function is to activate other neurotransmitters and to aid in exploratory and pleasure-seeking behaviors (thus balancing **serotonin**). A relative excess of dopamine is implicated in **schizophrenia** (although contradictory evidence suggests the connection is not simple), and its deficit is involved in **Parkinson's disease**.

dopaminergic system Parts of the nervous system activated by the **neurotransmitter dopamine**; involved in many functions, including the experience of reward.

dorsal horn of the spinal cord One of several sections of the spinal cord responsible for transmitting sensory input to the brain. These sections function as a "gate" that allows transmission of pain sensations if the stimulation is sufficiently intense.

double bind communication According to an obsolete, unsupported theory, the practice of transmitting conflicting messages that was thought to cause **schizophrenia**.

double depression Severe **mood disorder** typified by **major depressive episodes** superimposed over a background of **dysthymic disorder**.

double-blind control Procedure in **outcome research** that prevents bias by ensuring that neither the subjects nor the providers of the experimental treatment know who is receiving treatment and who is receiving a **placebo**.

Down syndrome Type of **intellectual disability** caused by a chromosomal aberration (chromosome 21) and involving characteristic physical appearance. Also known as *trisomy 21*.

dream analysis Psychoanalytic therapy method in which dream content is examined as symbolic of **id** impulses and **intrapsychic conflicts**.

duty to warn Mental health professional's responsibility to break confidentiality and notify the potential victim whom a client has specifically threatened.

dyslexia Learning disability involving problems in reading.

dysmorphophobia Literally, "fear of ugliness," an obsolete term for **body dysmorphic disorder**.

dyspareunia See **sexual pain disorder**.

dysphoric manic episode, See **mixed manic episode**.

dyssomnia A problem in getting to sleep or in obtaining sleep of sufficient quality.

dysthymic disorder **Mood disorder** involving persistently depressed **mood**, with low self-esteem, **withdrawal**, pessimism, or despair, present for at least 2 years, with no absence of symptoms for more than 2 months.

echolalia Repeating or echoing the speech of others, a normal intermediate step in the development of speech skills. Originally thought to be a unique symptom of **autism**, it is now seen as evidence of developmental delay involved in that disorder.

echopraxia Involuntary imitation of the movement of another person.

educable intellectual disability Term referring to a level of **intellectual disability** comparable to the *DSM-IV-TR* designation of **mild intellectual disability** that assumes the individual can learn basic academic skills.

effect size A statistical process that eliminates how large a change in measure occurred. Often used before and after a clinical treatment to determine its relative success.

ego In **psychoanalysis**, the psychic entity responsible for finding realistic and practical ways to satisfy **id** drives.

ego psychology Psychoanalytic theory that emphasizes the role of the **ego** in development and attributes **psychological disorders** to failure of the ego to manage impulses and internal conflicts. Also known as *self-psychology*.

egoistic suicide Suicide that occurs in the context of diminished social supports, as in the case of some elderly people who have lost friends and family contacts.

Electra complex In **psychoanalysis**, a young girl's intrapsychic desire to replace her mother, possess her father, and acquire a penis. The resolution of this complex results in development of the **superego**.

electrocardiogram Measure of electrical activity generated by heart muscle exertion used to detect and evaluate heart diseases.

electroconvulsive therapy (ECT) Biological treatment for severe, chronic depression involving the application of electrical impulses through the brain to produce seizures. The reasons for its effectiveness are unknown.

electroencephalogram (EEG) Measure of electrical activity patterns in the brain, taken through electrodes placed on the scalp.

electromyogram (EMG) Measure of muscle movement.

electrooculogram (EOG) Measure of eye muscle movement particularly relevant to detecting dream stages during sleep.

emotion Pattern of action elicited by an external event and a feeling state, accompanied by a characteristic physiological response.

emotion contagion Situation in which an emotional reaction spreads from one individual to others nearby.

empathy Condition of sharing and understanding the **emotions** of another person.

endocrine system Network of glands that affect bodily functions by releasing **hormones** into the bloodstream. Some endocrine activity is implicated in **psychological disorders**.

endogenous opioids Substance occurring naturally throughout the body that functions like a **neurotransmitter** to shut down pain sensation even in the presence of marked tissue damage. These opioids may contribute to psychological problems such as eating disorders. Also known as an *endorphin* or *enkephalin*.

endophenotype Genetic mechanism that contributes to the underlying problems causing the symptoms and difficulties experienced by people with **psychological disorders**.

endorphin See **endogenous opioid**.

enkephalin See **endogenous opioid**.

epidemiology **Psychopathology** research method examining the prevalence, distribution, and consequences of disorders in populations.

epigenetics The study of factors other than inherited DNA sequence, such as new learning or stress, that alter the phenotypic expression of **genes**.

episodic course Pattern of a disorder alternating between recovery and recurrence.

equifinality **Developmental psychopathology** principle that a behavior or disorder may have several causes.

erotomanic type Type of **delusional disorder** featuring the belief that another person, usually of higher status, is in love with the individual.

erotophobia Learned negative reaction to or attitude about sexual activity, perhaps developed as a result of a negative or even traumatic event, such as rape.

essential hypertension High blood pressure with no verifiable physical cause, which makes up the overwhelming majority of high blood pressure cases.

etiology Cause or source of a disorder.

event-related potential (ERP) Brain's electrical reaction to a psychologically meaningful environment event, as measured by the **electroencephalogram**. Also known as *evoked potential*.

evoked potential See **event-related potential (ERP)**.

exhibitionism A sexual gratification attained by exposing genitals to unsuspecting strangers.

exorcism Religious ritual that attributes disordered behavior to possession by demons and seeks to treat the individual by driving the demons from the body.

expectancy effect People's response to a substance on the basis of their beliefs about it, even if it contains no active ingredient. This phenomenon demonstrates that cognitive, as well as physiological, factors are involved in drug reaction and dependence.

experiment Research method that can establish causation by manipulating the variables in question and controlling for alternative explanations of any observed effects.

expert witness Person who because of special training and experience is allowed to offer opinion testimony in legal trials.

expressed emotion (EE) Hostility, criticism, and over-involvement demonstrated by some families toward a family member with a **psychological disorder**. This can often contribute to the person's **relapse**.

expressive language Communication with words.

expressive language disorder Individual's problems in spoken communication, as measured by significantly low scores on standardized tests of **expressive language** relative to nonverbal intelligence test scores. Symptoms may include a markedly limited vocabulary or errors in verb tense.

extensive support disability Intellectual disability level characterized by the long-term and regular care required for individuals with this degree of disability.

external validity Extent to which research findings generalize, or apply, to people and settings not involved in the study.

extinction Learning process in which a response maintained by **reinforcement** in **operant conditioning** or pairing in **classical conditioning** decreases when that reinforcement or pairing is removed; also the procedure of removing that reinforcement or pairing.

extrapyramidal symptom Serious side effect of **neuroleptic** medications resembling the motor difficulties of **Parkinson's disease**. Such symptoms include **akinesia** and **tardive dyskinesia**. Also known as a *parkinsonian symptom*.

extroversion One of the dimensions of the five-factor model of personality and individual differences, involving being talkative, assertive, and active as opposed to silent, passive, and reserved.

eye-tracking See **smooth-pursuit eye movement**.

facial agnosia Type of **agnosia** characterized by a person's inability to recognize even familiar faces.

factitious disorder Nonexistent physical or **psychological disorder** deliberately faked for no apparent gain except, possibly, sympathy and attention.

failure to thrive Stunted physical growth and maturation in children, often associated with psychosocial factors such as lack of love and nurturing.

false negative Assessment error in which no pathology is noted (that is, test results are negative) when one is actually present.

false positive Assessment error in which pathology is reported (that is, test results are positive) when none is actually present.

familial aggregation Extent to which a disorder would be found among a patient's relatives.

family studies Genetic study that examines patterns of traits and behaviors among relatives.

fatalistic suicide Suicide in the context of a person's hopelessness and loss of the feeling of control over personal destiny.

fear **Emotion** of an immediate alarm reaction to present danger or life-threatening emergencies.

fearlessness hypothesis One of the major theories of the **etiology** of **antisocial personality disorder**, stating that psychopaths are prone to **fear** and thus less inhibited from dangerous or illicit activities.

female orgasmic disorder The recurring delay or absence of orgasm in some women following a normal sexual excitement phase, relative to their prior experience and current stimulation. Also known as **inhibited orgasm** (female).

female sexual arousal disorder The recurrent inability in some women to attain or maintain adequate lubrication and sexual excitement swelling responses until completion of sexual activity.

fetal alcohol syndrome (FAS) A pattern of problems, including learning difficulties, behavior deficits, and characteristic physical flaws, resulting from heavy drinking by the victim's mother when she was pregnant with the victim.

fetishism Long-term, recurring, intense sexually arousing urges, fantasies, or behavior involving the use of nonliving, unusual objects, which cause distress or impairment in life functioning.

fight/flight system (FFS) **Brain circuit** in animals that when stimulated causes an immediate alarm-and-escape response resembling human **panic**.

fixation Psychoanalytic concept suggesting that clients stop at or concentrate on a psychosexual stage because of a lack of appropriate gratification at that stage.

flashback Sudden, intense reexperiencing of a previous, usually traumatic, event.

flat affect An apparently emotionless demeanor (including toneless speech and vacant gaze) when a reaction would be expected.

flight or fight response Biological reaction to alarming stressors that musters the body's resources (for example, blood flow and respiration) to resist or flee a threat.

fluoxetine **Serotonin-specific reuptake inhibitor** (trade name Prozac) that acts on the serotonergic system as a treatment for depression, **obsessive-compulsive disorder**, and **bulimia nervosa**.

flurazepam Long-acting medication for insomnia (trade name Dalmane) that may cause daytime sleepiness.

folie à deux See **shared psychotic disorder**.

forebrain Top section of the brain that includes the limbic system, **basal ganglia**, **caudate nucleus**, and **cerebral cortex**.

formal observation Structured recording of behaviors that are measurable and well defined.

fragile X syndrome Pattern of **abnormality** caused by a defect in the **X chromosome** resulting in **intellectual disability**, learning problems, and unusual physical characteristics.

free association Psychoanalytic therapy technique intended to explore threatening material repressed into the **unconscious**. The patient is instructed to say whatever comes to mind without censoring.

frenzy witchcraft Running frenzy disorder among the Navajo tribe that seems equivalent to **dissociative fugue**.

frontal lobe Forward section of each cerebral hemisphere most responsible for thinking, reasoning, memory, the experience of reward, and social behavior and thus most likely to be involved in a range of **psychopathologies**.

frotteurism **Paraphilia** in which the person gains sexual gratification by rubbing against unwilling victims in crowds from which they cannot escape.

functional communication training Teaching of speech or nonspeech communication skills to replace undesired behavior. The new skills are useful to the person and are maintained because of the effects they have on others.

functional genomics Study of how genes function to create changes in the organism.

GABA–benzodiazepine system Chemical **benzodiazepines** (minor tranquilizers) that facilitate the effects of the **neurotransmitter gamma-aminobutyric acid** in reducing anxiety. Such a system suggests the existence of natural benzodiazepines in the nervous system that have not yet been discovered.

gamma-aminobutyric acid (GABA) Neurotransmitter that reduces activity across the **synaptic cleft** and thus inhibits a range of behaviors and **emotions**, especially generalized **anxiety**.

gate control theory of pain View that psychological factors can enhance or diminish the sensation and perception of pain by influencing the transmission of pain impulses through the section of the spinal cord that acts as a "gate."

gender identity disorder A psychological dissatisfaction with biological gender, or a disturbance in the sense of identity as a male or female. The primary goal is not sexual arousal but rather to live the life of the opposite gender.

gender nonconformity Individuals expressing behavior and attitudes consistently characteristic of the opposite sex.

general adaptation syndrome (GAS) Sequence of reactions to sustained **stress** described by Hans Selye. These stages are alarm, resistance, and exhaustion, which may lead to death.

generalizability Extent to which research results apply to a range of individuals not included in the study.

generalized amnesia Loss of memory of all personal information, including identity.

generalized anxiety disorder (GAD) Anxiety disorder characterized by intense, uncontrollable, unfocused, chronic, and continuous worry that is distressing and unproductive, accompanied by physical symptoms of tenseness, irritability, and restlessness.

genes Long deoxyribonucleic acid (DNA) molecule, the basic physical unit of heredity that appears as a location on a chromosome.

genetic linkage analysis Study that seeks to match the inheritance pattern of a disorder to that of a **genetic marker**. This helps researchers establish the location of the **gene** responsible for the disorder.

genetic marker Inherited characteristic for which the chromosomal location of the responsible **gene** is known.

genome All of the hereditary information of an organism that is encoded in DNA.

genotype Specific genetic makeup of an individual.

globus hystericus Sensation of a lump in the throat causing the person difficulty in swallowing, eating, and talking. A conversion symptom or part of choking phobia.

glutamate Amino acid **neurotransmitter** that excites many different **neurons**, leading to action.

glutamate system Excitatory **neurotransmitter** system that may be the avenue by which **alcohol** affects cognitive abilities.

graduated extinction Monitoring of a desired behavior, such as sleeping or compliance by children, with decreasing frequency to encourage independence.

grandiose type Type of delusional disorder featuring beliefs of inflated worth, power, knowledge, identity, or a special relationship to a deity or famous person.

hallucinations A psychotic symptom of perceptual disturbance in which something is seen, heard, or otherwise sensed although it is not actually present.

hallucinogen Any **psychoactive substance**, such as **LSD** or **marijuana**, that can produce **delusions**, **hallucinations**, **paranoia**, and altered sensory perception.

hallucinogen use disorders Cognitive, biological, behavioral, and social problems associated with the use and abuse of hallucinogenic substances.

Halstead-Reitan Neuropsychological Battery Relatively precise instrument that helps identify and locate organic damage by testing various skills, including rhythm, grip, and tactile performance.

head trauma Injury to the head and, therefore, to the brain, typically caused by accidents; can lead to cognitive impairments, including memory loss.

health psychology Subfield of **behavioral medicine** that studies psychological factors important in health promotion and maintenance.

hebephrenia A silly and immature emotionality, a characteristic of some types of **schizophrenia**.

helper T cell T cell–type lymphocyte that enhances the **immune system** response by signaling **B cells** to produce **antibodies** and other **T cells** to destroy **antigens**.

hermaphrodite See **intersex individual**.

heterosexual behavior Sexual activity with members of the opposite gender.

hierarchy of needs Ranking of human necessities from basic food to self-actualization, proposed by Abraham Maslow.

high blood pressure See **hypertension**.

hindbrain Lowest part of the **brain stem**; regulates many automatic bodily functions, such as breathing and digestion, and includes the **medulla**, **pons**, and **cerebellum**.

hippocampus Part of the brain's **limbic system** that regulates **emotions** and the ability to learn and control impulses; figures prominently in some **psychopathology**.

histrionic personality disorder A cluster B (dramatic, emotional, or erratic) **personality disorder** involving a pervasive pattern of excessive emotionality and attention seeking.

homosexual behavior Sexual activity with members of the same gender.

hormone Chemical messenger produced by the endocrine glands.

human genome project Ongoing scientific attempt to develop a comprehensive map of all human **genes**.

human immunodeficiency virus type 1 (HIV-l) Disease that causes AIDS.

humor Bodily fluid (blood, black and yellow bile, or phlegm) that early theorists believed controlled normal and abnormal functioning.

humoral theory Ancient belief that **psychological disorders** were caused by imbalances in bodily **humors** or fluids.

Huntington's disease Genetic disorder marked by involuntary limb movements and progressing to **dementia**.

hypersomnia Abnormally excessive sleep. A person with this condition falls asleep several times a day.

hypertension Major risk factor for **stroke** and heart and kidney disease that is intimately related to psychological factors. Also known as *high blood pressure*.

hypnagogic hallucination Characteristic of **narcolepsy** involving a frightening and vivid experience during sleep that is visual, tactile, aural, and mobile.

hypoactive sexual desire disorder Apparent lack of interest in sexual activity or fantasy that would not be expected considering the person's age and life situation.

hypochondriasis Somatoform disorder involving severe **anxiety** over belief in having a disease process without any evident physical cause.

hypofrontality Relative deficiency in activity in the **frontal lobes** of the brains of people with **schizophrenia**; associated with the **negative symptoms** of the disorder.

hypomanic episode Less severe and less disruptive version of a **manic episode** that is one of the criteria for several **mood disorders**.

hypothalamic–pituitary–adrenocortical (HPA) axis Brain–endocrine system connection implicated in some **psychological disorders**.

hypothalamus Part of the brain that lies beneath the **thalamus** and is broadly involved in the regulation of behavior and **emotion**.

hypothesis Educated guess or statement to be tested by research.

hypoventilation Reduced or labored breathing—for example, during sleep.

id In **psychoanalysis**, the **unconscious** psychic entity present at birth representing basic drives.

idea of reference Person's **delusion** that the actions, thoughts, laughter, and meaningless activities of others are directed toward or refer to that person.

idiographic strategy A close and detailed investigation of an individual emphasizing what makes that person unique. (Compare with **nomothetic strategy**.)

illness phobia Extreme **fear** of the possibility of contracting a disease (as opposed to the belief in already having it), combined with irrational behaviors to avoid contracting it.

imaginal exposure Presentation or **systematic exposure** of **emotions** or fearful or traumatic experiences in the imagination.

imipramine One of the **tricyclic antidepressant** drugs affecting the serotonergic and noradrenergic **neurotransmitter** systems. It blocks **panic attacks** but not more generalized **anxiety** and causes side effects such as dry mouth, dizziness, and occasionally, **sexual dysfunction**; effective in some **mood** and **anxiety** disorders, as well as other disorders.

immune system Body's means of identifying and eliminating any foreign materials (for example, bacteria, parasites, and even transplanted organs) that enter.

impacted grief reaction See **pathological grief reaction**.

implicit memory Condition of memory in which a person cannot recall past events despite acting in response to them.

impulse-control disorders A disorder in which a person acts on an irresistible, but potentially harmful, impulse.

inappropriate affect An emotional display that is improper for the situation.

incest A deviant sexual attraction (**pedophilia**) directed toward a family member; often the attraction of a father toward a daughter who is maturing physically.

incidence Number of new cases of a disorder appearing during a specific period (compare with **prevalence**).

independent variable Phenomenon manipulated by the experimenter in a study and expected to influence the **dependent variable**.

inferiority complex Feeling of being inferior to others while striving for superiority.

informal observation, Attention paid to behavior but without defining or recording it in any systematic fashion.

information transmission Warnings about the feared object repeated so often that the person develops a **phobia** solely on the basis of hearing them.

informed consent Ethical requirement whereby research subjects agree to participate in a study only after they receive full disclosure about the nature of the study and their own role in it.

inhibited orgasm An inability to achieve orgasm despite adequate sexual desire and arousal; commonly seen in women but relatively rare in men.

insanity Legal rather than psychological or medical concept involving both a **psychological disorder** and an inability to know or appreciate the wrongfulness of criminal acts.

insanity defense Legal plea that a defendant should not be held responsible for a crime because that person was mentally ill at the time of the offense.

insidious onset Development of a disorder that occurs gradually over an extended period (contrast with **acute onset**).

insight In **psychoanalysis**, recognition of the causes of emotional distress.

insulin shock therapy Dangerous biological treatment involving the administration of large doses of insulin to induce seizures.

intellectual disability A diagnosis received when one achieves a significantly below-average score on a test of intelligence and by limitations in the ability to function in areas of daily life. Significantly subaverage intellectual functioning paired with deficits in adaptive functioning such as self-care or occupational activities, appearing before age 18.

intelligence quotient (IQ) Score on an intelligence test estimating a person's deviation from average test performance.

intermittent explosive disorder The episodes during which a person acts on aggressive impulses that result in serious assaults or destruction of property.

intermittent support disability Intellectual **disability** level characterized by the need for only episodic special care—for example, during crises and difficult life changes.

internal validity Extent to which the results of a study can be attributed to the **independent variable** after confounding alternative explanations have been ruled out.

interoceptive avoidance Avoidance of situations or activities, such as exercise, that produce internal physical arousal similar to the beginnings of a **panic attack**.

interpersonal psychotherapy (IPT) Brief treatment approach that emphasizes resolution of interpersonal problems and stressors, such as role disputes in marital conflict, forming relationships in marriage, or a new job. It has demonstrated effectiveness for such problems as depression.

interrater reliability Degree to which two or more observers make the same ratings or measurements.

intersex individual Person born with ambiguous genitalia and hormonal abnormalities. Such a person is assigned a gender at birth and then often provided **hormones** and surgery to complete the correspondence. Also known as *hermaphrodite*.

intrapsychic conflicts In psychoanalytic theory, a struggle among the **id**, **ego**, and **superego**.

introjection In **object relations** theory, the process of incorporating memories and values of individuals who are important and close to the person.

introspection Early, nonscientific approach to the study of psychology involving systematic attempts to report thoughts and feelings that specific stimuli evoked.

inverse agonist In **neuroscience**, a chemical substance that produces effects opposite those of a particular **neurotransmitter**.

isolated sleep paralysis Period upon going to sleep or upon awakening during which a person cannot perform voluntary movements.

ischemia Narrowing of arteries caused by plaque buildup within the arteries.

jealous type Type of **delusional disorder** featuring **delusions** that the individual's sexual partner is unfaithful.

jet lag type of circadian rhythm sleep disorder Disorder in which sleepiness and alertness patterns conflict with local time and occur after recent or repeated travel across time zones.

kleptomania A recurrent failure to resist urges to steal things not needed for personal use or their monetary value.

koro In Malaysia, a condition of **mass hysteria** or group **delusion** in which people believe their genitals are retracting into their bodies.

la belle indifférence Lack of distress shown by some individuals presenting **conversion**, **somatization**, or **amnestic disorders**.

labeling Applying a name to a phenomenon or a pattern of behavior. The label may acquire negative connotations or be applied erroneously to the person rather than that person's behaviors.

large fiber Nerve fiber in the **dorsal horns of the spinal cord** that regulates the pattern and intensity of pain sensations. Large fibers close the gate, decreasing the transmission of painful stimuli.

lateral ventricle Naturally occurring cavity in the brain filled with cerebrospinal fluid. Some individuals with **schizophrenia** have enlarged ventricles, probably resulting from insufficient development or atrophy of surrounding tissue.

law of effect Edward Thorndike's principle that behaviors are strengthened or weakened by the environmental events that follow them.

learned helplessness theory of depression Martin Seligman's theory that people become anxious and depressed when they make an attribution that they have no control over the **stress** in their lives (whether or not they actually have control).

learning disorder Reading, mathematics, or written expression performance substantially below the level expected relative to the person's age, **intelligence quotient** score, and education.

Lesch-Nyhan syndrome X-linked gene disorder characterized by **intellectual disability**, signs of cerebral palsy, and **self-injurious** behavior.

leukocyte White blood cell of one of several types that plays a specialized role in the **immune system** to fight viral and parasitic infections.

level Degree of behavior change with different interventions (for example, high or low).

libido In **psychoanalysis**, the energy within the **id** that drives people toward life and fulfillment.

life-span developmental psychopathology Study of **psychological disorders** over the entire age range.

limbic system Part of the **forebrain** involved in **emotion**, the ability to learn and to control impulses, and the regulation of sex, hunger, thirst, and aggression drives. This system figures prominently in much of **psychopathology**.

limited support disability Intellectual **disability** level characterized by the special care needed on a consistent although time-limited basis—for example, during employment training.

lithium carbonate Common salt used in substantial doses to treat bipolar disorder. Clients often discontinue its use because they enjoy the manic periods, and **relapse** rates are high. The mechanism for its effects is unknown.

localized or selective amnesia Memory loss limited to specific times and events, particularly traumatic events.

locus coeruleus Area in the **hindbrain** that is part of a noradrenergic (norepinephrine-sensitive) circuit. It is involved in emergency and alarm reactions and may be related to **panic** states.

longitudinal course Time patterns among **mood disorders** (for example, prior **dysthymic disorder** or **cyclothymic disorder rapid cycling** and **seasonal pattern**) that may suggest their **course**, treatment, and **prognosis**.

longitudinal design Systematic study of changes in the same individual or group examined over time (contrast with **cross-sectional design**).

loose association Deficits in logical continuity of speech, with abrupt movement between ideas, characteristic of **schizophrenia**. Also called *derailment*.

LSD (*d*-lysergic acid diethylamide) The most common hallucinogenic drug; a synthetic version of the grain fungus ergot.

Luria-Nebraska Neuropsychological Battery Relatively precise instrument that helps identify and locate organic damage by testing various skills.

lysergic acid amide Naturally occurring **hallucinogen** found in the seeds of the morning glory plant.

magnetic resonance imaging (MRI) Procedure using radio signals generated in a strong magnetic field and passed through body tissue to produce detailed, even layered, images of its structure.

maintenance of sameness Necessity among people with **autism** for their familiar environment to remain unchanged. They become upset when changes are introduced.

maintenance treatment Combination of continued **psychosocial treatment**, medication, or both designed to prevent **relapse** following therapy.

major depressive disorder, single or recurrent episode Mood disorder involving one **major depressive episode**; **mood disorder** involving multiple (separated by at least 2 months without depression) **major depressive episodes**.

major depressive episode Most common and severe experience of depression, including feelings of worthlessness, disturbances in bodily activities such as sleep, loss of interest, and inability to experience pleasure, persisting at least 2 weeks.

male erectile disorder The recurring inability in some men to attain or maintain adequate penile erection until completion of sexual activity.

male orgasmic disorder The recurring delay in or absence of orgasm in some men following a normal sexual excitement phase, relative to age and current stimulation. Also known as **inhibited orgasm** (male).

malingering Deliberate faking of a physical or **psychological disorder** motivated by gain.

mania Period of abnormally excessive elation or euphoria associated with some **mood disorders**.

manic episode Period of abnormally elevated or irritable **mood** that may include inflated self-esteem, decreased need for sleep, pressured speech, flight of ideas, agitation, or self-destructive behavior.

marijuana (Cannabis sativa) The dried part of the hemp plant *(Cannabis sativa);* a **hallucinogen** that is the most widely used illegal substance.

marital therapy Interventions for the relationship problems of couples, whether married or not.

mass hysteria Phenomenon in which people in groups share the same **fear**, **delusion**, **abnormal behavior**, or even physical symptoms as a result of psychological processes and suggestion.

mathematics disorder Mathematics performance significantly below the standard for that age level.

medroxyprogesterone Medication that helps stimulate respiration and is used in treatment of **obstructive sleep apnea**.

medulla Part of the **hindbrain** that regulates such automatic bodily functions as breathing and digestion.

melatonin Hormone produced by the pineal gland that is activated by darkness to control the body's biological clock and to induce sleep. It is implicated in **seasonal affective disorder** and may be used in treatments for **circadian rhythm sleep disorder**.

memory B cell Specialized lymphocyte created after an **antigen** is neutralized to help the **immune system** fight off new invasions by that antigen more rapidly. Memory B cells account for the effectiveness of inoculations.

mental age Score a person achieves on an intelligence test representing the highest age-equivalent items passed.

mental hygiene movement Mid-19th-century effort to improve care of the mentally disordered by informing the public of their mistreatment.

mental illness Term formerly used to mean **psychological disorder** but less preferred because it implies that the causes of the disorder can be found in a medical disease process.

mental status exam Relatively coarse preliminary test of a client's judgment, orientation to time and place, and emotional and mental state; typically conducted during an initial interview.

mescaline Naturally occurring **hallucinogen** found in the peyote cactus plant.

methadone **Opiate agonist** used as a treatment for heroin **addiction**. It initially provides the analgesic and sedative effects of heroin. After extended use, these effects diminish and **tolerance** develops. Methadone is an effective treatment for some when combined with counseling.

methylphenidate **Stimulant** medicine (trade name Ritalin) used to treat **hypersomnia** (by keeping the person awake during the day); **narcolepsy**, including that with sudden onset (by suppressing **rapid eye movement sleep**); and **attention deficit/hyperactivity disorder**.

microsleeps The short, seconds-long period of sleep that occurs when someone has been deprived of sleep.

midbrain Section of the brain that coordinates movement with sensory input and contributes to the processes of arousal and tension.

migraine headache Debilitating, throbbing, or pulsing head pain with rapid onset, usually occurring on one side of the head.

mild intellectual disability Level of **intellectual disability** defined by **intelligence quotient** scores between 50–55 and 70.

Minnesota Multiphasic Personality Inventory (MMPI) Empirically derived standardized personality test that provides scales for assessing such abnormal functioning as depression and **paranoia**. One of the most widely used and heavily researched assessment instruments.

mixed manic episode or dysphoric manic episode Condition in which the individual experiences both elation and depression or **anxiety** at the same time. Also known as *dysphoric manic episode*.

mixed sleep apnea Combination of **obstructive sleep apnea** and **central sleep apnea**, such as brief interruptions in breathing during sleep caused by a blocked air passage and by cessation in respiratory activity.

modeling Learning through observation and imitation of the behavior of other individuals and consequences of that behavior.

moderate intellectual disability Level of **intellectual disability** defined by **intelligence quotient** scores between 35–40 and 50–55.

monoamine oxidase (MAO) inhibitor Medication that treats depression and severe social **anxiety** by blocking an enzyme that breaks down the **neurotransmitters norepinephrine** and **serotonin**.

mood Enduring period of emotionality.

mood disorders One of a group of disorders involving severe and enduring disturbances in emotionality ranging from elation to severe depression.

mood-stabilizing drug A medication used in the treatment of **mood disorders**, particularly bipolar disorder, that is effective in preventing and treating pathological shifts in mood.

moral therapy Psychosocial approach in the 19th century that involved treating patients as normally as possible in normal environments.

moral weakness model of chemical dependence View that substance abusers should be blamed because their behavior results from lack of self-control, character, or moral fiber.

morphine **Opiate** medication used as an analgesic (pain reliever) and narcotic that is sometimes a substance of abuse.

multiaxial system Categorization system, such as in *DSM-IV-TR*, employing several dimensions or **axes**, each used for differentiating among the categories.

multidimensional integrative approach Approach to the study of **psychopathology** that holds **psychological disorders** are always the products of multiple interacting causal factors.

multiple baseline **Single-case experimental design** in which measures are taken on two or more behaviors or on a single behavior in two or more situations. A particular intervention is introduced for each at different times. If behavior change is coincident with each introduction, this is strong evidence the intervention caused the change.

multiple infarctions More than one area or incident of death to tissue (for example, in the brain or heart) because of blockage of blood flow.

multiple personality disorder Outdated term for **dissociative identity disorder (DID)**.

myocardial infarction Death of heart tissue when its blood supply artery is blocked by plaque or a blood clot.

myocardium Heart muscle.

naltrexone Most widely used opiate-antagonist drug. It produces immediate **withdrawal** and, thus, a great deal of discomfort. It may also contribute to the treatment of **alcohol** abuse but is not as successful for either substance as was originally hoped.

narcissistic personality disorder A cluster B (dramatic, emotional, or erratic) **personality disorder** involving a pervasive pattern of grandiosity in fantasy or behavior, need for admiration, and lack of **empathy**.

narcolepsy Sleep disorder involving sudden and irresistible **sleep attacks**.

natural environment phobia Fear of situations or events in nature, especially heights, storms, and water.

negative affect Emotional symptoms that are part of the definition of both **anxiety** and depression but are not specific to either of these. Also, **substance abuse** may be maintained because the substance causes an escape from unpleasant circumstances, responsibilities, or, especially, feelings.

negative correlation Association between two variables in which one increases as the other decreases.

negative schema Automatic, enduring, and stable negative cognitive bias or belief system about some aspect of life.

negative symptom A less outgoing symptom, such as **flat affect** or poverty of speech, displayed by some people with **schizophrenia**.

negativistic personality disorder Pervasive pattern of resisting routine requests and expectations and adopting a contrary attitude; considered for, but not included in, *DSM-IV*. Corresponds to former category known as **passive–aggressive personality disorder**.

nervous breakdown Lay term for a severe psychological upset that has no meaning in scientific or professional **psychopathology**.

neuritic plaque See **amyloid plaque**.

neurofibrillary tangles Brain damage in the form of large numbers of strandlike filaments found during autopsy in people with **Alzheimer's disease**.

neurohormones Hormone that affects the brain and is increasingly the focus of study in **psychopathology**.

neuroimaging Sophisticated computer-aided procedure that allows nonintrusive examination of nervous system structure and function.

neuroleptic Major antipsychotic medication, a **dopamine antagonist**, that diminishes **delusions**, **hallucinations**, and aggressive behavior in psychotic patients but may also cause serious side effects.

neuromodulator Hormone secreted into the blood to transmit brain messages throughout the body. Also known as a *neuropeptide*.

neuron Individual nerve cell responsible for transmitting information.

neuropeptide See **neuromodulator**.

neuropsychological testing Assessment of brain and nervous system functioning by testing an individual's performance on behavioral tasks.

neuroscience Study of the nervous system and its role in behavior, thoughts, and **emotions.**

neurosis (neuroses *plural*) Obsolete psychodynamic term for a **psychological disorder** thought to result from an **unconscious** conflict and the **anxiety** it causes. Plural is *neuroses*.

neuroticism One of the dimensions of the five-factor model of personality and individual differences, involving being even-tempered as opposed to nervous, moody, and temperamental.

neurotransmitters Chemical that crosses the **synaptic cleft** between nerve cells to transmit impulses from one **neuron** to the next. Relative excess or deficiency of neurotransmitters is involved in several **psychological disorders**.

nicotine Toxic and addictive substance found in tobacco leaves.

nicotine gum Chewing gum that delivers **nicotine** to smokers without the carcinogens in cigarette smoke. This substitute may help people stop smoking, especially when combined with counseling.

nicotine patch Patch placed on the skin that delivers **nicotine** to smokers without the carcinogens in cigarette smoke. Somewhat more successful than nicotine gum because it requires less effort by the wearer and delivers the drug more consistently; should be coupled with counseling to stop smoking and avoid **relapse**.

nicotine use disorders Cognitive, biological, behavioral, and social problems associated with the use and abuse of **nicotine**.

night eating syndrome Consuming a third or more of daily food intake after the evening meal and getting out of bed at least once during the night to have a high-calorie snack. In the morning, individuals with night eating syndrome are not hungry and do not usually eat breakfast. These individuals do not **binge** during their night eating and seldom purge.

nightmare A frightening and anxiety-provoking dream occurring during **rapid eye movement sleep**. The individual recalls the bad dream and recovers alertness and orientation quickly.

nocturnal penile tumescence (NPT) Erection of the penis during sleep, usually **rapid eye movement sleep.** If this normal reaction occurs in a man with erectile problems in the waking state, his problems may be assumed to have psychological origins.

nomenclature In a naming system or **nosology**, the actual labels or names that are applied. In **psychopathology**, these include **mood disorders** and eating disorders.

nomothetic strategy Identification and examination of large groups of people with the same disorder to note similarities and develop general laws.

nondemand pleasuring Procedure to reestablish sexual arousal involving fondling and caressing while intercourse is forbidden. This method avoids the **anxiety** provoked by the need to perform sexually.

nondisjunction In **Down syndrome**, the failure of two of the 21st chromosomes to divide, thus creating one cell with one copy that dies and one cell with three copies that continue to divide.

nonrapid eye movement (NREM) sleep Periods in the sleep cycle, divided into four substages, when the body may be active while the brain is relatively less active and dreaming does not occur.

noradrenaline See **norepinephrine**.

norepinephrine Neurotransmitter active in the **central** and **peripheral nervous systems**, controlling heart rate, blood pressure, and respiration, among other functions. Because of its role in the body's alarm reaction, it may also contribute generally and indirectly to **panic attacks** and other disorders. Also known as *noradrenaline*.

nosology **Classification** and naming system for medical and psychological phenomena.

obesity An excess of body fat resulting in a body mass index (a ratio of weight to height) of 30 or more.

object relations Modern development in psychodynamic theory involving the study of how children incorporate the memories and values of people who are close and important to them.

observational learning See modeling.

obsessions Recurrent intrusive thought or impulse the client seeks to suppress or neutralize while recognizing it is not imposed by outside forces.

obsessive-compulsive disorder (OCD) **Anxiety** disorder involving unwanted, persistent, intrusive thoughts and impulses, as well as repetitive actions intended to suppress them.

obsessive-compulsive personality disorder A cluster C (anxious or fearful) **personality disorder** featuring a pervasive pattern of preoccupation with orderliness, perfectionism, and mental and interpersonal control at the expense of flexibility, openness, and efficiency.

obstructive sleep apnea Snoring and brief interruptions in breathing during sleep caused by blockage of the airway.

occipital lobe Section of each cerebral hemisphere that integrates and makes sense of visual inputs.

Oedipus complex In **psychoanalysis**, the intrapsychic struggle within a young boy between his lust for his mother and his **fear** of castration because of it. The resolution of this complex results in development of the **superego**.

operant conditioning Fundamental behavioral learning process in which responses are modified by their consequences (reinforcers, punishers, **extinction**, and so on).

operational definition Delineation of a concept on the basis of the operation used to measure it.

opiate An addictive **psychoactive substance** such as heroin, **opium**, or **morphine** that causes temporary euphoria and analgesia (pain reduction).

opioid One of a family of substances including **opiates** and **endorphins**, as well as synthetic variants such as **methadone**, that have a narcotic effect.

opioid use disorders Cognitive, biological, behavioral, and social problems associated with the use and abuse of **opiates** and their synthetic variants.

opioid-releasing neuron Nerve cell that releases an **endogenous opioid** and plays a role in the brain's pleasure pathway, controlling the experience of reward.

opium Naturally occurring compound from the poppy plant that is a strong narcotic, having pain-relieving and sleep- and euphoria-inducing effects. Its derivatives include **morphine** and heroin.

opponent-process theory Explanation of drug **tolerance** and dependence suggesting that when a person experiences positive feelings these are followed shortly by negative feelings, and vice versa. Eventually, the motivation for drug taking shifts from a desire for the euphoric high to a need to relieve the increasingly unpleasant feelings that follow drug use. A vicious cycle develops: The drug that makes a person feel terrible is the one thing that can eliminate the pain.

orgasmic reconditioning The learning procedure to help clients strengthen appropriate patterns of sexual arousal by pairing appropriate stimuli with the pleasurable sensations of masturbation.

oriented times three Patients are aware of, or oriented to, their identity, location, and time (person, place, and time).

outcome research Studies examining the effectiveness and results, positive or negative, of treatment procedures.

pain behavior Observable manifestation of the private experience of pain. Such behaviors may include wincing or other facial expressions, verbal complaints of distress, and avoidance of activities that increase pain sensations.

pain disorder **Somatoform disorder** featuring true pain but for which psychological factors play an important role in onset, severity, or maintenance.

panic Sudden, overwhelming fright or terror.

panic attack Abrupt experience of intense **fear** or discomfort accompanied by several physical symptoms, such as dizziness or heart palpitations.

panic control treatment (PCT) Cognitive–behavioral treatment for **panic attacks**, involving gradual exposure to feared somatic sensations and modification of perceptions and attitudes about them.

panic disorder with agoraphobia (PDA) **Fear** and avoidance of situations the person believes might induce a dreaded **panic attack**.

panic disorder without agoraphobia (PD) **Panic attacks** experienced without development of **agoraphobia**.

papaverine Vasodilating medication used to treat **male erectile disorder** by dilating blood vessels, increasing blood flow to the penis to form an erection. The medication must be injected, and the procedure can be painful. It is so intrusive that it is often declined or discontinued by patients.

paranoia People's irrational beliefs that they are especially important **(delusions of grandeur)** or that other people are seeking to do them harm.

paranoid personality disorder A cluster A (odd or eccentric) **personality disorder** involving pervasive distrust and suspiciousness of others such that their motives are interpreted as malevolent.

paranoid type of schizophrenia A type of **schizophrenia** in which symptoms primarily involve **delusions** and **hallucinations**; speech and motor and emotional behavior are relatively intact.

paraphilias A sexual disorder or deviation in which sexual arousal occurs almost exclusively in the context of inappropriate objects or individuals.

parasomnia An **abnormal behavior** such as a **nightmare** or **sleepwalking** that occurs during sleep.

parasympathetic nervous system Part of the **autonomic nervous system** that regulates bodily systems (for example, digestion) while activity level is low and that balances **sympathetic nervous system** activity.

parens patriae Latin term (state or country as the parent) used to describe when the government takes on the role of guardian for a minor or person incapacitated.

parietal lobe Section of each cerebral hemisphere responsible for recognizing touch sensations.

parkinsonian symptom See **extrapyramidal symptom**.

Parkinson's disease Degenerative brain disorder principally affecting motor performance (for example, tremors and stooped posture) associated with reduction in **dopamine**. **Dementia** may be a result as well.

passive–aggressive personality disorder Former diagnostic category not included in *DSM-IV-TR* for lack of sufficient research. See the similar category **negativistic personality disorder**.

pathological gambling A persistent and recurrent maladaptive gambling behavior.

pathological or impacted grief reaction Extreme reaction to the death of a loved one that involves psychotic features, **suicidal ideation**, or severe loss of weight or energy or that persists more than 2 months. Also known as an *impacted grief reaction*.

patient uniformity myth Tendency to consider all members of a category as more similar than they are, ignoring their individual differences.

pedophilia **Paraphilia** involving strong sexual attraction toward children.

penile prosthesis Surgical treatment for **male erectile disorder** involving the insertion of a prosthesis that may be a semirigid silicone rod or an inflatable tube.

penile strain gauge Psychophysiological monitoring device that measures male sexual arousal by changes in penis circumference.

performance scale In the Wechsler group of intelligence tests, a subtest that assesses psychomotor and nonverbal reasoning skills and the ability to learn new relationships.

peripheral nervous system Neural networks outside the brain and spinal cord, including the **somatic nervous system**, which controls muscle movement, and the **autonomic nervous system**, which regulates cardiovascular, endocrine, digestion, and regulation functions.

persecutory type Form of **delusion** that involves believing oneself (or someone close) is being malevolently treated in some way.

personality disorder An enduring maladaptive pattern for relating to the environment and self, exhibited in a range of contexts that cause significant functional impairment or subjective distress.

personality inventory Self-report questionnaire that assesses personal traits by asking respondents to identify descriptions that apply to themselves.

personality trait Enduring tendency to behave in particular predisposed ways across situations.

person-centered therapy Therapy method in which the client, rather than the counselor, primarily directs the course of discussion, seeking self-discovery and self-responsibility.

pervasive developmental disorder not otherwise specified Wide-ranging, significant, and long-lasting dysfunctions that appear before the age of 18.

pervasive developmental disorders One of several wide-ranging, significant, and long-lasting dysfunctions that appear before the age of 18.

pervasive support disability Intellectual **disability** level characterized by the constant, intensive care needed by the individual in all environments.

phencyclidine (PCP) Dangerous synthetic **hallucinogen**, also called angel dust, that may cause agitated or violent behavior, disorientation, convulsions, coma, and even death.

phenotype Observable characteristics or behaviors of an individual.

phenylketonuria (PKU) **Recessive gene** disorder involving the inability to break down a food chemical whose buildup causes **intellectual disability**, seizures, and behavior problems. PKU can be detected by infant screening and prevented by a specialized diet.

phii pob Thailand's version of dissociative trance states.

phobia **Psychological disorder** characterized by marked and persistent **fear** of an object or situation.

phobic avoidance Extreme shunning of feared objects or situations displayed by people with **phobias**.

phototherapy Treatment of **seasonal affective disorder** with large doses of exposure to bright light.

Pick's disease Rare neurological disorder that results in **presenile dementia**.

pivloktoq Running frenzy disorder among native peoples of the Arctic that seems equivalent to **dissociative fugue**.

placebo Nonactive treatment that is successful due to suggestion.

placebo control group In **outcome research**, a **control group** that does not receive the experimental manipulation but is given a similar procedure with an identical expectation of change, allowing the researcher to assess any **placebo effect**.

placebo effect Behavior change resulting from the person's expectation of change rather than from the experimental manipulation itself.

pleasure principle Tendency to seek pleasure and minimize discomfort.

polysomnographic (PSG) evaluation An assessment of sleep disorders in which a client sleeping in the lab is monitored for heart, muscle, respiration, brain wave, and other functions.

polysubstance use The use of multiple mind- and behavior-altering substances, such as drugs.

pons Part of the hindbrain that controls such automatic bodily functions as breathing and digestion.

positive correlation Association between two variables in which one increases as the other increases.

positive symptom A more overt symptom, such as a **delusion** or **hallucination**, displayed by some people with **schizophrenia**.

positron emission tomography (PET) scan Imaging procedure in which a radioactive tracer that binds to blood glucose is detected as the glucose is metabolized during brain activity. This allows nonintrusive localization and observation of brain activity.

posttraumatic stress disorder (PTSD) Enduring, distressing emotional disorder that follows exposure to a severe helplessness- or fear-inducing threat. The victim reexperiences the trauma, avoids stimuli associated with it, and develops a numbing of responsiveness and an increased vigilance and arousal.

predictive validity Degree to which an assessment instrument accurately predicts a person's future behavior. See also **criterion validity**.

premature ejaculation A recurring ejaculation before the person wishes it, with minimal sexual stimulation.

prepared learning Ability adaptive for evolution, allowing certain associations to be learned more readily than others.

presenile dementia Dementia that appears before old age, between 40 and 60 years.

presenting problem Original complaint reported by the client to the therapist. The actual treated problem may be a modification derived from the presenting problem.

prevalence Number of people displaying a disorder in the total population at any given time (compare with **incidence**).

primary gain Freudian notion that **anxiety** reduction is the principal reinforcement obtained for the display of psychological symptoms.

primary insomnia A difficulty in initiating, maintaining, or gaining from sleep; not related to other medical or psychological problems.

primary process In psychodynamic theory, the **id**'s characteristic mode of thinking, which is emotional, irrational, and preoccupied with sex, aggression, and envy.

proband In genetics research, the individual displaying the trait or characteristic being studied.

prodromal stage Period of 1 to 2 years before serious symptoms of **schizophrenia** occur but when less severe yet unusual behaviors start to appear.

profound intellectual disability Level of **intellectual disability** defined by **intelligence quotient** scores below 20–25 and extremely limited communication and self-help skills.

prognosis Predicted development of a disorder over time.

progressive muscle relaxation Set of exercises to teach people to become aware of and actively counteract muscle tension to induce relaxation or drowsiness.

projective tests Psychoanalytically based measure that presents ambiguous stimuli to clients on the assumption that their responses can reveal their **unconscious** conflicts. Such tests are inferential and lack high **reliability** and **validity**.

prototypical approach System for categorizing disorders using both essential, defining characteristics and a range of variation on other characteristics.

psilocybin Naturally occurring **hallucinogen** found in certain species of mushrooms.

psychiatric nurse Person with nursing training who specializes in care and treatment of psychiatric patients, usually in a hospital setting.

psychiatric social worker Person who has earned a master of social work (M.S.W.) degree or, occasionally, a doctor of social work (D.S.W.) degree and is trained to work with social agencies to help psychologically disordered clients and their families.

psychiatrist Person who has earned an M.D. degree and then has specialized in psychiatry during residency training. Such a person is trained to investigate primarily the biological nature and causes of psychiatric disorders and to diagnose and treat them.

psychoactive substances Substances, such as a drug, that alter **mood** or behavior.

psychoanalysis Assessment and therapy pioneered by Sigmund Freud that emphasizes exploration of, and insight into, **unconscious** processes and conflicts.

psychoanalyst Therapist who practices **psychoanalysis** after earning either an M.D. or a Ph.D. degree and receiving additional specialized postdoctoral training.

psychoanalytic model Complex and comprehensive theory originally advanced by Sigmund Freud that seeks to account for the development and structure of personality, as well as the origin of **abnormal behavior**, based primarily on inferred inner entities and forces.

psychodynamic psychotherapy Contemporary version of **psychoanalysis** that still emphasizes **unconscious** processes and conflicts but is briefer and more focused on specific problems.

psychological autopsy Postmortem psychological profile of a suicide victim constructed from interviews with people who knew the person before death.

psychological disorder Psychological dysfunction associated with distress or impairment in functioning that is not a typical or culturally expected response.

psychological model Explanation of human behavior and its dysfunction that emphasizes the influence of the social environment and early experience.

psychomotor disability Deficits in motor activity and coordination development.

psychoneuroimmunology (PNI) Study of psychological influences on the neurological responding involved in the body's immune response.

psycho-oncology Study of psychological factors involved in the course and treatment of **cancer**.

psychopathology Scientific study of **psychological disorders**.

psychopathy A non-*DSM-IV-TR* category similar to **antisocial personality disorder** but with less emphasis on overt behavior. Indicators include superficial charm, lack of remorse, and other personality characteristics.

psychopharmacogenetics Study of how genetic makeup can affect individual reactions to drugs.

psychophysiological assessment Measurement of changes in the nervous system reflecting psychological or emotional events such as **anxiety**, **stress**, and sexual arousal.

psychophysiological disorder Outdated term, similar to **psychosomatic medicine**, for the study of psychological and social factors influencing a physical disorder. The term is misleading because it falsely implies that other psychological problems, such as **mood disorders**, do not have significant biological components.

psychosexual stages of development Psychoanalytic concept of the sequence of phases a person passes through during development. Each stage is named for the location on the body where **id** gratification is maximal at that time.

psychosis Group of severe **psychological disorders**, including **schizophrenia**, featuring **delusions** and **hallucinations**.

psychosocial treatment Treatment practices that focuses on social and cultural factors (such as family experience), as well as psychological influences. These approaches include cognitive, behavioral, and interpersonal methods.

psychosomatic medicine See **behavioral medicine**.

psychosurgery Biological treatment involving neurosurgery, such as lobotomy, for a **psychological disorder**. For example, a specific surgical lesion to the cingulate bundle may be an effective last-resort treatment for **obsessive-compulsive disorder**.

psychotic behavior A severe **psychological disorder** category characterized by **hallucinations** and loss of contact with reality.

pure categorical approach See **classical categorical approach**.

purging technique In the eating disorder **bulimia nervosa**, the self-induced vomiting or laxative abuse used to compensate for excessive food ingestion.

pyromania An **impulse-control disorder** that involves having an irresistible urge to set fires.

randomization Method for placing individuals into research groups that assures each an equal chance of being assigned to any group, thus eliminating any systematic differences across groups.

rapid cycling Temporal **course** of a bipolar disorder when transitions between **mania** and depression are quick, occurring four or more times in 1 year.

rapid eye movement (REM) sleep The periodic intervals of sleep during which the eyes move rapidly from side to side, and dreams occur, but the body is inactive.

Rauwolfia serpentina More commonly known as *reserpine*, an early medication derived from the snakeroot plant that helps control the agitation and aggressiveness of some psychotic patients.

Raynaud's disease Cardiovascular disease involving blockage of blood circulation to the extremities, with resultant pain and cold sensations in the hands and feet.

reactivity Changes in one person's behavior as a result of observing the behavior in another.

reading disorder Reading performance significantly below the standard for that age level.

reality principle In psychodynamic theory, the logical reasoning style of the **ego** that ensures actions are practical and realistic.

rebound insomnia In a person with insomnia, the worsened sleep problems that can occur when medications are used to treat insomnia and then withdrawn.

receptive language Communicated material that is understood.

receptor Location on a nerve cell **dendrite** that receives chemical impulses for transmission through the **neuron**.

recessive gene Gene that must be paired with another recessive gene to determine a trait.

reciprocal gene–environment model Hypothesis that people with a genetic predisposition for a disorder may also have a genetic tendency to create environmental risk factors that promote the disorder.

regulated-breathing method Intervention for **stuttering** in which the person is instructed to stop and take a deep breath whenever a stuttering episode begins.

reinforcement In **operant conditioning**, consequences for behavior that strengthen it or increase its frequency. Positive reinforcement involves the contingent delivery of a desired consequence. Negative reinforcement is the contingent escape from an aversive consequence. Unwanted behaviors may result from reinforcement of those behaviors or the failure to reinforce desired behaviors.

relapse Reappearance of or return to problem behaviors after treatment or recovery.

relapse prevention The extending therapeutic progress by teaching the client how to cope with future troubling situations.

relaxation response Active components of meditation methods, including repetitive thoughts of a sound to reduce distracting thoughts and closing the mind to other intruding thoughts, that decrease the flow of **stress hormones** and **neurotransmitters** and cause a feeling of calm.

reliability Degree to which a measurement is consistent—for example, over time or among different raters.

repeated measurement When responses are measured on more than two occasions (not just before and after intervention) to assess **trends**.

replication Confirming the results of a study by repeating it, often by a separate, independent researcher.

repression In psychoanalytic theory, a process that forces unwanted material from the conscious to the **unconscious**.

research design Plan of experimentation used to test a **hypothesis**.

reserpine See **rauwolfia serpentina**.

residual type of schizophrenia A diagnostic category for people who have experienced at least one episode of **schizophrenia** and who no longer display its major symptoms but still show some bizarre thoughts or social **withdrawal**.

retarded ejaculation Male orgasmic disorder in which ejaculation is delayed; thus, the patient is unable to reach orgasm with his partner, although he is able to ejaculate during masturbation.

reticular activating system Section of the **midbrain** responsible for tension and arousal processes, including sleep and wakefulness.

retrograde ejaculation Condition in which ejaculatory fluids travel backward into the bladder, usually as a result of certain drugs or a medical condition. This is not considered a *DSM-IV-TR* **male orgasmic disorder**.

retrospective information Literally "the view back;" data collected by examining records or recollections of the past. It is limited by the accuracy, **validity**, and thoroughness of the sources.

Rett's disorder Progressive neurological developmental disorder featuring constant hand-wringing, **intellectual disability**, and impaired motor skills.

reuptake Action by which a **neurotransmitter** is quickly drawn back into the discharging **neuron** after being released into a **synaptic cleft**.

rheumatoid arthritis Painful, degenerative disease in which the **immune system** essentially attacks itself, resulting in stiffness, swelling, and even destruction of the joints. **Cognitive–behavioral treatments** can help relieve pain and stiffness.

Rhythm Test Subtest of the **Halstead-Reitan Neuropsychological Battery** that asks respondents to compare rhythmic beats to assess sound recognition, attention, and concentration.

Rorschach inkblot test Projective test that uses irregular patterns of ink as its ambiguous stimuli.

sadistic personality disorder Pervasive pattern of deriving pleasure by inflicting pain on others; proposed as a category for *DSM-III-R* but not included in *DSM-IV-TR*.

sakit gila Disorder reported in Malaysia, similar to **schizophrenia** but different in important ways that may illuminate details of both disorders.

schedule of reinforcement In **operant conditioning**, the pattern of consequences following a behavior based on the number of responses emitted or the intervals between them.

scheduled awakening For children who wake frequently at night, awakening them about 30 minutes before their usual episodes and from a deeper sleep than usual to help them learn to fall asleep on their own.

schizoaffective disorder A psychotic disorder featuring symptoms of both **schizophrenia** and major **mood disorder**.

schizoid personality disorder A cluster A (odd or eccentric) **personality disorder** featuring a pervasive pattern of detachment from social relationships and a restricted range of expression of **emotions**.

schizophrenia A devastating psychotic disorder that may involve characteristic disturbances in thinking **(delusions)**, perception **(hallucinations)**, speech, **emotions**, and behavior.

schizophreniform disorder A psychotic disorder involving the symptoms of **schizophrenia** but lasting less than 6 months.

schizophrenogenic mother According to an obsolete, unsupported theory, a cold, dominating, and rejecting parent who was thought to cause **schizophrenia** in her offspring.

schizotypal personality disorder A cluster A (odd or eccentric) **personality disorder** involving a pervasive pattern of interpersonal deficits featuring acute discomfort with, and reduced capacity for, close relationships, as well as cognitive or perceptual distortions and eccentricities of behavior.

scientist–practitioner Mental health professional expected to apply scientific methods to his or her work. A scientist–practitioner must know the latest research on **diagnosis** and treatment, must evaluate his or her methods for effectiveness, and may generate research to discover information about disorders and their treatment.

script theory Theory of sexual functioning that suggests people's sexual behavior and attitudes are guided by scripts reflecting social and cultural expectations. Negative scripts may increase **vulnerability** to the development of **sexual dysfunction**.

seasonal affective disorder (SAD) Mood disorder involving a cycling of episodes corresponding to the seasons of the year, typically with depression occurring during the winter.

seasonal pattern Temporal **course** of bipolar or recurrent **major depressive disorders** in which episodes occur during particular seasons of the year.

secondary gain Additional reinforcers beyond **primary gain** that a person may obtain by the display of symptoms. These may include attention, sympathy, and avoidance of unwanted responsibilities.

selective amnesia See **localized amnesia**.

selective mutism Developmental disorder characterized by the individual's consistent failure to speak in specific social situations despite speaking in other situations.

self-actualizing Process emphasized in humanistic psychology in which people strive to achieve their highest potential against difficult life experiences.

self-defeating personality disorder Pervasive pattern of being overly passive and accepting the pain and suffering imposed by others. A category proposed for *DSM-III-R* but not included in *DSM-IV-TR* for lack of research.

self-efficacy Perception of having the ability to cope with **stress** or challenges.

self-injurious Dangerous actions, including head-banging and hitting and biting oneself, seen in many children with **autism**.

self-medication Process by which some individuals may abuse substances in attempting to use them to relieve other problems such as **anxiety**, pain, or sleeplessness.

self-monitoring Action by which clients observe and record their own behaviors as either an assessment of a problem and its change or a treatment procedure that makes them more aware of their responses. Also known as *self-observation*.

self-observation See **self-monitoring**.

self-psychology See **ego psychology**.

semistructured interview Interview that employs preplanned, standardized questions to elicit information in a consistent way.

sensate focus Sex therapy in which couples concentrate on pleasurable sensations from caressing and fondling. Intercourse is forbidden to prevent focus on sexual performance and the **anxiety** it may provoke.

sensorium Person's general awareness of the surroundings, including time and place.

separation anxiety disorder Excessive, enduring **fear** in some children that harm will come to them or their parents while they are apart.

septum Part of the **limbic system** that regulates **emotions** and the ability to learn and control impulses, as well as such drives as sex, hunger, thirst, and aggression.

sequential design Combination of **cross-sectional** and **longitudinal designs** involving repeated study of different **cohorts** over time.

serotonin **Neurotransmitter** involved in processing of information and coordination of movement, as well as inhibition and restraint. It also assists in the regulation of eating, sexual, and aggressive behaviors, all of which may be involved in different **psychological disorders**. Its interaction with **dopamine** is implicated in **schizophrenia**.

serotonin-specific reuptake inhibitor (SSRI) One of a class of medications for depression (including Prozac) that act on the serotonergic system by inhibiting the **reuptake** of the **neurotransmitter serotonin**.

severe intellectual disability Level of **intellectual disability** defined by **intelligence quotient** scores between 20–25 and 35–40 and with somewhat limited communication, self-help, social, and vocational skills. Also a term used in the education system referring to a similar level of **intellectual disability** that assumes the individual would not benefit from academic or vocational instruction.

sex ratio Percentage of men and women with a disorder.

sex reassignment surgery A surgical procedure to alter a person's physical anatomy to conform to that person's psychological gender identity.

sexual aversion disorder An extreme and persistent dislike of sexual contact or similar activities.

sexual dysfunction A sexual disorder in which the client finds it difficult to function adequately while having sex.

sexual masochism **Paraphilia** in which sexual arousal is associated with experiencing pain or humiliation.

sexual pain disorders (dyspareunia) A recurring genital pain in either males or females before, during, or after sexual intercourse. Also known as *dyspareunia*.

sexual sadism **Paraphilia** in which sexual arousal is associated with inflicting pain or humiliation.

shaping In **operant conditioning**, the development of a new response by reinforcing successively more similar versions of that response. Both desirable and undesirable behaviors may be learned in this manner.

shared psychotic disorder (folie à deux) A psychotic disturbance in which individuals develop a **delusion** similar to that of a person with whom they share a close relationship. Also known as *folie à deux*.

shift work type of circadian rhythm sleep disorder Disorder characterized by insomnia during sleep time and sleepiness during wake time because of late-shift work or frequent work shift changes.

silver nitrate Chemical that can be used in gum or lozenges to make subsequent smoking aversive by producing a bad taste in the mouth. Research indicates this treatment approach is not particularly effective.

single photon emission computed tomography (SPECT) **Neuroimaging** procedure similar to a **positron emission tomography (PET) scan**, although less accurate, less complex, and less costly.

single-case experimental design Research tactic in which an **independent variable** is manipulated for a single individual, allowing cause-and-effect conclusions but with limited **generalizability** (contrast with **case study method**).

sinoaortic baroreflex arc Body mechanism to compensate for sudden blood pressure increases by decreasing pressure. This reaction causes some people to faint and may lead them to develop **phobias**.

situational phobia Anxiety involving enclosed places (for example, claustrophobia) or public transportation (for example, **fear** of flying).

situationally bound panic attack **Panic attack** for which the triggering circumstances are known to the client.

situationally predisposed panic attack Circumstance that increases the likelihood a **panic attack** may be triggered.

sleep apnea Disorder involving brief periods when breathing ceases during sleep.

sleep attack Unexpected episode of falling asleep during the day.

sleep efficiency (SE) The percentage of time actually spent sleeping of the total time spent in bed.

sleep hygiene Psychological treatment for insomnia that teaches clients to recognize and eliminate environmental obstacles to sleep. These include the use of **nicotine**, caffeine, certain medications, and **alcohol**, as well as ill-timed exercise.

sleep paralysis Brief and frightening period at the beginning or end of sleep when the individual cannot move or speak; sometimes mistaken for nocturnal **panic attack**.

sleep restriction Treatment for insomnia that involves limiting time in bed to the actual amount spent sleeping so that the bed is associated with sleep and no other competing activities.

sleep stress Environmental events, such as ingesting excess caffeine, that can affect sleep negatively.

sleep terror An episode of apparent awakening from sleep, accompanied by signs of **panic** and followed by disorientation and amnesia for the incident. Sleep terrors occur during **nonrapid eye movement sleep** and so do not involve frightening dreams.

sleepwalking (somnambulism) **Parasomnia** that involves leaving the bed during **nonrapid eye movement sleep**. See also **somnambulism**.

slow wave sleep See **delta wave**.

small fiber Nerve fiber in the **dorsal horns of the spinal cord** that regulates the pattern and intensity of pain sensations. Small fibers open the gate, increasing the transmission of painful stimuli.

smooth-pursuit eye movement Ability to follow moving targets visually. Deficits in this skill can be caused by a single **gene** whose location is known. This problem is associated with **schizophrenia** and, thus,

may serve as a **genetic marker** for this disorder. Also known as *eye-tracking*.

social phobia Extreme, enduring, irrational **fear** and avoidance of social or performance situations.

somatic nervous system Part of the **peripheral nervous system** that controls muscle movement.

somatic type **Delusion** built on a false and unfounded belief about the body—for example, that parts are rotting or turning to stone.

somatization disorder **Somatoform disorder** involving extreme and long-lasting focus on multiple physical symptoms for which no medical cause is evident.

somatoform disorder Pathological concern of individuals with the appearance or functioning of their bodies, usually in the absence of any identifiable medical condition.

somnambulism Repeated **sleepwalking** that occurs during **nonrapid eye movement sleep** and so is not the acting out of a dream. The person is difficult to waken and does not recall the experience.

specific phobia Unreasonable **fear** of a specific object or situation that markedly interferes with daily life functioning.

specifier In **mood disorders**, a pattern of characteristics that sometimes accompany **major depressive** or **manic episodes** and may help predict their **course** and **prognosis**. Specifiers include psychotic, melancholic, atypical, catatonic, and chronic.

standardization Process of establishing specific norms and requirements for a measurement technique to ensure it is used consistently across measurement occasions. This includes instructions for administering the measure, evaluating its findings, and comparing these to data for large numbers of people.

Stanford-Binet test Early standardized intelligence test designed to identify children likely to experience academic difficulties by assessing their attention, perception, reasoning, and comprehension.

statistical significance Small probability of obtaining the observed research findings by chance.

stereotyped and ritualistic behavior, Usually movements of the body or limbs that are repeated in nonfunctional ways and often assumed to occur because of their sensory consequences.

stimulant A **psychoactive substance** that elevates **mood**, activity, and alertness; such substances include **amphetamines**, caffeine, **cocaine**, and **nicotine**.

stimulus control Deliberate arrangement of the environment so that it encourages desired behaviors and discourages problem behaviors. For example, insomnia may be combated by limiting time in, and associations with, the bed.

stress Body's physiological response to a stressor, which is any event or change that requires adaptation.

stress hormone One of a group of **hormones** involved in the body's physiological **stress** response.

stress physiology Study of the body's response to stressful events.

stroke Temporary blockage of blood vessels supplying the brain, or a rupture of vessels in the brain, resulting in temporary or permanent loss of brain functioning.

stuttering Disturbance in the fluency and time patterning of speech (for example, sound and syllable repetitions or prolongations).

subcortical dementia Disease affecting the inner areas of the brain below the cortex. It differs from **dementia of the Alzheimer's type** in that it involves impaired recall but normal recognition, more severe depression and **anxiety**, slowed motions, and impaired coordination but no **aphasia**.

sublimation Psychodynamic **defense mechanism** in which the person redirects energy from conflict and **anxiety** into more constructive outlets, such as work.

substance abuse A pattern of **psychoactive substance** use leading to significant distress or impairment in social and occupational roles and in hazardous situations.

substance dependence A maladaptive pattern of substance use characterized by the need for increased amounts to achieve the desired effect, negative physical effects when the substance is withdrawn, unsuccessful efforts to control its use, and substantial effort expended to seek it or recover from its effects. Also known as *addiction*.

substance intoxication A physiological reaction, such as impaired judgment and motor ability, as well as **mood** change, resulting from the ingestion of a **psychoactive substance**.

substance-related disorder One of a range of problems associated with the use and abuse of drugs such as **alcohol**, **cocaine**, heroin, and other substances people use to alter the way they think, feel, and behave. These are extremely costly in human and financial terms.

suicidal attempts Effort made to kill oneself.

suicidal ideation Serious thoughts about committing suicide.

suicide plans The formulation of a specific method of killing oneself.

superego In **psychoanalysis**, the psychic entity representing the internalized moral standards of parents and society.

supernatural model Explanation of human behavior and its dysfunction that posits important roles for spirits, demons, grace, sin, and so on.

susceptibility In genetics, **genes** that only slightly increase the risk of developing the disorder, but in contrast to the **deterministic** genes, these are more common in the population.

sympathetic nervous system Part of the **autonomic nervous system** that prepares the body for activity or to respond to stressors—for instance, by increasing heart rate and blood flow to muscles.

symptom substitution Psychodynamic assertion that if overt problem behavior (the symptom) is treated without eliminating the underlying conflict thought to be causing it, that conflict can reemerge in the form of new, perhaps worse, symptoms.

synaptic cleft Space between nerve cells where chemical transmitters act to move impulses from one **neuron** to the next.

systematic desensitization Behavioral therapy technique to diminish excessive **fears**, involving gradual exposure to the feared stimulus paired with a positive coping experience, usually relaxation.

systemic perspective View that the many contributing causes of **abnormal behavior** form a system involving biology, behavior, cognition, **emotion**, culture, and society. Each component of the system affects all other components.

systolic blood pressure Blood pressure generated when the heart is at work pumping blood.

T cell Lymphocyte produced in bone marrow, developed in the thymus gland, and operating in the cellular branch of the **immune system**. Some T cells attack **antigens** directly; others help regulate the immune system.

Tactile Performance Test Subtest of the **Halstead-Reitan Neuropsychological Battery** that asks the respondent to insert wooden shapes into a hidden form board, allowing the examiner to assess the subject's learning and memory skills.

taijin kyofusho Japanese variant of **social phobia**. In many cases, individuals avoid social interaction because they believe they have terrible body or breath odor.

tangentiality Characteristic of the loose cognitive and verbal associations seen in **schizophrenia** in which the person fails to answer questions and quickly moves the conversation to unrelated topics.

tardive dyskinesia Extrapyramidal **symptom** and sometimes irreversible side effect of long-term **neuroleptic** medication, involving involuntary motor movements, especially in the face and tongue.

task analysis Method for evaluating a skill to be learned, breaking it down into its component parts.

taxonomy System of naming and **classification** (for example, of specimens) in science.

temporal lobe Section of each cerebral hemisphere associated primarily with sight and sound recognition and with long-term memory storage.

temporal patterning Course modifier for **mood disorders** describing their time sequences, including recurrence, recovery, and alternation.

tension headache Bilateral head pain characterized by a dull ache, usually starting at the front or back of the head.

tension reduction Negative reinforcement motivation account for **substance abuse**, suggesting it is maintained because it allows people to escape **anxiety**.

testability Ability of a **hypothesis**, for example, to be subjected to scientific scrutiny and to be accepted or rejected, a necessary condition for the hypothesis to be useful.

test–retest reliability Degree to which results of two administrations of one test to the same person are similar.

tetrahydrocannabinol (THC) Most common active chemical in **marijuana** responsible for its ability to alter **mood** and behavior.

thalamus Small region deep inside the brain broadly associated with regulation of behavior and **emotion**.

thanatos Freudian concept of a human drive toward death and destruction.

Thematic Apperception Test (TAT) Projective test in which the respondent is asked to tell stories about a series of ambiguous drawings.

tic Sudden, rapid, and recurrent involuntary motor movement or vocalization.

tic disorder Disruption in early development involving involuntary motor movements or vocalizations.

time-limited course Condition in which a disorder improves on its own in a relatively brief period.

time-management training Instruction that teaches patients to deal with **stress** by establishing priorities among activities and demands and paying less attention to the less important ones.

token economy A social learning behavior modification system in which individuals earn items they can exchange for desired rewards by displaying appropriate behaviors.

tolerance The need for increased amounts of a substance to achieve the desired effect, and a diminished effect with continued use of the same amount.

Tourette's disorder Developmental disorder featuring multiple dysfunctional motor and vocal **tics**.

trainable intellectual disability Term referring to a level of **intellectual disability** comparable to the *DSM-IV-TR* designation of **moderate intellectual disability** that suggests the individual can learn rudimentary vocational but not academic skills.

transcendental meditation Technique for focusing attention by softly repeating a single syllable (mantra); often accompanied by slow and regular breathing.

transference Psychoanalytic concept suggesting that clients may seek to relate to the therapist as they do to important authority figures, particularly their parents.

transinstitutionalization Movement of people with severe **mental illness** from large psychiatric hospitals to smaller group residences.

transsexualism Obsolete term for **gender identity disorder**.

transvestic fetishism Paraphilia in which individuals, usually males, are sexually aroused or receive gratification by wearing clothing of the opposite sex.

trend Direction of change of a behavior or behaviors (for example, increasing or decreasing).

triazolam Short-acting **benzodiazepine** medication (trade name Halcion) used to treat insomnia. Possible negative side effects include drowsiness, dependence, short-term memory loss, or rebound.

trichotillomania People's urge to pull out their own hair from anywhere on the body, including the scalp, eyebrows, and arm.

tricyclic antidepressant Most common treatment for depression. Such medications include **imipramine** and amitriptyline that block the **reuptake** of **neurotransmitters**, principally **serotonin** and **norepinephrine**, at the **synaptic cleft**. The drugs are effective for some **anxiety** disorders and **mood disorders**. They are also used to treat **obstructive sleep apnea** because they help maintain respiratory muscle tone to assist breathing during **rapid eye movement sleep**. Positive effects are delayed, and negative side effects may include dizziness and even death, so close monitoring is required. **Relapse** rates range from 20% to 50% when the drug is stopped.

trisomy 21 See **Down syndrome**.

tuberous sclerosis Rare **dominant gene** disorder characterized by bumps on the skin and sometimes **intellectual disability** and seizures.

twin studies In genetics research, the comparison of twins with unrelated or less closely related individuals. If twins, particularly monozygotic twins who share identical **genotypes**, share common characteristics such as a disorder, even if they were reared in different environments, then strong evidence of genetic involvement in those characteristics exists.

type A behavior pattern Cluster of behaviors including excessive competitiveness, time-pressured impatience, accelerated speech, and anger, originally thought to promote high risk for heart disease.

type B behavior pattern Cluster of behaviors including a relaxed attitude, indifference to time pressure, and less forceful ambition; originally thought to promote low risk for heart disease.

unconditional positive regard Acceptance by the counselor of the client's feelings and actions without judgment or condemnation.

unconditioned response (UCR) In **classical conditioning**, the natural or unlearned reaction to the **unconditioned stimulus**.

unconditioned stimulus (UCS) Environmental event that would elicit a response in almost anyone and requires no learning. In **classical conditioning**, it is paired with a neutral stimulus that, after training, may become a **conditioned stimulus**.

unconscious Part of the psychic makeup that is outside the awareness of the person.

unconscious vision See **blindsight**.

underarousal hypothesis Theory of the **etiology** of **antisocial personality disorder** suggesting psychopaths engage in dangerous or illicit behavior to stimulate the underaroused **cerebral cortex** in their brains.

undifferentiated somatoform disorder Somatization disorder with fewer than eight symptoms but still causing distress and impaired functioning.

undifferentiated type of schizophrenia A category for individuals who meet the criteria for **schizophrenia** but not for one of the defined subtypes.

unexpected panic attack **Panic attack** that has no identified triggering circumstance.

unipolar mood disorder **Mood disorder** characterized by depression or **mania** but not both. Most cases involve unipolar depression.

unshared environment Term indicating that even identical twins living in the same home may have different prenatal and family experiences.

vacuum device therapy Mechanical treatment for **male erectile disorder** that employs a vacuum cylinder to draw blood into the penis, where it is held by a ring placed at the base of the penis.

vaginal photoplethysmograph Light-sensitive psychophysiological monitoring device that measures female sexual arousal reflected by blood flow to the vagina.

vaginismus A recurring involuntary muscle spasm in the outer third of the vagina that interfere with sexual intercourse.

validity Degree to which a technique measures what it purports to measure.

variability Degree of change in a phenomenon over time.

vascular Pertaining to the vessels that transport blood and other fluids in the body.

vascular dementia Progressive brain disorder involving loss of cognitive functioning, caused by blockage of blood flow to the brain, that appears concurrently with other neurological signs and symptoms.

vasovagal syncope Fainting because of low blood pressure in the head and brain.

ventral tegmental area **Midbrain** region that includes part of the "pleasure pathway" responsible for the experience of reward.

verbal scale Section of the Wechsler series of intelligence tests that assesses vocabulary, memory, reasoning skills, and information facts.

vinvusa Nigerian variant of dissociative trance states.

visuospatial skill Ability to see, recognize, orient within, and negotiate between objects in space.

voyeurism **Paraphilia** in which sexual arousal is derived from observing unsuspecting individuals undressing or naked.

vulnerability **Susceptibility** or tendency to develop a disorder.

waxy flexibility Characteristic of **catatonia** in which the person remains in bodily postures positioned by another person.

Wechsler Adult Intelligence Scale—3rd Edition (WAIS-III) Intelligence test for adults, assessing a range of verbal and performance abilities.

Wechsler Intelligence Scale for Children—4th Edition (WISC-IV) Intelligence test for children assessing a range of verbal and performance abilities.

Wechsler Preschool and Primary Scale of Intelligence—3rd Edition (WPPSI-III) Intelligence test for young children that measures a range of performance, verbal, and preverbal abilities.

Wernicke-Korsakoff syndrome Organic brain syndrome resulting from prolonged heavy **alcohol** use, involving confusion, unintelligible speech, and loss of motor coordination. It may be caused by a deficiency of thiamine, a vitamin metabolized poorly by heavy drinkers.

withdrawal A severely negative physiological reaction to removal of a **psychoactive substance**, which can be alleviated by the same or a similar substance.

withdrawal delirium (delirium tremens/DTs) The frightening hallucinations and body tremors that result when a heavy drinker withdraws from **alcohol**. Also known as *delirium tremens (DT)*.

withdrawal design Removing a treatment to note whether it has been effective. In **single-case experimental designs**, a behavior is measured **(baseline)**, an **independent variable** is introduced (intervention), and then the intervention is withdrawn. Because the behavior continues to be measured throughout (**repeated measurement**), any effects of the intervention can be noted.

X chromosome One of the two sex chromosomes that determine gender; females have two and males have one, contributed by the mother. X chromosome abnormalities are implicated in some physical and cognitive problems.

X-linked gene Gene on the X chromosome.

Y chromosome One of the two sex chromosomes that determine gender; its presence, contributed by the father, determines that the offspring is male.

Yerkes-Dodson curve Inverted U-shaped graphical relationship between arousal and performance. Optimal performance occurs at intermediate levels of arousal. Psychopaths may engage in stimulus-seeking behavior to increase their low arousal to more useful levels.

REFERENCES

Aarsland, D., & Kurz, M. W. (2010). The epidemiology of dementia associated with Parkinson disease. *Journal of the Neurological Sciences, 289*(1–2), 18–22.

Abad, V., & Guilleminault, C. (2009). Treatment options for obstructive sleep apnea. *Current Treatment Options in Neurology, 11*(5), 358–367.

Abbey, S. E., & Garfinkel, P. E. (1991). Neurasthenia and chronic fatigue syndrome: The role of culture in the making of a diagnosis. *American Journal of Psychiatry, 148*, 1638–1646.

Abbott, D. W., de Zwaan, M., Mussell, M. P., Raymond, N. C., Seim, H. C., Crow, S. J., ... Mitchell J. E. (1998). Onset of binge eating and dieting in overweight women: Implications for etiology, associated features and treatment. *Journal of Psychosomatic Research, 44*, 367–374.

Abel, G. G. (1989). Behavioral treatment of child molesters. In A. J. Stunkard & A. Baum (Eds.), *Perspectives in behavioral medicine: Eating, sleeping and sex* (pp. 223–242). Hillsdale, NJ: Erlbaum.

Abel, G. G., Becker, J. V., Cunningham-Rathner, J., Mittelman, M., & Rouleau, J. L. (1988). Multiple paraphilic diagnoses among sex offenders. *Bulletin of the American Academy of Psychiatry and Law, 16*, 153–168.

Abel, G. G., Becker, J. V., Mittelman, M., Cunningham-Rathner, J., Rouleau, J. L., & Murphy, W. E. (1987). Self-reported sex crimes of nonincarcerated paraphiliacs. *Journal of Interpersonal Violence, 2*, 3–25.

Abela, J. R., & Skitch, S. A. (2007). Dysfunctional attitudes, self-esteem, and hassles: Cognitive vulnerability to depression in children of affectively ill parents. *Behaviour Research and Therapy, 45*(6), 1127–1140.

Abramson, L. Y., Metalsky, G. I., & Alloy, L. B. (1989). Hopelessness depression: A theory-based subtype of depression. *Psychological Review, 96*(2), 358–372.

Abramson, L. Y., Seligman, M. E. P., & Teasdale, J. D. (1978). Learned helplessness in humans: Critique and reformulation. *Journal of Abnormal Psychology, 87*, 49–74.

Adachi, Y., Sato, C., Nishino, N., Ohryoji, F., Hayama, J., & Yamagami, T. (2009). A brief parental education for shaping sleep habits in 4-month-old infants. *Clinical Medicine & Research, 7*(3), 85–92. doi:10.3121/cmr.2009.814

Adair, R., Bauchner, H., Philipp, B., Levenson, S., & Zuckerman, B. (1991). Night waking during infancy: Role of parent presence at bedtime. *Pediatrics, 87*, 500–504.

Addington v. Texas, 99 S. Ct. 1804 (1979).

Addis, M. E. (2008). Gender and depression in men. *Clinical Psychology: Science and Practice, 15*(3), 153–168.

Ader, R., & Cohen, N. (1975). Behaviorally conditioned immunosuppression. *Psychosomatic Medicine, 37*, 333–340.

Ader, R., & Cohen, N. (1993). Psychoneuroimmunology: Conditioning and stress. *Annual Review of Psychology, 44*, 53–85.

Adler, C. M., Côte, G., Barlow, D. H., & Hillhouse, J. J. (1994). *Phenomenological relationships between somatoform, anxiety, and psychophysiological disorders.* Unpublished manuscript.

Afari, N., & Buchwald, D. (2003). Chronic fatigue syndrome: A review. *American Journal of Psychiatry, 160*, 221–236.

Agatisa, P., Matthews, K., Bromberger, J., Edmundowicz, D., Chang, Y., & Sutton-Tyrell, K. (2005). Coronary and aortic calcification in women with major depression history. *Archives of Internal Medicine, 165*, 1229–1236.

Agras, W. S. (1982). Behavioral medicine in the 1980s: Nonrandom connections. *Journal of Consulting and Clinical Psychology, 50*, 797–803.

Agras, W. S. (1987). *Eating disorders: Management of obesity, bulimia, and anorexia nervosa.* Elmsford, NY: Pergamon Press.

Agras, W. S. (2001). The consequences and costs of eating disorders. *Psychiatric Clinics of North America, 24*, 371–379.

Agras, W. S., Barlow, D. H., Chapin, H. N., Abel, G. G., & Leitenberg, H. (1974). Behavior modification of anorexia nervosa. *Archives of General Psychiatry, 30*, 279–286.

Agras, W. S., Schneider, J. A., Arnow, B., Raeburn, S. D., & Telch, C. F. (1989). Cognitive-behavioral and response-prevention treatments for bulimia nervosa. *Journal of Consulting and Clinical Psychology, 57*, 215–221.

Agras, W. S., Sylvester, D., & Oliveau, D. (1969). The epidemiology of common fears and phobia. *Comprehensive Psychiatry, 10*, 151–156.

Agras, W. S., Telch, C. F., Arnow, B., Eldredge, K., & Marnell, M. (1997). One-year follow-up of cognitive-behavioral therapy of obese individuals with binge eating disorder. *Journal of Consulting and Clinical Psychology, 65*, 343–347.

Agras, W. S., Walsh, B. T., Fairburn, C. G., Wilson, G. T., & Kraemer, H. C. (2000). A multicenter comparison of cognitive-behavioral therapy and interpersonal psychotherapy for bulimia nervosa. *Archives of General Psychiatry, 57*, 459–466.

Aigner, M., & Bach, M. (1999). Clinical utility of DSM-IV pain disorder. *Comprehensive Psychiatry, 40*(5), 353–357.

Aikins, D. E., & Craske, M. G. (2001). Cognitive theories of generalized anxiety disorder. *Psychiatric Clinics of North America, 24*, 57–74.

Åkerstedt, T., & Wright, K. P., Jr. (2009). Sleep loss and fatigue in shift work and shift work disorder. *Sleep Medicine Clinics, 4*(2), 257–271. doi:10.1016/j.jsmc.2009.03.001

Akiskal, H. (2006). Special issue on circular insanity and beyond: Historic contributions of French psychiatry to contemporary concepts and research on bipolar disorder. *Journal of Affective Disorders, 96*, 141–143.

Akiskal, H. S. (2009). Dysthymia, cyclothymia, and hyperthymia. In M. G. Gelder, N. C. Andreasen, J. J. López-Ibor, Jr., & J. R. Geddes (Eds.), *New Oxford textbook of psychiatry* (2nd ed., Vol. 1, pp. 680–692). Oxford, UK: Oxford University Press.

Akiskal, H. S., & Cassano, G. B. (Eds.) (1997). *Dysthymia and the spectrum of chronic depressions.* New York, NY: Guilford Press.

Akiskal, H. S., & Pinto, O. (1999). The evolving spectrum: Prototypes I, II, III, and IV. *The Psychiatric Clinics of North America, 22*(3), 517–534.

al'Absi, M., & Wittmers, L. E., Jr. (2003). Enhanced adrenocortical responses to stress in hypertension-prone men and women. *Annals of Behavioral Medicine, 25*, 25–33.

Alarcon, R. D., Bell, C. C., Kirmayer, L. J., Ling, K., Bedirhan, U., & Wisner, K. L. (2002). Beyond the funhouse mirrors: Research agenda on culture and psychiatric diagnosis. In D. Kupfer, M. First, & D. Regier (Eds.), *A research agenda for DSM-V* (pp. 219–281). Washington, DC: American Psychiatric Association.

Albano, A., Pincus, D. B., Tracey, S., & Barlow, D. H. (in preparation). Cognitive behavioral group treatment of social phobia in adolescents: Importance of parent inclusion in treatment. Manuscript in preparation.

Albano, A. M., & Barlow, D. H. (1996). Breaking the vicious cycle: Cognitive-behavioral group treatment for socially anxious youth. In E. D. Hibbs & P. S. Jensen (Eds.), *Psychosocial treatment research and adolescent disorders* (pp. 43–62). Washington, DC: APA Press.

Albano, A. M., Chorpita, B. F., & Barlow, D. H. (1996). Childhood anxiety disorders. In E. J. Mash & R. A. Barkley (Eds.), *Child psychopathology* (pp. 196–241). New York, NY: Guilford Press.

Albano, A. M., DiBartolo, P. M., Heimberg, R. G., & Barlow, D. H. (1995). Children and adolescents: Assessment and treatment. In R. G. Heimberg, M. R. Liebowitz, D. A. Hope, & F. Schneier (Eds.), *Social phobia: Diagnosis, assessment and treatment.* New York, NY: Guilford Press.

Albano, A. M., & Hack, S. (2004). Children and adolescents. In R. G. Heimberg, C. L. Turk, & D. S. Mennin (Eds.), *Generalized anxiety disorder: Advances in research and practice* (pp. 383–408). New York, NY: Guilford Press.

Albano, A. M., Miller, P. P., Zarate, R., Côté, G., & Barlow, D. H. (1997). Behavioral assessment and treatment of PTSD in prepubertal children: Attention to development factors and innovative strategies in the case study of a family. *Cognitive and Behavioral Practice, 4,* 245–262.

Albert, C., Chae, C., Rexrode, K., Manson, J., & Kawachi, I. (2005). Phobic anxiety and risk of coronary heart disease and sudden cardiac among women. *Circulation, 111,* 480–487.

Alessi, S. M., Roll, J. M., Reilly, M. P., & Johanson, C. E. (2002). Establishment of a diazepam preference in human volunteers following a differential- conditioning history of placebo versus diazepam choice. *Experimental and Clinical Psychopharmacology, 10,* 77–83.

Alexander, F. G. (1939). Emotional factors in essential hypertension: Presentation of a tentative hypothesis. *Psychosomatic Medicine, 1,* 175–179.

Alexander, F. G. (1950). *Psychosomatic medicine.* New York, NY: Norton.

Alexander, F. G., & Selesnick, S. T. (1966). *The history of psychiatry: An evaluation of psychiatric thought and practice from prehistoric times to the present.* New York, NY: Harper & Row.

Alexopoulos, G., Katz, I., Bruce, M., Heo, M., Have, T., Raue, P., Reynolds, C. F., III, (2005). Remission in depressed geriatric primary care patients: A report from the PROSPECT study. *American Journal of Psychiatry, 162,* 718–724.

Alim, T. N., Feder, A., Graves, R. E., Wang, Y., Weaver, J., Westphal, M., ... Charney, D. S. (2008). Trauma, resilience, and recovery in a high-risk African-American population. *The American Journal of Psychiatry, 165*(12), 1566–1575.

Allen, J., DeMyer, M., Norton, J., Pontius, W., & Yang, G. (1971). Intellectuality in parents of psychotic, subnormal, and normal children. *Journal of Autism and Childhood Schizophrenia, 1,* 311–326.

Allen, J. J., & Movius, H. L. (2000). The objective assessment of amnesia in dissociative identity disorder using event-related potentials. *International Journal of Psychophysiology, 38,* 21–41.

Allen, L. A., Woolfolk, R. L., Escobar, J. I., Gara, M. A., & Hamer, R. M. (2006). Cognitive-behavioral therapy for somatization disorder: A randomized controlled trial. *Archives of Internal Medicine, 166*(14), 1512–1518.

Allen, L. B., White, K. S., Barlow, D. H., Shear, M. K., Gorman, J. M., & Woods, S. W. (2010). Cognitive-behavior therapy (CBT) for panic disorder: Relationship of anxiety and depression comorbidity with treatment outcome. *Journal of Psychopathology & Behavioral Assessment, 32*(2), 185–192.

Allen, L. S., & Gorski, R. A. (1992). Sexual orientation and the size of the anterior commissure in the human brain. *Proceedings of the National Academy of Science, 89,* 7199–7202.

Allen, N. J., & Barres, B. A. (2009). Neuroscience: Glia—more than just brain glue. *Nature, 457*(7230), 675–677.

Aller, R., & Aller, G. (1997). An institutional response to patient/family complaints. In A. E. Shamoo (Ed.), *Ethics in neurobiological research with human subjects: The Baltimore Conference on Ethics* (pp. 155–172). Amsterdam, The Netherlands: Gordon and Breach Publishers OPA.

Allin, M., Streeruwitz, A., & Curtis, V. (2005). Progress in understanding conversation disorder. *Neuropsychiatric Disease and Treatment, 3,* 1–5.

Alloy, L., & Abramson, L. (2001). Cyclothymic personality. In W. E. Craighead & C. B. Nemeroff (Eds.), *The Corsini encyclopedia of psychology and behavioral science* (3rd ed., pp. 417–418). New York, NY: Wiley & Sons.

Alloy, L., & Abramson, L. (2006). Prospective incidence of first onsets and recurrences of depression individuals at high and low cognitive risk for depression. *Journal of Abnormal Psychology, 115,* 145–156.

Alloy, L., Abramson, L., Safford, S., & Gibb, B. (2006). The cognitive vulnerability to depression (CVD) project: Current findings and future directions. In L. B. Alloy & J. H. Riskind (Eds.), *Cognitive vulnerability to emotional disorders* (pp. 33–61). Hillsdale, NJ: Erlbaum.

Alloy, L., Abramson, L. Y., Hogan, M. E., Whitehouse, W. G., Rose, D. T., Robinson, M. S., ... Lapkin, J. B. (2000). The Temple-Wisconsin cognitive vulnerability to depression project: Lifetime history of axis I psychopathology in individuals at high and low cognitive risk for depression. *Journal of Abnormal Psychology, 109,* 403–418.

Alloy, L., Kelly, K. A., Mineka, S., & Clements, C. M. (1990). Comorbidity of anxiety and depressive disorders: A helplessness–hopelessness perspective. In J. D. Maser & C. R. Cloninger (Eds.), *Comorbidity of mood and anxiety disorders* (pp. 499–543). Washington, DC: American Psychiatric Press.

Alloy, L. B., & Abramson, L. Y. (2010). The role of the behavioral approach system (BAS) in bipolar spectrum disorders. *Current Directions in Psychological Science, 19*(3), 189–194.

Alloy, L. B., Abramson, L. Y., Urosevic, S., Bender, R. E., & Wagner, C. A. (2009). Longitudinal predictors of bipolar spectrum disorders: a behavioral approach system (BAS) perspective. *Clinical Psychology* (New York), *16*(2), 206–226.

Altarac, M., & Saroha, E. (2007). Lifetime prevalence of learning disability among U.S. children. *Pediatrics, 119*(Suppl. 1), S77–S83.

Althof, S. (2006). The psychology of premature ejaculation: Therapies and consequences. *Journal of Sexual Medicine, 3,* 324–331.

Althof, S. E. (2007). Treatment of rapid ejaculation: Psychotherapy, pharmacotherapy, and combined therapy. In S. R. Leiblum (Ed.), *Principles and practice of sex therapy* (4th ed., pp. 212–240). New York, NY: Guilford Press.

Altshuler, L. L., Kupka, R. W., Hellemann, G., Frye, M. A., Sugar, C. A., McElroy, S. L., ... Suppes, T. (2010). Gender and depressive symptoms in 711 patients with bipolar disorder evaluated prospectively in the Stanley Foundation bipolar treatment outcome network. *American Journal of Psychiatry, 167*(6), 708–715.

Alvino, C., Kohler, C., Barrett, F., Gur, R., Gur, R., & Verma, R. (2007). Computerized measurement of facial expression of emotions in schizophrenia. *Journal of Neuroscience Methods, 163*(2), 350–361.

Alzheimer's Association. (2010). 2010 Alzheimer's disease facts and figures. *Alzheimer's & Dementia* (Vol. 6). Chicago, IL: Alzheimer's Association.

Amat, J., Baratta, B. V., Paul, E., Bland, S. T., Watkins, L. R., & Maier, S. F. (2005). Medial prefrontal cortex determines how stressor controllability affects behavior and dorsal raphe nucleus. *Nature Neuroscience, 8,* 365–371.

American Bar Association Standing Committee on Association Standards for Criminal Justice. (1984). *Criminal justice and mental health standards.* Chicago, IL: Author.

American Cancer Society (2007). Prevention and early detection: Cigarette smoking. Retrieved from http://www.cancer.org/acs/groups/cid/documents/webcontent/002967-pdf.pdf

American Law Institute. (1962). *Model penal code: Proposed official draft.* Philadelphia, PA: Author.

American Psychiatric Association. (1980). *Diagnostic and statistical manual of mental disorders* (3rd ed.). Washington, DC: Author.

American Psychiatric Association. (1983). American Psychiatric Association statement on the insanity defense. *American Journal of Psychiatry, 140,* 681–688.

American Psychiatric Association. (1987). *Diagnostic and statistical manual of mental disorders* (3rd ed. rev.). Washington, DC: Author.

American Psychiatric Association. (1994). *Diagnostic and statistical manual of mental disorders* (4th ed.). Washington, DC: Author.

American Psychiatric Association. (2000). *Diagnostic and statistical manual of mental disorders* (4th ed., text revision). Washington, DC: Author.

American Psychiatric Association. (2000). Substance use disorders: Alcohol, cocaine, opioids. In Practice guideline for the treatment of psychiatric disorders: Compendium 2000 (pp. 139–238). Washington, DC: Author.

American Psychiatric Association. (2003). Practice guideline for the assessment and treatment of patients with suicidal behaviors. *American Journal of Psychiatry, 160*(Suppl.), 1–44.

American Psychiatric Association. (2004). Practice guideline for the treatment of patients with schizophrenia (2nd ed.). *American Journal of Psychiatry, 161*(Suppl.), 1–56.

American Psychiatric Association. (2006). Practice guideline for the psychiatric evaluation of adults (2nd ed.). *American Journal of Psychiatry, 163*(Suppl.), 1–36.

American Psychiatric Association. (2007). Practice guidelines for the treatment of patients with substance use disorders (2nd ed.). *American Journal of Psychiatry, 164*(Suppl.), 1–14.

American Psychiatric Association. (2010a). APA practice guidelines for treatment of patients with eating disorders (3rd ed.). Retrieved from http://www.psychiatryonline.com/content .aspx?aID5138866

American Psychiatric Association. (2010b). *DSM-5 development: Personality and personality disorders.* Retrieved from http://www.dsm5.org/ProposedRevisions/Pages/PersonalityandPersonalityDisorders.aspx

American Psychiatric Association. (2010c). *DSM-5 development: Schizophrenia and other psychotic disorders.* Retrieved from http://www.dsm5.org/ProposedRevisions/Pages/SchizophreniaandOtherPsychotic Disorders.aspx

American Psychiatric Association. (2010d). *DSM-5 development: Autistic disorder.* Retrieved from http://www.dsm5.org/ProposedRevisions/Pages/proposedrevision .aspx?rid594#

American Psychiatric Association. (2010f). *DSM-5 Development: Proposed revisions.* Retrieved from http://www.dsm5.org/ProposedRevisions/Pages/Default.aspx

American Psychiatric Association Practice Guideline. (2000a). Substance use disorders: Alcohol, cocaine, opioids. In Practice guideline for the treatment of psychiatric disorders: Compendium 2000 (pp. 139–238). Washington, DC: Author.

American Psychiatric Association Practice Guideline. (2000b). Practice guideline for the treatment of patients with major depressive disorder (revision). *American Journal of Psychiatry, 157*(Suppl. 4), 49.

American Psychiatric Association Practice Guideline. (2000c). *Practice guideline for the treatment of patients with Alzheimer's disease and other dementias of late life: Compendium 2000.* Washington, DC: Author.

American Psychological Association. (2002a). Ethical principles of psychologists and code of conduct. *American Psychologist, 57,* 1060–1073.

American Psychological Association. (2002b). Criteria for practice guideline development and evaluation. *American Psychologist, 57,* 1048–1059.

American Psychological Association. (2010a). 2010 Amendments to the 2002 "Ethical principles of psychologists and code of conduct." *American Psychologist, 65*(5), 493–493.

American Psychological Association. (2010b). Report of the ethics committee, 2009. *American Psychologist, 65*(5), 483–492.

American Psychological Association Board of Professional Affairs Task Force on Psychological Intervention Guidelines (1995). *Template for developing guidelines: Interventions for mental disorders and psychosocial aspects of physical disorders.* Approved by APA Council of Representatives, February 1995. Washington, DC: American Psychological Association.

American Psychological Association Presidential Task Force. (2006). Evidence-based practice in psychology. *American Psychologist, 61,* 271–285.

American Psychological Association Task Force on Gender Identity and Gender Variance. (2008). Report of the Task Force on Gender Identity and Gender Variance. Washington, DC: Author.

American Society for Metabolic & Bariatric Surgery. (2010). Fact Sheet. Retrieved from http://www.asmbs.org/Newsite07/media/ASMBS_Metabolic_Bariatric_Surgery_Overview _FINAL_09.pdf

Amir, N., Cashman, L., & Foa, E. B. (1997). Strategies of thought control and obsessive-compulsive disorder. *BRAT, 35,* 775–777.

Anastopoulos, A., Sommer, J., & Schatz, N. (2009). ADHD and family functioning. *Current Attention Disorders Reports, 1*(4), 167–170. doi:10.1007/s12618-009-0023-2

Ancoli-Israel, S., & Ayalon, L. (2009). Diagnosis and treatment of sleep disorders in older adults. *Focus: The Journal of Lifelong Learning in Psychiatry, 7*(1), 98–105.

Andersen, B. L. (1992). Psychological interventions for cancer patients to enhance the quality of life. Special issue: Behavioral medicine: An update for the 1990s. *Journal of Consulting and Clinical Psychology, 60*(4), 552–568.

Andersen, B. L., & Cyranowski, J. M. (1994). Women's sexual self-schema. *Journal of Personality and Social Psychology, 67*(6), 1079–1100.

Andersen, B. L., Cyranowski, J. M., & Espindle, D. (1999). Men's sexual self-schema. *Journal of Personality and Social Psychology, 76*(4), 645–661.

Andersen, B. L., Farrar, W. B., Golden-Kreutz, D., Emery, C. F., Glaser, R., Crespin, T., & Carson, W. E., III. (2007). Distress reduction from a psychological intervention contributes to improved health for cancer patients. *Brain, Behavior, and Immunity, 21,* 953–961.

Andersen, B. L., Yang, H., Farrar, W. B., Golden-Kreutz, D. M., Emery, C. F., Thornton, L. M., ... Carson, W. E., III. (2008). Psychologic intervention improves survival for breast cancer patients: A randomized clinical trial. *Cancer, 113,* 3450–3458.

Anderson, D. J., Noyes, R., & Crowe, R. R. (1984). A comparison of panic disorder and generalized anxiety disorder. *American Journal of Psychiatry, 141,* 572–575.

Anderson-Fye, E. (2009). Cross-cultural issues in body image among children and adolescents. In L. Smolak & J. K. Thompson (Eds.), *Body image, eating disorders, and obesity in youth: Assessment, prevention, and treatment* (2nd ed., pp. 113–133). Washington, DC: American Psychological Association.

Andrasik, F. (2000). Biofeedback. In D. I. Mostofsky & D. H. Barlow (Eds.), *The management of stress and anxiety in medical disorders* (pp. 66– 83). Needham Heights, MA: Allyn & Bacon.

Andrews, G., Hobbs, M. J., Borkovec, T. D., Beesdo, K., Craske, M. G., Heimberg, R. G., ... Stanley, M. A. (2010). Generalized worry disorder: A review of DSM-IV generalized anxiety disorder and options for DSM-V. *Depression and Anxiety, 27*(2), 134–147.

Aneshensel, C. S., Pearlin, L. I., Mullan, J. T., Zarit, S. H., & Whitlatch, C. J. (1995). *Profiles in caregiving: The unexpected career.* San Diego, CA: Academic Press.

Angst, A., Angst, F., Gerber-Werder, R., & Gamma, A. (2005). Suicide in 406 mood disordered patients with and without long-term medication: A 40 to 44 years'

follow-up. *Archives Suicide Research, 9,* 279–300.

Angst, J. (1988). Clinical course of affective disorders. In T. Helgason & R. J. Daly (Eds.), *Depressive illness: Prediction of course and outcome* (pp. 1–44). Berlin, Germany: Springer-Verlag.

Angst, J. (2009). Course and prognosis of mood disorders. In M. G. Gelder, N. C. Andreasen, J. J. López-Ibor, Jr., & J. R. Geddes (Eds.), *New Oxford textbook of psychiatry* (2nd ed., Vol. 1, pp. 665–669). Oxford, UK: Oxford University Press.

Angst, J., & Preizig, M. (1996). Course of a clinical cohort of unipolar, bipolar, and schizoaffective patients: Results of a prospective study from 1959 to 1985. *Schweizer Archiv fur Neurologie und Psychiatrie, 146,* 1–16.

Angst, J., & Sellaro, R. (2000). Historical perspectives and natural history of bipolar disorder. *Biological Psychiatry, 48*(6), 445–457.

Ansell, E., Sanislow, C., McGlashan, T., & Grilo, C. (2007). Psychosocial impairment and treatment utilization by patients with borderline personality disorder, other personality disorders, mood and anxiety disorders, and a healthy comparison group. *Comprehensive Psychiatry, 48*(4), 329–336.

Anton, R. F., O'Malley, S. S., Ciraulo, D. A., Cisler, R. A., Couper, D., Donovan, D. M., ... Zweben, A. for the COMBINE Study Research Group. (2006). Combined pharmacotherapies and behavioral interventions for alcohol dependence: The COMBINE Study: A randomized controlled trial. *JAMA: Journal of the American Medical Association, 295,* 2003–2017.

Antoni, M. H., Cruess, D. G., Cruess, S., Lutgendorf, S., Kumar, M., Ironson, G., ... Schneiderman, N. (2000). Cognitive-behavioral stress management intervention effects on anxiety, 24-hr urinary norepinephrine output, and T-cytotoxic/suppressor cells over time among symptomatic HIV-infected gay men. *Journal of Consulting and Clinical Psychology, 68,* 31–45.

Antoni, M. H., Lechner, S., Diaz, A., Vargas, S., Holley, H., Phillips, K., ... Blombery, B. (2009). Cognitive behavioral stress management effects on psychosocial and psychological adaptation in women undergoing treatment for breast cancer. *Brain, Behavior, and Immunity, 23,* 580–591.

Antoni, M. H., Lechner, S., Kazi, A., Wimberly, S., Sifre, T., Urcuyo, K., ... Carver, C.S. (2006). How stress management improves quality of life after treatment for breast cancer. *Journal of Consulting and Clinical Psychology, 74,* 1143–1152.

Antoni, M. H., & Lutgendorf, S. (2007). Psychosocial factors and disease progression in cancer. *Current Directions in Psychological Science, 16,* 42–46.

Antony, M. M., & Barlow, D. H. (2002). Specific phobias. In D. H. Barlow, *Anxiety and its disorders: The nature and treatment of anxiety and panic* (2nd ed.). New York, NY: Guilford Press.

Antony, M. M., & Barlow, D. H. (Eds.). (2010). *Handbook of assessment and treatment planning for psychological disorders* (2nd ed.). New York, NY: Guilford Press.

Antony, M. M., Brown, T. A., & Barlow, D. H. (1997a). Heterogeneity among specific phobia types in DSM-IV. *Behavior Research and Therapy, 35,* 1089–1100.

Antony, M. M., Brown, T. A., & Barlow, D. H. (1997b). Response to hyperventilation and 5.5% CO_2 inhalation of subjects with types of specific phobia, panic disorder, or no mental disorder. *American Journal of Psychiatry, 154,* 1089–1095.

Antony, M. M., Craske, M. G., & Barlow, D. H. (2006). *Mastering your fears and phobias: Workbook.* New York, NY: Oxford University Press.

Aouizerate, B., Rotge, J., Martin-Guehl, C., Cuny, E., Rougier, A., Guehl, D., ... Tignol, J. (2006). A systematic review of psychsurgical treatments for obsessive-compulsive disorder: Does deep brain stimulation represent the future trend in psychosurgery? *Clinical Neuropsychiatry, 3*(6), 391–403.

Apfelbaum, B. (2000). Retarded ejaculation: A much misunderstood syndrome. In S. R. Leiblum & R. C. Rosen (Eds.), *Principles and practice of sex therapy* (3rd ed., pp. 205–241). New York, NY: Guilford Press.

Apple, R. F., Lock, J., & Peebles, R. (2006). *Preparing for weight loss surgery.* New York, NY: Oxford University Press.

Arai, J. A., Li, S., Hartley, D. M., & Feig, L. A. (2009). Transgenerational rescue of a genetic defect in long-term potentiation and memory formation by juvenile enrichment. *The Journal of Neuroscience, 29*(5), 1496–1502.

Arenas, E. (2010). Towards stem cell replacement therapies for Parkinson's disease. *Biochemical and Biophysical Research Communications, 396*(1), 152–156.

Arenkiel, B. R., & Ehlers, M. D. (2009). Molecular genetics and imaging technologies for circuit-based neuroanatomy. *Nature, 461*(7266), 900–907.

Armbruster, D., Mueller, A., Moser, D. A., Lesch, K. P., Brocke, B., & Kirschbaum, C. (2009). Interaction effect of D4 dopamine receptor gene and serotonin transporter promoter polymorphism on the cortisol stress response. *Behavioral Neuroscience, 123*(6), 1288–1295.

Arrindell, W. A., Eisemann, M., Richter, J., Oei, T. P. S., Caballo, V. E., van der Ende, J., ... Hudson, B. L. (2003a). Phobic anxiety in 11 nations part I: Dimensional constancy of the five-factor model. *Behaviour Research and Therapy, 41,* 461–479.

Arrindell, W. A., Eisemann, M., Richter, J., Oei, T. P. S., Caballo, V. E., van der Ende, J., ... Zaldívar, F. (2003b). Masculinity–femininity as a national characteristic and its relationship with national agoraphobic fear levels: Fodor's sex role hypothesis revitalized. *Behaviour Research and Therapy, 41,* 795–807.

Arseneault, L., Cannon, M., Witton, J., & Murray, R. M. (2004). Causal association between cannabis and psychosis: Examination of the evidence. *British Journal of Psychiatry, 184,* 110–117.

Asberg, M., Nordstrom, P., & Traskman-Bendz, L. (1986). Cerebrospinal fluid studies in suicide: An overview. *Annals of the American Academy of Science, 487,* 243–255.

Aschoff, J., & Wever, R. (1962). Spontanperiodik des Menschen die Ausschulus aller Zeitgeber. *Die Naturwissenschaften, 49,* 337–342.

Asmal, L., & Stein, D. J. (2009). Anxiety and culture. In M. M. Antony & M. B. Stein (Eds.), *Oxford handbook of anxiety and related disorders.* (pp. 657–664). New York, NY: Oxford University Press.

Asmundson, G. J., & Carleton, R. N. (2009). Fear of pain. In M. M. Antony & M. B. Stein (Eds.), *Oxford handbook of anxiety and related disorders* (pp. 551–561). Oxford, UK: Oxford University Press.

Attia, E., Haiman, C., Walsh, B. T., & Flater, S. R. (1998). Does fluoxetine augment the inpatient treatment of anorexia nervosa? *American Journal of Psychiatry, 155*(4), 548–551.

Attia, E., & Roberto, C. A. (2009). Should amenorrhea be a diagnostic criterion for anorexia nervosa? *International Journal of Eating Disorders, 42*(7), 581–589.

Attie, I., & Brooks-Gunn, J. (1995). The development of eating regulation across the life span. In D. Cicchetti & D. J. Cohen (Eds.), *Developmental psychopathology* (Vol. 2, pp. 332–368). New York, NY: Wiley.

Auyeng, B., Baron-Cohen, S., Ashwin, E., Knickmeyer, R., Taylor, K., Hackett, G., & Hines, M. (2009). Fetal testosterone predicts sexually differentiated childhood behavior in girls and boys. *Psychological Science, 20,* 144–148.

Axelson, D., Birmaher, B., Strober, M., Gill, M. K., Valeri, S., Chiappetta, L., ... Keller, M. (2006). Phenomenology of children and adolescents with bipolar spectrum disorders. *Archives of General Psychiatry, 63*(10), 1139–1148.

Ayala, E. S., Meuret, A. E., & Ritz, T. (2009). Treatments for blood-injury-injection phobia: A critical review of current evidence. *Journal of Psychiatric Research, 43*(15), 1235–1242.

Ayearst, L. E., & Bagby, R. M. (2010). Evaluating the psychometric properties of psychological measures. In M. M. Antony & D.H. Barlow (Eds.), *Handbook of assessment and treatment planning for psychological disorders* (2nd ed., pp. 23–61). New York, NY: Guilford Press.

Ayers, C. R., Thorp, S. R., & Wetherell, J. L. (2009). Anxiety disorders and hoarding in older adults. In M. M. Antony & M. B. Stein (Eds.), *Oxford handbook of anxiety and related disorders.* (pp. 625–635). New York, NY: Oxford University Press.

Ayllon, T., & Azrin, N. H. (1968). *The token economy: A motivational system for therapy and rehabilitation.* New York, NY: Appleton-Century-Crofts.

Azmitia, E. C. (1978). The serotonin-producing neurons of the midbrain median and dorsal raphe nuclei. In L. Iverson, S. Iverson, & S. Snyder (Eds.), *Handbook of psycho pharmacology: Vol. 9. Chemical pathways in the brain* (pp. 233–314). New York, NY: Plenum Press.

Baasher, T. A. (2001). Islam and mental health. *Eastern Mediterranean Health Journal, 7,* 372–376.

Babyak, M., Blumenthal, J. A., Herman, S., Khatri, P., Doraiswamy, M., Moore, K., ... Krishnan, K. R. (2000). Exercise treatment for major depression: Maintenance of therapeutic benefit at 10 months. *Psychosomatic Medicine, 62,* 633–638.

Bach, A. K., Barlow, D., & Wincze, J. (2004). The enhancing effects of manualized treatment for erectile dysfunction among men using slidenafil: A preliminary investigation. *Behaviour Therapy, 35,* 55–73.

Bach, A. K., Brown, T. A., & Barlow, D. H. (1999). The effects of false negative feedback on efficacy expectancies and sexual arousal in sexually functional males. *Behavior Therapy, 30,* 79–95.

Bach, A. K., Wincze, J. P., & Barlow, D. H. (2001). Sexual dysfunction. In D. H. Barlow (Ed.), *Clinical handbook of psychological disorders: A step-by-step treatment manual* (3rd ed., pp. 562–608). New York, NY: Guilford Press.

Bailey, J. A. (2009). Addressing common risk and protective factors can prevent a wide range of adolescent risk behaviors. *Journal of Adolescent Health, 45*(2), 107–108.

Bailey, J. M., & Benishay, D. S. (1993). Familial aggregation of female sexual orientation. *American Journal of Psychiatry, 150*(2), 272–277.

Bailey, J. M., & Pillard, R. C. (1991). A genetic study of male sexual orientation. *Archives of General Psychiatry, 48,* 1089–1096.

Bailey, J. M., Pillard, R. C., Dawood, K., Miller, M. B., Farrer, L. A., Trivedi, S., & Murphy, R. L. (1999). A family history study of male sexual orientation using three independent samples. *Behavior Genetics, 29,* 79–86.

Bailey, J. M., Pillard, R. C., Neale, M. C., & Agyei, Y. (1993). Heritable factors influence sexual orientation in women. *Archives of General Psychiatry, 50,* 217–223.

Baker, A., van Kesteren, P. J., Gooren, L. J. G., & Bezemer, P. D. (1993). The prevalence of transsexualism in The Netherlands. *Acta Psychiatrica Scandinavica, 87,* 237–238.

Baker, C. D., & DeSilva, P. (1988). The relationship between male sexual dysfunction and belief in Zilbergeld's myths: An empirical investigation. *Sexual and Marital Therapy, 3*(2), 229–238.

Bakkevig, J. F., & Karterud, S. (2010). Is the Diagnostic and Statistical Manual of Mental Disorders, Fourth Edition, histrionic personality disorder category a valid construct? *Comprehensive Psychiatry.* doi:10.1016/j.comppsych.2009.11.009

Bakshi, S. (2004). A comparative analysis of hijras and drag queens: The subversive possibilities and limits of parading effeminacy and negotiating masculinity. *Journal of Homosexuality, 46,* 211–223.

Baldessarini, R., Pompili, M., & Tondo, L. (2006). Suicidal risk in antidepressant drug trials. *Archives General Psychiatry, 63,* 246–248.

Baldwin, J. D., & Baldwin, J. I. (1989). The socialization of homosexuality and heterosexuality in a non-Western society. *Archives of Sexual Behavior, 18,* 13–29.

Baldwin, R. (2009). Mood disorders in the elderly. In M. G. Gelder, N. C. Andreasen, J. J. López-Ibor, Jr., & J. R. Geddes (Eds.), *New Oxford textbook of psychiatry* (2nd ed., Vol. 2, pp. 1550–1558). Oxford, UK: Oxford University Press.

Ball, J., & Links, P. (2009). Borderline personality disorder and childhood trauma: Evidence for a causal relationship. *Current Psychiatry Reports, 11*(1), 63–68. doi:10.1007/s11920-009-0010-4

Balon, R. (2006). SSRI-associated sexual dysfunction. *American Journal of Psychiatry, 163,* 1504–1512.

Balon, R., Segraves, R., & Clayton, A. (2007). Issues for DSM-V: Sexual dysfunction, disorder, or variation along normal distribution—Toward rethinking DSM criteria of sexual dysfunctions. *American Journal of Psychiatry, 164,* 198–200.

Bancroft, J. (1989). *Human sexuality and its problems* (2nd ed.). New York, NY: Churchill Livingstone.

Bancroft, J. (1994). Homosexual orientation: The search for a biological basis. *British Journal of Psychiatry, 164,* 437–440.

Bancroft, J. (1997). Sexual problems. In D. M. Clark & C. G. Fairburn (Eds.), *Science and practice of cognitive behavior therapy* (pp. 243–257). New York, NY: Oxford University Press.

Bancroft, J., Loftus, J., & Long, J. S. (2003). Distress about sex: A national survey of women in heterosexual relationships. *Archives of Sexual Behavior, 32,* 193–208.

Bandelow, B., Krause, J., Wedekind, D., Broocks, A., Hajak, G., & Ruther, E. (2005). Early traumatic life events, parental attitudes, family history, and birth risk factors in patients with borderline personality disorder and healthy controls. *Psychiatry Research, 134,* 169–179.

Bandura, A. (1973). *Aggression: A social learning analysis.* Englewood Cliffs, NJ: Prentice Hall.

Bandura, A. (1986). *Social foundations of thought and action: A social cognitive theory.* Englewood Cliffs, NJ: Prentice Hall.

Bandura, A., O'Leary, A., Taylor, C. B., Gauthier, J., & Gossard, D. (1987). Perceived self-efficacy and pain control: Opioid and nonopioid mechanisms. *Journal of Personality and Social Psychology, 53,* 563–571.

Bankert, E. A., & Amdur, R. J. (2006). *Institutional Review Board: Management and function.* Boston, MA: Jones and Bartlett Publishers.

Barbaree, H. E., & Seto, M. C. (1997). Pedophilia: Assessment and treatment. In D. R. Laws & W. O. O'Donohue (Eds.), *Sexual deviance: Theory, assessment, and treatment* (pp. 175– 193). New York, NY: Guilford Press.

Barger, L. K., Wright, K. P., & Czeisler, C. A. (2008). Sleep and sleep-promoting medication use in shuttle crewmembers. *Aviation, Space, and Environmental Medicine, 79*(3), 266.

Bargh, J. A., & Chartrand, T. L. (1999). The unbearable automaticity of being. *American Psychologist, 54,* 462–479.

Barkley, R. A. (1990). *Attention-deficit hyperactivity disorder: A handbook for diagnosis and treatment.* New York, NY: Guilford Press.

Barkley, R. A. (2006a). ADHD in adults: Developmental course and outcome of children with ADHD, and ADHD in clinic-referred adults. In R. A. Barkley (Ed.), *Attention-deficit hyperactivity disorder: A handbook for diagnosis and treatment* (3rd ed., pp. 248–296). New York, NY: Guilford Press.

Barkley, R. A. (2006b). Primary symptoms, diagnostic criteria, prevalence, and gender differences. In R. A. Barkley (Ed.), *Attention-deficit hyperactivity disorder: A handbook for diagnosis and treatment* (3rd ed., pp. 76–121). New York, NY: Guilford Press.

Barlow, D. H. (1986). Causes of sexual dysfunction: The role of anxiety and cognitive interference. *Journal of Consulting and Clinical Psychology, 54,* 140–148.

Barlow, D. H. (1988). *Anxiety and its disorders: The nature and treatment of anxiety and panic.* New York, NY: Guilford Press.

Barlow, D. H. (1991). Disorders of emotion. *Psychological Inquiry, 2*(1), 58–71.

Barlow, D. H. (1993). Covert sensitization for paraphilia. In J. R. Cautela & A. J. Kearney (Eds.), *Covert conditioning casebook* (pp. 187–198). Pacific Grove, CA: Brooks/Cole.

Barlow, D. H. (2000). Unraveling the mysteries of anxiety and its disorders from the perspective of emotion theory. *American Psychologist, 55,* 1245–1263.

Barlow, D. H. (2002). *Anxiety and its disorders: The nature and treatment of anxiety and panic* (2nd ed.). New York: Guilford Press.

Barlow, D. H., Allen, L. B., & Basden, S. (2007). Psychological treatments for panic disorders, phobias, and generalized anxiety disorder. In P. E. Nathan & J. M. Gorman (Eds.), *A guide to treatments that work* (3rd ed.). New York, NY: Oxford University Press.

Barlow, D. H., Allen, L. B., & Choate, M. L. (2004). Toward a unified treatment for emotional disorders. *Behavior Therapy, 35,* 205–230.

Barlow, D. H., Becker, R., Leitenberg, H., & Agras, W. S. (1970). A mechanical strain gauge for recording penile circumference change. *Journal of Applied Behavior Analysis, 3,* 73–76.

Barlow, D. H., Brown, T. A., & Craske, M. G. (1994). Definitions of panic attacks and panic disorder in DSM-IV: Implications for research. *Journal of Abnormal Psychology, 103,* 553–554.

Barlow, D. H., Chorpita, B. F., & Turovsky, J. (1996). Fear, panic, anxiety, and disorders of emotion. In D. A. Hope (Ed.), *Perspectives on anxiety, panic, and fear* (The 43rd Annual Nebraska Symposium on Motivation) (pp. 251– 328). Lincoln, NE: Nebraska University Press.

Barlow, D. H., & Craske, M. G. (2007). *Mastery of your anxiety and panic* (4th ed.). New York, NY: Oxford University Press.

Barlow, D. H., Ellard, K. K., Fairholme, C. P., Farchione, T. J., Boisseau, C. L. Allen, L. B. & Ehrenreich-May, J. (2011-b). *Unified Protocol for the Transdiagnostic Treatment of Emotional Disorders (Workbook).* New York, NY: Oxford University Press.

Barlow, D. H., Farchione, T. J., Fairholme, C. P., Ellard, K. K., Boisseau, C. L. Allen, L. B. & Ehrenreich-May, J. (2011-a). *Unified protocol for the transdiagnostic treatment of emotional disorders (Therapist Guide).* New York, NY: Oxford University Press.

Barlow, D. H., Gorman, J. M., Shear, K. M., & Woods, S. W. (2000). Cognitive-behavioral therapy, imipramine, or their combination for panic disorder: A randomized controlled trial. *JAMA: Journal of the American Medical Association, 283*(19), 2529–2536.

Barlow, D. H., Hayes, S. C., & Nelson, R. O. (1984). *The scientist practitioner: Research and accountability in clinical and educational settings.* Boston, MA: Allyn & Bacon.

Barlow, D. H., & Lehman, C. L. (1996). Advances in the psychosocial treatment of anxiety disorders: Implications for national health care. *Archives of General Psychiatry, 53,* 727–735.

Barlow, D. H., Levitt, J. T., & Bufka, L. F. (1999). The dissemination of empirically supported treatments: A view to the future. *Behaviour Research and Therapy, 37*(Suppl. 1), S147–162.

Barlow, D. H., & Liebowitz, M. R. (1995). Specific and social phobias. In H. I. Kaplan & B. J. Sadock (Eds.), *Comprehensive textbook of psychiatry: VI* (pp. 1204–1217). Baltimore, MD: Williams & Wilkins.

Barlow, D. H., Moscovitch, D. A., & Micco, J. A. (2004). Psychotherapeutic interventions for phobias: A review. In M. Maj, H. S. Akiskal, J. L. Lopez-Ibor, & A. Okasha (Eds.), *Phobias.* (pp. 179–210). Hoboken, NJ: John Wiley & Sons.

Barlow, D. H., Nock, M. K., & Hersen, M. (2009). *Single case experimental designs: Strategies for studying behavior change* (3rd ed.). New York, NY: Allyn & Bacon.

Barlow, D. H., Pincus, D. B., Heinrichs, N., & Choate, M. (2003). Anxiety disorders: A lifespan developmental perspective. In I. Weiner (Ed.), *Comprehensive Handbook of Psychology* (Vol. 8, pp. 119–147) New York, NY: John Wiley.

Barlow, D. H., Rapee, R. M., & Reisner, L. C. (2001). *Mastering stress 2001: A lifestyle approach.* Dallas, TX: American Health.

Barlow, D. H., & Wincze, J. P. (1980). Treatment of sexual deviations. In S. R. Leiblum & L. A. Pervin (Eds.), *Principles and practice of sex therapy* (pp. 347–375). New York, NY: Guilford Press.

Barnard, A. (2000, September 12). When plastic surgeons should just say "no." *Boston Globe,* pp. E1, E3.

Barnes, G. M., Hoffman, J. H., Welte, J. W., Farrell, M. P., & Dintcheff, B. A. (2006). Effects of parental monitoring and peer deviance on substance use and delinquency. *Journal of Marriage and the Family, 68,* 1084–1104.

Barnes, J., Bowman, E. P., & Cullen, J. (1984). Biofeedback as an adjunct to psychotherapy in the treatment of vaginismus. *Biofeedback and Self-Regulation, 9,* 281–289.

Barrera, Á., McKenna, P., & Berrios, G. (2009). Formal thought disorder, neuropsychology, and insight in schizophrenia. *Psychopathology, 42*(4), 264–269.

Barrett, L. F. (2009). Variety is the spice of life: A psychological construction approach to understanding variability in emotion. *Cognition and Emotion, 23*(7), 1284–1306.

Barrett, R., Loa, P., Jerah, E., Nancarrow, D., Chant, D., & Mowry, B. (2005). Rates of treated schizophrenia and its clinical and cultural features in the population isolate of the Iban of Sarawak: A tri-diagnostic approach. *Psychological Medicine, 35,* 281–293.

Barsky, A. J., & Ahern, D. K. (2005). Cognitive behavior therapy for hypochondriasis: A randomized controlled trial. *JAMA: Journal of the American Medical Association, 291,* 1464–1470.

Barsky, A. J., Frank, C. B., Cleary, P. D., Wyshak, G., & Klerman, G. L. (1991). The relation between hypochondriasis and age. *American Journal of Psychiatry, 148,* 923–928.

Barsky, A. J., Orav, E., & Bates, D. (2005). Somatization increases medical utilization and costs independent of psychiatric and medical comorbidity. *Archives of General Psychiatry, 62,* 903–910.

Barsky, A. J., & Wyshak, G. (1990). Hypochondriasis and somatosensory amplification. *British Journal of Psychiatry, 157,* 404–409.

Barsky, A. J., Wyshak, G., & Klerman, G. L. (1986). Hypochondriasis: An evaluation of the DSM-III criteria in medical outpatients. *Archives of General Psychiatry, 43,* 493–500.

Bartlett, N., & Vasey, P. (2006). A retrospective study of childhood gender-atypical behavior in Samoan Fa'afafine. *Archives of Sexual Behavior, 35,* 695–666.

Bartlik, B., & Goldberg, J. (2000). Female sexual arousal disorder. In S. R. Leiblum & R. C. Rosen (Eds.), *Principles and practice of sex therapy* (3rd ed., pp. 85–117). New York, NY: Guilford Press.

Basson, R. (2007). Sexual desire/arousal disorders in women. In S. R. Leiblum (Ed.), *Principles and practice of sex therapy* (4th ed., pp. 25–53). New York, NY: Guilford Press.

Bateson, G. (1959). Cultural problems posed by a study of schizophrenic process. In A. Auerback (Ed.), *Schizophrenia: An integrated approach.* (pp. 125–148) New York, NY: Ronald Press.

Battaglia, M., Bertella, S., Bajo, S., Politi, E., & Bellodi, L. (1998). An investigation of the cooccurrence of panic and somatization disorders through temperamental variables. *Psychosomatic Medicine, 60*(6), 726–729.

Baxter, L. R., Jr., Schwartz, J. M., Bergman, K. S., Szuba, M. P., Guze, B. H., Mazziotta, J. C., et al. (1992). Caudate glucose metabolic rate changes with both drug and behavior therapy for obsessive-compulsive disorder. *Archives of General Psychiatry, 49,* 681–689.

Baylé, F. J., Caci, H., Millet, B., Richa, S., & Olié, J. P. (2003). Psychopathology and comorbidity of psychiatric disorders in patients with kleptomania. *American Journal of Psychiatry, 160,* 1509–1513.

Beach, S. R. H., Jones, D. J., & Franklin, K. J. (2009). Marital, family, and interpersonal therapies for depression in adults. In I. H. Gotlib & C. L. Hammen (Eds.), *Handbook of depression* (2nd ed., pp. 624–641). New York, NY: Guilford Press.

Beach, S. R. H., Sandeen, E. E., & O'Leary, K. D. (1990). Depression in marriage: A model for etiology and treatment. In D. H. Barlow (Ed.), *Treatment manuals for practitioners* (pp. 53–86). New York, NY: Guilford Press.

Beals, J., Manson, S., Whitesell, N., Mitchell, C., Novins, D., Simpson, S., & Spicer, P. (2005). Prevalence of major depressive episode in two American Indian reservation populations: Unexpected findings with a structured interview. *American Journal of Psychiatry, 162,* 1713–1722.

Bebbington, P., Cooper, C., Minot, S., Brugha, T., Jenkins, R., Meltzer, H., Dennis, M. (2009). Suicide attempts, gender, and sexual abuse: Data from the 2000 British Psychiatric Morbidity Survey. *American Journal of Psychiatry, 166*(10), 1135.

Bebbington, P. E., Brugha, T., MacCarthy, B., Potter, J., Sturt, E., Wykes, T., ... McGuffin, P. (1988). The Camberwell Collaborative Depression Study: I. Depressed probands: Adversity and the form of depression. *British Journal of Psychiatry, 152,* 754–765.

Bech, P. (2009). Clinical features of mood disorders and mania. In M. G. Gelder, N. C. Andreasen, J. J. López-Ibor, Jr., & J. R. Geddes (Eds.), *New Oxford textbook of psychiatry* (2nd ed., Vol. 1, pp. 632–637). Oxford, UK: Oxford University Press.

Beck, A. T. (1967). *Depression: Clinical, experimental, and theoretical aspects.* New York, NY: Harper & Row.

Beck, A. T. (1976). *Cognitive therapy and the emotional disorders.* New York, NY: International Universities Press.

Beck, A. T. (1986). Hopelessness as a predictor of eventual suicide. *Annals of the New York Academy of Science, 487,* 90–96.

Beck, A. T., Epstein, N., & Harrison, R. (1983). Cognitions, attitudes and personality dimensions in depression. *British Journal of Cognitive Psychotherapy, 1*(1), 1–16.

Beck, A. T., & Freeman, A. (1990). *Cognitive therapy of personality disorders.* New York, NY: Guilford Press.

Beck, A. T., Freeman, A., & Davis, D. D. (2007). *Cognitive therapy of personality disorders* (2nd ed.). New York, NY: Guilford Press.

Beck, A. T., Hollon, S. D., Young, J. E., Bedrosian, R. C., & Budenz, D. (1985). Treatment of depression with cognitive therapy and amitriptyline. *Archives of General Psychiatry, 42,* 142–148.

Beck, A. T., Steer, R., Kovacs, M., & Garrison, B. (1985). Hopelessness and eventual suicide: A 10-year prospective study of patients hospitalized with suicidal ideation. *American Journal of Psychiatry, 142,* 559–563.

Beck, A. T., & Young, J. E. (1985). Depression. In D. H. Barlow (Ed.), *Clinical handbook of psychological disorders* (pp. 206–244). New York, NY: Guilford Press.

Beck, J. G. (1993). Vaginismus. In W. O'Donohue & J. H. Geer (Eds.), *Handbook of sexual dysfunctions: Assessment and treatment* (pp. 381–397). Boston, MA: Allyn & Bacon.

Beck, J. G., & Averill, P. M. (2004). Older adults. In R. G. Heimberg, C. L. Turk, & D. S. Mennin (Eds.), *Generalized anxiety disorder: Advances in research and practice* (pp. 409–433). New York, NY: Guilford Press.

Beck, J. G., & Stanley, M. A. (1997). Anxiety disorders in the elderly: The emerging role of behavior therapy. *Behavior Therapy, 28,* 83–100.

Becker, A. E., Burwell, R. A., Cilman, S. E., Herzog, D. B., & Hamburg, P. (2002). Eating behaviours and attitudes following prolonged exposure to television among ethnic Fijian adolescent girls. *British Journal of Psychiatry, 180,* 509–514.

Becker, C. B., Smith, L. M., & Ciao, A. C. (2005). Reducing eating disorder risk factors in sorority members: A randomized trial. *Behavior Therapy, 36,* 245–253.

Becker, D. (1997). *Through the looking glass: women and borderline personality disorder.* Boulder, CO: Westview Press.

Becker, J. V. (1990). Treating adolescent sexual offenders. *Professional Psychology: Research and Practice, 21,* 362–365.

Beech, H. (2008, July 7). Where the 'Ladyboys' Are. *TIME,* Retrieved from *http://www.time.com/time/world/article/0,8599,1820633,00.html*

Beekman, A. T., Geerlings, S. W., Deeg, D. J., Smit, J. H., Schoevers, R. S., de Beurs, E., ... van Tilberg, W. (2002). The natural history of late-life depression: A 6-year prospective study in the community. *Archives of General Psychiatry, 59,* 605–611.

Beets, M. W., Flay, B. R., Vuchinich, S., Li, K. K., Acock, A., & Snyder, F. J. (2009). Longitudinal patterns of binge drinking among first year college students with a history of tobacco use. *Drug and Alcohol Dependence, 103*(1–2), 1–8.

Belger, A., & Dichter, G. (2006). Structural and functional neuroanatomy. In J. A. Lieberman, T. S. Stroup, & D. O. Perkins (Eds.), *The American Psychiatric Publishing textbook of schizophrenia* (pp. 167–185). Washington, DC: American Psychiatric Publishing.

Bell, I. R. (1994). Somatization disorder: Health care costs in the decade of the brain. *Biological Psychiatry, 35,* 81–83.

Bellak, L. (1975). *The thematic apperception test, the children's apperception test, and the senior apperception technique in clinical use* (3rd ed.). New York, NY: Grune & Stratton.

Ben Itzchak, E., Lahat, E., Burgin, R., & Zachor, A. D. (2008). Cognitive, behavior and intervention outcome in young children with autism. *Research in Developmental Disabilities, 29*(5), 447–458.

Benbadis, R. R., & Allen-Hauser, W. (2000). An estimate of the prevalence of psychogenic non-epileptic seizures. *Seizure, 9*(4), 280–281.

Bender, D. S. (2005). Therapeutic alliance. In J. M. Oldham, A. E. Skodol, & D. S. Bender (Eds.), *Textbook of personality disorders* (pp. 405– 420). Washington, DC: American Psychiatric Publishing.

Bender, E. (2004). Data show wide variation in addiction treatment costs. *Psychiatric News, 39,* 11.

Benedetti, A., Perugi, G., Toni, C., Simonetti, B., Mata, B., & Cassano, G. B. (1997). Hypochondriasis and illness phobia in panic-agoraphobic patients. *Comprehensive Psychiatry, 38,* 124–131.

Benedetti, F., Colombo, C., Serretti, A., Lorenzi, C., Pontiggia, A., Barbini, B., & Smeraldi, E. (2003). Antidepressant effects of light therapy combined with sleep deprivation are influenced by a functional polymorphism within the promoter of the serotonin transporter gene. *Biological Psychiatry, 54,* 687–692.

Benowitz, N. (2008). Neurobiology of nicotine addiction: Implications for smoking cessation treatment. *The American Journal of Medicine, 121*(4A), S3–S10.

Benson, H. (1975). *The relaxation response.* New York, NY: William Morrow.

Benson, H. (1984). *Beyond the relaxation response.* New York, NY: Times Books.

Ben-Zeev, D., Ellington, K., Swendson, J., & Granholm, E. (2010). Examining a cognitive model of persecutory ideation in the daily life of people with schizophrenia: A computerized experience sampling study. *Schizophrenia Bulletin.*

Berenbaum, H., & Oltmanns, T. F. (1992). Emotional experience and expression in schizophrenia and depression. *Journal of Abnormal Psychology, 101,* 37–44.

Berenbaum, H., Thompson, R. J., Milanak, M. E., Boden, M. T., & Bredemeier, K. (2008). Psychological trauma and schizotypal personality disorder. *Journal of Abnormal Psychology, 117*(3), 502–519.

Berghöfer, A., Pischon, T., Reinhold, T., Apovian, C. M., Sharma, A. M., & Willich, S. N. (2008). Obesity prevalence from a European perspective: A systematic review. *BMC Public Health, 8,* 200.

Bergman, R. L., & Lee, J. C. (2009). Selective mutism. In B. J. Sadock, V. A. Sadock, & P. Ruiz (Eds.), *Kaplan & Sadock's comprehensive textbook of psychiatry* (9th ed., Vol. II, pp. 3694–3698). Philadelphia, PA: Lippincott Williams & Wilkins.

Berkman, L. F., & Syme, S. L. (1979). Social networks, host resistance, and mortality: A nine-year follow-up study of Alameda county residents. *American Journal of Epidemiology, 109,* 186.

Berkowitz, R. I., Wadden, T. A., Tershakovec, A. M., & Cronquist, J. L. (2003). Behavior therapy and Sibutramine for the treatment of adolescent obesity: A randomized controlled trial. *JAMA: Journal of the American Medical Association, 289,* 1805–1812.

Berlin, I. N. (1987). Suicide among American Indian adolescents: An overview. *Suicide and Life Threatening Behavior, 17*(3), 218–232.

Berman, A. L. (2009). Depression and suicide. In I. H. Gotlib & C. L. Hammen (Eds.), *Handbook of depression* (2nd ed., pp. 510–530). New York, NY: Guilford Press.

Berman, J. R., Berman, L. A., Toler, S. M., Gill, J., Haughie, S., for the Sildenafil Study Group. (2003). Safety and efficacy of sildenafil citrate for the treatment of female sexual arousal disorder: A double-blind, placebo controlled study. *The Journal of Urology, 170,* 2333–2338.

Berman, A. L., & Jobes, D. A. (1991). *Adolescent suicide: Assessment and intervention.* Washington, DC: American Psychological Association.

Berman, K. F., & Weinberger, D. R. (1990). Lateralization of cortical function during cognitive tasks: Regional cerebral blood flow studies of normal individuals and patients with schizophrenia. *Journal of Neurology, Neurosurgery and Psychiatry, 53,* 150–160.

Bernat, J. A., Calhoun, K. S., & Adams, H. E. (1999). Sexually aggressive and nonaggressive men: Sexual arousal and judgments in response to acquaintance rape and consensual analogues. *Journal of Abnormal Psychology, 108,* 662–673.

Bernstein, D. M., & Loftus, E. F. (2009). How to tell if a particular memory is true or false. *Perspectives on Psychological Science, 4*(4), 370–374.

Bernstein, D. P., & Useda, J. (2007). Paranoid personality disorder. In W. O'Donohue, K. Fowler, & S. Lilienfeld (Eds.), *Personality disorders: Toward the DSM-V* (pp. 41–62). Thousand Oaks, CA: Sage.

Bertelsen, M., Jeppesen, P., Petersen, L., Thorup, A., Ohlenschlaeger, J., le Quach, P., et al. (2008). Five-year follow-up of a randomized multicenter trial of intensive early intervention vs standard treatment for patients with a first episode of psychotic illness: the OPUS trial. *Archives of General Psychiatry, 65*(7), 762–771.

Bettelheim, B. (1967). *The empty fortress.* New York, NY: Free Press.

Bettens, K., Sleegers, K., & Van Broeckhoven, C. (2010). Current status on Alzheimer disease molecular genetics: From past, to present, to future. *Human Molecular Genetics, 19*(R1), R4–11.

Bhagwanjee, A., Parekh, A., Paruk, Z., Petersen, I., & Subedar, H. (1998). Prevalence of minor psychiatric disorders in an adult African rural community in South Africa. *Psychological Medicine, 28,* 1137–1147.

Bharucha, A., Anand, V., Forlizzi, J., Dew, M., Reynolds, C., III, Stevens, S., Wactlar, H. (2009). Intelligent assistive technology applications to dementia care: Current capabilities, limitations, and future challenges. *The American Journal of Geriatric Psychiatry: Official Journal of the American Association for Geriatric Psychiatry, 17*(2), 88.

Bhasin, T., & Schendel, D. (2007). Sociodemographic risk factors for autism in a U.S. metropolitan area. *Journal of Autism and Developmental Disorders, 37,* 667–677.

Biederman, J., Faraone, S. V., Wozniak, J., Mick, E., Kwon, A., Cayton, G. A., & Clark, S. V. (2005). Clinical correlates of bipolar disorder in a large, referred sample of children and adolescents. *Journal of Psychiatric Research, 39*(6), 611–622.

Biederman, J., Mick, E., Faraone, S. V., & Burback, M. (2001). Patterns of remission and symptom decline in conduct disorder: A four-year prospective study of an ADHD sample. *Journal of the American Academy of Child and Adolescent Psychiatry, 40,* 290–298.

Biederman, J., Mick, E., Faraone, S. V., Spencer, T., Wilens, T. E., & Wozniak, J. (2000). Pediatric mania: A developmental subtype of bipolar disorder? *Biological Psychiatry, 48*(6), 458–466.

Biederman, J., Rosenbaum, J. F., Hirschfeld, D. R., Faraone, S. V., Bolduc, E. A., Gersten, M., ... Reznick, J. S. (1990). Psychiatric correlates of behavioral inhibition in young children of parents with and without psychiatric disorders. *Archives of General Psychiatry, 47,* 21–26.

Biederman, J., Spencer, T., Wilens, T., & Greene, R. (2001). Attention-deficit/hyperactivity disorder. In G. O. Gabbard (Ed.), *Treatment of psychiatric disorders* (3rd ed., Vol. 1, pp. 145–176). Washington, DC: American Psychiatric Publishing.

Bierut, L. J., Heath, A. C., Bucholz, K. K., Dinwiddie, S. H., Madden, P. A., Statham, D. J., ... Martin, N. G. (1999). Major depressive disorder in a community-based twin sample: Are there different genetic and environmental contributions for men and women? *Archives of General Psychiatry, 56*(6), 557–563.

Billy, J. O. G., Tanfer, K., Grady, W. R., & Klepinger, D. H. (1993). The sexual behavior of men in the United States. *Family Planning Perspectives, 25,* 52–60.

Binder, E. B., Bradley, R. G., Liu, W., Epstein, M. P., Deveau, T. C., Mercer, K. B., ... Ressler, K. J. (2008). Association of FKBP5 polymorphisms and childhood abuse with risk of posttraumatic stress disorder symptoms in adults. *JAMA: Journal of the American Medical Association, 299*(11), 1291–1305.

Binik, Y. (2005). Should dyspareunia be retained as a sexual dysfunction in DSM-V? A painful classification decision. *Archives of Sexual Behavior, 34,* 11–21.

Binik, Y. M. (2010). The DSM diagnostic criteria for dyspareunia. *Archives of Sexual Behavior, 39,* 292–303.

Binik, Y. M., Bergeron, S., & Khalifé, S. (2000). Dyspareunia. In S. R. Leiblum & R. C. Rosen (Eds.), *Principles and practice of sex therapy* (3rd ed., pp. 154–180). New York, NY: Guilford Press.

Binik, Y. M., Bergeron, S., & Kalifé, S. (2007). Dyspareunia and vaginismus: So-called sexual pain. In S. R. Leiblum (Ed.), *Principles and practice of sex therapy* (4th ed., pp. 124–156). New York, NY: Guilford Press.

Binzer, M., Andersen, P. M., & Kullgren, G. (1997). Clinical characteristics of patients with motor disability due to conversion disorder: A prospective control group study. *Journal of Neurology, Neurosurgery, and Psychiatry, 63*(1), 83–88.

Birley, J., & Brown, G. W. (1970). Crisis and life changes preceding the onset or relapse of acute schizophrenia: Clinical aspects. *British Journal of Psychiatry, 16,* 327–333.

Birmaher, B., Axelson, D., Goldstein, B., Strober, M., Gill, M. K., Hunt, J., ... Keller, M. (2009). Four-year longitudinal course of children and adolescents with bipolar spectrum disorders: The Course and Outcome of Bipolar Youth (COBY) study. *American Journal of Psychiatry, 166*(7), 795–804.

Birmaher, B., Axelson, D., Strober, M., Gill, M. K., Valeri, S., Chiappetta, L., ... Keller, M. (2006). Clinical course of children and adolescents with bipolar spectrum disorders. *Archives of General Psychiatry, 63*(2), 175–183.

Biron, M., Risch, N., Hamburger, R., Mandel, B., Kushner, S., Newman, M., ... Belmaker, R. H (1987). Genetic linkage between X-chromosome markers and bipolar affective illness. *Nature, 326,* 289–292.

Bisson, M. A., & Levine, T. R. (2009). Negotiating the friends with benefits relationship. *Archives of Sexual Behavior, 38,* 66–73.

Bjorntorp, P. (1997). Obesity. *Lancet, 350,* 423–426.

Bjorvatn, B., & Pallesen, S. (2009). A practical approach to circadian rhythm sleep disorders. *Sleep Medicine Reviews, 13*(1), 47–60. doi:10.1016/j. smrv.2008.04.009

Blackburn, I. M., & Moore, R. G. (1997). Controlled acute and follow-up trial of cognitive therapy and pharmacotherapy in outpatients with recurrent depression. *British Journal of Psychiatry, 171,* 328–334.

Blacker, D. (2005). Psychiatric rating scales. In B. J. Sadock & V. A. Sadock (Eds.), *Kaplan & Sadock's comprehensive textbook of psychiatry* (pp. 929–955). Philadelphia, PA: Lippincott Williams & Wilkins.

Blagys, M. D., & Hilsenroth, M. J. (2000). Distinctive features of short-term psychodynamic–interpersonal psychotherapy: A review of the comparative psychotherapy process literature. *Clinical Psychology: Science and Practice, 7,* 167–188.

Blair, K., Shaywitz, J., Smith, B. W., Rhodes, R., Geraci, M., Jones, M., ... Pine, D. S. (2008). Response to emotional expressions in generalized social phobia and generalized anxiety disorder: Evidence for separate disorders. *American Journal of Psychiatry, 165*(9), 1193–1202.

Blakemore, S. J., Oakley, D. A., & Frith, C. D. (2003). Delusions of alien control in the normal brain. *Neuropsychologia, 41*(8), 1058–1067.

Blanchard, E. B. (1987). Long-term effects of behavioral treatment of chronic headache. *Behavior Therapy, 18*, 375–385.

Blanchard, E. B. (1992). Psychological treatment of benign headache disorders. Special issue: Behavioral medicine: An update for the 1990s. *Journal of Consulting and Clinical Psychology, 60*(4), 537–551.

Blanchard, E. B., & Andrasik, F. (1982). Psychological assessment and treatment of headache: Recent developments and emerging issues. *Journal of Consulting and Clinical Psychology, 50*(6), 859–879.

Blanchard, E. B., Andrasik, F., Ahles, T. A., Teders, S. J., & O'Keefe, D. (1980). Migraine and tension headache: A meta-analytic review. *Behavior Therapy, 11*, 613–631.

Blanchard, E. B., & Epstein, L. H. (1977). *A biofeedback primer.* Reading, MA: Addison-Wesley.

Blanchard, R. (2008). Sex ration of older siblings in heterosexual and homosexual, right-handed and non-right-handed men. *Archives of Sexual Behavior, 37*, 977–981.

Blanchard, R. (2010). The DSM diagnostic criteria for pedophilia. *Archives of Sexual Behavior, 39*, 304–314.

Blanchard, R., & Bogaert, A. (1996). Homosexuality in men and number of older brothers. *American Journal of Psychiatry, 153*, 27–31.

Blanchard, R., & Bogaert, A. (1998). Birth order in homosexual versus heterosexual sex offenders against children, pubescents, and adults. *Archives of Sexual Behavior, 27*(6), 595–603.

Blanchard, R., & Steiner, B. W. (1992). *Clinical management of gender identity disorders in children and adults.* Washington, DC: American Psychiatric Press.

Blanco, C., Heimberg, R. G., Schneier, F. R., Fresco, D. M., Chen, H., Turk, C. L., ... Liebowitz, M. R. (2010). A placebo-controlled trial of phenelzine, cognitive behavioral group therapy, and their combination for social anxiety disorder. *Archives of General Psychiatry, 67*(3), 286–295.

Bland, R. C. (1997). Epidemiology of affective disorders: A review. *Canadian Journal of Psychiatry, 42*, 367–377.

Blanes, T., Burgess, M., Marks, I., & Gill, M. (2009). Dream anxiety disorders (nightmares): A review. *Behavioural and Cognitive Psychotherapy, 21*(01), 37–43.

Blascovich, J., & Tomaka, J. (1996). The biopsychosocial model of arousal regulation. *Advances in Experimental Social Psychology, 28*, 1–51.

Blashfield, R. K., & Livesley, W. J. (1991). Metaphorical analysis of psychiatric classification as a psychological test. *Journal of Abnormal Psychology, 100*(3), 262–270.

Blazer, D. G., George, L., & Hughes, D. (1991). The epidemiology of anxiety disorders: An age comparison. In C. Salzman & B. Liebowitz (Eds.), *Anxiety disorders in the elderly* (pp. 17–30). New York, NY: Springer.

Blazer, D. G., & Hybels, C. F. (2009). Depression in later life: Epidemiology, assess-

ment, impact, and treatment. In I. H. Gotlib & C. L. Hammen (Eds.), *Handbook of depression* (2nd ed., pp. 492–509). New York, NY: Guilford Press.

Bleiberg, K. L., & Markowitz, J. C. (2008). Interpersonal psychotherapy for major depressive disorder. In D. H. Barlow (Ed.), *Clinical handbook of psychological disorders* (4th ed.). New York, NY: Guilford Press.

Bleuler, E. (1908). Die prognose der dementia praecox (schizophreniegruppe). *Allgemeine Zeitschrift für Psychiatrie, 65*, 436–464.

Bleuler, E. (1911). *Dementia praecox or the group of schizophrenias* (J. Zinkin, Trans.). New York, NY: International Universities Press.

Bleuler, E. (1924). *Textbook of psychiatry* (A. A. Brill, Trans.). New York, NY: Macmillan.

Bliss, E. L. (1984). A symptom profile of patients with multiple personalities including MMPI results. *Journal of Nervous and Mental Diseases, 172*, 197–211.

Bliss, E. L. (1986). *Multiple personality allied disorders and hypnosis.* New York, NY: Oxford University Press.

Bloch, M. H., Landeros-Weisenberger, A., Rosario, M. C., Pittenger, C., & Leckman, J. F. (2008). Meta-analysis of the symptom structure of obsessive-compulsive disorder. *American Journal of Psychiatry, 165*(12), 1532–1542.

Block, J. J. (2008). Issues for DSM-V: Internet addiction. *American Journal of Psychiatry, 165*(3), 306–307. doi:10.1176/appi.ajp.2007.07101556

Bloom, F. E., & Kupfer, D. J. (1995). *Psychopharmacology: The fourth generation of progress.* New York, NY: Raven Press.

Bloom, F. E., Nelson, C. A., & Lazerson, A. (2001). *Brain, mind, & behavior* (3rd ed.). New York, NY: Worth Publishers.

Blumenthal, J. A., Sherwood, A., Babyak, M., Watkins, L., Waugh, R., Georgiades, A., ... Hinderliter, A. (2005). Effects of exercise and stress management training on markers of cardiovascular risk in patients with ischemic heart disease. *JAMA: Journal of the American Medical Association, 293*, 1626–1634.

Blumenthal, S. J. (1990). An overview and synopsis of risk factors, assessment, and treatment of suicidal patients over the life cycle. In S. J. Blumenthal & D. J. Kupfer (Eds.), *Suicide over the life cycle: Risk factors, assessment and treatment of suicidal patients* (pp. 685–734). Washington, DC: American Psychiatric Press.

Blumenthal, S. J., & Kupfer, D. J. (1988). Clinical assessment and treatment of youth suicide. *Journal of Youth and Adolescence, 17*, 1–24.

Blundell, J. E. (2002). The psychobiological approach to appetite and weight control. In K. D. Brownell & C. G. Fairburn (Eds.), *Eating disorders and obesity: A comprehensive handbook* (2nd ed., pp. 13–20). New York, NY: Guilford Press.

Bockoven, J. S. (1963). *Moral treatment in American psychiatry.* New York, NY: Springer.

Bodlund, O., & Kullgren, G. (1996). Transsexualism—General outcome and prognostic factors: A five-year follow-up study of nineteen transsexuals in the process of changing sex. *Archives of Sexual Behavior, 25*, 303–316.

Bogart, A. F. (2010). Physical development and sexual orientation in men and

women: An analysis of NATSL-2000. *Archives of Sexual Behavior, 39*, 110–116.

Bögels, S. M., Alden, L., Beidel, D. C., Clark, L. A., Pine, D. S., Stein, M. B., ...Voncken, M. (2010). Social anxiety disorder: Questions and answers for the DSM-V. *Depression and Anxiety, 27*(2), 168–189.

Bohman, M., Cloninger, C. R., von Knorring, A. L., & Sigvardsson, S. (1984). An adoption study of somatoform disorders: III. Cross-fostering analysis and genetic relationship to alcoholism and criminality. *Archives of General Psychiatry, 41*, 872–878.

Boland, R. J., & Keller, M. B. (2009). Course and outcome of depression. In I. H. Gotlib & C. L. Hammen (Eds.), *Handbook of depression* (2nd ed., pp. 23–43). New York, NY: Guilford Press.

Bonanno, G. (2006). Is complicated grief a valid construct? *Clinical Psychology Science Practice, 13*, 129–134.

Bonanno, G., & Kaltman, S. (1999). Toward an integrative perspective on bereavement. *Psychological Bulletin, 125*(6), 1004–1008.

Bonanno, G., Wortman, C., & Nesse, R. (2004). Prospective patterns of resilience and maladjustment during widowhood. *Psychology and Aging, 19*, 260–271.

Bond, A., & Lader, M. L. (1979). Benzodiazepines and aggression. In M. Sandler (Ed.), *Psychopharmacology of aggression.* New York, NY: Raven Press.

Bongaarts, J., & Over, M. (2010). Global HIV/AIDS policy in transition. *Science, 328*, 1359–1360.

Booij, L., & Van der Does, A. J. (2007). Cognitive and serotonergic vulnerability to depression: Convergent findings. *Journal of Abnormal Psychology, 116*(1), 86–94.

Boon, S., & Draijer, N. (1991). Diagnosing dissociative disorders in the Netherlands: A pilot study with the Structured Clinical Interview for DSM-III-R dissociative disorders. *American Journal of Psychiatry, 148*, 458–462.

Borckardt, J. J., Nash, M. R., Murphy, M. D., Shaw, D., O'Neil, P., & Moore, M. (2008). Clinical practice as natural laboratory for psychotherapy research: A guide to case-based time-series analysis. *American Psychologist, 63*(2), 77–95.

Borge, F. M., Hoffart, A., Sexton, H., Martinsen, E., Gude, T., Hedley, L. M., ... Abrahamsen, G. (2010). Pre-treatment predictors and in-treatment factors associated with change in avoidant and dependent personality disorder traits among patients with social phobia. *Clinical Psychology & Psychotherapy, 17*(2), 87–99.

Borkovec, T. D., Alcaine, O. M., & Behar, E. (2004). Avoidance theory of worry and generalized anxiety disorder. In R. G. Heimberg, C. L. Turk, & D. S. Mennin (Eds.), *Generalized anxiety disorder: Advances in research and practice* (pp. 77–108). New York, NY: Guilford Press.

Borkovec, T. D., & Hu, S. (1990). The effect of worry on cardiovascular response to phobic imagery. *Behaviour Research and Therapy, 28*, 69–73.

Borkovec, T. D., Newman, M. G., Pincus, A. L., & Lytle, R. (2002). A component analysis of cognitive-behavioral therapy for generalized anxiety disorder and the role of interpersonal problems. *Journal of Consulting and Clinical Psychology, 70*, 288–298.

Borkovec, T. D., Shadick, R., & Hopkins, M. (1991). The nature of normal and pathological worry. In R. M. Rapee & D. H. Barlow (Eds.), *Chronic anxiety, generalized anxiety disorder, and mixed anxiety depression.* New York, NY: Guilford Press.

Bornstein, R. F. (1992). The dependent personality: Developmental, social, and clinical perspectives. *Psychological Bulletin, 112,* 3–23.

Borodinsky, L. N., Root, C. M., Cronin, J. A., Sann, S. B., Gu, X., & Spitzer, N. C. (2004). Activity-dependent homeostatic specification of transmitter expression in embryonic neurons. *Nature, 429,* 523–530.

Boskind-Lodahl, M. (1976). Cinderella's stepsisters: A feminist perspective on anorexia nervosa and bulimia. *Signs, 2,* 342–356.

Bothe, A. K., Davidow, J. H., Bramlett, R. E., & Ingham, R. J. (2006). Stuttering treatment research 1970–2005: I. Systematic review incorporating trial quality assessment of behavioral, cognitive, and related approaches. *American Journal of Speech-Language Pathology, 15*(4), 321–341.

Bouchard, C. (2002). Genetic influences on body weight and shape. In K. D. Brownell & C. G. Fairburn (Eds.), *Eating disorders and obesity: A comprehensive handbook* (2nd ed., pp. 21–26). New York, NY: Guilford Press.

Bouchard, M. F., Bellinger, D. C., Wright, R. O., & Weisskopf, M. G. (2010). Attention-deficit/hyperactivity disorder and urinary metabolites of organophosphate pesticides. *Pediatrics, 125*(6), e1270–e1277.

Bouchard, T. J., Jr., Lykken, D. T., McGue, M., Segal, N. L., & Tellegen, A. (1990). Sources of human psychological differences: The Minnesota study of twins reared apart. *Science, 250,* 223–228.

Bourgeois, J. A., Seaman, J. S., & Servis, M. E. (2003). Delirium, dementia, and amnestic disorders. In R. E. Hales & S. C. Yudofsky (Eds.), *Textbook of clinical psychiatry* (4th ed., pp. 259– 308). Washington, DC: American Psychiatric Publishing.

Bourgeois, J. A., Seaman, J. S., & Servis, M. E. (2008). Delirium, dementia, and amnestic and other cognitive disorders. In R. E. Hales, S. C. Yudofsky, & G. O. Gabbard (Eds.), *The American Psychiatric Publishing textbook of psychiatry* (5th ed., pp. 303–364). Arlington, VA: American Psychiatric Publishing, Inc.

Bourgeois, M. S. (1992). Evaluating memory wallets in conversations with persons with dementia. *Journal of Speech and Hearing Research, 35,* 1344–1357.

Bourgeois, M. S. (2007). *Memory books and other graphic cuing systems: Practical communication and memory aids for adults with dementia.* Baltimore, MD: Health Professions Press.

Bouton, M. E. (2005). Behavior systems and the contextual control of anxiety, fear, and panic. In L. Feldman Barrett, P. Niedenthal, & P. Winkielman (Eds.), *Emotion: Conscious and unconscious* (pp. 205–227). New York, NY: Guilford Press.

Bouton, M. E., Mineka, S., & Barlow, D. H. (2001). A modern learning-theory perspective on the etiology of panic disorder. *Psychological Review, 108,* 4–32.

Bower, G. H. (1981). Mood and memory. *American Psychologist, 36,* 129–148.

Bower, J. E., Moskowitz, J. T., & Epel, E. (2009). Is benefit finding good for your health? Pathways linking positive life changes after stress and physical health outcomes. *Current Directions in Psychological Science, 18,* 337–341.

Bowers, J. S., & Marsolek, C. J. (2003). *Rethinking implicit memory.* New York, NY: Oxford University Press.

Bowlby, J. (1977). The making and breaking of affectionate bonds. *British Journal of Psychiatry, 130,* 201–210.

Boyer, P., & Liénard, P. (2008). Ritual behavior in obsessive and normal individuals: Moderating anxiety and reorganizing the flow of action. *Current Directions in Psychological Science, 17*(4), 291–294.

Bradford, A., & Meston, C. M. (2011). Sex and gender disorders. In D. H. Barlow (Ed.), *Oxford handbook of clinical psychology* (pp. 446–468). New York, NY: Oxford University Press.

Bradford, J. (1997). Medical interventions in sexual deviance. In D. R. Laws & W. O'Donohue (Eds.), *Sexual deviance: Theory, assessment and treatment* (pp. 449–464). New York, NY: Guilford Press.

Bradley, B. P., Mogg, K., White, J., Groom, C., & de Bono, J. (1999). Attentional bias for emotional faces in generalized anxiety disorder. *British Journal of Clinical Psychology, 38,* 267–278.

Bradley, R., Danielson, L., & Hallahan, D. P. (Eds.). (2002). *Identification of learning disabilities: Research to practice.* Mahwah, NJ: Erlbaum.

Bradley, R. G., Binder, E. B., Epstein, M. P., Tang, Y., Nair, H. P., Liu, W.,...Ressler, K. J. (2008). Influence of child abuse on adult depression: Moderation by the corticotropin-releasing hormone receptor gene. *Archives of General Psychiatry, 65*(2), 190–200.

Brady, J. P., & Lind, D. L. (1961). Experimental analysis of hysterical blindness. *Archives of General Psychiatry, 4,* 331–339.

Braff, D., Schork, N. J., & Gottesman, I. I. (2007). Endophenotyping schizophrenia. *American Journal of Psychiatry, 164,* 705–707.

Braga, R., & Petrides, G. (2005). The combined use of electroconvulsive therapy and antipsychotics in patients with schizophrenia. *The Journal of ECT, 21*(2), 75.

Brand, B., Classen, C., Lanins, R., Loewenstein, R., McNary, S., Pain, C., & Putnam, F. (2009). A naturalistic study of dissociative identity disorder and dissociative disorder not otherwise specified patients treated by community clinicians. *Psychological Trauma: Theory, Research, Practice, and Policy, 1*(2), 153–171.

Brannigan, G. G., & Decker, S. L. (2006). The Bender-Gestalt II. *American Journal of Orthopsychiatry, 76*(1), 10–12.

Brannon, L., & Feist, J. (1997). *Health psychology: An introduction to behavior and health.* Pacific Grove, CA: Brooks/Cole.

Brawman-Mintzer, O. (2001). Pharmacologic treatment of generalized anxiety disorder. *Psychiatric Clinics of North America, 24,* 119–137.

Bremner, J. D. (1999). Does stress damage the brain? *Biological Psychiatry, 45,* 797–805.

Bremner, J. D., Licinio, J., Darnell, A., Krystal, A. H., Owens, M. J., Southwick, S. M., ... Charney, D. S. (1997). Elevated CSF corticotropin-releasing factor concentrations in posttraumatic stress disorder. *American Journal of Psychiatry, 154,* 624–629.

Bremner, J. D., Randall, P. R., Scott, T. M., Bronen, R. A., Seibyl, J. P., Southwick, S. M., ... & Innis, R. R. (1995). MRI-based measurement of hippocampal volume in patients with combat-related posttraumatic stress disorder. *American Journal of Psychiatry, 152,* 973–981.

Bremner, J. D., Vermetten, E., Southwick, S. M., Krystal, J. H., & Charney, D. S. (1998). Trauma, memory, and dissociation: An integrative formulation. In J. D. Bremner & C. Marmar (Eds.), *Trauma, memory, and dissociation.* Washington, DC: American Psychiatric Press.

Brener, N. D., Hassan, S. S., & Barrios, L. C. (1999). Suicidal ideation among college students in the United States. *Journal of Consulting & Clinical Psychology, 67,* 1004–1008.

Brenner, D. E., Kukull, W. A., van Belle, G., Bowen, J. D., McCormick, W. C., Teri, L., & Larson, E. B. (1993). Relationship between cigarette smoking and Alzheimer's disease in a population-based case-control study. *Neurology, 43,* 293–300.

Brent, D. & Birmaher, B. (2009). Paediatric mood disorders. In M. G. Gelder, N. C. Andreasen, J. J. López-Ibor, Jr., & J. R. Geddes (Eds.), *New Oxford textbook of psychiatry* (2nd ed., Vol. 2, pp. 1669–1680). Oxford, UK: Oxford University Press.

Brent, D., Emslie, G., Clarke, G., Wagner, K. D., Asarnow, J. R., Keller, M., ... Zelazny, J. (2008). Switching to another SSRI or to venlafaxine with or without cognitive behavioral therapy for adolescents with SSRI-resistant depression: The TORDIA randomized controlled trial. *JAMA: Journal of the American Medical Association, 299*(8), 901–913.

Brent, D., Melhem, N., Donohoe, M. B., & Walker, M. (2009). The incidence and course of depression in bereaved youth 21 months after the loss of a parent to suicide, accident, or sudden natural death. *American Journal of Psychiatry, 166*(7), 786–794.

Brent, D. A., & Kolko, D. J. (1990). The assessment and treatment of children and adolescents at risk for suicide. In S. J. Blumenthal & D. J. Kupfer (Eds.), *Suicide over the life cycle: Risk factors, assessment and treatment of suicidal patients.* Washington, DC: American Psychiatric Press.

Brent, D. A., Oquendo, M., Birmaher, B., Greenhill, L., Kolko, D., Stanley, B., ... Mann, J. J. (2002). Familial pathways to early-onset suicide attempt risk for suicidal behavior in offspring of mood-disordered suicide attempters. *Archives of General Psychiatry, 59,* 801–807.

Brent, D. A., Oquendo, M., Birmaher, B., Greenhill, L., Kolko, D., Stanley, B., ... Mann, J. J. (2003). Peripubertal suicide attempts in offspring of suicide attempters with siblings concordant for suicidal behavior. *American Journal of Psychiatry, 160,* 1486–1493.

Brent, D. A., Perper, J. A., Goldstein, C. E., Kolko, D. J., Allan, M. J., Allman, C. J., & Zellenak, J. P. (1988). Risk factors for adolescent suicide: A comparison of adolescent suicide victims with suicidal inpatients. *Archives of General Psychiatry, 45,* 581–588.

Brentjens, M. H., Yeung-Yue, K. A., Lee, P. C., & Tyring, S. K. (2003). Recurrent genital herpes treatments and their impact on quality of life. *Pharmacoeconomics, 21,* 853–863.

Breslau, N., Davis, G. C., & Andreski, M. A. (1995). Risk factors for PTSD-related traumatic events: A prospective analysis. *American Journal of Psychiatry, 152,* 529–535.

Breslau, N., Lucia, V. C., & Alvarado, G. F. (2006). Intelligence and other predisposing factors in exposure to trauma and posttraumatic stress disorder. *Archives of General Psychiatry, 63,* 1238–1245.

Breuer, J., & Freud, S. (1957). *Studies on hysteria.* New York, NY: Basic Books. (Original work published 1895).

Brewer, S., Gleditsch, S. L., Syblik, D., Tietjens, M. E., & Vacik H. W. (2006). Pediatric anxiety: Child life intervention in day surgery. *Journal of Pediatric Nursing, 21,* 13–22.

Brewin, C. R., Andrews, B., & Gotlib, I. H. (1993). Psychopathology in early experience: A reappraisal of retrospective reports. *Psychological Bulletin, 113,* 82–98.

Britton, J. C. & Rauch, S. L. (2009). Neuroanatomy and neuroimaging of anxiety disorders. In M. M. Antony & M. B. Stein (Eds.), *Oxford handbook of anxiety and related disorders* (pp. 97–110). Oxford, UK: Oxford University Press.

Brody, A. L., Saxena, S., Stoessel, P., Gillies, L. A., Fairbanks, L. A., Alborzian, S., ... Baxter, L. R., Jr. (2001). Regional brain metabolic changes in patients with major depression treated with either paroxetine or interpersonal therapy. *Archives of General Psychiatry, 48,* 631–640.

Brody, M. J., Walsh, B. T., & Devlin, M. J. (1994). Binge eating disorder: Reliability and validity of a new diagnostic category. *Journal of Consulting and Clinical Psychology, 62,* 381–386.

Broft, A., Berner, L. A., & Walsh, B. T. (2010). Pharmacotherapy for bulimia nervosa. In C. M. Grilo & J. E. Mitchell (Eds.), *The treatment of eating disorders: A clinical handbook.* (pp. 388–401). New York, NY: Guilford Press.

Brondolo, E., Rieppi, R., Erickson, S. A., Bagiella, E., Shapiro, P. A., McKinley, P., & Sloan, R. P. (2003). Hostility, interpersonal interactions, and ambulatory blood pressure. *Psychosomatic Medicine, 65,* 1003–1011.

Brotto, L. A. (2006). Psychologic-based desire and arousal disorders: Treatment strategies and outcome results. In I. Goldstein, C. M. Meston, S. R. Davis, & A. M. Traish (Eds.), *Women's sexual function and dysfunction: Study, diagnosis, and treatment* (pp. 441–448). New York, NY: Taylor and Francis.

Brotto, L. A. (2010a). The DSM diagnostic criteria for hypoactive sexual desire disorder in women. *Archives of Sexual Behavior, 39,* 222–239.

Brotto, L. A. (2010b). The DSM diagnostic criteria for sexual aversion disorder. *Archives of Sexual Behavior, 39,* 271–277.

Broude, G. J., & Greene, S. J. (1980). Cross-cultural codes on 20 sexual attitudes and practices. In H. Barry, III, & A. Schlegel (Eds.), *Cross-cultural samples and codes*

(pp. 313–333). Pittsburgh, PA: University of Pittsburgh Press.

Broughton, R., Billings, R., & Cartwright, R. (1994). Homicidal somnambulism: A case report. *Sleep, 17,* 253–264.

Broughton, R. J. (2000). NREM arousal parasomnias. In M. H. Kryger, T. Roth, & W. C. Dement (Eds.), *Principles and practice of sleep medicine* (3rd ed., pp. 693–706). Philadelphia, PA: W. B. Saunders.

Brown, D. R., Ahmed, F., Gary, L. E., & Milburn, N. G. (1995). Major depression in a community sample of African Americans. *American Journal of Psychiatry, 152,* 373–378.

Brown, G. K., Beck, A. T., Steer, R. A., & Grisham, J. R. (2000). Risk factor for psychiatric outpatients: A 20-year perspective study. *Journal of Consulting and Clinical Psychology, 63*(3), 371–377.

Brown, G. K., Have, T., Henriques, G., Xie, S., Hollander, J., & Beck, A. (2005). Cognitive therapy for the prevention of suicide attempts: A randomized controlled trial. *JAMA, 294,* 563–570.

Brown, G. W. (1959). Experiences of discharged chronic schizophrenic mental hospital patients in various types of living group. *Millbank Memorial Fund Quarterly, 37,* 105–131.

Brown, G. W. (1989a). Depression. In G. W. Brown & T. O. Harris (Eds.), *Life events and illness* (pp. 49–93). New York, NY: Guilford Press.

Brown, G. W. (1989b). Life events and measurement. In G. W. Brown & T. O. Harris (Eds.), *Life events and illness* (pp. 3–48). New York, NY: Guilford Press.

Brown, G. W., & Birley, J. L. T. (1968). Crisis and life change and the onset of schizophrenia. *Journal of Health and Social Behavior, 9,* 203–214.

Brown, G. W., & Harris, T. O. (1978). *Social origins of depression: A study of psychiatric disorder in women.* London, UK: Tavistock.

Brown, G. W., Harris, T. O., & Hepworth, C. (1994). Life events and endogenous depression. *Archives of General Psychiatry, 51,* 525–534.

Brown, G. W., Monck, E. M., Carstairs, G. M., & Wing, J. K. (1962). Influence of family life on the course of schizophrenic illness. *British Journal of Preventive and Social Medicine, 16,* 55–68.

Brown, J., & Finn, P. (1982). Drinking to get drunk: Findings of a survey of junior and senior high school students. *Journal of Alcohol and Drug Education, 27,* 13–25.

Brown, P. L. (2006, December 2). Supporting boys or girls when the line isn't clear. *New York Times.* Retrieved from http://www .nytimes.com/2006/12/02/us/02child.html

Brown, T. A., & Barlow, D. H. (2002). Classification of anxiety and mood disorders. In D. H. Barlow (Ed.), *Anxiety and its disorders: The nature and treatment of anxiety and panic.* (2nd ed., pp. 292–327). New York, NY: Guilford Press.

Brown, T. A., & Barlow, D. H. (2005). Dimensional versus categorical classification of mental disorders in the fifth edition of the diagnostic and statistical manual of mental disorders and beyond: Comment on the special section. Special issue: Toward a dimensionally based taxonomy of psychopathology. *Journal of Abnormal Psychology, 114*(4), 551–556.

Brown, T. A., & Barlow, D. H. (2009). A proposal for a dimensional classification system based on the shared features of the DSM-IV anxiety and mood disorders: Implications for assessment and treatment. *Psychological Assessment, 21*(3), 256–271.

Brown, T. A., Campbell, L. A., Lehman, C. L., Grisham, J. R., & Mancill, R. B. (2001). Current and lifetime comorbidity of the DSM-IV anxiety and mood disorders in a large clinical sample. *Journal of Abnormal Psychology.*

Brown, T. A., Chorpita, B. F., & Barlow, D. H. (1998). Structural relationships among dimensions of the DSM-IV anxiety and mood disorders and dimensions of negative affect, positive affect, and autonomic arousal. *Journal of Abnormal Psychology, 107*(2), 179–192.

Brown, T. A., Marten, P. A., & Barlow, D. H. (1995). Discriminant validity of the symptoms comprising the DSM-III-R and DSM-IV associated symptom criterion of generalized anxiety disorder. *Journal of Anxiety Disorders, 9,* 317–328.

Brown, T. E. (Ed.). (2009). *ADHD comorbidities: Handbook for ADHD complications in children and adults.* Arlington, VA: American Psychiatric Publishing.

Brown, W. M., Finn, C. J., Cooke, B. M., & Breedlove, S. M. (2002). Differences in finger length ratios between self-identified "butch" and "femme" lesbians. *Archives of Sexual Behavior, 31,* 123–127.

Brownell, K. D. (1991). Dieting and the search for the perfect body: Where physiology and culture collide. *Behavior Therapy, 22,* 1–12.

Brownell, K. D. (2002). Eating disorders in athletes. In K. D. Brownell & C. G. Fairburn (Eds.), *Eating disorders and obesity: A comprehensive handbook* (2nd ed., pp. 191–196). New York, NY: Guilford Press.

Brownell, K. D. (2003). *Food fight: The inside story of the food industry, America's obesity crisis and what we can do about it.* New York, NY: McGraw-Hill.

Brownell, K. D., & Fairburn, C. G. (Eds.) (1995). *Eating disorders and obesity: A comprehensive handbook.* New York, NY: Guilford Press.

Brownell, K. D., & Fairburn, C. G. (2002). *Eating disorders and obesity: A comprehensive handbook* (2nd ed.). New York, NY: Guilford Press.

Brownell, K. D., Hayes, S. C., & Barlow, D. H. (1977). Patterns of appropriate and deviant sexual arousal: The behavioral treatment of multiple sexual deviations. *Journal of Consulting and Clinical Psychology, 45*(6), 1144–1155.

Brownell, K. D., Kersh, R., Ludwig, D. S., Post, R. C., Puhl, R. M., Schwartz, M. B., & Willett, W. C. (2010). Personal responsibility and obesity: A constructive approach to a controversial issue. *Health Affairs, 29*(3), 379–387.

Brownell, K. D., & Rodin, J. (1994). The dieting maelstrom: Is it possible and advisable to lose weight? *American Psychologist, 49*(9), 781–791.

Brownmiller, S. (1984). *Femininity.* New York, NY: Ballantine Books.

Bruce, M. L. (2002). Psychosocial risk factors for depressive disorders in late life. *Biological Psychiatry, 52,* 175–184.

Bruce, M. L., & Kim, K. M. (1992). Differences in the effects of divorce on major depression in men and women. *American Journal of Psychiatry, 149*(7), 914–917.

Bruce, S. E., Vasile, R. G., Goisman, R. M., Salzman, C., Spencer, M., Machan, J. T., & Keller, M. B. (2003). Are benzodiazepines still the medication of choice for patients with panic disorder with or without agoraphobia? *American Journal of Psychiatry, 160*, 1432–1438.

Bruce, S. E., Yonkers, K. A., Otto, M. W., Eisen, J. L., Weisberg, R. B., Pagano, M., ... Keller, M. B. (2005). Influence of psychiatric comorbidity on recovery and recurrence in generalized anxiety disorder, social phobia, and panic disorder: A 12-year prospective study. *American Journal of Psychiatry, 162*, 1179–1187.

Bruch, H. (1973). *Eating disorders: Obesity, anorexia nervosa, and the person within.* New York, NY: Basic Books.

Bruch, H. (1985). Four decades of eating disorders. In D. M. Garner & P. E. Garfinkel (Eds.), *Handbook of psychotherapy for anorexia nervosa and bulimia* (pp. 7–18). New York, NY: Guilford Press.

Bruch, M. A., & Heimberg, R. G. (1994). Differences in perceptions of parental and personal characteristics between generalized and non-generalized social phobics. *Journal of Anxiety Disorders, 8*, 155–168.

Bruck, M., Ceci, S., Francouer, E., & Renick, A. (1995). Anatomically detailed dolls do not facilitate preschoolers' reports of a pediatric examination involving genital touching. *Journal of Experimental Psychology: Applied, 1*, 95–109.

Bryant, R. A., Moulds, M. L., & Nixon, R. V. D. (2003). Cognitive behavior therapy of acute stress disorder: A four-year follow-up. *Behaviour Research and Therapy, 41*, 489–494.

Buchanan, R. W., & Carpenter, W. T. (2005). Schizophrenia and other psychotic disorders. In B. J. Sadock & V. A. Sadock (Eds.), *Kaplan & Sadock's comprehensive textbook of psychiatry* (pp. 1329–1345). Philadelphia, PA: Lippincott Williams & Wilkins.

Buchwald, A. M., & Rudick-Davis, D. (1993). The symptoms of major depression. *Journal of Abnormal Psychology, 102*(2), 197–205.

Buffum, J. (1982). Pharmacosexology: The effects of drugs on sexual function—A review. *Journal of Psychoactive Drugs, 14*, 5–44.

Bulik, C. M., Sullivan, P. F., & Kendler, K. S. (2000). An empirical study of the classification of eating disorders. *American Journal of Psychiatry, 157*(6), 886–895.

Bulik, C. M., Sullivan, P. F., Tozzi, F., Furberg, H., Lichtenstin, P., & Pederson, N. L. (2006). Prevalence, heritability, and prospective risk factors, for anorexia nervosa. *Archives of General Psychiatry, 63*, 305–312.

Bumpass, E. R., Fagelman, F. D., & Brix, R. J. (1983). Intervention with children who set fires. *American Journal of Psychotherapy, 37*(3), 328–345.

Burleson, J. A., & Kaminer, Y. (2005). Self-efficacy as a predictor of treatment outcome in adolescent substance use disorders. *Addictive Behaviors, 30*, 1751–1764.

Burnette, M. M., Koehn, K. A., Kenyon-Jump, R., Hutton, K., & Stark, C. (1991). Control of genital herpes recurrences using progressive muscle relaxation. *Behavior Therapy, 22*, 237–247.

Burns, J. (2009). Dispelling a myth: Developing world poverty, inequality, violence, and social fragmentation are not good for outcome in schizophrenia. *African Journal of Psychiatry, 12*(3), 200–205.

Burns, J. W., Glenn, B., Bruehl, S., Harden, R. N., & Lofland, K. (2003). Cognitive factors influence outcome following multidisciplinary chronic pain treatment: A replication and extension of a cross-lagged panel analysis. *Behaviour Research and Therapy, 41*, 1163–1182.

Burton, R. (1977). *Anatomy of melancholy.* (Reprint edition). New York, NY: Random House. (Original work published 1621).

Buscher, A. L., & Giordano, T. P. (2010). Gaps in knowledge in caring for HIV survivors long-term. *JAMA: Journal of the American Medical Association, 304*, 340–341.

Bushman, B. J. (1993). Human aggression while under the influence of alcohol and other drugs: An integrative research review. *Psychological Science, 2*, 148–152.

Butcher, J. N. (2009). Clinical personality assessment: History, evolution, contemporary models, and practical applications. In J. N. Butcher (Ed.), *Oxford handbook of personality assessment* (pp. 5–21). New York: Oxford University Press.

Butcher, J. N., & Perry, J. N. (2008). *Personality assessment in treatment planning: Use of the MMPI-2 and BTPI.* New York: Oxford University Press.

Butler, B. (2006). NGRI revisited: Venirepersons' attitudes toward the insanity defense. *Journal of Applied Social Psychology, 36*, 1833–1847.

Butler, L. D., Duran, R. E. F., Jasiukaitis, P., Koopman, C., & Spiegel, D. (1996). Hypnotizability and traumatic experience: A diathesis stress model of dissociative symptomatology. *American Journal of Psychiatry, 153*, 42–63.

Buysse, D. J., Reynolds, C. F., & Kupfer, D. J. (1993). Classification of sleep disorders: A preview of the DSM-IV. In D. L. Dunner (Ed.), *Current psychiatric therapy* (pp. 360–361). Philadelphia, PA: W. B. Saunders.

Buysse, D. J., Strollo, P. J., Black, J. E., Zee, P. G., & Winkelman, J. W. (2008). Sleep disorders. In R. E. Hales, S. C. Yudofsky, & G. O. Gabbard (Eds.), *The American Psychiatric Publishing Textbook of Psychiatry* (5th ed., pp. 921–969). Arlington, VA: American Psychiatric Publishing.

Bye, E. K. (2007). Alcohol and violence: Use of possible confounders in a time-series analysis. *Addiction, 102*, 369–376.

Byers, A. L., Yaffe, K., Covinsky, K. E., Friedman, M. B., & Bruce, M. L. (2010). High occurrence of mood and anxiety disorders among older adults: The National Comorbidity Survey Replication. *Archives of General Psychiatry, 67*(5), 489–496.

Byne, W., Lasco, M. S., Kemether, E., Edgar, M. A., Morgello, S., Jones, L. B., & Tobet, S. (2000). The interstitial nuclei of the human anterior hypothalamus: An investigation of sexual variation in volume and cell size, number and density. *Brain Research, 856*, 254–258.

Byne, W., & Parsons, B. (1993). Human sexual orientation: The biologic theories reappraised. *Archives of General Psychiatry, 50*, 228–239.

Byrne, D., & Schulte, L. (1990). Personality dispositions as mediators of sexual responses. *Annual Review of Sex Research, 1*, 93–117.

Byrne, M., Agerbo, E., Bennedsen, B., Eaton, W. W., & Mortensen, P. B. (2007). Obstetric conditions and risk of first admission with schizophrenia: A Danish national register based study. *Schizophrenia Research, 97*(1–3), 51–59. doi:10.1016/j.schres.2007.07.018

Byrne, Z., & Hochwarter, W. (2006). I get by with a little help from my friends: The interaction of chronic pain and organizational support and performance. *Journal of Occupational Health Psychology, 11*, 215–227.

Caballero, B. (2007). The global epidemic of obesity: An overview. *Epidemiologic Reviews, 29*, 1–5.

Cacioppo, J. T., Amaral, D. G., Blanchard, J. J., Cameron, J. L., Carter, C. S., Crews, D., ... Quinn, K. J. (2007). Social neuroscience: Progress and implications for mental health. *Perspectives on Psychological Science, 2*(2), 99–123.

Cadoret, R. J. (1978). Psychopathology in the adopted-away offspring of biologic parents with antisocial behavior. *Archives of General Psychiatry, 35*, 176–184.

Cadoret, R. J., Yates, W. R., Troughton, E., Woodworth, G., & Stewart, M. A. (1995). Genetic–environment interaction in the genesis of aggressivity and conduct disorders. *Archives of General Psychiatry, 52*, 916–924.

Cafri, G., Yamamiya, Y., Brannick, M., & Thompson, J. K. (2005). The influence of sociocultural factors on body image: A meta-analysis. *Clinical Psychology: Science and Practice, 12*, 421–433.

Cain, A. S., Epler, A. J., Steinley, D., & Sher, K. J. (2010). Stability and change in patterns of concerns related to eating, weight, and shape in young adult women: A latent transition analysis. *Journal of Abnormal Psychology, 119*(2), 255–267.

Calabrese, J., Shelton, M, Rapport, D., Youngstrom, E., Jackson, K., Bilali, S., ... Findling, R. L. (2005). A 20-month, double-blind, maintenance trial of lithium versus divalproex, in rapid-cycling bipolar disorder. *American Journal of Psychiatry, 162*, 2152–2161.

Calamari, J. E., Wiegartz, P. S., Riemann, B. C., Cohen, R. J., Greer, A., Jacobi, D. M., ... Carmin, C. (2004). Obsessive-compulsive disorder subtypes: An attempted replication and extension of symptom-based taxonomy. *Behavior Research and Therapy, 42*, 647–670.

Callahan, L. A., McGreevy, M. A., Cirincione, C., & Steadman, H. (1992). Measuring the effects of the guilty but mentally ill (GBMI) verdict: Georgia's 1982 GBMI reform. *Law and Human Behavior, 16*, 447–462.

Callicott, J. H., Mattay, V. S., Verchinski, B. A., Marenco, S., Egan, M. F., & Weinberger, D. R. (2003). Complexity of prefrontal cortical dysfunction in schizophrenia: More than up or down. *American Journal of Psychiatry, 160*, 2209–2215.

Cameron, N. M., Champagne, F. A., Parent, C., Fish, E. W., Ozaki-Kuroda, K., & Meaney, M. J. (2005). The programming of individual differences in defensive responses and reproductive strategies in the rat through variations in maternal care. *Neuroscience and Biobehavioral Reviews, 29,* 843–865.

Campbell, J. M., & Oei, T. P. (2010). A cognitive model for the intergenerational transference of alcohol use behavior. *Addictive Behaviors, 35*(2), 73–83. doi:10.1016/j.addbeh.2009.09.013

Campbell-Sills, L., & Barlow, D. H. (2007). Incorporating emotion regulation into conceptualization and treatment of anxiety and mood disorders. In J. J. Gross (Ed.), *Handbook of emotion regulation* (pp. 542–560). New York, NY: Guilford Press.

Cannon, T. D., Barr, C. E., & Mednick, S. A. (1991). Genetic and perinatal factors in the etiology of schizophrenia. In E. F. Walker (Ed.), *Schizophrenia: A life-course developmental perspective* (pp. 9–31). New York, NY: Academic Press.

Cannon, T. D., Cadenhead, K., Cornblatt, B., Woods, S. W., Addington, J., Walker, E., et al. (2008). Prediction of psychosis in youth at high clinical risk: A multisite longitudinal study in North America. *Archives of General Psychiatry, 65*(1), 28–37.

Cannon, W. B. (1929). *Bodily changes in pain, hunger, fear, and rage* (2nd ed.). New York, NY: Appleton-Century-Crofts.

Cannon, W. B. (1942). Voodoo death. *American Anthropologist, 44,* 169–181.

Cantor, J. M., Blanchard, R., Paterson, A. D., & Bogaert, A. F. (2002). How many gay men owe their sexual orientation to fraternal birth order? *Archives of Sexual Behavior, 31,* 63–71.

Capobianco, D. J., Swanson, J. W., & Dodick, D. W. (2001). Medication-induced (analgesic rebound) headache: Historical aspects and initial descriptions of the North American experience. *Headache, 41,* 500–502.

Cardeña, E. A., & Gleaves, D. H. (2003). Dissociative disorders: Phantoms of the self. In M. Hersen & S. M. Turner (Eds.), *Adult Psychopathology and Diagnosis* (4th ed., pp. 476–404). Hoboken, NJ: John Wiley & Sons.

Cardeña, E., Lewis-Fernández, R., Bear, D., Pakianathan, I., & Spiegel, D. (1996). Dissociative disorders. In T. A. Widiger, A. J. Frances, H. A. Pincus, R. Ross, M. B. First, & W. W. Davis (Eds.), *DSM-IV sourcebook* (Vol. 2, pp. 973–1005). Washington, DC: American Psychiatric Press.

CARE Study Group. (2008). Maternal caffeine intake during pregnancy and risk of fetal growth restriction: A large prospective observational study. *BMJ, 337,* 1334–1338.doi:10.1136/bmj. a2332

Carlat, D. J., Camargo, C. A., Jr., & Herzog, D. B. (1997). Eating disorders in males: A report on 135 patients. *American Journal of Psychiatry, 154,* 1127–1132.

Carlson, E. B., & Putnam, F. W. (1989). Integrating research on dissociation and hypnotizability: Are there two pathways to hypnotizability? *Dissociation, 2,* 32–38.

Carlson, G. A. (1990). Annotation: Child and adolescent mania—Diagnostic considerations. *Journal of Child Psychology and Psychiatry, 31*(3), 331–341.

Caron, C., & Rutter, M. (1991). Comorbidity in childhood psychopathology: Concepts, issues, and research strategies. *Journal of Child Psychology and Psychiatry, 32,* 1063–1080.

Carr, E. G., & Durand, V. M. (1985). Reducing behavior problems through functional communication training. *Journal of Applied Behavior Analysis, 18,* 111–126.

Carrico, A. W., & Antoni, M. H. (2008). Effects of psychological interventions on neuroendocrine hormone regulation and immune states in HIV-positive persons: A review of randomized controlled trials. *Psychosomatic Medicine, 70,* 575–584.

Carrier, S., Brock, G. B., Pommerville, P. J., Shin, J., Anglin, G., Whittaker, S., & Beasley, C. M., Jr. (2005). Efficacy and safety of oral tadalafil in the treatment of men in Canada with erectile dysfunction: A randomized, double-blind, parallel, placebo-controlled clinical trial. *Journal of Sexual Medicine, 2,* 685–698.

Carroll, A. (2009). Are you looking at me? Understanding and managing paranoid personality disorder. *Advances in Psychiatric Treatment, 15*(1), 40.

Carroll, B. C., McLaughlin, T. J., & Blake, D. R. (2006). Patterns and knowledge of nonmedical use of stimulants among college students. *Archives of Pediatrics and Adolescent Medicine, 160,* 481–485.

Carroll, E. M., Rueger, D. B., Foy, D. W., & Donahoe, C. P. (1985). Vietnam combat veterans with posttraumatic stress disorder: Analysis of marital and cohabitating adjustment. *Journal of Abnormal Psychology, 94,* 329–337.

Carroll, K. M. (2008). Cognitive-behavioral therapies. In M. Galanter & H. D. Kleber (Eds.), *The American Psychiatric Publishing Textbook of Substance Abuse Treatment* (4th ed., pp. 349–360). Arlington, VA: American Psychiatric Publishing.

Carroll, R. A. (2007). Gender dysphoria and trans-gender experiences. In S. R. Leiblum (Ed.), *Principles and practice of sex therapy* (4th ed., pp. 477–508). New York, NY: Guilford Press.

Carson, R. C. (1991). Discussion: Dilemmas in the pathway of DSM-IV. *Journal of Abnormal Psychology, 100,* 302–307.

Carson, R. C. (1996). Aristotle, Galileo, and the *DSM* taxonomy: The case of schizophrenia. *Journal of Consulting and Clinical Psychology, 64*(6), 1133–1139.

Carstensen, L. L., Charles, S. T., Isaacowitz, D., & Kennedy, Q. (2003). Life-span personality development and emotion. In R. J. Davidson, K. Scherer & H. H. Goldsmith (Eds.), *Handbook of affective sciences* (pp. 931–951). Oxford, UK: Oxford University Press.

Carter, J. C., & Fairburn, C. G. (1998). Cognitive-behavioral self-help for binge eating disorder: A controlled effectiveness study. *Journal of Consulting and Clinical Psychology, 66,* 616–623.

Carter, J. C., McFarlane, T. L., Bewell, C., Olmsted, M. P., Woodside, D. B., Kaplan, A. S., & Crosby, R. D. (2009). Maintenance treatment for anorexia nervosa: A comparison of cognitive behavior therapy and treatment as usual. *International Journal of Eating Disorders, 42*(3), 202–207.

Carter, J. S., Garber, J., Cielsa, J., & Cole, D. (2006). Modeling relations between hassles and internalizing and externalizing symptoms in adolescents: A four-year prospective study. *Journal of Abnormal Psychology, 115,* 428–442.

Carter, R. M., Wittchen, H. U., Pfister, H., & Kessler, R. C. (2001). One-year prevalence of subthreshold and threshold DSM-IV generalized anxiety disorder in a nationally representative sample. *Depression & Anxiety, 13,* 78–88.

Cartwright, R. D. (2006). Sleepwalking. In T. Lee-Chiong (Ed.), *Sleep: A comprehensive handbook* (pp. 429–433). Hoboken, NJ: John Wiley & Sons.

Carver, C. S., Johnson, S. L., & Joormann, J. (2009). Two-mode models of self-regulation as a tool for conceptualizing effects of the serotonin system in normal behavior and diverse disorders. *Current Directions in Psychological Science, 18*(4), 195–199.

Casper, R. C. (1982). Treatment principles in anorexia nervosa. *Adolescent Psychiatry, 10,* 431–454.

Caspi, A., McClay, J., Moffitt, T. E., Mill, J., Martin, J., Craig, I. W., & Poulton, R. (2002). Role of genotype in the cycle of violence in maltreated children. *Science, 297,* 851–853.

Caspi, A., Sugden, K., Moffitt, T. E., Taylor, A., Craig, I. W., Harrington, H.,...Poulton, R. (2003). Influence of life stress on depression: Moderation by a polymorphism in the 5-HTT gene. *Science, 301,* 386–389.

Cassano, G., Rucci, P., Frank, E., Fagiolini, A., Dell'Osso, L., Shear, K., & Kupfer, D. J. (2004). The mood spectrum in unipolar and bipolar disorder: Arguments for a unitary approach. *American Journal Psychiatry, 161,* 1264–1269.

Cassidy, F., Forest, K., Murry, E., & Carroll, B. J. (1998). A factor analysis of the signs and symptoms of mania. *Archives of General Psychiatry, 55,* 27–32.

Castonguay, L. G., Eldredge, K. L., & Agras, W. S. (1995). Binge eating disorder: Current state and directions. *Clinical Psychology Review, 15,* 815–890.

Catania, J. A., Morin, S. F., Canchola, J., Pollack, L., Chang, J., & Coates, T. J. (2000). U.S. priorities—HIV prevention. *Science, 290,* 717.

Cautela, J. R. (1966). Treatment of compulsive behavior by covert sensitization. *Psychological Record, 16,* 33–41.

Cautela, J. R. (1967). Covert sensitization. *Psychological Reports, 20,* 459–468.

Ceci, S. J. (1995). False beliefs: Some developmental and clinical considerations. In D. L. Schacter (Ed.), *Memory distortion: How minds, brains, and societies reconstruct the past* (pp. 91–125). Cambridge, MA: Harvard University Press.

Ceci, S. J. (2003). Cast in six ponds and you'll reel in something: Looking back on 25 years of research. *American Psychologist, 58,* 855–867.

Celio, A. A., Winzelberg, A. J., Dev, P., & Taylor, C. B. (2002). Improving compliance in on-line, structured self-help programs: Evaluation of an eating disorder prevention program. *Journal of Psychiatric Practice, 8,* 14–20.

Celio, A. A., Zabinski, M. F., & Wilfley, D. E. (2002). African American body images. In T. F. Cash & T. Pruzinsky (Eds.), *Body image: A handbook of theory, research, and clinical practice* (pp. 234–242). New York, NY: Guilford Press.

Centers for Disease Control and Prevention. (2003a). Deaths: Final data for 2001. *National Vital Statistics Reports, 52*(3). Hyattsville, MD: National Center for Health Statistics.

Centers for Disease Control and Prevention. (2003b). Deaths, percent of total deaths, and death rates for the 15 leading causes of death in 5-year age groups, by race and sex: United States, 2000. Centers for Disease Control and National Center for Health Statistics, National Vital Statistics System. Hyattsville, MD: National Center for Health Statistics.

Centers for Disease Control and Prevention. (2005). Prevalence of diagnosis and medication treatment for attention-deficit/hyperactivity disorder: United States, 2003. *Morbidity and Mortality Weekly Report, 54,* 842–847.

Centers for Disease Control and Prevention. (2006). Nonfatal, unintentional medication exposures in young children—United States, 2001–2003. *Morbidity and Mortality Weekly Report* [serial online]; 55, 1–5. Retrieved from http://www.cdc.gov/mmwr/preview/mmwrhtml/mm5501a1.htm

Centers for Disease Control and Prevention. (2007). Cigarette smoking among adults—United States, 2006. *Morbidity and Mortality Weekly Report* [serial online]; 56(44): 1157–1161. Retrieved from http://www.cdc.gov/mmwr/preview/mmwrhtml/mm5644a2.htm

Centers for Disease Control and Prevention. (2008). Annual smoking-attributable mortality, year, and potential life lost, and productivity losses—United States, 2000–2004. *Morbidity and Mortality Weekly Report* [serial online]; 57(45): 1226–1228. Retrieved from http://www.cdc.gov/mmwr/preview/mmwrhtml/mm5745a3.htm

Centers for Disease Control and Prevention. (2009). Prevalence of autism spectrum disorders—autism and developmental disabilities monitoring network—United States, 2006. *Morbidity and Mortality Weekly Report, 58*(SS10), 1–20.

Centers for Disease Control and Prevention. (2010a). Diagnosis of HIV infection and AIDS in the United States and dependent areas, 2008. *HIV Surveillance Report, 20.* Retrieved from http://www.cdc.gov/hiv/surveillance/resources/reports/2008report/index.htm

Centers for Disease Control and Prevention. (2010b). Fatal injury data. Retrieved from http://www.cdc.gov/injury/wisqars/fatal.html

Cha, C. B., Najmi, S., Park, J. M., Finn, C. T., & Nock, M. J. (2010). Attentional bias toward suicide-related stimuli predicts suicidal behavior. *JAMA: Journal of Abnormal Psychology, 119,* 616–622.

Chakrabarti, S., & Fombonne, E. (2001). Pervasive developmental disorders in preschool children. *JAMA: Journal of the American Medical Association, 285,* 3093–3099.

Chalder, T., Cleare, A., & Wessely, S. (2000). The management of stress and anxiety in chronic fatigue syndrome. In D. I. Mostofsky & D. H. Barlow (Eds.), *The management of stress and anxiety in medical disorders* (pp. 160–179). Needham Heights, MA: Allyn & Bacon.

Chamberlain, S. R., Menzies, L., Sahakian, B. J., & Fineberg, N. A. (2007). Lifting the veil on trichotillomania. *American Journal of Psychiatry, 164,* 568–574.

Chaouloff, F., & Groc, L. (2010). Temporal modulation of hippocampal excitatory transmission by corticosteroids and stress. *Frontiers in Neuroendocrinology.* Advance online publication. doi:10.1016/j.yfrne.2010.07.004

Charland, L. C. (2008). A moral line in the sand: Alexander Crichton and Philippe Pinel on the psychopathology of the passions. In L. C. Charland & P. Zachar (Eds.), *Fact and value in emotion* (pp. 15–34). Amsterdam, The Netherlands: John Benjamins Publishing Company.

Charland, L. C. (2010). Science and morals in the affective psychopathology of Philippe Pinel. *History of Psychiatry, 21*(1), 38–53.

Charles, S. T., & Carstensen, L. L. (2010). Social and emotional aging. *Annual Review of Psychology, 61,* 383–409.

Charney, D. S. (2004). Psychobiological mechanisms of resilience and vulnerability: Implications for successful adaptation to extreme stress. *The American Journal of Psychiatry, 161*(2), 195–216.

Charney, D. S., Barlow, D. H., Botteron, K., Cohen, J. D., Goldman, D., Raquel, E. G., ... Zalcman, S. J. (2002). Neuroscience research agenda to guide development of a pathophysiologically based classification system. In D. J. Kupfer, M. B. First, & D. A. Regier (Eds.), *A research agenda for DSM-V* (pp. 31–83). Washington, DC: American Psychiatric Association.

Charney, D. S., Deutch, A. Y., Krystal, J. H., Southwick, S. M., & Davis, M. (1993). Psychobiological mechanisms of posttraumatic stress disorder. *Archives of General Psychiatry, 50,* 294–305.

Charney, D. S., & Drevets, W. C. (2002). Neurobiological basis of anxiety disorders. In K. L. Davis, D. Charney, J. T. Coyle, & C. Nemeroff (Eds.), *Neuropsychopharmacology: The fifth generation of progress* (pp. 901–951). Philadelphia, PA: Lippincott Williams & Wilkins.

Chassin, L., Pillow, D. R., Curran, P. J., Molina, B. S. G., & Barrera, M. (1993). Relation of parental alcoholism to early adolescent substance use: A test of three mediating mechanisms. *Journal of Abnormal Psychology, 102,* 3–19.

Chassin, L., Presson, C. C., Rose, J. S., & Sherman, S. J. (2001). From adolescence to adulthood: Age-related changes in beliefs about cigarette smoking in a Midwestern community sample. *Health Psychology, 20*(5), 377–386.

Chassin, L., Presson, C. C., Rose, J., Sherman, S. J., Davis, M. J., & Gonzalez, J. L. (2005). Parenting style and smoking-specific parenting practices as predictors of adolescent smoking onset. *Journal of Pediatric Psychology, 30*(4), 333–344.

Chavez, M., & Insel, T. R. (2007). Eating disorders: National Institute of Mental Health perspective. *American Psychologist, 62,* 159–166.

Check, J. R. (1998). Munchausen syndrome by proxy: An atypical form of child abuse. *Journal of Practical Behavioral Health, 4,* 340–345.

Chen, M. C., Hamilton, J. P., & Gotlib, I. H. (2010). Decreased hippocampal volume in healthy girls at risk of depression. *Archives of General Psychiatry, 67*(3), 270–276.

Chesney, M. A. (1986, November). *Type A behavior: The biobehavioral interface.* Keynote address presented at the annual meeting of the Association for Advancement of Behavior Therapy, Chicago.

Chida, Y., and Mao, X. (2009). Does psychosocial stress predict symptomatic herpes simplex virus recurrence? A meta-analytic investigation on prospective studies. *Brain, Behavior, and Immunity, 23,* 917–925.

Chivers, M. L., & Bailey, J. M. (2000). Sexual orientation of female-to-male transsexuals: A comparison of homosexual and nonhomosexual types. *Archives of Sexual Behavior, 29*(3), 259–279.

Chivers, M. L., Rieger, G., Latty, E., & Bailey, M. (2004). A sex difference in the specificity of sexual arousal. *Psychological Science, 15,* 736–744.

Cho, H. J., Lavretsky, H., Olmstead, R., Levin, M. J., Oxman, M. N., & Irwin, M. R. (2008). Sleep disturbance and depression recurrence in community-dwelling older adults: a prospective study. *American Journal of Psychiatry, 165*(12), 1543–1550.

Choate, M. L., Pincus, D. B., Eyberg, S. M., & Barlow, D. B. (2005). Parent–child interaction therapy for treatment of separation anxiety disorder: A pilot study. *Cognitive and Behavioral Practice, 12*(1), 126–135.

Chobanian, A. V., Bakris, G. L., Black, H. R., Cushman, W. C., Green, L. A., Izzo, J. L., ... National High Blood Pressure Education Program Coordinating Committee. (2003). Seventh report of the Joint National Committee on prevention, detection, evaluation, and treatment of high blood pressure. *Hypertension, 42,* 1206–1252.

Chodoff, P. (1974). The diagnosis of hysteria: An overview. *American Journal of Psychiatry, 131,* 1073–1078.

Chodoff, P. (1982). Hysteria in women. *American Journal of Psychiatry, 139,* 545–551.

Chorpita, B. F., & Barlow, D. H. (1998). The development of anxiety: The role of control in the early environment. *Psychological Bulletin, 124*(1), 3–21.

Chorpita, B. F., Brown, T. A., & Barlow, D. H. (1998). Perceived control as a mediator of family environment in etiological models of childhood anxiety. *Behavior Therapy, 29,* 457–476.

Chosak, A., Marques, L., Greenberg, J. L., Jenike, E., Dougherty, D. D., & Wilhelm, S. (2008). Body dysmorphic disorder and obsessive-compulsive disorder: Similarities, differences, and the classification debate. *Expert Review of Neurotherapeutics, 8*(8), 1209–1218.

Christakis, N. A., & Fowler, J. H. (2007). The spread of obesity in a large social network over 32 years. *New England Journal of Medicine, 357*(4), 370–379.

Christiansen, B. A., Smith, G. T., Roehling, P. V., & Goldman, M. S. (1989). Using alcohol expectancies to predict adolescent drinking behavior after one year. *Journal of Consulting and Clinical Psychology, 57,* 93–99.

Christodoulou, G., Margariti, M., Kontaxakis, V., & Christodoulou, N. (2009). The delusional misidentification syndromes: Strange, fascinating, and instructive. *Current Psychiatry Reports, 11*(3), 185–189.

Chronis, A. M., Lahey, B. B., Pelham, W. E., Jr., Williams, S. H., Baumann, B. L., Kipp, H., ... Rathouz, P.J. (2007). Maternal depression and early positive parenting predict future conduct problems in young children with attention deficit/hyperactivity disorder. *Developmental Psychology, 43,* 70–82.

Chung, S. Y., Luk, S. L., & Lee, P. W. H. (1990). A follow-up study of infantile autism in Hong Kong. *Journal of Autism and Developmental Disorders, 20,* 221–232.

Cicchetti, D. (1991). A historical perspective on the discipline of developmental psychopathology. In J. Rolf, A. S. Masten, D. Cicchetti, K. H. Nuechterlein, & S. Weintraub (Eds.), *Risk and protective factors in the development of psychopathology* (pp. 2–28). New York, NY: Cambridge University Press.

Cipani, E. (1991). Educational classification and placement. In J. L. Matson & J. A. Mulick (Eds.), *Handbook of mental retardation* (2nd ed., pp. 181–191). Elmsford, NY: Pergamon Press.

Ciraulo, D. A., & Sarid-Segal, O. (2009). Sedative-, hypnotic-, or anxiolytic-related disorders. In B. J. Sadock, V. A. Sadock, & P. Ruiz (Eds.), *Kaplan & Sadock's comprehensive textbook of psychiatry* (9th ed., Vol. I, pp. 1397–1418). Philadelphia, PA: Lippincott Williams & Wilkins.

Citrome, L., Lieb, K., Vollm, B., Rücker, G., Timmer, A., & Stoffers, J. (2010). Pharmacotherapy for borderline personality disorder. *British Journal of Psychiatry, 196,* 4–12.

Clark, D. A., & O'Connor, K. (2005). Thinking is believing: Ego-dystonic intrusive thoughts in obsessive-compulsive disorder. In D. A. Clark (Ed.), *Intrusive thoughts in clinical disorders* (pp. 145–174). New York, NY: Guilford Press.

Clark, D. A., & Rhyno, S. (2005). Unwanted intrusive thoughts in nonclinical individuals: Implications for clinical disorders. In D. A. Clark (Ed.), *Intrusive thoughts in clinical disorders* (pp. 1–29). New York, NY: Guilford Press.

Clark, D. M. (1986). A cognitive approach to panic. *Behaviour Research and Therapy, 24,* 461–470.

Clark, D. M. (1996). Panic disorder: From theory to therapy. In P. Salkovskis (Ed.), *Frontiers of cognitive therapy* (pp. 318–344). New York, NY: Guilford Press.

Clark, D. M., Ehlers, A., Hackman, A., McManus, F., Fennell, M., Grey, N., ... Wild, J. (2006). Cognitive therapy versus exposure and applied relaxation in social phobia: A randomized controlled trial. *Journal of Consulting and Clinical Psychology, 74,* 568–578.

Clark, D. M., Ehlers, A., McManus, F., Hackman, A., Fennell, M. J. V., Campbell, H., & Louis, B. (2003). Cognitive therapy versus fluoxetine in generalized social phobia: A randomized placebo-controlled trial. *Journal of Consulting and Clinical Psychology, 71,* 1058–1067.

Clark, D. M., Salkovskis, P. M., Hackmann, A., Middleton, H., Anastasiades, P., & Gelder, M. (1994). A comparison of cognitive therapy, applied relaxation, and imipramine in the treatment of panic disorder. *British Journal of Psychiatry, 164*(6), 759–769.

Clark, D. M., Salkovskis, P. M. N., Hackmann, A., Wells, A., Fennell, M., Ludgate, S., ... Gelder, M. (1998). Two psy-

chological treatments for hypochondriasis. *British Journal of Psychiatry, 173,* 218–225.

Clark, L. A. (1999). Introduction to the special section on the concept of disorder. *Journal of Abnormal Psychology, 108,* 371–373.

Clark, L. A. (2005). Temperament as a unifying basis for personality and psychopathology [Special issue]. *Journal of Abnormal Psychology, 114,* 505–521.

Clark, R. (2003). Parental history of hypertension and coping responses predict blood pressure changes in black college volunteers undergoing a speaking task about perceptions of racism. *Psychosomatic Medicine, 65,* 1012–1019.

Clarkin, J. F., Carpenter, D., Hull, J., Wilner, P., & Glick, I. (1998). Effects of psychoeducational intervention for married patients with bipolar disorder and their spouses. *Psychiatric Services, 49*(4), 531–533.

Clarkin, J. F., Howieson, D. B., & McClough, J. (2008). The role of psychiatric measures in assessment and treatment. In R. E. Hales, S. C. Yudofsky, & G. O. Gabbard (Eds.), *The American Psychiatric Publishing textbook of psychiatry* (5th ed., pp. 73–110). Arlington, VA: American Psychiatric Publishing, Inc.

Classen, C., Diamond, S., & Spiegel, D. (1998). Studies of life-extending psychosocial interventions. In J. Holland (Ed.), *Psycho-oncology* (pp. 653–836). Oxford, UK: Oxford University Press.

Clayton, P. J., & Darvish, H. S. (1979). Course of depressive symptoms following the stress of bereavement. In J. E. Barrett (Ed.), *Stress and mental disorder* (pp. 121–136). New York, NY: Raven.

Cleckley, H. M. (1982). *The mask of sanity* (6th ed.). St. Louis, MO: Mosby. (Original work published 1941.)

Cleghorn, J. M., & Albert, M. L. (1990). Modular disjunction in schizophrenia: A framework for a pathological psychophysiology. In A. Kales, C. N. Stefanis, & J. A. Talbot (Eds.), *Recent advances in schizophrenia* (pp. 59–80). New York, NY: Springer-Verlag.

Cleghorn, J. M., Franco, S., Szechtman, B., Kaplan, R. D., Szechtman, H., Brown, G. M., ... Garnett, E. S. (1992). Toward a brain map of auditory hallucinations. *American Journal of Psychiatry, 149,* 1062–1069.

Clement, U. (1990). Surveys of heterosexual behavior. *Annual Review of Sex Research, 1,* 45–74.

Clementz, B. A., & Sweeney, J. A. (1990). Is eye movement dysfunction a biological marker for schizophrenia? A methodological review. *Psychological Bulletin, 108,* 77–92.

Cloninger, C. R. (1978). The link between hysteria and sociopathy: An integrative model of pathogenesis based on clinical, genetic, and neurophysiological observations. In H. S. Akiskal & W. L. Webb (Eds.), *Psychiatric diagnosis: Exploration of biological predictors* (pp. 189–218). New York, NY: Spectrum.

Cloninger, C. R. (1987). A systematic method for clinical description and classification of personality variants: A proposal. *Archives of General Psychiatry, 44,* 573–588.

Cloninger, C. R. (1989). Establishment of diagnostic validity in psychiatric illness:

Robins and Guze's method revisited. In L. N. Robins & J. E. Barrett (Eds.), *The validity of psychiatric diagnosis* (pp. 9–16). New York, NY: Raven Press.

Cloninger, C. R. (1996). Somatization disorder. Literature review for DSM-IV sourcebook. Washington, DC: American Psychiatric Press.

Cloninger, C. R., & Svakic, D. M. (2009). Personality disorders. In B. J. Sadock, V. A. Sadock, & P. Ruiz (Eds.), *Kaplan & Sadock's comprehensive textbook of psychiatry* (9th ed., Vol. II, pp. 2197–2240). Philadelphia, PA: Lippincott Williams & Wilkins.

Closser, M. H. (1992). Cocaine epidemiology. In T. R. Kosten & H. D. Kleber (Eds.), *Clinician's guide to cocaine addiction: Theory, research, and treatment* (pp. 225-240). New York, NY: Guilford Press.

Coates, T. J. (1990). Strategies for modifying sexual behavior for primary and secondary prevention of HIV disease. *Journal of Consulting and Clinical Psychology, 58*(1), 57–69.

Cobb, S. (1976). Social support as a moderator of life stress. *Psychosomatic Medicine, 38,* 300.

Coccaro, E., & McCloskey, M. (2010). Intermittent explosive disorder: Clinical aspects. In E. Aboujaoude & L. M. Koran (Eds.), *Impulse control disorders* (pp. 221–232). New York, NY: Cambridge University Press.

Coderre, T. J., Katz, J., Vaccarino, A. L., & Melzack, R. (1993). Contribution of central neuroplasticity to pathological pain: Review of clinical and experimental evidence. *Pain, 52,* 259–285.

Cohen, J. (2002). Confronting the limits of success. *Science, 296,* 2320–2324.

Cohen, J. (2006). The overlooked epidemic. *Science Magazine, 313,* 468–469.

Cohen, J. B., & Reed, D. (1985). Type A behavior and coronary heart disease among Japanese men in Hawaii. *Journal of Behavioral Medicine, 8,* 343–352.

Cohen, L., Soares, C., Vitonis, A., Otto, M., & Harlow, B. (2006). Risk for new onset of depression during the menopausal transition. *Archive General Psychiatry, 63,* 385–390.

Cohen, S. (1996). Psychological stress, immunity, and upper respiratory infections. *Current Directions in Psychological Science, 5,* 86–90.

Cohen, S. P., Doyle, W. J. P., Alper, C. M. M. D., Janicki-Deverts, D. P., & Turner, R. B. M. D. (2009). Sleep habits and susceptibility to the common cold. *Archives of Internal Medicine January, 169*(1), 62–67.

Cohen, S., Doyle, W. J., & Skoner, D. P. (1999). Psychological stress, cytokine production, and severity of upper respiratory illness. *Psychosomatic Medicine, 61,* 175–180.

Cohen, S., Doyle, W. J., Skoner, D. P., Fireman, P., Gwaltney, J. M., Jr., & Newsome, J. T. (1995). State and trait negative affect as predictors of objective and subjective symptoms of respiratory viral infections. *Journal of Personality and Social Psychology, 68,* 159–169.

Cohen, S., Doyle, W. J., Turner, R., Alper, C. M., & Skoner, D. P. (2003). Sociability and susceptibility to the common cold. *Psychological Science, 14*(5), 389–395.

Cohen, S., & Herbert, T. B. (1996). Health psychology: Psychological factors and physical disease from the perspective of human psychoneuroimmunology. *Annual Review of Psychology, 47,* 113–142.

Cohen, S., & Janicki-Deverts, D. (2009). Can we improve our physical health by altering our social networks? *Perspectives on Psychological Science, 4,* 375–378.

Cohen, S., Tyrrell, D. A., & Smith, A. P. (1991). Psychological stress and susceptibility to the common cold. *New England Journal of Medicine, 325,* 606–612.

Cohen, S., Tyrrell, D. A., & Smith, A. P. (1993). Negative life events, perceived stress, negative affect, and susceptibility to the common cold. *Journal of Personality and Social Psychology, 64*(1), 131–140.

Cohen-Kettenis, P. T., & Pfäfflin, F. (2010). The DSM diagnostic criteria for gender identity disorder in adolescents and adults. *Archives of Sexual Behavior, 39,* 499–513.

Coker, L. H., Espeland, M. A., Rapp, S. R., Legault, C., Resnick, S. M., Hogan, P., ... Shumaker, S. A. (2010). Postmenopausal hormone therapy and cognitive outcomes: The Women's Health Initiative Memory Study (WHIMS). *The Journal of Steroid Biochemistry and Molecular Biology, 118*(4–5), 304–310.

Cole, J. T., Mitala, C. M., Kundu, S., Verma, A., Elkind, J. A., Nissim, I., & Cohen, A. S. (2010). Dietary branched chain amino acids ameliorate injury-induced cognitive impairment. *Proceedings of the National Academy of Sciences, 107,* 366–371.

Cole, M., Winkelman, M. D., Morris, J. C., Simon, J. E., & Boyd, T. A. (1992). Thalamic amnesia: Korsakoff syndrome due to left thalamic infarction. *Journal of the Neurological Sciences, 110,* 62–67.

Cole, M. G., Ciampi, A., Belzile, E., & Zhong, L. (2009). Persistent delirium in older hospital patients: A systematic review of frequency and prognosis. *Age and Ageing, 38*(1), 19–26.

Cole, S. W. (2008). Psychosocial influences on HIV-1 disease progression: Neural, endocrine, and virologic mechanisms. *Psychosomatic Medicine, 70,* 562–568.

Coleman, E., Bockting, W. O., & Gooren, L. (1993). Homosexual and bisexual identity in sex-reassigned female-to-male transsexuals. *Archives of Sexual Behavior, 22,* 37–50.

Coleman, E., Colgan, P., & Gooren, L. (1992). Male cross-gender behavior in Myanmar (Burma): A description of the acault. *Archives of Sexual Behavior, 21*(3), 313–321.

Collinge, J., Whitfield, J., McKintosh, E., Beck, J., Mead, S., Thomas, D. J., Alpers, M. P. (2006). Kuru in the 21st century: An acquired human prion disease with very long incubation periods. *Lancet, 367*(9528), 2068–2074.

Collins, W. A., Maccoby, E. E., Steinberg, L., Hetherington, E. M., & Bornstein, M. H. (2000). Contemporary research on parenting: The case for nature and nurture. *American Psychologist, 55,* 218–232.

Colman, I., Murray, J., Abbott, R., Maughan, B., Kuh, D., Croudace, T., ... Jones, P. B. (2009). Outcomes of conduct problems in adolescence: 40-year follow-up of national cohort. *British Medical Journal, 338,* a2981.

Colp, R. (2009). History of psychiatry. In B. J. Sadock, V. A. Sadock, & P. Ruiz (Eds.), *Kaplan & Sadock's comprehensive textbook of psychiatry* (9th ed., Vol. II, pp. 4474–4509). Philadelphia, PA: Lippincott Williams & Wilkins.

Comas-Diaz, L. (1981). Puerto Rican *espiritismo* and psychotherapy. *American Journal of Orthopsychiatry, 51*(4), 636–645.

Compas, B. E., Boyer, M., Stanger, C., Colletti, R., & Thomsen, A. (2006). Latent variable analysis of coping, anxiety/depression, and somatic symptoms in adolescents with chronic pain. *Journal of Consulting and Clinical Psychology, 74,* 1132–1142.

Compas, B. E., Forehand, R., Keller, G., Champion, J. E., Rakow, A., Reeslund, K. L., ... Cole, D. A. (2009). Randomized controlled trial of a family cognitive-behavioral preventive intervention for children of depressed parents. *Journal of Consulting and Clinical Psychology, 77*(6), 1007–1020.

Compas, B. E., Oppedisano, G., Connor, J. K., Gerhardt, C. A., Hinden, B. R., Achenbach, T. M., & Hammen, C. (1997). Gender differences in depressive symptoms in adolescence: Comparison of national samples of clinically referred and nonreferred youths. *Journal of Consulting and Clinical Psychology, 65,* 617–626.

Condon, W., Ogston, W., & Pacoe, L. (1969). Three faces of Eve revisited: A study of transient microstrabismus. *Journal of Abnormal Psychology, 74,* 618–620.

Conduct Problems Prevention Research Group. (2010). The effects of a multiyear universal social-emotional learning program: The role of student and school characteristics. *Journal of Consulting and Clinical Psychology, 78*(2), 156–168.

Conn. Gen. Stat. Ann., 319: Part II, 17a-495 (1992).

Conners, C. K., March, J. S., Frances, A., Wells, K. C., & Ross, R. (2001). Treatment of attention-deficit/hyperactivity disorder: Expert consensus guidelines. *Journal of Attention Disorders, 4*(Suppl. 1), 7–128.

Connor, D. F. (2006). Stimulants. In R. A. Barkley (Ed.), *Attention-deficit hyperactivity disorder: A handbook for diagnosis and treatment* (3rd ed., pp. 608–647). New York, NY: Guilford Press.

Constantino, J., Abbacchi, A., Lavesser, P., Reed, H., Givens, L., Chiang, L., ... Todd, R. D. (2009). Developmental course of autistic social impairment in males. *Development and psychopathology, 21*(01), 127–138.

Conti, C. R., Pepine, C. J., & Sweeney, M. (1999). Efficacy and safety of sildenafil citrate in the treatment of erectile dysfunction in patients with ischemic heart disease. *American Journal of Cardiology, 83,* 29C–34C.

Conwell, Y., Duberstein, P. R., & Caine, E. D. (2002). Risk factors for suicide in later life. *Biological Psychiatry, 52,* 193–204.

Conwell, Y., Duberstein, P. R., Cox, C., Hermmann, J. H., Forbes, N. T., & Caine, E. D. (1996). Relationships of age and axis I diagnoses in victims of completed suicide: A psychological autopsy study. *American Journal of Psychiatry, 153,* 1001–1008.

Cook, E. W., III, Hodes, R. L., & Lang, P. J. (1986). Preparedness and phobia: Effects of stimulus content on human visceral conditioning. *Journal of Abnormal Psychology, 95,* 195–207.

Cook, P. J. (1993). The matter of tobacco use. *Science, 262,* 1750–1751.

Cookson, C. (2009). Confronting our fear: Legislating beyond battered woman syndrome and the law of self-defense in Vermont. *Vermont Law Review, 34,* 415.

Coolidge, F., Thede, L., & Young, S. (2002). The heritability of gender identity disorder in a child and adolescent twin sample. *Behavior Genetics, 32,* 251–257.

Coons, P. M. (1994). Confirmation of childhood abuse in child and adolescent cases of multiple personality disorder not otherwise specified. *Journal of Nervous & Mental Disease, 182,* 461–464.

Cooper, A. J. (1988). Sexual dysfunction and cardiovascular disease. *Stress Medicine, 4,* 273–281.

Cooper, A. M., & Ronningstam, E. (1992). Narcissistic personality disorder. In A. Tasman & M. B. Riba (Eds.), *Review of psychiatry* (Vol. 11, pp. 80–97). Washington, DC: Psychiatric Press.

Cooper, J., Kapur, N., Webb, R., Lawlor, M., Guthrie, E., Mackway-Jones, K., & Appleby, L. (2005). Suicide after deliberate self-harm: A 4-year cohort study. *American Journal of Psychiatry, 162,* 297–303.

Cooper, N. S., Feder, A., Southwick, S. M., & Charney, D. S. (2007). Resilience and vulnerability to trauma: Psychobiological mechanisms. In D. Romer & E. F. Walker (Eds.), *Adolescent psychopathology and the developing brain: Integrating brain and prevention science* (pp. 347–372). New York, NY: Oxford University Press.

Cooperberg, J., & Faith, M. S. (2004). Treatment of obesity II: Childhood and adolescent obesity. In J. K. Thompson (Ed.), *Handbook of eating disorders and obesity* (pp. 443–450). New York, NY: John Wiley.

Cope, M. B., Fernandez, J. R., & Allison, D. (2004). Genetic and biological risk factors. In J. K. Thompson (Ed.), *Handbook of eating disorders and obesity* (pp. 323–338). New York, NY: John Wiley.

Copeland, W., Shanahan, L., Costello, E., & Angold, A. (2009). Childhood and adolescent psychiatric disorders as predictors of young adult disorders. *Archives of General Psychiatry, 66*(7), 764.

Coplan, J. D., Andrews, M. W., Rosenblum, L. A., Owens, M. J., Friedman, S., Gorman, J. M., & Nemeroff, C. B. (1996). Persistent elevations of cerebrospinal fluid concentrations of corticotropin-releasing factor in adult nonhuman primates exposed to early life stressors: Implications for the pathophysiology of mood and anxiety disorders. *Proceedings of the National Academy of Sciences, 93,* 1619–1623.

Coplan, J. D., Trost, R. C., Owens, M. J., Cooper, T. B., Gorman, J. M., Nemeroff, C. B., & Rosenblum, L. A. (1998). Cerebrospinal fluid concentrations of somatostatin and biogenic amines in grown primates reared by mothers exposed to manipulated foraging conditions. *Archives of General Psychiatry, 55,* 473–477.

Corcoran, C. M., Kimhy, D., Stanford, A., Khan, S., Walsh, J., Thompson, J., ... Malaspina, D. (2008). Temporal association of cannabis use with symptoms in individuals at clinical high risk for psychosis. *Schizophrenia Research, 106,* 286–293.

Coryell, W., Endicott, J., Maser, J. D., Keller, M. B., Leon, A. C., & Akiskal, H. S. (1995). Long-term stability of polarity distinctions in the affective disorders. *American Journal of Psychiatry, 152,* 385–390.

Coryell, W., Solomon, D. A., Fiedorowicz, J. G., Endicott, J., Schettler, P. J., & Judd, L. L. (2009). Anxiety and outcome in bipolar disorder. *American Journal of Psychiatry, 166*(11), 1238–1243.

Costa, E. (1985). Benzodiazepine–GABA interactions: A model to investigate the neurobiology of anxiety. In A. H. Tuma & J. D. Maser (Eds.), *Anxiety and the anxiety disorders.* Hillsdale, NJ: Erlbaum.

Costa e Silva, J. A., & De Girolamo, G. (1990). Neurasthenia: History of a concept. In N. Sartorius, D. Goldberg, G. De Girolamo, J. A. Costa e Silva, Y. Lecrubier, & U. Wittchen (Eds.), *Psychological disorders in general medical settings* (pp. 699–81). Toronto, Canada: Hogrefe and Huber.

Costello, E. J., Foley, D. L., & Angold, A. (2006). 10-year research update review: The epidemiology of child and adolescent psychiatric disorders: II. Developmental epidemiology. *Journal of the American Academy of Child and Adolescent Psychiatry, 45*(1), 8–25.

Côté, G., O'Leary, T., Barlow, D. H., Strain, J. J., Salkovskis, P. M., Warwick, H. M. C., ... Rasmussen, S. A. (1996). Hypochondriasis. In T. A. Widiger, A. J. Frances, H. A. Pincus, R. Ross, M. B. First, & W. W. Davis (Eds.), *DSM-IV sourcebook* (Vol. 2, pp. 933–947). Washington, DC: American Psychiatric Association.

Cotugno, A. (2009). Social competence and social skills training and intervention for children with autism spectrum disorders. *Journal of Autism and Developmental Disorders, 39*(9), 1268–1277.

Cowley, G., & Springen, K. (1990, March). The promise of Prozac. *Newsweek,* p. 38.

Cox, A., Rutter, M., Newman, S., & Bartak, L. (1975). A comparative study of infantile autism and specific developmental receptive language disorder: II. Parental characteristics. *British Journal of Psychiatry, 126,* 146–159.

Cox, A. C., Weed, N. C., & Butcher, J. N. (2009). The MMPI-2: History, interpretation, and clinical issues. In J. N. Butcher (Ed.), *Oxford handbook of personality assessment* (pp. 250–276). New York: Oxford University Press.

Coyne, J. C., Stefanek, M., & Palmer, S. C. (2007). Psychotherapy and survival in cancer: The conflict between hope and evidence. *Psychological Bulletin, 133,* 367–394.

Coyne, M., Zipoli, R., Chard, D., Faggella-Luby, M., Ruby, M., Santoro, L., Baker, S. (2009). Direct instruction of comprehension: instructional examples from intervention research on listening and reading comprehension. *Reading and Writing Quarterly, 25,* 2(3), 221–245.

Cozanitis, D. A. (2004). One hundred years of barbiturates and their saint. *Journal of the Royal Society of Medicine, 97,* 594–598.

Crabbe, J. C., Wahlsten, D., & Dudek, B. C. (1999). Genetics of mouse behavior: Interactions with laboratory environment. *Science, 284,* 1670–1672.

Craddock, N., & Jones, I. (2001). Molecular genetics of bipolar disorder. *British Journal of Psychiatry, 41,* 128–133.

Crago, M., Shisslak, C. M., & Estes, L. S. (1997). Eating disturbances among American minority groups: A review. *The International Journal of Eating Disorders, 19,* 239–248.

Craig, M. C., & Murphy, D. G. M. (2009). Alzheimer's disease in women. *Best Practice & Research Clinical Obstetrics & Gynaecology, 23*(1), 53–61.

Craighead, W. E., Hart, A. B., Craighead, L. W., & Ilardi, S. S. (2002). Psychosocial treatments for major depressive disorder. In P. E. Nathan & J. M. Gorman (Eds.), *A guide to treatments that work* (2nd ed., pp. 245–261). New York, NY: Oxford University Press.

Craighead, W. E., Ilardi, S. S., Greenberg, M. P., & Craighead, L. W. (1997). Cognitive psychology: Basic theory and clinical implications. In A. Tasman, J. Key, & J. A. Lieberman (Eds.), *Psychiatry* (Vol. 1, pp. 350–368). Philadelphia, PA: W. B. Saunders.

Craske, M. G. (1999). *Anxiety disorders: Psychological approaches to theory and treatment.* Boulder, CO: Westview Press.

Craske, M. G., Antony, M. M., & Barlow, D. H. (2006). *Mastering your fears and phobias: Therapist guide.* New York, NY: Oxford University Press.

Craske, M. G., & Barlow, D. H. (1988). A review of the relationship between panic and avoidance. *Clinical Psychology Review, 8,* 667–685.

Craske, M.G., & Barlow, D.H. (2006). *Mastery of your anxiety and worry.* New York, NY: Oxford University Press.

Craske, M. G., & Barlow, D. H. (2008). Panic disorder and agoraphobia. In D. H. Barlow (Ed.), *Clinical handbook of psychological disorders: A step-by-step treatment manual* (4th ed.). New York, NY: Guilford Press.

Craske, M. G., Barlow, D. H., Clark, D. M., Curtis, G. C., Hill, E. M., Himle, J. A., ... Warwick, H. M. C. (1996). Specific (simple) phobia. In T. A. Widiger, A. J. Frances, H. A. Pincus, R. Ross, M. B. First, & W. W. Davis (Eds.), *DSM-IV sourcebook* (Vol. 2, pp. 473–506). Washington, DC: American Psychiatric Association.

Craske, M. G., Brown, T. A., & Barlow, D. H. (1991). Behavioral treatment of panic disorder: A two-year follow-up. *Behavior Therapy, 22,* 289–304.

Craske, M. G., Golinelli, D., Stein, M. B., Roy-Byrne, P., Bystritsky, A., Sherbourne, C. (2005). Does the addition of cognitive behavioral therapy improve panic disorder treatment outcome relative to medication alone in the primary-care setting? *Psychological Medicine, 35*(11), 1645–1654.

Craske, M. G., Hermans, D., & Vansteenwegen, D. (2006). *Fear and learning.* Washington, DC: American Psychological Association.

Craske, M. G., Kircanski, K., Epstein, A., Wittchen, H.-U., Pine, D. S., Lewis-Fernández, R., & Hinton, D. (2010). Panic disorder: A review of DSM-IV panic disorder and proposals for DSM-V. *Depression and Anxiety, 27*(2), 93–112.

Craske, M. G., Lang, A. J., Mystkowski, J. L., Zucker, B. G., & Bystritsky, A. (2002). Does nocturnal panic represent a more se-

vere form of panic disorder? *Journal of Nervous and Mental Disease, 190,* 611–618.

Craske, M. G., Rapee, R. M., & Barlow, D. H. (1988). The significance of panic expectancy for individual patterns of avoidance. *Behavior Therapy, 19,* 577–592.

Craske, M. G., & Rowe, M. K. (1997). Nocturnal panic. *Clinical psychology: Science & practice, 4,* 153–174.

Creed, F., & Barsky, A. (2004). A systematic review of the epidemiology of somatisation disorder and hypochondriasis. *Journal of Psychosomatic Research, 56,* 391–408.

Creese, I., Burt, D. R., & Snyder, S. H. (1976). Dopamine receptor binding predicts clinical and pharmacological potencies of antischizophrenic drugs. *Science, 192,* 481–483.

Cremniter, D., Jamin, S., Kollenbach, K., Alvarez, J. C., Lecrubier, Y., Gilton, A., ... Spreux-Varoquaux, O. (1999). CSF 5-HIAA levels are lower in impulsive as compared to nonimpulsive violent suicide attempts and control subjects. *Biological Psychiatry, 45*(12), 1572–1579.

Crerand, C., Sarwer, D., Magee, L., Gibbons, L., Lowe, M., Bartlett, S., ... Whitaker, L. A. (2004). Rate of body dysmorphic disorder among patients seeking facial plastic surgery. *Psychiatric Annals, 34,* 958–965.

Crichton, P., & Morey, S. (2003). Treating pain in cancer patients. In D. C. Turk & R. J. Gatchel (Eds.), *Psychological approaches to pain management: A practitioner's handbook* (2nd ed., pp. 501–514). New York, NY: Guilford Press.

Crisp, A. H., Callender, J. S., Halek, C., & Hsu, L. K. G. (1992). Long-term mortality in anorexia nervosa: A 20-year follow-up of the St. George's and Aberdeen cohorts. *British Journal of Psychiatry, 161,* 104–107.

Critelli, J. W., & Bivona, J. M. (2008). Women's erotic rape fantasies: An evaluation of theory and research. *Journal of Sex Research, 45,* 57–70.

Critser, G. (2003). *Fat land: How Americans became the fattest people in the world.* Boston, MA: Houghton Mifflin.

Crow, S. J., Mitchell, J. E., Roerig, J. D., & Steffen, K. (2009). What potential role is there for medication treatment in anorexia nervosa? *International Journal of Eating Disorders, 42*(1), 1–8.

Crow, S. J., Thuras, P., Keel, P. K., & Mitchell, J. E. (2002). Long-term menstrual and reproductive function in patients with bulimia nervosa. *American Journal of Psychiatry, 159,* 1048–1050.

Crowe, L. C., & George, W. H. (1989). Alcohol and human sexuality: Review and integration. *Psychological Bulletin, 105*(3), 374–386.

Crowe, R. R. (1974). An adoption study of antisocial personality. *Archives of General Psychiatry, 31,* 785–791.

Crowley, P. H., Hayden, T. L., & Gulati, D. K. (1982). Etiology of Down syndrome. In S. M. Pueschel & J. E. Rynders (Eds.), *Down syndrome: Advances in biomedicine and behavioral sciences* (pp. 89–131). Cambridge, MA: Ware Press.

Crowley, T., Richardson, D., & Goldmeir, D. (2006). Recommendation for the management of vaginismus: BASHH special interest group for sexual dysfunction. *International Journal of STD and AIDS, 17,* 14–18.

Cummings, J. L. (Ed.). (1990). *Subcortical dementia*. New York, NY: Oxford University Press.

Curatolo, P., Bombardieri, R., & Jozwiak, S. (2008). Tuberous sclerosis. *The Lancet, 372*(9639), 657–668.

Currier, J. M., Neimeyer, R. A., & Berman, J. S. (2008). The effectiveness of psychotherapeutic interventions for bereaved persons: a comprehensive quantitative review. *Psychological Bulletin, 134*(5), 648–661.

Curtis, G. C., Hill, E. M., & Lewis, J. A. (1990). *Heterogeneity of DSM-III-R simple phobia and the simple phobia/agoraphobia boundary: Evidence from the ECA study*. Preliminary report to the Simple Phobia subcommittee of the DSM-IV Anxiety Disorders Work Group.

Curtis, G. C., Himle, J. A., Lewis, J. A., & Lee, Y-J. (1989). *Specific situational phobias: Variant of agoraphobia?* Paper requested by the Simple Phobia subcommittee of the DSM-IV Anxiety Disorders Work Group.

Cyranowski, J. M., Aarestad, S. L., & Andersen, B. L. (1999). The role of sexual self-schema in a diathesis-stress model of sexual dysfunction. *Applied & Preventative Psychology, 8*, 217–228.

Cyranowski, J. M., Frank, E., Young, E. & Shear, M. K. (2000). Adolescent onset of the gender difference in lifetime rates of major depression. *Archives of General Psychiatry, 57*, 21–27.

Dagan, Y., Dela, H., Omer, H., Hallis, D., & Dar, R. (1996). High prevalence of personality disorders among circadian rhythm sleep disorders (CRSD) patients. *Journal of Psychosomatic Research, 41*, 357–363.

Dalack, G. W., Glassman, A. H., & Covey, L. S. (1993). Nicotine use. In D. L. Dunner (Ed.), *Current psychiatric therapy* (pp. 114–118). Philadelphia, PA: W. B. Saunders.

Dana, R. H. (1996). The Thematic Apperception Test (TAT). In C. S. Newmark (Ed.), *Major psychological assessment instruments* (pp. 166–205). Boston, MA: Allyn & Bacon.

Daniel, S. S., Walsh, A. K., Goldston, D. B., Arnold, E. M., Reboussin, B. A., & Wood, F. B. (2006). Suicidality, school dropout, and reading problems among adolescents. *Journal of Learning Disabilities, 39*, 507–514.

Daniels, A., Adams, N., Carroll, C., & Beinecke, R. (2009). A conceptual model for behavioral health and primary care integration: Emerging challenges and strategies for improving international mental health services. *International Journal of Mental Health, 38*(1), 100–112.

Darcangelo, S. (2008). Fetishism: Psychopathology and theory. In D. R. Laws & W. T. O'Donohue (Eds.), *Sexual deviance: Theory, assessment, and treatment* (2nd ed., pp. 108–118). New York, NY: Guilford Press.

Darwin, C. R. (1872). *The expression of emotions in man and animals*. London, UK: John Murray.

Dassori, A. M., Miller, A. L., & Saldana, D. (1995). Schizophrenia among Hispanics: epidemiology, phenomenology, course, and outcome. *Schizophr Bull, 21*(2), 303–312.

Davey, G. (2006). Cognitive mechanisms in fear acquisition and maintenance. In M. G. Craske, D. Hermans, & D. Vansteenwegen (Eds.), *Fear and learning from basic processes to clinical implications*. (pp. 99–116). Washington, DC: American Psychological Association.

Davidson, A. J., Sellix, M. T., Daniel, J., Yamazaki, S., Menaker, M., & Block, G. D. (2006). Chronic jet-lag increases mortality in aged mice. *Current Biology, 16*, R914–R916.

Davidson, J., Swartz, M., Storck, M., Krishnan, R. R., & Hammett, E. (1985). A diagnostic and family study of posttraumatic stress disorder. *American Journal of Psychiatry, 142*, 90–93.

Davidson, J. R. T., Foa, E. B., & Huppert, J. D. (2004). Fluoxetine, comprehensive Cognitive behavioral therapy, and placebo in generalized social phobia. *Archives of General Psychiatry, 61*, 1005–1013.

Davidson, J. R. T., Hughes, D. L., Blazer, D. G., & George, L. K. (1991). Posttraumatic stress in the community: An epidemiological study. *Journal of Psychological Medicine, 21*, 713–721.

Davidson, K., MacGregor, M. W., Stuhr, J., Dixon, K., & MacLean, D. (2000). Constructive anger verbal behavior predicts blood pressure in a population-based sample. *Health Psychology, 19*, 55–64.

Davidson, M., Keefe, R. S. E., Mohs, R. C., Siever, L. J., Losonczy, M. F., Horvath, T. B., & Davis, K. L. (1987). L-Dopa challenge and relapse in schizophrenia. *American Journal of Psychiatry, 144*, 934–938.

Davidson, R. J. (1993). Cerebral asymmetry and emotion: Methodological conundrums. *Cognition and Emotion, 7*, 115–138.

Davidson, R. J., Pizzagalli, D. A., & Nitschke, J. B. (2009). Representation and regulation of emotion in depression: Perspectives from affective neuroscience. In I. H. Gotlib & C. L. Hammen (Eds.), *Handbook of depression* (2nd ed., pp. 218–248). New York, NY: Guilford Press.

Davila, J., Stroud, C. B., & Starr, L. R. (2009). Depression in couples and families. In I. H. Gotlib & C. L. Hammen (Eds.), *Handbook of depression* (2nd ed., pp. 467–491). New York, NY: Guilford Press.

Davis, C., Katzman, D. K., Kaptein, S., Krish, C., Brewer, H., Kalmbach, K., ... Kaplan, A. S. (1997). The prevalence of high-level exercise in the eating disorders: Etiological implications. *Comprehensive Psychiatry, 38*, 321–326.

Davis, M. (1992). The role of the amygdala in fear and anxiety. *Annual Review of Neuroscience, 15*, 353–375.

Davis, M. (2002). Neural circuitry of anxiety and stress disorders. In K. L. Davis, D. Charney, J. T. Coyle, & C. Nemeroff (Eds.), *Neuropsychopharmacology: The fifth generation of progress* (pp. 901–930). Philadelphia, PA: Lippincott Williams & Wilkins.

Davison, G. C. (1968). Elimination of a sadistic fantasy by a client-controlled counter-conditioning technique: A case study. *Journal of Abnormal Psychology, 73*, 91–99.

Dawson, D. A., Grant, B. F., Stinson, F. S., Chou, P. S., Huang, B., & Ruan, W. J. (2005). Recovery from DSM-IV alcohol dependence: United States, 2001–2002. *Addiction, 100*, 281–292.

Dawson, G., Toth, K., Abbott, R., Osterling, J., Munson, J., Estes, A., Liaw, J. (2004). Early social attention impairments in autism: Social orienting, joint attention, and attention to distress. *Developmental Psychology, 40*, 271–283.

Dawson, M., Mottron, L., & Gernsbacher, M. (2008). Learning in autism. In J. H. Byrne & H. L. Roediger (Eds.), *Learning and memory: A comprehensive reference: Vol. 2. Cognitive psychology* (pp. 759–772). New York, NY: Elsevier.

Day, R., Nielsen, J. A., Korten, A., Ernberg, G., Dube, K. C., Gebhart, J., ... Olatawura, M. (1987). Stressful life events preceding the acute onset of schizophrenia: A cross-national study from the World Health Organization. *Cultural Medicine and Psychiatry, 11*, 123–205.

de Almeidia-Filho, N., Santana, V. S., Pinto, I. M., & de Carvalho-Neto, J. A. (1991). Is there an epidemic of drug misuse in Brazil? A review of the epidemiological evidence (1977–1988). *International Journal of the Addictions, 26*, 355–369.

De Backer, G., Kittel, F., Kornitzer, M., & Dramaix, M. (1983). Behavior, stress, and psychosocial traits as risk factors. *Preventative Medicine, 12*, 32–36.

de Boo, G. M., & Prins, P. J. M. (2007). Social incompetence in children with ADHD: Possible moderators and mediators in social-skills training. *Clinical Psychology Review, 27*, 78–97.

De Brito, S. A., & Hodgins, S. (2009). Antisocial personality disorder. In M. McMurran & R. C. Howard (Eds.), *Personality, personality disorder and violence: An evidence based approach* (pp. 133–154). New York, NY: Wiley.

de Lissovoy, V. (1961). Head banging in early childhood. *Child Development, 33*, 43–56.

de Zwaan, M., Roerig, J. L., & Mitchell, J. E. (2004). Pharmacological treatment of anorexia nervosa, bulimia nervosa, and binge eating disorder. In J. K. Thompson (Ed.), *Handbook of eating disorders and obesity* (pp. 186–217). New York, NY: John Wiley.

Deakin, J. F. W., & Graeff, F. G. (1991). Critique: 5-HT and mechanisms of defence. *Journal of Psychopharmacology, 5*(4), 305–315.

Deale, A., Chalder, T., Marks, I., & Wessely, S. (1997). Cognitive behavior therapy for chronic fatigue syndrome: A randomized controlled trial. *American Journal of Psychiatry, 154*, 408–414.

Deale, A., Husain, K., Chalder, T., & Wessely, S. (2001). Long-term outcome of cognitive behavioral therapy versus relaxation therapy for chronic fatigue syndrome: A 5-year follow-up study. *American Journal of Psychiatry, 158*, 2038–2042.

Dean, R. R., Kelsey, J. E., Heller, M. R., & Ciaranello, R. D. (1993). Structural foundations of illness and treatment: Receptors. In D. L. Dunner (Ed.), *Current psychiatric therapy*. Philadelphia, PA: W. B. Saunders.

Debruyne, H., Portzky, M., Van den Eynde, F., & Audenaert, K. (2009). Cotard's syndrome: A review. *Current Psychiatry Reports, 11*(3), 197–202.

Degenhardt, L., Chiu, W. T., Sampson, N., Kessler, R. C., Anthony, J. C., Angermeyer, M., et al. (2008). Toward a global view of alcohol, tobacco, cannabis, and cocaine use: findings from the WHO

World Mental Health Surveys. *PLoS Medicine, 5*(7), e141.

DeKosky, S. T., Williamson, J. D., Fitzpatrick, A. L., Kronmal, R. A., Ives, D. G., Saxton, J. A., ... Furberg, C. D. (2008). Ginkgo biloba for prevention of dementia: A randomized controlled trial. *JAMA: Journal of the American Medical Association, 300*(19), 2253–2262.

Del Parigi, A., Panza, F., Capurso, C., & Solfrizzi, V. (2006). Nutritional factors, cognitive decline, and dementia. *Brain Research Bulletin, 69*(1), 1–19.

DeLamater, J., & Sill, M. (2005). Sexual desire in later life. *Journal of Sex Research, 42*, 138–149.

Delano-Wood, L., & Abeles, N. (2005). Late-life depression: Detection, risk, reduction, and somatic intervention. *Clinical Psychology Science Practice, 12*, 207–217.

DeLisi, L. E., Maurizio, A., Yost, M., Papparozzi, C. F., Fulchino, C., Katz, C. L., ... Stevens, P. (2003). A survey of New Yorkers after the Sept. 11, 2001, terrorist attacks. *American Journal of Psychiatry, 160*, 780–783.

Delizonna, L. L., Wincze, J. P., Litz, B. T., Brown, T. A., & Barlow, D. H. (2001). A comparison of subjective and physiological measures of mechanically produced and erotically produced erections. (Or, is an erection an erection?) *Journal of Sex and Marital Therapy, 27*, 21–31.

Dell, P. F., & O'Neil, J. A. (Eds.). (2009). *Dissociation and the dissociative disorders*. New York, NY: Routledge.

Dembroski, T. M., & Costa, P. T., Jr. (1987). Coronary prone behavior: Components of the type A pattern and hostility. *Journal of Personality, 55*(2), 211–235.

Dembroski, T. M., MacDougall, J. M., Costa, P. T., & Grandits, G. A. (1989). Components of hostility as predictors of sudden death and myocardial infarction in the multiple risk factor intervention trial. *Psychosomatic Medicine, 51*(5), 514–522.

Dent, M. F., & Bremner, J. D. (2009). Pharmacotherapy for posttraumatic stress disorder and other trauma-related disorders. In M. M. Antony & M. B. Stein (Eds.), *Oxford handbook of anxiety and related disorders.* (pp. 405–416). New York, NY: Oxford University Press.

Denzin, N. K. (1987). *The recovering alcoholic*. Newbury Park, CA: Sage.

Depression Guideline Panel. (1993, April). *Depression in primary care: Vol. 1. Detection and diagnosis* (AHCPR Publication No. 93–0550). Clinical practice guideline, No. 5. Rockville, MD: U.S. Department of Health and Human Services, Public Health Service, Agency for Health Care Policy and Research.

Deptula, D., & Pomara, N. (1990). Effects of antidepressants on human performance: A review. *Journal of Clinical Psychopharmacology, 10*, 105–111.

Depue, R. A., & Spoont, M. R. (1986). Conceptualizing a serotonin trait: A behavioral dimension of constraint. *Annals of the New York Academy of Sciences, 487*, 47–62.

Depue, R. A., Luciana, M., Arbisi, P., Collins, P., & Leon, A. (1994). Dopamine and the structure of personality: Relation of agonist-induced dopamine activity to positive emotionality. *Journal of Personality and Social Psychology, 67*, 485–498.

Depue, R. A., & Zald, D. (1993). Biological and environmental processes in nonpsychotic psychopathology: A neurobehavioral system perspective. In C. Costello (Ed.), *Basic issues in psychopathology*. New York, NY: Guilford Press.

Dersh, J., Polatin, P. B., & Gatchel, R. J. (2002). Chronic pain and psychopathology: Research findings and theoretical considerations. *Psychosomatic Medicine, 64*, 773–786.

DeRubeis, R., Gelfand, L. A., Tang, T. Z., & Simons, A. D. (1999). Medications versus cognitive behavior therapy for severely depressed outpatients: Mega-analysis of four randomized comparisons. *American Journal of Psychiatry, 156*, 1007–1013.

DeRubeis, R., Hollon, S., Amsterdam, J., Shelton, R., Young, P., ... Gallop, R. (2005). Cognitive therapy vs. medications in the treatment of moderate to severe depression. *Archives of General Psychiatry, 62*, 409–416.

Desantis, A., & Hane, A. (2010). "Adderall is definitely not a drug": Justifications for the illegal use of ADHD stimulants. *Substance Use & Misuse, 45*(1–2), 31–46.

Devanand, D. P. (2002). Comorbid psychiatric disorders in late life depression. *Biological Psychiatry, 52*, 236–242.

Deveci, A., Taskin, O., Dinc, G., Yilmaz, H., Demet, M. M., Erbay-Dundar, P., Ozman, E. (2007). Prevalence of pseudoneurologic conversion disorder in an urban community in Manisa, Turkey. *Social Psychiatry and Psychiatric Epidemiology, 42*(11), 857–864.

DeWall, C. N., MacDonald, G., Webster, G. D., Masten, C. L., Baumeister, R. F., Powell, C., ... Eisenberger, N. I. (2010). Acetaminophen reduces social pain: Behavioral and neural evidence. *Psychological Science, 21*, 931–937.

DeWitt, D. J., Adlaf, E. M., Offord, D. R., & Ogborne, A. C. (2000). Age at first alcohol use: A risk factor for the development of alcohol disorders. *American Journal of Psychiatry, 157*, 745–750.

Dhawan, N., Kunik, M. E., Oldham, J., & Coverdale, J. (2010). Prevalence and treatment of narcissistic personality disorder in the community: A systematic review. *Comprehensive Psychiatry*. doi:10.1016/j.comppsych.2009.09.003

Diamond, L. M. (2007). A dynamical systems approach to the development and expression of female same-sex sexuality. *Perspectives on Psychological Science, 2*, 142–161.

Diamond, L. M., Butterworth, M. R., & Savin-Williams, R. C. (2011). Working with sexual-minority individuals. In D. H. Barlow (Ed.), *Oxford handbook of clinical psychology* (pp. 837–867). New York, NY: Oxford University Press.

Diamond, M. (1995). Biological aspects of sexual orientation and identity. In L. Diamant & R. D. McAnulty (Eds.), *The psychology of sexual orientation, behavior, and identity*. Westport, CT: Greenwood Press.

Diamond, M., & Sigmundson, K. (1997). Sex reassignment at birth: Long-term review and clinical implications. *Archives of Pediatric and Adolescent Medicine, 151*, 298–304.

Dick, D. M., Aliev, F., Wang, J. C., Grucza, R. A., Schuckit, M., Kuperman, S., ... Goate, E. (2008). Using dimensional models of externalizing psychopathology to aid in gene identification. *Archives of General Psychiatry, 65*(3), 310–318. doi:10.1001/archpsyc.65.3.310

Dickersin, K. (2010). To reform U.S. health care, start with systematic reviews. *Science, 329*, 516.

Diener, E. (2000). Subjective well-being: The science of happiness, and a proposal for a national index. *American Psychologist, 55*, 34–43.

Diener, E., Oishi, S., & Lucas, R. E. (2003). Personality, culture, and subjective well-being: Emotional and cognitive evaluations of life. *Annual Review of Psychology, 54*, 403–425.

Dimberg, U., & Öhman, A. (1983). The effects of directional facial cues on electrodermal conditioning to facial stimuli. *Psychophysiology, 20*, 160–167.

Dimidjian, S., Martell, C. R., Addis, M. E., & Herman-Dunn, R. (2008). Behavioral activation for depression. In D. H. Barlow (Ed.), *Clinical handbook of psychological disorders: A step-by-step treatment manual* (4th ed., pp. 328–364). New York, NY: Guilford Press.

DiNardo, P. A., Brown, T. A., & Barlow, D. H. (1994). *Anxiety disorders interview schedule for DSM-IV (ADIS-IV)*. Albany, NY: Oxford University Press.

DiNardo, P. A., Guzy, L. T., Jenkins, J. A., Bak, R. M., Tomasi, S. F., & Copeland, M. (1988). Etiology and maintenance of dog fears. *Behaviour Research and Therapy, 26*, 241–244.

Dinnel, D. L., Kleinknecht, R. A., & Tanaka-Matsumi, J. (2002). A cross-cultural comparison of social phobia symptoms. *Journal of Psychopathology and Behavioral Assessment, 24*, 75–82.

Dishion, T. J., Patterson, G. R., & Reid, J. R. (1988). Parent and peer factors associated with drug sampling in early adolescence: Implications for treatment. In E. R. Rahdert & J. Gabowski (Eds.), *Adolescent drug abuse: Analyses of treatment research* (NIDA Research Monograph No. 77, DHHS Publication No. ADM88-1523, pp. 69–93). Rockville, MD: National Institute on Drug Abuse.

Distel, M. A., Trull, T. J., & Boomsma, D. I. (2009). Genetic epidemiology of borderline personality disorder. In M. H. Jackson & L. F. Westbrook (Eds.), *Borderline personality disorder: New research* (pp. 1–31). Hauppage, NY: Nova Science Publishers.

Dixon, L. B., & Lehman, A. F. (1995). Family interventions for schizophrenia. *Schizophrenia Bulletin, 21*, 631–643.

Djernes, J. K. (2006). Prevalence and predictors of depression in populations of elderly: A review. *Acta Psychiatrica Scandinavica, 113*(5), 372–387.

Docter, R. F., & Prince, V. (1997). Transvestism: A survey of 1032 cross-dressers. *Archives of Sexual Behavior, 26*, 589–605.

Doğan, S. (2009). Vaginismus and accompanying sexual dysfunctions in a Turkish clinical sample. *Journal of Sexual Medicine, 6*, 184–192.

Doğan, S., & Doğan, M. (2006). Possible gender identity disorder in an extremely religious Muslim family. *Archives of Sexual Behavior, 35,* 645–646.

Dohrenwend, B. P., & Dohrenwend, B. S. (1981). Socioenvironmental factors, stress, and psychopathology. *American Journal of Community Psychology, 9*(2), 128–164.

Dohrenwend, B. P., & Egri, G. (1981). Recent stressful life events and episodes of schizophrenia. *Schizophrenia Bulletin, 7,* 12–23.

Dohrenwend, B. P., Turner, J. B., & Turse, N. A. (2006). The psychological risks of Vietnam for U.S. veterans: A revisit with new data and methods. *Science, 313,* 979–982.

Dolan, M., & Völlm, B. (2009). Antisocial personality disorder and psychopathy in women: A literature review on the reliability and validity of assessment instruments. *International Journal of Law and Psychiatry, 32*(1), 2–9.

Donaldson, K. (1976). *Insanity inside out.* New York, NY: Crown.

D'Onofrio, B. M., Turkheimer, E., Emery, R. E., Slutske, W. S., Heath, A. C., Madden, P. A., & Martin, N. G. (2006). A genetically informed study of the processes underlying the association between parental marital instability and offspring adjustment. *Developmental Psychology, 42,* 486–499.

Dougherty, D. D., Baer, L., Cosgrove, G. R., Cassem, E. H., Price, B. H., Nierenberg, A. A., ... Ruach, S. L. (2002). Prospective long-term follow-up of 44 patients who received cingulotomy for treatment-refractory obsessive-compulsive disorder. *The American Journal of Psychiatry, 159*(2), 269–275.

Douglas, K. S., Guy, L. S., & Hart, S. D. (2009). Psychosis as a risk factor for violence to others: A meta-analysis. *Psychological Bulletin, 135*(5), 679–706. doi:10.1037/a0016311

Douglas, K. S., Vincent, G. M., & Edens, J. F. (2006). Psychopathy and substance use disorders. In C. J. Patrick (Ed.), *Handbook of psychopathy* (pp. 533–554). New York, NY: Guilford Press.

Dowling, N., Smith, D., & Thomas, T. (2007). A comparison of individual and group cognitive-behavioural treatment for female pathological gambling. *Behaviour Research and Therapy, 45*(9), 2192–2202.

Draguns, J. G. (1990). Normal and abnormal behavior in cross-cultural perspective: Specifying the nature of their relationship. In J. Berman (Ed.), *Cross-cultural perspectives: Nebraska symposium on motivation 1989* (pp. 235–277). Lincoln: University of Nebraska Press.

Draguns, J. G. (1995). Cultural influences upon psychopathology: Clinical and practical implications. *Journal of Social Distress and the Homeless, 4,* 79–103.

Drummond, K. D., Bradley, S. J., Peterson-Badali, M., & Zucker, K. J. (2008). A follow-up study of girls with gender identity disorder. *Developmental Psychology, 44,* 34–45.

Dubovsky, S. L. (1983). Psychiatry in Saudi Arabia. *American Journal of Psychiatry, 140,* 1455–1459.

Dulit, R. A., Marin, D. B., & Frances, A. J. (1993). Cluster B personality disorders. In D. L. Dunner (Ed.), *Current psychiatric therapy* (pp. 405– 411). Philadelphia, PA: W. B. Saunders.

Duman, R. (2004). Depression: A case of neuronal life and death? *Biological Psychiatry, 56,* 140–145.

Dunlop, B. W., & Nemeroff, C. B. (2007). The role of dopamine in the pathophysiology of depression. *Archives of General Psychiatry, 64*(3), 327–337.

Durand, V. M. (1990). *Severe behavior problems: A functional communication training approach.* New York, NY: Guilford Press.

Durand, V. M. (1998). Good sleep habits. In V. M. Durand (Ed.), *Sleep better: A guide to improving sleep for children with special needs* (p. 60). Baltimore, MD: Paul H. Brookes.

Durand, V. M. (1999). Functional communication training using assistive devices: Recruiting natural communities of reinforcement. *Journal of Applied Behavior Analysis, 32*(3), 247–267.

Durand, V. M. (2001). Future directions for children and adolescents with mental retardation. *Behavior Therapy, 32,* 633–650.

Durand, V. M. (2006). Sleep terrors. In J. E. Fisher & W. T. O'Donohue (Eds.), *Evidence-based psychotherapy* (pp. 654–659). Reno, NV: Springer.

Durand, V. M. (2008). *When children don't sleep well: Interventions for pediatric sleep disorders, therapist guide.* New York, NY: Oxford University Press.

Durand, V. M. (2011). Disorders of development. In D. H. Barlow (Ed.), *Oxford handbook of clinical psychology* (pp. 551–573). New York, NY: Oxford University.

Durand, V. M. (in press). Functional communication training to reduce challenging behavior. In P. Prelock & R. McCauley (Eds.), *Treatment of autism spectrum disorders: Evidence-based intervention strategies for communication & social interaction.* Baltimore, MD: Paul H. Brookes.

Durand, V. M., & Carr, E. G. (1992). An analysis of maintenance following functional communication training. *Journal of Applied Behavior Analysis, 25,* 777–794.

Durand, V. M., & Hieneman, M. (2008). *Helping parents with challenging children: Positive family intervention, facilitator's guide.* New York, NY: Oxford University Press.

Durand, V. M., Hieneman, M., Clarke, S., & Zona, M. (2009). Optimistic parenting: Hope and help for parents with challenging children. In W. Sailor, G. Dunlap, G. Sugai, & R. H. Horner (Eds.), *Handbook of positive behavior support* (pp. 233–256). New York, NY: Springer.

Durand, V. M., & Mindell, J. A. (1999). Behavioral intervention for childhood sleep terrors. *Behavior Therapy, 30,* 705–715.

Durand, V. M., & Wang, M. (in press). Clinical trials. In J. C. Thomas & M. Hersen (Eds.), *Understanding research in clinical and counseling psychology.* New York, NY: Routledge.

Durham v. United States, 214 F.2d, 862, 874-875 (D.C. Cir., 1954).

Durham, M. L., & La Fond, J. Q. (1985). The empirical consequences and policy implications of broadening the statutory criteria for civil commitment. *Yale Law and Policy Review, 3,* 395–446.

Durkheim, E. (1951). *Suicide: A study in sociology.* (J. A. Spaulding & G. Simpson, Trans.). New York, NY: Free Press.

Dusky v. United States, 362 U.S. 402 (1960).

Dusseldorp, E., van Elderen, T., Maes, S., Meulman, J., & Kraaij, V. (1999). A meta-analysis of psychoeducational programs for coronary heart disease patients. *Health Psychology, 18,* 506–519.

Dustin, M. L., & Long, E. O. (2010). Cytotoxic immunological synapses. *Immunological Review, 235,* 24–34.

Dvorak-Bertscha, J., Curtin, J., Rubinstein, T., & Newman, J. (2009). Psychopathic traits moderate the interaction between cognitive and affective processing. *Psychophysiology, 46*(5), 913.

Eagles, J. M., Johnston, M. I., Hunter, D., Lobban, M., & Millar, H. R. (1995). Increasing incidence of anorexia nervosa in the female population of northeast Scotland. *American Journal of Psychiatry, 152,* 1266–1271.

Eaker, E. D., Pinsky, J., & Castelli, W. P. (1992). Myocardial infarction and coronary death among women: Psychosocial predictors from a 20-year follow-up of women in the Framingham study. *American Journal of Epidemiology, 135,* 854–864.

Eaton, W. W., Kessler, R. C., Wittchen, H. U., & Magee, W. J. (1994). Panic and panic disorder in the United States. *American Journal of Psychiatry, 151,* 413–420.

Eaton, W. W., Shao, H., Nestadt, G., Lee, H. B., Bienvenu, O. J., & Zandi, P. (2008). Population-based study of first onset and chronicity in major depressive disorder. *Archives of General Psychiatry, 65*(5), 513–520.

Ebben, M., & Spielman, A. (2009). Non-pharmacological treatments for insomnia. *Journal of Behavioral Medicine, 32*(3), 244–254.

Ebigno, P. (1982). Development of a culture-specific screening scale of somatic complaints indicating psychiatric disturbance. *Culture, Medicine, and Psychiatry, 6,* 29–43.

Ebigno, P. O. (1986). A cross-sectional study of somatic complaints of Nigerian females using the Enugu Somatization Scale. *Culture, Medicine, and Psychiatry, 10,* 167–186.

Eckman, T. A., Wirshing, W. C., Marder, S. R., Liberman, R. P., Johnston-Cronk, K., Zimmermann, K., & Mintz, J. (1992). Techniques for training schizophrenic patients in illness self-management: A controlled trial. *American Journal of Psychiatry, 149,* 1549–1555.

Eddy, K. T., Dorer, D. J., Franko, D. L., Tahilani, K., Thompson-Brenner, H., & Herzog, D. B. (2008). Diagnostic crossover in anorexia nervosa and bulimia nervosa: Implications for DSM-V. *American Journal of Psychiatry, 165*(2), 245–250.

Eddy, K. T., Keel, P. K., Dorer, D. J., Delinsky, S. S., Franko, D. L., & Herzog, D. B. (2002). A longitudinal comparison of anorexia nervosa subtypes. *International Journal of Eating Disorders, 31,* 191–201.

Edelson, M. G. (2006). Are the majority of children with autism mentally retarded? *Focus on Autism and other Developmental Disabilities, 21,* 66–83.

Edens, J. F., Marcus, D. K., & Morey, L. C. (2009). Paranoid personality has a dimensional latent structure: Taxometric analyses of community and clinical samples. *Journal of Abnormal Psychology, 118*(3), 545–553. doi:10.1037/a0016313

Edwards, A. J. (1994.). *When memory fails: Helping the Alzheimer's and dementia patient.* New York, NY: Plenum Press.

Edwards, R. R., Campbell, C., Jamison, R. N., & Wiech, K. (2009). The neurobiological underpinnings of coping with pain. *Current Directions in Psychological Science, 18,* 237–241.

Eelen, P., & Vervliet, B. (2006). Fear conditioning and clinical implications: What can we learn from the past? In M. G. Craske, D. Hermans, & D. Vansteenwegen, *Fear and learning: From basic processes to clinical implications* (pp. 17– 35). Washington, DC: American Psychological Association.

Efon, S. (1997, October 19). Tsunami of eating disorders sweeps across Asia. *San Francisco Examiner,* p. A27.

Egan, B. M., Zhao, Y., & Axon, R. N. (2010). US trends in prevalence, awareness, treatment, and control of hypertension. *JAMA: Journal of the American Medical Association, 303,* 2043–2050.

Egeland, J. A., Gerhard, D. S., Pauls, D. L., Sussex, J. N., Kidd, K. K., Allen, C. R., et al. (1987). Bipolar affective disorders linked to DNA markers on chromosome 11. *Nature, 325*(6107), 783–787.

Ehlers, A., & Clark, D. M. (2003). Early psychological interventions for adult survivors of trauma: A review. *Biological Psychiatry, 53,* 817–826.

Ehlers, A., Clark, D. M., Hackmann, A., McManus, F., Fennell, M., Herbert, C., ... Mayou, R. (2003). A randomized controlled trial of cognitive therapy, a self-help booklet, and repeated assessments as early interventions for posttraumatic stress disorder. *Archives of General Psychiatry, 60,* 1024–1032.

Ehlers, C., Gizer, I., Vieten, C., Gilder, D., Stouffer, G., Lau, P., & Wilhemsen, K. C. (2010). Cannabis dependence in the San Francisco Family Study: Age of onset of use, DSM-IV symptoms, withdrawal, and heritability. *Addictive Behaviors, 35*(2), 102–110.

Ehrhardt, A. A., & Meyer-Bahlburg, H. F. L. (1981). Effects of prenatal sex hormones on gender-related behavior. *Science, 211,* 1312–1318.

Ehrhardt, A. A., Meyer-Bahlburg, H. F. L., Rosen, L. R., Feldman, J. F., Veridiano, N. P., Zimmerman, I., & McEwen, B. (1985). Sexual orientation after prenatal exposure to exogenous estrogen. *Archives of Sexual Behavior, 14*(1), 57–77.

Eisen, J., Mancebo, M., Chiappone, K., Pinto, A., & Rasmussen, S. (2008). Obsessive-compulsive personality disorder. In J. S. Abramowitz, D. McKay, & S. Taylor (Eds.), *Clinical handbook of obsessive-compulsive disorder and related problems* (pp. 316–334). Baltimore, MD: Johns Hopkins University Press.

Eisen, J., & Steketee, G. (1998). Course of illness in obsessive-compulsive disorder. In L. J. Dickstein, M. B. Riba, & J. M. Oldham (Eds.), *Review of psychiatry* (Vol. 16). Washington, DC: American Psychiatric Press.

Eisler, I., Dare, C., Hodes, M., Russell, G. F. M., Dodge, E., & Le Grange, D. (2000). Family therapy for adolescent anorexia nervosa: The results of a controlled comparison of two family interventions. *Journal of Child Psychology and Psychiatry, 41,* 727–736.

Eisler, I., Dare, C., Russell, G. F. M., Szmukler, G., le Grange, D., & Dodge, E. (1997). Family and individual therapy in anorexia nervosa: A five-year follow-up. *Archives of General Psychiatry, 54,* 1025–1030.

Ekstrand, M. L., & Coates, T. J. (1990). Maintenance of safer sexual behaviors and predictors of risky sex: The San Francisco men's health study. *American Journal of Public Health, 80,* 973–977.

Elbogen, E., & Johnson, S. (2009). The intricate link between violence and mental disorder: Results from the National Epidemiologic Survey on Alcohol and Related Conditions. *Archives of General Psychiatry, 66*(2), 152.

Eldevik, S., Hastings, R., Hughes, J., Jahr, E., Eikeseth, S., & Cross, S. (2009). Meta-analysis of early intensive behavioral intervention for children with autism. *Journal of Clinical Child & Adolescent Psychology, 38*(3), 439–450.

Eldevik, S., Jahr, E., Eikeseth, S., Hastings, R. P., & Hughes, C. J. (2010). Cognitive and adaptive behavior outcomes of behavioral intervention for young children with intellectual disability. *Behavior Modification, 34*(1), 16–34.

Ellard, K. K., Fairholme, C. P., Boisseau, C. L., Farchione, T., & Barlow, D. H. (2010). Unified protocol for the transdiagnostic treatment of emotional disorders: Protocol development and initial outcome data. *Cognitive and Behavioral Practice, 17*(1), 88–101.

Ellason, J. W., & Ross, C. A. (1997). Two-year follow up of inpatients with dissociative identity disorder. *American Journal of Psychiatry, 154,* 832–839.

Ellicott, A. G. (1988). *A prospective study of stressful life events and bipolar illness.* Unpublished doctoral dissertation, University of California, Los Angeles.

Elliott, R., Rubinsztein, J. S., Sahakian, B. J., & Dolan, R. J. (2002). The neural basis of mood-congruent processing biases in depression. *Archives of General Psychiatry, 59,* 597–604.

Elovainio, M., Kivimaki, M., Viikari, J., Ekelund, J., & Keltikangas-Jarvinen, L. (2005). The mediating role of novelty seeking in the association between the type 4 dopamine receptor gene polymorphism and cigarette-smoking behavior. *Personality and Individual Differences, 38,* 639–645.

Emery, C. F., Anderson, D. R., & Andersen, B. L. (2011). Psychological interventions in health care settings. In D. H. Barlow (Ed.), *Oxford handbook of clinical psychology* (pp. 701–716). New York, NY: Oxford University Press.

Engle, P., Black, M., Behrman, J., de Mello, M., Gertler, P., Kapiriri, L., ... Young, M. (2007). Child development in developing countries 3: Strategies to avoid the loss of developmental potential in more than 200 million children in the developing world. *Lancet, 369,* 229–242.

Epstein, D. H., Marrone, G. F., Heishman, S. J., Schmittner, J., & Preston, K. L. (2010). Tobacco, cocaine, and heroin: Craving and use during daily life. *Addictive Behaviors, 35*(4), 318–324. doi:10.1016/j.addbeh.2009.11.003

Epstein, L. H., Myers, M. D., Raynor, H., & Saelens, B. E. (1998). Treatment of pediatric obesity. *Pediatrics, 101,* 554–570.

Eranti, S., Mogg, A., Pluck, G., Landau, S., Purvis, R., Brown, R. G., ... McLoughlin, D. M. (2007). A randomized, controlled trial with 6-month follow-up of repetitive transcranial magnetic stimulation and electroconvulsive therapy for severe depression. *American Journal of Psychiatry, 164*(1), 73–81.

Erath, S. A., Bierman, K. L., & Conduct Problems Prevention Research Group. (2006). Aggressive marital conflict, maternal harsh punishment, and child aggressive-disruptive behavior: Evidence for direct and mediated relations. *Journal of Family Psychology, 20,* 217–226.

Erikson, E. (1982). *The life cycle completed.* New York, NY: Norton.

Ernst, C., & Angst, J. (1995). Depression in old age: Is there a real decrease in prevalence? A review. *European Archives of Psychiatry and Clinical Neuroscience, 245*(6), 272–287.

Eron, L., & Huesmann, R. (1990). The stability of aggressive behavior: Even unto the third generation. In M. Lewis & S. Miller (Eds.), *Handbook of developmental psychopathology* (pp. 147– 156). New York, NY: Plenum.

Escobar, J. I., & Canino, G. (1989). Unexplained physical complaints: Psychopathology and epidemiological correlates. *British Journal of Psychiatry, 154,* 24–27.

Eser, D., Schule, C., Baghai, T. C., Romeo, E., & Rupprecht, R. (2006). Neuroactive steroids in depression and anxiety disorders: Clinical studies. *Neuroendocrinology, 84*(4), 244–254.

Eslinger, P. J., & Damasio, A. R. (1985). Severe disturbance of higher cognition after bilateral frontal lobe ablation: Patient EVR. *Neurology, 35,* 1731–1741.

Esposito, C. L., & Clum, G. A. (2003). The relative contribution of diagnostic and psychosocial factors in the prediction of adolescent suicidal ideation. *Journal of Clinical Child and Adolescent Psychology, 32,* 386–395.

Essex, M. J., Klein, M. H., Slattery, M. J., Goldsmith, H. H., & Kalin, N. H. (2010). Early risk factors and developmental pathways to chronic high inhibition and social anxiety disorder in adolescence. *American Journal of Psychiatry, 167*(1), 40–46.

Eth, S. (1990). Posttraumatic stress disorder in childhood. In M. Hersen & C. G. Last (Ed.), *Handbook of child and adult psychopathology: A longitudinal perspective.* Elmsford, NY: Pergamon Press.

Etter, J. (2009). Dependence on the nicotine gum in former smokers. *Addictive Behaviors, 34*(3), 246–251.

Ettinger, A. B., Devinsky, O., Weisbrot, D. M., Ramakrishna, R. K., & Goyal, A. (1999). A comprehensive profile of clinical, psychiatric, and psychosocial characteristics of patients with psychogenic nonepileptic seizures. *Epilepsia, 40*(9), 1292–1298.

Euling, S. Y., Selevan, S. G., Pescovitz, O. H., & Skakkebaek, N. E. (2008). Role of environmental factors in the timing of puberty. *Pediatrics, 121,* S167-S171.

Evans, M. D., Hollon, S. D., DeRubeis, R. J., Pinsecki, J. M., Grove, W. M., Garvey, J. J., & Tuason, V. B. (1992). Differential relapse following cognitive therapy and pharmacotherapy for depression. *Archives of General Psychiatry, 49*(10), 802–808.

Evans, R. M., Emsley, C. L., Gao, S., Sahota, A., Hall, K. S., Farlow, M. R., Hendrie, H. (2000). Serum cholesterol, APOE genotype, and the risk of Alzheimer's disease: A population-based study of African Americans. *Neurology, 54,* 240–242.

Exeter-Kent, H. A., & Page, A. C. (2006). The role of cognitions, trait anxiety, and disgust sensitivity in generating faintness around blood–injury phobic stimuli [Special issue]. *Journal of Behavior Therapy and Experimental Psychiatry, 37,* 41–52.

Exner, J. E. (2003). *The Rorschach: A comprehensive system. Basic foundations and principles of interpretation* (4th ed.). New York, NY: Wiley.

Eysenck, H. J. (Ed.) (1967). *The biological basis of personality.* Springfield, IL: Charles C. Thomas.

Eysenck, M. W. (1992). *Anxiety: The cognitive perspective.* Hove, UK: Erlbaum.

Ezzel, C. (1993). On borrowed time: Long-term survivors of HIV-l infection. *JAMA: Journal of NIH Research, 5,* 77–82.

Fagan, P. J., Wise, T. N., Schmidt, C. W., & Berlin, M. D. (2002). Pedophilia. *JAMA: Journal of the American Medical Association, 288,* 2458–2465.

Failer, J. L. (2002). *Who qualifies for rights? Homelessness, mental illness, and civil commitment.* Ithaca, NY: Cornell University Press.

Fairburn, C. G. (1985). Cognitive-behavioral treatment for bulimia. In D. M. Garner & P. E. Garfinkel (Eds.), *Handbook of psychotherapy for anorexia nervosa and bulimia* (pp. 160–192). New York, NY: Guilford Press.

Fairburn, C. G., Agras, W. S., & Wilson, G. T. (1992). The research on the treatment of bulimia nervosa: Practical and theoretical implications. In G. H. Anderson & S. H. Kennedy (Eds.), *The biology of feast and famine: Relevance to eating disorders* (pp. 317–340). New York, NY: Academic Press.

Fairburn, C. G., & Bohn, K. (2005). Eating disorder NOS (EDNOS): An example of the troublesome 'not otherwise specified' (NOS) category in DSM-IV. *Behaviour Research and Therapy, 43*(6), 691–701.

Fairburn, C. G., & Cooper, Z. (1993). The eating disorder examination. In C. G. Fairburn & G. T. Wilson (Eds.), *Binge eating: Nature, assessment, and treatment.* (pp. 317–360). New York, NY: Guilford Press.

Fairburn, C. G., Cooper, Z., Bohn, K., O'Connor, M. E., Doll, H. A., & Palmer, R. L. (2007). The severity and status of eating disorder NOS: Implications for DSM-V. *Behavior Research and Therapy, 45,* 1705–1715.

Fairburn, C. G., Cooper, Z., & Cooper, P. J. (1986). The clinical features and maintenance of bulimia nervosa. In K. D. Brownell & J. P. Foreyt (Eds.), *Handbook of eating disorders: Physiology, psychology, and treatment of obesity, anorexia, and bulimia* (pp. 389–404). New York, NY: Basic Books.

Fairburn, C. G., Cooper, Z., Doll, H. A., & Davies, B. A. (2005). Identifying dieters who will develop an eating disorder: A prospective, population-based study. *American Journal of Psychiatry, 162,* 2249–2255.

Fairburn, C. G., Cooper, Z., Doll, H. A., Norman, P., & O'Connor, M. (2000). The natural course of bulimia nervosa and binge eating disorder in young women. *Archives of General Psychiatry, 57,* 659–665.

Fairburn, C. G., Cooper, Z., Doll, H. A., O'Connor, M. E., Bohn, K., Hawker, D. M., ... Palmer, R. L. (2009). Transdiagnostic cognitive-behavioral therapy for patients with eating disorders: A two-site trial with 60-week follow-up. *American Journal of Psychiatry, 166*(3), 311–319.

Fairburn, C. G., Cooper, Z., Doll, H. A., & Welch, S. L. (1999). Risk factors for anorexia nervosa. Three integrated case-control comparisons. *Archives of General Psychiatry, 56,* 468–476.

Fairburn, C. G., Cooper, Z., & Shafran, R. (2003). Cognitive behavior therapy for eating dis orders: A "transdiagnostic" theory and treatment. *Behaviour Research and Therapy, 41,* 509–528.

Fairburn, C. G., Cooper, Z., Shafran, R., Bohn, K., Hawker, D. M., Murphy, R., ... Straebler, S. (2008). Enhanced cognitive behavior therapy for eating disorders: The core protocol. In C. G. Fairburn (Ed.), *Cognitive Behavior Therapy and Eating Disorders.* New York, NY: Guilford Press.

Fairburn, C. G., Cooper, Z., Shafran, R., & Wilson, G. T. (2008). Eating disorders: A transdiagnostic protocol. In D. H. Barlow (Ed.), *Clinical handbook of psychological disorders: A step-by-step treatment manual* (4th ed., pp. 578–614). New York, NY: Guilford Press.

Fairburn, C. G., Cowen, P. J., & Harrison, P. J. (1999). Twin studies and the etiology of eating disorders. *International Journal of Eating Disorders, 26*(4), 349–358.

Fairburn, C. G., Doll, H. A., Welch, S. L., Hay, P. J., Davies, B. A., & O'Connor, M. E. (1998). Risk factors for binge eating disorder. *Archives of General Psychiatry, 55,* 425–432.

Fairburn, C. G., Jones, R., Peveler, R. C., Hope, R. A., & O'Connor, M. (1993). Psychotherapy and bulimia nervosa: The longer-term effects of interpersonal psychotherapy, behaviour therapy, and cognitive behaviour therapy. *Archives of General Psychiatry, 50,* 419–428.

Fairburn, C. G., Marcus, M. D., & Wilson, G. T. (1993). Cognitive behaviour therapy for binge eating and bulimia nervosa: A comprehensive treatment manual. In C. G. Fairburn & G. T. Wilson (Eds.), *Binge eating: Nature, assessment, and treatment.* New York, NY: Guilford Press.

Fairburn, C. G., Shafran, R., & Cooper, Z. (1999). A cognitive behavioural theory of anorexia nervosa. *Behaviour Research and Therapy, 37,* 1–13.

Fairburn, C. G., Stice, E., Cooper, Z., Doll, H. A., Norman, P. A., & O'Connor, M. E. (2003). Understanding persistence in bulimia nervosa: A 5-year naturalistic study. *Journal of Consulting and Clinical Psychology, 71,* 103–109.

Fairburn, C. G., Welch, S. L., Doll, S. A., Davies, B. A., & O'Connor, M. E. (1997). Risk factors for bulimia nervosa: A community-based case-control study. *Archives of General Psychiatry, 54,* 509–517.

Fairholme, C. P., Boisseau, C. L., Ellard, K. K., Ehrenreich, J. T., & Barlow, D. H. (2010). Emotions, emotion regulation, and psychological treatment: A unified perspective. In A. M. Kring & D. M. Sloan (Eds.), *Emotion regulation and psychopathology: A transdiagnostic approach to etiology and treatment* (pp. 283–309). New York, NY: Guilford Press.

Fakhoury, W., & Priebe, S. (2007). Deinstitutionalization and reinstitutionalization: Major changes in the provision of mental health-care. *Psychiatry, 6*(8), 313–316. doi:10.1016/j.mppsy.2007.05.008

Fallon, A. (1990). Culture in the mirror: Sociocultural determinants of body image. In T. F. Cash & T. Pruzinsky (Eds.), *Body images: Development, deviance, and change* (pp. 80–109). New York, NY: Guilford Press.

Fallon, A. E., & Rozin, P. (1985). Sex differences in perceptions of desirable body shape. *Journal of Abnormal Psychology, 94,* 102–105.

Fallon, B. A., Altamash, I., Qureshi, A. I., Schneier, F. R., Sanchez-Lacay, A., Vermes, D., ... Liebowitz, M. R. (2003). An open trial of fluvox-amine for hypochondriasis. *Psychosomatics, 44,* 298–303.

Falloon, I. R. H., Boyd, J. L., McGill, C. W., Williamson, M., Razani, J., Moss, H. B., ... Simpson, G.M.. (1985). Family management in the prevention of morbidity of schizophrenia. *Archives of General Psychiatry, 42,* 887–896.

Faraone, S. V., Biederman, J., Mick, E., Williamson, S., Wilens, T., Spencer, T., ... Zallen, B. (2000). Family study of girls with attention deficit hyperactivity disorder. *American Journal of Psychiatry, 157*(7), 1077–1108.

Fausto-Sterling, A. (2000a). The five sexes, revisited. *The Sciences, 40*(4), 19–23.

Fausto-Sterling, A. (2000b). *Sexing the body.* New York, NY: Basic.

Fava, G. A., Grandi, S., Rafanelli, C., Fabbri, S., & Cazzaro, M. (2000). Explanatory therapy in hypochondriasis. *Journal of Clinical Psychiatry, 61*(4), 317–322.

Fava, G. A., Grandi, S., Zielezny, M., Rafanelli, C., & Canestrari, R. (1996). Four-year outcome for cognitive behavioral treatment of residual symptoms in major depression. *American Journal of Psychiatry, 153,* 945–947.

Fava, G. A., Rafanelli, C., Grandi, S., Conti, S., & Belluardo, P. (1998). Prevention of recurrent depression with cognitive behavioral therapy: Preliminary finding. *Archives of General Psychiatry, 55*(9), 816–820.

Fava, G. A., Ruini, C., Rafanelli, C., Finos, L., Conti, S., & Grandi, S. (2004). Six-year outcome of cognitive behavior therapy for prevention of recurrent depression. *American Journal of Psychiatry, 161,* 1872–1876.

Fava, M. (2003). Can long-term treatment with antidepressant drugs worsen the course of depression? *The Journal of Clinical Psychiatry, 64,* 26–29.

Fava, M., & Rosenbaum, J. F. (1991). Suicidality and fluoxetine: Is there a relationship? *Journal of Clinical Psychiatry, 52*(3), 108–111.

Fava, M., Rush, A. J., Alpert, J. E., Balasubramani, G. K., Wisniewski, S. R., Carmin, C. N., ... Trivedi, M. H. (2008).

Difference in treatment outcome in outpatients with anxious versus non-anxious depression: a STAR*D report. *American Journal of Psychiatry, 165*(3), 342–351.

Fawzy, F. I., Cousins, N., Fawzy, N. W., Kemeny, M. E., Elashoff, R., & Morton, D. (1990). A structured psychiatric intervention for cancer patients: I. Changes over time in methods of coping and affective disturbance. *Archives of General Psychiatry, 47,* 720–728.

Fawzy, F. I., Kemeny, M. E., Fawzy, N. W., Elashoff, R., Morton, D., Cousins, N., & Fahey, J. L. (1990). A structured psychiatric intervention for cancer patients: II. Changes over time in immunological measures. *Archives of General Psychiatry, 47,* 729–735.

Fayyad, J., De Graaf, R., Kessler, R., Alonso, J., Angermeyer, M., DemyHenare, K., ... Jin, R. (2007). Cross-national prevalence and correlates of adult attention-deficit hyperactivity disorder. *British Journal of Psychiatry, 190,* 402–409.

Fazel, S., Khosla, V., Doll, H., & Geddes, J. (2008). The prevalence of mental disorders among the homeless in Western countries: Systematic review and meta-regression analysis. *PLoS Medicine, 5*(12), e225.

Fearing, M. A., & Inouye, S. K. (2009). Delirium. In D. G. Blazer & D. C. Steffens (Eds.), *The American Psychiatric Publishing textbook of geriatric psychiatry* (4th ed., pp. 229–242). Arlington, VA: American Psychiatric Publishing.

Fears, S. C., Mathews, C. A., & Freimer, N. B. (2009). Genetic linkage analysis of psychiatric disorders. In B. J. Sadock, V. A. Sadock, & P. Ruiz (Eds.), *Kaplan & Sadock's comprehensive textbook of psychiatry* (9th ed., Vol. I, pp. 320–333). Philadelphia, PA: Lippincott Williams & Wilkins.

Federoff, J. P., Fishell, A., & Federoff, B. (1999). A case series of women evaluated for paraphilic sexual disorders. *Canadian Journal of Human Sexuality, 8*(2), 127–140.

Feingold, B. F. (1975). *Why your child is hyperactive.* New York, NY: Random House.

Feinstein, C., & Phillips, J. M. (2006). Developmental disorders of communication, motor skills, and learning. In M. K. Dulcan & J. M. Wiener (Eds.), *Essentials of child and adolescent psychiatry* (pp. 203–231). Washington, DC: American Psychiatric Publishing.

Feldman, H. A., Goldstein, I., Hatzichristou, D. G., Krane, R. J., & McKunlay, J. B. (1994). Impotence and its medical and psychosocial correlates: Results of the Massachusetts Male Aging Study. *Journal of Urology, 151,* 54–61.

Feldman, M. B., & Meyer, I. H. (2007). Childhood abuse and eating disorders in gay and bisexual men. *International Journal of Eating Disorders, 40*(5), 418–423.

Ferber, R. (1985). *Solve your child's sleep problems.* New York, NY: Simon & Schuster.

Ferguson, C. (2010a). A meta-analysis of normal and disordered personality across the life span. *Journal of Personality and Social Psychology, 98*(4), 659–667.

Ferguson, C. (2010b). Genetic contributions to antisocial personality and behavior: A meta-analytic review from an evolutionary perspective. *The Journal of Social Psychology, 150*(2), 160–180.

Ferguson, S. G., & Shiffman, S. (2009). The relevance and treatment of cue-induced cravings in tobacco dependence. *Journal of Substance Abuse Treatment, 36*(3), 235–243.

Fergusson, D., Doucette, D., Glass, K., Shapiro, S., Healy, D., Herber, P., & Hutton, B. (2005). Association between suicide attempts and selective serotonin reuptake inhibitors: Systematic review of randomized controlled trials. *BMJ, 330,* 396–402.

Fergusson, D., Horwood, J., Ridder, E., & Beautrais, A. (2005). Subthreshold depression in adolescence and mental health outcomes in adulthood. *Archives General of Psychiatry, 62,* 66–72.

Fergusson, D., & Woodward, L. J. (2002). Mental health, educational, and social role outcomes of adolescents with depression. *Archives of General Psychiatry, 59,* 225–231.

Fernandez, F., Levy, J. K., Lachar, B. L., & Small, G. W. (1995). The management of depression and anxiety in the elderly. *Journal of Clinical Psychiatry, 56*(Suppl. 2), 20–29.

Ferreira, C. (2000). Serial killers: Victims of compulsion or masters of control? In D. H. Fishbein (Ed.), *The science, treatment, and prevention of antisocial behaviors: Application to the criminal justice system* (pp. 15-1–15-18). Kingston, NJ: Civic Research Institute.

Ferri, C. P., Prince, M., Brayne, C., Brodaty, H., Fratiglioni, L., Ganguli, M., ... Scazufca, M. (2005). Global prevalence of dementia: A Delphi consensus study. *The Lancet, 366*(9503), 2112–2117.

Ferster, C. B. (1961). Positive reinforcement and behavioral deficits of autistic children. *Child Development, 32,* 437–456.

Ferster, C. B., & Skinner, B. F. (1957). *Schedules of reinforcement.* New York, NY: Appleton-Century-Crofts.

Fertuck, E. A., Jekal, A., Song, I., Wyman, B., Morris, M. C., Wilson, S. T., ... Stanley, B. (2009). Enhanced 'Reading the Mind in the Eyes' in borderline personality disorder compared to healthy controls. *Psychological Medicine, 39*(12), 1979–1988.

Feuerstein, M., Labbe, E. E., & Kuczmierczyk, A. R. (1986). *Health psychology: A psychobiological perspective.* New York, NY: Plenum Press.

Feusner, J., Phillips, K, & Stein, D. (2010). Olfactory reference syndrome: Issues for DSM-V. *Depression and Anxiety.*

Ficks, C., & Waldman, I. (2009). Gene–environment interactions in attention-deficit/hyperactivity disorder. *Current Psychiatry Reports, 11*(5), 387–392. doi:10.1007/s11920-009-0058-1

Field, A. E., Camargo, C. A., Taylor, C. B., Bekey, C. S., Roberts, S. B., & Colditz, G. A. (2001). Peer, parent, and media influences on the development of weight concerns and frequent dieting among preadolescent and adolescent girls and boys. *Pediatrics, 107,* 54–60.

Field, A. E., Cheung, L., Wolf, A. M., Herzog, D. B., Gortmaker, S. L., & Colditz, G. A. (1999). Exposure to the mass media and weight concerns among girls. *Pediatrics, 103,* e36.

Fields, B. W., & Fristad, M. A. (2009). Assessment of childhood bipolar disorder. *Clinical Psychology: Science and Practice, 16*(2), 166–181.

Fincham, F. D., Beach, S. R. H., Harold, G. T., & Osborne, L. N. (1997). Marital satisfaction and depression: Different causal relationships for men and women? *Psychological Science, 8*(5), 351–357.

Fineberg, N. A., Potenza, M. N., Chamberlain, S. R., Berlin, H. A., Menzies, L., Bechara, A., ... Hollander, E. (2010). Probing compulsive and impulsive behaviors, from animal models to endophenotypes: A narrative review. *Neuropsychopharmacology, 35*(3), 591–604.

Finkenbine, R., & Miele, V. J. (2004). Globus hystericus: A brief review. *General Hospital Psychiatry, 26,* 78–82.

Finney, M. L., Stoney, C. M., & Engebretson, T. O. (2002). Hostility and anger expression in African American and European American men is associated with cardiovascular and lipid reactivity. *Psychophysiology, 39,* 340–349.

First, M. B., Bell, C. C., Cuthbert, B., Krystal, J. H., Malison, R., Offord, D. R., ... Wisner, K. L. (2002). Personality disorders and relational disorders: A research agenda for addressing crucial gaps in DSM. In D. J. Kupfer, M. B. First, & D. A. Regier (Eds.), *A research agenda for DSM-V* (pp. 123–199). Washington, DC: American Psychiatric Association.

First, M. B., & Pincus, H. A. (2002). The DSM-IV text revision: Rationale and potential impact on clinical practice. *Psychiatric Services, 53,* 288–292.

Fischer, M. (1971). Psychoses in the offspring of schizophrenic monozygotic twins and their normal co-twins. *British Journal of Psychiatry, 118,* 43–52.

Fishbain, D. A. (1987). Kleptomania as risk-taking behavior in response to depression. *American Journal of Psychotherapy, 41,* 598–603.

Fisher, P. L., & Wells, A. (2009). Psychological models of worry and generalized anxiety disorder. In M. M. Antony & M. B. Stein (Eds.), *Oxford handbook of anxiety and related disorders* (pp. 225–237). New York, NY: Oxford University Press.

Fiske, A., Wetherell, J. L., & Gatz, M. (2009). Depression in older adults. *Annual Review of Clinical Psychology, 5,* 363–389.

Fitts, S. N., Gibson, P., Redding, C. A., & Deiter, P. J. (1989). Body dysmorphic disorder: Implications for its validity as a DSM-III-R clinical syndrome. *Psychological Reports, 64,* 655–658.

Fitzgerald, P., Benitez, J., de Castella, A., Daskalakis, Z., Brown, T., & Kulkarni, J. (2006). A randomized controlled trial of sequential bilateral repetitive transcranial magnetic stimulation for treatment-resistant depression. *American Journal of Psychiatry, 163,* 88–94.

Fitzgerald, P. B., Brown, T. L., Marston, N. A., Daskalakis, J., De Castella, A., & Kulkarni, J. (2003). Transcranial magnetic stimulation in the treatment of depression: A double-blind, placebo-controlled trial. *Archives of General Psychiatry, 60,* 1002–1008.

Flaherty, J. H., Rudolph, J., Shay, K., Kamholz, B., Boockvar, K. S., Shaughnessy, M., ... Edes, T. (2007). Delirium is a serious and under-recognized problem: Why assessment of mental status should be the sixth vital sign. *Jour-*

nal of the American Medical Directors Association, 8(5), 273–275.

Flegal, K. M., Carroll, M. D., Ogden, C. L., & Curtin, L. R. (2010). Prevalence and trends in obesity among US adults, 1999–2008. JAMA: Journal of the American Medical Association, 303(3), 235–241.

Flegal, K. M., Graubard, B. I., Williamson, D. F., & Gail, M. H. (2005). Excess deaths associated with underweight, overweight, and obesity. JAMA: Journal of the American Medical Association, 293, 1861–1867.

Fletcher, J. M., Lyon, G. R., Fuchs, L. S., & Barnes, M. A. (2007). Learning disabilities: From identification to intervention. New York, NY: Guilford Press.

Fliers, E., Vermeulen, S., Rijsdijk, F., Altink, M., Buschgens, C., Rommelse, N., ... Franke, B. (2009). ADHD and poor motor performance from a family genetic perspective. Journal of the American Academy of Child & Adolescent Psychiatry, 48(1), 25–34.

Flint, A. (1994). Epidemiology and comorbidity of anxiety disorders in the elderly. American Journal of Psychiatry, 151, 640–649.

Flint, J. (2009). Molecular genetics. In M. G. Gelder, N. C. Andreasen, J. J. Lopez-Ibor, Jr., & J. R. Geddes (Eds.), New Oxford textbook of psychiatry (2nd ed., Vol. 1, pp. 222–233). Oxford, UK: Oxford University Press.

Foa, E. B., Jenike, M., Kozak, M. J., Joffe, R., Baer, L., Pauls, D., ...Turner, S. M. (1996). Obsessive-compulsive disorder. In T. A. Widiger, A. J. Frances, H. A. Pincus, M. R. Ross, M. B. First, & W. W. Davis (Eds.), DSM-IV sourcebook (Vol. 2, pp. 549– 576). Washington, DC: American Psychiatric Association.

Foa, E. B., Liebowitz, M. R., Kozak, M. J., Davies, S., Campeas, R., Franklin, M. E., ...Tu, X. (2005). Randomized, placebo-controlled trial of exposure and ritual prevention, clomipramine, and their combination in the treatment of obsessive-compulsive disorder. American Journal of Psychiatry, 162, 151–161.

Fogelson, D. L., Nuechterlein, K. H., Asarnow, R. A., Payne, D. L., Subotnik, K. L., Jacobson, K. C., ... Kendler, K. S. (2007). Avoidant personality disorder is a separable schizophrenia-spectrum personality disorder even when controlling for the presence of paranoid and schizotypal personality disorders: The UCLA family study. Schizophrenia Research, 91, 192–199.

Foley, E., Baillie, A., Huxter, M., Price, M., & Sinclair, E. (2010). Mindfulness-based cognitive therapy for individuals whose lives have been affected by cancer: A randomized controlled-trial. Journal of Consulting and Clinical Psychology, 78, 72–79.

Folks, D. G., Ford, C. U., & Regan, W. M. (1984). Conversion symptoms in a general hospital. Psychosomatics, 25(4), 285–295.

Follette, W. C., & Houts, A. C. (1996). Models of scientific progress and the role of theory in taxonomy development: A case study of the DSM. Journal of Consulting and Clinical Psychology, 64(6), 1120–1132.

Folsom, D. P., Hawthorne, W., Lindamer, L., Gilmer, T., Bailey, A., Golshan, S., ... Jeste, D. V. 2005). Prevalence and risk factors for homelessness and utilization of mental health services among 10,340 patients with serious mental illness in a large pub-

lic mental health system. American Journal of Psychiatry, 162, 370–376.

Ford, C., & Beach, F. (1951). Patterns of sexual behavior. New York, NY: Harper & Row.

Ford, C. V. (1985). Conversion disorders: An overview. Psychosomatics, 26, 371–383.

Ford, H., & Cortoni, F. (2008). Sexual deviance in females: Assessment and treatment. In D. R. Laws & W. T. O'Donohue (Eds.), Sexual deviance: Theory, assessment, and treatment (2nd ed., pp. 508–526). New York, NY: Guilford Press.

Ford, J., Roach, B., Jorgensen, K., Turner, J., Brown, G., Notestine, R., ... Lauriello, J. (2009). Tuning in to the voices: A multisite fMRI study of auditory hallucinations. Schizophrenia Bulletin, 35(1), 58.

Ford, M. R., & Widiger, T. A. (1989). Sex bias in the diagnosis of histrionic and antisocial personality disorders. Journal of Consulting and Clinical Psychology, 57, 301–305.

Fordyce, W. E. (1976). Behavioral methods in chronic pain and illness. St. Louis, MO: Mosby.

Fordyce, W. E. (1988). Pain and suffering: A reappraisal. American Psychologist, 43(4), 276–283.

Foti, D. J., Kotov, R., Guey, L. T., & Bromet, E. J. (2010). Cannabis use and the course of schizophrenia: 10-year follow-up after first hospitalization. American Journal of Psychiatry, 167(8), 987–993. Retrieved from http://ajp .psychiatryonline.org/cgi/content/abstract/appi.ajp.2010 .09020189v1. doi:10.1176/appi.ajp .2010.09020189

Fowles, D. C. (1988). Psychophysiology and psychopathy: A motivational approach. Psychophysiology, 25, 373–391.

Fowles, D. C. (1993). A motivational theory of psychopathology. In W. Spaulding (Ed.), Nebraska symposium on motivation: Integrated views of motivation, cognition, and emotion (Vol. 41, pp. 181–238). Lincoln, NE: University of Nebraska Press.

Fox, E., & Damjanovic, L. (2006) The eyes are sufficient to produce a threat superiority effect. Emotion, 6, 534–539.

Foy, D. W., Resnick, H. S., Sipprelle, R. C., & Carroll, E. M. (1987). Premilitary, military, and postmilitary factors in the development of combat related posttraumatic stress disorder. The Behavior Therapist, 10, 3–9.

Foy, D. W., Sipprelle, R. C., Rueger, D. B., & Carroll, E. M. (1984). Etiology of posttraumatic stress disorder in Vietnam veterans: Analysis of premilitary, military, and combat exposure influences. Journal of Consulting and Clinical Psychology, 52, 79–87.

Frances, A. (2009). Whither DSM-V? British Journal of Psychiatry, 195, 391–392.

Frances, A., & Widiger, T. A. (1986). Methodological issues in personality disorder diagnosis. In T. Millon & G. L. Klerman (Eds.), Contemporary directions in psychopathology: Toward the DSM-IV (pp. 381–400). New York, NY: Guilford Press.

Francis, D., Diorio, J., Liu, D., & Meaney, M. J. (1999). Nongenomic transmission across generations of maternal behavior and stress responses in the rat. Science, 286, 1155–1158.

Francis, D. D., Diorio, J., Plotsky, P. M., & Meaney, M. J. (2002). Environmental enrichment reverses the effects of maternal

separation on stress reactivity. Journal of Neuroscience, 22, 7840–7843.

Frank, E., Anderson, C., & Rubinstein, D. (1978). Frequency of sexual dysfunction in "normal" couples. New England Journal of Medicine, 299, 111–115.

Frank, E., Hlastala, S., Ritenour, A., Houck, P., Tu, X. M., Monk, T. H., ... Kupfer, D. J. (1997). Inducing lifestyle regularity in recovering bipolar disorder patients: Results from the Maintenance Therapies in Bipolar Disorder Protocol. Biological Psychiatry, 41, 1165–1173.

Frank, E., Kupfer, D. J., Perel, J. M., Cornes, C., Jarrett, D. B., Mallinger, A. G., ... Grochocinski, V. J. (1990). Three-year outcomes for maintenance therapies in recurrent depression. Archives of General Psychiatry, 47(12), 1093–1099.

Frank, E., Kupfer, D., Thase, M., Mallinger, A., Swartz, H., Eagiolini, A., ... Monk, T. (2005). Two-year outcomes for interpersonal and social rhythm therapy in individuals with bipolar I disorder. Archives of General Psychiatry, 62, 996–1004.

Frank, E., Swartz, H. A., Mallinger, A. G., Thase, M. E., Weaver, E. V., & Kupfer, D. J. (1999). Adjunctive psychotherapy for bipolar disorder: Effects of changing treatment modality. Journal of Abnormal Psychology, 108(4), 579–587.

Frankel, E. B., & Gold, S. (2007). Principles and practices of early intervention. In I. Brown & M. Percy (Eds.), A comprehensive guide to intellectual & developmental disabilities (pp. 451–466). Baltimore, MD: Paul H. Brookes.

Franklin, D. (1990). Hooked–Not hooked: Why isn't everyone an addict? Health, 4(6) 39–52.

Franklin, J. E., & Frances, R. J. (1999). Alcohol and other psychoactive substance use disorders. In R. E. Hales, S. C. Yudofsky, & J. A. Talbott (Eds.), Textbook of psychiatry (3rd ed., pp. 363–423). Washington, DC: American Psychiatric Press.

Franklin, M. E., & Foa, E. B. (2008). Obsessive-compulsive disorder. In D. H. Barlow (Ed.), Clinical handbook of psychological disorders: A step-by-step treatment manual (4th ed., pp. 164–215). New York, NY: Guilford Press.

Franko, D. L., Wonderlich, S. A., Little, D., & Herzog, D. B. (2004). Diagnosis and classification of eating disorders. In J. K. Thompson (Ed.), Handbook of eating disorders and obesity (pp. 58–80). New York, NY: John Wiley.

Frasure-Smith, N., & Lesperance, F. (2005). Depression and coronary heart disease: Complex synergism of mind, body, and environment. Current Directions in Psychological Science, 14, 39–43.

Frasure-Smith, N., Lesperance, F., Juneau, M., Talajic, M., & Bourassa, M. G. (1999). Gender, depression, and one-year prognosis after myocardial infarction. Psychosomatic Medicine, 61, 26–37.

Fratiglioni, L., Grut, M., Forsell, Y., Viitanen, M., Grafstrom, M., Holmen, K., ... Winblad, B. (1991). Prevalence of Alzheimer's disease and other dementias in an elderly urban population: Relationship with age, sex and education. Neurology, 41, 1886–1892.

Fratiglioni, L., Winblad, B., & von Strauss, E. (2007). Prevention of Alzheimer's disease and dementia: Major findings from the Kungsholmen Project. *Physiology & Behavior, 92*(1–2), 98–104.

Fredrikson, M., Annas, P., & Wik, G. (1997). Parental history, aversive exposure, and the development of snake and spider phobia in women. *Behavior Research and Therapy, 35,* 23–28.

Fredrikson, M., & Matthews, K. A. (1990). Cardiovascular responses to behavioral stress and hypertension: A meta-analytic review. *Annals of Behavioral Medicine, 12*(1), 30–39.

Freedman, M., King, J., & Kennedy, E. (2001). Popular diets: A scientific review. *Obesity Research, 9*(Suppl.), S1–S38.

Freeman, A., Pretzer, J., Fleming, B., & Simon, K. M. (1990). *Clinical applications of cognitive therapy*. New York, NY: Plenum Press.

Freeman, E., Sammel, M., Lin, H., & Nelson, D. (2006). Associations of hormones and menopausal status with depressed mood in women with no history of depression. *Archive General Psychiatry, 63,* 375–382.

Freud, S. (1957). Mourning and melancholia. In J. Strachey (Ed. and Trans.), *The standard edition of the complete psychological works of Sigmund Freud* (Vol. 14). London, UK: Hogarth Press. (Original work published 1917).

Freund, K., Seto, M. C., & Kuban, M. (1996). Two types of fetishism. *Behaviour Research and Therapy, 34,* 687–694.

Friedberg, F., & Sohl, S. (2009). Cognitive-behavior therapy in chronic fatigue syndrome: Is improvement related to physical activity? *Journal of Clinical Psychology, 65,* 423–442.

Friedl, M. C., & Draijer, N. (2000). Dissociative disorders in Dutch psychiatric inpatients. *American Journal of Psychiatry, 157*(6), 1012–1013.

Friedman, J. M. (2009). Obesity: Causes and control of excess body fat. *Nature, 459*(7245), 340–342.

Friedman, M., & Rosenman, R. H. (1959). Association of specific overt behavior pattern with blood and cardiovascular findings. *JAMA: Journal of the American Medical Association, 169,* 1286.

Friedman, M., & Rosenman, R. H. (1974). *Type A behavior and your heart*. New York, NY: Knopf.

Friedman, M. J. (2009). Phenomenology of posttraumatic stress disorder and acute stress disorder. In M. M. Antony & M. B. Stein (Eds.), *Oxford handbook of anxiety and related disorders* (pp. 65–72). New York, NY: Oxford University Press.

Friedman, S., Paradis, C. M., & Hatch, M. (1994). Characteristics of African American and white patients with panic disorder and agoraphobia. *Hospital & Community Psychiatry, 45,* 798–803.

Frohlich, C., Jacobi, F., & Wittchen, H. (2006). DSM-IV pain disorder in the general population: An exploration of the structure and threshold of medically unexplained pain symptoms. *European Archives of Psychiatry and Clinical Neuroscience, 256,* 187–196.

Fromm-Reichmann, F. (1948). Notes on the development of treatment of schizophren-

ics by psychoanalytic psychotherapy. *Psychiatry, 11,* 263–273.

Frost, R. O., Steketee, G., & Williams, L. (2002). Compulsive buying, compulsive hoarding, and obsessive-compulsive disorder. *Behavior Therapy, 33,* 201–214.

Fryar, C., Hirsch, R., Porter, K., Kottiri, B., Brody, D., & Louis, T. (2007). *Drug use and sexual behaviors reported by adults: United States, 1999–2002* (Advance data from Vital and Health Statistics, No. 384). Hyattsville, MD: National Center for Health Statistics.

Fu, S. Y., Anderson, D., & Courtney, M. (2003). Cross-cultural menopausal experience: Comparison of Australian and Taiwanese women. *Nursing and Health Sciences, 5,* 77-84.

Fugl-Meyer, A. R., & Sjogren Fugl-Meyer, K. (1999). Sexual disabilities, problems, and satisfaction in 18–74-year-old Swedes. *Scandinavian Journal of Sexology, 3,* 79–105.

Fukuda, K., Straus, S. E., Hickie, I., Sharpe, M. B., Dobbins, J. G., & Komaroff, A. L. (1994). Chronic fatigue syndrome: A comprehensive approach to its diagnosis and management. *Annals of Internal Medicine, 121,* 953–959.

Fullana, M. A., Mataix-Cols, D., Caspi, A., Harrington, H., Grisham, J. R., Moffitt, T. E., & Poulton, R. (2009). Obsessions and compulsions in the community: Prevalence, interference, help-seeking, developmental stability, and co-occurring psychiatric conditions. *American Journal of Psychiatry, 166*(3), 329–336.

Furberg, H., Olarte, M., Afari, N., Goldberg, J., Buchwald, D., & Sullivan, P. (2005). The prevalence of self-reported chronic fatigue in a U.S. twin registry. *Journal of Psychosomatic Research, 59,* 283–290.

Furnham, A., & Wong, L. (2007). A cross-cultural comparison of British and Chinese beliefs about the causes, behaviour manifestations, and treatment of schizophrenia. *Psychiatry Research, 151,* 123–138.

Furr, J. M., Tiwari, S., Suveg, C., & Kendall, P. C. (2009). Anxiety disorders in children and adolescents. In M. M. Antony & M. B. Stein (Eds.), *Oxford handbook of anxiety and related disorders* (pp. 636–656). New York, NY: Oxford University Press.

Fusar-Poli, P., & Politi, P. (2008). Paul Eugen Bleuler and the birth of schizophrenia (1908). *American Journal of Psychiatry, 165*(11), 1407. doi:10.1176/appi.ajp .2008.08050714

Fushimi, N., Wang, L., Ebisui, S., Cai, S., & Mikage, M. (2008). Studies of ephedra plants in Asia. Part 4.1. Morphological differences between Ephedra sinica Stapf and E. intermedia Schrenk et C.A.Meyer, and the botanical origin of Mahuang produced in Qinghai Province. *Journal of Traditional Medicines, 25*(3), 61–66.

Fyer, A., Liebowitz, M., Gorman, J., Compeas, R., Levin, A., Davies, S., et al. (1987). Discontinuation of alprazolam treatment in panic patients. *American Journal of Psychiatry, 144,* 303–308.

Fyer, A. J., Mannuzza, S., Chapman, T. F., Liebowitz, M. R., & Klein, D. F. (1993). A direct interview family study of social phobia. *Archives of General Psychiatry, 50,* 286–293.

Fyer, A. J., Mannuzza, S., Gallops, M. S., Martin, L. Y., Aaronson, C., Gorman, J. M., et al. (1990). Familial transmission of simple phobias and fears: A preliminary report. *Archives of General Psychiatry, 47,* 252–256.

Gagnon, J. H. (1990). The explicit and implicit use of the scripting perspective in sex research. *Annual Review of Sex Research, 1,* 1–43.

Galea, S., Ahern, J., Resnick, H., Kilpatrick, D., Bucuvalas, M., Gold, J., et al. (2002). Psychological sequelae of the September 11 terrorist attacks in New York City. *New England Journal of Medicine, 346,* 982–987.

Gallagher-Thompson, D., & Osgood, N. J. (1997). Suicide later in life. *Behavior Therapy, 28,* 23–41.

Gallagher-Thompson, D., Rabinowitz, Y., Tang, P., Tse, C., Kwo, E., Hsu, S., ... Thompson, L. W. (2006). Recruiting Chinese Americans for dementia caregiver intervention research: Suggestions for success. *American Journal of Geriatric Psych, 14*(8), 676.

Gallup, G. G., & Frederick, D. A. (2010). The science of sex appeal: An evolutionary perspective. *Review of General Psychology, 14,* 240–250.

Gansler, D. A., McLaughlin, N. C., Iguchi, L., Jerram, M., Moore, D. W., Bhadelia, R., et al. (2009). A multivariate approach to aggression and the orbital frontal cortex in psychiatric patients. *Psychiatry Research: Neuroimaging, 171*(3), 145–154.

Gao, Y., Raine, A., Venables, P. H., Dawson, M. E., & Mednick, S. A. (2010). Association of poor childhood fear conditioning and adult crime. *American Journal of Psychiatry, 167*(1), 56–60. doi:10.1176/appi .ajp.2009.09040499

Garb, H. N., Wood, J. M., Lilienfeld, S. O., & Nezworski, M. T. (2005). Roots of the Rorschach controversy. *Clinical Psychology Review, 25*(1), 97–118.

Garber, J., & Carter, J. S. (2006). Major depression. In R. T. Ammerman (Ed.), *Comprehensive handbook of personality and psychopathology. Vol. III: Child psychopathology* (pp. 165– 216). Hoboken, NJ: John Wiley & Sons.

Garber, J., Clarke, G. N., Weersing, V. R., Beardslee, W. R., Brent, D. A., Gladstone, T. R., ... Iyengar, S. (2009). Prevention of depression in at-risk adolescents: A randomized controlled trial. *JAMA: Journal of the American Medical Association, 301*(21), 2215–2224.

Garber, J., Gallerani, C. M., & Frankel, S. A. (2009). Depression in children. In I. H. Gotlib & C. L. Hammen (Eds.), *Handbook of depression* (2nd ed., pp. 405–443). New York, NY: Guilford Press.

Garcia, J., McGowan, B. K., & Green, K. F. (1972). Biological constraints on conditioning. In A. H. Black & W. F. Prokasy (Eds.), *Classical conditioning II: Current research and theory*. New York, NY: Appleton-Century-Crofts.

Garfield, A. F., & Zigler, E. (1993). Adolescent suicide prevention: Current research and social policy implications. *American Psychologist, 48*(2), 169–182.

Garfinkel, P. E. (1992). Evidence in support of attitudes to shape and weight as a diagnostic criterion of bulimia nervosa. *International Journal of Eating Disorders, 11*(4), 321–325.

Garfinkel, P. E., Moldofsky, H., & Garner, D. M. (1979). The heterogeneity of anorexia nervosa: Bulimia as a distinct subgroup. *Archives of General Psychiatry, 37,* 1036–1040.

Garlow, S., Boone, E., Li, W., Owens, M., & Nemeroff, C. (2005). Genetic analysis of the hypothalamic corticotrophin releasing factor system. *Endocrinology, 146,* 2362–2368.

Garlow, S., & Nemeroff, C. B. (2003). Neurobiology of depressive disorders. In R. J. Davidson, K. R. Scherer, & H. H. Goldsmith (Eds.)., *Handbook of affective sciences* (pp. 1021–1043). New York, NY: Oxford University Press.

Garmezy, N., & Rutter, M. (Eds.) (1983). *Stress, coping, and development in children.* New York, NY: McGraw-Hill.

Garner, D. M., & Fairburn, C. G. (1988). Relationship between anorexia nervosa and bulimia nervosa: Diagnostic implications. In D. M. Garner & P. E. Garfinkel (Eds.), *Diagnostic issues in anorexia nervosa and bulimia nervosa.* New York, NY: Brunner/Mazel.

Garner, D. M., Garfinkel, P. E., Rockert, W., & Olmsted, M. P. (1987). A prospective study of eating disturbances in the ballet. Ninth World Congress of the International College of Psychosomatic Medicine, Sydney, Australia. *Psychotherapy and Psychosomatics, 48,* 170–175.

Garrity, A. G., Pearlson, G. D., McKiernan, K., Lloyd, D., Kiehl, K. A., & Calhoun, V. D. (2007). Aberrant "default mode" functional connectivity in schizophrenia. *American Journal of Psychiatry, 164,* 450–457.

Gassen, M. D., Pietz, C. A., Spray, B. J., & Denney, R. L. (2007). Accuracy of Megargee's Criminal Offender Infrequency (FC) Scale in detecting malingering among forensic examinees. *Criminal Justice and Behavior, 34,* 493–504.

Gatchel, R. (2005). *Clinical essentials of pain management.* Washington, DC: American Psychological Association.

Gatchel, R. J., & Dersh, J. (2002). Psychological disorders and chronic pain: Are there cause-and- effect relationships? In D. C. Turk & R. J. Gatchel (Eds.), *Psychological approaches to pain management: A practitioner's handbook* (2nd ed., pp. 30–51). New York, NY: Guilford Press.

Gatchel, R. J., & Epker, J. (1999). Psychosocial predictors of chronic pain and response to treatment. In R. J. Gatchel & D. C. Turk (Eds.), *Psychosocial factors in pain: Critical perspectives* (pp. 412– 434). New York, NY: Guilford Press.

Gatchel, R. J., Peng, Y. B., Peters, M. L., Fuchs, P. N., & Turk, D. C. (2007). The biopsychosocial approach to chronic pain: Scientific advances and future directions. *Psychological Bulletin, 133,* 581–624.

Gatchel, R. J., Polatin, P. B., & Kinney, R. K. (1995). Predicting outcome of chronic back pain using clinical predictors of psychopathology: A prospective analysis. *Health Psychology, 14,* 415–420.

Gatchel, R. J., & Turk, D. C. (Eds.) (1999). *Psychosocial factors in pain: Critical perspectives.* New York, NY: Guilford Press.

Gatz, M. (2007). Genetics, dementia, and the elderly. *Current Directions in Psychological Science, 16,* 123–127.

Gavett, B., Stern, R., Cantu, R., Nowinski, C., & McKee, A. (2010). Mild traumatic brain injury: A risk factor for neurodegeneration. *Alzheimer's Research & Therapy, 2*(3), 18.

Gaw, A. C. (2008). Cultural issues. In R. E. Hales, S. C. Yudofsky, & G. O. Gabbard (Eds.), *The American Psychiatric Publishing textbook of psychiatry* (5th ed., pp. 1529–1547). Arlington, VA: American Psychiatric Publishing, Inc.

Ge, X., Conger, R., & Elder, G. (1996). Coming of age too early: Pubertal influences on girls' vulnerability to psychological distress. *Child Development, 67,* 3386–3400.

Gearhart, J. P. (1989). Total ablation of the penis after circumcision electrocautery: A method of management and long term follow-up. *Journal of Urology, 42,* 789–801.

Geer, J. H., Morokoff, P., & Greenwood, P. (1974). Sexual arousal in women: The development of a measurement device for vaginal blood volume. *Archives of Sexual Behavior, 3,* 559–564.

Gelernter, J., & Stein, M. B. (2009). Heritability and genetics of anxiety disorders. In M. M. Antony & M. B. Stein (Eds.), *Oxford handbook of anxiety and related disorders.* Oxford, UK: Oxford University Press.

Geller, B., Cooper, T. B., Graham, D. L., Fetaer, H. M., Marsteller, F. A., & Wells, J. M. (1992). Pharmacokinetically designed double blind placebo controlled study of nortriptyline in 6–12-year-olds with major depressive disorder: Outcome: Nortriptyline and hydroxy-nortriptyline plasma levels; EKG, BP and side effect measurements. *Journal of the American Academy of Child and Adolescent Psychiatry, 31,* 33–44.

Gellis, L. A., & Lichstein, K. L. (2009). Sleep hygiene practices of good and poor sleepers in the united states: An Internet-based study. *Behavior Therapy, 40*(1), 1–9.

Gendron, M., & Barrett, F. L. (2009). Reconstructing the past: A century of ideas about emotion in psychology. *Emotion Review, 1*(4), 316–339.

George, M. S., Lisanby, S. H., & Sakheim, H. A. (1999). Transcranial magnetic stimulation. *Archives of General Psychiatry, 56,* 300–311.

Geraerts, E., Lindsay, D. S., Merckelbach, H., Jelicic, M., Raymaekers, L., Arnold, M. M., & Schooler, J. S. (2009). Cognitive mechanisms underlying recovered memory experiences of childhood sexual abuse. *Psychological Science, 20,* 92–98.

Geraerts, E., & McNally, R. (2008). Forgetting unwanted memories: Directed forgetting and thought suppression methods. *Acta psychologica, 127*(3), 614–622.

Gerard, D. L. (1997). Chiarugi and Pinel considered: Soul's brain/person's mind. *Journal of the History of the Behavioral Sciences, 33*(4), 381–403.

Gershon, E. S. (1990). Genetics. In F. K. Goodwin & K. R. Jamison (Eds.), *Manic-depressive illness* (pp. 373–401). New York, NY: Oxford University Press.

Gershon, E. S., Kelsoe, J. R., Kendler, K. S., & Watson, J. D. (2001). It's time to search for susceptibility genes for major mental illnesses. *Science, 294,* 5.

Gerstein, D. R., Volberg, R. A., Toce, M. T., Harwood, H., Johnson, R. A., & Bule, T.,

... Tucker, A. (1999). *Gambling impact and behavior study: Report to the national gambling impact study commission.* Chicago, IL: National Opinion Research Center at the University of Chicago.

Gibbons, R., Hur, K., Bhaumik, D., & Mann, J. (2006). The relationship between antidepressant prescription rates and rate of early adolescent suicide. *American Journal of Psychiatry, 163,* 1898–1904.

Giedke, H., & Schwarzler, F. (2002). Therapeutic use of sleep deprivation in depression. *Sleep Medicine Reviews, 6,* 361–377.

Giesbrecht, T., Lynn, S. J., Lilienfeld, S. O., & Merckelbach, H. (2008). Cognitive processes in dissociation: An analysis of core theoretical assumptions. *Psychological Bulletin, 134*(5), 617–647.

Giesbrecht, T., Smeets, T., Leppink, J., Jelicic, M., & Merckelbach, H. (2007). Acute dissociation after 1 night of sleep loss. *Journal of Abnormal Psychology, 116*(3), 599–606.

Gifford, S. M. (1994). The change of life, the sorrow of life: Menopause, bad blood and cancer among Italian-Australian working class women. *Culture, Medicine, and Psychiatry, 18,* 299–319.

Gillberg, C. (1984). Infantile autism and other childhood psychoses in a Swedish urban region: Epidemiological aspects. *Journal of Child Psychology and Psychiatry, 25,* 35–43.

Gillespie, C. F., & Nemeroff, C. B. (2007). Corticotropin-releasing factor and the psychobiology of early-life stress. *Current Directions in Psychological Science, 16*(2), 85–89.

Gillham, J. E., Reivich, K. J., Jaycox, L. H., & Seligman, M. E. P. (1995). Prevention of depressive symptoms in schoolchildren: Two-year follow-up. *Psychological Science, 6*(6), 343–351.

Gillin, J. C. (1993). Clinical sleep–wake disorders in psychiatric practice: Dyssomnias. In D. L. Dunner (Ed.), *Current psychiatric therapy* (pp. 373–380). Philadelphia, PA: W. B. Saunders.

Gilmore, J. H. (2010). Understanding what causes schizophrenia: A developmental perspective. *American Journal of Psychiatry, 167*(1), 8–10. doi:10.1176/appi.ajp.2009.09111588

Ginovart, N., & Kapur, S. (2010). Dopamine receptors and the treatment of schizophrenia. In K. A. Neve (Ed.), *The dopamine receptors* (2nd ed., pp. 431–477). New York, NY: Humana Press.

Girault, J. A., & Greengard, P. (2004). The neurobiology of dopamine signaling. *Archives of Neurology, 61*(5), 641–644.

Girirajan, S. (2009). Parental-age effects in Down syndrome. *Journal of Genetics, 88*(1), 1–7. doi:10.1007/s12041-009-0001-6

Gitlin, M. J. (2009). Pharmacotherapy and other somatic treatments for depression. In I. H. Gotlib & C. L. Hammen (Eds.), *Handbook of depression* (2nd ed., pp. 554–585). New York, NY: Guilford Press.

Gitlin, M. J., Swendsen, J., Heller, T. L., & Hammen, C. (1995). Relapse and impairment in bipolar disorder. *American Journal of Psychiatry, 152,* 1635–1640.

Gladue, B. A., Green, R., & Hellman, R. E. (1984). Neuroendocrine response to estrogen and sexual orientation. *Science, 225,* 1496–1499.

Glatt, C. E., Tampilic, M., Christie, C., DeYoung, J., & Freimer, N. B. (2004). Re-screening serotonin receptors for genetic variants identifies population and molecular genetic complexity. *American Journal of Medical Genetics, 124,* 92–100.

Gleaves, D. H. (1996). The sociocognitive model of dissociative identity disorder: A reexamination of the evidence. *Psychological Bulletin, 120,* 42–59.

Gleaves, D. H., Lowe, M. R., Snow, A. C., Green, B. A., & Murphy-Eberenz, K. P. (2000). Continuity and discontinuity models of bulimia nervosa: A taxometric investigation. *Journal of Abnormal Psychology, 109*(1), 56–68.

Gleaves, D. H., Smith, S. M., Butler, L. D., & Spiegel, D. (2004). False and recovered memories in the laboratory and clinic: A review of experimental and clinical evidence. *Clinical Psychology: Science and Practice.*

Goater, N., King, M., Cole, E., Leavey, G., Johnson-Sabine, E., Blizard, R., & Hoar, A. (1999). Ethnicity and outcomes of psychosis. *British Journal of Psychiatry, 175,* 34–42.

Godart, N. T., Perdereau, F., Rein, Z., Berthoz, S., Wallier, J., Jeammet, P., & Falment, M. F. (2007). Comorbidity studies of eating disorders and mood disorders. Critical review of the literature. *Journal of Affective Disorders, 97*(1–3), 37–49.

Goering, P., Durbin, J., Sheldon, C. T., Ochocka, J., Nelson, G., & Krupa, T. (2006). Who uses consumer-run self-help organizations? *American Journal of Orthopsychiatry, 76,* 367–373.

Goff, D. C., & Coyle, J. T. (2001). The emerging role of glutamate in the pathophysiology and treatment of schizophrenia. *American Journal of Psychiatry, 158,* 1367–1377.

Gold, S. N., & Seibel, S. L. (2009). Treating dissociation: A contextual approach. In P. F. Dell & J. A. O'Neil (Eds.), *Dissociation and the dissociative disorders: DSM-V and beyond.* (pp. 625–636). New York, NY: Routledge/Taylor & Francis Group.

Goldberg, J. F., Harrow, M., & Grossman, L. S. (1995). Course and outcome in bipolar affective disorder: A longitudinal follow-up study. *American Journal of Psychiatry, 152,* 379–384.

Goldberg, J. F., Perlis, R. H., Bowden, C. L., Thase, M. E., Miklowitz, D. J., Marangell, L. B., Sachs, G. S. (2009). Manic symptoms during depressive episodes in 1,380 patients with bipolar disorder: Findings from the STEP-BD. *American Journal of Psychiatry, 166*(2), 173–181.

Golden, C. J., Hammeke, T. A., & Purisch, A. D. (1980). *The Luria-Nebraska Battery manual.* Palo Alto, CA: Western Psychological Services.

Goldfarb, W. (1963). Self-awareness in schizophrenic children. *Archives of General Psychiatry, 8,* 63–76.

Goldman, M. S., & Rather, B. C. (1993). Substance use disorders: Cognitive models and architecture. In K. S. Dobson & P. C. Kendall (Eds.), *Psychopathology and cognition* (pp. 245–292). New York, NY: Academic Press.

Goldman, S. J., D'Angelo, E. J., DeMaso, D. R., & Mezzacappa, E. (1992). Physical and sexual abuse histories among children with borderline personality disorder. *American Journal of Psychiatry, 149,* 1723–1726.

Goldmeier, D., Garvey, L., & Barton, S. (2008). Does chronic stress lead to increased rates of recurrences of genital herpes?—A review of the psychoneuroimmunilogical evidence. *International Journal of STD and AIDS, 19,* 359–362.

Goldschmidt, A. B., Hilbert, A., Manwaring, J. L., Wilfley, D. E., Pike, K. M., Fairburn, C. G., & Striegel-Moore, R. (2010). The significance of overvaluation of shape and weight in binge eating disorder. *Behaviour Research and Therapy, 48*(3), 187–193.

Goldstein, B. (1994). *Psychology,* Pacific Grove, CA: Brooks/Cole Publishing Company.

Goldstein, G., & Shelly, C. (1984). Discriminative validity of various intelligence and neuropsychological tests. *Journal of Consulting and Clinical Psychology, 52,* 383–389.

Goldstein, I., Lue, T. F., Padma-Nathan, H., Rosen, R. C., Steers, W. D., & Wicker, P. A., for the Sildenafil Study Group. (1998). Oral sildenafil in the treatment of erectile dysfunction. *New England Journal of Medicine, 338,* 1397–1404.

Goldstein, J. M., & Lewine, R. R. J. (2000). Overview of sex differences in schizophrenia: Where have we been and where do we go from here? In D. J. Castle, J. McGrath & J. Kulkarni (Eds.), *Women and schizophrenia* (pp. 111–143). Cambridge, UK: Cambridge University Press.

Goldstein, D., Reboussin, B., & Daniel, S. (2006). Predictors of suicide attempts: State and trait components. *Journal of Abnormal Psychology, 115,* 842–849.

Goldston, D. B., Molock, S. D., Whitbeck, L. B., Murakami, J. L., Zayas, L. H., & Hall, G. C. N. (2008). Cultural considerations in adolescent suicide prevention and psychosocial treatment. *American Psychologist, 63*(1), 14–31.

Gomez-Gil, E., Steva, I., Almaraz, M. C., Pasara, E., Segovia, S., & Guillamon, A. (2010). Familiality of gender identity disorder in non-twin siblings. *Archives of Sexual Behavior, 39,* 546–552.

Good, B. J., & Kleinman, A. M. (1985). Culture and anxiety: Cross-cultural evidence for the patterning of anxiety disorders. In A. H. Tuma & J. D. Maser (Eds.), *Anxiety and the anxiety disorders* (pp. 297–313). Hillsdale, NJ: Erlbaum.

Goodkin, K., Baldewicz, T. T., Asthana, D., Khamis, I., Blaney, N. T., Kumar, M., ... Shapshak, P. (2001). A bereavement support group intervention affects plasma burden of human immunodeficiency virus type 1. Report of a randomized controlled trial. *Journal of Human Virology, 4,* 44–54.

Goodman, G. S., Ghetti, S., Quas, J. A., Edelstein, R. S., Alexander, K. W., Redlich, A. D., Cordon, I. M., & Jones, D. P. H. (2003). A prospective study of memory for child sexual abuse: New findings relevant to the repressed/lost memory controversy. *Psychological Science, 14*(2), 113–118.

Goodman, S. H., & Gotlib, I. H. (1999). Risk for psychopathology in the children of de-pressed mothers: A developmental model for understanding mechanisms of transmission. *Psychological Review, 106*(3), 458–490.

Goodnough, A. (2002). Post-9/11 pain found to linger in young minds. Retrieved from http://www.nytimes.com/2002/05/02/health/02SCHO.html?todaysheadlines.

Goodwin, D. W., & Guze, S. B. (1984). *Psychiatric diagnosis* (3rd ed.). New York, NY: Oxford University Press.

Goodwin, F. K., Fireman, B., Simon, G. E., Hunkeler, E. M., Lee, J., & Revicki, D. (2003). Suicide risk in bipolar disorder during treatment with lithium and divalproex. *JAMA: Journal of the American Medical Association, 290,* 1467–1473.

Goodwin, F. K., & Ghaemi, S. N. (1998). Understanding manic-depressive illness. *Archives of General Psychiatry, 55*(1), 23–25.

Goodwin, F. K., & Jamison, K. R. (Eds.) (2007). *Manic depressive illness: Bipolar disorders and recurrent depression* (2nd ed.). New York, NY: Oxford University Press.

Goodwin, G. M. (2009). Neurobiological aetiology of mood disorders. In M. G. Gelder, N. C. Andreasen, J. J. Lopez-Ibor, Jr., & J. R. Geddes (Eds.), *New Oxford textbook of psychiatry* (2nd ed., Vol. 1, pp. 658–664). Oxford, UK: Oxford University Press.

Goodwin, P. J., Leszcz, M., Ennis, M., Koopmans, J., Vincent, L., Guther, H., ... Hunter, J. (2001). The effect of group psychosocial support on survival in metastatic breast cancer. *New England Journal of Medicine, 345,* 1719–1726.

Goos, L. M., Crosbie, J., Payne, S., & Schachar, R. (2009). Validation and extension of the endophenotype model in ADHD patterns of inheritance in a family study of inhibitory control. *American Journal of Psychiatry, 166*(6), 711–717.

Gordis, E. (2000). Alcohol, the brain, and behavior: Mechanisms of addiction. *Alcohol Research & Health, 24*(1), 12–15.

Gordon, J. A. (2002). Anxiolytic drug targets: Beyond the usual suspects. *Journal of Clinical Investigation, 110*(7), 915–917.

Gore-Felton, C., & Koopman, C. (2008). Behavioral mediation of the relationship between psychosocial factors and HIV disease progression. *Psychosomatic Medicine, 70,* 569–574.

Gorenstein, E. E., & Newman, J. P. (1980). Disinhibitory psychopathology: A new perspective and a model for research. *Psychological Review, 87,* 301–315.

Gotlib, I. H., & Beach, S. R. H. (1995). A marital/family discord model of depression: Implications for therapeutic intervention. In N. S. Jacobson & A. S. Gurman (Eds.), *Clinical handbook of couple therapy* (pp. 411–436). New York, NY: Guilford Press.

Gotlib, I. H., & Krasnoperova, E. (1998). Biased information processing as a vulnerability factor for depression. *Behavior Therapy, 29,* 603–617.

Gotlib, I. H., Kurtzman, H. S., & Blehar, M. C. (1997). Cognition and depression: Issues and future directions. *Cognition and Emotion, 11*(5/6), 663–673.

Gotlib, I. H., & MacLeod, C. (1997). Information processing in anxiety and depression: A cognitive-developmental perspective. In J. Burack & J. Enns (Eds.), *Attention, development, and psychopathology* (pp. 350–378). New York, NY: Guilford Press.

Gotlib, I. H., & Nolan, S. A. (2001). Depression. In A. S. Bellack & M. Hersen (Eds.), *Psychopathology in adulthood* (2nd ed., pp. 252–277). Boston, MA: Allyn & Bacon.

Gotlib, I. H., Roberts, J. E., & Gilboa, E. (1996). Cognitive interference in depression. In I. G. Sarason, G. R. Pierce, & B. R. Sarason (Eds.), *Cognitive interference: Theories, methods, and findings* (pp. 347–377). Mahwah, NJ: Erlbaum.

Gottesman, I. I. (1991). *Schizophrenia genesis: The origins of madness.* New York, NY: W. H. Freeman.

Gottesman, I. I. (1997). Twins: En route to QTLs for cognition. *Science, 276,* 1522–1523.

Gottesman, I. I., & Bertelsen, A. (1989). Dual mating studies in psychiatry: Offspring of inpatients with examples from reactive (psychogenic) psychoses. *International Review of Psychiatry, 1,* 287–296.

Gottfredson, L., & Saklofske, D. H. (2009). Intelligence: Foundations and issues in assessment. *Canadian Psychology/Psychologie canadienne, 50*(3), 183–195.

Gottlieb, G. (1998). Normally occurring environmental and behavioral influences on gene activity: From central dogma to probabilistic epigenesis. *Psychological Review, 105,* 492–802.

Gould, M. (1990). Suicide clusters and media exposure. In S. J. Blumenthal & D. J. Kupfer (Eds.), *Suicide over the life cycle: Risk factors, assessment, and treatment of suicidal patients* (pp. 517–532). Washington, DC: American Psychiatric Press.

Gould, M. S. (2001). Suicide and the media. *Annals of the New York Academy of Sciences, 932,* 200–221; discussion 221–204.

Gould, M. S., Greenberg, T., Velting, D. M., & Shaffer, D. (2003). Youth suicide risk and preventive interventions: A review of the past 10 years. *Journal of the American Academy of Child and Adolescent Psychiatry, 42*(4), 386–405.

Grabbe, K. L., & Bunnell, R. (2010). Reframing HIV prevention in sub-saharan Africa using couple-centered approaches. *JAMA: Journal of the American Medical Association, 304,* 346–347.

Grabe, H. J., Meyer, C., Hapke, U., Rumpf, H. J., Freyberger, H. J., Dilling, H., & John, U. (2003). Somatoform pain disorder in the general population. *Psychotherapy and Psychosomatics, 72,* 88–94.

Grabe, S., Ward, L. M., & Hyde, J. S. (2008). The role of the media in body image concerns among women: A meta-analysis of experimental and correlational studies. *Psychological Bulletin, 134*(3), 460–476.

Grados, M. A., Riddle, M. A., Samuels, J. F., Liang, K-Y., Hoehn-Saric, R., Bienvenu, O. J., ... Nestadt, J. (2001). The familial phenotype of obsessive-compulsive disorder in relation to tic disorders: The Hopkins OCD family study. *Biological Psychiatry, 50,* 559–565.

Graeff, F. G. (1987). The anti-aversive action of drugs. In T. Thompson, P. B. Dews, &

J. Barrett (Eds.), *Advances in behavioral pharmacology* (Vol. 6). Hillside, NJ: Erlbaum.

Graeff, F. G. (1993). Role of 5-HT in defensive behavior and anxiety. *Review in the Neurosciences, 4,* 181–211.

Graf, P., Squire, L. R., & Mandler, G. (1984). The information that amnesic patients do not forget. *Journal of Experimental Psychology: Learning, Memory, and Cognition, 10,* 164–178.

Graham, C. A. (2010). The DSM criteria for female orgasmic disorder. *Archives of Sexual Behavior, 39,* 256–270.

Granic, I., & Patterson, G. R. (2006). Toward a comprehensive model of antisocial development: A dynamic systems approach. *Psychological Review, 113,* 101–131.

Grant, B., Chou, S., Goldstein, R., Huang, B., Stinson, F., Saha, T., ... Pickering, R, P. (2008). Prevalence, correlates, disability, and comorbidity of DSM-IV borderline personality disorder: Results from the Wave 2 National Epidemiologic Survey on Alcohol and Related Conditions. *The Journal of Clinical Psychiatry, 69*(4), 533.

Grant, I., Patterson, T. L., & Yager, J. (1988). Social supports in relation to physical health and symptoms of depression in the elderly. *American Journal of Psychiatry, 145*(10), 1254–1258.

Grant, J. E., Correia, S., & Brennan-Krohn, T. (2006). White matter integrity in kleptomania: A pilot study. *Psychiatry Research: Neuroimaging, 147,* 233–237.

Grant, K. E., Compas, B. E., Thurm, A. E., McMahon, S. D., & Gipson, P. Y. (2004). Stressors and child and adolescent psychopathology: Measurement issues and prospective effects. *Journal of Clinical Child and Adolescent Psychology, 33*(2), 412–425.

Grant, J. E., & Kim, S. W. (2002). Temperament and early environmental influences in kleptomania. *Comprehensive Psychiatry, 43,* 223–229.

Gray, J. A. (1982). *The neuropsychology of anxiety.* New York, NY: Oxford University Press.

Gray, J. A. (1985). Issues in the neuropsychology of anxiety. In A. H. Tuma & J. D. Maser (Eds.), *Anxiety and the anxiety disorders* (pp. 5–25). Hillside, NJ: Erlbaum.

Gray, J. A. (1987). *The psychology of fear and stress* (2nd ed.). New York, NY: Cambridge University Press.

Gray, J. A., & Buffery, A. W. H. (1971). Sex differences in emotional and cognitive behavior in mammals including man: Adaptive and neural bases. *Acta Psychologica, 35,* 89–111.

Gray, J. A., & McNaughton, N. (1996). The neuropsychology of anxiety: Reprise. In D. A. Hope (Ed.), *Perspectives on anxiety, panic and fear* (The 43rd Annual Nebraska Symposium on Motivation) (pp. 61–134). Lincoln, NE: Nebraska University Press.

Gray, R., Mukherjee, R. A. S., & Rutter, M. (2009). Alcohol consumption during pregnancy and its effects on neurodevelopment: What is known and what remains uncertain. *Addiction, 104*(8), 1270–1273.

Graybar, S. R., & Boutilier, L. R. (2002). Nontraumatic pathways to borderline personality disorder. *Psychotherapy: Theory/Research/Practice/Training, 39,* 152–162.

Grazzi, L., Andrasik, F., D'Amico, D., Leone, M., Usai, S., Kass, S. J., & Bussone, G. (2002). Behavioral and pharmacologic treatment of transformed migraine with analgesic overuse: Outcome at 3 years. *Headache, 42,* 483–490.

Green, B. L., Grace, M. C., Lindy, J. D., Titchener, J. L., & Lindy, J. G. (1983). Levels of functional impairment following a civilian disaster: The Beverly Hills Supper Club fire. *Journal of Consulting and Clinical Psychology, 51,* 573–580.

Green, C. R., Ndao-Brumblay, S. K., & Hart-Johnson, T. (2009). Sleep problems in a racially diverse chronic pain population. *The Clinical Journal of Pain, 25*(5), 423–430.

Green, R. (1987). *The "sissy boy syndrome" and the development of homosexuality.* New Haven, CT: Yale University Press.

Green, R., & Fleming, D. T. (1990). Transsexual surgery follow-up: Status in the 1990s. *Annual Review of Sex Research, 1,* 163–174.

Green, R., & Money, J. (1969). *Transsexualism and sex reassignment.* Baltimore, MD: Johns Hopkins Press.

Greenberg, D. R., & LaPorte, D. L. (1996). Racial differences in body type preferences of men for women. *International Journal of Eating Disorders, 19,* 275–278.

Greenberg, H. R. (2005). Impulse-control disorders not elsewhere classified. In B. J. Sadock & V. A. Sadock (Eds.), *Kaplan & Sadock's comprehensive textbook of psychiatry* (8th ed., pp. 2035– 2054). Philadelphia, PA: Lippincott Williams & Wilkins.

Greenhill, L. L., & Hechtman, L. I. (2009). Attention deficit/hyperactivity disorder. In B. J. Sadock, V. A. Sadock, & P. Ruiz (Eds.), *Kaplan & Sadock's comprehensive textbook of psychiatry* (9th ed., Vol. II, pp. 3560–3572). Philadelphia, PA: Lippincott Williams & Wilkins.

Greenough, W. T., Withers, G. S., & Wallace, C. S. (1990). Morphological changes in the nervous system arising from behavioral experience: What is the evidence that they are involved in learning and memory? In L. R. Squire & E. Lindenlaub (Eds.), *The biology of memory, Symposia Medica Hoescht 23* (pp. 159–183). Stuttgart/New York, NY: Schattauer Verlag.

Greeven, A., Van Balkom, A., Visser, S., Merkelbach, J., Van Rood, Y., Van Dyck, R., ... Spinhoven, P. (2007). Cognitive behavior therapy and paroxetine in the treatment of hypochondriasis: A randomized controlled trial. *American Journal of Psychiatry, 164,* 91–99.

Gregoire, A. (1992). New treatments for erectile impotence. *British Journal of Psychiatry, 160,* 315–326.

Greist, J. H. (1990). Treatment of obsessive compulsive disorder: Psychotherapies, drugs, and other somatic treatments. *Journal of Clinical Psychiatry, 51,* 44–50.

Grice, S. J., Kuipers, E., Bebbington, P., Dunn, G., Fowler, D., Freeman, D., Garety, P. (2009). Carers' attributions about positive events in psychosis relate to expressed emotion. *Behaviour Research and Therapy, 47*(9), 783–789. doi:10.1016/j.brat.2009.06.004

Griffith, E. E. H., English, T., & Mayfield, U. (1980). Possession, prayer and testimony: Therapeutic aspects of the Wednesday night meeting in a black church. *Psychiatry, 43*(5), 120–128.

Griffiths, R., Richards, W., Johnson, M., McCann, U., & Jesse, R. (2008). Mystical-type experiences occasioned by psilocybin mediate the attribution of personal meaning and spiritual significance 14 months later. *Journal of Psychopharmacology, 22*(6), 621.

Griffiths, R. R., Richards, W. A., McCann, U., & Jesse, R. (2006). Psilocybin can occasion mystic-type experiences having substantial and sustained personal meaning and spiritual significance. *Psychopharmacology, 187*, 268–283.

Grilo, C. M., Masheb, R. M., & White, M. A. (2010). Significance of overvaluation of shape/weight in binge-eating disorder: Comparative study with overweight and bulimia nervosa. *Obesity, 18*, 499–504.

Grilo, C. M., Masheb, R. M., & Wilson, G. T. (2001). Subtyping binge eating disorder. *Journal of Consulting and Clinical Psychology, 69*, 1066–1072.

Grilo, C. M., Masheb, R. M., & Wilson, G. T. (2004). Efficacy of cognitive behavioral therapy and fluoxetine for the treatment of binge eating disorder: A randomized double-blind placebo-controlled comparison. *Biological Psychiatry, 57*, 301–309.

Grilo, C. M., Masheb, R. M., & Wilson, G. T. (2006). Rapid response to treatment for binge eating disorder. *Journal of Consulting and Clinical Psychology, 74*, 602–613.

Grinspoon, L., & Bakalar, J. B. (1980). Drug dependence: Non-narcotic agents. In H. I. Kaplan, A. M. Freedman, & B. J. Sadock (Eds.), *Comprehensive textbook of psychiatry* (3rd ed., pp. 1614– 1629). Baltimore, MD: Williams & Wilkins.

Grisham, J., Frost, R. O., Steketee, G., Kim, H. J., & Hood, S. (2006). Age of onset of compulsive hoarding. *Journal of Anxiety Disorders, 20*, 675–686.

Grisham, J. R., & Barlow, D. H. (2005). Compulsive hoarding: Current research and theory. *Journal of Psychopathology and Behavioral Assessment, 27*, 45–52.

Grob, G. N. (2009). *Mental institutions in America: Social policy to 1875*. New Brunswick, NJ: Transaction Publishers.

Gross, J. J. (Ed.). (2007). *Handbook of emotion regulation*. New York, NY: Guilford Press.

Grossardt, B. R., Bower, J. H., Geda, Y. E., Colligan, R. C., & Rocca, W. A. (2009). Pessimistic, anxious, and depressive personality traits predict all-cause mortality: The Mayo Clinic Cohort Study of Personality and Aging. *Psychosomatic Medicine, 71*, 491–500.

Grosz, H. J., & Zimmerman, J. (1965). Experimental analysis of hysterical blindness: A follow-up report and new experimental data. *Archives of General Psychiatry, 13*, 255–260.

Grosz, H. J., & Zimmerman, J. (1970). A second detailed case study of functional blindness: Further demonstration of the contribution of objective psychological laboratory data. *Behavior Therapy, 1*, 115–123.

Gruber, J., Johnson, S. L., Oveis, C., & Keltner, D. (2008). Risk for mania and positive emotional responding: Too much of a good thing? *Emotion, 8*(1), 23–33.

Grucza, R. A., Bucholz, K. K., Rice, J. P., & Bierut, L. J. (2008). Secular trends in the lifetime prevalence of alcohol dependence in the United States: A re-evaluation. *Alcohol Clin Exp Res, 32*(5), 763-770.

Grucza, R. A., Norberg, K., Bucholz, K. K., & Bierut, L. J. (2008). Correspondence between secular changes in alcohol dependence and age of drinking onset among women in the United States. *Alcohol Clin Exp Res*.

Guastella, A. J., Einfeld, S. L., Gray, K. M., Rinehart, N. J., Tonge, B. J., Lambert, T. J., Hickie, I. (2010). Intranasal oxytocin improves emotion recognition for youth with autism spectrum disorders. *Biological Psychiatry, 67*(7), 692–694.

Guedeney, N. (2007). Withdrawal behavior and depression in infancy. *Infant Mental Health Journal, 28*, 393–408.

Guilleminault, C. (1989). Clinical features and evaluation of obstructive sleep apnea. In M. H. Kryger, T. Roth, & W. C. Dement (Eds.), *Principles and practice of sleep medicine* (pp. 552–558). Philadelphia, PA: W. B. Saunders.

Gündel, H., O'Connor, M. F., Littrell, L., Fort, C., & Lane, R. D. (2003). Functional neuroanatomy of grief: An FMRI study. *American Journal of Psychiatry, 160*, 1946–1953.

Gunderson, J. G., Ronningstam, E., & Smith, L. E. (1991). Narcissistic personality disorder: A review of data on DSM-III-R descriptions. *Journal of Personality Disorders, 5*, 167–177.

Gunnar, M. R., & Fisher, P. A. (2006). Bringing basic research on early experience and stress neurobiology to bear on preventive interventions for neglected and maltreated children. *Development and Psychopathology, 18*(3), 651–677.

Gur, R. E., Nimgaonkar, V. L., Almasy, L., Calkins, M. E., Ragland, J. D., Pogue-Geile, M. F., ... Gur, R. C.. (2007). Neurocognitive endophenotypes in a multiplex multigenerational family study of schizophrenia. *American Journal of Psychiatry, 164*, 813–819.

Guralnik, O., Giesbrecht, T., Knutelska, M., Sirroff, B., & Simeon, D. (2007). Cognitive functioning in depersonalization disorder. *Journal of Nervous and Mental Disease, 195*(12), 983–988.

Guralnik, O., Schmeidler, J., & Simeon, D. (2000). Feeling unreal: Cognitive processes in depersonalization. *American Journal of Psychiatry, 157*(1), 103–109.

Gureje, O., Simon, G. E., Ustun, T. B., & Goldberg, D. P. (1997). Somatization in cross-cultural perspective: A World Health Organization study in primary care. *American Journal of Psychiatry, 154*, 989–995.

Gurvits, T. V., Shenton, M. E., Hokama, H., Ohta, H., Lasko, N. B., Gilbertson, M. W., ... Pitman, R. K. (1996). Magnetic resonance imaging study of hippocampal volume in chronic, combat-related post traumatic stress disorder. *Biological Psychiatry, 40*, 1091–1099.

Gusella, J. F., Wexler, N. S., Conneally, P. M., Naylor, S. L., Anderson, M. A., Tanzi, R. E., ... Martin, J. B. (1983). A polymorphic DNA marker genetically linked to Huntington's disease. *Nature, 306*, 234–239.

Gustad, J., & Phillips, K. A. (2003). Axis I comorbidity in body dysmorphic disorder. *Comprehensive Psychiatry, 44*, 270–276.

Guydish, J., Sorensen, J. L., Chan, M., Werdegar, D., & Acampora, A. (1999). A randomized trial comparing day and residential drug abuse treatment: 18-month outcomes. *Journal of Consulting and Clinical Psychology, 67*(3), 428–434.

Guyton, A. (1981). *Textbook of medical physiology*. Philadelphia, PA: W. B. Saunders.

Guze, S. B., Cloninger, C. R., Martin, R. L., & Clayton, P. J. (1986). A follow-up and family study of Briquet's syndrome. *British Journal of Psychiatry, 149*, 17–23.

Hackett, T. P., & Cassem, N. H. (1973). Psychological adaptation to convalescence in myocardial infarction patients. In J. P. Naughton, H. K. Hellerstein, & I. C. Mohler (Eds.), *Exercise testing and exercise training in coronary heart disease*. New York, NY: Academic Press.

Hadley, S., Kim, S., Priday, L., & Hollander, E. (2006). Pharmacologic treatment of body dysmorphic disorder. *Primary Psychiatry, 13*, 61–69.

Haenen, M. A., de Jong, P. J., Schmidt, A. J. M., Stevens, S., & Visser, L. (2000). Hypochondriacs' estimation of negative outcomes: Domain-specificity and responsiveness to reassuring and alarming information. *Behaviour Research and Therapy, 38*, 819–833.

Hall, A. C., Butterworth, J., Winsor, J., Gilmore, D., & Metzel, D. (2007). Pushing the employment agenda: Case study research of high performing States in integrated employment. *Intellectual and Developmental Disabilities, 45*, 182–198.

Hall, D. E., Eubanks, L., Meyyazhagan, S., Kenney, R. D., & Cochran Johnson, S. (2000). Evaluation of covert video surveillance in the diagnosis of Munchausen syndrome by proxy: Lessons from 41 cases. *Pediatrics, 6*, 1305–1312.

Hall, K. (2007). Sexual dysfunction and childhood sexual abuse: Gender differences and treatment implications. In S. R. Leiblum (Ed.), *Principles and practice of sex therapy* (4th ed., pp. 350– 378). New York, NY: Guilford Press.

Hall, L. S., & Love, C. T. (2003). Finger-length ratios in female monozygotic twins discordant for sexual orientation. *Archives of Sexual Behavior, 32*, 23–28.

Hall, W. D., & Degenhardt, L. (2009). Cannabis-related disorders. In B. J. Sadock, V. A. Sadock, & P. Ruiz (Eds.), *Kaplan & Sadock's comprehensive textbook of psychiatry* (9th ed., Vol. I, pp. 1309–1318). Philadelphia, PA: Lippincott Williams & Wilkins.

Hamer, D. H., Hu, S., Magnuson, V. L., Hu, N., & Pattatucci, A. M. (1993). A linkage between DNA markers on the X chromosome and male sexual orientation. *Science, 261*, 321–327.

Hammad, T., Laughren, T., & Racoosin, J. (2006). Suicidality in pediatric patients treated with antidepressant drugs. *Archives of General Psychiatry, 63*, 332–339.

Hammen, C. (2005). Stress and depression. *Annual Review of Clinical Psychology, 1*, 293–319.

Hammen, C. L. (2009). Children of depressed parents. In I. H. Gotlib & C. L. Hammen (Eds.), *Handbook of depression* (2nd ed., pp. 275–297). New York, NY: Guilford Press.

Hammer, S., Saag, M., Scheechter, M., Montaner, J., Schooley, R., Jacobsen, D., ... & the International AIDS Society-USA panel. (2006). Treatment for adult HIV infection: 2006 recommendations of the International AIDS Society-USA panel. *JAMA: Journal of the American Medical Association, 296,* 827–843.

Hampton, T. (2010). Depression care effort brings dramatic drop in large HMO population's suicide rate. *JAMA: Journal of the American Medical Association, 303*(19), 1903–1905.

Hankin, B. L., & Abramson, L. Y. (2001). Development of gender differences in depression: An elaborated cognitive vulnerability– transactional stress theory. *Psychological Bulletin, 127,* 773–796.

Hankin, B. L., Wetter, E., & Cheely, C. (2007). Sex differences in adolescent depression: A developmental psychopathological approach. In J. R. Z. Abela & B. L. Hankin (Eds.), *Handbook of depression in children and adolescents* (pp. 377– 414). New York, NY: Guilford Press.

Hanna, G. L. (1995). Demographic and clinical features of obsessive-compulsive disorder in children and adolescents. *Journal of the American Academy of Child and Adolescent Psychiatry, 34,* 19–27.

Hans, V. P. (1986). An analysis of public attitudes toward the insanity defense. *Criminology, 4,* 393–415.

Hanson, R. K., Gordon, A., Harris, A. J. R., Marques, J. K., Murphy, W., Quinsey, V. L., & Seto, M. C. (2002). First report on the collaborative outcome data project on the effectiveness of psychological treatment for sex offenders. *Sexual Abuse: A Journal of Research and Treatment, 14,* 169–194.

Hantouche, E., Akiskal, H., Azorin, J., Chatenet-Duchene, L., & Lancrenon, S. (2006). Clinical and psychometric characterization of depression in mixed mania: A report from the French National Cohort of 1090 manic patients. *Journal of Affective Disorders, 96,* 225–232.

Harbert, T. L., Barlow, D. H., Hersen, M., & Austin, J. B. (1974). Measurement and modification of incestuous behavior: A case study. *Psychological Reports, 34,* 79–86.

Harburg, E., Kaciroti, N., Gleiberman, L., Julius, M., & Schork, M. A. (2008). Marital pair anger- coping types may act as an entity to affect mortality: Preliminary findings from a prospective study (Tecumseh, Michigan, 1971–1988). *Journal of Family Communication, 8*(1), 44–61.

Hardie, T. L., Moss, H. B., & Lynch, K. G. (2006). Genetic correlations between smoking initiation and smoking behaviors in a twin sample. *Addictive Behaviors, 31*(11), 2030–2037.

Hare, R. D. (1970). *Psychopathy: Theory and research.* New York, NY: John Wiley.

Hare, R. D. (1993). *Without conscience: The disturbing world of the psychopaths among us.* New York, NY: Pocket Books.

Hare, R. D., McPherson, L. M., & Forth, A. E. (1988). Male psychopaths and their criminal careers. *Journal of Consulting and Clinical Psychology, 56,* 710–714.

Hare, R. D., & Neumann, C. S. (2006). The PCL-R assessment of psychopathology:

Development, structural properties, and new directions. In C. J. Patrick (Ed.), *Handbook of psychopathy* (pp. 58–88). New York, NY: Guilford Press.

Hariri, A. R., Mattay, V. S., Tessitore, A., Kolachana, B., Fera, F., Goldman, D., ... Weinberger, D. R. (2002). Serotonin transporter genetic variation and the response of the human amygdala. *Science, 297,* 400–402.

Harmer, C. J. (2008). Serotonin and emotional processing: Does it help explain antidepressant drug action? *Neuropharmacology, 55*(6), 1023–1028.

Harmer, C. J. (2010). Antidepressant drug action: A neuropsychological perspective. *Depression and Anxiety, 27*(3), 231–233.

Harmer, C. J., O'Sullivan, U., Favaron, E., Massey-Chase, R., Ayres, R., Reinecke, A., ... Cowen, P. J. (2009). Effect of acute antidepressant administration on negative affective bias in depressed patients. *The American Journal of Psychiatry, 166*(10), 1178–1184.

Harper, L. V. (2005). Epigenetic inheritance and the intergenerational transfer of experience. *Psychological Bulletin, 131,* 340–360.

Harpur, T. J., Hare, R. D., & Hakstian, A. R. (1989). Two-factor conceptualization of psychopathy: Construct validity and assessment implications. *Psychological Assessment: A Journal of Consulting and Clinical Psychology, 1,* 6–17.

Hart, S. D., Forth, A. E., & Hare, R. D. (1990). Performance of criminal psychopaths on selected neuropsychological tests. *Journal of Abnormal Psychology, 99,* 374–379.

Hartlage, S., & Gehlert, S. (2001). Differentiating premenstrual dysphoric disorder from premenstrual exacerbations of other disorders: A methods dilemma. *Clinical Psychology: Science and Practice, 8*(2), 242–253.

Harvey, A. G. (2008). Sleep and circadian rhythms in bipolar disorder: Seeking synchrony, harmony, and regulation. *The American Journal of Psychiatry, 165*(7), 820–829.

Harvey, A. G., & Bryant, R. A. (1998). The relationship between acute stress disorder and posttraumatic stress disorder: A prospective evaluation of motor vehicle accident survivors. *Journal of Consulting and Clinical Psychology, 66,* 507–512.

Harvey, A. G., Talbot, L. S., & Gershon, A. (2009). Sleep disturbance in bipolar disorder across the lifespan. *Clinical Psychology: Science and Practice, 16*(2), 256–277.

Harvey, L., Inglis, S. J., & Espie, C. (2002). Insomniacs' reported use of CBT components and relationship to long-term clinical outcome. *Behaviour Research and Therapy, 40,* 75–83.

Harvey, P., & Bellack, A. (2009). Toward a terminology for functional recovery in schizophrenia: Is functional remission a viable concept? *Schizophrenia Bulletin, 35*(2), 300–306.

Harvey, S. B., Wadsworth, M., Wessely, S., & Hotopf, M. (2008). Etiology of chronic fatigue syndrome: Testing popular hypotheses using a national birth cohort study. *Psychosomatic Medicine, 70,* 488–495.

Harvey, S. B., & Wessely, S. (2009). Chronic fatigue syndrome: Identifying zebras among the horses. *BMC Medicine, 7,* 58. doi:10.1186/1741-7015-7-58.

Hasin, D., Goodwin, R., Stinson, F., & Grant, B. (2005). Epidemiology of major depressive disorder. *Archives General Psychiatry, 62,* 1097–1106.

Haslam, J. (1976). *Observations on madness and melancholy.* New York, NY: Arno Press. (Original work published in 1809).

Hastings, J. (1990). Easy to get hooked on, hard to get off. *Health,* p. 37.

Hatfield, E., Cacioppo, J. T., & Rapson, R. L. (1994). *Emotional contagion.* Cambridge, UK: Cambridge University Press.

Hathaway, S. R., & McKinley, J. C. (1943). *Manual for the Minnesota Multiphasic Personality Inventory.* New York, NY: Psychological Corporation.

Hawkley, L. C., & Cacioppo, J. T. (2007). Aging and loneliness: Downhill quickly? *Current Directions in Psychological Science, 16,* 187–191.

Hawton, K. (1995). Treatment of sexual dysfunctions of sex therapy and other approaches. *British Journal of Psychiatry, 167,* 307–314.

Hawton, K., Houston, K., Haw, C., Townsend, E., & Harriss, L. (2003). Comorbidity of axis I and axis II disorders in patients who attempted suicide. *American Journal of Psychiatry, 160,* 1494–1500.

Hay, P. J., & Fairburn, C. (1998). The validity of the DSM-IV scheme for classifying bulimic eating disorders. *International Journal of Eating Disorders, 23,* 7–15.

Hay, P. J., & Hall, A. (1991). The prevalence of eating disorders in recently admitted psychiatric in-patients. *British Journal of Psychiatry, 159,* 562–565.

Hayes, S. C., Barlow, D. H., & Nelson-Gray, R. O. (1999). *The scientist–practitioner: Research and accountability in the age of managed care* (2nd ed.). Boston, MA: Allyn & Bacon.

Haynes, S. G., Feinleib, M., & Kannel, W. B. (1980). The relationship of psychosocial factors to coronary heart disease in the Framingham study: III. Eight-year incidence of coronary heart disease. *American Journal of Epidemiology, 111,* 37–58.

Haynes, S. G., & Matthews, K. A. (1988). Area review: Coronary-prone behavior: Continuing evolution of the concept: Review and methodologic critique of recent studies on type A behavior and cardiovascular disease. *Annals of Behavioral Medicine, 10*(2), 47–59.

Haynes, S. N., Yoshioka, D. T., Kloezeman, K., & Bello, I. (2009). Clinical applications of behavioral assessment. In J. N. Butcher (Ed.), *Oxford Handbook of Personality Assessment* (pp. 226– 249). New York, NY: Oxford University Press.

Hazell, P., O'Connell, D., Heathcote, D., Robertson, J., & Henry, D. (1995). Efficacy of tricyclic drugs in treating child and adolescent depression: A meta-analysis. *British Medical Journal, 8,* 897–901.

Heath, C. A., Cooper, S. A., Murray, K., Lowman, A., Henry, C., MacLeod, M. A., ... Will, R. G. (2010). Validation of diagnostic criteria for variant Creutzfeldt-Jakob disease. *Annals of Neurology, 67*(6), 761–770.

Hebert, L. E., Scherr, P. A., Bienias, J. L., Bennett, D. A., & Evans, D. A. (2003). Alzheimer disease in the U.S. population: Prevalence estimates using the 2000 Census. *Archives of Neurology, 60,* 1119–1122.

Heckers, S. (2009). Neurobiology of schizophrenia spectrum disorders. *Annals of the Academy of Medicine, Singapore, 38*(5), 431–432.

Heim, C., & Nemeroff, C. B. (1999). The impact on early adverse experiences on brain systems involved in the pathophysiology of anxiety and affective disorders. *Biological Psychiatry, 46*(11), 1509–1522.

Heim, C., Plotsky, P., & Nemeroff, C. (2004). Importance of studying the contributions of early adverse experience to neurobiological findings in depression. *Neuropsychopharmacology, 29*, 641–648.

Heim, C., Wagner, D., Maloney, E., Papanicolaou, D., Dimitris, A., Solomon, L., ... Reeves, W. C. (2006). Early adverse experience and risk for chronic fatigue syndrome. *Archives of General Psychiatry, 63*, 1258–1266.

Heiman, J. R. (2000). Orgasmic disorders in women. In S. R. Leiblum & R. C. Rosen (Eds.), *Principles and practice of sex therapy* (3rd ed., pp. 118–153). New York, NY: Guilford Press.

Heiman, J. R. (2007). Orgasmic disorders in women. In S. R. Leiblum (Ed.), *Principles and practice of sex therapy* (4th ed., pp. 84–123). New York, NY: Guilford Press.

Heiman, J. R., Gittelman, M., Costabile, R., Guay, A., Friedman, A., & Heard-Davison, A., ... Stephans, D. (2006). Topical alprostadil (PGE$_1$) for the treatment of female sexual arousal disorder: In clinic evaluation of safety and efficacy. *Journal of Psychosomatic Obstetrics & Gynecology, 27*, 31–41.

Heiman, J. R., & LoPiccolo, J. (1988). *Becoming orgasmic: A sexual and personal growth program for women* (rev. ed.). New York, NY: Prentice Hall.

Heiman, J. R., & Meston, C. M. (1997). Empirically validated treatment for sexual dysfunction. *Annual Review of Sex Research, 8*, 148–195.

Heimberg, R. G., Dodge, C. S., Hope, D. A., Kennedy, C. R., Zollo, L., & Becker, R. E. (1990). Cognitive behavioral group treatment for social phobia: Comparison to a credible placebo control. *Cognitive Therapy and Research, 14*, 1–23.

Heimberg, R. G., Liebowitz, M. R., Hope, D. A., Schneier, F. R., Holt, C. S., Welkowitz, L. A., ... Klien, D. F. (1998). Cognitive behavioral group therapy vs. phenelzine therapy for social phobia: 12-week outcome. *Archives of General Psychiatry, 55*, 1133–1141.

Heimberg, R. G., Salzman, D. G., Holt, C. S., & Blendell, K. A. (1993). Cognitive-behavioral group treatment for social phobia: Effectiveness at five-year follow-up. *Cognitive Therapy and Research, 17*, 325–339.

Helgeson, V. (2005). Recent advances in psychosocial oncology. *Journal of Consulting and Clinical Psychology, 73*, 268–271.

Heller, W., & Nitschke, J. B. (1997). Regional brain activity in emotion: A framework for understanding cognition in depression. *Cognition and Emotion, 11*(5–6), 737–661.

Helweg-Larsen, M., & Collins, B. E. (1997). A social psychological perspective on the role of knowledge about AIDS in AIDS prevention. *Current Directions in Psychological Science, 6*, 23–26.

Helzer, J. E., & Canino, G. (1992). Comparative analyses of alcoholism in 10 cultural regions. In J. Helzer & G. Canino (Eds.), *Alcoholism—North America, Europe, and Asia: A coordinated analysis of population data from ten regions* (pp. 131– 155). London, UK: Oxford University Press.

Helzer, J. E., Kraemer, H. C., Krueger, R. F., Wittchen, H.-U., Sirovatka, P. J., & Regier, D. A. (2008). *Dimensional approaches in diagnostic classification: Refining the research agenda for DSM-V*. Washington, DC: American Psychiatric Association.

Henderson, K. E., & Brownell, K. D. (2004). The toxic environment and obesity: Contribution and cure. In J. K. Thompson (Ed.), *Handbook of eating disorders and obesity* (pp. 339–348). New York, NY: John Wiley.

Henquet, C., Krabbendam, L., Spauwen, J., Kaplan, C., Lieb, R., Wittchen, H. U., van Os, J.. (2005). Prospective cohort study of cannabis use, predisposition for psychosis, and psychotic symptoms in young people. *British Medical Journal, 330*, 11.

Herbert, T. B., & Cohen, S. (1993). Depression and immunity: A meta-analytic review. *Psychological Bulletin, 113*(3), 472–486.

Herdt, G. H. (1987). *The Sambia: Ritual and gender in New Guinea*. New York, NY: Holt, Rinehart and Winston.

Herdt, G. H., & Stoller, R. J. (1989). Commentary to "The socialization of homosexuality and heterosexuality in a non-Western society." *Archives of Sexual Behavior, 18*, 31–34.

Herrick, J., Shecterle, L. M., & St. Cyr, J. A. (2009). D-ribose—an additive with caffeine. *Medical Hypotheses, 72*(5), 499–500. doi:10.1016/j.mehy.2008.12.038

Hershberger, S., & Segal, N. (2004). The cognitive, behavioral, and personality profiles of a male monozygotic triplet set discordant for sexual orientation. *Archives of Sexual Behavior, 33*, 497–514.

Herzog, D. B., Dorer, D. J., Keel, P. K., Selwyn, S. E., Ekeblad, E. R., Flores, A. T., ... Keller, M. B. (1999). Recovery and relapse in anorexia and bulimia nervosa: A 7.5-year follow-up study. *Journal of the American Academy of Child and Adolescent Psychiatry, 38*(7), 829–837.

Heshka, S., Anderson, J. W., Atkinson, R. L., Greenway, F. L., Hill, J. O., Phinney, S. D., ... Pi-Sunyer, F. X. (2003). Weight loss with self-help compared with a structured commercial program: A randomized trial. *JAMA: Journal of the American Medical Association, 289*, 1792–1798.

Hetherington, E. M., & Blechman, E. A. (Eds.) (1996). *Stress, coping, and resiliency in children and families*. Mahwah, NJ: Erlbaum.

Hetherington, M. M., & Cecil, J. E. (2010). Gene–environment interactions in obesity. *Forum of Nutrition, 63*, 195–203.

Hettema, J. M., Prescott, C. A., Myers, J. M., Neale, M. C., & Kendler, K. S. (2005). The structure of genetic and environmental risk factors for anxiety disorders in men and women. *Archives of General Psychiatry, 62*, 182–189.

Higgins, S. T., Heil, S. H., Dantona, R., Donham, R., Matthews, M., & Badger, G. J. (2006). Effects of varying the monetary value of voucher-based incentives on abstinence achieved during and following treatment among cocaine-dependent out patients. *Addiction, 102*, 271–281.

Higgins, S. T., Sigmon, S. C., & Heil, S. H. (2008). Drug abuse and dependence. In D. H. Barlow (Ed.), *Clinical handbook of psychological disorders* (4th ed., pp. 547–577). New York, NY: Gilford Press.

Higuchi, S., Matsushita, S., Imazeki, H., Kinoshita, T., Takagi, S., & Kono, H. (1994). Aldehyde dehydrogenase genotypes in Japanese alcoholics. *Lancet, 343*, 741–742.

Hilgard, E. R. (1992). Divided consciousness and dissociation. *Consciousness & Cognition, 1*, 16–31.

Hiller, W., Fichter, M. M., & Rief, W. (2003). A controlled treatment study of somatoform disorders including analysis of healthcare utilization and cost-effectiveness. *Journal of Psychosomatic Research, 54*, 369–380.

Hiller, W., Leibbrand, R., Rief, W., & Fichter, M. (2005). Differentiating hypochondriasis from panic disorder. *Journal of Anxiety Disorders, 19*, 29–49.

Hindmarch, I. (1986). The effects of psychoactive drugs on car handling and related psychomotor ability: A review. In J. F. O'Hanlon & J. J. Gier (Eds.), *Drugs and driving* (pp. 71–79). London, UK: Taylor & Francis.

Hindmarch, I. (1990). Cognitive impairment with anti-anxiety agents: A solvable problem? In D. Wheatley (Ed.), *The anxiolytic jungle: Where, next?* (pp. 49–61). Chichester, UK: John Wiley.

Hinshaw, S. P. (2002). Preadolescent girls with attention-deficit/hyperactivity disorder: I. Background characteristics, comorbidity, cognitive and social functioning, and parenting practices. *Journal of Consulting and Clinical Psychology, 70*, 1086–1098.

Hinshaw, S. P., & Stier, A. (2008). Stigma as related to mental disorders. *Annual Review of Clinical Psychology, 4*, 367–393.

Hinshelwood, J. A. (1896). A case of dyslexia: A peculiar form of word-blindness. *Lancet, 2*, 1451–1454.

Hinton, D. E., Chong, R., Pollack, M. H., Barlow, D. H., & McNally, R. J. (2008). Ataque de nervios: Relationship to anxiety sensitivity and dissociation predisposition. *Depression and Anxiety, 25*, 489–495.

Hinton, D. E., & Good, B. J. (Eds.). (2009). *Culture and panic disorder*. Stanford: Stanford University Press.

Hinton, D. E., Hofmann, S. G., Pitman, R. K., Pollack, M. H., Barlow, D. H. (2008). The panic attack-posttraumatic stress disorder model: Applicability to orthostatic panic among Cambodian refugees. *Cognitive Behavioral Therapy, 37*(2), 101–16.

Hinton, D. E., Lewis-Fernández, R., & Pollack, M. H. (2009). A model of the generation of ataque de nervios: The role of fear of negative affect and fear of arousal symptoms. *CNS Neuroscience Therapeutics, 15*(3), 264–275.

Hinton, D., Pich, V., Chhean, D., Pollack, M. H., & Barlow, D. H. (2004). Olfactory-triggered panic attacks among Cambodian refugees attending a psychiatric clinic. *General Hospital Psychiatry, 26*(5), 390–397.

Hinton, D., Pollack, M. H., Pich, V., Fama, J. M., & Barlow, D. H. (2005). Orthosatically induced panic attacks among Cambodian refugees: Flashbacks, catastrophic cognitions, and associated psychopathology. *Cognitive Behavioral Practice, 12,* 301–311.

Hinton, L., Guo, Z., Hillygus, J., & Levkoff, S. (2000). Working with culture: A qualitative analysis of barriers to the recruitment of Chinese American family caregivers for dementia research. *Journal of Cross-Cultural Gerontology, 15*(2), 119–137. doi:10.1023/A:1006798316654

Hirschfeld, D. R., Rosenbaum, J. F., Biederman, J., Bolduc, E. A., Farone, S. V., Snidman, N., ... Kagan, J. (1992). Stable behavioral inhibition and its association with anxiety disorder. *Journal of the American Academy of Child and Adolescent Psychiatry, 31,* 103–111.

Hirschfeld, R. M. A., Keller, M. M., Panico, S., Arons, B. S., Barlow, D., Davidoff, F., ... Wyatt, R. J. (1997). The National Depressive and Manic-Depressive Association consensus statement on the undertreatment of depression. *JAMA: Journal of the American Medical Association, 277*(4), 333–340.

Hirshkowitz, M., Seplowitz, R. G., & Sharafkhaneh, A. (2009). Sleep disorders. In B. J. Sadock, V. A. Sadock, & P. Ruiz (Eds.), *Kaplan & Sadock's Comprehensive Textbook of Psychiatry* (9th ed., Vol. I, pp. 2150–2177). Philadelphia, PA: Lippincott Williams & Wilkins.

Hitchcock, P. B., & Mathews, A. (1992). Interpretation of bodily symptoms in hypochondriasis. *Behaviour Research and Therapy, 30*(3), 223–234.

Hlastala, S. A., Kotler, J. S., McClellan, J. M., & McCauley, E. A. (2010). Interpersonal and social rhythm therapy for adolescents with bipolar disorder: Treatment development and results from an open trial. *Depression and Anxiety, 27*(5), 457–464.

Hobfoll, S. E., Canetti-Nisim, D., & Johnson, R. J. (2006). Exposure to terrorism, stress-related mental health symptoms, and defensive coping among Jews and Arabs in Israel. *Journal of Consulting and Clinical Psychology, 74,* 207–218.

Hoehn-Saric, R., McLeod, D. R., & Zimmerli, W. D. (1989). Somatic manifestations in women with generalized anxiety disorder: Psychophysiological responses to psychological stress. *Archives of General Psychiatry, 46,* 1113–1119.

Hoek, H. W. (2002). The distribution of eating disorders. In K. D. Brownell & C. G. Fairburn (Eds.), *Eating disorders and obesity: A comprehensive handbook* (2nd ed., pp. 207–211). New York, NY: Guilford Press.

Hofmann, S. G. (2004). Cognitive mediation of treatment change in social phobia. *Journal of Consulting and Clinical Psychology, 72,* 393–399.

Hofmann, S. G., Alpers, G. W., & Pauli, P. (2009). Phenomenology of panic and phobic disorders. In M. M. Antony & M. B. Stein (Eds.), *Oxford handbook of anxiety and related disorders* (pp. 34–46). New York, NY: Oxford University Press.

Hofmann, S. G., & Barlow, D. H. (2002). Social phobia (social anxiety disorder). In D. H. Barlow, *Anxiety and its disorders: The nature and treatment of anxiety and panic* (2nd ed.). New York, NY: Guilford Press.

Hofmann, S. G., Lehman, C. L., & Barlow, D. H. (1997). How specific are specific phobias? *Journal of Behavior Therapy and Experimental Psychiatry, 28,* 233–240.

Hofmann, S. G., Meuret, A. E., Smitts, J. A. J., Simon, N. M., Pollack, M. H., Eisenmenger, K., ... Otto, M. W. (2006). Augmentation of exposure therapy with D-cycloserine for social anxiety disorder. *Archives of General Psychiatry, 63,* 298–304.

Hofmann, S., Richey, J., Kashdan, T., & McKnight, P. (2009). Anxiety disorders moderate the association between externalizing problems and substance use disorders: Data from the National Comorbidity Survey-Revised. *Journal of Anxiety Disorders, 23*(4), 529–534.

Hofstede, G., & McCrae, R. R. (2004). Personality and culture revisited: Linking traits and dimensions of culture. *Cross-Cultural Research, 38,* 52–88.

Hogarty, G. E., Anderson, C. M., Reiss, D. J., Kornblith, S. J., Greenwald, D. P., Javna, C. D., & Madonia, M. J. (1986). Family psychoeducation, social skills training, and maintenance chemotherapy in the aftercare treatment of schizophrenia: I. One-year effects of a controlled study on relapse and expressed emotion. *Archives of General Psychiatry, 43,* 633–642.

Hogarty, G. E., Anderson, C. M., Reiss, D. J., Kornblith, S. J., Greenwald, D. P., Ulrich, R. F., Carter, M., & The Environmental–Personal Indicators in the Course of Schizophrenia (EPICS) Research Group. (1991). Family psychoeducation, social skills training, and maintenance chemotherapy in the aftercare treatment of schizophrenia. *Archives of General Psychiatry, 48,* 340–347.

Holden, C. (2005). Obesity in the east. *Science, 307,* 38.

Holder, H. D., Gruenewald, P. J., Ponicki, W. R., Treno, A. J., Grube, J. W., & Saltz, R. F., ... Roeper, P. (2000). Effect of community-based interventions on high-risk drinking and alcohol-related injuries. *JAMA: Journal of the American Medical Association, 284,* 2341–2347.

Holland, J. M., & Gallagher-Thompson, D. (2011). Interventions for mental health problems in later life. In D. H. Barlow (Ed.), *Oxford handbook of clinical psychology* (pp. 810–836). New York, NY: Oxford University Press.

Hollander, E., Allen, A., Kwon, J., Aronwoitz, B., Schmeidler, J., Wong, C., & Simeon, D. (1999). Clomipramine vs. desipramine crossover trial in body dysmorphic disorder: Selective efficacy of a serotonin reuptake inhibitor in imagined ugliness. *Archives of General Psychiatry, 56*(11), 1033–1039.

Hollander, E., Berlin, H. A., & Stein, D. J. (2009). Impulse-control disorders not elsewhere classified. In J. A. Bourgeois, R. E. Hales, J. S. Young, & S. C. Yudofsky (Eds.), *The American Psychiatric Publishing Board review guide for psychiatry* (pp. 469–482). Arlington, VA: American Psychiatric Publishing.

Hollifield, M., Katon, W., Spain, D., & Pule, L. (1990). Anxiety and depression in a village in Lesotho, Africa: A comparison with the United States. *British Journal of Psychiatry, 156,* 343–350.

Hollis, J. F., Connett, J. E., Stevens, V. J., & Greenlick, M. R. (1990). Stressful life events, type A behavior, and the prediction of cardiovascular and total mortality over six years. *Journal of Behavioral Medicine, 13*(3), 263–280.

Hollon, S. D., DeRubeis, R. J., Evans, M. D., Wiener, M. J., Garvey, M. J., Grose, W. M., & Tuason, V. B. (1992). Cognitive therapy and pharmacotherapy for depression: Singly and in combination. *Archives of General Psychiatry, 49*(10), 772–781.

Hollon, S. D., DeRubeis, R. J., Shelton, R. C., Amsterdam, J. D., Salomon, R. M., O'Reardon, J. P., ... Gallop, R. (2005). Prevention of relapse following cognitive therapy vs. medications in moderate to severe depression. *Archives of General Psychiatry, 62,* 417–422.

Hollon, S. D., & Dimidjian, S. (2009). Cognitive and behavioral treatment of depression. In I. H. Gotlib & C. L. Hammen (Eds.), *Handbook of depression* (2nd ed., pp. 586–603). New York, NY: Guilford Press.

Hollon, S. D., Kendall, P. C., & Lumry, A. (1986). Specificity of depressotypic cognitions in clinical depression. *Journal of Abnormal Psychology, 95,* 52–59.

Hollon, S. D., Shelton, R. C., & Loosen, P. T. (1991). Cognitive therapy and pharmacotherapy for depression. *Journal of Consulting and Clinical Psychology, 59*(1), 88–99.

Hollon, S. D., Stewart, M. O., & Strunk, D. (2006). Cognitive behavior therapy has enduring effects in the treatment of depression and anxiety. *Annual Review of Psychology, 57,* 285–315.

Holroyd, K. A., Andrasik, F., & Noble, J. (1980). A comparison of EMG biofeedback and a credible pseudotherapy in treating tension headache. *Journal of Behavioral Medicine, 3,* 29–39.

Holroyd, K. A., Nash, J. M., Pingel, J. D., Cordingley, G. E., & Jerome, A. (1991). A comparison of pharmacological (amitriptyline HCL) and nonpharmacological (cognitive-behavioral) therapies for chronic tension headaches. *Journal of Consulting and Clinical Psychology, 59*(3), 387–393.

Holroyd, K. A., & Penzien, D. B. (1986). Client variables in the behavioral treatment of current tension headache: A meta-analytic review. *Journal of Behavioral Medicine, 9,* 515–536.

Holroyd, K. A., Penzien, D. B., Hursey, K. G., Tobin, D. L., Rogers, L., Holm, J. E., ... Chila, A. G. (1984). Change mechanisms in EMG biofeedback training. Cognitive changes underlying improvements in tension headache. *Journal of Consulting and Clinical Psychology, 52,* 1039–1053.

Holt-Lunstad, J., Birmingham, W. A., & Light, K. C. (2008). Influence of a "warm touch" support enhancement intervention among married couples on ambulatory blood pressure, oxytocin, alpha amylase, & cortisol. *Psychosomatic Medicine, 70,* 976–985.

Holzman, P. S., & Levy, D. L. (1977). Smooth pursuit eye movements and functional psychoses: A review. *Schizophrenia Bulletin, 3,* 15–27.

Hook, E. B. (1982). Epidemiology of Down syndrome. In S. M. P. J. E. Rynders (Ed.), *Down syndrome: Advances in biomedicine and the behavioral sciences* (pp. 11–88). Cambridge, MA: Ware Press.

Hooley, J. M. (1985). Expressed emotion: A review of the critical literature. *Clinical Psychology Review, 5,* 119–139.

Hooley, J. M., & Campbell, C. (2002). Control and controllability: Beliefs and behaviour in high and low expressed emotion relatives. *Psychological Medicine, 32,* 1091–1099.

Hopwood, C., Morey, L., Markowitz, J., Pinto, A., Skodol, A., Gunderson, J., ... McGlashan, T. H. (2009). The construct validity of passive-aggressive personality disorder. *Psychiatry: Interpersonal & Biological Processes, 72*(3), 256–267.

Horan, W. P., Ventura, J., Mintz, J., Kopelowicz, A., Wirshing, D., Christian-Herman, J., Foy, D., & Liberman, R. P. (2007). Stress and coping responses to a natural disaster in people with schizophrenia. *Psychiatry Research, 151,* 77–86.

Horowitz, J., & Garber, J. (2006). The prevention of depressive symptoms in children and adolescents: A meta-analytic review. *Journal of Consulting and Clinical Psychology, 74,* 401–415.

Horowitz, M. J., Siegel, B., Holen, A., Bonanno, G. A., Milbrath, C., & Stinson, C. H. (1997). Diagnostic criteria for complicated grief disorder. *American Journal of Psychiatry, 154,* 904–910.

Horsfall, J., Cleary, M., Hunt, G., & Walter, G. (2009). Psychosocial treatments for people with co-occurring severe mental illnesses and substance use disorders (dual diagnosis): A review of empirical evidence. *Harvard Review of Psychiatry, 17*(1), 24–34.

Horwath, E., & Weissman, M. (1997). Epidemiology of anxiety disorders across cultural groups. In S. Friedman (Ed.), *Cultural issues in the treatment of anxiety* (pp. 21–39.) New York, NY: Guilford Press.

House, J. S., Landis, K. R., & Umberson, D. (1988). Social relationships and health. *Science, 241,* 540–545.

House, J. S., Robbins, C., & Metzner, H. M. (1982). The association of social relationships and activities with mortality: Prospective evidence from the Tecumseh community health study. *American Journal of Epidemiology, 116,* 123.

Houston, B. K., Chesney, M. A., Black, G. W., Cates, D. S., & Hecker, M. H. L. (1992). Behavioral clusters and coronary heart disease risk. *Psychosomatic Medicine, 54*(4), 447–461.

Houts, A. C. (2001). The diagnostic and statistical manual's new white coat and circularity of plausible dysfunctions: Response to Wakefield, Part I. *Behaviour Research and Therapy, 39,* 315–345.

Howe, M. L. (2007). Children's emotional false memories. *Psychological Science, 18*(10), 856–860.

Howes, O. D., & Kapur, S. (2009). The dopamine hypothesis of schizophrenia: version III—the final common pathway. *Schizophrenia Bulletin, 35*(3), 549–562. doi:10.1093/schbul/sbp006

Howland, R. H., Rush, A. J., Wisniewski, S. R., Trivedi, M. H., Warden, D., Fava, M., ... Gallop, R. (2009). Concurrent anxiety and substance use disorders among outpatients with major depression: Clinical features and effect on treatment outcome. *Drug and Alcohol Dependence, 99*(1-3), 248–260.

Hrabosky, J. I., Masheb, R. M., White, M. A., & Grilo, C. M. (2007). Overvaluation of shape and weight in binge eating disorder. *Journal of Consulting and Clinical Psychology, 75,* 175–180.

Hsu, L. K. G. (1990). *Eating disorders.* New York, NY: Guilford Press.

Hsu, L. K. G., & Zimmer, B. (1988). Eating disorders in old age. *International Journal of Eating Disorders, 7,* 133–138.

Huang, Y., Kotov, R., de Girolamo, G., Preti, A., Angermeyer, M., Benjet, C., ... Kessler, R. C. (2009). DSM-IV personality disorders in the WHO World Mental Health Surveys. *The British Journal of Psychiatry, 195*(1), 46–53. doi:10.1192/bjp.bp.108.058552

Hubert, N. C., Jay, S. M., Saltoun, M., & Hayes, M. (1988). Approach-avoidance and distress in children undergoing preparation for painful medical procedures. *Journal of Clinical Child Psychology, 17,* 194–202.

Hucker, S. J. (1997). Sexual sadism: Psychopathology and theory. In D. R. Laws & W. T. O'Donohue (Eds.), *Sexual deviance: Theory, assessment, and treatment* (pp. 194–209). New York, NY: Guilford Press.

Hucker, S. J. (2008). Sexual masochism: Psychopathology and theory. In D. R. Laws & W. T. O'Donohue (Eds.), *Sexual deviance: Theory, assessment, and treatment* (2nd ed., pp. 250–263). New York, NY: Guilford Press.

Hudson, C., & Vissing, Y. (2010). The geography of adult homelessness in the US: Validation of state and county estimates. *Health & Place, 16*(5), 828–837.

Hudson, J. I., Hiripi, E., Pope, H. G., Jr., & Kessler, R. C. (2007). The prevalence and correlates of eating disorders in the national comorbidity survey replication. *Biological Psychiatry, 61,* 348–358.

Hudson, J. I., Lalonde, J. K., Berry, J. M., Pindych, L. J., Bulik, C. M., Crow, S. J., ... Pope, H. G. (2006). Binge-eating disorder as a distinct familial phenotype in obese individuals. *Archives of General Psychiatry, 63,* 313–319.

Hudson, J. I., Mangweth, B., Pope, H. G., Jr., De Col, C., Hausmann, A., Gutweniger, S., ... Tsaung, M. T. (2003). Family study of affective spectrum disorder. *Archives of General Psychiatry, 60,* 170–177.

Hudson, J., Pope, H., Jonas, J. M., & Yurgelun-Todd, D. (1983). Family history study of anorexia nervosa and bulimia. *British Journal of Psychiatry, 142,* 133–138.

Hufford, M. R., Shields, A. L., Shiffman, S., Paty, J., & Balabanis, M. (2002). Reactivity to ecological momentary assessment: An example using undergraduate problem drinkers. *Psychology of Addictive Behaviors, 16,* 205–211.

Hughes, J. R. (2009). Nicotine-related disorders. In B. J. Sadock, V. A. Sadock, & P. Ruiz (Eds.), *Kaplan & Sadock's comprehensive textbook of psychiatry* (9th ed., Vol. I, pp. 1353–1360). Philadelphia, PA: Lippincott Williams & Wilkins.

Human Rights Campaign. History of National Coming Out Day. Retrieved from http://www.hrc.org/issues/3338.htm

Humphrey, L. L. (1986). Structural analysis of parent–child relationships in eating disorders. *Journal of Abnormal Psychology, 95,* 395–402.

Humphrey, L. L. (1988). Relationships within subtypes of anorexic, bulimic, and normal families. *Journal of the American Academy of Child and Adolescent Psychiatry, 27,* 544–551.

Humphrey, L. L. (1989). Observed family interactions among subtypes of eating disorders using structural analysis of social behavior. *Journal of Consulting and Clinical Psychology, 57,* 206–214.

Hunsley J. & Mash, E. J. (2011). Evidence based assessment. In D. H. Barlow (Ed.), *Oxford handbook of clinical psychology* (pp. 76–97). New York, NY: Oxford University Press.

Hunt, M. (2007). Borderline personality disorder across the life span. *Journal of Women & Aging, 19*(1), 173–191.

Hunt, W. A. (1980). History and classification. In A. E. Kazdin, A. S. Bellack, & M. Hersen (Eds.), *New perspectives in abnormal psychology.* New York, NY: Oxford University Press.

Hunter, E., Sierra, M., & David, A. (2004). The epidemiology of depersonalisation and derealisation: A systematic review. *Social Psychiatry and Psychiatric Epidemiology, 39,* 9–18.

Huntington's Disease Collaborative Research Group. (1993). A novel gene containing a trinucleotide repeat that is expanded and unstable on Huntington's disease chromosomes. *Cell, 72,* 971–983.

Huntjens, R. J., Peters, M., Woertman, L., Bovenschen, L., Loes, M., Martin, R., & Postma, A. (2006). Interidentity amnesia in dissociative identity disorder: A simulated memory impairment? *Psychological Medicine, 36,* 857–863.

Huntjens, R. J., Postma, A., Hamaker, E. L., Woertman, L., van der Hart, O., & Peters, M. (2002). Perceptual and conceptual priming in patients with dissociative identity disorder. *Memory & Cognition, 30,* 1033–1043.

Huntjens, R. J., Postma, A., Peters, M., Woertman, L., & van der Hart, O. (2003). Interidentity amnesia for neutral, episodic information in dissociative identity disorder. *Abnormal Psychology, 112,* 290–7.

Huppert, J. D. (2009). Anxiety disorders and depression comorbidity. In M. M. Antony & M. B. Stein (Eds.), *Oxford handbook of anxiety and related disorders* (pp. 576–586). New York, NY: Oxford University Press.

Hurt, S. W., Schnurr, P. P., Severino, S. K., Freeman, E. W., Gise, L. H., Rivera-Tovar, A., & Steege, J. F. (1992). Late luteal phase dysphoric disorder in 670 women evaluated for premenstrual complaints. *American Journal of Psychiatry, 149,* 525–530.

Hyman, S. E. (2009). How adversity gets under the skin. *Nature Neuroscience, 12*(3), 241–243.

Iacono, W. G., Bassett, A. S., & Jones, B. D. (1988). Eye tracking dysfunction is associated with partial trisomy of chromosome

5 and schizophrenia. *Archives of General Psychiatry, 45*(12), 1140–1141.

Imeri, L., & Opp, M. R. (2009). How (and why) the immune system makes us sleep. *Nature Reviews Neuroscience, 10*(3), 199–210.

Imhof, A., Kovari, E., von Gunten, A., Gold, G., Rivara, C.-B., Herrmann, F. R., ... Giannakopoulos, P. (2007). Morphological substrates of cognitive decline in nonagenarians and centenarians: A new paradigm? *Journal of the Neurological Sciences, 257*(1–2), 72–79.

Ingram, R., Miranda, J., & Segal, Z. (2006). Cognitive vulnerability to depression. In L. B. Alloy and J. H. Riskind (Eds.)., *Cognitive vulnerability to emotional disorders* (pp. 63–91). Mahwah, NJ: Lawrence Erlbaum Associates Publishers.

Inlow, J. K., & Restifo, L. L. (2004). Molecular and comparative genetics of mental retardation. *Genetics, 166*, 835–881.

Insel, T. R. (Ed.) (1984). *New findings in obsessive-compulsive disorder*. Washington, DC: American Psychiatric Press.

Insel, T. R. (1992). Toward a neuroanatomy of obsessive-compulsive disorder. *Archives of General Psychiatry, 49*, 739–744.

Insel, T. R. (2006). Beyond efficacy: The STAR*D trial. *American Journal of Psychiatry, 163*, 5–7.

Insel, T. R. (2009). Translating scientific opportunity into public health impact: A strategic plan for research on mental illness. *Archives of General Psychiatry, 66*(2), 128–133.

Insel, T. R., Scanlan, J., Champoux, M., & Suomi, S. J. (1988). Rearing paradigm in a nonhuman primate affects response to B-CCE challenge. *Psychopharmacology, 96*, 81–86.

Institute of Medicine. (1999). *Reducing the burden of injury: Advancing prevention and treatment*. Washington, DC: National Academy of Sciences.

Institute of Medicine. (2001). *Crossing the quality chasm: A new health system for the 21st century*. Washington, DC: National Academies Press.

Institute of Medicine. (2002). *Reducing suicide: A national imperative*. Washington, DC: National Academic Press.

Iribarren, C., Sidney, S., Bild, D. E., Liu, K., Markovitz, J. H., Roseman, J. M., & Matthews, K. (2000). Association of hostility with coronary artery calcification in young adults. *JAMA: Journal of the American Medical Association, 283*(19), 2546–2551.

Ironson, G., Taylor, C. B., Boltwood, M., Bartzokis, T., Dennis, C., Chesney, M., ... Segal, G. M. (1992). Effects of anger on left ventricular ejection fraction in coronary artery disease. *American Journal of Cardiology, 70*, 281–285.

Irvin, J. E., Bowers, C. A., Dunn, M. E., & Wang, M. C. (1999). Efficacy of relapse prevention: A meta-analytic review. *Journal of Consulting and Clinical Psychology, 67*(4), 563–570.

Isaacowitz, D., Smith, T. T., & Carstensen, L. L. (2003). Socioemotional selectivity, positive bias, and mental health among trauma survivors in old age. *Ageing International, 28*, 181–199.

Ivanov, I. (2009). Disulfiram and acamprosate. In B. J. Sadock, V. A. Sadock, & P. Ruiz (Eds.), *Kaplan & Sadock's compre-*

hensive textbook of psychiatry (9th ed., Vol. II, pp. 3099–3105). Philadelphia, PA: Lippincott Williams & Wilkins.

Iverson, L. (2006). Neurotransmitter transporters and their impact on the development of psychopharmacology. *British Journal of Pharmacology, 147*(Suppl. 1), S82–S88.

Izard, C. E. (1992). Basic emotions, relations among emotions, and emotion–cognition relations. *Psychological Review, 99*(3), 561–565.

Jablensky, A. (2009). Worldwide burden of schizophrenia. In B. J. Sadock, V. A. Sadock, & P. Ruiz (Eds.), *Kaplan & Sadock's comprehensive textbook of psychiatry* (9th ed., Vol. I, pp. 1451–1462). Philadelphia, PA: Lippincott Williams & Wilkins.

Jackson v. Indiana, 406 U.S. 715 (1972).

Jackson, C., Brown, J. D., & L'Engle, K. L. (2007). R-rated movies, bedroom televisions, and initiation of smoking by white and black adolescents. *Archives of Pediatrics & Adolescent Medicine, 161*, 260–268.

Jackson, G., Rosen, R., Kloner, R., & Kostis, J. (2006). The second Princeton consensus on sexual dysfunction and cardiac risk: New guidelines for sexual medicine. *Journal of Sexual Medicine, 3*, 28–36.

Jackson, S., Pretti-Frontczak, K., Harjusola-Webb, S., Grisham-Brown, J., & Romani, J. M. (2009). Response to intervention: Implications for early childhood professionals. *Language, Speech, and Hearing Services in Schools, 40*(4), 424–434.

Jacobi, W., & Winkler, H. (1927). Encephalographische studien an chronischen schizophrenen. *Archives fur Psychiarrie und Nervenkrunkheiten, 81*, 299–332.

Jacobs, S. (1993). *Pathologic grief: Maladaptation to loss*. Washington, DC: American Psychiatric Press.

Jacobs, S., Hansen, F., Berkman, L., Kasl, S., & Ostfeld, A. (1989). Depressions of bereavement. *Comprehensive Psychiatry, 30*(3), 218–224.

Jacobson, N. S., Dobson, K. S., Truax, P. A., Addis, M. E., Koerner, K., Gollan, J. K., ... Prince, S. E. (1996). A component analysis of cognitive-behavioral treatment for depression. *Journal of Consulting and Clinical Psychology, 64*, 295–304.

Jacobson, N. S., Martell, C. R., & Dimidjian, S. (2001). Behavioral activation treatment for depression: Returning to contextual roots. *Clinical Psychology: Science and Practice, 8*(3), 255–270.

Jamison, R. N., & Virts, K. L. (1990). The influence of family support on chronic pain. *Behaviour Research and Therapy, 28*(4), 283–287.

Jamner, L. D., Shapiro, D., Goldstein, I. B., & Hug, R. (1991). Ambulatory blood pressure and heart rate in paramedics: Effects of cynical hostility and defensiveness. *Psychosomatic Medicine, 53*, 393–406.

Jane, J. S., Oltmanns, T. F., South, S. C., & Turkheimer, E. (2007). Gender bias in diagnostic criteria for personality disorders: An item response theory analysis. *Journal of Abnormal Psychology, 116*, 166–175.

Jang, K. L. (2005). *The behavioral genetics of psychopathology: A clinical guide*. Mahwah, NJ: Lawrence Erlbaum Associates.

Jason, L. A., Fennell, P. A., & Taylor, R. R. (2003). *Handbook of chronic fatigue syndrome*. Hoboken, NJ: John Wiley.

Jason, L. A., Roesner, N., Porter, N., Parenti, B., Mortensen, J., & Till, L. (2010). Provision of social support to individuals with chronic fatigue syndrome. *Journal of Clinical Psychology, 66*, 249–258.

Jaspers, K. (1963). *General psychopathology* (J. Hoenig & M. W. Hamilton, Trans.). Manchester, UK: Manchester University Press.

Javitt, D. C., & Laruelle, M. (2006). Neurochemical theories. In J. A. Lieberman, T. S. Stroup, & D. O. Perkins (Eds.), *The American Psychiatric Publishing textbook of schizophrenia* (pp. 85– 116). Washington, DC: American Psychiatric Publishing.

Javitt, D. C., & Zukin, S. R. (2009). Phencyclidine (or Phencyclidine-like)-related disorders. In B. J. Sadock, V. A. Sadock, & P. Ruiz (Eds.), *Kaplan & Sadock's comprehensive textbook of psychiatry* (9th ed., Vol. I, pp. 1337–1397). Philadelphia, PA: Lippincott Williams & Wilkins.

Jay, S. M., Elliott, C. H., Ozolins, M., Olson, R. A., & Pruitt, S. D. (1985). Behavioral management of children's distress during painful medical procedures. *Behaviour Research and Therapy, 23*(5), 513–520.

Jellinek, E. M. (1946). Phases in the drinking histories of alcoholics. *Quarterly Journal of Studies on Alcohol, 7*, 1–88.

Jellinek, E. M. (1952). Phases of alcohol addiction. *Quarterly Journal of Studies on Alcohol, 13*, 673–684.

Jellinek, E. M. (1960). *The disease concept of alcohol*. New Brunswick, NJ: Hillhouse Press.

Jenike, M. A., Baer, L., Ballantine, H. T., Martuza, R. L., Tynes, S., Giriunas, I., ... Cassem, N. H. (1991). Cingulotomy for refractory obsessive-compulsive disorder: A long-term follow-up of 33 patients. *Archives of General Psychiatry, 48*, 548–555.

Jenkins, J. H., & Karno, M. (1992). The meaning of expressed emotion: Theoretical issues raised by cross-cultural research. *American Journal of Psychiatry, 149*, 9–21.

Jenkins, J. H., Kleinman, A., & Good, B. J. (1990). Cross-cultural studies of depression. In J. Becker & A. Kleinman (Eds.), *Psychosocial aspects of depression*. Hillsdale, NJ: Erlbaum.

Jennum, P., & Riha, R. L. (2009). Epidemiology of sleep apnoea/hypopnoea syndrome and sleep-disordered breathing. *European Respiratory Journal, 33*(4), 907–914. doi:10.1183/09031936.00180108

Jensen, E., Schmidt, E., Pedersen, B., & Dahl, R. (1991). Effect on smoking cessation of silver acetate, nicotine and ordinary chewing gum. *Psychopharmacology, 104*(4), 470–474.

Jensen, P. S., Hinshaw, S. P., Swanson, J. M., Greenhill, L. L., Conners, C. K., Arnold, L. E., ... Wigal, T. (2001). Findings from the NIMH Multimodal Treatment Study of ADHD (MTA): Implications and applications for primary care providers. *Journal of Developmental and Behavioral Pediatrics, 22*(1), 60–73.

Jeste, D., Palmer, B., Golshan, S., Eyler, L., Dunn, L., Meeks, T., ... Appelbaum, P. S. (2009). Multimedia consent for research in people with schizophrenia and normal subjects: A randomized controlled trial. *Schizophrenia Bulletin, 35*(4), 719.

Jilek, W. G. (1982). Altered states of consciousness in North American Indian ceremonials. *Ethos, 10*(4), 326–343.

Jindal, R. D., Thase, M. E., Fasiczka, A. L., Friedman, E. S., Buysse, D. J., Frank, E., & Kupfer, D.J. (2002). Electroencephalographic sleep profiles in single-episode and recurrent unipolar forms of major depression: II. Comparison during remission. *Biological Psychiatry, 1*, 230–236.

Jobe, T. H., & Harrow, M. (2005). Long-term outcome of patients with schizophrenia: A review. *Canadian Journal of Psychiatry, 50*, 892–900.

Jockin, V., McGue, M., & Lykken, D. T. (1996). Personality and divorce: A genetic analysis. *Journal of Personality and Social Psychology, 71*, 288–299.

Joe, S., Baser, R., Breeden, G., Neighbors, H., & Jackson, J. (2006). Prevalence of and risk factors for lifetime suicide attempts among blacks in the United States. *JAMA: Journal of the American Medical Association, 296*, 2112–2123.

Johnson, A. M., Wadsworth, J., Wellings, K., Bradshaw, S., & Field, J. (1992). Sexual lifestyles and HIV risk. *Nature, 360*, 410–412.

Johnson, J. G., Bromley, E., & McGeoch, P. G. (2005). Role of childhood experiences in the development of maladaptive and adaptive traits. In J. M. Oldham, A. E. Skodol, & D. S. Bender (Eds.), *Textbook of personality disorders* (pp. 209–221). Washington, DC: American Psychiatric Publishing.

Johnson, J. G., Cohen, P., Kasen, S., & Brook, J. S. (2002). Eating disorders during adolescence and the risk for physical and mental disorders during early adulthood. *Archives of General Psychiatry, 59*, 545–552.

Johnson, J. G., Cohen, P., Kasen, S., & Brook, J. S. (2006). Dissociative disorders among adults in the community, impaired functioning, and axis I and axis II comorbidity. *Journal of Psychiatric Research, 40*, 131–140.

Johnson, J. G., Cohen, P., Pine, D. S., Klein, D. F., Kasen, S., & Brook, J. S. (2000). Association between cigarette smoking and anxiety disorders during adolescence and early adulthood. *JAMA: Journal of the American Medical Association, 284*, 2348–2351.

Johnson, J. G., Weissman, M. M., & Klerman, G. L. (1990). Panic disorder, comorbidity, and suicide attempts. *Archives of General Psychiatry, 47*, 805–808.

Johnson, S. L., Cuellar, A. K., & Miller, C. (2009). Bipolar and unipolar depression: A comparison of clinical phenomenology, biological vulnerability, and psychosocial predictors. In I. H. Gotlib & C. L. Hammen (Eds.), *Handbook of depression* (2nd ed., pp. 142–162). New York, NY: Guilford Press.

Johnson, S. L., Cuellar, A. K., Ruggero, C., Winett-Perlman, C., Goodnick, P., White, R., & Miller, I. (2008). Life events as predictors of mania and depression in bipolar I disorder. *Journal of Abnormal Psychology, 117*(2), 268–277.

Johnson, S. L., Gruber, J. L., & Eisner, L. R. (2007). Emotion and bipolar disorder. In J. Rottenberg & S. L. Johnson (Eds.), *Emotion and psychopathology* (pp. 123–150).

Washington, DC: American Psychological Association.

Johnson, S. L., & Miller, I. (1997). Negative life events and time to recovery from episodes of bipolar disorder. *Journal of Abnormal Psychology, 106*(3), 449–457.

Johnson, S. L., Winett, C. A., Meyer, B., Greenhouse, W. J., & Miller, I. (1999). Social support and the course of bipolar disorder. *American Psychological Association, 180*(4), 558–566.

Johnson, W., Turkheimer, E., Gottesman, I. I., & Bouchard, T. J., Jr. (2009). Beyond heritability: Twin studies in behavioral research. *Current Directions in Psychological Science, 18*(4), 217–220.

Johnston, L., Bachman, J., & Schulenberg, J. (2005). *Monitoring the future national results on adolescent drug use: Overview of key findings, 2004*: Substance Abuse and Mental Health Services Administration.

Joiner, T., Kalafat, J., Draper, J., Stokes, H., Knudson, M., Berman, A. L., & McKeon, R. (2007). Establishing standards for the assessment of suicide risk among callers to the national suicide prevention lifeline. *Suicide and Life-Threatening Behavior, 37*(3), 353–365.

Joiner, T. E., Jr. (1997). Shyness and low social support as interactive diatheses, with loneliness as mediator: Testing an interpersonal–personality view of vulnerability to depressive symptoms. *Journal of Abnormal Psychology, 106*(3), 386–394.

Joiner, T. E., Jr. (1999). A test of interpersonal theory of depression in youth psychiatric inpatients. *Journal of Abnormal Child Psychology, 27*(1), 77–85.

Joiner, T. E., Jr., Heatherton, T. F., & Keel, P. K. (1997). Ten-year stability and predictive validity of five bulimia-related indicators. *American Journal of Psychiatry, 154*, 1133–1138.

Joiner, T. E., Jr., & Rudd, D. M. (1996). Toward a categorization of depression-related psychological constructs. *Cognitive Therapy and Research, 20*, 51–68.

Joiner, T. E., Jr., & Rudd, M. D. (2000). Intensity and duration of suicidal crises vary as a function of previous suicide attempts and negative life events. *Journal of Consulting and Clinical Psychology, 68*(5), 909–916.

Joiner, T. E., Jr., & Timmons, K. A. (2009). Depression in its interpersonal context. In I. H. Gotlib & C. L. Hammen (Eds.), *Handbook of depression* (2nd ed., pp. 322–339). New York, NY: Guilford Press.

Jones, B. E., & Gray, B. A. (1986). Problems in diagnosing schizophrenia and affective disorders in blacks. *Hospital and Community Psychiatry, 37*, 61–65.

Jones, J. C., & Barlow, D. H. (1990). The etiology of posttraumatic stress disorder. *Clinical Psychology Review, 10*, 299–328.

Jones, M. C. (1924a). The elimination of children's fears. *Journal of Experimental Psychology, 7*, 383–390.

Jones, M. C. (1924b). A laboratory study of fear. The case of Peter. *Pedagogical Seminary, 31*, 308–315.

Jones, P., Barnes, T., Davies, L., Dunn, G., Lloyd, H., Hayhurst, K., ... Lewis, S. W. (2006). Randomized controlled trial of the effect on quality of life of second- vs. first-generation antipsychotic drugs in schizo-

phrenia: Cost Utility of the Latest Antipsychotic Drugs in Schizophrenia Study (CUtLASS 1). *Archives of General Psychiatry, 63*(10), 1079.

Jones, R. T. (2009). Hallucinogen-related disorders. In B. J. Sadock, V. A. Sadock, & P. Ruiz (Eds.), *Kaplan & Sadock's comprehensive textbook of psychiatry* (9th ed., Vol. I, pp. 1331–1340). Philadelphia, PA: Lippincott Williams & Wilkins.

Jones, R. T., & Haney, J. I. (1984). A primary preventive approach to the acquisition and maintenance of fire emergency responding: Comparison of external and self-instruction strategies. *Journal of Community Psycho logy, 12*(2), 180–191.

Jones, R. T., & Kazdin, A. E. (1980). Teaching children how and when to make emergency telephone calls. *Behavior Therapy, 11*(4), 509–521.

Jones, R. T., & Ollendick, T. H. (2002). Residential fires. In A. M. La Greca, W. K. Silverman, E. Vernberg, & M. C. Roberts (Eds.), *Helping children cope with disasters and terrorism* (pp. 175–199). Washington, DC: American Psychological Association.

Joormann, J. (2009). Cognitive aspects of depression. In I. H. Gotlib & C. L. Hammen (Eds.), *Handbook of depression* (2nd ed., pp. 298–321). New York, NY: Guilford Press.

Jordan, B. D., Relkin, N. R., Ravdin, L. D., Jacobs, A. R., Bennett, A., & Gandy, S. (1997). Apolipoprotein E Epsilon 4 associated with chronic traumatic brain injury in boxing. *JAMA: Journal of the American Medical Association, 278*, 136–140.

Joshi, G., & Wilens, T. (2009). Comorbidity in pediatric bipolar disorder. *Child and Adolescent Psychiatric Clinics of North America, 18*(2), 291–319.

Joska, J. A., & Stein, D. J. (2008). Mood disorders. In R. E. Hales, S. C. Yudofsky & G. O. Gabbard (Eds.), *The American Psychiatric Publishing textbook of psychiatry* (5th ed., pp. 457–303). Arlington, VA: American Psychiatric Publishing.

Judd, L. L. (1997). The clinical course of unipolar major depressive disorders. *Archives of General Psychiatry, 54*, 989–991.

Judd, L. L. (2000). Course and chronicity of unipolar major depressive disorder: Commentary on joiner. *Child Psychology Science and Practice, 7*(2), 219–223.

Judd, L. L., Akiskal, H., Schettler, P., Coryell, W., Endicott, J., Maser, J., ... Keller, M. B. (2003). A prospective investigation of the natural history of the long-term weekly symptomatic status of the long-term weekly symptomatic status of bipolar II disorder. *Archives of General Psychiatry, 60*, 261–269.

Judd, L. L., Akiskal, H. S., Maser, J. D., Zeller, P. J., Endicott, J., Coryell, W., ... Keller, M. B. (1998). Major depressive disorder: A prospective study of residual subthreshold depressive symptoms as predictor of rapid release. *Journal of Affective Disorders, 50*, 97–108.

Judge, B., & Rusyniak, D. (2009). Illicit Drugs I: Amphetamines. In M. R. Dobbs (Ed.), *Clinical neurotoxicology: Syndromes, substances, environments, expert consult* (pp. 303–313). Philadelphia, PA: WB Saunders.

Juliano, L. M., & Griffiths, R. R. (2009). Caffeine-related disorders. In B. J. Sadock, V. A. Sadock, & P. Ruiz (Eds.), *Kaplan & Sadock's comprehensive textbook of psychiatry* (9th ed., Vol. I, pp. 1296–1309). Philadelphia, PA: Lippincott Williams & Wilkins.

Jummani, R., & Coffey, B. J. (2009). Tic disorders. In B. J. Sadock, V. A. Sadock, & P. Ruiz (Eds.), *Kaplan & Sadock's comprehensive textbook of psychiatry* (9th ed., Vol. II, pp. 3609–3623). Philadelphia, PA: Lippincott Williams & Wilkins.

Junginger, J. (1997). Fetishism: Assessment and treatment. In D. R. Laws & W. O'Donohue (Eds.), *Sexual deviance: Theory, assessment and treatment* (pp. 92–110). New York, NY: Guilford Press.

Kafka, M. P. (1997). A monoamine hypothesis for the pathophysiology of paraphilic disorders. *Archives of Sexual Behavior, 26*, 343–358.

Kafka, M. P., & Hennen, J. (2003). Hypersexual desire in males: Are males with paraphilias difference from males with paraphilia-related disorders? *Sexual Abuse: A Journal of Research & Treatment, 4*, 307–321.

Kagan, J. (1994). *Galen's prophesy.* New York, NY: Basic Books.

Kagan, J. (1997). Temperament and the reactions to unfamiliarity. *Child Development, 68*, 139–143.

Kagan, J., Reznick, J. S., & Snidman, N. (1988). Biological bases of childhood shyness. *Science, 240*, 167–171.

Kagan, J., & Snidman, N. (1991). Infant predictors of inhibited and uninhibited profiles. *Psychological Science, 2*, 40–44.

Kagan, J., & Snidman, N. (1999). Early childhood predictors of adult anxiety disorders. *Biological Psychiatry, 46*, 1536–1541.

Kahn, R. S., Khoury, J., Nichols, W. C., & Lanphear, B. P. (2003). Role of dopamine transporter genotype and maternal prenatal smoking in childhood hyperactive-impulsive, inattentive, and oppositional behaviors. *The Journal of Pediatrics, 143*(1), 104–110.

Kaiser, J. (2006). Differences in immune cell "brakes" may explain chimp–human split on AIDS. *Science Magazine, 312*, 672–673.

Kalaria, R., Maestre, G., Arizaga, R., Friedland, R., Galasko, D., Hall, K., … Potocnik, F. (2008). Alzheimer's disease and vascular dementia in developing countries: Prevalence, management, and risk factors. *Lancet Neurology, 7*(9), 812.

Kalat, J. W. (2009). *Biological Psychology* (10th ed.). Belmont, CA: Wadsworth.

Kalayasiri, R., Kranzler, H. R., Weiss, R., Brady, K., Gueorguieva, R., Panhuysen, C., & Malison, R. T. (2006). Risk factors for cocaine-induced paranoia in cocaine-dependent sibling pairs. *Drug and Alcohol Dependence, 84*, 77–84.

Kallmann, F. J. (1938). *The genetics of schizophrenia.* New York, NY: Augustin.

Kaminski, J. W., Valle, L., Filene, J., & Boyle, C. (2008). A meta-analytic review of components associated with parent training program effectiveness. *Journal of Abnormal Child Psychology, 36*(4), 567–589.

Kanayama, G., Barry, S., & Pope, H. G. (2006). Body image and attitudes toward male roles in anabolic–androgenic steroid users. *American Journal of Psychiatry, 163*, 697–703.

Kanayama, G., Brower, K. J., Wood, R. I., Hudson, J. I., & Pope, H. G., Jr. (2010). Treatment of anabolic–androgenic steroid dependence: Emerging evidence and its implications. *Drug and Alcohol Dependence, 109*(1–3), 6–13.

Kandel, D. B., Wu, P., & Davies, M. (1994). Maternal smoking during pregnancy and smoking by adolescent daughters. *American Journal of Public Health, 84*, 1407–1413.

Kandel, E. R. (1983). From metapsychology to molecular biology: Explorations into the nature of anxiety. *American Journal of Psychiatry, 140*, 1277–1293.

Kandel, E. R., Jessell, T. M., & Schacter, S. (1991). Early experience and the fine tuning of synaptic connections. In E. R. Kandel, J. H. Schwartz, & T. M. Jessell (Eds.), *Principles of neural science* (3rd ed., pp. 945–958). New York, NY: Elsevier.

Kandel, E. R., Schwartz, J., & Jessell, T. M. (2000). *Principles of neural science* (4th ed.). New York, NY: McGraw-Hill.

Kane, J. M. (2006). Tardive dyskinesia circa 2006. *American Journal of Psychiatry, 163*, 1316–1318.

Kane, J. M., Stroup, S., & Marder, S. R. (2009). Schizophrenia: Pharmacological treatment. In B. J. Sadock, V. A. Sadock, & P. Ruiz (Eds.), *Kaplan & Sadock's comprehensive textbook of psychiatry* (9th ed., Vol. I, pp. 1547–1556). Philadelphia, PA: Lippincott Williams & Wilkins.

Kanigel, R. (1988). Nicotine becomes addictive. *Science Illustrated, 2*, 19–21.

Kanner, L. (1943). Autistic disturbances of affective contact. *Nervous Child, 2*, 217–250.

Kanner, L. (1949). Problems of nosology and psychodynamics of early infantile autism. *American Journal of Orthopsychiatry, 19*, 416–426.

Kansas v. Hendricks, 117 S. Ct. 2072 (1997).

Kaplan, H. S. (1979). *Disorders of sexual desire.* New York, NY: Brunner/Mazel.

Kaplan, H. S. (1987). *Sexual aversion, sexual phobias, and panic disorder.* New York, NY: Brunner/Mazel.

Kaplan, M. (1983). A woman's view of DSM-III. *American Psychologist, 38*, 786–792.

Kaplan, S. A., Reis, R. B., Kohn, I. J., Ikeguchi, E. F., Laor, E., Te, A. E., & Martins, A. C. (1999). Safety and efficacy of sildenafil in postmenopausal women with sexual dysfunction. *Urology, 53*, 481–486.

Karno, M., & Golding, J. M. (1991). Obsessive-compulsive disorder. In L. N. Robins & D. A. Regier (Eds.), *Psychiatric disorders in America: The epidemiologic catchment area study* (pp. 204–219). New York, NY: Free Press.

Kasch, K. L., Rottenberg, J., Arnow, B. A., & Gotlib, I. H. (2002). Behavioral activation and inhibition systems and the severity and course of depression. *Journal of Abnormal Psychology, 111*, 589–597.

Kasindorf, J. (1988, May 2). The real story of Billie Boggs: Was Koch right—Or the civil libertarians? *New York,* pp. 36–44.

Kaslow, N. J., Davis, S. P., & Smith, C. O. (2009). Biological and psychosocial interventions for depression in children and adolescents. In I. H. Gotlib & C. L. Hammen (Eds.), *Handbook of depression* (2nd ed., pp. 642–672). New York, NY: Guilford Press.

Kass, D. J., Silvers, F. M., & Abrams, G. M. (1972). Behavioral group treatment of hysteria. *Archives of General Psychiatry, 26*, 42–50.

Kato, K., Sullivan, P., Evengard, B., & Pederson, N. (2006). Premorbid predictors of chronic fatigue. *Archives of General Psychiatry, 63*, 1267–1272.

Katon, W. (1993). Somatization disorder, hypochondriasis, and conversion disorder. In D. L. Dunner (Ed.), *Current psychiatric therapy* (pp. 314–320). Philadelphia, PA: W. B. Saunders.

Katon, W. J. (2003). Clinical and health services relationships between major depression, depressive symptoms, and general medical illness. *Biological Psychiatry, 54*, 216–226.

Katon, W., Lin, E., Von Korff, M., Russo, J., Lipscomb, P., & Bush, T. (1991). Somatization: A spectrum of severity. *American Journal of Psychiatry, 148*, 34–40.

Katon, W., & Roy-Byrne, P. P. (1991). Mixed anxiety and depression. *Journal of Abnormal Psychology, 100*(3), 337–345.

Katona, C., & Livingston, G. (2009). Depression and anxiety in dementia caregivers. In H. Herman, M. Maj, & N. Sartorius (Eds.), *Depressive disorders* (pp. 262–264). New York, NY: Wiley.

Katz, I. R. (1993). Delirium. In D. L. Dunner (Ed.), *Current psychiatric therapy* (pp. 65–73). Philadelphia, PA: W. B Saunders.

Kavale, K. A., & Forness, S. R. (1983). Hyperactivity and diet treatment: A metaanalysis of the Feingold hypothesis. *Journal of Learning Disabilities, 16*, 324–330.

Kavanagh, D. J. (1992). Recent developments in expressed emotion and schizophrenia. *British Journal of Psychiatry, 160*, 601–620.

Kawamura, K. Y. (2002). Asian American body images. In T. F. Cash & T. Pruzinsky (Eds.), *Body image: A handbook of theory, research and clinical practice* (pp. 243–249). New York, NY: Guilford Press.

Kaye, W. (2008). Neurobiology of anorexia and bulimia nervosa. *Physiology and Behavior, 94*(1), 121–135.

Kaye, W. H., Greeno, C. G., Moss, H., Fernstrom, J., Fernstrom, M., Lilenfeld, L. R., … Mann, J. J. (1998). Alterations in serotonin activity and psychiatric symptoms after recovery from bulimia nervosa. *Archives of General Psychiatry, 55*, 927–935.

Kaye, W. H., Weltzin, T. E., Hsu, L. K. G., McConaha, C. W., & Bolton, B. (1993). Amount of calories retained after binge eating and vomiting. *American Journal of Psychiatry, 150*(6), 969–971.

Kazak, A. E., Boeving, C. A., Alderfer, M. A., Hwang, W., & Reilly, A. (2005). Posttraumatic stress symptoms during treatment in parents of children with cancer. *Journal of Clinical Oncology, 23*, 7405–7410.

Kean, S. (2010). An indefatigable debate over chronic fatigue syndrome. *Science, 327*, 254–255.

Keane, T. M., & Barlow, D. H. (2002). Posttraumatic stress disorder. In D. H. Barlow, *Anxiety and its disorders: The nature and treatment of anxiety and panic* (2nd ed., pp. 418–453). New York, NY: Guilford Press.

Keane, T. M., Marx, B. P., & Sloan, D. M. (2011). Trauma, dissociation, and post-traumatic stress disorder. In D. H. Barlow (Ed.), *Oxford handbook of clinical psychology* (pp. 359–386). New York, NY: Oxford University Press.

Kearney, A. J. (2006). A primer of covert sensitization. *Cognitive and Behavioral Practice, 13*(2), 167–175. doi:10.1016/j.cbpra.2006.02.002

Kearney, C. (2010). *Helping children with selective mutism and their parents: A guide for school-based professionals.* New York, NY: Oxford University Press.

Kebir, O., Tabbane, K., Sengupta, S., & Joober, R. (2009). Candidate genes and neuropsychological phenotypes in children with ADHD: Review of association studies. *Journal of Psychiatry & Neuroscience: JPN, 34*(2), 88.

Keck, P. E., & McElroy, S. L. (2002). Pharmacological treatments for bipolar disorder. In P. E. Nathan & J. M. Gorman (Eds.), *A guide to treatments that work* (2nd ed., pp. 277–299). New York, NY: Oxford University Press.

Keefe, D. L. (2002). Sex hormones and neural mechanisms. *Archives of Sexual Behavior, 31*(5), 401–403.

Keefe, F. J., Dunsmore, J., & Burnett, R. (1992). Behavioral and cognitive-behavioral approaches to chronic pain: Recent advances and future directions. Special issue: Behavioral medicine: An update for the 1990s. *Journal of Consulting and Clinical Psychology, 60*(4), 528–536.

Keefe, F. J., & France, C. R. (1999). Pain: Biopsychosocial mechanisms and management. *Current Directions in Psychological Science, 8,* 137–141.

Keel, P. K., Dorer, D. J., Eddy, K. T., Franko, D., Charatan, D. L., & Herzog, D. B. (2003). Predictors of mortality in eating disorders. *Archives of General Psychiatry, 60,* 179–183.

Keel, P. K., Fichter, M., Quadflieg, N., Bulik, C. M., Baxter, M. G., Thornton, L., ... Kaye, W. H. (2004). Application of a latent class analysis to empirically define eating disorder phenotypes. *Archives of General Psychiatry, 61,* 192–200.

Keel, P. K., Heatherton, T. F., Dorer, D. J., Joiner, T, E., & Zalta, A. K. (2006). Point prevalence of bulimia nervosa in 1982, 1992, and 2002. *Psychological Medicine, 36,* 119–127.

Keel, P. K., & Klump, K. L. (2003). Are eating disorders culture-bound syndromes? Implications for conceptualizing their etiology. *Psychological Bulletin, 129*(5), 747–769.

Keel, P. K., & Mitchell, J. E. (1997). Outcome in bulimia nervosa. *American Journal of Psychiatry, 154,* 313–321.

Keel, P. K., Mitchell, J. E., Miller, K., B., Davis, T. L., & Crow, S. J. (1999). Long-term outcome of bulimia nervosa. *Archives of General Psychiatry, 56,* 63–69.

Keel, P. K., Mitchell, J. E., Miller, K. B., Davis, T. L., & Crow, S. J. (2000). Predictive validity of bulimia nervosa as a diagnostic strategy. *American Journal of Psychiatry 157*(1), 136–138.

Keilitz, I. (1987). Researching and reforming the insanity defense. *Rutgers Law Review, 39,* 289–322.

Keitner, G. I., Ryan, C. E., Miller, I. W., Kohn, R., Bishop, D. S., & Epstein, N. B. (1995). Role of the family in recovery and major depression. *American Journal of Psychiatry, 152,* 1002–1008.

Keller, M. B., Klein, D. N., Hirschfeld, R. M. A., Kocsis, J. H., McCullough, J. P., Miller, I., ... Marin, D. B. (1995). Results of the DSM-IV mood disorders field trial. *American Journal of Psychiatry, 152,* 843–849.

Keller, M. B., Lavori, P. W., Endicott, J., Coryell, W., & Klerman, G. L. (1983). "Double depression": Two-year follow-up. *American Journal of Psychiatry, 140*(6), 689–694.

Keller, M. B., McCollough, J. P., Klein, D. N., Arnow, B., Dunner, D. L., Gelenberg, A. J., ... Zajecka, J. (2000). A comparison of nefazodone, the cognitive behavioral-analysis system of psychotherapy, and their combination for the treatment of chronic depression. *New England Journal of Medicine, 342*(20), 1462–1470.

Keller, M. B., & Wunder, J. (1990). Bipolar disorder in childhood. In M. Hersen & C. G. Last (Eds.), *Handbook of child and adult psychopathology: A longitudinal perspective.* Elmsford, NY: Pergamon Press.

Keller, T. A., & Just, M. A. (2009). Altering cortical connectivity: Remediation-induced changes in the white matter of poor readers. *Neuron, 64*(5), 624–631.

Kellner, R. (1985). Functional somatic symptoms and hypochondriasis: A survey of empirical studies. *Archives of General Psychiatry, 42,* 821–833.

Kellner, R. (1986). *Somatization and hypochondriasis.* New York, NY: Praeger-Greenwood.

Kelly, B. D., Casey, P., Dunn, G., Ayuso-Mateos, J. L., & Dowrick, C. (2007). The role of personality disorder in "difficult to reach" patients with depression: Findings from the ODIN study. *European Psychiatry, 22,* 153–159.

Kelly, J. A., Murphy, D. A., Sikkema, K. J., McAuliffe, T. L., Roffman, R. A., Solomon, L. J., ... Community HIV Prevention Research Collaborative. (1997). Randomised, controlled community-level HIV-prevention intervention for sexual-risk behaviour among homosexual men in U.S. cities. *The Lancet, 350,* 1500–1505.

Kelly, J. F., Stout, R. L., Magill, M., Tonigan, J. S., & Pagano, M. E. (2010). Mechanisms of behavior change in alcoholics anonymous: Does Alcoholics Anonymous lead to better alcohol use outcomes by reducing depression symptoms? *Addiction, 105*(4), 626–636.

Kemeny, M. E. (2003). The psychobiology of stress. *Current Directions in Psychological Science, 12*(4), 124–129.

Kemp, S. (1990). *Medieval psychology.* New York, NY: Greenwood Press.

Kendall, P. C., & Comer, J. S. (2011). Research methods in clinical psychology. In D. H. Barlow (Ed.), *Oxford handbook of clinical psychology* (pp. 52–75). New York, NY: Oxford University.

Kendall, P. C., Flannery-Schroeder, E., Panichelli-Mindell, M., Southam-Gerow, M., Henin, A., & Warman, M. (1997). Therapy for youths with anxiety disorder: A second randomized clinical trial. *Journal of Consulting and Clinical Psychology, 65,* 366–380.

Kendell, R. (1985). Emotional and physical factors in the genesis of puerperal mental disorders. *Journal of Psychosomatic Research, 29,* 3–11.

Kendler, K., Kupfer, D., Narrow, W., Phillips, K., & Fawcett, J. (2009). *Guidelines for Making Changes to DSM-V (Revised 10/21/09).* Retrieved from http://www.dsm5.org/ProgressReports/Documents/Guidelines-forMaking-Changes-to-DSM_1.pdf

Kendler, K., & Walsh, D. (2007). Schizophreniform disorder, delusional disorder and psychotic disorder not otherwise specified: Clinical features, outcome and familial psychopathology. *Acta Psychiatrica Scandinavica, 91*(6), 370–378.

Kendler, K. S. (2001). Twin studies of psychiatric illness. *Archives of General Psychiatry, 58,* 1005–1013.

Kendler, K. S. (2005). Psychiatric genetics: A methodological critique. In N. C. Andreasen (Ed.), *Research advances in genetics and genomics: Implications for psychiatry* (pp. 5–25). Washington, DC: American Psychiatric Publishing.

Kendler, K. S. (2006). Reflections on the relationship between psychiatric genetics and psychiatric nosology. *American Journal of Psychiatry, 163,* 1138–1146.

Kendler, K. S., Czajkowski, N., Tambs, K., Torgersen, S., Aggen, S. H., Neale, M. C., ... Reichborn-Kjennerud, T.. (2006). Dimensional representations of DSM-IV cluster A personality disorders in a population-based sample of Norwegian twins: A multivariate study. *Psychological Medicine, 36,* 1583–1591.

Kendler, K. S., Gatz, M., Gardner, C. O., & Pedersen, N. L. (2007). Clinical indices of familial depression in the Swedish Twin Registry. *Acta Psychiatrica Scandinavica, 115*(3), 214–220.

Kendler, K. S., Heath, A. C., Martin, N. G., & Eaves, L. J. (1987). Symptoms of anxiety and symptoms of depression: Same genes, different environments? *Archives of General Psychiatry, 44*(5), 451–457.

Kendler, K. S., Hettema, J. M., Butera, F., Gardner, C. O., & Prescott, C. A. (2003). Life event dimensions of loss, humiliation, entrapment, and danger in the prediction of onsets of major depression and generalized anxiety. *Archives of General Psychiatry, 60,* 789–796.

Kendler, K. S., Jacobson, K. C., Prescott, C. A., & Neale, M. C. (2003). Specificity of genetic and environmental risk factors for use and abuse/dependence of cannabis, cocaine, hallucinogens, sedatives, stimulants, and opiates in male twins. *American Journal of Psychiatry, 160,* 687–695.

Kendler, K. S., Karkowski, L. M., & Prescott, C. A. (1999a). The assessment of dependence in the study of stressful life events: Validation using a twin design. *Psychological Medicine, 29*(6), 1455–1460.

Kendler, K. S., Karkowski, L. M., & Prescott, C. A. (1999b). Causal relationship between stressful life events and the onset of major depression. *American Journal of Psychiatry, 156*(6), 837–841.

Kendler, K. S., Kessler, R. C., Walters, E. E., MacLean, C., Neale, M. C., Heath, A. C., & Eaves, L. J. (1995). Stressful life events, genetic liability, and onset of an episode of major depression in women. *American Journal of Psychiatry, 152,* 833–842.

Kendler, K. S., Kuhn, J., Vittum, J., Prescott, C. A., & Riley, B. (2005). The interaction of stressful life events and a serotonin transporter polymorphism in the prediction of episodes of major depression. *Archives of General Psychiatry, 62,* 529–535.

Kendler, K. S., MacLean, C., Neale, M., Kessler, R., Heath, A., & Eaves, L. (1991). The genetic epidemiology of bulimia nervosa. *American Journal of Psychiatry, 148*(12), 1627–1637.

Kendler, K. S., Myers, J., & Prescott, C. A. (2005). Sex differences in the relationship between social support and risk for major depression: A longitudinal study of opposite-sex twin pairs. *American Journal of Psychiatry, 162,* 250–256.

Kendler, K. S., Myers, J., & Zisook, S. (2008). Does bereavement-related major depression differ from major depression associated with other stressful life events? *American Journal of Psychiatry, 165*(11), 1449–1455.

Kendler, K. S., Neale, M. C., Kessler, R. C., Heath, A. C., & Eaves, L. J. (1992a). Generalized anxiety disorder in women: A population-based twin study. *Archives of General Psychiatry, 49,* 267–272.

Kendler, K. S., Neale, M. C., Kessler, R. C., Heath, A. C., & Eaves, L. J. (1992b). Major depression and generalized anxiety disorder: Same genes, (partly) different environments? *Archives of General Psychiatry, 49,* 716–722.

Kendler, K. S., Neale, M. C., Kessler, R. C., Heath, A. C., & Eaves, L. J. (1993). A longitudinal twin study of 1-year prevalence of major depression in women. *Archives of General Psychiatry, 50,* 843–852.

Kendler, K. S., Neale, M. C., MacLean, C. J., Heath, A. C., Eaves, L. J., & Kessler, R. C. (1993). Smoking and major depression: A causal analysis. *Archives of General Psychiatry, 50,* 36–43.

Kendler, K. S., & Prescott, C. A. (2006). *Genes, environment, and psychopathology: Understanding the causes of psychiatric and substance use disorders.* New York, NY: Guilford Press.

Kennard, B. D., Clarke, G. N., Weersing, V. R., Asarnow, J. R., Shamseddeen, W., Porta, G., ... Brent, D. A. (2009). Effective components of TORDIA cognitive– behavioral therapy for adolescent depression: Preliminary findings. *Journal of Consulting and Clinical Psychology, 77*(6), 1033–1041.

Kennedy, S. (2000). Psychological factors and immunity in HIV infection: Stress, coping, social support, and intervention outcomes. In D. I. Mostofsky & D. H. Barlow (Eds.), *The management of stress and anxiety in medical disorders* (pp. 194–205). Needham Heights, MA: Allyn & Bacon.

Kennedy, S. H., Konarski, J. Z., Segal, Z. V., Lau, M. A., Bieling, P. J., McIntyre, R. S., & Mayberg, H. S. (2007). Differences in brain glucose metabolism between responders to CBT and venlafaxine in a 16-week randomized controlled trial. *The American Journal of Psychiatry, 164*(5), 778–788.

Kennedy, W. K., Leloux, M., Kutscher, E. C., Price, P. L., Morstad, A. E., & Carnahan, R. M. (2010). Acamprosate. *Expert Opinion on Drug Metabolism & Toxicology, 6*(3), 363–380.

Kerns, J. (2009). Distinct conflict resolution deficits related to different facets of schizophrenia. *Psychological Research, 73*(6), 786–793.

Kerns, R. D., Rosenberg, R., & Otis, J. D. (2002). Self-appraised problem solving and pain-relevant social support as predictors of the experience of chronic pain. *Annals of Behavioral Medicine, 24,* 100–105.

Keski-Rahkonen, A., Hoek, H. W., Susser, E. S., Linna, M. S., Sihvola, E., Raevuori, A., ... Rissanen, A. (2007). Epidemiology and course of anorexia nervosa in the community. *American Journal of Psychiatry, 164*(8), 1259–1265.

Kessler, R., Coccaro, E., Fava, M., Jaeger, S., Jin, R., & Walters, E. (2006). The prevalence and correlates of DSM-IV intermittent explosive disorder in the National Comorbidity Survey Replication. *Archives of General Psychiatry, 63*(6), 669.

Kessler, R. C. (1997). The effects of stressful life events on depression. *Annual Review of Psychology, 48,* 191–214.

Kessler, R. C. (2006). The epidemiology of depression among women. In C. Keyes, S. Goodman (Eds.), *A handbook for the social, behavioral, and biomedical sciences: Women and depression* (pp. 22–37). New York, NY: Cambridge University Press.

Kessler, R. C., Avenevoli, S., & Ries Merikangas, K. (2001). Mood disorders in children and adolescents: An epidemiologic perspective. *Biological Psychiatry, 49*(12), 1002–1014.

Kessler, R. C., Berglund, P., Borges, G., Nock, M., & Wang, P. (2005). Trends in suicide ideation, plans, gestures, and attempts in the United States, 1990–1992 to 2001–2003. *JAMA: Journal of the American Medical Association, 293,* 2487–2495.

Kessler, R. C., Berglund, P., Demler, O., Jin, R., & Walters, E. E. (2005). Lifetime prevalence and age-of-onset distributions of DSM-IV disorders in the National Comorbidity Survey replication. *Archives of General Psychiatry, 62,* 593–602.

Kessler, R. C., Berglund, P., Demler, O., Jin, R., Koretz, D., Merikangas, K. R., ... National Comorbidity Survey Replication. (2003). The epidemiology of major depressive disorder: Results from the National Comorbidity Survey Replication (NCS-R). *JAMA: Journal of the American Medical Association, 289,* 3095–3105.

Kessler, R. C., Chiu, W. T., Demler, O., & Walters, E. E. (2005). Prevalence, severity, and comorbidity of 12-month DSM-IV disorders in the National Comorbidity Survey replication. *Archives of General Psychiatry, 62,* 617–627.

Kessler, R. C., Chiu, W. T., Jin, R., Ruscio, A. M., Shear, K., & Walters, E. E. (2006). The epidemiology of panic attacks, panic disorder, and agoraphobia in the National Comorbidity Survey Replication. *Archives of General Psychiatry, 63*(4), 415–424.

Kessler, R. C., Galea, S., Jones, R. T., & Parker, H. A. (2006). *Mental illness and suicidality after Hurricane Katrina.* Bulletin of the World Health Organization (WHO Publication No. 06-033019).

Kessler, R. C., McGonagle, K. A., Zhao, S., Nelson, C. B., Hughes, M., Eshleman, S., ... Kendler, K. S. (1994). Lifetime and 12-month prevalence of DSM-III-R psychiatric disorders among persons aged 15–54 in the United States: Results from the national comorbidity survey. *Archives of General Psychiatry, 5,* 8–19.

Kessler, R. C., Sonnega, A., Bromet, E., Hughes, M., & Nelson, C. B. (1995). Posttraumatic stress disorder in the national comorbidity survey. *Archives of General Psychiatry, 52,* 1048–1060.

Kessler, R. C., & Wang, P. S. (2009). Epidemiology of depression. In I. H. Gotlib & C. L. Hammen (Eds.), *Handbook of depression* (2nd ed., pp. 5–22). New York, NY: Guilford Press.

Kety, S. S. (1990). Genetic factors in suicide: Family, twin, and adoption studies. In S. J. Blumenthal & D. J. Kupfer (Eds.), *Suicide over the life cycle: Risk factors, assessment, and treatment of suicidal patients* (pp. 127–133). Washington, DC: American Psychiatric Press.

Khachaturian, Z. S. (2007). Alzheimer's 101. *Alzheimer's and Dementia, 3,* 1–2.

Khan, S., King, A.P., Abelson, J.L., & Liberzon, I. (2009). Neuroendocrinology of anxiety disorders. In M. M. Antony & M. B. Stein (Eds.), *Oxford handbook of anxiety and related disorders.* Oxford, UK: Oxford University Press.

Khokhar, J., Ferguson, C., Zhu, A., & Tyndale, R. (2010). Pharmacogenetics of drug dependence: Role of gene variations in susceptibility and treatment. *Annual Review of Pharmacology and Toxicology, 50*(1), 39–61.

Kiecolt-Glaser, J. K., Loving, T., Stowell, J., Malarkey, W., Lemeshow, S., & Dickinson, S., & Glaser, R. (2005). Hostile marital interactions, proinflammatory cytokine production, and wound healing. *Archives of General Psychiatry, 62,* 1377–1384.

Kiecolt-Glaser, J. K., & Newton, T. L. (2001). Marriage and health: His and hers. *Psychological Bulletin, 127,* 475–503.

Kiesler, C. A., & Sibulkin, A. E. (1987). *Mental hospitalization: Myths and facts about a national crisis.* Beverly Hills, CA: Sage.

Kiesler, D. J. (1966). Some myths of psychotherapy research and the search for a paradigm. *Psychological Bulletin, 65,* 110–136.

Kihlstrom, J. F. (1992). Dissociation and dissociations: A commentary on consciousness and cognition. *Consciousness & Cognition, 1,* 47–53.

Kihlstrom, J. F. (2005). Dissociative disorders. In S. Nolen-Hoeksema, T. D. Cannon, & T. Widiger (Eds.), *Annual review of clinical psychology* (Vol. 1). Palo Alto, CA: Annual Reviews.

Kihlstrom, J. F., Barnhardt, T. M., & Tataryn, D. J. (1992). The psychological unconscious: Found, lost, and regained. *American Psychologist, 47*(6), 788–791.

Kihlstrom, J. F., Glisky, M. L., & Anguilo, M. J. (1994). Dissociative tendencies and dissociative disorders. *Journal of Abnormal Psychology, 103,* 117–124.

Killen, J. D. (1996). Development and evaluation of a school-based eating disorder symptoms prevention program. In L. Smolak, M. P. Levine, & R. Striegel-Moore (Eds.), *The developmental psychopathology of eating disorders: Implications for research, prevention, and treatment* (pp. 313– 339). Mahwah, NJ: Erlbaum.

Killen, J. D., Taylor, C. B., Hayward, C., Haydel, F., Wilson, D. M., Hammer, L. D., & Strachowski, D. (1996). Weight concerns influence the development of eating disorders: A four-year prospective study.

Journal of Consulting and Clinical Psychology, 64, 936–940.

Killen, J. D., Taylor, C. B., Hayward, C., Wilson, D. M., Hammer, L. D., Robinson, T. N., ... Kraemer, H. (1994). The pursuit of thinness and onset of eating disorder symptoms in a community sample of adolescent girls: A three-year prospective analysis. *International Journal of Eating Disorders, 16*, 227–238.

Killgore, W. D. S., Cotting, D. I., Thomas, J. L., Cox, A. L., McGurk, D., Vo, A. H., ... Hoge, C. W. (2008). Post-combat invincibility: Violent combat experiences are associated with increased risk-taking propensity following deployment. *Journal of Psychiatric Research, 42*(13), 1112– 1121. doi:10.1016/j.jpsychires.2008.01.001

Kilpatrick, D. G., Best, C. L., Veronen, L. J., Amick, A. E., Villeponteaux, L. A., & Ruff, G. A. (1985). Mental health correlates of criminal victimization: A random community survey. *Journal of Consulting and Clinical Psychology, 53*, 866–873.

Kilpatrick, D. G., Koenen, K. C., Ruggiero, K. J., Acierno, R., Galea, S., Resnick, H. S., ... Gelernter, J. (2007). The serotonin transporter genotype and social support and moderation of posttraumatic stress disorder and depression in hurricane-exposed adults. *The American Journal of Psychiatry, 164*(11), 1693–1699.

Kim, E. D., & Lipshultz, L. I. (1997, April 15). Advances in the treatment of organic erectile dysfunction. *Hospital Practice,* 101–120.

Kim, H. F., Schulz, P. E., Wilde, E. A., & Yudofsky, S. C. (2008). Laboratory testing and imaging studies in psychiatry. In R. E. Hales, S. C. Yudofsky, & G. O. Gabbard (Eds.), *The American Psychiatric Publishing textbook of psychiatry* (5th ed., pp. 19–72). Arlington, VA: American Psychiatric Publishing, Inc.

Kindon, S. L., Pain, R., & Kesby, M. (Eds.). (2007). *Participatory action research approaches and methods: Connecting people, participation, and place*. New York, NY: Routledge.

King, A. C., Taylor, C. B., Albright, C. A., & Haskell, W. L. (1990). The relationship between repressive and defensive coping styles and blood pressure responses in healthy, middle-aged men and women. *Journal of Psychosomatic Research, 34*, 461–471.

King, D. E., Mainous, A. G., III, & Geesey, M. E. (2007). Turning back the clock: Adopting a healthy lifestyle in middle age. *The American Journal of Medicine, 120*(7), 598–603.

King, D. W., King, L. A., Foy, D. W., & Gudanowski, D. M. (1996). Prewar factors in combat-related posttraumatic stress disorder: Structural equation modeling with a national sample of female and male Vietnam veterans. *Journal of Consulting and Clinical Psychology, 64*, 520–531.

King, M., & Wexler, D. (2010). Therapeutic jurisprudence. In J. M. Brown & E. A. Campbell (Eds.), *The Cambridge handbook of forensic psychology* (pp. 126–132). Cambridge, UK: Cambridge University Press.

King, S. A., & Strain, J. J. (1991). *Pain disorders: A proposed classification for DSM-IV.* Paper presented at the 144th annual meeting of the American Psychiatric Association, New Orleans.

Kinzie, J. D., Leung, P. K., Boehnlein, J., & Matsunaga, D. (1992). Psychiatric epidemiology of an Indian village: A 19-year replication study. *Journal of Nervous and Mental Disease, 180*(1), 33–39.

Kirmayer, L. J. (1991). The place of culture in psychiatric nosology: *Taijin kyofusho* and DSM-III-R. *Journal of Nervous and Mental Disease, 179*, 19–28.

Kirmayer, L. J., Looper, K. J., & Taillefer, S. (2003). Somatoform disorders. In M. Hersen & S. M. Turner (Eds.), *Adult psychopathology and diagnosis* (4th ed., pp. 420–475). New York, NY: John Wiley.

Kirmayer, L. J., & Robbins, J. M. (1991). Three forms of somatization in primary care: Prevalence, cooccurrence, and sociodemographic characteristics. *Journal of Nervous and Mental Disease, 179*, 647–655.

Kirmayer, L. J., & Sartorius, N. (2007). Cultural models and somatic syndromes. *Psychosomatic Medicine, 69*(9), 832–840.

Kirmayer, L. J., & Weiss, M. (1993). *On cultural considerations for somatoform disorders in the DSM-IV.* In Cultural proposals and supporting papers for DSM-IV. Submitted to the DSM-IV Task Force by the Steering Committee, NIMH-Sponsored Group on Culture and Diagnosis.

Kirov, G., & Owen, M. J. (2009). Genetics of schizophrenia. In B. J. Sadock, V. A. Sadock, & P. Ruiz (Eds.), *Kaplan & Sadock's comprehensive textbook of psychiatry* (9th ed., Vol. I, pp. 1462–1475). Philadelphia, PA: Lippincott Williams & Wilkins.

Kistner, J. A. (2009). Sex differences in child and adolescent psychopathology: An introduction to the special section: *Journal of Clinical Child and Adolescent Psychology, 38*(4), 453–459.

Kjernisted, K. D., Enns, M. W., & Lander, M. (2002). An open-label clinical trial of nefazodone in hypochondriasis. *Psychosomatics, 43*, 290–294.

Klein, D. F. (1989). The pharmacological validation of psychiatric diagnosis. In L. Robins & J. Barrett (Eds.), *Validity of psychiatric diagnosis*. New York, NY: Raven Press.

Klein, D. F. (1999). Harmful dysfunction, disorder, disease, illness, and evolution. *Journal of Abnormal Psychology, 108*, 421–429.

Klein, D. N. (2008). Classification of depressive disorders in the DSM-V: proposal for a two- dimension system. *Journal of Abnormal Psychology, 117*(3), 552–560.

Klein, D. N. (2010). Chronic depression: Diagnosis and classification. *Current Directions in Psychological Science, 19*(2), 96–100.

Klein, D. N., Lewinsohn, P. M., Rohde, P., Seeley, J. R., & Durbin, C. E. (2002). Clinical features of major depressive disorder in adolescents and their relatives: Impact on familial aggregation, implications for phenotype definition, and specificity of transmission. *Journal of Abnormal Psychology, 111*, 98–106.

Klein, D. N., Schwartz, J. E., Rose, S., & Leader, J. B. (2000). Five-year course and outcome of dysthymic disorder: A prospective, naturalistic follow-up study. *American Journal of Psychiatry, 157*(6), 931–939.

Klein, D. N., Shankman, S., & Rose, S. (2006). Ten-year prospective follow-up study of the naturalistic course of dysthymic disor-

der and double depression. *American Journal of Psychiatry, 163*, 872–880.

Klein, D. N., Taylor, E. B., Dickstein, S., & Harding, K. (1988). The early–late onset distinction in DSM-III-R dysthymia. *Journal of Affective Disorders, 14*(1), 25–33.

Kleinknecht, R. A., Dinnel, D. L., Kleinknecht, E. E., Hiruma, N., & Harada, N. (1997). Cultural factors in social anxiety: A comparison of social phobia symptoms and *taijin kyofusho. Journal of Anxiety Disorders, 11*, 157–177.

Kleinman, A. (2004). Culture and depression. *New England Journal of Medicine, 351*, 951–953.

Klerman, G. L., & Weissman, M. M. (1989). Increasing rates of depression. *JAMA: Journal of the American Medical Association, 261*, 2229–2235.

Klerman, G. L., Weissman, M. M., Rounsaville, B. J., & Chevron, E. S. (1984). *Interpersonal psychotherapy of depression.* New York, NY: Basic Books.

Klimas, N., Koneru, A. O., & Fletcher, M. A. (2008). Overview of HIV. *Psychosomatic Medicine, 70*, 523–530.

Klin, A., Jones, W., Schultz, R., Volkmar, F., & Cohen, D. (2002). Defining and quantifying the social phenotype in autism. *American Journal of Psychiatry, 159*, 895–908.

Klosko, J. S., Barlow, D. H., Tassinari, R., & Cerny, J. A. (1990). A comparison of alprazolam and behavior therapy in treatment of panic disorder. *Journal of Consulting and Clinical Psychology, 58*, 77–84.

Kluft, R. P. (1984). Treatment of multiple personality disorder. *Psychiatric Clinics of North America, 7*, 9–29.

Kluft, R. P. (1991). Multiple personality disorder. In A. Tasman & S. W. Goldinger (Eds.), *Review of psychiatry* (Vol. 10). Washington, DC: American Psychiatric Press.

Kluft, R. P. (1996). Treating the traumatic memories of patients with dissociative identity disorder. *American Journal of Psychiatry, 153*, 103–110.

Kluft, R. P. (1999). Current issues in dissociative identity disorder. *Journal of Practical Psychology and Behavioral Health, 5*, 3–19.

Kluft, R. P. (2009). A clinician's understanding of dissociation: Fragments of an acquaintance. In P. F. Dell & J. A. O'Neil (Eds.), *Dissociation and the dissociative disorders*. New York, NY: Routledge.

Klump, K. L., Kaye, W. H., & Strober, M. (2001). The evolving genetic foundations of eating disorders. *The Psychiatric Clinics of North America, 24*, 215–225.

Knight, R. A., & Prentky, R. A. (1990). Classifying sexual offenders: The development and corroboration of taxonomic models. In W. L. Marshall, D. R. Laws, & H. E. Barbaree (Eds.), *Handbook of sexual assault: Issues, theories, and treatment of the offender* (pp. 23–52). New York, NY: Plenum Press.

Knoll, B., Lassman, B., & Temesgen, Z. (2007). Current status of HIV infection: A review for non-HIV-treating physicians. *International Journal of Dermatology, 46*, 1219–1228.

Knoop, H., Prins, J. B., Moss-Morris, R., & Bleijenberg, G. (2010). The central role of cognitive processes in the perpetuation of chronic fatigue syndrome. *Journal of Psychosomatic Research, 68*, 489–494.

Knowles, J. (2010). Cognitive stimulation therapy: Why it deserves better awareness and availability. *Journal of Care Services Management, 4*(2), 188–194.

Ko, H-C., Lee, L-R., Chang, R-B., & Huang, K-E. (1996). Comorbidity of premenstrual depression and postpartum blues among Chinese women. *Biological Psychiatry, 39,* 648.

Kobau, R., DiIorio, C., Chapman, D., & Delvecchio, P. (2010). Attitudes about mental illness and its treatment: Validation of a generic scale for public health surveillance of mental illness associated stigma. *Community Mental Health Journal, 46*(2), 164–176.

Koch, P., Mansfield, P., Thurau, D., & Carey, M. (2005). "Feeling frumpy": The relationship between body image and sexual response changes in midlife women. *Journal of Sex Research, 42,* 215–223.

Kochanska, G., Aksan, N., & Joy, M. E. (2007). Children's fearfulness as a moderator of parenting in early socialization: Two longitudinal studies. *Developmental Psychology, 43,* 222–237.

Kochman, F. J., Hantouche, E. G., Ferrari, P., Lancrenon, S., Bayart, D., & Akiskal, H. S. (2005). Cyclothymic temperament as a prospective predictor of bipolarity and suicidality in children and adolescents with major depressive disorder. *Journal of Affective Disorders, 85,* 181–189.

Koen, L., Niehaus, D., Muller, J., & Laurent, C. (2008). Use of traditional treatment methods in a Xhosa schizophrenia population. *South African Medical Journal, 93*(6), 443.

Kogon, M. M., Biswas, A., Pearl, D., Carlson, R. W. L., & Spiegel, D. (1997). Effects of medical and psychotherapeutic treatment on the survival of women with metastatic breast carcinoma. *Cancer, 80,* 225–230.

Kohn, R., Wintrob, R. M., & Alarcón, R. D. (2009). Transcultural psychiatry. In B. J. Sadock, V. A. Sadock, & P. Ruiz (Eds.), *Kaplan & Sadock's comprehensive textbook of psychiatry* (9th ed., Vol. I, pp. 734–753). Philadelphia, PA: Lippincott Williams & Wilkins.

Kohut, H. (1971). *The analysis of self.* New York, NY: International Universities Press.

Kohut, H. (1977). *The restoration of the self.* Chicago, IL: University of Chicago Press.

Kolb, B., Gibb, R., & Gorny, G. (2003). Experience-dependent changes in dendritic arbor and spine density in neocortex vary qualitatively with age and sex. *Neurobiology of Learning & Memory, 79,* 1–10.

Kolb, B., Gibb, R., & Robinson, T. E. (2004). Brain plasticity and behavior. In J. Lerner & A. E. Alberts (Eds.), *Current directions in developmental psychology* (pp. 11–17).

Kolb, B., & Whishaw, I. Q. (1998). Possible regeneration of rat medial front cortex following neonatal frontal lesions. *Behavioral Brain Research, 91,* 127–141.

Kollins, S. (2008). ADHD, substance use disorders, and psychostimulant treatment: Current literature and treatment guidelines. *Journal of Attention Disorders, 12*(2), 115.

Kong, L. L., Allen, J. J., & Glisky, E. L. (2008). Interidentity memory transfer in dissociative identity disorder. *Journal of Abnormal Psychology, 117*(3), 686–692.

Koob, A. (2009). *The root of thought.* Upper Saddle River, NJ: FT Press.

Koocher, G. P. (1996). Pediatric oncology: Medical crisis intervention. In R. J. Resnick & R. H. Rozensky (Eds.), *Health psychology through the life span: Practice and research opportunities* (pp. 213–225). Washington, DC: American Psychological Association.

Kopelowicz, A., Liberman, R. P., & Zarate, R. (2006). Recent advances in social skills training for schizophrenia. *Schizophr Bull, 32*(Suppl. 1), S12–23.

Kopelowicz, A., Mintz, J., Liberman, R. P., Zarate, R., & Gonzalez-Smith, V. (2004). Disease management in Latinos with schizophrenia: A family-assisted, skills training approach. *Schizophrenia Bulletin, 29,* 211–227.

Koran, L. M., Abujaoude, E., Large, M. D., & Serpe, R. T. (2008). The prevalence of body dysmorphic disorder in the United States adult population. *CNS Spectrums, 13*(4), 316–322.

Korczyn, A. D., Kahana, E., & Galper, Y. (1991). Epidemiology of dementia in Ashkelon, Israel. *Neuroepidemiology, 10,* 100.

Korfine, L., & Hooley, J. M. (2000). Directed forgetting of emotional stimuli in borderline personality disorder. *Journal of Abnormal Psychology, 109,* 214–221.

Kosberg, J. I., Kaufman, A. V., Burgio, L. D., Leeper, J. D., & Sun, F. (2007). Family caregiving to those with dementia in rural Alabama: Racial similarities and differences. *Journal of Aging and Health, 19,* 3–21.

Koukoui, S. D., & Chaudhuri, A. (2007). Neuroanatomical, molecular genetic, and behavioral correlates of fragile X syndrome. *Brain Research Reviews, 53,* 27–38.

Kovacs, M., Akiskal, H. S., Gatsonis, C., & Parrone, P. L. (1994). Childhood-onset dysthymic disorder. *Archives of General Psychiatry, 51,* 365–374.

Kovacs, M., Goldston, D., & Gatsonis, C. (1993). Suicidal behaviors and childhood-onset depressive disorders: A longitudinal investigation. *Journal of the American Academy of Child and Adolescent Psychiatry, 32,* 8–20.

Kovacs, M., Rush, A. J., Beck, A. T., & Hollon, S. D. (1981). Depressed outpatients treated with cognitive therapy or pharmacotherapy: A one-year follow-up. *Archives of General Psychiatry, 38*(1), 33–39.

Koyama, E., Beitchman, J. H., & Johnson, C. J. (2009). Expressive language disorder. In B. J. Sadock, V. A. Sadock, & P. Ruiz (Eds.), *Kaplan & Sadock's comprehensive textbook of psychiatry* (9th ed., Vol. II, pp. 3509–3516). Philadelphia, PA: Lippincott Williams & Wilkins.

Kraepelin, E. (1898). *The diagnosis and prognosis of dementia praecox.* Paper presented at the 29th Congress of Southwestern German Psychiatry, Heidelberg.

Kraepelin, E. (1899). *Kompendium der psychiatrie* (6th ed.). Leipzig, Germany: Abel.

Kraepelin, E. (1913). *Psychiatry: A textbook for students and physicians.* Leipzig, Germany: Barth.

Kral, J. G. (2002). Surgical interventions for obesity. In K. D. Brownell & C. G. Fairburn (Eds.), *Eating disorders and obesity: A comprehensive handbook* (2nd ed., pp. 510–515). New York, NY: Guilford Press.

Krantz, D. S., & Deckel, A. W. (1983). Coping with coronary heart disease and stroke. In T. G. Burish & L. A. Bradley (Eds.), *Coping with chronic disease: Research and applications* (pp. 85–111). New York, NY: Academic Press.

Kring, A. M., & Sloan, D. M. (2010). Emotion regulation and psychopathology: A transdiagnostic *approach to etiology and treatment.* New York, NY: Guilford Press.

Kroenke, K. (2007). Efficacy of treatment for somatoform disorders: A review of randomized controlled trials. *Psychosomatic Medicine, 69*(9), 881–888.

Kroll, R., & Beitchman, J. H. (2009). Stuttering. In B. J. Sadock, V. A. Sadock, & P. Ruiz (Eds.), *Kaplan & Sadock's comprehensive textbook of psychiatry* (9th ed., Vol. II, pp. 3528–3533). Philadelphia, PA: Lippincott Williams & Wilkins.

Krueger, R. B. (2010). The DSM diagnostic criteria for sexual sadism. *Archives of Sexual Behavior, 39,* 325–345.

Krueger, R. F., Markon, K. E., Patrick, C. J., & Iacono, W. G. (2005). Externalizing psychopathology in adulthood: A dimensional-spectrum conceptualization and its implications for DSM-V. *Journal of Abnormal Psychology, 114*(4), 537– 550. doi:10.1037/0021-843x.114.4.537

Krueger, R. F., Skodol, A. E., Livesley, W. J., Shrout, P. E., & Huang, Y. (2008). Synthesizing dimensional and categorical approaches to personality disorders: Refining the research agenda for DSM-V axis II. In J. E. Helzer, H. C. Kraemer, R. F. Krueger, H. Wittchen, P. J. Sirovatka, & D. A. Regier (Eds.), *Dimensional approaches in diagnostic classification: Refining the research agenda for DSM-V* (pp. 85–100). Arlington, VA: American Psychiatric Association.

Krueger, R. F., Watson, D., & Barlow, D. H. (2005). Introduction to the special section: Toward a dimensionally based taxonomy of psychopathology [Special issue]. *Journal of Abnormal Psychology, 114,* 491–493.

Krug, E. G., Kresnow, M.-J., Peddicord, J. P., Dahlberg, L. L., Powell, K. E., Crosby, A. E., & Annest, J. L. (1998). Suicide after natural disasters. *New England Journal of Medicine, 338*(6), 373–378.

Krupitsky, E., & Blokhina, E. (2010). Longacting depot formulations of naltrexone for heroin dependence: A review. *Current Opinion in Psychiatry, 23*(3), 210.

Kuehn, B. M. (2010). Sibutramine warning. *JAMA: Journal of the American Medical Association, 303,* 322.

Kuiper, B., & Cohen-Kettenis, P. (1988). Sex reassignment surgery: A study of 141 Dutch transsexuals. *Archives of Sexual Behaviour, 17,* 439–457.

Kuno, E., & Rothbard, AB. (2002). Racial disparities in antipsychotic prescription patterns for individuals with schizophrenia. *American Journal of Psychiatry, 159*(4), 567.

Kuo, W. H., Gallo, J. J., & Tien, A. Y. (2001). Incidence of suicide ideation and attempts in adults: The 13-year follow-up of a community sample in Baltimore, Maryland. *Psychological Medicine, 31,* 1181–91.

Kupfer, D. J. (1995). Sleep research in depressive illness: Clinical implications—A tasting menu. *Biological Psychiatry, 38,* 391–403.

Kupfer, D. J., First, M. B., & Regier, D. A. (2002). *A research agenda for DSM-V.* Washington, DC: American Psychiatric Association.

Kurihara, T., Kato, M., Reverger, R., & Gusti Rai Tirta, I. (2006). Beliefs about causes of schizophrenia among family members: A community-based survey in Bali. *Psychiatric Services, 57*, 1795–1799.

Kushner, M. G., Abrams, K., & Borchardt, C. (2000). The relationship between anxiety disorders and alcohol use disorders: A review of major perspectives and findings. *Clinical Psychology Review, 20*, 149–171.

Kwok, T., Lee, J., Lam, L., & Woo, J. (2008). Vitamin B_{12} supplementation did not improve cognition but reduced delirium in demented patients with vitamin B_{12} deficiency. *Archives of Gerontology and Geriatrics, 46*(3), 273–282.

Kymalainen, J., & Weisman de Mamani, A. G. (2008). Expressed emotion, communication deviance, and culture in families of patients with schizophrenia: A review of the literature. *Cultural Diversity and Ethnic Minority Psychology, 14*(2), 85–91.

La Fond, J. Q. (2005). *Preventing sexual violence: How society should cope with sex offenders*. Washington, DC: American Psychological Association.

La Fond, J. Q., & Durham, M. L. (1992). *Back to the asylum: The future of mental health law and policy in the United States*. New York, NY: Oxford University Press.

La Greca, A. M., & Prinstein, M. J. (2002). Hurricanes and earthquakes. In A. N. La Greca, W. K. Silverman, & M. C. Roberts (Eds.), *Helping Children Cope with Disasters and Terrorism* (Vol. 1, pp. 107–138). Washington, DC: American Psychological Association.

Lacey, J. H. (1992). The treatment demand for bulimia: A catchment area report of referral rates and demography. *Psychiatric Bulletin, 16*, 203–205.

Lack, L. C., Gradisar, M., Van Someren, E. J. W., Wright, H. R., & Lushington, K. (2008). The relationship between insomnia and body temperatures. *Sleep Medicine Reviews, 12*(4), 307–317.

Ladd, C. O., Huot, R. L., Thrivikraman, K. V., Nemeroff, C. B., Meaney, M. J., & Plotsky, P. M. (2000). Long-term behavioral and neuroendocrine adaptations to adverse early experience. In E. A. Mayer & C. B. Saper (Eds.), *Progress in brain research: The biological basis for mind body interactions*. (Vol. 122, pp. 81–103). Amsterdam, The Netherlands: Elsevier.

Lader, M. H. (1975). *The psychophysiology of mental illness*. London, UK: Routledge & Kegan Paul.

Laing, R. D. (1967). *The politics of experience*. New York, NY: Pantheon.

Lakin, M. M., Montague, D. K., Vanderbrug Medendorp, S., Tesar, L., & Schover, L. R. (1990). Intracavernous injection therapy: Analysis of results and complications. *Journal of Urology, 143*, 1138–1141.

Lalumière, M. L., Blanchard, R., & Zucker, K. J. (2000). Sexual orientation and handedness in men and women: A meta-analysis. *Psychological Bulletin, 126*, 575–592.

Lam, D. H., Hayward, P., Watkins, E., Wright, K., & Sham, P. (2005). Relapse prevention in patients with bipolar disorder: Cognitive therapy outcome after 2 years. *American Journal of Psychiatry, 162*, 324–329.

Lam, D. H., Watkins, E. R., Hayward, P., Bright, J., Wright, K., Kerr, N., ... Sham, P.

(2003). A randomized controlled study of cognitive therapy for relapse prevention for bipolar affective disorder: Outcome of the first year. *Archives of General Psychiatry, 60*, 145–152.

Lamb, H. R. (2009). Reversing criminalization. *American Journal of Psychiatry, 166*(1), 8–10.

Lamb, H. R., & Weinberger, L. E. (2009). Criminalization of persons with severe mental illness. In B. J. Sadock, V. A. Sadock, & P. Ruiz (Eds.), *Kaplan & Sadock's comprehensive textbook of psychiatry* (9th ed., Vol. II, pp. 4380–4395). Philadelphia, PA: Lippincott Williams & Wilkins.

Lamberg, L. (2003). All night diners: Researchers take a new look at night eating syndrome. *JAMA: Journal of the American Medical Association, 290*, 1442.

Lambert, M. C., Weisz, J. R., Knight, F., Desrosiers, M., Overly, K., & Thesiger, C. (1992). Jamaican and American adult perspectives on child psychopathology: Further explorations of the threshold model. *Journal of Consulting and Clinical Psychology, 60*, 146–149.

Landis, S., & Insel, T. R. (2008). The "neuro" in neurogenetics. *Science, 322*, 821.

Landis, S. E., Earp, J. L., & Koch, G. G. (1992). Impact of HIV testing and counseling on subsequent sexual behavior. *AIDS Education and Prevention, 4*(1), 61–70.

Lang, P. J. (1985). The cognitive psychophysiology of emotion: Fear and anxiety. In A. H. Tuma & J. D. Maser (Eds.), *Anxiety and the anxiety disorders*. Hillsdale, NJ: Erlbaum.

Lang, P. J. (1995). The emotion probe: Studies of motivation and attention. *American Psychologist, 50*, 372–385.

Lang, P. J., Bradley, M. M., & Cuthbert, B. N. (1998). Emotion, motivation, and anxiety: Brain mechanisms and psychophysiology. *Biological Psychiatry, 44*, 1248–1263.

Långström, N., Rahman, Q., Carlström, E., & Lichtenstein, P. (2010). Genetic and environmental effects on same-sex sexual behavior: A population study of twins in Sweden. *Archives of Sexual Behavior, 39*, 75–80.

Långström, N., & Seto, M. (2006). Exhibitionistic and voyeuristic in a Swedish national population survey. *Archives of Sexual Behavior, 35*, 427–435.

Långström, N., & Zucker, K. (2005). Transvestic fetishism in the general population: Prevalence and correlates. *Journal of Sex & Marital Therapy, 31*, 87–95.

Lapierre, Y. D. (1994). Pharmacological therapy of dysthymia. *Acta Psychiatrica Scandinavica Supplemental, 89*(383), 42–48.

Latfi, R., Kellum, J. M., DeMaria, E. J., & Sugarman, H. J. (2002). Surgical treatment of obesity. In T. A. Wadden & A. J. Stunkard (Eds.), *Handbook of obesity treatment* (pp. 339–356). New York, NY: Guilford Press.

Laub, J. H., & Vaillant, G. E. (2000). Delinquency and mortality: A 50-year follow-up study of 1,000 delinquent and nondelinquent boys. *American Journal of Psychiatry, 157*, 96–102.

Laumann, E., Gagnon, J., Michael, R., & Michaels, S. (1994). *The social organization of sexuality: Sexual practices in the United States*. Chicago, IL: University of Chicago Press.

Laumann, E., Paik, A., & Rosen, R. C. (1999). Sexual dysfunction in the United States. Prevalence and predictors. *JAMA: Journal of the American Medical Association, 281*, 537–544.

Laumann, E. O., Nicolosi, A., Glasser, D. B., Paik, A., Gingell, C., Moreira, E., & Wang, T. (2005). Sexual problems among women and men aged 40–80 years: Prevalence and correlates identified by the Global Study of Sexual Attitudes and Behaviors. *International Journal of Impotence Research, 17*, 39–57.

Laws, D. R. (Ed.) (1989). *Relapse prevention with sex offenders*. New York, NY: Guilford Press.

Laws, D. R., & O'Donohue, W. (Eds.) (1997). *Sexual deviance: Theory, assessment and treatment*. New York, NY: Guilford Press.

Laxenaire, M., Ganne-Vevonec, M. O., & Streiff, O. (1982). Les problèmes d'identité chez les enfants des migrants. *Annales Medico-Psychologiques, 140*, 602–605.

Lazarus, R. A., & Folkman, S. (1984). *Stress, appraisal, and coping*. New York, NY: Springer.

Lazarus, R. S. (1968). Emotions and adaptation: Conceptual and empirical relations. In W. J. Arnold (Ed.), *Nebraska Symposium on Motivation* (Vol. 16). Lincoln: University of Nebraska Press.

Lazarus, R. S. (1991). Progress on a cognitive- motivational relational theory of emotion. *American Psychologist, 46*(8), 819–834.

Lazarus, R. S. (1995). Psychological stress in the workplace. In R. Crandall, P. L. Perrewe (Eds.), *Occupational stress: A handbook* (pp. 3–14). Philadelphia, PA: Taylor & Francis.

Le Foll, B., Gallo, A., Le Strat, Y., Lu, L., & Gorwood, P. (2009). Genetics of dopamine receptors and drug addiction: A comprehensive review. *Behavioural Pharmacology, 20*(1), 1–17.

Leamon, M. H., Wright, T. M., & Myrick, H. (2008). Substance-related disorders. In R. E. Hales, S. C. Yudofsky, & G. O. Gabbard (Eds.), *The American Psychiatric Publishing textbook of psychiatry* (5th ed., pp. 365–406). Arlington, VA: American Psychiatric Publishing.

LeBeau, R. T., Glenn, D., Liao, B., Wittchen, H.-U., Beesdo-Baum, K., Ollendick, T., & Craske, M. (2010). Specific phobia: A review of DSM-IV specific phobia and preliminary recommendations for DSM-V. *Depression and Anxiety, 27*(2), 148–167.

Lebedinskaya, K. S., & Nikolskaya, O. S. (1993). Brief report: Analysis of autism and its treatment in modern Russian defectology. *Journal of Autism and Developmental Disorders, 23*, 675–697.

Lechner, S., Antoni, M. (2004). Posttraumatic growth and group based intervention for persons dealing with cancer: What have we learned so far? *Psychological Inquiry, 15*, 35–41.

Leckman, J. F., Denys, D., Simpson, H. B., Mataix-Cols, D., Hollander, E., Saxena, S., ... Stein, D. (2010). Obsessive-compulsive disorder: A review of the diagnostic criteria and possible subtypes and dimensional specifiers for DSM-V. *Depression and Anxiety, 27*(6), 507–527.

Leckman, J. F., Grice, D. E., Boardman, J., Zhang, H., Vitali, A., Bondi, C., ... Pauls, D.

(1997). Symptoms of obsessive-compulsive disorder. *American Journal of Psychiatry, 154,* 911–917.

Lecrubier, Y., Bakker, A., Dunbar, G., & the Collaborative Paroxetine Panic Study Investigators. (1997). A comparison of paroxetine, clomipramine, and placebo in the treatment of panic disorder. *Acta Psychiatrica Scandinavica, 95,* 145–152.

Lecrubier, Y., Judge, R., & and the Collaborative Paroxetine Panic Study Investigators. (1997). Long-term evaluation of paroxetine, clomipramine, and placebo in panic disorder. *Acta Psychiatrica Scandinavica, 95,* 153–160.

LeDoux, J. E. (1996). *The emotional brain: The mysterious underpinnings of emotional life.* New York, NY: Simon & Schuster.

LeDoux, J. E. (2002). *Synaptic self: How our brains become who we are.* New York, NY: Penguin Books.

Lee, C. C., Czaja, S. J., & Schulz, R. (2010). The moderating influence of demographic characteristics, social support, and religious coping on the effectiveness of a multicomponent psychosocial caregiver intervention in three racial ethnic groups. *The Journals of Gerontology Series B: Psychological Sciences and Social Sciences, 65B(2),* 185–194.

Lee, C. K. (1992). Alcoholism in Korea. In J. Helzer & G. Canino (Eds.), *Alcoholism-North America, Europe, and Asia: A coordinated analysis of population data from ten regions* (pp. 247–262). London, UK: Oxford University Press.

Lee, K. (1992). Pattern of night waking and crying of Korean infants from 3 months to 2 years old and its relation with various factors. *Journal of Developmental & Behavioral Pediatrics, 13,* 326–330.

Lee, S. (1993). How abnormal is the desire for slimness? A survey of eating attitudes and behavior among Chinese undergraduates in Hong Kong. *Psychological Medicines, 23,* 437–451.

Lee, S. H., Han, D. H., Oh, S., Lyoo, I. K., Lee, Y. S., Renshaw, P. F., & Lukas, S. (2009). Quantitative electroencephalographic (qEEG) correlates of craving during virtual reality therapy in alcohol-dependent patients. *Pharmacology Biochemistry and Behavior, 91(3),* 393–397. doi:10.1016/j.pbb.2008.08.014

Lee, T. M., Chen, E. Y., Chan, C. C., Paterson, J. G., Janzen, H. L., & Blashko, C. A. (1998). Seasonal affective disorder. *Clinical Psychology: Science and Practice, 5,* 275–290.

Lefley, H. (2009). *Family psychoeducation in serious mental illness: Models, outcomes, applications.* New York, NY: Oxford University Press.

Lefrancois, G. R. (1990). *The lifespan* (3rd ed.). Belmont, CA: Wadsworth.

Leibbrand, R., Hiller, W., & Fichter, M. M. (2000). Hypochondriasis and somatization: Two distinct aspects of somatoform disorders? *Journal of Clinical Psychology, 56,* 63–72.

Leibenluft, E., & Rich, B. A. (2008). Pediatric bipolar disorder. *Annual Review of Clinical Psychology, 4,* 163–187.

Leiblum, S. R., & Rosen, R. C. (Eds.) (2000). *Principles and practice of sex therapy* (3rd ed.). New York, NY: Guilford Press.

Leitenberg, H., Detzer, M. J., & Srebnik, D. (1993). Gender differences in masturbation and the relation of masturbation experience in preadolescence and/or early adolescence to sexual behavior and sexual adjustment in young adulthood. *Archives of Sexual Behavior, 22*(2), 87–98.

Lejeune, J., Gauthier, M., & Turpin, R. (1959). Étude des chromosomes somatiques de neuf enfants mongoliens. *Comptes Rendus Hebdomadaires des Séances de l' Académie des Sciences. D: Sciences Naturelles (Paris), 248,* 1721–1722.

Lejoyeux, M., McLoughlin, M., & Ades, J. (2006). Pyromania. In E. Hollander & C. Stein (Eds.), *Clinical manual of impulse-control disorders* (pp. 229–250). Arlington, VA: American Psychiatric Publishing.

Lemay, M., & Landreville, P. (2010). Verbal agitation in dementia: The role of discomfort. *American Journal of Alzheimer's Disease and Other Dementias, 25*(3), 193-201. doi: 10.1177/1533317509356687.

Lenze, E. J., Miller, A. R., Munir, Z. B., Pornoppadol, C., & North, C. S. (1999). Psychiatric symptoms endorsed by somatization disorder patients in a psychiatric clinic. *Annals of Clinical Psychiatry, 11*(2), 73–79.

Lenzenweger, M. F., & Dworkin, R. H. (1996). The dimensions of schizophrenia phenomenology. Note one or two, at least three, perhaps four. *British Journal of Psychiatry, 168,* 432–440.

Lenzenweger, M. F., McLachlan, G., & Rubin, D. B. (2007a). Resolving the latent structure of schizophrenia endophenotypes using expectation- maximization-based finite mixture modeling. *Journal of Abnormal Psychology, 116,* 16–29.

Lenzenweger, M. F., Lane, M., Loranger, A., & Kessler, R. (2007b). DSM-IV personality disorders in the National Comorbidity Survey Replication. *Biological Psychiatry, 62*(6), 553–564.

Lesch, K.-P., Bengel, D., Heils, A., Sabol, S. Z., Greenberg, B. D., Petri, S., ... Murphy, D. (1996). Association of anxiety-related traits with a polymorphism in the serotonin transporter gene regulatory region. *Science, 274,* 1527–1531.

Leserman, J. (2008). Role of depression, stress, and trauma in HIV disease progression. *Psychosomatic Medicine, 70,* 539–545.

Leserman, J., Petitto, J. M., Golden, R. N., Gaynes, B. N., Gu, H., Perkins, D. O., ... & Evans, D.L. (2000). Impact of stressful life events, depression, social support, coping, and cortisol on progression to AIDS. *American Journal of Psychiatry, 157,* 1221–1228.

Lett, H., Blumenthal, J., Babyak, M., Strauman, T., Robins, C., & Sherwood, A. (2005). Social support and coronary heart disease: Epidemiologic evidence and implications for treatment. *Psychosomatic Medicine, 67,* 869–878.

Leucht, S., Komossa, K., Rummel-Kluge, C., Corves, C., Hunger, H., Schmid, F., ... Davis, J. M.. (2009). A meta-analysis of head-to-head comparisons of second-generation antipsychotics in the treatment of schizophrenia. *American Journal of Psychiatry, 166*(2), 152–163. doi:10.1176/appi.ajp.2008.08030368

Leuchter, A. F., Cook, I. A., Witte, E. A., Morgan, M., & Abrams, M. (2002). Changes in brain function of depressed subjects during treatment with placebo. *American Journal of Psychiatry, 159,* 122–129.

LeVay, S. (1991). A difference in hypothalamic structure between heterosexual and homosexual men. *Science, 253,* 1034–1037.

Levenston, G. K., Patrick, C. J., Bradley, M. M., & Lang, P. J. (2000). The psychopath as observer: Emotion and attention in picture processing. *Journal of Abnormal Psychology, 109,* 373–385.

Levin, F. R., Evans, S. M., Brooks, D. J., & Garawi, F. (2007). Treatment of cocaine-dependent treatment seekers with adult ADHD: Double-blind comparison of methylphenidate and placebo. *Drug and Alcohol Dependence, 87,* 20–29.

Levine, J. A., Lanningham-Foster, L. M., McCrady, S. K., Krizan, A. C., Olson, L. R., Kane, P. H., Jensen, M. D., & Clark, M. M. (2005). Interindividual variation in posture allocation: Possible role in human obesity. *Science, 307,* 584–586.

Levine, M. P., & Smolak, L. (1996). Media as a context for the development of disordered eating. In L. Smolak, M. P. Levine, & R. Striegel-Moore (Eds.), *The developmental psychopathology of eating disorders: Implications for research, prevention, and treatment* (pp. 235–257). Mahwah, NJ: Erlbaum.

Levinson, D. F. (2009). Genetics of major depression. In I. H. Gotlib & C. L. Hammen (Eds.), *Handbook of depression* (2nd ed., pp. 165–186). New York, NY: Guilford Press.

Levy, B. R., Slade, M. D., Kunkel, S. R., & Kasl, S. V. (2002). Longevity increased by positive self-perceptions of aging. *Journal of Personality and Social Psychology, 83,* 261–270.

Levy, K. B., O'Grady, K. E., Wish, E. D., & Arria, A. M. (2005). An in-depth qualitative examination of the ecstasy experience: Results of a focus group with Ecstasy-using college students. *Substance Use and Misuse, 40*(9–10), 1427– 1441. doi:10.1081/ja-200066886

Lewinsohn, P. M., Allen, N. B., Seeley, J. R., & Gotlib, I. H. (1999). First onset versus recurrence of depression: Differential processes of psychosocial risk. *Journal of Abnormal Psychology, 108*(3), 483–489.

Lewinsohn, P. M., & Rosenbaum, M. (1987). Recall of parental behavior by acute depressives, remitted depressives, and non-depressives. *Journal of Personality and Social Psychology, 52*(3), 611–619.

Lewis, B. A., Statt, E., & Marcus, B. H. (2011). Behavioral interventions in public health settings: Physical activity, weight loss, and smoking. In D. H. Barlow (Ed.), *Oxford handbook of Clinical Psychology* (pp. 717–738). New York, NY: Oxford University Press.

Lewis, G., Croft-Jeffreys, C., & Anthony, D. (1990). Are British psychiatrists racist? *British Journal of Psychiatry, 157,* 410–415.

Lewis, G., David, A., Andreasson, S., & Allsbeck, P. (1992). Schizophrenia and city life. *Lancet, 340,* 137–140.

Lewis, S., Escalona, R., & Keith, S. J. (2009). Phenomenology of schizophrenia. In B. J. Sadock, V. A. Sadock, & P. Ruiz (Eds.), *Kaplan & Sadock's comprehensive textbook of psychiatry* (9th ed., Vol. I, pp. 1433–1451). Philadelphia, PA: Lippincott Williams & Wilkins.

Lewis, S., & Lieberman, J. (2008). CATIE and CUtLASS: Can we handle the truth? *The British Journal of Psychiatry, 192*(3), 161.

Lewis, T. T., Everson-Rose, S. A., Powell, L. H., Matthews, K. A., Brown, C., ... Wesley, D. (2006). Chronic exposure to everyday discrimination and coronary artery calcification in African American women: The SWAN heart study. *Psychosomatic Medicine, 68*, 362–368.

Lewis-Fernández, R., Hinton, D. E., Laria, A. J., Patterson, E. H., Hofmann, S. G., Craske, M. G., & Liao, B. (2010). Culture and the anxiety disorders: Recommendations for DSM-V. *Depression and Anxiety, 27*(2), 212–229.

Leyfer, O. & Brown, T.A. (2011). The anxiety-depression spectrum. In D. H. Barlow (Ed.), *Oxford handbook of clinical psychology* (pp. 279–293). New York, NY: Oxford University Press.

Leykin, Y., & DeRubeis, R. J. (2009). Allegiance in psychotherapy outcome research: Separating association from bias. *Clinical Psychology: Science and Practice, 16*(1), 54–65.

Liberman, R., & Kopelowicz, A. (2009). Training skills for illness self-management in the rehabilitation of schizophrenia: A family-assisted program for Latinos in California. *Salud Mental, 31*, 93–105.

Liberman, R. P. (2007). Dissemination and adoption of social skills training: Social validation of an evidence-based treatment for the mentally disabled. *Journal of Mental Health, 16*, 595–623.

Lichtenthal, W., Cruess, D., & Prigerson, H. (2004). A case for establishing complicated grief as a distinct mental disorder in DSM-V. *Clinical Psychology Review, 24*, 637–662.

Liddell, H. S. (1949). The role of vigilance in the development of animal neurosis. In P. Hoch & J. Zubin (Eds.), *Anxiety*. New York, NY: Grune & Stratton.

Lieb, R., Wittchen, H-U., Hofler, M., Fuetsch, M., Stein, M. B., & Merikangas, K. R. (2000). Parental psychopathology, parenting styles, and the risk of social phobia in offspring. *Archives of General Psychiatry, 57*, 859–866.

Lieb, R., Zimmermann, P., Friis, R. H., Hofler, M., Tholen, S., & Wittchen, H. U. (2002). The natural course of DSM-IV somatoform disorders and syndromes among adolescents and young adults: A prospective-longitudinal community study. *European Psychiatry, 17*, 321–331.

Lieberman, J. A., Jody, D., Alvir, J. M. J., Ashtari, M., Levy, D. L., Bogerts, B., ... Cooper, T.. (1993). Brain morphology, dopamine, and eye-tracking abnormalities in first-episode schizophrenia. *Archives of General Psychiatry, 50*, 357–368.

Lieberman, J. A., Perkins, D., Belger, A., Chakos, M., Jarskog, F., Boteva, K., & Gilmore, J. (2001). The early stages of schizophrenia: Speculations on pathogenesis, pathophysiology, and therapeutic approaches. *Biological Psychiatry, 50*, 885.

Lieberman, J. A., Stroup, T. S., McEvoy, J. P., Swartz, M. S., Rosenheck, R. A., Perkins, D. O., ... Hsiao, J. K.; Clinical Antipsychotic Trials of Intervention Effectiveness (CATIE) Investigators. (2005). Effectiveness of antipsychotic drugs in patients with chronic schizophrenia. *New England Journal of Medicine, 353*, 1209–1223.

Liebeskind, J. (1991). Pain can kill. *Pain, 44*, 3–4.

Liebowitz, M. R., Heimberg, R. G., Schneier, F. R., Hope, D. A., Davies, S., Holt, C. S., ... Klein, D. (1999). Cognitive-behavioral group therapy versus phenelzine in social phobia: Long-term outcome. *Depression and Anxiety, 10*, 89–98.

Liebowitz, M. R., Salman, E., Jusino, C. M., Garfinkel, R., Street, L., Cardenas, D. L., ... Klein, D. (1994). Ataque de nervios and panic disorder. *American Journal of Psychiatry, 151*, 871–875.

Liebowitz, M. R., Schneier, F., Campeas, R., Hollander, E., Hatterer, J., Fyer, A., Gully, R. (1992). Phenelzine vs. atenolol in social phobia: A placebo-controlled comparison. *Archives of General Psychiatry, 49*, 290–300.

Liggett, J. (1974). *The human face.* New York, NY: Stein and Day.

Lilenfeld, L. R. R., Wonderlich, S., Riso, L. P., Crosby, R., & Mitchell, J. (2006). Eating disorders and personality: A methodological and empirical review. *Clinical Psychology Review, 26*, 299–320.

Lilienfeld, S. O. (1992). The association between antisocial personality and somatization disorders: A review and integration of theoretical models. *Clinical Psychology Review, 12*, 641–662.

Lilienfeld, S. O., & Hess, T. H. (2001). Psychopathic personality traits and somatization: Sex differences and the mediating role of negative emotionality. *Journal of Psychopathology and Behavioral Assessment, 23*, 11–24.

Lilienfeld, S. O., Kirsch, I., Sarbin, T. R., Lynn, S. J., Chaves, J. F., & Ganaway, G. K. (1999). Dissociative identity disorder and the sociocognitive model: Recalling the lessons of the past. *Psychological Bulletin, 125*(5), 507–523.

Lilienfeld, S. O., & Marino, L. (1995). Mental disorder as a Roschian concept: A critique of Wakefield's 'harmful dysfunction' analysis. *Journal of Abnormal Psychology, 104*(3), 411–420.

Lilienfeld, S. O., & Marino, L. (1999). Essentialism revisited: Evolutionary theory and the concept of mental disorder. *Journal of Abnormal Psychology, 108*, 400–411.

Lilienfeld, S. O., VanValkenburg, C., Larntz, K., & Akiskal, H. S. (1986). The relationship of histrionic personality to antisocial personality and somatization disorders. *American Journal of Psychiatry, 143*, 718–722.

Lin, N., & Ensel, W. M. (1984). Depression-mobility and its social etiology: The role of life events and social support. *Journal of Health and Social Behavior, 25*(1), 176–188.

Lincoln, M., Packman, A., & Onslow, M. (2006). Altered auditory feedback and the treatment of stuttering: A review. *Journal of Fluency Disorders, 31*, 71–89.

Lind, S., & Bowler, D. (2009). Delayed self-recognition in children with autism spectrum disorder. *Journal of Autism and Developmental Disorders, 39*(4), 643–650. doi:10.1007/s10803-008-0670-7

Linden, W., & Moseley, J. (2006). The efficacy of behavioral treatments for hypertension. *Applied Psychophysiology and Biofeedback, 31*, 51–63.

Lindenmayer, J. P., & Khan, A. (2006). Psychopathology. In J. A. Lieberman, T. S. Stroup, & D. O. Perkins (Eds.), *The American Psychiatric Publishing textbook of schizophrenia* (pp. 187– 221). Washington, DC: American Psychiatric Publishing.

Lindesay, J. (1991). Phobic disorders in the elderly. *British Journal of Psychiatry, 159*, 531–541.

Lindsey, M., Joe, S., Muroff, J., & Ford, B. (2010). Social and clinical factors associated with psychiatric emergency service use and civil commitment among African American youth. *General Hospital Psychiatry, 32*, 300–309.

Linehan, M., Comtois, K., Murray, A., Brown, M., Gallop, R., Heard, H., ... Lindenboim, N. (2006). Two-year randomized controlled trial and follow-up of dialectical behavior therapy vs. therapy by experts for suicidal behaviors and borderline personality disorder. *Archives of General Psychiatry, 63*(7), 757.

Linehan, M., Schmidt, H., Dimeff, L., Craft, J., Kanter, J., & Comtois, K. (1999). Dialectical behavior therapy for patients with borderline personality disorder and drug-dependence. *American Journal on Addictions, 8*(4), 279–292.

Linehan, M. M., & Dexter-Mazza, E. T. (2008). Dialectical behavior therapy for borderline personality disorder. In D. H. Barlow (Ed.), *Clinical handbook of psychological disorders* (4th ed., pp. 365–420). New York, NY: The Gilford Press.

Linehan, M. M., & Kehrer, C. A. (1993). Borderline personality disorder. In D. H. Barlow (Ed.), *Clinical handbook of psychological disorders: A step-by-step treatment manual* (pp. 396–441). New York, NY: Guilford Press.

Liotti, M., Mayberg, H. S., McGinnis, S., Brannan, S. L., & Jerabek, P. (2002). Unmasking disease-specific cerebral blood flow abnormalities: Mood challenge in patients with remitted unipolar depression. *American Journal of Psychiatry, 159*, 1807–1808.

Lipchik, G. L., Holroyd, K. A., & Nash, J. M. (2002). Cognitive-behavioral management of recurrent headache disorders: A minimal-therapist-contact approach. In D. C. Turk & R. J. Gatchel (Eds.), *Psychological approaches to pain management: A practitioner's handbook* (2nd ed.) (pp. 365–389). New York, NY: Guilford Press.

Lisspers, J., & Öst, L. (1990). Long-term follow-up of migraine treatment: Do the effects remain up to six years? *Behaviour Research and Therapy, 28*, 313–322.

Littauer, D. (2010, Dec. 9). Iranian honour killing: Trans murdered by her brothers in Tehran. Retrieved from http://gaymiddle-east.com/news/news%20224.htm

Litz, B. T., Gray, M. J., Bryant, R. A., & Adler, A. B. (2002). Early intervention for trauma: Current status and future directions. *Clinical Psychology: Science & Practice, 9*, 112–134.

Livesley, W. J., Jang, K. L., & Vernon, P. A. (1998). Phenotypic and genotypic structure of traits delineating personality disorder. *Archives of General Psychiatry, 55*, 941–948.

Livingston, E. H. (2010). Surgical treatment of obesity in adolescence. *JAMA: Journal of the American Medical Association, 303*(6), 559–560.

Lloyd, E. A. (2005). *The case of the female orgasm: Bias in the science of evolution.* Cambridge, MA: Harvard University Press.

Lock, J., le Grange, D., Agras, W. S., & Dare, C. (2001). *Treatment manual for anorexia nervosa: A family-based approach.* New York, NY: Guilford Press.

Loehlin, J., McFadden, D., Medland, S., & Martin, N. (2006). Population differences in finger-length ratios: Ethnicity or latitude? *Archives of Sexual Behavior, 35,* 739–742.

Loehlin, J. C. (1992). *Genes and environment in personality development.* Newbury Park, CA: Sage.

Loewenstein, R. J. (1991). An office mental status examination for complex chronic dissociative symptoms and multiple personality disorder. *The Psychiatric Clinics of North America, 14,* 567–604.

Loftus, E., & Davis, D. (2006). Recovered memories. *Annual Review of Clinical Psychology, 2,* 469–498.

Loftus, E. F. (2003). Make-believe memories. *American Psychologist, 58,* 867–873.

Loftus, E. F., Coan, J. A., & Pickrell, J. E. (1996). Manufacturing false memories using bits of reality. In L. Reder (Ed.), *Implicit memory and metacognition* (pp. 195–220). Mahwah, NJ: Erlbaum.

Logan, C. (2009). Sexual deviance in females: Psychopathology and theory. In D. R. Laws & W. T. O'Donohue (Eds.), *Sexual deviance: Theory, assessment, and treatment* (2nd ed., pp. 486–507). New York, NY: Guilford Press.

Logsdon, R., McCurry, S., Pike, K., & Teri, L. (2009). Making physical activity accessible to older adults with memory loss: A feasibility study. *The Gerontologist, 49*(S1), S94.

Lombardo, M. V., Chakrabarti, B., & Baron-Cohen, S. (2009). The amygdala in autism: Not adapting to faces? *American Journal of Psychiatry, 166*(4), 395–397.

Lonczak, H. S. P., Abbott, R. D. P., Hawkins, J. D. P., Kosterman, R. P., & Catalano, R. F. P. (2002). Effects of the Seattle Social Development Project on sexual behavior, pregnancy, birth, and sexually transmitted disease outcomes by age 21 years. *Archives of Pediatrics & Adolescent Medicine, 156*(5), 438–447.

Lopez, M. F., Compton, W. M., Grant, B. F., & Breiling, J. P. (2008). Dimensional approaches in diagnostic classification: A critical appraisal. In J. E. Helzer, H. C. Kraemer, R. F. Krueger, H. Wittchen, P. J. Sirovatka, & D. A. Regier (Eds.), *Dimensional approaches in diagnostic classification: Refining the research agenda for DSM-V* (pp. 1–4). Arlington, VA: American Psychiatric Association.

Lösel, F., & Schmucker, M. (2005). The effectiveness of treatment for sexual offenders: A comprehensive meta-analysis. *Journal of Experimental Criminology, 1,* 117–146.

Lovaas, O. I. (1977). *The autistic child: Language development through behavior Modification.* New York, NY: Irvington.

Lovaas, O. I. (1987). Behavioral treatment and normal educational and intellectual functioning in young autistic children. *Journal of Consulting and Clinical Psychology, 55,* 3–9.

Lovaas, O. I., Berberich, J. P., Perloff, B. F., & Schaeffer, B. (1966). Acquisition of imitative speech by schizophrenic children. *Science, 151,* 705–707.

Lovibond, P. (2006). Fear and avoidance: An integrated expectancy model. In M. G. Craske, D. Hermans, & D. Vansteenwegen, *Fear and learning: From basic processes to clinical implications* (pp. 117–132). Washington, DC: American Psychological Association.

Lowe, M. R., Miller-Kovach, K., Frie, N., & Phelan, S. P. (1999). An initial evaluation of a commercial weight loss program: Short-term effects on weight, eating behavior, and mood. *Obesity Research, 7,* 51–59.

Lubit, R. H. (2009). Ethics in psychiatry. In B. J. Sadock, V. A. Sadock, & P. Ruiz (Eds.), *Kaplan & Sadock's comprehensive textbook of psychiatry* (9th ed., Vol. II, pp. 4439–4448). Philadelphia, PA: Lippincott Williams & Wilkins.

Luby, J. L., Mrakotsky, C., Heffelfinger, A., Brown, K., Hessler, M., & Spitznagel, E. (2003). Modification of DSM-IV criteria for depressed preschool children. *American Journal of Psychiatry, 160,* 1169–1172.

Ludescher, B., Leitlein, G., Schaefer, J. E., Vanhoeffen, S., Baar, S., Machann, J., ... Eschweiler, G. (2009). Changes of body composition in bulimia nervosa: Increased visceral fat and adrenal gland size. *Psychosomatic Medicine, 71*(1), 93–97.

Ludwig, A., Brandsma, J., Wilbur, C., Bendfeldt, F., & Jameson, D. (1972). The objective study of a multiple personality. *Archives of General Psychiatry, 26,* 298–310.

Lundahl, B. W., Kunz, C., Brownell, C., Tollefson, D., & Burke, B. L. (2010). A meta-analysis of motivational interviewing: Twenty-five years of empirical studies. *Research on Social Work Practice, 20*(2), 137–160. doi:10.1177/1049731509347850

Lundgren, J. D., Allison, K. C., Crow, S., O'Reardon, J. P., Berg, K. C., Galbraith, J., ... Stunkard, A. (2006). Prevalence of the night eating syndrome in psychiatric population. *American Journal of Psychiatry, 163,* 156–158.

Lundh, L.-G., & Öst, L.-G. (1996). Recognition bias for critical faces in social phobics. *BRAT, 34,* 787–794.

Lundstrom, B., Pauly, I., & Walinder, J. (1984). Outcome of sex reassignment surgery. *Acta Psychiatrica Scandinavica, 70,* 289–294.

Lurigio, A., & Harris, A. (2009). Mental illness, violence, and risk assessment: An evidence-based review. *Victims & Offenders, 4*(4), 341–347.

Lussier, P., & Piché, L. (2008). Frotteurism: Psychopathology and theory. In D. R. Laws & W. T. O'Donohue (Eds.), *Sexual deviance: Theory, assessment, and treatment* (2nd ed., pp. 131–149). New York, NY: Guilford Press.

Lutgendorf, S., Costanzo, E., & Siegel, S. (2007). Psychosocial influences in oncology: An expanded model of biobehavioral mechanisms. In R. Ader, R. Glaser, N. Cohen, & M. Irwin (Eds.), *Psychoneuroimmunology* (4th ed., pp. 869–895). New York, NY: Academic Press.

Lutgendorf, S. K., Antoni, M. H., Ironson, G., Klimas, N., Kumar, M., Starr, K., ... Schneiderman, N. (1997). Cognitive-behavioral stress management decreases dysphoric mood and herpes simplex virus-type 2 antibody titers in symptomatic HIV-seropositive gay men. *Journal of Consulting and Clinical Psychology, 65,* 31–43.

Lydiard, R. B., Brawman-Mintzer, O., & Ballenger, J. C. (1996). Recent developments in the psychopharmacology of anxiety disorders. *Journal of Consulting & Clinical Psychology, 64,* 660–668.

Lyketos, C. G. (2009). Dementia and milder cognitive syndromes. In D. G. Blazer & D. C. Steffens (Eds.), *The American Psychiatric Publishing textbook of geriatric psychiatry* (4th ed., pp. 243–260). Arlington, VA: American Psychiatric Publishing.

Lyketsos, C. G., & Olin, J. (2002). Depression in Alzheimer's disease: Overview and treatment. *Biological Psychiatry, 52,* 243–252.

Lykken, D. T. (1957). A study of anxiety in the sociopathic personality. *Journal of Abnormal and Social Psychology, 55,* 6–10.

Lykken, D. T. (1982). Fearfulness: Its carefree charms and deadly risks. *Psychology Today, 16,* 20–28.

Lynch, S. K., Turkheimer, E., D'Onofrio, B. M., Mendle, J., Emery, R. E., Slutske, W. S., & Martin, N. G. (2006). A genetically informed study of the association between harsh punishment and offspring behavioral problems. *Journal of Family Psychology, 20,* 190–198.

Lynskey, M., & Hall, W. (2000). The effects of adolescent cannabis use on educational attainment: A review. *Addiction, 95,* 1621–1630.

Lyons, M. J., Eisen, S. A., Goldberg, J., True, W., Lin, N., Meyer, J. M., ... Tsuang, M. T. (1998). A registry-based twin study of depression in men. *Archives of General Psychiatry, 55,* 468–472.

Lyons, M. J., True, W. R., Eisen, S. A., Goldberg, J., Meyer, J. M., Faraone, S. V., ... Tsuang, M. (1995). Differential heritability of adult and juvenile antisocial traits. *Archives of General Psychiatry, 52,* 906–915.

Lyons, M. J., York, T. P., Franz, C. E., Grant, M. D., Eaves, L. J., Jacobson, K. C., ... Kremen, W. S. (2009). Genes determine stability and the environment determines change in cognitive ability during 35 years of adulthood. *Psychological Science, 20*(9), 1146–1152.

Lyubomirsky, S. (2001). Why are some people happier than others? The role of cognitive and motivational processes in well-being. *American Psychologist, 56,* 239–249.

MacDonald, R., Anderson, J., Dube, W. V., Geckeler, A., Green, G., Holcomb, W., ... Sanchez, J. (2006). Behavioral assessment of joint attention: A methodological report. *Research in Developmental Disabilities, 27,* 138–150.

MacDougall, J. M., Dembroski, T. M., Dimsdale, J. E., & Hackett, T. P. (1985). Components of type A, hostility, and anger-in: Further relationships to angiographic findings. *Health Psychology, 4*(2), 137–152.

Mace, C. J. (1992). Hysterical conversion II: A critique. *British Journal of Psychiatry, 161,* 378–389.

Maciejewski, P., Zhang, B., Block, S., & Prigerson, H. (2007). An empirical examination of the stage theory of grief. *JAMA: Journal of the American Medical Association, 297,* 716–723.

MacLeod, C., & Mathews, A. M. (1991). Cognitive-experimental approaches to the emotional disorders. In P. R. Martin (Ed.), *Handbook of behavior therapy and psychological science: An integrative approach* (pp. 116–150). Elmsford, NY: Pergamon Press.

MacLeod, C., Mathews, A., & Tata, P. (1986). Attentional bias in emotional disorders. *Journal of Abnormal Psychology, 95,* 15–20.

Macleod, J., Oakes, R., Copello, A., Crome, I., Egger, M., & Hickman, M., ... Davey Smith, G. (2004). Psychological and social sequelae of cannabis and other illicit drug use by young people: A systematic review of longitudinal, general population studies. *Lancet, 363,* 1579–1588.

Madsen, K. M., Hviid, A., Vestergaard, M., Schendel, D., Wohlfahrt, J., Thorsen, P., ... Melbye, M.. (2002). A population-based study of measles, mumps, and rubella vaccination and autism. *New England Journal of Medicine, 347,* 1477–1482.

Magee, W. J., Eaton, W. W., Wittchen, H.-U., McGonagle, K. A., & Kessler, R. C. (1996). Agoraphobia, simple phobia, and social phobia in the National Comorbidity Survey. *Archives of General Psychiatry, 53,* 159–168.

Magne-Ingvar, U., Ojehagen, A., & Traskman-Bendz, L. (1992). The social network of people who attempt suicide. *Acta Psychiatrica Scandinavica, 86,* 153–158.

Maher, B. A., & Maher, W. B. (1985a). Psychopathology: I. From ancient times to the eighteenth century. In G. A. Kimble & K. Schlesinger (Eds.), *Topics in the history of psychology* (pp. 251–294). Hillsdale, NJ: Erlbaum.

Maher, B. A., & Maher, W. B. (1985b). Psychopathology: II. From the eighteenth century to modern times. In G. A. Kimble & K. Schlesinger (Eds.), *Topics in the history of psychology* (pp. 295–329). Hillsdale, NJ: Erlbaum.

Maher, J. J. (1997). Exploring alcohol's effects on liver function. *Alcohol Health & Research World, 21,* 5–12.

Mahler, M. (1952). On childhood psychosis and schizophrenia: Autistic and symbiotic infantile psychosis. *Psychoanalytic Study of the Child, 7,* 286–305.

Mahoney, D. F., Purtilo, R. B., Webbe, F. M., Alwan, M., Bharucha, A. J., Adlam, T. D., ... Becker S. A. (2007). In-home monitoring of persons with dementia: Ethical guidelines for technology research and development. *Alzheimer's & Dementia, 3*(3), 217–226.

Mai, F. (2004). Somatization disorder: A practical review. *Canadian Journal of Psychiatry, 49,* 652–662.

Maier, S. F. (1997, September). *Stressor controllability, anxiety, and serotonin.* Paper presented at the National Institute of Mental Health Workshop on Cognition and Anxiety, Rockville, MD.

Maier, S. F., & Seligman, M. E. (1976). Learned helplessness: Theory and evidence. *Journal of Experimental Psychology: General, 105*(1), 3–46.

Maldonado, J. R., Butler, L. D., & Spiegel, D. (1998). Treatments for dissociative disorders. In P. E. Nathan & J. M. Gorman (Eds.), *A guide to treatments that work.* New York, NY: Oxford University Press.

Maletzky, B. (2002). The paraphilias: Research and treatment. In P. E. Nathan & J. M. Gorman (Eds.), *A guide to treatments that work* (2nd ed., pp. 525–557). New York, NY: Oxford University Press.

Maletzky, B. M. (1998). The paraphilias: Research and treatment. In P. E. Nathan & J. M. Gorman (Eds.), *A guide to treatments that work* (pp. 472– 500). New York, NY: Oxford University Press.

Manber, R., Edinger, J. D., Gress, J. L., San Pedro-Salcedo, M. G., Kuo, T. F., & Kalista, T. (2008). Cognitive behavioral therapy for insomnia enhances depression outcome in patients with comorbid major depressive disorder and insomnia. *Sleep, 31*(4), 489–495.

Mancuso, S., Knoesen, N., & Castle, D.J. (2010). Delusional vs. nondelusional body dysmorphic disorder. *Comprehensive Psychiatry.*

Mandalos, G. E., & Szarek, B. L. (1990). Dose-related paranoid reaction associated with fluoxetine. *Journal of Nervous and Mental Disease, 178*(1), 57–58.

Manicavasagar, V., Marnane, C., Pini, S., Abelli, M., Rees, S., Eapen, V., & Silove, D. (2010). Adult separation anxiety disorder– a disorder comes of age. *Current Psychiatry Reports, 12*(4), 290–297.

Mann, J., Apter, A., Bertolote, J., Beautrais, A., Currier, D., Haas, A., ... Hendin, H. (2005). Suicide prevention strategies: A systematic review. *JAMA: Journal of the American Medical Association, 294,* 2064–2074.

Mann, J. J., Brent, D. A., & Arango, V. (2001). The neurobiology and genetics of suicide and attempted suicide: a focus on the serotonergic system. *Neuropsychopharmacology, 24*(5), 467–477.

Mann, J. J., Malone, K. M., Diehl, D. J., Perel, J., Cooper, T. B., & Mintun, M. A. (1996). Demonstration in vivo of reduced serotonin responsivity in the brain of untreated depressed patients. *American Journal of Psychiatry, 153,* 174–182.

Mann, J. J., Waternaux, C., Haas, G. L., & Malone, K. M. (1999). Toward a clinical model of suicidal behavior in psychiatric patients. *American Journal of Psychiatry, 156*(2), 181–189.

Mann, K., Klingler, T., Noe, S., Röschke, J., Müller, S., & Benkert, O. (1996). Effects of yohimbine on sexual experiences and nocturnal penile tumescence and rigidity in erectile dysfunction. *Archives of Sexual Behavior, 25,* 1–16.

Manne, S. L., & Ostroff, J. S. (2008). *Coping with breast cancer: A couples-focused group intervention: Therapist guide.* New York, NY: Oxford University Press.

Manni, R., Ratti, M. T., & Tartara, A. (1997). Nocturnal eating: Prevalence and features in 120 insomniac referrals. *Sleep, 20,* 734–738.

Mannino, D. M., Klevens, R. M., & Flanders, W. D. (1994). Cigarette smoking: An independent risk factor for impotence? *American Journal of Epidemiology, 140,* 1003–1008.

Manson, J. E., Willett, W. C., Stampfer, M. J., Colditz, G. A., Hunter, D. J., Hankinson, S. E., ... Speizer, F. E. (1995). Body weight and mortality among women. *New England Journal of Medicine, 333,* 677–685.

Manson, S. M., & Good, B. J. (1993, January). *Cultural considerations in the diagnosis of DSM-IV mood disorders.* Cultural proposals and supporting papers for DSM-IV. Submitted to the DSM-IV Task Force by the Steering Committee, NIMH-Sponsored Group on Culture and Diagnosis.

Marangell, L., Rush, A., George, M., Sackheim, H., Johnson, C, Husain, M., ... Lisanby, S. H. (2002). Vagus nerve stimulation (VNS) for major depressive episodes: One-year outcomes. *Biological Psychiatry, 51,* 280–287.

March, J. S., & Vitiello, B. (2009). Clinical messages from the Treatment for Adolescents with Depression Study (TADS). *American Journal of Psychiatry, 166*(10), 1118–1123.

Marcopulos, B. A., & Graves, R. E. (1990). Antidepressant effect on memory in depressed older persons. *Journal of Clinical and Experimental Neuropsychology, 12*(5), 655–663.

Marcus, M. D., Wing, R. R., Ewing, L., Keern, E., Gooding, W., & McDermott, M. (1990). Psychiatric disorders among obese binge eaters. *International Journal of Eating Disorders, 9,* 69–77.

Marcus, M. D., Wing, R. R., & Hopkins, J. (1988). Obese binge eaters: Affect, cognitions, and response to behavioral weight control. *Journal of Consulting and Clinical Psychology, 3,* 433–439.

Maremmani, I., Pacini, M., Pani, P. P., Popovic, D., Romano, A., Maremmani, A. G. I., ... Perugi, G. (2009). Use of street methadone in Italian heroin addicts presenting for opioid agonist treatment. *Journal of Addictive Diseases, 28*(4), 382–388.

Marks, I. M. (1985). Behavioural treatment of social phobia. *Psychopharmacology Bulletin, 21,* 615–618.

Marlatt, G. A., & Gordon, J. R. (1985). *Relapse prevention: Maintenance strategies in the treatment of addictive behaviors.* New York, NY: Guilford Press.

Marlatt, G. A., Larimer, M. E., Baer, J. S., & Quigley, L. A. (1993). Harm reduction for alcohol problems: Moving beyond the controlled drinking controversy. *Behavior Therapy, 24,* 461–504.

Marmot, M. G., & Syme, S. L. (1976). Acculturation and coronary heart disease in Japanese Americans. *American Journal of Epidemiology, 104,* 225–247.

Marques, J. K., Wiederanders, M., Day, D. M., Nelson, C., & van Ommeren, A. (2005). Effects of a relapse prevention program on sexual recidivism: Final results from California's Sex Offender Treatment and Evaluation Project (SOTEP). *Sexual Abuse: A Journal of Research and Treatment, 17,* 79–107.

Marsella, A. J., & Kaplan, A. (2002). Cultural considerations for understanding, assessing, and treating depressive experience and disorder. In M. A. Reinecke & M. Davison (Eds.), *Comparative treatments of depression* (pp. 47–78). New York, NY: Springer.

Marsh, L., & Margolis, R. L. (2009). Neuropsychiatric aspects of movement disorders. In B. J. Sadock, V. A. Sadock, & P. Ruiz (Eds.), *Kaplan & Sadock's comprehensive textbook of psychiatry* (9th ed., Vol. I, pp. 481–503). Philadelphia, PA: Lippincott Williams & Wilkins.

Marshall, W. L. (1997). Pedophilia: Psychopathology and theory. In D. R. Laws & W. O'Donohue (Eds.), *Sexual deviance: Theory, assessment, and treatment* (pp. 152–174). New York, NY: Guilford Press.

Marshall, W. L., & Barbaree, H. E. (1990). An integrated theory of the etiology of sexual offending. In W. L. Marshall, D. R. Laws, & H. E. Barbaree (Eds.), *Handbook of sexual assault: Issues, theories, and treatment of the offender* (pp. 257–725). New York, NY: Plenum Press.

Marshall, W. L., Barbaree, H. E., & Christophe, D. (1986). Sexual offenders against female children: Sexual preferences for age of victims and type of behavior. *Canadian Journal of Behavioral Science, 18,* 424–439.

Marten, P. A., Brown, T. A., Barlow, D. H., Borkovec, T. D., Shear, M. K., & Lydiard, M. B. (1993). Evaluation of the ratings comprising the associated symptom criterion of DSM-III-R generalized anxiety disorder. *Journal of Nervous and Mental Disease, 181,* 676–682.

Martin, C. S., Chung, T., & Langenbucher, J. W. (2008). How should we revise diagnostic criteria for substance use disorders in the DSM-V? *Journal of Abnormal Psychology, 117*(3), 561–575. doi:10.1037/0021-843x.117.3.561

Martin, I. (1983). Human classical conditioning. In A. Gale & J. A. Edward (Eds.), *Physiological correlates of human behavior: Vol. 2. Attention and performance.* London, UK: Academic Press.

Martin, S. D., Martin, E., Rai, S. S., Richardson, M. A., & Royall, R. (2001). Brain blood flow changes in depressed patients treated with interpersonal psychotherapy or venlafaxine hydrochloride. *Archives of General Psychiatry, 58,* 641–648.

Martin, S. L., Ramey, C. T., & Ramey, S. L. (1990). The prevention of intellectual impairment in children of impoverished families: Findings of a randomized trial of educational daycare. *American Journal of Public Health, 80,* 844–847.

Maser, J. D. (1985). List of phobias. In A. H. Tuma & J. D. Maser (Eds.), *Anxiety and the anxiety disorders.* Hillsdale, NJ: Erlbaum.

Mason, F. L. (1997). Fetishism: Psychopathology and theory. In D. R. Laws & W. O'Donohue (Eds.), *Sexual deviance: Theory, assessment, and treatment* (pp. 75–91). New York, NY: Guilford Press.

Masona, T., Worsleyb, A., & Coylea, D. (2010). Forensic multidisciplinary perspectives of Tarasoff liability: A vignette study. *Journal of Forensic Psychiatry & Psychology, 21*(4), 549–554.

Master, S. L., Eisenberger, N. I., Taylor, S. E., Naliboff, B. D., Shirinyan, D., & Lieberman, M. D. (2009). A picture's worth: Partner photographs reduce experimentally induced pain. *Psychological Science, 20,* 1316–1318.

Masters, W. H., & Johnson, V. E. (1966). *Human sexual response.* Boston, MA: Little, Brown.

Masters, W. H., & Johnson, V. E. (1970). *Human sexual inadequacy.* Boston, MA: Little, Brown.

Mataix-Cols, D., Frost, R. O., Pertusa, A., Clark, L. A., Saxena, S., Leckman, J. F., ... Wilhelm, S. (2010). Hoarding disorder: A new diagnosis for DSM-V? *Depression and Anxiety, 27*(6), 556–572.

Mathew, S. J., & Hoffman, E. J. (2009). Pharmacotherapy for generalized anxiety disorder. In M. M. Antony & M. B. Stein (Eds.), *Oxford handbook of anxiety and related disorders* (pp. 350–363). New York, NY: Oxford University Press.

Mathews, A. (1997). Information processing biases in emotional disorders. In D. M. Clark & C. G. Fairburn (Eds.), *Science and practice of cognitive-behavior therapy* (pp. 47–66). Oxford, UK: Oxford University Press.

Mathews, A., & MacLeod, C. (1994). Cognitive approaches to emotion and emotional disorders. *Annual Review of Psychology, 45,* 25–50.

Mathews, A., Mogg, K., Kentish, J., & Eysenck, M. (1995). Effective psychological treatment on cognitive bias and generalized anxiety disorder. *Behavior Research and Therapy, 33,* 293–303.

Mathews, C.A. (2009). Phenomenology of obsessive-compulsive disorder. In M. M. Antony & M. B. Stein (Eds.), *Oxford handbook of anxiety and related disorders.* Oxford, UK: Oxford University Press.

Matsumoto, D. (1996). *Culture and psychology.* Pacific Grove, CA: Brooks/Cole.

Matthews, K. (2005). Psychological perspectives on the development of coronary heart disease. *American Psychologist, 60,* 780–796.

Matthews, K. A. (1988). Coronary heart disease and Type A behaviors: Update on and alternative to the Booth-Kewley and Friedman (1987) quantitative review. *Psychological Bulletin, 104*(3), 373–380.

Mattis, S. G., & Ollendick, T. H. (2002). Nonclinical panic attacks in late adolescence prevalence and associated psychopathology. *Journal of Anxiety Disorders, 16,* 351–367.

Mayberg, H., Lozano, A., Voon, V., McNeely, H., Seminowicz, D., Hanani, C., ... Kennedy, S. H. (2005). Deep brain stimulation for treatment-resistant depression. *Neuron, 45,* 651–660.

Mays, V. M., & Cochran, S. D. (1988). Issues in the perception of AIDS risk and risk reduction activities by black and Hispanic/Latino women. *American Psychologist, 43*(11), 949–957.

Mayville, S., Katz, R. C., Gipson, M. T., & Cabral, K. (1999). Assessing the prevalence of body dysmorphic disorder in an ethnically diverse group of adolescents. *Journal of Child and Family Studies, 8*(3), 357–362.

Mazure, C. M. (1998). Life stressors as risk factors in depression. *Clinical Psychology: Science and Practice, 5*(3), 291–313.

Mazure, C. M., Bruce, M. L., Maciejewski, P. K., & Jacobs, S. C. (2000). Adverse life events and cognitive-personality characteristics in the prediction of major depression and antidepressant response. *American Journal of Psychiatry, 157*(6), 896–903.

McCabe, R., Antony, M. M., Summerfeldt, L. J., Liss, A., & Swinson, R. P. (2003). Preliminary examination of the relationship between anxiety disorders in adults and self-reported history of teasing or bullying experiences. *Cognitive Behaviour Therapy, 32,* 187–193.

McCabe, M., & Wauchope, M. (2005). Behavioral characteristics of men accused of rape: Evidence for different types of rapists. *Archives of Sexual Behavior, 34,* 241–253.

McCaffrey, R. J., Lynch, J. K., & Westervelt, H. J. (2011). Clinical neuropsychology. In D. H. Barlow (Ed.), *Oxford handbook of clinical psychology* (pp. 680–700). New York: Oxford University.

McCann, D., Barrett, A., Cooper, A., Crumpler, D., Dalen, L., Grimshaw, K., ... Prince, E. (2007). Food additives and hyperactive behaviour in 3-year-old and 8/9-year-old children in the community: A randomised, double-blinded, placebo-controlled trial. *Lancet, 370*(9598), 1560–1567.

McCann, U. D., & Ricaurte, G. A. (2009). Amphetamine (or amphetamine-like)- related disorders. In B. J. Sadock, V. A. Sadock, & P. Ruiz (Eds.), *Kaplan & Sadock's comprehensive textbook of psychiatry* (9th ed., Vol. I, pp. 1288–1296). Philadelphia, PA: Lippincott Williams & Wilkins.

McCann, U. D., Sgambati, F. P., Schwartz, A. R., & Ricaurte, G. A. (2009). Sleep apnea in young abstinent recreational MDMA ("ecstasy") consumers. *Neurology, 73*(23), 2011–2017.

McClearn, G. E., Johansson, B., Berg, S., Pedersen, N. L., Ahern, F., Petrill, S. A., & Plomin, R. (1997). Substantial genetic influence on cognitive abilities in twins 80 or more years old. *Science, 276,* 1560–1563.

McClellan, J., & King, M. C. (2010). Genomic analysis of mental illness: A changing landscape. *JAMA: Journal of the American Medical Association, 303*(24), 2523–2524.

McClellan, J., Kowatch, R., & Findling, R. L. (2007). Practice parameter for the assessment and treatment of children and adolescents with bipolar disorder. *Journal of the American Academy of Child and Adolescent Psychiatry, 46*(1), 107–125.

McCloskey, M. S., Noblett, K. L., Deffenbacher, J. L., Gollan, J. K., & Coccaro, E. F. (2008). Cognitive-behavioral therapy for intermittent explosive disorder: A pilot randomized clinical trial. *Journal of Consulting and Clinical Psychology, 76*(5), 876–886.

McClure, M., Harvey, P., Goodman, M., Triebwasser, J., New, A., Koenigsberg, H., ... Siever, L. J. (2010). Pergolide treatment of cognitive deficits associated with schizotypal personality disorder: Continued evidence of the importance of the dopamine system in the schizophrenia spectrum. *Neuropsychopharmacology, 35,* 1356–1362.

McCrae, R. R. (2002). NEO PI-R data from 36 cultures: Further intercultural comparisons. In R. McCrae & J. Allik (Eds.), *The five-factor model of personality across cultures* (pp. 105–126). New York, NY: Kluwer Academic/Plenum Publishers.

McCrae, R., & Costa, P., Jr. (2008). The five-factor theory of personality. In O. P. John, R. W. Robins, & L. A. Pervin (Eds.), *Handbook of personality: Theory and research* (3rd ed., pp. 159–181). New York, NY: Guilford Press.

McCullough, J. P., Jr. (2000). *Treatment for chronic depression: Cognitive Behavioral Analysis System of Psychotherapy (CBASP).* New York, NY: Guilford Press.

McCullough, J. P., Jr., Klein, D. N., Keller, M. B., Holzer, C. E., III, Davis, S. M., Kornstein, S. G., ... Harrison, W. M. (2000). Comparison of DSM-III-R chronic major depression and major depression superimposed on dysthymia (double depression): Validity of the distinction. *Journal of Abnormal Psychology, 109,* 419–427.

McEachin, J. J., Smith, T., & Lovaas, O. I. (1993). Long-term outcome for children with autism who received early intensive behavioral treatment. *American Journal on Mental Retardation, 97,* 359–372.

McElroy, S. L., & Arnold, L. M. (2001). Impulse-control disorders. In G. O. Gabbard (Ed.), *Treatment of psychiatric disorders* (3rd ed., Vol. 1, pp. 2435–2471). Washington, DC: American Psychiatric Publishing.

McEwen, B. S. (1999). Stress and hippocampal plasticity. *Annual Review of Neuroscience, 22,* 105–122.

McEwen, B. S., & Magarinos, A. M. (2004). Does stress damage the brain? In J. M. Gorman, *Fear and anxiety: The benefits of translational research* (pp. 23–45). Washington, DC: American Psychiatric Publishing.

McFadden, D., Loehlin, J., Breedlove, S., Lippa, R., Manning, J., & Rahman, Q. (2005). A reanalysis of five studies on sexual orientation and the relative length of the 2nd and 4th fingers (the 2D:4D ratio). *Archives of Sexual Behavior, 34,* 341–356.

McGirr, A., Paris, J., Lesage, A., Renaud, J., & Turecki, G. (2009). An examination of DSM-IV borderline personality disorder symptoms and risk for death by suicide: A psychological autopsy study. *Canadian Journal of Psychiatry, 54*(2), 87.

McGoldrick, M., Loonan, R., & Wohlsifer, D. (2007). Sexuality and culture. In S. R. Leiblum (Ed.), *Principles and practice of sex therapy* (4th ed., pp. 416–441). New York, NY: Guilford Press.

McGough, J. J. (2005). Adult manifestations of attention-deficit/hyperactivity disorder. In B. J. Sadock & V. A. Sadock (Eds.), *Kaplan & Sadock's comprehensive textbook of psychiatry* (pp. 3198–3204). Philadelphia, PA: Lippincott Williams & Wilkins.

McGovern, M. P., Xie, H., Segal, S. R., Siembab, L., & Drake, R. E. (2006). Addiction treatment services and co-occurring disorders: Prevalence estimates, treatment practices, and barriers. *Journal of Substance Abuse Treatment, 31,* 267–275.

McGowin, D. F. (1993). *Living in the labyrinth: A personal journey through the maze of Alzheimer's.* New York, NY: Delacorte Press.

McGrath, J. (2010). Is it time to trial vitamin D supplements for the prevention of schizophrenia? *Acta Psychiatrica Scandinavica, 121*(5), 321–324.

McGrath, P., Marshall, P. G., & Prior, K. (1979). A comprehensive treatment program for a fire-setting child. *Journal of Behavior Therapy and Experimental Psychiatry, 10*(1), 69–72.

McGue, M., & Lykken, D. T. (1992). Genetic influence on risk of divorce. *Psychological Science, 3*(6), 368–373.

McGuffin, P., Katz, R., & Bebbington, P. (1988). The Camberwell Collaborative Depression Study: III. Depression and adversity in the relatives of depressed probands. *British Journal of Psychiatry, 152,* 775–782.

McGuffin, P., Rijsdijk, F., Andrew, M., Sham, P., Katz, R., & Cardno, A. (2003). The herita-

bility of bipolar affective disorder and the genetic relationship to unipolar depression. *Archives of General Psychiatry, 60,* 497–502.

McGuire, P. K., Shah, G. M. S., & Murray, R. M. (1993). Increased blood flow in Broca's area during auditory hallucinations in schizophrenia. *Lancet, 342,* 703–706.

McHugh, R. K., & Barlow, D. H. (2010). The dissemination and implementation of evidence-based psychological treatments: A review of current efforts. *American Psychologist, 65,* 73–84.

McKay, D., Todaro, J., Neziroglu, F., Campisi, T., Moritz, E. K., & Yaryura-Tobias, J. A. (1997). Body dysmorphic disorder: A preliminary evaluation of treatment and maintenance using exposure with response prevention. *Behaviour Research and Therapy, 35,* 67–70.

McKay, R., Langdon, R., & Coltheart, M. (2007). Models of misbelief: Integrating motivational and deficit theories of delusions. *Consciousness and Cognition, 16*(4), 932–941.

McKenzie, S. J., Williamson, D. A., & Cubic, B. A. (1993). Stable and reactive body image disturbances in bulimia nervosa. *Behavior Therapy, 24,* 195–207.

McLean, P., & Taylor, S. (1992). Severity of unipolar depression and choice of treatment. *Behaviour Research and Therapy, 30*(5), 443–451.

McLeod, J. D., Kessler, R. C., & Landis, K. R. (1992). Speed of recovery from major depressive episodes in a community sample of married men and women. *Journal of Abnormal Psychology, 101*(2), 277–286.

McNab, C., Haslam, N., & Burnett, P. (2007). Expressed emotion, attributions, utility beliefs, and distress in parents of young people with first episode psychosis. *Psychiatry Research, 151,* 97–106.

McNally, R. J. (1996). Cognitive bias in the anxiety disorders. In D. A. Hope (Ed.), *Perspectives on anxiety, panic, and fear* (The 43rd Annual Nebraska Symposium on Motivation) (pp. 211–250). Lincoln, NE: Nebraska University Press.

McNally, R. J. (1999). EMDR and mesmerism: A comparative historical analysis. *Journal of Anxiety Disorders, 13,* 225–236.

McNally, R. J. (2001). The cognitive psychology of repressed and recovered memories of childhood sexual abuse: Clinical implications. *Psychiatric Annals, 31,* 509–514.

McNally, R. J., & Geraerts, E. (2009). A new solution to the recovered memory debate. *Perspectives on Psychological Science, 4*(2), 126–134.

McNaughton, N., & Gray, J. H. (2000). Anxiolytic action on the behavioral inhibition system implies multiple types of arousal contribute to anxiety. *Journal of Affective Disorders, 61*(3), 161–176.

McNeil, T. F. (1987). Perinatal influences in the development of schizophrenia. In H. Helmchen & F. A. Henn (Eds.), *Biological perspectives of schizophrenia* (pp. 125–138). New York, NY: John Wiley.

Meaney, M. J., & Szyf, M. (2005). Maternal care as a model for experience-dependent chromatin plasticity? *Trends in Neurosciences, 28*(9), 456–463.

Means, M. K., & Edinger, J. D. (2006). Non-pharmacologic therapy of insomnia. In T. Lee-Chiong (Ed.), *Sleep: A comprehen-*

sive handbook (pp. 133–136). Hoboken, NJ: John Wiley & Sons.

Medina v. California, 112 S. Ct. 2575 (1992).

Mednick, S. A., & Schulsinger, F. (1965). A longitudinal study of children with a high risk for schizophrenia: A preliminary report. In S. Vandenberg (Ed.), *Methods and goals in human behavior genetics* (pp. 255–296). New York, NY: Academic Press.

Mednick, S. A., & Schulsinger, F. (1968). Some pre-morbid characteristics related to breakdown in children with schizophrenic mothers. *Journal of Psychiatric Research, 6,* 267–291.

Meehan, P. J., Lamb, J. A., Saltzman, L. E., & O'Carroll, P. W. (1992). Attempted suicide among young adults: Progress toward a meaningful estimate of prevalence. *American Journal of Psychiatry, 149*(1), 41–44.

Meehl, P. E. (1945). The dynamics of "structured" personality tests. *Journal of Clinical Psychology, 1,* 296–303.

Meehl, P. E. (1962). Schizotaxia, schizotypy, schizophrenia. *American Psychologist, 17,* 827–838.

Meehl, P. E. (1989). Schizotaxia revisited. *Archives of General Psychiatry, 46,* 935–944.

Mehler, P. S., Birmingham, L. C., Crow, S. J., & Jahraus, J. P. (2010). Medical complications of eating disorders. In C. M. Grilo & J. E. Mitchell (Eds.), *The treatment of eating disorders: A clinical handbook* (pp. 66–80). New York, NY: Guilford Press.

Melamed, B. G., & Siegel, L. J. (1975). Reduction of anxiety in children facing hospitalization and surgery by use of filmed modeling. *Journal of Consulting and Clinical Psychology, 43*(4), 511–521.

Melzack, R. (1999). From the gate to the neuromatrix. *Pain* (Suppl. 6), S121–S126.

Melzack, R. (2005). Evolution of the neuromatrix theory of pain. *Pain Practice, 5,* 85–94.

Melzack, R., & Wall, P. D. (1965). Pain mechanisms: A new theory. *Science, 150,* 971–979.

Melzack, R., & Wall, P. D. (1982). *The challenge of pain.* New York, NY: Basic Books.

Mendelson, W. (2005). Sleep disorders. In B. J. Sadock & V. A. Sadock (Eds.), *Kaplan & Sadock's comprehensive textbook of psychiatry* (pp. 2022–2034). Philadelphia, PA: Lippincott Williams & Wilkins.

Mennes, C. E., Ben Abdallah, A., & Cottler, L. B. (2009). The reliability of self-reported cannabis abuse, dependence, and withdrawal symptoms: Multisite study of differences between general population and treatment groups. *Addictive Behaviors, 34*(2), 223–226. doi:10.1016/j.addbeh .2008.10.003

Menza, M. (2006). STAR*D: The results begin to roll in. *American Journal of Psychiatry, 163,* 1123–1125.

Merens, W., Willem Van der Does, A. J., & Spinhoven, P. (2007). The effects of serotonin manipulations on emotional information processing and mood. *Journal of Affective Disorders, 103*(1–3), 43–62.

Merikangas, K. R., & Pato, M. (2009). Recent developments in the epidemiology of bipolar disorder in adults and children: Magnitude, correlates, and future directions. *Clinical Psychology: Science and Practice, 16*(2), 121–133.

Meyer, A. J., Nash, J. D., McAlister, A. L., Maccoby, M., & Farquhar, J. W. (1980).

Skills training in a cardiovascular health education campaign. *Journal of Consulting and Clinical Psychology, 2,* 129–142.

Meyer, B., & Carver, C. S. (2000). Negative childhood accounts, sensitivity, and pessimism: A study of avoidant personality disorder features in college students. *Journal of Personality Disorders, 14,* 233–248.

Meyer-Bahlburg, H., Dolezal, C., Baker, S., Carlson, A., Obeid, J., & New, M. (2004). Prenatal androgenization affects gender-related behavior but not gender identity in 5–12-year-old girls with congenital adrenal hyperplasia. *Archives of Sexual Behavior, 33,* 97–104.

Meyerowitz, B. E. (1983). Postmastectomy coping strategies and quality of life. *Health Psychology, 2,* 117–132.

Meyers, A. (1991). Biobehavioral interactions in behavioral medicine. *Behavior Therapy, 22,* 129–131.

Mezzich, J. E., Good, B. J., Lewis-Fernández, R., Guarnaccia, P., Lin, K. M., Parron, D., ... Hughes, C. (1993, September). *Cultural formulation guidelines.* Revised cultural proposals for DSM-IV. Submitted to the DSM-IV Task Force by the Steering Committee, NIMH-Sponsored Group on Culture and Diagnosis.

Mezzich, J. E., Kirmayer, L. J., Kleinman, A., Fabrega, H., Jr., Parron, D. L., Good, B. J., ... Manson, S. M. (1999). The place of culture in DSM-IV. *Journal of Nervous and Mental Disease, 187,* 457–464.

Mezzich, J. E., Kleinman, A., Fabrega, H., Jr., Good, B., Johnson-Powell, G., Lin, K. M., ... Parron, D. (1992). *Cultural proposals for DSM-IV.* Submitted to the DSM-IV Task Force by the Steering Committee, NIMH-Sponsored Group on Culture and Diagnosis.

Miaskowski, C. (1999). The role of sex and gender in pain perception and responses to treatment. In R. J. Gatchel & D. C. Turk (Eds.), *Psychosocial factors in pain: Critical perspectives* (pp. 401–411). New York, NY: Guilford Press.

Mick, E., Byrne, D., Fried, R., Monuteaux, M., Faraone, S., & Biederman, J. (2011). Predictors of ADHD persistence in girls at 5-year follow-up. *Journal of Attention Disorders, 15*(3), 183–192.

Middleton, W., Burnett, P., Raphael, B., & Martinek, N. (1996). The bereavement response: A cluster analysis. *British Journal of Psychiatry, 169,* 167–171.

Miklowitz, D. J. (2008). Adjunctive psychotherapy for bipolar disorder: State of the evidence. *The American Journal of Psychiatry, 165*(11), 1408–1419.

Miklowitz, D. J., George, E. L., Richards, J. A., Simoneau, T. L., & Suddath, R. L. (2003). A randomized study of family-focused psychoeducation and pharmacotherapy in the outpatient management of bipolar disorder. *Archives of General Psychiatry, 60,* 904–912.

Miklowitz, D. J., & Goldstein, M. J. (1997). *Bipolar disorder: A family-focused treatment approach.* New York, NY: Guilford Press.

Miklowitz, D. J., & Johnson, S. (2006). The psychopathology and treatment of bipolar disorder. In S. Nolen-Hoeksema, T. D. Cannon, & T. Widiger (Eds.), *Annual Review of Clinical Psychology* (pp. 199–235). Palo Alto, CA: Annual Reviews.

Miklowitz, D. J., Otto, M. W., Frank, E., Reilly-Harrington, N. A., Kogan, J. N., Sachs, G. S., ... Wisniewski, S. R. (2007). Intensive psychosocial intervention enhances functioning in patients with bipolar depression: Results from a 9-month randomized controlled trial. *The American Journal of Psychiatry, 164*(9), 1340–1347.

Millar, H. R., Qrdell, F., Vyvyan, J. P., Naji, S. A., Prescott, G. J., & Eagles, J. M. (2005). Anorexia nervosa mortality in northeast Scotland 1965– 1999. *American Journal of Psychiatry, 162,* 753–757.

Miller, A. L., McEvoy, J. P., Jeste, D. V., & Marder, S. R. (2006). Treatment of chronic schizophrenia. In J. A. Lieberman, T. S. Stroup, & D. O. Perkins (Eds.), *The American Psychiatric Publishing textbook of schizophrenia* (pp. 365–381). Washington, DC: American Psychiatric Publishing.

Miller, G., & Blackwell, E. (2006). Turning up the heat: Inflammation as a mechanism linking chronic stress, depression, and heart disease. *Current Directions in Psychological Science, 15,* 269–277.

Miller, I. W., & Norman, W. H. (1979). Learned helplessness in humans: A review and attribution-theory model. *Psychological Bulletin, 86*(1), 93–118.

Miller, I. W., Norman, W. H., & Keitner, G. I. (1989). Cognitive-behavioral treatment of depressed inpatients: Six- and twelve-month follow-up. *American Journal of Psychiatry, 146,* 1274–1279.

Miller, N. E. (1969). Learning of visceral and glandular responses. *Science, 163,* 434–445.

Miller, N. S., Gold, M. S., & Pottash, A. C. (1989). A 12-step treatment approach for marijuana (cannabis) dependence. *Journal of Substance Abuse Treatment, 6,* 241–250.

Miller, S. D. (1989). Optical differences in cases of multiple personality disorder. *Journal of Nervous and Mental Disease, 177*(8), 480–486.

Miller, T. Q., Smith, T. W., Turner, C. W., Guijarro, M. L., & Hallet, A. J. (1996). A meta-analytic review of research on hostility and physical health. *Psychological Bulletin, 119*(2), 322–348.

Miller, W. (2009). Motivational interviewing with problem drinkers. *Behavioural and Cognitive Psychotherapy, 11*(2), 147–172.

Miller, W. R., & Hester, R. K. (1986). Inpatient alcoholism treatment: Who benefits? *American Psychologist, 41,* 794–805.

Miller, W. R., & Rollnick, S. (2002). *Motivational interviewing: Lessons preparing people for change.* New York, NY: Guilford Press.

Millon, T. (1981). *Disorders of personality: DSM-III, axis II.* New York, NY: John Wiley.

Millon, T. (1991). Classification in psychopathology: Rationale, alternatives, and standards. *Journal of Abnormal Psychology, 100*(3), 245–261.

Millon, T. (2004). *Masters of the mind.* Hoboken, NJ: Wiley & Sons.

Millon, T., & Martinez, A. (1995). Avoidant personality disorder. In W. J. Livesley (Ed.), *The DSM-IV personality disorders* (pp. 218–233). New York, NY: Guilford Press.

Mills, P. J., Adler, K. A., Dimsdale, J. E., Perez, C. J., Ziegler, M. G., Ancoli-Israel, S., ... Grant, I. (2004). Vulnerable caregivers of

Alzheimer disease patients have a deficit in beta 2-adrenergic receptor sensitivity and density. *American Journal of Geriatric Psychiatry, 12,* 281–286.

Minagar, A., Alekseeva, N., Shapshak, P., & Fernandez, F. (2009). Neuropsychiatric aspects of prion disease. In B. J. Sadock, V. A. Sadock, & P. Ruiz (Eds.), *Kaplan & Sadock's comprehensive textbook of psychiatry* (9th ed., Vol. I, pp. 541–558). Philadelphia, PA: Lippincott Williams & Wilkins.

Mindell, J. A., & Owens, J. A. (2009). *A clinical guide to pediatric sleep: Diagnosis and management of sleep problems* (2nd ed.). Philadelphia, PA: Lippincott Williams & Wilkins.

Mineka, S. (1985). The frightful complexity of the origins of fears. In F. R. Bruch & J. B. Overmier (Eds.), *Affect, conditioning, and cognition: Essays on the determinants of behavior.* Hillsdale, NJ: Erlbaum.

Mineka, S., & Sutton, J. (2006). In M. G. Craske, D. Hermans, & D. Vansteenwegen, *Fear and learning: From basic processes to clinical implications* (pp. 75–97), Washington, DC: American Psychological Association.

Mineka, S., & Watson, D., & Clark, L. A. (1998). Comorbidity of anxiety and unipolar mood disorders. *Annual Review of Psychology, 49,* 377–412.

Mineka, S., & Zinbarg, R. (1996). Conditioning and ethological models of anxiety disorders: Stress-in-dynamic-context anxiety models. In D. A. Hope (Ed.), *Perspectives on anxiety, panic, and fear* (The 43rd Annual Nebraska Symposium on Motivation) (pp. 135–210). Lincoln, NE: Nebraska University Press.

Mineka, S., & Zinbarg, R. (1998). Experimental approaches to understanding the mood and anxiety disorders. In J. Adair (Ed.), *Advances in psychological research, Vol. 2. Social, personal, and cultural aspects* (pp. 429–454). Hove, UK: Psychology Press/Erlbaum.

Mineka, S., & Zinbarg, R. (2006). A contemporary learning theory perspective on the etiology of anxiety disorders. *American Psychologist, 61,* 10–26.

Minino, A. M., Arias, E., Kochanek, K. D., Murphy, S. L., & Smith, B. L. (2002). Deaths: Final data for 2000. *National Vital Statistics Reports, 50,* 1–119.

Minuchin, S., Rosman, B. L., & Baker, L. (1978). *Psychosomatic families.* Cambridge, MA: Harvard University Press.

Mirsky, A. F., Bieliauskas, L. A., French, L. M., van Kammen, D. P., Jonsson, E., & Sedvall, G. (2000). A 39-year follow-up of the Genain quadruplets. *Schizophrenia Bulletin, 26,* 699–708.

Mitchell, J. E., Cook-Myers, T., & Wonderlich, S. A. (2005). Diagnostic criteria for anorexia nervosa: Looking ahead to DSM-V [Special issue]. *International Journal of Eating Disorders, 37,* S95–S97.

Modahl, C., Green, L., Fein, D., Morris, M., Waterhouse, L., Feinstein, C., Levin, H.. (1998). Plasma oxytocin levels in autistic children. *Biological Psychiatry, 43,* 270–277.

Modinos, G., Mechelli, A., Ormel, J., Groenewold, N., Aleman, A., & McGuire, P. (2009). Schizotypy and brain structure: A voxel-based morphometry study. *Psychological Medicine, 40,* 1423–1431.

Moeller, F. G. (2009). Impulse-control disorders not elsewhere classified. In B. J. Sadock, V. A. Sadock, & P. Ruiz (Eds.), *Kaplan & Sadock's comprehensive textbook of psychiatry* (9th ed., Vol. I, pp. 2178–2186). Philadelphia, PA: Lippincott Williams & Wilkins.

Moffitt, T. E., Caspi, A., Rutter, M., & Silva, P. A. (2001). *Sex differences in antisocial behaviour: Conduct disorder, delinquency, and violence in the Dunedin longitudinal study*. Cambridge, UK: Cambridge University Press.

Mogg, K., Bradley, B. P., Millar, N., & White, J. (1995). A follow-up study of cognitive bias in generalized anxiety disorder. *BRAT, 33,* 927–935.

Mogg, K., Philippot, P., & Bradley, B. P. (2004). Selective attention to angry faces in clinical social phobia. *Journal of Abnormal Psychology, 113,* 160–165.

Mogil, J. S., Sternberg, W. F., Kest, B., Marek, P., & Liebeskind, J. C. (1993). Sex differences in the antagonism of swim stress-induced analgesia: Effects of gonadectomy and estrogen replacement. *Pain, 53,* 17–25.

Money, J., & Ehrhardt, A. (1972). *Man and woman, boy and girl.* Baltimore, MD: Johns Hopkins University Press.

Monroe, S. M., Imhoff, D. F., Wise, B. D., & Harris, J. E. (1983). Prediction of psychological symptoms under high-risk psychosocial circumstances: Life events, social support, and symptom specificity. *Journal of Abnormal Psychology, 92*(2), 338–350.

Monroe, S. M., Kupfer, D. J., & Frank, E. (1992). Life stress and treatment course of recurrent depression: I. Response during index episode. *Journal of Consulting and Clinical Psychology, 60*(5), 718–724.

Monroe, S. M., & Reid, M. W. (2009). Life stress and major depression. *Current Directions in Psychological Science, 18*(2), 68–72.

Monroe, S. M., Roberts, J. E., Kupfer, D. J., & Frank, E. (1996). Life stress and treatment course of recurrent depression: II. Postrecovery associations with attrition, symptom course, and recurrence over 3 years. *Journal of Abnormal Psychology, 105*(3), 313–328.

Monroe, S. M., Rohde, P., Seeley, J. R., & Lewinsohn, P. M. (1999). Life events and depression in adolescence: For first onset of major depressive disorder. *Journal of Abnormal Psychology, 108*(4), 606–614.

Monroe, S. M., Slavich, G. M., & Georgiades, K. (2009). The social environment and life stress in depression. In I. H. Gotlib & C. L. Hammen (Eds.), *Handbook of depression* (2nd ed., pp. 340–360). New York, NY: Guilford Press.

Montero, I., Hernandez, I., Asencio, A., Bellver, F., LaCruz, M., & Masanet, M. J. (2005). Do all people with schizophrenia receive the same benefit from different family intervention programs? *Psychiatry Research, 133*(2–3), 187–195.

Montero, I., Masanet, M. J., Bellver, F., & Lacruz, M. (2006). The long-term outcome of two family intervention strategies in schizophrenia. *Comprehensive Psychiatry, 47*(5), 362–367.

Moore, D. S. (2001). *The dependent gene: The fallacy of "nature vs. nurture."* New York, NY: Henry Holt and Company.

Moore, R. Y. (1999). Circadian rhythms: A clock for the ages. *Science, 284,* 2102–2103.

Moos, R. H., & Moos, B. S. (2007). Protective resources and long-term recovery from alcohol use disorders. *Drug and Alcohol Dependence, 86,* 46–54.

Morelli, G. A., Rogoff, B., Oppenheim, D., & Goldsmith, D. (1992). Cultural variation in infants' sleeping arrangements: Questions of independence. *Developmental Psychology, 28,* 604–613.

Morey, L. C., Alexander, G. M., & Boggs, C. (2005). Gender. In J. M. Oldham, A. E. Skodol, & D. S. Bender (Eds.), *Textbook of personality disorders* (pp. 541–559). Washington, DC: American Psychiatric Publishing.

Morey, L. C., Hopwood, C. J., & Klein, D. (2007). Depressive, passive-aggressive, and sadistic personality disorders. In W. O'Donohue, K. A. Fowler, & S. O. Lilienfeld (Eds.), *Personality disorders: Toward the DSM-V* (pp. 353–374). Thousand Oaks, CA: Sage Publications.

Morgan, H. W. (1981). *Drugs in America: A social history, 1800–1980.* Syracuse, NY: Syracuse University Press.

Morgenthaler, T. I., & Silber, M. H. (2002). Amnestic sleep-related eating disorder associated with zolpidem. *Sleep Medicine, 3,* 323–327.

Morokoff, P. J. (1993). Female sexual arousal disorder. In W. O'Donohue & J. H. Geer (Eds.), *Handbook of sexual dysfunctions: Assessment and treatment* (pp. 157–199). Boston, MA: Allyn & Bacon.

Morris, J. K., Cook, D. G., & Shaper, A. G. (1994). Loss of employment and mortality. *British Medical Journal, 308,* 1135–1139.

Morris, J. S., Öhman, A., & Dolan, R. J. (1998). Conscious and unconscious emotion learning in the human amygdala. *Nature, 393,* 467–470.

Morrow, G. R., & Dobkin, P. L. (1988). Anticipatory nausea and vomiting in cancer patients undergoing chemotherapy treatment: Prevalence, etiology, and behavioral interventions. *Clinical Psychology Review, 8,* 517–556.

Mosher, W. D., Chandra, A., & Jones, J. (2005). *Sexual behavior and selected health measures: Men and women 15–44 years of age, United States, 2002.* Advance data from vital and health statistics, no. 362. Hyattsville, MD: National Center for Health Statistics.

Mosko, S., Richard, C., & McKenna, J. C. (1997). Maternal sleep and arousals during bedsharing with infants. *Sleep, 20,* 142–150.

Moss, A. C., & Albery, I. P. (2009). A dual-process model of the alcohol-behavior link for social drinking. *Psychological Bulletin, 135*(4), 516–530. doi:10.1037/a0015991

Mostofsky, D. I., & Barlow, D. H. (Eds.) (2000). *The management of stress and anxiety in medical disorders.* Needham Heights, MA: Allyn & Bacon.

Moukas, G., Stathopoulou, A., Gourzis, P., Beratis, I., & Beratis, S. (2010). Relationship of "prodromal" symptoms with severity and type of psychopathology in the active phase of schizophrenia. *Comprehensive Psychiatry, 51*(1), 1–7.

Mucha, T. F., & Reinhardt, R. F. (1970). Conversion reactions in student aviators. *American Journal of Psychiatry, 127,* 493–497.

Mueller, T., Keller, M. B., Leon, A. C., Solomon, D. A., Shea, M. T., Coryell, W., & Endicott, J. (1996). Recovery after 5 years of unremitting major depressive disorder. *Archives of General Psychiatry, 53,* 794–799.

Mueser, K. T., & Berenbaum, H. (1990). Psychodynamic treatment of schizophrenia: Is there a future? *Psychological Medicine, 20,* 253–262.

Mueser, K. T., Liberman, R. P., & Glynn, S. M. (1990). Psychosocial interventions in schizophrenia. In A. Kales, C. N. Stefanis, & J. A. Talbott (Eds.), *Recent advances in schizophrenia* (pp. 213–235). New York, NY: Springer-Verlag.

Mueser, K. T., & Marcello, S. (2011). Schizophrenia. In D. H. Barlow (Ed.), *Oxford handbook of clinical psychology* (pp. 469–503). New York, NY: Oxford University Press.

Mufson, L., Pollack-Dorta, K., Wickramaratne, P., Nomura, Y., Olfson, M., & Weismann, M. (2004). A randomized effectiveness trial of interpersonal psychotherapy for depressed adolescents. *Archives General Psychiatry, 61,* 577–584.

Mulder, R., Frampton, C., Luty, S., & Joyce, P. (2009). Eighteen months of drug treatment for depression: Predicting relapse and recovery. *Journal of Affective Disorders, 114*(1–3), 263–270.

Mullen, P. (2010). The psychiatric expert witness in the criminal justice system. *Criminal Behaviour and Mental Health, 20*(3), 165–176.

Mumford, D. B., Whitehouse, A. M., & Platts, M. (1991). Sociocultural correlates of eating disorders among Asian schoolgirls in Bradford. *British Journal of Psychiatry, 158,* 222–228.

Munjack, D. J. (1984). The onset of driving phobias. *Journal of Behavior Therapy and Experimental Psychiatry, 15,* 305–308.

Muñoz, R. F. (1993). The prevention of depression: Current research and practice. *Applied and Preventative Psychology, 2,* 21–33.

Muñoz, R. F., Le, H.-N., Clarke, G. N., Barrera, A. Z., & Torres, L. D. (2009). Preventing first onset and recurrence of major depressive episodes. In I. H. Gotlib & C. L. Hammen (Eds.), *Handbook of depression* (2nd ed., pp. 533–553). New York, NY: Guilford Press.

Murdoch, D., Pihl, R. O., & Ross, D. (1990). Alcohol and crimes of violence: Present issues. *International Journal of the Addictions, 25,* 1065–1081.

Murphy, W. D., & Page, I. J. (2008). Exhibitionism: Psychopathology and theory. In D. R. Laws & W. T. O'Donohue (Eds.), *Sexual deviance: Theory, assessment, and treatment* (2nd ed., pp. 61–75). New York, NY: Guilford Press.

Murray, C. J. L. (1996). *Global health statistics.* Cambridge, MA: Harvard University Press.

Murray, C. J. L., & Lopez, A. (Eds.) (1996). *The global burden of disease.* Cambridge, MA: Harvard University Press.

Murray, R. M., & Bramon, E. (2005). Developmental model of schizophrenia. In B. J. Sadock & V. A. Sadock (Eds.), *Kaplan & Sadock's comprehensive textbook of psychi-*

atry (pp. 1381–1396). Philadelphia, PA: Lippincott Williams & Wilkins.

Must, A., Spadano, J., Coakley, E. H., Field, A. E., Colditz, G., & Dietz, W. H. (1999). The disease burden associated with overweight and obesity. *JAMA: Journal of the American Medical Association, 282,* 1523–1529.

Mustafa, G. (1990). Delivery systems for the care of schizophrenic patients in Africa-Sub-Sahara. In A. Kales, C. N. Stefanis, & J. A. Talbot (Eds.), *Recent advances in schizophrenia* (pp. 353–371). New York, NY: Springer-Verlag.

Mustanski, B. S., Bailey, J. M., & Kaspar, S. (2002). Dermatoglyphics, handedness, sex, and sexual orientation. *Archives of Sexual Behavior, 31,* 113–122.

Myers, J. K., Weissman, M. M., Tischler, C. E., Holzer, C. E., III, Orvaschel, H., Anthony, J. C., ... Stoltzman, R. (1984). Six-month prevalence of psychiatric disorders in three communities. *Archives of General Psychiatry, 41,* 959–967.

Myers, K., & Collett, B. (2006). Rating scales. In M. K. Dulcan & J. M. Wiener (Eds.), *Essentials of child and adolescent psychiatry* (pp. 81–97). Washington, DC: American Psychiatric Publishing.

Myin-Germeys, I., & Van Os, J. (2008). Adult adversity: Do early environment and genotype create lasting vulnerabilities for adult social adversity in psychosis? In C. Morgan, K. McKenzie, & P. Fearon (Eds.), *Society and Psychosis* (pp. 127–143). Cambridge, UK: Cambridge University Press.

Nachmias, M., Gunnar, M., Mangelsdorf, S., Parritz, R. H., & Buss, K. (1996). Behavioral inhibition and stress reactivity: The moderating role of attachment security. *Child Development, 67*(2), 508–522.

Nagel, D. B. (1991). Psychotherapy of schizophrenia: 1900–1920. In J. G. Howells (Ed.), *The concept of schizophrenia: Historical perspectives* (pp. 191–201). Washington, DC: American Psychiatric Press.

Najavits, L. M. (2007). Psychosocial treatments for posttraumatic stress disorder. In P. E. Nathan & J. M. Gorman (Eds.), *A guide to treatments that work* (3rd ed.). New York, NY: Oxford University Press.

Nanda, S. (1999). *The hijras of India: Neither man nor woman* (2nd ed.). Belmont, CA: Wadsworth.

Narr, K. L., Woods, R. P., Lin, J., Kim, J., Phillips, O. R., Del'Homme, M., ... Levitt, J. (2009). Widespread cortical thinning is a robust anatomical marker for attention-deficit/hyperactivity disorder. *Journal of the American Academy of Child & Adolescent Psychiatry, 48*(10), 1014–1022.

Nasser, M. (1988). Eating disorders: The cultural dimension. *Social Psychiatry and Psychiatric Epidemiology, 23,* 184–187.

National Collaborating Centre for Mental Health. (2009). *Borderline Personality Disorder: The NICE GUIDELINE on Treatment and Management, National Clinical Practice Guideline No. 78.* London, UK: British Psychological Society & Royal College of Psychiatrists.

National Institute of Mental Health. (2003). *Breaking ground, breaking through: The strategic plan for mood disorders research.* (NIH Publication No. 03-5121). Washington, DC: U.S. Government Printing Office.

National Institute on Drug Abuse. (2005). *NIDA research report: Marijuana abuse.* (NIH Publication No. 05-3859). Bethesda, MD: Author.

National Sleep Foundation. (2009). *2009 Sleep in America Poll.* Washington, DC: Author.

Navarrete, C. D., Olsson, A., Ho, A. K., Mendes, W. B., Thomsen, L., & Sidanius, J. (2009). Fear extinction to an out-group face: The role of target gender. *Psychological Science, 20*(2), 155–158.

Neal, A. M., Nagle-Rich, L., & Smucker, W. D. (1994). The presence of panic disorder among African American hypertensives: A pilot study. *Journal of Black Psychology, 20,* 29–35.

Neal-Barnett, A. M., & Smith, J., Sr. (1997). African Americans. In S. Friedman (Ed.), *Cultural issues in the treatment of anxiety* (pp. 154–174). New York, NY: Guilford Press.

Neimeyer, R. A., & Currier, J. M. (2009). Grief therapy: Evidence of efficacy and emerging directions. *Current Directions in Psychological Science, 18*(6), 352–356.

Nelles, W. B. N., & Barlow, D. H. (1988). Do children panic? *Clinical Psychology Review, 8*(4), 359–372.

Nelson, R. O., & Barlow, D. H. (1981). Behavioral assessment: Basic strategies and initial procedures. In D. H. Barlow (Ed.), *Behavioral assessment of adult disorders.* New York, NY: Guilford Press.

Nemeroff, C. (2004). Early-life adversity, CRF dysregulation, and vulnerability to mood and anxiety disorders. *Psychopharmacology Bulletin, 38,* 14–20.

Nemeroff, C. (2006). The burden of severe depression: A review of diagnostic challenges and treatment alternatives. *Journal of Psychiatric Research, 1–18.*

Nestadt, G., Romanoski, A., Chahal, R., Merchant, A., Folstein, M., Gruenberg, E., McHugh, P. R. (2009). An epidemiological study of histrionic personality disorder. *Psychological Medicine, 20*(2), 413–422.

Nestler, E. J., Hyman, S. E., & Malenka, R. C. (2008). *Molecular neuropharmacology* (2nd ed.). New York, NY: McGraw-Hill.

Neubauer, D. (2009). New directions in the pharmacologic treatment of sleep disorders. *Primary Psychiatry, 16*(2), 52–58.

Neugroschi, J. A., Kolevzon, A., Samuels, S. C., & Marin, D. B. (2005). Dementia. In B. J. Sadock & V. A. Sadock (Eds.), *Kaplan & Sadock's comprehensive textbook of psychiatry* (pp. 1068–1093). Philadelphia, PA: Lippincott Williams & Wilkins.

Neumann, C., Hare, R., & Newman, J. (2007). The superordinate nature of the Psychopathy Checklist-Revised. *Journal of Personality Disorders, 21*(2), 102–117.

Neumark-Sztainer, D., & Haines, J. (2004). Psychosocial and behavioral consequences of obesity. In J. K. Thompson (Ed.), *Handbook of eating disorders and obesity* (pp. 349–371). New York, NY: John Wiley.

Nevsimalova, S. (2009). Narcolepsy in childhood. *Sleep Medicine Reviews, 13*(2), 169–180. doi:10.1016/j.smrv.2008.04.007

New York Mental Hygiene Law § 1.03 (20) (1992).

Newman, J. P., Patterson, C. M., & Kosson, D. S. (1987). Response perseveration in psychopaths. *Journal of Abnormal Psychology, 96,* 145–148.

Newman, J. P., & Schmitt, W. A. (1998). Passive avoidance in psychopathic offenders: A replication and extension. *Journal of Abnormal Psychology, 107,* 527–532.

Newman, J. P., Widom, C. S., & Nathan, S. (1985). Passive-avoidance in syndromes of disinhibition: Psychopathy and extraversion. *Journal of Personality and Social Psychology, 50,* 624–630.

Neylan, T. C., Reynolds, C. F., III, & Kupfer, D. J. (2003). Sleep disorders. In R. E. Hales & S. C. Yudofsky (Eds.), *Textbook of clinical psychiatry* (4th ed., pp. 975–1000). Washington, DC: American Psychiatric Publishing.

Nezu, C. M., Nezu, A. M., Friedman, S. H., Houts, P. S., DelliCarpini, L., Bildner, C., & Faddis, S. (1999). Cancer and psychological distress: Two investigations regarding the role of social problem solving. *Journal of Psychosocial Oncology, 16*(3–4), 27–40.

Ng, B. Y., Yap, A. K., Su, A., Lim, D., & Ong, S. H. (2002). Personality profiles of patients with dissociative trance disorder in Singapore. *Comprehensive psychiatry, 43,* 121–126.

Nicassio, P. M., Meyerowitz, B. E., & Kerns, R. D. (2004). The future of health psychology interventions. *Health Psychology, 23,* 132–137.

Nicoletti, A. (2009). Teens and drug facilitated sexual assault. *Journal of Pediatric and Adolescent Gynecology, 22*(3), 187.

Nielsen, D., Barral, S., Proudnikov, D., Kellogg, S., Ho, A., Ott, J., & Kreek, M. J. (2008). TPH2 and TPH1: Association of variants and interactions with heroin addiction. *Behavior Genetics, 38*(2), 133–150.

Nierenberg, A. A., Fava, M., Trivedi, M. H., Wisniewski, S. R., Thase, M. E., McGrath, P. J., ... Rush, A. J. (2006). Comparison of lithium and T3 augmentation following two failed medication treatments for depression: A STAR*D report. *The American Journal of Psychiatry, 163*(9), 1519–1530.

Nijmeijer, J. S., Minderaa, R. B., Buitelaar, J. K., Mulligan, A., Hartman, C. A., & Hoekstra, P. J. (2008). Attention-deficit/hyperactivity disorder and social dysfunctioning. *Clinical Psychology Review, 28*(4), 692–708.

Nikolas, M., & Burt, S. (2010). Genetic and environmental influences on ADHD symptom dimensions of inattention and hyperactivity: A meta-analysis. *Journal of Abnormal Psychology, 119*(1), 1.

Nock, M., & Kessler, R. (2006). Prevalence of and risk factors for suicide attempts versus suicide gestures: Analysis of the national comorbidity survey. *Journal of Abnormal Psychology, 115,* 616–623.

Nock, M. K., Borges, G., Bromet, E. J., Alonso, J., Angermeyer, M., Beautrais, A., ... Williams, D. (2008). Cross-national prevalence and risk factors for suicidal ideation, plans, and attempts. *British Journal of Psychiatry, 192*(2), 98–105.

Nock, M. K., Borges, G., Bromet, E. J., Cha, C. B., Kessler, R. C., & Lee, S. (2008). Suicide and suicidal behavior. *Epidemiologic Reviews, 30,* 133–154.

Nock, M. K., Cha, C. B., & Dour, H. J. (2011). Disorders of impulse-control and self-harm. In D. H. Barlow (Ed.), *Oxford handbook of clinical psychology* (pp. 504–529). New York, NY: Oxford University.

Nock, M. K., Hwang, I., Sampson, N. A., & Kessler, R. C. (2009). Mental disorders, comorbidity, and suicidal behavior: Results from the National Comorbidity Survey Replication. *Molecular Psychiatry, 15,* 868–876.

Nock, M. K., Kazdin, A. E., Hiripi, E., & Kessler, R. C. (2006). Prevalence, subtypes, and correlates of DSM-IV conduct disorder in the National Comorbidity Survey Replication. *Psychological Medicine, 36*(05), 699–710.

Nock, M. K., Park, J. M., Finn, C. T., Deliberto, T. L., Dour, H. J., & Banaji, M. R. (2010). Measuring the suicidal mind: Implicit cognition predicts suicidal behavior. *Psychological Science, 21*(4), 511–517.

Nofzinger, E. A., Schwartz, C. F., Reynolds, C. F., Thase, M. E., Jennings, J. R., Frank, E., ... Kupfer, D. J. (1994). Affect intensity and phasic REM sleep in depressed men before and after treatment with cognitive-behavior therapy. *Journal of Consulting and Clinical Psychology, 62,* 83–91.

Nolen-Hoeksema, S. (1990). *Sex differences in depression.* Stanford, CA: Stanford University Press.

Nolen-Hoeksema, S. (2000). Further evidence for the role of psychosocial factors in depression chronicity. *Clinical Psychology: Science and Practice, 7*(2), 224–227.

Nolen-Hoeksema, S., Girgus, J. S., & Seligman, M. E. P. (1992). Predictors and consequences of childhood depressive symptoms: A 5-year longitudinal study. *Journal of Abnormal Psychology, 101*(3), 405–422.

Nolen-Hoeksema, S., & Hilt, L. M. (2009). Gender differences in depression. In I. H. Gotlib & C. L. Hammen (Eds.), *Handbook of depression* (2nd ed., pp. 386–404). New York, NY: Guilford Press.

Nolen-Hoeksema, S., Larson, J., & Grayson, C. (1999). Explaining the gender differences in depressive symptoms. *Journal of Personality and Social Psychology, 77*(5), 1061–1072.

Nolen-Hoeksema, S., Wisco, B. E., & Lyubomirsky, S. (2008). Rethinking rumination. *Perspectives on Psychological Science, 3*(5), 400–424.

Nolen-Hoeksema, S., Wolfson, A., Mumme, D., & Guskin, K. (1995). Helplessness in children of depressed and nondepressed mothers. *Developmental Psychology, 31,* 377–387.

Nordentoft, M., Thorup, A., Petersen, L., Ohlenschlaeger, J., Melau, M., Christensen, T. O., ... Jeppesen, P.. (2006). Transition rates from schizotypal disorder to psychotic disorder for first-contact patients included in the opus trial: A randomized clinical trial of integrated treatment and standard treatment. *Schizophrenia Research, 83,* 29–40.

Normile, D. (2009). Asia grapples with unexpected wave of HIV infections. *Science, 27,* 1174.

Norrholm, S. D., & Ressler, K. J. (2009). Genetics of anxiety and trauma-related disorders. *Neuroscience, 164*(1), 272–287.

Norton, G. R., Harrison, B., Hauch, J., & Rhodes, L. (1985). Characteristics of people with infrequent panic attacks. *Journal of Abnormal Psychology, 94,* 216–221.

Norton, M. C., Smith, K. R., Østbye, T., Tschanz, J. T., Corcoran, C., Schwartz, S., ... Welsh-Bohmer, K. A. (2010). Greater risk of dementia when spouse has dementia? The Cache County Study. *Journal of the American Geriatrics Society, 58*(5), 895–900.

Novak, B. (2010). Kleptomania and the law. In E. Aboujaoude (Ed.), *Impulse control disorders* (pp. 45–50). New York, NY: Cambridge University Press.

Noyes, R., Clarkson, C., Crowe, R. R., Yates, W. R., & McChesney, C. M. (1987). A family study of generalized anxiety disorder. *American Journal of Psychiatry, 144,* 1019–1024.

Noyes, R., Garvey, M. J., Cook, B., & Suelzer, M. (1991). Controlled discontinuation of benzodiazepine treatment for patients with panic disorder. *American Journal of Psychiatry, 148,* 517–523.

Noyes, R., Hoenk, P., Kuperman, S., & Slymen, D. (1977). Depersonalization in accident victims and psychiatric patients. *Journal of Nervous and Mental Disease, 164,* 401–407.

Noyes, R., & Kletti, R. (1977). Depersonalization in response to life-threatening danger. *Comprehensive Psychiatry, 18,* 375–384.

Noyes, R., Watson, D., Carney, C., Letuchy, E., Peloso, P., Black, D., & Doebbeling, B. N. (2004). Risk factors for hypochondriacal concerns in a sample of military veterans. *Journal of Psychosomatic Research, 57,* 529–539.

Noyes, R., Woodman, C., Garvey, M. J., Cook, B. L., Suelzer, M., Clancy, J., & Anderson, D. J. (1992). Generalized anxiety disorder vs. panic disorder: Distinguishing characteristics and patterns of comorbidity. *Journal of Nervous and Mental Disease, 180,* 369–379.

Noyes, R., Jr., Stuart, S. P., & Watson, D. B. (2008). A reconceptualization of the somatoform disorders. *Psychosomatics, 49*(1), 14–22.

Nugent, S. A. (2000). Perfectionism: Its manifestations and classroom-based interventions. *Journal of Secondary Gifted Education, 11,* 215–221.

Nunes, P., Wenzel, A., Borges, K., Porto, C., Caminha, R., & de Oliveira, I. (2009). Volumes of the hippocampus and amygdala in patients with borderline personality disorder: A metaanalysis. *Journal of Personality Disorders, 23*(4), 333–345.

Nurnberger, J. I., & Gershon, E. S. (1992). Genetics. In E. S. Paykel (Ed.), *Handbook of affective disorders* (pp. 126–145). New York, NY: Guilford Press.

Nyhan, W. L. (1978). The Lesch-Nyhan syndrome. *Developmental Medicine and Child Neurology, 20,* 376–387.

Oades, R. D. (1985). The role of noradrenaline in tuning and dopamine in switching between signals in the CNS. *Neuroscience and Biobehavioral Reviews, 9,* 261–282.

Oakley, D. A., & Halligan, P. W. (2009). Hypnotic suggestion and cognitive neuroscience. *Trends in Cognitive Sciences, 13*(6), 264–270.

O'Brien, M. E., Clark, R. A., Besch, C. L., Myers, L., & Kissinger, P. (2003). Patterns and correlates of discontinuation of the initial HAART regimen in an urban outpatient cohort. *Journal of Acquired Immune Deficiency Syndrome, 34*(4), 407–414.

O'Brien, P. E., Sawyer, S. M., Laurie, C., Brown, W. A., Skinner, S., Veit, F., ... Dixon, J. B. (2010). Laparoscopic adjustable gastric banding in severely obese adolescents: A randomized trial. *JAMA: Journal of the American Medical Association, 303*(6), 519–526.

O'Callaghan, E., Sham, P., Takei, N., Glover, G., & Murray, R. M. (1991). Schizophrenia after prenatal exposure to 1957 A2 influenza epidemic. *Lancet, 337,* 1248–1250.

O'Carroll, P. W. (1990). Community strategies for suicide prevention and intervention. In S. J. Blumenthal & D. J. Kupfer (Eds.), *Suicide over the life cycle: Risk factors, assessment, and treatment of suicidal patients.* Washington, DC: American Psychiatric Press.

Ochsner, K. N., Ray, R. R., Hughes, B., McRae, K., Cooper, J. C., Weber, J., ... Gross, J. J. (2009). Bottom-up and top-down processes in emotion generation: Common and distinct neural mechanisms. *Psychological Science, 20*(11), 1322–1331.

O'Connor v. Donaldson, 95 S. Ct. 2486 (1975).

Ogata, S. N., Silk, K. R., Goodrich, S., Lohr, N. E., Westen, D., & Hill, E. M. (1990). Childhood sexual and physical abuse in adult patients with borderline personality disorder. *American Journal of Psychiatry, 147,* 1008–1013.

Ogden, C. L., Carroll, M. D., Curtin, L. R., Lamb, M. M., & Flegal, K. M. (2010). Prevalence of high body mass index in US children and adolescents, 2007–2008. *JAMA: Journal of the American Medical Association, 303*(3), 242–249.

Ogden, C. L., Carroll, M. D., Curtin, L. R., McDowell, M. A., Tabak, C. J., & Flegal, K. M. (2006). Prevalence of overweight and obesity in the United States, 1999–2004. *JAMA: Journal of the American Medical Association, 295,* 1549–1555.

O'Hanlon, J. F., Haak, J. W., Blaauw, G. J., & Riemersma, J. B. J. (1982). Diazepam impairs lateral position control in highway driving. *Science, 27,* 79–81.

O'Hara, M. W., Stuart, S., Gorman, L. L., & Wenzel, A. (2000). Efficacy of interpersonal psychotherapy for postpartum depression. *Archives of General Psychiatry, 57,* 1039–1045.

Ohayon, M. M., & Schatzberg, A. F. (2003). Using chronic pain to predict depressive morbidity in the general population. *Archives of General Psychiatry, 60,* 39–47.

Öhman, A. (1986). Face the beast and fear the face: Animal and social fears as prototypes for evolutionary analyses of emotion. *Psychophysiology, 23,* 123–145.

Öhman, A. (1996). Preferential pre-attentive processing of threat in anxiety: Preparedness and attentional biases. In R. Rapee (Ed.), *Current controversies in the anxiety disorders* (pp. 253– 290). New York, NY: Guilford Press.

Öhman, A., & Dimberg, U. (1978). Facial expressions as conditioned stimuli for electrodermal responses: A case of preparedness? *Journal of Personality and Social Psychology, 36*(11), 1251–1258.

Öhman, A., Flykt, A., & Lundqvist, D. (2000). Unconscious emotion: Evolutionary perspective, psychophysiological data, and neuropsychological mechanisms. In R. Lane & L. Nadel (Eds.), *The cognitive neuroscience of emotion* (pp. 296–327). New York, NY: Oxford University Press.

Öhman, A., & Mineka, S. (2001). Fears, phobias, and preparedness: Toward an evolved model of fear and fear learning. *Psychological Review*.

Okazaki, S., Okazaki, M., & Sue, S. (2009). Clinical personality assessment with Asian Americans. In J. N. Butcher (Ed.), *Oxford handbook of personality assessment* (pp. 377–395). New York: Oxford University Press.

olde Hartman, T. C., Borghuis, M. S., Lucassen, P. L., van de Laar, F. A., Speckens, A. E., & van Weel, C. (2009). Medically unexplained symptoms, somatisation disorder, and hypochondriasis: Course and prognosis. A systematic review. *Journal of Psychosomatic Research, 66*(5), 363–377.

Olds, J. (1956). Pleasure centers in the brain. *Scientific American, 195,* 105–116.

Olds, J., & Milner, P. M. (1954). Positive reinforcement produced by electrical stimulation of septal area and other regions of rat brain. *Journal of Comparative and Physiological Psychology, 47,* 419–427.

Olfson, M., Marcus, S., & Schaffer, D. (2006). Antidepressant drug therapy and suicide in severely depressed children and adolescents. *Archives General Psychiatry, 63,* 865–872.

Olfson, M., Shaffer, D., Marcus, S. C., & Greenberg, T. (2003). Relationship between antidepressant medication treatment and suicide in adolescents. *Archives of General Psychiatry, 60,* 978–82.

Olin, S. S., Raine, A., Cannon, T. D., Parnas, J., Schulsinger, F., & Mednick, S. A. (1997). Childhood behavior precursors of schizotypal personality disorder. *Schizophrenia Bulletin, 23,* 93–103.

Olivardia, R., Pope, H. G., & Hudson, J. I. (2000). Muscle dysmorphia in male weightlifters: A case-control study. *American Journal of Psychiatry, 157,* 1291–1296.

Oliver, M. B., & Hyde, J. S. (1993). Gender differences in sexuality: A meta-analysis. *Psychological Bulletin, 114*(1), 29–51.

Olivier, P., Bertrand, L., Tubery, M., Lauque, D., Montastruc, J.-L., & Lapeyre-Mestre, M. (2009). Hospitalizations because of adverse drug reactions in elderly patients admitted through the emergency department: A prospective survey. *Drugs & Aging, 26*(6), 475–482.

Ollendick, T. H., & Huntzinger, R. M. (1990). Separation anxiety disorder in childhood. In M. Hersen & C. G. Last (Eds.), *Handbook of child and adult psychopathology: A longitudinal perspective.* Elmsford, NY: Pergamon Press.

Ollendick, T. H., & Shirk, S. R. (2011). Clinical interventions with children and adolescents: Current status, future directions. In D. H. Barlow (Ed.), *Oxford handbook of clinical psychology* (pp. 762–788). New York, NY: Oxford University.

Omalu, B. I., Ives, D. G., Buhari, A. M., Lindner, J. L., Schauer, P. R., Wecht, C. H., & Kuller, L. H. (2007). Death rates and causes of death after bariatric surgery for Pennsylvania residents, 1995 to 2004. *Archives of Surgery, 142*(10), 923–928; discussion 929.

Opjordsmoen, S. (1989). Delusional disorders: I. Comparative long-term outcome.

Acta Psychiatrica Scandinavica, 80, 603–612.

Oquendo, M., Galfalvy, H., Russo, S., Ellis, S., Grunebaum, M., Burke, A., & Mann, J. J. (2004). Prospective study of clinical predictors of suicidal acts after a major depressive episode in patients with major depressive disorder or bipolar disorder. *American Journal of Psychiatry, 161,* 1433–1441.

Orford, J., & Keddie, A. (2006). Abstinence or controlled drinking in clinical practice: A test of the dependence and persuasion hypotheses. *Addiction, 81*(4), 495–504.

Orne, M. T., Dinges, D. F., & Orne, E. C. (1984). On the differential diagnosis of multiple personality in the forensic context. *International Journal of Clinical and Experimental Hypnosis, 32,* 118–169.

Orsillo, S. M., Roemer, L., & Barlow, D. H. (2003). Integrating acceptance and mindfulness into existing cognitive-behavioral treatment for GAD: A case study. *Cognitive & Behavioral Practice, 10,* 222–230.

Orstavik, R. E., Kendler, K. S., Czajkowski, N., Tambs, K., & Reichborn-Kjennerud, T. (2007). The relationship between depressive personality disorder and major depressive disorder: A population-based twin study. *American Journal of Psychiatry, 164*(12), 1866–1872. doi:10.1176/appi.ajp.2007.07010045

Orth, U., Robins, R. W., Trzesniewski, K. H., Maes, J., & Schmitt, M. (2009). Low self-esteem is a risk factor for depressive symptoms from young adulthood to old age. *Journal of Abnormal Psychology, 118*(3), 472–478.

Ortiz, A., & Medicna-Mora, M. E. (1988). Research on drugs in Mexico: Epidemiology of drug abuse and issues among Native American populations. In Community Epidemiology Work Group Proceedings, December 1987. Contract No. 271-87-8321. Washington, DC: U.S. Government Printing Office.

Oslin, D. W., & Klaus, J. R. (2009). Drug and alcohol abuse. In B. J. Sadock & V. A. Sadock (Eds.), *Kaplan & Sadock's comprehensive textbook of psychiatry* (9th ed., Vol. 2, pp. 4088–4095). Philadelphia, PA: Lippincott Williams & Wilkins.

Öst, L. G. (1985). Mode of acquisition of phobias. *Acta Universitatis Uppsaliensis* (Abstracts of Uppsala Dissertations from the Faculty of Medicine), 529, 1–45.

Öst, L. G. (1987). Age at onset in different phobias. *Journal of Abnormal Psychology, 96,* 223–229.

Öst, L. G. (1989). *Blood phobia: A specific phobia subtype in DSM-IV.* Paper requested by the Simple Phobia subcommittee of the DSM-IV Anxiety Disorders Work Group.

Öst, L. G. (1992). Blood and injection phobia: Background and cognitive, physiological, and behavioral variables. *Journal of Abnormal Psychology, 101*(1), 68–74.

Öst, L. G., Ferebee, I., & Furmark, T. (1997). One session group therapy of spider phobia: Direct vs. indirect treatments. *BRAT, 35,* 721–732.

Öst, L. G., & Sterner, U. (1987). Applied tension: A specific behavioural method for treatment of blood phobia. *Behaviour Research and Therapy, 25,* 25–30.

Öst, L. G., Svensson, L., Hellström, K., & Lindwall, R. (2001). One-session treatment of specific phobia in youths: A randomized clinical trial. *Journal of Consulting and Clinical Psychology, 69,* 814–824.

Osterberg, E. (1986). Alcohol-related problems in cross-national perspectives: Results of the ISACE study. Special issue: Alcohol and culture: Comparative perspectives from Europe and America. (T. Babot, Ed.). *Annals of the New York Academy of Sciences, 472,* 10–20.

O'Sullivan, K. (1979). Observations on vaginismus in Irish women. *Archives of General Psychiatry, 36,* 824–826.

Otis, J., Macdonald, A., & Dobscha, A. (2006). Integration and coordination of pain management in primary care. *Journal of Clinical Psychology, 62,* 1333–1343.

Otis, J. D., & Pincus, D. B. (2008). Chronic pain. In B. A. Boyer & I. Paharia (Eds.), *Comprehensive handbook of clinical health psychology* (pp. 349–370). Hoboken, NJ: John Wiley & Sons.

Otis, J. D., Pincus, D. B., & Murawksi, M. E. (2011). Cognitive behavioral therapy in pain management. In R. D. Kerns & M. E. Eberts (Eds.), *Behavioral and psychopharmacological therapeutics in pain management.* New York, NY: Cambridge University Press.

Otto, M.W. & Applebaum, A.J. (2011). The nature and treatment of bipolar disorder and the bipolar spectrum. In D. H. Barlow (Ed.), *Oxford handbook of clinical psychology* (pp. 294–310). New York, NY: Oxford University Press.

Otto, M. W., Behar, E., Smits, J. A. J., & Hofmann, S. G. (2009). Combining pharmacological and cognitive behavioral therapy in the treatment of anxiety disorders. In M. M. Antony & M. B. Stein (Eds.), *Oxford handbook of anxiety and related disorders* (pp. 429–440). New York, NY: Oxford University Press.

Otto, M. W., Reilly-Harrington, N. A., Knauz, R. O., Henin, A., Kogan, J. N., & Sachs, G. S. (2008a). *Managing bipolar disorder: A cognitive- behavioral approach. (Therapist Guide).* New York, NY: Oxford University Press.

Otto, M. W., Reilly-Harrington, N. A., Knauz, R. O., Henin, A., Kogan, J. N., & Sachs, G. S. (2008b). *Managing bipolar disorder: A cognitive- behavioral approach. (Workbook).* New York, NY: Oxford University Press.

Otto, M. W., Tolin, D. F., Simon, N. M., Pearlson, G. D., Basden, S., Meunier, S. A., ... Pollack, M. H. (2010). Efficacy of D-cycloserine for enhancing response to cognitive-behavior therapy for panic dis order. *Biological Psychiatry, 67*(4), 365–370.

Ouellet-Morin, I., Boivin, M., Dionne, G., Lupien, S. J., Arsenault, L., Barr, R. G., ... Tremblay, R. E. (2008). Variations in heritability of cortisol reactivity to stress as a function of early familial adversity among 19-month-old twins. *Archives of General Psychiatry, 65*(2), 211–218.

Ovsiew, F. (2005). Neuropsychiatry and behavioral neurology. In B. J. Sadock & V. A. Sadock (Eds.), *Kaplan & Sadock's comprehensive textbook of psychiatry* (pp. 323–349). Philadelphia: Lippincott Williams & Wilkins.

Owen, J. J., Rhoades, G. K., Stanley, S. M., & Fincham, F. D. (2010). "Hooking up" among college students: Demographic and psychosocial correlates. *Archives of Sexual Behavior, 39*, 653–663.

Owens, J. A., Rosen, C. L., & Mindell, J. A. (2003). Medication use in the treatment of pediatric insomnia: Results of a survey of community-based pediatricians. *Pediatrics, 111*, 628–635.

Owens, M. J., Mulchahey, J. J., Stout, S. C., & Plotsky, P. M. (1997). Molecular and neurobiological mechanisms in the treatment of psychiatric disorders. In A. Tasman, J. Kay, & J. A. Lieberman (Eds.), *Psychiatry* (Vol. 1, pp. 210– 257). Philadelphia, PA: W. B. Saunders.

Oyama, O., & Andrasik, F. (1992). Behavioral strategies in the prevention of disease. In S. M. Turner, K. S. Calhoun, & H. E. Adams (Eds.), *Handbook of clinical behavior therapy* (2nd ed., pp. 397– 413). New York, NY: John Wiley.

Ozbay, F., Johnson, D. C., Dimoulas, E., Morgan, C. A., III, Charney, D., & Southwick, S. (2007). Social support and resilience to stress: From neurobiology to clinical practice. *Psychiatry, 4*(5), 35–40.

Page, A. C. (1994). Blood–injury phobia. *Clinical Psychology Review, 14*, 443–461.

Page, A. C. (1996). Blood–injury–injection fears in medical practice. *Medical Journal of Australia, 164*, 189.

Page, A. C., & Martin, N. G. (1998). Testing a genetic structure of blood–injury–injection fears. *American Journal of Medical Genetics (Neuropsychiatric Genetics), 81*, 377–384.

Page, G. G., Ben-Eliyahu, S., Yirmiya, R., & Liebeskind, J. C. (1993). Morphine attenuates surgery-induced enhancement of metastatic colonization in rats. *Pain, 54*(1), 21–28.

Pagel, J. F. (2006). Medications that induce sleepiness. In T. Lee-Chiong (Ed.), *Sleep: A comprehensive handbook* (pp. 175–182). Hoboken, NJ: John Wiley & Sons.

Pampallona, S., Bollini, P., Tibaldi, G., Kupelnick, B., & Munizza, C. (2004). Combined pharmacotherapy and psychological treatment for depression. *Archives of General Psychiatry, 61*, 714–719.

Pantaleo, G., Graziosi, C., & Fauci, A. S. (1993). The immunopathogenesis of human immunodeficiency virus infection. *New England Journal of Medicine, 328*, 327–335.

Papadopoulos, F. C., Ekbom, A., Brandt, L., & Ekselius, L. (2009). Excess mortality, causes of death, and prognostic factors in anorexia nervosa. *British Journal of Psychiatry, 194*(1), 10–17.

Papillo, J. F., & Shapiro, D. (1990). The cardiovascular system. In J. T. Cacioppo & L. G. Tassinaryo (Eds.), *Principles of psychophysiology: Physical, social, and inferential elements*. New York, NY: Cambridge University Press.

Paquette, V., Lévesque, J., Mensour, B., Leroux, J-M., Beudoin, G., Bourgouin, P., Beauregard, M. (2003). "Change the mind and you change the brain": Effects of cognitive-behavioral therapy on the neural correlates of spider phobia. *Neuroimage, 18*, 401–409.

Paradis, C. M., Friedman, S., & Hatch, M. (1997). Isolated sleep paralysis in African Americans with panic disorder. *Cultural Diversity & Mental Health, 3*, 69–76.

Pardini, D., Lochman, J., & Wells, K. (2004). Negative emotions and alcohol use initiation in high-risk boys: The moderating effect of good inhibitory control. *Journal of Abnormal Child Psychology, 32*, 505–518.

Paris, J. (2008). Clinical trials of treatment for personality disorders. *Psychiatric Clinics of North America, 31*(3), 517–526. doi:10.1016/j. psc.2008.03.013

Parish, W., Luo, Y., Stolzenberg, R., Laumann, E., Farrer, G., & Pan, S. (2007). Sexual practices and sexual satisfaction: A population-based study of Chinese urban adults. *Archives of Sexual Behavior, 36*, 5–20.

Park, C. L., Edmondson, D., Fenster, J. R., & Blank, T. O. (2008). Meaning making and psychological adjustment following cancer: The mediating roles of growth, life meaning, and restored just-world beliefs. *Journal of Consulting and Clinical Psychology, 76*, 863–875.

Parker, G., & Hadzi-Pavlovic, D. (1990). Expressed emotion as a predictor of schizophrenic relapse: An analysis of aggregated data. *Psychological Medicine, 20*, 961–965.

Parker, S., Schwartz, B., Todd, J., & Pickering, L. (2004). Thimerosal-containing vaccines and autistic spectrum disorder: A critical review of published original data. *Pediatrics, 114*(3), 793.

Parkinson, L., & Rachman, S. (1981a). Intrusive thoughts: The effects of an uncontrived stress. *Advances in Behaviour Research and Therapy, 3*, 111–118.

Parkinson, L., & Rachman, S. (1981b). Speed of recovery from an uncontrived stress. *Advances in Behaviour Research and Therapy, 3*, 119–123.

Parry-Jones, B., & Parry-Jones, W. L. (2002). History of bulimia and bulimia nervosa. In K. D. Brownell & C. G. Fairburn (Eds.), *Eating disorders and obesity: A comprehensive handbook* (2nd ed., pp. 145–150). New York, NY: Guilford Press.

Parsons, J., Kelly, B., & Weiser, J. (2007). Initiation into methamphetamine use for young gay and bisexual men. *Drug and Alcohol Dependence, 90*(2–3), 135–144.

Patrick, C. J. (Ed.), *Handbook of psychopathy*. New York, NY: Guilford Press.

Patrick, D., Althof, S., Pryor, J., Rosen, R., Rowland, D., Ho, K., ... Jamieson, C. (2005). Premature ejaculation: An observational study of men and their partners. *Journal of Sexual Medicine, 2*, 358–367.

Patterson, G. R. (1982). *Coercive family process*. Eugene, OR: Castalia.

Patterson, G. R. (1986). Performance models for antisocial boys. *American Psychologist, 41*, 432–444.

Patterson, G. R., DeBaryshe, B. D., & Ramsey, E. (1989). A developmental perspective on antisocial behavior. *American Psychologist, 44*, 329–335.

Patton, G. C., Johnson-Sabine, E., Wood, K., Mann, A. H., & Wakeling, A. (1990). Abnormal eating attitudes in London school girls—A prospective epidemiological study: Outcome at twelve-month follow-up. *Psychological Medicine, 20*, 383–394.

Paul, G. L., & Lentz, R. J. (1977). *Psychosocial treatment of chronic mental patients: Milieu versus social learning programs*. Cambridge, MA: Harvard University Press.

Paul, T., Schroeter, K., Dahme, B., & Nutzinger, D. O. (2002). Self-injurious behavior in women with eating disorders. *American Journal of Psychiatry, 159*, 408–411.

Pauli, P., & Alpers, G. W. (2002). Memory bias in patients with hypochondriasis and somatoform pain disorder. *Journal of Psychosomatic Research, 52*, 45–53.

Pavalko, E. K., Elder, G. H., Jr., & Clipp, E. C. (1993). Worklives and longevity: Insights from a life course perspective. *Journal of Health and Social Behavior, 34*, 363–380.

Paxton, S. J., Schutz, H. K., Wertheim, E. H., & Muir, S. L. (1999). Friendship clique and peer influences on body image concerns, dietary restraint, extreme weight-loss behaviors, and binge eating in adolescent girls. *Journal of Abnormal Psychology, 108*(2), 255–266.

Paykel, E. S. & Scott, J. (2009). Treatment of mood disorders. In M.G. Gelder, N.C. Andreasen, J.J. López-Ibor, Jr., & J.R. Geddes (Eds.), *New Oxford textbook of psychiatry* (2nd ed., Vol. 1, pp. 669–680). Oxford, UK: Oxford University Press.

Paykel, E. S., & Weissman, M. M. (1973). Social adjustment and depression: A longitudinal study. *Archives of General Psychiatry, 28*, 659–663.

Payne, K., Reissing, E., Lahaie, M., Binik, Y., Amsel, R., & Khalife, S. (2005). What is sexual pain? A critique of DSM's classification of dyspareunia and vaginismus. In D. Karasic & J. Drescher (Eds.), *Sexual and gender diagnoses of the Diagnostic and Statistical Manual (DSM): A reevaluation* (pp. 141–154). New York, NY: Haworth Press.

Pearson, C., Montgomery, A., & Locke, G. (2009). Housing stability among homeless individuals with serious mental illness participating in Housing First programs. *Journal of Community Psychology, 37*(3), 404–417.

Peat, C., Mitchell, J. E., Hoek, H. W., & Wonderlich, S. A. (2009). Validity and utility of subtyping anorexia nervosa. *International Journal of Eating Disorders, 42*(7), 590–594.

Pedersen, C. B., & Mortensen, P. B. (2006). Are the cause(s) responsible for urban-rural differences in schizophrenia risk rooted in families or in individuals? *American Journal of Epidemiology, 163*(11), 971–978.

Pedersen, N. L. (2010). Reaching the limits of genome-wide significance in Alzheimer disease: Back to the environment. *JAMA: Journal of the American Medical Association, 303*(18), 1864–1865.

Pehlivanturk, B., & Unal, F. (2002). Conversion disorder in children and adolescents: A 4-year follow-up study. *Journal of Psychosomatic Research, 52*, 187–191.

Pelham, W. E., Jr. (1999). The NIMH Multimodal Treatment Study for attention-deficit hyperactivity disorder: Just say yes to drugs alone? *Canadian Journal of Psychiatry, 44*, 981–990.

Pendery, M. L., Maltzman, I. M., & West, L. J. (1982). Controlled drinking by alcoholics? New findings and a reevaluation of a major affirmative study. *Science, 217*, 169–175.

Penedo, F. J., Antoni, M. H., & Schneiderman, N. (2008). *Cognitive-behavioral stress management for prostate cancer recovery:*

Facilitator guide. New York, NY: Oxford University Press.

Peng, T. (2008, November 23). Out of the Shadows. *Newsweek.*

Pennington, B., & Bishop, D. (2009). Relations among speech, language, and reading disorders. *Annual Review of Psychology, 60,* 283–306.

Pentz, M. A. (1999). Prevention. In M. Galanter & H. D. Kleber (Eds.), *Textbook of substance abuse treatment* (2nd ed., pp. 535–544). Washington, DC: American Psychiatric Press.

Peplau, L. A. (2003). Human sexuality: How do men and women differ? *Current Directions in Psychological Science, 12,* 37–40.

Pepper, C. M., Klein, D. N., Anderson, R. L., Riso, L. P., Ouimette, P. C., & Lizardi, H. (1995). DSM-III-R axis II comorbidity in dysthymia and major depression. *American Journal of Psychiatry, 152,* 239–247.

Perea, G., & Araque, A. (2007). Astrocytes potentiate transmitter release at single hippocampal synapses. *Science, 317,* 1083–1087.

Pereira, D. B., Antoni, M. H., Danielson, A., Simon, T., Efantis-Potter, J., Carver, C. S ... O'Sullivan, M. J. (2003). Stress as a predictor of symptomatic genital herpes virus recurrence in women with human immunodeficiency virus. *Journal of Psychosomatic Research, 54*(3), 237–244.

Pericak-Vance, M. A., Johnson, C. C., Rimmler, J. B., Saunders, A. M., Robinson, L. C., D'Hondt, E. G., ... Haines, J. L. (1996). Alzheimer's disease and apolipoprotein E-4 allele in an Amish population. *Annals of Neurology, 39,* 700–704.

Perlin, M. L. (2000). *The hidden prejudice: Mental disability on trial.* Washington, DC: American Psychological Association.

Perlis, M. L., Smith, L. J., Lyness, J. M., Matteson, S. R., Pigeon, W. R., Jungquist, C. R., & Tu, X. (2006). Insomnia as a risk factor for onset of depression in the elderly. *Behavioral Sleep Medicine, 4*(2), 104–113.

Perneczky, R., Wagenpfeil, S., Lunetta, K. L., Cupples, L. A., Green, R. C., DeCarli, C., … Kurz, A. (2009). Education attenuates the effect of medial temporal lobe atrophy on cognitive function in Alzheimer's disease: The MIRAGE Study. *Journal of Alzheimer's Disease, 17*(4), 855–862.

Perri, M. G., Nezu, A. M., McKelvey, W. F., Shermer, R. L., Renjilian, D. A., & Viegener, B. J. (2001). Relapse prevention training and problem-solving therapy in the long-term management of obesity. *Journal of Consulting and Clinical Psychology, 69,* 722–726.

Perron, B., & Howard, M. (2009). Adolescent inhalant use, abuse, and dependence. *Addiction, 104*(7), 1185–1192.

Perry, J. C. (1993). Longitudinal studies of personality disorders. *Journal of Personality Disorders, 7,* 63–85.

Person, D. C., & Borkovec, T. D. (1995, August). *Anxiety disorders among the elderly: Patterns and issues.* Paper presented at the 103rd annual meeting of the American Psychological Association. New York.

Peselow, E. D., Fieve, R. R., Difiglia, C., & Sanfilipo, M. P. (1994). Lithium prophylaxis of bipolar illness: The value of combination treatment. *British Journal of Psychiatry, 164,* 208–214.

Petersen, J. L., & Hyde, J. S. (2010). A meta-analytic review of research on gender differences in sexuality, 1993-2007. *Psychological Bulletin, 136,* 21–38.

Peterson, L., Farmer, J., & Kashani, J. H. (1990). Parental injury prevention endeavors: A function of health beliefs? *Health Psychology, 9*(2), 177–191.

Peterson, L., & Roberts, M. C. (1992). Complacency, misdirection, and effective prevention of children's injuries. *American Psychologist, 47*(8), 1040–1044.

Peterson, L., & Thiele, C. (1988). Home safety at school. *Child and Family Behavior Therapy, 10*(1), 1–8.

Petit, L., Azad, N., Byszewski, A., Sarazan, F. F. A., & Power, B. (2003). Non-pharmacological management of primary and secondary insomnia among older people: Review of assessment tools and treatments. *Age and Ageing, 32,* 19–25.

Petrill, S. A., Deater-Deckard, K., Thompson, L. A., DeThorne, L. S., & Schatschneider, C. (2006). Reading skills in early readers: Genetic and shared environmental influences. *Journal of Learning Disabilities, 39,* 48–55.

Phifer, J. F., & Murrell, S. A. (1986). Etiologic factors in the onset of depressive symptoms in older adults. *Journal of Abnormal Psychology, 95,* 282–291.

Philips, H. C., & Grant, L. (1991). Acute back pain: A psychological analysis. *Behaviour Research and Therapy, 29,* 429–434.

Phillips, K. A. (1991). Body dysmorphic disorder: The distress of imagined ugliness. *American Journal of Psychiatry, 148,* 1138–1149.

Phillips, K. A. (2005). *The broken mirror: Understanding and treating body dysmorphic disorder* (Rev. & expanded ed.). New York, NY: Oxford University Press.

Phillips, K. A., Albertini, R. S., & Rasmussen, S. A. (2002). A randomized placebo-controlled trial of fluoxetine in body dysmorphic disorder. *Evidence-Based Mental Health, 5,* 119.

Phillips, K. A., Dufresne, R. G., Wilkel, C. S., & Vittorio, C. C. (2000). Rate of body dysmorphic disorder in dermatology patients. *Journal of the American Academy of Dermatology, 42,* 436–441.

Phillips, K. A., Grant, J., Siniscalchi, J., & Albertini, R. S. (2001). Surgical and nonpsychiatric medical treatment of patients with body dysmorphic disorder. *Psychosomatics, 42,* 504–510.

Phillips, K. A., McElroy, S. L., Keck, P. E., Jr., Pope, H. G., Jr., & Hudson, J. I. (1993). Body dysmorphic disorder: 30 cases of imagined ugliness. *American Journal of Psychiatry, 150,* 302–308.

Phillips, K. A., Menard, W., & Fay, C. (2006). Gender similarities and differences in 200 individuals with body dysmorphic disorder. *Comprehensive Psychiatry, 47,* 77–87.

Phillips, K. A., Menard, W., Fay, C., & Pagano, M. E. (2005). Psychosocial functioning and quality of life in body dysmorphic disorder. *Comprehensive Psychiatry, 46*(4), 254–260.

Phillips, K. A., Menard, W., Fay, C., & Weisberg, R. (2005). Demographic characteristics, phenomenology, comorbidity, and family history in 200 individuals with body dysmorphic disorder. *Psychosomatics, 46,* 317–325.

Phillips, K. A., Menard, W., Pagano, M., Fay, C., & Stout, R. (2006). Delusional versus nondelusional body dysmorphic disorder: Clinical features and course of illness. *Journal of Psychiatric Research, 40,* 95–104.

Phillips, K. A., Pagano, M., Menard, W., & Stout, R. (2006). A 12-month follow-up study of the course of body dysmorphic disorder. *American Journal of Psychiatry, 163,* 907–912.

Phillips, K. A., & Stout, R. (2006). Association in the longitudinal course of body dysmorphic disorder with major depression, obsessive compulsive disorder, and social phobia. *Journal of Psychiatric Research, 40,* 360–369.

Phillips, K. A., Wilhelm, S., Koran, L. M., Didie, E., Fallon, B., Feusner, J., & Stein, D. J. (2010). Body dysmorphic disorder: Some key issues for DSM-V. *Depression and Anxiety.*

Phillips, L. J., Francey, S. M., Edwards, J., & McMurray, N. (2007). Stress and psychosis: Towards the development of new models of investigation. *Clinical Psychology Review, 27,* 307–317.

Phillips, M. R., Li, X., & Zhang, Y. (2002). Suicide rates in China, 1995–99. *Lancet, 359,* 835–840.

Phillips, M. R., Shen, Q., Liu, X., Pritker, S., Streiner, D., Conner, K., & Yang, G. (2007). Assessing depressive symptoms in persons who die of suicide in mainland China. *Journal of Affective Disorders, 98,* 73–82.

Piasecki, T. M., Hufford, M. R., Solhan, M., & Trull, T. J. (2007). Assessing clients in their natural environments with electronic diaries: Rationale, benefits, limitations, and barriers. *Psychological Assessment, 19,* 25–43.

Pihl, R. O., Peterson, J. B., & Lau, M. A. (1993). A biosocial model of the alcohol-aggression relationship. *Journal of Studies on Alcohol, 54*(Suppl. 11), 128–139.

Pike, K. M., Devlin, M. J., & Loeb, C. (2004). Cognitive-behavioral therapy in the treatment of anorexia nervosa and binge eating disorder. In J. K. Thompson (Ed.), *Handbook of eating disorders and obesity* (pp. 130–162). New York, NY: John Wiley.

Pike, K. M., Loeb, K., & Vitousek, K. (1996). Cognitive-behavioral therapy for anorexia nervosa and bulimia nervosa. In J. K. Thompson (Ed.), *Body image, eating disorders, and obesity* (pp. 253–302). Washington, DC: American Psychological Association.

Pike, K. M., & Rodin, J. (1991). Mothers, daughters, and disordered eating. *Journal of Abnormal Psychology, 100*(2), 198–204.

Pike, K. M., Walsh, B. T., Vitousek, K., Wilson, G. T., & Bauer, J. (2003). Cognitive behavior therapy in the post-hospitalization treatment of anorexia nervosa. *American Journal of Psychiatry, 160,* 2046–2048.

Pilowsky, I. (1970). Primary and secondary hypochondriasis. *Acta Psychiatrica Scandinavica, 46,* 273–285.

Pincus, D. B., Santucci, L. C., Ehrenreich, J. T., & Eyberg, S. M. (2008). The implementation of modified parent–child interaction therapy for youth with separation anxiety disorder. *Cognitive and Behavioral Practice, 15*(2), 118–125.

Pinel, P. (1962). *A treatise on insanity.* New York, NY: Hafner. (Original work published in 1801).

Pinel, P. H. (1809). *Traité medico-philosophique sur l'aliénation mentale.* Paris, France: Chez J. Ant Brosson.

Pinto, R., Ashworth, M., & Jones, R. (2008). Schizophrenia in black Caribbeans living in the UK: An exploration of underlying causes of the high incidence rate. *The British Journal of General Practice, 58*(551), 429.

Pithers, W. D., Martin, G. R., & Cumming, G. F. (1989). Vermont treatment program for sexual aggressors. In D. R. Laws (Ed.), *Relapse prevention with sex offenders* (pp. 292–310). New York, NY: Guilford Press.

Plant, M. L. (2008). The role of alcohol in women's lives: a review of issues and responses. *Journal of Substance Use, 13,* 155–191.

Plomin, R. (1990). The role of inheritance in behavior. *Science, 248,* 183–188.

Plomin, R., & Davis, O. S. P. (2009). The future of genetics in psychology and psychiatry: Microarrays, genome-wide association, and non-coding RNA. *Journal of Child Psychology and Psychiatry, 50*(1–2), 63–71.

Plomin, R., DeFries, J. C., McClearn, G. E., & Rutter, M. (1997). *Behavioral Genetics: A primer* (3rd ed.). New York, NY: Freeman.

Plomin, R., & Kovas, Y. (2005). Generalist genes and learning disabilities. *Psychological Bulletin, 131,* 592–617.

Plomin, R., McClearn, G. E., Smith, D. L., Skuder, P., Vignetti, S., Chorney, M. J., ... McGuffin, P. (1995). Allelic association between 100 DNA markers and high versus low IQ. *Intelligence, 21,* 31–48.

Polanczyk, G., de Lima, M. S., Horta, B. L., Biederman, J., & Rohde, L. A. (2007). The worldwide prevalence of ADHD: A systematic review and metaregression analysis. *American Journal of Psychiatry, 164,* 942–948.

Polanczyk, G., Zeni, C., Genro, J. P., Guimaraes, A. P., Roman, T., Hutz, M. H., Rohde, L. A.. (2007). Association of the adrenergic α-2A receptor gene with methylphenidate improvement of inattentive symptoms in children and adolescents with attention-deficit/hyperactivity disorder. *Archives of General Psychiatry, 64,* 218–224.

Polivy, J., & Herman, C. P. (2002). Dieting and its relation to eating disorder. In K. D. Brownell & C. G. Fairburn (Eds.), *Eating disorders and obesity: A comprehensive handbook* (2nd ed., pp. 83–86). New York, NY: Guilford Press.

Polivy, J. M., & Herman, C. P. (1993). Etiology of binge eating: Psychological mechanisms. In C. G. Fairburn & G. T. Wilson (Eds.), *Binge eating: Nature, assessment, and treatment.* New York, NY: Guilford Press.

Pollack, M. H. (2005). The pharmacotherapy of panic disorder. *Journal of Clinical Psychiatry, 66,* 23–27.

Pollack, M. H., & Simon, N. M. (2009). Pharmacotherapy for panic disorder and agoraphobia. In M. M. Antony & M. B. Stein (Eds.), *Oxford handbook of anxiety and related disorders* (pp. 295–307). New York, NY: Oxford University Press.

Polonsky, D. C. (2000). Premature ejaculation. In S. R. Leiblum & R. C. Rosen (Eds.), *Principles and practice of sex therapy* (3rd ed., pp. 305–332). New York, NY: Guilford Press.

Pomeroy, C. (2004). Assessment of medical status and physical factors. In J. K. Thompson (Ed.), *Handbook of eating disorders and obesity* (pp. 81–111). New York, NY: John Wiley.

Poorsattar, S., & Hornung, R. (2010). Tanning addiction: Current trends and future treatment. *Expert Review of Dermatology, 5*(2), 123–125.

Pope, C., Pope, H., Menard, W., Fay, C., Olivardia, R., & Phillips, K. (2005). Clinical features of muscle dysmorphia among males with body dysmorphic disorder. *Body Image, 4,* 395–400.

Pope, H. D., Jr., Oliva, P. S., Hudson, J. I., Bodkin, J. A., & Gruber, A. J. (1999). Attitudes toward DSM-IV dissociative disorders diagnoses among board-certified American psychiatrists. *American Journal of Psychiatry, 156*(2), 321–323.

Pope, H. G., & Brower, K. J. (2009). Anabolic-androgenic steroid-related disorders. In B. J. Sadock, V. A. Sadock, & P. Ruiz (Eds.), *Kaplan & Sadock's comprehensive textbook of psychiatry* (9th ed., Vol. I, pp. 1419–1431). Philadelphia, PA: Lippincott Williams & Wilkins.

Pope, H. G., Jr., Gruber, A. J., Mangweth, B., Bureau, B., deCol, C., Jouvent, R., & Hudson, J. I. (2000). Body image perception among men in three countries. *American Journal of Psychiatry, 157,* 1297–1301.

Pope, K. S. (1996). Memory, abuse, and science: Questioning claims about the false memory syndrome epidemic. *American Psychologist, 51,* 957–974.

Pope, K. S. (1997). Science as careful questioning: Are claims of a false memory syndrome epidemic based on empirical evidence? *American Psychologist, 52,* 997–1006.

Portenoy, R., & Mathur, G. (2009). Cancer pain. In S.-C. J. Yeung, C. P. Escalante, & R. F. Gagel (Eds.), *Medical care of the cancer patient* (pp. 60–71). Shelton, CT: PMPH USA Ltd.

Post, L., Page, C., Conner, T., & Prokhorov, A. (2010). Elder abuse in long-term care: Types, patterns, and risk factors. *Research on Aging, 32*(3), 323.

Post, R. M. (1992). Transduction of psychosocial stress into the neurobiology of recurrent affective disorder. *American Journal of Psychiatry, 149*(8), 999–1010.

Post, R. M., Rubinow, D. R., Uhde, T. W., Roy-Byrne, P. P., Linnoila, M., Rosoff, A., & Cowdry, R. (1989). Dysphoric mania: Clinical and biological correlates. *Archives of General Psychiatry, 46,* 353–358.

Potenza, M. N., Steinberg, M. A., Skudlarski, P., Fulbright, R. K., Lacadie, C. M., Wilber, M. K., ... Wexler, B. E. (2003). Gambling urges in pathological gambling: A functional magnetic resonance imaging study. *Archives of General Psychiatry, 60,* 828–836.

Powell, R. A., & Howell, A. J. (1998). Effectiveness of treatment for dissociative identity disorder. *Psychological Reports, 83,* 483–490.

Pratt, S. I., Mueser, K. T., Driscoll, M., Wolfe, R., & Bartels, S. J. (2006). Medication nonadherence in older people with serious mental illness: Prevalence and correlates. *Psychiatric Rehabilitation Journal, 29,* 299–310.

Prause, N., & Janssen, E. (2006). Blood flow: Vaginal photoplethysmography. In Goldstein, I., Meston, C. M., Davis, S. R., & Traish, A. M. (Eds.), *Women's sexual function and dysfunction: Study, diagnostic, and treatment* (pp. 359–367). New York, NY: Taylor and Francis.

Prelior, E. F., Yutzy, S. H., Dean, J. T., & Wetzel, R. D. (1993). Briquet's syndrome, dissociation and abuse. *American Journal of Psychiatry, 150,* 1507–1511.

Preskorn, S. H. (1995). Comparison of the tolerability of bupropion, fluoxetine, imipramine, nefazodone, paroxetine, sertraline, and venlafaxine. *Journal of Clinical Psychiatry, 56*(Suppl. 6), 12–21.

Presley, C. A., & Meilman, P. W. (1992). *Alcohol and drugs on American college campuses: A report to college presidents.* Carbondale, IL: Southern Illinois University Press.

Price, J. R., Mitchell, E., Tidy, E., & Hunot, V. (2008). Cognitive behaviour therapy for chronic fatigue syndrome in adults. *Cochrane Database of Systematic Reviews, 3,* CD001027. doi:10.1002/14651858.CD001027.pub2

Pridal, C. G., & LoPiccolo, J. (2000). Multi-element treatment of desire disorders: Integration of cognitive, behavioral and systemic therapy. In S. R. Leiblum & R. C. Rosen (Eds.), *Principles and practice of sex therapy* (3rd ed., pp. 57–81). New York, NY: Guilford Press.

Prien, R. F., & Potter, W. Z. (1993). Maintenance treatment for mood disorders. In D. L. Dunner (Ed.), *Current psychiatric therapy* (pp. 255–260). Philadelphia, PA: W. B. Saunders.

Prince, M. (1906–1907). Hysteria from the point of view of dissociated personality. *Journal of Abnormal Psychology, 1,* 170–187.

Prins, J., van der Meer, J., & Bleijenberg, G. (2006). Chronic fatigue syndrome. *Lancet, 367,* 346–355.

pro-ana-nation. (2010). Home page. Retrieved from http://www.pro-ana-nation.com/v1/index.php

Pruzinsky, T. (1988). Collaboration of plastic surgeon and medical psychotherapist: Elective cosmetic surgery. *Medical Psychotherapy, 1,* 1–13.

Pueschel, S. M., & Goldstein, A. (1991). Genetic counseling. In J. L. Matson & J. A. Mulick (Eds.), *Handbook of mental retardation* (2nd ed., pp. 279–291). Elmsford, NY: Pergamon Press.

Pugliese, M. T., Weyman-Daun, M., Moses, N., & Lifshitz, F. (1987). Parental health beliefs as a cause of nonorganic failure to thrive. *Pediatrics, 80,* 175–182.

Purcell, S., Wray, N., Stone, J., Visscher, P., O'Donovan, M., Sullivan, P., ... Morris, D. W. (2009). Common polygenic variation contributes to risk of schizophrenia and bipolar disorder. *Nature, 460,* 748–752.

Purdon, C. (1999). Thought suppression and psychopathology. *Behaviour Research and Therapy, 37,* 1029–1054.

Purdon, C. (2009). Psychological approaches to understanding obsessive-compulsive disorder. In M. M. Antony & M. B. Stein (Eds.), *Oxford handbook of anxiety and related disorders* (pp. 238–249). New York, NY: Oxford University Press.

Pury, C. L. S., & Mineka, S. (1997). Covariation bias for blood–injury stimuli and aversion outcomes. *Behavior Research and Therapy, 35*, 35–47.

Putnam, F. W. (1992). Altered states: Peeling away the layers of a multiple personality. *Sciences, 32*(6), 30–36.

Putnam, F. W., Guroff, J. J., Silberman, E. K., Barban, L., & Post, R. M. (1986). The clinical phenomenology of multiple personality disorder: Review of 100 recent cases. *Journal of Clinical Psychiatry, 47*, 285–293.

Quality Assurance Project. (1990). Treatment outlines for paranoid, schizotypal, and schizoid personality disorders. *Australian and New Zealand Journal of Psychiatry, 24*, 339–350.

Quay, H. C. (1993). The psychobiology of undersocialized aggressive conduct disorder: A theoretical perspective. *Development and Psychopathology, 5*, 165–180.

Quinsey, V. L. (2010). Coercive paraphilic disorder. *Archives of Sexual Behavior, 39*, 405–410.

Rabe, S., Zoellner, T., Beauducel, A., Maercker, A., & Karl, A. (2008). Changes in brain electrical activity after cognitive behavioral therapy for posttraumatic stress disorder in patients injured in motor vehicle accidents. *Psychosomatic Medicine, 70*(1), 13–19.

Rabins, P. V. (2006). *Guideline watch: Practice guidelines for the treatment of patients with Alzheimer's disease and other dementias of late life*. Washington, DC: American Psychiatric Association.

Rachman, S. (1978). *Fear and courage*. San Francisco: W. H. Freeman.

Rachman, S. (1991). Neo-conditioning and the classical theory of fear acquisition. *Clinical Psychology Review, 11*, 155–173.

Rachman, S. (2002). Fears born and bred: Non-associative fear acquisition? *Behaviour Research and Therapy, 40*, 121–126.

Rachman, S., & de Silva, P. (1978). Abnormal and normal obsessions. *Behaviour Research and Therapy, 16*, 233–248.

Rachman, S., & Hodgson, R. (1968). Experimentally induced "sexual fetishism": Replication and development. *Psychological Record, 18*(1), 25–27.

Radnitz, C. L., Appelbaum, K. A., Blanchard, E. B., Elliott, L., & Andrasik, F. (1988). The effect of self-regulatory treatment on pain behavior in chronic headache. *Behaviour Research and Therapy, 26*, 253–260.

Rado, S. (1962). Theory and therapy: The theory of schizotypal organization and its application to the treatment of decompensated schizotypal behavior. In S. Rado (Ed.), *Psychoanalysis of behavior* (Vol. 2, pp. 127–140). New York, NY: Grune & Stratton.

Rafii, M., & Aisen, P. (2009). Recent developments in Alzheimer's disease therapeutics. *BMC Medicine, 7*(1), 7.

Rahkonen, T., Eloniemi-Sulkava, U., Paanila, S., Halonen, P., Sivenius, J., & Sulkava, R. (2001). Systematic intervention for supporting community care of elderly people after a delirium episode. *International Psychogeriatrics, 13*(1), 37–49.

Rakison, D. H. (2009). Does women's greater fear of snakes and spiders originate in infancy? *Evolution and Human Behavior, 30*(6), 438–444.

Ramsawh, H. J., Morgentaler, A., Covino, N., Barlow, D. H., & DeWolf, W. C. (2005). Quality of life following simultaneous placement of penile prosthesis with radical prostatectomy. *Journal of Urology, 174*(4, Part 1 of 2), 1395–1398.

Ramsawh, H. J., Raffa, S. D., White, K. S., & Barlow, D. H. (2008). Risk factors for isolated sleep paralysis in an African American sample: A preliminary study. *Behavior Therapy, 39*(4), 386–397.

Ramsay, J. (2009). Evidence-based psychosocial treatments for adult ADHD: A review. *Current Attention Disorders Reports, 1*(2), 85–91. doi:10.1007/s12618-009-0012-5

Ranjith, G., & Mohan, R. (2004). Dhat syndrome: A functional somatic syndrome? (Letter to the editor). *British Journal of Psychiatry*, pp. 200–209.

Ranson, M. B., Nichols, D. S., Rouse, S. V., & Harrington, J. L. (2009). Changing or replacing an established psychological assessment standard: Issues, goals, and problems with special reference to recent developments in the MMPI-2. In J. N. Butcher (Ed.), *Oxford handbook of personality assessment* (pp. 112–139). New York: Oxford University Press.

Rao, U., Hammen, C., & Poland, R. (2009). Mechanisms underlying the comorbidity between depressive and addictive disorders in adolescents: Interactions between stress and HPA activity. *American Journal of Psychiatry, 166*(3), 361.

Rapee, R. M., & Melville, L. F. (1997). Recall of family factors in social phobia and panic disorder: Comparison of mother and offspring reports. *Depression and Anxiety, 5*, 7–11.

Rapee, R. M., Schniering, C. A., & Hudson, J. L. (2009). Anxiety disorders during childhood and adolescence: Origins and treatment. *Annual Review of Clinical Psychology, 5*, 311–341.

Rappaport, J., & Berger, J. (2010). Genetic testing and HIV dementia: Teasing out the molecular mechanisms of disease. *AIDS, 24*(10), 1585.

Rasmussen, S. A., & Eisen, J. L. (1990). Epidemiology of obsessive-compulsive disorder. *Journal of Clinical Psychiatry, 51*, 10–14.

Rasmussen, S. A., & Tsuang, M. T. (1984). The epidemiology of obsessive-compulsive disorder. *Journal of Clinical Psychiatry, 45*, 450–457.

Rasmussen, S. A., & Tsuang, M. T. (1986). Clinical characteristics and family history in DSM-III obsessive-compulsive disorder. *American Journal of Psychiatry, 143*, 317–322.

Rasmussen, A. M., Anderson, G. M., Krishnan-Sarin, S., Wu, R., & Paliwal, P. (2006). A decrease in plasma DHEA to cortisol ratio during smoking abstinence may predict relapse: A preliminary study. *Psychopharmacology, 186*, 473–480.

Rassin, E., & Koster, E. (2003). The correlation between thought–action fusion and religiosity in a normal sample. *Behaviour Research and Therapy, 41*, 361–368.

Rathod, N. H., Addenbrooke, W. M., & Rosenbach, A. F. (2005). Heroin dependence in an English town: 33-year follow-up. *British Journal of Psychiatry, 187*, 421–425.

Rauch, S. L., Phillips, K. A., Segal, E., Markis, N., Shin, L. M., Whalen, P. J., ... Kennedy, D. N. (2003). A preliminary morphometric magnetic resonance imaging study of regional brain volumes in body dysmorphic disorder. *Psychiatry Research, 122*, 13–19.

Ravussin, E., Valencia, M. E., Esparza, J., Bennett, P. H., & Schulz, L. O. (1994). Effects of a traditional lifestyle on obesity in Pima Indians. *Diabetes Care, 17*, 1067–1074.

Ray, W. A., Gurwitz, J., Decker, M. D., & Kennedy, D. L. (1992). Medications and the safety of the older driver: Is there a basis for concern? Special issue: Safety and mobility of elderly drivers: II. *Human Factors, 34*(1), 33–47.

Raymond, N. C., Coleman, E., Ohlerking, F., Christenson, G. A., & Miner, M. (1999). Psychiatric comorbidity in pedophilic sex offenders. *American Journal of Psychiatry, 156*, 786–788.

Razran, G. (1961). The observable unconscious and the inferable conscious in current Soviet psychophysiology: Interoceptive conditioning, semantic conditioning, and the orienting reflex. *Psychological Review, 68*, 81–150.

Rea, M., Tompson, M. C., & Miklowitz, D. J. (2003). Family-focused treatment versus individual treatment for bipolar disorder: Results of a randomized clinical trial. *Journal of Consulting and Clinical Psychology, 71*, 482–492.

Redd, W. H., & Andrykowski, M. A. (1982). Behavioral intervention in cancer treatment: Controlling aversion reactions to chemotherapy. *Journal of Consulting and Clinical Psychology, 50*, 1018–1029.

Reddy, L. A., Newman, E., De Thomas, C. A., & Chun, V. (2009). Effectiveness of school-based prevention and intervention programs for children and adolescents with emotional disturbance: A meta-analysis. *Journal of School Psychology, 47*(2), 77–99.

Regier, D. A., Narrow, W. E., Kuhl, E. A., & Kupfer, D. J. (2009). The conceptual development of DSM-V. *American Journal of Psychiatry, 166*(6), 645–650.

Reichardt, C. S. (2006). The principle of parallelism in the design of studies to estimate treatment effects. *Psychological Methods, 11*, 1–18.

Reichborn-Kjennerud, T., Czajkowski, N., Roysamb, E., Orstavik, R. E., Neale, M. C., Torgersen, S., Kendler, K. S.. (2009). Major depression and dimensional representations of DSM-IV personality disorders: A population-based twin study. *Psychological Medicine, 40*, 1475–1484 .

Reilly-Harrington, N. A., Alloy, L. B., Fresco, D. M., & Whitehouse, W. G. (1999). Cognitive styles and life events interact to predict bipolar and unipolar symptomatology. *Journal of Abnormal Psychology, 108*(4), 567–578.

Reilly-Harrington, N. A., Deckersbach, T., Knauz, R., Wu, Y., Tran, T., Eidelman, P., ... Nierenberg, A. A. (2007). Cognitive behavioral therapy for rapid-cycling bipolar disorder: A pilot study. *Journal of Psychiatric Practice, 13*(5), 291–297.

Reitan, R. M., & Davison, I. A. (1974). *Clinical neuropsychology: Current status and applications*. Washington, DC: V. H. Winston.

Rekers, G. A., Kilgus, M., & Rosen, A. C. (1990). Long-term effects of treatment for gender identity disorder of childhood. *Journal of Psychology & Human Sexuality, 3*(2), 121–153.

Report of the Advisory Panel on Alzheimer's Disease. (1995). *Alzheimer's disease and related dementias: Biomedical update.* U.S. Department of Health and Human Services. Washington, DC: U.S. Government Printing Office.

Repp, A. C., & Singh, N. N. (1990). *Perspectives on the use of nonaversive and aversive interventions for persons with developmental disabilities*. Sycamore, IL: Sycamore Publishing.

Rescorla, R. A. (1988). Pavlovian conditioning: It's not what you think it is. *American Psychologist, 43*(3), 151–160.

Resick, P. A., Monson, C. M., & Rizvi, S. L. (2008). Posttraumatic stress disorder. In D. H. Barlow (Ed.), *Clinical handbook of psychological disorders* (4th ed.). New York, NY: Guilford Press.

Resnick, H. S., Kilpatrick, D. G., Dansky, B. S., Saunders, B. E., & Best, C. L. (1993). Prevalence of civilian trauma in posttraumatic stress disorder in a representative national sample of women. *Journal of Consulting and Clinical Psychology, 61*, 984–991.

Reynolds, C. F., III. (2009). Prevention of depressive disorders: A brave new world. *Depression and Anxiety, 26*(12), 1062–1065.

Ricciardelli, L. A., & McCabe, M. P. (2004). A biopsychosocial model of disordered eating and the pursuit of muscularity in adolescent boys. *Psychological Bulletin, 130*, 170–205.

Rice, G., Anderson, C., Risch, N., & Ebers, G. (1999). Male homosexuality: Absence of linkage to microsatellite markers at Xq28. *Science, 284*, 665–667.

Rice, M. E., & Harris, G. T. (2002). Men who molest their sexually immature daughters: Is a special explanation required? *Journal of Abnormal Psychology, 111*, 329–339.

Richards, S. S., & Sweet, R. A. (2009). Dementia. In B. J. Sadock, V. A. Sadock, & P. Ruiz (Eds.), *Kaplan & Sadock's comprehensive textbook of psychiatry* (9th ed., Vol. I, pp. 1167–1198). Philadelphia, PA: Lippincott Williams & Wilkins.

Richardson, G. S. (2006). Shift work sleep disorder. In T. Lee-Chiong (Ed.), *Sleep: A comprehensive handbook* (pp. 395–399). Hoboken, NJ: John Wiley & Sons.

Rickels, K., Schweizer, E., Case, W. G., & Greenblatt, D. J. (1990). Long-term therapeutic use of benzodiazepines: I. Effects of abrupt discontinuation. *Archives of General Psychiatry, 47*, 899–907.

Riding, A. (1992, November 17). New catechism for Catholics defines sins of modern world. *New York Times*, pp. A1, A16.

Rief, W., Hiller, W., & Margraf, J. (1998). Cognitive aspects of hypochondriasis and the somatization syndrome. *Journal of Abnormal Psychology, 107*, 587–595.

Riemann, D., Berger, M., & Voderholzer, U. (2001). Sleep and depression—Results from psychobiological studies: An overview. *Biological Psychology, 57*, 67–103.

Riggins v. Nevada, 112 S. Ct. 1810 (1992).

Riggs, J. E. (1993). Smoking and Alzheimer's disease: Protective effect or differential survival bias? *Lancet, 342*, 793–794.

Ringel, J., Ellickson, P., & Collins, R. (2007). High school drug use predicts job-related outcomes at age 29. *Addictive Behaviors, 32*(3), 576–589.

Ritterband, L. M., Thorndike, F. P., Gonder-Frederick, L. A., Magee, J. C., Bailey, E. T., Saylor, D. K., Morin, C. M. (2009). Efficacy of an internet-based behavioral intervention for adults with insomnia. *Arch Gen Psychiatry, 66*(7), 692–698. doi: 10.1001/archgenpsychiatry.2009.66

Roberts, A., Cash, T., Feingold, A., & Johnson, B. (2006). Are black–white differences in females' body dissatisfaction decreasing? A meta-analytic review. *Journal of Consulting and Clinical Psychology, 74*, 1121–1131.

Roberts, L. W., Hoop, J. G., & Dunn, L. B. (2008). Ethical aspects of psychiatry. In R. E. Hales, S. C. Yudofsky, & G. O. Gabbard (Eds.), *The American Psychiatric Publishing textbook of psychiatry* (5th ed., pp. 1601–1636). Arlington, VA: American Psychiatric Publishing, Inc.

Roberts, R. E., Kaplan, G. A., Shema, S. J., & Strawbridge, W. J. (1997). Does growing old increase the risk for depression? *American Journal of Psychiatry, 154*, 1384–1390.

Roberts, R. E., Roberts, C. R., & Chen, I. G. (2000). Ethnocultural differences in sleep complaints among adolescents. *The Journal of Nervous and Mental Disease, 188*, 222–229.

Robertson, N. (1988). *Getting better: Inside Alcoholics Anonymous*. New York, NY: William Morrow.

Robins, L. N. (1966). *Deviant children grown up: A sociological and psychiatric study of sociopathic personality*. Baltimore, MD: Williams & Wilkins.

Robins, L. N. (1978). Sturdy childhood predictors of adult antisocial behavior: Replications from longitudinal studies. *Psychological Medicine, 8*, 611–622.

Robinson, G. E., Fernald, R. D., & Clayton, D. F. (2008). Genes and social behavior. *Science, 322*, 896–899.

Robinson, R. G., Jorge, R. E., Moser, D. J., Acion, L., Solodkin, A., Small, S. L., ... Arndt, S. (2008). Escitalopram and problem-solving therapy for prevention of poststroke depression: A randomized controlled trial: Correction. *JAMA: Journal of the American Medical Association, 301*(10).

Robles, T., Glaser, R., & Kiecolt-Glaser, J. (2005). Out of balance: A new look at chronic stress, depression, and immunity. *Current Directions in Psychological Science, 14*, 111–115.

Rockney, R. M., & Lemke, T. (1992). Casualties from a junior–senior high school during the Persian Gulf war: Toxic poisoning or mass hysteria? *Developmental and Behavioral Pediatrics, 13*(5), 339–342.

Rockwood, K., & Middleton, L. (2007). Physical activity and the maintenance of cognitive function. *Alzheimer's & Dementia: The Journal of the Alzheimer's Association, 3*(2), S38–S44.

Rodin, J., & Langer, E. J. (1977). Long-term effects of a controlled relevant intervention with the institutionalized aged. *Journal of Personality and Social Psychology, 35*(12), 897–902.

Rodin, J., & Salovey, P. (1989). Health psychology. *Annual Review of Psychology, 40*, 533–579.

Roelofs, K., Keijsers, G. P., Hoogduin, K. A., Naring, G. W., & Moene, F. C. (2002). Childhood abuse in patients with conversion disorder. *American Journal of Psychiatry, 159*, 1908–1913.

Roemer, L., & Borkovec, T. D. (1993). Worry: Unwanted cognitive activity that controls unwanted somatic experience. In D. M. Wegner & J. W. Pennebaker (Eds.), *Handbook of mental control*. Englewood Cliffs, NJ: Prentice Hall.

Roemer, L., & Orsillo, S. M. (2002). Expanding our conceptualization of and treatment for generalized anxiety disorder: Integrating mindfulness/acceptance-based approaches with existing cognitive-behavioral models. *Clinical Psychology: Science and Practice, 9*, 54–68.

Roemer, L., & Orsillo, S. M. (2007). An open trial of an acceptance-based behavior therapy for generalized anxiety disorder. *Behavior Therapy, 38*(1), 72–85.

Roemer, L., Orsillo, S. M., & Barlow, D. H. (2002). Generalized anxiety disorder. In D. H. Barlow, *Anxiety and its disorders: The nature and treatment of anxiety and panic* (2nd ed.). New York, NY: Guilford Press.

Rogers, S. J. (2009). What are infant siblings teaching us about autism in infancy? *Autism Research, 2*(3), 125–137.

Rogler, L. (2007). Framing research on culture in psychiatric diagnosis. In J. E. Mezzich & G. Caracci (Eds.), *Cultural formulation: A reader for psychiatric diagnosis* (pp. 151–166). Lanham, MD: Jason Aronson Inc.

Roid, G. H., & Pomplun, M. (2005). Interpreting the Stanford-Binet intelligence scales (5th ed.). In D. P. Flanagan & P. L. Harrison, (Eds.). *Contemporary intellectual assessment: Theories, tests, and issues* (2nd ed., pp. 325–343). New York, NY: Guilford Press.

Rojo, L., Conesa, L., Bermudez, O., & Livianos, L. (2006). Influence of stress in the onset of eating disorders: Data from a two-stage epidemiologic-controlled study. (2006). *Psychosomatic Medicine, 68*, 628–635.

Rollman, B. L., Belnap, B. H., & Mazumdar, S. (2005). A randomized trial to improve the quality of treatment for panic and generalized anxiety disorders in primary care. *Archives of General Psychiatry, 62*, 1332–1341.

Roma, P. G., Champoux, M., & Suomi, S. J. (2006). Environmental control, social context, and individual differences in behavioral and cortisol responses to novelty in infant rhesus monkeys. *Child Development, 77*, 118–131.

Romano, J. M., Jensen, M. P., Turner, J. A., Good, A. B., & Hops, H. (2000). Chronic pain patient–partner interactions: Further support for a behavioral model of chronic pain. *Behavior Therapy, 31*, 415–440.

Room, R., & Greenfield, T. (2006). Alcoholics Anonymous, other 12-step movements and psychotherapy in the US population, 1990. *Addiction, 88*(4), 555–562.

Root, T. L., Pinheiro, A. P., Thornton, L., Strober, M., Fernandez-Aranda, F., Brandt, H., ... Bulk, C. M.. (2010). Substance use disorders in women with anorexia nervosa. *International Journal of Eating Disorders, 43*(1), 14–21.

Rorschach, H. (1951). *Psychodiagnostics.* New York, NY: Grune & Stratton. (Original work published 1921).

Rosen, J. C., & Leitenberg, H. (1985). Exposure plus response prevention treatment of bulimia. In D. M. Garner & P. E. Garfinkel (Eds.), *Handbook of psychotherapy for anorexia nervosa and bulimia* (pp. 193–209). New York, NY: Guilford Press.

Rosen, J. C., Reiter, J., & Orosan, P. (1995). Cognitive-behavioral body image therapy for body dysmorphic disorder. *Journal of Consulting Clinical Psychology, 63,* 263–269.

Rosen, L. W., Shafer, C. L., Dummer, G. M., Cross, L. K., Deuman, G. W., & Malmberg, S. R. (1988). Prevalence of pathogenic weight-control behaviors among Native American women and girls. *International Journal of Eating Disorders, 7*(6), 807–811.

Rosen, R. C. (2000). Medical and psychological interventions for erectile dysfunction: Toward a combined treatment approach. In S. R. Leiblum & R. C. Rosen (Eds.), *Principles and practice of sex therapy* (3rd ed., pp. 276–304). New York, NY: Guilford Press.

Rosen, R. C. (2007). Erectile dysfunction: Integration of medical and psychological approaches. In S. R. Leiblum (Ed.), *Principles and practice of sex therapy* (4th ed., pp. 277–312). New York, NY: Guilford Press.

Rosen, R. C., & Beck, J. G. (1988). *Patterns of sexual arousal: Psychophysiological processes and clinical applications.* New York, NY: Guilford Press.

Rosen, R. C., & Leiblum, S. R. (1995). Treatment of sexual disorders in the 1990s: An integrated approach. *Journal of Consulting and Clinical Psychology, 63,* 877–890.

Rosen, R., Wing, R., Schneider, S., & Gendrano, N. (2005). Epidemiology of erectile dysfunction: The role of medical comorbidities and lifestyle factors. *Urological Clinics of North America, 32,* 403–417.

Rosenbaum, M. (2000). Psychogenic seizures—Why women? *Psychosomatics, 41*(2), 147–149.

Rosenberg, R. N., Richter, R. W., Risser, R. C., Taubman, K., Prado-Farmer, I., Ebalo, E., ... Schellenberg, G. D. (1996). Genetic factors for the development of Alzheimer's disease in the Cherokee Indian. *Archives of Neurology, 53,* 997–1000.

Rosengren, A., Tibblin, G., & Wilhelmsen, L. (1991). Self-perceived psychological stress and incidence of coronary artery disease in middle-aged men. *American Journal of Cardiology, 68,* 1171–1175.

Rosenman, R. H., Brand, R. J., Jenkins, C. D., Friedman, M., Straus, R., & Wurm, M. (1975). Coronary heart disease in the Western Collaborative Group Study: Final follow-up experience of 8 years. *JAMA: Journal of the American Medical Association, 233,* 872–877.

Rosenthal, D. (Ed.). (1963). *The Genain quadruplets: A case study and theoretical analysis of heredity and environment in schizophrenia.* New York, NY: Basic Books.

Ross, A. O., & Pelham, W. E. (1981). Child psychopathology. *Annual Review of Psychology, 32,* 243–278.

Ross, C. A. (1997). *Dissociative identity disorder.* New York, NY: John Wiley.

Ross, C. A. (2009). Dissociative amnesia and dissociative fugue. In P. F. Dell & J. A. O'Neil (Eds.), *Dissociation and the dissociative disorders* (pp. 429–434). New York, NY: Routledge.

Ross, C. A., Anderson, G., Fleisher, W. P., & Norton, G. R. (1991). The frequency of multiple personality disorder among psychiatric inpatients. *American Journal of Psychiatry, 148,* 1717–1720.

Ross, C. A., Miller, S. D., Reagor, P., Bjornson, L., Fraser, G. A., & Anderson, G. (1990). Structured interview data on 102 cases of multiple personality disorder from four centers. *American Journal of Psychiatry, 147,* 596–601.

Ross, M. W., Walinder, J., Lundstrom, B., & Thuwe, I. (1981). Cross-cultural approaches to transsexualism: A comparison between Sweden and Australia. *Acta Psychiatrica Scandinavica, 63,* 75–82.

Rothblum, E. D. (2002). Gay and lesbian body images. In T. F. Cash & T. Pruzinsky (Eds.), *Body image: A handbook of theory, research and clinical practice* (pp. 257–265). New York, NY: Guilford Press.

Rottenberg, J., Gross, J. J., Wilhelm, F. H., Najmi, S., & Gotlib, I. H. (2002). Crying threshold and intensity in major depressive disorder. *Journal of Abnormal Psychology, 111,* 302–312.

Rottenberg, J., Gross, J., & Gotlib, I. (2005). Emotion content insensitivity in major depressive disorder. *Journal of Abnormal Psychology, 114,* 627–639.

Rottenberg, J., & Johnson, S. L. (2007). *Emotion and psychopathology: Bridging affective and clinical science.* Washington, DC: American Psychological Association.

Rouff, L. (2000). Schizoid personality traits among the homeless mentally ill: A quantitative and qualitative report. *Journal of Social Distress and the Homeless, 9,* 127–141.

Roush, W. (1997). Herbert Benson: Mind–body maverick pushes the envelope. *Science, 276,* 357–359.

Rowe, J. B. (2010). Conversion disorder: Understanding the pathogenic links between emotion and motor systems in the brain. *Brain, 133*(Pt. 5), 1295–1297.

Roy-Byrne, P. P., & Katon, W. (2000). Anxiety management in the medical setting: Rationale, barriers to diagnosis and treatment, and proposed solutions. In D. I. Mostofsky & D. H. Barlow (Eds.), *The management of stress and anxiety in medical disorders* (pp. 1–14). Needham Heights, MA: Allyn & Bacon.

Rubin, R. T. (1982). Koro (Shook Yang): A culture-bound psychogenic syndrome. In C. T. H. Friedmann & R. A. Fauger (Eds.), *Extraordinary disorders of human behavior* (pp. 155–172). New York, NY: Plenum Press.

Ruchkin, V., Schwab-Stone, M., Jones, S., Cicchetti, D. V., Koposov, R., & Vermeiren, R. (2005). Is posttraumatic stress in youth a culture-bound phenomenon? A comparison of symptom trends in selected U.S. and Russian communities. *American Journal of Psychiatry, 162,* 538–544.

Rück, C., Karlsson, A., Steele, J. D., Edman, G., Meyerson, B. A., Ericson, K., ... Svanborg, P. (2008). Capsulotomy for obsessive-compulsive disorder: Long-term follow-up of 25 patients. *Archives of General Psychiatry, 65*(8), 914–921.

Rudaz, M., Craske, M. G., Becker, E. S., Ledermann, T., & Margraf, J. (2010). Health anxiety and fear of fear in panic disorder and agoraphobia vs. social phobia: A prospective longitudinal study. *Depression and Anxiety, 27,* 404–411.

Rudd, M. D., Joiner, Y., & Rajab, M. H. (2001). *Treating suicidal behavior.* New York, NY: Guilford Press.

Rudd, M. D., Rajab, M. H., Orman, D. T., Stulman, D. A., Joiner, T., & Dixon, W. (1996). Effectiveness of an outpatient intervention targeting suicidal young adults: Preliminary results. *Journal of Consulting and Clinical Psychology, 64,* 179–190.

Rudolph, K. D. (2009). Adolescent depression. In I. H. Gotlib & C. L. Hammen (Eds.), *Handbook of depression* (2nd ed., pp. 444–466). New York, NY: Guilford Press.

Rudolph, K. D., & Conley, C. S. (2005). The socioemotional costs and benefits of social-evaluative concerns: Do girls care too much? *Journal of Personality, 73*(1), 115–137.

Rupprecht, R., Rammes, G., Eser, D., Baghai, T. C., Schule, C., Nothdurfter, C., ... Kucher, K. (2009). Translocator protein (18 kD) as target for anxiolytics without benzodiazepine-like side effects. *Science, 325*(5939), 490–493.

Rush, A. (2007). STAR*D: What have we learned? *American Journal of Psychiatry, 164,* 201–204.

Rush, A. J., Erman, M. K., Giles, D. E., Schlesser, M. A., Carpenter, G., Vasavada, N., & Roffwarg, H. P. (1986). Polysomnographic findings in recently drug-free and clinically remitted depressed patients. *Archives of General Psychiatry, 43,* 878–884.

Russell, G. F. M. (1979). Bulimia nervosa: An ominous variant of anorexia nervosa. *Psychological Medicine, 9,* 429–448.

Russo, S. J., Mazei-Robison, M. S., Ables, J. L., & Nestler, E. J. (2009). Neurotrophic factors and structural plasticity in addiction. *Neuropharmacology, 56*(Suppl. 1), 73–82. doi:10.1016/j.neuropharm.2008.06.059

Rutter, M. (2002). The interplay of nature, nurture, and developmental influences: The challenge ahead for mental health. *Archives of General Psychiatry, 59,* 996–1000.

Rutter, M. (2006). *Genes and behavior: Nature–nurture interplay.* Oxford, UK: Blackwell.

Rutter, M. (2010). Gene–environment interplay. *Depression and Anxiety, 27*(1), 1–4.

Rutter, M., & Giller, H. (1984). *Juvenile delinquency: Trends and perspectives.* New York, NY: Guilford Press.

Rutter, M., Moffitt, T. E., & Caspi, A. (2006). Gene–environment interplay and psychopathology: Multiple varieties but real effects. *Journal of Child Psychology and Psychiatry, 47,* 226–261.

Ryan, W. D. (1992). The pharmacologic treatment of child and adolescent depression. *Psychiatric Clinics of North America, 15,* 29–40.

Ryder, A. G., Yang, J., Zhu, X., Yao, S., Yi, J., Heine, S. J., & Bagby, R. M. (2008). The cultural shaping of depression: Somatic symptoms in China, psychological symptoms in North America? *Journal of Abnormal Psychology, 117*(2), 300–313.

Saab, P. G., Llabre, M. M., Hurwitz, B. E., Frame, C. A., Reineke, I., Fins, A. I., ... Schneiderman, N. (1992). Myocardial and peripheral vascular responses to behavioral challenges and their stability in black and white Americans. *Psychophysiology, 29*(4), 384–397.

Sachs, G. S., & Rush, A. J. (2003). Response, remission, and recovery in bipolar disorders: What are the realistic treatment goals? *Journal of Clinical Psychiatry, 64*, 18–22.

Sachs, G. S., Nierenberg, A. A., Calabrese, J. R., Marangell, L. B., Wisniewski, S. R., Gyulai, L., ... Thase, M. E. (2007). Effectiveness of adjunctive antidepressant treatment for bipolar depression. *New England Journal of Medicine, 356*(17), 1711–1722.

Sackeim, H., Haskett, R., Mulsant, B., Thase, M., Mann, J., Pettinati, H., ... Prudic, J. (2001). Continuation pharmacotherapy in the prevention of relapse following electroconvulsive therapy: A randomized controlled trial. *JAMA: Journal of the American Medical Association, 285*, 1299–1307.

Sackeim, H. A., & Devanand, D. P. (1991). Dissociative disorders. In M. Hersen & S. M. Turner (Eds.), *Adult psychopathology & diagnosis* (2nd ed., pp. 279–322). New York, NY: John Wiley.

Sackeim, H. A., Nordlie, J. W., & Gur, R. C. (1979). A model of hysterical and hypnotic blindness: Cognition, motivation and awareness. *Journal of Abnormal Psychology, 88*, 474–489.

Sackett, D. L., Strauss, S. E., Richardson, W. S., Rosenberg, W., & Haynes, R. B. (2000). *Evidence-based medicine: How to practice and teach EBM* (2nd ed.). London, UK: Churchill Livingstone.

Sahler, O., Fairclough, D., Phipps, S., Mukhern, R., Dolgin, M., & Noll, R. (2005). Using problem-solving skills training to reduce negative affectivity in mothers of children with newly diagnosed cancer: Report of a multisite randomized trial. *Journal of Consulting and Clinical Psychology, 73*, 272–283.

Saigh, P. A. (1984). Pre- and postinvasion anxiety in Lebanon. *Behavior Therapy, 15*, 185–190.

Sakai, J. T., & Crowley, T. J. (2009). Inhalant-related disorders. In B. J. Sadock, V. A. Sadock, & P. Ruiz (Eds.), *Kaplan & Sadock's comprehensive textbook of psychiatry* (9th ed., Vol. 1, pp. 1341–1353). Philadelphia, PA: Lippincott Williams & Wilkins.

Sakel, M. (1958). *Schizophrenia*. New York, NY: Philosophical Library.

Sakheim, D. K., Barlow, D. H., Abrahamson, D. J., & Beck, J. G. (1987). Distinguishing between organogenic and psychogenic erectile dysfunction. *Behaviour Research and Therapy, 25*, 379–390.

Saleh, F., Malin, H., Grudzinskas, A., Jr., & Vitacco, M. (2010). Paraphilias with comorbid psychopathy: The clinical and legal significance to sex offender assessments. *Behavioral Sciences & the Law, 28*(2), 211–223.

Salekin, R. T. (2006). Psychopathy in children and adolescents: Key issues in conceptualization and assessment. In C. J. Patrick (Ed.), *Handbook of psychopathy* (pp. 389–414). New York, NY: Guilford Press.

Salekin, R. T., Rogers, R., & Sewell, K. W. (1997). Construct validity of psychopathy in a female offender sample: A multitrait–multimethod evaluation. *Journal of Abnormal Psychology, 106*(4), 576–585. doi:10.1037/0021-843x.106.4.576

Salkovskis, P., Shafran, R., Rachman, S., & Freeston, M. H. (1999). Multiple pathways to inflated responsibility beliefs in obsessional problems: Possible origins and implications for therapy and research. *Behaviour Therapy and Research, 37*, 1055–1072.

Salkovskis, P., Warwick, H., & Deale, A. (2003). Cognitive-behavioral treatment for severe and persistent health anxiety. *Brief Treatment and Crisis Intervention, 3*, 353–367.

Salkovskis, P. M., Atha, C., & Storer, D. (1990). Cognitive-behavioural problem solving in the treatment of patients who repeatedly attempt suicide: A controlled trial. *British Journal of Psychiatry, 157*, 871–876.

Salkovskis, P. M., & Campbell, P. (1994). Thought suppression induces intrusion in naturally occurring negative intrusive thoughts. *Behaviour Research and Therapy, 32*(1), 1–8.

Salkovskis, P. M., & Clark, D. M. (1993). Panic disorders and hypochondriasis. Special issue: Panic, cognitions, and sensations. *Advances in Behavioral Research and Therapy, 5*, 23–48.

Saln-Pascual, R. J., Castao, A., Shiromani, P. J., Valencia-Flores, M., & Campos, R. M. (2006). Caffeine challenge in insomniac patients after total sleep deprivation. *Sleep Medicine, 7*, 141–145.

Salzman, C. (1991). Pharmacologic treatment of the anxious elderly patient. In C. Salzman & B. D. Lebowitz (Eds.), *Anxiety in the elderly: Treatment and research* (pp. 149–173). New York, NY: Springer.

Samuels, J., Bienvenu, O. J., III, Riddle, M. A., Cullen, B. A. M., Grados, M. A., Liang, K.-Y., ... Nestadt, G. (2002). Hoarding in obsessive compulsive disorder: Results from a case-control study. *Behaviour Research Therapy, 40*, 517–528.

Sanders, M. H., & Givelber, R. J. (2006). Overview of obstructive sleep apnea in adults. In T. Lee-Chiong (Ed.), *Sleep: A comprehensive handbook* (pp. 231–240). Hoboken, NJ: John Wiley & Sons.

Sanders, M. R. (1992). Enhancing the impact of behavioural family intervention with children: Emerging perspectives. *Behaviour Change, 9*, 115–119.

Sanderson, W. C., & Barlow, D. H. (1990). A description of patients diagnosed with DSM-III-R generalized anxiety disorder. *Journal of Nervous and Mental Disease, 178*, 588–591.

Sandin, B., Chorot, P., Santed, M., & Valiente, R. (2004). Differences in negative life events between patients with anxiety disorders, depression and hypochondriasis. *Anxiety, Stress & Coping: An International Journal, 17*, 37–47.

Sandys, J. (2007). Work and employment for people with intellectual and developmental disabilities. In I. Brown & M. Percy (Eds.), *A comprehensive guide to intellectual & developmental disabilities* (pp. 527–543). Baltimore, MD: Paul H. Brookes.

Sankey, A., Hill, C., Brown, J., Quinn, L., & Fletcher, A. (2006). A follow-up study of chronic fatigue syndrome in children and adolescents: Symptoms persistence and school absenteeism. *Clinical Child Psychology and Psychiatry, 11*, 126–138.

Sano, M., Ernesto, C., Thomas, R. G., Klauber, M. R., Schafer, K., Grundman, M., ... Thal, L. J. (1997). A controlled trial of selegiline, alpha-tocopherol, or both as treatment for Alzheimer's disease. *New England Journal of Medicine, 336*, 1216–1222.

Santarelli, L., Saxe, M., Gross, C., Surget, A., Battaglia, F., Dulawa, S., ... Hen, R. (2003). Requirement of hippocampal neurogenesis for the behavioral effects of antidepressants. *Science, 301*, 805–809.

Santosh, P. J. (2009). Medication for children and adolescents: Current issues. In M. G. Gelder, N. C. Andreasen, J. J. Lopez-Ibor, Jr. & J. R. Geddes (Eds.), *New Oxford textbook of psychiatry* (2nd ed., Vol. 2, pp. 1793–1798). Oxford, UK: Oxford University Press.

Santucci, L. C., Ehrenreich, J. T., Trosper, S. E., Bennett, S. M., & Pincus, D. B. (2009). Development and preliminary evaluation of a one-week summer treatment program for separation anxiety disorder. *Cognitive and Behavioral Practice, 16*, 317–331.

Sapolsky, R. (2004). Is impaired neurogenesis relevant to the affective symptoms of depression? *Biological Psychiatry, 56*, 137–139.

Sapolsky, R. M. (2000a). Genetic hyping. *The Sciences, 40*(2), 12–15.

Sapolsky, R. M. (2000b). Glucocorticoids and hippocampal atrophy in neuropsychiatric disorders. *Archives of General Psychiatry, 57*, 925–935.

Sapolsky, R. M. (2002). *A primate's memoir*. New York, NY: Simon & Schuster.

Sapolsky, R. M. (2007). Stress, stress-related disease, and emotional regulation. In J. J. Gross (Ed.), *Handbook of emotion regulation* (pp. 606–615). New York, NY: Guilford Press.

Sapolsky, R. M., & Meaney, M. J. (1986). Maturation of the adrenal stress response: Neuroendocrine control mechanisms and the stress hyporesponsive period. *Brain Research Review, 11*, 65–76.

Sapolsky, R. M., & Ray, J. C. (1989). Styles of dominance and their endocrine correlates among wild, live baboons. *American Journal of Primatology, 18*(1), 1–13.

Sarbin, T., & Mancuso, J. (1980). *Schizophrenia: Medical diagnosis or moral verdict?* Elmsford, NY: Pergamon Press.

Sarwer, D. B., & Durlak, J. A. (1997). A field trial of the effectiveness of behavioral treatment for sexual dysfunctions. *Journal of Sex and Marital Therapy, 23*, 87–97.

Sarwer, D. B., Foster, G. D., & Wadden, T. A. (2004). Treatment of obesity I: Adult obesity. In J. K. Thompson (ed.). *Handbook of eating disorders and obesity* (pp. 421–442). New York, NY: John Wiley.

Sass, K. J., Sass, A., Westerveld, M., Lencz, T., Novelly, R. A., Kim, J. H., & Spender, D. D. (1992). Specificity in the correlation of verbal memory and hippocampal neuron loss: Dissociation of memory, language, and verbal intellectual ability. *Journal of Clinical and Experimental Neuropsychology, 14*(5), 662–672.

Saudino, J. J., Pedersen, N. L., Lichenstein, P., McClearn, G. E., & Plomin, R. (1997). Can personality explain genetic influence on life events? *Journal of Personality & Social Psychology, 72*(1), 196–206.

Saudino, K. J., & Plomin, R. (1996). Personality and behavioral genetics: Where have we been and where are we going? *Journal of Research in Personality, 30,* 335–347.

Saudino, K. J., Plomin, R., & DeFries, J. C. (1996). Tester-rated temperament at 14, 20, and 24 months: Environmental change and genetic continuity. *British Journal of Developmental Psychology, 14,* 129–144.

Savard, J., Savard, M.-H., & Morin, C. M. (2010). Insomnia. In M. M. Antony & D. H. Barlow (Eds.), *Handbook of assessment and treatment planning for psychological disorders* (2nd ed.). New York, NY: Guilford.

Savin-Williams, R. (2006). Who's gay? Does it matter? *Current Directions in Psychological Science, 15,* 40–44.

Saxe, G. N., Stoddard, F., Hall, E., Chawla, N., Lopez, C., Sheridan, R., ... Yehuda, R. (2005). Pathways to PTSD: Part I. Children with burns. *American Journal of Psychiatry, 162,* 1299–1304.

Saxe, G. N., van der Kolk, B. A., Berkowitz, R., Chinman, G., Hall, K., Leiberg, G., & Schwartz, J. (1993). Dissociative disorders in psychiatric inpatients. *American Journal of Psychiatry, 150,* 1037–1042.

Saxena, S., & Prasad, K. (1989). DSM-III subclassifications of dissociative disorders applied to psychiatric outpatients in India. *American Journal of Psychiatry, 146,* 261–262.

Scarmeas, N., Albert, S. M., Manly, J. J., & Stern, Y. (2006). Education and rates of cognitive decline in incident Alzheimer's disease. *Journal of Neurology, Neurosurgery, and Psychiatry, 77*(3), 308–316.

Schacter, D. L. (Ed.) (1995). *Memory distortion: How minds, brains, and societies reconstruct the past.* Cambridge, MA: Harvard University Press.

Schacter, D. L., Chiu, P., & Ochsner, K. N. (1993). Implicit memory: A selective review. *Annual Review of Neuroscience, 16,* 159–182.

Schatzberg, A., Rush, J., Arnow, B., Banks, P., Blalock, J., Borian, F., Howland, R., ... Keller, M. B. (2005). Chronic depression: Medication (Nefazodone) or psychotherapy (CBASP) is effective when the other is not. *Archives of General Psychiatry, 62,* 513–520.

Scheerenberger, R. C. (1983). *A history of mental retardation.* Baltimore, MD: Paul H. Brookes.

Scheidt, P. C., Overpeck, M. D., Trifiletti, L. B., & Cheng, T. (2000). Child and adolescent injury research in 1998: A summary of abstracts submitted to the Ambulatory Pediatrics Association and the American Public Health Association. *Archives of Pediatrics and Adolescent Medicine, 154,* 442–445.

Scheier, M. F., Matthews, K. A., Owens, J. F., Magovern, G. J., Sr., Lefebvre, R. C., Abbott, R. A., & Carver, C. S. (1989). Dispositional optimism and recovery from coronary artery bypass surgery: The beneficial effects on physical and psychological well-being. *Journal of Personality and Social Psychology, 57*(6), 1024–1040.

Schiavi, R. C. (1990). Chronic alcoholism and male sexual dysfunction. *Journal of Sex and Marital Therapy, 16,* 23–33.

Schiavi, R. C., White, D., Mandeli, J., & Levine, A. C. (1997). Effect of testosterone administration on sexual behavior and mood in men with erectile dysfunction. *Archives of Sexual Behavior, 26,* 231–241.

Schiffer, B., Peschel, T., Paul, T., Gizewski, E., Forsting, M., Leygraf, N., ... Krueger, T. H. C. (2007). Structural brain abnormalities in the frontostriatal system and cerebellum in pedophilia. *Journal of Psychiatric Research, 41,* 753–762.

Schiffman, J., Walker, E., Ekstrom, M., Schulsinger, F., Sorensen, H., & Mednick, S. (2004). Childhood videotaped social and neuromotor precursors of schizophrenia: A prospective investigation. *American Journal of Psychiatry, 161*(11), 2021–2027.

Schildkraut, J. J. (1965). The catecholamine hypothesis of affective disorders: A review of supporting evidence. *American Journal of Psychiatry, 122,* 509–522.

Schlundt, O. G., & Johnson, W. G. (1990). *Eating disorders: Assessment and treatment.* Boston, MA: Allyn & Bacon.

Schmaling, K. B., Fiedelak, J. I., Katon, W. J., Bader, J. O., & Buchwald, D. S. (2003). Prospective study of the prognosis of unexplained chronic fatigue in a clinic-based cohort. *Psychosomatic Medicine, 65,* 1047–1054.

Schmitz, D., Netzer, C., & Henn, W. (2009). An offer you can't refuse? Ethical implications of non-invasive prenatal diagnosis. *Nature Reviews Genetics,10*(8), 515. doi:10.1038/nrg2631

Schneiderman, N. (2004). Psychosocial, behavioral, and biological aspects of chronic diseases. *Current Directions in Psychological Science, 13,* 247–251.

Schneier, F. R., Liebowitz, M. R., Beidel, D. C., Fyer, A. J., George, M. S., Heimberg, R. G., ... Versiani, M. (1996). Social phobia. In T. A. Widiger, A. J. Frances, H. A. Pincus, R. Ross, M. B. First, & W. W. Davis (Eds.), *DSM-IV sourcebook* (Vol. 2, pp. 507–548). Washington, DC: American Psychiatric Association.

Schnell, K., & Herpertz, S. C. (2007). Effects of dialectic-behavioral-therapy on the neural correlates of affective hyperarousal in borderline personality disorder. *Journal of Psychiatric Research, 41,* 837–847.

Schoenbach, V. J., Kaplan, B. H., Fredman, L., & Kleinbaum, D. G. (1986). Social ties and mortality in Evans County, Georgia. *American Journal of Epidemiology, 123,* 577.

Schoeneman, T. J. (1977). The role of mental illness in the European witchhunts of the sixteenth and seventeenth centuries: An assessment. *Journal of the History of the Behavioral Sciences, 13,* 337–351.

Schoenmakers, B., Buntinx, F., & DeLepeleire, J. (2010). Supporting the dementia family caregiver: The effect of home care intervention on general well-being. *Aging & Mental Health, 14*(1), 44–56.

Schover, L. R., & Jensen, S. B. (1988). *Sexuality and chronic illness: A comprehensive approach.* New York, NY: Guilford Press.

Schreiber, F. R. (1973). *Sybil.* Chicago, IL: Regnery.

Schreiner-Engel, P., & Schiavi, R. C. (1986). Lifetime psychopathology in individuals with low sexual desire. *Journal of Nervous and Mental Disease, 174,* 646–651.

Schuckit, M. A. (1994). Low level of response to alcohol as a predictor of future alcoholism. *American Journal of Psychiatry, 151,* 184–189.

Schuckit, M. A. (1998). Biological, psychological, and environmental predictors of alcoholism risk: A longitudinal study. *Journal of Studies on Alcohol, 59,* 485–494.

Schuckit, M. A. (2009). Alcohol-use disorders. *Lancet, 373*(9662), 492–501.

Schuckit, M. A. (2009a). Alcohol-related disorders. In B. J. Sadock, V. A. Sadock, & P. Ruiz (Eds.), *Kaplan & Sadock's comprehensive textbook of psychiatry* (9th ed., Vol. I, pp. 1268–1288). Philadelphia, PA: Lippincott Williams & Wilkins.

Schuckit, M. A. (2009b). Alcohol-use disorders. *Lancet, 373*(9662), 492–501.

Schuckit, M. A., Smith, T. L., Anthenelli, R., & Irwin, M. (1993). Clinical course of alcoholism in 636 male inpatients. *American Journal of Psychiatry, 150,* 786–792.

Schulberg, H. C., Block, M. R., Madonia, M. J., Scott, C. P., Rodriguez, E., Imber, S. D., ... Coulehan, J. L. (1996). Treating major depression in primary care practice: Eight-month clinical outcomes. *Archives of General Psychiatry, 53,* 913–919.

Schulsinger, F., Kety, S. S., & Rosenthal, D. (1979). A family study of suicide. In M. Schou & E. Stromgren (Eds.), *Origin, prevention, and treatment of affective disorders.* New York, NY: Academic Press.

Schultz, R. T., Romanski, L. M., & Tsatsanis, K. D. (2000). Neurofunctional models of autistic disorder and Asperger syndrome: Clues from neuroimaging. In A. Klin, F. R. Volkmar, & S. S. Sparrow (Eds.), *Asperger syndrome* (pp. 172–209). New York, NY: Guilford Press.

Schumacher, J., Jamra, R. A., Becker, T., Klopp, N., Franke, P., Jacob, C., ... Nöthen, M.M. (2005). Investigation of the DAOA/G30 locus in panic disorder. *Molecular Psychiatry, 10,* 428–429.

Schumann, C. M., & Amaral, D. G. (2006). Stereological analysis of amygdala neuron number in autism. *Journal of Neuroscience, 26,* 7674–7679.

Schutter, D. J. (2009). Antidepressant efficacy of high-frequency transcranial magnetic stimulation over the left dorsolateral prefrontal cortex in double-blind sham-controlled designs: A metaanalysis. *Psychological Medicine, 39*(1), 65–75.

Schwalberg, M. D., Barlow, D. H., Alger, S. A., & Howard, L. J. (1992). Comparison of bulimics, obese binge eaters, social phobics, and individuals with panic disorder or comorbidity across DSM-III-R anxiety. *Journal of Abnormal Psychology, 101,* 675–681.

Schwartz, A. J., & Whitaker, L. C. (1990). Suicide among college students: Assessment, treatment, and intervention. In S. J. Blumenthal & D. J. Kupfer (Eds.), *Suicide over the life cycle: Risk factors, assessment, and treatment of suicidal patients* (pp. 303–340). Washington, DC: American Psychiatric Press.

Schwartz, G. E., & Weiss, S. M. (1978). Behavioral medicine revisited: An amended definition. *Journal of Behavioral Medicine, 1,* 249–252.

Schwartz, J. M., Stoessel, P. W., Baxter, L. R., Martin, K. M., & Phelps, M. E. (1996). Systematic changes in cerebral glucose metabolic rate after successful behavior modification treatment of obsessive compulsive disorder. *Archives of General Psychiatry, 53,* 109–113.

Schwartz, M. B., & Brownell, K. D. (2007). Actions necessary to prevent childhood obesity: Creating the climate for change. *Journal of Law, Medicine, & Ethics, 35,* 78–89.

Schwartz, M. S., & Andrasik, F. (Eds.) (2003). *Biofeedback: A practitioner's guide* (3rd ed.). New York, NY: Guilford Press.

Schwartz, R., & Feisthamel, K. (2009). Disproportionate diagnosis of mental disorders among African American versus European American clients: Implications for counseling theory, research, and practice. *Journal of Counseling & Development, 87*(3), 295–301.

Schwartz, R. P., Jaffe, J. H., O'Grady, K. E., Das, B., Highfield, D. A., & Wilson, M. E. (2009). Scaling-up interim methadone maintenance: Treatment for 1,000 heroin-addicted individuals. *Journal of Substance Abuse Treatment, 37*(4), 362–367. doi:10.1016/j.jsat.2009.04.002

Schwarz, A. (2007, March 14). Wives united by husband's post-NFL trauma, *New York Times,* p. A1. Retrieved from http://www.nytimes.com

Scott, C. L., Hilty, D. M., & Brook, M. (2003). Impulse-control disorders not elsewhere classified. In R. E. Hales & S. C. Yudofsky (Eds.), *Textbook of clinical psychiatry* (4th ed., pp. 781–802). Washington, DC: American Psychiatric Publishing.

Scott, C. L., Quanbeck, C. D., & Resnick, P. J. (2008). Assessment of dangerousness. In R. E. Hales, S. C. Yudofsky, & G. O. Gabbard (Eds.), *The American Psychiatric Publishing textbook of psychiatry* (5th ed., pp. 1655–1672). Arlington, VA: American Psychiatric Publishing, Inc.

Scott, J. (1995). Psychotherapy for bipolar disorder. *British Journal of Psychiatry, 167,* 581–588.

Scott, J. E., & Dixon, L. B. (1995). Psychological interventions for schizophrenia. *Schizophrenia Bulletin, 21,* 621–630.

Sechi, G., & Serra, A. (2007). Wernicke's encephalopathy: New clinical settings and recent advances in diagnosis and management. *Lancet Neurology, 6*(5), 442–455.

Secko, D. (2005). Depression: More than just serotonin. *Canadian Medical Association Journal, 172,* 1551.

Sedlak, T. W., & Kaplin, A. I. (2009). Novel neurotransmitters. In B. J. Sadock, V. A. Sadock, & P. Ruiz (Eds.), *Kaplan & Sadock's comprehensive textbook of psychiatry* (9th ed., Vol. I, pp. 102–118). Philadelphia, PA: Lippincott Williams & Wilkins.

Seeman, P., Lee, T., Chau Wong, M., & Wong, K. (1976). Antipsychotic drug doses and neuroleptic/dopamine receptors. *Nature, 261,* 717–719.

Segal, N. (2006). Two monozygotic twin pairs discordant for female to male transsexualism. *Archives of Sexual Behavior, 35,* 347–358.

Segerstrom, S. C., & Sephton, S. E. (2010). Optimistic expectancies and cell-mediated immunity: The role of positive affect. *Psychological Science, 21,* 448–455.

Segraves, R., & Althof, S. (1998). Psychotherapy and pharmacotherapy of sexual dysfunctions. In P. E. Nathan & J. M. Gorman (Eds.), *A guide to treatments that work* (pp. 447–471). New York, NY: Oxford University Press.

Segraves, R., & Woodard, T. (2006). Female hypoactive sexual desire disorder: History and current status. *Journal of Sexual Medicine, 3,* 408–418.

Seligman, M. E. P. (1971). Phobias and preparedness. *Behavior Therapy, 2,* 307–320.

Seligman, M. E. P. (1975). *Helplessness: On depression, development, and death.* San Francisco, CA: W. H. Freeman.

Seligman, M. E. P. (1998). *Learned optimism* (2nd ed.). New York, NY: Simon & Schuster.

Seligman, M. E. P. (2002). *Authentic happiness: Using the new positive psychology to realize your potential for lasting fulfillment.* New York, NY: Free Press/Simon & Schuster.

Selye, H. (1936). A syndrome produced by diverse noxious agents. *Nature, 138,* 32.

Selye, H. (1950). *The physiology and pathology of exposure to stress.* Montreal, Canada: Acta.

Semans, J. H. (1956). Premature ejaculation: A new approach. *Southern Medical Journal, 49,* 353–358.

Seshadri, S., Fitzpatrick, A. L., Ikram, M. A., DeStefano, A. L., Gudnason, V., Boada, M., ... Breteler, M. M. (2010). Genome-wide analysis of genetic loci associated with Alzheimer disease. *JAMA: Journal of the American Medical Association, 303*(18), 1832–1840.

Setlik, J., Bond, G. R., & Ho, M. (2009). Adolescent prescription ADHD medication abuse is rising along with prescriptions for these medications. *Pediatrics, 124*(3), 875–880.

Seto, M., Cantor, J., & Blanchard, R. (2006). Child pornography offenses are a valid diagnostic indicator of pedophilia. *Journal of Abnormal Psychology, 115,* 610–615.

Seto, M. C. (2009). Pedophilia. In S. Nolen-Hoeksema, T. D. Cannon, & T. Widiger, T. (Eds.), *Annual review of clinical psychology* (Vol. 5, pp. 391–408). Palo Alto, CA: Annual Reviews.

Sevy, S., Robinson, D. G., Napolitano, B., Patel, R. C., Gunduz-Bruce, H., Miller, R., ... Kane, J. (2010). Are cannabis use disorders associated with an earlier age at onset of psychosis? A study in first episode schizophrenia. *Schizophrenia Research, 120*(1–3), 101–107.

Shaffer, D., Garland, A., Vieland, V., Underwood, M., & Busner, C. (1991). The impact of curriculum-based suicide prevention programs for teenagers. *Journal of the American Academy of Child and Adolescent Psychiatry, 30*(4), 588–596.

Shaffer, D., Leibenluft, E., Rohde, L. A., Sirovatka, P., & Regier, D. A. (Eds.). (2009). *Externalizing disorders of childhood: Refining the research agenda for DSM-V.* Arlington, VA: American Psychiatric Association.

Shaffer, D. R. (1993). *Developmental psychology: Childhood and adolescence* (3rd ed.). Pacific Grove, CA: Brooks/Cole.

Shafran, R., Lee, M., Payne, E., & Fairburn, C. G. (2006). The impact of manipulating personal standards on eating attitudes and behaviour. *Behaviour Research and Therapy, 44,* 897–906.

Shapiro, D. A., Rees, A., Barkham, M., Hardy, G., Reynolds, S., & Startup, M. (1995). Effects of treatment duration and severity of depression on the maintenance of gains after cognitive-behavioral and psychodynamic-interpersonal psychotherapy. *Journal of Consulting and Clinical Psychology, 63,* 378–387.

Shapiro, E. S., & Lentz, F. E. (1991). Vocational-technical programs: Follow-up of students with learning disabilities. *Exceptional Children, 58,* 47–59.

Shapiro, J. R., Berkman, N. D., Brownley, K. A., Sedway, J. A., Lohr, K. N., & Bulik, C. M. (2007). Bulimia nervosa treatment: A systematic review of randomized controlled trials. *International Journal of Eating Disorders, 40*(4), 321–336.

Sharp, T. (2009). Neurotransmitters and signalling. In M. G. Gelder, N. C. Andreasen, J. J. Lopez-Ibor, Jr., & J. R. Geddes (Eds.), *New Oxford textbook of psychiatry* (2nd ed., Vol. 1, pp. 168–176). Oxford, UK: Oxford University Press.

Sharpe, M. (1992). Fatigue and chronic fatigue syndrome. *Current Opinion in Psychiatry, 5,* 207–212.

Sharpe, M. (1993). *Chronic fatigue syndrome* (pp. 298–317). Chichester, UK: John Wiley.

Sharpe, M. (1997). Chronic fatigue. In D. M. Clark & C. G. Fairburn (Eds.), *Science and practice of cognitive behavior therapy* (pp. 381–414). Oxford, UK: Oxford University Press.

Sharpe, M., Clements, A., Hawton, K., Young, A., Sargent, P., & Cowen, P. (1996). Increased prolactin response to buspirone in chronic fatigue syndrome. *Journal of Affective Disorders, 41,* 71–76.

Shatkin, J. P., & Ivanenko, A. (2009). Pediatric sleep disorders. In B. J. Sadock, V. A. Sadock & P. Ruiz (Eds.), *Kaplan & Sadock's comprehensive textbook of psychiatry* (9th ed., Vol. I, pp. 3903–3908). Philadelphia, PA: Lippincott Williams & Wilkins.

Shattuck, P. T. (2006). The contribution of diagnostic substitution to the growing administrative prevalence of autism in U.S. special education. *Pediatrics, 117,* 1028–1037.

Shaw, D. S., Dishion, T. J., Supplee, L., Gardner, F., & Arnds, K. (2006). Randomized trial of a family-centered approach to the prevention of early conduct problems: 2-year effects of the family checkup in early childhood. *Journal of Consulting and Clinical Psychology, 74,* 1–9.

Shaw, C., & Proctor, G. (2005). Women at the margins: A critique of the diagnosis of borderline personality disorder. *Feminism and Psychology, 15,* 483-490.

Shaywitz, S. (2003). *Overcoming dyslexia: A new and complete science-based program for overcoming reading problems at any level.* New York, NY: Knopf.

Shaywitz, S. E., Mody, M., & Shaywitz, B. A. (2006). Neural mechanisms in dyslexia. *Current Directions in Psychological Science, 15,* 278–281.

Shear, K. (2006). Adapting imaginal exposure to the treatment of complicated grief. In Rothbaum, B. (Ed.), *Pathological anxiety: Emotional processing in etiology and treatment* (pp. 215–226). New York, NY: Guilford Press.

Shear, K., Frank, E., Houck, P., & Reynolds, C. (2005). Treatment of complicated grief: A randomized controlled trial. *JAMA: Jour-*

nal of the American Medical Association, 293, 2601–2608.

Shear, K., Jin, R., Ruscio, A. M., Walters, E. E., & Kessler, R. C. (2006). Prevalence and correlates of estimated DSM-IV child and adult separation anxiety disorder in the National Comorbidity Survey Replication. American Journal of Psychiatry, 163(6), 1074–1083.

Shear, M. K., Brown, T. A., Barlow, D. H., Money, R., Sholomskas, D. E., Woods, S. W., ... Papp, L.A. (1997). Multicenter collaborative panic disorder severity scale. American Journal of Psychiatry, 154, 1571–1575.

Sheffield, J. K., Spence, S. H., Rapee, R. M., Kowalenko, N., Wignall, A., Davis, A., & McLoone, J. (2006). Evaluation of universal, indicated, and combined cognitive-behavioral approaches to the prevention of depression among adolescents. Journal of Consulting and Clinical Psychology, 74, 66–79.

Sheikh, J. I. (1992). Anxiety and its disorders in old age. In J. E. Birren, K. Sloan, & G. D. Cohen (Eds.), Handbook of mental health and aging (pp. 410–432). New York, NY: Academic Press.

Shenton, M. E., & Kubicki, M. (2009). Structural brain imaging in schizophrenia. In B. J. Sadock, V. A. Sadock, & P. Ruiz (Eds.), Kaplan & Sadock's comprehensive textbook of psychiatry (9th ed., Vol. I, pp. 1494–1507). Philadelphia, PA: Lippincott Williams & Wilkins.

Sher, K. J., Martinez, J. A., & Littlefield, A. K. (2011). Alcohol use and alcohol use disorders. In D. H. Barlow (Ed.), Oxford handbook of clinical psychology (pp. 405–445). New York, NY: Oxford University.

Sherbourne, C. D., Hays, R. D., & Wells, K. B. (1995). Personal and psychosocial risk factors for physical and mental health outcomes and course of depression among depressed patients. Journal of Consulting and Clinical Psychology, 63, 345–355.

Shimizu, M., Kubota, Y., Toichi, M., & Baba, H. (2007). Folie à deux and shared psychotic disorder. Current Psychiatry Reports, 9(3), 200–205. doi:10.1007/s11920-007-0019-5

Shin, L. M., Lasko, N. B., Macklin, M. L., Karpf, R. D., Milad, M. R., Orr, S. P., ... Pitman, R. K. (2009). Resting metabolic activity in the cingulate cortex and vulnerability to posttraumatic stress disorder. Archives of General Psychiatry, 66(10), 1099–1107.

Shin, L. M., Shin, P. S., Heckers, S., Krangel, T. S., Macklin, M. L., Orr, S. P., ... Rauch, S. L. (2004). Hippocampal function in posttraumatic stress disorder. Hippocampus, 14, 292–300.

Shneidman, E. S. (1989). Approaches and commonalities of suicide. In R. F. W. Diekstra, R. Mariss, S. Platt, A. Schmidtke, & G. Sonneck (Eds.), Suicide and its prevention: The role of attitude and imitation. Advances in Suicidology (Vol. 1). Leiden, Netherlands: E. J. Brill.

Shneidman, E. S., Farberow, N. L., & Litman, R. E. (Eds.) (1970). The psychology of suicide. New York, NY: Science House.

Shulman, K. I., Cohen, C. A., Kirsh, F. C., Hull, I. M., & Champine, P. R. (2007). Assessment of testamentary capacity and vulnerability to undue influence. American Journal of Psychiatry, 164(5), 722–727.

Shumaker, S. A., Legault, C., Kuller, L., Rapp, S. R., Thal, L., Lane, D. S., ... Coker, L. H. & Women's Health Initiative Memory Study. (2004). Conjugated equine estrogens and incidence of probable dementia and mild cognitive impairment in postmenopausal women: Women's Health Initiative Memory Study. JAMA: Journal of the American Medical Association, 291, 3005–3007.

Sidani, S., Miranda, J., Epstein, D. R., Bootzin, R. R., Cousins, J., & Moritz, P. (2009). Relationships between personal beliefs and treatment acceptability, and preferences for behavioral treatments. Behaviour Research and Therapy, 47(10), 823–829.

Sierra, M., & Berrios, G. E. (1998). Depersonalization: Neurobiological perspectives. Society of Biological Psychiatry, 44, 898–908.

Siever, L. J. (1992). Schizophrenia spectrum personality disorders. In A. T. M. B. Riba (Ed.), Review of psychiatry (Vol. 11, pp. 25–42). Washington, DC: American Psychiatric Press.

Siever, L. J., & Davis, K. L. (2004). The pathophysiology of schizophrenia disorders: Perspectives from the spectrum. American Journal of Psychiatry, 161, 398–413.

Siever, L. J., Davis, K. L., & Gorman, L. K. (1991). Pathogenesis of mood disorders. In K. Davis, H. Klar, & J. T. Coyle (Eds.), Foundations of psychiatry. Philadelphia, PA: W. B. Saunders.

Siffre, M. (1964). Beyond time (H. Briffaul, Trans.). New York, NY: McGraw-Hill.

Sigafoos, J., Arthur-Kelly, M., & Butterfield, N. (2006). Enhancing everyday communication for children with disabilities. Baltimore, MD: Paul H. Brookes.

Sigafoos, J., Green, V. A., Schlosser, R., O'Reilly, M. F., Lancioni, G. E., Rispoli, M., Lang, R.. (2009). Communication intervention in Rett syndrome: A systematic review. Research in Autism Spectrum Disorders, 3(2), 304–318.

Sigvardsson, S., Cloninger, C. R., Bohman, M., & von-Knorring, A. L. (1982). Predisposition to petty criminality in Swedish adoptees. Archives of General Psychiatry, 39, 1248–1253.

Sikich, L. (2009). Early onset psychotic disorders. In B. J. Sadock, V. A. Sadock, & P. Ruiz (Eds.), Kaplan & Sadock's comprehensive textbook of psychiatry (9th ed., Vol. II, pp. 3699–3706). Philadelphia, PA: Lippincott Williams & Wilkins.

Silove, D. M., Marnane, C. L., Wagner, R., Manicavasagar, V. L., & Rees, S. (2010). The prevalence and correlates of adult separation anxiety disorder in an anxiety clinic. BMC Psychiatry, 10, 21.

Silver, E., Cirincione, C., & Steadman, H. J. (1994). Demythologizing inaccurate perceptions of the insanity defense. Law and Human Behavior, 18, 63–70.

Silverman, W. K., & La Greca, A. M. (2002). Children experiencing disasters: Definitions, reactions, and predictors of outcomes. In A. N. La Greca, W. K. Silverman, & M. C. Roberts (Eds.), Helping Children Cope with Disasters and Terrorism (Vol. 1, pp. 11–33). Washington, DC: American Psychological Association.

Silverman, W. K., & Rabian, B. (1993). Simple phobias. Child and Adolescent Psychiatric Clinics of North America, 2, 603–622.

Silverstone, T. (1985). Dopamine in manic depressive illness: A pharmacological synthesis. Journal of Affective Disorders, 8(3), 225–231.

Simeon, D. (2009). Neurobiology of depersonalization disorder. In P. F. Dell & J. A. O'Neil (Eds.), Dissociation and the dissociative disorders (pp. 367–372). New York, NY: Routledge.

Simeon, D., Guralnik, O., Hazlett, E. A., Spiegel-Cohen, J., Hollander, E., & Buchsbaum, M. S. (2000). Feeling unreal: A PET study of depersonalization disorder. American Journal of Psychiatry, 157, 1782–1788.

Simeon, D., Guralnik, O., Knutelska, M., Hollander, E., & Schmeidler, J. (2001). Hypothalamic–pituitary–adrenal axis dysregulation in depersonalization disorder. Neuropsychopharmacology, 25, 793–795.

Simeon, D., Knutelska, M., Nelson, D., & Guralnik, O. (2003). Feeling unreal: A depersonalization disorder update of 117 cases. Journal of Clinical Psychiatry, 64, 990–997.

Simmons, R., & Blyth, D. (1987). Moving into adolescence: The impact of pubertal change and school context. New York, NY: Aldine de Gruyter.

Simon, G. (2006). How can we know whether antidepressants increase suicide risk? American Journal of Psychiatry, 163, 1861–1863.

Simon, G. E., Gureje, O., & Fullerton, C. (2001). Course of hypochondriasis in an international primary care study. General Hospital Psychiatry, 23, 51–55.

Simon, R. I., & Shuman, D. W. (2008). Psychiatry and the law. In R. E. Hales, S. C. Yudofsky, & G. O. Gabbard (Eds.), The American Psychiatric Publishing textbook of psychiatry (5th ed., pp. 1555–1599). Arlington, VA: American Psychiatric Publishing.

Simon, R. I., & Shuman, D. W. (2009). Clinical-legal issues in psychiatry. In B. J. Sadock, V. A. Sadock, & P. Ruiz (Eds.), Kaplan & Sadock's comprehensive textbook of psychiatry (9th ed., Vol. II, pp. 4427–4439). Philadelphia, PA: Lippincott Williams & Wilkins.

Simoneau, T. L., Miklowitz, D. J., Richards, J. A., Saleem R., & George, E. L. (1999). Bipolar disorder and family communication: Effects of a psychoeducational treatment program. Journal of Abnormal Psychology, 108, 588–597.

Simons, A. D., Murphy, G. E., Levine, J. L., & Wetzel, R. D. (1986). Cognitive therapy and pharmacotherapy for depression: Sustained improvement over one year. Archives of General Psychiatry, 43(1), 43–48.

Simons, J. S., Dvorak, R. D., & Lau-Barraco, C. (2009). Behavioral inhibition and activation systems: Differences in substance use expectancy organization and activation in memory. Psychology of Addictive Behaviors, 23(2), 315–328. doi:10.1037/a0015834

Singer, M., & Flannery, D. J. (2000). The relationship between children's threats of violence and violent behaviors. Archives of Pediatrics and Adolescent Medicine, 154, 785–790.

Singh, M. K., DelBello, M. P., Kowatch, R. A., & Strakowski, S. M. (2006). Co-occurrence of bipolar and attention-deficit hyperactivity disorders in children. Bipolar Disorders, 8(6), 710–720.

Sivertsen, B., Omvik, S., Pallesen, S., Bjorvatn, B., Havik, O. E., Kvale, G., ... Nordhus, I. H. (2006). Cognitive behavioral therapy vs. zopiclone for treatment of chronic primary insomnia in older adults: A randomized controlled trial. *JAMA: Journal of the American Medical Association, 295*(24), 2851–2858. doi: 10.1001/jama.295.24.2851

Skhiri, D., Annabi, S., Bi, S., & Allani, D. (1982). Enfants d'immigrés: Facteurs de liens ou de rupture? *Annales Medico-Psychologiques, 140*, 597–602.

Skidmore, W., Linsenmeier, J., & Bailey, J. (2006). Gender nonconformity and psychological distress in lesbians and gay men. *Archives of Sexual Behavior, 35*, 685–697.

Skinner, B. F. (1948). *Walden two.* New York, NY: Macmillan.

Skinner, B. F. (1971). *Beyond freedom and dignity.* New York, NY: Knopf.

Skinner, M. D., & Aubin, H.-J. (2010). Craving's place in addiction theory: Contributions of the major models. *Neuroscience and Biobehavioral Reviews, 34*(4), 606–623. doi:10 .1016/j .neubiorev.2009.11.024

Skodol, A. E. (2005). Manifestations, clinical diagnosis, and comorbidity. In J. M. Oldham, A. E. Skodol, & D. S. Bender (Eds.), *Textbook of personality disorders* (pp. 57–87). Washington, DC: American Psychiatric Publishing.

Skodol, A. E., & Gunderson, J. G. (2008). Personality disorders. In R. E. Hales, S. C. Yudofsky, & G. O. Gabbard (Eds.), *The American Psychiatric Publishing textbook of psychiatry* (5th ed., pp. 821–860). Arlington, VA: American Psychiatric Publishing.

Skodol, A. E., Oldham, J. M., Bender, D. S., Dyck, I. R., Stout, R. L., & Morey, L. C., ... Gunderson, J. (2005). Dimensional representations of DSM-IV personality disorders: Relationships to functional impairment. *American Journal of Psychiatry, 162*, 1919–1925.

Sleet, D. A., Hammond, R., Jones, R., Thomas, N., & Whitt, B. (2003). Using psychology for injury and violence prevention in the community. In R. H. Rozensky, N. G. Johson, C. D. Goodheart, & R. Hammond (Eds.), *Psychology builds a healthy world* (pp. 185–216). Washington, DC: American Psychological Association.

Smeets, G., de Jong, P. J., & Mayer, B. (2000). If you suffer from a headache, then you have a brain tumour: Domain-specific reasoning "bias" and hypochondriasis. *Behaviour Research and Therapy, 38*, 763–776.

Smeets, I., Tan, E., Vossen, H., Leroy, P., Lousberg, R., van Os, J., Schieveld, J. (2010). Prolonged stay at the paediatric intensive care unit associated with paediatric delirium. *European Child & Adolescent Psychiatry, 19*(4), 389–393. doi:10.1007/s00787-009-0063-2

Smith, B. H., Barkley, R. A., & Shapiro, C. J. (2006). Combined child therapies. In R. A. Barkley (Ed.), *Attention-deficit hyperactivity disorder: A handbook for diagnosis and treatment* (3rd ed., pp. 678–691). New York, NY: Guilford Press.

Smith, D. E., Marcus, M. D., & Kaye, W. (1992). Cognitive-behavioral treatment of obese binge eaters. *International Journal of Eating Disorders, 12*, 257–262.

Smith, G. A., & Hall, J. A. (1982). Evaluating Michigan's guilty but mentally ill verdict: An empirical study. *Journal of Law Reform, 16*, 75–112.

Smith, G. P., & Gibbs, J. (2002). Peripheral physiological determinants for eating and body weight. In K. D. Brownell & C. G. Fairburn (Eds.), *Eating disorders and obesity: A comprehensive handbook* (2nd ed., pp. 8–12). New York, NY: Guilford Press.

Smith, G. T., & Oltmanns, T. F. (2009). Scientific advances in the diagnosis of psychopathology: Introduction to the special section. *Psychological Assessment, 21*(3), 241–242.

Smith, G. T., Simmons, J. R., Flory, K., Annus, A. M., & Hill, K. K. (2007). Thinness and eating expectancies predict subsequent binge-eating and purging behavior among adolescent girls. *Journal of Abnormal Psychology, 116*, 188–197.

Smith, P. M., Kraemer, H. C., Miller, N. H., DeBusk, R. F., & Taylor, C. B. (1999). In-hospital smoking cessation programs: Who responds, who doesn't? *Journal of Consulting and Clinical Psychology, 67*(1), 19–27.

Smith, T. W. (1992). Hostility and health: Current status of a psychosomatic hypothesis. *Health Psychology, 11*(3), 139–150.

Smith, W., Noonan, C., & Buchwald, D. (2006). Mortality in a cohort of chronically fatigued patients. *Psychological Medicine, 36*, 1301–1306.

Smolak, L., & Levine, M. P. (1996). Adolescent transitions and the development of eating problems. In L. Smolak, M. P. Levine, & R. Striegel-Moore (Eds.), *The developmental psychopathology of eating disorders: Implications for research, prevention, and treatment* (pp. 207–233). Mahwah, NJ: Erlbaum.

Smoller, J. W., Yamaki, L. H., & Fagerness, J. A. (2005). The corticotropin-releasing hormone gene and behavioral inhibition in children at risk for panic disorder. *Biological Psychiatry, 57*, 1485–1492.

Snelling, J., Sahai, A., & Ellis, H. (2003). Attitudes of medical and dental students to dissection. *Clinical Anatomy, 16*, 165–172.

Snowdon, D. A., Kemper, S. J. , Mortimer, J. A., Greiner, L. H., Wekstein, D. R., & Markesbery, W. R. (1996). Linguistic ability in early life and cognitive function and Alzheimer's disease in late life: Findings from the nun study. *JAMA: Journal of the American Medical Association, 275*(7), 528–532.

Snyder, S. H. (1976). The dopamine hypothesis of schizophrenia: Focus on the dopamine receptor. *American Journal of Psychiatry, 133*, 197–202.

Snyder, S. H. (1981). Opiate and benzodiazepine receptors. *Psychosomatics, 22*(11), 986–989.

Snyder, S. H., Burt, D. R., & Creese, I. (1976). Dopamine receptor of mammalian brain: Direct demonstration of binding to agonist and antagonist states. *Neuroscience Symposia, 1*, 28–49.

Sobell, M. B., & Sobell, L. C. (1978). *Behavioral treatment of alcohol problems.* New York, NY: Plenum Press.

Sobell, M. B., & Sobell, L. C. (1993). *Problem drinkers: Guided self-change treatment.* New York, NY: Guilford Press.

Society for Research in Child Development. (2007). Ethical Standards for Research with Children. Retrieved from www.srcd .org/ethicalstandards. html.

Soderstrom, H., Sjodin, A.-K., Carlstedt, A., & Forsman, A. (2004). Adult psychopathic personality with childhood-onset hyperactivity and conduct disorder: A central problem constellation in forensic psychiatry. *Psychiatry Research, 121*, 271–280.

Sohn, C., & Lam, R. (2005). Update on the biology of seasonal affective disorder. *CNS Spectrums, 10*, 635–646.

Sohn, M., & Bosinski, H. A. G. (2007). Gender identity disorders: Diagnostic and surgical aspects. *Journal of Sexual Medicine, 4*, 1193–1208.

Solai, L. K. K. (2009). Delirium. In B. J. Sadock, V. A. Sadock, & P. Ruiz (Eds.), *Kaplan & Sadock's comprehensive textbook of psychiatry* (9th ed., Vol. I, pp. 1153–1167). Philadelphia, PA: Lippincott Williams & Wilkins.

Soloff, P. H., Lynch, K. G., Kelley, T. M., Malone, K. M., & Mann, J. J. (2000). Characteristics of suicide attempts of patients with major depressive episode and borderline personality disorder: A comparative study. *American Journal of Psychiatry, 157*(4), 601–608.

Solomon, D. A., Leon, A. C., Endicott, J., Coryell, W. H., Mueller, T. I., Posternak, M. A., & Keller, M. B. (2003). Unipolar mania over the course of a 20-year follow-up study. *American Journal of Psychiatry, 160*, 2049–2051.

Solomon, R. L. (1980). The opponent-process theory of acquired motivation: The costs of pleasure and the benefits of pain. *American Psychologist, 35*, 691–712.

Solomon, R. L., & Corbit, J. D. (1974). An opponent process theory of motivation: I. Temporal dynamics of affect. *Psychological Review, 81*, 119–145.

Soreca, I., Frank, E., & Kupfer, D. J. (2009). The phenomenology of bipolar disorder: What drives the high rate of medical burden and determines long-term prognosis? *Depression and Anxiety, 26*(1), 73–82.

South, S. C., Oltmanns, T. F., & Krueger, R. F. (2011). The spectrum of personality disorders. In D. H. Barlow (Ed.), *Oxford handbook of clinical psychology* (pp. 530–550). New York, NY: Oxford University.

Spangler, D. L., Simons, A. D., Monroe, S. M., & Thase, M. E. (1997). Comparison of cognitive models of depression: Relationships between cognitive constructs and cognitive diathesis-stress match. *Journal of Abnormal Psychology, 106*, 395–403.

Spanos, N. P., Weeks, J. R., & Bertrand, L. D. (1985). Multiple personality: A social psychological perspective. *Journal of Abnormal Psychology, 92*, 362–376.

Spector, I. P., & Carey, M. P. (1990). Incidence and prevalence of the sexual dysfunctions: A critical review of the empirical literature. *Archives of Sexual Behavior, 19*(4), 389–408.

Spencer, T. J., Biederman, J., & Mick, E. (2007). Attention-deficit/hyperactivity disorder: Diagnosis, lifespan, comorbidities, and neurobiology. *Ambulatory Pediatrics, 7*(1, Suppl. 1), 73–81.

Spiegel, D. (1995). Hypnosis and suggestion. In D. L. Schacter (Ed.), *Memory distortion: How minds, brains, and societies reconstruct the past.* Cambridge, MA: Harvard University Press.

Spiegel, D. (2010). Dissociation in DSM-5. *Journal of Trauma and Dissociation.*

Spiegel, D., Bloom, J. R., Kramer, H. C., & Gotheil, E. (1989). Effect of psychosocial treatment on survival of patients with metastatic breast cancer. *Lancet, 14,* 888–891.

Spiegel, D., & Cardeña, E. (1991). Disintegrated experience: The dissociative disorders revisited. *Journal of Abnormal Psychology, 100*(3), 366–378.

Spiegel, D., Wiegel, M., Baker, S. L., & Greene, K. A. I. (2000). Pharmacological management of anxiety disorders. In D. I. Mostofsky & D. H. Barlow (Eds.), *The management of stress and anxiety in medical disorders* (pp. 36–65). Needham Heights, MA: Allyn & Bacon.

Spielberger, C. D., & Frank, R. G. (1992). Injury control: A promising field for psychologists. *American Psychologist, 47*(8), 1029–1030.

Spielman, A. J., & Glovinsky, P. (1991). The varied nature of insomnia. In P. J. Hauri (Ed.), *Case studies in insomnia* (pp. 1–15). New York, NY: Plenum Press.

Spinella, M. (2005). Mood in relation to subclinical symptoms. *International Journal of Neuroscience, 115,* 433–443.

Spinelli, M. G., & Endicott, J. (2003). Controlled clinical trial of interpersonal psychotherapy versus parenting education program for depressed pregnant women. *American Journal of Psychiatry, 160,* 555–562.

Spinelli, S., Chefer, S., Suomi, S. J., Higley, J. D., Barr, C. S., & Stein, E. (2009). Early-life stress induces long-term morphologic changes in primate brain. *Archives of General Psychiatry, 66*(6), 658–665.

Spira, A., Bajos, N., Bejin, A., Beltzer, N., Bozon, M., Ducot, M., ... Touzard, H. (1992). AIDS and sexual behavior in France. *Nature, 360,* 407–409.

Spitzer, R. L. (1999). Harmful dysfunction and the DSM definition of mental disorder. *Journal of Abnormal Psychology, 108,* 430–432.

Spitzer, R. L., Devlin, M. J., Walsh, B. T., Hasin, D., Wing, R., Marcus, M. D., ... Nonas, C. (1991). Binge eating disorder: To be or not to be in DSM-IV. *International Journal of Eating Disorders, 10,* 627–629.

Spitzer, R. L., Yanovski, S. Z., Wadden, T., Wing, R., Marcus, M., Stunkard, A., ... Horne, R. L. (1993). Binge eating disorder: Its further validation in a multi-site study. *International Journal of Eating Disorders, 13,* 137–153.

Spoont, M. R. (1992). Modulatory role of serotonin in neural information processing: Implications for human psychopathology. *Psychological Bulletin, 112*(2), 330–350.

Sprock, J. (2000). Gender-typed behavioral examples of histrionic personality disorder. *Journal of Psychopathology and Behavioral Assessment, 22,* 107–122.

Spurrell, E. B., Wilfley, D. E., Tanofsky, M. B., & Brownell, K. D. (1997). Age of onset for binge eating: Are there different pathways to binge eating? *International Journal of Eating Disorders, 21,* 55–65.

Staal, W. G., Pol, H. E. H., Schnack, H. G., Hoogendoorn, M. L. C., Jellema, K., & Kahn, R. S. (2000). Structural brain abnormalities in patients with schizophrenia and their healthy siblings. *American Journal of Psychiatry, 157,* 416–421.

Stahl, S. M. (2008). *Stahl's essential psychopharmacology* (3rd ed.). New York, NY: Cambridge University Press.

Stall, R., McKusick, L., Wiley, J., Coates, T. J., & Ostrow, D. G. (1986). Alcohol and drug use during sexual activity and compliance with safe sex guidelines for AIDS. *Health Education Quarterly, 13,* 359–371.

Stanley, B., & Brodsky, B. (2009). *Dialectical behavior therapy.* Arlington, VA: American Psychiatric Publishing.

Stanley, M. A., Beck, J. G., Novy, D. M., Averill, P. M., Swann, A. C., Diefenbach, G. J., & Hopko, D. R. (2003). Cognitive-behavioral treatment of late-life generalized anxiety disorder. *Journal of Consulting and Clinical Psychology, 71*(2), 309–319.

Stanley, M. A., Wilson, N. L., Novy, D. M., Rhoades, H. M., Wagener, P. D., Greisinger, A. J., ... Kunik, M. E. (2009). Cognitive behavior therapy for generalized anxiety disorder among older adults in primary care: a randomized clinical trial. *JAMA: Journal of the American Medical Association, 301*(14), 1460–1467.

State v. Campanaro, Nos. 632-79, 1309-79, 1317-79, 514-80, & 707-80 (S. Ct. N.J. Criminal Division, Union County 1980).

Stathopoulou, G., Powers, M. B., Berry, A. C., Smits, J. A. J., & Otto, M. W. (2006). Exercise interventions for mental health: A quantitative and qualitative review. *Clinical Psychology: Science and Practice, 13*(2), 179–193.

Steiger, A. (2008). Hormones and sleep. In S. R. Pandi-Perumal & J. Verster (Eds.), *Sleep disorders: Diagnosis and therapeutics* (pp. 457–466). Boca Raton, FL: Taylor & Francis.

Stein, M. B., Liebowitz, M. R., Lydiard, R. B., Pitts, C. D., Bushnell, W., & Gergel, I. (1998). Paroxetine treatment of generalized social phobia (social anxiety disorder). A randomized clinical trial. *JAMA: Journal of the American Medical Association, 280,* 708–713.

Stein, M. B., Schork, N. J., & Gelernter, J. (2007). Gene-by-environment (serotonin transporter and childhood maltreatment) interaction for anxiety sensitivity, an intermediate phenotype for anxiety disorders. *Neuropsychopharmacology, 33*(2), 312–319.

Stein, M. I. (1978). Thematic apperception test and related methods. In B. B. Wolman (Ed.), *Clinical diagnosis of mental disorders: A handbook* (pp. 179–235). New York, NY: Plenum Press.

Steinberg, A. B., & Phares, V. (2001). Family functioning, body image, and eating disturbances. In J. K. Thompson & L. Smolak (Eds.), *Body image, eating disorders, and obesity in youth: Assessment, prevention, and treatment* (pp. 127–147). Washington, DC: American Psychological Association.

Steinberg, M. (1991). The spectrum of depersonalization: Assessment and treatment. *Annual Review of Psychiatry, 10,* 223–247.

Steinglass, J. E., Sysko, R., Glasofer, D., Albano, A. M., Simpson, H. B., & Walsh, B. T. (2010). Rationale for the application of exposure and response prevention to the treatment of anorexia nervosa. *International Journal of Eating Disorders.* Advance online publication. doi:10.1002./eat.20784

Steketee, G., & Barlow, D. H. (2002). Obsessive-compulsive disorder. In D. H. Barlow, *Anxiety and its disorders: The nature and treatment of anxiety and panic* (2nd ed.). New York, NY: Guilford Press.

Steketee, G., & Frost, R. O. (2007a). *Compulsive hoarding and acquiring: Client workbook.* New York, NY: Oxford University Press.

Steketee, G., & Frost, R. O. (2007b). *Compulsive hoarding and acquiring: Therapist guide.* New York, NY: Oxford University Press.

Steketee, G., Quay, S., & White, K. (1991). Religion and guilt in OCD patients. *Journal of Anxiety Disorders, 5,* 359–367.

Stenvall, M., Olofsson, B., Lundstrom, M., Svensson, O., Nyberg, L., & Gustafson, Y. (2006). Inpatient falls and injuries in older patients treated for femoral neck fracture. *Archives of Gerontology and Geriatrics, 43*(3), 389–399.

Stepanski, E. J. (2006). Causes of insomnia. In T. Lee-Chiong (Ed.), *Sleep: A comprehensive handbook* (pp. 99–102). Hoboken, NJ: John Wiley & Sons.

Stern, Y. (2009). Cognitive reserve. *Neuropsychologia, 47*(10), 2015–2028.

Sterzer, P. (2010). Born to be criminal? What to make of early biological risk factors for criminal behavior. *American Journal of Psychiatry, 167*(1), 1–3. doi:10.1176/appi.ajp.2009.09111601

Stewart, S., Cutler, D., & Rosen, A. (2009). Forecasting the effects of obesity and smoking on US life expectancy. *The New England Journal of Medicine, 361*(23), 2252.

Stewart, S. E., Jenike, E., & Jenike, M. A. (2009). Biological treatment for obsessive-compulsive disorder. In M. M. Antony & M. B. Stein (Eds.), *Oxford handbook of anxiety and related disorders* (pp. 375–390). New York, NY: Oxford University Press.

Stice, E., Agras, W. S., Telch, C. F., Halmi, K. A., Mitchell, J. E., & Wilson, G. T. (2001). Sub-typing binge eating disordered women along dieting and negative affect dimension. *International Journal of Eating Disorders, 30,* 11–27.

Stice, E., Akutagawa, D., Gaggar, A., & Agras, W. S. (2000). Negative affect moderates the relation between dieting and binge eating. *International Journal of Eating Disorders, 27,* 218–229.

Stice, E., Cameron, R. P., Killen, J. D., Hayward, C., & Taylor, C. B. (1999). Naturalistic weight-reduction efforts prospectively predict growth in relative weight and onset of obesity among female adolescents. *Journal of Consulting and Clinical Psychology, 67,* 967–974.

Stice, E., Marti, C. N., Shaw, H., & Jaconis, M. (2009). An 8-year longitudinal study of the natural history of threshold, sub-threshold, and partial eating disorders from a community sample of adolescents. *Journal of Abnormal Psychology, 118*(3), 587–597.

Stice, E., Ng, J., & Shaw, H. (2010). Risk factors and prodromal eating pathology. *Journal of Child Psychology and Psychiatry and Allied Disciplines, 51*(4), 518–525.

Stice, E., Presnell, K., Shaw, H., & Rohde, P. (2005). Psychological and behavioral risk factors for obesity onset in adolescent girls: A prospective study. *Journal of Consulting and Clinical Psychology, 73,* 195–202.

Stice, E., Shaw, H., & Marti, C. N. (2007). A metaanalytic review of eating disorder prevention programs: Encouraging findings. *Annual Review of Clinical Psychology, 3,* 207–231.

Stock, W. (1993). Inhibited female orgasm. In W. O'Donohue & J. H. Geer (Eds.), *Handbook of sexual dysfunctions: Assessment and treatment* (pp. 253–277). Boston, MA: Allyn & Bacon.

Stoller, R. J. (1976). Two feminized male American Indians. *Archives of Sexual Behavior, 5,* 529–538.

Stone, G. C. (1987). The scope of health psychology. In G. C. Stone, S. M. Weiss, J. D. Matarazzo, N. E. Miller, J. Rodin, D. D. Belar, M. J. Follick, & J. E. Singer (Eds.), *Health psychology: A discipline and a profession.* Chicago, IL: University of Chicago Press.

Stone, J., Carson, A., Aditya, H., Prescott, R., Zaubi, M., Warlow, C., Sharpe, M. (2009). The role of physical injury in motor and sensory conversion symptoms: A systematic and narrative review. *Journal of Psychosomatic Research, 66*(5), 383–390.

Stone, J., Carson, A., Duncan, R., Coleman, R., Roberts, R., Warlow, C., et al. (2009). Symptoms 'unexplained by organic disease' in 1144 new neurology out-patients: How often does the diagnosis change at follow-up? *Brain, 132*(Pt. 10), 2878–2888.

Stone, J., LaFrance, W. C., Levenson, J. L., & Sharpe, M. (2010). Issues for DSM-5: Conversion disorder. *American Journal of Psychiatry, 167,* 626–627.

Stone, M. H. (1993). Cluster C personality disorders. In D. L. Dunner (Ed.), *Current psychiatric therapy* (pp. 411–417). Philadelphia, PA: W. B. Saunders.

Stone, R. (2000). Stress: The invisible hand in eastern Europe's death rates. *Science, 288,* 1732–1733.

Strain, E. C. (2009). Substance-related disorders. In B. J. Sadock, V. A. Sadock, & P. Ruiz (Eds.), *Kaplan & Sadock's comprehensive textbook of psychiatry* (9th ed., Vol. I, pp. 1237–1268). Philadelphia, PA: Lippincott Williams & Wilkins.

Strain, E. C., Lofwall, M. R., & Jaffe, J. H. (2009). Opioid-related disorders. In B. J. Sadock, V. A. Sadock, & P. Ruiz (Eds.), *Kaplan & Sadock's comprehensive textbook of psychiatry* (9th ed., Vol. I, pp. 1360–1387). Philadelphia, PA: Lippincott Williams & Wilkins.

Straus, S. E., Tosato, G., Armstrong, G., Lawley, T., Preble, O. T., Henle, W., ... Blaese, R. M. (1985). Persisting illness and fatigue in adults with evidence of Epstein Barr virus infection. *Annals of Internal Medicine, 102,* 7–16.

Strauss, J. L., Hayes, A. M., Johnson, S. L., Newman, C. F., Brown, G. K., Barber, J. P., ... Beck, A.T. (2006). Early alliance, alliance ruptures, and symptom change in a nonrandomized trial of cognitive therapy for avoidant and obsessive-compulsive personality disorders. *Journal of Consulting and Clinical Psychology, 74,* 337–345.

Stravynski, A., Elie, R., & Franche, R. L. (1989). Perception of early parenting by patients diagnosed with avoidant personality disorder: A test of the overprotection hypothesis. *Acta Psychiatrica Scandinavica, 80,* 415–420.

Strickland, B. R. (1992). Women and depression. *Current Directions in Psychological Science, 1*(4), 132–135.

Striegel-Moore, R., Rosselli, F., Wilson, G., Perrin, N., Harvey, K., & DeBar, L. (2010). Nocturnal eating: Association with binge eating, obesity, and psychological distress. *Clinical Psychology & Psychotherapy, 11,* 13.

Striegel-Moore, R. H., Cachelin, F. M., Dohm, F. A., Pike, M., Wilfley, D. E., & Fairburn, C. G. (2001). Comparison of binge eating disorder and bulimia nervosa in a community sample. *International Journal of Eating Disorders, 29,* 157–165.

Striegel-Moore, R. H., Dohm, F. A., Kaemer, H. C., Taylor, C. B., Daniels, S., Crawford, P. B., & Schreiber, G. B. (2003). Eating disorders in white and black women. *American Journal of Psychiatry, 160,* 1326–1331.

Striegel-Moore, R. H., & Franko, D. L. (2002). Body image issues among girls and women. In T. F. Cash & T. Pruzinsky (Eds.), *Body image: A handbook of theory, research and clinical practice* (pp. 183–191). New York, NY: Guilford Press.

Striegel-Moore, R. H., & Franko, D. L. (2008). Should binge eating disorder be included in the DSM-V? A critical review of the state of the evidence. *Annual Review of Clinical Psychology, 4,* 305–324.

Striegel-Moore, R. H., Franko, D. L., & Garcia, J. (2009). The validity and clinical utility of night eating syndrome. *International Journal of Eating Disorders, 42*(8), 720–738.

Striegel-Moore, R. H., Silberstein, L. R., & Rodin, J. (1986). Toward an understanding of risk factors for bulimia. *American Psychologist, 3,* 246–263.

Striegel-Moore, R. H., Silberstein, L. R., & Rodin, J. (1993). The social self in bulimia nervosa: Public self-consciousness, social anxiety, and perceived fraudulence. *Journal of Abnormal Psychology, 102*(2), 297–303.

Striegel-Moore, R. H., Wilson, G. T., DeBar, L., Perrin, N., Lynch, F., Rosselli, F., & Kraemer, H.C. (2010). Cognitive behavioral guided self-help for the treatment of recurrent binge eating. *Journal of Consulting and Clinical Psychology, 78*(3), 312–321.

Strike, P. C., & Steptoe, A. (2005). Behavioral and emotional triggers of acute coronary syndromes: A systematic review and critique. *Psychosomatic Medicine, 67,* 179–186.

Strober, M. (2002). Family–genetic perspectives on anorexia nervosa and bulimia nervosa. In K. D. Brownell & C. G. Fairburn (Eds.), *Eating disorders and obesity: A comprehensive handbook* (2nd ed., pp. 212–218). New York, NY: Guilford Press.

Strober, M., Freeman, R., Lampert, C., Diamond, J., & Kaye, W. (2000). Controlled family study of anorexia nervosa and bulimia nervosa: Evidence of shared liability and transmission of partial syndromes. *American Journal of Psychiatry, 157,* 393–401.

Strober, M., & Humphrey, L. L. (1987). Familial contributions to the etiology and course of anorexia nervosa and bulimia. Special issue: Eating disorders. *Journal of Consulting and Clinical Psychology, 55*(5), 654–659.

Stroebe, M., Stroebe, W., & Abakoumkin, G. (2005). The broken heart: Suicidal ideation in bereavement. *American Journal of Psychiatry, 162,* 2178–2180.

Stroup, T. S., & Lieberman, J. A. (Eds.). (2010). *Antipsychotic trials in schizophrenia: The CATIE project.* Cambridge, UK: Cambridge University Press.

Stunkard, A., Allison, K., & Lundgren, J. (2008). Issues for DSM-V: Night eating syndrome. *American Journal of Psychiatry, 165*(4), 424.

Suarez, E. C., Lewis, J. G., & Kuhn, C. (2002). The relation of aggression, hostility, and anger to lipopolysaccharide-stimulated tumor necrosis factor (TNF) by blood monocytes from normal men. *Behavior and Immunity, 16,* 675–684.

Suárez, L., Bennett, S., Goldstein, C., & Barlow, D. H. (2009). Understanding anxiety disorders from a "triple vulnerabilities" framework. In M. M. Antony & M. B. Stein (Eds.), *Oxford handbook of anxiety and related disorders* (pp. 153–172). New York, NY: Oxford.

Substance Abuse and Mental Health Services Administration, Office of Applied Studies. (2002). *Emergency department trends from the Drug Abuse Warning Network, final estimates 1994–2001.* (DAWN Series D-21, DHHS Publication No. (SMA) 02-3635). Rockville, MD: Author.

Substance Abuse and Mental Health Services Administration, Office of Applied Studies. (2006). Results from the 2005 national survey on drug use and health: National findings *NSDUH Series H–30, DHHS Publication No. SMA 06–4194.* Rockville, MD: Author.

Substance Abuse and Mental Health Services Administration, Office of Applied Studies. (2009). *Results from the 2008 National Survey on Drug Use and Health: National Findings* (NSDUH Series H-36, DHHS Publication No. (SMA) 09-4434). Rockville, MD: Author.

Sugiyama, T., & Abe, T. (1989). The prevalence of autism in Nagoya, Japan: A total population study. *Journal of Autism and Developmental Disorders, 19,* 87–96.

Sullivan, G. M., Kent, J. M., & Coplan, J. D. (2000). The neurobiology of stress and anxiety. In D. I. Mostofsky & D. H. Barlow (Eds.), *The management of stress and anxiety in medical disorders* (pp. 15–35). Needham Heights, MA: Allyn & Bacon.

Sullivan, G. M., & LeDoux, J. E. (2004). Synaptic self: Conditioned fear, developed adversity, and the anxious individual. In J. M. Gorman (Ed.), *Fear and anxiety: The benefits of translational research* (pp. 1–22). Washington, DC: American Psychiatric Publishing.

Sullivan, S. S., & Guilleminault, C. (2009). Emerging drugs for insomnia: New frontiers for old and novel targets. *Expert Opinion on Emerging Drugs, 14*(3), 411–422.

Suls, J., & Bunde, J. (2005). Anger, anxiety, and depression as risk factors for cardiovascular disease: The problems and implications of overlapping affective dispositions. *Psychological Bulletin, 131,* 260–300.

Summerfeldt, L. J., Kloosterman, P. H., & Antony, M. M. (2010). Structured and semi-structured interviews. In M. M. Antony & D. H. Barlow (Eds.), *Handbook of assessment and treatment planning for psychological disorders* (2nd ed.). New York, NY: Guilford Press.

Suomi, S. J. (1999). Attachment in rhesus monkeys. In J. Cassidy & P. Shaver (Eds.), *Handbook of attachment: Theory, research, and clinical applications* (pp. 181–197). New York, NY: Guilford Press.

Suomi, S. J. (2000). A biobehavioral perspective on developmental psychopathology. In A. J. Sameroff, J. Lewis, & S. M. Miller (Eds.), *Handbook of developmental psychopathology* (pp. 237–256). New York, NY: Kluwer Academic/Plenum.

Suvisaari, J., Perälä, J., Saarni, S., Juvonen, H., Tuulio-Henriksson, A., & Lönnqvist, J. (2009). The epidemiology and descriptive and predictive validity of DSM-IV delusional disorder and subtypes of schizophrenia. *Clinical Schizophrenia & Related Psychoses, 2*(4), 289–297.

Suvrathan, A., Hoeffer, C. A., Wong, H., Klann, E., & Chattarji, S. (2010). Characterization and reversal of synaptic defects in the amygdala in a mouse model of fragile X syndrome. *Proceedings of the National Academy of Sciences, 107*(25), 11591–11596.

Svartberg, M., Stiles, T. C., & Seltzer, M. H. (2004). Randomized, controlled trial of the effectiveness of short-term dynamic psychotherapy and cognitive therapy for cluster C personality disorders. *American Journal of Psychiatry, 161,* 810–817.

Svetkey, L. P., Stevens, V. J., Brantley, P. J., Appel, L. J., Hollis, J. F., Loria, C. M., ... Aicher, K. (2008). Comparison of strategies for sustaining weight loss: The weight loss maintenance randomized controlled trial. *JAMA: Journal of the American Medical Association, 299*(10), 1139–1148.

Swanda, R. M., & Haaland, K. Y. (2009). Clinical neuropsychology and intellectual assessment of adults. In B. J. Sadock, V. A. Sadock, & P. Ruiz (Eds.), *Kaplan & Sadock's comprehensive textbook of psychiatry* (9th ed., Vol. I, pp. 935–951). Philadelphia, PA: Lippincott Williams & Wilkins.

Swartz, M. S., Lauriello, J., & Drake, R. E. (2006). Psychosocial therapies. In J. A. Lieberman, T. S. Stroup, & D. O. Perkins (Eds.), *The American Psychiatric Publishing textbook of schizophrenia* (pp. 327–340). Washington, DC: American Psychiatric Publishing.

Swartz, M., Blazer, D., George, L., & Landerman, R. (1986). Somatization disorder in a community population. *American Journal of Psychiatry, 143,* 1403–1408.

Swedo, S., Thorsen, P., & Pine, D. (2008, February 3–5). *Autism and Other Pervasive Developmental Disorders Conference.* Paper presented at The Future of Psychiatric Diagnosis: Refining the Research Agenda, Sacramento, CA.

Sweet, R. A. (2009). Cognitive disorders: Introduction. In B. J. Sadock, V. A. Sadock, & P. Ruiz (Eds.), *Kaplan & Sadock's comprehensive textbook of psychiatry* (9th ed., Vol. I, pp. 1152–1153). Philadelphia, PA: Lippincott Williams & Wilkins.

Sylvers, P., Ryan, S., Alden, S., & Brennan, P. (2009). Biological factors and the development of persistent criminality. In J. Savage (Ed.), *The Development of Persistent Criminality* (pp. 141–162). New York, NY: Oxford University Press.

Sysko, R. & Wilson, G.T. (2011). Eating disorders. In D. H. Barlow (Ed.), *Oxford handbook of clinical psychology* (pp. 387–404). New York, NY: Oxford University Press.

Szasz, T. (1961). *The myth of mental illness: Foundations of a theory of personal conduct.* New York, NY: Hoeber-Harper.

Tafti, M. (2009). Genetic aspects of normal and disturbed sleep. *Sleep Medicine, 10*(Suppl. 1), S17–S21. doi: 10.1016/j.sleep.2009.07.002

Tager-Flusberg, H., Rogers, S., Cooper, J., Landa, R., Lord, C., Paul, R., ... Yoder, P. (2009). Defining spoken language benchmarks and selecting measures of expressive language development for young children with autism spectrum disorders. *Journal of Speech, Language, and Hearing Research, 52*(3), 643–652.

Takahasi, T. (1989). Social phobia syndrome in Japan. *Comprehensive Psychiatry, 30,* 45–52.

Takei, N., Lewis, S., Jones, P., Harvey, I., & Murray, R. M. (1996). Prenatal exposure to influenza and increased cerebrospinal fluid spaces in schizophrenia. *Schizophrenia Bulletin, 22,* 521–534.

Tamminga, C. A. (2009). Schizophrenia and other psychotic disorders: Introduction and overview. In B. J. Sadock, V. A. Sadock, & P. Ruiz (Eds.), *Kaplan & Sadock's comprehensive textbook of psychiatry* (9th ed., Vol. I, pp. 1432–1433). Philadelphia, PA: Lippincott Williams & Wilkins.

Tan, E. S. (1980). Transcultural aspects of anxiety. In G. D. Burrows & B. Davies (Eds.), *Handbook of studies on anxiety.* Amsterdam, The Netherlands: Elsevier/North-Holland.

Tannock, R. (2009a). Mathematics disorder. In B. J. Sadock, V. A. Sadock, & P. Ruiz (Eds.), *Kaplan & Sadock's comprehensive textbook of psychiatry* (9th ed., Vol. II, pp. 3485–3493). Philadelphia, PA: Lippincott Williams & Wilkins.

Tannock, R. (2009b). Reading disorder. In B. J. Sadock, V. A. Sadock, & P. Ruiz (Eds.), *Kaplan & Sadock's comprehensive textbook of psychiatry* (9th ed., Vol. II, pp. 3475–3485). Philadelphia, PA: Lippincott Williams & Wilkins.

Tarasoff v. Regents of University of California ("Tarasoff I"), 529 P.2d 553 (Cal. S. Ct. 1974).

Tarasoff v. Regents of University of California ("Tarasoff II"), 551 P.2d 334 (Cal. S. Ct. 1976).

Tardiff, K. J. (2003). Violence. In R. E. Hales & S. C. Yudofsky (Eds.), *Textbook of clinical psychiatry* (4th ed., pp. 1485–1509). Washington, DC: American Psychiatric Publishing.

Tau, G. Z., & Peterson, B. S. (2010). Normal development of brain circuits. *Neuropsychopharmacology, 35*(1), 147–168.

Taylor, C. B., Sheikh, J., Agras, W. S., Roth, W. T., Margraf, J., Ehlers, A., ... Gossard, D. (1986). Self-report of panic attacks: Agreement with heart rate changes. *American Journal of Psychiatry, 143,* 478–482.

Taylor, G. T., Maloney, S., Dearborn, J., & Weiss, J. (2009). Hormones in the mentally disturbed brain: Steroids and peptides in the development and treatment of psychopathology. *Central Nervous System Agents in Medicinal Chemistry, 9,* 331–360.

Taylor, J., & Lang, A. R. (2006). Psychopathy and substance use disorders. In C. J. Patrick (Ed.), *Handbook of psychopathy* (pp. 495–511). New York, NY: Guilford Press.

Taylor, R. R., Jason, L. A., Richman, J. A., Torres-Harding, S. R., King, C., & Song, S. (2003). Epidemiology. In L. A. Jason, P. A. Fennell, & R. R. Taylor (Eds.), *Handbook of chronic fatigue syndrome* (pp. 3–25). Hoboken, NJ: John Wiley.

Taylor, S. (1996). Meta-analysis of cognitive behavioral treatment for social phobia. *Journal of Behavior Therapy and Experimental Psychiatry, 27,* 1–9.

Taylor, S., & Asmundson, G. J. (2009). Hypochondriasis and health anxiety. In M. M. Antony & M. B. Stein (Eds.), *Oxford handbook of anxiety and related disorders* (pp. 525–540). Oxford, UK: Oxford University Press.

Taylor, S., & Asmundson, J. G. (2004). *Treating health anxiety: A cognitive behavioral approach.* New York, NY: Guilford Press.

Taylor, S., Asmundson, G., & Coons, M. (2005). Current directions in the treatment of hypochondriasis. *Journal of Cognitive Psychotherapy: An International Quarterly, 19,* 285–304.

Taylor, S., & Koch, W. J. (1995). Anxiety disorders due to motor vehicle accidents: Nature and treatment. *Clinical Psychology Review, 15,* 721–738.

Taylor, S., Thordarson, D. S., Jang, K. L., & Asmundson, G. J. (2006). Genetic and environmental origins of health anxiety: A twin study. *World Psychiatry, 5*(1), 47–50.

Taylor, S. E. (2002). *The tending instinct: How nurturing is essential to who we are and how we live.* New York, NY: Henry Holt and Company.

Taylor, S. E. (2006). Tend and befriend: Biobehavioral bases of affiliation under stress. *Current Directions in Psychological Science, 15*(6), 273–277.

Taylor, S. E. (2009). *Health psychology* (7th ed.). New York, NY: McGraw-Hill.

Taylor, S. E., Klein, L. C., Lewis, B. P., Gruenewald, T. L., Gurung, R. A. R., & Updegraff, J. A. (2000). Biobehavioral responses to stress in females: Tend-and-befriend, not fight-or-flight. *Psychological Review, 107,* 411–429.

Taylor, S. E., Repetti, R. L., & Seeman, T. (1997). Health psychology: What is an unhealthy environment and how does it get under the skin? *Annual Review of Psychology, 48,* 411–447.

Teasdale, J. D. (1993). Emotion and two kinds of meaning: Cognitive therapy and applied cognitive science. *Behaviour Research and Therapy, 31*(4), 339–354.

Teasdale, J. D., Segal, Z. V., Williams, J. M., Ridgeway, V. A., Soulsby, J. M., & Lau, M. A. (2000). Prevention of relapse/recurrence in major depression by mindfulness-based cognitive therapy. *Journal of Consulting and Clinical Psychology, 4,* 615–623.

Teh, C. F., Zaslavsky, A. M., Reynolds, C. F., & Cleary, P. D. (2009). Effect of depression treatment on chronic pain outcomes. *Psychosomatic Medicine, 72,* 61–67.

Teicher, M. H., Glod, C., & Cole, J. O. (1990). Emergence of intense suicidal preoccupation during fluoxetine treatment. *American Journal of Psychiatry, 147*(1), 207–210.

Telch, C. F., & Agras, W. S. (1993). The effects of a very low calorie diet on binge eating. *Behavior Therapy, 24,* 177–193.

Telch, C. F., Agras, W. S., & Rossiter, E. M. (1988). Binge eating increases with increasing adiposity. *International Journal of Eating Disorders, 7,* 115–119.

Telch, M. J., Lucas, J. A., & Nelson, P. (1989). Nonclinical panic in college students: An investigation of prevalence and symptomatology. *Journal of Abnormal Psychology, 98,* 300–306.

Temoshok, L. R., Wald, R. L., Synowski, S., & Garzino-Demo, A. (2008). Coping as a multisystem construct associated with pathways mediating HIV-relevant immune function and disease progression. *Psychosomatic Medicine, 70,* 555–561.

Temple, E., Deutisch, G. K., Poldrack, R. A., Miller, S. L., Tallal, P., Merzenich, M. M., Gabrieli, J.. (2003). Neural deficits in children with dyslexia ameliorated by behavioral remediation: Evidence from functional MRI. *Proceedings of the National Academy of Sciences, 100,* 2860–2865.

Tenhula, W. N., Bellack, A. S., & Drake, R. E. (2009). Schizophrenia: Psychosocial approaches. In B. J. Sadock, V. A. Sadock, & P. Ruiz (Eds.), *Kaplan & Sadock's comprehensive textbook of psychiatry* (9th ed., Vol. I, pp. 1557–1572). Philadelphia, PA: Lippincott Williams & Wilkins.

ter Kuile, M., van Lankveld, J., Jacques, J., de Groot, E., Melles, R., Neffs, J., & Zanbergen, M. (2007). Cognitive-behavioral therapy for women with lifelong vaginismus: Process and prognostic factors. *Behaviour Research and Therapy, 45,* 359–373.

Teri, L., Gibbons, L. E., McCurry, S. M., Logsdon, R. G., Buchner, D. M., Barlow, W. E., … Larson, E. B. (2003). Exercise plus behavioral management in patients with Alzheimer disease: A randomized controlled trial. *JAMA: Journal of the American Medical Association, 290*(15), 2015–2022.

Terman, M., & Terman, J. S. (2006). Controlled trial of naturalistic dawn simulation and negative air ionization for seasonal affective disorder. *American Journal of Psychiatry, 163*(12), 2126–2133.

Testad, I., Ballard, C., Brønnick, K., & Aarsland, D. (2010). The effect of staff training on agitation and use of restraint in nursing home residents with dementia: A single-blind, randomized controlled trial. *The Journal of Clinical Psychiatry, 71*(1), 80.

Thaker, G. K., & Avila, M. (2003). Schizophrenia, V: Risk markers. *American Journal of Psychiatry, 160,* 1578.

Thapar, A., & McGuffin, P. (2009). Quantitative genetics. In M. G. Gelder, N. C. Andreasen, J. J. Lopez-Ibor, Jr. & J. R. Geddes (Eds.), *New Oxford textbook of psychiatry* (2nd ed., Vol. 1, pp. 212–221). Oxford, UK: Oxford University Press.

Thase, M. (2005). Major depressive disorder. In F. Adrasik (Ed.), *Comprehensive handbook of personality and psychopathology. Vol. 2. Adult psychopathology* (pp. 207–230). New York, NY: Wiley.

Thase, M. E. (2009). Neurobiological aspects of depression. In I. H. Gotlib & C. L. Hammen (Eds.), *Handbook of depression* (2nd ed., pp. 187–217). New York, NY: Guilford Press.

Thase, M. E., & Denko, T. (2008). Pharmacotherapy of mood disorders. *Annual Review of Clinical Psychology, 4,* 53–91.

Thase, M. E., & Kupfer, D. J. (1996). Recent developments in the pharmacotherapy of mood disorders. *Journal of Consulting and Clinical Psychology, 64,* 646–659.

Thayer, J. F., Friedman, B. H., & Borkovec, T. D. (1996). Autonomic characteristics of generalized anxiety disorder and worry. *Biological Psychiatry, 39,* 255–266.

The evolving insanity defense. (2006). *ABA Journal, 92,* 37.

The Treatment for Adolescents with Depression Study Team (TADS). (2004). Fluoxetine, cognitive-behavioral therapy, and their combination for adolescents with depression. *JAMA: Journal of the American Medical Association, 292,* 807–820.

The Treatment for Adolescents with Depression Study Team. (2009). The Treatment for Adolescents with Depression Study (TADS): Outcomes over 1 year of naturalistic follow-up. *American Journal of Psychiatry, 166,* 1141–1149.

Theander, S. (1985). Outcome and prognosis in anorexia nervosa and bulimia: Some results of previous investigations, compared with those of the Swedish long-term study. *Journal of Psychiatric Research, 19,* 493–508.

Thies-Flechtner, K., Muller-Oerlinghausen, B., Seibert, W., Walther, A., & Greil, W. (1996). Effect of prophylactic treatment on suicide risk in patients with major affective disorders: Data from a randomized prospective trial. *Pharmacopsychiatry, 29,* 103–107.

Thirthalli, J., & Rajkumar, R. P. (2009). Statistical versus clinical significance in psychiatric research—An overview for beginners. *Asian Journal of Psychiatry, 2*(2), 74–79.

Thomas, C. R. (2009). Oppositional defiant disorder and conduct disorder. In M. K. Dulcan (Ed.), *Dulcan's textbook of child and adolescent psychiatry* (pp. 223–239). Arlington, VA: American Psychiatric Publishing.

Thompson v. County of Alameda, 614 P.2d 728 (Cal. S. Ct. 1980).

Thompson, J. K., & Kinder, B. (2003). Eating disorders. In M. Hersen & S. Turner (Eds.), *Handbook of adult psychopathology* (4th ed., pp. 555–582). New York, NY: Plenum.

Thompson, J. K., & Stice, E. (2001). Thinidea internalization: Mounting evidence for a new risk factor for body-image disturbance and eating pathology. *Current Directions in Psychological Science, 11,* 181–183.

Thompson, J. R., Bradley, V. J., Buntinx, W. H. E., Schalock, R. L., Shogren, K. A., Snell, M. E., … Yeager, M. (2009). Conceptualizing supports and the support needs of people with intellectual disability. *Intellectual and Developmental Disabilities, 47*(2), 135–146.

Thompson, M. A., Aberg, J. A., Cahn, P., Montaner, J. S. G., Rizzardini, G., Telenti, A … Schooley, R. T. (2010). Antiretroviral treatment of adult HIV infection. *JAMA: Journal of the American Medical Association, 304,* 321–333.

Thompson-Brenner, H., Glass, S., & Westen, D. (2003). A multidimensional meta-analysis of psychotherapy for bulimia nervosa. *Clinical Psychology: Science and Practice, 10,* 269–287.

Thomson, A. B., & Page, L. A. (2007). Psychotherapies for hypochondriasis. *Cochrane Database of Systematic Reviews*(4), CD006520.

Thoresen, C. E., & Powell, L. H. (1992). Type A behavior pattern: New perspectives on theory, assessment, and intervention. Special issue: Behavioral medicine: An update for the 1990s. *Journal of Consulting and Clinical Psychology, 60*(4), 595–604.

Thorpe, G. L., & Burns, L. E. (1983). *The agoraphobic syndrome.* New York, NY: John Wiley.

Thurston, R. C., & Kubzansky, L. D. (2009). Women, loneliness, and incident coronary heart disease. *Psychosomatic Medicine, 71*(8), 836–842.

Tienari, P. (1991). Interaction between genetic vulnerability and family environment: The Finnish adoptive family study of schizophrenia. *Acta Psychiatrica Scandinavica, 84,* 460–465.

Tienari, P., Wahlberg, K.-E., & Wynne, L. C. (2006). Finnish adoption study of schizophrenia: Implications for family interventions. *Families, Systems & Health, 24,* 442–451.

Tienari, P., Wynne, L. C., Laksy, K., Moring, J., Nieminen, P., & Sorri, A., … Wahlberg, K. E.. (2003). Genetic boundaries of the schizophrenia spectrum: Evidence from the Finnish Adoptive Family Study of Schizophrenia. *American Journal of Psychiatry, 160,* 1567–1594.

Tienari, P., Wynne, L. C., Moring, J., Lahti, I., Naarala, M., Sorri, A., … Moring, J. (1994). The Finnish adoptive family study of schizophrenia: Implications for family research. *British Journal of Psychiatry, 23*(Suppl. 164), 20–26.

Tiggemann, M. (2002). Media influences on body image development. In T. F. Cash & T. Pruzinsky (Eds.), *Body image: A handbook of theory, research and clinical practice* (pp. 91–98). New York, NY: Guilford Press.

Tiggemann, M., & Lynch, J. E. (2001). Body image across the life span in adult women: The role of self-objectification. *Developmental Psychology, 37,* 243–253.

Tinbergen, E. A., & Tinbergen, N. (1972). *Early childhood autism: An ethological approach.* Berlin, Germany: Parey.

Tingelstad, J. B. (1991). The cardiotoxicity of the tricyclics. *Journal of the American Academy of Child and Adolescent Psychiatry, 30,* 845–846.

Tjio, J. H., & Levan, A. (1956). The chromosome number of man. *Hereditas, 42,* 1–6.

Tondo, L., Jamison, K. R., & Baldessarini, R. J. (1997). Effect of lithium maintenance on suicidal behavior in major mood disorders. In D. M. Stoff & J. J. Mann (Eds.), *The neurobiology of suicide: From the bench to the clinic* (Vol. 836, pp. 339–351). New York, NY: Academy of Sciences.

Toomey, R., Faraone, S. V., Simpson, J. C., & Tsuang, M. T. (1998). Negative, positive, and disorganized symptom dimensions in schizophrenia, major depression, and bipolar disorder. *Journal of Nervous and Mental Disorders, 186,* 470–476.

Torgensen, S., Kringlen, E., & Cramer, V. (2001). The prevalence of personality disorders in a community sample. *Archives of General Psychiatry, 58,* 590–596.

Torgersen, S. (1986). Genetics of somatoform disorder. *Archives of General Psychiatry, 43,* 502–505.

Torrey, E., Eslinger, S., Lamb, R., & Pavle, J. (2010). *More mentally ill persons are in jails and prisons than hospitals: A survey of the states*. Arlington, VA: Treatment Advocacy Center.

Torry, Z., & Billick, S. (2010). Overlapping universe: Understanding legal insanity and psychosis. *Psychiatric Quarterly*, 1–10.

Toth, K., & King, B. H. (2010). Intellectual disability (mental retardation). In M. K. Dulcan (Ed.), *Dulcan's textbook of child and adolescent psychiatry* (5th ed., pp. 151–172). Arlington, VA: American Psychiatric Publishing.

Trivedi, M., Rush, A., Wisniewski, S., Nierenberg, A., Warden, D., Ritz, L., ... STAR*D Study Team. (2006). Evaluation of outcomes with citalopram for depression using measurement-based care in STAR*D: Implications for clinical practice. *American Journal of Psychiatry, 163*, 28–40.

True, W. R., Rice, J., Eisen, S. A., Heath, A. C., Goldberg, J., Lyons, M. J., & Nowak, J. (1993). A twin study of genetic and environmental contributions to liability for posttraumatic stress symptoms. *Archives of General Psychiatry, 50*, 257–264.

Tsai, G. E., Condie, D., Wu, M. T., & Chang, I. W. (1999). Functional magnetic resonance imaging of personality switches in a woman with dissociative identity disorder. *Harvard Review of Psychiatry, 7*(2), 119–122.

Tsao, J. C. I., Mystkowski, J. L., Zucker, B. G., & Craske, M. G. (2002). Effects of cognitive-behavioral therapy for panic disorder on comorbid conditions: Replication and extension. *Behavior Therapy, 33*, 493–509.

Tuchman, B. (1978). *A distant mirror*. New York, NY: Ballantine Books.

Tucker, J. A., Murphy, J. G., & Kertesz, S. G. (2010). Substance use disorders. In M. Antony & D. H. Barlow (Eds.), *Handbook of assessment and treatment planning for psychological disorders* (2nd ed., pp. 529–570). New York, NY: Guilford.

Tuma, A. H., & Maser, J.D. (Eds.) (1985). *Anxiety and the anxiety disorders*. Hillsdale, NJ: Erlbaum.

Turk, C. L., Heimberg, R. G., & Magee, L. (2008). Social anxiety disorder. In D. H. Barlow (Ed.), *Clinical handbook of psychological disorders: A step-by-step treatment manual* (4th ed., pp. 123–163). New York, NY: Guilford Press.

Turk, D. C., & Gatchel, R. J. (1999). Psychosocial factors and pain: Revolution and evolution. In R. J. Gatchel & D. C. Turk (Eds.), *Psychosocial factors in pain: Critical perspectives* (pp. 481–493). New York, NY: Guilford Press.

Turk, D. C., & Monarch, E. S. (2002). Biopsychosocial perspective on chronic pain. In D. C. Turk & R. J. Gatchel (Eds.), *Psychological approaches to pain management: A practitioner's handbook* (2nd ed., pp. 3–29). New York, NY: Guilford Press.

Turkheimer, E., Haley, A., Waldron, M., D'Onofrio, B., & Gottesman, I. I. (2003). Socioeconomic status modifies heritability of IQ in young children. *Psychological Science, 14*, 623–628.

Turkheimer, E., & Waldron, M. C. (2000). Nonshared environment: A theoretical, methodological, and quantitative review. *Psychological Bulletin, 126*, 78–108.

Turner, J., Mancl, L., & Aaron, L. (2006). Short- and long-term efficacy of brief cognitive behavioral therapy for patients with chronic temporomandibular disorder pain: A randomized, controlled trial. *Pain, 121*, 181–194.

Turovsky, J., & Barlow, D. H. (1996). Generalized anxiety disorder. In J. Margraf (Ed.), *Textbook of behavior therapy* (pp. 87–106). Berlin, Germany: Springer-Verlag.

Tushnet, M. (2008). Who qualifies for rights? [Review of the book Homelessness, mental illness and civil commitment]. *The Journal of Politics, 66*(02), 626–628.

Tyas, S. L., Salazar, J. C., Snowdon, D. A., Desrosiers, M. F., Riley, K. P., Mendiondo, M. S., Kryscio, R. J. (2007). Transitions to mild cognitive impairments, dementia, and death: Findings from the nun study. *American Journal of Epidemiology, 165*(11), 1231–1238.

Tynes, L. L., White, K., & Steketee, G. S. (1990). Toward a new nosology of obsessive-compulsive disorder. *Comprehensive Psychiatry, 31*, 465–480.

Uchino, B. N. (2009). Understanding the link between social support and physical health: A life-span perspective with emphasis on the separability of perceived and received support. *Perspectives on Psychological Science, 4*, 236–255.

Uebelacker, L., & Whisman, M. (2006). Moderators of the association between relationship discord and major depression in a national population-based sample. *Journal of Family Psychology, 20*, 40–46.

Uhde, T. (1994). The anxiety disorder: Phenomenology and treatment of core symptoms and associated sleep disturbance. In M. Kryger, T. Roth, & W. Dement (Eds.), *Principles and practice of sleep medicine* (pp. 871–898). Philadelphia, PA: Saunders.

Uhde, T., Cortese, B., & Vedeniapin, A. (2009). Anxiety and sleep problems: Emerging concepts and theoretical treatment implications. *Current Psychiatry Reports, 11*(4), 269–276.

Uleman, J. S., Saribay, S. A., & Gonzalez, C. M. (2008). Spontaneous inferences, implicit impressions, and implicit theories. *Annual Review of Psychology, 59*, 329–360.

Ullman, S., Najdowski, C., & Filipas, H. (2009). Child sexual abuse, post-traumatic stress disorder, and substance use: Predictors of revictimization in adult sexual assault survivors. *Journal of Child Sexual Abuse, 18*(4), 367–385.

UNAIDS (2009). *AIDS epidemic update 2009*. Geneva: Joint United Nations Programme on HIV/AIDS (UNAIDS). Retrieved from http://www.who.int/hiv/pub/epidemiology/epidemic/en/index.html

Ungvari, G. S., Goggins, W., Leung, S.-K., & Gerevich, J. (2007). Schizophrenia with prominent catatonic features ('catatonic schizophrenia'). II. Factor analysis of the catatonic syndrome. *Progress in Neuro-Psychopharmacology and Biological Psychiatry, 31*, 462–468.

Unutzer, J., Katon, W., Callahan, C. M., Williams, J. W., Hunkeler, E., Harpole, L., ... Langston, C. (2002). Collaborative care management of late-life depression in the primary care setting: A randomized controlled trial. *JAMA: Journal of the American Medical Association, 288*, 2836–2845.

Urbszat, C., Herman, C. P., & Polivy, J. (2002). Eat, drink, and be merry, for tomorrow we diet: Effects of anticipated deprivation on food intake in restrained and unrestrained eaters. *Journal of Abnormal Psychology, 11*, 396–401.

U.S. Department of Energy Office of Science. (2009). Human Genome Project Information. Retrieved from http://www.ornl.gov/sci/techresources/Human_Genome/home.shtml

U.S. Department of Health and Human Services. (1991). *Health and behavior research*. National Institutes of Health: Report to Congress.

U.S. General Accounting Office. (1995). *Prescription drugs and the elderly: Many still receive potentially harmful drugs despite recent improvements*. (GOA/HEHS-95-152). United States General Accounting Office: Report to Congress.

Vachon, D., Sellbom, M., Ryder, A., Miller, J., & Bagby, R. (2009). A five-factor model description of depressive personality disorder. *Journal of Personality Disorders, 23*(5), 447–465.

Vahia, I. V., & Cohen, C. I. (2009). Schizophrenia and delusional disorders. In B. J. Sadock, V. A. Sadock, & P. Ruiz (Eds.), *Kaplan & Sadock's comprehensive textbook of psychiatry* (9th ed., Vol. II, pp. 4073–4081). Philadelphia, PA: Lippincott Williams & Wilkins.

Vaillant, G. E. (1979). Natural history of male psychological health. *New England Journal of Medicine, 301*, 1249–1254.

Valera, E. M., Faraone, S. V., Murray, K. E., & Seidman, L. J. (2007). Meta-analysis of structural imaging findings in attention-deficit/hyperactivity disorder. *Biological Psychiatry, 61*, 1361–1369.

Valtonen, H. M., Suominen, K., Mantere, O., Leppämäki, S., Arvilommi, P., & Isometsä, E. (2007). Suicidal behaviour during different phases of bipolar disorder. *Journal of Affective Disorders, 97*, 101–107.

Van Ameringen, M., Mancini, C., Patterson, B., & Simpson, W. (2009). Pharmacotherapy for social anxiety disorder: An update. *The Israel Journal of Psychiatry and Related Sciences, 46*(1), 53–61.

van Beijsterveldt, C., Hudziak, J., & Boomsma, D. (2006). Genetic and environmental influences on cross-gender behavior and relation to behavior problems: A study of Dutch twins at ages 7 and 10 years. *Archives of Sexual Behavior, 35*, 647–658.

van der Hart, O., & Nijenhuis, E. R. S. (2009). Dissociative disorders. In P. H. Blaney & T. Millon (Eds.), *Oxford textbook of psychopathology* (2nd ed., pp. 452–481). New York, NY: Oxford University Press.

van Duijil, M., Cardena, E., & de Jong, J. (2005). The validity of DSM-IV dissociative disorders in southwest Uganda. *Transcultural Psychiatry, 42*, 219–241.

van Goozen, S. H. M., Fairchild, G., Snoek, H., & Harold, G. T. (2007). The evidence for a neurobiological model of childhood antisocial behavior. *Psychological Bulletin, 133*, 149–182.

van Hoeken, D., Veling, W., Sinke, S., Mitchell, J. E., & Hoek, H. W. (2009). The validity and utility of subtyping bulimia nervosa. *International Journal of Eating Disorders, 42*(7), 595–602.

van Kammen, D. P., Docherty, J. P., & Bunney, W. E. (1982). Prediction of early relapse after pimozide discontinuation by response to d-amphetamine during pimozide treatment. *Biological Psychiatry, 17*, 223–242.

van Laar, M., Volkerts, E., & Verbaten, M. (2001). Subchronic effects of the GABA-agonist lorazepam and the 5-HT2A/2C antagonist ritanserin on driving performance, slow wave sleep, and daytime sleepiness in healthy volunteers. *Psychopharmacology (Berlin), 154*, 189–197.

Van Orden, K. A., Witte, T. K., Cukrowicz, K. C., Braithwaite, S. R., Selby, E. A., & Joiner, T. E., Jr. (2010). The interpersonal theory of suicide. *Psychological Review, 117*(2), 575–600.

van Os, J., & Allardyce, J. (2009). The clinical epidemiology of schizophrenia. In B. J. Sadock, V. A. Sadock, & P. Ruiz (Eds.), *Kaplan & Sadock's comprehensive textbook of psychiatry* (9th ed., Vol. I, pp. 1475–1487). Philadelphia, PA: Lippincott Williams & Wilkins.

Van Praag, H. M., & Korf, J. (1975). Central monoamine deficiency in depressions: Causative of secondary phenomenon? *Pharmakopsychiatr Neuropsychopharmakol, 8*, 322–326.

Vander Wal, J. S., & Thelen, M. H. (2000). Predictors of body image dissatisfaction in elementary-age school girls. *Eating Behaviors, 1*, 105–122.

Vanitallie, T. B., & Lew, E. A. (1992). Assessment of morbidity and mortality risk in the overweight patient. In T. A. Wadden and T. B. Vanitallie (Eds.) *Treatment of the seriously obese patient*. New York, NY: Guilford Press.

van't Veer-Tazelaar, P. J., van Marwijk, H. W. J., van Oppen, P., van Hout, H. P. J., van der Horst, H. E., Cuijpers, P., ... Beekman, A. T. (2009). Stepped-care prevention of anxiety and depression in late life: A randomized controlled trial. *Archives of General Psychiatry, 66*(3), 297–304.

Veale, D. (2000). Outcome of cosmetic surgery and "DIY" surgery inpatients with body dysmorphic disorder. *Psychiatric Bulletin, 24*(6), 218–221.

Veale, D., Boocock, A., Gournay, K., Dryden, W., Shah, F., ... Walburn, J. (1996). Body dysmorphic disorder: A survey of 50 cases. *British Journal of Psychiatry, 169*, 196–201.

Veale, D., Ennis, M., & Lambrou, C. (2002). Possible association of body dysmorphic disorder with an occupation or education in art and design. *American Journal of Psychiatry, 159*, 1788–1790.

Veale, D., Gournay, K., Dryden, W., Boocock, A., Shah, F., Willson, R., & Walburn, J. (1996). Body dysmorphic disorder: A cognitive behavioral model and pilot randomized control trial. *Behaviour Research and Therapy, 34*, 717–729.

Veale, D., & Riley, S. (2001). Mirror, mirror on the wall, who is the ugliest of them all? The psychopathology of mirror gazing in body dysmorphic disorder. *Behaviour Research and Therapy, 39*, 1381–1393.

Venables, P. H. (1996). Schizotypy and maternal exposure to influenza and to cold temperature: The Mauritius study. *Journal of Abnormal Psychology, 105*, 53–60.

Venkatagiri, H. S. (2005). Recent advances in the treatment of stuttering: A theoretical perspective. *Journal of Communication Disorders, 38*, 375–393.

Ventura, S. L., Peters, K. D., Martin, J. A., & Mauer, J. D. (1997). Births and deaths: United States, 1996. *Monthly Vital Statistics Report, 46*(Suppl. 2) 1–41.

Vermetten, E., Schmahl, C., Lindner, S., Loewenstein, R., & Bremner, J. (2006). Hippocampal and amygdala volumes in dissociative identity disorder. *American Journal of Psychiatry, 163*, 630–636.

Vernberg, E. M., LaGreca, A. M., Silverman, W. K., & Prinstein, M. J. (1996). Prediction of posttraumatic stress symptoms in children after Hurricane Andrew. *Journal of Abnormal Psychology, 105*, 237–248.

Vinkers, D., de Vries, S., van Baars, A., & Mulder, C. (2010). Ethnicity and dangerousness criteria for court ordered admission to a psychiatric hospital. *Social Psychiatry and Psychiatric Epidemiology, 45*(2), 221–224.

Virag, R. (1999). Indications and early results of sildenafil (Viagra) in erectile dysfunction. *Urology, 54*, 1073–1077.

Vitiello, B., & Lederhendler, I. (2000). Research on eating disorders: Current status and future prospects. *Biological Psychiatry, 47*, 777–786.

Vitousek, K., Watson, S., & Wilson, G. T. (1998). Enhancing motivation for change in treatment-resistant eating disorders. *Clinical Psychological Review, 18*, 391–420.

Vogel, S. A., & Reder, S. (1998). Educational attainment of adults with learning disabilities. In S. A. Vogel & S. Reder (Eds.), *Learning disabilities, literacy, and adult education* (pp. 5–28). Baltimore, MD: Paul H. Brookes.

Vohs, K. D., Bardone, A. M., Joiner, T. E., Jr., Abramson, L. Y., & Heatherton, T. F. (1999). Perfectionism, perceived weight status, and self-esteem interact to predict bulimic symptoms: A model of bulimic symptom development. *Journal of Abnormal Psychology, 108*, 695–700.

Voigt, K., Nagel, A., Meyer, B., Langs, G., Braukhaus, C., & Lowe, B. (2010). Towards positive diagnostic criteria: A systematic review of somatoform disorder diagnoses and suggestions for future classification. *Journal of Psychosomatic Research, 68*(5), 403–414.

Volkmar, F. R., Klin, A., & Schultz, R. T. (2005). Pervasive developmental disorders. In B. J. Sadock & V. A. Sadock (Eds.), *Kaplan & Sadock's comprehensive textbook of psychiatry* (pp. 3164–3182). Philadelphia, PA: Lippincott Williams & Wilkins.

Volkmar, F. R., Klin, A., Schultz, R. T., & State, M. W. (2009). Pervasive developmental disorders. In B. J. Sadock, V. A. Sadock, & P. Ruiz (Eds.), *Kaplan & Sadock's comprehensive textbook of psychiatry* (9th ed., Vol. II, pp. 3540–3559). Philadelphia, PA: Lippincott Williams & Wilkins.

Volkow, N. D., Wang, G. J., Kollins, S. H., Wigal, T. L., Newcorn, J. H., Telang, F., ... Swanson, J. M. (2009). Evaluating dopamine reward pathway in ADHD: Clinical implications. *JAMA: Journal of the American Medical Association, 302*(10), 1084–1091.

Voon, V., Gallea, C., Hattori, N., Bruno, M., Ekanayake, V., & Hallett, M. (2010). The involuntary nature of conversion disorder. *Neurology, 74*(3), 223–228.

Waddell, J., Morris, R. W., & Bouton, M. E. (2006). Effects of bed nucleus of the stria terminalis lesions on conditioned anxiety: Aversive conditioning with long-duration conditional stimuli and reinstatement of extinguished fear. *Behavioral Neuroscience, 120*, 324–336.

Wadden, T. A., Berkowitz, R. I., Womble, L. G., Sarwer, D. B., Phelan, S., Cato, R. K., ... Stunkard, A. J. (2005). Randomized trial of lifestyle modification and pharmacotherapy for obesity. *New England Journal of Medicine, 353*(20), 2111–2120.

Wadden, T. A., Brownell, K. D., & Foster, G. D. (2002). Obesity: Responding to the global epidemic. *Journal of Consulting and Clinical Psychology, 70*, 510–525.

Wadden, T. A., & Osei, S. (2002). The treatment of obesity: An overview. In T. A. Wadden & A. J. Stunkard (Eds.), *Handbook of obesity treatment* (pp. 229–248). New York, NY: Guilford Press.

Wade, T. D., Bulik, C. M., Neale, M., & Kendler, K. S. (2000). Anorexia nervosa and major depression: Shared genetic and environmental risk factors. *American Journal of Psychiatry, 157*, 469–471.

Wager, T. (2005). The neural bases of placebo effects in pain. *Current Directions in Psychological Science, 14*, 175–179.

Wagner, B. M. (1997). Family risk factors for child and adolescent suicidal behavior. *Psychological Bulletin, 121*, 246–298.

Wagner, K. D., & Pliszka, S. R. (2009). Treatment of child and adolescent disorders. In A. F. Schatzberg & C. B. Nemeroff (Eds.), *The American Psychiatric Publishing textbook of psychpharmacology* (4th ed., pp. 1309–1372). Arlington, VA: American Psychiatry Publishing.

Wahl, O. (1995). *Media madness: Public images of mental illness*. New Brunswick, NJ: Rutgers University Press.

Wakefield, J. C. (1992). The concept of mental disorder: On the boundary between biological facts and social values. *American Psychologist, 47*, 373–388.

Wakefield, J. C. (1999). Evolutionary versus prototype analyses of the concept of disorder. *Journal of Abnormal Psychology, 108*, 3, 374–399.

Wakefield, J. C. (2003). Dysfunction as a factual component of disorder. *Behavior Research and Therapy, 41*, 969–990.

Wakefield, J. C. (2009). Mental disorder and moral responsibility: Disorders of personhood as harmful dysfunctions, with special reference to alcoholism. *Philosophy, Psychiatry, & Psychology, 16*(1), 91–99.

Waldman, I. D., & Gizer, I. R. (2006). The genetics of attention deficit hyperactivity disorder. *Clinical Psychology Review, 26*(4), 396–432.

Waldman, I. D., & Rhee, S. H. (2006). Genetic and environmental influences on psychopathy and antisocial behavior. In C. J. Patrick (Ed.), *Handbook of psychopathy* (pp. 205–228). New York, NY: Guilford Press.

Walker, D. L., Ressler, K. J., Lu, K.-T., & Davis, M. (2002). Facilitation of conditioned fear extinction by systemic administration or intra-amygdala infusions of D-cycloserine assessed with fear-potentiated startle. *Journal of Neuroscience, 22*, 2343–2351.

Walkup, J. T., Albano, A. M., Piacentini, J., Birmaher, B., Compton, S. N., Sherrill, J. T., ... Kendall, P. C. (2008). Cognitive behavioral therapy, sertraline, or a combination in childhood anxiety. *New England Journal of Medicine, 359*(26), 2753–2766.

Wallace, C. S., Kilman, V. L., Withers, G. S., & Greenough, W. T. (1992). Increases in dendritic length in occipital cortex after 4 days of differential housing in weanling rats. *Behavioral and Neural Biology, 58,* 64–68.

Wallace, J., & O'Hara, M. W. (1992). Increases in depressive symptomatology in the rural elderly: Results from a cross-sectional and longitudinal study. *Journal of Abnormal Psychology, 101*(3), 398–404.

Waller, N. G., Putnam, F. W., & Carlson, E. B. (1996). Types of dissociation and dissociative types: A taxometric analysis of dissociative experiences. *Psychological Methods, 1,* 300–321.

Waller, N. G., & Ross, C. A. (1997). The prevalence and biometric structure of pathological dissociation in the general population: Taxometric and behavior genetic findings. *Journal of Abnormal Psychology, 106,* 499–510.

Walsh, B. T. (1991). Fluoxetine treatment of bulimia nervosa. *Journal of Psychosomatic Research, 35,* 471–475.

Walsh, B. T. (1995). Pharmacotherapy of eating disorders. In K. D. Brownell & C. G. Fairburn (Eds.), *Eating disorders and obesity: A comprehensive handbook* (pp. 313–317). New York, NY: Guilford Press.

Walsh, B. T. (2010). Eating disorders in DSM-V: Review of existing literature (Part 3). *International Journal of Eating Disorders, 43*(2), 97.

Walsh, B. T., Agras, W. S., Devlin, M. J., Fairburn, C. G., Wilson, G. T., Kahn, C., & Chally, M. K. (2000). Fluoxetine for bulimia nervosa following poor response to psychotherapy. *American Journal of Psychiatry, 157,* 1332–1334.

Walsh, B. T., Hadigan, C. M., Devlin, M. J., Gladis, M., & Roose, S. P. (1991). Long-term outcome of antidepressant treatment of bulimia nervosa. *Archives of General Psychiatry, 148,* 1206–1212

Walsh, B. T., Kaplan, A. S., Attia, E., Olmsted, M., Parides, M., Carter, J. C., ... Rockert, W. (2006). Fluoxetine after weight restoration in anorexia nervosa. *JAMA: Journal of the American Medical Association, 295,* 2605–2612.

Walsh, B. T., Wilson, G. T., Loeb, K. L., Devlin, M. J., Pike, K. M., Roose, S. P., Fleiss, J., & Waternaux, C. (1997). Medication and psychotherapy in the treatment of bulimia nervosa. *American Journal of Psychiatry, 154,* 523–531.

Walsh, J. K., Mayleben, D., Guico-Pabia, C., Vandormael, K., Martinez, R., & Deacon, S. (2008). Efficacy of the selective extrasynaptic GABA$_A$ agonist, gaboxadol, in a model of transient insomnia: A randomized, controlled clinical trial. *Sleep Medicine, 9*(4), 393–402.

Walters, E. E., & Kendler, K. S. (1995). Anorexia nervosa and anorexia-like syndromes in a population based female twin sample. *American Journal of Psychiatry, 152,* 64–71.

Wampold, B. E., Minami, T., Tierney, S. C., Baskin, T. W., & Bhati, K. S. (2005). The placebo is powerful: Estimating placebo effects in medicine and psychotherapy from randomized clinical trials. *Journal of Clinical Psychology, 61*(7), 835–854.

Wan, M., Abel, K., & Green, J. (2008). The transmission of risk to children from mothers with schizophrenia: A developmental psychopathology model. *Clinical Psychology Review, 28*(4), 613–637.

Wan, Y. Y. (2010). Multitasking of helper T cells. *Immunology, 130,* 166–171.

Wang, P. S., Aguilar-Gaxiola, S., Alonso, J., Angermeyer, M. C., Borges, G., Bromet, E. J., et al. (2007). Use of mental health services for anxiety, mood, and substance disorders in 17 countries in the WHO world mental health surveys. *Lancet, 370*(9590), 841–850.

Wang, P. S., Berglund, P., Olfson, M., Pincus, H. A., Wells, K. B., & Kessler, R. C. (2005). Failure and delay in initial treatment contact after first onset of mental disorders in the national comorbidity survey replication. *Archives of General Psychiatry, 62,* 603–613.

Wang, P. S., Bohn, R. L., Glynn, R. J., Mogun, H., & Avorn, J. (2001). Hazardous benzodiazepine regimens in the elderly: Effects of half-life, dosage, and duration on risk of hip fracture. *American Journal of Psychiatry, 158,* 892–898.

Wang, S. (2006). Contagious behavior. *Psychological Science, 19,* 22–26.

Wang, T., Collet, J.-P., Shapiro, S., & Ware, M. A. (2008). Adverse effects of medical cannabinoids: A systematic review. *Canadian Medical Association Journal, 178*(13), 1669–1678. doi:10.1503/cmaj .071178

Wang, X., Wang, D., & Shen, J. (2006). The effects of social support on depression in the aged. *Chinese Journal of Clinical Psychology, 14,* 73.

Wang, Z., Neylan, T. C., Mueller, S. G., Lenoci, M., Truran, D., Marmar, C. R., ... Schuff, N. (2010). Magnetic resonance imaging of hippocampal subfields in posttraumatic stress disorder. *Archives of General Psychiatry, 67*(3), 296–303.

Ward, M. M., Swan, G. E., & Chesney, M. A. (1987). Arousal-reduction treatments for mild hypertension: A meta-analysis of recent studies. *Handbook of Hypertension, 9,* 285–302.

Ward, T., & Beech, A. R. (2008). An integrated theory of sexual offending. In D. R. Laws & W. T. O'Donohue (Eds.), *Sexual deviance: Theory, assessment, and treatment* (2nd ed., pp. 21–36). New York, NY: Guilford Press.

Warwick, H. M., & Salkovskis, P. M. (1990). Hypochondriasis. *Behavior Research Therapy, 28,* 105–117.

Watson, D. (2005). Rethinking the mood and anxiety disorders: A quantitative hierarchical model for DSM-V [Special issue]. *Journal of Abnormal Psychology, 114,* 522–536.

Watson, J. B. (1913). Psychology as a behaviorist views it. *Psychology Review, 20,* 158–177.

Way, B. M., & Taylor, S. E. (2010). Social influences on health: Is serotonin a critical mediator? *Psychosomatic Medicine, 72,* 107–112.

Weaver, J. C. G., Cervoni, N., Champagne, F. A., D'Alessio, A. C., Charma, S., Seckl, J., ... Meaney, M. J. (2004). Epigenetic programming by maternal behavior. *Nature Neuroscience, 7,* 847–854.

Weems, C. F., Silverman, W. K., & La Greca, A. M. (2000). What do youths referred for anxiety problems worry about? Worry and its relation to anxiety and anxiety disorders in children and adolescents. *Journal of Abnormal Child Psychology, 28,* 63–72.

Wegner, D. (1989). *White bears and other unwanted thoughts.* New York, NY: Viking.

Weighs, K. L., Enright, T. M., & Simmens, S. J. (2008). Close relationships and emotional processing predict decreased mortality in women with breast cancer: Preliminary evidence. *Psychosomatic Medicine, 70,* 117–124.

Weight Watchers International. (2010). Company overview. Retrieved from http://www .weightwatchersinternational.com/ phoenix.zhtml?c5130178&p5irol-irhome

Weinberger, D. R., Berman, K. F., & Chase, T. N. (1988). Mesocortical dopaminergic function and human cognition. *Annals of the New York Academy of Sciences, 537,* 330–338.

Weiner, D. B. (1979). The apprenticeship of Philippe Pinel: A new document, 'Observations of Citizen Pussin on the insane.' *The American Journal of Psychiatry, 136*(9), 1128–1134.

Weiner, D. N. (1996). *Premature ejaculation: An evaluation of sensitivity to erotica.* Unpublished doctoral dissertation, State University of New York, Albany.

Weiner, J. M. (2000). Integration of nature and nurture: A new paradigm for psychiatry. *American Journal of Psychiatry, 157,* 1193–1194.

Weiner, M. F., Hynan, L. S., Beekly, D., Koepsell, T. D., & Kukull, W. A. (2007). Comparison of Alzheimer's disease in American Indians, whites, and African Americans. *Alzheimer's & Dementia, 3*(3), 211–216.

Weiner, M. W., Aisen, P. S., Jack, C. R., Jr., Jagust, W. J., Trojanowski, J. Q., Shaw, L., ... Schmidt, M. (2010). The Alzheimer's Disease Neuroimaging Initiative: Progress report and future plans. *Alzheimer's and Dementia, 6*(3), 202–211, e207.

Weinshilboum, R. (2003). Inheritance and drug response. *New England Journal of Medicine, 348,* 529–537.

Weisburg, R. B., Brown, T. A., Wincze, J. P., & Barlow, D. H. (2001). Causal attributions and male sexual arousal: The impact of attributions for a bogus erectile difficulty on sexual arousal, cognitions, and affect. *Journal of Abnormal Psychology, 110*(2), 324–334.

Weisfeld, G. E., & Woodward, L. (2004). Current evolutionary perspectives on adolescent romantic relations and sexuality. *Journal of the American Academy of Child and Adolescent Psychiatry, 43,* 11-19.

Weiskrantz, L. (1980). Varieties of residual experience. *Quarterly Journal of Experimental Psychology, 32,* 365–386.

Weiskrantz, L. (1992, September/October). Unconscious vision: The strange phenomenon of blindsight. *The Sciences,* pp. 23–28.

Weisman de Mamani, A. G., Kymalainen, J. A., Rosales, G. A., & Armesto, J. C. (2007). Expressed emotion and interdependence in white and Latino/Hispanic family members of patients with schizophrenia. *Psychiatry Research, 151,* 107–113.

Weiss, B., & Garber, J. (2003). Developmental differences in the phenomenology of depression. *Development and Psychopathology, 15,* 403–430.

Weiss, R. D., & Iannucci, R. A. (2009). Cocaine-related disorders. In B. J. Sadock, V. A. Sadock, & P. Ruiz (Eds.), *Kaplan & Sadock's comprehensive textbook of psychiatry* (9th ed., Vol. I, pp. 1318–1331). Philadelphia, PA: Lippincott Williams & Wilkins.

Weisse, C. S. (1992). Depression and immunocompetence: A review of the literature. *Psychological Bulletin, 111*(3), 475–489.

Weissman, M. (1995). *Mastering depression: A patient's guide to interpersonal psychotherapy.* New York, NY: Oxford University Press.

Weissman, M., Bland, R., Canino, G., Greenwald, S., Hwo, H., Lee, C., ... Eng-Kung, Y. (1994). The cross national epidemiology of obsessive compulsive disorder. *Journal of Clinical Psychiatry, 55,* 5–10.

Weissman, M. M., Bruce, M. L., Leaf, P. J., Florio, L. P., & Holzer, C. (1991). Affective disorders. In L. N. Robins & D. A. Regier (Eds.), *Psychiatric disorders of America: The epidemiologic catchment area study* (pp. 53–80). New York, NY: Free Press.

Weissman, M. M., & Klerman, G. L. (1977). Sex differences and the epidemiology of depression. *Archives of General Psychiatry, 34,* 98–111.

Weissman, M. M., & Olfson, M. (1995). Depression in women: Implications for health care research. *Science, 269,* 799–801.

Weissman, M. M., Wolk, S., Wickramaratne, P., Goldstein, R. B., Adams, P., Greenwald, S., ... Steinberg, D. (1999). Children with prepubertal-onset major depressive disorder and anxiety grow up. *Archives of General Psychiatry, 56,* 794–801.

Weitze, C., & Osburg, S. (1996). Transsexualism in Germany: Empirical data on epidemiology and application of the German transsexuals' act during its first ten years. *Archives of Sexual Behavior, 25,* 409–465.

Welham, J., Scott, J., Williams, G., Najman, J., Bor, W., O'Callaghan, M., McGrath, J. (2008). Emotional and behavioural antecedents of young adults who screen positive for non-affective psychosis: A 21-year birth cohort study. *Psychological Medicine, 39*(4), 625–634.

Wells, B., & Twenge, J. (2005). Changes in young people's sexual behavior and attitudes, 1943–1999: A cross-temporal meta-analysis. *Review of General Psychology, 9,* 249–261.

Wender, P. H., Kety, S. S., Rosenthal, D., Schlusinger, F., Ortmann, J., & Lunde, I. (1986). Psychiatric disorders in the biological and adoptive families of adopted individuals with affective disorders. *Archives of General Psychiatry, 43,* 923–929.

Wermter, A.-K., Kamp-Becker, I., Hesse, P., Schulte-Körne, G., Strauch, K., & Remschmidt, H. (2010). Evidence for the involvement of genetic variation in the *oxytocin receptor gene* (*OXTR*) in the etiology of autistic disorders on high-functioning level. *American Journal of Medical Genetics Part B: Neuropsychiatric Genetics, 153B*(2), 629–639.

Westen, D. (1991). Social cognition and object relations. *Psychological Bulletin, 109,* 429–455.

Wetherell, J. L., Gatz, M., & Craske, M. G. (2003). Treatment of generalized anxiety disorder in older adults. *Journal of Consulting and Clinical Psychology, 71,* 31–40.

Wetherell, J. L., Lenze, E. J., & Stanley, M. (2005). Evidence-based treatment of geriatric anxiety disorders. *Psychiatric Clinics of North America, 28,* 871–896.

Wetherell, J. L., Thorp, S. R., Patterson, T. L., Golshan, S., Jeste, D. V., & Gatz, M. (2004). Quality of life in geriatric generalized anxiety disorder: A preliminary investigation. *Journal of Psychiatric Research, 38,* 305–312.

Wexler, N. S., & Rawlins, M. D. (2005). Prejudice in a portrayal of Huntington's disease. *Lancet, 366*(9491), 1069–1070.

Wheeler, J., Newring, K. A. B., Draper, C. (2008). Transvestic fetishism: Psychopathology and theory. In D. R. Laws & W. T. O'Donohue (Eds.), *Sexual deviance: Theory, assessment, and treatment* (2nd ed., pp. 286–304). New York, NY: Guilford Press.

Whisman, M., Weinstock, L., & Tolejko, N. (2006). Marriage and depression. In L. M. Corey & S. Goodman (Eds.), *A handbook for the social, behavioral, and biomedical sciences* (pp. 219–240). Boulder, CO: Cambridge University Press.

Whitbourne, S. K., & Skultety, K. M. (2002). Body image development: Adulthood and aging. In T. M. Cash & T. Pruzinsky (Eds.), *Body image: A handbook of theory, research, and clinical practice* (pp. 83–90). New York, NY: Guilford Press.

White, J. L., Moffitt, T. E., & Silva, P. A. (1989). A prospective replication of the protective effects of IQ in subjects at high risk for juvenile delinquency. *Journal of Consulting and Clinical Psychology, 57,* 719–724.

White, K. S. & Barlow, D. H. (2002). Panic disorder and agoraphobia. In D. H. Barlow (Ed.) *Anxiety and its disorders: The nature and treatment of anxiety and panic* (2nd ed.). New York, NY: Guilford Press.

White, K. S., Brown, T. A., Somers, T. J., & Barlow, D. H. (2006). Avoidance behavior in panic disorder: The moderating influence of perceived control. *Behaviour Research and Therapy, 44,* 147–157.

White, W., & Kurtz, E. (2008). Twelve defining moments in the history of Alcoholics Anonymous. In M. Galanter & L. A. Kaskutas (Eds.), *Research on Alcoholics Anonymous and spirituality in addiction recovery: The twelve-step program model, spiritually oriented recovery, twelve-step membership, effectiveness and outcome research* (pp. 37–57). New York, NY: Springer Verlag.

Whitnam, F. L., Diamond, M., & Martin, J. (1993). Homosexual orientation in twins: A report on 61 pairs and three triplet sets. *Archives of Sexual Behavior, 22*(3), 187–206.

Whittal, M. L., Agras, W. S., & Gould, R. A. (1999). *Behavior Therapy, 30,* 117–135.

WHO World Mental Health Survey Consortium (2004). Prevalence, severity, and unmet need for treatment of mental disorders in the World Health Organization world mental health surveys. *JAMA: Journal of the American Medical Association, 291*(21), 2581–2590.

Whooley, M. A., de Jonge, P., Vittinghoff, E., Otte, C., Moos, R., Carney, R. M., ... Browner, W. S. (2008). Depressive symptoms, health behaviors, and risk of cardiovascular events in patients with coronary heart disease. *JAMA: Journal of the American Medical Association, 300,* 2379–2388.

Widaman, K. F. (2009). Phenylketonuria in children and mothers: Genes, environments, behavior. *Current Directions in Psychological Science, 18*(1), 48–52.

Widiger, T., & Trull, T. (2007). Plate tectonics in the classification of personality disorder: Shifting to a dimensional model. *American Psychologist, 62*(2), 71.

Widiger, T. A. (1997). Mental disorders as discrete clinical conditions: Dimensional versus categorical classification. In S. M. Turner & M. Hersen (Eds.), *Adult psychopathology and diagnosis* (3rd ed., pp. 3–23). New York, NY: John Wiley.

Widiger, T. A. (2006). Psychopathy and DSM-IV psychopathology. In C. J. Patrick (Ed.), *Handbook of psychopathy* (pp. 156–171). New York, NY: Guilford Press.

Widiger, T. A. (2007). An empirically based classification of personality pathology: Where we are now and where do we go. *Clinical Psychology: Science and Practice, 14,* 94–98.

Widiger, T. A., & Coker, L. A. (2003). Mental disorders as discrete clinical conditions: Dimensional versus categorical classification. In M. Hersen & S. M. Turner (Eds.), *Adult psychopathology and diagnosis* (4th ed., pp. 3–35). New York, NY: John Wiley.

Widiger, T. A., & Edmundson, M. (2011). Diagnoses, dimensions, and DSM-V. In D. H. Barlow (Ed.), *Oxford handbook of clinical psychology* (pp. 254–278). New York, NY: Oxford University Press.

Widiger, T. A., Frances, A. J., Pincus, H. A., Ross, R., First, M. B., Davis, W., & Kline, M. (Eds.) (1998). *DSM-IV sourcebook* (Vol. 4). Washington, DC: American Psychiatric Association.

Widiger, T. A., Livesley, W. J., & Clark, L. A. (2009). An integrative dimensional classification of personality disorder. *Psychological Assessment, 21*(3), 243–255.

Widiger, T. A., & Samuel, D. B. (2005). Diagnostic categories or dimensions? A question for the diagnostic and statistical manual of mental disorders (5th ed.). *Journal of Abnormal Psychology, 114,* 494–504.

Widiger, T. A., & Sankis, L. M. (2000). Adult psychopathology: Issues and controversies. *Annual Review of Psychology, 51,* 377–404.

Widiger, T. A., & Spitzer, R. L. (1991). Sex bias in the diagnosis of personality disorders: Conceptual and methodological issues. *Clinical Psychology Review, 11,* 1–22.

Widiger, T. A., Frances, A. J., Pincus, H. A., Ross, R., First, M. B., & Davis, W. W. (Eds.) (1996). *DSM-IV sourcebook* (Vol. 2). Washington, DC: American Psychiatric Association.

Widom, C. S. (1977). A methodology for studying noninstitutionalized psychopaths. *Journal of Consulting and Clinical Psychology, 45,* 674–683.

Widom, C. S. (1984). Sex roles, criminality, and psychopathology. In C. S. Widom (Ed.), *Sex roles and psychopathology* (pp. 183–217). New York, NY: Plenum Press.

Widom, C. S., Czaja, S. J., & Paris, J. (2009). A prospective investigation of borderline personality disorder in abused and neglected children followed up into adulthood. *Journal of Personality Disorders, 23*(5), 433–446.

Wiegel, M. (2008). *Women who sexually abuse minors: Description and instrument validation.* (Unpublished doctoral dissertation). Boston University, Boston, MA.

Wiegel, M., Scepkowski, L., & Barlow, D. (2006). Cognitive and affective processes in female sexual dysfunctions. In I. Goldstein, C. Meston, S. Davis, & A. Traish (Eds.), *Women's sexual function and dysfunction: Study, diagnosis and treatment* (pp. 85–92). London, UK: Taylor & Francis.

Wiegel, M., Wincze, J. P., & Barlow, D. H. (2010). Sexual dysfunction. In M. M. Antony & D. H. Barlow (Eds.), *Handbook of assessment and treatment planning for psychological disorders* (pp. 481–522). New York, NY: Guilford Press.

Wiers, R. W., Schoenmakers, T., Houben, K., Thush, C., Fadardi, J. S., & Cox, W. M. (2008). Can problematic alcohol use be trained away? New behavioural treatments aimed at changing and moderating implicit cognitive processes in alcohol abuse. In C. R. Martin (Ed.), *Identification and treatment of alcohol dependency* (pp. 334–358). Keswick, UK: M&K Publishing.

Wiggins, R. (2009). Prion stability and infectivity in the environment. *Neurochemical Research, 34*(1), 158–168.

Wilamowska, Z. A., Thompson-Hollands, J., Fairholme, C. P., Ellard, K. K., Farchione, T. J., & Barlow, D. H. (2010). Conceptual background, development, and preliminary data from the Unified Protocol for the Transdiagnostic Treatment of Emotional Disorders. *Depression and Anxiety, 27*(10), 882–890.

Wilcox, H. C., Storr, C. L., & Breslau, N. (2009). Posttraumatic stress disorder and suicide attempts in a community sample of urban American young adults. *Archives of General Psychiatry, 66*(3), 305–311.

Wilfley, D. E., Welch, R., Stein, R. I., Spurrell, E. B., Cohen, L. R., Saelens, B. E., ... Matt, G. E. (2002). A randomized comparison of group cognitive-behavioral and group interpersonal psychotherapy for treatment of overweight individuals with binge-eating disorder. *Archives of General Psychiatry, 59*, 713–721.

Wilhelm, S., Otto, M. W., Lohr, B., & Deckersbach, T. (1999). Cognitive behavior group therapy for body dysmorphic disorder: A case series. *Behaviour Research and Therapy, 37*, 71–75.

Williams, C. J., & Weinberg, M. S. (2003). Zoophilia in men: A study of sexual interest in animals. *Archives of Sexual Behavior, 32*, 523–535.

Williams, J., Hadjistavropoulos, T., & Sharpe, D. (2006). A meta-analysis of psychological and pharmacological treatments for body dysmorphic disorder. *Behaviour Research and Therapy, 44*, 99–111.

Williams, J., Wake, M., Hesketh, K., Maher, E., & Waters, E. (2005). Health-related quality of life of overweight and obese children, *JAMA: Journal of the American Medical Association, 293*, 70–76.

Williams, L. (1994). Recall of childhood trauma: A prospective study of women's memories of child sexual abuse. *Journal of Consulting and Clinical Psychology, 62*, 1167–1176.

Williams, R. B., Barefoot, J. C., & Schneiderman, N. (2003). Psychosocial risk factors for cardiovascular disease; More than one culprit at work. *JAMA: Journal of the American Medical Association, 290*, 2190–2192.

Williams, R. B., & Schneiderman, N. (2002). Resolved: Psychosocial interventions can improve clinical outcomes in organic disease (Pro). *Psychosomatic Medicine, 64*, 552–557.

Williams, R. B., Marchuk, D. A., Gadde, K. M., Barefoot, J. C., Grichnik, K., Helms, M. J., ... Siegler, I.C. (2001). Central nervous system serotonin function and cardiovascular responses to stress. *Psychosomatic Medicine, 63*, 300–305.

Williams, R. B., Jr., Haney, T. L., Lee, K. L., Kong, V., & Blumenthal, J. A. (1980). Type A behavior, hostility, and coronary atherosclerosis. *Psychosomatic Medicine, 42*, 529–538.

Willwerth, J. (1993, August 30). Tinkering with madness, *Time*, pp. 40–42.

Wilson, G. T., & Fairburn, C. G. (2002). Treatments for eating disorders. In P. E. Nathan, & J. M. Gorman (Eds.), *A guide to treatments that work* (2nd ed., pp. 559–592). New York, NY: Oxford University Press.

Wilson, G. T., Grilo, C. M., & Vitousek, K. M. (2007). Psychological treatment of eating disorders. *American Psychologist, 62*, 199–216.

Wilson, G. T., Loeb, K. L., Walsh, B. T., Labouvie, E., Petkova, E., Liu, S., & Waternaux, C. (1999). Psychological versus pharmacological treatments of bulimia nervosa: Predictors and processes of change. *Journal of Consulting and Clinical Psychology, 67*, 451–459.

Wilson, G. T., Wilfley, D. E., Agras, W. S., & Bryson, S. W. (2010). Psychological treatments of binge eating disorder. *Archives of General Psychiatry, 67*(1), 94–101.

Wilson, R. S., Aggarwal, N. T., Barnes, L. L., Mendes de Leon, C. F., Hebert, L. E., & Evans, D. A. (2010). Cognitive decline in incident Alzheimer disease in a community population. *Neurology, 74*(12), 951–955.

Wimo, A., Winblad, B., & Jonsson, L. (2007). An estimate of the total worldwide societal costs of dementia in 2005. *Alzheimer's and Dementia, 3*(2), 81–91.

Winchel, R. M., Stanley, B., & Stanley, M. (1990). Biochemical aspects of suicide. In S. J. Blumenthal & D. J. Kupfer (Eds.), *Suicide over the life cycle: Risk factors, assessment, and treatment of suicidal patterns* (pp. 97–126). Washington, DC: American Psychiatric Press.

Wincze, J. P. (2009). *Enhancing sexuality: A problem-solving approach to treating dysfunction: Therapist Guide* (2nd ed.). New York, NY: Oxford University Press.

Wincze, J. P., Bach, A., & Barlow, D. H. (2008). Sexual dysfunction. In D. H. Barlow (Ed.), *Clinical handbook of psychological disorders: A step-by-step treatment manual* (4th ed., pp. 615–661). New York, NY: Guilford Press.

Wincze, J. P., & Carey, M. P. (2001). *Sexual dysfunction: A guide for assessment and treatment*. New York, NY: Guilford Press.

Windgassen, K. (1992). Treatment with neuroleptics: The patient's perspective. *Acta Psychiatrica Scandinavica, 86*, 405–410.

Wing, J. K., Cooper, J. E., & Sartorius, N. (1974). *The measurement and classification of psychiatric symptoms*. Cambridge, UK: Cambridge University Press.

Winkelman, J. W. (2006). Efficacy and tolerability of open-label topiramate in the treatment of sleep-related eating disorder: A retrospective case series. *Journal of Clinical Psychiatry, 67*, 1729–1734.

Winter, A. (1998). *Mesmerized powers of mind in Victorian Britain*. Chicago, IL: University of Chicago Press.

Winters, R. W., & Schneiderman, N. (2000). Anxiety and coronary heart disease. In D. I. Mostofsky & D. H. Barlow (Eds.), *The management of stress and anxiety in medical disorders* (pp. 206–219). Needham Heights, MA: Allyn & Bacon.

Winzelberg, A. J., Eppstein, D., Eldredge, K. L., Wilfley, D., Dasmahapatra, R., Dev, P., & Taylor, C. B. (2000). Effectiveness of an Internet-based program for reducing risk factors for eating disorders. *Journal of Consulting and Clinical Psychology, 68*, 346–350.

Winzelberg, A. J., Taylor, C. B., Sharpe, T., Eldredge, K. L., Dev, P., & Constantinou, P. S. (1998). Evaluation of a computer-mediated eating disorder intervention program. *International Journal of Eating Disorders, 24*, 339–349.

Wise, M. G., Hilty, D. M., & Cerda, G. M. (2001). Delirium due to a general medical condition, delirium due to multiple etiologies, and delirium not otherwise specified. In G. O. Gabbard (Ed.), *Treatment of psychiatric disorders* (3rd ed., Vol. 1, pp. 387–412). Washington, DC: American Psychiatric Publishing.

Wiseman, F. K., Alford, K. A., Tybulewicz, V. L. J., & Fisher, E. M. C. (2009). Down syndrome—recent progress and future prospects. *Human Molecular Genetics, 18*(R1), R75–83.

Wisner, K. L., Sit, D. K., Hanusa, B. H., Moses-Kolko, E. L., Bogen, D. L., Hunker, D. F., ... Singer, L. T. (2009). Major depression and antidepressant treatment: Impact on pregnancy and neonatal outcomes. *American Journal of Psychiatry, 166*(5), 557–566.

Wisocki, P. A. (1988). Worry as a phenomenon relevant to the elderly. *Behavior Therapy, 19*, 369–379.

Witherington, R. (1988). Suction device therapy in the management of erectile impotence. *Urologic Clinics of North America, 15*, 123–128.

Witkiewitz, K., & Marlatt, G. A. (2004). Relapse prevention for alcohol and drug problems: That was Zen, this is Tao. *American Psychologist, 59*, 224–235.

Wittchen, H. U., Gloster, A. T., Beesdo-Baum, K., Fava, G. A., & Craske, M. G. (2010). Agoraphobia: A review of the diagnostic classificatory position and criteria. *Depression and Anxiety, 27*(2), 113–133.

Wittchen, H. U., Knäuper, B., & Kessler, R. C. (1994). Lifetime risk of depression. *British Journal of Psychiatry, 165*(Suppl. 26), 116–122.

Wittchen, H. U., Zhao, S., Kessler, R. C., & Eaton, W. W. (1994). DSM-III-R generalized anxiety disorder in the national comorbidity survey. *Archives of General Psychiatry, 51*, 355–364.

Wittstein, I., Thiemann, D., Lima, J., Baughman, K., Sculman, S., Gerstenblith, G., ... Champion, H. C. (2005). Neurohumoral features of myocardial stunning due to sudden emotional stress. *New England Journal of Medicine, 352*, 539–548.

Wolf, M. M. (1978). Social validity: The case for subjective measurement or how applied behavior analysis is finding its heart. *Journal of Applied Behavior Analysis, 11,* 203–214.

Wolfe, B. M., & Morton, J. M. (2005). Weighing in on bariatric surgery. *JAMA: Journal of the American Medical Association, 294,* 1960–1963.

Wolf-Maier, K., Cooper, R. S., Banegas, J. R., Giampaoli, S., Hense, H., Joffres, M., ... Vescio, F. (2003). Hypertension prevalence and blood pressure levels in 6 European countries, Canada, and the United States. *JAMA: Journal of the American Medical Association, 289,* 2362–2369.

Wolitzky-Taylor, K. B., Castriotta, N., Lenze, E. J., Stanley, M. A., & Craske, M. G. (2010). Anxiety disorders in older adults: A comprehensive review. *Depression and Anxiety, 27*(2), 190–211.

Wolpe, J. (1958). *Psychotherapy by reciprocal inhibition.* Stanford, CA: Stanford University Press.

Wonderlich, S. A., Gordon, K. H., Mitchell, J. E., Crosby, R. D., & Engel, S. G. (2009). The validity and clinical utility of binge eating disorder. *International Journal of Eating Disorders, 42*(8), 687–705.

Woodman, C. L., Noyes, R., Black, D. W., Schlosser, S., & Yagla, S. J. (1999). A 5-year follow-up study of generalized anxiety disorder and panic disorder. *Journal of Nervous and Mental Disease, 187,* 3–9.

Woods, E. R., Lin, Y. G., Middleman, A., Beckford, P., Chase, L., & DuRant, R. H. (1997). The associations of suicide attempts in adolescents. *Pediatrics, 99,* 791–796.

Woods, S. W., Miller, T. J., Davidson, L., Hawkins, K. A., Sernyak, M. J., & McGlashan, T. H. (2001). Estimated yield of early detection of prodromal or first episode patients by screening first-degree relatives of schizophrenic patients. *Schizophrenia Research, 52,* 21–27.

Woodside, M. R., & Legg, B. H. (1990). Patient advocacy: A mental health perspective. *Journal of Mental Health Counseling, 12,* 38–50.

Woolfolk, R. L., & Allen, L. A. (2011). Somatoform and physical disorders. In D. H. Barlow (Ed.), *Oxford handbook of Clinical Psychology* (pp. 334–358). New York, NY: Oxford University Press.

Worell, J., & Remer, P. (1992). *Feminist perspectives in therapy: An empowerment model for women.* New York, NY: John Wiley.

World Health Organization. (1998). *Obesity: Preventing and managing the global epidemic.* Geneva, Switzerland: World Health Organization.

World Health Organization. (2000). Women and HIV/AIDS: Fact sheet no. 242. Retrieved from http://www.who.int/inf-fs/en/fact242.html

World Health Organization. (2001). *Mental health: New understanding, new hope.* Geneva, Switzerland: World Health Organization.

World Health Organization. (2003). Global summary of the HIV/AIDS epidemic. Retrieved from http://www.who.int/hiv/pub/epidemiology/epi2003/en

World Health Organization. (2010). Mental health. Retrieved from http://www.who.int/mental_health/en

Wray, N. R., & Visscher, P. M. (2010). Narrowing the boundaries of the genetic architecture of schizophrenia. *Schizophrenia Bulletin, 36*(1), 14–23. doi:10.1093/schbul/sbp137

Wright, J. (2009). *Address unknown: The homeless in America.* New Brunswick, NJ: Transaction Publishers.

Wu, E., Birnbaum, H., Shi, L., Ball, D., Kessler, R., Moulis, M., Aggarwal, J.. (2005). The economic burden of schizophrenia in the United States in 2002. *Journal of Clinical Psychiatry, 66*(9), 1122–1129.

Wu, L., Parrott, A., Ringwalt, C., Patkar, A., Mannelli, P., & Blazer, D. (2009). The high prevalence of substance use disorders among recent MDMA users compared with other drug users: Implications for intervention. *Addictive Behaviors, 34*(8), 654–661.

Wulfert, E., Franco, C., Williams, K., Roland, B., & Maxson, J. H. (2008). The role of money in the excitement of gambling. *Psychology of Addictive Behaviors, 22*(3), 380–390.

Wulfert, E., Maxson, J., & Jardin, B. (2009). Cue-specific reactivity in experienced gamblers. *Psychology of Addictive Behaviors, 23*(4), 731–735. doi:10.1037/a0017134

Wyatt v. Stickney, 344 F. Supp. 373 (Ala. 1972).

Wyllie, E., Glazer, J. P., Benbadis, S., Kotagal, P., & Wolgamuth, B. (1999). Psychiatric features of children and adolescents with pseudoseizures. *Archives of Pediatrics and Adolescent Medicine, 153,* 244–248.

Wynne, L. C., Tienari, P., Nieminen, P., Sorri, A., Lahti, I. O., Moring, J., ... Miettunen, J.. (2006). I. Genotype–environment interaction in the schizophrenia spectrum: Genetic liability and global family ratings in the Finnish Adoption Study. *Family Process, 45*(4), 419–434.

Xing, G., Zhang, L., Russell, S., & Post, R. (2006). *Schizophrenia Research, 84,* 36–56.

Yamada, K., Watanabe, K., Nemoto, N., Fujita, H., Chikaraishi, C., Yamauchi, K., ... Kanba, S. (2006). Prediction of medication noncompliance in outpatients with schizophrenia: 2-year follow-up study. *Psychiatry Research, 141,* 61–69.

Yamamoto, J., Silva, A., Sasao, T., Wang, C., & Nguyen, L. (1993). Alcoholism in Peru. *American Journal of Psychiatry, 150,* 1059–1062.

Yan, L. L., Liu, K., Matthews, K. A., Daviglus, M. L., Ferguson, T. F., & Kiefe, C. I. (2003). Psychosocial risk factors and risk of hypertension: The coronary artery risk development in young adults (CARDIA) study. *JAMA: Journal of the American Medical Association, 290,* 2138–2148.

Yanez, B., Edmondson, D., Stanton, A. L., Park, C. L., Kwan, L., Ganz, P. A., & Blank, T. O. (2009). Facets of spirituality as predictors of adjustment to cancer: Relative contributions of having faith and finding meaning. *Journal of Consulting and Clinical Psychology, 77,* 730–741.

Yates, P. M., Hucker, S. J., & Kingston, D. A. (2008). Sexual sadism: Psychopathology and theory. In D. R. Laws & W. T. O'Donohue (Eds.), *Sexual deviance: Theory, assessment, and treatment* (2nd ed., pp. 213–230). New York, NY: Guilford Press.

Yatham, L., Kennedy, S., O'Donovan, C., Parikh, Sagar, V., MacQueen, G.,...Beaulieu, S. (2006). Canadian Network for Mood and Anxiety Treatments (CANMAT) guidelines for the management of patients with bipolar disorder: Update 2007. *Bipolar Disorders, 8,* 721–739.

Ye, X., Mitchell, M., Newman, K., & Batshaw, M. L. (2001). Prospects for prenatal gene therapy in disorders causing mental retardation. *Mental Retardation and Developmental Disabilities Research Review, 7,* 65–72.

Yeaton, W. H., & Bailey, J. S. (1978). Teaching pedestrian safety skills to young children: An analysis and one-year follow-up. *Journal of Applied Behavior Analysis, 11,* 315–329.

Yeh, S.-R., Fricke, R. A., & Edwards, D. H. (1996). The effect of social experience on serotonergic modulation of escape circuit of crayfish. *Science, 271,* 355–369.

Yen, S., Johnson, J., Costello, E., & Simpson, E. (2009). A 5-day dialectical behavior therapy partial hospital program for women with borderline personality disorder: Predictors of outcome from a 3-month follow-up study. *Journal of Psychiatric Practice, 15*(3), 173.

Yerkes, R. M., & Dodson, J. D. (1908). The relation of strength of stimulus to rapidity of habit-formation. *Journal of Comparative Neurology and Psychology, 18,* 459–482.

Yonkers, K. A., Warshaw, M., Massion, A. O., & Keller, M. B. (1996). Phenomenology and course of generalized anxiety disorder. *British Journal of Psychiatry, 168,* 308–313.

Young, A. M., & Herling, S. (1986). Drugs as reinforcers: Studies in laboratory animals. In S. R. Goldberg & I. P. Stolerman (Eds.), *Behavioral analysis of drug dependence* (pp. 9–67). Orlando, FL: Academic Press.

Young, J., Rygh, J., Weinberger, A., & Beck, A.T. (2008). Cognitive therapy for depression. In Barlow, D. H. (Ed.), *Clinical handbook of psychological disorders* (4th ed.) (pp. 250–305). New York, NY: Guilford Press.

Youngberg v. Romeo, 457 U.S. 307 (1982).

Youngstrom, E., Youngstrom, J. K., & Starr, M. (2005). Bipolar diagnoses in community mental health: Achenbach child behavior checklist profiles and patterns of comorbidity. *Biological Psychiatry, 58*(7), 569–575.

Youngstrom, E. A. (2009). Definitional issues in bipolar disorder across the life cycle. *Clinical Psychology: Science and Practice, 16*(2), 140–160.

Yung, A. R., Phillips, L. J., Yuen, H. P., & McGorry, P. D. (2004). Risk factors for psychosis in an ultra high-risk group: Psychopathology and clinical features. *Schizophrenia Research, 67,* 131–142.

Zadra, A., & Donderi, D. C. (2000). Nightmares and bad dreams: Their prevalence and relationship to well-being. *Journal of Abnormal Psychology, 109,* 273–281.

Zajonc, R. B. (1984). On the primacy of affect. *American Psychologist, 39*(2), 117–123.

Zajonc, R. B. (1998). Emotions. In D. Gilbert, S. T. Fiske, & G. Lindzey (Eds.), *Handbook of social psychology* (Vol. 1, 4th ed., pp. 591–632). New York, NY: McGraw-Hill.

Zanarini, M. C., Frankenburg, F. R., Hennen, J., Reich, D. B., & Silk, K. R. (2006). Prediction of the 10-year course of borderline personality disorder. *American Journal of Psychiatry, 163,* 827–832.

Zanarini, M. C., Reichman, C. A., Frankenburg, F. R., Reich, D. B., & Fitzmaurice, G. (2010). The course of eating disorders in patients with borderline personality disorder: A 10-year follow-up study. *International Journal of Eating Disorders, 43*(3), 226–232.

Zapf, P., Zottoli, T., & Pirelli, G. (2009). Insanity in the courtroom: Issues of criminal responsibility and competency to stand trial. In D. A. Krauss & J. D. Lieberman (Eds.), *Psychological expertise in court: Psychology in the courtroom* (pp. 79–101). Surrey, England: Ashgate Publishing.

Zautra, A., Johnson, L., & Davis, M. (2005). Positive affect as a source of resilience for women in chronic pain. *Journal of Consulting and Clinical Psychology, 73*, 212–220.

Zigler, E., & Hodapp, R. M. (1986). *Understanding mental retardation*. Cambridge, UK: Cambridge University Press.

Zilbergeld, B. (1999). *The new male sexuality*. New York, NY: Bantam Books.

Zilboorg, G., & Henry, G. (1941). *A history of medical psychology*. New York, NY: W. W. Norton.

Zimmerman, M., & Mattia, J. I. (1998). Body dysmorphic disorder in psychiatric outpatients: Recognition, prevalence, comorbidity, demographic, and clinical correlates. *Comprehensive Psychiatry, 39*(5), 265–270.

Zimmerman, M., Rothschild, L., & Chelminski, I. (2005). The prevalence of DSM-IV personality disorders in psychiatric outpatients. *American Journal of Psychiatry, 162*, 1911–1918.

Zinbarg, R. E., Craske, M. G., & Barlow, D. H. (2006). *Mastery of your anxiety and worry: Therapist guide*. New York, NY: Oxford University Press.

Zingmond, D. S., McGory, M. L., & Ko, C. Y. (2005). Hospitalization before and after gastric bypass surgery. *JAMA: Journal of the American Medical Association, 294*, 1918–1924.

Zipfel, S., Lowe, B., Deter, H. C., & Herzog, W. (2000). Long-term prognosis in anorexia nervosa: Lessons from a 21-year follow-up study. *Lancet, 355*, 721–722.

Zonana, H., & Buchanan, A. (2009). Ethical issues in the treatment of sex offenders. In F. M. Saleh, A. J. Grudzinskas, J. M. Bradford, & D. J. Brodsky (Eds.), *Sex offenders: Identification, risk assessment, treatment, and legal issues* (pp. 425–440). New York, NY: Oxford University Press.

Zubieta, J., Bueller, J., Jackson, L., Scott, D., Xu, Y., & Koeppe, R., ... Stohler, C. S. (2005). Placebo effects mediated by endogenous opioid activity on μ-opioid receptors. *Journal of Neuroscience, 25*, 7754–7762.

Zubin, J., Steinhauer, S. R., & Condray, R. (1992). Vulnerability to relapse in schizophrenia. *British Journal of Psychiatry, 161*, 13–18.

Zuccato, C., & Cattaneo, E. (2009). Brain-derived neurotrophic factor in neurodegenerative diseases. *Nature Reviews Neurology, 5*(6), 311–322.

Zuchner, S., Cuccaro, M. L., Tran-Viet, K. N., Cope, H., Krishnan, R. R., Pericak-Vance, M. A., ... Ashley-Koch, A. (2006). SLITRK1 mutations in trichotillomania. *Molecular Psychiatry, 11*, 887–889.

Zucker, K. J. (2005). Measurement of psychosexual differentiation. *Archives of Sexual Behavior, 34*, 375–388.

Zucker, K. J. (2010). The DSM diagnostic criteria for gender identity disorder in children. *Archives of Sexual Behavior, 39*, 477–498.

Zwahlen, M., & Egger, M. (2006). Progression and mortality of untreated HIV-positive individuals living in resource-limited settings: Update of literature review and evidence synthesis (UNAIDS Obligation HQ/05/42204). Retrieved from http://data.unaids.org/pub/periodical/2006/zwahlen_unaids_hq_05_422204_2007_en.pdf

NAME INDEX

Aarestad, S. L., 333
Aaron, L., 274
Aarsland, D., 519, 524
Abad, V., 316, 319
Abakoumkin, G., 207
Abbey, S. E., 269
Abbott, D. W., 291
Abbott, R., 106
Abdallah, A., 389
Abe, T., 498
Abel, G. G., 303, 355, 362
Abel, K., 468
Abela, J. R., 222
Abeles, N., 213, 227
Abelson, J. L., 120
Ables, J. L., 397
Abrahamson, D. J., 348
Abrams, G. M., 438
Abrams, K., 120
Abrams, M., 51
Abramson, 221
Abramson, L., 209, 219–220, 225
Abramson, L. Y., 55, 219–223, 299
Abujaoude, E., 179
Acampora, A., 400
Adachi, Y., 320
Adair, R., 312–313
Adams, H. E., 357
Adams, N., 105
Addenbrooke, W. M., 388
Addis, M. E., 223, 231
Ader, R., 256
Ades, J., 404
Aditya, H., 174, 176
Adlaf, E. M., 380
Adler, A. B., 150
Adler, C. M., 168
Afari, N., 269–270
Agatisa, P., 264
Agerbo, E., 469
Agras, W. S., 147, 250, 285, 288, 290–291, 295, 299–300, 302–303, 347
Agyei, Y., 334
Ahern, D. K., 169
Ahles, T. A., 271
Ahmed, F., 211
Aigner, M., 173
Aikins, D. E., 125
Aisen, P., 523
Åkerstedt, T., 317
Akiskal, H., 202, 209
Akiskal, H. S., 206, 209, 417
Aksan, N., 431
Akutagawa, D., 291
al'Absi, M., 262
Alarcón, R. D., 90, 108, 396
Albano, A. M., 124, 127, 138, 142, 144, 146, 155
Albert, C., 264
Albert, S. M., 517
Albertini, R. S., 181–182

Albery, I. P., 395
Albright, C. A., 262
Alcaine, O. M., 125
Alden, S., 429
Alder, A., 18, 20
Alderfer, M. A., 260
Alekseeva, N., 311
Alessi, S. M., 394
Alexander, F. G., 7, 11–12, 249, 262
Alexander, G. M., 417
Alexopoulos, G., 228
Alford, K. A., 507
Allardyce, J., 469–470
Allen, J., 499
Allen, J. J., 188
Allen, L. A., 165–167, 171–172, 177, 179, 182
Allen, L. B., 59, 126, 232
Allen, L. S., 334
Allen, N. B., 218
Allen-Hauser, W., 176
Aller, G., 551
Allin, M., 176
Allison, D., 306
Allison, K., 305
Alloy, L., 209, 219–220, 222, 225
Alloy, L. B., 219
Allsbeck, P., 62
Alonso, J., 237, 239
Alper, C. M., 254, 309
Alpers, G. W., 136, 168
Altarac, M., 492
Althof, S., 343–344, 346, 349–350, 352–353
Altshuler, L. L., 211
Alvarado, G. F., 149
Amaral, D. G., 500
Amat, J., 149
Amir, N., 155
Anastopoulos, A., 489
Ancoli-Israel, S., 98
Andersen, B. L., 258–259, 274, 333
Andersen, P. M., 177
Anderson, C., 335
Anderson, D., 268
Anderson, D. J., 124
Anderson, D. R., 258
Anderson, G., 189
Anderson, G. M., 386
Anderson-Fye, E., 292
Andrasik, F., 251, 271, 274
Andreasson, S., 62
Andreski, M. A., 149
Andrews, B., 192
Andrews, G., 125
Andrykowski, M. A., 21
Aneshensel, C. S., 525
Angold, A., 211, 406
Angst, F., 210
Angst, J., 202–204, 206, 209–210
Anguilo, M. J., 190
Annabi, S., 435

Annas, P., 55
Annus, A. M., 293
Ansell, E., 435
Anthony, D., 462
Anton, B., 94
Antoni, M. H., 258–260
Antony, M. M., 32, 71, 74, 136–138, 140–141, 143
Aouizerate, B., 51
Apfelbaum, B., 345
Appelbaum, K. A., 274
Apple, R. F., 308
Applebaum, A. J., 209, 234
Arai, J. A., 39
Arango, V., 216
Arbisi, P., 47
Arenas, E., 523
Arenkiel, B. R., 46
Armbruster, D., 48
Armesto, J. C., 471
Arnds, K., 432
Arnold, L. M., 405
Arnow, B., 299, 302
Arnow, B. A., 202
Arria, A. M., 384
Arrindell, W. A., 120, 129, 138, 140
Arseneault, A. M., 469
Arthur-Kelly, M., 509
Asberg, M., 238
Aschoff, J., 317
Ashworth, M., 463
Asmal, L., 130
Asmundson, G. J. G., 166–167, 169, 172–173
Asmundson, J. G., 168, 169
Atha, C., 241
Attia, E., 290, 300
Attie, I., 293, 297
Aubin, H.-J., 394–395
Audenaert, K., 454
Auyeng, B., 334, 338
Avenevoli, S., 211
Averill, P. M., 124
Avorn, J., 126
Axelson, D., 213
Axon, R. N., 261
Ayala, E. S., 32, 141
Ayalon, L., 98
Ayearst, L. E., 71
Ayers, C. R., 124, 138
Ayllon, T., 474
Ayuso-Mateos, J. L., 421
Azad, N., 320
Azmitia, E. C., 48
Azorin, J., 203
Azrin, N. H., 474

Baasher, T. A., 108
Baba, H., 460
Babyak, M., 231
Bach, A., 342, 351
Bach, A. K., 347, 352, 354

Bach, M., 173
Bachman, J., 388
Bader, J. O., 269
Baer, J. S., 401
Bagby, R., 418
Bagby, R. M., 71
Baghai, T. C., 47
Bailey, J., 338
Bailey, J. A., 106
Bailey, J. M., 334–336
Bailey, J. S., 275
Bailey, M., 333
Baillie, A., 260
Bajo, S., 172
Bakalar, J. B., 385
Baker, A., 336
Baker, C. D., 351
Baker, L., 298
Baker, S. L., 132
Bakker, A., 132–133
Bakkevig, J. F., 438
Bakshi, S., 337
Balabanis, M., 76
Baldessarini, R., 227
Baldessarini, R. J., 229
Baldwin, J. D., 360
Baldwin, J. I., 360
Baldwin, R., 213
Ball, J., 435
Ballard, C., 524
Ballenger, J. C., 155
Balon, R., 341, 349
Bancroft, J., 334, 339, 346, 351–352, 355
Bandelow, B., 435
Bandura, A., 55, 254, 266–267
Banegas, J. R., 262
Bankert, E. A., 110
Barban, L., 188
Barbaree, H. E., 360, 362
Bardone, A. M., 299
Barefoot, J. C., 250
Barger, L. K., 310
Bargh, J. A., 56
Barkley, R. A., 486–487, 489–490
Barksy, 171
Barlow, D. H., 4, 9, 32, 54–60, 71, 73, 83, 85–86, 90–91, 100, 117–119, 121–122, 124–131, 133–134, 136–151, 153, 155, 156–157, 168–169, 183, 203, 219–220, 222, 224–225, 232, 242, 251, 253, 264, 272–273, 303, 342, 347–350, 352, 354–356, 360–361, 435, 552
Barnard, A., 182
Barnes, G. M., 395
Barnes, J., 347
Barnes, M. A., 492
Barnhardt, T. M., 56
Baron-Cohen, S., 500
Barr, C. E., 469
Barrera, Á., 457

Barrera, A. Z., 232
Barrera, M., 394
Barrett, L. F., 58
Barrett, R., 108
Barrios, L. C., 237
Barry, S., 295
Barsky, A., 166, 171
Barsky, A. J., 166–169, 172
Bartak, L., 499
Bartels, S. J., 474
Bartlett, N., 339
Bartlik, B., 344
Barton, S., 251
Basden, S., 126
Baser, R., 239
Baskin, T. W., 99
Bassett, A. S., 465
Basson, R., 343–344, 347, 353
Bates, D., 171
Bateson, G., 470
Batshaw, M. L., 510
Battaglia, M., 172
Bauchner, H., 312
Bauer, J., 300
Baxter, L. R., 51
Baylé, F. J., 404
Beach, F., 333
Beach, S. R. H., 222, 224, 232
Beals, J., 211, 214, 236
Beardslee, W. R., 240
Beauducel, A., 51
Beautrais, A., 213
Bebbington, P., 435
Bebbington, P. E., 38
Bech, P., 202–203
Beck, A. T., 21, 220–221, 230,
    232–233, 239, 421, 435–437,
    438, 441–442
Beck, J. G., 124, 347–348, 353
Becker, A. E., 293
Becker, C. B., 303
Becker, D., 434
Becker, J. V., 362
Becker, R., 347
Bedrosian, R. C., 232
Beech, A. R., 360
Beech, H., 337
Beekly, D., 518
Beekman, A. T., 213
Beesdo-Baum, K., 128
Beets, M. W., 96
Behar, E., 133
Behar, E., 125
Beinecke, R., 105
Beitchman, J. H., 494
Belger, A., 468
Bell, I. R., 171
Bellack, A., 462
Bellack, A. S., 474
Bellak, L., 87
Bellinger, D. C., 489
Bello, I., 75
Bellodi, L., 172
Bellver, F., 476
Belnap, B. H., 126
Belzile, E., 512
Ben Itzchak, E., 499
Benbadis, R. R., 176
Benbadis, S., 176
Bender, D. S., 421, 423
Bender, E., 400
Bender, R. E., 219
Bendfeldt, F., 187
Benedetti, A., 167
Benedetti, F., 309
Ben-Eliyahu, S., 270
Benishay, D. S., 334

Bennedsen, B., 469
Bennett, D. A., 515
Bennett, P. H., 306
Bennett, S., 121, 253, 435
Bennett, S. M., 141
Benowitz, N., 386
Benson H., 272
Ben-Zeev, D., 455
Beratis, I., 462
Beratis, S., 462
Berberich, J. P., 501
Berenbaum, H., 424, 456, 474
Berger, J., 519
Bergeron, S., 346–347
Berglund, P., 124, 129, 138, 147,
    155, 237
Bergman, R. L., 494
Berkman, L. F., 62
Berkowitz, R. I., 308
Berlin, H. A., 404
Berlin, I. N., 236
Berlin, M. D., 358
Berman, A. L., 227, 236–239,
    241
Berman, J. R., 354
Berman, J. S., 207
Berman, K. F., 469
Bermudez, O., 299
Bernat, J. A., 357
Berner, L. A., 301
Bernstein, D. M., 191
Bernstein, D. P., 420
Berrios, G., 457
Berrios, G. E., 184
Berry, A. C., 231
Bertella, S., 172
Bertelsen, A., 465
Bertelsen, M., 477
Bertrand, L. D., 188
Besch, C. L., 258
Bettelheim, B., 499
Bettens, K., 521
Bezemer, P. D., 336
Bharucha, A., 524
Bhasin, T., 499
Bhati, K. S., 99
Bhaumik, D., 227
Bi, S., 435
Biederman, J., 143, 210, 428,
    487, 491
Bienias, J. L., 515
Bierut, L. J., 215–216, 381
Billick, S., 546
Billings, R., 322
Binet, A., 79
Bini, L., 12
Binik, Y., 347
Binik, Y. M., 346–347, 353
Binzer, M., 177
Birley, J., 470
Birley, J. L. T., 470
Birmaher, B., 209, 211–212, 217
Birmingham, L. C., 288
Birmingham, W. A., 262
Bishop, D., 492
Bisson, M. A., 333
Biswas, A., 259
Bivona, J. M., 331
Bjorvatn, B., 319
Blaauw, G. J., 126
Black, D. W., 124
Black, G. W., 264
Black, J. E., 309
Blackburn, I.-M., 232
Blacker, D., 76
Blackwell, E., 250, 255
Blair, K., 143

Blake, D. R., 383
Blakemore, S. J., 75
Blanchard, E. B., 271, 274
Blanchard, R., 335, 339, 358
Bland, R. C., 222
Blanes, T., 320
Blank, T. O., 260
Blascovich, J., 254
Blashfield, R. K., 87
Blazer, D., 171
Blazer, D. G., 124, 138, 147,
    212–214, 228
Blechman, E. A., 64
Blehar, M. C., 221
Bleiberg, K. L., 232
Bleijenberg, G., 270
Blendell, K. A., 144
Bliss, E. L., 188, 190
Bloch, M. H., 152–153
Block, 119
Block, J. J., 406
Block, S., 207
Blokhina, E., 399
Bloom, F. E., 46–47
Bloom, J. R., 259
Blumenthal, J. A., 59, 273
Blumenthal, S. J., 236, 240
Blundell, J. E., 306
Blyth, D., 223
Bockoven, J. S., 12–14
Bockting, W. O., 336
Boden, M. T., 424
Bodkin, J. A., 189
Bodlund, O., 339
Boehnlein, J., 214
Boeving, C. A., 260
Bogaert, A., 335
Bogaert, A. F., 335
Bogart, A. F., 335
Bögels, S. M., 141
Boggs, C., 417
Bohman, M., 171, 430
Bohn, K., 323
Bohn, R. L., 126
Boisseau, C. L., 58
Boland, R. J., 204–206
Bollini, P., 233
Bolton, B., 288
Bombardieri, R., 506
Bonanno, G., 207
Bond, A., 48
Bond, G. R., 490
Bongaarts, J., 257
Boocock, A., 179
Booij, L., 225
Boomsma, D., 337
Boomsma, D. I., 434
Boon, S., 184
Boone, E., 215
Borchardt, C., 120
Borckardt, J. J., 95
Borge, F. M., 441
Borges, G., 236–239
Borkovec, T. D., 124–126
Bornstein, R. F., 441
Borodinsky, L. N., 46
Bosinski, H. A. G., 336
Boskind-Lodahl, M., 291
Bouchard, C., 306
Bouchard, M. F., 489
Bouchard, T. J., Jr., 35, 104
Bourgeois, J. A., 519, 526
Bourgeois, M. S., 524
Boutilier, L. R., 435
Bouton, M. E., 54, 119, 121, 131
Bower, G. H., 60
Bower, J. E., 260

Bower, J. H., 264
Bowers, C. A., 402
Bowers, J. S., 56
Bowlby, J., 441
Bowler, D., 499
Bowman, E. P., 347
Boyer, P., 154
Boyle, C., 432
Bradford, A., 341, 360
Bradford, J., 363
Bradley, B. P., 125–126, 143
Bradley, M. M., 57, 430
Bradley, R., 492
Bradley, R. G., 215, 217
Bradley, S. J., 339
Bradshaw, S., 332
Brady, J. P., 177
Braff, D., 463–466
Braga, R., 472
Bramon, E., 462
Brand, B., 193
Brandsma, J., 187
Brandt, L., 285
Brannan, S. L., 225
Brannick, M., 294
Brannigan, G. G., 81
Brannon, L., 261
Brawman-Mintzer, O., 126, 155
Bredemeier, K., 424
Breeden, G., 239
Breedlove, S. M., 335
Breiling, J. P., 444
Bremner, J., 191
Bremner, J. D., 149–151
Brenner, N. D., 237, 239
Brennan, P., 429
Brennan-Krohn, T., 404
Brenner, D. E., 520
Brent, D., 207, 211–212, 216–217,
    232, 238
Brent, D. A., 216, 239
Brentjens, M. H., 250
Breslau, N., 148–149
Breuer, J., 15–16, 56
Brewer, S., 260
Brewin, C. R., 192
Briquet, P., 170
Britton, J. C., 120–121, 216
Brix, R. J., 404
Brodsky, B. S., 436
Brody, A. L., 51
Brody, M. J., 291
Broft, A., 301
Bromet, E., 148
Bromet, E. J., 236–239, 470
Bromley, E., 423
Brondolo, E., 262
Brønnick, K., 524
Brook, J. S., 184, 303
Brook, M., 404
Brooks, D. J., 394
Brooks-Gunn, J., 293, 297
Brotto, L. A., 342–343, 353
Broughton, R., 322
Brower, K. J., 391
Brown, D. R., 211
Brown, G. K., 210, 242
Brown, G. W., 218, 224,
    470–471
Brown, J., 269
Brown, J. D., 395
Brown, P. L., 364
Brown, T. A., 74, 86, 89, 91,
    117–118, 121, 122, 124, 136,
    156–157, 203, 347, 354
Brown, T. E., 488
Brown, W. M., 335

SUBJECT INDEX

Blindsight, 56
Blood, fear and, 57
Blood pressure
    description of, 261–262
    vasovagal syncope and, 32
Blood–injury–injection phobia, 1, 32–33,
        136–137, 141
Bloodletting, 11
Body dysmorphic disorder (BDD), 178–182,
        198
    causes of, 181
    clinical description of, 178–179
    statistics about, 179–181
    treatment of, 181–182
Body image, eating disorder and, 297, 299
Body weight
    anorexia nervosa and, 289–290
    social dimensions of, 294–298
Bombing, 148
Borderline personality disorder, 415, 433–
        436, 449
    DSM-IV-TR description of, 415
    statistics about, 416
    suicide and, 240–241
Bradykinesia, 519
Brain
    alcohol effects on, 378
    in Alzheimer's disease, 520
    anatomy of, 44, 46
    anxiety disorder and, 119–120
    attention deficit/hyperactivity disorder and,
        488–489
    autistic disorder and, 499–500
    borderline personality disorder and, 435
    Broca's area of, 456
    in dementia, 522
    in dissociative disorder, 191
    environment and, 36
    immune system and, 256
    learning disorder and, 493
    mood disorders and, 216
    neuroimaging of, 81–82
    in obsessive-compulsive disorder, 50–51, 155
    placebo effects and, 278
    in posttraumatic stress disorder, 149–150
    psychosocial factors and, 51–53
    reward center of, 393
    schizophrenia and, 468–469
    spinal cord and, 40–41
    stress and, 252–253
    structure of, 42–45
    surgery on, 51
Brain circuit, 46–47
Brain imaging, 455–456
Brain stem, 42
Brain wave, 83, 217
Breast, gynecomastia and, 339
Breathing-related sleep disorder, 310, 315–
        316, 318, 329
Brief Psychiatric Rating Scale, 76
Brief psychotic disorder, 460–461
Briquet's syndrome, 170
Broca's area, 456, 493
Bromides, 12
2-(4-bromo-2,5-dimethoxy-phenyl)-
        ethylamine, 391
Bulimia nervosa, 286–289, 328
    binge-eating disorder and, 291
    case study of, 286–287
    clinical description of, 287–288
    gender and, 61
    statistics about, 291–292
    treatment of, 301–302

C fibers, 267
Caffeine use disorder, 387
Cambodian patient, panic disorder in, 130

Cancer, 258–260, 282
Cannabinoid, 388–390
Capgras syndrome, 454
Capsulotomy, 156
CARDIA study, 262
Cardiac artery, 262
Cardiovascular disease, 260–264, 282
Case study method
    description of, 95–96
    single case experiment vs, 101–102
Castration anxiety, 18
Catalepsy, 207
Cataplexy, 315, 318
Catatonia, 451
Catatonic immobility, 458–460
Catatonic type of schizophrenia, 458
Categorical approach, classical, 85
Category, of personality disorder, 414
Catharsis, 15, 150
Caudate nucleus, 43
Causation, correlation and, 96
Centers for Disease Control and Prevention,
        331
Central nervous system, 40–45
    brain structure, 42–45
    components of, 40–41
    psychosocial factors and, 51–53
Central sleep apnea, 316
Cerebellum, 42
Cerebral cortex, 43
Cerebrospinal fluid, 468
Cerebrovascular accidents, 260–261
CFS. *See* Chronic fatigue syndrome
Chang and Eng, 39
Chemical dependence, 395
Chemical transporter, 37
Child. *See also* Adolescent
    anxiety disorder and, 121
    bipolar disorder in, 212–213
    conduct disorder in, 428, 432
    conversion disorder and, 177
    developmental disorder in. *See*
        Developmental disorder
    dissociative disorder in, 190
    false memories and, 192
    gender nonconformity in, 363–364
    hypochondriasis and, 169
    incest and, 358
    insomnia and, 312
    mood disorder in, 211–213
        prevention of, 232–233
        treatment of, 228
    obesity treatment in, 308
    pedophilia and, 358–359
    personality disorder in, 415
    phobias in, 138
    posttraumatic stress disorder in, 146, 149
    schizoid personality disorder in, 422–423
    separation anxiety in, 137
    sleep terrors in, 130, 321
Child abuse
    in borderline personality disorder, 435
    dissociative disorder and, 189–190
    false memories and, 192
    Munchausen syndrome by proxy vs,
        174–175
Childhood disintegrative disorder, 496–497,
        533
Chinese patient
    hypochondriasis and, 167
    phobias in, 138–139
    suicide in, 236–237
Choleric personality, 11
Cholinesterase inhibitors, 523
Chorionic villus sampling, 507
Chromosomal abnormality
    Alzheimer's disease and, 520

Down syndrome, 506–507
    fragile X syndrome, 507–508
Chromosome, 34
Chronic course, 5
Chronic disease. *See* Physical disorder
Chronic fatigue syndrome, 268–270
Chronic negative emotion, 262
Chronic pain, 264–268, 282
Chronic stress
    description of, 252
    posttraumatic. *See* Posttraumatic stress
        disorder
Chronic traumatic encephalopathy, 518, 522
Cigarette smoking
    Alzheimer's disease and, 520
    anxiety disorder and, 121
    quitting, 399
Cingulate gyrus, 43
Cingulotomy, 156
Circadian rhythm
    mood disorders and, 217
    sleep disorder and, 310, 316–317
Circuit, brain, 46–47
Circumcision accident, 338
Civil commitment, 538–543, 554
    changes affecting, 540–542
    criteria for, 538–540
    overview of, 538, 542–543
    Supreme Court and, 540
Classical categorical approach, 85
Classical conditioning, 20–21
Classification, 84–85
Cleft, synaptic, 40
Clergy, pedophilia and, 358
Clinical assessment, 70–71
Clinical description, 5
Clinical efficacy axis, 552–553
Clinical interview
    mental status examination in, 72–75
    semistructured, 74–75
Clinical practice guidelines, 551–552,
        554–555
Clinical psychologist, 4
Clinical trial, 98
Clinical utility axis, 552–553
Clomipramine, 181
Clonidine, 399
Cluster A personality disorder, 415, 419–425,
        444, 448
    paranoid, 419–421
    schizoid, 421–423
    schizotypal, 423–425
Cluster B personality disorder, 415, 425–439,
        444, 449
    antisocial, 425–432
    borderline, 433–436
    histrionic, 436–438
    narcissistic, 438–439
Cluster C personality disorder, 415, 440–443,
        445, 448–449
    avoidant, 440–441
    dependent, 441–442
    obsessive-compulsive, 442–443
Cocaine use disorder
    description of, 384–386
    sexual dysfunction and, 349
Coefficient, correlation, 96–97
Cognition, 58
Cognitive disorder, 511–526, 528, 534
    amnestic, 526–527
    delirium, 512–513
    dementia, 514–525. *See also* Dementia
Cognitive factors
    in borderline personality disorder, 435
    in mood disorder, 246
    in schizophrenia, 482
    in substance use disorder, 394–395

Dependent personality disorder, 441–442, 448
  DSM-IV-TR description of, 415
  statistics about, 416
Dependent variable, 92
Depersonalization disorder, 183–184
Depressant, 376–377, 410–411
Depression, 246–247
  in adolescent, 201–202
  age and, 206
  in AIDS, 258
  anorexia nervosa and, 291
  anxiety and, 122
  bulimia nervosa and, 288
  clinical description of, 204
  cognitive vulnerability for, 221–222
  coronary heart disease and, 264
  cultural differences in symptoms of, 108
  definition of, 60
  double, 205
  duration of, 206–207
  in elderly, 213–214
  grief and, 207
  lack of control and, 55
  learned helplessness and, 220
  mania and, 203–204
  marital relationship and, 222
  onset of, 206–207
  schizotypal personality disorder and, 424
  stress and, 253–254
  stressful live events and, 218–219
Depressive cognitive triad, 221
Depressive personality disorder, 418. *See also* Depression
Deprivation, maternal, 39
Derailment, 73
Derealization, 183
Description, clinical, 5
Design, research
  comparative treatment, 99
  cross-sectional, 106
  group experimental, 98–99
  longitudinal, 106–107
  multiple baseline, 103
  sequential, 107
  single-case experimental, 99–103
  withdrawal, 100–101
Designer drug, 391, 490–491
Desire disorder, sexual, 342–343, 353
Deterministic gene, 521
Development, psychosexual stages of, 18
Developmental disorder, 485–511, 527
  attention deficit/hyperactivity disorder
    causes of, 488–490
    clinical description of, 486–487
    statistics about, 487–488
    treatment of, 490–491
  integrating treatment of, 502
  intellectual disability, 502–510
  learning disorder, 491–495
  overview of, 485–486
  pervasive, 496–502
    Asperger's, 500–501
    autistic, 496–500
    disintegrative, 497
    Rett's, 497
    unspecified, 497
  prevention of, 510–511
Developmental factors
  in antisocial personality disorder, 431
  in phobia, 33
  in schizophrenia, 462
Developmental psychology, 5
Developmental psychopathology, 64
Developmental psychotherapy, 5
Dhat, 167
Diagnosis, 84–91, 112

classification issues in, 85–86
current trends in, 90
definition of, 70–71
DSM-IV-TR in, 86–87
overview of, 84–85
reliability of, 86–87
validity of, 87
Diagnostic and Statistical Manual of Mental Disorders. See also DSM-IV-TR criteria
  changes in, 86
  criticisms of, 89
  DSM-III, 87–88
  DSM-III-R, 87–88
  DSM-5, 88, 154
  multiaxial format of, 88
  new approach to, 90–91
  new edition of, 90–91
  on panic attacks, 118–119
  on personality disorder, 413–415
  reliability and validity of, 86–87
  social and cultural considerations in, 89
  on somatoform disorders, 194
Dialectical behavioral therapy, 436
Diastolic blood pressure, 261
Diathesis, 219
Diathesis–stress model, 36–37
Diet, phenylketonuria and, 506
Dietary restraint, 297
Dieting
  anorexia nervosa and, 289
  eating disorder and, 295–296
  in obesity, 306–307
Dilator for vaginismus, 353
Dimension of personality disorder, 414
Dimensional approach, 85–86
Diminished capacity, 544–545
Directionality, 96–97
Disability, 90
Discrimination training, 501
Disease. *See* Physical disorder
Disease conviction, 167
Disease model of chemical dependence, 395
Disorder of written expression, 492–493
Disorganized schizophrenia, 457–458
Disorganized speech, 457
Disorganized symptoms, of schizophrenia, 454, 457–458
Displacement, 17
Dissociative disorder, 165, 183–199
  causes of, 189–192
  clinical description of, 187–189
  depersonalization disorder as, 183–184
  dissociative amnesia as, 184–185, 199
  fugue state as, 185–186, 199
  identify disorder as, 187–193, 199
  statistics about, 189
  trance disorder as, 186–187, 199
  treatment of, 192–193
Distress, personal, 2
Disulfiram, 399
Diversity. *See also* Cultural factors
  anxiety disorder and, 120
  eating disorders and, 294
  fear and, 60
  gender identity disorder and, 337
  suicide and, 239
Divorce, 38
DNA molecule, 34
Dog phobia, 139
Domestic violence, 380
Dominant gene, 34, 506
Donepezil, 523
Dopamine
  mood disorders and, 216
  as neurotransmitter, 48–49
  schizophrenia and, 466–468
Dopamine antagonist, 472

Dopamine D_4 receptor gene, 488
Double bind communication, 470
Double helix, 34
Double-blind control, 99
Down syndrome, 506–507
Dracula hormone, 317
Dream analysis, 19
Dream sleep, nightmares in, 320–321
Driving phobia, 139
Drug abuse. *See* Substance-related disorder
Drug therapy
  addictiveness of, 375
  in AIDS, 258
  attention deficit/hyperactivity disorder treated with, 490–491
  body dysmorphic disorder treated with, 181
  chronic fatigue syndrome treated with, 270
  delirium caused by, 512–513
  dementia treated with, 523–524
  development of, 12
  generalized anxiety disorder treated with, 126
  headache and, 274
  hypochondriasis treated with, 169
  mood disorder treated with, 227–229, 233, 247
  obsessive-compulsive disorder treated with, 155–156
  panic attack and, 132–133
  paraphilia treated with, 363
  schizophrenia and, 472–474
  sexual dysfunction treated with, 353–354
  sleep disorder treated with, 318–319
  social phobia treated with, 144–145
DSM-III, 87–88
DSM-III-R, 87–88
DSM-IV-TR criteria
  Alzheimer's disease, 518
  anorexia nervosa, 290
  attention deficit/hyperactivity disorder, 488
  autistic disorder, 498
  bipolar II disorder, 208
  body dysmorphic disorder, 178
  bulimia nervosa, 288
  conduct disorder, 429
  cyclothymic disorder, 210
  delirium, 512
  delusional disorder, 460
  dissociative fugue, 186
  dysthymic disorder, 205
  generalized anxiety disorder, 124
  hypoactive sexual desire disorder, 342
  hypochondriasis, 168
  identity disorder
    dissociative, 188
    gender, 337
  intellectual disability, 504
  intoxication
    amphetamine, 383–384
    caffeine, 387
    cannabis, 390
    cocaine, 384
    hallucinogen, 390
    sedative, hypnotic, or anxiolytic, 382
    substance, 373
  major depressive episode, 86, 203
  manic episode, 204
  narcolepsy, 315
  nicotine withdrawal, 386
  opioid withdrawal, 388
  personality disorder
    antisocial, 427
    avoidant, 440
    borderline, 434
    dependent, 442

Fluoxetine. *See also* Prozac
 body dysmorphic disorder treated with, 181
 description of, 228
 mood disorders treated with, 227
fMRI, 82
Folie à deux, 460
Food additive, 489
Forebrain, 42
Formal observation, 76
Four humors, 11
Fragile X syndrome, 507–508
Framingham Heart Study, 263
Fraternal twins, 104
Free association, 19
Freud, Sigmund
 case study method and, 95
 on conversion disorder, 176
 psychoanalytic theory of, 15–18
"Friends with benefits," 333
Frontal lobe
 function of, 45
 schizophrenia and, 469
Frotteurism, 355
Fugue state, 199
Functional communication training, 102
Functional genomics, 393
Functional magnetic resonance imaging, 82
Fusion, thought–action, 155

GABA. *See* Gamma-aminobutyric acid
GABA-benzodiazepine system, 119
GAD. *See* Generalized anxiety disorder
Galantamine, 523
Galen, 10–11
Galvanic skin response (GSR), 83
Gambling, pathological, 404–405, 411
Gamma-aminobutyric acid (GABA)
 alcohol and, 378
 anxiety disorder and, 119
 as neurotransmitter, 47–48
Gamma-hydroxybutyrate (GHB), 318, 392
Ganglion, basal, 43–44
GAS. *See* General adaptation syndrome
Gate control theory of pain, 267
Genain quadruplets, 464
Gender
 agoraphobia and, 129
 attention deficit/hyperactivity disorder and, 487
 body dysmorphic disorder and, 179
 conversion disorder and, 176
 eating disorder and, 286–287, 291, 295
 generalized anxiety disorder and, 124
 histrionic personality disorder and, 437
 hypochondriasis and, 167
 hysteria and, 11
 insomnia and, 312
 mood disorder and, 215–216, 222–223
 orgasmic disorder and, 345–346
 pain and, 267–268
 paraphilia and, 359
 personality disorder and, 417
 posttraumatic stress disorder and, 149
 psychopathology and, 61–62
 sexual arousal disorders and, 343–344
 sexual behavior and, 332–334
 sexual desire disorder and, 342–343
 sexual orientation and, 334–335
 social phobias and, 142
 somatization disorder and, 171
 suicide and, 236
Gender identity disorder, 335–340, 363
 causes of, 336–339
 definition of, 335
 description of, 331
 treatment of, 339–340
Gender nonconformity, 338–339, 363–364

Gene. *See also* Genetics
 attention deficit/hyperactivity disorder and, 488–489
 behavior and, 35
 definition of, 34–35
 intellectual disability and, 506
 nature of, 34–35
Gene-environmental model, reciprocal, 37–38
General adaptation syndrome (GAS), 252–253
General paresis, 11
Generalizability, 94
Generalization, stimulus, 21
Generalized amnesia, 184–185
Generalized anxiety disorder (GAD), 123–127, 163
Generalized social phobia, 142
Generalized vulnerability
 to anxiety disorder, 126
 description of, 122, 131
Genetic linkage analysis, 104–105
Genetic marker, 104–105
Genetic predisposition, 39
Geneticist, behavioral, 36, 39
Genetics, 34–40
 adoption studies in, 104
 Alzheimer's disease and, 521
 antisocial personality disorder and, 429
 anxiety disorder and, 119
 attention deficit/hyperactivity disorder and, 488–489
 autistic disorder and, 499–500
 behavior and, 35
 body dysmorphic disorder and, 181
 borderline personality disorder and, 434
 eating disorder and, 298
 environment and, 36–38
 hypertension and, 261
 intellectual disability and, 506
 in mood disorders, 215–216
 narcolepsy and, 316
 nature of genes and, 34–35
 nongenomic "inheritance" and, 38–40
 obesity and, 306
 phobias and, 140
 research and, 103–105, 112
 schizoid personality disorder and, 423
 of schizophrenia, 463–466
 schizotypal personality disorder and, 424
 social phobia and, 143
 stressful life events and, 219
 substance-related disorder and, 392–393
 twin studies and, 104
Genital examination, 192
Genital surgery, 339–340
Genome, 35
Genotype, 103
GHB. *See* Gamma-hydroxybutyrate
Ginkgo biloba, 523
Global incidence of psychological disorder, 63
Globus hystericus, 174
Glutamate
 alcohol and, 378
 as neurotransmitter, 47–48
Graduated extinction for insomnia, 319
Grandiose delusion, 460
Grandiosity, 439
Grief reaction, 207
Group, control, 93, 98–99
Group experimental design, 98–99
Group therapy, for social phobia, 144–145
Guided imagery relaxation, 319
Guidelines
 clinical practice, 551–552, 554–555
 ethical, 111
Guilty but mentally ill, 546–547

Gum, nicotine, 399
Gynecomastia, 339
Gyrus, cingulate, 43

HAART. *See* Highly active antiretroviral treatment
Habit, sleep, 320
Hair-pulling, 405, 411
Hallucination
 definition of, 73, 207
 hypnagogic, 315
 in schizophrenia, 455–456
Hallucinogen, 376–377, 388–390, 410
Hallucinogen use disorder, 388–389
Halstead-Reitan Neuropsychological Battery, 81
Hara-kiri, 238
Harm, psychological, research and, 110
Head trauma
 dementia with, 519
 in dissociative disorder, 191
Health
 description of, 250–251
 social relationships and, 62–63
Health psychology, 250–251
Health-related behavior, 250–251
Hearing, 57
Heart, 58–59
Heart attack, 262
Heart disease, 260–264
Hebephrenia, 451
Hebephrenic schizophrenia, 458
Helix, double, 34
Helper T cell, 255
Helplessness, learned, 54–55
Hemisphere of brain, 44, 493
Heritability of behavior, 35–36. *See also* Genetics
Heterosexual behavior, 332
Hierarchy of needs, 20
High expressed emotion, 471
Highly active antiretroviral treatment (HAART), 258
Hillside Strangler, 188
Hindbrain, 42
Hippocampus, 43
 mood disorders and, 217
 stress and, 252–253
Hippocrates, 10–11
Hispanic patient, eating disorders in, 292
Histrionic personality disorder, 436–438, 449
 DSM-IV-TR description of, 415
 gender bias and, 417
 statistics about, 416
HIV infection. *See* Human immunodeficiency virus infection
Hoarding, 153–154
Home visit, 75
Homelessness, 540–541
Homosexual behavior, 332
Homosexuality
 biological determination of, 334–335
 gender identity disorder and, 336
 hormone exposure and, 334–335
"Hooking up," 333
Hormone
 definition of, 46–47
 Dracula, 317
 sexual orientation and, 334–335
Host identity, 187
Hostility, 262
Human genome project, 103
Human immunodeficiency virus infection (HIV)
 dementia and, 519
 description of, 257–258
 prevention of, 275–276

Humanistic psychology, 20
Humanistic theory, 20
Humoral immune system, 255
Humoral theory, 10–11
Huntington's disease, 519–520
Hygiene, mental, 14–15
Hyperactivity disorder, 486–491
Hyperplasia, congenital adrenal, 337–338
Hypersomnia, primary, 310, 314–315, 329
Hypertension, 261–262
Hypnagogic hallucination, 315
Hypnosis
    faking of, 188
    unconscious vision in, 56
Hypnotic use disorder, 380–382
Hypoactive sexual desire disorder, 342–343
Hypochondriasis, 166–169, 198
    causes of, 168–169
    clinical description of, 166–167
    statistics about, 167–168
    treatment of, 169
Hypofrontality, 469
Hypomanic episode, 203
Hypothalamic-pituitary-adrenal axis, 46
    mood disorders and, 216
    stress and, 252–253
Hypothalamus, 42
Hypothesis
    cognitive reserve, 517
    description of, 92–93
    underarousal, 429
Hypothesis testing, 231
Hypoventilation, 316
Hysteria
    history of, 11
    mass, 8–9

Id, 16–17
Ideas of reference, 73, 422
Ideation, suicidal, 237, 239
Identical twins
    description of, 39, 104
    mood disorders in, 215
Identity
    host, 187
    search for, 185–186
Identity disorder
    dissociative, 187–193, 199
    gender, 331, 335–340
Illness. See Physical disorder
Image, body, 295, 297
Imagery, guided, 319
Imaginal exposure, 150
Imaging, 81–83
    borderline personality disorder evaluations,
        434–435
    brain, 81–82
    dissociative identity disorder evaluations,
        189
    hallucinations and, 455–456
    learning disorder evaluations, 495
    neuroimaging, 81–82
Immobility, catatonic, 458–459
Immune response, 254–257
Immune system, 254–257
Immunizations, 500
Immunoglobulin, 255
Impacted grief reaction, 207
Impairment, personal, 2
Implant, penile, 354
Implicit memory, 56
Impulse-control disorder, 371, 403–406, 411
Impulsivity
    in attention deficit/hyperactivity disorder,
        486–487
    somatization disorder and, 172
Inadequate coping, 225

Inappropriate affect, 457, 459
Inattention, 486
Incest, 358–359
Incidence, 5
Independent living skills program, 475
Independent variable, 92–93
Indicated prevention, 106
Individual case study, 95
Infant
    failure to thrive in, 295
    gender reassignment in, 338
    shyness in, 143
Inference, arbitrary, 221
Inferiority complex, 18
Informal observation, 76
Information
    retrospective, 106–107
    transmission of, 139
Inhalant, 391
Inheritance. See Genetics
Inhibited orgasm, 345
Injury control, 275
Inkblot test, 77
Inpatient treatment of substance abuse, 400
Insanity defense, 545–547
Insanity Defense Reform Act, 544
Insidious onset, 5
Insomnia
    drug therapy for, 318
    primary, 310–314, 329
    psychological treatment of, 319–320
    rebound, 313–314
Institute of Medicine, 241
Institutionalization
    civil commitment and, 538–543
    criminal commitment and, 542–547
Insulin shock therapy, 12
Integrative approach
    antisocial personality disorder managed
        with, 431
    anxiety disorder managed with, 122
    Asperger's disorder managed with, 502
    borderline personality disorder managed
        with, 436
    eating disorders managed with, 299
    insomnia managed with, 313–314
    mood disorders managed with, 224–225
    psychopathology, 23, 31–68
        behavioral and cognitive science in,
            53–56
        cultural, social, and interpersonal factors
            in, 61–63
        emotions and, 57–60
        genetics and, 34–40
        life-span development in, 64–65
        multidimensional model of, 32–34
        neuroscience in, 40–53. See also
            Neuroscience
    schizophrenia managed with, 476
    substance use disorder managed with,
        396–397
Intellectual disability, 502–510, 528, 533
    causes of, 505–508
    clinical description of, 503–505
    educable, 505
    mild, 504
    moderate, 504
    overview of, 502
    profound, 504
    severe, 504–505
    statistics about, 505
    trainable, 505
    treatment of, 508–510
Intellectual function, 73
Intelligence
    autism and, 498–499
    intellectual disability and, 505

Intelligence testing, 79–80
Interceptive avoidance, 128
Intermittent explosive disorder, 403, 411
Internal validity, 92–93
International Classification of Diseases,
    87–88
Interpersonal psychotherapy
    bulimia nervosa treated with, 301
    description of, 232
    mood disorder treated with, 247
Interpersonal relationship, 62–63
Intersexuality, 339–340
Intoxication
    amphetamine, 383
    caffeine, 387
    cannabis, 390
    cocaine, 384
    definition of, 373
    hallucinogen, 390
    opioid, 388
Intrapsychic conflict, 17
Introjection, 18
Introspection, 21
Intrusive thought, 154
Inventory, personality, 78
Inverse agonist, 47
IQ
    autism and, 498–499
    intellectual disability and, 505
IQ test, 79–80
Isolated sleep paralysis, 130–131

Jackson v. Indiana, 548
Japanese patient
    body dysmorphic disorder and, 181
    eating disorders in, 293
    social phobia in, 143
Jealous type of delusion, 460
Jet lag, 313, 316–317
Job loss, 218
Jurisprudence, therapeutic, 547–549

Kansas v. Hendricks, 542
Khmer patient, panic disorder in, 130
Killer T cell, 255
King Charles VI of France, 8
Kleptomania, 403–405, 411
Koro, 60, 167
Kuru, 522

La belle indifférence, 177
Labeling, 89–90
Language
    in autistic disorder, 501
    echolalia and, 486
Language disorder, 493–494, 532
Law
    civil commitment, 538–543
    criminal commitment and, 542–547, 554
    patients' rights and, 550–553
Law of effect, 22
L-dopa
    mood disorders and, 216
    schizophrenia and, 466
Learned alarm, 131
Learned helplessness
    depression and, 220
    description of, 54–55
Learned optimism, 55
Learned response, 169
Learning, 55
Learning disorder, 532
    causes of, 493–494
    clinical description of, 492
    definition of, 491
    statistics about, 492–493
    treatment of, 494–495

prevalence of, 138
situational, 136–137
social. *See* Social phobia
social influences of, 33
specific, 135–136
statistics about, 137–139
treatment of, 140–141
Photoplethysmograph, vaginal, 347
Phototherapy, 319
Physical disorder, 248–283
AIDS, 257–258
anorexia nervosa and, 290
bulimia nervosa and, 288
cancer, 258–260
cardiovascular, 260–264
chronic fatigue syndrome, 268–270
chronic pain, 264–268
definition of, 249
health behaviors and, 250–251
psychological treatment of, 270–278
behavior modification, 274–277
biofeedback, 271
denial and, 274
drugs and, 274
relaxation and meditation, 272
stress and pain reduction, 272–274
sexual dysfunction and, 349
stress and, 251–257. *See also* Stress;
Stressful life event
Physical examination, 75
Pick's disease, 520–521
Pituitary gland
function of, 46
mood disorders and, 216
Placebo
brain and, 278
control group and, 98–99
in panic disorder study, 134–135
treatment delay or withdrawal and, 109
Placebo effect, 98–99
Plaque, 520
Plastic surgery, 182
Pleasure center, 393
Pleasure principle, 16
Pleasuring, nondemand, 352
Polygenic trait, 35
Polysomnographic evaluation, 309
Polysubstance use, 371
Pons, 42
Poppies, 387–388
Positive correlation, 96–97
Positive regard, unconditional, 20–21
Positive reinforcement, 394
Positive symptoms, of schizophrenia,
454–456
Positron emission tomography (PET) scan,
82
Possession, 186
Posttraumatic stress disorder, 145–151, 163
causes of, 148–150
clinical description of, 146–147
dissociative disorder and, 190
DSM criteria for, 147
statistics about, 147–148
symptoms of, 146–147
treatment of, 150–151
Practice guidelines, 551–552, 554–555
Predictive validity, 87
Predisposition, genetic, 39
Pregnancy, schizophrenia and, 469
Premarital sex, 334
Premature ejaculation, 346, 352–353
Prenatal influences in schizophrenia,
469–470
Prepared learning, 55–56
Presenting problem, 5
Prevalence, 5

Prevention
accident, 275
of AIDS, 275–276
of antisocial personality disorder, 432
of delirium, 513
of dementia, 525
of eating disorder, 303–304
exposure and ritual, 51, 155–156
of mood disorder, 232–233
of schizophrenia, 477
of sleep disorder, 320
of substance use disorder, 402, 410
Prevention research, 105–107
Primary gain in conversion disorder, 176
Primary hypersomnia, 310, 314–315, 329
Primary insomnia, 310–314, 329
Primary process, 16
Primate study, 252
Principle, reality, 16
Privileged communication, 74
Proband, 104
Problem, presenting, 5
Problem-solving for suicidal patient,
241–242
Process research, 99
Prodromal stage of schizophrenia, 462
Professional, mental health, 4
Prognosis, 5
Progressive muscle relaxation, 272, 319
Projection, 17
Projective test, 77–78
Prosthesis, penile, 354
Prototype, 3
Prototypical approach, 86
Prozac, 48. *See also* Fluoxetine
body dysmorphic disorder treated with,
181
sexual dysfunction and, 349
social phobia treated with, 145
suicide risk and, 227
Psyche, 6
Psychiatric social worker, 4
Psychiatrist, 4
Psychoactive substance, 372–373
Psychoanalysis, 14–15
Psychoanalyst, 19
Psychoanalytic model, 16–17
Psychoanalytic theory, 15–20
defense mechanisms in, 17
later developments in, 18–19
psychosexual stages of development in, 18
psychotherapy in, 19–20
structure of mind in, 16–17
Psychodynamic psychotherapy, 19
Psychological autopsy of suicide, 238
Psychological dimensions of mood disorder,
217–222
cognitive vulnerability, 221–222
learned helplessness, 220
negative cognitive style, 220–221
stressful life events, 218–219
Psychological disorder
definition of, 1
suicide and, 239
Psychological dysfunction, 2–3
Psychological experience, early, 52
Psychological factors
in antisocial personality disorder, 430–431
in anxiety disorder, 121
in attention deficit/hyperactivity disorder,
489–490
in autistic disorder, 499
brain function and, 51–53
in dementia, 522
in eating disorder, 298–299
influencing health, 249–257, 278, 282
in insomnia, 312

in intellectual disability, 508
in mood disorder, 246
neurotransmitters and, 52
in paranoid personality disorder, 420–421
in schizophrenia, 470–471
in sexual dysfunction, 349–350
in substance use disorder, 393–394
Psychological harm, 110
Psychological model, of abnormal
behavior, 6
Psychological test, 111
of intelligence, 79–80
neuroimaging in, 81–82
neuropsychological, 81
personality inventory, 78–79
projective, 77–78
psychophysiological, 82–83
Psychological tradition of psychopathology
asylum reform in, 14–15
behavioral model in, 20–23
humanistic theory in, 20
moral therapy in, 13–23
psychoanalytic theory in, 15–20. *See also*
Psychoanalytic theory
Psychological treatment. *See also*
Psychosocial treatment
for cancer, 258–260
for generalized anxiety disorder, 126–127
for mood disorder, 230–233
bipolar, 234–235
cognitive-behavioral therapy, 230–232
combined, 233
interpersonal, 232
preventive, 232–233
of obesity, 308
for panic disorder, 133–134
for paraphilia, 361–363
of sleep disorder, 319–320
of substance use disorder, 399–402
Psychological vulnerability.
See Vulnerability
Psychologist, 4
Psychology
developmental, 5
health, 250–251
humanistic, 20
Psychomotor retardation, 73
Psychoneuroendocrinology, 46
Psychoneuroimmunology, 256–257
Psychopath. *See* Antisocial personality
disorder
Psychopathology
biological tradition of, 10–13
causation in, 6
clinical description of, 5
definition of, 3
emotion and, 59–60
integrative approach to, 31–68. *See also*
Integrative approach
psychological tradition of, 13–23
science of, 4–6
scientific method in, 23
scientist-practitioner of, 4
supernatural tradition and, 6–10
treatment in, 6
types of disorders, 2–3
Psychopathy, 427, 429. *See also* Antisocial
personality disorder
Psychopharmacogenetics, 490
Psychophysiological assessment, 82–83,
111–112
Psychophysiological disorders, 249
Psychosexual stages of development, 18
Psychosis. *See also* Psychotic disorder
cultural factors in treatment of, 477
syphilis causing, 11–12
Psychosocial approach, 13

Self-observation, 76
Self-schema, sexual, 333
Semen, 334
Semistructured clinical interview, 74–75
Senile plaque, 520
Sensitization
    covert, 361–362
    for paraphilia, 361–363
Sensorium, 73
Separation anxiety, 137, 141
September 11 attack, 97
Sequential design, 107
Serotonin. *See also* Selective serotonin reup-
        take inhibitor
    borderline personality disorder and, 434
    mood disorders and, 216
    as neurotransmitter, 48
    in obsessive-compulsive disorder, 50
Serotonin transporter gene, 435
Severe intellectual disability, 505
Sex chromosome, 34
Sex differences. *See* Gender
Sex offender, 542
Sex reassignment surgery, 339
Sexual arousal disorder
    distraction and, 351
    psychosocial treatment of, 352–353
Sexual arousal in paraphilia, 360
Sexual aversion disorder, 342–343
Sexual behavior, 172
Sexual desire disorder, 342, 353
Sexual dysfunction, 340–355, 365. *See also*
        Paraphilia
    of arousal, 343–344
    causes of, 348–351
    of desire, 342–343
    orgasmic, 345–346
    pain disorder, 346–347
    treatment of, 351–354
    types of, 342
Sexual orientation, 334–335
Sexual pain disorder, 346–347
Sexual response cycle, 341
Sexual revolution, 334
Sexual self-schema, 333
Sexuality
    cultural differences in, 334
    gender differences in, 332–334
    myths of, 351
    normal, 331–335, 364
Sexually transmitted disease
    prevention of HIV, 275–276
    syphilis, 11–12
Shaping
    in autistic disorder, 501
    in behavior therapy, 22
Shared psychotic disorder, 460–461
Shift work, 317
Shinkeishitsu, 143
Shoplifting, 404
Shyness, 142
    in infant, 143
    schizoid personality disorder and, 422
Siamese twins, 39
Significance, statistical vs clinical, 94
Significantly subaverage intellectual function-
        ing, 504
Sildenafil, 353–354
Silver nitrate, 399
Simulated amnesia, 188
Simulation, 75
Single photon emission computed tomogra-
        phy, 82–83
Sinoaortic baroreflex arc, 33
Situational phobia, 136–137

Situationally bound panic attack, 118–119
Situationally predisposed panic attack,
        118–119
Size, effect, 94
Skill, intellectual disability and, 509
Sleep
    mood disorders and, 217
    nocturnal panic and, 130
    rapid eye movement, 309
Sleep apnea, 316–317
Sleep attack, 316
Sleep disorder, 309–322, 329
    breathing-related, 310, 315–316
    circadian rhythm in, 310, 316–317
    narcolepsy, 310, 315–316, 329
    overview of, 309–311
    parasomnia and, 309–310, 320–322
    prevention of, 320
    primary hypersomnia, 310, 314–315
    primary insomnia, 311–314
    treatment of, 318–320
Sleep efficiency, 310–311
Sleep habits, 320
Sleep paralysis, 315
Sleep terrors, 130, 310, 321, 329
Sleepiness, 315–316
Sleep–wake schedule disorder. *See* Circadian
        rhythm; Sleep disorder
Sleepwalking, 310, 321–322, 329
Slow wave sleep, 217
Smoking
    Alzheimer's disease and, 520
    anxiety disorder and, 121
Smoking cessation, 399
Smooth-pursuit eye movement, 465
Snoring, 316
Social anxiety disorder, 141
Social factors
    in antisocial personality disorder,
        430–431
    in anxiety disorder, 121
    in attention deficit/hyperactivity disorder,
        489–490
    in autistic disorder, 497–499
    in chronic pain, 265–267
    in conversion disorder, 177
    in dementia, 522
    in *Diagnostic and Statistical Manual of
        Mental Disorders*, 89
    in eating disorder, 294–298
    health affected by, 249–257, 278, 282
    in mood disorder, 222–224
    in phobia, 33
    in posttraumatic stress disorder, 149
    in schizophrenia, 470–471, 482
    in sexual dysfunction, 350–351
    in stress, 252–253
    in substance use disorder, 395
Social learning, 55
Social norm, 2–3
Social phobia, 141–145, 163
    body dysmorphic disorder and, 181
    bulimia nervosa and, 288
    causes of, 143–144
    clinical description of, 141–142
    statistics about, 142–143
    treatment of, 144–145
Social relationships, 62–63
Social stigma, 63
Social support
    mood disorder and, 224
    pain and, 267
Social validity, 94
Society for Research in Child Development,
        111

Somatic delusion, 460
Somatic symptoms, 169
Somatization disorder, 170–172, 198
    causes of, 171–172
    clinical description of, 170
    statistics about, 170–171
    treatment of, 172
Somatoform disorder, 165–182, 198
    body dysmorphic disorder as, 178–182
    conversion disorder as, 173–177
    historical descriptions of, 11
    hypochondriasis as, 166–169
    pain disorder as, 172–173
    somatization disorder as, 170–172
    undifferentiated, 171
Somnambulism, 321–322
Soul, 6
Spasm in vaginismus, 347
Specific phobia, 135–136, 163
SPECT imaging, 82–83
Speech
    in autistic disorder, 501
    development of, 486
    disorganized, 457
Spinal cord, 40
Splitting, associative, 452–453
Squeeze technique for premature ejaculation,
        352
SS allele, 37
SSRI. *See* Selective serotonin reuptake
        inhibitor
Standardization of assessment, 72–73
Stanford Three Community Study, 276–277
Stanford-Binet test, 79
State v. Campanaro, 545
Statistical significance, 94
Stereotypical female, 417
Steroid, anabolic–androgenic, 391
Stimulant, 410
    attention deficit/hyperactivity disorder
        treated with, 490
    definition of, 376–377
Stimulant use disorder
    amphetamine, 383–384
    caffeine, 387
    cocaine, 384–386
    nicotine, 386
Stimulus
    for anxiety disorder, 121
    conditioned, 21
    for hypochondriasis, 168
    unconditioned, 21
Stimulus generalization, 21
Stress, 251–257
    anxiety and, 253–254
    in cancer patient, 260
    chronic fatigue syndrome and, 269
    contributions to, 252–253
    conversion disorder and, 177
    definition of, 253
    depression and, 253–254
    gender and, 61
    heart disease and, 262–263
    hypertension and, 262–263
    immune response and, 254–257
    insomnia and, 312
    management of, 272–274
    melancholy and, 7–8
    nature of, 251–252
    panic and, 131
    physiology of, 252
    posttraumatic, 145–151. *See also*
        Posttraumatic stress disorder
    schizophrenia and, 470
    tolerance for, 39